House of Commons

Laws under which monies are raised by Grand Jury presentments

House of Commons

Laws under which monies are raised by Grand Jury presentments

ISBN/EAN: 9783741105098

Manufactured in Europe, USA, Canada, Australia, Japa

Cover: Foto ©ninafisch / pixelio.de

Manufactured and distributed by brebook publishing software (www.brebook.com)

House of Commons

Laws under which monies are raised by Grand Jury presentments

REPORT

FROM THE

SELECT COMMITTEE

ON THE

GRAND JURY PRESENTMENTS (IRELAND);

TOGETHER WITH THE

PROCEEDINGS OF THE COMMITTEE,

MINUTES OF EVIDENCE,

AND APPENDIX.

Ordered, by The House of Commons, to be Printed,
6 *July* 1868.

Tuesday, 17th March 1868.

Ordered, THAT a Select Committee be appointed to inquire into the several Laws under which Monies are now raised by Grand Jury Presentments in Ireland, and into the nature and incidence of all charges levied under such Presentments, with the view of ascertaining what alterations might beneficially be made in those Laws.

Friday, 20th March 1868.

Ordered, THAT the Committee do consist of Seventeen Members.

Committee nominated of—

The O'Conor Don.
The Earl of Mayo.
Mr. Chichester Fortescue.
Mr. Dawson.
Sir Charles Lanyon.
Mr. Maguire.
Colonel Forde.
Mr. Leader.
Mr. Blake.
Mr. Gregory.
Sir Colman O'Loghlen.
General Dunne.
Colonel Cooper.
Lord John Browne.
Mr. Kendall.
Mr. Knatchbull-Hugessen.
Mr. Herbert.

Ordered, THAT the Committee have power to send for Persons, Papers, and Records.

Ordered, THAT Five be the quorum of the Committee.

Wednesday, 1st April 1868.

Ordered, THAT Lord John Browne be discharged from further attendance on the Committee.

Ordered, THAT Colonel French be added to the Committee.

Monday, 6th July 1868.

Ordered, THAT the Committee have power to Report their Observations, together with the Minutes of Evidence taken before them, to The House.

R E P O R T.

THE SELECT COMMITTEE appointed to inquire into the several LAWS under which Monies are now Raised by GRAND JURY PRESENTMENTS in *Ireland*, and into the Nature and Incidence of all Charges levied under such Presentments, with the view of ascertaining what Alterations might beneficially be made in those LAWS;——HAVE considered the Matters to them referred, and have agreed to the following REPORT:

1. THE whole question of the working of the Irish Grand Jury Laws was inquired into in 1842 by a Royal Commission, and as the constitution and functions of the different county bodies are very fully set forth in the Report of that Commission, your Committee do not believe it necessary to enter into any lengthened detail upon these points. Nevertheless a brief recapitulation may be desirable.

2. The present county fiscal system of Ireland is, in the main, worked under 6 & 7 Will. 4, c. 116, known as the Grand Jury Act, and although numerous Acts have been since passed modifying, more or less, the provisions of that statute, yet on the whole it is still the foundation of the system.

By the Act 6 & 7 Will. 4, c. 116, the functions or fiscal powers of grand juries were very much limited, and practically those bodies now form courts of appeal from the decisions arrived at at the presentment sessions. They have no power except in a few limited cases, to which allusion will be made hereafter, to initiate any taxation, nor even to alter any presentments sent up to them from the sessions, and they stand in relation to the sessions much in the same position as the House of Lords occupies on Money Bills in relation to the House of Commons. The grand jury is still constituted at the discretion of the high sheriff, with this limitation, that he is bound to call, first, on his panel, a representative from each barony, but that obligation is fulfilled by placing the name on the panel, and, whether the individual called attends or not, the obligation is equally complied with.

3. The presentment sessions are the tribunals where all steps are taken for initiating presentments, with the slight exceptions referred to in the preceding paragraph. All proposals for county works come before them, and cannot be legally sanctioned unless with their approval. Each presentment sessions is composed of the magistrates of the county and of a certain number of cesspayers, who are associated with the magistrates for the transaction of the fiscal business. In every barony there are held two presentment sessions in each year at a certain time before each assize. The number of cesspayers to be associated with the magistrates is fixed by the grand jury as well as the time for their meeting. The mode in which the cesspayers are selected is the following: the county cess or rate collectors are obliged to return to the grand jury at each assize the names of 100 of the highest cesspayers from each barony, and out of these 100 names the grand jury select double the number that they have fixed upon as the proper number to be associated with the magistrates at the sessions. This list, thus formed by the grand jury, contains the names of those who are eligible to sit at the succeeding sessions, and from it those who are to act are selected by ballot at the

meeting of the sessions. It is the first duty of the court, after having appointed a chairman, who must be a magistrate, to ballot for the cesspayers, and the persons whose names are first drawn out of the ballot are those who are entitled to act with the magistrates. In addition to the presentment sessions for each barony, there is also held a general presenting sessions for the county at large, at which matters affecting the whole county are considered. The county at large sessions is composed also of the magistrates and of one cesspayer selected at each baronial sessions.

4. From the presentment sessions and the grand juries emanate all the county taxation of Ireland, and having briefly stated the constitution and functions of these two bodies, your Committee next proceed to consider the objections raised against them. The chief objection urged is, that neither is representative in its character. It is asserted that the grand jury, being named to a certain extent at the discretion of an individual, cannot, under any circumstances, be considered a representative body, although in practice it is generally composed of the chief landed proprietors. As far as your Committee have been able to ascertain, there appears to be no qualification required for a grand juror, who, with the exception of the representative of the barony, need not have any connection either by residence or property with the county. The presentment sessions, on the other hand, it is urged, possess but a semblance of representation, although in their establishment, under the Grand Jury Act, it was evidently intended that they should be representative. The chief objections raised to the constitution of the presentment sessions by the different witnesses were the following: that the cesspayers to be associated at sessions are selected by the grand jury, and are not real representatives of the taxpayers of the county; that in consequence of there being a ballot at the sessions, even those cesspayers placed on the list by the grand jury cannot be certain of being called on to act, as no individual amongst them can be sure that his name will be one of those first drawn out from the ballot box; that even when the full number attend they may be out-voted by the magistrates, whose number is not limited, and who may come from any part of the county to attend at a particular sessions; that, in consequence of this, the attendance of the selected cesspayers is very irregular, and that when they do attend, they have no responsibility, and are too often guided by their own private interest.

5. To meet these objections, two courses seem open for adoption, either to do away altogether with the present powers of grand juries and presentment sessions, and to establish other machinery for carrying on the county work, or to improve the existing system by giving to it more of a representative character. Both courses have been advocated by different witnesses before your Committee. In favour of the former course, it was urged that the present system is unpopular, that it is indefensible in theory, that it has been already condemned by various Commissions and Committees which have inquired into the subject, and that the principle of taxation and representation going together requires a total alteration in the constitution of the taxing bodies in county matters. The substitution of baronial and county boards for the presentment sessions and grand jury was therefore recommended, and the poor-law system of mixed boards, composed of elected guardians and magistrates, was proposed as a model. On the other hand, many of the witnesses examined before your Committee held that, by some important modifications, the present system could be rendered satisfactory, and that it would be better to take existing institutions and adapt them to the circumstances of the times, rather than to inaugurate a totally new system, of the working of which only a conjecture could be formed. To these different recommendations your Committee have given a great deal of attention, and for the purpose of arriving at a correct conclusion regarding them, they desire to analyse the practical difference between them. Nearly all the witnesses agree that the present constitution of the presentment sessions is objectionable. The practice in different parts of Ireland regarding it is very different, and the law upon the subject seems doubtful. In some counties the grand juries think themselves obliged to place on the list of associated cesspayers the highest rated out of the 100 cesspayers returned to them; in other counties they consider themselves at liberty to select those they desire out of that list of the 100 names. Both courses have been stated to your Committee to be highly objectionable. On the one hand, if the names selected be those who pay the highest rates,

rates, it is possible, and in many cases very probable, that the majority of them will be residents in one or two portions of the barony, and that the other portions will be wholly unrepresented. On the other hand, a simple selection by the grand jury does away with even the appearance of representation. The change in this respect most strongly recommended, seems to be in favour of having the cesspayers who are to be associated with the magistrates at the presentment sessions for the barony, elected by the cesspayers of the barony, and those associated at the sessions for the county, elected by the baronial sessions. Were these proposals carried out, it seems to your Committee that, practically, baronial and county boards would be formed, differing undoubtedly in certain important particulars from the county and baronial boards before alluded to. The main difference between the two proposals of course consists in the maintenance of the controlling power of the grand jury in the one case, and its abrogation in the other.

6. Such are the principal objections to the existing system, but, having carefully considered the whole of the evidence, your Committee have come to the conclusion that, however open to objection certain portions of the grand jury system may be in theory, its administration has generally been pure and economical. The large increase in the amount of grand jury cess has been alluded to by several witnesses, but the exact nature of that increase is not easily arrived at, and still less can it be shown that it was owing to the extravagance or carelessness of the sessions or grand juries. As a matter of fact, the amount of the grand jury cess was less last year than it was in the year 1840, and the poundage of the rate, in consequence of the increase in the value of property, was still lower. Yet from this, very fallacious conclusions might be drawn. In comparing the amount of the cess at different times, it is essential to remember that the charges upon this rate have not been at all periods similar. A comparison between the rate at one period and that at another is thus not likely to lead to correct conclusions. There can be no doubt that in those particulars where grand juries and sessions have had real control, there has been a considerable increase in the expenditure: but this cannot be a matter for surprise, when it is recollected that the wages of labour have so much increased during the last quarter of a century; that a great many miles of new road have been constructed, and have now to be maintained in every county; and that all turnpike roads have been abolished, and the cost of maintaining the same transferred to the counties. Your Committee cannot say that any increase was shown to be due to the extravagance of the present acting bodies. Under these circumstances they do not consider it necessary to recommend the abolition of the existing system, believing that it can be so far modified as to do away with all the just objections raised to it.

7. It appears to your Committee, that to render the presentment sessions a satisfactory tribunal, two conditions are essential: it should be independent of the grand jury, who should have no control over its nomination; and it ought, as far as possible, to represent the ratepayers of the barony, and of all portions of the barony. Two methods of accomplishing this have been recommended: one, to have the baronies divided into electoral districts, each of which should elect a representative to sit at the baronial sessions, the election to be similar to that for poor-law guardians; the other, that the collectors should be obliged to send in from each parish, or other approved-of district, the names of a limited number of the highest cesspayers, and that out of this number a ballot should be taken at the assizes, and those whose names were first drawn should be associated with the magistrates at the sessions.

8. Your Committee recommend the adoption of the former course as the more straightforward, direct, and generally satisfactory. The election of the cesspayers is, no doubt, open to several objections; it may cause trouble and expense; it may lead to having the same individuals acting at the sessions time after time, and, under certain circumstances, it may degenerate into nomination by the great landed proprietors, or even, in some instances, to corrupt elections promoted by contractors, or expectant contractors. Nevertheless, having considered the arguments on both sides, your Committee believe that the principle of direct elective representation is the right one, and if abuses then arise it will be the fault of the ratepayers themselves. With respect to the baronial

baronial presentment sessions, they therefore recommend that each barony should be divided into districts, each of which should return a qualified representative to sit at the sessions, elected on the same principle and in the same manner as are the poor-law guardians; and as abuses have arisen from there being no limit to the number of magistrates, they further recommend that the number of magistrates qualified to act at any sessions should not exceed the number of elected cesspayers, and that no magistrate should be qualified to act who does not reside in, or who has not or does not represent property to a certain amount in the barony. With respect to the presentment sessions of the county at large, they would recommend that each baronial sessions should elect out of their own body an equal number of magistrates and cesspayers to represent the barony. The county-at-large sessions thus formed would also become a representative body.

9. As to the grand jury, your Committee do not believe that it would be desirable to do away with its fiscal powers, and they do not think that any necessity exists for any great alteration in its constitution. It appears from the evidence that, as a general rule, the grand jury represents the landed property of the county, and your Committee think it eminently desirable that there should be some such body to control and check the transactions of the sessions. It is to be remembered that the Poor Law Commissioners often exercise a most wholesome control over the different boards of guardians, and without some check outside the immediate locality, local influences might lead to extra-

Mr. Balmer, 4464. vagance. To obtain this desirable supervision, some witnesses have recom-

Mr. Adams, 7072. mended the appointment of a public commission, corresponding to that of the Poor Law, whilst Lord John Browne, one of the witnesses, recommends that a body elected out of the magistrates of the county by the magistrates might

Mr. Downing, 4984. be substituted for the grand jury. Your Committee do not see that there is any reason for such a change, especially as even the witnesses most desirous to

Mr. Adams, 7103. take from the grand juries their fiscal powers recognise the fact that they have discharged their duties satisfactorily.

10. Your Committee, however, consider that no person should be eligible to serve as a grand juror who is not connected, either by residence or property, with the county; that a sufficient qualification should be fixed by statute; that lists of all qualified persons of each barony should be prepared; and that no barony should have two representatives on the grand jury, until one representative had answered from each of the other baronies, or until the list of all the qualified persons therein had been exhausted.

11. This retention of the controlling power over all presentments by the grand jury, and the exercise of co-equal authority by the magistrates at the sessions, seem intimately connected with another important proposal made to your Committee, viz.: the division of the direct payment of the county rates between landlord and tenant. Recognising fully the fact that all peculiar charges on land are in the end paid in their entirety by the owner, and not the occupier, yet your Committee believe that, in respect of all future lettings, a direct payment of half the assessment should be made by the landlord. They recommend this for the following reasons: first, because though theoretically true that all taxes on land are paid by the owner, either directly as the tithe rentcharge, or indirectly, in the shape of a diminished rent, as the county cess, yet it cannot be expected that this will be generally seen or understood by the great mass of the people of the country. They only see and recognise the fact that at each levy they are called on to pay to the tax collector the full amount of the tax, and they naturally conclude that they are the sole losers by its imposition. That this is the general belief, even of most intelligent persons, the evidence abundantly proves, and so long as it exists it is impossible to expect that the county financial system can be regarded with satisfaction. At present the landed proprietors have entire control on the grand juries; they can exercise a monopoly of power at the sessions, and yet, except where they are occupiers, they pay directly none of the taxation which they themselves impose. The natural result of this is, that the occupiers believe they pay all the tax, and believing this, are dissatisfied with the system under which they have to pay all, and have little control over the expenditure. As your Committee deem it desirable that the owners of property should still continue to exercise, at least, an equal

control

control at the sessions, and that the grand jury should retain its fiscal functions, they consider a direct payment of half the rate by the owners essential to render this state of things satisfactory. In the next place, although it is true that all charges on land are in the end borne by the landlord, yet it is not true that this is the case immediately and in every particular instance. The owner when letting his farm may get less on account of the occupier having to pay the whole county rate, but when once the rent is fixed, he gets no more nor less in consequence of the rate falling or rising. He has, therefore, no direct interest in every alteration in the rate, and no direct interest in promoting economy in particular instances. That he should have this direct interest in all changes in the rate, your Committee believe to be highly desirable, and without wishing to express an opinion that the proprietors encourage extravagance or undue expenditure, the reverse of which they believe, in most cases, to be the fact, your Committee still consider that a direct payment of half the rate would lead to more attention to all matters of detail, whilst it would entitle the owners to that extended power of control over all county expenditure, which your Committee deem it desirable that they should possess.

12. Whilst admitting, in principle, the justice and expediency of this division of the payment of the rate, your Committee have confined their recommendations regarding it to the cases of future lettings, for the following reasons. It would be both absolutely and relatively unjust to extend the proposed change to any existing leasehold tenancy. The lease being made and the rent fixed on the understanding that whatever the county charges were they should be borne by the tenant, it would be unjust to remove this obligation without at least giving the option to the owner to cancel the lease. To divide the payment of the cess, in cases of existing leases, without this option, would be therefore an absolute injustice; but its relative injustice is still more apparent; were a general enactment passed for the division of the payment of the county cess, those who had let their lands on lease on the most moderate terms, allowing full margin to the tenant for the payment of the county rates, would then have to pay this tax twice over; they would pay it first through a diminished rent from the tenant; they would pay it, secondly, directly to the collector. In this, their position would be much worse than that of those who had refused to give leases, and had let their lands at the highest figure that competition could enforce; these latter could immediately reimburse themselves for any additional charge placed on them by re-adjusting the rent, and thus would be relatively in a better position than those who had granted leases. Abstracting from the injustice of this proceeding, your Committee believe it would be very impolitic to place this penalty on owners who had granted leases, as it could not but have the effect of deterring others from acting similarly in future. The case of other existing contracts is not so clear. The extension of the principle of the divided payment of the rate to these contracts could be justified on the ground that the owners had it in their power to re-consider and alter the contracts; but if this were generally acted upon, it might lead to great confusion, and in many instances to great hardship to the occupiers, therefore your Committee believe it safer to confine the operation of the change to all future lettings, whether by lease or otherwise.

13. That as considerable difficulty often arises in the collection of the county cess from the occupiers of very small tenements, and as that class is composed of the poorest portion of the community, often little removed from pauperism, your Committee believe that the occupiers of all tenements rated at or below 4 *l.* should be exempted from the payment of the county cess, which in such cases should be paid, like the poor rates, by the immediate lessors. If this recommendation were adopted, care should be taken to except from its operation such small tenements as might, at the time of the passing of an amended Grand Jury Act, be held under a lease.

14. Questions have been raised as to what ought to be the exact fiscal powers of the grand jury; at present their powers, in most instances, are restricted either to ratifying or rejecting the decisions of the sessions. There are, however, some exceptions to this; it would appear that they appoint some of the county officers, that they fix the amount of remuneration to be given to the collectors

collectors of the county cess, the amounts to be paid to certain officers for particular expenses incurred, and the presentments for building or repairing diocesan schools, as well as several other matters of no great importance. Your Committee believe that in some instances an extension, in others a restriction, of their functions is desirable. At present the grand jury have no power to make any provision for the maintenance of a road or other public work, for which a tender has been accepted at the sessions, except by ratifying that tender. It sometimes happens that an improper tender has been accepted at the sessions, and if the road or work for which this tender has been accepted be of importance, the grand jury must either ratify that tender which they believe to be improper, or otherwise leave the work neglected. This difficulty has been alluded to by several witnesses, but especially by Mr. Brett; and your Committee believe that the powers of the grand jury ought, in this instance, to be extended, and that they should be competent to annul an extravagant or improper contract, and make temporary provision until the next assizes for the care of the road or public work. This power should be limited to works of maintenance, and should not be exercised a second time with respect to the same contract, if a second presentment sessions approved of it; beyond this, your Committee believe that the powers of the grand jury should be limited as much as possible to the ratification or rejection of the presentments passed at the sessions. The county officers at present appointed by them are not numerous, and, with the exception of the secretary, none of these appointments should rest exclusively in their hands.

15. A considerable amount of evidence has been received upon the question, whether it would be advisable to appoint standing or finance committees of the grand juries or the sessions, to transact certain business between one assize and another. It has been represented that occasional inconvenience arises from the ephemeral character of the present county tribunals. The advantages of having some continuing body between one assize and another appear to be the following: such a body would be a check and control over the county officers; to it the collectors of the rate could be made responsible, and obliged to bring in their accounts periodically; through it advances to contractors during the progress of the works could be made, and finally to it the different accounts of the public institutions could be referred for examination, before the meeting of the grand jury. Were its functions strictly confined to these matters, your Committee believe the establishment of such a body would be very useful. It is to be apprehended, however, that unless carefully guarded against, these functions would, in practice, be much extended, and that such a committee would eventually control the grand jury, and in fact become a substitute for it. For many years such a committee has existed in the county of Dublin, and according to the evidence of Mr. Baker and Mr. Roche, that committee is practically the grand jury of that county. Moreover, it has not been shown that much practical good has arisen in the county of Dublin in consequence of this committee; the county cess has nearly doubled since its appointment, the contracts do not appear to be taken at a lower figure than in other counties, and the rate paid for the collection of the cess is as high as in any county in Ireland. Your Committee are far from implying that these results are the consequences of the existence of this standing body; they merely mention them to show that no comparatively great advantage has been proved to exist in Dublin county, and that therefore it would be fallacious to hope for any great or extended good result from the adoption of this system in other counties. Again, the county of Dublin can hardly be taken as a fair standard for the rest of Ireland, in the matter of the attendances at each meeting of the members of this committee. Were such a body to be appointed in other counties, it is to be feared that its management would fall into the hands of a few gentlemen resident near the county town. In the county of Dublin all the members of the finance committee reside in or near the city, and can with ease attend each meeting at the Four Courts. In a large country district this would be very different, and the working of such a committee would be necessarily in the hands of a few. For these reasons, if such a committee were appointed, it should not have very extended jurisdiction. If strictly limited to checking the county accounts, and having a supervision over the county officers, it could be made useful; and, so far, your Committee would recommend its appointment.

16. The

16. The recommendations of your Committee on the main principles submitted to them may be therefore set out as follows:—

They recommend—

That the authority of the grand juries in county fiscal matters should not be done away with.

That no one should be eligible to serve on a grand jury who had not a property or residential qualification, to be fixed by statute.

That the sheriff should be obliged, as far as possible, to secure the representation of each barony on the grand jury.

That the baronial sessions should be composed of a limited number of magistrates and cesspayers, the former connected by property with the barony, the latter elected by the general body of the cesspayers therein.

That at the sessions the magistrates and cesspayers should be placed in all respects on a footing of equality.

That from the presentment sessions thus formed all presentments affecting the barony should originate.

That, for considering all presentments affecting the county at large, there should be a county-at-large sessions, and that it should consist of an equal number of magistrates and cesspayers, elected by each baronial sessions.

That in all future lettings, the payment of the county cess should be equally divided between the owners and occupiers of land.

That, subject to such exceptions as may be found necessary, the payment of the county cess should be made by the immediate lessor in the case of tenements rated at or below 4 *l.*; and, lastly,

That a standing committee, with strictly limited powers, should be appointed by each grand jury to transact certain business between one assize and another.

17. The details in which the present grand jury laws require alteration are very numerous, and can be but lightly touched upon in this Report. Your Committee propose, in the first instance, to deal with the cases of the county officers. The principal county officers at present are, the treasurer, the secretary of the grand jury, the county surveyors and their assistants, the clerks of the Crown and peace, the coroners, the barony cess collectors, and the local inspectors of prisons.

18. *The Treasurer.*—By an Act passed in the last Session of Parliament, this, as a distinct office, has been prospectively abolished, and upon the death or resignation of the present treasurers, the principal duties of the office will devolve on the secretaries of the grand juries. The Act has been so short a time in operation, that it has taken effect only in three or four counties in Ireland, but there seems no reason to believe that it will not work satisfactorily.

19. *The Secretary of the Grand Jury* is at present one of the principal county officers, and if the recommendations of your Committee be carried out, his duties and responsibilities will be largely increased. The secretary is appointed by the grand jury, but holds office only at the pleasure of that body, and may be dismissed without any reason being assigned. This has been represented to your Committee as a cause of complaint on the part of the grand jury secretaries, who seek to be placed in an equal position with the treasurers, and to hold their office during good behaviour. There seems to be much reason in this complaint, and prospectively your Committee would recommend the placing of the secretaries on the same footing as the treasurers, especially as they may be called upon at any time to discharge the duties of the latter office, and to give the required securities. The secretaries are at present paid by salaries and fees. The salaries are fixed by the schedule to the Grand Jury Act, and the fees, which depend on the number of presentments, are of two descriptions; recognised or legal fees, and customary payments for particular services rendered to contractors. The only legally recognised fees to which the secretaries are entitled are, 6 *d.* on each blank form of tender, and 1 *s.* for each unfilled bond. These form a very small amount of the payments they receive, the customary payments by contractors being in some instances far more than the salary and all the other fees put together. The chief customary payments made to the secretaries are for filling up these and other forms and notices. The rate at

which these documents are charged for varies in different counties, and the amount received through them is very considerable. It appears to your Committee that the payment of the secretaries through these fees ought to be abolished. There are many objections to it. As long as it continues, it is the interest of the secretaries to have as many contracts and tenders as possible, and, consequently, to cut up contracts, and to have them entered into for very short periods. It also renders the secretary's remuneration uncertain and unknown. Your Committee therefore recommend that the secretaries' salaries should be of a fixed amount, and should not be dependent upon these fees. As has been before observed, most of these payments are now made for particular services rendered in filling up the necessary notices and other documents for the contractors, and it does not appear desirable either that those services should be rendered gratuitously, or that the secretaries should be prohibited from rendering them. Your Committee believe that these small charges or fees are not felt as any burden by the contractors, and in no way enhance the rate of the contracts, whilst they form some test of the *bonâ fide* intentions of the parties seeking the forms. On the other hand, were the secretaries not permitted to issue and fill up those necessary documents, the contractors, in many instances illiterate men, would be obliged to go to an attorney or other person, and have the forms filled-in at much greater expense. Your Committee would therefore recommend the legalisation of all these fees at a uniform rate all over Ireland, the receipts to go, not to the secretaries, but to the credit of the county. They would recommend that the secretaries of the grand juries should be obliged to furnish these forms filled up to all persons applying for the same, each complete form to be stamped, for which stamp a certain small sum should be paid, and the receipts thereof credited to the county funds. Were these additional duties thrown on the secretaries, and their receipts from fees abolished, a readjustment of their salaries would of course become necessary. Under any circumstances such a readjustment seems called for, as the duties of the office have much increased since 1838, and are likely to go on increasing. Prospectively, all the duties of the treasurer devolve on the secretary, and amongst them that of aplotting the county cess. For this duty at present there appears to be no fixed system of payment, and apparently whatever the treasurer demands for it is paid. It varies in the most irregular way in the different counties; in some of the very small ones being much greater than in those of the largest extent, and generally it appears to be much in excess of what it should be. In any readjustment of the secretary's salary, this duty should be taken into consideration, and in all cases it should at once be transferred to the secretary. A new classification of counties appears also to be required. The circumstances of several of the counties of Ireland have very much altered since the passing of the Grand Jury Act in 1838, and the classification then arranged is no longer a fair one. Were the salaries of the secretaries of the grand juries readjusted, as proposed, your Committee believe they might very well be called upon to discharge all the duties recommended to be imposed upon them in this Report.

20. *The County and Assistant Surveyors.*—The county surveyors' duties and remuneration have been fixed by a much later Act of Parliament than those of the other county officers. In the year 1857, a Committee was appointed to inquire into their duties, and into the best mode of carrying out the supervision of the county works. Upon the recommendation of that Committee the salaries of those officers were largely increased, the mode of appointment altered, and the system of assistants approved of. A considerable amount of evidence of a rather contradictory character has been received upon the question whether it would be more beneficial to appoint district surveyors rather than assistants. Your Committee do not think it necessary to make any recommendation on this subject, as it was very fully investigated in 1857, when the system at present in force was unanimously recommended. As the assistants are now appointed by the county surveyors, and as the latter are responsible for them in every respect, it would seem desirable that the county surveyors should have authority also to dismiss them. Your Committee are of opinion that with reference to the mode of appointment of county surveyors, some alteration is desirable. The existing Act provides for the competitive examination of candidates whenever a vacancy occurs. This arrangement would necessarily create considerable

considerable delay in filling up the appointment. Your Committee therefore recommend that there always should be the names of two candidates (certified as provided in the Act by the examiners) in the hands of the Government ready for filling the appointment immediately on its becoming vacant.

21. *The Clerks of the Crown and Peace.*—These two offices your Committee believe ought to be amalgamated. As far back as the year 1836, this amalgamation was recommended by a committee which inquired into the different duties of the county officers, and since then a similar recommendation has been the result of every inquiry, yet up to the present day these recommendations have had no result. This, in some measure, may be due to the fact that these two officers are appointed by different authorities;—the clerk of the Crown by the Government, the clerk of the peace by the "custos rotulorum" of the different counties. The duties of the two offices are very similar, the one discharging at the assizes the same functions as the other at the quarter sessions. Neither officer has much to do in connection with the fiscal business of the county. The clerk of the Crown keeps the county records, countersigns the cheques issued by the treasurer, and swears the grand jury. The clerk of the peace in case of death, or unavoidable absence of the secretary of the grand jury, takes his place until a new appointment is made, or until the recovery of the secretary; he also arranges and is responsible for the registration of Parliamentary voters. All the other duties of both officers are connected with the criminal and civil business in the courts of assize and quarter sessions. Your Committee believe that the custody of the county records should be vested in the secretary of the grand jury, that the countersigning of the cheques should be the duty of the finance committee, with whom should also rest the temporary appointment of a substitute for the secretary in case of illness or death; and that the grand jury should be sworn by the sub-sheriff. The expense of registration of Parliamentary voters being now separately paid for, all the fiscal duties of the clerks of the Crown and peace would be thus disposed of, and your Committee believe that for the criminal and civil business in the courts the two officers ought to be united, and the counties altogether relieved from the payment of the salary of this new officer, who should be paid in the same manner and from the same sources as the Crown solicitors, the chairman of quarter sessions, and other legal functionaries. The criminal business in the different courts of Ireland has enormously diminished during the last 30 years, and as there are fees charged for all the civil business transacted by the clerks of the Crown and peace, your Committee believe that the salary of one of these officers might be completely saved by this amalgamation. It appears from the evidence that in 24 of the counties of Ireland the duties of the clerks of the peace are discharged by deputies, and your Committee cannot express too strongly their condemnation of this practice. It should be incumbent upon the new officer to reside in the county, to be a professional man, and to discharge his duties in person and not by deputy, and being as much the officer of the court as the Crown solicitor, he should be appointed by the Government.

22. *The Coroner.*—With respect to this office, which is one of the most ancient in connection with the grand jury laws, it appears to your Committee that it ought not to be filled up as at present. Some professional qualification ought to be required from the candidate, and the appointment should rest either with the grand jury or the magistracy of the county, subject to the approval of the Lord Lieutenant. The present system of election by all the Parliamentary voters in the district is in many respects objectionable. There is no guarantee that a fit person will be elected, as the only qualification required is, that the candidate should be a 50 *l.* freeholder or 100 *l.* leaseholder, and the expense, where there are contests, is heavy. Evidence was received from Dr. Hayes on behalf of the coroners of Ireland, who seek a payment of a fixed salary instead of fees on each inquest. To this change there appears to be no objection, provided the salary be fixed in proportion to the average number of inquests held during a certain number of preceding years. To the proposal to have one uniform salary for every district in Ireland your Committee see many objections, and they think it would be manifestly unequal, as the coroner's work in some districts is much greater than in others.

23. The *Barony Cess Collectors* are now appointed by the grand juries for the

collection of the county rates from one assizes to another. They hold the appointment only for this limited period, and are, if reappointed, obliged to enter into new securities at each assizes. For the collection of the cess, it appears they receive a much larger poundage than do the collectors of the poor rates, who discharge almost precisely the same duties. The practice almost universally is, that the barony cess collector appoints deputies, who collect the cess for about half the amount which he is paid. In most counties in Ireland the rate of payment for this collection seems to be 9 *d.* in the pound; in several it is 1 *s.*; and considering that the poor rates are collected for 4 *d.*, 5 *d.*, and 6 *d.*, your Committee believe that the payment made for the collection of the county cess is in most cases excessive. It has been suggested that the two collections might be amalgamated and carried on by the one individual, but as there might be some difficulties in carrying this out in some parts of Ireland, your Committee do not recommend its adoption in all cases, although they do not see any reason why the same person might not be appointed cess collector, who is now poor-rate collector. Your Committee, therefore, do not recommend the absolute abolition of the office of county-cess collector, but they consider that the payment made for the collection is excessive, and the appointment of the collectors unsatisfactory. This was almost the only direct charge of extravagance brought against the grand jury by any of the witnesses, and it is evidently a source of dissatisfaction to the ratepayers. The collectors ought to be appointed, and the rate of remuneration fixed, by the presentment sessions and not by the grand jury, and tenders for the collection should be received in the same way as they are now for the collection of the poor rates. The office of cess collector is, even at the present time, essentially a baronial one, and the magistrates and cesspayers at the sessions are far more likely to know the position and solvency of the securities offered for the collection than are the grand jury. Moreover, as difficulties might sometimes arise in getting securities for so large an amount as the collection of a whole barony, if the baronies be divided into electoral districts, collectors might be appointed for one or more districts of the barony as the sessions should think proper. Your Committee believe, that if this principle be adopted, a great saving will be effected in the collection of the rate, whilst a source of dissatisfaction with the grand juries will be removed. Of course, under this proposal, the present rate collectors would be eligible for reappointment were they willing to undertake the duties for a fair remuneration. Your Committee further recommend that the barony cess collectors should be obliged to lodge their receipts every month, and to bring in their accounts to the finance committee, for, from the want of some supervision of this description, the present enactment, that collectors should lodge their receipts when they amount to 100 *l.*, appears to be inoperative.

24. *The Local Inspectors of Prisons.*—A recommendation in favour of the abolition of this office has been made by previous committees and commissions, but particularly by the Royal Commission which inquired into the Grand Jury Laws in 1842. The local inspectors are appointed by the board of superintendence of each gaol, and the remuneration given appears to be fixed upon no principle, and to be quite at the discretion of the grand jury. The duties of this office have been fully set forth by Mr. Lentaigne, and most of them appear to be duties which really belong to the governors of these institutions. Mr. Lentaigne, although admitting this, expresses his opinion that some sort of inspection is required, but your Committee are of opinion that the retention of this officer can be more properly considered when the general question of prisons in Ireland becomes the subject of legislation.

25. *The County Gaols.*—It has been shown to your Committee that a great portion of the county taxation is raised for the county institutions and other imperative presentments. According to the evidence and returns given by Mr. Lentaigne, it appears that great and unnecessary expense is incurred in the maintenance of the county gaols of Ireland. The average number of prisoners in some of these gaols is very trifling, and the cost of each prisoner to the county is proportionately increased. Your Committee are happy to remark that there is visible in Ireland a large diminution in the number of criminals, and they believe that great economy would be effected, and also much public good accomplished, by the establishment of district instead of county gaols. The latter might still be continued, with a diminished

diminished staff, for receiving untried prisoners and those sentenced to short terms of imprisonment. The exact saving which in this way might be effected, your Committee are not able to determine, but they have no doubt it would be considerable, besides which, the district gaols being under a uniform management, uniformity in punishment, all over Ireland, would be secured.

26. *The Lunatic Asylums* are another source of great and increasing expense to the counties. These institutions have already cost for their erection nearly 1,000,000 *l.* sterling, of which about one-half has been already paid by the counties, and the other half is in course of repayment. The history of these asylums and how their expense came to be defrayed out of the county rates, has been fully given in the evidence of Dr. Nugent. They originated before the establishment of the poor-laws in Ireland, and the county rate was then the only one out of which all local charges were defrayed. The money for their erection was, in the first instance, advanced out of the Consolidated Fund, to be repaid by 28 half-yearly instalments, and the Lord Lieutenant had authority, by a special Act of Parliament, to order the erection of one of these buildings in any district he thought proper. There are, at present, 23 asylums in Ireland, and unless some alteration be made as to the class of persons sent to them, a considerable number of new asylums will have to be erected. The present annual charge of these institutions for maintenance is 120,000*l.*, and no charge on the county cess has so enormously increased within the last 20 years. This maintenance charge alone now amounts to 3 *d.* in the pound on the valuation of all Ireland. To enable your Committee to recommend any mode of reducing this very heavy expenditure would have required a complete examination of the whole system of lunatic asylums in Ireland, which your Committee have not been able to undertake.

Mr. Nugent, 3580 and 5616.

Mr. Nugent, 5574.

27. *The Annual Revision of the Valuation.*—The only other important presentment of an imperative character to which it is necessary to make particular allusion, is that for the expense of the annual revision of the valuation. Upon this subject your Committee have not had time, owing to the lateness of the Session, to take much evidence; but they find this to be an increasing expenditure over which neither the grand jury nor any local body has any control; and they are satisfied that while the general valuation of Ireland has been conducted with much ability, and has conferred great advantages on the country, yet its annual revision requires a more careful investigation than they have been able to give to it. They also believe that more detailed information of the sources of expense should be furnished to the Poor Law unions, to be by them remitted to the grand jury, and thus the correctness of the charge would be submitted to local investigation.

28. *Malicious Injuries.*—Presentments are at present granted to persons as compensation for losses sustained by reason of malicious injury done to their property. Applications for these presentments must come before the presentment sessions, the grand jury, and finally the judge of assize; but the decision of either, or both, of the first tribunals is not final; the application may be thrown out by the sessions, thrown out by the grand jury, and yet be passed before the judge, or it may be passed by the grand jury, and sessions, and yet rejected before the judge. Conflicting evidence has been taken before your Committee on the subject of these presentments for malicious injuries; on the one side it has been contended that by this system of compensation, the innocent may be made to pay for the guilty, and that as the injured person looks forward to be indemnified for the loss he has sustained, the detection of the offender becomes a matter of small importance to him. On the other hand it is urged by witnesses of great experience that the present state of the law does away with inducements to commit malicious injuries, which generally result from the ill-will of neighbours. It is manifest that a man will be likely to abstain from acts of destruction towards the property of his neighbour, when he is aware that not only will the person injured be, in all probability, indemnified for his loss, but that he, the offender, may have to contribute to that indemnity. All the neighbours have thus an interest in preventing malicious injury to property, and your Committee are of opinion that to do away with the present system, guarded as it is from abuse by the various checks above referred to, would be injurious to the

Lord J. Browne.
Mr. Baister.
Mr. Redkin.

the security of property, more especially of the farming classes in Ireland. Your Committee recommend, therefore, the retention of the present system, subject to the following alterations, viz., that no larger sum than 100 *l.* be given as compensation for injuries to buildings by fire, and also that the holding of the injured person shall be exempted from the compensation rate.

29. Several other defects in the details of the grand jury laws have been pointed out to your Committee. Most of them will be found noticed in the evidence and suggestions of Mr. Hill, Mr. Tate, and Mr. Brett. They refer chiefly to the taking and enforcing of contracts, and the apportionment of payments between different baronies and counties.

30. Your Committee recommend that the principle of accepting the lowest tender should be adhered to.

31. That further facilities should be given for suing defaulting contractors and their sureties.

32. That the principle of Section 17 of 19 & 20 Vict. c. 63, should be extended to works of maintenance as well as contracts.

33. That where security is now required for double the amount of the tender it should be given instead for double the amount approved of at sessions.

34. That the bonds for the performance of contracts should be entered into, not to the Crown, but to the secretary of the grand jury, and that any penalty recovered should go to the credit of the county.

35. That power should be given, under restrictions, to one barony or county to subscribe to the expenditure on works situated in another.

36. That the powers of grand juries in dividing or uniting baronies should be extended.

37. That the half payment of the maintenance of post roads by the county at large should be abolished, and that all roads should be maintained by their respective baronies.

38. That grand juries should not have the power to present any work to the county surveyor, unless a work of maintenance, and that of pressing importance.

39. That superannuation may be given, at the option of the grand jury, to county officers who have employed their whole time in the service of the county, but not otherwise, and that such superannuation shall be regulated on the scale laid down by the Civil Service Superannuation Act.

40. That it is desirable to have the treasurers' accounts audited in their respective counties. Your Committee recommend that this duty should be performed by the auditors employed under the Poor Law.

41. For carrying out the recommendations of your Committee, a total remodelling of the Grand Jury Act will be necessary. Already the statutes under which presentments are made are extremely numerous, confusing, and complex, and your Committee would therefore recommend, as far as possible, the embodiment of all their provisions in the one Act. The preamble of the Act of 6 & 7 Will. 4, c. 116, appears to have again become true, and your Committee would therefore recommend that a similar course should now be adopted to that followed in 1836.

PROCEEDINGS OF THE COMMITTEE.

Tuesday, 24th *March* 1868.

MEMBERS PRESENT:

The O'Conor Don.
Mr. Kendall.
Mr. Blake.
Lord John Browne.
Colonel Cooper.
Sir Charles Lanyon.
Colonel Forde.
General Dunne.
Mr. Leader.
Mr. Dawson.
Mr. Chichester Fortescue.
Mr. Herbert.

The O'Conor Don was called to the Chair.

The Committee deliberated.

[Adjourned to Friday next, at Twelve o'clock.

Friday, 27th *March* 1868.

MEMBERS PRESENT:

The O'Conor Don in the Chair.

Colonel Forde.
Lord John Browne.
Mr. Herbert.
Mr. Kendall.
Mr. Blake.
Colonel Cooper.
Sir Charles Lanyon.
General Dunne.
Mr. Chichester Fortescue.
Mr. Leader.
Mr. Gregory.

Mr. *Peter Burrowes Sharkey* examined.

[Adjourned to Tuesday next, at Twelve o'clock.

Tuesday, 31st *March* 1868.

MEMBERS PRESENT:

The O'Conor Don in the Chair.

Colonel Forde.
Mr. Herbert.
Mr. Kendall.
Mr. Leader.
General Dunne.
Sir Charles Lanyon.
Colonel Cooper.
Mr. Blake.
Mr. Dawson.
Mr. Gregory.
Lord John Browne.
Sir Colman O'Loghlen.
Mr. Maguire.

Mr. *John Hill* and Mr. *William Johnson* were severally examined.

[Adjourned to Friday next, at Twelve o'clock.

Friday, 3rd *April* 1868.

MEMBERS PRESENT:

The O'Conor Don in the Chair.

Colonel Forde.
Mr. Herbert.
Sir Charles Lanyon.
Mr. Kendall.
Colonel French.
Colonel Cooper.
Mr. Blake.
Mr. Leader.
General Dunne.
Sir Colman O'Loghlen.
Mr. Gregory.
Mr. Maguire.
Mr. Dawson.
Mr. Chichester Fortescue.

Mr. *William Johnson* further examined.

Mr. *Daniel Cronin Coltsmann* examined.

[Adjourned to Tuesday, 28th April, at Twelve o'clock.

Tuesday, 28th *April* 1868.

MEMBERS PRESENT:

Mr. Chichester Fortescue.
Colonel French.
Mr. Herbert.
Sir Charles Lanyon.
Sir Colman O'Loghlen.
Colonel Cooper.
Mr. Kendall.
Colonel Forde.
Mr. Maguire.
Mr. Blake.
Mr. Dawson.
Mr. Gregory.
The Earl of Mayo.

In the absence of The O'Conor Don, Mr. Chichester Fortescue was called to the Chair.

Mr. *Alexander Tait*, examined.

The Committee deliberated.

[Adjourned to Friday next, at Twelve o'clock.

Friday, 1st *May* 186[illegible]

MEMBERS PRESENT:

Mr. CHICHESTER FORTESCUE in the Chair.

Colonel French.
Colonel Forde.
Mr. Blake.
Mr. Gregory.
Mr. Kendall.
Mr. Herbert.
Mr. Dawson.
Mr. Maguire.
Sir Charles Lanyon.
Sir Colman O'Loghlen.
The Earl of Mayo.

Mr. *Francis A. Leigh* examined.

The Committee deliberated.

[Adjourned to Tuesday next, at Twelve o'clock.

Tuesday, 5th May 1868.

MEMBERS PRESENT:

Mr. CHICHESTER FORTESCUE in the Chair.

Colonel French.
Colonel Forde.
Sir Colman O'Loghlen.
Mr. Maguire.
Sir Charles Lanyon.
Mr. Blake.
Colonel Cooper.
Mr. Kendall.
Mr. Leader.
Mr. Herbert.
The Earl of Mayo.

Mr. *William D'Esterre Parker* examined.

[Adjourned to Friday next, at Twelve o'clock.

Friday, 8th May 1868.

MEMBERS PRESENT:

Mr. CHICHESTER FORTESCUE in the Chair.

Colonel French.
Colonel Cooper.
Mr. Maguire.
Mr. Gregory.
Mr. Blake.
Mr. Kendall.
The Earl of Mayo.
Colonel Forde.
Mr. Herbert.
Mr. Leader.
Sir Charles Lanyon.
Mr. Dawson.

Mr. *Uniacke Ramsay Mackey* and Lord *John Browne*, a Member of the House, were severally examined.

[Adjourned to Tuesday next, at Twelve o'clock.

Tuesday, 12th May 1868.

MEMBERS PRESENT:

Mr. CHICHESTER FORTESCUE in the Chair.

Colonel French.
Sir Charles Lanyon.
Mr. Herbert.
Colonel Forde.
Colonel Cooper.
Mr. Dawson.
Mr. Blake.
Mr. Kendall.
Mr. Maguire.
Sir Colman O'Loghlen.
The Earl of Mayo.
Mr. Gregory.

In the absence of Mr. Chichester Fortescue, Colonel Forde was called to the Chair.

Lord *John Browne*, a Member of the House, further examined.

[Adjourned to Friday next, at Twelve o'clock.

Friday, 15th *May* 1868.

MEMBERS PRESENT:

The O'Conor Don in the Chair.

Colonel French.
Sir Charles Lanyon.
General Dunne.
Colonel Forde.
Mr. Blake.
Mr. Kendall.
Colonel Cooper.
Mr. Dawson.
Sir Colman O'Loghlen.
Mr. Maguire.
The Earl of Mayo.
Mr. Chichester Fortescue.
Mr. Herbert.
Mr. Leader.

Mr. *Peter B. Sharkey* examined.

The Committee deliberated.

Mr. *Henry E. Wynne* examined.

[Adjourned to Tuesday next, at Twelve o'clock.

Tuesday, 19*th May* 1868.

MEMBERS PRESENT:

The O'Conor Don in the Chair.

Colonel French.
Mr. Kendall.
Mr. Blake.
Mr. Leader.
Sir Charles Lanyon.
Mr. Dawson.
Colonel Cooper.
Mr. Maguire.
Mr. Herbert.
General Dunne.
Mr. Chichester Fortescue.

Mr. *Edwin Sadleir* examined.

The Committee deliberated.

Mr. *Henry Brett* examined.

[Adjourned to Friday next, at Twelve o'clock.

Friday, 22*nd May* 1868.

MEMBERS PRESENT:

The O'Conor Don in the Chair.

Colonel French.
Colonel Cooper.
Mr. Gregory.
Mr. Dawson.
Mr. Leader.
Mr. Kendall.
Mr. Maguire.
General Dunne.
Mr. Chichester Fortescue.
Mr. Blake.
Sir Charles Lanyon.
Mr. Herbert.
Colonel Forde.

Mr. *William Bolster* and Mr. *John Lanigan* were severally examined.

[Adjourned to Tuesday next, at Twelve o'clock.

Tuesday, 26th May 1868.

MEMBERS PRESENT:

The O'Conor Don in the Chair.

Mr. Gregory.	Colonel Cooper.
Colonel French.	General Dunne.
Mr. Herbert.	Mr. Dawson.
Mr. Maguire.	Sir Charles Lanyon.
Mr. Blake.	Sir Colman O'Loghlen.

Mr. *McCarthy Downing* and Mr. *Wm. Wentworth Fitz-William Dick*, a Member of the House, were severally examined.

[Adjourned to Friday, 5th June, at Twelve o'clock.

Friday, 5th June 1868.

MEMBERS PRESENT:

The O'Conor Don in the Chair.

Mr. Gregory.	Mr. Chichester Fortescue.
Colonel French.	General Dunne.
Colonel Cooper.	Mr. Leader.
Colonel Forde.	The Earl of Mayo.
Mr. Blake.	

Mr. *Neal Davis* and Mr. *John Nugent*, M.D., were severally examined.

[Adjourned to Tuesday next, at Twelve o'clock.

Tuesday, 9th June 1868.

MEMBERS PRESENT:

The O'Conor Don in the Chair.

Mr. Blake.	General Dunne.
Colonel Cooper.	Sir Charles Lanyon.
Colonel French.	The Earl of Mayo.
Mr. Leader.	Mr. Kendall.
Mr. Gregory.	

Mr. *Henry Baker*, Mr. *John Edmund Beach*, and Mr. *Robert S. Hayes*, M.D., were severally examined.

[Adjourned to Friday next, at Twelve o'clock.

Friday, 12th *June* 1868.

MEMBERS PRESENT:

The O'CONOR DON in the Chair.

Mr. Blake.
Colonel French.
Mr. Dawson.
General Dunne.
Mr. Kendall.
Sir Charles Lanyon.
Mr. Leader.
Mr. Maguire.
Mr. Gregory.

Mr. *John Duiguan M'Dermot*, Mr. *John O'Reilly*, and Mr. *William Malcolmson*, were severally examined.

[Adjourned to Tuesday next, at Twelve o'clock.

Tuesday, 16th *June* 1868.

MEMBERS PRESENT:

The O'CONOR DON in the Chair.

Mr. Dawson.
Colonel French.
Mr. Blake.
Mr. Leader.
Mr. Gregory.
Colonel Forde.
General Dunne.
Mr. Kendall.
Mr. Maguire.
The Earl of Mayo.

Mr. *Robert Bellis* and Mr. *John Adams* were severally examined.

[Adjourned to Friday next, at Twelve o'clock.

Friday, 19th *June* 1868.

MEMBERS PRESENT:

The O'CONOR DON in the Chair.

Colonel French.
Colonel Cooper.
Mr. Leader.
Sir Charles Lanyon.
General Dunne.
Mr. Blake.
Colonel Forde.
Mr. Gregory.
Mr. Maguire.

Mr. *John Ball Greene* and Mr. *John Hardiman* were severally examined.

The Committee deliberated.

[Adjourned to Tuesday, 30th June, at Twelve o'clock.

Tuesday, 30th June 1868.

MEMBERS PRESENT:

The O'Conor Don in the Chair.

Mr. Kendall.	Colonel Cooper.
Colonel French.	Mr. Dawson.
Sir Charles Lanyon.	Mr. Chichester Fortescue.
General Dunne.	Mr. Leader.
Colonel Forde.	Sir Colman O'Loghlen.
Mr. Blake.	Mr. Maguire.
Mr. Gregory.	The Earl of Mayo.

DRAFT REPORT proposed by the Chairman, read the first time, as follows:—

"1. The whole question of the working of the Irish Grand Jury Laws was inquired into in 1842 by a Royal Commission, and as the constitution and functions of the different county bodies are very fully set forth in the Report of that Commission, your Committee do not believe it necessary to enter into any lengthened detail upon these points. Nevertheless a brief recapitulation may be desirable.

"2. The present county fiscal system of Ireland is, in the main, worked under 6 & 7 Will. 4, c. 116, known as the Grand Jury Act, and although numerous Acts have been since passed modifying, more or less, the provisions of that statute, yet on the whole it is still the foundation of the system.

"By the Act 6 & 7 Will. 4, c. 116, the functions or fiscal powers of grand juries were very much limited, and practically those bodies now form courts of appeal from the decisions arrived at at the presentment sessions. They have no power except in a few limited cases, to which allusion will be made hereafter, to initiate any taxation, nor even to alter any presentments sent up to them from the sessions, and they stand in relation to the sessions much in the same position as the House of Lords occupies on Money Bills in relation to the House of Commons. The grand jury is still constituted at the discretion of the high sheriff, with this single limitation, that he is bound to call, first, on his panel, a representative from each barony, but that obligation is fulfilled by placing the name on the panel, and, whether the individual called attends or not, the obligation is equally complied with.

"3. The presentment sessions are the tribunals where all steps are taken for initiating presentments. All proposals for county works come before them, and cannot be legally sanctioned unless with their approval. Each presentment sessions is composed of the magistrates of the county and of a certain number of cesspayers, who are associated with the magistrates for the transaction of the fiscal business. In every barony there are held two presentment sessions in each year at a certain time before each assize. The number of cesspayers to be associated with the magistrates is fixed by the grand jury as well as the time for their meeting. The mode in which the cesspayers are selected is the following: the county cess or rate collectors are obliged to return to the grand jury at each assize the names of 100 of the highest cesspayers from each barony, and out of these 100 names the grand jury select double the number that they have fixed upon as the proper number to be associated with the magistrates at the sessions. This list, thus formed by the grand jury, contains the names of those who are eligible to sit at the succeeding sessions, and from it those who are to act are selected by ballot at the meeting of the sessions. It is the first duty of the court, after having appointed a chairman, who must be a magistrate, to ballot for the cesspayers, and the persons whose names are first drawn out of the ballot are those who are entitled to act with the magistrates. In addition to the presentment sessions for each barony, there is also held a general presenting sessions for the county at large, at which matters affecting the whole county are considered. The county at large sessions is composed also of the magistrates and of one cesspayer selected at each baronial sessions.

"4. From the presentment sessions and the grand juries emanate all the county taxation of Ireland, and having briefly stated the constitution and functions of these two bodies, your Committee next proceed to consider the objections raised against them. The chief objection is, that neither is representative in its character. The grand jury, being named almost exclusively at the discretion of an individual, cannot, under any circumstances, be considered a representative body, although practically it is generally composed of the chief landed proprietors. As far as your Committee have been able to ascertain, there appears to be no qualification required for a grand juror, who need not have any connection either by residence or property with the county. The presentment sessions, on the other hand, possess a semblance of representation. In their establishment, under the Grand Jury Act, it was evidently intended that they should be representative, but practically they have failed to be so. The chief objections raised to the constitution of the presentment sessions by the different witnesses were the following: that the cesspayers to be associated at sessions are selected by the grand jury, and are not real representatives of the taxpayers of the county;

that in consequence of there being a ballot at the sessions, even those cesspayers placed on the list by the grand jury cannot be certain of sitting at the sessions, as no individual amongst them can be sure that his name will be one of those first drawn out from the ballot box; that even when the full number attend they may be out-voted by the magistrates whose number is not limited, and who may come from any part of the county to attend at a particular sessions; that in consequence of this, the attendance of the selected cesspayers is very irregular, and that when they do attend, they have no responsibility, and are guided solely by their own private interest.

*5. To meet these objections, two courses seem open for adoption, either to do away altogether with the present powers of grand juries and presentment sessions, and to establish other machinery for carrying on the county work, or to improve the existing system by giving to it more of a representative character. Both courses have been advocated by different witnesses before your Committee. In favour of the former course, it is urged that the present system is unpopular, that it is indefensible in theory, that it has been already condemned by various Commissions and Committees which have inquired into the subject, and that the principle of taxation and representation going together requires a total alteration in the constitution of the taxing bodies in county matters. The substitution of baronial and county boards for the presentment sessions and grand jury is therefore recommended, and the poor-law system of mixed boards composed of elected guardians and magistrates is taken as a model. On the other hand, many of the witnesses before your Committee hold that by a few, though not unimportant modifications, the present system can be rendered satisfactory, and that it is better to take existing institutions and adapt them to the circumstances of the times, rather than to inaugurate a totally new system, of the working of which, only a conjecture can be formed. To these different recommendations your Committee have given a great deal of attention, and for the purpose of arriving at a correct conclusion regarding them, they desire to analyse the practical difference between them. Nearly all the witnesses agree that the present constitution of the presentment sessions is indefensible. The practice in different parts of Ireland regarding it is very different, and the law upon the subject seems doubtful. In some counties the grand juries think themselves obliged to place on the list of associated cesspayers the highest rated out of the 100 cesspayers returned to them; in other counties they consider themselves at liberty to select those they desire out of that list of the 100 names. Both courses have been stated to your Committee to be highly objectionable. On the one hand, if the names selected be those who pay the highest rates, it is possible, and in many cases very probable, that the majority of them will be residents in one or two portions of the barony, and that the other portions will be wholly unrepresented. On the other hand, a simple selection by the grand jury does away with even the appearance of representation. The change in this respect most strongly recommended, seems to be in favour of having the cesspayers who are to be associated with the magistrates at the presentment sessions for the barony, elected by the cesspayers of the barony, and those associated at the sessions for the county, elected by the baronial sessions. Were these proposals carried out, it seems to your Committee that, practically, baronial and county boards would be formed, differing undoubtedly in certain important particulars from the county and baronial boards before alluded to. The main difference between the two proposals of course consists in the maintenance of the controlling power of the grand jury in the one case, and its abrogation in the other.

*6. Such are the principal objections to the existing system, and, having carefully considered the whole of the evidence, your Committee have come to the conclusion that however indefensible portions of the grand jury system are in theory, yet in practice it has not worked so badly as is often asserted. The large increase in the amount of grand jury cess has been alluded to by several witnesses, but what that really is, is not easily arrived at, and still less can it be shown that it was owing to the extravagance or carelessness of the sessions or grand juries. As a matter of fact, the amount of the grand jury cess was less last year than it was in the year 1840, and the poundage of the rate, in consequence of the increase in the value of the property, was still lower. Yet from this, very fallacious conclusions might be drawn. In comparing the amount of the cess at different times it is essential to remember that the charges upon this rate have not been at all periods similar. For instance, in 1840, the charge for the constabulary, now a very formidable charge, and paid out of the Consolidated Fund, was then placed on the county rates. On the other hand, the expenses for such public institutions as lunatic asylums, have enormously increased since 1840, and yet over these the grand juries and sessions have no control whatever. A comparison between the rate at one period and that at another, is thus not at all likely to lead to correct conclusions. There can be no doubt that in those particulars where grand juries and sessions have had real control there has been a considerable increase in the expenditure; but this cannot be a matter for surprise when it is recollected that the wages of labour have so much increased during the last quarter of a century. Your Committee cannot say that any increase was shown to be due to the extravagance of the present acting bodies. Under these circumstances they do not consider it necessary to recommend the total abolition of the existing system, believing that it can be so far modified as to do away with all the just objections raised to it. As before observed, the presentment sessions was evidently intended, by the Act of Will. 4, to be a representative body; but this intention has been defeated.

*7. To render it at all a satisfactory tribunal, two conditions are essential. It should be perfectly

perfectly independent of the grand jury, who should have no control over its nominations, and it ought, as far as possible, to represent the ratepayers of the barony, and of all portions of the barony. Two methods of accomplishing this have been recommended. One, to have the baronies divided into electoral districts, each of which should elect a representative to act at the baronial sessions, the election to be similar to that for poor law guardians. The other, that the collectors should be obliged to send in from each parish, or other appointed district, the names of a limited number of the highest cesspayers, and that out of this number a ballot should be taken at the sessions, and those whose names were first drawn should be associated with the magistrates at the sessions.

"8. Your Committee recommend the adoption of the former course, as the more straightforward, direct, and generally satisfactory. The election of the cesspayers is, no doubt, open to several objections; it may cause unnecessary trouble and expense; it may lead to having the same individuals acting at the sessions time after time, and, under certain circumstances, it may degenerate into simple nomination by the great landed proprietors, or even, in some instances, to corrupt elections promoted by contractors, or expectant contractors. Nevertheless, having considered the arguments on both sides, your Committee believe that the principle of direct elective representation is the right one, and if abuses then arise it will be the fault of the ratepayers themselves. With respect to the baronial presentment sessions, they therefore recommend that each barony should be divided into districts, each of which should return a representative to sit at the sessions, elected on the same principle as are the poor law guardians; and as abuses have arisen from there being no limit to the number of magistrates, they further recommend that the number of magistrates qualified to act at any sessions should not exceed the number of elected cesspayers, and that no magistrate should be qualified to act who did not reside in, or who had not property to a certain amount in the barony. With respect to the presentment sessions of the county at large, they would recommend that each baronial sessions should elect out of their own body one magistrate and one cesspayer to represent the barony. The county at large sessions thus formed would also become a representative body.

"9. As to the grand jury, your Committee do not believe that it would be desirable to do away altogether with its fiscal powers, unless some other similar body were substituted, and they do not think any necessity exists for any great alteration in its constitution. It appears from the evidence that, as a general rule, the grand jury represents the landed property of the county, and your Committee think it eminently desirable that there should be some such body to control and check the transactions of the sessions. It is to be remembered that the Poor Law Commissioners often exercise a most wholesome control over the different boards of guardians, and without some check outside the immediate locality your Committee fear that, in some instances, local influences would lead to extravagance. To obtain this desirable supervision some witnesses have recommended the appointment of a public commission, corresponding to that of the Poor Law, whilst Lord John Browne, one of the witnesses, recommends that a body elected out of the magistrates of the county by the magistrates might be substituted for the grand jury. Your Committee do not see that there is any reason for this. The evidence has shown to them that, on the whole, the grand jury represents the property of the county; and even the witnesses most desirous to take from them their fiscal powers recognise that they have discharged their duties satisfactorily.

"10. The retention of the controlling power over all presentments by the grand jury, and the exercise of co-equal authority by the magistrates at the sessions, seem intimately connected with another important proposal made to your Committee, viz.: the division of the direct payment of the county cess between landlord and tenant. Recognising fully the fact that all peculiar charges on land are in the end paid in their entirety by the owner, and not the occupier, yet your Committee believe that a direct payment of at least half the assessment should be made by the landlord. They recommend this for the following reasons: first, because though theoretically true that all taxes on land are paid by the owner, either directly as the tithe rentcharge, or indirectly, in the shape of a diminished rent, as the county cess, yet it cannot be expected that this will be generally seen or understood by the great mass of the people of the country. They only see and recognise the fact that at each levy they are called on to pay to the tax collector the full amount of the tax, and they naturally conclude that they are the sole losers by its imposition. That this is the general belief, even of most intelligent persons, the evidence abundantly proves, and so long as it exists it is impossible to expect that the county financial system can be regarded with satisfaction. At present the landed proprietors have entire control on the grand juries; they have a practical monopoly of power at the sessions, and yet, except where they are occupiers, they pay directly none of the taxation which they themselves impose. The natural result of this is, that the occupiers believe they pay all the tax, and believing this, are dissatisfied with the system under which they have to pay all, and have little control over the expenditure. As your Committee deem it desirable that the owners of property should still continue to exercise, at least, an equal control at the sessions, and that the grand jury should retain its fiscal functions, they consider a direct payment of half the rate by the owners essential to render this state of things satisfactory. In the next place, although it is true that all charges on land are in the end borne by the landlord, yet it is not true that this is the case immediately and in every particular instance. The owner when letting his farm may get less on account of the occupier having to pay the whole county rate, but when once the rent is fixed, he gets no more

more nor less in consequence of the rate falling or rising. He has, therefore, no direct interest in promoting economy in particular instances. That he should have this direct interest in all changes in the rate, your Committee believe highly desirable, and without wishing to express an opinion that the proprietors are at present those who encourage extravagance or undue expenditure, the reverse of which they believe, in most cases, to be the fact, your Committee still consider that a direct payment of half the rate would lead to more attention to all matters of detail, whilst it would entitle the owners to that extended power of control over all county expenditure, which your Committee deem it desirable that they should possess.

"11. Admitting the abstract justice and expediency of this division of the payment of the rate, the question next arises how far it should be put into immediate operation; evidently it would be unjust to extend it to all, binding existing contracts of a continuous character. To charge the owner of land, let on lease for a number of years, with half the county rates, would be to treat him absolutely and relatively unfairly. The lease being made and the rent fixed on the understanding that whatever the county charges were they should be borne by the tenant, it would be clearly unjust to remove this obligation without at least giving the option to the owner to cancel the lease altogether. To divide the payment of the cess, in cases of existing leases, without this option, would be therefore an absolute injustice; but its relative injustice is still more apparent; were a general enactment passed for the division of the payment of the county cess, those who had let their lands on lease on the most moderate terms, allowing full margin to the tenant for the payment of the county rates, would then have to pay the tax twice over; they would pay it, secondly, directly to the collector. In this, their position would be much worse than that of those who had refused to give leases, and had let their lands at the highest figure that competition could enforce; these latter could immediately reimburse themselves for any additional charge placed on them by re-adjusting the rent, and thus would be relatively in a better position than those who had granted leases. Abstracting from the injustice of this proceeding, your Committee believe it would be very impolitic to place this penalty on owners who had granted leases, as it could not but have the effect of deterring others from acting similarly in future; they therefore do not recommend any attempt to divide the rate in cases of existing contracts of a continuous character. With respect to other tenancies and all future lettings, whether by lease or otherwise, your Committee would recommend the division of the rate. They would also recommend that the occupiers of all lands or tenements rated at or below 4 *l.* should be exempted from any direct payment of the county cess, and that in this respect the county rates and poor rates should be assimilated in their incidence.

"12. Questions have been raised as to what ought to be the exact fiscal powers of the grand jury; at present their powers, in most instances, are restricted either to ratifying or rejecting the decisions of the sessions. There are, however, some exceptions to this; it would appear that they appoint some of the county officers, that they fix the amount of remuneration to be given to the collectors of the county cess, the amount to be paid to certain officers for particular expenses incurred, and the presentments for building or repairing diocesan schools, as well as several other matters of not much importance. Your Committee believe that in some instances an extension, in others a restriction, of their functions is desirable. At present the grand jury have no power to make any provision for the maintenance of a road or other public work, for which a tender has been accepted at the sessions, except by ratifying that tender. It sometimes happens that an improper tender has been accepted at the sessions, and if the road or work for which this tender has been accepted be of importance, the grand jury are placed in this difficulty, that they must either ratify that tender, which they believe to be improper, or otherwise leave the work neglected. This difficulty has been alluded to by several witnesses, but especially by Mr. Brett, and your Committee believe that the powers of the grand jury ought, in this instance, to be extended, and that they should be competent to annul an extravagant or improper contract, and make temporary provision until the next sessions for the care of the road or public work. This power should be limited to works of maintenance, and should not be exercised a second time with respect to the same contract, if a second presentment sessions approved of it; and beyond this, your Committee believe that the powers of the grand jury should be limited as much as possible to the ratification or rejection of the presentments passed at the sessions. The county officers at present appointed by them are not numerous, and, with the exception of the secretary, none of these appointments should rest exclusively in their hands.

"13. Your Committee, however, consider that no person should be eligible to serve as a grand juror, who was not connected either by residence or property with the county; and that lists of all qualified persons of each barony should be prepared, and that no barony should have two representatives on the grand jury, until one representative had answered from each of the other baronies, or until the list of all the qualified persons therein had been exhausted.

"14. A considerable amount of evidence has been received upon the question, whether it would be advisable to appoint standing or finance committees of the grand juries or the sessions, to transact certain business between one assize or another. It has been represented that occasional inconvenience arises from the ephemeral character of the present county tribunals. The advantages of having some continuing body between one assize and another, appear

appear to be the following; such a body would be a check and control over the county officers; to it the collectors of the rate could be made responsible, and obliged to bring in accounts every month; through it advances to contractors during the progress of the works could be made, and finally to it the different accounts of the public institutions could be referred for examination, before the meeting of the grand jury. Were its functions strictly confined to these matters, your Committee believe the establishment of such a body would be very useful. It is to be apprehended, however, that unless carefully guarded against, these functions would, in practice, be much extended, and that such a committee would eventually control the grand jury, and in fact become a substitute for it. For many years such a committee has existed in the county of Dublin, and according to the evidence of Mr. Baker and Mr. Roache, that committee is practically the grand jury of Dublin. Moreover, it has not been shown that much practical good has arisen in Dublin in consequence of this committee; the county cess has nearly doubled since its appointment; the contracts do not appear to be taken at a lower figure than in other counties, and the rate paid for the collection of the cess is as high as in any county in Ireland. Your Committee are far from implying that these results are the consequences of the existence of this standing body; they merely mention them to show that no comparatively great advantage has been proved to exist in Dublin county, and that therefore it would be fallacious to hope for any great or extended good result from the adoption of that system in other counties. Again, the county of Dublin can hardly be taken as a fair standard for the rest of Ireland, in the matter of the attendances at each meeting of the members of this committee. Were such a body to be appointed in other counties, it is to be feared that its management would fall into the hands of a few gentlemen resident near the county town. In Dublin all the members of the finance committee reside in or near the city, and can with ease attend each meeting at the Four Courts. In a large county district this would be very different, and the working of such a committee would be necessarily in the hands of a few. For these reasons if such a committee were appointed, it should not have very extended jurisdiction. If strictly limited to checking the county accounts, and having a supervision over the county officers, it could be made useful, and, so far, your Committee would recommend its appointment.

"15. The recommendations of your Committee on the main principles submitted to them may be therefore set out as follows:—

They recommend—

That the authority of the grand juries on county fiscal matters should not be done away with.

That no one should be eligible to serve on a grand jury who had not a property or residential qualification of a certain amount, to be fixed by statute.

That the sheriff should be obliged, as far as possible, to have each barony really represented on the grand jury.

That the baronial sessions should be composed of a limited number of magistrates and cesspayers, the former connected by property with the barony, the latter elected by the general cesspayers thereon.

That at the sessions the magistrates and cesspayers should be placed in all respects on a footing of equality.

That from the presentment sessions thus formed all presentments affecting the barony should originate.

That, for considering all presentments affecting the county at large, there should be a county-at-large sessions, and that it should consist of one magistrate and one cesspayer, elected by each baronial sessions.

That, with the exception of cases of existing leases, the payment of the county cess should be divided between the owners and occupiers of land.

That occupiers rated at or below 4 l. should be altogether exempted from the payment of the rate; and, lastly,

That a standing committee, with strictly limited powers, should be appointed by each grand jury, to be a check and control over the county officers between one assizes and another.

"16. The details in which the present grand jury laws require alteration are very numerous, and can be but lightly touched upon in this report. Your Committee propose, in the first instance, to deal with the cases of the different county officers. The principal county officers at present are, the treasurer, the secretary of the grand jury, the county surveyors and their assistants, the clerks of the Crown and peace, the coroners, the barony cess collectors, and the local inspectors of prisons.

"17. *The Treasurer.*—By an Act passed in the last Session of Parliament, this, as a distinct office, has been prospectively abolished, and upon the death or resignation of the present treasurers, the principal duties of the office will devolve on the secretaries of the grand juries. The Act has been so short a time in operation, that it has taken effect only in three or four counties in Ireland, but there seems no reason to believe that it will not work satisfactorily.

"18. *The Secretary of the Grand Jury* is at present one of the principal county officers, and if the recommendations of your Committee be carried out, his duties and responsibilities will be largely increased. The Secretary is appointed by the grand jury, but holds office only at the pleasure of that body, and may be dismissed without any reason being assigned. This has been represented to your Committee as a cause of complaint on the part of the grand jury secretaries, who seek to be placed in an equal position with the treasurers, and to hold their office during good behaviour. There seems to be much reason in this complaint, and prospectively your Committee would recommend the placing of the secretaries on the same footing as the treasurers, especially as they may be called upon at any time to discharge the duties of the latter office, and to give the required securities. The secretaries are at present paid by salaries and fees. The salaries are fixed by the schedule to the Grand Jury Act, and the fees, which depend on the number of presentments, are of two descriptions: recognised or legal fees, and customary payments for particular services rendered to contractors. The only legally recognised fees to which the secretaries are entitled are, 1 s. on each blank form or tender, and 1 s. for each unfilled bond. These form a very small amount of the payments they receive, the customary payments by contractors being in some instances far more than the salary and all the other fees put together. The chief customary payments made to the secretaries are for filling up these and other forms and notices. The rate at which these documents are charged for varies in different counties, and the amount received through them is very considerable. It appears to your Committee that the payment of the secretaries through these fees ought to be abolished. There are many objections to it. As long as it continues, it is the interest of the secretaries to have as many contracts and tenders as possible, and, consequently, to cut up contracts, and to have them entered into for very short periods. It also renders the secretary's remuneration uncertain and unknown. Your Committee therefore recommend that the secretaries' salaries should be of a fixed amount, and should not be dependent upon these fees. As has been before observed, most of these payments are now made for particular services rendered in filling up the necessary notices and other documents for the contractors, and it does not appear desirable either that these services should be rendered gratuitously, or that the secretaries should be prohibited from rendering them. Your Committee believe that these small charges or fees are not felt as any burden by the contractors, and in no way enhance the rate of the contracts, whilst they form some test of the *bonâ fide* intentions of the parties seeking the forms. Were these forms furnished gratuitously, this would lead to no reduction in the rate of the contracts, and in many instances would result in applications being made where there was no intention of carrying out any work whatever. On the other hand, were the secretaries not permitted to issue and fill up these necessary documents, the contractors, in many instances illiterate men, would be obliged to go to some country attorney or other person, and have the forms filled in at much greater expense. Your Committee would therefore recommend the legalisation of all these fees at a uniform rate all over Ireland, the receipts to go, not to the secretaries, but to the credit of the county. They would recommend that the secretaries of the grand juries should be obliged to furnish these forms filled up to all persons applying for the same, each complete form to be stamped, for which stamp a certain small sum should be paid, and the receipts thereof credited to the county funds. Were these additional duties thrown on the secretaries, and their receipts from fees abolished, a readjustment of their salaries would of course become necessary. Under any circumstances such a re-adjustment seems called for, as the duties of the office have much increased since 1836, and are likely to go on increasing. Prospectively, all the duties of the treasurer devolve on the secretary, and amongst them that of applotting the county cess. For this duty at present there appears to be no fixed system of payment, and apparently whatever the treasurer demands for it is paid. It varies in the most irregular way in the different counties; in some of the very small ones being much greater than in those of the largest extent, and in all it appears to be much in excess of what it should be. In any readjustment of the secretary's salary, this duty should be taken into consideration, and in all cases it should at once be transferred to the secretary. A new classification of counties appears also to be required. The circumstances of several of the counties of Ireland have very much altered since the passing of the Grand Jury Act in 1836, and the classification then arranged is no longer a fair one. Were the salaries of the secretaries of the grand juries readjusted, as proposed, your Committee believe they might very well be called upon to discharge all the duties recommended to be imposed upon them in this Report.

"19. *The County and Assistant Surveyors.*—The county surveyors' duties and remuneration have been fixed by a much later Act of Parliament than those of the other county officers. In the year 1857, a Committee was appointed to inquire into their duties, and into the best mode of carrying out the supervision of the county works. Upon the recommendation of that Committee the salaries of these officers were largely increased, the mode of appointment altered, and the system of assistants approved of. A considerable amount of evidence of a rather contradictory character has been received upon the question whether it would be more beneficial to appoint district surveyors rather than assistants. Your Committee do not think it necessary to make any recommendations on this subject, as it was very fully investigated in 1857, when the system at present in force was unanimously recommended. As the assistants are now appointed by the county surveyors, and as the latter are responsible for them in every respect, it would seem desirable that the county surveyors should have authority also to dismiss them.

"20. The

"30. *The Clerks of the Crown and Peace.*—These two offices your Committee believe ought to be amalgamated. As far back as the year 1836, this amalgamation was recommended by a committee which inquired into the different duties of the county officers, and since then a similar recommendation has been the result of every inquiry, yet up to the present day these recommendations have had no result. This, in some measure, may be due to the fact that these two officers are appointed by different authorities. The clerk of the Crown by the Government, the clerk of the peace by the "custos rotulorum" of the different counties. The duties of the two offices are very similar, the one discharging at the assizes the same functions as the other at the quarter sessions. Neither officer has much to do in connection with the fiscal business of the county. The clerk of the Crown keeps the county records, countersigns the cheques issued by the treasurer, and swears the grand jury. The clerk of the peace in case of death, or unavoidable absence of the secretary of the grand jury, takes his place until a new appointment is made, or until the recovery of the secretary; he also arranges and is responsible for the registration of Parliamentary voters. All the other duties of both officers are connected with the criminal and civil business in the courts of assize and quarter sessions. Your Committee believe that the custody of the county records should be vested in the secretary of the grand jury; that the countersigning of the cheques should be the duty of the finance committee, with whom should also rest the temporary appointment of a substitute for the secretary in case of illness or death; and that the grand jury should be sworn by the sub-sheriff. The expense of registration of Parliamentary voters being now separately paid for, all the fiscal duties of the clerks of the Crown and peace would be thus disposed of, and your Committee believe that for the criminal and civil business in the courts the two offices ought to be united, and the counties altogether relieved from the payment of the salary of this new officer, who should be paid in the same manner and from the same sources as the Crown solicitors, the chairmen of quarter sessions, and other legal functionaries. The criminal business in the different courts of Ireland has enormously diminished during the last 20 years, and as there are fees charged for all the civil business transacted by the clerks of the Crown and peace, your Committee believe that the salary of one of these officers might be completely saved by this amalgamation. The new officer being as much the officer of the court as the Crown solicitor, he should be appointed by the Government. It should be incumbent on him to reside in the county, to be a professional man, and to discharge his duties in person and not by deputy. In order to bring about this proposed amalgamation as soon as possible, it should be compulsory on one or other of the present officers to retire on a superannuation allowance, the other officer discharging for the future the duties of both. It appears from the evidence that in 28 of the counties of Ireland the duties of the clerks of the peace are discharged by deputies, and a claim has been put forward by these deputies for compensation in case the office be abolished. It is not very easy to see what claim these deputies have upon the public, or what vested interest they possess. They hold their appointments at the will and pleasure of their principals, and may be dismissed at any moment. Moreover their arrangements, as regards remuneration, with the clerks of the peace, are not known, and it would be very difficult for any public department to provide for their compensation. It may no doubt seem a hardship, whereas these men have been really discharging all the duties of the office for many years, that on the abolition of the office they should receive no compensation, whilst their principals, who never discharged any active duty, should be entitled to receive a superannuation allowance. Were the present holders of the existing offices permitted to retain them for their lives, and allowed to act by deputy, this difficulty would be got over, but your Committee believe it would be a more satisfactory arrangement if a certain proportion of the superannuation allowance could be made payable to the deputies in all cases where the principals had never acted themselves.

"31. *The Coroner.*—With respect to the duties of this office, which is one of the most ancient in connection with the grand jury laws, it appears that not much alteration is required if the office be at all retained. It seems to your Committee that the holding of inquests in all county districts might very well be transferred to the stipendiary magistrates, and, in their absence, to any two justices of the peace. The stipendiary magistrates would certainly be far more competent to preside at inquests than the class of men from whom the coroners are usually elected. If the office be retained as a separate one, it ought not to be filled up as at present. Some personal qualification ought to be required from the candidate, and the appointment ought to rest either with the Government, the grand jury, or the magistracy of the county. The present system of election by all the Parliamentary voters in the district is in many respects objectionable. There is no guarantee that a fit person will be elected, as the only qualification required is, that the candidate should be a 50 *l.* freeholder or 100 *l.* leaseholder, and the expense, where there are contests, is heavy. Evidence was received from Dr. Hayes on behalf of the coroners of Ireland, who seek a payment of a fixed salary instead of fees on each inquest. To this change there appears to be no objection, provided the salary was fixed in proportion to the average number of inquests held during a certain number of preceding years. To the proposal to have one uniform salary for every district in Ireland, your Committee see many objections, and they think it would be manifestly unequal, as the coroner's work in some districts is much greater than in others.

"32. *The Barony Cess Collectors* are now appointed by the grand juries for the collection of the county rates from one assize to another. They hold the appointment only for this limited

limited period, and are, if re-appointed, obliged to enter into new securities at each sessions. For the collection of the cess, it appears they receive a much larger poundage than do the collectors of the poor rates, who discharge almost precisely the same duties. The practice almost universally is, that the barony cess collector appoints deputies, who collect the cess for about half the amount which he is paid. In most counties in Ireland the rate of payment for this collection seems to be 9 d. in the pound; in several it is 1 s.; and, considering that the poor rates are collected for 4 d., 5 d., and 6 d. a year, your Committee believe that the payment made for the collection of the county cess is in most cases excessive. It has been suggested that the two collections might be amalgamated and carried on by one individual, but as there might be some difficulties in carrying this out in some parts of Ireland, your Committee do not recommend its adoption in all cases, although they do not see any reason why the same person might not be appointed cess collector, who is now poor-rate collector. Your Committee, therefore, do not recommend the absolute abolition of the office of county cess collector, but they consider that the payment made for the collection is excessive, and the appointment of the collectors unsatisfactory. This was almost the only direct charge of extravagance brought against the grand jury by any of the witnesses, and it is evidently a source of dissatisfaction to the ratepayers. The collectors ought to be appointed, and the rate of remuneration fixed, by the presentment sessions and not by the grand jury, and tenders for the collection should be received in the same way as they are now for the collection of the poor rates. The office of cess collector is, even at the present time, essentially a baronial one, and the magistrates and cesspayers at the sessions are far more likely to know the position and solvency of the securities offered for the collection than are the grand jury. Moreover, as difficulties might sometimes arise in getting securities for so large an amount as the collection of a whole barony, if the baronies be divided into electoral districts, collectors might be appointed for one or more districts of the barony as the sessions should think proper. Your Committee believe, that if this principle be adopted, a great saving will be effected in the collection of the rate, whilst a source of dissatisfaction with the grand juries will be removed. Of course, under this proposal, the present rate collectors would be eligible for reappointment were they willing to undertake the duties for a fair remuneration. Your Committee further recommend that the barony cess collectors should be obliged to lodge their receipts every month, and to bring in their accounts to the finance committee, for, from the want of some supervision of this description, the present enactment, that collectors should lodge their receipts when they amount to 300 l., appears to be inoperative.

"33. *The Local Inspectors of Prisons.*—A recommendation in favour of the abolition of this office has been made by previous committees and commissions, but particularly by the Royal Commission which inquired into the Grand Jury Laws in 1842. The office, as at present constituted, is objectionable and useless. The local inspectors are appointed by the board of superintendence of each gaol, and the remuneration given appears to be fixed upon no principle, and to be quite at the discretion of the grand jury. The duties of this office have been fully set forth by Mr. Lentaigne, and most of them appear to be duties which really belong to the governors of these institutions. Mr. Lentaigne, although admitting this abuse, expresses his opinion that some sort of inspection is required, but your Committee agree with him in thinking that that inspection should be made by an officer wholly independent of the board of superintendence, and that a separate inspector for each gaol is by no means required. They, therefore, concur with the Commission of 1842, in recommending the abolition of the office of local inspector, and they agree with Mr. Lentaigne in recommending the appointment of district inspectors, four of whom, he states, would be sufficient for the whole of Ireland. These inspectors, your Committee believe, ought to be paid, as in England, out of the Consolidated Fund, but even were their salaries charged on the counties, yet there would, by the adoption of this proposal, be a saving of at least half the present expense.

"34. *The County Gaols.*—It has been shown to your Committee that a great portion of the county taxation is raised for the county institutions and other imperative presentments. According to the evidence and returns given by Mr. Lentaigne, it appears that great and unnecessary expense is gone to in the maintenance of the county gaols of Ireland. The average number of prisoners in some of these gaols is very trifling, and the cost of each prisoner to the county is proportionately increased. In some gaols each individual prisoner costs as large a sum as 81 l., in others not half that amount. Your Committee are happy to remark that there is visible in Ireland a very great diminution in the number of criminals, and they believe that great economy would be effected, and also great public good accomplished by the establishment of district instead of county gaols. The latter might still be continued, with a greatly diminished staff, for receiving untried prisoners and those sentenced to very short terms of imprisonment. The exact saving which in this way might be effected, your Committee are not able to determine, but they have no doubt it would be considerable, besides which, the district gaols being under a uniform management, uniformity in punishment, all over Ireland, would be secured.

"35. *The Lunatic Asylums* are another source of great and increasing expense to the counties. These institutions have already cost for their erection nearly 1,000,000 l. sterling, of which about one-half has been already paid by the counties, and the other half is in course of repayment. The history of these asylums, and how their expenses came to be defrayed out of the county rates, has been fully given in the evidence of Dr. Nugent. They originated before the establishment of the Poor Laws in Ireland,

Ireland, and the county rate was then the only one out of which all local charges were defrayed. The money for their erection was, in the first instance, advanced out of the Consolidated Fund, to be repaid by 20 half-yearly instalments, and the Lord Lieutenant had authority, by a special Act of Parliament, to order the erection of one of these buildings in any district he thought proper. There are, at present, 22 asylums in Ireland, and unless some alteration be made as to the class of persons sent to them, a considerable number of new asylums will have to be erected. The present annual charge of these institutions for maintenance is 120,000 *l.*, and no charge on the county cess has so enormously increased within the last 20 years. This maintenance charge alone now amounts to 3 *d.* in the pound on the valuation of all Ireland. County lunatic asylums, as explained to Dr. Nugent, are kept up for those persons who are either paupers or too poor to pay for themselves in private asylums. The persons relieved through them are essentially the same class as that relieved by the Poor Laws and Medical Charities Acts, and your Committee have no doubt that, had the Poor Law system been in force when these institutions were established, their expense would have been fixed upon the poor rates. They recommend, therefore, that the maintenance charges for lunatic asylums should at once be transferred to the poor rates. The objects of these asylums are analogous to those for which the poor rates are at present paid; they are institutions for the relief of the poor though not strictly confined to actual paupers. Moreover, several advantages would arise from having each union charged with the cost of its own lunatics. The cost of supporting a lunatic in an asylum is more than double that of a pauper in a workhouse, and, according to the evidence of Dr. Nugent, there are now maintained in many of the asylums individuals, imbeciles, idiots, and other incurables who could be just as well kept at half the expense in the workhouse. At present the guardians of each union object to receive these persons; they believe they free themselves from a charge by transferring them to an asylum, but were they obliged to pay for the maintenance and proportionate establishment charges for each lunatic sent from their union to the asylum, greater care would be taken that none but proper persons should be sent there. Again, by transferring these charges to the poor rates, you would transfer them to a rate the guardians over which would have some control and interest in the expenditure. At present the grand juries have no jurisdiction whatever in the matter. The presentment comes before them as an imperative one; they cannot ascertain its correctness; they cannot diminish its amount; their duty regarding it is merely ministerial; they are obliged to pass it. Were the payment of the rate transferred to each union, the guardians would look narrowly into it and would see that no persons sent from their union were unnecessarily kept there, and thus that evil to which Dr. Nugent alludes as a growing and a formidable one would cease. Your Committee, therefore, recommend that all maintenance charges for asylums should be transferred to the poor rates. Unless some such system be adopted, it is to be feared that the lunatic asylums will require to be multiplied. Probably, in order to provide for the due care of those lunatics who could as well be kept in the workhouses, separate wards should be set apart for their use, either in every workhouse, or in a certain workhouse in the province; but this is a matter of detail which would soon be arranged were the charge transferred as recommended. Your Committee also believe that poor persons, unable to pay for their support in a private asylum, but able to pay for it in a public one, ought to be admitted into the latter, but only on the condition of paying for their support, and that none should be admitted free except absolute paupers.

"26. *County Infirmaries.*—Upon this subject your Committee have not taken much evidence. It appears that the amount of annual subscriptions falls very short of the amount paid by the counties, yet the subscribers, as governors, have all the appointments. The amount paid for these institutions is very considerable, and their utility, now that there are so many good workhouse hospitals, has greatly decreased. This is also a charge more properly belonging to the poor rates, and your Committee recommend that it should be transferred to them.

"27. The only other important presentment of an imperative character to which it is necessary to make particular allusion, is that for the expense of the annual revision of the valuation. Upon this subject your Committee have not had time, owing to the lateness of the Session, to take much evidence; the expense of the annual revision of the valuation is a large and increasing one; the original estimate for it was about 16,000 *l.*; it now amounts to 25,000 *l.*, and according to the evidence it must go on increasing for many years until the officers attain their maximum salaries. It has been proved to your Committee, by Mr. Green, the Superintendent of the Valuation Office, that more than 19-20ths of this expenditure is a permanent and increasing charge, practically independent of the fluctuations in the number of changes of occupancy in Ireland; over this expenditure neither the grand juries nor any county body had any control whatsoever. The presentment for it is an imperative one, its amount cannot be disputed or its accuracy investigated. Proposals have been made by several witnesses that the revision should be carried on by local officers; and whilst your Committee believe that were that system adopted a saving of more than one-half of the expenditure could be effected, yet, as there are many advantages in having one uniform system for all Ireland, they are not prepared, without further investigation, to recommend the change. At the same time, they believe that the present system requires to be thoroughly investigated. They cannot think that a system under which seven months of the year are spent in repairing the damage done to the maps and documents in the other five is a satisfactory one, yet this is the description given of the present duties of the official Green, [illegible]

staff

Greene, 7563. staff of the Valuation Office by Mr. Greene. Under these circumstances, your Committee believe that the subject requires a much more careful investigation than they are able to give it, it coming only incidentally before them. They also believe that much more detailed information of the sources of expense should be furnished to the local authorities, either grand juries, or Poor Law unions, and that the correctness of the charge should thus be open to local investigation.

"28. *Malicious Injuries.*—Presentments are at present granted to persons as compensation for losses sustained by reason of malicious injury done to their property. Applications for these presentments must come before the presentment sessions, the grand jury, and finally the judge of assize; but the decision of either, or both, of the first tribunals is not final; the application may be thrown out by the sessions, thrown out by the grand jury, and yet be passed before the judge, or it may be passed before the grand jury and sessions, and yet rejected before the judge. The principle of these presentments your Committee believe to be objectionable; it is the principle of making the parish, barony, or county responsible for the acts of its inhabitants; except under certain circumstances where a criminal act is the work of a large body, such as in cases of riot, this principle has been long ago abandoned in every part of the United Kingdom except Ireland. Every witness examined before your Committee admitted that its continuance in that country does not lead to the discovery of the particular criminals in these cases, and most of the witnesses seem to think that it had the opposite effect. Naturally, it can have no other result; the person injured directs his whole energy and attention to making out a case for compensation, and takes very little trouble to discover the offender; whilst in many parts of Ireland there is a belief that were the criminal discovered, the case for compensation could not be upheld.

M'Dermott, 6367.

"29. The only argument urged in favour of the retention of the system is, that it tends to the repression of these offences. This your Committee does not believe to be substantiated, but, even had it this effect in some cases, yet this would hardly justify the continuance of this exceptional legislation for Ireland. Your Committee believe that many applications for compensation are made in cases where injury has resulted from purely accidental causes. They particularly believe this to be the case where buildings have been destroyed by fire; and even should it be thought desirable in certain cases to preserve the system of granting compensation out of the public funds for injuries of a malicious character, they concur with the Royal Commission of 1842 in recommending that no such compensation should be given for injuries by fire to buildings of greater value than 50 *l.* The proper provision against such injuries is by insurance, and as it is next to impossible, in many cases, to tell whether a fire was accidental or otherwise, these are the cases in which the greatest frauds are attempted to be perpetrated. They also consider that if the system of granting compensation for injuries suffered through the criminal acts of an individual or individuals, is thought at all desirable, the applications for that compensation should be tried before a regularly constituted legal tribunal, such as the quarter sessions or assize courts, and that it should not be left to the decision of parties who are themselves directly or indirectly interested in deciding it in a certain way. If the recommendations of your Committee be carried out, the presentment sessions will represent those who will have to pay the damages, in case the claim for compensation is allowed, and it is manifestly contrary to the principles of the British law that they should have the decision of the case, and thus be judges of their own cause. Moreover, these claims for compensation involve questions intimately mixed up with the criminal law. Each claim involves the charge of criminality against an individual or a district, and the presentment sessions and the grand juries are not the proper tribunals for deciding such questions. Your Committee, therefore, recommend that, under no circumstances, should compensation be granted for damages by fire to buildings of greater value than 50 *l.*, and that in all other cases, in which it is thought desirable to retain this right of seeking compensation from the public for malicious injuries, the applications should be tried before the quarter sessions or the judge of assize.

Collum. M'Carthy Downing.

"30. Several other defects in the details of the grand jury laws have been pointed out to your Committee. Most of them will be found noticed in the evidence and suggestions of Mr. Hill, Mr. Tate, and Mr. Barry. They refer chiefly to the taking and enforcing of contracts, and the apportionment or payment between different baronies and counties.

"31. Your Committee strongly recommend that the principle of accepting the lowest tender should be adhered to.

"32. They recommend that further facilities should be given for suing defaulting contractors and their sureties.

"33. That Section 17 of 16 & 17 Vict. c. 64, should be extended to works of maintenance as well as contracts.

"34. That surety should be given for double the amount approved of for any work, instead of for double the amount of tender.

"35. That the bonds for the performance of contracts should be entered into, not to the Crown, but to the secretary of the grand jury.

"36. That

"36. That power should be given, under certain restrictions, to one barony or county to subscribe to the expenditure on works situated in another.

"37. That the powers of grand juries in dividing or uniting baronies should be extended.

"38. That the county of Cork should be divided for grand jury purposes.

"39. That the half-payment of post roads by the county at large should be abolished, and that either all roads should be paid for by their respective baronies, or otherwise classified according to their importance, and that only works of first-class importance should be charged on the county at large.

"40. That grand juries should not have the power to present any work to the county surveyor, unless a work of maintenance, and that of pressing importance.

"41. For carrying out these and the other recommendations of your Committee, a total remodelling of the Grand Jury Act will be necessary. Already the statutes under which presentments are made are extremely numerous, confusing, and complex, and your Committee would therefore recommend, as far as possible, the embodiment of all their provisions in the one Act. The preamble of the Act 6 & 7 Will. 4, c. 116, appears to have again become true, and your Committee would therefore recommend that a similar course should now be adopted to that followed in 1836."

Draft Report proposed by the Chairman, read a second time, paragraph by paragraph.

Paragraph 1, *agreed to*.

Paragraph 2.—Amendment made.—Another Amendment proposed, in line 18, after the words "from each barony," to leave out the word "but," in order to insert the word "and"—(*General Dunne*).—Question, "That the word 'but' stand part of the paragraph,"—put, and *agreed to*.—Paragraph, as amended, *agreed to*.

Paragraph 3, amended, and *agreed to*.

Paragraph 4.—Amendments made.—Another Amendment proposed, in line 5, to leave out the words "almost exclusively," in order to insert the words "to a certain extent"—(*General Dunne*)—instead thereof.—Question, "That the words proposed to be left out stand part of the paragraph,"—put, and negatived.—Question, That the words "to a certain extent" be there inserted.—The Committee divided:

Ayes, 8.	Noes, 5.
Earl of Mayo.	Mr. Chichester Fortescue.
Mr. Dawson.	Colonel Forde.
Sir Charles Lanyon.	Mr. Blake.
Mr. Leader.	Mr. Gregory.
General Dunne.	Sir Colman O'Loghlen.
Colonel Cooper.	
Mr. Kendall.	
Colonel French.	

Other Amendments made.—Paragraph, as amended, *agreed to*.

Paragraph 5, amended, and *agreed to*.

Paragraph 6.—Amendments made.—Another Amendment proposed, after the words "pure and economical," at the end of the last Amendment, to insert the words "and in practice has worked satisfactorily"—(*Sir Charles Lanyon*).—Question put, "That those words be there inserted."—The Committee divided:

Ayes, 6.	Noes, 7.
Earl of Mayo.	Mr. Chichester Fortescue.
Sir Charles Lanyon.	Mr. Dawson.
Colonel Forde.	Mr. Maguire.
Colonel Cooper.	Mr. Leader.
Mr. Kendall.	Mr. Blake.
Colonel French.	Mr. Gregory.
	Sir Colman O'Loghlen.

Paragraph 6.—Other Amendments made.—Another Amendment proposed, to leave out from the words, "taxing bodies," in line 22, to the end of the paragraph, in order to insert the following words: "Nevertheless, your Committee believe that it would be most desirable that the fiscal should be altogether separated from the criminal business of grand juries, and therefore recommend that the sheriff, as at present, should summon a body for the discharge of the former, but that for the performance of fiscal duties, a special body should be constituted, to be appointed by the magistrates

magistrates and the ratepayers, one-half to be elected by the magistrates and the other half by the ratepayers, as proposed in the Bill introduced by the Government in 1849 and again in a Bill introduced in 1860. The Committee recommend that the Board thus formed should be a continuous one, half to go out by rotation each year, but to be eligible for re-election, and that Peers should be competent to serve. Very considerable advantages would result from this change, in the opinion of the Committee.

"In the first place, they submit that it is just in principle that a body charged with such important functions should be appointed by the ratepayers and not by an almost irresponsible officer like the High Sheriff. Benefit, they think, would also result from the body so formed being permanent, instead of its existence terminating at the end of each assizes, as occasions might arise between one assizes and another, often an interval of eight months, when it would be desirable to summon such a Board for the discussion of matters which might arise connected with the fiscal affairs of the county."—(Mr. *Blake*)—instead thereof.—Question put, That the words "under these circumstances, they do not consider it necessary to recommend the," stand part of the paragraph.—The Committee divided:

Ayes, 11.	Noes, 2.
Earl of Mayo.	Mr. Maguire.
Mr. Chichester Fortescue.	Mr. Blake.
Mr. Dawson.	
Sir Charles Lanyon.	
Colonel Forde.	
Mr. Leader.	
Mr. Gregory.	
Sir Colman O'Loghlen.	
General Dunne.	
Colonel Cooper.	
Colonel French.	

Other Amendments made.—Paragraph, as amended, *agreed to*.

Paragraph 7, amended, and *agreed to*.

Paragraph 8.—Amendment proposed, in line 1, to leave out the word "former," in order to insert the word "latter"—(General *Dunne*)—instead thereof.—Question put, that the word "former" stand part of the paragraph.—The Committee divided:

Ayes, 12.	Noes, 1.
Earl of Mayo.	General Dunne.
Mr. Chichester Fortescue.	
Mr. Dawson.	
Sir Charles Lanyon.	
Mr. Maguire.	
Colonel Forde.	
Mr. Leader.	
Mr. Blake.	
Mr. Gregory.	
Sir Colman O'Loghlen.	
Colonel Cooper.	
Colonel French.	

Other Amendments made.—Another Amendment proposed, in line 14, after the words "at any session," to leave out the words "should not exceed the number of elected cesspayers"—(General *Dunne*).—Question put, That the words proposed to be left out stand part of the paragraph.—The Committee divided:

Ayes, 11.	Noes, 2.
Earl of Mayo.	Sir Charles Lanyon.
Mr. Chichester Fortescue.	General Dunne.
Mr. Dawson.	
Mr. Maguire.	
Colonel Forde.	
Mr. Leader.	
Mr. Blake.	
Mr. Gregory.	
Sir Colman O'Loghlen.	
Colonel Cooper.	
Colonel French.	

Further consideration of paragraph 8, *postponed*.

[Adjourned to Thursday next, at Twelve o'clock.

Thursday, 2nd July 1868.

MEMBERS PRESENT:

The O'Conor Don in the Chair.

Mr. Gregory.	Colonel Cooper.
Colonel Forde.	Mr. Blake.
Colonel French.	Earl of Mayo.
Mr. Dawson.	Mr. Kendall.
General Dunne.	Mr. Chichester Fortescue.
Sir Colman O'Loghlen.	Sir C. Lanyon.
Mr. Leader.	Mr. Maguire.

Paragraph 8, as amended, further considered.

Another Amendment made.—Another Amendment proposed, in line 18, after the words "their own body," to insert the words "an equal number of magistrates and cess-payers"—(*Colonel Cooper*).—Question put, That those words be there inserted.—The Committee divided:

Ayes, 8.	Noes, 2.
Earl of Mayo.	General Dunne.
Mr. Dawson.	Colonel French.
Colonel Forde.	
Mr. Leader.	
Mr. Gregory.	
Sir Colman O'Loghlen.	
Colonel Cooper.	
Mr. Kendall.	

Paragraph, as amended, agreed to.

Paragraph 9.—Amendments made.—Another Amendment proposed, in line 5, after the words "efficient in its construction," to leave out the words, "it appears from the evidence that, as a general rule, the grand jury represents the landed property of the county, and your Committee think it eminently desirable that there should be some such body to control and check the transactions of the Sessions"—(*General Dunne*).—Question put, That the words proposed to be left out stand part of the paragraph.—The Committee divided:

Ayes, 12.	Noes, 1.
Earl of Mayo.	General Dunne.
Mr. Chichester Fortescue.	
Mr. Dawson.	
Sir Charles Lanyon.	
Colonel Forde.	
Mr. Leader.	
Mr. Blake.	
Mr. Gregory.	
Sir Colman O'Loghlen.	
Colonel Cooper.	
Mr. Kendall.	
Colonel French.	

Other Amendments made.—Another Amendment proposed, to leave out from the words, "lead to extravagance," in line 11, down to words, "the evidence," in line 16—(*General Dunne*).—Question put, That the words "To obtain this desirable supervision, some witnesses have recommended the appointment of a public commission, corresponding to that of the Poor Law; whilst Lord John Browne, one of the witnesses, recommended that a body elected out of the magistrates of the county by the magistrates might be substituted for the Grand Jury. Your Committee do not see that there is any reason for" stand part of the paragraph.—The Committee divided:

Ayes, 11.	Noes, 3.
Earl of Mayo.	General Dunne.
Mr. Chichester Fortescue.	Mr. Kendall.
Mr. Dawson.	Colonel French.
Sir Charles Lanyon.	
Mr. Maguire.	
Colonel Forde.	
Mr. Leader.	
Mr. Blake.	
Mr. Gregory.	
Sir Colman O'Loghlen.	
Colonel Cooper.	

Other Amendments made.—Paragraph, as amended, agreed to.

Amendment proposed, after paragraph 9, to insert paragraph 13—(*The Chairman*).—Paragraph read, as follows: "Your Committee, however, consider that no person should be eligible to serve as a grand juror who was not connected, either by residence or property, with the county; that lists of all qualified persons of each barony should be prepared, and that no barony should have two representatives on the Grand Jury until one representative had answered from each of the other baronies, or until the list of all the qualified persons therein had been exhausted."

Amendment proposed in line 2, after word "connected," to leave out the word "either," and after the words "by residence," to leave out the words "or property"—(*Sir Colman O'Loghlen*).—Question put, "That the words proposed to be left out stand part of the paragraph."—The Committee divided:

Ayes, 12.	Noes, 2.
Earl of Mayo.	Mr. Maguire.
Mr. Chichester Fortescue.	Sir Colman O'Loghlen.
Mr. Dawson.	
Sir Charles Lanyon.	
Colonel Forde.	
Mr. Leader.	
Mr. Blake.	
Mr. Gregory.	
General Dunne.	
Colonel Cooper.	
Mr. Kendall.	
Colonel French.	

Amendment made—Paragraph, as amended, *agreed to*, and inserted.

Paragraph 10.—Amendment proposed, in line 5, after the words "fact that," to insert the words, "as a general rule"—(*Mr. Chichester Fortescue*).—Question put, "That those words be there inserted."—The Committee divided:

Ayes, 5.	Noes, 8.
Mr. Chichester Fortescue.	Earl of Mayo.
Mr. Dawson.	Sir Charles Lanyon.
Mr. Maguire.	Colonel Forde
Mr. Blake.	Mr. Leader.
Sir Colman O'Loghlen.	Mr. Gregory.
	General Dunne.
	Colonel Cooper
	Colonel French.

Another Amendment proposed, in line 6, after the words "by the owner," to insert the following words:—"That it is a matter of much doubt, whether dividing the rate would in any manner benefit the tenant, inasmuch as it would increase the pecuniary demands on them as ratepayers. The Committee do not deem it advisable to recommend such division"—(*Colonel French*).—Question put, "That those words be there inserted."—The Committee divided:

Ayes, 2.	Noes, 11.
General Dunne.	Earl of Mayo.
Colonel French.	Mr. Chichester Fortescue.
	Mr. Dawson.
	Sir Charles Lanyon.
	Mr. Maguire.
	Colonel Forde.
	Mr. Leader.
	Mr. Blake.
	Mr. Gregory.
	Sir Colman O'Loghlen.
	Colonel Cooper.

Another Amendment proposed, in line 6, after the words "believe that," to insert the words, "in respect of all future lettings"—(*Earl of Mayo*).—Question put, "That those words be there inserted."—The Committee divided:

Ayes, 9.	Noes, 4.
Earl of Mayo.	Mr. Chichester Fortescue.
Mr. Dawson.	Mr. Maguire.
Sir Charles Lanyon.	Mr. Blake.
Colonel Forde.	Sir Colman O'Loghlen.
Mr. Leader.	
Mr. Gregory.	
General Dunne.	
Colonel Cooper.	
Colonel French.	

Word

Words *inserted*.—Another Amendment made.—Another Amendment proposed, in line 21, after the words, "of the country," to insert the words, "or that in cases of excessive competition such a result will always follow"—(Mr. *Chichester Fortescue*).—Question put, "That those words be there inserted."—The Committee divided:

Ayes, 5.	Noes, 8.
Mr. Chichester Fortescue.	Earl of Mayo.
Mr. Maguire.	Mr. Dawson.
Mr. Blake.	Sir Charles Lanyon.
Mr. Gregory.	Colonel Forde.
Sir Colman O'Loghlen.	Mr. Leader.
	General Dunne.
	Colonel Cooper.
	Colonel French.

Other Amendments made.—Paragraph, as amended, *agreed to*.

Paragraph 11, *postponed*.

Paragraph 12, amended, and *agreed to*.

Paragraph 14, amended, and *agreed to*.

Paragraph 15.—Amendments made.—Another Amendment proposed, in line 7, after the word "alone," to insert the words "and a residence in Ireland."—(Sir *Colman O'Loghlen*).—Question put, "That those words be there inserted."—The Committee divided:

Ayes, 5.	Noes, 8.
Mr. Maguire.	Earl of Mayo.
Mr. Blake.	Mr. Chichester Fortescue.
Sir Colman O'Loghlen.	Mr. Dawson.
General Dunne.	Sir Charles Lanyon.
Colonel French.	Colonel Forde.
	Mr. Leader.
	Mr. Gregory.
	Colonel Cooper.

Other Amendments made.—Another Amendment proposed, after the words, "occupiers of land," in line 21, to leave out the following words, "That occupiers rated at or below 4*l*. should be altogether exempted from the payment of the rate"—(Colonel *French*).—Question put, "That the word 'that' stand part of the paragraph."—The Committee divided:

Ayes, 11.	Noes, 2.
Earl of Mayo.	Colonel Forde.
Mr. Chichester Fortescue.	Colonel French.
Mr. Dawson.	
Sir Charles Lanyon.	
Mr. Maguire.	
Mr. Leader.	
Mr. Blake.	
Mr. Gregory.	
Sir Colman O'Loghlen.	
General Dunne.	
Colonel Cooper.	

Other Amendments made.—Paragraph, as amended, *agreed to*.

[Adjourned to To-morrow, at Twelve o'clock.

Paragraph 16, amended, and *agreed to.*

Paragraph 17, *agreed to.*

Paragraph 18, amended, and *agreed to.*

Postponed paragraph 11, amended, and *agreed to.*

Amendment proposed, after paragraph 11, to insert the following paragraph:—"That, as considerable difficulty often arises in the collection of the county cess from the occupiers of very small tenements, and as that class is composed of the poorest portion of the community, often little removed from paupers, your Committee believe that the occupiers of all tenements rated at or below 4 *l.* should be exempted from the payment of the county cess, which, in such cases, should be paid like the poor rates, by the immediate lessor. If this recommendation were adopted, care should be taken to except from its operation such small tenements as might at the time of the passing of an amended Grand Jury Act be held under a lease"—(The *Chairman*).—Question proposed, "That the paragraph be inserted in the proposed Report."—Amendment proposed, to leave out from the word "that," in line 1, to the end of the proposed paragraph, in order to add the following words:—"The exemption of all persons rated at or below 4 *l.* would largely add to the pecuniary demands of the small tenantry by the addition to their rents, which the landlord would, to recoup himself, of course make. That it must materially tend to the ejectment of small holders, which in the present state of emigration from Ireland is not advisable, and that it would brand as paupers a large class of the present cesspayers, and stand as a bar in future to them of acquiring the electoral franchise, even for associated cesspayers, and therefore it is not recommended by your Committee"—(Colonel *French*)—instead thereof.—Question put, "That the words proposed to be left out stand part of the proposed paragraph,"—put, and *agreed to.*

Main Question put, and *agreed to.*

Paragraph 19, *postponed.*

Paragraph 20.—Amendment proposed, in line 2, to leave out the words "ought to," in order to insert the word, "might,"—(Colonel *French*)—instead thereof.—Question put, "That the words proposed to be left out stand part of the paragraph."—The Committee divided:

Ayes, 9.	Noes, 2.
Earl of Mayo.	Sir Colman O'Loghlen.
Mr. Chichester Fortescue.	Colonel French.
Mr. Dawson.	
Sir Charles Lanyon.	
Colonel Forde.	
Mr. Blake.	
Mr. Gregory.	
General Dunne.	
Colonel Cooper.	

Other Amendments made.—Paragraph, as amended, *agreed to.*

Paragraph 21.—Amendment proposed, in line 2, to leave out from the words, "It appears," down to the words "be filled up," in line 7, in order to insert the following words: "to your Committee that"—(Earl of *Mayo*)—instead thereof.—Question put, "That the words proposed to be left out stand part of the paragraph."—The Committee divided:

Ayes, 2.	Noes, 9.
Mr. Blake.	Earl of Mayo.
Mr. Gregory.	Mr. Chichester Fortescue.
	Mr. Dawson.
	Sir Charles Lanyon.
	Colonel Forde.
	Sir Colman O'Loghlen.
	General Dunne.
	Colonel Cooper.
	Colonel French.

Words inserted.—Other Amendments made.—Paragraph, as amended, *agreed to.*

Paragraphs 22, 23, and 24, amended, and *agreed to.*

Paragraph 25.—Amendment proposed, to leave out from the words "all Ireland," in line 16, to end of the paragraph, in order to add the following words: "To enable your Committee to recommend any mode of reducing this very heavy expenditure would have required a complete examination of the whole system of lunatic asylums in Ireland, which your Committee have not been able to undertake"—(Sir *Colman O'Loghlen*.)—Question put, "That the words proposed to be left out stand part of the paragraph"—The Committee divided:

Ayes, 1.	Noes, 9.
Colonel French.	Earl of Mayo.
	Mr. Chichester Fortescue.
	Sir Charles Lanyon.
	Mr. Maguire.
	Colonel Forde.
	Mr. Blake.
	Mr. Gregory.
	Sir Colman O'Loghlen.
	General Dunne.

Word inserted.—Paragraph as amended, *agreed to.*

Paragraph 26, negatived.

[Adjourned to Monday next, at Twelve o'clock.

Monday, 6th *July* 1868.

MEMBERS PRESENT:

The O'Conor Don in the Chair.

Colonel French.	Mr. Leader.
Colonel Forde.	Mr. Dawson.
Sir Charles Lanyon.	Mr. Maguire.
The Earl of Mayo.	Mr. Gregory.
Colonel Cooper.	Mr. Blake.
Mr. Chichester Fortescue.	Sir Colman O'Loghlen.

Proposed paragraph 19.—Amendment proposed at the end of the paragraph to add the following words: "Your Committee are of opinion that with reference to the mode of appointment of county surveyors some alteration is desirable. The existing Act provides for the competitive examination of candidates whenever a vacancy occurs. This arrangement would necessarily create considerable delay in filling up the appointment. Your Committee, therefore, recommend that there always should be the names of two candidates (certified as provided in the Act by the examiners) in the hands of the Government ready for filling the appointment immediately on its becoming vacant"—(*Sir Charles Lanyon*).—Amendment proposed to proposed amendment to leave out the words "names of two" in order to insert "name of one"—(*Colonel French*)—instead thereof.—Question put, "That the words proposed to be left out stand part of the proposed amendment."—The Committee divided:

Ayes, 5.	Noes, 4.
Mr. Dawson.	Earl of Mayo.
Sir Charles Lanyon.	Mr. Chichester Fortescue.
Mr. Leader.	Colonel Forde.
Mr. Gregory.	Colonel French.
Colonel Cooper.	

Main Question put, and *agreed to.*

Paragraph, as amended, *agreed to.*

Paragraph 27.—Amendment proposed to leave out from the word "evidence" in line 4, down to the word "requires" in line 23, in order to insert the following words: "But they find this to be an increasing expenditure over which neither the grand jury nor any local body have any control, and they are satisfied that, while the general valuation of Ireland has been conducted with great ability, and has conferred great advantages on the country, yet its annual revision"—(Mr. *Chichester Fortescue*)—instead thereof.—Question put, "That the words proposed to be left out stand part of the paragraph"—put, and negatived.

Words inserted.—Other amendments made.—Paragraph, as amended, *agreed to.*

Paragraph 28.—Amendment proposed in line 7, to leave out from the words "before the judge" to the end of the paragraph in order to insert the following words:—"Conflicting evidence has been taken before your Committee on the subject of these presentments for malicious injuries; on the one side it has been contended that by this system of compensation, the innocent may be made to pay for the guilty, and that as the injured person looks forward to be indemnified for the loss he has sustained, the detection of the offender becomes a matter of small importance to him. On the other hand, it is urged by witnesses of great experience, that the present state of the law does away with inducements to commit malicious injuries, which generally result from the ill-will of neighbours. It is manifest Lord J. Browne, Mr. Bolster, Mr. Baldwin.

that a man will be likely to abstain from acts of destruction towards the property of his neighbour, when he is aware that not only will the person injured be, in all probability, indemnified for his loss, but that he, the offender, may have to contribute to that indemnity. All the neighbours have thus an interest in preventing malicious injury to property, and your Committee are of opinion that to do away with the present system, guarded as it is from abuse by the various checks above referred to, would be injurious to the security of property, more especially of the farming classes in Ireland. Your Committee recommend, therefore, the retention of the present system, subject to the following alterations, viz., that no larger sum than 300l. be given as compensation for injuries to buildings by fire, and also that the holding of the injured person shall be exempted from the compensation rate"—(Mr. *Gregory*)—instead thereof.

Question put, "That the words proposed to be left out stand part of the paragraph."—The Committee divided:

Ayes, 2.	Noes, 10.
Mr. Dawson.	Earl of Mayo.
Sir Colman O'Loghlen.	Mr. Chichester Fortescue.
	Sir Charles Lanyon.
	Mr. Maguire.
	Colonel Forde.
	Mr. Leader.
	Mr. Blake.
	Mr. Gregory.
	Colonel Cooper.
	Colonel French.

Question proposed, "That the proposed words be there added."—Amendment proposed to proposed Amendment, to leave out the words, "Guarded as it is from abuse by the various checks above referred to"—(*Sir Colman O'Loghlen*).

Question put, "That the words proposed to be left out stand part of the proposed Amendment."—The Committee divided:

Ayes, 8.	Noes, 4.
Earl of Mayo.	Mr. Dawson.
Mr. Chichester Fortescue.	Mr. Maguire.
Sir Charles Lanyon.	Mr. Blake.
Colonel Forde.	Sir Colman O'Loghlen.
Mr. Leader.	
Mr. Gregory.	
Colonel Cooper.	
Colonel French.	

Another Amendment proposed to proposed Amendment, to leave out the words, "no larger sum than 300l. be given as compensation for injuries to buildings by fire, and also that"—(Earl of *Mayo*).

Question put, "That the words 'no larger sum than 300l. be given as compensation for injuries to buildings by fire,' stand part of the proposed Amendment."—The Committee divided:

Ayes, 6.	Noes, 6.
Mr. Chichester Fortescue.	Earl of Mayo.
Mr. Dawson.	Sir Charles Lanyon.
Colonel Forde.	Mr. Maguire.
Mr. Gregory.	Mr. Leader.
Sir Colman O'Loghlen.	Mr. Blake.
Colonel French.	Colonel Cooper.

Whereupon the *Chairman* declared himself with the Ayes.

Another Amendment proposed to proposed Amendment, after the words "buildings by fire," to insert the words, "provided that the parties could have protected themselves by insurance"—(Mr. *Blake*).—Question put, "That those words be there inserted in the proposed Amendment."—The Committee divided:

Ayes, 3.	Noes, 8.
Mr. Maguire.	Earl of Mayo.
Mr. Leader.	Mr. Chichester Fortescue.
Mr. Blake.	Sir Charles Lanyon.
	Colonel Forde.
	Mr. Gregory.
	Sir Colman O'Loghlen.
	Colonel Cooper.
	Colonel French.

Original Question, "That the proposed words be there added,"—put, and agreed to.

Question

Question put, "That this paragraph, as amended, stand part of the proposed Report." —The Committee divided:

Ayes, 8.	Noes, 3.
Earl of Mayo.	Mr. Maguire.
Mr. Chichester Fortescue.	Mr. Leader.
Sir Charles Lanyon.	Mr. Blake.
Colonel Forde.	
Mr. Gregory.	
Sir Colman O'Loghlen.	
Colonel Cooper.	
Colonel French.	

Paragraph 29, *disagreed to.*

Paragraph 30, *agreed to.*

Paragraphs 31 and 32, amended, and *agreed to.*

Paragraph 33 amended, and *agreed to.*

Paragraphs 34, 35, and 36, amended, and *agreed to.*

Paragraph 37, *agreed to.*

Paragraph 38, *disagreed to.*

Paragraph 39.—Amendments made.

Another Amendment proposed, to leave out from the words, "respective baronies," in line 8, to the end of paragraph.—(*Earl of Mayo*.)—Question put, "That the words proposed to be left out stand part of the paragraph."—The Committee divided:

Ayes, 5.	Noes, 5.
Mr. Chichester Fortescue.	Earl of Mayo.
Mr. Maguire.	Sir Charles Lanyon.
Sir Colman O'Loghlen.	Colonel Forde.
Colonel Cooper.	Mr. Blake.
Colonel French.	Mr. Gregory.

Whereupon the *Chairman* declared himself with the Noes.

Paragraph, as amended, *agreed to.*

Paragraph 40.—Amendment proposed, in line 8, to leave out the words "and that," in order to insert "or"—(*Sir Colman O'Loghlen*)—instead thereof.—Question put, "That the words proposed to be left out stand part of the paragraph."—The Committee divided:

Ayes, 7.	Noes, 3.
Earl of Mayo.	Mr. Chichester Fortescue.
Sir Charles Lanyon.	Sir Colman O'Loghlen.
Mr. Maguire.	Colonel Cooper.
Colonel Forde.	
Mr. Blake.	
Mr. Gregory.	
Colonel French.	

Paragraph, as amended, *agreed to.*

Amendment proposed, after paragraph 40, to insert the following paragraph:—"That superannuation may be given, at the option of the grand jury, to county officers who have employed their whole time in the service of the county, but not otherwise, and that such superannuation shall be regulated on the scale laid down by the Civil Service Superannuation Act"—(*Mr. Gregory*).—Question, "That this paragraph be inserted in the proposed Report,"—put, and *agreed to.*

Amendment proposed, after the last paragraph, to insert the following paragraph:—"That it is desirable to have the treasurers' accounts audited in their respective counties. Your Committee recommend that this duty should be performed by the auditors employed under the Poor Law"—(*Colonel Forde*).—Question, "That this paragraph be inserted in the proposed Report,"—put, and *agreed to.*

Paragraph 41, *agreed to.*

Ordered, To Report, together with the Minutes of Evidence and Appendix.

EXPENSES OF WITNESSES.

Name of Witness.	Profession or Condition.	From whence Summoned.	Number of Days Absent from Home, under Orders of Committee.	Expenses of Journey to London and back.	Allowance during Absence from Home.	Total Expenses allowed to Witness.
				£. s. d.	£. s. d.	£. s. d.
Mr. John Hill - - -	Civil Engineer	Ennis - -	3	6 – –	9 9 –	15 9 –
Mr. William Johnson - -	Solicitor - -	Cork - -	9	5 15 –	16 16 –	22 12 –
Mr. Daniel Cronin Coltsmann	Justice of the Peace	Kerry - -	3	6 – –	3 3 –	9 3 –
Mr. Alexander Tate - -	Civil Engineer -	Belfast (twice) -	9	9 15 –	20 4 –	24 19 –
Mr. Francis A. Leigh - -	Justice of the Peace	Wexford - -	4	6 – –	4 4 –	10 4 –
Mr. Wm. D'Esterre Parker -	Solicitor - -	Cork - -	5	5 – –	10 10 –	15 10 –
Mr. Uniacke [illegible] Mackey	Gentleman - -	Cork - -	8	5 5 –	8 8 –	13 11 –
Mr. Henry E. Wynne - -	Secretary to the Grand Jury.	Wexford - -	5	6 5 –	5 5 –	11 10 –
Mr. Edwin Sadleir - -	Secretary to the Grand Jury.	Tipperary -	6	7 15 –	6 6 –	14 1 –
Mr. Henry Brett - - -	Civil Engineer -	Detained in London.	3	- -	9 9 –	9 9 –
Mr. Wm. Bolster - -	Agriculturist -	Limerick - -	5	5 10 –	5 5 –	10 15 –
Mr. John Lentaigne - -	Inspector General of Prisons.	Dublin - -	5	5 10 –	5 5 –	10 15 –
Mr. Macarthy Downing -	Solicitor - -	Skibbereen (Co. Cork).	7	9 11 10	14 14 –	24 5 10
Mr. Paul Davis - - -	Solicitor -	Edinburgh -	4	6 – –	8 8 –	14 8 –
Dr. John Nugent - - -	M.D. - - -	Dublin - -	5	5 10 –	5 5 –	11 15 –
Mr. Henry Baker - -	Gentleman - -	Dublin - -	4	5 10 –	4 4 –	9 14 –
Mr. J. E. Roach - - -	Solicitor - -	Dublin - -	4	5 10 –	8 8 –	13 18 –
Mr. Robert A. Hayes - -	M.D. - - -	[illegible] - -	4	6 – –	12 12 –	18 12 –
Mr. John O'Reilly - -	Surveyor - -	Dublin - -	4	5 – –	8 8 –	13 8 –
Mr. John MacDermott -	Solicitor - -	Boyle - -	5	10 – –	7 – –	17 10 –
Mr. John Adams - - -	[illegible] - -	Ballymoney -	5	8 – –	2 5 –	10 5 –
Mr. John Hamilton - -	Deputy Clerk of Peace.	Limerick - -	6	6 – –	5 5 –	11 5 –
					Total - - - £.	323 1 10

MINUTES OF EVIDENCE.

LIST OF WITNESSES.

Friday, 27th March 1868.

MEMBERS PRESENT:

Mr. Blake.	Mr. Gregory.
Lord John Browne.	Mr. Herbert.
Colonel Cooper.	Mr. Kendall.
General Dunne.	Sir Charles Lanyon.
Colonel Forde.	Mr. Leader.
Mr. Chichester Fortescue.	The O'Conor Don.

THE O'CONOR DON IN THE CHAIR.

MR. P. BURROWES SHARKEY, called in; and Examined.

Mr. *P. Burrowes Sharkey.* — 27 March 1868.

1. *Chairman.*] YOU are a Solicitor and Parliamentary Agent, I believe?—I am.

2. And you reside in London, do you not?—I reside in London.

3. You have had some acquaintance with the operation of the grand jury laws in Ireland, have you not?—Yes, I have had many years' experience of the working of the Act of 1836, the Grand Jury Code, since that period.

4. You acted as secretary to the grand jury for the county of Roscommon, under your father, I believe, for several years?—I was acting secretary of the grand jury for the county of Roscommon for, I think, 8 or 10 years.

5. Your father held that office for a very long period, did he not?—My father held the office up to his death. He was for 53 years, I think, the secretary to the grand jury for the county of Roscommon.

6. And at one time he was also the clerk of the peace, was he not?—At one time he discharged the double duties of secretary of the grand jury, and clerk of the peace.

7. Will you describe to the Committee the practical working of the grand jury laws; first, as to the mode of obtaining a presentment, they have to go through two courses, have they not?—I propose to describe to the Committee, in a popular narrative, as much as possible divested of Act of Parliament language, the present working of the grand jury system in Ireland; and with that view I have, both for the convenience of the Committee and for my own, subdivided the subject, and put it under three heads. Under the first head I deal with the grand jury, the mode in which the grand jury is constituted, and its functions, both fiscal and criminal; under the next head I propose to deal with the constitution of the baronial presentment sessions, and also with its functions; under the next head I propose to deal with the county at large presentment sessions, and with its functions; and under the next head I propose to describe to the Committee the adjourned sessions, and its constitution, both in baronies and in counties at large, and the duties which are discharged by it. I then propose to point out to the Committee the evils or defects of the present system; and, with the sanction of the Committee, respectfully to suggest such remedial measures as occur to me to be desirable.

8. Will you proceed with the first head of the subject, as to the constitution of the grand juries?—I will. The sheriff having regard to the business to be transacted at the assizes, fixes a day for the empannelling of the grand jury previous to the opening of the commission, such day not being more than five clear days, nor less than one; and he summons a sufficient number of persons qualified according to law to serve as grand jurors to attend upon the day so fixed. The persons so summoned are required by the statute to attend under penalties and forfeitures, and they are also required to serve, subject to the like penalties and forfeitures, until they are discharged. On the day appointed for the empannelling of the grand jury the sheriff, aided by the clerk of the Crown, proceeds to empannel and to swear the grand jury. I now come to the mode in which that body is constituted: The Act of Parliament regulating it, is the 6 & 7 Will. 4, c. 116, s. 31, amended in some slight particulars by the 7 Will. 4 & 1 Vict. c. 2, s. 9. The sheriff in framing the panel is required to place first on the panel for each barony the name of either a 50 *l.* freeholder, or a 100 *l.* leaseholder, so that one fit and competent person having lands of the

Mr. P. Baronne Sherley.

27 March 1868.

the value mentioned and resident in each barony, if the same can be found therein, shall be placed upon the panel. Under the first Act the sheriff was obliged to follow the rule laid down for him in cases where the county consisted of nine baronies. The subsequent Act of Parliament applied it to the case of all counties irrespective of the number of baronies, and at this stage, with a view to a subject, which I shall bring before the Committee subsequently, I would direct their attention to the fact that the sheriff is only required under the statute which I have named to go through the form of calling representatives for each barony; he is not bound to go on calling until he gets a representative. He complies with the law by placing a representative on his panel for each barony, irrespective of the question whether or not that gentleman attends to discharge his duties. Having thus selected one fit and proper person for each of the baronies, he then proceeds to complete the panel in the language of the Act of Parliament (and I believe it is the only time when I need quote the language of the Act of Parliament) "in such a manner as now by law authorised and directed."

9. The grand jury existed as a legal body before this Act was passed, did it not?—The grand jury existed under an Act of very old date, for the purpose of the criminal business of the county, and it existed irrespective of the fiscal business. The Act under which it existed for criminal business was the 54 Geo. 3, c. 67; but it existed for the double purpose of civil and criminal duties long prior to the Act which I am now discussing. It existed under an Act of the 59 Geo. 3, c. 84, but all the prior Acts relating to the grand juries were repealed by the first section of the 6 & 7 Will. 4, c. 116. The preamble of this Act goes on to say, that "it is desirable that a uniform system of raising money by the presentment of grand juries should be established in all counties in Ireland;" and then, by implication, it goes on through its various sections to repeal all the previously existing Grand Jury Acts. But I may mention that there are certain sections of those former Acts which are saved. Then the persons so placed upon the panel are called in open Court, and those answering, having been sworn by the clerk of the Crown, constitute the grand jury or the grand inquest of the county. That is the manner in which the grand jury is at present selected and constituted. I now proceed to call the attention of the Committee to the functions of the grand jury so constituted. The Act regulating in very great detail the duties of the grand jury is the Act of 6 & 7 Will. 4, c. 116, as amended by the Act of 7 Will. 4, c. 2; and so amended, I may state to the Committee, that it constitutes the general law by which all grand juries, except those of the county of the city of Dublin, are now governed in the discharge of their fiscal duties. The grand jury, when empanelled and sworn as mentioned, proceed with the fiscal business, which must be concluded before the opening of the commission. In practice they then proceed with the presentments for public money which come before them. Having disposed of these duties they then proceed to fix the time and place for holding the presentment sessions of the various baronies and of the county at large prior to the next assizes. They direct the number of copies of the schedule of applications to be printed and distributed, and fix the number of persons within the limits of twelve and five to be associated with the justices at the baronial presentment sessions, of which I have previously spoken. The grand jury then proceeds to make out (from a list of 100 names previously delivered in to their secretary by the high constable of each barony), a list of double the number of persons, previously determined upon, to form the list of associated cesspayers at the succeeding baronial sessions; and in making out that list, they are bound to have regard to the persons who have paid the highest sums for grand jury rates under the last applotment, and to strike out of the high constable's return the names of one-half the persons nominated at the previous sessions, and who acted at the previous presentment sessions, in order to prevent the same persons serving a second time as associated cesspayers.

10. Sir *Charles Lanyon*.] Are you aware that grand juries act differently in different counties upon that section?—I believe that in different counties there are various readings of that section. The next duty that devolves upon the grand jury is to open tenders, and to declare contracts for works exceeding 100 *l.*, where the presentment sessions has referred to the grand jury that duty. It is the practice in the county with which I have familiar acquaintance, that in all cases where the works exceed 100 *l.* the duty is cast upon the grand jury of opening the tenders. At this stage it may be well to call attention upon this point to an Act of Parliament which was subsequently passed, and which bears immediately upon that question of opening the tenders in certain cases by the grand jury. It is an Act of 20 & 21 Vict. c. 15, and it provides for the case which very frequently happens, of there being no persons at the adjourned sessions desirous of taking contracts, or of entering into contracts for the completion of works previously approved of; and the amendment of the law in that regard saves those cases where, previously to the passing of that Act, when no contractor offered, the works so approved of and sanctioned at the baronial sessions fell to the ground.

11. *Chairman*.] Under that Act the county surveyor is enabled to take a contract, is he not?—In the second contingency he is. The first contingency is, that if there are no contractors at the presentment sessions the works are then referred to the grand jury, and then if before the grand jury a contractor does not offer, the grand jury by an order can throw the obligation of executing the works in question upon the county surveyor. The next duty that devolves upon the grand jury is in the case of new roads, where an application is made for a new road involving the compulsory taking of land for the purpose, which has been approved of at presentment sessions. The grand jury goes through a formal duty in certifying the application. It has not under the statute any discretion at this stage of the proceedings. The application comes up from the baronial sessions approved of, and the foreman is bound to certify; the effect of that certification being to send back the application to the then ensuing baronial sessions to be a second time dealt with upon its merits. The next duty which we come to is the presentment of money by the grand jury, and this is one of the cases where the grand jury exercise the power of paying away public money without any previous application to presentment sessions. I may here mention that there are very few cases where the

the grand jury are vested with that authority irrespective of the will or the wish of the ratepayers. The grand jury transacts there, in general terms, all business relating to presentments for raising money to public works, contracts, and the local concerns of the county: and they consider and decide upon all applications made at sessions; and receive and obtain all legal and pertinent evidence tendered for or against the making of any presentment, or in any way relating thereto; and they are specially prevented from making a presentment for any work, unless the application for that work has been previously approved of at the sessions. They are, however, authorised to make presentments for the levy of public money without previous application to the sessions, in cases which I shall mention to the Committee hereafter; the applications for officers' salaries, with the exception of two, do not go before the presentment sessions; the application for them is made to the grand jury, and the grand jury, without any previous application to the presentment sessions, are authorised to make presentments for those salaries. It has also the power, without previous application at presentment sessions, to make presentments for money which has been certified by the executive Government in a form prescribed, money expended by the Commissioners of Public Works in Ireland. It has also the power to present, without any application to presentment sessions, all monies for the maintenance and the support of lunatic asylums, and in certain other specified cases. The grand jury are by law precluded from making any presentment for any work which has not previously been approved of at the presentment sessions.

11. Is it not the case that those presentments which you say the grand jury can make without application at the present sessions are imperative upon the grand jury, and that they have no discretion with regard to them?—They would fall within that category.

12. *Lord John Browne.*] Then the grand jury have no power to originate those presentments? —They have no power to originate them; they are mere machines. In fact, the functions of the grand jury, in respect to applications made to presentment sessions, are limited to the approval or rejection of the same as approved of or modified at the sessions, and to the presentment of such sums or the annulling of them. In point of fact, they must either reject or accept the decision of the sessions in those matters in its integrity.

13. *Chairman.*] They cannot alter a presentment made by the presentment sessions?—They cannot. There are other cases, which I may as well mention here, which come within the 20 & 21 Vict., where the county surveyor is required to put roads in repair, where a contractor does not tender to do it. There the grand jury make a presentment for the work in question; but the work has been previously approved of. Although no contractor has been selected at the sessions, still the grand jury have the power of making a presentment in favour of the county surveyor, to enable him to execute the work in question.

14. *Lord John Browne.*] Do you mean in accordance with orders from the Post Office?—No.

15. Then the money has been passed at sessions previously?—The money has been passed at sessions previously. To put it beyond all doubt except in the cases referred to, the grand jury have no power in law to present public money, and to tax the ratepayers for any purpose whatever, which has not previously received the sanction of the ratepayers at the baronial, or the county at large presentment sessions.

Mr. *P. Barrows Sharkey.*

17 March 18[illegible].

16. *Chairman.*] Excepting in those cases of imperative presentments to which you have alluded, where they have no discretion?—Exactly; the grand jury appoint a secretary, whom they may remove at any time without assigning a reason, and it presents money certified to have been expended by the Public Works Commissioners, in putting small coach roads into repair; that would be an imperative presentment. There is another case where they are authorised to make presentment without application to presentment sessions; it is a very small matter, it is for providing fire and candle-light for the various session houses throughout the county; and in those cases the grand jury do present, but it is generally a fixed and well-ascertained sum, and would come perhaps within the same class of cases as officer's salaries. The grand jury present sums for the maintenance of the county infirmary upon applications approved of at sessions, and also sums for the maintenance of lunatic asylums, and for the maintenance of the county gaol, and it makes presentments for sums in reimbursement for malicious injuries; they appoint the high constables, or the collectors of the grand jury cess; and at the time of the appointment they fix their salaries, which is a poundage allowance on the amount to be collected by those officers. I now come to the second head of the subject, namely, the presentment sessions for baronies, the mode of its constitution, and its functions. The magistrates of every county are required to assemble at the places and times previously appointed by the grand jury, and they are there and then, with the associated cesspayers, to hold the presentment sessions for each barony. When the magistrates assemble at the place appointed, their first duty is to choose a chairman, and then they proceed to select by ballot the number of associated cesspayers from the list made out by the previous grand jury, a copy of which list is handed on the opening of the sessions to the chairman by the secretary of the grand jury. In practice each of the persons upon that list receives from the secretary, prior to the sessions, a notification that he has been named and selected by the previous grand jury, and placed upon the list of associated cesspayers, from which list the requisite number will, on the meeting of the sessions, be selected by ballot, so that they all have notice to attend.

17. The number on the list is twice the number of those selected, is it not?—Yes. The grand jury determine the number of associate cesspayers who shall sit with the magistrates, and in so determining they have regard to a variety of circumstances relating to each barony, such as, for instance, the length and breadth of the barony and its area. All those matters enter into the consideration of the grand jury in determining the number. In the county of Roscommon, I think, in my experience, the number has always remained the same at each sessions. Although the form is gone through of appointing the number, it is always done upon the previous number, and in only one instance do I ever recollect that upon an application from the barony was the

Mr. P. Burrowes Shapley.

27 March 1868.

the number increased. The grand jury generally attend to well-founded suggestions coming from the ratepayers. When the associated ratepayers are so selected by ballot, and with the justices present, sign, or subscribe, a declaration which is given as one of the forms in the schedule to the statute, they jointly constitute the presentment sessions of the barony, and are authorised to exercise all power and authority in the business of the sessions. If, as frequently happens in the county with which I am acquainted the ratepayers do not attend, the magistrates are authorised to proceed with the business of the sessions in the same way, exactly as if they had attended. If, after the sessions is so constituted, any magistrate of the county comes in subsequent to the proceedings being commenced, he is eligible to sit and discharge the duties of the sessions; if an associated cesspayer comes in late and the ballot is closed he is precluded from sitting and discharging the duties of the sessions.

18. Although the number of cesspayers be not filled up?—Although the number of cesspayers be not filled up. In practice it often occurs that there is an appeal *ad misericordiam* to the sessions that the rule should be relaxed; and invariably, if there is not a sufficient number of ratepayers, the sessions relax the rule, and admit the ratepayer so coming late to the sessions.

19. Lord *John Browne*.] Do you think that they have power by law to do that?—I do not think so. I think that the question as to a magistrate coming late has formed the subject of a judicial decision, and that case has been decided in favour of the magistrate.

20. Colonel *Forde*.] What is the section of the Act under which the ratepayers are selected?—The sections of the Act under which the ratepayers are selected are the 5th and 6th sections.

21. *Chairman*.] As soon as the Presentment Sessions Court is constituted, what do they proceed to do?—In some counties their first duty (though in other counties it is done last) is to select, from the associated ratepayers present, one person to attend the county at large presentment sessions, and at that sessions to represent the barony. I may anticipate suggestions which I intend to make upon the fourth branch of the subject, by stating that the intention of the legislature in that respect is but very imperfectly given effect to, and that in the County at large presentment sessions the ratepayers so selected do not take the trouble, or incur the expense, of attending the county at large presentment sessions.

22. Practically, you find that the cesspayers selected at the presentment sessions do not attend the county at large sessions?—Practically it is so.

23. Lord *John Browne*.] Is there often a dispute about the selection of representatives at the county at large sessions?—I have never, in my experience, known a case in which there was a dispute. On the contrary, the ratepayers are generally anxious to shirk the responsibility, and cast it from one to the other. I hold in my hand a schedule of applications considered at the last sessions of the county of Roscommon, which contains, at the head of each barony, the list of associated ratepayers who attended; and, in the case of the county at large presentment sessions, I find that out of the ten baronies which compose the county, and for each of which a ratepayer had been selected at the baronial sessions to attend, there was only one who attended, and he happened to live within three or four miles of the town where those sessions were holden. There is a moral obligation, but there is no legal obligation whatever involving a penalty upon the persons selected at the baronial sessions to attend the county at large sessions, and generally you find that those persons will give precedence to their own business over the public business upon the day in question. If they have business to attend to, such as a fair or a market, they will attend to it in preference.

24. Mr. *Kendall*.] I understand that out of the 10 associated ratepayers, only one attended; how many magistrates attended?—Only one at the particular sessions to which I refer.

25. How many could have attended?—I should say that the county of Roscommon has, of magistrates who could attend without very great trouble, 50 or 60 at least; that is to say, it was possible for 50 or 60 without any great inconvenience to attend, and one attended; and I may repeat that at those sessions some very important presentments, or applications for presentments, are generally submitted and disposed of.

26. Mr. *Chichester Fortescue*.] Can you tell us what business those two gentlemen transacted on that occasion?—In the first place they approved of an application for 576 *l.* 9 *s.* 9 *d.* to defray the expenses of extra constabulary force.

27. *Chairman*.] Before you go into a detail of all the presentments which they made at that particular sessions, it will be well for the Committee to understand what is the nature of the presentments made at the county at large presentment sessions?—The presentments made at the county at large presentment sessions in general are grants of money for the maintenance of county establishments.

28. Are those imperative presentments?—I do not think that they are imperative. I do not think that the presentment for the maintenance of the county infirmary is imperative; for it is sometimes submitted for a much larger sum than that allowed by the opinion of the sessions; and therefore I take that out of the category of imperative presentments; and I think that you will find that in some instances they approve of a shilling. I think the case was referred to one of the learned judges in Ireland, and he held that, in the case of a presentment by sessions presenting a shilling, he had no power to compel them. It was the case, I think, of a lunatic asylum or dispensary in the county of Wicklow, given in Foot. Those cases do not come within the class of imperative presentments. If they were imperative presentments there would be no necessity for submitting them to the ratepayers.

29. Lord *John Browne*.] Can you give us the case in Foot to which you refer?—The case to which I referred is the case of a dispensary in the county of Wicklow; but they are now transferred to the Poor Law Department.

30. *Chairman*.] Can you state, as a fact, that the presentments for county infirmaries are not imperative?—They are not so imperative as the cases which come under a sealed order from the Lord Lieutenant, or from the Privy Council, directing the money to be presented; and, if it is not presented, authorising the judge of assize to make an order for the presentment; and, failing

Mr. *P. Burrowes Sharkey.* 27 March 1868.

ing the judge, directing the treasurer to insert it in his warrant. Those I call imperative presentments, and they are not submitted to the ratepayers.

31. Lord *John Browne.*] Have you ever known a case of a presentment for a county infirmary having been reduced or rejected by the sessions?—Certainly; I have known numerous cases of sums being reduced.

32. Mr. *Kendall.*] They cannot increase it, can they?—No, but it frequently has occurred in the county of Roscommon, that the ratepayers on the one hand, considering that the maintenance of the county infirmary ought not to be entirely put upon them, have, through their representatives at the county at large sessions, reduced the amount applied for.

33. Lord *John Browne.*] Was that for the maintenance of the infirmary?—For the maintenance fund, to enable them to provide for the support and maintenance thereof; and I shall show the Committee why it is quite within their power to reduce the amount. It is only presented as a fund. Whatever sum is approved of at the sessions, and presented by the grand jury, is only presented as a fund to meet the current expenses of the next half year. It may so happen that, during that half year, the expenses of the county infirmary are not so great as they were on a former half year, and they will have a balance in hand; and then the form of presentment, which was framed under the late Judge Perrin's directions, is in these terms: "To the treasurer of the county infirmary, as a fund towards the support and maintenance thereof for one half year, ending summer 1868." At the end of the half year he may have a balance in hand, and therefore it would not be necessary that the same amount should be granted at the next presentment sessions. The accounts are before the next presentment sessions, and they see by the previous expenditure what is likely to be wanted for the ensuing period; and if the treasurer, or the managing authorities ask too large a sum, the ratepayers have power to reduce it.

34. Mr. *Chichester Fortescue.*] According to the Report of the Commissioners of 1842, it apparently goes even farther than that; the law leaves it optional with grand juries to present, or not, for county fever hospitals?—Yes.

35. *Chairman.*] Would you state what other description of presentments came before that county at large sessions?—The county at large presentment sessions on this occasion dealt with the salaries of the officers of the county prison, and they also dealt with the sum applied for the maintenance of the prison.

36. Lord *John Browne.*] Are these imperative?—No; they fall within the same class of cases as that which I mentioned; in some instances the ratepayers reduce the amount. I have never known the amount refused, but I have known the amount asked for cut down. Then the next class of cases is salary to the county infirmary surgeons, and also to the surgeons and medical officers of the county prison; salaries to the various court keepers and sessions-house keepers throughout the county; and then a remunerating or reimbursing presentment to the clerk of the peace of the county for the trouble imposed upon him, in giving effect to the Parliamentary Voters Act. Certain additional duties are thrown upon him, and the grand jury are authorised, under the 13 & 14 Vict. c. 69, to reimburse him for that additional trouble.

37. Is not that imperative?—It is so far imperative that they are bound to give him some remuneration.

38. They are bound to give him a proper amount?—Yes.

39. What is a proper amount?—In the county of Roscommon I think they give him 40 *l.* a year, exclusive of printing. One of the Parliamentary boroughs (Athlone) is situated in two counties, Westmeath and Roscommon, and the clerk of the peace of Westmeath is also paid, and so is the town clerk of Athlone for giving effect to the Parliamentary Voters Act in that borough. Then there is an application for a sum of money for putting the courthouse in order, 100 *l.* Without going farther into detail, the sessions in question dealt with presentments to the amount of 3,500 *l.*

40. *Chairman.*] But most of these presentments were ordinary routine presentments, were they not, which come on every year, and which are generally of the same amount?—Yes, they are generally of the same amount.

41. Lord *John Browne.*] And most of them were imperative?—Yes, in the same way as I have mentioned that the sessions could have refused a part.

42. *Chairman.*] Could you put in a return of the amount of those presentments which were not imperative?—I could.

43. The presentments for the making of roads which come before the county at large presentment sessions have all been previously approved at the baronial sessions, have they not?—In the case of coach or mail car roads, the law authorises half the amount of expense to be levied upon the barony, and the other half to be levied upon the county at large. Generally speaking, those various cases are considered at the baronial sessions, and they only come before the county at large sessions as a mere matter of form.

44. Lord *John Browne.*] There is no discretion, I think, about their coming before the baronial sessions?—They must come first before the baronial sessions. It is a mere matter of routine and detail as to the portion of the sum necessary to be levied off the county at large.

45. Sir *Charles Lanyon.*] Is it necessary that they should come before the county at large?—In the county of Roscommon they do.

46. Colonel *French.*] In the case of new roads, for instance, in which half the cost would be thrown on the county, those would come before the county at large sessions, and would be there discussed upon their merits the same as in the courts below, would they not?—Not unless they are mail coach roads. If half is on the county, they come before the county at large sessions.

47. And are subject to approval or rejection?—Certainly.

48. So, therefore, the county at large sessions are responsible for them?—For new works. The 52nd section of the Act of 6 & 7 Will. 4, c. 116, contains the law on the subject. "Provided always, that in the case of any road upon which his Majesty's mails are or shall be carried in mail carriages, one half of the expenses of such repairs shall be levied off the county, and the other half off any barony or baronies in which such road or any part thereof may be locally situate."

49. Sir *Charles Lanyon.*] That does not say that a portion of the expense shall be brought before the county at large sessions?—It does not.

In

Mr. P. [illegible] [illegible]. 27 March 18[illegible].

in the county of Roscommon. I see that the practice is to bring it formally both before the county at large sessions and the baronial sessions. If hills to be cut down or bridges to be built, happen to be on a mail car road, they also come before the county at large sessions.

50. Colonel *French*.] The grand jury are empowered to cut down hills, and to throw half the expense upon the county where it can be proved that the county at large will get the benefit of it, even though they are not on a mail coach road; and, in that case, it comes before the county at large sessions for approval, does it not?—No doubt.

51. *Chairman*.] Will you return to the proceedings of the baronial presentment sessions?—I think I diverged at the point where the associated ratepayer is selected for the purpose of representing the barony at the county at large presentment sessions.

52. What is the next proceeding of the presentment sessions after having selected the representative to attend at the county at large sessions?—They then proceed to the business of the session, and that can be described shortly in these terms: they take into consideration all applications for expenditure of public money upon baronial works, applications for those works having been previously deposited with the secretary of the grand jury, who makes an abstract of them, and places that abstract before the chairman of the sessions, accompanied by the applications. The sessions then proceed to examine into the posting and serving of notices of all applications, where the law requires notice to be given, and it inquires into the merits of each application, and the conformity thereof with the provisions of the Act of Parliament. The Act of Parliament requires certain specified particulars to be stated in the application, and also requires the application to set out the section of the Act of Parliament authorising the sessions to deal with it; and if in any of those particulars the application should be defective, the sessions reject those applications. However, road contractors, and other persons interested in these matters, take very good care not to leave themselves open to a casual point of that kind, and the applications are invariably prepared in strict conformity with the Act of Parliament. Having inquired into the merits of each application, and examined witnesses, if necessary, the presentment sessions decide by the majority of votes upon each application, and they *determine* whether the same ought to be adopted or rejected, either wholly, or in part; and they also invariably limit the amount, if the application is for a sum of money. If, on conferring with the county surveyor, they find that the application is a reasonable application, they approve of it; if it should be an excessive application, they generally restrict the amount by saying, "Approved; the expense not to exceed 6 s. a perch," or "50 *l*.," or a given sum, according to the nature of the work. If it is a new road to be made, or a road to be repaired, not kept under contract, they generally limit the price to so much a perch. If it is a road to be maintained for a period of years, they limit the period and the price per perch. If it is for a bridge, and the application they think is larger than it ought to be, they mark "Approved" on the back of the application; "the expense not to exceed" a certain limited amount. Having gone through that duty, they then direct the county surveyor to prepare specifications, maps, plans, &c., for the works which have been so approved of; and the county surveyor prepares those specifications, and lodges them with the secretary of the grand jury, within a limited time. Having endorsed the application in the way I mention, the chairman hands it back to the secretary.

53. Mr. *Chichester Fortescue*.] By whom are the applications made?—The law requires them to be made by two ratepayers. The Act of 6 & 7 Will. 4 directs how, and by whom, those applications are to be made.

54. May they be made by the county surveyor?—They may be made by the county surveyor, but in practice in the county of Roscommon that very seldom occurs. The county surveyor has enough to do to inspect the works for which notice is given, and that portion of the Act has fallen into desuetude in the county of Roscommon. The sessions are then supposed to give directions as to the form of advertising those works so approved of; that is, advertising for contractors and tenders, and their secretary gives effect to their wishes, and then, as the final act of the presentment sessions, they adjourn their sitting to a future day.

55. *Chairman*.] But before they adjourn the sessions to a future day, do they not consider the applications of contractors for payment?—They do. I have omitted that. Having disposed of the applications for works requiring fresh expenditure of money, they then come to what is called the accounting applications; and I would, with a view to base a suggestion hereafter upon this branch of the case, call the attention of Honourable Members to the working of this portion of the system. The accounting applications, or, as I think the law calls them, the applications for payment, are lodged with the secretary of the grand jury 10 days before the first sessions of the county, at the same time exactly as the applications for new works. The Committee will not understand me to mean by new works, works to be done for the first time, but rather works upon which a fresh expenditure of money is required, either on new contracts, or repairs of by-roads. I do not at all mean such a case as new works, or a new bridge, or a new road; I confine myself merely to works requiring a fresh expenditure of money. Those applications are scheduled in the same manner as the first-mentioned applications by the secretary, and they are read before the presentment sessions, and each case is taken up and considered *seriatim*, and upon its own merits. The form of that application is, in effect, setting out the time of the contract, or when the original authority to do the work was given; it then goes on to recite that the work has been done, and having been done application is made for payment; hence they are called applications for payment; the presentment sessions proceed to consider each of these cases, and in doing so they are very much, if not entirely, guided by the opinion of the county surveyor, who sits generally upon the bench with the magistrates and cesspayers; but previously to lodging the application for payment the contractor is required to give notice to the county surveyor that his work has been done, and that he means to apply for payment to the next sessions; and the duty is cast upon the county surveyor of inspecting those works so said to have been executed, with a view to his giving an opinion

opinion to the presentment sessions, as to whether or not the case was one in which the contractor was entitled to have his application for payment allowed. If the county surveyor, having inspected the work, or having taken other means to inform himself upon the subject, is of opinion that the contractor is entitled to payment, he so reports or certifies to the sessions.

56. Mr. *Kendall*.] How does he take those means of satisfying himself?—He has assistants; in the county of Roscommon there are two assistants; in other counties there are more, according to the size and extent of the county, but he generally takes all due and proper means to satisfy himself; there is no very defined rule for his guidance, but he takes such means as he thinks he ought to take in the interests of the county, whose officer he is, to satisfy himself that the application is a proper one, and that it ought, or ought not, to be allowed; I think the assistants must be qualified; they have to go through some examination. Upon that point I may perhaps hereafter direct the attention of the Committee to the very insufficient salaries which these assistants receive. The county surveyor, then, is in a position at the presentment sessions to advise the sessions whether or not this application for payment ought to be allowed or disallowed, and thereupon the magistrate endorses the opinion of the sessions in the words "Allowed," if the man is entitled to payment, or "Disallowed," if he is not entitled to payment; that is, if the work has not been executed according to the wishes of the county surveyor.

57. Lord *John Browne*.] The sessions have no power to allow it without a certificate from the county surveyor, have they?—It is necessary that the county surveyor should give a certificate.

58. *Chairman*.] And practically, the certificate of the county surveyor is always respected, is it not?—I have scarcely known an instance in which the presentment sessions, disregarding the certificate of the county surveyor, have allowed an application. I have known struggles to take place out of consideration for Pat This or Tom That, on the ground of his being a poor man, to get the county surveyor to grant a certificate.

59. General *Dunne*.] Are the sessions bound by law to reject it, if the county surveyor's certificate is not given?—I think by law they are so bound; but everything at presentment sessions is not done according to law.

60. *Chairman*.] Do you mean to say that by law they are obliged to allow the payment, if the county surveyor's certificate is given?—They are.

61. Then, their duties legally are merely ministerial?—If a magistrate on the bench happened, on his way to the sessions, to pass, for instance, a bridge for which payment had been applied, and saw a breach in it, he might say, in the discharge of his duties, "I passed that bridge this morning and saw one of the parapets down," and then, of course, the county surveyor would withhold or withdraw his certificate; and if it was a case of sudden damage, or malicious injury, the sessions might take a considerate view and say, "We will allow your application provisionally, but the county surveyor must go and inspect the work again; and if he should then be of opinion that you have not performed your contract, your application will be disallowed by the grand jury;" thus keeping in their own hands the power, when it went before the grand jury, to have it disallowed, if the state of things warranted it.

Mr. *P. Barrow Sharkey.*

17 March 1868.

62. But the case you put is the case in which the county surveyor certifies it for the time being? He certifies it for the time anterior to the information given by the magistrate or by the associated ratepayer.

63. But without the certificate they could not certify that the presentment should be paid?—They could not do so legally.

64. Mr. *Chichester Fortescue*.] And with that certificate they are bound to do so?—They are, I think; the law appears to be very clear upon that point.

65. Lord *John Browne*.] Have not the sessions power to refuse to order a warrant to pay a man, though he has obtained the county surveyor's certificate; and do you not know cases in which that power has been exercised?—They have the power and may exercise it occasionally; but I have known no instance where they have exercised it. The section bearing upon it is very clear, and I do not think that any doubt has ever arisen upon it. It is the 120th section.

66. *Chairman*.] Then are the Committee to understand that the presentment sessions have no power legally to order payment for any work which has not been certified by the county surveyor, but on the other hand that they can refuse to order payment for a work, although it has been certified by the county surveyor?—The section of the Act of Parliament is so short and so clear, that I would ask permission to relieve myself from the difficulty of expressing an opinion until I place before the Committee the section of the Act of Parliament. The 180th section of the 6th & 7th Will. 4, c. 116, says: "That every person who may contract for the execution of any work under this Act shall, on the completion of the work for which he may have contracted, or whensoever by the terms of such contract he may be entitled to payment, give notice to the surveyor of the county ten days at the least before the day appointed for the holding of the first presentment sessions in the county after every assizes or presenting term of his intention to make application as hereinafter provided, and require of such surveyor a certificate of the due execution of such work or performance of such contract." Now that portion of the section was subsequently amended. It is not necessary before he lodges his application to have the certificate of the county surveyor. The 7th of Will. 4, which amends this Act, gives the county surveyor power to give a certificate when the application comes before the sessions. The section proceeds as follows: "And such contractor shall lodge with the secretary of the grand jury, within the period hereinbefore limited for the lodgment of notices of applications for presentments for public works, a notice of his intention to apply for payment of the sum contracted for by him, together with such certificates to be obtained from the said surveyor" (that, as pointed out, is repealed). "And the secretary to the grand jury shall arrange in like manner as he has been hereinbefore directed to arrange applications for presentments, all such notices and certificates, and annex to each the number." Thus a certain routine duty is cast upon the secretary of bringing forward those applications to the sessions, and the duty of the sessions is described in these terms: "And the justices and cesspayers at such sessions shall examine into all such applications for payment on the part

Mr. *P. Burrowes Sharkey.*

17 March 1902.

part of such contractors, and inspect the works thereof and the certificates aforesaid, and examine the surveyor or surveyors, and all other persons whom they may think it necessary to examine for the purpose of ascertaining the due execution of the work or matter contracted for, and shall therein have and exercise all such powers and authorities, as in the case of applications for presentments, and in like manner determine and decide upon all such applications for payment by majority of votes; and the chairman at such sessions shall, on every application which may be approved, indorse the word "Allowed" and on every application which shall not be approved he shall indorse the word "Disallowed;" and the reason of such disallowance, and a note of or reference to the particulars of the execution of the work which may have caused such disallowance; and all such applications, with the notices and certificates thereto belonging, shall be delivered to the secretary of the grand jury, to be laid before them at the next ensuing assizes; and such grand jury shall take such applications as have been approved into consideration, and allow or disallow the same according to their discretion; but it shall not be lawful for such grand jury, or for the Court, to allow any application which shall not have been approved of at such sessions; and no such contractor shall be entitled to payment who shall not have given such notice and made such application; nor unless such application shall have been approved and allowed as aforesaid." It is clear upon reading that section of the Act of Parliament that the baronial sessions are quite free to deal with the question of applications coming before them for payment with or without the certificate of the county surveyor, as they may think fit.

67. *Sir Charles Lenyon.*] But can the magistrates and cesspayers approve of an application from a contractor without a certificate?—The county surveyor, without good reason, may withhold his certificate.

68. Then the remedy is as mentioned, that it must be by mandamus?—In practice I may tell you that the grand jury of the county of Roscommon, and indeed I may speak generally of the grand juries throughout Ireland, as long as they have a public officer in whom they repose the utmost confidence, they invariably support his decisions throughout.

69. *Chairman.*] But your reading of that section would be that the presentment sessions were perfectly free either to grant or to refuse approval of the presentment, whether it was certified by the county surveyor or not?—It gives them such extensive power that I think that it would be open to them to do so.

70. They are merely to examine the county surveyor as a witness as to the state of the road? —Yes, and I think that the policy of the law is that it should be so; what would be the necessity for baronial sessions if the *ipse dixit* of the county surveyor was to be final.

71. Having determined upon what payments should be made, and what certificates should be granted to contractors, do the presentment sessions then adjourn?—The practice is that they then adjourn to a day not later than 30 days from the day upon which the adjournment takes place; and that brings us in the order of my narrative to the adjourned presentment sessions. To lead up to that and to the better understanding of the question before the Committee, I shall interpose shortly a portion of the duties that are cast in the meantime upon the secretary. The secretary of the grand jury, having received back the applications from the sessions, advertises in certain papers, and also by sending to each of the associated ratepayers, and to the justices of the district, a printed list, setting out in much detail the particulars of each of the works which have been approved of at the sessions. The applications for payment allowed or disallowed drop out of consideration until the meeting of the grand jury. I am now dealing with the applications for the expenditure of money in putting roads, &c. in repair, or in the construction of bridges, and so on. Having advertised these matters, and sent handbills round the district, generally, to the leading contractors, or persons who are likely to tender for them, the adjourned sessions takes place, and the constitution of that sessions is exactly the same as the presentment sessions. In theory it is so, but in practice it is very different. At the baronial sessions you are aware that the associated cesspayers and the justices constitute the tribunal, which ought to be the same at the adjourned sessions; but, in very many instances which I could mention, the justices and associated cesspayers, after the termination of the presentment sessions, lose all interest in the proceedings, and do not attend the adjourned sessions. It often happens that there can be no magistrate found to attend to open the proceedings of the adjourned sessions; and it seldom occurs that the associated ratepayers attend at the adjourned sessions; it not unfrequently becomes a very great trouble for the secretary to send messengers all about the country to try and get a magistrate to come in and open the tenders, and thus save the whole of the previous sessions' work from falling to the ground.

72. *Lord John Browne.*] And in many cases it does fall to the ground?—Well, in law it does fall to the ground, but the secretary (I have done it myself when acting in that position) sooner than allow the proceedings up to that point to become inoperative, will perhaps adjourn the sessions.

73. But that is quite illegal, is it not?—It is quite illegal.

74. And if any single cesspayer in the county chooses to traverse the whole of these presentments before a judge, they must of necessity be rejected?—They must. However, it is not so with us in Roscommon; those interested rather favour that perhaps illegal, but equitable proceeding.

75. *Chairman.*] If at the adjourned sessions there be cesspayers present, but no magistrate present, can the sessions be held?—It cannot.

76. *Lord John Browne.*] Nobody can take the chair, except a magistrate?—Nobody can take the chair, except a magistrate.

77. Colonel *Forde.*] Is it not the case that it must be one of the magistrates who attended at the first sessions should take the chair at the adjourned sessions?—It does not follow. I think that the decision referred to in Foot would lead to a conclusion that it being the same sessions any magistrate coming in who was not at the first sessions, and duly qualifying, would be entitled to discharge the duties.

78. *Chairman.*] Then the duty of these adjourned sessions is to open the tenders for the works which have been allowed?—Yes. Then assuming

Mr. *P. Borrowes Sharkey.* — 27 March 1868.

assuming that the sessions is constituted, their duty then is (and it is a very important duty), to receive the tenders which are supposed to be previously deposited with the secretary. On the adjourned sessions being opened those tenders are laid before the justices and associated cesspayers present, and they are opened according to the number appearing on the list. They are sent in previously filled in a certain form prescribed by practice, but I think not by law; and the secretary produces them to the bench, and the details of the particular work in question are read from the application, or from the abstract made, and the tenders which are numbered according to the number of that application are then opened by the magistrates, and if the magistrate is of opinion that it is a *bonâ fide* tender, and that the persons offered as sureties are solvent persons, and that there is no fraud, he is bound to accept the lowest tender. Having so accepted the tender, he endorses a statement to that effect upon it, and having proceeded then through all the other numbers upon the book and opened the tenders for them, a bond, or obligation to the Queen is entered into by the person whose tender has been accepted, and his sureties. Now a word upon that obligation, for the purpose of showing the inconvenience which often arises from putting that obligation in suit. It is a bond binding the person making it and his sureties to the Queen in a certain specified sum; and when you come to sue upon that bond, you must apply to the Attorney General for his sanction. There are, I think, certain fees payable to the Attorney General upon his *fiat* in all those matters; and, in point of fact, the amount of trouble involved in the obtaining of his permission on the part of the Queen to sue renders the suing upon those bonds wholly inoperative; and that has now become so well known throughout the county of Roscommon, and I dare say in other counties, that the contractors' bonds are very seldom sued upon.

79. Mr. *Gregory.*] Do you know what the fee is?—I think it is a fee of five guineas for each bond. He is entitled to it; it is one of his perquisites, and he generally exacts it.

80. [Lord *John Browne.*] Then the proceedings must be taken as he directs?—The proceedings cannot be taken by an officer of the grand jury. I think that the late Attorney General (or the present one, I am not quite certain which) has issued an order that his *fiat* shall not be given, unless the proceedings are carried on by an officer named by himself. That officer is generally the sessional Crown solicitor, and he, in all those cases, represents the Crown.

81. And the result is that these legal proceedings are taken in the most expensive possible mode?—In the most expensive mode possible; being first of all reached by a most expensive and roundabout proceeding, and then carried out in a more expensive manner.

82. Mr. *Gregory.*] Do you know whether there is any particular policy in hampering these proceedings in this manner?—I think that there is no particular policy, except that at the time it was instituted its practical working could not be known; but now that it has been some 30 years and upwards in practice, it is very easy to point out defects in that respect.

83. *Chairman.*] Are you quite sure that that is the present state of the law?—The 17th section of the 19 & 20 Vict. c. 63, is in these words: "If in the opinion of the county surveyor, the contractor for the repair of any road shall be guilty of neglect or inattention in the performance of his contract, it shall be lawful for such surveyor to summon the said contractor and his sureties before the justices at petty sessions of the district in which such work may be situate; and if such charge of neglect or inattention be established before such justices, it shall be lawful for them to make an order, directing the said contractor and his sureties to execute his contract within a period to be stated in such order; and if at the expiration of such order the county surveyor shall still see reason for being dissatisfied with the manner in which such work has been executed, it shall be lawful for him again to summon the contractor and his sureties before the justices at petty sessions; and the justices thereupon shall proceed to inquire into, and finally adjudicate upon the complaint; and if it shall appear that such work has been insufficiently executed, or contrary to the terms of the contract, it shall be lawful for such justices, having ascertained the amount which it may require for the completion of such work according to the contract, to authorise such surveyor to complete the same, and to levy such amount by warrant of distress upon the goods of such contractor or his sureties, not exceeding the amount of the recognizance or bond of such sureties; does not that section meet the case of contractors for the repair of roads?—It gives great facilities for the suing of contractors and their sureties; but the law upon that point, I take it, is far from being settled: I will read the note to that section in Foot, "At the Westport quarter sessions, January 1860, upon an appeal by a contractor for keeping a public road in repair for a certain number of years, from an order made under the above section, the chairman of the county Mayo (Sir Colman O'Loghlen) quashed the order, upon the ground that the above section applied only to the case of contractors for specific works, *i. e.*, the repair of a road, and that, therefore, the appellant was entitled to the 10 days' notice directed to be given in 6 & 7 Will. 4, c. 116, s. 54 (exp.) Higgins, app. Brewster, resp.; *et relatione*. When the county surveyor had obtained an order under this section against a defaulting contractor, and the surety of the latter, in compliance with the order, performed the work, Hayes, J., held that the surety was not entitled to have the presentment which had been made in favour of the contractor at the last assizes handed over to him, but left him to his action." This is a statement (*handed to the Witness by Lord John Browne*) of the report of the grand jury and road contractors, at the last Clonmel assizes held in March 1867. Mr. Shaw gives an opinion upon a case submitted to him; he was the Castle adviser at the time, and he states: "It was decided by Sir C. O'Loghlen, while chairman of quarter sessions for the county of Mayo, that the 17th section applied only to contracts for specific works, and not to maintenance contracts (Higgins *v.* Brewster, Foot's G. J. Acts, page 526). This decision has been followed by Judge O'Brien in a recent case."

84. But as far as contracts for specific works are concerned, there is an easier mode of coming at contractors than going to Queen's Bench, is there not?—This section would give a facility for imposing a penalty upon a contractor for not discharging his obligation.

0.59. B

85. Lord

Mr. F. [illegible] [illegible].

[illegible] March [illegible].

85. *Lord John Browne.*] But it does not apply to continuous contracts?—It does not apply to continuous contracts.

86. There are some of the most important in the county, are they not?—They are.

87. *Chairman.*] Does it not seem to be an oversight in the section that it should be confined to particular contracts?—Having regard to the judge who decided the point I should think that it was an omission from the section.

88. *Lord John Browne.*] That section which you have been reading only refers to the repair of roads, and not to specific works?—Quite so.

89. *Chairman.*] You have now described the different functions of the grand jury, the presentment sessions, the county at large sessions, and the adjourned sessions, is there any other point upon which you can furnish the Committee with any information?—The next and last head of my narrative will be the constitution of the presentment sessions for the county at large, and it will be very short, inasmuch as it was anticipated at an earlier stage of the proceedings; and I shall then add a word upon the functions of the presentment sessions. I will dismiss that in one or two words to complete the narrative.

90. From your practical experience, do you see any defects in the constitution of the grand jury at present?—I approach this subject with very great diffidence indeed, and if it were at all open to the Committee to grant me the indulgence which I am about to ask from them, I would claim it. I have had considerable trouble in refreshing my recollection of the various matters with which I have occupied the time of the Committee up to the present, and I have not had sufficient time to fully consider, or at least to digest the views that I would venture humbly to put before the Committee as to the remedial measures which I would suggest; and if I got until the next meeting of the Committee, the time would not be ill-spent, and I should then place before them my views upon the subjects I have mentioned; first of all, I shall point out the evils or defects of the present system, and then, with the sanction of the Committee, humbly suggest what I would consider to be remedial measures.

91. *Chairman.*] Having been acting as secretary to a grand jury for so many years, could you state in a short way to the Committee what are the general duties of secretaries of grand juries in Ireland?—The general duties of secretaries of grand juries in Ireland are to carry on all correspondence between the grand jury and the executive government and the various public departments. The grand jury, it will be recollected, cease to exist when once they are discharged by the judge. In addition to all those duties he has to attend the various presentment sessions; to attend at the adjourned sessions; to receive applications for works and also applications for payment; to schedule or make out a list of all those applications which are approved of and allowed at sessions, and to circulate them through the county; to invite tenders from contractors; to make out the bonds for the contractors, to prepare a schedule of all those applications to be laid before the judge and the grand jury at the following assizes; to attend the grand jury at all their sittings, and the various committees of that body; and to assist and guide them in their inquiries and deliberations, with his practical experience and knowledge of the law.

92. How is the secretary paid?—He is paid by a very small salary.

93. Has he not fees in addition?—The only legal fees to which he is entitled, are 1*s.* for filling up the bond, and 1*s.* for a copy of the specification, which is prepared by the surveyor, in case it should be required by any person; but in practice the amount received for that service is comparatively trifling, because all necessary details are set out so fully in the presentment book, such as the number of feet wide that the road is to be, and the number of tons of stone to be put upon it, and so on; in fact, the requirements of the county surveyor are so fully set out, that the secretary is seldom called upon to supply a specification. There are cases of bridges, &c., where there is a good deal of complication, and where there are plans and sections, and the work being large, it is worth while to the contractor to pay 1*s.*, or more, according to the amount of labour to get the specifications in those cases; but the fee he is authorised to charge for this work produces a comparatively small sum.

94. In practice, are you not aware that the secretaries of grand juries do charge several fees to contractors?—I am aware that they charge for certain services rendered by them, irrespectively altogether of their position as secretaries of grand juries, and wholly outside the Act of Parliament. As secretaries there is no obligation to render those services, and on the other hand there is no legal authority to charge for them, but the practice is this: I spoke in my evidence of the system of lodging the applications for payment, and also applications for the expenditure of money upon works, and I also directed the attention of the Committee to certain technical points that are often raised against contractors, if certain requirements of the statute are not complied with; I called them nonsuit points upon which they might be turned over after great expense had been incurred; to avoid that contingency, and to facilitate business, the secretaries, generally speaking, throughout Ireland, previous to the presentment sessions, go round to certain districts of their county and hold what is called a preparatory sessions; that is, they open an office, and they go provided with forms of applications and accompanied by clerks; and then for any person desirous of making an application for work, the clerk, acting for such person, fills up the application in proper form; in return for that service, in the county of Roscommon, I think the secretary charges the sum of 1*s.* 6*d.*; and for a similar service rendered in the case of applications for payment, he charges a similar fee of 1*s.* 6*d.*; but if he does not do the work he is not entitled to the payment; and if he is obliged to sue for it, he can only sue as any other person could sue for work and labour done. He is not entitled to the fee by statute. If I chose to go into his shop and deal with him in the way of getting him to fill up a form, I ask his price, and if I feel it is too high, I say, "I will not deal with you, but go elsewhere."

95. But do you not believe that, practically, contractors deem it essential to go to the secretary of the grand jury, because otherwise, they would fear that their application would be rejected on some technical ground?—There is a popular notion that the secretary is a man of influence with the grand jury, and that it is better to go into court with the secretary upon your side than otherwise.

96. General

Mr. *P. Barrytton Sharkey.*

27 March 1868.

96. General *Dunne.*] A man may fill it up himself; but it is the dread of informality which makes him go to the secretary?—I was trying to impress that upon the Committee.

97. Mr. *Chichester Fortescue.*] Is there a real necessity, generally, on the part of these road contractors, to apply to the secretary for these services?—I do not think there is an absolute necessity; but it is more convenient to them. When they prepare their own applications they are never certain that they are prepared in accordance with law until the last moment.

98. But they are very often old hands who have been contracting for years, are they not?—They are.

99. And they ought to know, ought they not?—They ought, certainly; and I have known certain instances in which contractors threw the Secretary over altogether, and filled their own forms, and he was bound where they were filled properly, to put them forward; but the dread of the contractors is that, inasmuch as the Secretary is vested with the power of suppressing any application that is informal, no questions being asked, he will regard with a more critical eye applications prepared by the contractors than those prepared in his own office, and they think that he would suppress their applications for but slight cause, and they therefore find it to their interest to deal with him.

100. Can a secretary suppress the application without bringing it before the sessions?—Yes, he need not bring it forward unless it is in form according to the Act of Parliament; but I need not tell the Committee that a secretary will be careful not to do that, unless it is clearly not conformable to the law.

101. May not a contractor traverse that?—No, he may make a complaint to the sessions; and the secretary would be bound then, in defence of the charge against his character, to produce the application to the sessions and point out why he did not bring it forward.

102. Colonel *Forde.*] Is it not really the case that the secretary is obliged to bring these cases forward and to report to the sessions that such an application is informal?—In point of law he is not bound to go so far; but as a matter of expediency he would certainly do so.

103. As a matter of practice, is it not always done?—Not in my county.

104. Lord *John Browne.*] In practice what does the man pay for the application?—The payment for all forms of application is 1 *s.* 6 *d.*

105. And then does he pay 1 *s.* 6 *d.* for filling it up?—No.

106. Then what does he pay for the specification?—One shilling, unless it involves plans and sections, and then he must pay in addition the charges of a draughtsman.

107. Then what does he pay for a tender?—Sixpence.

108. The payment for the bond is at the adjourned sessions, is it not?—That is at the adjourned sessions.

109. That makes, altogether, 4 *s.*, does it not?—Yes.

110. Colonel *Forde.*] Then do you pay the county surveyor for the certificate?—No; he is bound to give the certificate gratuitously. It is a verbal certificate to the sessions that is given, and by the time the sessions come on it is a written certificate.

111. Then for filling up what is the payment?—For each half year he pays 1 *s.* 6 *d.*

112. But the contractor pays a sum to the secretary of the grand jury for making out his account with the treasurer, does he not?—He does not with us.

113. Does he not pay for taking out his account from the schedule and returning that to the county treasurer for payment?—He gets 1 *s.* 6 *d.* for the application for payment at the accounting sessions. When the contractor has done his work, and he desires to apply for payment, he deals with the secretary for the application for payment.

114. *Chairman.*] When you say that the sum of 1 *s.* 6 *d.* is charged for this form of application for payment, you are speaking of a particular county. There is no fixed charge throughout the country, is there?—No.

115. The secretaries of the grand juries have different charges in different counties, have they not?—Quite so, and they need not be dealt with at all. There is opposition in many counties. Discarded clerks and others set up an opposition shop very often.

116. Lord *John Browne.*] But they must get the form from the secretary, must they not?—Not at all. The form is given in the schedule to the statute. I recollect my father having very serious trouble or at least he considered it serious trouble, (though I do not) with the county printer. The county printer took it into his head that the secretary did not favour his views before the grand jury as to the printing contract; and he gave notice in his paper, to all contractors, and others concerned, that the applications which were charged 1 *s.* 6 *d.* for in the secretary's office, would be sold by him for 1 *d.* That continued for a long time, and I think it did to a certain extent diminish the Secretary's emoluments—ultimately the county printer withdrew his notice, and the competition ceased.

117. Colonel *Forde.*] The secretary of the grand jury provides those printed forms which he fills up at his own expense, I suppose?—Yes. He would get 100 of them for about 2 *s.*

118. Lord *John Browne.*] You said that if the representatives of the baronies did not attend, as only one was called for each barony, the barony was not in that case represented?—Yes.

119. Is it not customary for the sheriff in most counties to send a notice to the gentleman whom he proposes to call as the representative of the barony?—He is bound under the Act of Parliament to summon them.

120. Then he generally receives a reply from the gentleman who is to be the representative of the barony, as to whether he will serve or not?—I cannot speak of the duties of the sheriff at all upon that point, but my impression is, that a courteous letter inviting him to attend would be answered by a courteous reply.

121. So that, practically, he really knows that he has representatives of each barony on the grand jury?—In many instances that I could mention, that portion of the law is not carried into effect. In the case of a struggle for the appointment of secretary in the county of Roscommon, the gentlemen who would have supported a certain candidate for the office who should have been called as the representatives of their respective baronies, were not so called, but were called so low that they were not sworn on the jury, and the candidate

date whom they had previously promised to support had not the benefit of their vote.

122. General *Dunne*.] Is not the Act of Parliament imperative that the sheriff shall call first on the list a 50*l.* freeholder for each barony?—It is imperative that he shall call them, but it is not imperative that he shall require them to attend.

123. Lord *John Browne*.] But he does notice them beforehand, and notifies them?—I should say in practice it would be so.

124. *Chairman*.] But it is in the power of the sheriff always to call some one for the barony who he knows cannot attend?—It is in his power to call some one who he knows cannot attend, and he frequently does it; and in the case which I mentioned, where the appointment of secretary was about to be vacant, the sheriff pursued that course; and in doing so he strictly complied with the letter of the Act of Parliament.

125. Lord *John Browne*.] With reference to choosing the associated cesspayers, is the same practice followed in every county?—I have not the general knowledge that would enable me to speak as to that. I think the law, generally, is administered, and its requirements complied with, equally in all counties.

126. Are you aware that difference of opinion prevails as to the meaning of the section under which associated ratepayers are chosen on the part of grand jurors and country gentlemen?—I believe there is some doubt in their minds; but it has never formed the subject of judicial decision.

127. Are you aware that in many counties the grand juries are of opinion that they have no discretion whatever, and that they are obliged to take the highest cesspayers out of the list?—My reading of the statute would leave no doubt whatever that they were bound in making out the list of associated cesspayers to select the highest.

128. So that really they have no discretion?—In that respect I think the law gives them no discretion.

129. Are you aware that that practice is followed in the county of Mayo?—I am not aware of that, though I have no doubt that it is so if you state it.

130. You are fully aware that the other practice prevails in other counties?—It may be so.

131. With reference to taking the contracts at the adjourned sessions, you say that the sessions are bound to take the lowest contract. Have you read the note in Foot's book, at page 19, which gives the decision of Chief Justice Doherty?—I see there is a note to the 23rd section, that "Contracts cannot be invalidated for technical errors. Where, of five tenders sent in, the grand jury accepted the highest, and the person who had made the lowest tender applied to the court to direct the grand jury to accept it, undeniable security having been offered, Doherty, C. J. held that the grand jury had a discretion to deal with the different tenders, and that as they had exercised that discretion, he had no authority to interfere." It would appear that in that case the tender was accepted at the assizes; but my evidence was directed to the point, that justices at baronial sessions had no jurisdiction, except in case of fraud (that I especially excepted), to take any but the lowest tender, provided they were satisfied as to the solvency of the parties.

132. Does not the same remark apply to the sessions as to the assizes?—If you direct my attention to the section I will endeavour to answer the question.

133. Is not this a note relating to the proceedings at the sessions, and not at the assizes?—It is; but the case where this particular decision was given evidently was a case where the grand jury dealt with it.

134. And you think that it does not go nearer?—It is difficult to give an absolute opinion.

135. Do you not think that it is desirable that the sessions should have a discretion?—I think it is most desirable that they should have a discretion.

136. Is it not the case that a contractor very often plays very clever tricks, such as putting in three or four tenders in different names?—It is. I will take a case which is mentioned in the Report of 1842, and I will put it before the Committee as there stated, because I have seen similar cases take place over and over again. Take a bridge to be built for 50*l.*, there is a competition, and a contractor who is anxious to get it knows that he is about to be opposed; he will put in two tenders, he will put in one say at 40*l.*, and he will put in one at 35*l.* The man who is opposing him will put in a tender say at 45*l.* The position then is, that there is a tender for 45*l.*, a tender for 40*l.*, and a tender for 35*l.* When the tenders come to be opened the lowest is the 35*l.*, but the same person who put in the 35*l.* tender put in the 40*l.* tender, but in a different name; and when he is called in court he does not answer, nobody seems to know anything about him, or his sureties, and then the next highest tender, which was put in in his interest, becomes the lowest, and the sessions is bound to accept it.

137. Mr. *Gregory*.] That would be a case of fraud, would it not?—Yes, but you cannot tell; it is done in another man's name.

138. Lord *John Browne*.] Are not three or four tenders sometimes put in different men's names in that way?—Yes.

139. Practically, does not that put an end to all competition, unless the sessions have the power of making a selection to meet that case?—Certainly; I should think if the sessions were constituted, with a little more of the rate-paying element in it, it might be entrusted with larger discretionary power.

140. Sir *Charles Lanyon*.] With regard to that question of taking the lowest tender, do you not think that the difficulties of taking the lowest tender would be very much diminished if there was a better power of dealing with defaulting contractors?—Certainly; it would be contingent very much upon that.

141. Do you not think that if defaulting contractors could be dealt with immediately on the default taking place, it would be very much better to leave the question of accepting the lowest tender just where it is?—I would rather be inclined to think that better results would come from entrusting baronial sessions with a discretion; in fact, all public bodies, I think, ought to have a certain amount of discretion in the management of their own affairs; as a principle, I would lay that down.

142. Do you not think that it would leave the matter open to a great deal of jobbing in giving works to favourite contractors, if you once broke through the rule of accepting the lowest tender?—I think that, if the present system, were continued it would leave matters open to an infinity

of

Mr. *P. Dorrance Sheeby*.

27 March 1868.

of jobbing; but under an improved system, which I hope will come into operation, the gentlemen who compose the sessions should be intrusted with ample discretionary power.

143. *Lord John Browne.*] Have you ever known the case of a man tendering for work for a sum notoriously insufficient to perform it?—Yes; solely and entirely for the purpose of preventing another person from getting it.

144. And without the slightest intention of even executing the work?—Without the slightest intention of even executing it.

145. Then, if the sessions must take the lowest tender, they must take that man?—They must take that man.

146. And the sureties are only for double the amount of his tender?—Yes.

147. Then, if he offers to do for a shilling, what would require 50 *l.*, he is only required to give securities for 2 *s.*?—No; because the amount of security is calculated on the amount required. His recognizance would be 50 *l.* to the Queen.

148. Suppose there is a bridge to be built for which, in the county surveyor's opinion 50 *l.* is required, and a man is anxious that another contractor should not perform the work, he therefore tenders to perform it for 1 *s.*, and produces securities for 2 *s.*, and the only remedy which you have against him is to proceed against him for the 2 *s.*; is not that so?—No; that case is met by the Act of Parliament. The tender is made for an unfair purpose, and, therefore the sessions would be perfectly justified, under the authority of the Act of Parliament, in rejecting it.

149. Is there not a practical difficulty in drawing the line where a man tenders for 50 *l.* instead of 1 *s.*?—Of course there is; and no doubt large discretionary power should be given to the sessions, protected in such a manner as to guard against any abuse of such power.

150. You are aware of the fact, that in the case of a notorious defaulter the sessions are obliged to take him as a contractor?—If you speak of the law, I think that they are bound to do it.

151. Do you think that it is desirable that the sessions should have no discretion to refuse to take a notorious defaulter?—That leads to a very large question as to what is a notorious defaulter, and these matters are so thoroughly bound up the one with the other, that I would hesitate to answer the question immediately. What might be my notion as to what is a notorious defaulter might not be yours, and so on. It would be very difficult to provide by Act of Parliament that a notorious defaulter should not be accepted without giving a definition of a notorious defaulter.

152. Supposing a man had been declared to be so by the grand jury?—If you like you might put it in this form: That a contractor who, for a certain number of times, was found to be a defaulter in the completion of his contracts, should not be eligible in future for contracts in the county. If you despotically call a man a defaulting contractor, and under that designation preclude him from entering into contracts, that would be rather severe; but if you provide, as I have suggested, that a man who has, for a certain number of times, been declared a defaulter, or found a defaulter, or has had judgment passed against him as a defaulter, should be ineligible as a contractor, I think it would be more in accordance with the spirit of the law that he should be so precluded from being permitted to tender for contracts, and then the question arises how long you would keep the disqualification hanging over him. Would you prevent him for the remainder of his life from tendering for public works, or would you prevent him from doing so for a term of years?

153. Would it not be a much more simple course, instead of all that more complicated legislation, to give a discretion?—Yes, certainly.

154. And you are in favour of giving a discretion to meet all difficulties?—Certainly I am in favour of giving a discretion as much as possible.

155. And you would give an appeal to a judge?—Yes; I think that the tendency of modern legislation is in favour of an appeal from all decisions, and that there ought to be an appeal from every decision of the sessions or grand jury to a judge of assize, or to the Privy Council.

156. Sir *Charles Lanyon.*] With regard to that case you have just mentioned, of 1 *s.* and 50 *l.*, supposing that a man took a contract for a bridge, for which the sum of 50 *l.* would be a fair equivalent, would he not be obliged to give sureties to the amount of 50 *l.* each for the fulfilment of that contract?—He would.

157. Therefore, if the law was so amended, that in the case of a man not proceeding with his work, either not efficiently, or not within the time, he might be without difficulty proceeded against, the county would be preserved by the solvency of the sureties?—No doubt.

158. Therefore, if the law was so altered is it likely that that man would become a defaulter a second time?—I think not.

159. Nor would others be so likely to do the same?—I think that they would be deterred.

160. Therefore would not such an amendment of the Act with reference to facilities for procedure prevent that difficulty to which my noble Lord, the member for the county of Mayo, has referred with regard to the sessions approving the lowest tender; would it not altogether vanish if facilities were given by the amendment of the law in that particular?—Yes, I think if facilities were given by an amendment of the law as to instituting immediate proceedings against defaulting contractors, it would be a very great improvement upon the present state of things; but I do not think that it would lead me to alter my opinion as to giving the baronial sessions full discretion, particularly when you come to consider that, in doing so, you are entrusting them with discretion in the management of their own affairs.

161. Colonel *French.*] Do you not think that that might be equally open to abuse?—I think that under the present system it would be open to abuse; but under the system which I shall be prepared to put before the Committee, I think that would in a great measure be controlled.

162. General *Dunne.*] What are the class of men who generally attend baronial sessions?—In the county of Roscommon, which is an agricultural county, the ratepayers have very large holdings, and they are, generally speaking, a very respectable class of country farmers.

163. Do you find that they generally attend the sessions?—I find that unless there is a whip, for or against a job, they have so many claims on their own time, that they do not attend.

164. Are they not generally either connected with contractors or contractors themselves?—I think they are not, generally speaking, contractors. I do not think that the ratepayers

Mr. *P. Burrowes Sharkey.* 27 March 1868.

selected in compliance with the law, are in any way connected with the contractors.

165. *Chairman.*] When you say that the cesspayers generally are not very punctual in their attendance, does not that partially arise from the fact that they are in doubt whether they will have to serve or not, in consequence of the ballot?—Yes. They are in a state of doubt as to whether or not they will be called upon to serve until the moment that the ballot takes place; and having travelled perhaps 10 or 12 miles on a cold winter's day, a cesspayer may find on arriving at the court-house, that he is not drawn in the ballot; there is, therefore, a great disinclination to attend, on the part of persons selected to fill that office, because of the great uncertainty attending their selection.

166. *General Dunne.*] I understand you to say, that where a job is to be done, or where they are personally interested, they generally do go?—That depends; they are very often jobbers themselves, and their landlord sometimes has a little road to be repaired, or some drains to be covered at the county expense.

167. Can drains be done at the county expense for private individuals?—Yes, if they run parallel to roads.

168. Then it is in reference to roads, and not to drainage?—It may improve the property on one side or the other.

169. Do you think that the ratepayers are generally acted upon by their landlords?—They do not like to go against their landlords.

170. Is it not because their interests are mutual?—They are so in a great measure; but not in this instance, I think.

171. Do you not think that the landlords are the people to correct these little jobs, and do they correct them generally in Roscommon?—In Roscommon the duties are very fairly discharged, both by the associated ratepayers and by the magistrates; of course there are exceptional instances.

172. The general tendency of the magistrates and cesspayers is to make the rates as low as possible, is it not?—I do not know their tendency, but the practical result is that the rates have gone up considerably since 1836.

173. In Roscommon alone?—In every county in Ireland, I believe. On the whole they have considerably increased. There may be exceptional cases where public works and the expenditure upon public works are cut down; I cannot name any one case; but as a general result the taxation under the county cess has risen considerably since the year 1836.

174. Could you furnish the Committee with a return as to the increase of the rates for the county of Roscommon?—Yes.

Tuesday, 31st March 1868.

MEMBERS PRESENT:

Mr. Blake.	Mr. Herbert.
Lord John Browne.	Mr. Kendall.
Colonel Cooper.	Sir Charles Lanyon.
Mr. Dawson.	Mr. Leader.
General Dunne.	Mr. Maguire.
Colonel Forde.	The O'Conor Don.
Mr. Gregory.	Sir Colman O'Loghlen.

THE O'CONOR DON, IN THE CHAIR.

Mr. JOHN HILL, called in; and Examined.

Mr. J. Hill.

31 March 1868.

175. *Chairman*.] You are at present County Surveyor for the county of Clare, are you not?—I am.

176. You previously held that office in King's County, did you not?—I did.

177. For how long a time have you held that office?—Twelve years in the King's County.

178. And how long in the county of Clare?—I was 10 years in Clare, before, and a year since.

179. By whom are the county surveyors appointed?—By the Lord Lieutenant.

180. Is there any previous examination required?—There is. There was formerly an examination, which has been altered since; it is to be in future an examination by the Civil Service Commission.

181. Have you any assistants in Clare?—I have four assistants.

182. By whom are they appointed?—By me, or by the surveyor in office at the time.

183. And have you the power of removing them?—No.

184. Who has the power of removing them?—The grand jury.

185. What is their salary?—They are paid 80 *l.* a-year as the maximum salary in the county of Clare.

186. Do they undergo any previous examination?—They do.

187. By whom?—By the same examiners who examine the county surveyors in Dublin, at the Board of Works.

188. Could you state to the Committee what are the duties of the county surveyor, in the first place, with respect to presentments applied for?—He is obliged to examine them, estimate for them, and be prepared to advise the sessions on their propriety.

189. How long before the sessions does the county surveyor get notice of an application for presentments?—Only 10 days.

190. Do you believe that during those 10 days he has time to examine all the presentments that are applied for?—Not at all; he must have examined the county previously to be of any service whatever to the presentment sessions. It would be wholly out of his power to examine sufficiently in that time.

191. In addition to the examination of works applied for, has the county surveyor to see where works are required in different places which may not be applied for?—He is obliged to do so, and to make application for them, if he considers them necessary.

192. He has also to inspect all the works for which application for payment is to be made at the sessions, has he not?—He has.

193. How long before the sessions does he make this examination of the works?—During the latter part of the half-year previous to the sessions for works of maintenance, and, for special works, as near the sessions as is in his power.

194. After the works are approved of at the sessions, what is the duty of the county surveyor?—To prepare forms of tender and contract, and such specifications of the works, maps and plans, and elevations as may be necessary.

195. He has to do that before the adjourned sessions?—He has.

196. What is generally the length of time between the first sessions and the adjourned sessions?—In Clare it is about five or six weeks.

197. The county surveyor has also similar duties before the grand jury, has he not?—He has.

198. He has also to inspect all roads and bridges which may be suddenly damaged, and to specify and estimate the probable expense of repairs, has he not?—He has.

199. He has also to inspect and report upon sudden damages occurring between the sessions and the assizes?—He has.

200. And to execute the works for their repairs, if ordered by the grand jury?—He has.

201. Although those works are not certified at presentment sessions?—There is a special enactment for the purpose. Where it is proved on oath to the grand jury that the works could not be delayed until the ordinary presentments without danger or inconvenience to the public, they are empowered to make a presentment for the works, and to have them executed.

202. Is it the duty of the county surveyor to prosecute in case of a contractor neglecting his work?—It is.

203. Do you believe the law at present in that respect to be satisfactory?—I have found

no difficulty in prosecuting road contractors under the present law before the chairman of sessions.

201. Have you power to prosecute contractors before the petty sessions for all sorts of works?—No.

202. Would you explain to the Committee the works as to which you have that power?—Only for the repair of roads, not for either the maintenance of roads, or for the construction of bridges, or for hill cuttings and several other works, as to which it would be most desirable that that power should be given to the magistrates.

206. But as regards the repair of roads, you consider the present law is amply sufficient?—I do not as to prosecution before the magistrates. It is a very tedious process requiring two summonses; and it is really more a punishment on the surveyor than it is on the defaulting contractor.

207. In what way would you propose that it should be amended?—To shorten the proceedings and to make it applicable to all works, both of maintenance and construction, such as bridges and other works usually presented by the grand jury.

208. It is to the 10 day's notice then that you object chiefly?—I object to the two summonses, and the non-application of it to any works but the mere repair of roads.

209. Are you obliged to keep an office in the county?—I am.

210. Will you explain to the Committee what is the course of proceeding of a person applying for a presentment?—He would have to lodge an application with the secretary of the grand jury, and to serve notices, by posting them on the police barracks, and to serve a notice on the clerk of petty sessions of the district in which the work is situate, and a notice on the county surveyor; and applicants have then to attend before the sessions to advocate, or to explain the nature of the application which they make.

211. You stated just now that you believed that it was not possible for the county surveyor to examine all the works applied for?—No.

212. How then is he able to give an opinion to the magistrates and cesspayers at presentment sessions?—From his previous knowledge of the county, and from information derived from his assistants, and from partial examination also.

213. Do you believe that the system of assistants is a good one; do you think that the class of men whom you have as assistants are of a very high description?—They are not.

214. And the county surveyor is obliged to rely a good deal upon what they report to him, is he not?—He is; but I cannot conceive that any county surveyor would entrust them with matters requiring skill beyond their powers. What I employ them for is the mere details of the works, such as serving notice on contractors, measuring materials, and works of that nature.

215. Colonel *Forde*.] Do you not appoint your own deputies?—We do.

216. Lord *John Browne*.] Do you do it yourself; does not the grand jury do it?—The surveyor himself does it.

217. Colonel *Forde*.] Do you not take care to have as good a class of men as you can?—I have the best I can get.

218. *Chairman*.] But the salary is very small, is it not, and you cannot get a very superior man for 90 *l.* a year?—Certainly not.

219. Mr. *Leader*.] Has there been any improvement in the character and position of the assistants since their salary was raised, as it was authorized to be by Act of Parliament some three or four years ago?—A considerable improvement, both in their efficiency and in the character of the men offering, has been the result.

220. In your county did you change your staff after the augmentation of the salary was authorized?—It changed in the King's County where I was employed, not by the dismissal of men, but one man died, and another resigned his office.

221. How many assistants would there be for the county of Cork?—I think that there are only nine, which is a wholly inadequate number for such a county.

222. *Chairman*.] When applications for payment are made at the presentment sessions, you give your opinion as to whether these applications are justified or not, do you not?—I do.

223. Is the sessions obliged to approve of them if you certify them?—No.

224. And they can certify them although you disapprove of them?—I do not think that they can, nor do I know of any instance in which they have done so.

225. Practically they never approve of an application which has not been certified by you?—I have never known an instance of it.

226. After the application for payment is approved of at sessions, is any payment made until the assizes?—There is now.

227. Will you explain in what instances that occurs?—In several instances; in the county of which I have lately taken charge, I found that there was a very poor class of men as road contractors, and I made an application to Master Fitzgibbon, who is the receiving master, having the audit of the treasurer's accounts; and I laid before him the state of the case in a letter which I will hand to the Committee if they think proper, and he advised that the treasurer would be justified in paying three-fourths of the amount of the contract, on my certificate before the assizes, to the contractor, for the purpose of assisting him in the execution of the work.

228. Lord *John Browne*.] Was that without any previous order from the grand jury to that effect?—There must be a resolution of the grand jury authorizing it to be done.

229. *Chairman*.] But might not the succeeding grand jury refuse to approve of those presentments?—They might refuse to allow that proceeding to continue.

230. Colonel *Forde*.] How would the necessary funds be provided by the treasurer?—In the county of Clare I made an investigation, and we had over 7,000 *l.* that might have been available for such a purpose.

231. Was that in Exchequer Bonds?—Some was in Exchequer Bonds, and some in the hands of the treasurer.

232. *Chairman*.] But the grand jury have always the power of refusing to allow the payment for presentments, although the payment had been approved of at the sessions, have they not?—They have.

233. Then supposing this payment had been previously made by the county surveyor, and that the grand jury afterwards thought that this work

work had not been satisfactorily done, and refused to certify it or to mark it "approved," what would happen with respect to the payment made by the county surveyor?—I think that portion of the presentment would be legally discharged, whether the grand jury discharged it or not, if certified by the surveyor and paid by the treasurer.

234. *Sir Charles Lanyon.*] On the order of the the grand jury in the first instance?—On the previous order of the grand jury.

235. *Chairman.*] Do you see any good result from having this double application for payment, first to the presentment sessions, and secondly to the grand jury?—I do.

236. What good results from it?—It gives a very adequate control by the grand jury. For instance, it might occur that the sessions, whom we always look upon as an irresponsible body, passed accounts without a certificate of the surveyor. There would be no mode of checking such an abuse as that, excepting the control of the grand jury.

237. Do you consider the sessions to be an irresponsible body?—I do at present.

238. Do you consider the grand jury to be a responsible body?—Their interest is too large in the county for them to be considered an irresponsible body. They are the men having the largest interest in each county, and I look upon them as a much more responsible body than the sessions.

239. In what way do you mean that they are more responsible?—That they have a greater interest in the well being and in the proper conduct of the affairs of the county.

240. The presentment sessions is generally a court composed of all the magistrates of the county, and of a certain number of the highest cesspayers, is it not?—It is very frequently composed of one magistrate. I have attended, I suppose, 20 sessions in my life with but one magistrate to do the business.

241. Colonel *French.*] Do your cesspayers attend pretty regularly?—They do in the county of Clare; but in the county I was in before, in several baronies we would never have more than one or two cesspayers.

242. *Chairman.*] How are the cesspayers selected in Clare?—There is a list of 100 of the highest cesspayers, furnished by the barony constable, and that list is handed to the grand jury secretary to strike off the names of those who served the previous sessions. Invariably, in Clare, the grand jury take the first names that occur on the list, omitting those that are marked as having attended the previous sessions.

243. They take the highest rated cesspayers, do they not?—They take the highest rated cesspayers.

244. Colonel *French.*] Irrespective of their position as living in the barony for which they are chosen?—They take them on the list; but, as far as I recollect, they are all resident in the barony.

245. But are they taken irrespective of their position in the barony?—They do not make any selection of that nature in Clare. They consider that they are bound to select the highest.

246. Do you not think that it would be advisable that such an arrangement should be made?—I would rather the cesspayers themselves should do that.

247. But do you not think it advisable that the cesspayers should be scattered over the barony from which they come?—It would be most advisable.

248. *Chairman.*] How long is a contractor out of pocket now for expenditure on a road?—He would be, under the late regulations, out of pocket for a half year in Clare. Now, he need be only out of pocket half a year for one-fourth of the amount of his contract, if he acquits himself so as to deserve it.

249. But, I presume, that is only an exceptional case; it is not the general rule to pay contractors three-fourths, is it?—It is.

250. Where do you get the money to pay so large a portion as that?—In every county that I know there is a large balance in the hands of the treasurer.

251. Sufficiently large to pay three-fourths of the expenses of the roads?—There is.

252. Colonel *French.*] Is your county cess collected after the assizes at which the levy is granted, or is it only collected immediately before the assizes before which the works come?—Some of it is paid up three months before the assizes.

253. That will give you funds, of course?—Yes; but it is not necessary.

254. Is that the case in all counties?—No.

255. *Chairman.*] How many miles of road have you under your charge now?—1,700, and odd.

256. Could you state how many there were in the year 1847, in Clare?—I think in 1813 there were 1,400, and odd.

257. Are there many applications now for new roads?—No.

258. You think the county is sufficiently supplied with works?—Clare is not sufficiently supplied yet.

259. Is the same the case with respect to King's County?—No; it is adequately supplied with roads.

260. Do you think the expenses of new roads, and the repairs of roads, have increased of late years?—They have.

261. Have they much increased?—In some counties they have very considerably increased.

262. To what do you attribute the increase?—Principally to the social change that is taking place in the country; the increase in the rate of wages, and the increased difficulty in procuring contractors.

263. But, on the other hand, ought there not to be a diminution in consequence of the county being now tolerably well supplied with roads?—There is a diminution, so far as the expense of new works or construction is concerned, but the expense of maintenance, which is what I alluded to, has considerably increased.

264. You say there is a difficulty found in procuring contractors?—Great difficulty.

265. Has the grand jury in Clare been much in the habit of giving works to the county surveyor to execute?—They gave none to my predecessor; but they gave some to me in charge at the last assizes.

266. Have you heard any complaint in Clare of the incidence of the county cess being all paid by the occupiers?—I have.

267. Mr. *Leader.*] Among what class of persons?—Principally amongst the middle class of cesspayers.

268. *Chairman.*] Do you believe that if some portion were paid by the landowners, it would, on one hand, give them a greater interest in county works, and on the other, allay that feeling of

Mr. J. Hill.

31 March 1868.

Mr. *J. Hill.*

31 March 1852.

of dissatisfaction?—I do not think it would apply to the first part of the question, because most of our grand jurors are large cesspayers themselves; but as regards the second part, no doubt it would give great satisfaction to the body of cesspayers of the county. As regards the permanent works of the county, such as buildings like the lunatic asylum that has been lately built, and court-houses and gaols, they think that it is a great hardship that they should be altogether paid for by the occupiers; but they would have no objection whatever to pay for the maintenance of the whole of the roads.

269. You have stated that the cesspayers and magistrates attended very irregularly at those sessions in King's county; to what do you attribute that?—In King's county they were satisfied that things were going on very well, and there was the other thing, that no man was sure that he would be balloted for. The two motives operated, for I inquired of them frequently; I said I should rather see a larger number of cesspayers attending, and they said they saw everything going on to their satisfaction, and that they did not want to give themselves any trouble.

270. Do you not think the uncertainty of the ballot leads to many not attending?—I am sure it does.

271. You also stated, did you not, that the magistrates in that county also attended very irregularly?—They always made an arrangement that one attended, and we very frequently had but that one.

272. General *Dunne.*] One must attend, I believe?—One must attend to be chairman of the sessions, and we very frequently had but that one.

273. *Chairman.*] And, perhaps, only one or two cesspayers?—Sometimes.

274. Do you not think that if a portion of the county cess were directly paid by the landlord, that would lead to the magistrates attending more regularly at the sessions?—I do not think it would in the county which I have mentioned. Of the magistrates and cesspayers, I do not know more than three or four that are not large cesspayers themselves, and some of them are very much the largest in the county.

275. And yet they leave to one individual, or, perhaps, two, the whole initiative of all the works of the county?—They do very frequently.

276. Mr. *Lowder.*] Have you heard of any dissatisfaction about the way in which the associated cesspayers are now nominated?—I have heard of it.

277. Among what classes?—Amongst the cesspayers themselves.

278. In what way would they prefer them to be chosen?—They would prefer to have them chosen by an election similar to that of the Poor Law Guardians.

279. *Chairman.*] Is the county cess high in Clare?—It is.

280. What is the rate in the pound in the half year?—It is up to 1 *s.* 5 *d.* in the pound half yearly in some of the baronies in Clare.

281. What is the average on the whole county?—I have here a paper which has reference to the expense of roads alone; then there is to be added to this the county charges.

282. And, the other charges being added to those charges, it amounts in some baronies, you say, to 1 *s.* 5 *d.* in the pound?—Yes.

283. Is each barony put down separately in the county books?—Yes, every charge is put down separately.

284. Some baronies, in fact, pay a much greater rate in the pound than others, do they not?—Very considerably so.

285. Do some of them even pay twice as much?—They do.

286. At presentment sessions, if there be no magistrate present, although there be a sufficient number of cesspayers, can the sessions be held?—They cannot.

287. Do you believe that to be a good system?—I do not.

288. Do you think that the cesspayers ought to be permitted to elect a chairman if a magistrate be not present?—I do.

289. Do you think it desirable that all the magistrates of the county should have the power of attending at a presentment sessions for a particular barony?—I never saw any objection to it; I mean that I never saw any impropriety arising from it. I have heard of some such instances, in which there is a great dissatisfaction on the subject, and it would be better to allay that and to allow no magistrate, except he had property in the barony, to act in it.

290. Have you any observation to make with regard to the notices which have to be given before session?—I consider that it would be most desirable that, instead of serving a 10 days' notice, they should be served at least 21 days, and that instead of the applicants posting those notices they should be printed on a list, and that list should be sent to each magistrate and associated cesspayer, and also posted in the usual place for posting notices.

291. You think that 10 days' notice is not sufficient to give to the county surveyor and the persons interested?—It is not, and I should say, too, that the sort of notices which are posted are not such as are easily deciphered by the people interested; they are little printed notices, and they are stuck up, and that is all that is known about them.

292. On whom would you throw the duty of promulgating those notices?—On the secretary of the grand jury.

293. Have you any observation to make with respect to the county surveyors applying for a work if no contractor applies?—His duty is circumscribed to works which are not applied for, and it often happens that an informal application is made, or that there is some defect in it; and it would be most judicious if it was in his power to remedy it by a new application.

294. At present if any application is made for a work, if that application be informal, the county surveyor cannot then apply himself?—Not according to the law.

295. The sessions are obliged, are they not, to take the lowest tender?—They are.

296. Are you aware that that sometimes leads to attempts at fraud on the part of contractors?—I am.

297. Would you explain how that arises?—In several places there is a system of fraud; in each case when a man wishes to tender for a road he puts in perhaps two or three tenders, and at different rates; if he happens to be the lowest tenderer, and he finds that there is no one between him and his higher tender, he withdraws the lower one and gets the highest; and there is a system of selling the tenders to one another, and a great many fraudulent transactions.

298. How

298. How would you provide against that?—I see no remedy, except to insist upon the strict and proper fulfilment of the contracts.

299. Do you think the security at present offered is sufficient?—It is quite adequate for a maintenance contract, and more than adequate for the special works; it is excessive for those works.

300. The present security is twice the amount of presentment, is it not?—Yes.

301. *Lord John Browne.*] Supposing 60 *l.* is granted for a work, and a man tenders to do it for 60 *l.*, it is twice 30 *l.* and not twice 50 *l.*, is it not?—It is, but that would be the presentment afterwards.

302. *Chairman.*] Do you propose any alteration in cases where roads are neglected by contractors?—I would propose that, upon the provisions of the 29th section of the Grand Jury Act, the provisions of the Act enabling them to be summoned should be engrafted, and that the proceedings of summoning them should be shortened; that instead of having two summonses there should be but one summons; that there should be a summons served after the expiration of one notice, and that the magistrates should adjudicate upon that; and I think that it would be most desirable that the magistrates should have the power of putting an end to the contract in case of a gross breach of it.

303. Would you propose that any additional power should be given for advancing money to contractors before the assizes?—I would like to see the Act of Parliament explicit to carry out what the Master in Chancery has at present sanctioned; because it is a confused section under which the grants are made, and that the 109th section should be made more explicit.

304. In what way would you propose that it should be altered; would you give power to the county surveyor on all occasions to advance this money if he thought proper?—Not without a previous order of the grand jury; but if he had the sanction of the grand jury it is a most beneficial thing to do, and then the treasurer would be bound to advance it out of the funds "applicable to the general purposes of the county," instead of the words which are in the section now "applicable to the purpose." Some of the treasurers who have an interest in retaining the money consider that, as being the money only that is raised and levied for the purpose of the presentment.

305. With regard to traverses for presentments, how are they carried on at present?—There must be a notice served two days after the day of the sessions, and I consider that almost a bar to the exercise of that most important privilege of traversing for improper presentments.

306. What would you propose in place of it?—A notice of ten days before the assizes would be quite enough.

307. Have you any proposal to make with respect to the re-presenting of monies?—I have. The section under which the grand jury represent monies at present is not very clear or explicit. It is considered by some lawyers that they have no power to re-present the money to the credit of the denomination for which it was raised; but that they must apply it to the completion of the works, which is often inexpedient, and in some cases impracticable. Power should be given to them where a work is not executed from any cause, at their discretion to re-present that money to the credit of the denomination from which it was originally levied.

308. What do you mean by "the denomination from which it was originally levied"?—The barony or the county at large. Mr. J. Hill.

31 March 1868.

309. You propose that it should be re-presented to that barony, or county at large, for any other work?—Yes, in aid of the next levy of the cess.

310. At present there are certain presentments which are levied half on the county at large, and half on the barony, are there not?—Yes.

311. What presentments are those?—For roads on which Her Majesty's mails are carried.

312. Do you think that a desirable way of levying presentments?—It is, so far as it goes. The post-roads previous to the construction of railways in Ireland did represent the principal or main lines of the country, and I think that it would be most beneficial and desirable that all the roads which are similar to what the post-roads were formerly should be charged, half on the county at large and half on the baronies. They are excessively heavy on some of the baronies now for those main lines of communication through the counties.

313. With respect to sudden damages which occur, at present two justices may order the damage to be repaired, may they not?—Yes.

314. Must they view the damage?—They must view it according to the present law.

315. And they must also have the approval of the county surveyor, must they not?—They need not.

316. Do you approve of that?—No; I would propose, that on the requisition of the county surveyor, the two justices should be empowered to give the order, without going to view the place.

317. Would you take away from them the power of ordering these repairs in case the county surveyor had not certified that the work ought to be done?—I would not, although it is practically taken away from them in the county of Clare. There is a resolution of the grand jury, that the county surveyor, or his assistant, must certify for every work of sudden damage before the magistrates give an order.

318. It might often be very inconvenient, might it not, if the county surveyor were obliged to view cases of sudden damage?—His assistant could do it.

319. County surveyors are paid a regular salary, are they not?—They are.

320. And they receive no fees?—They receive no fees.

321. The secretaries of the grand juries receive a salary and also fees, do they not?—They do.

322. Are you aware what fees are paid to the secretaries of grand juries?—I am not.

323. Do you think the system of fees a good one?—I think it a very bad one.

324. You are aware, I suppose, that in most counties the contractors consider themselves obliged to pay fees to the secretaries of the grand juries for drawing up their applications, and different other forms?—They do.

325. In that way are not a great many fees paid which are not exactly legal?—There is no law for them; they are established by old usage; but it is a very objectionable course.

326. Do you think that if the secretaries of grand juries were paid regular and increased salaries, and these fees were done away with, still the contractors would continue to pay them for forms and for clerkship work?—If they were paid

Mr. *J. Hill.*

21 March [illegible].

paid adequate salaries, I would be very glad to see a penalty inflicted upon them for receiving any fees.

327. If the secretaries got an extra salary for the abolition of those fees, do you not think that they ought then to be obliged to fill up the applications for the contractors?—I do not think so. I do not think that there is any necessity whatever for their filling the applications. The contractors would get that done themselves. They should give them the forms, and there is no difficulty whatever in filling them.

328. What description of presentments come before the county at large sessions?—There is the building and repair of the court houses; and I think that the construction of mile-posts and things of that nature should also come before them, and the salaries of the court-house keepers.

329. Are not the majority of cases which come before the county at large sessions, almost imperative, or matter of course presentments?—Nearly all.

330. Do you see much utility in those county at large sessions?—I never did.

331. Do you think that they might be done away with?—Perfectly, without the slightest inconvenience or injury to the country.

332. Do you find that the cesspayers selected at the baronial sessions are very regular in attendance on the county at large sessions?—They are very irregular.

333. Colonel *Forde*.] You stated in the early part of your examination, that you were obliged to keep an office; is not that provided for you in the county court house?—It is provided.

334. You have no rent to pay for it?—I have no rent to pay for it.

335. As regards the posting of those notices which you talked about, does not the secretary post those notices now on the different police barracks and the different court houses which are required?—No; he posts only the notices which are promulgated after the sessions, and not the notices for applications for works. Those are posted by the applicants themselves.

336. This (*handing a paper to Witness*) is a notice posted by the secretary of the grand jury in the County of Down before the sessions?—This is a schedule of the applications which have been made, and they are printed here and posted, and that is what I propose to have done.

337. That is done in some counties?—It is not done compulsorily.

338. And a form of application such as that is always posted in the usual way, and sent to the magistrates, and to all the associated cesspayers who are on the list to attend the sessions?—That is the proceeding which I have recommended, and which I consider most desirable.

339. As to the fees, you stated, did you not, you were against fees to the secretary, and that you would give him a higher salary for the loss of those fees?—Yes.

340. Why are you against the secretary having those fees?—There are many objections to it; the principal one is that they are irregular and uncertain. In some counties they are very high, and in others they are moderate; in addition to that it gives the secretary a vested interest in the number of presentments in the county, which may often be a very inconvenient and very improper thing.

341. How could the secretary affect that?—He might influence it.

342. In what way?—In the first place, if it is known that his income is considerably dependent on it, it precludes his brother officer from perhaps taking the course of consolidating contracts, or arranging them in a different way.

343. Or from refusing an application which he thinks ought to be refused?—His interest would be to multiply the applications.

344. But your interest as county surveyor might clash with his, and you might wish to stop an application, but you would not like to do it?—I do not think it would go that extent with any surveyor; but there is often a very desirable consolidation of contracts.

345. Would you get the contractors to take a contract at less money, provided those fees were not payable?—I think so.

346. The amount of fees on each contract is not more than four or five shillings; do you think that the county would get the benefit of that four or five shillings?—No. As I stated before, I purposely abstained, during my whole time in office, from knowing anything directly about the fees paid to secretaries; but I believe that it comes to 10 *s.* or to 12 *s.* generally on small contracts in some places.

347. If those fees are so good, would there not be always other people who would get the advantage, if the secretary had not it, of the filling up of those documents?—The other person would have to do it by agreement between himself and the contractor; but when the secretary monopolises it, he can charge a considerable amount.

348. Is it the case that he can monopolise it?—He can practically monopolise it.

349. But the contractor can now fill up his own application himself, can he not?—He can.

350. And it is only for his own convenience that he goes to the secretary?—It is practically a monopoly in the whole of the West of Ireland.

351. Do you think in your county, or in the county in which you were before, no other person fills up those applications except the secretary of the grand jury?—Not one in the county in which I was before. The secretary there did it himself, and he charged very small fees. I understand that occasionally some people start up and do it in Clare; but the great majority are filled up by the clerk of the secretary, and not by himself.

352. I understand you to state that you thought the county would derive benefit if those fees were done away with, and not charged to the contractor?—I do.

353. Lord *John Browne*.] Will you state, from Parliamentary Return, No. 456 of last Session, the amount of fees received by the secretary of the County of Down, and the amount of his salary?—The amount of salary was 202 *l.*, and the amount of fees, 482 *l.* 18 *s.* 1 *d.*

354. Will you give the Committee the same information as regards the County of Tipperary?—The secretary's salary is stated here as 232 *l.*, and the fees at 390 *l.*

355. What were the amounts in the County of Wexford?—The salary was 140 *l.*, and the amount of fees 220 *l.*

356. If a tender is informal, the secretary is not obliged to bring it before the road sessions, is he?—He is not.

357. And is it not the case that if the tenders are not filled up by the secretary, they are very frequently informal?—No; it is a very simple proceeding to fill up the tenders.

358. But

358. But, practically, are they not frequently informed, and do they not fall to the ground in consequence?—I never knew one instance.

359. Why do you suppose that these large sums are paid to the contractors, unless it be for some such reason as that?—I cannot tell what is the reason they are paid, but I think it a very objectionable course.

360. Have you a small class of contractors in your county?—We have.

361. With presentments frequently of 10 *l.* and 20 *l.*?—Yes, we have.

362. Is it your practice to pay three-fourths of those amounts on a certificate from the county surveyor?—They must be over 20 *l.*

363. Some members of the Committee wanted to know where the treasurer obtained funds to make those payments. Will you look at the last column but one in that return, and see what was the amount that is invested in Exchequer Bills for the last five years, for the counties of Tipperary and Tyrone?—In Tyrone there are 29,000 *l.* stated to be invested, and in Tipperary 41,000 *l.*

364. Does not that system of paying the contractors three-fourths of their money before the sessions, practically deprive the sessions and the grand jury of any control over the completion of the works?—It would if it was abused.

365. It leaves it entirely in the hands of the county surveyor, does it not?—It does, but the grand jury have the power of controlling it by not passing the resolution. It must be passed every assizes.

366. In your county there is a general resolution at every assizes which authorises all payments to be made in this way?—Yes.

367. You stated, did you not, that you had an office in the County Court House?—Yes.

368. That is not always the case, I believe?—It is not.

369. A great many county surveyors have to pay for their own offices, have they not?—They have.

370. You said that you think no magistrate ought to attend at the sessions, unless he has property in the barony?—Yes.

371. Are you aware that there are in Ireland some magistrates who pay 5,000 *l.* and 7,000 *l.* a year rent, but who own no property?—I would consider that person as having property, he being in the possession of it in the barony.

372. Then do you consider any man who occupies land to be in the same position as a man who owns land?—I think so, for the purposes of that duty.

373. Has it come to your knowledge that in many cases magistrates have not attended adjourned sessions, and that the adjourned sessions have consequently fallen to the ground?—It has been so in some instances.

374. Is there any possible means of executing any repairs in a barony in which that occurs under those circumstances?—There is; the action can be taken by the grand jury under the 20 & 21 Vict., where no adjourned sessions are held; there is a great objection to that, but it can be done.

375. What is the general attendance of magistrates now at the sessions?—In Clare both magistrates and cess-payers attend very largely.

376. In your opinion, when cess-payers do not attend, is it because they have confidence in the proceedings of the magistrates?—That is what we always considered to be the case in King's County.

Mr. J. Hill.

31 March 1868.

377. And their non-attendance you think arises chiefly from that cause?—Entirely.

378. *Chairman.*] Is it your opinion that their non-attendance arises entirely from their confidence in the magistrates?—I am wrong in saying entirely, because there is some uncertainty as to their being balloted for; but the general non-attendance in King's County entirely arose from the confidence that things were going on satisfactorily, and that it was not necessary for them to go.

379. They have confidence in the magistrates?—They have confidence in the magistrates.

380. But you stated before, did you not, that the magistrates themselves did not attend regularly?—By one magistrate the business was often as well conducted as by a larger attendance. There is very little to be done in that and many other midland counties but the maintenance of the roads.

381. *Lord John Browne.*] Are you talking now of the sessions, or of the adjourned sessions?—Of the adjourned sessions.

382. Have you often known but one magistrate attend without any cesspayers?—Very often.

383. With regard to the prosecutions, you said you were satisfied with the present power of prosecution with a slight alteration?—I am.

384. Supposing a man is to be prosecuted, is not the matter obliged to be referred to the Attorney General, and does not he direct proceedings to be taken by the Crown solicitor, and are not those proceedings the most expensive that can possibly be devised?—I am not aware that any reference whatever is made to the Attorney General. I never knew it, nor is it the case in the counties with which I am acquainted. I give instructions to the local attorney, and the process is filled up forthwith, and served upon the man.

385. Is it not the case that when those prosecutions are ordered by the grand jury, very heavy bills of costs come in, and no money is recovered from the contractors?—It is very often the case, but the costs are generally levied on the contractors.

386. Are you aware that the Attorney General is entitled to a fee of five guineas on every proceeding which is taken?—I am sure it is not claimed.

387. We had it in evidence from Mr. Sharkey, that it was?—He must be mistaken. I know the practice in six or seven counties, and there is no such thing known.

388. Would you be surprised to hear that, in the County of Mayo, we paid hundreds of pounds of costs without recovering more than 3 or 4 per cent. of the amount from the contractors; those proceedings being taken in the way that I have described under the authority, and by the directions of, the Attorney General for Ireland?—I would not be surprised at it, but no such thing has occurred within my experience.

389. Will you read Question 79 of Mr. Sharkey's evidence?—(*Q.*) "Do you know what the fee is?—(*A.*) I think it is a fee of five guineas for each bond. He is entitled to it; it is one of his perquisites, and he generally exacts it." There is no such thing in the eight counties that I am aware of.

390. Then Mr. Sharkey was wrong in giving that evidence?—He must be under a mistake.

391. Do

Mr. J. Hill.

[illegible] March [illegible].

391. Do you undertake to say that the proceedings must not be taken under the authority of the Attorney General for Ireland?—I do not know anything about that; but all I know is, that if I give instructions to the local Crown solicitor, he invariably fills the processes, and has them issued at once.

392. Will you read Questions 80 and 81 of Mr. Sharkey's evidence?—(Q.) "Then the proceedings must be taken as he" (that is, the Attorney General) "directs?—(A.) The proceedings cannot be taken by an officer of the grand jury. I think that the late Attorney General (or the present one, I am not quite certain which) has issued an order that his fiat shall not be given unless the proceedings are carried on by an officer named by himself; that officer is generally the sessional Crown solicitor, and he, in all those cases, represents the Crown; and therefore the Attorney General felt that this, which is Crown business, ought to be carried on by him."

393. Is not the recognizance of every contractor made to the Crown?—It is.

394. And is it not for that reason that the Attorney General interferes?—I believe so.

395. Now read the next Question if you please?—"The result is, that these legal proceedings are taken in the most expensive possible mode?" The answer is, "In the most expensive mode possible, being first of all reached by a most expensive and roundabout proceeding, and then carried out in a more expensive manner." That is not the fact in either Clare, King's County, Limerick, Meath, Westmeath, or in Queen's County.

396. *Chairman.*] In Question 82, the 17th section of the 19 & 20 Vict., c. 63, is given, which alters the law in a certain respect?—It does not alter the other remedy a bit; but it gives another remedy for one class of presentments alone, that is, for the repair of roads.

397. But is it your opinion, that irrespective of that section of the 19 & 20 Vict. c. 63, proceedings can be taken against a contractor without going through this expensive form mentioned by Mr. Sharkey?—It is not an expensive form; there must be some mistake about it; it may be made expensive in some counties; but the whole expense is, I think, about 1 *l.*

398. The whole expense is about 1 *l.*, you say, for a breach of contract, for instance, for building a bridge?—I think so.

399. *Lord John Browne.*] The county surveyor has no fund in hand, has he, for taking proceedings under the 19 and 20 Vict. c. 63?—He has no public funds.

400. So that if he takes proceedings against a defaulting contractor, if he is beaten on any technical points he has to pay the costs out of his own pocket?—He has.

401. Is not that an impediment to the exercise of the power conveyed by that Act?—I think it is a great hardship.

402. You spoke of assistants; are you in favour of the county surveyors having assistants generally?—I think that they could not discharge their duties with any effect without assistants.

403. You are aware, are you not, that in some counties they are very much disapproved of, and not allowed?—I am aware that that is the case in Galway; that is the only one that I know of, and I think they have but four assistants for a very large county.

404. Has a case ever come under your knowledge of a county surveyor's assistant taking bribes?—Never.

405. Are you in favour of a county surveyor being allowed to practise professionally?—I am too much interested in that question myself to give a very useful answer, but I am in favour of it.

406. Colonel *French.*] What does your county say about it?—I think that they would be perfectly satisfied that I would not neglect my duty for any other business.

407. Lord *John Browne.*] In travelling about to attend to your private business, you go over a great many of the county roads, do you not?—I have no private business, but one small drainage at present.

408. A man who had private business would naturally travel over the roads of the county, would he not?—He would.

409. And that would give him an opportunity of seeing those roads?—It would.

410. Do the assistants in your county, or in other counties that you are acquainted with, keep shops, or perform any other business?—They do not keep shops, or perform any business of that sort; but some of them farm, and I have one assistant at present who transacts business as a civil engineer and land agent.

411. Mr. *Gregory.*] Your roads have always been so admirably kept that I should like to ask you how far you consider yourself bound to go over those roads personally every year?—In a large county like Clare, once a year is as often as I can possibly say that I would be able to go over every road.

412. But do you go over every road in the course of the year?—I think I would be neglecting my duty very much if I did not. In King's County I went over them twice a year regularly.

413. Lord *John Browne.*] You expressed an opinion that certain works should be charged half on the county at large; has your attention ever been attracted to the case of large bridges?—Yes.

414. Are you aware that the largest rivers in Ireland are generally the boundaries between two counties, or between two baronies?—They are very frequently.

415. Is it then your opinion that the expense of a large bridge connecting two counties, or baronies, should all be charged on the barony?—I think it is a very great hardship to charge it upon the barony.

416. For instance, in any two counties between which the river Shannon is running, the bridge would be of an expensive character, would it not?—Even in the case of a bridge very much smaller than that, it is a very great hardship.

417. Practically, those bridges are for the benefit of the whole county, are they not, and not for the benefit of the barony itself?—Yes.

418. By the existing law, the barony may put the whole cost of such bridge on the county at large, or the whole on the barony?—They may.

419. But they cannot put half on the barony and half on the county?—They can do so, at least Judge Keogh ruled so. I am under the impression that it was argued before him, and I believe that it is a very fair interpretation of the law, that the grand jury can put half on the barony and half on the county.

420. Do you know where that was?—It was in Ennis, the assizes before last; last spring assizes.

421. And

Mr. *J. Hill*.

31 March 1868.

421. And up to that time there was a doubt about it?—There was a doubt about it. I was under the impression myself that they could only put the whole on the county at large, or the whole on the barony, and that they could not divide it. They did divide it, and it was brought before Mr. Justice Keogh, and argued, and he decided that they exercised a very proper discretion in putting half on the county at large.

422. Was that in the county of Clare?—Yes.

423. In your opinion, should it be left discretionary with the grand jury as to whether a bridge over a large river like the Shannon should be put wholly on the locality, or not?—I think that in the case of such a bridge as has been alluded to over the Shannon, there should be no discretion to any party, and that it should not be contemplated to levy the money on the adjoining barony at all.

424. Do you know the River Moy?—I do.

425. A bridge over that must be of a very expensive character, must it not?—It must.

426. Do you think that in a case of that sort the grand jury should have the power to put the whole cost upon the barony?—I think not.

427. Where would you draw the line, at 500 *l.* or 1,000 *l.*?—Something like that. I think that a bridge costing 500 *l.* is a very severe thing to throw on a barony.

428. Are you aware that these bridges are frequently in poor mountain districts, where the cess is very high, and where sometimes they are liable to be swept away by floods; and generally speaking, is not a small and poor barony badly represented on the grand jury?—It is sometimes the case, but in the county in which I transact business now, the baronies are very fairly represented.

429. You stated that you wished to have a larger extent of roads, half on the county at large?—I would.

430. How would you define them?—The leading roads from market towns to market towns, and from market towns to points of importance upon the sea coast, such as for shipping, fishing, or bathing.

431. How would you define what is a leading road, because every little village is a market town on occasions?—Wherever there are market towns, is quite a sufficient definition; it should be that the one direct or principal road between two market towns.

432. Colonel *Forde*.] Do you find any inconvenience from the fact that you are obliged to hold the sessions in a town in the barony for which you are holding the sessions?—I have never found any inconvenience in that.

433. There is no inconvenience in your county?—No, nor in the other county in which I was employed; it is changed from town to town.

434. Do you not think that in some cases it might be an advantage to give the grand jury the power of allowing the sessions to be held in a town which was not in the immediate barony, which was more convenient both for the cess-payers and magistrates and contractors?—There might possibly be some inconvenience, but I know of none whatever myself.

435. Lord *John Browne*.] When I asked you if no adjourned sessions were held, you said that the grand jury could take the contracts?—They can.

436. And you stated to me your authority for saying that, where the adjourned sessions fell to the ground, the grand jury could pass the presentment?—They could open the tenders and deal with them.

437. Will you read from the Act of Parliament the words which you think authorise that course of procedure?—The case of no tenders is provided for by the 20th & 21st Victoria, which, after reciting, "That great loss and inconvenience has arisen to the public from the want of proper contractors to tender at adjourned sessions for the execution of works previously sanctioned at the first sessions; and whereas it is expedient in such cases to make further provision for the repair, maintenance, and construction of such public works," enacts that (sec. 1), "when any application for the repair, maintenance, or construction of any public work or road shall have been approved of at road sessions, and duly advertised for tenders in the manner directed and provided for in the said recited Act, if no proper contractor shall tender at the adjourned sessions, or if no proposal shall be made or accepted for such work, the grand jury at the next assizes shall have power and authority to present for such work of repair, maintenance, or construction, or the re-building of any bridge or gullet, any sum of money in such case necessary, not exceeding the amount approved of at road sessions, and to enter into any contract for its execution."

438. Is not that in the case when an adjourned sessions shall have been held, and nobody has tendered at those adjourned sessions?—It does not follow at all; there is no contract in reality when the adjourned sessions is not held; and the grand jury, provided that the work is approved of at the first sessions, have power to deal with it, and to enter into contracts for its execution.

439. But I call your attention to the words you have read; "if no proper contractor shall tender at the adjourned sessions," does not that clearly refer to the case of adjourned sessions having been held?—But if they have not been held there no contract is tendered. There might be a question of law, but the practice is as I state.

440. Mr. *Herbert*.] You have a very large county to look after, have you not?—I have.

441. How many assistants have you?—I have four assistants.

442. In fact, you could not do the work without those four assistants?—I could not do the detail work of measurements of materials, and a great many other duties connected with it.

443. I believe that the grand jury have the power of giving to the county surveyor any works that are not contracted for?—They have.

444. Do you think that it would be a good thing if the grand jury were to give very many of these works into your hands?—It would not. I believe that the number of them given into the surveyor's hands should be only as an alternative, in case of failure in obtaining a contractor.

445. And you think it would be a very bad system if the grand jury were to give a great many of those contracts into the hands of the county surveyor, and that he would in fact not have time to look after the business?—He would not.

446. Would you limit the amount of works to be given to the county surveyor?—I do not know that I should like to see it limited by any statute, because that would be just perhaps stopping at the place where it would be most desirable to give it. I think that the feeling of all

Mr. *J. Hill.*

31 March 1852.

all the country gentlemen in Ireland is that the less the county surveyor has to do with it the better; and every county surveyor that I know has the same feeling also.

447. In your county do the magistrates generally attend well at the road sessions?—They attend very well in Clare.

448. Did you not state that there was often only one magistrate?—I referred to another county entirely, namely, King's County.

449. Did you ever find any abuse arising from the fact of only one magistrate attending?—Certainly not.

450. In fact you have generally found magistrates most anxious for the public good and for the county's good?—Particularly so.

451. Sir *Charles Lanyon.*] Do you not think that if there was any very great dissatisfaction, that would be the very cause why both magistrates and cesspayers would attend in large numbers?—Certainly.

452. And where public opinion generally is in favour of the works in the county being carried out fairly and equitably, it is only on that account that the attendance is small?—That is the principal reason.

453. With reference to the opening of tenders at the sessions, your statement, I think, merely referred to the case of lapse at the adjourned sessions?—To a case of a lapse of the adjourned sessions.

454. Then in the case of the first sessions lapsing, what occurs?—There is no remedy whatever.

455. Do you not think it very important that a remedy should be provided for the lapsing of the first sessions?—In answer to the honourable Chairman, I said that one of the remedies would be to enable the cesspayers to choose a chairman and to hold the sessions without the attendance of a magistrate; and I think that there would be very little chance of a lapse if that provision was made.

456. The difficulty of the lapse of adjourned sessions is met by the provisions of the Act; but has the difficulty of the lapse of a first sessions ever been met?—That would remedy it, I think, sufficiently; but it never has been met at present. The road contractors' payments cannot be passed at present unless a first sessions is held.

457. Has it been the custom in your county to present all bridges, costing above 50 *l.*, to the county at large?—It has not.

458. With reference to the large bridges to which the noble lord referred just now, are you not aware that, with reference to the mode of assessing the costs of those bridges upon the baronies, or districts, there is power of appeal to the Lord Lieutenant to appoint a commission to decide how the same shall be apportioned, either to one county, or to two counties, or to any neighbouring county?—I was not aware of that; I understood that that was always done under special Acts applying to the particular bridges themselves.

459. As to works which are applied for on the county at large, what works in your county are generally applied for on the county at large?—Nothing but the repairs of court-houses.

460. Where are the applications made for cutting hills and building bridges which are intended to be charged upon the county at large?—Upon the baronies.

461. Do you not think that it would be very desirable to alter that law; have you not observed considerable inconvenience arising from the application being made for cutting hills and building bridges at the county at large sessions, in that they never receive that investigation which they ought to receive, because the parties at the baronies do not represent the parties who have to pay the expense of the cutting of those hills, or the building of those bridges, when they amount to a large sum?—I have known no inconvenience or error arising from it; practically the county at large sessions, I consider, are not of the slightest use; I would abolish them altogether.

462. In the case of those works, after having undergone the preliminary investigation at the sessions, taking the instance of an application for building a bridge for 1,000 *l.* being approved of at the baronial sessions, it is approved to be raised off the county at large, is it not?—They cannot do that; it is the grand jury who have the power of fixing it.

463. The application comes in the first instance for the money to be raised off the county at large, and it is approved by the sessions to be raised off the county at large; it goes afterwards before the grand jury, but it never comes before the county at large sessions, so that the cesspayers, who ought to be the parties to consider this large presentment, never have the opportunity of doing so; what I want to ascertain from you (though it may not be the custom in your county) is, whether supposing an application for 1,000 *l.* is made for the building of a bridge on the county at large, and that application is brought before the sessions and is approved of by the sessions for the county, the expenditure being over 1,000 *l.*, you do not think it desirable that the application should go before the county at large sessions as well as the baronial sessions, at which it is first investigated?—I should not think it would make any practical difference in any of the counties with which I am acquainted; I think that the general interests of the county are fully protected by the action of the grand jury, and that there is sufficient consideration given to such works. In Clare such cases as cuttings would be all levied on the barony if they were passed.

464. Do you not think that it would be desirable that all applications for the cutting of hills should be levied on the barony?—Yes, unless they were on post-roads, or on roads analogous to post-roads.

465. With regard to sudden damage, I think from observations which you made that you consider that the requisitions of the county surveyor for the repair of a sudden damage should supersede the necessity of the visit of the magistrates?—Yes.

466. Mr. *Lender.*] Do you think that the sum which the magistrates have now the power of ordering is sufficient in the case of sudden breaches?—The sum is limited by the 6th and 7th of William the Fourth, but it is increased by another Act, which was passed last Session, to 50 *l.*

467. Is that sufficient at this moment to meet a heavy work?—I think it is; I think that heavier amounts than that should be submitted to the cesspayers, and that their sanction should be got for it.

468. Sir *Charles Lanyon.*] Do you not consider that the powers given under the 64th section of the Act of William the Fourth are very good?

good?—I do not; I do not approve of them. I consider that the power itself is too arbitrary to be placed in the hands of the surveyor, and I would like to see embodied with it the power of summoning the contractor instead of superseding him, as the surveyor is enabled to do if he had money under that section.

469. With regard to the power of compelling contractors to proceed with their work under the 54th section, is it not a most desirable thing?—Most desirable.

470. Do you not think that it would be very desirable to modify that section in the way in which you have just referred?—Very desirable, and to provide funds to carry it into execution.

471. Do you not think it more essential, in order to the proper carrying out of that section, that funds should be provided for the purpose of enabling you to proceed with work where there was a defaulting contractor?—It is absolutely essential, it could not be done without.

472. Would not that be one of the greatest improvements which could be effected in the Grand Jury Act?—It would be the greatest improvement with reference to the maintenance of roads.

473. With reference to accepting the lowest tenders, do you not think that the most desirable way of remedying the evils which at present arise from the acceptance of the lowest tender will be by the carrying out of those clauses which I have placed in your hands, which would enable you to deal with defaulting contractors in a sub-summary way?—Undoubtedly.

474. Would that not be better than interfering with the great principle of adopting the lowest tender at the sessions?—I would recommend that there should be no interference with that principle at all; it would be very dangerous.

475. It is your decided opinion that, rather than interfere with the principle of accepting the lowest tender, such an arrangement as that which these sections propose would be much better, and would be perfectly satisfactory in preventing those evils which at present arise?—I am sure it would, if it were carried out.

476. Mr. *Kendall*.] Did I understand from you that the county surveyor has the power of appointing assistants, but that he has not the power of dismissing them?—That is so.

477. Do you think that is a good plan, and that he ought to have the power of dismissing them?—I think that he ought to have the power of dismissing them.

478. Did you ever know an instance where a county surveyor had occasion to find fault with his assistant, and it was reported to those who had the power of dismissal, and it was not attended to?—I have not known such an instance, but there are some.

479. Do you not think that those who have the power of appointment should have the power of dismissal?—Decidedly; it is an invidious thing to bring a charge before a grand jury, and have it argued before any popular body.

480. With regard to the secretary, I gathered just now that from your experience, though contractors, when they send in their tenders, are told that they can fill up the form of tender, yet generally they go to the secretary?—They do.

481. Do they go there because they think the secretary has some influence as regards the contract?—They have a vague idea of that kind.

482. Is there any reason at all for that?—Not the least.

483. They have no power at all?—Not the least.

484. And therefore it is under a false impression that they go there?—It is.

485. And you would do away with all fees to secretaries?—I would.

486. As I understand, now the grand jury in certain counties do permit the county surveyor to give a certificate to the county treasurer, and the county treasurer advances money on the contract as it progresses?—Yes.

487. Do I understand from you that, instead of leaving it in the hands of the grand jury, you would wish to see a law by which you would make it imperative on the county treasurer to advance such monies as he, on certificate, should think it safe to advance?—I think that the discretion should be altogether vested in the grand jury, to give that power to the surveyor or not, as they thought fit.

488. You would have it done annually?—It is done annually now, or it should be done so.

489. And you would let that stand entirely as it is now?—I would.

490. You would not make it the law that the county treasurer should advance money on the certificate of the county surveyor?—Not further than it is the law at present, except to enable him to advance money out of the general funds applicable to the general purposes of the county.

491. Did I understand that any two magistrates can, without the county surveyor, give an order for the repair of certain parts of roads?—They can, provided it is a sudden breach, or a sudden damage.

492. Lord *John Browne*.] I think that is limited to 10 *l.* for a road, and 20 *l.* for a bridge?—It is, and then there are three magistrates for 50 *l.* There is a further protection, that money will not be paid without the certificate of the county surveyor. He must go and measure and value the work.

493. *Chairman*.] The magistrate can do it even without viewing it, can he not?—No, he must go and view it.

494. Lord *John Browne*.] And he must do it at petty sessions, must he not?—It must be done at petty sessions.

495. Sir *Colman O'Loghlen*.] I believe the county surveyor is entitled to no fees at all, to nothing but his salary?—None whatever.

496. Do you get any allowance for a clerk?—We get 50 *l.* a year for the expenses of the office and the clerk.

497. Is that sufficient for a clerk; can you get a skilled person for 50 *l.* a year?—No.

498. In preparing plans for bridges, are you obliged to prepare all the plans yourself?—Either to prepare them myself, or to pay an assistant out of my own pocket to do so.

499. Supposing you have to advertise contracts for bridges, and contractors wish to get copies of those plans, have you any fund by which you can give them copies of those plans?—No, the contractors are obliged to procure them at their own expense.

500. Do you think that 50 *l.* a year is a sufficient allowance for office expenses, considering the extent of work that must be done in your office?—It is not, nor nearly so.

501. What would you suggest yourself as being sufficient?—I think it would take double the amount

Mr. J. Hall.

31 March [illegible].

[illegible] to pay it. The postage alone in my office at present is 1 *l.* a month.

502. And then, independent of the clerk's expenses, there is stationery; and many other things connected with the office?—Yes.

503. And you cannot get a skilled clerk for the salary given at present?—Certainly not.

504. You get no allowance for travelling expenses, do you?—None whatever.

505. If you have to sleep out at a distance to inspect a road, you have no additional allowance for it?—No additional allowance.

506. I believe county surveyors are not entitled to any retiring allowance?—They are not.

507. Is there any feeling among the county surveyors as to getting superannuation allowances?—There is a strong feeling.

508. Have you known, in your own experience, an instance where a subscription has been made for an old county surveyor, in consequence of his being suddenly afflicted with illness and being obliged to give up work?—We are supporting one poor man, that was in the county of Donegal, at present.

509. Assistants to county surveyors are not entitled, I believe, to any compensation?—They are not.

510. Are you, yourself, aware of persons who are extremely old and almost unfit for the discharge of their duties, being kept on as assistants by grand juries, because the grand jury have no power to give superannuation allowances?—I know such instances.

511. In your opinion, would it conduce to the efficiency of the public service if power was given to grand juries to grant superannuation allowances to county surveyors and their assistants?—I think so.

512. With regard to bridges: is it not the fact that there is no power under the Grand Jury Act to present for an iron bridge?—There is no such power.

513. And where iron bridges have been erected they are erected in defiance of the law, or by connivance?—Quite so. It is not a proper state to have the law in.

514. I believe, under the 56th section the only power is to erect bridges or gullets in stone or wood?—Yes.

515. In fact, when the Grand Jury Act was passed, iron bridges were unknown?—They were.

516. Have you known, in your experience, cesspayers refuse works of utility which ought to be carried on, such as the erection of sea-walls, or bridges, or things of that kind?—I cannot call to my recollection a single instance of the kind in 25 years.

517. Were you never in the county of Mayo?—Yes, I have been there; but I do not know the proceedings there.

518. Do you think there ought to be any appeal to any court, from a refusal to do what might be considered a necessary work, such as, for instance, a refusal on the part of the cesspayers to erect a bridge on the boundary between two counties?—I think there should be such an appeal in such a case.

519. Would you suggest an appeal to the Board of Works, or to the Court of Queen's Bench?—I think there should be such an appeal, although I never knew an instance myself in which it was necessary.

520. Do you consider that it would be advisable to make any change with respect to applications for repairs to court-houses; would you be inclined to give the grand jury the power to make presentments without going before the presentment sessions for repairs of court-houses?—I would not.

521. Do you think the law should be left as it is at present; that repairs of public buildings and court-houses should be obliged to go before the presentment sessions?—I think there are ample provisions for its being done at present.

522. With respect to fences upon roads; you are aware that very often very good fences are made when new roads are made in counties; is there any provision in the Grand Jury Act, that you are aware of, by which the contractor contracts with the parties for keeping the road, as well as the fences, in repair?—In every contract I know of in Ireland the fences are included.

523. Is there any power in the Act to include the fences as well as the roads?—There is; the *fence* is part of the road.

524. Is the contractor bound to keep the fences in repair as much as the roads?—He is just as much bound to do that as to perform any other part of the contract, but it is not very often observed.

525. With regard to the expenses of prosecutions, I believe what you alluded to was suing upon the contractors' bonds at quarter sessions?—It was.

526. And what you stated to the noble lord, as to the Attorney-General's fiat not being necessary, related to quarter sessions proceedings, did it not?—Entirely.

527. You are aware that under the Act that jurisdiction is confined to proceedings under 100 *l.*?—I am.

528. Do you think it would be an advantage to extend the jurisdiction of the chairman to all contracts?—I do not see any practical good in limiting it.

529. I believe the expenses of proceedings in superior courts are very heavy?—I believe that is the case, but I never instituted any proceedings in the superior courts. If the penalty ought to be above 100 *l.* I would sue the contractor in the inferior courts, rather than go to the expense, and put him to the expense, of proceeding in the superior court.

530. Do you know whether there is any power in the Grand Jury Act to give compensation for consequential injury; supposing there is a hollow in a road which is filled up, and the entrances of houses on the road are left in the hollow, and the houses are thereby injured, is there any power to give consequential injury as there is in railway Acts?—I do not think there is. There is no power for giving compensation for anything unless the land or house is taken.

531. Is there any power of giving consequential injury for any work done under the grand jury system?—No.

532. You spoke of having power to advance money to stewards to do the works; do you think that would be an advantage?—It would.

533. In reference to what you said about the county surveyor having the power to advance money to enable stewards whom he may appoint to complete the work, would it be any advantage to have a permanent committee of the grand jury to act from session to session, as far as public works are concerned, like a Board of Superintendence?

business?—I do not see any great advantage in it. I really do not see a sufficiency of duties in any of the counties that I am connected with to render such an organization desirable.

534. (*Chairman.*) You do not see any disadvantage arising from the transitory character of the grand jury at present?—At present I do not.

535. (*Sir Colman O'Loghlen.*) Is there anybody at all, at present, to see that the county cess collectors lodge the money in the Bank according as they collect?—I do not think there is.

536. In fact, according to the present system, a grand jury cess collector may collect the whole money immediately after he gets his warrant, and keep the money in his pocket until the next assizes, may he not?—I believe he does that.

537. And if there was a committee of the grand jury who met once a month, of course that could be obviated?—Yes, or the treasurer could obviate it at present, or the person who acts for the treasurer.

538. (*Colonel Forde.*) It could be made compulsory on them to lodge the money as soon as they receive it, could it not; the same as under the poor law?—It might, and the secretary might discharge that duty.

539. (*Mr. Gregory.*) Do you think that the effect of a standing committee would be to place the business of the county in the hands of a small clique and keep it there?—There would be a danger of such a thing; but really I do not see the objection to be a grave one, nor do I see any particular advantage in the proposal.

540. (*Chairman.*) Are you aware that at present the collector is bound to lodge the money in the bank if it exceeds 100 *l.*?—I am.

541. And in spite of that law do you mean to say that the collectors do keep more than 100 *l.* in their own possession?—I am sure they do.

542. (*General Dunne.*) There is no enforcement of that lodging of the money, is there?—There is not.

543. You say that the attendance of cesspayers in the two counties you know is different; that in King's County they do not attend, and that in Clare they generally do attend?—They do attend in Clare, and in several of the baronies in King's County they do not attend.

544. Do you think that any tendency to extravagance which may exist is rather in the cesspayers than in the magistrates?—Certainly; the tendency of the cesspayers would be, if unchecked, to have small insignificant jobs extended all through the county.

545. Are not the magistrates a check upon that?—They are the greatest possible check in every county that I know of.

546. Do you not think that that tendency would be increased if the cess was taken off that class of which the cesspayers is composed?—I do not think it would; they look upon those small roads as a convenience to themselves which they are to be paying for themselves, and I do not think that it would make any practical difference.

547. The interests of the grand jurors and the magistrates are of course much larger than the interests of the cesspayers in keeping down extravagance, are they not?—They are very much larger.

548. Do you not think that the non-attendance of magistrates, and sometimes of cesspayers, is the cause that the business of many road sessions is merely formal?—It was merely formal in the places where there was that non-attendance to which I alluded, and if there was any knowledge or any opinion that anything was wrong, or appeared to be wrong, there would be a full attendance. It was entirely because it was only a formal proceeding, and that they had perfect confidence in those who were transacting the business.

549. Would iron bridges be legal if erected by presentment of the grand jury?—It is a legal question; but there is no mention of them in the Act of Parliament.

550. Have you ever known them erected?—I have; I have had them erected myself.

551. And therefore, unless they are traversed, there is no difficulty about it?—There was one traversed in Clare, and the court of Queen's Bench fined the presentment.

552. If any work is thrown out by the presentment sessions, there is no possibility for the grand jury to put it in, is there?—No.

553. Consequential damages, you say, cannot be given by the grand jury?—I think not under the Grand Jury Acts.

554. But could not an action be taken, by a person who was injured, against the county, if damages should ensue in consequence of such works?—I could not give an opinion upon that point.

555. Have you ever known such a case?—I have never known such a case.

556. Have you ever known it under the Board of Works Acts?—Yes.

557. And would not the powers be analogous?—I think that there would be greater difficulty in suing a county than in suing a corporation.

558. Cannot a county be sued as a corporation?—I am not aware.

559. If there was a permanent board, would you entrust the powers now given to the magistrates to that board, of repairing sudden breaches and damages?—It would be one of the most important duties which could be entrusted to such a board. I do not see any inconvenience from the present state of the law in that case.

560. You could entrust them with larger expenditure, could you not?—You could; but I do not see that it would be desirable to entrust a larger expenditure without going through the sessions.

561. Have you never seen sudden damages, which magistrates could not repair, remaining until further damage ensued, and consequently a larger expense was incurred?—Not to my knowledge; three magistrates can now give up to 50 *l.*, and that sum would be sufficient to secure any ordinary works, except in some very extraordinary instances; when there are very much larger works, it cannot be done all at once, as people imagine, and the amount of time between the sessions and the assizes would not be a very serious delay.

562. And therefore the want of a permanent board is not an injury to the country?—I do not see an injury, nor would I see any objection to it if it were thought desirable.

563. Do you think that it would supplement in any way the works going on in the country?—I do not think so.

564. In all works such as gaols and lunatic asylums, is the county surveyor always the person to make the plans?—No.

565. Is it at the pleasure of the grand jury that they should take his plans, or pay for others?

Mr. J. Hill.

31 March 1868.

Mr. J. Hill.

3d March [illegible]

others?—The Board of Superintendence have the option.

566. For the bridges he makes all the plans, does he not?—For the bridges he makes all the plans.

567. And they may choose other plans, may they not?—They must take his plans for bridges.

568. And court-houses?—No, only the sessions court-houses, not county court-houses.

569. Colonel *French*.] Did I understand you to say that the Board of Superintendence have the power to appoint an architect for gaols?—They can employ an architect if they like and pay him for it.

570. General *Dunne*.] In the case of lunatic asylums it is always done by the Government, is it not?—So I understand.

571. You have never known a county surveyor employed in making plans for a lunatic asylum, unless specially employed?—He must be specially employed. In the county in which I am employed now, the county surveyor was the architect of the lunatic asylum, with another.

572. Lord *John Browne*.] The Board of Control in Dublin have always an architect for lunatic asylums, have they not?—Yes.

573. General *Dunne*.] Taking altogether the whole grand jury system connected with the presenting session, do you think that the system could be well conducted at a cheaper rate to the country?—I do not think that there can be any great saving of expenditure at present, by any system that could be adopted.

574. Then you think that the administration is a cheap one?—I do.

575. Have you any idea of what the whole amount of the presentments in Ireland are?—I have.

576. Do you know the per-centage of expenditure for administration upon it?—Not except on county surveyors' expenditure.

577. Could you put in a return giving the amount of per-centage for the administration on the amount expended?—I can; it was prepared in 1858; 19,918 *l.* was the cost of superintendence, for surveyors and assistants, on 400,000 *l.* The cost of superintendence was 4½ per cent. on the expenditure.

578. You have no account of the whole administration of the grand jury presentments, have you?—I have not.

579. Could you give that in, or could you guess at it?—I think I could make it out from the documents which I have; I will make it out in two counties, King's County and Clare.

580. Have you ever compared the administration of the grand jury laws with the administration of the poor law; and, if so, which do you consider to be the more expensive?—I have no real personal knowledge of what the expense of the poor law administration is.

581. *Sir Colman O'Loghlen*.] With regard to encroachments on public roads, by making fences or building houses, is not there a time limited now within which the surveyor can alone proceed to cause an abatement of those encroachments, by proceedings before the magistrates?—It is limited to six months.

582. Is it your opinion that that time ought to be extended?—I think it ought.

583. The surveyors may not ascertain the encroachments under six months?—They may not.

584. Would you fix any period, or would you leave it generally?—I would leave it generally.

585. That you think would be an improvement on the present system?—I do.

586. Mr. Lo[redacted].] How many baronies are there in the County of Clare?—There are 11 baronies.

587. And then, of course, there are 11 road sessions?—There are.

588. Do you think that the number could be increased or diminished advantageously?—I do not know of any advantage that would arise from interference with them.

589. How many poor law unions are there in that county?—There are five poor law unions wholly in Clare, and there is part of the Union of Limerick, and part of the Union of Scariff, and part of the Union of Gort.

590. Are all the baronies in the County of Clare compact?—They are not.

591. Do you think that that is disadvantageous?—It is disadvantageous; but it would be very hard to change it now without great difficulty.

592. But supposing that Parliament should think it advisable to alter the boundaries and the extent of the present baronies, and to change them into districts, do you think that that could be advantageously done?—I do not.

593. In the county of Cork, where there are 23 baronies, some of which consist of 8,000 or 10,000 acres, and others of 2,000 or 3,000 acres, do you not think that some change might be made with great advantage?—A change might be made there with great advantage; but in the county about which the Honourable Member asked me before, they have altered baronies under some Act of Parliament, and made them as convenient as they thought fit; they are greatly altered now from what they were originally. In the county of Clare, there was the barony of Tulla, of nearly 200,000 acres; that is divided into two, and another barony Bunratty, also is divided into two.

594. The poor law unions seem to me to be double the size of the baronies; do you think that they would be inconveniently large districts for administering the road sessions?—I think so; our baronies vary from 50,000 to 90,000 acres; 90,000 acres is very large, and 50,000 acres is small enough.

595. Then you think that the proper limit would be from 50,000 to 90,000 acres?—I think that about 70,000 acres for a barony is a very convenient district.

596. Mr. *Herbert*.] You stated, in answer to the honourable Chairman, that you considered the associated cesspayers were an irresponsible body; does that irresponsibility, in your opinion, arise from their not being elected by the cesspayers?—It was not that so much which I referred to, although I called them an irresponsible body; what I meant in reality was, that they had not so large an interest in the county as the grand jury, nor were they so much under the control of public opinion.

597. But would you consider it desirable to have them elected by the cesspayers, instead of being nominated by the grand jury?—I would. They are not nominated exactly by the grand jury; but I would have them so elected.

598. It amounts to the same thing, does it not?—It does not amount to anything like nomination.

599. You spoke of the attendance of those cesspayers being very often of an irregular character;

character; do you think that the attendance would be better if they were sent directly to the cesspayers?—I think it would.

600. Does it not often arise that a cesspayer has to ride some 10 or 12 miles to the sessions, and on his arrival finds that he is not one of the parties elected?—Precisely; I gave that as one of the reasons.

601. Would not some advantage arise from the grand jury being a continuous instead of a terminating body?—I do not know any advantage which would arise from that.

602. With regard to the division of the rates, you stated, in answer to the gallant general, that the landlord has as much interest as the tenant in keeping down the rates; in the case of a large proprietor, who may sometimes cover a fourth of the whole barony, is not his interest rather the other way; in fact, to get as much work as possible constructed at the cost of the tenant?—I am speaking from experience, and I can state that in King's County the magistrates and the grand jurors were far more careful of the expenditure of the public money, and looked after it a great deal more earnestly, than any other class in the county.

603. But, generally speaking, is there not an absolute bonus to the landlord to get as much expenditure as he possibly can in the barony in which his property is, as the tenant has to pay for it all, and he has the benefit of the permanent works?—I am not aware that that occurs in practice, but that is evidently the inference.

604. May not tenants, by paying for the construction of these works over which they have no control, be leading the way to enhancing the value of their farm, and increasing their own rent?—They may eventually increase their rent by it.

605. Therefore the principle is bad, is it not?—I think so.

606. In the county to which you belong, there are several fishery harbours constructed by the Board of Works, are there not?—There are some.

607. Does it form part of your duty to report upon the state of those harbours if they want repairs, and does it occur, when you so report, that the grand jury have them put into an efficient state of repair?—Most of them which have been erected in Clare have been by private subscriptions, aided by some grant from the Board of Works; and with them the grand jury have nothing to do. They must be kept in repair by the parties who originally built them. I think that there are only three small piers which are under the charge of the grand jury.

608. But surely when the pier is once constructed, partly by the contributions of the locality and partly by a contribution given by the Board of Works, the future maintenance of that harbour falls upon the grand jury, does it not?—No; except there is a presentment in aid of it.

609. It came out very distinctly last year that, when once these works are constructed, it is the duty of the grand jury to repair them, and in one case it has been so?—We have not had a shilling expended upon them in the county of Clare at all. We had no charge of them, excepting three small piers, which are very old ones.

610. Have you ever been in a county where there is a lunatic asylum?—Yes.

611. When that lunatic asylum requires repairs, or enlargement, have you ever been called in to give your opinion?—No.

612. It is always done by the Board of Works, under the superintendence of the Board of Control of Lunatic Asylums, is it not?—I believe so.

613. Would it not be desirable that a county work like that should be more directly under the control of the grand jury than it is at present?—I think it should be more directly under the control of the grand jury than it is at present.

614. You stated, did you not, that you thought it desirable that the county-at-large sessions should be abolished?—I do not see the least use for it. Any transaction done in it could be done in the baronial sessions.

615. *Mr. Lowther.*] Even large bridges?—They never come before the sessions of the county for the county at large.

616. If you were told now that some important bridges, costing several thousand pounds, were voted by the adjoining barony, the whole county at large paying for them, would you think that that was a fair arrangement?—At present they are presented for in the barony in which they are locally situate.

617. And they tax the county at large for them?—They do; that is to say, if it is allowed by the grand jury; but the present sessions for the county at large have no check or control over it.

618. *Chairman.*] You consider the check of the grand jury sufficient in such cases?—I do.

619. *Colonel Cooper.*] With regard to a statement which you made about paying the contractors a certain proportion before the grand jury approves of the contract, does it pass the presentment sessions before you pay the contractor, or do you do it simply on your own certificate?—On my own certificate.

620. It does not go before the presentment sessions?—No.

621. Do you not think that it would be desirable in any of those payments to have the sanction of the presentment sessions?—I do not think that in that particular, in making advances, it would be so; on the contrary, I think that any interference of the sessions with the action of the surveyors on the advances would be anything but desirable.

622. Do you find that contracts are taken at all lower, and that the county gets any advantage from these payments before the assizes?—I know that it has got an advantage in the county in which I was formerly employed, and I am quite confident that there will be a very important advantage in the county in which I am employed now.

623. And you think that if that system was more freely adopted the county would get the advantage of the ready money transaction?—I think so.

624. Do you think it promotes competition amongst the contractors?—It ought to do so; but in King's County, when I left, there was very little competition amongst contractors; and in the county where I am now up to this time there has been undue competition amongst the contractors.

625. *Lord John Browne.*] What do you call undue competition?—They take the contracts at prices wholly inadequate to the performance of the works.

626. *Colonel Cooper.*] In the counties with which you are acquainted, if the cesspayers come into

Mr. *J. Hill.*

21 March [illegible]

late and the full number is not complete, are they excluded from taking part in the proceedings?—They are.

627. In both King's County and in the county of Clare?—Yes, in King's County and in the county of Clare, and in all the counties which I know of, I believe that they consider it is the law, that if a man does not answer when he is called on the ballot, he is not legally qualified to sit as a cesspayer.

628. Did I understand you to say that the county surveyor has no right to put in an application for repairs if no other application is made?—In case two cesspayers make an application in the ordinary way, if that is refused, or if it is informal, or if it in any way fails, there is no power there for the county surveyor to make an application for any work. It is only in the case where no application has been made, that he has authority under that section to make an application at all.

629. Lord *John Browne.*] But, if the application is informal, it is no application at all?—I have done it myself repeatedly; but I would like to see the law distinct upon it.

630. You say that if that application is informal, it is no application?—That is what we say; but I have done it repeatedly myself.

631. And it has never been traversed or objected to?—Not in my case; but I know it has been in other cases.

632. And was it considered irregular?—It was considered irregular.

633. And the application was quashed?—It was quashed.

634. Colonel *Cooper.*] If a person wishes to lay out a road, is it not very frequently the case that he applies to the county surveyor for a plan, and pays him for it?—It may be so; but I took care that it never should be the case where I was concerned; I never received any payment for any work connected with the county in any shape, nor would I permit anyone in my employ to do so.

635. But have you known any such instances?—I cannot say I have known such instances; but I believe there have been such instances.

636. That would at once come under the head of fees, would it not?—It would.

637. You admit, I think, that there is an appeal if an application is twice refused consecutively?—Yes.

638. That very often works inconveniently, does it not?—I do not know that of my own knowledge, but it has been suggested to me that it has done so.

639. Have you ever known an instance in which a road of some five or six miles long in which two baronies are interested has been stopped, because for half a mile or so in the centre it passes through a third barony very little interested; and have you ever known applications refused for such a road?—I have; but it cannot stop a new road. The barony in which the greater portion of the work is situate has the power of making the presentment for the whole road, and it becomes compulsory on the smaller portion; but for repairs of roads, I have found the inconvenience which the honourable Member suggests.

640. And unless it is refused twice consecutively there is no appeal?—There is no appeal unless it is refused twice consecutively.

641. But the removal of that word "consecutively" would remedy that entirely, would it not?—Entirely.

642. I believe the treasurer may issue the warrants to the barony collectors directly after the assizes?—He does issue them very shortly after.

643. Is that the case in all the counties you know of?—In all the counties I know of.

644. Lord *John Browne.*] What do you call "very shortly"?—Certainly within three months.

645. *Chairman.*] Is he not bound to issue them within two months?—I believe he is; but it is very seldom that he is able to do it, because he has much heavier business to do than people imagine; it is an exceedingly heavy job.

646. Colonel *Cooper.*] With regard to the question of dividing the cess between the landlord and the tenant, I think I understood that the tenants in the counties with which you are acquainted do not object to pay for roads and local improvements?—They say to me that they have no objection whatever to pay for the maintenance of the roads; they look upon that as a thing which directly benefits them; but what they object to is for building large establishments.

647. And you think that they make no objection to paying for roads and bridges and gullets in their own neighbourhood?—Not a bit.

648. And that in fact they wished to encourage the making of roads in their own neighbourhood rather more than grand juries like?—A great deal more.

649. And at the same time they are quite willing to pay the expense?—They are; they look upon that as the only benefit they get from the grand jury cess, but dividing it would just about do what is required.

650. Mr. *Maguire.*] Do you mean to say that they would not prefer the division of the rate to having the whole burden of it to bear for any purpose?—It is their general feeling that they are willing to pay for the whole of the baronial cess.

651. Colonel *Cooper.*] And half of the county-at-large cess?—No.

652. Mr. *Maguire.*] Is that what you call a division?—Yes.

653. They are in favour of the principle of dividing equally between the occupier and the landlord, are they not?—Very strongly.

654. So that your statement is that there is an anxiety on the part of occupiers to divide the cess equally between landlord and tenant?—A very great anxiety, and there is no objection on the part of the proprietors so far as I know.

655. But there is a strong feeling that the rate is not equitably imposed at present, and that it ought to be divided?—A very strong feeling.

656. Is that feeling universal amongst that class?—I think it is.

657. Mr. *Herbert.*] Do you not think it would be a fair thing to put it upon tenancies that are to be, and not upon existing tenancies?—That is a question the details of which I, as an officer employed under the counties, do not think is a proper subject for me to give an opinion upon.

658. Mr. *Kendall.*] Would not the rent be raised in consequence?—I am not aware, but I think that very few proprietors would take up a thing of the sort to raise the rents.

659. Sir *Charles Lanyon.*] Irrespectively altogether of the question of the dividing of cess between landlord and tenant, what is your

opinion

Mr. J. Hill.

31 March 1868.

opinion as to the general view of the public as to the working of the grand jury laws?—I think, in a great many counties of Ireland, the system is most beneficially worked, and is very satisfactory to the people.

660. You having had experience in several counties, what is your view of public opinion generally as to the working of the grand jury laws being considered satisfactory or otherwise? —I think it is satisfactory in most of the counties that I know.

661. *Colonel Cooper.*] Upon whom do you think the satisfactory working chiefly depends, the county surveyor or the grand jury?—I think it depends very mainly upon the county surveyor.

662. With regard to the division of the county cess, do the cesspayers consider that they derive no advantage from the infirmary and the lunatic asylum, which are kept up from the county cess? —The farming class look upon the roads as the advantage which they derive from the expenditure of the county cess. They put very little value on the other establishments of the county.

663. Do they not consider that the advantages of the road depend in a great measure upon the county surveyor's services?—They do.

664. Do they object to pay for that?—I do not think they do; they do not look upon the large establishments of the county as being so much to their direct benefit as the roads; they look upon them as their direct benefit, and they are very well satisfied with them.

665. *Colonel Forde.*] For whose benefit is it, if not for theirs?—Of course it is for the general benefit of the public, but that is their strong feeling.

666. *General Dunne.*] In fact, all people of that class have a general feeling, have they not, that they object to pay anything?—It is paid very freely and very easily.

667. *Mr. Maguire.*] The suggestion given in the question of the gallant general does not at all represent the feeling of the people; I believe they are anxious to bear their fair share of the common burden, are they not?—They pay it very freely.

668. *Chairman.*] You say that you do not see any advantage likely to arise from having any permanent body existing, such as the committee of the grand jury?—I do not see any advantage.

669. Do you know anything about the working of the grand jury laws in the County of Dublin? —Not much; but I know a little about it.

670. Are you aware that they have in the county of Dublin an existing body appointed from the grand jury called a finance committee? —I am.

671. Are you able to give any information as to how that works?—I have not sufficient knowledge of its working to give a proper opinion upon that.

672. You stated, did you not, in answer to some questions from the honourable Member for Clare, that the amount of money paid to you for office expenses and travelling expenses was not adequate?—I am not paid anything for travelling expenses; even the 50 *l.* a year given to me is inadequate; I pay the whole of that 50 *l.* to a clerk, and I think that is rather less than he should get; and then there is the expense of stationery and other expenses.

673. What is your present salary?—600 *l.* a year.

674. Has not that salary been very largely increased of late years?—It has.

675. Was not that increase intended to meet all these calls for travelling expenses and office expenses?—The 50 *l.* a year is distinctly stated to be for the purpose of covering the office expenses, and the expenses of a clerk.

676. Although the amount of 50 *l.* a year may be distinctly stated to be paid for office and clerk expenses, at the same time, if your general salary has been largely increased, do you not think that that that is a very strong reason for not having a further increase for office expenses?—I am not making any claim, or complaint.

677. Comparatively speaking, your salary as county surveyor is the largest county salary now, is it not?—It is the largest now.

678. Is it not much the largest?—It is; but if the travelling expenses were taken out of it, it would not be much the largest.

679. *Colonel Forde.*] You said something about the applications being lodged; you have to lodge in the secretary's office your applications that you make to the county ten days before the time, have you not?—No; I may make them at the sessions.

680. Do you not think that the secretary should have a notice of what was going on, so that he might be prepared for the application before the sessions?—It would be very desirable; and that the applications made by the surveyors should be printed, the same as other applications, so that they should not come by surprise, and I arrange to have that done always.

681. You have a power of refusing a certified work that comes before you, have you not, when it comes before the next road sessions?—The sessions have a power of refusal.

682. You have a power to object as the county surveyor, have you not?—Yes, to advise them against it if I saw any objection.

683. Do you not think that the county surveyor should be obliged to state his objection at the time, and at the same time to show the sessions what he would consider a better line if it was for a new road, at the time when he made the objection, so that the different notices should be served, and so on?—My recollection and certainly the practice, so far as I know about it, is this; that where a new road would be certified at one sessions I would look upon it as my duty to go and have that work re-surveyed, and if I saw any alteration that was necessary in it, to make those alterations, and to bring them before the next sessions.

684. And that you ought at once to serve the necessary notice?—Yes, if there were complaints.

685. And to give notice to the promoters of the work, which you are not now bound to do? —We are not, but practically I would do it.

686. But it is not necessarily done at present, is it?—It is not necessarily done.

687. *Lord John Browne.*] Do you know the mode in which the bonds of the high constable's securities are taken?—Nothing more than from seeing them taken in the grand jury room.

688. Has it come to your knowledge that great practical difficulties arise in consequence of the two services being obliged to be present before the grand jury or the quarter sessions?—In the county of Clare I do not recollect any difficulty, and in King's County there was one instance where it was usually taken at the quarter ses-

Mr. J. Hill.

21 March 1868.

duce, but I am not aware that any inconvenience ever arose.

689. By law, two sureties must be taken, either at the assizes or at the quarter sessions?—Yes.

690. But if the high constable is living in Dublin, he is obliged to come down to the assizes or quarter sessions for that purpose, is he not?—He is.

691. Have you not known difficulties to arise in consequence of that?—I have not.

692. In your counties are the grand jury particular about the security they get from the high constables?—Very particular.

693. And the high constable is always obliged to get good sureties in the county?—He is.

694. Mr. *Herbert*.] You give a report to the grand jury every time it meets, do you not?—Yes.

695. Do you not think it would be very advisable if that report was drawn up by you, and printed and circulated to the members of the grand jury before they meet?—Indeed it would.

696. *Chairman*.] Have you any statistics or papers which you would like to put in?—I have not.

Mr. William Johnson, called in; and Examined.

Mr. W. Johnson.

697. *Chairman*.] You are the Secretary of the Grand Jury for the County of Cork, are you not?—I am.

698. How long have you held that office?—For 27 years.

699. I believe Cork is a very exceptional county?—It is the largest county in Ireland.

700. How many baronies are there in that county?—Twenty-three.

701. And you have consequently 23 road sessions to attend?—Yes.

702. Would you explain, as briefly as you can, the duties of the secretary of a grand jury?—I have read the evidence of Mr. Sharkey, and the duties are exactly the same as in his county.

703. Are you obliged to keep an office?—Yes.

704. What is your salary?—£. 334.

705. In addition to that you receive certain fees, do you not?—Yes.

706. Would you state what the amount of those fees is?—The fees which I receive under the Act of Parliament are for the recognizances, and for the forms of tender. The recognizances amount to about 48 *l.* in the year, and the forms of tender to 18 *l.* I am entitled, under the Act of Parliament, for the blank form of tender to 6 *d.* on each. For the last year those blank tenders amounted to 18 *l.*; but my clerk, in addition, receives a fee for filling the tender, what was called just now the customary fee, which has been established by usage. There are also fees received on the presentments, which I can explain to the Committee, but those fees have all been given in the different returns.

707. In the return that has been furnished of the amount of fees paid to the secretaries of grand juries, are the fees or payments returned which are made by the contractors?—Not in the return which the Honourable Chairman has before him. When I made that return, I thought I was only bound to return the salary and legal fees; I did not return the customary fees.

708. In addition to those legal fees the secretaries of grand juries or their clerks receive certain other fees from the contractors, do they not?—Precisely.

709. Could you state in a rough way what they amount to in the County of Cork?—They amount to a very large sum in the County of Cork. The fees for filling the applications for supplying the forms of sudden breaches, and for making payments to contractors, amount altogether to about 500 *l.* a year.

710. In what way are the cesspayers selected in the county of Cork, for attendance at the presentment sessions?—A list of the hundred highest cesspayers is returned to the grand jury by the high constable; from that list the grand jury select, omitting, in the first instance, the names of those who have served at the previous sessions, whatever number they think proper, according to the size of the barony, differing from 10 to 24, and they spread them over the entire barony, in whatever way the grand juror of the barony thinks proper. He makes that selection, and that list is then read out before the grand jury.

711. He selects any names out of the hundred that he likes?—Yes. In so large a county as the county of Cork, it is necessary to leave that entirely to the juror who represents the barony, as the other grand jurors know nothing whatever of that barony.

712. You are aware that, by the Act of Parliament, the grand jury are obliged to select the highest rated cesspayers?—The opinion of the Judge was taken upon that point, and that opinion was, that if you are bound to take the highest, you would not be able to spread the selection over the entire barony, but you would be confined to the first 24.

713. So that, practically, in the county of Cork, the selection of cesspayers is at the discretion of some particular grand juror, who is asked to perform that duty?—Precisely.

714. Do you find that the cesspayers attend well to the presentment sessions?—Yes, very well, particularly in the large baronies.

715. Do you generally have a greater number in attendance than the number that can sit?—Yes, very often; very often the entire number attend; sometimes there is not a very great attendance, but that may be caused by several circumstances.

716. Do the magistrates attend well?—Yes, very well, in the large baronies particularly.

717. All the magistrates for the county can attend at any particular baronial sessions, can they not?—Yes.

718. Do you think that is a good system?—No, not at all. I think it very objectionable.

719. You would prefer the attendance to be confined exclusively to the magistrates who either have property in the district, or who reside in the district?—Certainly.

720. Have you ever known any instance of magistrates coming out of one barony into another barony, such magistrate not having property in the barony, and attending presentment sessions, in order to carry some particular works which would be objected to in the barony itself, but which would be of use to other baronies?—Not lately; but I have heard of such cases.

721. Do you not think that that is a very objectionable

objectionable state of things?—Certainly; but very few magistrates would do so.

722. Would you describe to the Committee the course of proceeding with respect to the applotment of the county cess?—That is more in the province of the treasurer. I have no knowledge whatever of the treasurer's office.

723. Have you any knowledge of the duties of the collectors of the county cess?—Not officially.

724. You are aware that under an Act which was passed last year, this applotment of the county cess and other duties will be thrown upon the secretary?—I am sorry to say that I am.

725. I presume that you do not know anything about the audit of the county accounts?—I do not.

726. Are you aware of what is done with the balances in the hands of the county treasurer?—The treasurer receives the interest upon them, having been appointed previous to the Act which took away the interest from the treasurer.

727. Are you acquainted at all with the duties of the clerk of the peace and clerk of the Crown?—I am not officially acquainted with those duties; although my brother is clerk of the peace for the county.

728. Would you state to the Committee what are his duties?—I could hardly undertake to describe them.

729. Are you aware that presentments are made in Ireland for what are called malicious injuries?—Yes.

730. Those presentments can be passed by the grand jury although rejected by the presentment sessions, can they not?—Yes.

731. And they can finally be passed by the judge, although they may have been refused both by the grand jury and the presentment sessions?—Not unless a petty jury hear the case.

732. But they can be passed on trial before a petty jury?—Yes, if the judge thinks proper to empanel a jury.

733. Do you consider this system of granting presentments for malicious injuries a good one in the way in which it is carried out?—I think that there are many deficiencies in the present law. I have known some instances in which a man made out a very fair case of malicious injury, and it passed the presentment sessions and the grand jury unanimously; and on a point being raised before the judge, the judge, very reluctantly, was obliged to reject it. All the judges construe the Act very strictly, and one of the points which I allude to was that the property was not included in the section of the Act of Parliament, and the other was that the notice had not been posted at the police barracks. The process server and the applicant, when they went to the police barracks, were prevented by the police constable from posting the notice. He said that he would receive the notice, but that he would not allow them to attach it either to the barracks or to the door. The point was brought before the Chief Justice Monahan, and he very reluctantly nilled the presentment.

734. That was on technical grounds?—That was on technical grounds.

735. But with regard to the principle of having presentments made by the grand jury for special malicious injuries, do you believe it to be a good principle that the grand jury, or the presentment sessions, should have the power of granting money to any individual as compensation for what he endeavours to show to be a malicious injury?—I think that they are both about the fittest tribunals before which an applicant can go.

736. Has not your experience led you to the belief, that when the application made is for a small sum, and when it is proposed to levy it over a large area, both the presentment sessions and the grand jury are very indifferent about granting it?—I think that if a fair case is made out, both the sessions and the grand jury are always ready to grant a presentment.

737. Do you not think that they are too ready to grant it?—Certainly not. There is nothing that comes before the sessions which is so closely investigated as the malicious injuries. I have known one case occupy an entire day.

738. Was that case, which you say occupied an entire day, for a large or a small sum?—It was for a very large sum; it was the burning of a mill.

739. Is it not the fact that when the sum is large the grand jury and the presentment sessions are very loth to grant it, and inquire very strictly into it, but that when the sum is small they inquire very little with regard to it?—It is immaterial whether the sum is large or small; I think that they investigate each case very carefully.

740. But do you not think that this power of obtaining compensation for malicious injuries in this way leads to many applications being made for accidental loss and damage?—That may occur, but it is a very difficult thing to prove a malicious injury, such as a man's house being burnt during the night, for instance; and unless they make out a very strong and good case, it is rejected.

741. These applications as to malicious injuries may be rejected by the presentment sessions and by the grand jury, and finally they have to go before the judge; would it not be a better and fairer course to have them tried at once before the judge and a sworn jury?—Whether they are granted or rejected, they may be brought before a judge.

742. But do you not think that it would be better to have but the one tribunal, and to bring them immediately before the judge?—I think not; I prefer the present system.

743. Why do you prefer it?—Because I think that they are inquired into very carefully. I see no objection to the present system.

744. Are you aware whether presentments are made at present for the maintenance of deserted children by the grand jury?—No, that has ceased; the Act has been repealed, I think, about three years since. They are all transferred to the Poor Law Board.

745. By what Act was that repealed?—I think it was three or four years ago.

746. Do you remember by what Act it was repealed?—I do not remember.

747. Have you found any feeling to exist in your county in favour of a division of the payment of the county cess between the landlord and the tenant?—That is a point upon which, if I give an opinion, it must be as an individual, and not as secretary to the grand jury; but I would rather not give an opinion upon the point.

748. The question I put to you was this, whether you are aware that such an opinion exists in the country?—There is a great difference of opinion. Of course, every tenant thinks it ought

Mr. W. Johnson.

31 March 1868.

ought

Mr. *W. Johnson.*

27 March 1868.

ought to be divided, and every landlord thinks it ought not.

749. Is there any other point upon which you would like to give information to the Committee?—There are one or two matters which I would have taken the liberty of suggesting, but I was not aware that I should be allowed to offer any suggestions until to-day, and I am not prepared to do so at present.

750. Colonel *Forde.*] With regard to magistrates attending the sessions, could you offer any opinion as to the limit of the property that they should hold in the barony?—I should not think that any man should attend the sessions unless he has a very good property in the barony.

751. *Chairman.*] What do you mean by "a very good property"?—I should think that a man ought at least to possess 400 *l.* or 500 *l.* a year; but very few men do attend out of their own barony.

752. Colonel *Forde.*] In the case of a magistrate being an agent, would you impose any restriction?—I do not think I would allow any agent to act as magistrate at presentment sessions if his principal resided in the barony or in the county, and had the opportunity of attending those sessions.

753. But he might be ill, or something of that sort?—Of course, if he was unable to do so, the agent might attend.

754. But you mean that the agent and the principal should not sit on the same presentment sessions?—Certainly not.

755. And of course that would be equally applicable to the county at large sessions?—Yes.

756. What is the notice that you get of the different applications to be made; how long before the time is it necessary for those applications to be left in your office?—They must be all lodged 10 days previous to the first presentment sessions for the county.

757. Do you think that that is a long enough time?—Certainly not; it is very inconvenient.

758. I suppose that you would like to have 18 days' notice on all events?—At least 18 days.

759. I asked the county surveyor of Clare as to the notices that the county surveyors were obliged to give for the applications which they mean to bring forward at the presentment sessions; and whether it was not desirable that they should be obliged to serve such notices on you a certain number of days before the road sessions, as well as a common promoter of a road: do you think that it would be an advantage if the county surveyor were obliged to serve such notice on the secretary, and each case brought before the road sessions in the usual manner?—In my county the county surveyor scarcely ever makes what we call a special application under the 11th section. There is a rule of the grand jury prohibiting him from doing so. If an application has been lodged with the secretary and rejected, they have no power then to apply.

760. The county surveyor can make an application?—Yes.

761. He is not bound to lodge the application with you?—No.

762. Do you think it advisable that he should be obliged to lodge that application with you?—I think it would be so certainly, because the public would have notice of it; all applications which are lodged with me are printed and circulated to every magistrate in the barony, and every cesspayer selected by the grand jury to act at presentment sessions; they receive those applications at least a week in each barony before the sessions, that gives full time to inquire into every work, and to see it if necessary, and I think that it would be well if the public saw the county surveyor's applications as well as those lodged by the public.

763. From the adjourned sessions you are obliged by law now not to exceed 20 days, are you not?—Yes.

764. Is that a sufficient time?—Certainly not; I hold the first sessions on the very last day that the law allows me; from the size of the county of Cork and the number of baronies, I have only one day between the last county at large sessions and the first adjourned sessions.

765. You think that it would be advisable to increase the number of days in a large county?—Clearly.

766. *Chairman.*] Would you think it desirable to have the county of Cork divided into two ridings?—There is a great difference of opinion in the county upon that point. I at one time was very much in favour of dividing the county. It is a very difficult thing now to select a grand jury, and it throws a very difficult and unpleasant duty upon the high sheriff. There are 23 baronies and 23 grand jurors, and consequently many gentlemen who ought to be on the grand jury are excluded from it, which sometimes causes a great deal of annoyance in the county.

767. The high sheriff is obliged to summon some one from each barony, is he not?—They are not summoned in Cork, they are invited. Some of the baronies are so large that 23 men could be got out of one barony alone.

768. Lord *John Browne.*] There is a Parliamentary return presented here, in which I see the secretary of the grand jury of the county of Cork has 324 *l.* a year?—Yes.

769. And the average amount of the annual fees and other payments is 145 *l.* 11 *s.*?—Those are only the legal fees.

770. You stated, did you not, that the other receipts amounted to about 500 *l.* a year?—About 500 *l.* a year.

771. That makes 969 *l.*; but could you state it more particularly, giving the exact amount, and hand it to the Committee at their next meeting?—I can do so.

772. What are the fees to the secretary on the payments to the contractors, which you mentioned just now?—Every contractor who is entitled to payment must lodge an application with the secretary; and it is for filling up those applications for payment at the sessions that the fee is charged.

773. What is the amount of that fee that he pays?—The highest fee paid for any application is 2 *s.*; it varies according to the amount; they are not charged 2 *s.* for each application; it depends entirely upon the amount; if it is a very small amount they pay 6 *d.*, and for the larger ones pay 1 *s.*, and for the highest 2 *s.*

774. Colonel *Forde.*] You post the notices after you receive them, at the police barracks, do you not?—I heard Mr. Hill's evidence, and it would be utterly impossible to do so; there are four notices required by the Act to be posted for every application, and if I had a staff of 100 men I do not think I could do it in so large a county as Cork.

775. This (*handing a paper to the Witness*) is a schedule which the county of Down use, and the

the secretary posts that on the police barracks, and he serves it on the magistrate of the barony and the cesspayers who are to be associated with them, for their information, a few days before the session: what is your opinion as to the desirability of such a procedure?—I thought the Honourable Member meant to ask whether notice was required to be posted on the police barrack, &c.; I send the same application at this round to every magistrate and cesspayer always.

776. In the county of Clare it was not done, I believe?—No, I am not obliged to do so.

777. The present mode of selecting the roads which are to be chargeable on the county is to take the mail car lines, is it not?—Yes.

778. Those on account of railways, &c., are not now the roads which have the greatest traffic on them; what would you recommend in that case?—There are some baronies through which no mail cars pass at all, and the people in those baronies think it a hardship to be paying half the expense of all the mail car roads in the county. There are not very many post roads at present for the reasons which the Honourable Member has stated.

779. Would you suggest that some other mode of testing what roads should be supported half by the county, should be adopted?—I am not prepared to make any suggestion.

780. Then you would say, let each barony support its own roads?—I think it would be much the better way. Our baronies are very unequally divided; some of them are very large, and others are very small.

781. Have you ever found any inconvenience from the fact that the place in which it has been arranged by the grand jury, that your sessions should be held, is not the most convenient place, but that a more convenient place could be had outside the barony in an adjoining barony?—No, I think not. The grand jury have the power of fixing any place they choose, but it must be within the barony.

782. But in your county, have you found any inconvenience in that respect?—I think not.

783. (Lord *John Browne*.) Do you know the way in which the bonds of high constables are taken?—Yes.

784. Has it ever come within your experience that there has been some practical inconvenience in consequence of the two sureties being obliged to be present?—No; because if a gentleman who has been sent into the grand jury for approval, cannot attend, there is nothing to prevent his substituting another name, and that has always been done.

785. In the county of Cork, do they never get a security, who is living, say in Dublin, or in some distant place?—Never. The high constable always returns the names of the two persons whom he intends to propose as sureties to the treasurer, and the treasurer lays the names before a committee of the grand jury, which is called the finance committee, to which all financial matters are referred, and it is part of their duty to approve or to disapprove of the security offered. I have known a gentleman appointed the first day, and if he found that he could not attend, another name was submitted and approved of.

786. Is the name submitted to the treasurer for approval or for disapproval?—No; he has no control over it whatever, it is entirely for the grand jury.

787. Why is it submitted to him?—It is not submitted to him, but the names are sent in through him.

Mr. *W. Johnson*.

21 March 1868.

788. In the county of Cork, I suppose you have never had a case of adjourned sessions falling to the ground for want of magistrates?—It was the case once in a very remote barony. It would have been almost an impossibility to have taken the contracts before the grand jury, for the district was so remote that the contractors and their sureties would not have come up to the assizes. That was at Castletown and Bearhaven, 90 miles from Cork, and one of the cesspayers acted as chairman, and the contracts were entered into. I reported the matter to the grand jury, and they thought it better, if no objection was made by any other person as to the illegality of it, not to raise any question about it, as it was the winter half year, and all the roads would have fallen out of repair.

789. They carried out justice at the expense of law?—Yes.

790. Do you not think it is desirable that there should be a general power that any cesspayer may take the chair if no magistrate be present?—Certainly.

791. (General *Dunne*.) In the case of malicious injuries, I understood you to say that they could not be entertained by the sessions if they were rejected by the grand jury?—Quite so. I think it is the only presentment the grand jury have any control over, unless it passes the sessions.

792. Is it not the case that local circumstances very often have influence upon the local sessions?—Yes, I look upon the grand jury as a court of appeal from all decisions of the sessions.

793. Would it not be very injudicious to allow a judge to put a tax upon any locality; does it not require local knowledge to know how a district should be taxed?—Certainly.

794. If a judge had that kind of power, would it not be very injurious, unless it was attended by the judgment of a jury confirming it?—I doubt if a judge would ever use the power.

795. In fact he would always commit it to a jury?—I should think so.

796. In any case of an appeal from the decision of the grand jury, he may empanel a jury if the decision is challenged, may he not?—He may.

797. The cesspayers in the county of Cork, I suppose, are a much higher class of men than in other counties?—They vary in different baronies; in some baronies they are a very superior class of men, in some others they are the farmers of the district.

798. It does not follow, does it, that men who have the largest property will be the largest cesspayers?—It does not.

799. Very often a gentleman has not very much land in the district in his own hands, and the farmer pays the highest cess?—Most of the gentry in the county of Cork are in the commission of the peace.

800. The magistrates, you say, attend pretty well?—Very well indeed, except in some small baronies.

801. And the cesspayers attend equally well?—The cesspayers attend equally well.

802. Is there generally a sufficient accord and agreement between them?—I cannot state so that; they do very often differ.

803. But not as a class?—Certainly not.

804. In the case of the grand jury of the county of Cork, there is some difficulty in con-

Mr. W. Johnson.

31 March 1862.

stituting it, is there not?—There are 23 grand jurors and 23 baronies.

605. They must call a 50 *l.* freeholder for each barony, must they not?—They are not called; the sheriff invites them, and he knows the day before they are empanelled whether they will attend or not.

606. But is he not directed by law to call a 50 *l.* freeholder for each barony?—Every man he invites must either be a 50 *l.* freeholder, or a 100 *l.* leaseholder.

607. But whether a man answers or not, must he not call a 50 *l.* freeholder?—I never knew them not answer; they always attend.

608. But is not the law imperative upon the sheriff to call a 50 *l.* freeholder first on the list?—I think that if he selects one from each barony, he complies with the Act of Parliament.

609. Is there not a great change in the grand jury in the county of Cork; are there very few men who are continually grand jurors?—There are a few good working-men who are put on very often.

610. Is there not this inconvenience practically found in the county of Cork; that the grand jurors have a little experience from the frequent changes, that you have not men who have been accustomed to the administration of the law so much as could be wished?—I think not. There are always men on the grand jury who have been frequently been on before, and they understand the working very well.

611. Do you not think that the reasons which you have given would make it desirable to divide the county of Cork into two ridings?—I am in favour of it, but I should be almost afraid of it. It would be a dangerous thing to do, because if the county was divided it should be divided for every purpose, and it would put the county to great expense in building gaols and other county buildings. In the West Riding there is no gaol, and I am afraid that there would be a great difference of opinion as to where the assizes should be held. If I was sure that the assizes for both ridings would be held in Cork I should not mind.

612. Is there not a great difficulty in bringing jurors from, say, Castletown to Cork?—Not since the railways were established. We have now railways from all parts of the country, coming into Cork, and it would be better for the people to come into Cork than into any such towns as Skibbereen, for instance.

613. How far is Castletown from Cork?—It is a very long distance, but Castletown would be always a long distance from any assize town.

614. Do not magistrates vote at some of those sessions who have no property at all in the barony?—Very seldom, but I have known such instances.

615. Is not that extremely objectionable?—I think it is.

616. Lord *John Browne.*] Do you mean that they do not occupy land either?—Not in the barony.

617. General *Dunne.*] Have you ever known an instance where they attended when they had no property in the county?—I have.

618. And they have voted?—They have voted.

619. Was not there a law some time ago requiring a qualification?—There was.

620. And that has been repealed?—It has been repealed.

621. And the injury of that appeal now appears in those arrangements?—It does.

622. Lord *John Browne.*] You have stated (and correctly so far as my experience goes) that the grand jury has power to present for malicious injury, even though it has been rejected at presentment sessions?—Yes.

623. Will you read the note at page 107 of Fost's book, and say if that does not show that there is a doubt about the law of the matter?—"Where an application for compensation for malicious injury was endorsed 'rejected,' at presentment sessions, held that the grand jury had not power to present in such cases." I am aware of that decision.

624. Is not that apparently contrary to the law as generally understood?—Yes.

625. Mr. *Leader.*] I suppose that you have given some consideration to the size of the baronies in the county of Cork?—Yes; the baronies are very unequally divided.

626. Have you found the business better or worse done in the large baronies than in the small ones; in which is the fairest consideration given to the different matters which come before the secretary?—I think it is just as well done in the one as in the other. If there is any distinction, I think that it is better done in some of the large baronies.

627. The barony of Barrymore, which I suppose is the largest, is it not?—I think Duhallow is the largest.

628. Do you find that you have sufficient time there to take the presentments?—No; in Duhallow I have known it occupy the whole day to take them.

629. Why have not those defects been remedied under the Grand Jury Acts?—Because it is difficult to divide a barony; each barony must contain a certain number of acres, and cannot contain more than a certain number of acres.

630. Was there not some memorial from the grand jury lately, expressing a wish that an alteration should be made in the present Act of Parliament?—Yes.

631. Have you that memorial?—I have not.

632. That points out how the present Act is inapplicable to the county of Cork?—Yes; it would be much better if the baronies were altered. In fact, I would substitute unions, which I think would work a great deal better than baronies.

633. Did you hear the evidence of Mr. Hill?—I did.

634. And do you agree with him that the unions are rather too large for the purpose?—I think not. I do not think that there is any union larger than the barony of Duhallow at present.

635. Do you think that the unions would be suitable for rating divisions instead of baronies?—At present I think not.

636. With regard to the amount of your salary, what expenses have you to pay out of it?—I have to pay all my travelling expenses out of it. The sessions in the county of Cork last four months in the year, and I have to pay all my own expenses and the expenses of my clerk. I never travel without a clerk. I could not do the business without him.

637. Are there any other deductions?—There are the salaries of two clerks all the year round.

638. You say that, for a lengthened period, you did not receive what you call the customary fees?—No; I was for more than 20 years in office,

office, and all I received was the legal fees which, as I stated just now, amounted to 48 l. and 18 l. It left me a very little over 200 l. a year.

639. How many sessions in the year have you to attend?—Ninety-four.

640. Mr. *Blake*.] Was that outside the expenses of your clerks?—After deducting all the expenses.

641. Mr. *Leader*.] Under this new Act which is coming into operation, supposing the duties of treasurer were added to those of the secretary, how do you think your remuneration would be affected?—If the office of treasurer became vacant in the county of Cork to-morrow, I should have all the duties which the present treasurer performs, and I should have the responsibility of paying about 60,000 l. a year, and all I should receive for it would be about 80 l., for I should have to pay 100 l. to the clerk, who is now in the treasurer's office, since without him I could never do my duty.

642. Mr. *Blake*.] I presume that, under those circumstances, you would rather do without it?—Certainly I would.

643. Mr. *Maguire*.] You say that you would prefer unions to baronies?—I think they are better understood.

644. But do you not think that if the county cess were divided, just as the poor rate is divided now, that would render the new arrangement more feasible and more acceptable?—I do not see how dividing the rate would make it easier to substitute the unions for the baronies.

645. With regard to this 500 l. a year, Mr. Murphy does not get the 500 l. a year now, does he?—No; I was not aware until his illness that these fees amounted to anything like what they were, and when I ascertained the large amount of them I decided on doing what every other secretary in Ireland did, and I now receive these fees myself, paying him an annuity out of them.

646. But that must be taken into consideration, must it not, when you estimate the remuneration attached to the office?—I now consider it as part of the payment for my office.

647. *Chairman*.] Was Mr. Murphy your clerk?—Yes; I found him in the office before I was appointed, and I did not disturb any arrangements which my predecessor had made.

648. Mr. *Maguire*.] Do you remember a case within recent years where magistrates came from other baronies and literally swamped the local magistrates and the local cesspayers?—It has not occurred recently; it is a great many years ago since it occurred.

649. How many years ago is it?—I think it must be 20 years ago.

650. Do you remember no case since that?—No, I do not; but perhaps I am going too far in saying that it was 20 years ago.

651. Do you not remember any case attracting public notice in the county, where magistrates came from other baronies, and where the local magistrates, and the local cesspayers, protested against it?—Not where a large number of them came; one or two might come, but I do not take any particular notice of them.

652. Has the law since then changed?—No; the law is the same.

653. Do you not think that that is a bad principle?—Certainly.

654. It is an abuse, you think, of the exercise of the power given by the law?—Certainly.

655. Do you not think it desirable for the satisfaction of the public that the law should be altered?—I think it ought; but as I said before there are very few magistrates who would ever do so; I have known magistrates attend at presentment sessions and refuse to interfere or to vote.

Mr. W. Adamson.

31 March 1868.

656. No doubt; but some have done it, and the law gives power to anybody to do it?—No doubt.

657. And what you believe to be an abuse and what the public believe to be an abuse ought, in your opinion, to be altered?—Certainly.

658. How are the high sheriffs appointed?—By the judges.

659. Who suggests their names to the judges?—The judge may return any person he chooses to the Government, but generally the course which is adopted is, that the outgoing high sheriff gives a list to the judge, from which list the judge may select or not, just as he may think proper.

660. Does any other person suggest a name to the judge?—No.

661. Are you certain of that?—I am certain of that.

662. Does the sub-sheriff never give any name to the judge?—He may do so.

663. Does the judge go beyond that list which is given to him?—Frequently he does.

664. How many names does the sheriff suggest to the judge?—The sheriff gives three names to the judge, and of course out of those three names the judge can only select one.

665. Is there no larger list than that given to the judge?—No, I think not.

666. Who suggests the additional names, then?—The high sheriff.

667. But you say that the list only contains three names, and that the judge often goes outside that?—The high sheriff returns three names to judges; but the judge is not bound to select any of those three.

668. Does any other person suggest a name to the judge, save the outgoing high sheriff?—I think not; but it may be done without my knowledge of course.

669. Then, the judge having that list in his hand, he may go outside and select whom he pleases?—He may, and it has been done very often.

670. But does he consult any local person?—That I cannot tell.

671. Is not the inconvenience in consequence of the extent of the county of Cork obviated by the arrangement of the judges now taking the first batch of jurors from one place, and the second from another?—There are two matters which have been arranged lately in the county of Cork, from which great convenience has arisen; one is, the power of dividing the panel, and the other is, for holding the assizes for the county and the city separately.

672. Do I understand that if the treasurer of the county of Cork died to-morrow the duties would have to be performed by you?—Yes.

673. And there is no sufficient provision made for payment in proportion to the responsibility?—The present treasurer receives about 1,100 l. a year, and all that I could possibly receive would be 184 l., out of which I should have to pay a clerk 100 l., and be responsible for the payment of 60,000 l. a year.

674. Is that fixed by Act of Parliament?—It was

Mr. *W. Johnson.*

31 March 1868.

was fixed by an Act of Parliament which was passed last Session.

875. Is there any discretion?—There is no discretion whatever.

876. As a mere matter of fact, is there not a very strong feeling on the part of what you would term the cesspayers throughout the country, that the county cess should be divided, whatever the feeling of the landlords may be?—I think it is so.

877. There is no doubt about it?—I think not.

878. Mr. *Blake.*] Is it not the theory that the associated ratepayers are intended to be a check upon the grand jury?—I suppose that was the intention when the Act was passed.

879. But the practice is that the grand jury nominate them?—I think the magistrates are a check upon the ratepayers at sessions; but, so far as my experience goes, I think that the ratepayers are much more likely to pass presentments than the magistrates.

880. Is it not the case that it is the body over whom the associated ratepayers are supposed to have the check who actually appoint them?—The grand jury select the names from the 100 highest ratepayers.

881. Is it your opinion that it would be more desirable to have these cesspayers elected by the ratepayers?—It is not; because, in the first place, I think that it would be a very expensive proceeding. The election of guardians costs a great deal of money, and if the cesspayers were to be elected in the same way it would be a great expense.

882. But in principle would it not be the more correct and juster way?—That is not the mode which I would suggest for selecting the cesspayers. The mode I would suggest would be this: I would have 100 names returned, and I would have the ballot take place at the assizes, and would let the number decided upon to sit at the sessions be balloted for and selected at the assizes, and not at the sessions.

883. Would you not let the cesspayer who bears the rates have a voice in the selection of them in the same way as poor law guardians are elected now?—If the baronies were abolished and unions substituted, I should see no objection whatever to allow the selected guardian for the year in the union to be the associated cesspayer at the sessions; that would be a very simple way, or you might have a certain number of them.

884. Colonel *Forde.*] Is it not the case that when a guardian is once elected it is very seldom that he is displaced, and in that case would it be advisable that that guardian should be the continual associated cesspayer at the sessions?—I think there is that objection.

885. Mr. *Blake.*] Do you consider it desirable that the grand jury should be a continuous body?—I see no use whatever in it; I do not know what duty they would have to perform between assizes and assizes.

886. Might it not be desirable on some occasions to call together such a body as the grand juries between one assizes and another?—I do not think so.

887. General *Dunne.*] In point of fact, if the grand jury take from the list of 100 ratepayers the first, they have not choice at all about it?—If they have to select the 24 highest ratepayers there is no use in returning more than the 24.

888. But they cannot be said to appoint them when they are merely the executive of the law?—My experience is, that when the grand jury are selecting the 24 ratepayers, they select the men most likely to attend, and the most intelligent.

889. But in that case it is a selection by the grand jury, is it not?—It is.

890. But if they take the 24 first, and consider it imperative that they can make no selection, surely you can hardly call it a selection?—Certainly not; the law would select them.

891. *Chairman.*] But that is not the practice in the county of Cork?—It is not.

892. General *Dunne.*] Then, again, if 100 are returned, and they are balloted for by the grand jury, the jury cannot be said to select them in the way you propose?—Certainly not.

893. Have you any doubt that the selection of grand jurors generally, is the most judicious that could possibly be made?—I have no doubt of it.

894. Colonel *Forde.*] Do not the grand jury dot them about the barony?—They do; they select the men most likely to attend.

895. *Chairman.*] What is your present salary?—£ 324.

896. And according to the return of last year, what are the legal fees?—I think the return which the noble Lord had is nearly an accurate return of what I am legally entitled to.

897. And that, in addition to the 500 *l.* a year, makes it nearly 1,000 *l.* a year?—Yes.

898. And if you got the treasurer's work, that would make over 1,200 *l.* a year?—Yes.

899. Do you think that 1,200 *l.* a year is not sufficient remuneration for discharging those duties?—With regard to those fees, I would much rather that they were taken from me altogether, provided I got compensation for them; because the way in which they are received is very disagreeable. Although the applicants reckon they get full value for them, still I would much rather be relieved of them altogether. I think that it would be much better to have them collected in the nature of stamps, and to have them handed over to the credit of the county.

Friday, 3rd April 1868.

MEMBERS PRESENT:

Mr. Blake.	Mr. Gregory.
Colonel Cooper.	Mr. Herbert.
Mr. Dawson.	Mr. Kendall.
General Dunne.	Sir Charles Lanyon.
Colonel Forde.	Mr. Leader.
Mr. Chichester Fortescue.	Mr. Maguire.
Colonel French.	Sir Colman O'Loghlen.

THE O'CONOR DON, IN THE CHAIR.

Mr. WILLIAM JOHNSON recalled; and further Examined.

Mr. W. Johnson. 3 April 1868.

900. *Chairman.*] I BELIEVE you wish to explain a statement which you made on the last day of the sitting of the Committee, respecting the amount of fees which you received for filling up tenders, and which you stated in answer to a question from me, to be 18 *l.* only?—I think I made a mistake. The fees which I returned as 18 *l.*, were for their blank forms of tenders, which were sold to any party applying for them, for which the secretary is entitled to sixpence. The average fees for the last 18 months for the filling of tenders have been 104 *l.* 4 *s.* I should have divided that of course, because I was entitled to 6 *d.* for the blank form, and to 4 *d.* for filling it. Consequently, I should have put the blank tenders at 18 *l.* and 50 *l.* 2 *s.*

901. You should have included in the legal fees the 6 *d.* which you charge upon the filled tenders?—Precisely.

902. Your legal fees are upon blank tenders and recognizances only, are they not?—They are upon blank tenders and recognizances only.

903. The return then which was presented to Parliament, is not even strictly correct as regards the legal fees, because you omitted the legal fees upon those tenders, upon which you charge another fee for filling up?—Yes, I find that is so.

904. You stated on the last day of the meeting of the Committee, that the amount of extra legal fees was over 300 *l.*, did you not?—Somewhere about 500 *l.*

905. And that you allow your clerk to receive?—That my clerk always received up to the year 1861.

906. So that, in fact, during that time your clerk was receiving a larger salary than yourself?—Double; which I was not aware of.

907. As far as you were personally concerned, you stated on the last day the Committee sat, that you would wish the system of fees to be done away with, did you not?—I think it would be much better.

908. Do you think that although done away with as regards the secretary, the fees ought still to be exacted from the contractor?—I think that somebody ought to be appointed to do the duty, otherwise great public inconvenience would be felt. There would be no person to fill up those forms properly, and it might create a constant conflict between me and parties lodging applications, if they were not formally done; and they would be driven elsewhere, and probably would have those forms filled up at very great expense.

909. Would the abolition of the fees altogether, and the refusal of the secretary to fill up the forms, lead to the contractors taking the contracts at a lower figure than they do now?—Not at all. I do not think that the fee of 1 *s.* guides them in the least in estimating the amount of the tender.

910. Do you not think that those fees might be received and paid to the benefit of the county?—Certainly, and that is the general opinion.

911. And if the secretary's salary were increased, and he were obliged to fill up the tenders, those fees might be paid to the benefit of the county, might they not?—I would suggest that they should be collected in stamps and handed over to the credit of the county.

912. With respect to the County of Cork, do you not find considerable difficulty in attending to all the different sessions, and is not a deputy in the County of Cork very often required?—At the present moment I have two duties to perform; and I am expected to be at two places at the same time. For instance, the first adjournment sessions must be within 30 days from the first presentment sessions; there are 22 baronies, as I stated before, and the county at large makes 24, and four Sundays, which make 28. While the adjourned sessions are going on, there are preparations making in the office for the next days' business. It requires great secrecy and great confidence, and since this gentleman has left me on account of illness, I am obliged to attend to that duty myself. Consequently, for the last seven or eight years, I have seldom attended an adjourned sessions. I never attend an adjourned sessions until towards the end, when the receiving of tenders in the office is over. When that duty is finished, I attend the remaining adjourned sessions. In all other counties, an interval elapses between the county at large sessions and the first adjourned sessions. During that interval, the secretary is employed in making preparations and receiving tenders for adjourned sessions; in small counties there is ample time to do that, but in mine there is not.

913. Do you consider that your attendance

Mr. W. *Johnson.*

9 April [illegible].

at your office to receive the tenders is of more importance than your attendance at the adjourned sessions?—Of much more importance. I conceive that my duty at the adjourned sessions is very trifling indeed. I only attend there in custody of tenders and hand them to the magistrates and ratepayers. My duty, or rather my clerk's duty, is merely to fill up the blanks in the recognizances.

914. Under an Act of last year you have power to appoint a deputy, in certain cases, have you not?—I have.

915. Do you think that is sufficient?—No; I think that it is clogged with a very inconvenient restriction, that is, the approval of the Lord Lieutenant. Now, last winter I had occasion to appoint a deputy, from illness. On Saturday evening I wrote to Sir Thomas Larcom, asking his approval. I appointed my son but I was able to resume my duties about three days afterwards, and I did not receive Sir Thomas Larcom's reply until long after I had been able to perform my duties myself and return to the sessions.

916. The county of Cork is a peculiar county in many respects, is it not, it being so very large? —Yes.

917. Do you not believe that it might be divided?—There is a great difference of opinion about that. I should be, myself, for dividing the county, if I was certain that the assizes would be held in Cork.

918. The great objection to dividing the county of Cork, is that from all parts of the county, the city of Cork is the most convenient place for holding the assizes?—Certainly.

919. Should you see any impracticability in dividing the county and still having both assizes held in the City of Cork?—None whatever. I think that it would be the most convenient and the most proper place.

920. If the county were divided and both assizes held, one after the other, in the city of Cork, would it not be a great convenience both to the jurors and the officers of the county?—A vast convenience, and I conceive that Cork would be a much more convenient place for holding the assizes than any town in the West Riding, and I fear that there would be a constant struggle as to what town should be appointed in the West Riding.

921. How many surveyors are there appointed in the county of Cork?—Three.

922. What are their salaries?—The East Riding is divided into two divisions; and there are two county surveyors for that Riding, and one for the West. The salary of the county surveyor of the one division is 450 *l.* a year; that includes the salary of a clerk; it is 200 *l.* every half year, and 25 *l.* every half year for a clerk. The salary of the county surveyor of the West Riding is 225 *l.* every half year, and 25 *l.* for a clerk.

923. The annual salary is 400 *l.*, is it not?—The annual salary of the county surveyor for the West Riding is 500 *l.*, including the salary of a clerk; the surveyors for the other two divisions have 450 *l.*, including the salary of a clerk.

924. Have the grand jury in any county of Ireland the power of appointing as many county surveyors as they think proper?—I think so; the question was argued before Justice Keogh, and he decided that they had.

925. Giving to each county surveyor the maximum salary for the county?—That was the decision of Justice Keogh, and it was argued by counsel before him.

926. So that a divisional additional county surveyor may, in fact, receive a much larger salary than the surveyor for an entire county; for instance, a divisional surveyor in a first-class county can receive legally a larger salary than the surveyor for an entire second-class county can legally receive?—I think so, according to that decision.

927. Have you anything like a standing grand jury committee in the county of Cork?—Yes; our court-house has been built a long time, and it requires constant repair, and the grand jury some years ago appointed a committee of 12 of their own body to see to it. That has been a permanent committee, and has continued up to the present time. A sum is granted to them when required, never exceeding 100 *l.*, to be a floating sum in their hands to keep the court-house in repair. They also make a presentment for a further sum for the expense of repairing the weights and measures when necessary, when called on by the constabulary; and they have also a third sum presented to them for the cost of suing defaulting contractors. Under the opinion of the law adviser, the magistrates at petty sessions can only give costs on the second summons, not on the first; and it was conceived to be a hardship that the county surveyor should pay those costs out of his own pocket; and, consequently, the finance committee pay the cost actually incurred for the summons and the travelling expenses to the petty sessions, either of the county surveyor, or his deputies. It amounts to very little.

928. This standing finance committee is different from the board of superintendence, is it not?—They are quite a different body, although they happen to be the same individuals, with a few exceptions; there is a change every new board of superintendence, and some of the gentlemen on the present board of superintendence are not on the finance committee.

929. Do you think that the presentments to this finance committee are legal?—I have very great doubts about it; I think not, but I am not a lawyer; I think if they were traversed it would be very doubtful; but they are very useful I must say.

930. Have you any statement to make to the Committee with respect to the presentments in the county of Cork being entered on parchment? —Yes, every presentment of the grand jury, no matter what it is, either a resolution, or otherwise, is engrossed when passed by the grand jury on skins of parchment, each skin of parchment being very large; those skins are very expensive; it is done under the impression that a presentment is something in the nature of an indictment, and there is an Act of Parliament requiring all indictments to be put on parchment. I understand it is not done in other counties; those parchments we call the county roll; there are 300 pages in it, and I think it costs the county from 80 *l.* to 100 *l.* a-year, according to the size of the parchment roll.

931. And you believe in the county of Cork, that you are obliged by law to have the presentments entered on parchment in this manner?—It is considered so, and it has been the practice for the last 30 years.

932. Colonel *French.*] Under what law, and under

Mr. W. Johnson. — 3 April [illegible].

under what section?—I do not remember under what section the indictments have to be so entered.

933. (General *Dunne*.) Are those the presentments that go up to the grand jury to be passed and fiated, or the presentment book in which all are entered?—It is what we call the presentment book; it is parchment, and the whole of it is bound up in the shape of a very large book; I believe in other counties they call the schedule the county book.

934. Are you aware that in Queen's County the presentments come up on paper very like the ordinary paper for the tenders; but they are all entered in a county book, and that county book is signed by 12 or 13 jurors?—The last parchment sheet of this roll is signed by every member of the grand jury.

935. Colonel *Verner*.] The book that you talk of would be what you present to the judge, that is to say, the judges' book?—No; the book that we present to the judge is something in the nature of this book that I have here. What is presented to the judge is the schedule of all applications that have been approved of at the Sessions and not this large parchment roll.

936. Does the judge sign that?—He does not; that is the book which is handed over to the Clerk of the Crown; the Clerk of the Crown is bound to make a copy of that within a week from the assizes, and to hand that to the treasurer, verified by affidavit, on which the treasurer makes his applotment.

937. But does not the judge sign the county book?—No, in our county the judge never signs any document.

938. (General *Dunne*.) How does he express a fiat then?—He makes no observation at all, unless there is opposition to it; the Clerk of the Crown calls out,—"Does any person object to any presentment in the barony of so-and-so?" and so he passes that on; if no person makes any objection, or has any application to make, the presentments are fiated as a matter of course.

939. Do no members of the grand jury go to the judge and sit with him and go over them?—Always.

939. Colonel *French*.] Is not each presentment read separately before the judge?—They are so very numerous that it would occupy almost the entire day; I have here the schedule of the present period and also the schedule for a half year in 1833, previous to the present Grand Jury Act coming into operation; the contract rolls in the county have increased by perhaps three-fourths.

940. *Chairman*.] The baronies in the county of Cork are very inconveniently divided, are they not?—Very.

941. Do you believe that the grand jury have the power of altering baronies?—Yes, they have, but they cannot contain more than a certain number of acres; I do not exactly remember the number, but it is in Foot's Book; I think it is 45,000 acres.

942. Do you think that the substitution of the area of the acres for the baronies would be beneficial?—I think so; but I have had conversations with some gentlemen within the last couple of days who differ from me as to that.

943. But you think that some alteration ought to be made in the division of the baronies in the county of Cork?—Certainly.

944. Why has not that alteration been made, if the grand jury have the power of making it at present?—In consequence of the restriction in the section. I have not read the section lately. It is a section I have had very little occasion to refer to, but it is a very short section, "and be it further enacted, that it shall and may be lawful for the grand jury of any county by presentment, to divide any barony or half barony thereof into one or more subdivisions, each whereof shall, for the purposes of this Act, and for all purposes relating to the presenting, raising, and levying of money for any matter or thing for which presentment may be lawfully made by grand juries, be deemed and taken to be a barony or half barony, as such grand jury shall present the same; provided such barony shall contain forty-five thousand acres, but not otherwise; and it shall be lawful for any grand jury to unite any two baronies, or any barony or any portion of any barony or baronies, into one, for the purposes of this Act, provided the baronies or portions so united shall not contain more than forty thousand acres."

945. Does not that appear to leave it completely in the power of the grand jury to alter the state of things which you say is so disadvantageous in the county of Cork?—They conceive not. There was a resolution passed at one of the baronial sessions last circuit, recommending that the unions should be adopted, but unfortunately I did not bring it with me.

946. Are the expenses of bridges in the county of Cork paid partially by the county at large, or by the barony?—There is a standing rule of the grand jury, that no presentment shall be made for a bridge unless the barony contribute one-fourth of the expense, and they adhere very strictly to that rule.

947. But the presentments for those bridges are all voted at the baronial sessions only?—Yes; at the baronial sessions.

948. Do you believe that the check of the grand jury over those presentments is a sufficient one?—I think so. The baronial sessions are very careful in passing an application; they reduce it as much as they can, because they know that unless they give some inducement they have very little chance of getting the presentments passed before the grand jury.

949. At present a bridge, which is partially in one county and partially in another, can be presented for by both counties, can it not?—Yes.

950. Have you any suggestion to make respecting the case of a bridge which, though situate in one county, might be as convenient to an adjoining county as to the county in which it is situate?—Yes, there is a case at present, the Youghal bridge. There was an Act of Parliament passed last session, upon which the grand jury are not very much inclined to act, as they appear to be more anxious to abandon the present old bridge and to build the bridge a little higher up the river. Both sides of the river where they proposed to build the new bridge are in the county of Waterford, and the county of Cork will be willing to pay half that expense; but there is a doubt as to whether they possess the power to make a presentment for a bridge where no portion of it will be in their own county. It is about a quarter of a mile outside the boundary of the county. The county of Waterford and the county of Cork join quite close to where the bridge is intended to be built.

951. Mr. *Blake*.] Is the Youghal bridge wholly in

in the county of *Waterford*?—The present bridge is not, but the intended bridge will cross a little higher up, at both sides in the county of Waterford.

952. Colonel *French*.] When a presentment is passed in a county where the larger portion of the proposed work is to be executed, is it not imperative on the adjoining county to pass that presentment?—I am not aware that it is so as to counties, but it is so as to baronies. I do not remember that there is any such power in this Grand Jury Act, but there is as to baronies. That is the case that we have a doubt about.

953. The whole of the bridge, according to your statement, is in one county?—Yes, in the county of Waterford. If we were to build a new bridge on the very site of the present bridge we would not require any change in the law.

954. *Chairman*.] But you would approve of empowering a grand jury to contribute towards the expense of a bridge in an adjoining county? —Where the whole was in another county.

955. Do you approve of the system of the county at large road presentments; do you approve of having certain roads paid partially by the county at large, and partially by the baronies?—I think not. There is a great complaint in some of the baronies, that they are obliged to contribute a part of the county at large expenses for post roads, where several of the baronies have no post roads at all, and through which no post is carried, or if carried, carried by a man on foot.

956. Colonel *French*.] They would not be charged on the county at large, if the post were only carried by a footman?—They would not; but the baronies through which only a man carries the mail on foot have to contribute their proportion towards the other mail carriage roads in other baronies, and that they think is not fair; I think it would be much fairer if each barony paid for its own roads.

957. But the mail coach roads are so much wider, and so much more expensive to keep, that that is the reason that the additional expense has to be borne by the county at large, is it not?—Some of what we call the mail-carriage roads are very unimportant, and very minor roads. There are a great number of them.

958. Sir *Charles Lanyon*.] Is it not the case now, that the leading mail coach roads have been superseded by railways, and that consequently, in many counties, if not in Cork, the leading coach roads which were mail coach roads, have been superseded by railways?—Yes; and in the county of Cork that is the case.

959. Then, the expense of maintaining those roads is now thrown upon the baronies, is it not? —Entirely.

960. Then there are many other roads throughout the county which are minor roads, which are still mail car roads, and roads of very much less consequence than the roads which have been superseded by the railways; and yet those roads are maintained half by the barony and half by the county?—Yes.

961. That is a very anomalous state of things, is it not?—I think so.

962. And would it not be desirable that some arrangement should be made, by which all the roads of a particular class should be put upon the barony, and that the words "mail coach road," or "mail car road" should be superseded, and that all roads should be put upon the barony; or else, if any of them are repaired, half by the barony or half by the county, all the leading lines of road between market town and market town should be so denominated as to secure an equal adjustment of rates in the county?—That is what I would suggest. No coach runs on any road now; there is nothing more than a one-horse car upon any road; in fact we should not consider them as mail carriage roads at all.

963. *Chairman*.] Does not almost every road in the country lead to a market town directly or indirectly?—Not at all. There are hundreds of cross roads which are very fine roads. Some of the best roads which we have do not lead directly from one town to another.

964. But where would you draw the line, between a road leading from market town to market town; if a law were passed that all roads leading from market town to market town should be on the county at large?—I think that that could be easily ascertained.

965. There is only the shortest road from one market town to another that could be put on the county at large?—I would not put any on the county at large. I would let each barony pay for its own roads.

966. I understood you to say, in answer to the Honourable Member for *Belfast*, that you would be in favour of putting all the roads which lead from one market town to another upon the county at large?—I would put every road upon its own barony. I would abolish the county at large proportion altogether.

967. General *Dunne*.] At this moment when you apply for a road, is there not a fiction?—I think that was under the old law, but that has been changed, and does not exist at present.

968. But it did exist, did it not?—It did exist under the old law of George the Third.

969. *Chairman*.] Then I understand you to differ from Mr. Hill, who gave evidence on the last day in favour of putting more roads upon the county at large?—Certainly.

970. You do not agree with him on that point? —I do not.

971. Did you hear Mr. Hill's evidence with respect to advances to contractors for works in progress?—Yes.

972. Do you believe that those advances can legally be made, except there be a direct order of the grand jury upon each presentment to that effect?—Certainly not.

973. You do not think that a general order of the grand jury is sufficient?—Certainly not; I should think that the order ought to be made when the presentment is passing. I think it refers entirely to presentments, and not to contracts.

974. When there is no tender for a contract at adjourned sessions, is it in the power now of the grand jury to make over that presentment to the county surveyor, is it not?—Either to take the tender themselves or to hand it over to the county surveyor.

975. Do you believe that such presentments ought to be handed over to the county surveyor, in the cases of new works?—I never knew it done in the case of a new work, only in case of a contract for works of maintenance, and that only when no tender could be obtained at the assizes, after having been properly advertised for, and where the road was such a road as could not be allowed to get out of order; and then it was only

Mr. W. Johnson.

3 April 1868.

only for the winter half-year; they very seldom adopt it for the summer half-year.

976. Would you not think it a very objectionable system to make over those roads to the county surveyor in cases where there is no imperative necessity for having the work immediately done, in the case of both presentments and contracts?—They never hand over a presentment to the county surveyor, only contracts. When a presentment is not executed, and some time elapses after the period appointed for finishing the work, the enquiry is what we call "transferred" (not re-presented) to another person, to be executed under the direction of the county surveyor. Formerly they used to transfer them to the county surveyor himself; but they thought that it was much better to transfer them to a contractor, who would finish them under the county surveyor's supervision.

977. Are you now speaking of the practice in the county of Cork?—Yes.

978. What I am asking you is with respect to the present law; you are aware that at present the grand jury have the power of making over a presentment to the county surveyor, both for a new work and for repairs, in case no tender appears before the grand jury?—Yes.

979. Do you not believe it to be most objectionable to make those presentments to the county surveyor in all cases, except where there is an imperative necessity that the work should be immediately done?—Certainly; and they never do so.

980. They never do so in the county of Cork?—They never do, except in case of great necessity.

981. But you may not, perhaps, be aware that in other counties they have the power to do so, and that they do so?—I was not aware of that.

982. Colonel French.] Then you transfer a presentment from men who have given security to men who have given no security at all?—Yes; that is the omission in the Act of Parliament. They cannot compel the new person appointed to give security.

983. General Dunne.] How do they pay the new contractor?—Out of the monies in hand. They can only transfer the balance.

984. How do they recover the balance expended?—For a great many years we have not had a prosecution in the county of Cork, either in the superior court, or the quarter sessions; for we found that the bills of costs which were brought in were so large that, as we got no returns, we have given up the expense altogether of prosecuting.

985. Are you aware of a decision lately come to by the assistant barristers and judges that the county cannot recover unless they prove a money loss?—I have not heard that.

986. Chairman.] You are aware that, under the present law, the barony cess-collectors are obliged to lodge their receipts when they amount to 100 l.?—Yes.

987. Do you think that there is any check over them?—In the county of Cork they do it, but the treasurer watches them very strictly. When they lodge the money they bring the Bank receipts to the treasurer, and it is a matter which he looks after very closely.

988. The treasurer in the county of Cork has a direct interest in seeing that this money is immediately lodged, has he not?—Yes; but I think that it would be a great breach of duty, and a neglect on the part of the treasurer, if he did not do so, even though he had no direct interest in the matter. The present treasurer has a direct personal interest, because he gets the interest of the county moneys.

989. He is one of the treasurers appointed before the present Act of Parliament was passed, is he not?—He was appointed before the Act passed.

990. Colonel French.] Then if he had been appointed since the Act, he would not have had any personal interest in the matter?—He would not.

991. Chairman.] With regard to the treasurers who held their offices at the time of the passing of the Act of 1836, their interest in the county money was preserved by that Act, was it not?—Yes.

992. Before the passing of the Act of 1836 the treasurers had the right to receive, as a portion of their emoluments, the interest upon the county moneys?—They had.

993. And as far as the existing treasurers were concerned, that was preserved to them?—Yes.

994. But all treasurers appointed after the Act was passed, were to be deprived of that interest?—Yes, and it was to go to the county.

995. Do you believe that a standing body of the grand jury would be able to control the barony cess-collectors, and to make them pay in this 100 l. as soon as it was raised?—No, I do not think there would be any necessity for it, because I think that if the treasurer reported it to the grand jury at the next assizes, the collectors would not be re-appointed.

996. You consider that in all cases, even where the treasurer has no direct personal interest in the matter, he is a sufficient check on the barony cess-collector?—I think so; it is his duty.

997. What do they give in the county of Cork for the collection of the cess?—Ninepence.

998. Are you aware what is given for the collection of the poor-rates?—It varies in different unions.

999. What is the average?—The only union of which I have any personal knowledge is my own union, where it is sixpence and fourpence.

1000. Do you continue your collectors constantly?—Yes, there is only an election when a vacancy occurs.

1001. Chairman.] Do you not think that the barony cess collection might be made by the poor-rate collectors?—I suppose it could.

1002. And at the same rate at which they collect the poor rates?—I think it is possible.

1003. Colonel French.] The barony cess collector had the option of collecting the poor rate, formerly if he pleased, had he not?—Yes.

1004. Chairman.] How do you select the cesspayers in the county of Cork?—A hundred names are returned to the grand jury for each barony, or rather to me. Those lists are laid before the grand jury, and they select (omitting in the first instance those persons' names who have been at the previous presentment sessions) from that list any number not less than 10, or more than 24, dividing them as carefully as they can over the barony. Generally speaking, what they look to principally, is to select the men who are most likely to attend.

1005. They do not select the highest names on the list?—No.

1006. Is not this mode of selection very often a source of difficulty to the grand jury and of dissatisfaction,

Mr. W. Johnson.

3 April 1868.

dissatisfaction, though it may be very justly done; and are there not often complaints?—There are, but I really think these complaints are unfair.

1007. But still it is a subject upon which complaint is sometimes made?—I have heard complaints, but, in my opinion, they are groundless.

1008. Do you not think that it would be better to take away this source of dissatisfaction?—I think that the grand jury would be very glad to be relieved of it themselves.

1009. How would you propose that the cesspayers should be selected?—At one time I thought that it would be better for the grand jury to ballot out of the 100 highest names at the sessions, but I have been since considering the matter, and if there were a sufficient number, I think that it would be better that any elected guardian in the barony should be entitled to sit at the baronial sessions and to allow the grand jury to ballot from these guardians at the assizes, if there were a sufficient number; because, in point of fact, they are very nearly the same individuals. The persons who act at the presentment sessions with the magistrates and the elected guardians are generally the same persons.

1010. You would not approve of having a special election of those cesspayers?—I think not.

1011. Why not?—In the first place, I think that it would be very expensive to select them on the same principle as the elected guardians. In the county of Cork it would be a very expensive thing from the size of the county and the extent of the baronies.

1012. Do you believe that, without any special election, the elected guardians might be taken as a body from the cesspayers?—I see no objection to that.

1013. Mr. *Maguire*.] Can you say what the expense would be?—I am not prepared to say what the expense would be; but judging by experience of the election of guardians in each union in the county of Cork, I should say it would be expensive.

1014. But you said that it would be a very large expense. Give me, if you can, an idea of what is the expense of electing the local guardians, or what justifies your saying that it is a very large expense?—I have no means of giving the information, but I always understood that the expense of the annual elections for the guardians is very great; I have no idea what it is.

1015. Is it 1,000 *l.*, or is it 5 *l.*?—I cannot say; I have no conception whatever.

1016. *Chairman*.] Generally speaking, is there a contest for the election of those elected guardians?—There is.

1017. General *Dunne*.] Do you think that if there were an election, anybody except some contractor or other person who had some ulterior interest, would set himself up as a cesspayer, for the mere pleasure of being a cesspayer?—I do not think they would.

1018. Colonel *French*.] Should you think that such a change would promote economy, or would they be playing into each other's hands; for instance, do you think that if elected guardians were the parties selected in place of the cesspayers appointed by the grand jury under certain regulations, the change by putting it into the hands of the elected guardians would tend to economy in the expenses of the county?—I do not think it would, because I think that they would be very nearly the same persons; very often the cesspayers who act at the presentment sessions are some of the elected guardians in the union.

1019. *Chairman*.] Do you find from your experience that the magistrates or the cesspayers are the most watchful of presentments at sessions?—Certainly; the magistrates.

1020. Cesspayers coming in late at the presentment sessions cannot sit upon them?—No.

1021. But a magistrate can?—A magistrate can.

1022. Do you not think that they ought to be placed upon an equality in that respect?—Certainly.

1023. Colonel *French*.] Have you ever known that point decided?—I have known it decided; no cesspayer makes a declaration, or, at least, very seldom. I have infringed the law a little myself in that respect. When they apply to me, when a man comes in a little late, and they have only just commenced, and he is very anxious to be on, and the list was not filled up, I have given him the declaration, although it was not strictly according to law.

1024. *Chairman*.] But you think that restriction ought to be abolished?—Yes, certainly.

1025. At present the sessions are obliged to take the lowest tender, are they not?—Yes.

1026. Are you aware that frauds sometimes exist in consequence of this?—I certainly would not alter the system of taking the lowest tender. I think it would be a most dangerous thing to alter.

1027. Could you suggest any mode by which those fraudulent proceedings on the part of contractors might in some way be prevented?—I am afraid that it would be very difficult.

1028. Will you state why you would consider it dangerous to alter the system of taking the lowest tenders?—I think that if there was a discretion given to the magistrates and ratepayers an influential contractor, who would be certain to be the highest tenderer, may (though I do not say he would) use interest to get some of his friends to attend, and if the door was opened once it would be very hard to say where it would end. I think the law is the best guide in the case.

1029. Before the passing of the Grand Jury Act of William the Fourth it was in the power of the grand jury to make presentments to any parties whom they thought proper, was it not?—Yes.

1030. And there were great complaints about that time about certain contractors being favoured?—I have had no experience of the time; but I have always understood that that was the case.

1031. And you think it would be very undesirable to leave the door open for such transactions?—Certainly.

1032. You are one of the governors of the lunatic asylum in the county of Cork, are you not?—I am.

1033. This asylum is paid for wholly out of the county rates, is it not?—It is supported out of the county rates. I have been only very recently appointed, so that I cannot give very much information as to the working of the establishment.

1034. The governors are appointed, not by the county, but by the Government, are they not?—They are appointed by the Government.

1035. The inmates are paupers, are they not?—With a few exceptions. There are a few paying patients; but the amount which they pay is very

very small. If the governors find that the family of the patient are able to contribute any portion, they require something to be paid for the maintenance of the patient; but, generally speaking, they are paupers.

1036. Do you not therefore consider that this charge ought rather to be upon the poor rate than upon the county rate?—I think so.

1037. Neither the grand jury nor the sessions have any control whatever in the management or direction of those establishments, have they?—They are bound to make a half-yearly presentment; I think it is some 4,000 *l.* or 5,000 *l.* It is an imperative presentment on the certificate of the chief or under secretary.

1038. Has the expense of the lunatic asylum in Cork increased very much of late years?—No; it has been the same for some years. There will be an increase now, because they are about to enlarge the asylum, and they are about to build an infirmary.

1039. Is there any great increase in the number of lunatics?—No, they are generally the same. A good many are discharged as cured, and some die. There is not very much mortality in the establishment, but of course out of so large a number, there are cases of death.

1040. Do you know anything about the government of the county gaol?—The grand jury appoint the board of superintendence.

1041. Is there not an officer called the local inspector?—Yes.

1042. Do you believe his office to be a very necessary one?—From my own personal knowledge, I do not think that I could give any evidence about that matter.

1043. Then you do not know his duties?—I do not.

1044. You stated on the last day of the sitting of the Committee, in answer to a question which I asked you, that the presentments for deserted children were abolished by an Act passed two or three years ago, do you understand that that Act prevents the grand jury from making any presentments after the date of that Act for deserted children?—It is some time now since I read the Act, but I think that there was power in the Act to make a presentment up to a certain time, where the amount was due, because those presentments generally were not made in advance, but I cannot very well explain it, unless I have the Act of Parliament. I know there were presentments made in our county after the Act passed.

1045. And are you aware that even up to last year in many counties, presentments for that purpose were made?—After the sessions, there appeared to be some moneys due to some persons who had care of the children, or to the churchwardens, and the grand jury thought it fair and right to pay them what was due, but no farther.

1046. The children who were under their care, after the passing of the Act, were to be transferred to the poor-house, were they not?—Yes; the parties did not apply, and as well as I remember they were poor people, and were not generally aware of the change in the law. They generally made their application yearly, and after the Act had been passed they came in six months, perhaps, or longer, to the sessions and made applications; and although the Act had been repealed, the grand jury thought it only just to pay them.

1047. Colonel *French.*] With regard to tenders, they are taken at the adjourned sessions, are they not?—They are. Mr. W. Johnson.

1048. There is only one magistrate present at the adjournment sessions, is there?—Very often, though not always, there is a greater number of magistrates at the adjourned sessions than at the first sessions. 3 April 1868.

1049. Do the associated cesspayers attend the adjourned sessions?—They do.

1050. And it is with them that the acceptance of the tenders lies, is it not?—Yes; it is discretionary with them.

1051. You have stated that you would not like the clause repealed in which the lowest tender is bound to be taken?—Certainly not.

1052. On the last meeting of the Committee, during the course of your examination by the honourable Member for Waterford as to the Poor Law Guardians being the associated cesspayers, I asked you this question, No. 884, "Is it not the case, that when a guardian is once elected, it is very seldom that he is displaced, and in that case would it be advisable that that guardian should be the continual associated cesspayer at the sessions?" and your answer was, "I think that there is that objection." You have stated now, in answer to the honourable Chairman, that you would not object to see the Poor Law Guardians the associated cesspayers, have you not?—Yes, because I think they are.

1053. But then if you made it an enactment that the Poor Law Guardians should necessarily be the associated cesspayers, virtually from that question which I asked you, and your reply, you would always have the same men associated with the magistrates for the baronial sessions?—If there was not a change in the elected guardians, of course there would be no change in the associated cesspayers.

1054. Do you not know that there is very seldom a change in the elected guardians?—In my union there is very often a change in the elected guardians.

1055. At all events, you do not think that it would be proper that the associated cesspayers should always be the same?—No; I think that would be objectionable.

1056. Would there not be a chance of that by making the guardians virtually the associated cesspayers?—There certainly would.

1057. Have you had any experience in other parts of Ireland as to guardians, because I think it generally happens that if a man is once an elected guardian, he is nearly always an elected guardian, unless he chooses to give it up himself?—I know nothing whatever about that matter, except as regards the Cork union alone, which is my own union; I happen to be a guardian in my own union.

1058. You said something about the Poor Law union, or it was suggested by the honourable Chairman, that the Poor Law union should be the area of taxation; do you consider that that would be more advisable than the present baronies?—I think it would; because the divisions are so much better understood, and the others are so very unequal; in fact, no person can ascertain what guided those when they were arranging those baronies, they are arranged in such an extraordinary manner.

1059. Is not the Poor Law union, generally speaking, a very large district?—Yes; it is. There are 17 Poor Law unions in our county.

Mr. W. Johnson.

3 April 1858.

1060. Would it not be very cumbersome?—I think not.

1061. Of course, only that part would be appropriated for taxation, which would be in the county?—Just so; in one county there is only one union that goes into another county; or rather, one union of another which comes into ours, and that is part of the county of Limerick.

1062. Is it not the Board of Superintendence which always has charge of the county court-houses from assizes to assizes?—No; not of the court-houses; they have the charge of the bridewells.

1063. Is it necessary for the grand jury to appoint a committee each time to take charge of the court-house?—No; it is a permanent committee, which was appointed some years ago, and it continued without any change.

1064. Is it not usual that the Board of Superintendence is the Board for the management of the court-house?—They happen to be the same gentlemen, with one or two exceptions. There is a change made sometimes on the Board of Superintendence, and some of the present members of the Board of Superintendence, in consequence, are not members of the Court House committee, but the majority of them are.

1065. You stated, did you not, that you could very seldom attend at the adjourned sessions, owing to having to remain in your office to take the tenders for the sessions which are abroad?—Yes; when this gentleman who was in my office before I was appointed, and who had had a very long experience, and in whom there was great confidence by the grand jury and the public, was there, there was, of course, no necessity for me to remain there, and I always attended the adjourned sessions myself; but I did not like to appoint any person in his place, as I knew that it would give him great annoyance, and I thought it of much more importance that I should remain and do that duty myself, and receive those tenders myself, because sometimes there is a little uneasiness on the part of some contractors when they do not get a contract, and they fancy their tenders have been disclosed, or may be disclosed. There was, some years ago, that feeling, though it does not exist at present; and therefore I thought it much better to perform that duty myself, and I accordingly appointed the deputy clerk of the peace, who always did duty for me at the adjourned sessions.

1066. I think that I asked you a question on the last day of the meeting of the Committee, as to that very subject, as to extending the time between the sessions and the adjourned sessions; it is at present limited only to 30 days, is it not?—Yes.

1067. Do you not think that if that time was extended to, say 40 days, it would enable you to do your duty, which you are now unable to do?—If the county is divided, 30 days would be sufficient, because then I should do the duty as for two separate counties; but if the county is not divided, I think 40 days would not be sufficient.

1068. If it was more than 40 days between the spring and summer sessions, would you have time to do it?—I fear not, but I would run the chance, because by getting additional clerks, and working harder, I might be able to have the business ready: for instance, about half the book must be abridged after the adjourned sessions have ceased and before the grand jury. That book is never ready until the night before the grand jury are empannelled.

1069. At all events you would recommend that a longer time should elapse between the sessions and the adjourned sessions?—In case the county is not divided.

1070. But in any large county you would recommend it?—Certainly.

1071. As to the filling of those applications, you recommended that it should be done by means of stamps; what officer would you appoint for that purpose?—I suppose the secretary to the grand jury, or whoever does the duty.

1072. Then, if he does not get the income which he now gets by fees, you must give him a larger amount of salary?—Yes, but I would require him to do the duty. I think some person ought to be appointed to do the duty for the public.

1073. If the secretary of the grand jury was allowed a sum of money now to pay for a clerk (which he is not allowed), could not that clerk do the duty for the county, and act as other clerks as the secretary's clerk as well?—Yes, I suppose he could; but I think that would be rather objectionable, because it would make him independent of the secretary, which would not be advisable.

1074. I mean, that you should have a clerk paid for you by the county, and that the clerk should be the party who should do this work of filling up those applications, and receiving the stamps in the way in which you propose it to be done?—I think it would be better to let the secretary do the duty, and let him be responsible for it. The suggested arrangement would make the clerk responsible and not the secretary.

1075. But he would be virtually your clerk, and he is responsible to you for all he does. I would not give you a clerk now unless it was understood that he was to do that duty, and to collect the stamps?—I would let the secretary do it himself, if he chose, and give him a salary, allowing him what would be sufficient for a clerk; the secretary himself could not possibly do it without his clerk; but I would let the secretary be the responsible man; I would not recognise the clerk at all in the Act of Parliament.

1076. *Chairman.*] In point of fact, you would prefer having an actual increase to your salary to having an increase nominally for a clerk?—I fear it would make the clerk independent of the secretary.

1077. *Mr. [illegible].*] The secretaries of grand juries are differently paid in different counties; can you tell me exactly how the salaries of secretaries of grand juries were originally fixed?—They are in the schedule; that schedule was not fixed by the Act 6 & 7 Will. 4; but by 4 Geo. 4, c. 43, before there were any adjourned sessions, and when the sessions were allowed to be held for two or three or more baronies in the same place, and on the same day; for instance, in the county Cork the sessions only occupied 16 days, whereas they now occupy 34 days; there were no adjourned sessions then, but there are now, of course, 34 adjourned sessions, doubling both those numbers makes 68. In the year 1829 my predecessor attended only 15 sessions altogether, every half-year, making 30 in the year, and I have now 68; but the same salary still continues, and that is what the secretaries of grand juries thought was a very great hardship; that while the Act of 1837 was putting

them

these additional duties upon the officers, no remuneration was allowed for the additional travelling, and the additional expense incurred.

1078. Colonel *North*.] But were there not a greater extent of subjects in which new fees would be given?—Yes, but we conceive that those were so very small that they did not at all compensate for the additional trouble and expense.

1079. They amounted in your county to 700 *l.* or 800 *l.* a year, did they not?—Not the legal fees, though the same customary fees existed then. The gentleman who was assisting me in the duties of the office until lately, was in that year, and long before then, receiving the customary fees. My predecessor was appointed in the year 1816, and that gentleman was appointed by him at the same time. His customary fees that now amount to so large a sum (I must say entirely by his good management) existed then.

1080. Mr. *Herbert*.] Do you not think it would be an advisable thing to have the report of the county surveyor printed before the grand jury meets, in order for it to be circulated among the members?—I think it would, and I see no objection to it. I think they would be very willing to do so if they were so asked. It is the very first thing done in our county, and I think it would be advisable.

1081. *Chairman*.] How could the report of the county surveyor be sent to the grand jury beforehand, when it is not known who the grand jury are?—In our county there would be no difficulty, because it is known.

1082. Sir *Charles Lanyon*.] Are you not aware that, under the Act of 6 & 7 Will. 4, the fees were 2 *s.* 6 *d.* for filling the recognizances?—They were; there was an Act passed previous to 6 & 7 Will. 4, which only continued in force a few years.

1083. New duties were imposed upon the secretary, which it was supposed that this fee of 2 *s.* 6 *d.* would be enough to cover?—I was not in office then, so I cannot speak as to that.

1084. The law was afterwards altered, and the duties were still continued to the secretary?—I think under 3 & 4 Will. 4, the fee was 2 *s.* 6 *d.*

1085. When the law was changed, this 2 *s.* 6 *d.* for the recognizance was supposed to pay the secretary for his extra duty, was it not?—But it amounts to very little. It does not always follow that there are the same number of recognizances as applications, because a great many works are not tendered for at all; and, of course, there would be no recognizances. Even though the applications may be approved of, there may be no tenders for them, and then there can be no recognizances. If the 2 *s.* 6 *d.* was given under the present law, I do not think it would be any remuneration for the additional duty by any means.

1086. With regard to applications for any new works, have you ever thought of the desirability of having a presentment for new works once a year, and that no application for repairing a road should be for less than in a year, and that one sessions only for applications should be required; that is, say that a presentment sessions should be held once a year, dividing the sums approved of into equal instalments at each sessions, which would equalize the cess and would save an immense amount of trouble? Then the question arises, how the contractors would be paid.

1087. I am merely speaking now of applications for new works, and works of maintenance, without reference to payment?—I have never considered that point.

1088. One very great advantage resulting from it would be, that you could apportion the cess, either equally at each sessions, for all works, or else you could put a larger sum at one sessions, when the cesspayers were more able to pay for it than at the other?—In our county the levy at each sessions is very nearly the same.

1089. With reference to the lowest tender, you stated, did you not, that any alteration might lead to large contractors, and so forth, making application amongst their brethren to get their tenders approved. Do you not think it would also lead to a very great amount of dissatisfaction generally with reference to the road contractors themselves, and that it would tend very much to reduce competition?—I think it would.

1090. Do you not think that the rejection of the lowest tender would add very materially to the expenses of the county?—It would increase the taxation very much. You would not have the present class of contractors tendering, because they would say, "It is no use my tendering; I have not sufficient influence to get the contract."

1091. Do you not think that all the difficulties which at present arise from the approval of the lowest tender would be got rid of by obligations which would make the defaulting contractors perform their work properly?—If I could I would put a penalty on any man putting in a tender if he withdrew from it.

1092. I think you misunderstood my question; my question is not with reference to a penalty upon a man for putting in a wrong tender, but do you think that people would put in tenders at too low a price if they thought that they would be compelled by law to perform that work properly?—But they can be compelled at present by law to perform the work properly if they enter into recognizances.

1093. They cannot, because the difficulties connected with proceedings against defaulting contractors prevent the county surveyor frequently from putting the law into force against them?—That difficulty does not exist in our county. Mr. Hill said that he never prosecutes at the petty sessions any but contractors, for the repair of roads by presentments. In our county the practice is the very reverse. The county surveyor in Cork never prosecutes any contractor, but for works of maintenance. What we call our annual contracts.

1094. The fact of a judge not giving the case against a defaulting contractor, if no money is lost to the country from his neglect, has operated very seriously against the prosecution of road contractors at quarter sessions, has it not?—We never prosecute at quarter sessions. We have not done so for a great many years, either at quarter sessions, or in the superior courts.

1095. You spoke of the ballot for the cesspayers, do you not think that the ballot for the cesspayers would be prejudicial, inasmuch as all the cesspayers happen to be from the same locality?—Yes.

1096. Do you not think it is very important that all the cesspayers at baronial sessions should represent the different districts throughout the barony, so that from their local knowledge, they may be acquainted with all the works brought before them?—Certainly.

1097. Under those circumstances, would it not be

Mr. W. Johnson.

3 April 1868.

Mr. W. Johnson.

2 April 1852.

be better that the selection of the cesspayers instead of being as it now is, should be from each poor law union, or from each parish in each barony, so as to ensure a representation of the whole barony?—Then there would be that objection of the expense to which I alluded just now.

1098. But how would it make a difference of a single fraction in the expense?—Would you elect them in the same way as the guardians are now elected?

1099. I am not speaking of elections at all. If the cesspayers were selected by the grand jury, instead of being taken from the first 100 cesspayers on the list, they should be bound to make out the list, making the selection from the highest ratepayers in each Poor Law Electoral Divisions, or in each parish in the barony?—From what list would you select them?

1100. From the baronial constable's list?—They could do that now.

1101. Can they do it according to law?—I think, in our county, the grand juror selects them all over the barony as equally as he can.

1102. Then the cesspayers in your county are first of all illegally selected, and on the other hand they are taken at the option of the grand juror. The grand juror, according to what you say, who represents the barony may take any man he pleases from the list that is handed into the grand jury by the barony constable?—Yes, because he is the only man in the room who has any knowledge of them.

1103. Then he acts contrary to the Act of Parliament?—We do it under the opinion of the judge. He said, "If the grand jury are bound to the 24 highest names where is the necessity of returning more than the number required." The 50th man could never be selected according to the argument of the Honourable Member.

1104. What I propose is this, that instead of there being 100 of the highest cesspayers returned, there should be the names of five or six of the highest cesspayers in each Poor Law Union, or in each parish of the barony returned by the high constable?—I think that would be an improvement on the present system.

1105. Would not that insure a fair representation of the whole barony at the sessions?—I think it would.

1106. Colonel *French*.] Would it not lead to an accusation of unfairness of selection on the part of the grand jury, and add greatly to the discontent?—It strikes me that it might put too much power in the hands of the high constable. At present the high constable has no discretion whatever in the matter. I think the Honourable Member's project would give him more power than would be desirable, or perhaps than he would wish himself.

1107. Sir *Charles Lemon*.] I cannot understand what power it would give him if, instead of making out a list of 100 of the highest cesspayers taken from the whole barony, he made out his list of the 100 highest cesspayers in each Poor Law electoral division?—That might be done.

1108. Is there not very frequently a very great disadvantage arising from the attendance of cesspayers from one district, instead of the whole barony being represented at the sessions?—I do not think that ever arises in our county.

1109. You have stated that new cess-collectors are only appointed when vacancies occur; are you not aware that they are appointed at every assizes?—They are re-appointed; there is a new appointment every assizes.

1110. They must be appointed every assizes?—Yes.

1111. And the grand jury have the power, at each assizes, of appointing new cess-collectors, have they not?—Yes.

1112. With reference to the mail-coach road presentments, does it not frequently happen now that the most leading lines of road in the county are repaired at baronial expense, consequent upon railways having prevented the running of mail coaches over post roads?—Not the most leading lines of road; I do not think all the leading lines have been affected by the railways, though some have been so affected, of course.

1113. Are not many of the most leading lines of road in the county repaired now at the expense of the baronies themselves?—Yes.

1114. Consequent upon the substitution of railways for the conveyance of mails?—The mails are not carried by all the railways that pass through the country; for instance the mail to Killarney is not carried by train, or at any rate it was not till lately; there are mails that are not carried by railways.

1115. May it not be likely that a leading line of road which was formerly repaired half by the county and half by the barony, is now repaired altogether at the expense of the barony, consequently upon the withdrawal of the mail?—Yes, certainly, the county surveyor takes care to ascertain that.

1116. And are there not many lines of road which are not leading lines of road, and which are very useful to the barony which are repaired half at the expense of the county, and half at the expense of the barony, consequent upon the mail car running over them?—Yes, I think so.

1117. Then would it not be desirable that there should be some arrangement by which those roads should all come under the same rule as to the mode of their expense of maintenance being charged upon the baronies?—I think so; I would put them all upon the baronies.

1118. Sir *Colman O'Loghlen*.] Can you state what is the amount of the presentments on an average at the Cork Assizes for the last 20 years?—The whole levy is about 80,000 *l.* a year.

1119. Forty thousand pounds each assizes?—Yes.

1120. It is only four days I believe that the grand jury have to consider the presentments of that 40,000 *l.*, they are sworn four days before the assizes commence, are they not?—They can have five days by law, but the majority of these presentments are compulsory upon them: they have no control over them.

1121. In round numbers, how much of the 40,000 *l.* are not compulsory presentments?—I am afraid it would take me some time to answer the question. I have the whole levy here, in which each is set out separately.

1122. Do you not think it would be an advantage in the case of such a large county as Cork, to have it divided for the purpose of enabling the grand jury to have more time to consider the presentments?—Yes.

1123. Would you see any objection at all to having two grand juries for the County of Cork, provided that the assizes for both divisions of the county, were held in the City of Cork?—None whatever.

1124. Do you think it would be satisfactory

to

to the County of Cork to have two grand juries?—I do.

1125. I believe there are so many gentry in the County of Cork, that you could form four or five grand juries, if necessary?—That is the case. There are several baronies in the county of Cork from which a grand jury could be very easily obtained; and it would be the means of putting gentlemen on the grand juries who have never been on, and who ought to be on.

1126. With regard to the trial of cases, and the summoning of juries, would it not be an advantage to divide the county into two divisions?—Clearly. The business of a riding might be done in two or three days, and allow all those engaged in it to return home, and then you might take the business of the other riding.

1127. If the assizes for the two ridings were held in the city of Cork, there would be no necessity for additional gaols and additional court-houses, would there?—Certainly not. I would make it compulsory that the two assizes should be held in Cork, otherwise there would be a great struggle between the different towns in the county.

1128. At present, in consequence of the different railways, Cork would be the most convenient place for the assizes, would it not?—More so than any town in the west riding.

1129. I believe the fees you receive are very few of them legal; most of them being customary fees, as you call them?—The larger proportion of them are not legal fees.

1130. Would you have any objection to see all those customary fees made legal fees?—Certainly not.

1131. Would you see any objection to the fees now paid to the secretary of the grand jury being paid to the grand jury; and that the secretary should be made accountable to the treasurer for those fees in aid of the rates of the county?—Certainly not; and I think that is the opinion generally of the grand jury.

1132. You are entitled, I believe, to no superannuation?—No.

1133. In your opinion, would it conduce to public advantage if the county officers were entitled to superannuation?—I think it would be only just.

1134. Is there a feeling amongst the county officers in favour of superannuation?—There is.

1135. Colonel French.] With regard to the amount of cess collected in the county of Cork, what is the average cess of the county; how much in the pound?—It varies in the different baronies. That is more in the province of the treasurer, but I have it here.

1136. It is about 1 s. 6 d. in the pound, is it not?—I think it is.

1137. Out of that rate of 1 s. 6 d. in the pound, all the expenses of the compulsory presentments, lunatic asylums, and 50,000 miles of road, or whatever the number of your share of them is in Cork, are paid?—It is all paid out of the rate of 1 s. 6 d. in the pound; and within late years we have had the turnpike roads handed over to us.

1138. You have had this thrown upon you; and the charge made upon the county for money due for bonds, and things belonging to the old trusts?—Yes; and the repair of the piers. There are a good many piers built by the Board of Works which have been lately handed over to the county, and they are now repaired by each barony.

1139. That will account for some additional expenses in the sum total of the money levied for roads in Ireland?—Yes.

1140. With regard to the fees; are you aware that very great dissatisfaction is felt throughout the country, both on the part of the contractors, and on the part of the general public, as to the fees levied upon them for presentments?—I think they are paid very readily, and very willingly.

1141. You charge 1 s., as you are entitled to do by law, for a single paper that does not stand you in a fraction of a halfpenny; and, after that, there is a payment for filling it up?—There is great responsibility in filling it up, if you mean the recognizances.

1142. But what responsibility is there, I should like to know, because the Act of Parliament is so clear that I cannot see any?—If there was anything wrong, or any miscalculation in the recognizances, it would be a serious thing.

1143. The Act of Parliament is clear as to what you are bound to put in, and what excuse is there for charging more than you are absolutely out of pocket for the papers giving to the people who are competing to fulfil a public duty at the lowest terms they possibly can?—The Act of Parliament gives it.

1144. The Act of Parliament gives it, but that Act of Parliament which gave it was supposed to give it as a compensation for the additional duty put upon the secretaries of the grand juries?—It amounts to a very small sum in the year. In our county it only amounts to 48 l. a year.

1145. Under what law, is anything charged except the 1 s.?—Sixpence for the blank form of tender.

1146. But 6 d. is far beyond the value of the blank form; a farthing would pay for the blank form. You state that you are required to attend the adjourned sessions; what object is there in your attending; is your presence in any way necessary?—It is not. I have nothing whatever to do; it is a mere matter of form. I merely attend in custody of the tenders.

1147. The chairman opens the tenders, and they are obliged by law to accept the lowest tender, proper security being given?—Yes.

1148. Some tenders are reserved for the grand jury, are they not?—If there is no tender at the sessions, the grand jury can take one.

1149. Do you consider that objectionable, as the grand jury have no power to inquire into the solvency of the securities tendered at the sessions?—Certainly; I think the local tribunal is the proper judge.

1150. The division of the county of Cork, as you propose, appears to me to be a strange one, because you think it necessary that the assizes should be held at the city of Cork, which would be out of one of the divisions of the county; does it not strike you that it would be necessary if you divided the county of Cork to have a second staff?—I think not; there is not a second staff in Tipperary; Tipperary has been divided into two ridings for assize purposes, and the same officers do the duty in both ridings.

1151. Chairman.] Is not the city of Cork a county in itself?—It is a borough.

1152. For fiscal purposes it is a county in itself, is it not?—Under a special Act of Parliament the court-house is a part of the county for all purposes, both civil and criminal.

Mr. W. Adams.

3 April 1868.

Mr. W. Johnson.

3 April 1868.

1153. But there is a grand jury for the city of Cork, is there not?—There is.

1154. At present then the assizes for the county of Cork are held in a county which is outside the county of Cork itself?—Yes, under a special Act of Parliament.

1155. Colonel *French*.] Then you would then have the business of three assizes transacted in the court-house of Cork?—Yes, there are two separate assizes transacted at present in Cork; but the assizes for the city and the county are not held at present at the same time, and that is a great convenience, which has only lately been adopted.

1156. You stated, did you not, that you thought it would be an improvement that the cesspayers should be the same parties as the Poor Law Guardians?—I see no objection to it, although I do not know that a better plan may not be devised.

1157. Your reason, it appears to me, was that there would be no expense of election, those men having been already elected?—I think so.

1158. But you are aware that in many cases in Ireland the union consists of divisions that are not in the same county?—That is the case.

1159. So that it would be necessary to make some selection, and so to confine them to the county to which they themselves belong?—There would not be much difficulty with regard to that in our county, for there is only a very small portion of our county in a union belonging to the county of Limerick.

1160. You will recollect that the Poor Law Guardians are elected by certain votes given in accordance with the amount of property held, and that they are elected by men who give their votes by voting papers; would you bring all that alteration into the grand jury system?—I would not. The only reason why I take advantage of the election of guardians is that it would be so inexpensive, and that, from my own personal knowledge, I generally see the same persons acting as cesspayers at presentment sessions, whom I know to be guardians in the union.

1161. But are there reasons which would make you not so strongly in favour of that change?—Yes.

1162. The honourable Member for Kerry asked you a question as to the report of the surveyor of the county with regard to the state of the roads being delivered before the grand jury was summoned; what is your view on that point?—There is no difficulty in their doing so in our county, because the grand jury are not summoned; they are invited, and invited perhaps some days before the assizes; and the county surveyor can just as easily send a copy of his report to those gentlemen, as he can hand it in the first day of the assizes.

1163. Are you aware that, in several of the counties in Ireland, it is the habit to publish in the county book the report of the grand jury?—It is always printed in what we call the schedule of grants.

1164. Sir *Charles Lanyon*.] Is not that after the assizes?—Yes.

1165. Colonel *French*.] In many counties the works agreed to are passed at each presentment sessions before they are put up to tender, and are printed and distributed, in order that both the contractors and the county generally may know what the work proposed to be done at the sessions is; is that the arrangement in your county?—We never do it in our county; it would be utterly impossible, because the two sessions follow so quickly after each other.

1166. Then how do we do it in the county of Roscommon?—Because there is an interval, I take it for granted, between the last county at large sessions and the first county adjourned sessions.

1167. General *Dunne*.] With regard to the weights and measures, did you not say that you had a committee to look after them?—Yes.

1168. Have not the constables at each station, or within reach of a station, a set of weights and measures?—Every police station is supplied with them.

1169. How are they compared with the standard weights?—They are compared by the sub-inspector of constabulary, who is provided with copies of the standard weights and measures from London.

1170. You said that there was a rule of the grand jury as to bridges; that they would not grant them unless the barony agreed to subscribe a quarter of the expense; do you think they can do that legally as a rule?—As well as I can remember, the words of the Act are these; "either on the barony or on the county at large," and we interpret that rather freely, and conceive that we have the power of putting it on both.

1171. Is it not a very free interpretation?—Perhaps it is, but it works well.

1172. Colonel *Forde*.] As to the county surveyor sending in his report to the grand jury before they meet, by that plan you would insist upon the sheriff sending his panel to the county surveyor for approval?—No, it is very objectionable, I think to have the names of the grand jury made public, until they are actually sworn; and what I propose to do, if it is thought desirable, is that they should have the report prepared, that the county surveyor should send the report to the sheriff, and that the high sheriff should forward the report himself to each member of the grand jury.

1173. Mr. *Gregory*.] Would you have him forward a copy to each member of the panel?—To every gentleman whom he had invited. We have no panel in our county. The panel merely consists of the 23 gentlemen who have accepted the invitation of the high sheriff, there being 23 grand jurors and 23 baronies.

1174. General *Dunne*.] Would not that merely be applicable to the county of Cork, and totally inapplicable to every other county?—I suppose it would.

1175. Mr. *Leader*.] Do you think they get sufficient information at present?—I think they have full information at present.

1176. Mr. *Maguire*.] With regard to the question of the lowest tenders, I think you said that you do not have recourse to the law in reference to a fraudulent contractor, and I believe you gave as your reason, that the process would be too expensive?—It was not with regard to fraudulent contractors that I made that answer; it was only with regard to defaulting contractors.

1177. You say that you are in favour of the lowest tender?—Certainly.

1178. If the law were inexpensive, would you appeal to it oftener than you do now?—There is no law with regard to the lowest tender. The laws as to prosecutions are only with regard to a contractor who has taken a contract and who neglects it.

1179. As

1179. As to works, you say that you receive the lowest tender by law, and that that is a right system?—Yes.

1180. Would you say that that system is equally good as applied to large works, heavy works, and to small works?—I think so.

1181. Do you never find that when you receive the lowest tender the work is not done, and that the person who contracts with you throws himself on the mercy of the grand jury?—Yes; such a case may arise.

1182. But do not such things happen very frequently?—Yes.

1183. And is not that in consequence of receiving the lowest tender?—I think it is in consequence of not receiving sufficient security. The magistrates and cesspayers are sometimes a little careless in the amount which they take.

1184. Is it within your experience that the most reckless person generally puts in the lowest tender, and does not much care to perform the work for which he contracts?—I do not think that that is very often so.

1185. Your experience is quite different then?—It may occur, and sometimes does occur, but not often.

1186. Have you any knowledge of the state of things in the city of Cork; and do you not know that appeals are very frequently made to the corporation to free men from the contracts into which they have entered on the lowest tender system?—Very frequently applications are made to the grand jury to release men from contracts, and they are invariably refused; except in a case where a contractor may have taken a road, and the traffic since he got the contract may have been greatly increased by many causes. In that case they think it is hard to keep the contractor to his bond, and they release him.

1187. Supposing that a bridge is carried away and it has to be rebuilt, do you consider that it is a wise plan to receive the lowest tender in that case?—I think it is if they get ample security. It may save the barony a very large amount.

1188. Are you very careful about the securities?—In some baronies they are most careful; but in others they are not so careful as I would wish them to be.

1189. Have you sought to recover from the securities when the contractor has failed to carry out his contract?—Not since the Act of the 19 & 20 Vict. was passed. We think it much better to summon the contractor at the petty sessions: it is a more summary and more inexpensive procedure.

1190. Suppose the case of a large work, and the man has not the means to do it—what would you do with the security?—I would sue the security in that case.

1191. Have you sued the securities in any cases lately?—We have not had a prosecution lately.

1192. Mr. *Blake*.] Is not your chief objection against the election of associated cesspayers, by the cesspayers, founded upon the question of expense?—I think that the less elections we have the better, and the expense guides me.

1193. Might not that objection be obviated by having those associated cesspayers elected at the same time as the guardians; the police at present go about with voting papers; could not they put out a set of voting papers for the associated ratepayers as well?—Yes; I suppose they could.

1194. There was an objection urged by an honourable Member against making the guardians the associated ratepayers, on the ground that the same men are usually elected every year, might not that be obviated in the case of the associated ratepayers by having one-third or one-half of them go out annually so that you would get a fresh set every year?—That might be done. Mr. *W. Johnson*. 3 April 1868.

1195. Colonel *Cooper*.] Have you expressed any opinion upon the county at large sessions as to whether they might be abolished?—Certainly not, there is a great deal of important business to be done at the county at large sessions.

1196. But it is chiefly routine work, is it not?—A great deal of money is passed at county at large sessions which is discretionary.

1197. You think that the county at large sessions ought to be continued?—Certainly.

1198. You stated, did you not, that the county surveyor does not print the notices and post them in your county?—It is not necessary for the county surveyor under the 18th section to give any notice.

1199. And he does not do so?—He does not.

1200. In your county you say that presentment sessions have never failed; you have always had an attendance?—There never was an instance but once where a magistrate did not attend at the sessions and that was at an adjourned sessions in a very remote district.

1201. As a rule do the magistrates or the cesspayers attend more regularly?—In some baronies there are very few magistrates, and of course in that case there is a much larger attendance of cesspayers.

1202. But do you think that it might be well, if the sessions failed, to have a second day for holding them, and to have some machinery therefor?—If the first presentment sessions failed for want of attendance of magistrates and ratepayers, I would certainly adjourn them; but I do not see any absolute necessity for adjourning the adjourned sessions, because under the 20th and 21st Vict. the grand jury can take the contracts.

1203. But then they have not the means of inquiring into the securities?—No, that is better done in the locality.

1204. Do you not think that it would be also better to adjourn the adjourned sessions if they fail?—All the parties who attend the first sessions may not come to the second sessions.

1205. Do you hear any complaints in the county of Cork as to the way in which the grand jury laws work?—I think that that is a matter of opinion. Some think that the grand jury laws work uncommonly well in the county of Cork, and others think not.

1206. Is there any strong feeling against the present law?—I do not think that there is.

1207. Do you think that houses which are for a certain time unoccupied should be exempted from the county cess?—In our county, if the high constable is unable to levy either from waste or unoccupied houses, under a rule of the grand jury, he attends at presentment sessions with a list. They examine very carefully into that list, and they strike out any they think he is not entitled to and allow the remainder. He then brings that before the finance committee of the grand jury, and whatever they approve of is handed to the grand jury; and the high constable or his deputy must swear that he is unable to collect the cess, stating his reasons.

1208. And then what cannot be collected is represented?

Mr. W. [illegible]. [illegible] April [illegible]

presented?—Yes; but the high constable is obliged, whatever the amount may be, to pay it out of his own pocket, and to get a fresh presentment for the amount from the grand jury, which he is not repaid until the following session.

1209. But, as a rule, do the grand jury exempt un-occupied houses?—Yes.

1210. Does the Cork grand jury appoint a committee to examine the charitable institution's accounts?—Yes, they appoint four committees, I think. They appoint a finance committee, which consists of five members, to whom every matter of finance of every kind is referred; they appoint a committee to visit the lunatic asylum, and they appoint another committee to visit the gaol, and another to visit the county infirmary.

1211. That gives them a certain check upon the accounts, does it not?—I think so.

1212. And if they saw any extravagance, they would comment upon it or disallow it, would they not?—I am not sure that it is a check upon the accounts, for I do not think that they examine the accounts. They go through the establishment, and see that everything is properly conducted, and in order.

1213. Do you think that they examine the accounts?—I am almost sure that they do not, for in their reports to the grand jury which those gentlemen make, they never refer to the accounts.

1214. Mr. *Dawson*.] And they have to give in their report before the grand jury is dissolved?—Yes, they have.

1215. Colonel *Cooper*.] But they examine the coroner's accounts, do they not?—No; the finance committee do that.

1216. But do the finance committee examine the charitable institution's accounts?—No.

1217. You have never seen an instance in which the books of the lunatic asylum have been brought before the grand jury?—Yes; the books of the asylum and the books of the county infirmary are all sent in the first day of the session, and laid on the table for the grand jury to inspect.

1218. But does not the finance committee look into those books?—They do not; the grand jury do that themselves, that is not referred to the finance committee, not being a money question.

1219. But it is so far a money question, that if they thought there was extravagance, they could object to any items, could they not?—There is a separate book given to each grand juror, and they can examine them if they choose.

1220. When a contractor's security is taken in the grand jury room, any cesspayer present can challenge that security, can he not?—Certainly.

1221. That gives some protection, I suppose?—Yes, it does; but I think it is much better to do it at the sessions if possible, and it is never acted on, as I said before, but in cases of great necessity.

1222. You said that possibly the county cess might be collected by the poor-rate collectors, but you gave no opinion upon it; do you think that that would be a good change?—I should be inclined to leave it in the hands of the present men.

1223. To have the high constables and rate collectors separate?—I much prefer having the present barony constables; it is a mere matter of pounds, shillings, and pence.

1224. Did you state that the county cess amounted to 1 s. 6 d. in the year, or on each levy?—In the year.

1225. Your county cess in Cork is only 1 s. 6 d. in the year, is it?—Yes, it varies in different baronies.

1226. But is that about the average?—It is.

1227. Mr. *Dawson*.] Are you aware that, in the county of Dublin, there is a separate system of a finance committee composed of members of the grand jury, sitting from one assize to the other?—Yes.

1228. Do you think that an advantageous arrangement?—I do not see any necessity for it. The reason they did so in Dublin, I think, was because the treasurer's office was abolished, and the secretary of the grand jury now under the direction of the finance committee pay the contractors.

1229. Then you do not think that it would be necessary to extend that system to the other counties of Ireland, and that there is no want of it?—I think not. I understand that there is no great advantage gained by it.

1230. And they have peculiar functions, have they not; they take cognizance of sudden breaches, and they have extraordinary power, I believe, to find additional funds beyond what the magistrates can find under their own order?—Yes.

1231. Are not those powers of the magistrate sometimes deficient?—I think not, since the Act of last session. There was an Act of Parliament passed last session extending the power of magistrates to 50 *l.*, and if it exceeds 50 *l.* then a sessions can be called, and I think that that is quite sufficient. The magistrates are very careful, I think, in giving those orders.

1232. With regard to the baronial collectors, their securities have to attend at the assizes in person, have they not?—Yes.

1233. Do you not think that that is almost unnecessary, and causes a great deal of inconvenience, and that their securities might file affidavits, and the securities might be received by the grand jury without their personal attendance?—The personal attendance must be very little inconvenient; if a gentleman who has been approved of by the grand jury, or by the finance committee cannot attend, there is no difficulty in substituting another. The high constables in our county have no difficulty whatever in getting security; they are all gentlemen of high position, and they have no difficulty in getting security.

1234. You were kind enough to give an opinion about the best way in which a fresh nomination of associated cesspayers should take place; is there any objection or dissatisfaction among the associated cesspayers themselves as to the present system of their appointment?—I have heard it; but I think the complaint is groundless.

1235. Have you ever found that it interfered with their attendance?—Certainly not.

1236. Mr. *Chichester Fortescue*.] Do you not think that if the associated cesspayers were elected for the purpose of looking after the county rates, in the same way as the Poor Law Guardians are elected to look after the poor rates, there would be far more probability of their attending and doing their business than under the present system?—I think not.

1237. Why not?—Because I do not think the attendance of the Poor Law Guardians at the workhouse is a bit better, not perhaps as good as the attendance of the associated cesspayers at the presentment sessions under the present mode of election.

1238. Is

Mr. W. Johnson.

2 April 1868.

1238. Is that your experience in your county?—I think so.

1239. But do you not think upon general grounds, that it is probable that persons who are elected by a large body of ratepayers to do a certain duty, will be more apt to perform their duty, than where they are selected by a totally different body in the haphazard way which now prevails?—It may be so; but the attendance of cesspayers at presentment sessions in my county is very good; just as good as the attendance of the Guardians at the workhouse.

1240. It is the case, is it not, that the presentment sessions go on no matter if there is only a single magistrate present?—Yes.

1241. And there need be no representative of the cesspayers?—It is not necessary.

1242. Do you think that a satisfactory system?—It never occurs in my county.

1243. Do you think that a satisfactory state of the law under which there need be no representative of the ratepayers present, and under which the quorum of the meeting consists of a single person?—It would be better to have it so than to have the whole business fall to the ground, the contractors could not be paid, they would lose half their yearly monies; the grand jury could not pay them, even though the judge ordered it unless their applications for payment had been approved at the sessions.

1244. But you are aware that upon almost all other occasions which one knows of, a quorum is required to constitute a meeting; why should not a quorum be required in the case of a presentment sessions?—I do not see any objection to it, but it may cause inconvenience.

1245. (Chairman.] You stated that you would prefer having the present barony cess collectors rather than having the poor rate collectors, might I ask you why you would prefer them?—I think that it is very immaterial which is the officer; it is a mere matter of pounds, shillings and pence.

1246. But the barony cess collectors charge sixpence, whereas the poor rate collectors would do it for sixpence?—Probably the barony cess collector would do it for less too; it is a mere matter of account.

1247. Mr. *Leader*.] At one time it was reduced to sixpence, was it not?—It was; for a great many years it was sixpence.

1248. *Chairman*.] But supposing the barony cess collectors are to continue to get ninepence, would you not consider it in that case desirable to transfer it to the poor rate collectors if they undertook to do it for sixpence?—Certainly, if it was a saving to the country.

1249. Mr. *Dawson*.] Do you not think that there would be an advantage in getting it together, and having it collected at the same time?—Yes.

1250. Chairman.] Do you not think that the poor rate collectors could afford to collect it at a cheaper rate than any other persons; they being already going about collecting the poor rate, could they not collect the county cess with very little additional inconvenience, and therefore collect it at a cheaper rate than anybody else?—I suppose they could, they having a staff already provided.

1251. If you saw any advantage in the way of cheap collection, you would see no objection to transferring it from the present collector to the poor rate collectors?—I see no objection.

1252. You stated that you were very strongly against the abolition of the county at large sessions?—I am, because there is a great deal of important business to be done there.

1253. Are you aware of any considerable number of presentments being rejected at those county at large sessions?—Frequently.

1254. Of what class?—Building bridewells, rebuilding or repairing court-houses; the county surveyors' salaries and those of their assistants all come before them, and they never reduce them, though they have the power of doing so. They have also the gaol presentment, the petty sessions rents (they very often reduced these; they cannot exceed 10 *l*.), the constabulary; the printing, which is a very large item; bills of costs for suing contractors, or anything of that kind. Bills of costs for suing defaulting contractors and bills of costs for opposing traverses.

1255. Are those presentments which are generally examined into and curtailed or rejected at the county at large sessions?—Yes, there is no other tribunal to whom you could refer them.

1256. Except the grand jury?—But then you take it away from the control of the ratepayer.

1257. Do you find that the county at large sessions are well attended by magistrates and ratepayers?—Very well by magistrates; there can only be one cesspayer from each barony.

1258. Does he generally attend?—They do pretty well, except from some of the remote districts.

1259. Colonel *Forde*.] With regard to the county cess being collected by the poor rate collectors; the poor rates are collected only once a year?—Yes.

1260. The county is collected twice a year, is it not?—In my union the poor rate is collected twice a year. There are two rates struck in the Cork Union in the year, but it is not the same in all unions. There are 17 unions in the county, and I think that of the 17 the Cork union is the only one in which the poor rate is collected twice a year.

1261. Then in every other of those unions the difficulty would be, the collection of the county cess being for one year, how to get at the sum which would be required to be collected?—I think there would be that difficulty.

1262. And there would be a large sum collected and placed to the credit of the county, virtually going to loss and unproductive?—Yes; unless they were compelled in some way to lodge the money as they collected it, as they are at present.

1263. You say that your treasurer gets the benefit of it?—Yes; our treasurer takes very good care that they must lodge it when they have collected 100 *l*.

1264. Then he would have a greater interest now, because he would have a year in hand instead of half a year?—Of course he would.

1265. And then the ratepayers would have to lose that money?—Yes.

1266. And that, you conceive, would be the greatest difficulty in allowing the county cess to be collected with the poor rate?—Yes.

1267. Chairman.] Do you see any absolute necessity why, if the collection of the county cess was transferred to the poor rate collector, it should be collected only once a year?—I do not see why he should not collect it twice a year.

1268. Colonel *Cooper*.]. Then he would not collect

Mr. W. Johnson.

3 April 1868.

collect it at the same rate if he had to go twice round, would he?—He would not.

1269. That is a good reason why the allowance should be larger to the barony constable than to the rate collector?—Yes; he would not be collecting the two rates at the same time.

1270. *Chairman.*] You do not think that a poor rate collector would undertake to collect the county cess twice a year for a less sum than the barony cess collector?—I cannot say; probably he might not, as he would not be collecting the two at the same time.

1271. Colonel *Cooper.*] If there was a power to adjourn the sessions to a future day, would it not be as well to establish a quorum?—If there was power to adjourn the sessions in my county, I think it would be a very inconvenient thing, and almost an impossibility.

1272. But taking Ireland generally, would it be desirable or otherwise?—I am afraid that if you required a quorum it would cause inconvenience.

1273. Mr. *Fortescue.*] Can you state what is the usual number of associated cesspayers who attend at presentment sessions in your county?—That all depends upon the size of the barony; in some of the large baronies 24 attend, for instance, as the barony of Dubhallow, which is one of the largest, 24 men attend regularly, and they are very much disappointed if they do not come out in the ballot; and in some of the smaller baronies they attend equally well.

1274. In what proportion are the ratepayers, generally, to the magistrates?—In some baronies there is only one magistrate; it is very seldom, however, that the majority are magistrates.

DANIEL CRONIN COLTSMANN, Esq., called in; and Examined.

D. C. Coltsmann, Esq.

1275. *Chairman.*] You are a magistrate and grand juror of the county of Kerry, are you not?—Yes.

1276. Have you paid any attention to the working of the grand jury law?—A good deal.

1277. How are the cesspayers selected in Kerry?—The associated cesspayers are selected in Kerry in the same way as Mr. Johnson, the last witness, told the committee; that is to say, that the barony collector sends in the hundred highest names, and then the grand juror who represents the barony, consulting the other grand jurors on the grand jury who may happen to be connected with the barony by either residence or property, selects the number out of the hundred to act at the sessions.

1278. Does he select them in any way he thinks proper?—The universal rule is to select them, as far as possible, from different parts of the barony.

1279. You do not take the highest names on the list?—No.

1280. Do the cesspayers, as a general rule, attend well in Kerry?—Very fairly.

1281. Do the magistrates attend the best?—There is an excellent attendance of magistrates in that portion of the county with which I am acquainted.

1282. Do you believe the present system of selection by the grand jury to be a good one?—I think that, theoretically speaking, it is bad; and I think that the feeling of the country is against giving any one, or two, or three, individuals the power of selecting parties at all.

1283. Would you think a system of election better?—I have great doubts whether, looking to the practical results, it would be an advantage so far as my county is concerned.

1284. Would you propose any alteration in the present system of selection?—If there were to be an alteration, assuming that the baronial area remains as it is, and that the machinery of the grand jury law remains unaltered, I think the best course to obviate that objection of their being nominated by any individual, would be to have those names, as they are sent in, balloted for.

1285. You would propose a ballot out of the 100 names?—Out of the 100 names.

1286. Would you approve of the system of having a ballot at the sessions?—A ballot at the sessions would probably be more convenient, but I am afraid that if 100 men had to attend the sessions on the chance of 12 of them being selected out of the 100, they would be so very often out of it, that, practically speaking, they would cease to come.

1287. Do you approve of the present system of having men balloted for at the presentment sessions; do you think that that leads to a non-attendance of the cesspayers?—I think it does not, for this reason, that the number for whom the ballot is intended are few. Not less than five, or more than 12, can sit at the road sessions; and those five, or those 12, as the case may be, are selected from a comparatively small number of persons, as contradistinguished from the proposition to select them from the 100.

1288. Do you think that the present uncertainty of sitting on the bench leads many cesspayers not to attend at sessions?—I do not.

1289. Do you find that there is a larger attendance of cess-payers at the sessions than the number which can sit?—Frequently.

1290. At present all the magistrates of the county can take part at presentment sessions whether they have property in the barony or not?—Yes.

1291. Do you think that that is a proper state of the law?—I consider it most objectionable.

1292. Do you think that no magistrate should be permitted to attend except those having an interest in the barony?—No magistrate except one residing in the barony or connected with it by property.

1293. If a magistrate comes late to sessions he may take his seat?—Yes he does, he makes his declaration.

1294. But if a cesspayer comes in late he cannot take his seat?—I will not say that he cannot, but in practice he does not.

1295. Do you think that that ought to be altered?—I do.

1296. Have you formed any opinion as to the proposed division of the payment of the county cess between landlord and tenant?—Yes; I should not have the slightest objection that the county cess should be divided between the landlord and the tenant always saving existing contracts or leases; I think that it would be most unjust to put the county cess upon the landlord when the tenant had covenanted by lease to pay it.

1297. But in all future railings you believe that it would be a better system?—In all future railings

village or in cases of townships where there are no leases.

1298. Do you think that dissatisfaction exists in the county at present from all the taxation being borne by the tenant?—I do.

1299. Do you believe that an alteration in the direct incidence of the tax would lead to more attention, on the part of the landowners, to presentments?—It naturally ought to have that effect where their pockets are touched; but in my county the attention of the landowners and of the magistrates to the fiscal matters of the county is very good indeed.

1300. As to the collection of the rate in Kerry, what do you pay in the pound?—We pay ninepence.

1301. And what is paid for the poor rate collection?—In the Killarney union, of which I am chairman, we pay sixpence.

1302. Do you think that the collection of the poor rate and the county cess might be united?—I do.

1303. Do you think that such a union would lead to the county cess being collected at a lower rate?—I think that the fact of the two rates being united would enable a party for lower remuneration to collect both, and even then he would be better paid; and I also think that the fewer the parties going to the tenantry for rates the better.

1304. You think that it would be a convenience to the ratepayers to pay both rates to one party at the same time?—Yes; and I think that the one party would probably get it easier.

1305. You are aware, I suppose, that the barony cess collectors are obliged to lodge their receipts in the bank when they amount to the sum of 100 *l.*?—I am.

1306. Is there any way of enforcing those lodgments?—It is very difficult, for this reason; first, the treasurer in our county has no personal interest in looking after it, because he does not receive any interest on balances to the credit of the county. In the next place, I cannot see what authority exists to call upon the barony collector between one assizes and another, and to ask whether he has 100 *l.* in hand, or not. I think that that is one of the results of the absence of a good finance committee, which should always exist between one assizes and another.

1307. You are in favour of having a standing committee of the grand jury between one assizes and another?—I am strongly of opinion that it would be greatly to the advantage of all the counties; and in my county I would recommend it, from my knowledge, to be constituted of the Board of Superintendence. If there were always existing a finance committee between one assizes and another, on them would devolve the duty of having the barony collectors appear regularly before them at their monthly meetings, with their block books to be examined, which examination would show to the baronial sessions, if they appoint the finance committee, the state of their collection and how far they had got into funds.

1308. Do you not fear that, if such a standing committee were appointed, a great deal of the responsibility of the grand jury would be transferred to them?—I think that, as regards financial matters, the investigation into the accounts, the state of the fever hospital accounts, the infirmary accounts, and the collector's accounts, as a matter of course, would to a certain extent be handed over to that committee, because they would be looked upon as being responsible for those accounts; but the grand jury can never do that in the short period during which they meet together. I have observed that when the grand jury are sitting, if they appoint committees of their body to retire into the other room to go into these sort of accounts, they are most unwilling to do so, because it takes them away from the general business of the grand jury, and very often matters are done in the grand jury room in their absence which they would have been very anxious to attend to; and therefore in my county we have great difficulty in getting a sub-committee to act in those financial matters.

D. G. [illegible], Esq.

2 April 18[illegible].

1309. You would not apprehend that when these sub-committees are appointed, if any difficult question arose before the grand jury, it would be referred to this committee, and that the decision of this committee would be practically the decision of the grand jury?—I do not apprehend that.

1310. Have you never found amongst grand jurors the feeling of trying to shove off the difficult questions to a committee appointed at the time being, or to any other body that might get them out of the trouble of examining the question?—I think that occasionally it has been so, but it is so with all public bodies.

1311. You are not afraid then that these finance committees would practically become for all time to come the grand jury on all controverted questions?—No; I think they are principally to check the accounts, to see the vouchers, and to watch how the public money goes, and to see that the monies are lodged. In fact, I would look upon them as a strictly financial body.

1312. You would not apprehend any other functions being forced upon them?—No.

1313. You are aware that presentments are granted in Ireland by grand juries as compensation for a certain class of losses which are called malicious injuries?—Yes.

1314. Do you believe that these presentments are sound in principle?—I do not; I may state that the county of Kerry grand jury some years since unanimously petitioned Parliament to do away with the Malicious Injuries Compensation clause in the Grand Jury Acts altogether; the grand jury think it vicious in principle, and applicable to a period which is passed; apparently the motive was by putting a tax upon a district to make it their interest to discover the perpetrators of this class of crime; we think that the very opposite result has been attained, that when a party has a house burnt, whether it be maliciously or accidentally, invariably the attempt is made to recover the loss from the county; it is a class of cases which we consider most difficult to deal with, and most unsatisfactory, it being almost impossible to prove malice, and generally what is proved is a negative, that is to say, they endeavour to prove that it could not have occurred by accident; the result of these applications is, that when the party's house is burnt, and he receives compensation, he takes very little further trouble to try and find out who the perpetrator of that burning was.

1315. You do not think that it leads to the discovery of the criminal?—I think that it leads to the reverse, and in my part of the country among the lower orders, there is an idea that if they were to disclose the name of the party, even if

D. C. Coltsman, Esq.

5 April [illegible].

if they knew this it would militate against the recovery of compensation.

1316. Do you think that it prevents the commission of those outrages to any extent?—Not in the slightest degree, in my opinion.

1317. Does it lead, in your opinion, to men coming forward and representing as malicious what has been accidental?—Undoubtedly.

1318. And that leads to much perjury?—It does, in my opinion. If the Committee will allow me, I will mention a singular case in connexion with one malicious injury which came before us; there was a very valuable store and premises in the county town of Tralee, which was destroyed by fire. The case came on for investigation before a large bench of magistrates and ratepayers at the county sessions, and was there investigated and refused; it was subsequently brought before the grand jury, and after investigation there, was also refused. The amount was 700 l., and on investigation before the grand jury, the party looking for the damage was obliged to admit, when examined upon oath, that the insurance company with which his premises were insured, had put a clause into the insurance, that if the injury was malicious they were not to pay; and he was obliged further to admit, that he would not have brought the application before us in the first instance, except that he was obliged, before he would receive the money from the insurance company, to have the verdict of the road sessions as to whether it was malicious or not. The road sessions negatived its being malicious, and after survey, the insurance company paid him 400 l., his damage having been 700 l. Having been paid the 400 l. he, under the Act, came before the grand jury for the difference, and on the investigation before the grand jury he admitted, that if they passed the presentment for the 300 l. the difference between the 400 l. and the 700 l., it was to go into the pockets of the insurance company. I mention that as an illustration of the great abuses which may be committed under the Act of Parliament.

1319. At present, in your experience, many abuses exist, and you do not see any principle for these compensations being made by the public?—I do not.

1320. Supposing this compensation were good in principle, do you think that the grand jury and the sessions are the right tribunals to try it?—The grand jury and the sessions both give very great attention to those cases and examine them very closely; but when the amount is small and the party in a humble position in life, it is generally easy to get the presentments; where the amount is large and the ratepayers are alarmed at the extent of it, they generally fee counsel and fight the matter out.

1321. The sessions and the grand jury are supposed to represent the parties who are to pay the damage, are they not?—They are interposed, I take it, between the applicant and the parties who are to pay the damage; that is, the ratepayers.

1322. But they are under the present law supposed to represent the ratepayers, are they not?—No, I think they are more in the light of judges, to act impartially by all parties with regard to malicious injuries and the compensation sought therefor.

1323. But as a tribunal the sessions and the grand jury represent the ratepayers?—Certainly.

1324. Do you believe that it is in accordance with the principles of English law to make people judges in their own case, as they are in this matter?—I should say certainly not.

1325. And you have stated that, in your experience, when the sum asked for is large, the case is very minutely sifted, and it is not very easy to get a presentment?—I think that that is the result.

1326. But when the sum is small it is given as a sort of charity?—As a sort of charity; I think that there is generally a feeling of consideration which induces many perhaps, if they are not quite satisfied that the injury is malicious, to stretch a point and give compensation.

1327. Are you aware whether anything like compensation for this sort of offence exists in England?—It does not.

1328. Do you see any reason why there should be any peculiarity in Ireland upon this point?—I do not; I think that the proper course is to provide by insurance for the results of accidents.

1329. There are some cases, are there not, for which compensation is given in England in cases of riots?—Yes, but that is quite a different thing, that is under a different Act altogether.

1330. That is the only description of compensation for malicious damage which you would wish to see preserved in Ireland?—That is all; I am very much opposed to the present law.

1331. And in that case it would be tried before a judge and a regularly empannelled jury?—Yes.

1332. Are you aware that the grand jury, in investigating claims for malicious injury, are allowed to hear only one side of the case, and that they cannot take evidence against the claim?—That was so ruled formerly, but it has since been ruled otherwise, and they now, in the counties of Kerry and Cork, invariably go into the case both pro and con. There have been conflicting decisions upon that point.

1333. The Act appears, therefore, to be not very distinct upon that point?—No; I am aware that the judges have decided differently upon it, and I am aware that the practice is now to hear both sides.

1334. Is the county of Kerry conveniently divided into baronies?—The baronies are large. Our county is the fifth in Ireland in point of extent, and we have but eight baronies, so that they must be necessarily very large.

1335. Do you think that they are well laid out?—I think they are as well laid out as they can be, geographically looking at the peculiarity of the formation of the county.

1336. Did you hear Mr. Johnson's evidence with respect to the substitution of the area of the union for the barony?—I did.

1337. Would you approve of that?—It is a question which involves considerable difficulty; I think that as regards the materials, an area selected from the Poor Law Union, or its component electoral divisions, would give you a very intelligent class to act with the magistrates; but, on the other hand, it would give you an area much larger than the existing baronies.

1338. Do you think it would be too large?—I think that it would be too large, unless some modification were effected by law, so as to group the electoral divisions. Take, for example, the Kenmare union, it contains 33 electoral divisions. By law, under the grand jury Act, only 12 cesspayers can sit with magistrates at the road sessions, for the barony. Now, out of those 33

electoral

electoral divisions, containing the Poor Law area to be taken, would you select 12 cesspayers.

1339. Of course, if the union be selected in place of the barony, it is not necessary that the number of ratepayers should be limited as now? —There you must consider what proportion the number of cesspayers bears to the county magistrates.

1340. How many county surveyors have you in Kerry?—One.

1341. How many assistants has he?—Four.

1342. Do you approve of the system of the county surveyor having assistants?—No; I would strongly ask that the grand jury should have the power, if they think proper, to have their county divided into one or two districts, each to have a county surveyor. We have not that power. The Lord Lieutenant has the power, but the grand jury has not; and I would ask for that power to be given to the grand jury. As regards my own county, I consider that if we had two county surveyors at 300*l.* a year instead of one county surveyor at 600*l.* a year, the result would be, that the work would be much more efficiently done, and would enable us to do away with the deputy assistants, in whom the public do not place confidence.

1343. Would not the Lord Lieutenant appoint a second county surveyor if the grand jury applied to him to do so?—I am not quite certain. There would be a good deal of circumlocution, and a good many letters to be written, and a good many interviews before the thing could be effected.

1344. Has the grand jury of the county of Kerry ever applied to the Lord Lieutenant for a division of the county between two surveyors? —No; the Kerry grand jury would certainly not do it during the term of office of the present holder; they would not think it just that a man who had been 20 years or so in possession of the one office, should at the end of his service be compelled to select either one-half of the county or the other, and we should make no move during his lifetime. I am sure that would be the feeling of the county.

1345. But you are in favour, as I understand you, of doing away with the system of assistants? —I do not think that there is that confidence in the assistants which there ought to be; I do not think that they are that class of persons in whom the public have confidence, and I think that two professional men as county surveyors would do the work just as well, and bring much more experience and ability to the work than one surveyor with a number of deputies.

1346. Deputies receive but 60*l.* a year, in your county?—They receive 50*l.* a year; and it must be clear, I think, that you cannot get men of any eminence or standing for that figure. Lately they receive 75*l.* a year in Kerry.

1347. Do you approve of granting presentments generally to the county surveyor directly? —No, with this qualification I never would present to him any new work; I would present to him in substance the tenders for existing works where, in the event of repairs being required and no tender being forthcoming, the county would be considerable sufferers, and the works deteriorate very much in value.

1348. But you would confine presentments to the county surveyor to those necessary works?— I would; I would never allow the county surveyor any power to originate a new work himself. One result of that would be to deprive the ratepayers of the necessity for 15 days' notice, which they always receive for new works when they are initiated in the regular way, by an application on behalf of two cesspayers. Every occupier whose land is to be affected, gets 15 days' notice of the intention to do such work, whereas in the case of the county surveyor the Act dispenses with any such notice.

1349. When an application is presented to the county surveyor for a certain sum, if the work afterwards exceeds that sum, there is no remedy for the county but to pay whatever he asks to finish it?—There is no other remedy.

1350. But, in case a contractor takes a work at a fixed sum, he and his securities are bound to fulfil it?—He and his securities are bound to fulfil it, notwithstanding what the loss may be to them.

1351. Are you aware of many works having been presented to the county surveyor?—The Act of the 21 & 22 Vict., which was the Act that recently enabled the grand jury to give works in charge to the county surveyor, in the absence of tenders, either at the road sessions or before the grand jury, had been adopted so extensively in my county, that at the assizes the matter was discussed at considerable length by the grand jury, and we consider that it had reached a point which called upon us to interfere; and we thereupon determined, in future, not to avail ourselves of that Act, except in cases of the greatest possible emergency.

1352. Do you not think that works which are presented to the county surveyor are generally more costly than those which are contracted for? —I think that they are more expensively done. Another great thing is this, that I think it entirely destroys the position which the county surveyor occupies as being the officer who interposes between the county and the contractor; it being his duty to watch the construction of the works; to see that proper materials are used, and that the works are executed properly; and if you remove him from his position in that way, and make him as it were a contractor himself, it strikes at the root of all competition. In our county it was fast coming to this, that we could get no contractors at all, as the grand jury were handing over everything to the county surveyor, and giving him a great amount of patronage, in employing every class of mechanics, such as masons, carpenters, &c. I suppose that one-fourth of the work of the county was beginning to be done, under the supervision of the county surveyor, in that way.

1353. Do you not think, therefore, that the Act of Parliament should be so altered as to leave it out of the power of the grand jury to present to the county surveyor, except in cases where great necessity exists for the work being immediately done?—I am of that opinion. I may mention that our late honoured member, Colonel Herbert, said that he was instrumental in getting the Act of the 20th and 21st of Victoria passed.

1354. Are you a governor of the lunatic asylum of Kerry?—I am.

1355. The governors of the lunatic asylum are not appointed by the grand jury, or in any way under their control, are they?—No.

1356. The inmates of the lunatic asylum are chiefly paupers, are they not?—Nearly all of them are so.

D. C. Coltsmann, Esq.

2 April 1868.

1357. And

D. C. Coltsmann, Esq.

3 April 1868.

1357. And the whole expense of this lunatic asylum is borne by the county cess?—It is.

1358. Do you not think that it would be more appropriate that the expense of those lunatic paupers should be borne by the poor rates?—I do; if the rate is not immediately collected under the operation of the Poor Law, the principle of having half paid by the tenant, and half by the landlord, ought to be applied to lunatic asylums.

1359. At present, though the whole is paid by the county rates, neither the presentment sessions nor the grand jury have any control whatever over those asylums?—No; they have not. A detailed report of the governors of the asylum is always laid before the grand jury of the state of the institution, and the working of it, during the half-year; but, I take it, that is merely for their information.

1360. The presentment comes to them as a compulsory presentment, does it not?—The presentment is mandatory, because, in the first instance, the funds are advanced by the Government, and then a mandatory presentment comes down to the grand jury to recoup the Government.

1361. Are you a member of the Board of Superintendence?—I am.

1362. Do you know anything about an officer called a local inspector?—I do.

1363. Do you believe that to be an office which is of any practical utility?—I really think that the chaplains of the gaol would carry out all the duties which a local inspector is supposed to do. The Board of Superintendence meet regularly once a month in our county, and look very carefully after matters.

1364. There is an expense annually charged in Ireland for the revision of the valuation on the counties, is there not?—There is.

1365. Is not that a very large charge?—It is a very large charge, and it very much complained of.

1366. Do you not think that that revision of the valuation, if left to the counties, could be done at a much lower rate than is charged by the valuation office?—I do.

1367. Can you state what was the amount charged in Kerry last year?—I think, taking one year with another, it comes up to 500 *l.* or 600 *l.* a year. There is no addition to the value of the lands; it is merely a re-adjustment of the valuation. Supposing three farms are made into two, the officer comes down, and he apportions the existing valuation which was upon the three over the two; or, if there are new houses built, he brings them into the valuation; but as regards the value of the land itself, he cannot touch it at all; so that we consider it a very expensive charge, and we consider it a charge which ought to be paid by the Government, because they use that valuation to an immense extent.

1368. Are you aware that half of it is paid by the Government?—Yes; but I think the whole ought to be, as they use it very extensively for Imperial purposes.

1369. The fact is that if the county authorities were allowed to appoint their own officers, to make this revision, you think that it could be done at a much lower rate?—I am certain it could, and we could get competent persons to do it; what they have to do is very trifling.

1370. How long does it take in a year; one or two days?—It takes more than that in a large county; they come down generally once a year about this time.

1371. How long do they remain down?—I should think that in our county they must remain certainly from three weeks to a month; all changes of occupancy come under their supervision, together with the names of the parties.

1372. Most of the changes are mere clerical changes of names?—Yes, in fact as to certain classes of property, such as the produce of mines, fisheries, or new houses, which have been built recently; the valuation of these is liable to annual revision and alteration, that no land remains the same; they do not touch the valuation itself at all; they merely re-adjust it.

1373. *Colonel French.*] With regard to lunatic asylums, I do not understand you to say that you would recommend that the lunatic asylums should be managed by the Poor Law Commissioners, as the law is now?—Not by the Poor Law Commissioners, but that the expense of the lunatic asylums should be borne in the same way as under the Medical Charities Act.

1374. And then you would recommend that the grand jury should appoint the governors instead of the Government's doing so?—I think that the board of governors are the first men in the county, and are both connected with it by property and by residence, and that there is no complaint to make of the appointments which are made by the Lord Lieutenant.

1375. But do you not think that as the county are obliged to pay the expense of the lunatics, it would be only right that the county should have the appointment of those who manage the institution?—That would be carrying out the representative system.

1376. With regard to unions being taken as the area instead of baronies, you cited Kanturk union; how many baronies does the Kanturk union comprise?—I think it comprises portions of two baronies, and that it does not comprise the entire baronies. The main portion of Kanturk union consists of the barony of Duhallow, and I think it also contains a portion of Orrery and Kilmore; but I think it does not contain all the barony of Duhallow.

1377. How would you manage the representation at the road sessions from that union, so that the barony should be properly represented?—If you go to the poor law area, I think you must come down to the electoral divisions which are contained within the barony, forming a portion of the union of Kanturk, for instance. You must take only those electoral divisions in that union which belong to the barony as it now exists, and then you must in some way at the road sessions select representatives from those electoral divisions of the Kanturk union which belong to the barony. Of course, you could not allow electoral divisions belonging to other baronies to come in.

1378. Still you would have the taxation to a certain extent upon the barony?—You would.

1379. What would be the use of going to the Poor Law to divide it in that way, and coming back to the barony again?—If you assume new areas altogether, and make them areas the Poor Law unions, you make them much larger than the existing baronial areas.

1380. And not so convenient?—When they are so large they are not so convenient, no doubt. For instance, there are 23 baronies in the county of Cork; the barony of Duhallow, for instance, is larger than the entire county of Carlow or Leitrim. If you abandon the baronies and fall back upon the Poor Law unions, you have only 17 Poor Law unions, and consequently the area covered by the 17 Poor Law unions must be much more extensive than that covered by the 23 baronies.

1381. What objection would there be against dividing that barony of Duhallow, for instance, into four districts?—The honourable Member is doubtless aware that the Act requires that in dividing baronies they must consist, at the least, of 45,000 acres, or, if you unite two baronies, curiously enough, they cannot consist of more than 40,000 acres; and if you took 45,000 acres as your guide, and divided the barony of Duhallow, you would probably have to divide the barony into four divisions.

1382. There is no law against that, is there?—No, but it would multiply the number of districts most inconveniently for fiscal purposes.

1383. Would it not rather be the contrary; and would you not then have a better representation for the smaller districts?—Of course, by dividing one existing barony into four, you would have a representation of the smaller districts.

1384. In the county of Down there are four baronies, one of which has four divisions in it, so that the objection could be obviated of which you speak?—Certainly, if you divide it; but you have already 23 baronies in the county of Cork, and you can have only 23 grand jurors.

1385. Then, as suggested by the honourable Chairman, the county of Cork might be divided into two ridings. As to the guardians being selected, do you not see this difficulty; that a guardian being so very often re-elected for each electoral division, it would virtually come to this, that the same men would always be on the list?—Undoubtedly. Practically speaking, they are nearly always the same, particularly in rural unions.

1386. Do you not see great objection to that?—It would vest taxation for practical purposes always in the same men.

1387. And these men are not divided round the barony in the way which you think pleasant?—I think I heard you say that in your barony you dotted the cesspayers round, so that you should have a representation?—I think that if you selected from the electoral divisions it would really represent the barony. A barony consists, in Ireland, of so many parishes; and, when we are selecting the associated cesspayers, we endeavour to select, as far as we can, a member from each parish; and therefore to represent, as far as we can, the entire barony.

1388. Would you get that, supposing the Poor Law guardian was to be the representative?—I think that you would get that equally in electoral divisions, because they are spread all over the barony.

1389. As to malicious injuries; if any man has a spite against his neighbour, or owes him a grudge in any way, what is to prevent him from going and putting a match to his neighbour's property, and thereby doing a great deal of damage, for which he would have no power of getting any compensation; you do not think that having that Malicious Injury Act is a check upon anything of that sort?—Not in the least; if a man is malicious or wicked enough to destroy his neighbour's property, he would not be deterred by the consideration that that neighbour might, after a considerable time, recoup himself at the expense of the county.

D. C. Coltsmann, Esq.

8 April 1868.

1390. Are not these cases generally very closely looked after and investigated, both at sessions and by grand juries?—Most undoubtedly they are, in any part of the country.

1391. And if, as the law at present is, the sessions refuse, and the grand jury also refuse, it is in the power of the promoters of that presentment to go before a judge, and to essay a jury?—It is.

1392. Do you not generally find, or is it not often found, that that jury reverses the decision, both of the sessions and of the grand jury?—It frequently occurs, and that is, I think, one of the evil results of the clause, that a party goes before a petty jury and employs counsel, and has the case put, of course, as strongly and as favourably as he can, and the cesspayers or the grand jury of the county are seldom or never represented.

1393. Has he generally appears before the sessions of the grand jury by counsel as well, does he not?—He does.

1394. And his case is clearly put before them?—It is clearly put before them.

1395. And they investigate it, as you say, equally clearly?—Yes.

1396. And they come to the determination that that burning was not malicious, and then by law it goes before a judge and 12 other persons, who cannot possibly go into the case as strictly as was done by the other two courts, and who reversed their decision?—Yes; that is, the applicant may take it before the judge and a jury of 12.

1397. That is a part of the law which you think objectionable?—I do; and I think that it is appealing to an inferior tribunal from a better one.

1398. Would you approve of the finance committee, of which you have spoken, having the power of distributing money or anything of that sort?—Yes, I would give them the power to sign cheques upon the treasurer for county works, as the works went on under certain sections of the Act. There is a certain section of the Act which enables a grand jury, where the amount of the work exceeds a certain figure, 30 l., to put a direction on the presentment that, as the work proceeds upon the certificate of the county surveyor, money may be advanced to the contractor not exceeding in the whole three quarters of the cost of the entire work. That is a very useful section, and one result of it is that it enables men who may not have sufficient capital to undertake large and expensive works, such as large bridges, and to come in and compete, because they know that if they do the work satisfactorily they will get from time to time advances from the county. I would allow those advances to be made by that financial board, if it was in existence; but the primary object of this board in my mind would be to examine minutely all the accounts connected with the gaols, bridewells, infirmaries, county fever hospitals, and things of that sort, which never get proper or full investigation before either the road sessions or the grand juries.

1399. You say yourself that there is power to advance the money on the certificate of the county surveyor; why do you want a financial committee to assist him in that, because a finance committee could only pay the money on the certificate of the county surveyor, as it is now?—The certificate of the county surveyor is of course re-

D. G. Coltsmann, Esq.

8 April 1858.

quired in order to enable the contractor to get the money, but I would not allow the certificate of the county surveyors to be made the instrument for getting money; I would have a regular responsible body in existence, the same as under the Poor Law, which would be a check upon the treasurer, and enable the contractor to draw his money.

1400. Then would you insist upon the finance committee going and inspecting each work before they paid the money?—I would not; I think that the state of the work is ascertained by the certificate of the responsible officer, the county surveyor.

1401. You say that the finance committee could not work without the certificate of the county surveyor; they cannot work now without it; the contractor cannot get his money without that certificate, can he?—He can; I have seen the sessions grant the money.

1402. Therefore the county surveyor would be responsible all the same?—In ordinary contracts the contractor cannot get his money without the certificate of the county surveyor; even if the county surveyor refuses his certificate at the sessions and the sessions choose to pass the presentment, notwithstanding the refusal of the certificate, the money is paid to the contractor; that is the decision of the judges.

1403. Is that often acted upon?—I know that it has been the decision of the judges very recently.

1404. That may be, but is it often acted upon?—I should say, myself, that it would be better for the interests of the county if that certificate were made a *sine quâ non* in the first instance; but I know, myself, that latterly they have overruled the county surveyor's decisions very frequently, though not always granting the full amount asked for. In order to meet the county surveyor half way when a man is refused his certificate and has applied for 50 *l.* they have only given him 25 *l.*, and fined him the difference.

1405. As to the collection of the cess, do the baronial constables commence immediately after each assizes to collect the cess?—No. As a general rule they do not get their warrants probably for a month or six weeks; and, for practical purposes, I think that they seldom put their collections in force until a considerable period has elapsed as between one assizes and the other.

1406. Virtually, until just before the assizes, when they have to lodge the money?—I think that is the practice with the collectors. It is a tax so well understood by the people, and so cheerfully paid, that they do not go to them until the last moment.

1407. In case of any alteration in the law as to advances to contractors the cess must be collected at once, must it not?—No.

1408. Then where would you get the funds?—We are always in funds in our county, because we present an advance for all works. Some years ago we found that, if contractors were paid quickly, as a natural result they would undertake works at a cheaper rate, and we presented a sum of money in advance which put us in funds, and we have always large balances to the credit of the county of Kerry in the treasurer's hands which enable us to pay those parties.

1409. How did you manage to get those presentments put on the levy?—We put it on the levy ourselves.

1410. What did the judge say?—He sanctioned it.

1411. *Chairman.*] Did you present it for any specific work?—We presented a sum of money to enable us to do what I state to you, as the several works came before us.

1412. For no specific work, but for general purposes?—For general purposes as well as specific works.

1413. Mr. *Dawson.*] Is that a usual thing in the county of Kerry?—We are always in funds in that way; when you do it once it is not necessary to repeat it; it is just like a man always having a balance at the credit side with his banker.

1414. *Chairman.*] But is not the treasurer obliged by Act of Parliament to invest in exchequer bills any balance in hand to the credit of the county?—I rather think not; I think that that only applies to an old Act; I do not think that our monies are invested at all.

1415. I see by the return that they are not invested?—They are not; of course, I am only speaking from recollection; but I think that you will find that the Act which required the money to be invested in exchequer bonds has been repealed.

1416. Colonel *Forde.*] Your county is losing the interest of all that money at this time?—No, I think that we receive the interest from the bank on current account.

1417. With regard to the fees paid to the secretary to the grand jury for filling up applications, &c., do you know anything about them?—I know that they are collected.

1418. Do you think that that is an advisable system?—No, I think that the system of fees is bad altogether; I would always pay a man a salary, and not allow fees to form any part of his remuneration.

1419. Would you do away with those fees altogether, or would you still continue them, and credit them to the county by means of stamps, as Mr. Johnson suggested?—When I made my answer it was with reference to the mode of paying the officer; I would always prefer paying an officer a salary, but I do not see any objection to the public paying some small fees for certain services rendered to them, and which would go to the county exchequer.

1420. And you think that that would be a better plan than is adopted at present?—I do.

1421. You have of course great information from attending road sessions; what is your opinion as to whether the lowest tender should be taken or not?—There are advantages *pro and con*, but on the whole I would rather that the present system was adhered to. Sometimes I think that the terms of the section afford considerable advantage to the road sessions in dealing with a small class of contractors, because the words used are that they must take the lowest tender, unless it be for an unfair or fraudulent purpose. For instance, a person may put in a double tender, that is to say he may put in a tender at a figure something like what the work really ought to cost, and then he may put in a much lower one, in order that if he finds no opponents he may withdraw the lower one and take the contract at the higher figure, but if he finds opponents he may withdraw the higher one and take the lower. Where we find that there is in any case of double tender, or that the party has been in any way connected with a double tender

tender on examination on oath, we reject that tender altogether, and we find that that is very much checking that system.

1422. And the grand jury has given orders to their secretary to bring those cases before the grand jury?—At baronial sessions we swear the parties; we reject them there.

1423. But is such notice brought before the grand jury to account for your not taking the lowest tender?—No, the baronial sessions are not accountable to the grand jury at all; we do that of our own authority.

1424. Would you give to the sessions the power to reject any contractor, no matter whether he was the lowest tenderer or not, if he had been a defaulter on a former contract; that is to say, a man who had to be prosecuted by the county surveyor for the non-performance of his work?—I think that I would give a discretion to the road sessions to do it or not as they thought proper; it might be a severe penalty to exclude him for ever.

1425. We have not that power now?—You have not that power.

1426. I think I understand you to say that you would not allow the county surveyor to originate all presentments?—No new works.

1427. But you would allow any cesspayer to approve any work he chose?—Yes; that is to originate, not approve.

1428. You would not give that power to the county surveyor?—No.

1429. Mr. *Herbert.*] I believe the grand jury at the present moment has a right to settle where the county surveyor may live?—Yes; that is to say, if he refused they could suspend him.

1430. Do you not think it would be advisable to put it out of the power of the grand jury to compel by law that the county surveyor should live in the most central part of the district?—When there is only one county surveyor for a county, as a matter of course, he ought to be resident in the county town, because he is allowed by law, in addition to his salary, 50 *l.* a year for his office, and his clerk, and he is supposed to be in his office if any one wishes to consult him.

1431. Do you not think that it would be advisable that there should be the same system if there were two county surveyors?—Certainly; they should reside in the most convenient portion of the district and in the principal town of the district.

1432. Do you think it advisable that the county surveyor should be allowed to have private business?—Until recently we were not able to give professional men of their position, education, and eminence, adequate salaries; but now we can give them very remunerative salaries; I think it stands to common sense that if a man is allowed to take private business he must neglect public business; the temptation is so great.

1433. In point of fact, in a county like your own, you think the county surveyor has quite enough to do without any private business?—I do.

1434. Mr. *Dawson.*] What is his salary?—£. 600; that is the maximum.

1435. Mr. *Herbert.*] Has it not been generally remarked that owing to the grand jury giving a great many works to the county surveyor, those works have not been properly executed, and have cost more than they should have cost?—I should not like to say that they had not been properly executed; but I have no hesitation in saying that my belief is (and others whose opinion I value have arrived at the same conclusion) that the works have been more expensive.

1436. Owing to the necessity of the appointment of men as stewards?—Owing to the appointment of stewards; in our county the system went to such an extent that the surveyor had a regular staff on pay during the year; it gives a great amount of patronage to the county surveyor, and in my mind draws him away from what are the essential and proper duties of a county surveyor.

1437. With regard to the appointment of the collectors of the county cess, should not the appointment be confined to the officers of the barony where the collector is to be appointed?—Certainly; I think it is not right that where you appoint for a barony, and only for that barony, magistrates from a distant barony should come and put in a man totally opposed to the man that the cesspayers of the barony wished to put in. At present the appointment between assize and assize rests with the magistrates of the county, and I think the appointment ought to rest with the magistrates connected by residence and property with the barony.

1438. You said that no magistrate ought to vote at the road sessions except a magistrate having property in that barony; for what reason?—I think for a very distinct and clear reason; that the taxation which they are about to vote upon is supposed to be either granted or refused by those who have to bear it; and I think that the magistrates of the barony residing in it, or having property in it, with the associated cesspayers, are the proper parties to control that taxation, and not men from a distance who may come and vote for those works towards which they will not have to contribute one single shilling, and perhaps out-vote men who have to pay the tax.

1439. Have you ever known that to be the case?—I think the good feeling of the gentry is in advance of the law; latterly, no magistrate has ever come into a district with which he is not connected either by residence or property. It has occurred, but it is very rare.

1440. With regard to the board of superintendence, do you not think it would be very advisable that half should be compelled by law to resign their appointments, and that fresh appointments should be made every year?—I do; I do not think the board of superintendence ought to be the same body at different assizes; they consist of 13, and it is a very invidious thing, of course, for the grand jury to strike off any particular one of the 13; even if a gentleman is not a good attendant, because he is liable to be huffed a little if his name is left out. I know one of the late judges, Judge Perrin, on one occasion remonstrated with the Kerry grand jury, and he said "Gentlemen, you ought occasionally to infuse some new blood into your board." The answer was, that "no one gentleman liked to undertake what would give offence," and practically the same board always continued. I think it would be a very desirable change in the law to have half the body at each assizes retire, to be replaced by new men, leaving half who are acquainted with the business remaining, to carry on the business as before.

1441. Mr. *Dawson.*] By your suggestion, the whole body would be changed in the course of the

D. C. Coltsmann, Esq.

8 April 1868.

the year?—Precisely so. I would put six out at one session, and six out the next session. I would make the county gentlemen take their fair share of the work.

1442. Colonel *French*.] Would you not practically find a very great deal of difficulty in getting men from the far end of so large a county as yours to attend each month at the baronial sessions?—No doubt there would be great difficulty in getting men from remote portions of the county to do it; but a great portion of the county is now connected with the county town by railway; and as regards the gentry who live very numerously about Killarney, for instance, there would be no difficulty whatever. In fact at this moment, the board of superintendence of our gaol consists entirely of gentlemen connected with the county town; and the town of Killarney for the very reason you speak of. From the more remote portions of the county they could not come once a month to attend a board, but you would get the six men I speak of, with comparative comfort to themselves.

1443. And you would reduce the number of those in the immediate vicinity of your gaol, to a number who could practically work the whole business of your gaol?—You would have practically in the immediate neighbourhood of the gaol enough for a meeting.

1444. Is it not better to have six men for a certainty than 12 men for an uncertainty?—I think you might always substitute six men in our county who would attend.

1445. Mr. *Herbert*.] Do you think that charitable institutions ought to be liable to county cess, or not?—My own feeling would be to include every property; but if the decision be otherwise, I would take a liberal view of all charitable institutions. I would not take a narrow view of what are charitable institutions, but I think the sounder and better principle is to include all descriptions of property.

1446. Mr. *Dawson*.] Is it your opinion that advantage would arise from a financial committee composed of the grand jury sitting from one assizes to the other?—I think it is a great advantage to have a permanent financial body, such as the board of superintendence would constitute.

1447. The objection which has been urged in the House of Commons to that which was part of the plan of a Bill which I introduced last year, was, that it would be the most difficult thing in the world to procure the attendance of those gentlemen in the interval, and that it would be left in the hands of one or two persons, and that therefore it would be a jobbing irresponsible body; do you think that objection is tenable?—No, for this reason, that you have a finance committee ready made to your hand in the board, who are a very efficient body, and who do not necessarily consist exclusively of the grand jury, as you are aware. There may be other men of intelligence outside the grand jury on the board, and that is the case, and I think the board would make an admirable finance committee.

1448. Would you give that committee or board discretionary power over the county officers to see that they were acting according to their duties?—I would not; I do not think it is necessary for them to go into those cases at all.

1449. Do you know that there is such a board working in the county of Dublin, sitting by special Act of Parliament?—I am aware that there is a special Act regulating the county of Dublin, but I am not aware of the existence of that board.

1450. Is there any objection in the county of Kerry to the manner in which the associated cesspayers are at present nominated or chosen?—I think the objection is a theoretical and not a practical one, as I mentioned before.

1451. Mr. *Blake*.] On principle, I understand you are in favour of the associated ratepayers being elected by the cesspayers?—I think, as I said before, that, theoretically, there is an objection to their being nominated by an individual grand juror or by two or three grand jurors. The difficulty is to have them nominated by the cesspayers without entailing twice a year a meeting of all the cesspayers of a large barony, and, in fact, a regular re-election, which would involve a great deal of trouble and annoyance to the parties.

1452. Did you ever read Sir William Somerville's Bill for the reform of the grand jury laws?—I have read his Bill.

1453. Do you remember his plan of having voting papers the same as for the guardians?—Yes.

1454. Might not the trouble and expense be saved for one half year at least in that way?—No doubt it would.

1455. But your only objection is on the question of expense?—I think myself that it is just and right and fair that those who pay the tax should nominate their own representatives. The only thing is how to do it, and whether you would obtain a better class of men.

1456. As the grand jury have extensive powers of taxation, would you not, upon the same principle, have the county fiscal board elected by the ratepayers?—No.

1457. Why not?—Because in my opinion you would not get so good a board in any county if you gave the selection of that board to the county ratepayers. Would you have the election in the county town?

1458. I propose that at the same time that they vote for a member of the baronial board, of a certain qualification, they should also vote for a member of the county board, with a certain qualification; say, for instance, he is assessed for the value of 50 *l.* in the county, either by occupation or property; supposing that to be his qualification, and that you also enact that a person voting for him shall have a certain qualification also, is not the person so elected likely to be as good a person to perform the county business as the person nominated at the discretion of the high sheriff?—I should say that your mode, theoretically, would be the constitutional one; but in practice it would not produce as efficient a body as that now nominated by the grand jury.

1459. I am not speaking of the body constituted by the grand jury, but of the body that is constituted by the sheriff, namely, the grand jury itself?—I do not think that any system that you could substitute would get a more efficient body than, or as good a body, in the shape of a fiscal board, as the grand jury in the county of Kerry. In practical working out, I think the high sheriffs of Kerry select the best men. I only give my own opinion as regards the county I know.

1460. Do you know how the suggestion is now made to the Lord Lieutenant as to the appointment of governors of lunatic asylums; how does he know the persons that ought to be appointed?
—I think

D. C. Coltsmann, Esq.

3 April 1868.

—I think when the lunatic asylums were originally built (there is a new asylum), it was very much the medical gentlemen, the inspectors, who took the trouble to ascertain who the gentry were in the county that ought to be put upon that board; and I think that subsequent appointments which have been made in our county have been made at the suggestion of the board themselves, asking the Lord Lieutenant to add so-and-so and so-and-so to their body.

1461. Does it not very often occur that the suggestion of the appointment of governors of lunatic asylums comes from the Inspector General's office?—Not with us, I think.

1462. Would it not be infinitely better that the grand jury should appoint, than the Lord Lieutenant, who is unacquainted with the district?—It might be better for the grand jury to appoint, but the Kerry Asylum is located at Killarney, and practically speaking, though we have about 40 governors selected from every part of the county, not a single man has ever attended the institution from the day of its opening till now, except those resident within three or four miles of the asylum, and those gentlemen perform the duty entirely.

1463. Supposing the local inspectors of prisons were discontinued, would it not be desirable to have a more frequent Government inspection of the prisons?—I think it would do no harm; I think the inspection of prisons by Government officers a very good thing.

1464. Would it not be likely to be more efficient than if it were performed by county gentlemen who have no previous knowledge of the subject?—I think so; if the Committee will allow me, I will just mention one thing, which is this, that I think it would be advisable to give power to counties on fair terms, to borrow from time to time monies from the Consolidated Fund.

1465. Chairman.] For what purpose?—Take a case like our county; we had this year one flood which destroyed 8,000 *l.* worth of bridges, and that was, of course, an immense addition to come quite suddenly upon the county funds irrespective of the ordinary expenditure.

1466. Is there not the power of making advances to counties for building bridges?—I am not aware of that; there is one other matter with regard to the rating of unoccupied houses and their liability to the county cess; there have been conflicting decisions given, some exempting them, and others not, and I think in any Grand Jury Act that was passed, it would be advisable to assimilate the law to that which now regulates the rating of unoccupied houses to the poor rates. If a house becomes occupied subsequent to the issue of the warrant, the party should pay for the house proportionately for the time he occupies the house; that is the present poor law system if a house is vacant when they strike the rate.

1467. You heard Mr. Johnston's evidence with regard to the charge for mail coach roads, did you not?—I did.

1468. What is your view upon that point?—I would do away with all distinction upon that point?—I would make them all baronial, and I would put all bridges upon the county altogether.

Tuesday, 28th *April* 1868.

MEMBERS PRESENT:

Mr. Blake.	Mr. Herbert.
Colonel Cooper.	Mr. Kendall.
Mr. Dawson.	Sir Charles Lanyon.
Colonel Forde.	Mr. Maguire.
Mr. Chichester Fortescue.	Earl of Mayo.
Colonel French.	Sir Colman O'Loghlen.
Mr. Gregory.	

MR. CHICHESTER FORTESCUE, IN THE CHAIR.

ALEXANDER TATE, Esq., C.E., called in; and Examined.

A. Tate, Esq., C.E. — 28 April 1868.

1469. *Chairman*.] YOU are the County Surveyor of the County Antrim?—I am.

1470. *Sir Charles Lanyon*.] How long have you been surveyor for the county of Antrim?—Since the beginning of 1862.

1471. What office did you hold previous to that?—The office of one of the district surveyors in the county of Dublin.

1472. For how many years?—For 17 years previous to that.

1473. In what respect do you think the grand jury laws require amendment with reference to your department, or the department of the execution of Public Works?—The principal points in which I think it requires amendment are in reference to the power of enforcing the fulfilment of contracts and proceeding against defaulting contractors. The next point that I would mention as, in my opinion, of considerable importance, is the means of providing prompt payment. These are the two principal points, but there are a number of minor points.

1474. Colonel *French*.] The law in Dublin is not the same as in the rest of Ireland, I believe?—It is not.

1475. Sir *Charles Lanyon*.] Do you refer to prompt payment on account, or prompt payment after the execution of the work?—Prompt payment in certain cases, when the work is partly fulfilled; in other cases, when the terms of the contract entitle the contractor to payment at the expiration of the half years, for maintenance contracts.

1476. I think in the year 1866 you drew up certain sections for a new Grand Jury Bill, which you submitted to me. You have since seen that document as having been handed in by Mr. Hill?—Yes, I understand that the document was placed in Mr. Hill's hands, and handed in by him during his examination.

1477. The sections set forth in that document would, in your mind, principally avoid the difficulties that you at present find in carrying out the public works of the county?—In so far as it regards the proceedings against contractors. As well as I remember, it did not deal much with the question of providing prompt payment. It simply provided that the payments should be made by the Treasurer out of the funds in his hands applicable to the general purposes of the county. That appears to me to be the most desirable way in which the prompt payment can be made. I believe that in all the counties in Ireland there is a sum of money to the credit of the county, which would be sufficient to meet all claims of this kind which would be likely to come against the county. In the county of Antrim, in which I am at present placed, it certainly is so.

1478. Colonel *French*.] Is not the money always presented in advance?—I am not sure that I understand the question.

1479. I mean this; there is a contract, and before the man begins to work there is a presentment made for his payment, which money he receives, if he has accounted for it, at the next assizes?—I believe so. If he has executed the works, supposing the works to be presented at the spring assizes in the year, and it might be a maintenance contract; if he has executed that work satisfactorily, he would be paid at once at the summer assizes.

1480. Sir *Charles Lanyon*.] The proceeding against defaulting contractors is at present under the 34th section of the 6 & 7 Will. 4, c. 116?—That is so so far as it regards maintenance contracts. That section merely refers to the contracts for keeping roads in repair, and it provides that after the service of a ten days' notice by the surveyor, if at the expiration of that time he still has reason to be dissatisfied with the state of the road, he may employ other persons to repair it.

1481. Will you state what have been found the difficulties in getting works properly executed under that section?—The want of prompt means of payment. If the law were amended so that the surveyor would be empowered to give a certificate in respect of a contract of that nature, and the treasurer bound to pay it out of the general funds of the county, in my opinion it would provide a fitting means of meeting the difficulty.

1482. What Act is it that specifies the mode of procedure under the recognizance against defaulting contractors?—It is the 6 & 7 Will. 4, c. 116, s. 166.

1483. Are

A. Tate, Esq., C.E.

19 April 1868.

1483. Are there not great difficulties in proceeding against contractors under that section? —There are difficulties. The mode of procedure varies according to the amount which is at stake. If the amount be under 100*l.* the proceedings would be at quarter sessions; if over 100*l.* they must necessarily be in a superior court, and it is a very troublesome, a very difficult, and a very expensive process. I understand that there are also difficulties as to the employment of the money, if it be recovered; that the law is not explicit in stating how it is to be applied.

1484. Is there not a great difficulty in carrying out the provisions of the Act, that where works exceed 100*l.* in value, the proceeding must be taken in the higher court of Dublin?—I think so.

1485. Would it not be desirable that all proceedings should be taken at the quarter sessions for any sum, and not in the higher courts in Dublin?—I think it would; and I myself do not see any disadvantage that would result from that course being adopted, there being a power of appeal to the judge at the assizes.

1486. Are there not also great inconveniences with reference to the mode of summoning defaulting contractors or sureties?—There are.

1487. Will you state what those difficulties are?—The 19 & 20 Vict. c. 63, s. 18, is a section which provides for the case of contracts for repair of roads and by the decisions which have been come to with reference to that section, its powers are restricted to the cases of presentments for repair of roads; which are of inconsiderable extent and importance as compared with many other works. On the first complaint of the county surveyor, the magistrates at petty sessions are empowered to order execution within a limited time. On the second complaint, if there has been a failure to execute, they are empowered to make an order to authorise the levy of the estimated costs, not exceeding the amount of the recognizance. The inconveniences of that section are, first of all, its being restricted to the case of presentments for the repair of roads. In Foot's Grand Jury Laws, page 390, there is a note which refers to that, and Sir Colman O'Loghlen has given a judgment on the subject, which is referred to in page 528 of Foot. The other deficiencies of that section are the insufficiency of the provisions for the levy, and further, the case of no proceeds from the levy order has not been provided for at all.

1488. *Chairman.*] That is the distress levy?—Precisely.

1489. *Sir Charles Lanyon.*] Is there not also a further difficulty, supposing the work is ordered to be carried out by the surveyor, in getting that order executed?—Unquestionably.

1490. On what grounds?—The county surveyor may be suddenly required to take up a work in a distant part of the county, without having any suitable machinery for the purpose of carrying it out; he has to provide that machinery at an inconvenience; he may attempt to get another contractor to undertake the work, but he will commonly find that there is great indisposition on the part of other contractors to do so; and if he does enter into a contract with another contractor, it is generally the case that he has to pay an excessively high price for the doing of the work.

1491. In fact, is it not the case, and very frequently, that where works are taken out of the contractor's hands, you can get no contractor to take them up; and the only mode in which you can get those works performed is by giving the surveyor power to carry them out, and obtain funds from the treasurer for the purpose?—It is a constant occurrence that the surveyor has a difficulty in getting works contracted for which he has in his own hands, except, as I have already mentioned, at excessive rates. It is also a matter of very great difficulty for him, in an isolated district, where the system is not prevalent in the adjoining districts; where he has not many works of a similar kind going on, and a staff already in existence which he can transfer from one place to another, it always will be difficult for a county surveyor, on a sudden emergency, to undertake work of that kind in an advantageous way, or in such a way as he could do if the system of works being in charge of the county surveyor had been in extensive operation.

1492. Would not you recommend that the levies in the case of defaulting contractors should be made by the constabulary, and immediately lodged in the treasurer's hands to the credit of the county?—I think that would be a convenient way to do it, and also that the county surveyor should be altogether free from any connection with the duties attendant upon the levying of the order; that it should be an order made by the Petty Sessions Court, and that the county surveyor should know nothing whatever about it, except to be aware that the funds were obtained. I mention this because, in my own case, I have found difficulties to occur in which the police (who, I have been informed, are not obliged to undertake those duties, but upon being asked have done so) have required me or my assistant to go with them, and point out the property belonging to the contractor and his sureties; and if it were not pointed out to him, by me or my assistant, they would not interfere at all. That, in my opinion, is a position in which the county surveyor ought in no possible circumstances to be placed.

1493. *Mr. Dawson.*] Would not you believe that the police officers generally would very much object to the employment of the police for those purposes?—Well, I really do not know.

1494. *Colonel French.*] When you have pointed out the lands, was not the money levied under a decree of the petty sessions?—It was a levy order, made by the magistrates.

1495. *Sir Charles Lanyon.*] Supposing the case of a levy for a work not being sufficient for the maintenance of a line of road for the period for which it has been contracted; how would you provide for the funds which would be necessary under those circumstances; would you consider it desirable that the act of proceeding against the contractor should be the means of quashing the presentment?—I should hesitate to go to the length of that, except in extreme cases. I am aware that the practice in some localities is to make a regular provision in the contract by which, upon payment of a half year's amount being stopped from the contract, that fact in itself determines the contract; I should hesitate myself to recommend that.

1496. Have you not found some difficulties with reference to the amount of money to be recovered from the contractors; has it not, at the quarter sessions, been deemed necessary to prove a certain money loss to the county, by the works not being carried out by defaulting contractors?

—I have

—I have not had immediate experience of that myself; my knowledge is only from hearsay. I have heard that, in many cases, the chairman of quarter sessions requires to have a money apportionment of the damage which the county has sustained by the default of the contractor; and that is a thing which it is very difficult to do before the work has been executed, and while it is uncertain what the cost of it is.

1497. Have you found any difficulty from the limitation of the cost of stone depôts to 1*l.* in the Act?—I have.

1498. Do you not think it desirable either to put a larger maximum or to leave the sum undefined?—I should leave the sum undefined. I can conceive no reason why it is to be supposed that a worse judgment would be exercised as to the amount to be paid for stone depôts than for any other work which the grand jury have power to present; I should leave it altogether undefined. It is a subject of very considerable importance, and the limitation at the present time has the effect of creating a state of things through a part of Ireland which is the reverse of satisfactory. You are obliged, if you want to have the quantity of the stones accurately ascertained, to tolerate a state of things which may be productive of danger to the traffic, and which certainly is inconvenient.

1499. Colonel *French.*] By stone depôts do you mean quantities of stone laid at the side of the road?—I mean a recess made for the purpose of holding stone.

1500. Or, if there is no recess, on the part of the road not used?—Well, even there it is to a considerable extent subject to disadvantage on a dark night, if there be a small margin. It is a structure usually built of stone, as a recess from the road, for the purpose of holding stone, and of a rectangular form.

1501. Sir *Charles Lanyon.*] Have you found any difficulty with reference to the cutting of hills and filling hollows; have you at any time found difficulty in not being able to carry out the work consequent on not being able to take possession of the ground from want of notice having been served on the occupiers?—There have been cases which have arisen in my experience, not only in connection with hill cuttings but also other works, such as the making of footpaths, where the widening of the road was absolutely necessary in order to carry out the work, that no notice has been served; and where it has been held by a great number of the judges that unless the presentment in express terms is for widening or for making a new road, there is no power to admit a traverse. I think in all cases in which the public, for the execution of a public work, require to encroach upon the ground of the adjoining occupiers or owners, notice ought to be given to those parties, in order that they may be in a position to traverse the presentment for damages and have a legal right to do so.

1502. In fact you would apply the operation of the Act in reference to serving notices for making new roads, but it should also be applied in all cases of widening or hill cutting where new ground is required to be taken?—Quite so.

1503. Have you found any difficulty with reference to the power of obtaining materials for the repair of roads, or for the execution of any public works?—Not myself directly, but I am aware that difficulties do occur in the case of contractors throughout the county.

1504. Would it not be desirable that the wording of the Act should be altered, so as to include other materials beside stone or gravel?—I think it would.

1505. For instance, supposing a hollow was required to be filled, for which there were no appropriate cuttings, would it not be desirable to provide the means of getting spoil, which would be necessary for filling the hollows?—I think it would be desirable to extend the provisions of that Act, so that it would include all materials which would properly be required, and would necessarily be required for the execution of county works.

1506. *Chairman.*] What is the section?—Section 103 of 6 & 7 William 4th, chapter 116.

1507. Colonel *French.*] There are certain places which you cannot go to for material at all?—There are.

1508. And others for which you require an order of the justices?—Quite so; in that section, page 148 of Foot; and the opinion of the law adviser of the Crown was lately taken by the resident magistrate in the county of Antrim in reference to the scope of the words, "any gravel, stone, sand, or other materials." The purport of the opinion given by him, as I understand it, was, that according to the proper mode of interpreting words of that kind, where certain things are specified, the larger term, (such as, in this case,) "or other materials," is limited by the specific words which have preceded it.

1509. Sir *Charles Lanyon.*] In fact, that if you want earth, or sods, or any materials of that kind, you could not, under that section, obtain it?—Just so. That opinion has been acted upon by the different benches in the county of Antrim lately, and it has impeded the execution of the works very considerably. It was prominently brought before the notice of the grand jury at the last assizes. I may mention another point of difficulty in that section, which is this. You will find that in nominating the three householders, there is a power to compel the surveyor or contractor to nominate his. The magistrates can nominate theirs, but there is no power whatever to compel the person into whose land you want to enter to nominate one upon his part; and proceedings in consequence of that may be rendered nugatory.

1510. Colonel *French.*] Are you aware of any case where that has occurred?—I am.

1511. Sir *Charles Lanyon.*] Do you think it is necessary to have any further control to prevent injudicious and unwarrantable interference with roads and fences?—I certainly do. It is a matter of very considerable importance in such a district as I have the charge of now, where in the neighbourhood of a rising town like Belfast, the suburbs are extending, and where land, which previously had been quite a rural district, has been now turned into use for building purposes, the power of preventing injudicious interference is, in my opinion, quite insufficient, and the words of the Summary Jurisdiction Act in reference to one class of interferences are extremely vague, and want to be made more explicit.

1512. *Chairman.*] You refer to encroachments?—Yes.

1513. Sir *Charles Lanyon.*] Will you refer to the Act?—It is page 134, of Foot, 14 & 15 Vict. c. 92, s. 9, clause 3, "Any person who shall scour, deepen, widen, or fill up any ditch or drain on the side of any public road, or who shall alter the

the fences of any public road, or who shall build any wall or make any ditch, drain, or watercourse, or dig any pit or hollow, on any public road, or within 30 feet of the centre thereof, save upon or within any ancient fence adjoining such road," and so on. Now, those last words which I have just read, which are parenthetical, constitute the principal difficulty, because it is impossible to know what precise interpretation to put upon them. The public are directly interested in two things in reference to the ordinary fences which you have at the side of a road. The drainage of the road is one, and there being an adequate fence is another; these apart from the question of encroachment on the road. Take the ordinary case of a country new road. You have a grass kerb adjoining the road, and inside that you have a grip, which answers for the purpose of drainage. Under that section there would appear to be a considerable difficulty in preventing a person, or in substantiating a complaint against a person who had built a wall upon that fence at the side of the road, even upon any part of it. If a demesne wall were built there (and there are cases in which this is actually occurring) you cannot tell what takes place with reference to the grip; if you go inside you become a trespasser.

1514. *Chairman.*] Do you mean that before the building of the wall the drain or grip is under the control of the county surveyor?—I do.

1515. But after the building of the wall, it is taken out of his power?—It seems to me so; as I read the Act of Parliament, in reference to drains, the county have full control over the grip at the side of the road, and they have no power to call upon the occupier or landowner to clean it out or to repair it; they must accept the responsibility of that themselves: their power in reference to drains and watercourses is altogether confined to those which lead from the road, which are of importance for the purpose of clearing out the water which otherwise might stagnate at the side of the road.

1516. Sufficient openings through the wall connecting the road with the drain behind would meet the difficulty, and in any case there must be openings through the bank which had existed previously?—Certainly; but you cannot insist upon their being openings in the wall; and if there be, how can you know, if the person wishes to plant, as persons constantly do, and to do away with the grip altogether and to substitute a drain which would be altogether unsuitable for proper drainage purposes? You have no control over them in that case.

1517. Colonel *French.*] The wall could not have been built without a presentment?—If it could not, you get rid of a great deal of this difficulty; but I apprehend that it could be built under this section.

1518. Sir *Charles Lanyon.*] I wish to ask you whether the best mode of providing for the difficulty would be that no walls should be built without a shilling presentment from the grand jury?—I think it would be very desirable; and that you should go further and provide this; that persons who desire to interfere and alter the present position of the road for their own private convenience should be obliged, as they are in all towns and under the Towns Improvement Act, to submit to the officer acting on behalf of the public a plan or a proper and sufficient statement of what it is they propose to do.

1519. Would not the effect of a shilling presentment be exactly what you have described as a desirable arrangement?—Not necessarily so; if you make provision in connection with the shilling presentment that with all shilling presentments for such purposes as have been referred to it shall be obligatory on the persons who seek to make those changes to submit with their applications a proper map explaining what it is they propose to do; I think that would answer the purpose. I would press upon the Committee the importance on the part of the public of having not merely in vague terms "a map," which might be got rid of by making a sketch which would be practically of no sufficient value. The honourable Member who has put the question to me must be perfectly aware that the section of the Act with reference to new roads, which requires a map to be lodged, together with the application, is one which is not by any means sufficiently explicit; that you ought to require that a document should be produced which would show plainly what it is intended to do, and, if there be an encroachment, the extent of it.

1520. Colonel *French.*] Would it not be your duty, as the county surveyor, if a wall were built within the prescribed limits, to level it on your own authority?—I conceive that under that section, as it is now, if the wall were built within the limits of the present fence, I should be prevented from interfering, and that they would have, under that section, a sufficient case against me. I should have no power to interfere.

1521. Have you ever heard of the county surveyor several times knocking down a wall that has been built in defiance of the law, within the given distance of the side of the road?—I have; and there are many cases in which even now, and with that section in existence, he can do so. But if you take the case of a wall which is built upon and within the limits of an ancient fence adjoining the road, I conceive he would have no power to do so.

1522. Sir *Charles Lanyon.*] Is there any other limitation in that section 9 of the 14 & 15 Vict., which you would think is desirable to dispense with?—Yes; I certainly think that that six months' limitation should not be in the Act.

1523. Will you refer to that limitation?—I think that is in the general Act, if I remember right. There is a provision that proceedings cannot be taken in reference to encroachments which have been made, if the term of six months after they have been made is allowed to expire. That limitation, I think, is not desirable, and should be removed. There is also in that section a question about building houses. No part of a house can be built within 30 feet of the centre of any public road, except in the streets of corporate or market towns, or where a house now stands; and there is a fine imposed not exceeding 10 *l.* In practice, the working of that section is too stringent. It is at page 133. The words are, "except in the case of corporate or market towns." There are many towns which are neither the one nor the other, where there have been old buildings at either side of a vacant space, for a considerable distance; and if a person proposed to build in line with the houses at each side, according to the strict interpretation of that section, he would be prevented from doing so.

1524. Do you not think it would be desirable to prevent the lapse of sessions by the non-attendance of magistrates?—Certainly.

A. Tew, Esq., Q.C.

13 April 1868.

1525. What would you propose as a substitute for the chairman?—In the event of there being one of the associated cess-payers present, I think it would be very proper to empower him to act, rather than that the sessions should lapse.

1526. Do you know of any instance where the obligation to appoint sessions to be held in any particular barony has been found very inconvenient, and where it would be desirable to give the grand jury the power of appointing sessions to be held in an adjoining barony, as being more convenient than any place that could be found in the barony itself?—I have heard of many cases, and within my own experience there is one barony in the county, Antrim, where, in my opinion, it would be a convenience to the public to hold the sessions in the adjoining barony, in which there is a good court-house; I allude to the barony of Lower Massereene, in Antrim. The sessions, at present, are held in the town of Crumlin, which is not in the barony of Lower Massereene, but being in the barony of Upper Massereene, it was felt that it was a sufficient compliance with the law. However, it is an inconvenient place to get to, and there have been, even since I came to the county, two or three instances in which if something illegal had not been done, the sessions would have lapsed. The town of Antrim, as you are aware, in which there is a very good court-house, is only separated from the barony of Massereene by the river.

1527. In fact, it would be for the public advantage to enable the grand jury to appoint the sessions in an adjoining barony in some few cases?—If a sufficient case were made for doing so.

1528. Colonel *French*.] But that the grand jury should have the appointment with the prior approval of the sessions?—I see no objection to limiting it to that approval.

1529. *Sir Charles Lanyon*.] You are aware of the power of repairing post roads under the Act of Parliament, half at the expense of the barony, and half at the expense of the county?—I am.

1530. Are you not aware that since the introduction of railways the most leading post roads of the country are no longer post roads?—I am.

1531. Are you not aware that in many districts the post roads which are repaired, half at the expense of the county, and half at the expense of the barony, are roads which have very little thoroughfare and very little traffic?—There are some of them which are, comparatively speaking, of much less importance than many other roads which are not made half county and half barony.

1532. Would not it be desirable, therefore, in order to effect a proper assessment of the county, that the post roads should be abandoned as post roads; I mean that the repair of them, half at the expense of the county, and half at the expense of the barony, should be abandoned, or else that all the leading lines of road in the county, the direct leading lines of road between market town and market town, should now be considered the same as if they were post roads?—I should myself prefer your latter alternative, and I think it would be very desirable if there is to be an apportionment of the cost of maintenance of any road in the county that it should be a general one over the entire county, endeavouring to obtain roads of a certain class of leading importance.

1533. At all events the present power is an unfair one, so far as the county generally is concerned, consequent upon the change that has taken place in the general lines of communication of the country?—Undoubtedly, there are some baronies which are deriving at present an advantage which others do not derive; some baronies have post roads, but others have none.

1534. And, therefore, it would be extremely desirable to amend the law in that respect?—I think so.

1535. Colonel *French*.] Was it not necessary to widen those roads in order to make them common coach roads, which you would think much wider than would be necessary for the use of the barony, or for the common traffic of the country?—In many cases, no doubt, that is so.

1536. A power has been given to the Post Office to keep these roads in repair?—There is an especial power given to the Post Office in reference to roads on which mail carriages travel, which does not exist with reference to any other road. If the road gets out of repair the Post Office can send a remonstrance or statement to the Board of Works of the fact, and the Board of Works have the power of having money expended on that road at the cost of the county.

1537. *Sir Charles Lanyon*.] I think the question which Colonel French has put with reference to the width of roads refers to an old Act of Parliament, before the introduction of the 6 & 7 William 4th, chap. 116. Under the old Act of George it was necessary to make post roads of a certain width, but under the 6 & 7 William 4, the Grand Jury Law now in force, it is not necessary that the road should be of a certain width in order to be a post road?—I believe that is so. I know as a matter of fact that there are many roads now, upon which mail carriages of any kind (including in that term mail cars) travel, which originally were not of leading importance. Leading lines are often provided for by the railways and now the post roads, or any that are in that position, in many instances are branch lines, and are not of the class of mail coach roads.

1538. Colonel *French*.] Can you state the exact number of miles of mails carried entirely by cars?—I cannot.

1539. *Sir Charles Lanyon*.] You mentioned just now that it would be desirable to appoint one of the associated cess-payers as chairman of the sessions in case of the non-attendance of magistrates; have you known any difficulty to arise in your country from the representation of the cess-payers not being a fair representation of every locality in the barony; are they not frequently drawn from one particular district of the country, consequent upon their being the highest cess-payers, and living in a certain locality in the barony; many of the important mountain districts being entirely unrepresented in the sessions?—I cannot say that it has come under my knowledge that that is so; at the same time I can readily believe it is possible that, where cess-payers are selected because they are the highest cess-payers in the barony, the district in the barony, which would require representation probably more than any other district in that barony, might not be adequately represented. In mountain districts to which you have referred, works of improvement are more needed than when you get down to the plain districts, and mountain land being of less value than the plain land it frequently happens that you may not have an adequate representation, if you are strictly confined to the very highest cess-payer in the barony.

1540. Can

A. Tate, Esq., C.E.

18 April 1868.

1540. Can you suggest any means for selecting the cess-payers of the district, so as to secure the superintendence of the whole barony at the sessions?—I have seen the evidence which has been given in reference to that subject, and that the attention of the Committee was directed to it. I have therefore given some consideration to it; but while appreciating the importance of representing every portion of each district, I have found a difficulty in determining in my own mind how to get a subdivision that would practically be found a convenient one for the purpose. The object of representing the entire of the barony unquestionably is a desirable one.

1541. Do you think that the representation by electoral divisions, a cess-payer having to be selected from each electoral division in the barony, in the first instance, would be a desirable mode of meeting the difficulty?—It may be so, but I have not examined the question sufficiently to give an expression of opinion to which I should like to tie myself. You see, if you adopt the electoral divisions, then comes the question of the number of cess-payers that would belong to that particular district; and if you assume that six would be the number of cess-payers for the particular district, and you found that ten would be the number of electoral divisions, you at once get into a difficulty; it is a very difficult matter to obtain a sub-denomination that will meet all purposes. The object in question is a most desirable one, but the exact mode of attaining it I am not prepared to suggest.

1542. Colonel *French*.] The electoral divisions and the barony divisions are not the same?—I think not.

1543. Sir *Charles Lanyon*.] At all events you agree in the propriety of some arrangement being made, if possible, for a selection of the cess-payers, not from one particular district, but in order to obtain a fair representation of the whole of the barony?—Most fully.

1544. Colonel *French*.] If there was an option of that kind given, would it not cause remarks to be made of the unfairness of the selection in departing from the given lines as at present; if you allowed the grand jury, for instance, to select A, B, and C out of a certain number instead of selecting the highest cess-payer, would it not very likely occasion remarks to be made that these men were selected for particular purposes?—Perhaps the best answer I can give to your question would be to state the system that obtains in the county of Dublin, with which I am familiar, which differs from that which obtains elsewhere in Ireland, and which, in my opinion, is a very considerable improvement; it is this, if the grand jury appoint six as the proper number of cess-payers to be associated for a particular barony, they select out of the list of 100 cess-payers 18, that is, three times the number to be finally associated, and a ballot is made by the foreman of the grand jury for the six who are to be the associated cess-payers for that district. That, in my opinion, is a very great improvement upon the system which obtains in the counties generally. You get rid of two objections which may be raised to it; first of all, to a considerable extent, the objection of their being nominees, and the other objection as to the uncertainty which would attend the mind of any cess-payer, after he has been nominated under the Grand Jury Act. You are aware if six be the number ultimately to sit, 12 persons will be apprised that they may have the privilege of sitting, and the uncertainty which attends the fact whether they will be called upon to act even if they go to the trouble of driving a considerable distance to the sessions would no doubt act to deter some from going. You get rid of that objection if you adopt the system which is in use in the county of Dublin, and, in my opinion, it would be a desirable change.

1545. The only difference in Dublin is that the ballot takes place at the grand jury; in the other counties in Ireland it takes place at the baronial sessions?—The difference is further this, that in the counties you have double the number of cess-payers.

1546. You have 100 to select from?—You have 100 in the other case to select your 18 from, and you have the other difficulty got rid of, of the uncertainty which attends the cess-payer not knowing if he does go that he will have the privilege of sitting.

1547. May not that uncertainty be made into a certainty of jobbing among themselves?—I do not see that.

1548. Sir *Charles Lanyon*.] Do you know that the doubt as to whether cess-payers will be appointed to act at the sessions when they have to travel perhaps many miles for the purpose of attending there, and losing their day's work very often, prevents them from attending under the present system?—It necessarily must do so, I think.

1549. In order to secure that representation which I speak of as the representation of the whole barony, do you not think that it would be desirable that the barony cess collectors, instead of returning their lists of 100 cess-payers in the whole barony, should return their lists under the head of 20 of the highest cess-payers in each electoral division?—Well, I really have hardly given sufficient consideration to that question, as to the subdivision of the barony, to enable me to give an opinion on that subject.

1550. At all events, you consider that the mode of selecting the cess-payers in the county of Dublin is a very much better one than that adopted in the other counties?—I do.

1551. Supposing the law to be amended in the way you have pointed out, as to the prosecution of defaulting contractors, do you think it would be desirable to alter the law in reference to the compulsory acceptance of the lowest tender?—I think that in general the lowest tender should be adopted; I can conceive circumstances in which it might be desirable to place a discretion in the road sessions, and in the grand jury, in reference to it.

1552. Would not that discretion be rendered very much less important by the alterations which you have suggested in the mode of dealing with contractors than what it is at the present time?—It would.

1553. Have you any difficulty in obtaining the assistance in your district of men of sufficient information and intelligence?—Very considerable.

1554. To what do you attribute that?—To the smallness of the remuneration afforded to the office and the facility for any person of good character and skill obtaining employment.

1555. They are all bound to undergo a certain examination before the Board of Public Works, are they not?—They are bound to undergo an examination, and at present it is conducted by the Board of Works, but under the change in the law

A. Tate, Esq., C.E.

[illegible]

law which has taken place, I imagine it would be transferred from their hands into the hands of the Civil Service Commissioners.

1556. Do you not think that it is a very important part of the Grand Jury Act, the provision of proper and efficient superintendence of the public works of the county?—A most important one.

1557. Unless the assistants are people of very good character, the greatest amount of peculation and deception may be carried on?—Unquestionably, unless they are persons of good character, there are very considerable opportunities for fraud in connection with the discharge of their duties.

1558. Do you think that the present salaries are insufficient to obtain that class of men that you consider necessary for the superintendence of the public?—I do; I gave evidence to that effect before the Committee upon County and District Surveyors, in the year 1857, and at that time the whole scope of the evidence which was given upon the subject by a number of witnesses, by Sir John Burgoyne, by Sir Richard Griffith, by yourself, by myself, and by a number of other witnesses, all tended to make what is the maximum now the minimum. I may describe the general scope of the evidence then to be, that the salaries should range from 80 *l.* to 120 *l.* a year. 80 *l.* then was certainly more valuable than 80 *l.* now.

1559. You think it would be desirable to raise the salaries of the assistants; to give the grand juries the power, at all events, of raising the salaries?—I do, most certainly.

1560. Can you say what is the present cost of the superintendence of all the public works of Antrim at the present time?—I have a statement here which has been deduced from statistics in Thom's Almanac.

1561. What per-centage is it upon the total cost of the works?—It amounts to a little over three per cent. in the county of Antrim.

1562. That is including all the expenses of office and everything else?—It is; the expenses of office and assistants, county surveyor's salary, the allowance for office, clerks, and deputies.

1563. Do you know what it averages in Ireland generally, in other counties besides Antrim?—I have made a calculation in reference to the entire of Ireland, and it is a little over five per cent., or about five per cent. It is to be borne in mind, in reference to any statement as to the per-centage of cost for superintendence, that the class of works which are superintended are a multitude of small contracts spread in 5 *l.* and 10 *l.* amounts, generally over the entire face of the country, and that it by no means is the measure of the amount of superintendence executed by the county surveyor; because all the works which have heretofore been executed, and which may not be under presentment at the moment, all the county buildings, and a variety of other matters which he has to advise the grand jury upon, are all provided for in that same sum which I have stated as the per-centage.

1564. Do you think any improvement could be made in the manner in which the county surveyors are appointed?—The present law in reference to the appointment and the examination of the county surveyors is, I believe, about to come into force, and it will be the first operation of the new law upon the subject.

1565. What Act is that?—It was passed two or three years ago. I have not the exact Act at present.

1566. At all events, this new Act provides for a different arrangement to the former one?—It does.

1567. And it now provides that no appointment, nor examination for the appointment, of county surveyor can take place until a vacancy occurs; is that the case?—I believe so.

1568. Supposing a vacancy to occur immediately before the commencement of the session, in what state would the county be placed consequent upon that vacancy?—Supposing a vacancy to occur at this moment, it would be about the most disadvantageous time it could occur, immediately preceding the spring sessions. There would be no certificate given for any works at the spring sessions, and the result of that would be that the contractors might be without payment for 10 months. The provision for examination, as I understand it, is this; it is to be in the hands of the Civil Service Commissioners. There is to be an examination for every vacancy. When a vacancy occurs, there is to be a public notification in the public prints, and any person who chooses to present himself will be examined.

1569. Colonel *French*.] A competitive examination?—A competitive examination. The examiners may return any number of persons as qualified whom they find to be, in their opinion, qualified for the office. The Lord Lieutenant has the power of appointment, subject to the approval of the grand jury.

1570. Should another vacancy occur, is it not necessary to have another examination?—If the law be attended to, and carried out, in my opinion it would be.

1571. Sir *Charles Lanyon*.] The list that is prepared by these examiners merely answers the purpose of the vacancy of the moment?—Just so.

1572. And that list is not kept as a record at the Castle, of persons who are qualified for the position, and from which the selections would afterwards be made, but a fresh examination must again take place for the next vacancy?—That is as I understand it. From one examination you can only provide for one appointment, and that appointment is to be made by the Lord Lieutenant in the first instance, subject to the approval of the grand jury. The result of that, in my opinion, would be this; that it would deter the most desirable candidates from competing at the examination at all. The amount of contingencies to which they would be subjected is considerable; for even supposing they found themselves to be quite competent to be A 1 in the examination, after being A 1 possibly they might not get the appointment, and they would subject themselves to all the annoyance of the examination fruitlessly; and in alluding to persons who are the most qualified for the office, I certainly say that unless a person has attained a position, and has acquired some experience in the conduct and management of works, and is not merely a person who is fresh from college, or from college classes, you will not get the most desirable person, and that a person who has acquired any position in his profession, and has been at actual work as a member of the profession, would be deterred from submitting himself to an examination of the character of that which is provided by the present law.

1573. In fact, the present law is totally at variance with all similar examinations under the competitive system?—I am not so fully aware of that. In the competitive examinations ordinarily, you have

have several prizes; here you have but one prize. Take the *Royal* Engineers, the Artillery, or any Indian Civil Service appointments, there are a number of prizes there; here you have but one, and no certainty whatever that the person who stands A 1 shall be appointed.

1574. That is what I would conceive to be at variance with the principle of competitive examination?—Yes, in those respects.

1575. Under the ordinary system of competitive examination, the man obtaining the highest marks obtains the prize?—He does.

1576. Under this system it might not be the case?—It might not.

1577. Do you consider it would be desirable that the first person on the list should obtain the appointment?—If there is to be but one appointment, and an examination for each vacancy, I certainly do; but my opinion is, that a modification of the two systems, a medium course between the present law and that which obtained formerly, would be the most desirable, and thus a limited list be obtained by which you would have in reserve an officer to put into any vacancy which may occur.

1578. That would be the modification you would recommend?—That would be the modification I would recommend; to have a list of, perhaps, three persons kept. There is this other point in reference to that question in which I am interested, and it is the only way in which I am interested, except in having my brother officials who may be appointed hereafter such as they ought to be; it is this; that county surveyors, under the present law have a power under certain circumstances of appointing a deputy; that deputy must be appointed from the list of persons who obtain the qualification for county surveyor. If this examination be conducted as now, there would be no person whom I could appoint as a deputy under any circumstances.

1579. What is the modification or medium system which you would propose?—Formerly the examiners returned a list of as many persons as they considered qualified for the office out of a particular examination. It might have been six, it might have been 10 or 12. That list was returned to Dublin Castle, and until it was exhausted no further examination was held. If that list was a very long one, as sometimes it was, the vacancies occurring but seldom, it might be that when you came to the bottom of that list, so long a space of time would have elapsed that the person might possibly have turned to some other occupation in the meantime, and not have followed his profession. He would, however, have a right to obtain the appointment if he chose to accept of it, and that I think might operate to the disadvantage of the public. I would make the list a limited one; but I am clearly of opinion that it ought not to be restricted to a single appointment for each vacancy.

1580. You would think it desirable, in fact, that there should be a list at the Castle, from which appointments might be filled up at any moment they occurred?—I do; a limited list.

1581. Supposing a vacancy to occur, must there not, under the present arrangement, be a very considerable delay before the appointment could be filled up; first of all from the advertisement, then from the examination, and thirdly from the decision of the Lord Lieutenant on the list sent to him?—Unquestionably.

1582. Have you ever thought it desirable, with reference to applications as to works at sessions, that the applications should be made by the county surveyors themselves for all leading and important roads, not leaving it open to the present desultory mode in which the applications are made?—I think it would be very desirable that in regard to applications for the maintenance of roads, they should be regarded almost in the light of imperative presentments; and that the only question from time to time occurring on the expiration of the contract, should be the determining of the account proper to be presented for the purpose; that it would be desirable carefully to arrange the system of road contracts in any particular barony, in what was considered the most desirable manner; and that then, as a matter of course, on the expiry of the contracts, the applications should be brought forward by some officer, such as the secretary, as a matter of course.

A. Tate, Esq., C.E.

28 April 1868.

1583. Do you not think it would be desirable also to do away with the system of fees at the present time?—I certainly do; I think it would be much better that the system of fees should be abolished.

1584. If the fees were abolished, compensation would have to be made to the county officers for the amount of those fees?—Yes, very considerable compensation in the large counties.

1585. Do you not think it desirable that all the tenders and all the papers should be filled by the secretary and by his officer?—I think it would be manifestly for the public advantage and convenience that they should be filled up in a regular and systematic way, and not be subjected to the chances of being filled up by any of the road contractors or persons of that kind; documents which have to go through several courts, to the Road Sessions Court, and to the grand jury with all the endorsements upon them, and eventually before the judge.

1586. There are fees to be paid upon every application and upon every presentment, whether the application is made by the county surveyor or otherwise, the recognisances to be entered into by the contractor; the application being made by the county surveyor merely relieves those fees which are consequent upon the application itself; is not that the case?—I believe so; but really I am very indifferently informed as to the fees in connexion with the secretary's office.

1587. As to the charges for the cutting of hills, and building of bridges, do you not think that in some cases there is a very great hardship in putting those works upon the county at large?—The cutting of hills upon local roads certainly, in my opinion, ought to be local baronial charges.

1588. The Act is indefinite upon that point at present, as to the mode of charging for the cutting of hills?—It gives a power to place the charge for cutting hills and filling hollows, either upon the county at large or upon the barony; and I believe it has been ruled by the judges, that they may divide it between the two, and the practice has been to divide it between the two in many cases.

1589. Are you not aware that very frequently at the sessions for the barony, an application for the cutting of a hill receives the approval of the sessions, consequent upon its being a county at large charge, and not a baronial charge?—I can conceive cases, and cases do occur in which presentments for large amounts for the cutting of hills are approved of, in all probability, through there being an expectation that at least a portion of

A. Tate, Esq., C.E.

28 April 1857.

of the charge would be placed upon the county at large. I have never known an instance, I believe, in which it has been made absolutely obligatory upon the grand jury to make them a county at large charge. In my experience, I think it has only gone the length of placing it as a recommendation, that it be made a county at large charge. The cost of cutting hills has very frequently in the county of Antrim been divided between the county and the barony. I believe the question has been argued before the judges, and they have ruled that it may be divided.

1590. Will you refer to the section under which the county at large pays for the cutting of hills?—The section is at page 47 of Foot, No. 68, and after describing a number of works, it says, at the close of the section, "to be raised either off the county or off the barony or baronies in which the same may be locally situate." The practice has obtained in the county of Antrim in many cases to apportion the charge between the county and the barony according to a certain principle.

1591. Do you not think in principle that it is unfair to give the baronial sessions the power of approving of a work which is to be charged upon the county at large?—To a certain extent it is, but there is the power of revision by the whole grand jury, eventually.

1592. I know that; but I mean to say in the first instance it must be approved of by the baronial sessions, and do you not think that it is unreasonable to give the sessions, which merely represents the barony, the power of presenting for the cutting of a hill or the building of a bridge, the total cost of which shall be levied off the county at large?—Theoretically, according to the general law, you should certainly give the cess-payers for the county at large a power of approval in the matter, but practically in the county of Antrim the attendance at the county at large sessions of associated cess-payers has always been so extremely limited that I do not think it would have affected the question.

1593. Do you not think it would be desirable, at all events, that any application so approved of at the baronial sessions should be referred to the county at large sessions for subsequent approval, the county at large sessions always occurring after the baronial sessions?—I see no objection to its being so done.

1594. Is there any other matter which you wish to give evidence upon?—No, I think not.

1595. Colonel *French*.] You stated that it would be advisable for the payment of contractors and for the convenience of the county works, that the surveyor should have a certain sum of money in hand; you stated that there should be a power to draw on the treasurer for whatever he thought ought to be paid according to the amount of work done under the contract; for instance, if the contract was 10*l.*, and half of the work was done, the man should be authorised to get 5*l.* by the order of the county surveyor?—I should not descend to sums of so low an amount as that.

1596. But that is the principle; now, as you admitted, if all the presentments which were passed at the preceding sessions were accounted for at the time they were bound to be accounted for according to the contracts, there would be no money whatever in the hands of the treasurer to pay any such order?—In all my experience in connexion with the county matters, I have never known a case in which, in my opinion, there would be a difficulty in meeting any claims that, I think, would properly be brought against the general fund.

1597. That is not exactly an answer to my question?—Practically, I do not think the inconvenience would arise.

1598. You do not think it would arise, but it might arise; there is no doubt it must arise under the circumstances I refer to; if all the presentments were accounted for and paid, I wish to know whether you would propose that a given sum of money at each assizes should be presented to the credit of the county surveyor; do you think it advisable that 100*l.* or 200*l.*, or any given sum, according to the estimate of the county surveyor, should be left subject to certificates signed by him, as to the progress of the works contracted for?—I think that that might be a very desirable and convenient course to adopt; for instance, if this fund to which I referred were to be used for the purpose, a portion of it would be in Exchequer Bills, and it would be desirable that there should be some general estimate made of the sum which would probably be called for.

1599. You mentioned difficulties which the county surveyor had to deal with in the case of contractors neglecting their work; you said you found difficulties, and I believe there are difficulties in getting other contractors to undertake them; there is usually a combination amongst them?—Yes.

1600. If the county surveyor had money at his disposal, could not he purchase a certain quantity, whatever he considered necessary, of broken stones, hire cars, and put them to it at once, under the direction of one of his subordinate officers?—Even there, in getting the materials, considerable difficulties are in the way. In my county, in which the number of assistants in proportion to the extent of the county is nearly as great as in any county in Ireland, I have myself found very considerable difficulties in connexion with road maintenance contracts, in getting persons to undertake the provision of broken stones except at excessive rates.

1601. There are certain limitations to the power of the county surveyor or of the contractor to enter into lands for materials for stone or gravel; for instance, you cannot go into pleasure grounds, nor can you go into a walled demesne?—There are, but practically the county surveyor is seldom in connexion with works in that position, that he requires to take advantage of that power at all unless the system of giving works in charge of the county surveyor be largely used. I think the cases would be of extremely rare occurrence in which the county surveyor himself, as the officer on behalf of the county, would have occasion to take advantage of that section.

1602. If the case were brought before petty sessions, how could you decide where the nearest material for the road could be got by the contractor without the assistance of the county surveyor?—The magistrates would know from their own knowledge of the district, and from the evidence they would get from the county surveyor or his assistant.

1603. From that evidence he could point out where the contractor had a right to go for material, and where, when he estimated the cost of that work, he supposed the contractor would go?—There are certain cases in which the contractor would

would be bound to go to a particular place for a particular material. The importance of maintaining a very leading and important road in a district in which good material for the purpose was scarce and difficult to be got, would, in some cases, render it necessary for a contractor to go to a distance of eight or nine miles. When I was in the county of Dublin, for the maintenance of the roads in the same neighbourhood, we had to go to the extreme end of Howth, for instance.

1604. You stated that you thought it would be advisable to collect the county cess by means of the constabulary?—No, that was not the purport of my answer. If I conveyed that impression to your mind it was not what I intended to convey; what I did intend to convey with reference to that was merely in regard to the cases in which proceedings against a contractor under the 19 & 20 Vict. c. 63, should require to be pushed to extremity, and then, if the magistrates gave an order under that section, then for the levying of that order the assistance of the constabulary might be called in.

1605. Do you consider that the constabulary have any such duty as to keep the roads clear; that they should keep pigs off the road?—I certainly think they should.

1606. Do you know whether it is the law or not, whether they are bound to do it?—I am aware it is differently acted upon. I am not a lawyer, but to me it seems that the law has imposed upon them that duty. I know the answer is frequently given that they have so many other duties to discharge, that they cannot give proper attention to those duties, but under the Summary Jurisdiction Act it appears to me that the constabulary have imposed upon them the duty of taking charge of road nuisances. In my opinion they would form the most efficient means of controlling those nuisances.

1607. Mr. *Maguire.*] How long have you been in your present position?—Since the beginning of the year 1862.

1608. Before that were you connected with this kind of works?—I was acting in the county of Dublin for the previous 17 years.

1609. In those two counties had you an opportunity of knowing how the feeling of the people generally was about the burden of the tax?—No, I cannot say I have.

1610. You have never heard anything about it?—I have hardly ever heard anything said on the subject.

1611. It was out of your way altogether?—Yes.

1612. I would simply ask you, do you think there would be more satisfaction if the burden of the tax were divided equally between the occupier and the owner of the land?—I think, in reference to a certain class of the county expenditure, the expenditure for the county at large, charges for works of large improvement, probably it would.

1613. You have no doubt as to that?—No.

1614. As to the equity and justice of that division?—No.

1615. Do you mean gaols, or hospitals, or bridges?—Yes; as to the bridges, the cesspayers of the county have a direct interest in them.

1616. You divided them into classes, by that I suppose you mean the occupiers; those who do pay the cess are the occupiers, are they not?—Yes.

1617. They have a direct interest in the construction and maintenance of a bridge?—They have.

1618. And I suppose you say in the construction and maintenance of roads?—Yes.

1619. Have they a greater interest in it than the owner of the property through which the river runs, or through which the road passes?—I have really given very little attention to the subject.

1620. Do answer me that question; from your own knowledge, have they?—That, I think, would depend on the nature of their interest in the land.

1621. If the nature of their interest were at all precarious, certainly the gentleman who owned the land would have a more direct, immediate, and permanent interest than the man who simply had a temporary holding, would he not?—He would.

1622. Do not you think it would be a fair thing to divide the burden between them, and with satisfaction to the occupying classes. What do you think of it yourself. If you do not wish to give an opinion, I will not press you?—I have really not considered the subject.

1623. At any rate you go this length, there are certain works of great public utility, the burden of establishing or maintaining which you think ought to be borne equally by the occupier and the owner?—Yes.

1624. As to the question of selection and nomination, inasmuch as the cesspayer is the person who has to support the burden of all those public works, and pay for them, do not you think he ought to have some right of nominating the person who is to represent him, or, in plain words, to elect the person to represent him?—Yes, in theory, I think it would be so.

1625. In practice, do you not think it would work well?—I think in practice it might not. It might be attended with very considerable difficulty. That seems to me the stumbling-block in the way of it.

1626. Have you any knowledge how the Poor Law works in Ireland?—No, I cannot say that I have.

1627. Have you ever heard any complaints made that the system of election did not work well?—I have not.

1628. Saving the name, is there any difference between poor rate and county cess. Practically, is there any difference between the one rate and the other?—There is certainly very considerable difference. The rates are raised for entirely different purposes.

1629. Are not they raised from the same classes. Is not the occupier a taxpayer, paying the county rate just as well as the poor rate?—Yes.

1630. Why then should a person who represents the cesspayer, or the ratepayer, in one instance, be nominated by some irresponsible person, and in the other case be deliberately selected by the ratepayer. Is there any reason that you can see?—I do not see any reason why they should not be elected, if it be found a convenient arrangement to do so.

1631. Then your objection would merely be one of expediency, or as to whether the machinery would work well; but in the abstract, as a matter of justice and equity, you think it would be right and fair, do you not?—Yes.

1632. Mr. *Blake.*] Contractors for works at present

A. Tate, Esq., C.E.

[illegible] April 18[illegible].

present give security direct to the Crown, do they not?—They do.

1633. In the event of the contractor being either a defaulter, or not able to fulfil his contract, it rests with the grand jury altogether whether he should be proceeded against?—It does.

1634. From your experience, do you think it would not be more desirable that a contractor should be proceeded against directly by the Crown for the fulfilment of his contract, instead of leaving him to endeavour to get off by any interest he may bring to bear on the grand jury?—No; I think that the grand jury, who are conversant with the circumstances, and have the opportunity of hearing all about each case, form a proper court to determine whether proceedings shall be taken or not.

1635. Does not it often occur that a man's getting off a bad contract, or not fulfilling one, will be dependent on the interest he is able to bring to bear on the grand jury?—I really have never been aware of any instance in which anything of the kind occurred.

1636. Could not any mitigating circumstances be as well discussed before the Judge of Assize, or the Chairman of Quarter Sessions, if he were directly proceeded against for the fulfilment of the bond by the Crown?—I certainly do not think that in carrying out the law generally it would be desirable under all possible circumstances to proceed against contractors who should be in default.

1637. Now with regard to your own position as county surveyor, are you not liable to be summarily removed to another county, and to an inferior class, without any reason whatever being assigned for your removal?—Well, there has been one case which has occurred in Ireland lately, which would seem to show that county surveyors are possibly subject to a contingency of that kind. There was one case of a removal of an officer which was represented to me by some of the gentlemen of the district.

1638. What class are you in?—The first class.

1639. May not the Lord Lieutenant without giving any explanation whatever, to-morrow remove you to a third class county?—I believe it is possible. There is a general section in the Act of Parliament, whether it has been repealed by the recent laws I cannot tell, but there is a provision in the 6 & 7 Will. 4, which appears to say that the Lord Lieutenant has the power of removing surveyors from county to county, and he does not appear to be responsible to anybody how he exercises that power.

1640. Has it not occurred before now that a surveyor has been removed, without any reason being assigned?—No, I believe not; I think there has been only one single case of a removal that I have heard of, which was done without the knowledge of the county surveyor, until he was told, "you are to remove from this county to another;" I believe that is the only case in which that has occurred.

1641. The county surveyor is liable, without being aware of what the reason of his removal is, to be summarily removed, is he not?—It would appear to be so, but it is a power that one can hardly contemplate.

1642. As a matter of fact, such is the case, is it not?—I think so.

1643. Do you think it is a desirable power?—I certainly do not.

1644. From your long experience as a county surveyor, do you think it is the best thing in justice to the surveyors themselves and for the benefit of the public service, that the appointment should be in the hands of the Lord Lieutenant; or do you think it would be better to have them appointed by the county grand jury, and to be removed in the same way, certain qualifications being essential in the first instance as to capacity?—From my long acquaintance with the office, and my experience with the way in which the power has been exercised, which until now you may say has rested in the Lords Lieutenant of Ireland to appoint to the office of county surveyor, I am aware that that power has been exercised strictly in the order of merit, with, I believe, two exceptions, and those two exceptions only virtually prove the admirable way in which the power has been used; there were amply sufficient reasons when the strict order of which was departed from; one of them occurred thus: Sir John Young was Chief Secretary for Ireland at the time; the county surveyor who was appointed did not enter upon his duties at the moment; he appointed from the list of qualified persons one as his deputy; that deputy had acted in the county for several months to the satisfaction of the grand jury, and on the subsequent retirement of the principal, the grand jury by unanimous resolution requested Sir John Young, as Secretary for Ireland, to use his influence with the Lord Lieutenant to have the deputy appointed to the county, and in doing that I believe he was only put over the head of one person. That and one other case, which I am not familiar with, are the only instances since the year 1832, in which the Lords Lieutenant have not taken the very head of the list.

1645. Would you suggest any change either in the mode of appointment or in the peremptory power of removal without assigning a reason or giving an opportunity to a person like yourself, of knowing the reason of removal, and of defending himself from the charge brought against him?—I think it is an arbitrary power.

1646. Is there anything which you could suggest in the way of improvement?—I have not previously given consideration to the question, but what occurs to me at the moment is, that the Lord Lieutenant ought to be put in motion upon the subject by the grand jury of the county; that if there was any expression of opinion on the part the grand jury of the county in reference to the officer holding office in that county, the Lord Lieutenant should be put in motion.

1647. But not otherwise?—No.

1648. (Mr. Dawson.) It was given in evidence by a very intelligent witness at the commencement of these proceedings, that it would be desirable that the county surveyor should be entirely responsible for all the works of the county. Of course his position would have to be ameliorated as regards his salary, but he proposed that there should be no such thing as an assistant surveyor. Do you think such a plan as that could be carried out?—I think it would be a perfectly monstrous plan, if you take into consideration the entire of Ireland, and the varying circumstances of the different counties, to subdivide the entire of Ireland into small districts, into which it would be necessary to divide it; in order to enable a county surveyor, with proper regard to the interests of the public, to discharge his duty, you would require to make those districts so extremely limited that it would multiply the offices; it would entail a

great

great deal of cost, and at the same time it would be subject to the disadvantage, that unless you lowered the class of officers altogether whom you would appoint, you would require them to be exercising duties which you should not expect from educated gentlemen.

1649. I suppose, in a county like Antrim, which is a very large county, such a proposition would be inadmissible; it could not be done?—I think so.

1650. The evidence of the county surveyor of Clare, I think, was to the effect, that the great difficulty once in each year, in going over the roads of the county, that there is a great portion of the roads in county Clare, that he had not the opportunity of seeing once in each year. Can you manage to see all the roads between the different sessions in Antrim?—No, nor do I think it absolutely necessary that it should be so; I think to attain that you may get into great difficulty and great disadvantage. In the county of Antrim, which is the largest county surveyors' district in Ireland, there are constantly springing up a class of works of improvement in the most remote districts; and in giving attention to these while they are being executed, in visiting them and inspecting them when the applications are originally being brought forward, I am brought at times, when no person expects me, into every part of the county, into the most remote part of the county. Those whom I control never can tell when I may come. If you have a system regularly organised under which the reports from assistants are sent in a systematic way, and under which you have precise returns in the most explicit terms, for instance, the dimensions and position of every heap of stones in the county, and the insertion of those particulars in the district books, when inspections are made it is easy to see if the measurements made are correct, and if you do detect anything which manifestly cannot be accounted for through a mistake, or something of that kind, as it would lead to dismissal, I think you provide all that is necessary; and one result of such a system is this, that in the county of Antrim the percentage of expenditure, though there are in it 10 assistants, is very little over three per cent. I doubt if you can show me any way in which you can provide for the superintendence of so large an amount of works as there is to be superintended in the county of Antrim by any other system more advantageously than by the present. That very subject which you have entered upon was considered very largely before the Select Committee upon County and District Surveyors. There it was a question between county and district surveyors, and before that Committee I gave very lengthened evidence upon that subject; I formed the opinion I have here stated from the very first, and my further experience in county duties has only tended to confirm me in the opinion which I first formed.

1651. *Chairman.*] In what year was that Committee?—In 1857.

1652. *Mr. Dawson.*] The next question I shall ask is a general one which I put to all the witnesses, and it is not connected with your profession. Does there appear to you to be dissatisfaction, or the contrary, among the associated cesspayers about the manner in which they are at present nominated?—I have never heard any expression of dissatisfaction in the county of Antrim.

1653. Is there any deficiency of attendance on their part at the different road sessions?—I observed that questions had been put upon that subject, and out of curiosity I had a statement made of the attendance of the magistrates and cesspayers in the county of Antrim at every sessions since I first held office in it, I found there were 611 magistrates and 615 cess-payers at every sessions since I entered into office in the county Antrim since 1842, being six and a half years.

1654. Have you ever made any objections on the same grounds as to the necessary attendance of baronial collectors at the time of the sessions; have you heard that it causes much inconvenience, and that it is considered unnecessary?—I have not, as a matter of fact, heard it, but I am aware that they do attend, and I can readily understand that it is inconvenient, and it seems to me to be unnecessary to put them to that expense.

1655. Very often people are brought up to whom it is excessively inconvenient to attend?—Without having actually heard it, I can readily see that it is an inconvenience to which it is unnecessary to subject them.

1656. Have you heard that it would be desirable in any way to alter the laws relative to the payment of coroners; I am speaking as to your general knowledge?—No; I have not.

1657. To put them at a fixed salary instead of the sliding scale which now exists, in regard to their payment at grand juries?—I have not.

1658. *Colonel Cooper.*] Do you think it an equitable arrangement that part of the cess should be levied on the county at large, and part on the baronies for the maintenance of the main roads?—I do for the leading roads; to make it a general thing all over the county.

1659. That as to certain leading roads, the expense should be divided between them?—I think so.

1660. And not thrown entirely on the local cess?—I think so. There are some cases in which it may so happen, owing to the position of the barony, that a road of very considerable importance is of very little benefit to the particular barony, so there are cases which have occurred in which roads, which entail large cost to maintain them, are rather stinted in their maintenance in consequence of the charge being placed upon a barony which has, comparatively speaking, but little interest in them.

1661. I asked that question because some of the witnesses thought that the locality should keep the whole of the roads, and I wanted to get your opinion on it; what is the average amount of county cess in Antrim?—According to the statement in Thom's Directory, I find that for the six years for new roads, confining it merely to works to which I apprehend your question addresses itself.

1662. Works exclusive of the institutions?—For new roads and bridges, and for the repair of roads, it has amounted in the county of Antrim to 526,422 *l.*, which brings it to the average of 87,737 *l.* per annum for works alone.

1663. How much in the pound?—The poundage rate varies in the different baronies; I can give you the poundage rates too, if you wish to have them; the poundage rates in the half-year.

1664. Have you got the general average?—I have not made out the general average; it varies.

1665. What is the highest, and what is the lowest?

lowest?—The highest seems to be 1 s. per half-year, and the lowest 7½ d.

1666. That does not include the institutions?—Yes; that does include everything.

1667. The average would be something about 10 d. or 11 d. round the county each half-year?—Yes, it would be, I should say, something about that.

1668. *Earl of Mayo.*] With regard to the payment for roads, do you not think it is rather an absurd distinction now to make any difference in the payment for the maintenance of a road, because a mail cart happens to travel over it?—I have already given evidence that, in my opinion, inasmuch as the mail carts travel over but few roads, and those few not the most important, it is anomalous in the present state of things, but I think it would be advantageous if all the leading roads of a certain class in the county were apportioned between the county and the barony, in a similar manner to that which obtained with reference to the mail car roads.

1669. How would you make that distinction?—The single leading road from one town to another; you would probably define it to be a town of a certain amount of population; roads leading from a town to a harbour, or to a bathing place at the sea side, should also be included.

1670. By whose authority would you propose that that distinction should be made; by the grand jury or by the Government?—By the grand jury.

1671. By whose authority should those roads be defined, the maintenance of which is to be divided equally between the county at large and the barony?—It should be done by the county, and I see no disadvantage, if it were thought desirable, in submitting the roads to be considered as such to a baronial sessions, subject afterwards to be confirmed by the grand jury.

1672. As in the ordinary presentments?—Yes.

1673. *Colonel Forde.*] I do not think you explained, at least I do not quite understand you with reference to the prompt payment, how you would get sufficient funds to pay the contractors before the money was raised, as at present, from the county cess?—In the county of Antrim there is a sum which amounts, I think, to 13,000 *l.* In most of the counties in Ireland there are sums which vary from 13,000 *l.* down to 6,000 *l.* or 8,000 *l.* That is to the credit of the county, and there is a somewhat equal sum to that constantly lying by, some portion of it bearing interest at the rate of 2½ per cent., or some small per-centage in exchequer bills, and another portion of it in the hands of the treasurer, subject to his control. That would furnish more than an ample sum for the charges.

1674. How is it that in Antrim it is such a large account as that, while in the treasurer's accounts for the county Down I see that the balance with the treasurer is 2,987 *l.* 16 s. 7 d., with a balance in exchequer bills of 4,200 *l.*, which together is about 7,000 *l.* That would not defray your payments between one assize and another?—I do not at all propose to defray the entire payments, only to provide for those cases in which it would be desirable to do it.

1675. You have the power now to do so?—No; there is the power to make an order, but you may not have the money to make the payment with.

1676. Do not the grand jury make the order that it is to be paid out of the surplus funds?—That is precisely what I want to do. There has been an expression of opinion on the subject that the treasurers may do so, but it is open to some measure of doubt, and what is desirable is to remove any question of doubt there may be on the matter, and to make it quite plain by law that there is to be this power.

1677. We consider in the County Down that we have that power, and we do it as far as practicable. Do not you think that it would be advantageous to other counties supposing they could in most instances give, we will say, two-thirds payment between the assizes, say, on the certificate of the county surveyor. Could not contracts be got at a cheaper rate on those terms than they are now, contractors having to wait for the money for so long a time?—You have that power, under the present law, where the amount exceeds 20 *l.* The grand jury, at the time they make the presentment, may, if they please, make an order directing the treasurer to pay on the certificate of a county surveyor to the amount of three-fourths of the contract. Then all you want is, that there shall be funds to meet such certificates, and in any county under the present law there is the means in respect to contracts of an amount above 20 *l.*, of paying between the assizes to the extent of three-fourths, the county surveyor certifying that more than the amount of the works certified has been executed.

1678. Would it not be an advantage to the county to have that more defined, and more used?—They have the power, and though it is a slumbering power now, they may use it if they please.

1679. Except that the money is not sufficient at present?—If there be any doubt as to there being in any county money sufficient for the purpose, that could be met by some power to maintain a kind of floating sum. If in any county, owing to the way in which it is managed, there should not be funds sufficient to carry out the intermediate payments to the extent which was in that county considered desirable, I should see no objection to there being a power to make a presentment, which would be, as it were, to keep up a floating balance in the county of the amount considered desirable.

1680. In your county, how soon do they commence, after each assize, to collect the county cess?—I really do not know.

1681. If the money were collected immediately after the assizes for which the levy is made and lodged in the treasurer's hands, would not that place the county in funds to meet the demands which would, on the suggestion I gave you, be necessary?—No doubt, it would.

1682. Do you think it would be an advantage or not?—Yes, I certainly think it would.

1683. Would it be a corresponding advantage; would you get the contracts taken at a less amount?—There is no doubt whatever that if a contractor knows, should he perform his contract faithfully and well, that a provision has been made by which he can obtain prompt payment, and without waiting for the money for a length of time, no doubt the result would be eventually a diminution of the cost.

1684. You think a power given in any new law that would be proposed would be an advantage?—I do.

1685. I need not ask you about holding sessions outside the particular barony, for your opinion was distinct that that power should be given to the

the grand jury, having been approved of before at the sessions?—Yes. I have already given an opinion that upon a proper case being made out, it would be desirable that there should be that power.

1686. Lord Mayo asked you a question about who should determine which should be the leading roads; that was the great difficulty in my mind in your proposition as to half to the county and half to the barony?—I have already mentioned that I think it might be subjected to the determination and approval at the sessions, and confirmation by the grand jury, with a power of revising it from time to time as occasion might arise.

1687. *Sir Charles Lanyon.*] You also said with reference to population?—Yes. If you say from market town to market town, there are a great number of towns not market towns, which might as fairly be included as many which are market towns.

1688. Colonel *Forde.*] In the course of your examination as to assistant surveyors, you threw out a suggestion that they would require a larger salary than they get now, which is an augmented one by the last Act?—Yes.

1689. Do you consider that that augmentation of their salaries is not sufficient?—I do; the whole of the evidence given in the Select Committee to which I have referred is in that direction.

1690. On those recommendations they got that augmentation?—The evidence of Sir Richard Griffith, for instance, is that it should be from 80*l.* to 120*l.* per annum.

1691. You said something about a county surveyor originating new works?—No, I think not.

1692. I understood you in your direct examination by Sir Charles Lanyon to say that the county surveyor should originate new works?—No.

1693. Do you think that the county surveyor should originate new works?—What do you mean by new works?

1694. New roads?—Certainly not.

1695. Nor cutting down hills, and filling hollows?—No; I think that the county surveyor, in reference to any of the important improvements of that kind, naturally would be consulted, as I have recently been in my county, in reference to the improvement of one, the leading road from Ballymena to Glenarm, by persons desirous of having it improved. I gave them my opinion on the subject, and they brought forward the application.

1696. You would not think it advisable that the county surveyor should be empowered to originate those new works?—Situated as the country now is, I certainly do not. It might have been a question originally when the grand jury was first introduced into the country, but not in the state in which the works are now in Antrim, all the leading works having been executed.

1697. You would confine them to simple things which were forgotten at the road sessions?—Yes, works in which the people have a direct interest; works of importance, which are indispensably required.

1698. As to the fees, you said you thought it would be right that the fees to the secretaries of the grand jury should be discontinued?—I think it would be an advantage that they should get salaries commensurate with the duties of their offices. In the large counties their expenses are very considerable. In the county of Antrim the salaries are comparatively very small, and the outgoings from the office are very considerable.

1699. It was suggested by one witness that the fees should still be the same as at present, but collected by stamps to go to the credit of the county, and the secretaries of the grand jury should be paid an extra salary for the loss of their present fees. Would that meet the difficulty do you think?—That is really collecting money from the contractors with one hand, to be returned with the other. I do not see any great advantage in it.

1700. Do you think you would get a contract one half-penny less by not having those fees than you do now by having them, and is it not a great means of keeping out parties from contracting which the sessions and grand jury would not like to have as contractors?—Well, it may be of use in that point of view.

1701. I think I understood you to say that you would make the secretary in his office fill up all the different forms, the same as is done now, only without the fees?—There are a certain number of forms which it appears to me, in the interest of the public, should be brought in in a regular and proper form, and in such a way as that they would be fit to be presented before the different courts, and not be subject to the chances to which they would be subject if they were filled up by any person in the country.

1702. And that that should rest as at present in the secretary's office?—I think so.

1703. Earl of *Mayo.*] There was an Act passed, I think, in 1862, to amend the laws with regard to the appointment of county surveyors?—Yes.

1704. By that Act it is provided that "whenever a vacancy shall occur in the office of county surveyor, an examination of all persons desirous to fill the appointment shall be held in Dublin by the Civil Service Commissioners;" do you think that is a good mode of testing the qualifications of the various candidates?—Does your question refer to the Board of Examiners or to the mode in which the examination is to be held?

1705. I should like to have your opinion upon both those points?—I have already mentioned that in my opinion the examination which is provided there would be extremely inconvenient, there being one examination for each vacancy, it being competent for the examiners to return a list of as many persons out of that examination as they may consider qualified for the office, while ultimately the appointment is to be made by the Lord Lieutenant out of that list, his appointment being subject to the approval of the grand jury. I mentioned that if a vacancy occurred at this time of the year, prior to the spring assizes, the result of that might be that there would be no officer to certify the accounts at the spring assizes, the contractors would, in consequence, not be entitled to payment, and there would be no power of providing payment for them virtually for a period of 10 months.

1706. Then you think it would be desirable to alter the Act in this way: that whenever a vacancy takes place, an examination should be held for the next vacancy, so that there would be always a candidate for the office ready to take it at a moment's notice?—I would go even further than that; I would provide that there should be a limited list, but would not go to the extreme of of having a very long list; it would be to the advantage of the public that there should be a limited list in many points of view; you would get a far better class of persons to come forward to compete if they are not simply competing for a single prize. If you calculate the average of chances as to the vacancies in the office, you would find that that list, if limited to three or four, would not last more than a couple of years. You cannot suppose that a person who would be found fully qualified at an examination of that kind would cease to be qualified at the end of two or three years, which time it would be at the outside before he would be reached; you would get a far greater number of desirable persons to compete. If as at present, as I apprehend, you are restricted to a single appointment from each examination, and if that appointment is not to be from the head of the list but is to be subject to a number of contingencies, the persons whom you ought to desire to see come forward as candidates, those persons who have qualified themselves well by their previous education for the profession, and who have practised the profession for some time and gained some practical experience, will not come forward to the examination at all.

1707. Do not you think that if the appointment is to be by competition, in that case the best answerer ought always to get the appointment?—Certainly; if it is to be a competitive examination, and there is to be only one prize, certainly the person who is at the head of the list ought to get the appointment; but I do say in reference to the appointment and the examination for the office of county surveyor, that it is not desirable for the public that there should be an examination to which there would be only one prize, even supposing that you remove from the law all uncertainty as to the person at the top of the list getting the appointment.

1708. Surely you could not hold a competitive examination except the result of it was to be that the qualifications of the best man should be tested and determined, and that he should be placed at the head of the list. You do not propose then to hold a general examination, which would last for some years?—I would limit it to what you suppose would provide for two or three years; even if you had only three upon the list I would certainly go to that extent.

1709. Why do you think that there should be a difference made in competitive examinations for the appointment of a county surveyor and a competitive examination for any other office; I quite understand your reason in point of time, that there should always be one man in reserve, because the county surveyor may die immediately before the assizes, and great public inconvenience might ensue, unless there was an immediate power to fill up the appointment in the course of a few days, but I cannot understand your reason for making the result of this competitive examination with regard to the county surveyor different from the result of the competitive examination for any other office?—For most of the other offices, for a great number of them certainly, it is not the case that there is but one prize, for instance, for the civil service of India, and for the Royal Engineers' Department.

1710. Why do you think you would get a greater number of candidates for a list, such as you refer to, than for one appointment?—Because their chance of a prize is greater, the chance of recompense for submitting themselves to the ordeal, which an examination of that kind is, is greater; you do not want to get for county surveyors persons fresh from Trinity College or any other college; such persons you would have reason to suppose would not be in a position to go at once into the charge of a county as county surveyor, which office probably requires as much as any other, not mere book knowledge, or the knowledge which is to be obtained of theoretical matters, but practical knowledge and experience in dealing with men, and the management of works.

1711. *Chairman.*] You would not have it depend merely upon the result of a competitive examination?—I should not in that point of view.

1712. *Earl of Mayo.*] Your opinion I gather is that there should be a testing examination held at stated intervals, and that from the number of candidates properly tested and qualified, the Lord Lieutenant should select a county surveyor according to his discretion; is that the way you think county surveyors ought to be appointed?—Yes; the list should be a limited one; I should say a list of three. There is one other point, with reference to the necessity of having a list, which I have not referred to, and that is that county surveyors under the present law are provided with the means of providing a deputy in the case of illness; that deputy must be a person who has obtained a qualification for the office of county surveyor. If that power of appointing a deputy, under certain circumstances, is to be retained, you must either give the county surveyor the power of appointing a person who has not obtained that qualification, or you must maintain at least a list of a moderate amount.

1713. That was under the old Act?—That was under the old Act, but it is unrepealed.

1714. It is not in this Act?—But it has not been repealed.

1715. You propose to go back very much to the old system of keeping a list of a certain number. The objection you have to the old system is that the list was too numerous, and that therefore men were very often old men, and past their work, before it came to be their turn to be appointed?—It may be so; I think you might get a better person by having an examination at a regular period before the list would be exhausted; but with the greater inducement that you afford to proper persons to come to the examination by having three prizes instead of one, I am satisfied the result would be to give you a better class of officers, and you would get rid of these two difficulties, the one as to being able to put an officer at once into office when a vacancy occurs, and of having a person to provide for the contingency of a county surveyor being temporarily ill, which I think is a very reasonable provision.

1716. Do not you think that if a Government, in selecting these county surveyors, were to depart from the qualifications of merit, as returned by the Civil Service Commissioners, and appoint to a county surveyorship a man who had not passed as good an examination as another, you would give rise to very great jealousy and very great objections, and that the man who had answered best being left out would have a very just cause of complaint?—It would surely get rid of that difficulty if you made it a positive enactment that without the intervention of the Lord Lieutenant at all, if the Civil Service Commissioners returned 1, 2, 3, that they should be the persons to receive appointments, if they are willing to accept them.

them, in the order of these numbers as vacancies occurred.

1717. I apprehend that the reason that the Act was framed in this way was that it was never intended or contemplated that the Government should not take the best answerer, but that it left to the Lord Lieutenant a discretion to reject a man on the score of character, or want of health, or some cause of that kind. In ordinary competitive examinations they are by a nomination. The Government nominates the candidates, and then the best answerer is selected, as a matter of course; but here the examination is open to the whole world; no original nomination is required, and therefore some discretion must be left with the Government to prevent men who may have answered well, but who still may otherwise be ineligible, from being appointed?—Yes; that did not strike me at the time, but, unquestionably, it is a very fair view.

1718. Therefore I apprehend that no Government would ever feel themselves satisfied in departing from the rule of merit unless there was some very strong objection to the candidate in point of character or of health?—Yes.

1719. The new system, I believe, has not yet come into operation?—It has not.

1720. Do you know whether there is still a name on the old list?—There is not.

1721. *Chairman*.] How has the old system been worked in reference to that point which Lord Mayo has just referred to; has it been a matter of course to appoint those who have passed the test examination hitherto when their turn came, when a vacancy offered?—It has.

1722. Irrespective of other considerations?—I believe that with two exceptions the list has been strictly adhered to in the order of merit.

1723. Have there been no cases in which persons have been set aside upon other grounds?—None whatever, I believe.

1724. Your proposal, as I understand it, is not that all of the candidates offering themselves who should come up to a certain standard should obtain a certificate, because that would bring it back to the old system in fact, but that out of all the candidates the three best answerers should obtain those professional certificates?—Yes.

1725. And should be appointed to vacancies in the order of their merit, I suppose?—Yes. I fully appreciate the importance of having a power residing in the Lord Lieutenant to reject a person as to whom there was something objectionable, inasmuch as there has been no nomination for the candidature; I think if disqualifying circumstances were brought to the knowledge of the Lord Lieutenant, he should have a power of exercising a discretion in the matter.

1726. Under the old system has there been any practical nomination for examination beforehand?—None whatever.

1727. Of course another method might be that such nomination should take place, and that before the candidate is permitted to enter the examination before the Civil Service Commissioners he should satisfy the Lord Lieutenant of his character, health, and so on?—Of course.

1728. What class of persons have you as assistants in the county Antrim?—Some of them at the present time are persons who have been in office for a very considerable length of time who were overseers in connection with the new works being executed in the county; there are several of that class; there are some who have been appointed by me in later times, persons of better education since the increase of the amount of the salary.

A. Tate, Esq., C.E.

[illegible] April 1868.

1729. Do you find much difficulty in obtaining properly qualified assistants?—I do; I have frequently put advertisements in the newspapers for the purpose of getting them, and I find I can get plenty of persons whom you must regard only as birds of passage, who have very high educational qualifications without practical experience; those, in my opinion, are not the class of persons from whom desirable assistants can be obtained. They only look to the appointment as a stepping stone to something better, and take it as a temporary expedient while looking for something better. No change in the office of an assistant in a county can take place, no matter if it is to get a better officer, but at the time of the change there will be a disadvantage. The transfer from the one officer to the other is always attended with disadvantage, therefore any frequent changes in the office would be extremely undesirable.

1730. You would wish to obtain persons who would make it their permanent employment?—Yes.

1731. *Earl of Mayo*.] But you would hardly be able to get men for the salary which the county would be willing to give to an assistant surveyor, who would be competent and qualified hereafter to get on to be a county surveyor?—Certainly not.

1732. Therefore the recommendation that was made, that the assistant surveyor should be a sort of apprentice, and a man in the position to fill the county surveyorship afterwards, could not be carried out?—It could not; it is not the class of persons from which to get assistants at all. I have over and over again applications from persons of that kind, some of whom have got their C.E. diploma at Trinity College, and perhaps the degree of A.B., who would be glad to get an appointment to qualify them to go forward for the examination for county surveyor. No doubt it would be a desirable thing for them to obtain it, but it would generally be against the interests of the public.

1733. The man who is the best for an assistant county surveyor, I should apprehend, is a better class of pretty well educated steward or bailiff?—Just so; who has experience in the management of men, and who has a limited amount of education.

1734. But it is not necessary that an assistant surveyor should be an engineer?—There are some particular districts in which a greater amount of engineering knowledge is requisite than in others. If you take a plain district, where the new works are but seldom occurring, you do not require a person of that class. There are other districts, where a considerable amount of new work would be going on, where you would require such a person.

1735. *Chairman*.] You draw a wide distinction between an assistant and a deputy surveyor?—The assistant is often called a deputy surveyor, but there is no such permanent office as deputy surveyor.

1736. What class of persons have you as contractors, generally speaking, in the county Antrim?—Well, for the road maintenance, they are from the class of small farmers. For the works of improvement they are persons of a better class, who are able to take contracts of a considerable amount, up to 7,000 *l.* and 8,000 *l.* sometimes. At present there are two contracts, each of the amount of of 8,300 *l*. The contractors who come forward for those works have now in their charge probably works to the amount of 12,000 *l*. or 14,000 *l*.

1737. Have you found any difficulty in obtaining proper contractors?—At times there has been rather a difficulty of late years. Owing to the impetus that was given to the growth of flax in the north, and the prosperity of the linen trade, it has been rather more difficult during the last three years to obtain contractors, greater indisposition to tender. They have found more profitable work elsewhere; and then again the value of labour makes a difference.

1738. Have you many roads in your own hands, as county surveyor?—Very few indeed.

1739. Do you approve of that system, of the county surveyor taking charge of roads?—I think it should only be to meet a public convenience. As the law is one that provides for a contract system that it should be the exception, and the exception is simply to prevent what would otherwise be a public inconvenience. The county surveyor cannot with advantage take charge of county works, if it is to be done in a desultory manner, here and there, he cannot do it without disadvantage to the public. He may come forward to prevent an inconvenience occurring, but he is not in a favourable position; certainly not in anything like the favourable position in which he would be, if the system obtained general currency in any district, where, from any circumstances whatever, he had a large amount of work in his hands, then he could raise up machinery to have them executed in a beneficial way to the county.

1740. Do you find that you repair these roads at cost greater or less than the cost at which they would be repaired under the contract system?—If I had the management of an entire district, I could maintain them certainly at very much less cost, with prompt payment, and more efficiently than the contract system now. That is my opinion and my experience in reference to it, for I had a very large amount of it at one time; but if it is to be a case where the contract system generally prevails, with here and there isolated works in the charge of the surveyor, and with no machinery ready for the purpose, then it would be unquestionably attended with disadvantage.

1741. I want to ask a question about the law and the system as to the obtaining of materials: what compulsory power has a contractor to obtain materials?—Certain lands being excepted within which he has no power to go, he may go into any place, or he may propose to go into any place, for the purpose of raising materials; if he can agree with the occupier of the ground, he may do so. If he cannot agree, he may go to the petty sessions court of the district, to any neighbouring magistrate, and say to him, "I require to enter this land for the purpose of obtaining materials for this county work, as the contractor for it." If he satisfies the magistrate that that is the proper place for him to go to, and that the materials cannot be conveniently got elsewhere, the magistrate may give him an order. Then the further process is that there are to be three appraisers, one nominated by the magistrate, one by the occupier of the ground, and one by the contractor or surveyor. There is a compulsory power on the part of the land occupier or land owner to require a surveyor or contractor to nominate his appraiser; but there is no corresponding power on the part of the contractor, and in consequence of that deficiency the section may work badly in a variety of cases.

1742. Earl of *Mayo*.] Is there much difficulty about it?—Yes, frequently. There is this further difficulty, which I alluded to before, that the words "and other materials," are held to be not sufficient to embrace all the materials which are required for county works, and it would be desirable to use terms which shall not be ambiguous.

1743. *Chairman*.] The magistrates, then, can prohibit a contractor from quarrying at a certain spot, or in a certain field, if they thought it advisable or fair to the occupier?—They can; there is this other phrase in connection with that power, which I think also would be better expressed more explicitly. It is this, "Quarries heretofore drained, with liberty to work." There are words of that kind which may prevent a surveyor or contractor from having power to enter lands for that purpose, and in certain cases they do not work advantageously. There may be, as it were, an advantage taken, by means of that phrase, for the purpose of rendering the Act powerless.

1744. Earl of *Mayo*.] I suppose those cases generally arise in new works; they do not arise often with regard to the repairs of the old roads?—Not so frequently, but they do from time to time; it is of very great importance in certain districts where quarries of commercial value are frequent.

1745. Colonel *Forde*.] With reference to the appraiser; if the man whose land it is refuses to appoint an appraiser, how would you propose that that appraiser should be appointed; would you leave it in the power of the magistrate to appoint one in his behalf?—I think so.

1746. To remove the difficulty which you speak of?—Yes; I think that would be the better way if there should be a disagreement between the two.

1747. Colonel *Cooper*.] Do you think the contract system an expensive one for keeping up roads?—I think it would be possible to devise a system which would be less expensive.

1748. Is it generally suited to Ireland, throughout the country?—No; I think the tendency of the country and the disposition is against such an extent of centralisation as would be necessary in carrying out that system; but, nevertheless, I am quite satisfied that if you had a system of centralisation and a system of competent engineers, with subordinates under them, and trained workmen all over the country, and funds to provide payment for them on a scale of economy and efficiency, you might have the thing better done than at present.

1749. And cheaper?—And cheaper.

1750. Is there a different system at Dublin; where did you get your experience?—Partly in the county of Dublin, because I was there at the time that its present Grand Jury Law was introduced in the first instance. Owing to there being a total change in the system, there were no persons who came forward for a considerable length of time to undertake contracts at all; and virtually the county surveyors had to take charge of the entire works; otherwise, I also had the experience in it by having been the surveyor to several turnpike trusts in connection with which that system prevailed, where there were fortnightly payments; I was acting as engineer on the road from Dublin to Dunleer, on the Malahide road, and the Howth road, on each of them I had that system at work.

1751. And

1751. And you think those roads were maintained cheaper than they have subsequently been?—Certainly.

1752. *Earl of Mayo.*] Do you mean to say, from your experience, turnpike trusts were able to maintain their roads in good order, cheaper than they would have been under the contract system adopted by the counties?—I certainly do; I think, if you have prompt payments, which the turnpike laws gave, for the accounts were paid fortnightly, and proper officers to have the maintenance carried out, and trained overseers and trained workmen, you would have it better done and cheaper done; I am perfectly certain of that, for I had practical demonstration of it.

1753. You think if the grand jury system were so altered that payment might be made immediately on the completion of the work, there would be a great saving to the county?—Yes; but that would still be carrying on a contract system. With the law now so clearly for the contract system, and with the temper of the country, you never could have a general system which requires so much centralisation. But at the same time my opinion is clear that, with good officers, you could have cheaper and more efficient work, if you had prompt payments and regular trained assistants.

A. Tate, Esq., C.E.

[illegible] April [illegible].

1754. *Sir Charles Lanyon.*] With reference to the apportioning of the grand jury cess at each assizes, at the present time the grand juries generally present about equal sums at each assizes. Now it would be very much to the advantage of the cess-payers if that amount were differently proportioned. For instance, supposing a certain sum were raised for the repair of a road by the year, say 100 *l.* a year, that two-fifths of that should should be raised at the spring assizes, and three-fifths at the summer assizes, to make it press very much easier upon the cess-payers of the district?—I think it is very likely that it would.

1755. And it would not interfere in any shape or way with public interests, because the men generally are never entitled to half the money at the summer assizes. At the summer assizes the men are not prepared to receive half their salaries. You very frequently have to give the two half years at the spring assizes?—Yes, you can provide what you propose under the present law. It is so arranged, I believe, in the county of Down, or something similar.

Friday, 1st *May* 1868.

MEMBERS PRESENT:

Mr. Blake.	Mr. Herbert.
Mr. Dawson.	Mr. Kendall.
Colonel Forde.	Sir Charles Lanyon.
Mr. Chichester Fortescue.	Mr. Maguire.
Colonel French.	Earl of Mayo.
Mr. Gregory.	Sir Colman O'Loghlen.

Mr. CHICHESTER FORTESCUE, IN THE CHAIR.

FRANCIS AUGUSTINE LEIGH, Esq., called in; and Examined.

F. A. Leigh, Esq.

1 May 1868.

1756. *Chairman*.] I BELIEVE you were last year the High Sheriff of the county of Wexford?—Yes.

1757. I believe a few years ago you were a member of an association for the purpose of procuring a reform of the grand jury laws?—I was.

1758. The report of that association which was printed in the year 1862, was signed by you as chairman of the meeting?—Yes; I was chairman of the meeting when the resolutions were drawn up.

1759. I believe you are of opinion that very considerable alterations ought to take place in the present system of grand jury laws?—I am.

1760. What is your opinion as to the desirability of separating the criminal from the fiscal functions of the grand jury?—I think it is most necessary and desirable that the grand jury should be confined to their originally intended functions, which were to examine into the different criminal matters and the indictments, as I believe is the case in England.

1761. What kind of body would you propose to substitute for the grand jury in its fiscal functions?—A county board.

1762. How would you propose to constitute such board?—On the same principle, very nearly, as the Poor Law Boards are constituted; so many magistrates, the highest rated magistrates in a barony, joined with the same number of elected cesspayers rated at a certain amount.

1763. Do you consider that the ratepayers are now sufficiently represented at the baronial presentment sessions?—I do not.

1764. What is your reason for so thinking?—One reason is, that they can be swamped by the attendance of magistrates from all parts of the county; magistrates not connected with that particular barony have the power of attending.

1765. The number of magistrates who may attend is unlimited?—It is.

1766. What alteration would you propose in the constitution of the baronial sessions?—As at present.

1767. Yes?—I would propose that a certain number of magistrates, the number to be decided upon by the Lord Lieutenant, should be named in each barony, and that an equal number, not the highest rated cesspayers, but, of cesspayers rated above a certain amount, should be chosen in the same way that they are chosen at present for the Board of Guardians, by election in conjunction with them.

1768. What is your experience, as a magistrate, of the working of presentment sessions?—There is rather an indifference on the part of the cesspayers. They do not feel that they have sufficient power.

1769. Do the cesspayers attend regularly and fully in your county?—Some do and some do not. I have a presentment list here.

1770. As a general rule, do you consider their attendance good or bad?—It depends very much on circumstances, but I know they are very much deterred by the uncertainty of their being called.

1771. How do you find the attendance of magistrates to be in your county?—Very good.

1772. Do you know what amount of attendance of magistrates and cesspayers there is in your county at the county at large sessions?—I see by reference to this last presentment that the attendance has been very small, but I have known large numbers of magistrates attend. In November 1867 there were five magistrates and four cesspayers.

1773. *Colonel French*.] How many baronies have you?—Ten.

1774. *Chairman*.] Is there any amount of county expenditure which never comes before the associated cesspayers at presentment sessions?—About one-half.

1775. What is the nature of that expenditure?—A great many of them of course are imperative, such as the money paid for the support of buildings and salaries. There is a poundage given to collectors. Cesspayers have no voice in that matter. I would place under that head malicious injuries, increase of salaries, support of county infirmary, county lunatic asylums, and building and repairing our diocesan schools. Under those heads it is about one-half, I think, in Ireland, and the same in my county, and roads are about one-half. They are the only things which come before the cesspayers, in fact.

1776. Among these items how many are

not imperative presentments?—Salaries are imperative, but fixing the amount is left with the grand jury. The section is Section 41 of the Act. Under that Act our county surveyor's salary, which I give as an instance, not that he did not deserve it, was doubled. Now the cesspayers have not a voice in that matter.

1777. I asked you how many of those items did not come under the head of compulsory presentments?—Salaries, because they have been increased; poundage to collectors, malicious injuries, and county infirmary. I must correct myself. The county infirmary comes before the county sessions.

1778. Colonel *French*.] But lunatic asylums do not?—No. The county infirmary only comes before the county at large.

1779. *Chairman*.] When you say that the grand jury can increase the salaries of the county officers, you mean within the maximum fixed by the Act of Parliament?—Yes, but not in the case of poundage to collectors.

1780. What is your opinion with regard to the present incidence of the county rate?—I think, as at present, it is unjust. You allude, I suppose, to the division of the rate between them?

1781. I allude to the mode in which it is levied?—Under the present system I think it is unjust.

1782. What change are you in favour of?—That will depend on the change in the law. If the system is to remain as it is, I would suggest the system which is carried out in Scotland, which is, that the tenant pays half the expense of the roads. The feeling of the county is that they would have no objection to pay for the roads, but where the cess can be increased at the will of the grand jury, and the landlords are not obliged to pay the cess, they are dissatisfied.

1783. Mr. *Blake*.] Do you mean to say the grand jury can increase the cess?—No; I want to convey that it is not entirely the grand jury that pay the cess. The landlord need not pay any of the cess if he is not an occupier.

1784. *Chairman*.] Did you intend to draw a distinction between the two different classes of expenditure; the expenditure upon roads, and the expenditure upon permanent works and buildings?—The system in Scotland is that the tenant pays half on the roads only. I am given to understand so.

1785. The landlords, the heritors, paying the whole of the rate for other county purposes?—Exactly.

1786. Is that the system you would desire to introduce throughout Ireland?—If no change is made; but if a change is made so that the cesspayer has a voice in the levying of the money, I should say half should be paid by the landlord.

1787. That is, if a change such as you contemplate, were made?—Yes.

1788. Are there any other observations which you wish to address to the Committee?—I would only make this statement, that there is another class unrepresented by the present system, which is the property of Peers. A Peer has no representative on the grand jury, nor at presentment sessions.

1789. Colonel *French*.] Has he not an agent?—He is not necessarily a member of the grand jury.

1790. *Chairman*.] I do not think you have fully explained to the Committee the mode in which you would propose to constitute the county board which you suggest. Having described the baronial boards, such as you would propose them, will you tell the Committee how you propose to constitute the central county board?—Supposing the number appointed by the Lord Lieutenant to be four magistrates in each barony, there would therefore be four cesspayers elected, and from them I would take two magistrates and two cesspayers to form the County Board. That County Board would form themselves into a finance committee, superintendents of the jail, and governors of the lunatic asylum.

F. A. Leigh, Esq.

4 May 18[illegible].

1791. Then the County Board would consist of one-half of the Baronial Boards?—Yes; that is a mere matter of detail that might be settled; but I suppose that four magistrates would be named, that would be eight of each; taking 10 as the number of baronies, it would be 80. That might be too many. It would entirely depend on the number of magistrates the Lord Lieutenant would choose to make.

1792. Would you propose that each Baronial Board should elect a fixed number of representatives for the County Board?—Yes.

1793. The number of elected and *ex officio* members being always the same; that is your meaning?—Yes, it is.

1794. Colonel *French*.] How would you elect the Baronial Board itself?—By voting papers.

1795. The same as under the Poor Law?—Very similar to it.

1796. Mr. *Blake*.] You are in favour, you stated, of separating the fiscal from the criminal business of the grand jury, and leaving the grand juries as at present to be nominated by the sheriff for criminal purposes?—Precisely so.

1797. Then you would elect the Baronial Board in the first instance, by allowing the ratepayers of a certain qualification to send representatives into the County Board?—Precisely.

1798. And the magistrates of a certain qualification also to have representatives on the Board; is that not so?—Yes, the same number of representatives that the elected cesspayers have.

1799. How would you have the cesspayers elected; would it be by voting papers?—By voting papers, the same as the elected guardians.

1800. They to nominate from themselves two magistrates and two cesspayers to act on the County Board?—Supposing the number was eight.

1801. In your own county, for instance, how many would you have upon the County Board. How many baronies are there in your county?—There are 10 baronies; allowing eight for each barony, it would be 80.

1802. That is 80 for each Baronial Board?—No, for the County Board.

1803. If only four were sent in, only two magistrates and two cesspayers, it would be 40 instead of 80?—Yes.

1804. Have you settled in your own mind what the qualification should be for the voters; you have got Sir William Somerville's Bill?—Yes.

1805. And the Bill founded upon that Bill, which was subsequently brought in by myself?—Yes.

1806. Do you concur in the qualification contained in the schedule of that Bill at page 8?—That would be giving cumulative votes according to

F. A. Leigh, Esq.

1 May 1868.

to property. I do not see any objection to it; I will not pledge myself to that; it is a question I cannot enter upon.

1807. Would you have the County Board so formed a continuous Board?—Certainly.

1808. How would you have the members go out; would it be by rotation?—By one-half or one-third retiring every year.

1809. What do you consider would be the advantage of having a continuous Board. Would there be work for them to begin with?—Yes, as constituting the Highway Board, the superintendents of the gaol and governors of the lunatic asylum, which are at present continuous, and in case of any sudden thing arising in the county, such as the washing away of a bridge, which happened in my county lately, they would be there on the spot to refer to. They could also countersign the checks of the Baronial Boards, so as to advance money to the surveyor to carry on works or pay for works when completed; I see those advantages in it.

1810. If such a plan as you mentioned were carried out, you would still have the division of the rate between the landlord and the tenant in the case of the poor rates?—Yes, that would not be retrospective.

1811. Can you give any instance in your own county of the unsatisfactory working of the present system from your own experience?—You mean of the grand jury system?

1812. Yes; of the Baronial Sessions, for instance?—Not beyond what occurs in all parts of Ireland. I have known of magistrates coming from other parts and overwhelming the cesspayers in order to carry a point. There is one thing comes to my recollection, which is, that some years ago the cesspayers were dissatisfied with the amount of poundage that we paid, which, by the way, was contrary to the Act, section 148. We paid a shilling in the pound, and the cesspayers found fault with that, and formed an association to try and get it reduced. We took all the proper steps, and got counsel to argue the question.

1813. Colonel *French*.] It is a higher rate than usual?—That is the reason I referred you to section 148, because there 9 *d.* is the maximum, and we pay 1 *s.* I mention this as an instance. The cesspayers were rather indignant at this, and to prove that the thing could be done even lower than 1 *s.*, we got most unexceptionable collectors that could not be found fault with, with undeniable security, and they offered to do it all over the county at 6 *d.*, which is more than is paid for the collection of the poor rates or income tax, which is done at 5 *d.* We brought forward men capable and willing, and with ample security, to do it for 6 *d.*

1814. Under the 19th and 20th Victoria, you will find it can be increased to 1 *s.*?—I was not aware of that. This certainly was in force before the 19th and 20th Victoria.

1815. *Chairman*.] What is the date of the occurrence to which you refer?—As far back as 1860. The agitation against it was in 1860, but we paid it for years before. That I am positive of. Whether it was allowed or not by Act of Parliament, the cesspayers were dissatisfied with it, and we brought forward men willing to do it at 6 *d.* A compromise was made by the grand jury and the associated cess-payers, and it was agreed that it should be left at 9 *d.* as a final arrangement. Well, since then, it has been raised, without appealing to the cesspayers, to 1 *s.*

1816. Mr. *Blake*.] That is clearly against the Act of Parliament?—That is one proof how things can be done. It was raised to 1 *s.*, and the cesspayers were never consulted on the subject. That makes a difference of 450 *l.* a year in my county.

1817. Could you have got any eligible parties to perform it for a less sum?—Certainly. We brought men, one of whom is at present a baronial constable and collector of the cess, who offered to do it for 6 *d.*, and he was forced to take 9 *d.* Since then, as another proof, I may say that a baronial constable has taken another barony, and in the face of that they have raised it to 1 *s.*

1818. That is one instance?—That is an instance in which it comes to my knowledge that the cesspayers have not been consulted.

1819. Although the initiative of the expenditure must commence with the associated ratepayers, yet you state that in that and in other questions it is in the power of the grand jury afterwards to increase the expenditure considerably without any reference to the cesspayers at all?—Just so.

1820. Is it not also in their power to increase the size of gaols, and make considerable alterations in court houses without a reference to the cesspayers?—I am under the impression that that should come before the county at large sessions, but at the county at large sessions the matter is still more in the hands of the magistrates than it is at presentment sessions, for the number of cesspayers there cannot exceed 10, who must come from all parts of the county, whereas I have seen as many as 20 magistrates, and they can, of course, act together in a point of that sort.

1821. In your county is it the practice for the grand jury of a barony to select the highest rated cesspayers, or is it the practice to select, at their discretion, whom they choose to act in the presentment session of the barony?—Opinions are divided on that subject; some appoint the highest, that is leaving out those who served on the last occasion, and then they take the highest, thinking that is the law. I am aware that others do not think so. Opinions are divided as to the law on the subject.

1822. In your county do you find that the elected cesspayers act generally at the baronial sessions, or is it left very much in the hands of the magistrates?—They come, but I repeat what I said before, that there is a general feeling that the uncertainty of being called deters a great many from attending.

1823. Colonel *Forde*.] That is the baronial presentment sessions?—Yes.

1824. Because the county at large sessions is appointed by the baronial?—Yes, but I have answered that by stating that they can only number 10 coming from all parts of the county.

1825. Mr. *Blake*.] Being an active member of the Grand Jury Reform Association, you have been able to generally ascertain the opinions of the cesspayers of Ireland. Is it your opinion that the present system causes dissatisfaction among the ratepayers?—Yes, very great; I doubt whether there is any question that could be decided that would give more satisfaction generally to the people of Ireland, the cesspayers, than the settlement of the grand jury system.

1826. By having them elected?—By making such

such a change as would give them a fair share in the representation.

1827. Do you consider that the present system works so unsatisfactorily that a change such as you suggest is called for?—Such is my opinion, and such is the general opinion.

1828. Mr. *Dease*.] Of course, your system would do away altogether with the election of associated cess-payers, excepting through these baronial boards?—Yes, it would entirely take it out of the hands of the grand jury.

1829. Do you see any objection to those who are elected poor law guardians acting in the same capacity as associated cess-payers?—I have read that Bill, and I do not like it myself, nor was it adopted by the association with which I was mixed up.

1830. Do not you see any objection to having a plurality of elections in the same county?—It may add a little to the expense; it would be very trifling. The attendance would not be so constant and annoying as attending weekly at the board of guardians, and I think you would get a better class of men who would be glad to act in a baronial session.

1831. Of course, it would depend very much upon the grand jury of the county, but do you think you could secure a good attendance at the county sessions from that class; do you think there would be a sufficient attendance at the county sessions?—I can only speak of my own county, which is very well peopled; I cannot refer to the mountainous parts of Ireland.

1832. Do you know anything about the county of Londonderry?—I do not.

1833. Do you think that the collection of county cess and poor rates may be made by the same collector, and thereby cause a saving to the public?—As it is at present done in the county, it is collected very much by the same class of people. We have the baronial constables that we pay 1 s. to, and who only pay their deputies 4 d., in fact it is collected for 4 d. and the remainder he puts into his pocket. He is of a superior class to the generality, of course, but I doubt if he is above the class of men who collect our poor rates. I am speaking of our own county; in fact our poor rate collector collects our income-tax.

1834. Both kinds of public rates may be collected by the same individuals?—Yes, at a saving of one-half.

1835. And at the same time?—Yes.

1836. As you are in the habit of attending assizes regularly, I will ask you, have you heard many objections made to the attendance of the securities of baronial collectors, and do you consider it unnecessary?—To get their warrants signed?

1837. Yes?—I have heard objections.

1838. Do you think it is actually necessary that they should be present?—I have known cases in which they have not been present, and other people have been called upon immediately to do it, to make the thing in form and not to have delay.

1839. You do not think there is any hardship inflicted?—No, in our case particularly not, because our collectors pay the money in before the assizes.

1840. Have you heard any objections made at your grand jury as to the way in which coroners are at present paid, by a sliding scale of fees instead of a fixed salary?—No, I have not heard an objection made to it.

F. A. Leigh, Esq.

1 May 1868.

1841. The law is different in Ireland?—I am aware of the law.

1842. I suppose these matters are generally referred to a committee, to examine the coroner's account?—Yes, I have never heard an objection made.

1843. There is a strong feeling among the coroners themselves that they should have a fixed salary?—I daresay they would like it better, because their salary of course must be dependent very much upon circumstances, but I have not heard any objection.

1844. Are you satisfied with the law as it at present exists with regard to malicious injury, and the recovery?—No, that is one of the points to which I referred in answer to the question of the Chairman, that the grand jury have a power of ordering payments of money that do not come before the Presentment Sessions, and malicious injury is one instance.

1845. Do you think there is too wide a field at present for recovery of malicious injuries?—Malicious injury as the law stands at present only comes before the Presentment Sessions, I may say, as a matter of form, to see that the forms are complied with. If you refer to the section you will see that is the fact; I have not the number of the section, but I am positive of what I state.

1846. Colonel *French*.] To see that the notices are served regularly?—Yes; the words are, that they should endorse their opinion on the Bill. Suppose the forms are proved to have been complied with, but on its merits it is rejected at the Presentment Sessions; it then comes before the grand jury, and is passed; I have known cases of it.

1847. Mr. *Dease*.] I suppose there are not many flax scutching mills in the county of Wexford, are there?—Not many. There are some.

1848. It has been stated in evidence that the charges for the county lunatic asylum would be more properly borne by the poor rate than the county cess; have you formed any opinion on the subject?—There is an injustice in it for this reason; a pauper goes into the workhouse and he costs about 10 *l.* a-year, of which the landlord pays half, that is 5 *l.* Then the man becomes a lunatic, and he is sent to the lunatic asylum. He costs, we will say, 24 *l.* a-year, and the tenant pays all, which is a manifest injustice.

1849. Mr. *Maguire*.] What is the cost in the lunatic asylum?—I am not exactly binding myself; 20 *l.* or 24 *l.*

1850. Do you see any reason whatever, expediency or justice, why the tax should not be equally divided between the two parties?—No, I do not.

1851. Are you of opinion that a tax including all purposes should be divided equally between the occupier and the owner?—For all purposes of poor rate and cess.

1852. For all purposes of county cess, are you of opinion that this rate which is applicable to all purposes, such as roads, bridges, gaols, or whatever it may be, should be equally divided, unreservedly divided, between the owner and the occupier?—I see no objection. In that case the owner would have an advantage, for as I have stated before, nearly one half in every county all over Ireland goes to permanent improvements, so that

F. A. Leigh, Esq.

1 May 1868.

that even at half the landlord would be a gainer, the balance would be in his favour.

1853. Do you, in any item of expenditure, see any reason why there should be an exception made, and the charge not equally divided between the owner and occupier?—No, I do not.

1854. You think that they are equally interested, and that they should bear their share of the common burden?—Yes.

1855. That is your opinion?—Yes.

1856. Well now as to the feeling which exists, what means have you of knowing the feeling that prevails amongst the occupying classes who are the payers of this rate, at the present moment?—I was very much mixed up in this matter some six or eight years ago, on account of the agitation got up in my own county against the payment of this poundage; we had large meetings. I have here the headings of one of the petitions; we presented petitions to Parliament. This petition was signed by every cesspayer in this county. This refers to the county Wexford alone.

1857. When was this meeting held?—In 1862.

1858. That is the petition which emanated from the meeting?—Yes, and the general expression of the feeling over the county Wexford. It was signed by magistrates, and people of all classes.

1859. Was that petition numerously signed?—Very numerously.

1860. It was signed by different classes?—By all classes.

1861. What do you think was the number of signatures it had; had it a large number?—Very large; the petitions were presented by Mr. Macmahon. There were some thousands of signatures.

1862. Did it fairly represent the opinion of those who objected to the taxes throughout the county?—Most certainly. It was signed by grand jurors, and people of all classes.

1863. Now, will you read it?—This is the petition: "That within the last few years the sums annually levied for county cess in the County of Wexford have been quadrupled both in amount and in rate." I must correct that a little. It has not been quadrupled, because the county cess in the County Wexford, in 1850, was 23,000 *l.* a year; in 1862, it was about 36,000 *l.* "That the annual amount even exceeds 36,000 *l.*, and is increasing; that the system whereby county cess in Ireland is collected and expended by the grand jury, a body in the nomination of which the cesspayers have no voice, and who are not responsible to them, is most unfair to the cesspayers, and opposed to the first principles of the Constitution. That the ancient common law functions and mode of nomination of grand juries are wholly incompatible with any control over, or management of, public money by the same body. That the introduction through a *free* election of the popular element into the constitution of grand juries as forming part of a criminal court would be as dangerous to the lives and liberties of the people as the non-introduction thereof into their constitution as managers of public taxes is unjust to those by whom such taxes are paid. That the imposition of the county cess only upon the occupier of land is also both unfair and grievous. Your petitioners, therefore, most humbly pray your Lordships that it may be enacted, that the functions of all grand juries in Ireland be restricted to the limits within which alone they can usefully be exercised, and which alone appertained to them at common law, as part of a criminal court, and that all their other functions, including especially the levying, collecting, and expending of the county cess, be vested in one or more local Boards, elected by and responsible to the cesspayers; and also, that the liability to pay the county cess be henceforth imposed on the owners as well as the occupiers of land, in just proportion to their respective interests therein."

1864. Has the feeling represented in that petition in any way died away since then?—It still exists, but it has not manifested itself in any way. We took all the steps we could, and we gained nothing by it.

1865. As to the fact, has the feeling changed since?—No, it has not.

1866. Is the feeling as strong as ever?—As strong as ever.

1867. Is the conviction of what they imagine the injustice to be, as strong as when that petition was drawn up?—I think so.

1868. Does that fairly express the opinions of the occupiers who do pay this rent all through your county?—I pledge myself that is done.

1869. There is no exaggeration on your part, when you say the feeling is unanimous on the part of that body against the present system?—No.

1870. Can you see any possible evil that would result from the substitution of election for nomination; *free* election by those who pay the rates, instead of nomination?—I do not see any objection; the elective element would be kept in check by the magistrates, the rated occupiers.

1871. Do you see any reason why the one rate, the county cess, should not be divided as well as the poor-rate?—I do not.

1872. No particular evil results from the division in that latter case?—No.

1873. Have you heard complaints made that elected guardians did not perform their duties faithfully to those whom they represent under the Poor Law administration; do they perform their duties properly?—Yes, they do.

1874. You have heard no complaints against them?—It may be for non-attendance, or something of that sort; if by "faithfully" you mean honestly, I never did hear any complaints.

1875. I mean faithfully and honestly?—Yes.

1876. They wisely and justly administered the funds entrusted to their care?—Yes; I never heard any complaints, except for non-attendance.

1877. You talk of non-attendance, but is it not a fact that on the average the elected guardians attend better than the *ex officio* guardians?—Undoubtedly.

1878. You would not anticipate a failure of attendance if election were substituted for nomination in this case?—I would not.

1879. And you would take the fact that the elected guardians attend even better than the *ex officio* guardians, as a fair guarantee that the others would attend if appointed in the same way?—Yes, I do.

1880. As to elections, would there be any great difficulty in getting these people elected?—A trifling expenditure in sending round voting papers.

1881. There is no enormous expense?—It might be done by the constabulary for nothing. It is a question of detail.

1882. The elections at the present moment under

P. A. Leigh, Esq.

1 May 1868.

under the poor law are not very expensive?—They seldom occur.

1883. Even when they do occur, they are not expensive. Is it not a trifling matter altogether?—Yes, a few shillings.

1884. Is it worth taking into consideration?—No, I do not pledge myself to the amount.

1885. It is a small matter?—Yes.

1886. Not to be contrasted for a moment with the great object in view?—No.

1887. An honourable Member seemed to imply that there would be a general ferment; do you think that apprehension is justified, and that there would be this constant ferment occasioned by elections similar to those now under the poor law. Would there be constant ferment, *excitement*, or turmoil, or any inconvenience of the kind?—I never witnessed any ferment. Elections are very rare now in the poor law.

1888. But even when they do occur?—It may occur in towns.

1889. Suppose they do occur according to your experience, is there any particular excitement?—No.

1890. They are done very quietly?—Very quietly.

1891. Mr. *Dawson*.] I suppose there is some ferment attending all elections, Parliamentary elections, and other elections, is there not?—I only speak from my knowledge.

1892. Mr. *Maguire*.] Can there for a moment be any possible analogy between a contested Parliamentary election, and an election of a similar character to that of a poor law guardian?—I should think not.

1893. None whatever?—No.

1894. Mr. *Gregory*.] With regard to the county cess, the memorial which you have read proposes that it should be divided equally between the landlord and the tenant?—It does. That is the general feeling in my county.

1895. Is that irrespective of arrangements which are existing between the landlord and the tenant?—No, it is not to be retrospective.

1896. But in all future arrangements?—In all future arrangements. I express the feeling of the cesspayers, not my own opinion as a landlord.

1897. It contemplates that any arrangements which ought to take place with regard to the division of the county cess ought to have reference solely to future agreements?—To future agreements; to start from the time the Bill becomes law.

1898. I wish to ask you a question about those Boards; I think you propose that a baronial Board should be, as it were, the unit of representation?—Exactly.

1899. Then you propose that that Board shall be composed of four magistrates and four elected cesspayers?—I said the number was to be decided by, we will say, the Lord Lieutenant.

1900. You say that the magistrates should be named by the Lord Lieutenant?—I said the Lord Lieutenant, because it is in our report, but I do not pledge myself to it exactly.

1901. It is very important to know exactly the plan suggested; do you not think there would be rather a danger in a country where politics and religious differences run so high, if the magistrates upon Boards were to be named by the Lord Lieutenant?—I must correct myself; I stated that they should be rated above a certain amount; that would be a check.

1902. But even presuming that they were rated above a certain amount, do not you think there would be a danger of very considerable dissatisfaction if magistrates were chosen by the Lord Lieutenant, all of the same politics, even presuming them to be men of, perhaps, the highest position in the county?—Not more so than the nomination of the present magistrates, which can be turned to a political object; as it is, the nomination of magistrates may be made a political question; I do not anticipate that it would be more so, and I do not confine myself to nomination by the Lord Lieutenant.

1903. Supposing the Lord Lieutenant is to nominate, is he to nominate upon any particular principle, upon any special ground?—It might be done in this way; the highest rated magistrate.

1904. Then you might take that without the interference of the Lord Lieutenant?—Certainly; I mentioned the Lord Lieutenant because he is mentioned in Mr. Blake's Bill, but suppose it be taken exactly on the system of the poor law for the highest occupiers, I consider that would answer.

1905. *Chairman*.] Why should not a body of magistrates elect their own representatives out of their own number, supposing such a plan as yours were to be adopted?—I should say take the four highest, the number to be chosen to be settled by the Lord Lieutenant.

1906. Mr. *Gregory*.] If you take an arbitrary selection of that kind, and if the Lord Lieutenant were obliged to select the highest magistrates, might not you fall into the misfortune of having perhaps a number of absentees placed upon the Board?—Not more so than in the case of the *ex officio* magistrates at a Poor Law Board now.

1907. Quite so, but with regard to the *ex officio* magistrates there is always a number of magistrates, but in a baronial division might you not have two magistrates selected for that division who were absentees?—It might be so.

1908. And then the magistrates would not be represented at all?—It is open to that objection, of course. I would make them occupiers, not owners of land.

1909. What test of occupation would you give?—Paying cess.

1910. But still a man might pay cess personally and be an absentee?—That is true; it is open to that objection. I suppose he would not accept it then.

1911. Do you propose that the whole body of the magistrates and all the elected cesspayers in each barony should form a portion of the County Board or only a portion of them?—A portion of them. It would be too numerous if they were all included.

1912. How would you make the division in the Baronial Board, of who should form the County Board?—I would say either by election or by lot.

1913. You would have another election?—Well, say the ballot.

1914. Mr. *Blake*.] The Bill says "by lot"?—Yes.

1915. Mr. *Gregory*.] You say there are 10 baronies in the county; I suppose you can hardly have less than four from each barony go up to the County Board?—No.

1916. Two magistrates and two cesspayers?—Yes.

1917. Then you would have your County Board composed of 40?—Yes.

1918. Do you think that would be a very unwieldable

F. A. Leigh, Esq.

1 May 1868.

ageable Board?—Forty is the usual number of an elected Board of Guardians.

1919. Where would you have this board meet? —The county board should meet at the assize town, certainly during the time of the assizes, for the purpose of appealing or referring any question to the judge. It might be a question afterwards whether they should not meet at a more central spot between the assizes.

1920. That is a question of detail; you propose that this county board shall be in permanent sitting, do you not; that is to say, that it shall be permanent and liable to be occasionally called upon?—Yes; just so.

1921. Do you think you would find 40 elected cess-payers disposed to come from extreme ends of a large county to attend this board occasionally?—A quorum could be formed. They are not all obliged to attend.

1922. Do not you think the quorum that would be formed would be more likely to be formed of rich men, of the magistrates, rather than of the poorer classes who are the cess-payers?—No, I do not think so. I am alluding to my own county, the cess-payers in my own county.

1923. Yours is a smaller and more compact county, but in large and wild counties do you think these cess-payers would be able to give that attendance to the board that would be necessary to keep up their equality of influence?—They attend very regularly; they attend better than the *ex officio* members of the board of guardians.

1924. Then, again, you would divide these county boards into committees, would you not?—Exactly so.

1925. And you would have one portion of one committee for the gaols and another for the lunatic asylums?—Just so.

1926. I presume you would have the cess-payers also to take charge of the lunatic asylums? —A certain number.

1927. I presume the cess-payers all over the country have a great interest in the management of the lunatic asylums?—As they pay for it, undoubtedly they have.

1928. Therefore, you would not confine the superintendence of the lunatic asylums merely to cess-payers who lived in the neighbourhood of it, would you?—The subject would be in the hands of the committee in the same manner as the board of guardians choose their sub-committee of finance, house visiting, and other things. It would be in the hands of the committee, and naturally they would choose people who resided in the neighbourhood.

1929. The county Board would then select their own committees?—Yes.

1930. A committee, I presume, half and half? —Yes, certainly.

1931. I think one of the complaints you have made with regard to the present system is the liability of cess-payers to be swamped by the magistrates at Presentment Session?—It is open to that objection.

1932. Do you not think that with this county Board, the cess-payers having to come from these very great distances, would be more liable to be swamped by the magistrates?—I can only refer again to the Board of Guardians in which the attendance of elected members is better and more numerous than that of the *ex officio* members.

1933. Is not the area of a union very much smaller than the area of a very large county?—Certainly.

1934. I think you say that the cess-payers have no voice in malicious injuries, and you mention that all they had to inquire into was the subject of the form of procedure?—That is so.

1935. Are you not aware that in an Act of Parliament the Presentment Sessions are specially to inquire actually into the merits of the case?—Yes.

1936. Well then, have the cess-payers in this Presentment Session no voice in determining on the merits of the case; Section 134 is this, "And the Presentment shall examine into the serving and posting the notices of such application, and into the merits of the same, and the Chairman shall endorse their opinion thereon"?—Yes, that is all; I believe I am borne out in my interpretation of the Act.

1937. Are the Presentment Sessions desired by Act of Parliament to examine into the merits of the case?—Certainly, but their decision is not final.

1938. It goes up to the grand jury?—Yes.

1939. Have not the cess-payers still an appeal from the grand jury to the judge?—Certainly, but the objection to that is this, if you will allow me to give an instance. A case comes before the Presentment Session, which is argued as to the serving of the notice. All that the Presentment Session have to do is to certify that these notices have been served, or else it falls to the ground, and the chairman endorses their opinion as to the merits. But supposing they reject it, it comes before the grand jury and it is there argued; I have known it to be argued by counsel; and the cess-payers are unrepresented unless one of them chooses to put his hand into his pocket and pay for it. I know counsel have been employed, and a presentment passed for a large amount which has been rejected by the cess-payers; of course there is an appeal, but an appeal must be brought by a cess-payer, who must go to the trouble and expense of attending, and I think he must lodge 20 *l.*

1940. Do you approve of the principle, when a vacancy takes place for a barony constable, that the election for a new barony constable is to be in the barony in which the first quarter sessions are held, no matter how far that may be from the barony in which the vacancy occurred; or do you think it would be better that the election should take place in the barony in which the vacancy has occurred?—Yes; in that barony.

1941. Or at the quarter sessions nearest to the barony?—Certainly; I remember a case in which that put us to a very great deal of trouble.

1942. Colonel *Forde*.] As to the salary of the county surveyor; you say that his salary can be increased or diminished by the grand jury, irrespective of the voice of the associated cess-payers? —Yes; they are not called upon to give an opinion on the subject; they are not consulted.

1943. Where shall we find that?—It is Section 41 of the Act of Will. 4; I was not aware of a change in the Act.

1944. Even under the old Act of Will. 4, did not you know that the counties were classified, and attached to the Act, and the salaries according to classification settled in the Act which were to be given to each class of the county?—The words are, "The grand juries are hereby authorised and required to fix the amount of such salary for his

one

own proper county ?" the amount of salary is fixed by the grand jury.

1945. You say you did not know of the late Act ?—No; I am under a mistake; I was referred to the 6 & 7 Will. 4.

1946. Do you not know that within the last three years or so there has been a new Act passed, regulating the salary of the county surveyors and their assistants, and re-classifying the counties ?—Yes.

1947. And that before the salary could be increased, even under that Act, that the application should be made, in the first instance, to the grand jury at the summer assizes, that that application, if it was approved of, should go before the county at large sessions to be approved of there, and that approval being brought before the following assizes, to be finally approved of by the grand jury ?—Very well; admitting that is so, I do not consider that the cess-payer can get proper representation at the county at large sessions.

1948. Why not ?—Because there are only 10 considered to attend, and the magistrates come from all parts, and, as I have known, come to the number of 30.

1949. But they can come and express an opinion ?—Certainly.

1950. Do you mean to say that the opinion of the cess-payers would be over-ridden in that way, both by the magistrates and by the grand jury eventually ?—I have known instances of it; I have known every cess-payer except one, nine out of ten, object to an expense which was passed by the magistrates and then by the grand jury; that I can pledge myself to.

1951. Then you think that even now the cess-payers have not what you consider a sufficient voice in the raising of the salary of their county surveyor ?—I do not consider that even under the present Act they have.

1952. In your baronial sessions you propose by any new law to make the proprietors, or I will call them for shortness landlords, pay half the county cess ?—I see no objection to it.

1953. You will not give them, as I may say, half of the representation in the baronial sessions ?—They will get half of the representation, as much as they have under the Poor Law system; you cannot well divide it altogether.

1954. You limit the number of magistrates, and the number of cess-payers in each barony ?—Yes.

1955. So that therefore all the magistrates would not be taken in ?—No, they would not; no more are they on the board of guardians.

1956. Pretty nearly ?—I am speaking of my own county, where they are not.

1957. Look at the area of an electoral division, or a Poor Law union, and then look at the area of a barony. The area of an electoral division is a smaller area than that of a barony, most likely, whereas there is a tremendous representation ?—Not in my county; a poor law union generally extends over two baronies; I know of one that equals three baronies in extent; the number we will say is to be decided by the Lord Lieutenant.

1958. You go out of the principle of the Poor Law because you give the representation as much as you can ?—The representation of the Poor Law is settled as to the number; it is the magistrates that are named afterwards, according to the number of the elected Poor Law guardians. The only change would be that it would be naming the magistrates first; it might be settled equally well by the Lord Lieutenant, or a board naming the number of cess-payers, and then the magistrates being made equal. If the principle is carried, that is all I advocate, I do not pledge myself to the details of it.

F. A. Leigh, Esq.

1 May 18[illegible].

1959. Colonel *French*.] On what principle do you propose to bring the Lord Lieutenant into it ?—I do not pledge myself to state why the Lord Lieutenant should be the person named; I was asked to name somebody, and I referred to Mr. Blake's Bill, which names him.

1960. I put the question, because the Executive Government does not in any way contribute to the expenses of the county ?—No.

1961. Mr. *Blake*.] I wish to correct you in one thing; you referred to the Bill; you are under the erroneous impression that the mode laid down by that Bill was, that the Lord Lieutenant was to name the justices; that is not in the Bill. The Lord Lieutenant is to say how many cess-payers, and how many magistrates, and the magistrates were to elect their own representatives ?—Yes, that is so.

1962. Colonel *French*.] You commenced your evidence by stating, that in your opinion the criminal and fiscal business now discharged by the grand jury, should be separated ?—I did.

1963. That the criminal business should be left as at present to the grand jury, and you proposed to substitute a board for the grand jury which now discharges the fiscal business ?—Yes.

1964. Is it not your opinion, that at present the great economy which is one of the most remarkable features of the grand jury system, is owing to your having the first people resident in the county encouraged to discharge fiscal duties without any expense whatever ?—I will answer that in this way; I do not see that this would entail increased expenses on the county, and the increase of county cess in Ireland for the last 40 years, justifies me in thinking that the present system is not the correct one.

1965. Generally speaking your reasons for wishing to change the system is the experience of the last 40 years ?—Yes; and that there is taxation without representation. On the general principle.

1966. Now you propose to make a permanent County Board and permanent Baronial Boards ?—Baronial Boards to act as permanent Highway Boards to look after the roads.

1967. Do you expect that the persons appointed on the County Board, and on these Highway Boards, will take upon them to discharge the duties attached to them without any remuneration ?—You have the elected Board of Guardians as a proof that such can be done.

1968. Would it not be necessary to appoint secretaries to keep anything in business-like order, and other officers, that these baronial matters would require to carry out their views ?—You have a secretary at present who would act as secretary; you have a treasurer which it is contemplated to do away with; a treasurer would not be required.

1969. You have one secretary for the entire fiscal business of the county, but in this case you would have a number of secretaries ?—I do not see why it should increase the expense, or that the number of secretaries should be increased.

1970. Do you intend the secretary to go round to all the baronies as well as to discharge the permanent duties of the County Board ?—Not more

F. A. Leigh, Esq.

1 May 1868.

than he does at present at the presentment sessions.

1971. One of the principal objections you have made to the present system of cess-payers chosen by lot out of the list given by the grand jury is, that they are liable to be swamped by the magistrates?—In the first place there is an uncertainty about their being named, which reduces the attendance, and they have that feeling; I know that feeling exists that they can be swamped.

1972. When there is double the number, the doubts as to whether they will be taken by ballot in your opinion prevents them attending?—Yes, certainly.

1973. And in addition to that there is the fear in any measures that are necessary for the public business of the county of their being out-voted or overruled by the magistrates?—Yes, and especially at county at large sessions.

1974. Is it your experience that the attendance of the magistrates tends more to economy than to wasteful expenditure?—I am not inclined to express an opinion on the subject.

1975. Would not your objection be met by an alteration in the law; a short alteration that no magistrate should attend a session out of his district; would not that meet the entire of your objection as to the cess-payers being out-voted by magistrates?—It would as to baronial sessions.

1976. You have stated that there is a power in the grand jury to increase the county cess. You must be aware that the grand jury have no power to make any presentment that is not sent up to them by the baronial sessions, with the exception of the compulsory presentments on the subjects you have named?—I have named poundage and malicious injuries. The infirmary comes before the county at large sessions. I confine myself to the poundage and the malicious injuries.

1977. As to the malicious injuries, the expenditure cannot be said to be incurred by the grand jury. It comes first before the presentment sessions?—I think as to the merits, and to put their opinion on it.

1978. Well, there is nothing but the merits?—And the form.

1979. And according to the formula?—Yes.

1980. If the chairman at the sessions writes, "Disapproved. No malice," that does not bar the claimant?—No.

1981. He can go on to the grand jury?—Yes.

1982. And the foreman of the jury endorses the opinion on the back of the paper given by the baronial sessions, "No malice. Disapproved?"—He may do that, or not. The grand jury may either confirm or overrule the view of the presentment sessions.

1983. Is the judgment of the grand jury final?—No, it comes before the judge by appeal.

1984. Then by traverse, it can be tried before the judge?—Yes.

1985. That is final and conclusive?—Yes.

1986. Now you seem to be of opinion that the cess-payers have not sufficient power to control the expenditure. I want to ask you some questions in relation to the respective powers of the cess-payers and the grand jury. Is it not the case that any two cess-payers may originate a presentment for the repairs of any work, roads, or bridges, in the barony where they reside?—Yes, the application is bound to be made by two cess-payers.

1987. It is submitted to a court consisting of the associated cess-payers and the magistracy?—It is.

1988. The associated cess-payers have a double interest, have they not, in the consideration of each application made to them as farmers resident in it; it is material to their interests that the road should be in good order to get their produce to market?—Yes, certainly.

1989. And it is also material to them, as the cess is to be paid by them, that the work should be executed as economically as possible?—Yes.

1990. So that they have, as I say, this double interest in considering such demand upon them?—Certainly.

1991. They have the professional assistance of the county surveyor to state, first, whether the work is required; and, secondly, the amount of money that, in his opinion, would be sufficient to execute the works asked for?—Allow me to answer that question by saying, that the county surveyors object to that system. They do not get sufficient warning from the cess-payers to be able to report upon the necessity of some of these works.

1992. The want of sufficient warning is a question which ought, in any alteration of the law, to be fairly considered?—Certainly.

1993. Is it in your county the habit to print, for circulation, all the works proposed to be considered at the baronial sessions?—It is.

1994. If approved of by the cess-payers and associated magistrates, the work itself is not given to any particular person?—No; it is put to competition.

1995. The work, as arranged by the county surveyor, is put up to public tender?—Yes.

1996. The cess-payers or the magistrates have no power to appoint any particular person to execute that work?—By law, it is the lowest tender, except in cases of fraud.

1997. The law says, that the lowest tender, giving proper and sufficient security, has a right to undertake those works?—So it is stated.

1998. There is no favouritism which can exist under these circumstances to any particular person by the court of magistrates and cess-payers?—No.

1999. It is followed, then, by a second meeting; a meeting of the cess-payers to open the tenders?—Yes.

2000. And there they are obliged to declare the lowest tender and to submit the security for their approval?—Yes.

2001. If, then, all that preliminary has been carried out, it then, for the first time, comes before the grand jury at the assizes?—Yes.

2002. They have the professional advantage of the presence of the county surveyor. They have the advantage of all persons resident in the neighbourhood who know the nature of the work demanded, and whether it is required or not?—Yes.

2003. There is no necessity to summon any of those persons as witnesses. They are there on the criminal business. They are summoned the day or two before upon criminal business, and you have all their evidence without any expense being incurred?—If required, certainly.

2004. If a road is to be made near your place, you are there to say, "Well, I have seen that work, and it really requires to be done very much," or to say, "It does not require it"?—Yes.

2005. After the presentment has been laid before

before the grand jury and approved by the sessions, it is to be brought before the judge to, what they call, file the presentment?—Yes.

2006. Is it not in the power of any person, without employing any counsel, to get up his own account and challenge either the legality or the necessity of the work?—I believe he must deposit some 5 *l*. A person can do it.

2007. The question as to the legality of the presentment rests with the judge?—Yes.

2008. If he decides that the presentment is not legal he refuses to fiat it?—Yes.

2009. If the question comes on the merits it is decided by the petty jury?—Yes, I believe so.

2010. And their decision is final?—Yes.

2011. You have been asked some questions about the lunatic asylums, are you aware that the expenses of lunatic asylums are obliged to be levied by a compulsory order from Dublin Castle, by the grand jurors?—I am aware of that; that is for the building.

2012. For the building or for the maintenance?—Yes.

2013. And they have no power as a grand jury, as a body, of knowing how this expenditure is being carried on?—I believe not.

2014. Whether they approved of it or not, they must present?—Yes.

2015. Do not you think it is very inadvisable to continue that system of compulsory presentments?—I do.

2016. And in any alteration of the law, would it be your opinion that it would be advisable to modify or do away with that power altogether?—Certainly. I may state an instance in my own county in which it was proposed to devote a building to the purpose of a lunatic asylum, and it was the opinion of a great number of the magistrates and cess-payers that it should be done, and we were overruled.

2017. *Earl of Mayo*.] By whom?—I am not aware; it being compulsory, I cannot state the exact person it came from, whether from Government.

2018. What county was it?—County Wexford.

2019. When was it?—When the lunatic asylum was ordered to be built.

2020. Was the proposition, then, that you should have two lunatic asylums?—No.

2021. What was the proposal made by the county?—I did not say by the county, I said by a large body of the cess-payers and magistrates.

2022. What was proposed?—That two or three, I forget which, of our unions should be amalgamated, so that one of the poorhouses should be used as a lunatic asylum.

2023. *Colonel French*.] In answer to a question put you by the honourable Member for Cork, you stated that there was great unanimity of opinion amongst the cess-payers, but if half the cess was thrown upon the landlords it would be a relief to them; they would, I presume, be equally in favour of taking off the entire of it?—Certainly, more so.

2024. Do you believe that that would be the slightest advantage to them in a pecuniary way if half were taken?—That goes into a question of future settlements of land.

2025. You said you would not propose to interfere with existing arrangements?—No.

2026. Do you not think that the landlords would impose an additional rent in order to cover the charge even more than the amount that was paid by them, if they paid the entire of the county cess?—I cannot answer that.

2027. *Earl of Mayo*.] To revert to the case of the lunatic asylum in the county of Wexford, as I understand, you state now that the proposal made was that one of the poor-houses should be appropriated to the purposes of an asylum, with the view, I suppose, of saving the expense of building the new institution in Enniscorthy; is that so?—The idea was suggested, and it was started by a great number of the cess-payers and ratepayers, but it was found that it would not act, and it was overruled. We supposed it would not act, because the suggestion was overruled.

2028. By whom?—I am not prepared to state.

2029. Are you aware that such a principle as that could not be carried out without legislation?—I am not aware of it.

2030. Then the board of guardians, or the Poor-law Commissioners, or the Government, have no power whatever, without an Act of Parliament, to alienate the property of unions for any other purpose except that for which they were originally built?—I was not aware of it, but I will take it so since you state it.

2031. *Chairman*.] That sufficiently accounts for the failure of the application to which you refer?—Yes; that is the first answer I have heard to it.

2032. *Mr. Herbert*.] You attend the Poor Law Board in Wexford, do you?—In New Ross.

2033. Do many of the *ex-officio* members attend there regularly?—Yes, there is a fair attendance.

2034. What proportion of the rural guardians?—They are outnumbered by the poor law guardians; they are not so regular in their attendance as the elected guardians.

2035. Could you tell us the difference in number?—I could not.

2036. Is it not a proverbial thing, generally, I will not say in your union, that the rural guardians attend very well when there is a job, and not when that is not the case?—No, that is not the case in Wexford; not in any of the unions of county Wexford. They attend very regularly.

2037. *Sir Charles Lanyon*.] I did not hear the whole of your examination, but I think I understood you to say that there is very great dissatisfaction on the part of the cesspayers in your county against the present law?—Yes.

2038. And that you advocated a change in the law consequent upon that dissatisfaction?—We did.

2039. And that dissatisfaction principally arises from the power of the grand jury to present matters over which the cesspayers have no control?—Rather from the cesspayers feeling that they were not represented sufficiently; that there was not sufficient representation; that it was not commensurate with the taxation.

2040. Did you not state that the great dissatisfaction was owing to the grand jury having power to present matters over which the cesspayers had no control?—That was not the entire reason of the dissatisfaction.

2041. I think you must be aware from what has since passed with reference to the malicious injuries, that the cesspayers have a power of expressing an opinion?—Only expressing an opinion. If they report, it can be passed by the grand jury.

R. A. Leigh, Esq.

4 May 1868.

2042. Are you not aware that there is very great difficulty in getting an expression of opinion in favour of a malicious injury from the presentment sessions?—I have never seen it; I am not aware of it.

2043. Mr. *Dawson*.] The grand jury have the power of allocating the taxation?—Yes, I have seen the sum increased; I have seen instances in which the application has been rejected, in which the same has been given by the presentment sessions, and increased by the grand jury.

2044. *Chairman*.] You are speaking of malicious injury only?—Yes.

2045. *Sir Charles Lanyon*.] Will you show me the section under which the sessions can at all interfere with the sum applied for for a malicious injury. You say that you are aware of the sum given at the sessions being increased by the grand jury?—I do not know whether they acted under a certain section, but I have known an instance. At the late presentment sessions in my county, the application which was for 15*l*., was knocked by the chairman in these words, "Service being proved, we consider the sum of 5*l*. is sufficient." That went to the grand jury, and the sum of 15*l*. was given by the grand jury.

2046. Are you aware that the sessions have no right to interfere with the sum applied for?—I was not aware of that.

2047. They have no right to inquire into the sum applied for; that is a question for evidence before the grand jury?—Yes.

2048. You said, with reference to the attendance of magistrates and cesspayers at sessions, that the cesspayers were apt to be swamped by the magistrates?—It is possible that they can be.

2049. I want to know whether you have had any experience of such swamping of cesspayers?—Yes; I have known instances of that.

2050. What particular case can you mention?—I am not prepared at this moment to give day and date, but I pledge myself that I can do so; you allude to the presentment sessions.

2051. Yes?—I can give instances of that.

2052. Is it not generally the case that the cesspayers are much more numerous than the magistrates?—I refer to the presentment sessions of my county; I think they are about equal.

2053. If they attend in the number in which they have the power of attending, would not they be more numerous than the magistrates?—I have already said that they are deterred from attending by the uncertainty of being called.

2054. Supposing they did attend as they are empowered by the Act to attend, would not they, generally speaking, be more numerous than the magistrates?—Yes, in some places, generally.

2055. Then, if the magistrates are more numerous than the cesspayers at the sessions, it is generally owing to the cesspayers not availing themselves of the opportunity of attending?—To a certain extent.

2056. *Chairman*.] The magistrates, if they chose to attend, could always overrule the cesspayers?—Yes, they could.

2057. The number of cesspayers being limited, and the number of magistrates capable of attending being unlimited, is not that the case?—It is; I was wrong in the answer I gave just now; I thought it was the magistrates in the barony to which Sir Charles Lanyon alluded; of course the baronial cesspayers could not be as numerous as the magistrates, who may come from all parts of the county.

2058. Colonel *French*.] Would not a simple restriction in the Act confining magistrates to their own barony do away with your objection?—I have already answered that in the affirmative.

2059. *Chairman*.] But the number of magistrates in the barony itself may still easily outnumber the cesspayers of that barony?—That would depend on the local circumstances.

2060. They might?—If it was a well-inhabited barony they might, and in some they might not.

2061. If no numbers were fixed, equality would not be secured?—It would not be secured.

2062. Mr. *Dawson*.] Do you think the magistrate ought to have a qualification?—I would qualify him as an occupier.

2063. Or if he represented a certain amount of property, supposing he was acting as agent for a large proprietor at a distance?—If he represented property in that barony.

2064. *Sir Charles Lanyon*.] That would get rid of the point you speak of, with reference to the outnumbering of the cesspayers by the magistrates?—It would to a great extent.

2065. Would it not also be desirable to limit the attendance of magistrates who are agents for property, unless they represent a certain amount in the barony?—You allude to their being magistrates.

2066. I allude to their being magistrates; and occupiers, but agents?—That, I believe, I have answered already; I do consider that that would be advisable.

2067. You spoke about the increase of the grand jury cess; are you aware of any particular causes that have lately increased the grand jury cess in Ireland?—Mileage of roads has increased, and also the public buildings, lunatic asylums, and different things have increased it during the last 40 years about 25 per cent.

2068. Is it not a matter of necessity that the county cess must increase as the prosperity of the county advances?—Yes.

2069. Have you not repairs of harbours placed under grand jury cess, which you never had before?—Yes.

2070. Have you not turnpike roads under grand jury cess, which you never had before?—I believe it is not so in my county, but it is the case in other counties.

2071. Therefore there are evident reasons for the increase of the county taxation?—Yes.

2072. Will you state what the advantages of the County Boards and Baronial Boards would be over the present system?—With the Baronial Boards the roads would be better looked after; there would be more direct interest in looking after the roads. The Baronial Board would act as a sort of Highway Board, as in England, and help the surveyor to see that the contractors and assistant surveyors did their duty.

2073. Are you aware that the highway system in England is about the worst possible system upon which any highway can be maintained?—I have heard different opinions on the subject.

2074. Is not that the general opinion, and that our system is a very much better one?—I am not prepared to say that it is the general opinion; I have heard opinions on both sides.

2075. From what you say, I suppose you intend to give some responsibility to these local Boards, in the inspection of works?—Yes, they might

F. A. Leigh, Esq.

1 May 1868.

might see that the assistant surveyors did their duty, and see to the removal of nuisances, sudden breaches, and things of that sort.

2076. In what way would that be different from the present constitution of magistrates and cesspayers?—In the present system there is nobody actually appointed to do it, it is nobody's actual business to do it, and therefore it is not done.

2077. Would not that be going back entirely to the old system before the introduction of county surveyors?—I would not interfere with the duty of county surveyors, I consider it would be an assistance.

2078. Do you know anything of the mode in which the roads were repaired prior to the introduction of the 6 & 7 Will. 4?—No, that is before my time; I do not recollect it.

2079. Mr. *Maguire*.] The honourable Member on the other side was endeavouring to show that the interests of the occupiers was sufficiently protected, and you were asked whether you did not apprehend that in case the burden was divided between the occupier and the owner, it would not be attended with any pecuniary advantage to the occupier, inasmuch as his rent would be raised; do you think that is a question we have to deal with, or is not the question for us rather to do what is fair than to consider what may happen afterwards?—Certainly.

2080. Is not that generally the feeling of the cesspayers. What they demand is the division of the rate?—It is.

2081. And they are ready to take their chance as to the result?—Yes.

2082. Do you think so badly of the landlords of the county of Wexford, as if Parliament divided the cess equally between the landlord and occupier, that they would violate the spirit of that by not only putting it on in the shape of rent, but even adding to it over and above it?—I do not think they would.

2083. At any rate, whether they would or would not, the first thing you think is to divide the burden equally?—I do.

2084. If the associated cesspayer be so vigilant in protecting the interests of his class now, is there any reason why, if he were an elected cesspayer, elected by a constituency of the barony, that he would not do it quite so well?—No, I do not see why.

2085. He would be just the same person with the same interests?—Yes.

2086. And just as vigilant?—Yes.

2087. Mr. *Blake*.] Mr. Gregory suggested that it might be, and probably would be, a matter of great inconvenience to a poor cesspayer, to come a distance and attend the County Board. Is it your view that this County Board should meet oftener than the present grand jury meet, unless they are called together for a particular occasion?—No; I think it would be sufficient to call them at the assizes. They could name their Board of Superintendence and Lunatic Board at once, which should meet perhaps monthly, as is done at present; I do not see that they themselves, unless in a case of a bridge being washed away or something of that sort, need attend so often.

2088. Generally speaking, there will be no occasion for their meeting more than twice a year?—I think that would be sufficient.

2089. Is it not also your view that the persons to be elected in the County Board should be assessed in the value of 50 *l.*, that every person elected by the ratepayers should be an owner or occupier of land assessed at the value of 50 *l.* What qualification would you have for a member of the County Board?—Say 50 *l.*

2090. Would not persons assessed at that value be likely to be of a class that would not be much inconvenienced by attending upon such occasions?—Certainly.

2091. With regard to your remark about the justices to be associated with the elected cesspayers at the County Board being elected by the Lord Lieutenant, did I understand you that you yourself objected to this election by the Lord Lieutenant, that that was a suggestion of your own, or that you would have representative justices elected by themselves?—I corrected myself by saying that the number should be stated by the Lord Lieutenant.

2092. Then would you have the justices to act on the County Board selected by themselves?—I see no objection to that.

2093. Would you prefer that course to their being nominated, as you were at first understood to say, by the Lord Lieutenant?—I said I stated that under an impression that it was in your Bill.

2094. You would leave it with the Lord Lieutenant to say what the number of cesspayers upon each of the Baronial Boards were to be?—Yes.

2095. And also to appoint the time and place for the election?—Yes.

2096. And the districts?—The districts would be baronies.

2097. The same baronies as they are now?—Yes; I would prefer baronies to electoral divisions.

2098. You would make no change in that way?—No; I would make no change.

Tuesday, 4th May 1868.

MEMBERS PRESENT:

Mr. Blake.	Mr. Headlam.
Colonel Cooper.	Sir Charles Lanyon.
Mr. Dawson.	Mr. Leader.
Colonel Forde.	Mr. Maguire.
Mr. Chichester Fortescue.	Earl of Mayo.
Colonel French.	Sir Colman O'Loghlen.
Mr. Herbert.	

MR. CHICHESTER FORTESCUE, IN THE CHAIR.

WILLIAM D'ESTERRE PARKER, Esq., called in; and Examined.

W. D'Esterre Parker, Esq.

4 May 1868.

2099. Mr. *Maguire*.] WHERE do you reside?—In Passage West, county Cork.

2100. That is within a few miles of the City of Cork?—Yes.

2101. Have you a practical knowledge of the working of the grand jury laws?—Yes.

2102. Have you made it a subject of special interest to you for years past?—Yes, for a number of years.

2103. I will ask you generally, are you satisfied with the principle of the law with its machinery, or with its operation?—I am not.

2104. That is your general answer?—Yes.

2105. Do you consider that the main objections to the present system arise from the want of representation and the non-division of the rate between the owner and occupier of the property?—Most decidedly.

2106. We will deal first with the taxation. In the first place I ask you, do you think it a fair thing that the tax should be borne alone by the occupier?—I do think it most unfair.

2107. Why do you think it unfair?—Because the landlord has power through the grand jury of making improvements in his property, while the tenant is bound to pay for the entire improvement, except when the landlord is occupier. Where the landlord is occupier he contributes in the same manner as an ordinary occupier; but with regard to the property not in his possession he contributes nothing towards the improvements of the country.

2108. In the first place, do you not think that the owner of property has as great an interest in all the improvements effected by the county expenditure as the occupier?—He has a much greater interest.

2109. We will take it item by item, and I will ask you as to the relative interests of the different classes of occupiers and owners. One of the items of expenditure is for prisons, gaols, bridewells, and reformatories?—Yes.

2110. Is it your opinion that the owners of property have as much interest in the maintenance of these institutions as the occupiers?—Most decidedly.

2111. Is there any doubt in your mind that the owner of property has to say the least as strong an interest in their maintenance as the occupier?—Not only as he as strong an interest, but he ought to have a stronger interest, for they tend to protect and secure his own property.

2112. Now we will come to the hospitals; do you think that the richer portion of the community are morally as much bound to support the charities of the country as the humbler classes?—Unquestionably.

2113. The owners of property, I take it as a rule, are the richer portion?—Yes.

2114. And the occupiers are the poorer, or the least richer?—Yes.

2115. Another item of expenditure is coroners; I suppose the owners of property have as much interest in the institution of coroners as the other class?—No doubt.

2116. Suppose a revision of the valuation; there is a large expenditure for that?—Very large.

2117. The one class has as much interest in it as the other?—Unquestionably.

2118. As to lunatic asylums under the head of charities, or under what other head they come, the support of lunatic asylums in the county Cork is a very great burden?—It is.

2119. What is the cost, up to this moment, of the lunatic asylums for the county and city of Cork, confining yourself to the county portion of the burden?—The original charge for building the lunatic asylum was 80,000 *l.*; since then there has been a considerable outlay on it. I understand the different outlays from year to year have amounted to upwards of 100,000 *l.*

2120. And that, or such portion as has been already paid, has been raised entirely from the occupiers, and none from the owners of property?—The 80,000 *l.* has been raised entirely in the county, from the occupiers; a portion of the other may have been raised by the city. As you are aware, it is a joint hospital.

2121. What is the proportion paid by the county for the annual maintenance of that institution; is it 6,000 *l.* a year?—I think about that.

2122. I believe the number in the Eglinton Lunatic Asylum, if I mistake not, is about 550?—I am not quite aware on that point.

2123. It is over 600, is it not?—Yes.

2124. From your knowledge, what proportion of these are paying inmates?—I should think at the

W. D'Esterre Parker, Esq.

6 May 1868.

the outside about 20, and they only pay a proportion of their expenses.

2125. Certainly, they are under 50?—Yes.

2126. Nine-tenths at least are of the poorer class of the community, are they not?—Yes.

2127. Who, if they were poor, would be received into the workhouse?—Yes.

2128. And if received into the workhouse, the burden of their support would be equally divided between the landlord and the occupier?—Precisely.

2129. But because they happen to be insane, and are kept in another building, the entire burden of their support is thrown on the poorer classes of the community?—Just so.

2130. Do you think that is right?—I do not think it at all right. It is one of the many causes of complaint against the grand jury laws.

2131. Is it considered to be a very serious cause of complaint?—Of course it is a very serious cause of complaint.

2132. Is it felt and represented in that light by what I may call the occupying class?—It is. The governors of the lunatic asylum are appointed by the Lord Lieutenant. The ratepayers have no control in the management of it in any way, and they consider it very unfair that they should be charged in support of a building as to the expenditure of which they have no voice.

2133. Suppose the burden of the support were equally divided between occupiers and owners, and that the rate-payers were represented, there would then be no objection?—There could be no objection to that.

2134. Nor to any fair and legitimate item of expenditure under the grand jury system. The occupier would have no objection if he were fairly represented, and if he paid what he considered a fair proportion of the rate?—No objection whatever.

2135. Now, as to the roads and bridges, the expenses of maintenance and construction of roads and bridges is entirely borne by the occupiers?—By the occupiers.

2136. Will you give your opinion to the Committee why the rate should be equally divided between the two classes?—I consider the rate should be equally divided between the two classes because, in the first instance, both parties benefit by the expenditure of the money. The landlord benefits by the making of a new road through his property, and by the keeping in repair of the present roads. His property, in many instances, would be of little or no value were it not for the communication made by the public roads.

2137. You think that the owner of the property, in as much as he has a permanent interest, has, to say the least, and without exaggeration, as great an interest as that of the man who has a temporary occupation and a temporary interest?—Without the slightest exaggeration, his interest is much larger. The man holding by the year may be dismissed to-morrow; and, after paying for the making of the new road, he loses all his money, while the landlord gains by the expenditure of it.

2138. Suppose the resident landlord holding 20,000 acres of land, and occupying 200 or 300 in his own domain, he only pays upon that 200 or 300 while the occupiers pay upon the remaining thousands?—Yes.

2139. And only as occupier does he pay a single farthing of the rate?—Only as occupier.

2140. As owner he pays nothing?—Nothing.

2141. As to the present system, by which the entire burden is thrown on the occupier, is there to your knowledge a strong feeling against that system?—A very strong feeling for many years, in fact the feeling has been existing from generation to generation since the first enactment of the grand jury system.

2142. Has it been expressed on various occasions to your knowledge?—Yes, at several public meetings.

2143. Expressed by public proclamation against it as well as by petitions to Parliament?—Yes, petitions were brought forward last Session.

2144. If I mistake not you are a member of a body lately formed called "The Cork Farmers' Club"?—Yes.

2145. Are you in the way of knowing what is the opinion of those who, in that club, represent the occupiers of the county?—Intimately.

2146. You are in the way of knowing what their feeling is as to what they consider the unjust burden of this rate?—Yes.

2147. Which I may say is a very great burden on the county generally, is it not?—A very great burden.

2148. Last year I believe it was over a million?—Yes, it has been for many years over a million.

2149. Now suppose that the law was changed, and that the rate was divided equally between the two classes of whom I speak, have you any apprehension as to what the result would be; do you believe that the landlords would not give the tenants or occupiers the advantage which the law contemplated, and that they would make them pay in rent what was deducted from the landlord in the way of the division of the tax?—I have too high an opinion of the landlords to think for a moment that they would do anything of the kind; I am certain they would not do anything so unfair.

2150. There may be an individual instance where a landlord may act wrongly?—Yes, you may have a black sheep in every flock, but it would be a very rare instance.

2151. Do you believe that the landlords of the county make the tenants pay the entire of the poor rate?—I do not believe any such thing.

2152. There are cases, I suppose?—There are isolated cases of oppression which may exist, but they are very isolated.

2153. No doubt there are a few cases where they do make them pay it?—Yes.

2154. But as a rule, nothing of the kind is done?—No.

2155. Do you imagine that if the grand jury cess were treated in the same way as the poor rate, and divided equally between the occupier and the owner, there is any real ground for an apprehension of the kind?—No ground whatever.

2156. You have no such apprehension?—No; and I have a very intimate knowledge of the country.

2157. Assuming that the law was changed, you would have its operation prospective, not retrospective?—Prospective.

2158. You would not interfere with the old bargains and leases?—Not at all.

2159. You would rather things continue?—Yes.

2160. In your opinion, would any benefit arise from the division of the tax?—I think a very great benefit; I think the funds would be managed much more economically. I think the landlords would take a much greater interest in the management of their own affairs. I think the

W. H. [illegible] Parker, Esq.

5 May 1868.

the tenants would have a greater interest in it also. I think where the taxation is divided between them both, there would be a mutual obligation on the part of both to protect one another.

2161. Can you point out how the taxation under the Poor Law differs from that under the grand jury system?—Under the grand jury taxation, the baronial constables, that is, the rate collectors, are paid 5 per cent. for collecting the county rates. The county rates in county Cork are upwards of 80,000 *l.* a year. They are paid about 4,000 *l.* a year, while the rate collectors, under the poor rate, get only 2½ per cent., and in some cases 1 per cent. The poor rate is managed by the landlords and the tenants; the county cess is not.

2162. That is only one item?—Yes.

2163. Generally speaking, do you think it would be more economically managed under a system analogous to that of the Poor Law?—I am perfectly satisfied it would, for many reasons.

2164. Will you give us those reasons?—I should think the principal reason is, that all parties take an interest where they have to bear the burden of the taxation; I think that is the most natural inference.

2165. Now as to representation, you are in favour of a change from the present system, which is one of nomination, to the system of representation?—Yes.

2166. I suppose you know that is the constitutional principle that those who are taxed should be represented?—Yes.

2167. Has not the principle of representation been thoroughly and satisfactorily tested by the operation of the Poor Law system?—Most thoroughly.

2168. According to your idea, is the grand jury system one of total irresponsibility, that is, that the grand jurors are irresponsible, that the magistrates who may go from one part of the county to the other are irresponsible, and that the cesspayers are more or less irresponsible, is that your idea?—Quite so; they are all irresponsible.

2169. How is the grand jury irresponsible?—The grand jury, you are aware, is elected by the county sheriff, who chooses whom he likes; they remain in office on fiscal matters for three days, when their office ceases; we know no more of them. They may possibly be chosen next year, or they may not, but we know nothing of them up to the time of the sitting of the grand jury at the end of that period.

2170. And if the grand jury, according to your opinion, be irresponsible, you would say that the magistrate who may come at any time to vote in any barony on any subject within the purview of the law is also irresponsible?—Yes.

2171. And the associated cesspayer, inasmuch as he represents no one, is merely a person nominated by an irresponsible person, and he is also, in your opinion, irresponsible?—Quite so.

2172. Assuming that they all kept within the limit of the law, that is, that they acted legally, you are of opinion that they are not responsible to anybody?—Yes.

2173. And you would be in favour, then, of a system of representation?—Representation for the associated cesspayers, and representation for the grand jury of the barony.

2174. You would have the grand jury of the barony elected by the ratepayers?—By the ratepayers of the barony.

2175. And you would have the associated cesspayers, or a person of the same character, also elected?—Also elected.

2176. You do not mean to interfere in any way with the criminal jurisdiction?—Not at all, merely the fiscal matters.

2177. Now the associated cesspayers are nominated by the grand juror of the barony?—Practically so.

2178. He may select whom he likes, may he not?—Yes, out of one hundred names sent to him by the high constable.

2179. Do you know a case where, in a barony extending over a very large area, a grand juror has selected those who represented his immediate neighbourhood, in preference to selecting men from all parts, so as to have a thorough representation of the entire barony?—I do.

2180. Have you a case in point to illustrate that abuse?—I can mention the case of my own barony, the Barony of *Kerricurrihy*; I may divide the barony into three electoral divisions, one is the Carrigaline, the other the Monkstown electoral division, and the other is the Ballygarvan; dividing the barony into three electoral divisions, and taking into consideration also their valuation, one would expect that there would be some attention paid to the interests of the ratepayers in each division; the grand juror belongs to the Carrigaline district; well, the Act of Parliament gave him the power of naming 24 cesspayers, 12 of whom would be selected at the road sessions; he only selected 18, and at the road session nine of those would be selected; out of that number he gave 14 for the electoral division of Carrigaline, two for Ballygarvan, and two for the electoral division of Monkstown, which is nearly as large as that of Carrigaline; I consider that a very great abuse, and very unfair; on a former occasion I represented to the very same gentleman the injustice of his having done so, and his reply was this; "He thought it an extraordinary thing to mention such a matter to him; he did not consider it his duty, as a grand juror, to represent the interests of the barony, and that he should take care of his own." I said, "I look upon it as if you were a member of Parliament, if one of your constituents have a complaint they have a right to make it to you, and you should attend to it." However, on the present occasion he has given Monkstown no representation; at the road session when the names are called out, it is almost impossible for a ratepayer, either from Ballygarvan or Monkstown to be represented, and the entire cesspayers would be in the hands of the Carrigaline portion of the cesspayers.

2181. There can be no doubt as to the veracity of that document?—No; it is an official document. Now with regard to another barony, the barony of Cork, which is a very large one, there are only six cesspayers selected there. That barony is one of the largest baronies in the county; a number of magistrates reside in the neighbourhood. It would be absurd for the ratepayers to attend the road session there, because their voice would be nowhere among the large bench of magistrates; and the same remark applies to a number of other baronies.

2182. *Chairman.*] Can you tell the Committee upon what principle apparently the grand juror proceeded in selecting the cesspayers for that barony? You are aware that some of the grand

jurors

jurors consider themselves bound by the Act of 6 & 7 Will. 4, to take those cesspayers, one after another, who pay the highest amount of cess; can you tell the Committee whether the grand jurors proceed upon that principle in selecting the cesspayers?—The cesspayers selected here, from my own knowledge, are all large ratepayers; but whether they are the largest ratepayers I cannot say, not having the list before me.

2183. You cannot say for certain whether the grand jury may have proceeded upon that supposed interpretation of the Act?—The grand jury do not choose the cesspayers; it is the grand juror of the barony; the individual grand juror has the names of 100 large cesspayers, and he selects whom he likes, irrespective of the amount of their rates or locality.

2184. Mr. *Maguire.*] But within the barony?—Yes.

2185. *Chairman.*] You may be aware of that as a matter of practice; but, of course, in the eye of the law the persons selected out of the list of 100 returned by the barony constable are the nominees of the jury as a whole?—They are presumed so by law; but in practice they are not.

2186. You cannot tell the Committee for certain upon what interpretation of the Act of 6 & 7 Will. 4, the grand jury proceeded in the selection from the constable's list?—I think it is a matter entirely dependent on the grand juror; from my own knowledge, he selects as he thinks proper, and he chooses those whom he likes.

2187. Mr. *Maguire.*] Does he always confine himself to the highest ratepayers?—He does not, and I think it would be very unfair if he did.

2188. In point of fact, in those cases to which you refer, you complain that all portions of the barony have not been fairly represented?—Precisely.

2189. And that it is within the power of the grand juror of the barony to do as he pleases?—Precisely.

2190. To appoint whom he pleases belonging to any locality that he prefers?—No doubt.

2191. Do you understand that the one grand juror appoints for all the baronies?—No, for the barony he represents.

2192. You think if there were a system of representation that evil or abuse would be put an end to?—Yes.

2193. And that all districts would be equally represented?—Yes, the barony being divided into districts.

2194. Do you know of any other baronies in which the same abuse exists?—I cannot speak as to other baronies, for I have not the same knowledge as of my own; but, judging from the numbers selected by the grand juror, they invariably fall short, or with few exceptions, of the number allowed by the Act of Parliament; for instance, there are seven, eight, and nine selected at the road sessions, where the number would be 12. In some large baronies it depends on the feeling of the grand juror whether he would wish to have a large number of associated cesspayers or a small number; I think the smallest number allowed by the Act of Parliament is five, and I think the largest is twelve.

2195. Colonel *French.*] You say that the grand juror who has charge of and who selects those associated cesspayers sometimes does not nominate a sufficient number by law allowed to represent the barony?—Precisely.

W. D'Esterre Parker, Esq.

5 May 1868.

2196. I understood you to say twenty-four was the number in your barony, and that sometimes only twelve were elected?—Twenty-four is the number allowed in any barony. Out of that twenty-four, at the road sessions, twelve are elected by ballot. In many of the baronies they only give 16, 15, or 14, or similar numbers.

2197. Mr. *Maguire.*] Will you take that paper and read the number that are selected?—They are as follows:—Barretts, 6; Barrymore, 12; Condons and Clongibbons, 18; Cork, 6; Duhallow, 10; Fermoy, 18; Imokilly, 10; Kerricurrihy, 8; Kinalea, 8; Kinnatalloon, 7; Kinsale, 8; East Muskerry, 9; Orrery and Kilmore, 8.

2198. Is not Cork a large barony?—A very large and wealthy barony.

2199. There are 6 selected there?—But 6. In the western district it is even more remarkable. They are as follows:—Bantry, 6; Bear, 8; E. D. E. Carbery, 10; W. D. E. Carbery, 8; E. D. W. Carbery, 12; W. D. W. Carbery, 9; Courceys, 7; Ibane and Barryroe, 8; Kinalmeaky, 18; West Muskerry, 7. They all vary in their numbers. Very few are up to the full number, and a great many are below it.

2200. Is that in the discretion of the grand juror of the barony?—Yes; the grand jury, as a body, do not interfere with any individual member of the grand jury. The grand juror of the barony is supposed to have the best local information as to the wants of the barony. The grand jury, as a body, do not know much about the individual barony.

2201. Is there a complaint of this, that the magistrates can at any time swamp the cesspayers, and render their influence, in fact, of no avail?—Yes.

2202. Do you know any cases where magistrates have come from a distance and have carried what they pleased against the local feeling?—I have known instances.

2203. Have you often heard complaints of it?—Many; under the law the magistrates of the county are allowed to sit at any road sessions that they deem proper as their interests or wishes may suggest, quite irrespective of their having property in the barony or not. That is another matter of very serious complaint. We think it very unfair that a gentleman who has no property in the barony should come and vote away our money, merely to gratify a brother magistrate.

2204. A magistrate, if he wished, could now come from the remotest part of the county of Cork to the other end of it, to carry a job if he so pleased?—Decidedly.

2205. You do not say that he does, but the law allows of his doing it?—Yes.

2206. Do you not think that the law that permits such an abuse ought to cease to exist?—Unquestionably.

2207. Would you be in favour of confining the vote of a magistrate within his own barony?—Unquestionably.

2208. You would not give him power to vote unless he had property in the barony?—He should have property to a certain amount in the barony.

2209. You being in favour of elections, and there being some idea that elections would be attended with great expense and turmoil, I want to have

W. D'Esterre Parker, Esq.

5 May 18[illegible].

have some information on that point, and I ask you in the first place, would an election, supposed to be carried on as that for the Poor Law Guardians is, be attended with much expense?—Very trifling.

2210. I believe you have some knowledge of contests as a Poor Law Guardian?—Yes.

2211. Is there a year scarcely that you are not in for an election?—No.

2212. So that you thoroughly understand it?—Quite so.

2213. You are able to speak as to the expense of a contested election?—Yes.

2214. Will you give an idea of what is the average expense of even a contested election for poor law guardians?—The average expense of a contested election in one of the Cork electoral divisions would be 6 *l.* or 7 *l.*

2215. That is the utmost?—The average.

2216. What is the utmost you have ever paid, or that has ever been incurred?—I think about 10 *l.* It depends upon the number of voting papers and the numbers of distributors.

2217. Is that private or public expense?—Public expense; there is no private expense.

2218. What are the items of expenditure?—They are the printing of the voting papers; the delivery of them at each ratepayer's house, and the collecting of them again. The returning officer gets an annual salary for the entire union of 30 *l.* a-year; generally speaking we have very few contests. There are 50 elected guardians.

2219. What do you say is the salary of the returning officer?—*L.* 30 a-year for his duties as returning officer.

2220. For the whole union?—Yes.

2221. *Chairman.*] Who is the returning officer?—The clerk of the union, generally speaking.

2222. *Mr. Meynier.*] Am I to understand that the entire expense for the election, where two persons contest the representation of the particular electoral district is 10 *l.*?—That would be the outside; the very outside; and it must be a large electoral division. In the division I speak of, there were over 1,000 voting papers.

2223. And it is a very extensive division?—Yes.

2224. What would be the expense for a contested election in an average sized district?—From 6 *l.* to 7 *l.*

2225. That is the maximum?—The maximum.

2226. As a rule, I believe contests are rather unfrequent?—They occur very seldom; for instance, there are 50 elected guardians for the union of Cork, and I should think there are not more than six or seven contests.

2227. That is a very small proportion?—Very small.

2228. The expense would not be a cause of alarm to you?—It would be infinitesimal on the rates. The papers are sometimes issued by the constabulary, sometimes by paid men. The constabulary are paid for issuing them.

2229. Something small?—One shilling a day.

2230. And if other persons are employed, they are paid something more?—Perhaps 4 *s.* or 5 *s.* a day.

2231. Is it not nearly always the constabulary who issue these voting papers, and collect them again?—Invariably, except in a town like Queenstown.

2232. I am speaking generally?—I speak of my own district.

2233. Never mind an individual case; we are dealing with the whole country. Where the constabulary do issue these papers and collect them again, then the cost is not so great?—It is much less.

2234. Putting aside altogether these isolated cases, and dealing with the question generally, and assuming that the constabulary do issue these papers and return them again, under these circumstances, what would you say would be the expense of a contested election?—It would reduce it, perhaps, ten shillings or a pound. If the baronies were divided into districts, and the clerk of the petty sessions appointed a returning officer, living in the district, the expense would be still less, because at present some of the electoral divisions are a distance from Cork, and the persons who distribute papers have to go there, which causes an additional expense, which would be done away with by having a local returning officer.

2235. Under any circumstances, it brings down the costs of a contested election for Poor Law Guardians to about 4 *l.*?—I suppose so.

2236. It is not a thing to be apprehensive of?—No; if there was any apprehension about it, it might be divided between the candidates.

2237. Would not it be far better than it should not?—Yes.

2238. Inasmuch, as out of 50 elections at the present moment, there are but five or six contested; you do not apprehend, if the same system were adopted, there would be very much expense incurred by a contested election?—No.

2239. Well, now as to excitement and turmoil, is there any whatever?—Not the slightest; the elections are managed with the most perfect quietness.

2240. Is it not almost done in secret?—Yes.

2241. Imperceptibly to the community at large?—Yes.

2242. Is there anything further that you wish to say as to these two questions of the representation and division of the rates?—I can say nothing further than what I have said about the division of the rates, but as to the representation I think, in regard to the baronies, in the first instance, that some are too large and some too small; I am speaking of Cork. I think a more equal distribution of the baronies would be better; I think the baronies should be divided into districts. The number of the cesspayers to be elected by the ratepayers should correspond to the number of magistrates in the district. With regard to magistrates, it is very different now to what it was years ago, when first the grand jury laws were made. We have many magistrates who live in the barony, but have no property there; I think in place of the word "magistrate" in the Act of Parliament, it ought to be the word "landlord." I think the landlord is the legitimate party to have a voice in the expenditure or in the improvement of public property.

2243. Provided he pays half?—Of course, I take for granted that he pays half. The number of ratepayers in the district should correspond with the number of magistrates or landlords living in the district, so that the landlords or others should not be outvoted by the ratepayers; and, on the other hand, the ratepayers should have an equal right with the landlord; that is the principal thing as regards the cesspayer. I think the qualification of the cesspayer might be the

Poor

Poor Law qualification, 25 *l.* a year; that would be a fair qualification for the cesspayer.

2244. The members of the Board of Guardians are highly respectable, are they not?—Highly so.

2245. And they discharge their duties in the most satisfactory manner?—No complaint is ever made of them, none whatever.

2246. If there be cause of complaint against an individual guardian, the matter could very easily be settled, by his being ejected at the next election?—Unquestionably; that is the great benefit arising from the election.

2247. And there is no such control over the associated cesspayer?—Yes.

2248. Even if he has a fault or is extravagant, or, in other words, is objectionable, there is no reason why he may not be again and again put to administer the affairs of the county?—Yes, the great qualification with many cesspayers is their non-attendance at the Road Sessions. With regard to the grand jurors, I certainly think it would be very wise to have the grand jurors of the barony selected by the ratepayers of the barony, that grand juror to have a property qualification of such an amount as would answer for his perfect respectability and perfect competency; I think the present system of selecting them by the high sheriff is an abuse which is very much felt, for many highly respectable ratepayers, and gentlemen are passed over by the grand jurors and the high sheriff from year to year; I think it is very wrong; I think the landlord is above all other persons to be associated at the Road Sessions with the cesspayers, and that a magistrate, having no property in the barony, should not be allowed to sit at the barony.

2249. Will you now state anything you desire to suggest as to the county secretary?—I think with regard to the county secretary, it is a mistake to have his salary augmented by fees; I think they are most objectionable in many instances, because the fees in small matters would nearly amount to as much as the cost of doing the work itself. I speak of matters which require to be done in small towns.

2250. You have a practical knowledge of what you are saying?—Yes.

2251. Personal experience?—Yes; the fees received by the county secretary amount to 6 *s.*; the first fee is on making an application for any public works; no matter what the amount would be, you pay 2 *s.* for that; it is not actually allowed by Act of Parliament, but it is allowed by usage, for the salary of the county secretary is considered very small, and the grand jurors allow his salary to be augmented in this manner by fees. There is a shilling for putting in the tender for the works, there is a shilling in signing the bond, and there are 2 *s.* paid at the Road Sessions for getting an order for payment.

2252. Is there no duty done by the secretary or his assistants for any portion of that money?—For all those payments there are certain papers filled up; that is really the duty which is performed. We consider that when he is paid a salary, he ought to do those duties without being paid extra.

2253. Do you mean to say every contractor who puts in a tender which is accepted has to pay 6 *s.*?—Yes, he has to pay 6 *s.* before he gets his money; before he is paid.

2254. No matter how small the contract?—Yes, the contract might be 1 *l.*; he would have to pay 6 *s.* for that, irrespective of the trouble all and bother of attending road sessions, and everything else.

2255. Do you know of your own knowledge that that has been paid?—I have paid it myself.

2256. Just state what you did pay, and under what circumstances it was paid?—Some seven or eight years ago, for the purpose of getting full information into the practical working of the grand jury laws, I took up a small contract for making a footpath in my own town; the footpath was badly wanted. I paid 2 *s.* on application, and 1 *s.* in tendering for the work; of course, there were many other parties tendered besides, who also paid 1 *s.* The tender was granted to me, and I paid 1 *s.* on signing the bond for performance of the work. I had to pay 2 *s.* for getting the payment paper at the road session.

2257. You were the accepted person?—Yes.

2258. There were many others put in tenders?—Yes.

2259. Had all these people to pay the preliminary charge?—They had all to pay for the tenders.

2260. *Chairman.*] That is to say, for the printed tender paper, properly filled up by the secretary?—Yes.

2261. Mr. *Maguire.*] How many were there tendering for that?—I could not say exactly; there might be four, or five, or a dozen. It was the first work I undertook, and it gave me more insight into the working of the grand jury laws than anything else.

2262. You had other contracts after that?—Yes.

2263. And the same thing occurred?—Yes.

2264. The same expense?—Yes.

2265. You object to that?—I think it would be well to have these fees removed, and to have the county secretary paid by salary.

2266. Have you any other suggestion to make?—The only suggestion I have to make is this. His salary would be reduced; that is a matter which ought to be taken into account; and I think the grand jury should have the power of appointing an assistant secretary.

2267. You speak of the county Cork, which is a very large county?—Yes.

2268. An immense county, in fact?—It is about one-tenth or one-eleventh of Ireland.

2269. As to the county surveyor, or his duties, have you any suggestion to make?—Yes; with regard to the county surveyor, I think he should be bound to reside in his district, I think he should also be bound to devote his entire time to the duties of his office.

2270. I ask for information; as a matter of fact now, in the county of Cork, do the surveyors reside in their respective districts?—I think they do now.

2271. You would wish for the public benefit that they should reside?—I think so.

2272. As to their devoting their entire attention to their duties, do they do so?—They do not.

2273. Do you know that as a fact?—I do, they take up private matters.

2274. You would have them devote their entire attention to the county duties?—I think so.

2275. Inasmuch as you think they are of sufficient importance to demand all their energy?—Yes, within the last few years we had two county surveyors at a salary of 300 *l.* a year each; that was before the railways were established, then the

W. D'Esterre Parker, Esq.

6 May 18[illegible].

W. D'Esterre Parker, Esq.

5 May 1868.

the railways have been established a third county surveyor has been put on the county, and the salaries of the three have been raised to 400 *l.* a-year; we are now paying 1,200 *l.* a-year for what we formerly paid 600 *l.* a-year for.

2276. If they devoted all their time to county duties you would not think that too much?—No.

2277. You do not object to their being well paid providing they give their undivided attention?—Decidedly, let them give their undivided attention to the interests of the county.

2278. Have you any other suggestion to make with reference to that?—I consider the county surveyor should, before the road sessions, attend a meeting of ratepayers in any town not under the Towns' Improvement Act, in any populous district so as to give his advice and services.

2279. Advice as to what?—As to any public work or the repair of any work before the application is put in at the road sessions; very often at the road sessions when the applications are put in we have little or no information about them.

2280. You think as he ought to have official information of everything connected with the county, he ought to be the person to advise what work should be undertaken, and what expenditure is to be incurred?—Unquestionably, that would save a good deal of trouble and do a good deal of good.

2281. Preliminary advice would be important?—Precisely so; it would save the applications being put in.

2282. As to the towns, I think you are anxious that they should be rendered independent of the counties, and conduct their own affairs?—Yes.

2283. You have given that subject some consideration?—Yes; previously to the uniform Grand Jury Assessment Act, the houses did not pay county cess. In 1838 the law was extended to houses under the Uniform Grand Jury Law, and all houses now pay county cess. They do not derive any additional benefit. They are very peculiarly situated with regard to baronial works. Invariably I may say the ratepayers on house property are not selected at the road sessions, and the consequence is, that the householders have no voice at the road sessions. When an individual ratepayer attends at the road sessions to support the work, he is generally silenced by the Bench, not being an associated cesspayer, and finds a very great difficulty on that account in getting any improvements done in towns that have not adopted the Towns' Improvement Act. Many of those towns that have adopted that Act considered it a great grievance to pay for their town rates, and pay their baronial rates. They had to go to considerable expense in Parliament to get a Private Bill exempting them from baronial rates, and giving them the power to repair the streets and the roads in their own towns. That has been done in many instances, and the law is working very well. The towns contribute their proportion to the county at large charges, but they are exempt from the baronial charges. They find they can repair their streets with much more economy than under the grand jury laws, with much more comfort to the inhabitants. Queenstown has been separated from the barony of Barrymore. I think it would be most important if a permissive Bill were put into the new Bill to enable all towns that adopt the Towns' Improvement Act to be relieved from baronial taxation, and to take charge of their own roads at their own expense.

2284. *Chairman.*] You speak of a private Act, what is it?—I speak of Kingstown, Queenstown, Dungarvan, and several other towns in Ireland, that had to come before Parliament for a private Bill to enable them to be separated from the grand jury system.

2285. Mr. *Maguire.*] A private public Bill?—Yes.

2286. That is always done at very great cost, 600 *l.* or 700 *l.*?—About 600 *l.*

2287. Ranging from that to 1,000 *l.*?—Yes.

2288. That is too much for a small town to bear?—Decidedly.

2289. You would wish to have permissive power given?—Yes; there is nothing which would more promote the improvement of the towns, either as regards the proper repair of their streets, or in a sanitary point of view, than giving them the power, for at present they are almost helpless.

2290. I believe you contemplate sanitary improvements as one of the results of that arrangement?—A very great result.

2291. You would think the locality would of course take a greater interest in what affected the health and life of its inhabitants than the barony?—Unquestionably. The barony at large cares nothing for us.

2292. It is not very natural that they should?—No.

2293. They do not feel the inconvenience?—No, and they do not care about us.

2294. As to unoccupied houses, have you any suggestions to make?—Yes; I think it unfair that unoccupied houses should be liable to the grand jury tax. At present the law does not exempt them; but the grand jury of the county Cork, seeing the injustice of it, allowed the rate collector to return unoccupied houses as waste. Practically they are exempt, but it is contrary to law. I think, with regard to houses under 4 *l.* a year, labourers' cottages, they should be exempt altogether from the grand jury tax. I think it is very hard to charge a poor labouring man with the expenses of the county. I think it would be a great boon to the labourer. It would induce landlords to have better cottages for them if they were not taxed for improving those cottages. At present the cottages are in a very wretched condition.

2295. What is the limitation of taxation; where does it commence?—At 10 *s.* a year, and less.

2296. For the county?—Yes; a house of any amount would be taxed. I think the removal of the tax from these houses would be a great boon to the labourer, and an inducement to the landlord to improve them. If the labourer improves his cottage by keeping it neat and in order, the reviser puts an additional value on it. I think it would be very desirable to have it removed altogether.

2297. Have you any suggestions to make with regard to malicious injuries?—With regard to malicious injuries, the law at present allows them to be charged on the county, on the barony, on the parish, or on the town lands. I think it is hard either on the parish or on the town lands. Under the present law the party whose property would be destroyed would have to pay the greater portion of it himself. The law punishes the owner of the property

W. H. Roberts Parker, Esq.

6 May 1868.

property as well as the innocent party who lives alongside of him. Malicious injuries are generally done by strangers, not by one's own neighbours, and they have a right to be paid for; but I think they should be contributed for by the county at large in the same way as the prosecution of criminals, where the expenses have to be paid for by the county at large. I think a proportion should be borne by the county, not by the town lands or the parish.

2298. As to public nuisances; have you anything to suggest?—I think, with regard to them, it would be most important to have them extended to the towns under the Public Health Act, and in the place of having them as they are now in the care of the Board of Guardians, that they should be put into the charge of the constabulary, who are a most efficient body; they are continually passing by these nuisances on the roads when they are out, and it would be very little trouble to them.

2299. Will you define what you call public nuisances?—Dunghills; filth in public places.

2300. Affecting the health of the inhabitants?—Yes, any nuisance affecting the health of the inhabitants. I think those should be placed under the control of the constabulary. At present the Sanatory Act—the Public Health Act is almost a dead letter in consequence of not having an effective governing body to see it carried out—neighbours do not like to complain against neighbours, and nothing is done unless a violent epidemic breaks out, which they make a great stir about, and the moment that ceases all relapses into its former state.

2301. You prefer perpetual vigilance to spasmodic efforts?—Yes, nothing will save the rates more, and nothing will preserve the public health more.

2302. Would it be giving an invidious or odious duty to the constabulary?—I think it would be a very proper duty to discharge; it is merely the duty of protecting the public health; they are already bound to protect it from aggression one way, and this is merely protecting it from aggression another way.

2303. In fact they want an efficient administration of a very important law?—Yes.

2304. Now, as to the coroner, have you any observations to make?—Yes, with regard to them, I think that every coroner should be bound to have a legal education. I think it is a mistake in the law electing coroners who are not legally educated; the office of a coroner is a most important one, and I think he should be perfectly educated in the law which he is bound to carry out. With regard to the coroners' juries, they are generally composed of a very inferior class; the present law says, that a ratepayer over 4 *l.* is eligible for a coroner's jury; if he cannot be found, they may take any one they like that they may meet in the street. To save trouble passers by are generally called in, and many of them are illiterate parties, who can neither read nor write, and who do not know the difference between right and wrong. Coroners' juries in the county I speak of are in a very great measure a mistake. I think the jurors in a populous town should be selected from a higher class of ratepayers, and that we ought to have men of more intellect on the jury. I think the constabulary should be furnished with a list of the jurors; at present they have no list to guide them, and they are not to blame.

2305. Mr. *Dawson.*] With regard to coroners, do you think there is any alteration of the law necessary as to the way in which they are paid; they are now paid by a sliding scale?—Thirty shillings an inquest, I think.

2306. They are very anxious to have a fixed salary; do you think that would accord more with justice; that it is desirable that they should be placed on a fixed salary?—I think the payment on each inquest is a very proper mode of paying them; I should not be at all disposed to alter that arrangement.

2307. Mr. *Maguire.*] You might, perhaps, pay them a little more liberally, but you would like to pay them by the job, as it were?—Yes; I think the present payment is too small if they have to come a distance.

2308. Mr. *Dawson.*] They can make a charge for mileage?—Yes.

2309. Mr. *Maguire.*] As to the division of baronies, I think you have already spoken of that?—Yes.

2310. As to petty sessions houses and locks up, for temporary detention of prisoners before conviction, have you anything to say?—The petty sessions houses in county Cork are of a most miserable character; wretched rooms, more like barns than anything else, with miserable accommodation. The grand jury have no power to build or to pay a higher rent than 10 *l.* a year. We went before the grand jury to see if we could get one built in the town in which I reside, and they said they had no power.

2311. Passage is a place where there is a considerable business?—Yes, a large shipping place; it is most important, not alone as regards the magistrates in their criminal proceedings, but in the road sessions, to have a room where the cesspayers can sit down with any ordinary degree of comfort; at present it is hardly a room fit for the magistrates let alone for the cesspayers; the cesspayers and the public at large are crowded in this room.

2312. You do not feel, if their powers were extended, and a discretion given to the magistrates, that they would abuse it by building expensive structures?—I am certain they would not, but I think the law might limit either the rent or the structures.

2313. The present limit is absurd?—It is; it is bringing justice into contempt.

2314. Now as to the locks up?—They are of an equally inferior description. The one attached to the Passage police barracks is a small cellar in the yard about eight feet long and five feet wide; it is supposed to be a lock up for men and women; there are no separate apartments, and the policemen are obliged to put the females in their own apartments.

2315. In fact, it is a dog-hole?—Well, it is even worse, for the floor of it is flagged, and they have not so much as straw to lay on.

2316. Have not the grand jury power to make a provision for that?—They have no power to build these locks up; they are generally rented along with the police barracks; I made a complaint of it to the local government, but nothing was done. I think that there should be some proper place for the temporary confinement of prisoners; it is a wretched thing to have men imprisoned for 24 hours on the cold flags on a winter's night.

2317. Is there any other suggestion which you wish

W. H. Edward Parker, Esq.

4 May 1868.

wish to make to the Committee in reference to the grand jury system?—With reference to the sudden breach orders; where breaches take place in walls or bridges, I think those sudden breaches ought to be first inspected by the county surveyor, that he should estimate the cost of having them done, and again the application should be made in open court at the petty sessions for the magistrates to sign.

2318. How are they done at the present moment?—A sudden breach is made; the contractor goes to a magistrate. First of all he goes to the county secretary and gets a sudden breach order in blank filled up; he goes before a magistrate, and gets it signed; he gets one magistrate to sign it, and then gets another, he executes the work, and the county surveyor goes and looks at it after the magistrates; the contractor practically speaking regulates the price of the work, and he puts down any sum under 10 *l.* for a wall; 20 *l.* is allowed for a bridge. The work is executed and there is no more said about it. I think the county surveyor ought to be the proper officer to inspect the work in the first instance; to estimate; and any sum over 5 *l.* should be tendered for as any other tender; that would prevent abuse.

2319. If the work is to be suddenly done, how could you have those tenders put in?—It would be immediately tendered for by local people.

2320. You would have the county surveyor decide?—Yes.

2321. Would not a deputy do as well?—Yes.

2322. Earl of *Mayo*.] In case of a county surveyor being called upon in the way you suggest, would you think it desirable to extend the limit of the amount which could be ordered for the sudden breach?—I think it would be very desirable, for in many instances 10 *l.* is too small for the sudden breach of a wall.

2323. To what limit would you propose to go?—If the limit were made at 20 *l.* for the ordinary breach of a wall, I think that would meet it.

2324. Mr. *Maguire*.] Suppose a huge piece had been carried away by the sea?—That would be almost unlimited. It might be some hundreds of pounds. A good deal should be left to the judgment of the county surveyor, for he really is the proper person to judge.

2325. Would you not leave him a larger discretion than within the limits of 20 *l.*?—It might be desirable. I think so; I think where the county surveyor is the acknowledged, paid, and responsible officer of the county, there should be a discretion left with him. I think with regard to contractors the law is rather imperfect at present. The grand jury have no power to annul a contract, no matter how bad the contractor may be. I think that it may be desirable that the grand jury should have power to annul the contract in case of a report made by the county surveyor, that the contractor has not properly performed the contract; and then, as a protection to the contractor, that he should have an appeal to the going judge of assize.

2326. Mr. *Blake*.] You stated you were in favour of the entire separation of the fiscal and criminal business of the grand juries?—Yes.

2327. You would have a county board much the same as the grand jury at present?—Yes.

2328. Elected by the ratepayers?—You mean as the Poor Law Board is?

2329. Yes?—Yes, elected by the ratepayers in the barony.

2330. You would have baronial boards for the purposes of the barony?—Yes.

2331. And you would have a county board for the purposes of the county at large?—Yes.

2332. The same as the grand jury is at present; you would have each of these boards elected by the ratepayers?—Yes.

2333. Have you any idea as to whether you would have the county board elected by the baronial board, or one member for the county board to be sent in directly by the ratepayers. Perhaps I can better explain it to you by telling you the evidence of the preceding witness, Mr. Leigh; he was in favour of having a certain number of ratepayers elected upon the baronial board, and they were then to elect representatives from themselves to go upon the county board. Would you be in favour of that plan, or would you have the ratepayers of each barony in addition to sending members to the baronial board, also sending a representative to the county board?—May I ask what you mean by a county board?

2334. I mean the county at large board, the same as the present grand jury?—What is conveyed to my mind by the county at large board, is the county at large sessions. You speak of the grand jury board; you wish to know as to how the grand jury of the barony should be chosen.

2335. I mean the representative on the county board answering to the present grand jury for the county, how would you have him elected?—He should have a certain qualification in the barony, and he should be elected by the ratepayers of the barony.

2336. You would have the members of the baronial board elected, I suppose, in the same way?—Yes.

2337. Would you have both the baronial boards and the county at large boards a continuous board; a certain number of members to go out by rotation, one-third every year, and the others to remain?—Most unquestionably; it is one the most desirable points, for at present the grand jury are merely in existence for three days, and they are gone. We know no more of them. We have no opportunity of making our complaints known to them, advising with them, or seeing them as to what they ought to do, and it would be most desirable that they should remain in office, at least, for a year; eligible for re-election in the same way as the elected board of guardians.

2338. By having the nomination the same as with regard to the Poor Law Board; an election in each instance might not be necessary?—It might not be necessary. In all probability it would not be necessary; but as long as gentlemen attend to their business, the ratepayers are satisfied with them, and they never think of choosing any in their place.

2339. Might not the barony constable hold a meeting in the district, and receive the nominations, and if those nominations did not exceed the necessary number, there would not be a necessity for any election at all?—Precisely; he would be a very proper person to appoint in that way.

2340. You would, if I understand you correctly, have an equal number of magistrates on the county board, as well as on the baronial board?—Yes.

2341. Would you have these magistrates elected by themselves, or would you have the highest rated magistrates residing in the district

for

for the baronial board, for instance?—I should hardly like to offer an opinion upon that point. Either way would be very good; some magistrates may not wish to attend, and they may prefer some one to go in their place; some have a taste for business, and others have not.

2342. You have no suggestions to offer as to the mode of electing magistrates?—No; except that they should be owners of property in the barony to a certain amount.

2343. Under the present system of the occupier paying the entire of the rates, is there not a positive bonus offered to a landlord, supposing him to be a grand juror of the district, to put as much as possible on the occupier for improvements?—Undoubtedly.

2344. If those improvements occur, and are made by the tenants' money, may it not often happen, that the tenant by reason of the outlay of his own money, would be an instrument for raising the rent on himself?—Decidedly; unquestionably an instrument for raising the rent. "If he does not pay, turn him out."

2345. Mr. *Dawson.*] Did you ever know a case where that took place?—No, I did not, but it stands to reason.

2346. Mr. *Blake.*] Did you ever know an instance where a tenant at will has improved his land, and by reason of that, the rent has been raised?—No, I cannot bring to mind any particular case.

2347. Is it not one of the great disadvantages which the tenant labours under, that that amount is uncertain; that he has no control over the outlay?—Decidedly.

2348. With regard to the lunatics; are you aware in the union you belong to, what the charge is for maintaining paupers in the workhouse; it is about 10*l.* a year, I think?—About 10*l.* a year is the average charge. In the Cork union it is estimated at about 12*l.*; that is more expensive than others.

2349. Are you aware that according to the last report of the lunatic asylum for the county of Cork, that the charge for the maintenance of the insane paupers there is about 24*l.* a year?—It is very probable, but I am not aware of it.

2350. In consequence of the present system, has not the occupier to pay just four times as much on the county of Cork for the maintenance of an insane pauper as he has to pay for the maintenance of a sane pauper?—Yes.

2351. He pays the whole of the 24*l.* for the insane pauper, and he pays but 6*l.* for the sane pauper?—Yes.

2352. That is a manifest injustice?—Of course it is.

2353. Could you offer any opinion with regard to the desirability of the continuance or discontinuance of the inspectors of county prisons?—No, I have not made any note of that.

2354. Does it not often occur that county gentlemen are appointed with no previous knowledge of the duties?—Yes.

2355. Would it not strike you, who have paid a good deal of attention to these subjects, that it would be infinitely better that an inspection of that kind should be carried on by a properly qualified Government officer?—I should say so. I know gentlemen have been appointed who knew nothing whatever about it.

2356. The fiscal duties which the clerk of the Crown and the clerk of the peace have to perform are very different now, I believe?—I am not prepared to answer that.

2357. In your experience, do you find those offices very often combined in one officer?—No, not in my county, which is so very large.

W. D'Esterre Parker, Esq.

5 May 1868.

2358. From your knowledge of the fiscal duties necessary to be performed by some public officers, do you think the secretaries of grand juries could conveniently perform all the fiscal duties that might be required under the system you propose, of the separation of the fiscal from the criminal business of the grand juries?—I think so; there is a large portion of the year during which the county secretary is in a measure unemployed.

2359. He could, you think, perform those duties?—Yes.

2360. You consider that if the system you suggest be carried into operation, there should be another division, other than the present baronial division; that the counties ought to be divided into districts?—The counties ought to be divided into districts more equally divided. Some of the baronies are very small, and some are very large. I think it would be desirable to have them more equally divided.

2361. With regard to coroners, do you not think, considering the class of persons now generally appointed as coroners, the magistrates could hold inquests just as well as the coroner?—Of course they could, there is nothing to prevent them; and it would be more convenient.

2362. Did you ever hear of instances where, owing to the absence of a coroner, the inquest has very often to stand over for a week or more?—No, I have not; they have sometimes been delayed.

2363. Do you not think the charge for a coroner might be dispensed with altogether by the magistrate of the district, in which an inquest was to be held, holding it?—Yes; I think you would find a difficulty in getting the magistrate to take correct notes of the evidence, as the coroner is bound to do; that duty could of course be done by the clerk of the petty sessions, otherwise I think the magistrates would be quite able to preside at a coroner's inquest.

2364. Mr. *Dawson.*] Do you think the magistrates would willingly undertake the duties of holding inquests, being an unpaid body, it not being a very agreeable duty; do you think they would like to undertake the responsibility as well as all the consequences of holding an inquest?—I invariably found the magistrates most anxious for responsibility, and very desirous to perform any public duty placed upon them.

2365. Do you think it would be desirable that the coroner should generally be a medical man?—I think his legal education has more to do with it than his medical education.

2366. Mr. *Maguire.*] Would you assume that the magistrates would have a legal education?—The magistrates are presumed as judges to know the law.

2367. Mr. *Blake.*] Would you have him both a lawyer and a doctor?—I think the doctor is unnecessary; I think the lawyer would be the best; they invariably call in the medical officer of the dispensary, or whoever is in the district, but I think it is right that he should have a legal education.

2368. Mr. *Dawson.*] Do you think from your knowledge of the grand jury laws that when the baronial constables at each assizes have to produce

W. D'Esterre Parker, Esq.

5 May 1858.

dure their securities, that could be done without the presence of those securities by affidavit and by proof that they were in solvent circumstances, and living?—It could be done by affidavit, of course, but I think it would be desirable that the securities should attend. On that point, if you will allow me to suggest it is absolutely necessary that the bonds of the baronial constables and their securities should be registered; at present they are not registered, and I think that is a mistake.

2269. Colonel *Cooper*.] In regard to the incidence of the grand jury cess, does the cess in your county vary much each year?—Not very much; sometimes more, sometimes less; it entirely depends upon the expenditure upon new works.

2270. It has been given in evidence that your cess amounts to about 1 *s.* 6 *d.* in the pound in the year?—On an average; sometimes more, sometimes less.

2271. A tenant, therefore, taking a farm can tell within a penny or so what he will have to pay?—He makes an approximate idea of it, but at the same time it is very uncertain, for new works may be carried out immediately after his taking the farm, and the cess may be doubled.

2272. Have you ever known an instance of that?—There must be several instances.

2273. When it was anything like doubled?—I should say so; several instances.

2274. I should like to know something more particularly about that?—The cess in some parishes varies; in the barony of B   it is 1 *s.* 1 *d.* in the pound, while in the barony of B   it is only 7 *d.*

2275. That is not what I wanted to know; does it vary in *your* barony *from year to year*?—I cannot say that, because I have not the returns.

2276. You say you have taken an interest in the subject?—Yes.

2277. What is your barony?—Kerricurrihy.

2278. Has your cess varied much within the last ten years?—The cess at the last assizes was 8 *d.* in the pound; it is sometimes more, sometimes less, but within a penny or two-pence.

2279. Was it ever sixteen-pence?—Not for the half-year, not within the few years you speak of.

2280. Not within the last 20 years?—I could not say that.

2281. At all events you admit that a man taking land in your barony can, generally speaking, form an estimate within a penny or two of what he will have to pay?—He can form some estimate of that, but new works may be executed a year or two after he takes the farm which he had no idea of; there may be 4,000 *l.* or 5,000 *l.* laid out which would raise the rate for that year. I know many instances of it.

2282. Will *you give one*?—The lunatic asylum.

2283. The Government advances money for that, and it is repaid in a series of *years*?—Yes.

2284. Therefore the cess does not vary very much; it does not raise the cess much?—Yes, it does.

2285. To a certain extent, but not very much?—The paying for the building raises the cess, but the maintenance of the patients and the staff afterwards continues a permanent raising of the cess, as well as I can recollect; our county cess was four or five pence in the pound a number of years ago, and now it is 1 *s.* 6 *d.*; these additional things have been put on.

2286. It is a very gradual thing, farmers can see if they change their farm what they will have to pay?—To be candid with you, farmers do not take into account what rates they have to pay, no matter what is offered for the farm, they must take it.

2287. You think they never consider what poor rates they may have to pay?—Never.

2288. You are aware the poor rates vary very much in some of the electoral divisions?—Yes.

2289. In poor electoral divisions the poor rate is very high?—That does not follow.

2290. In some districts?—In the city districts it is high, and in the rural districts low.

2291. You think that does not affect the value of a farm?—I do not think it does.

2292. Is there such very great competition for land?—Very great. The farmer must take the land, no matter what rates he has to pay; or, I may almost add, no matter what rent he has to pay; either that or leave the country; it is a choice between the two evils.

2292.* You say the jury and the presentment sessions are irresponsible; I do not quite understand what you mean by that?—What I mean by that is this; they are not responsible for their acts to any person; they may vote for or against a work as they think proper.

2293. Surely you must be aware that anybody can traverse a presentment?—I am perfectly aware of that.

2294. If the grand jury pass a presentment which the people object to, any cesspayer can traverse that presentment?—Yes.

2295. That gives him a protection?—It does to a certain extent.

2296. You are also, I suppose, aware that if the grand jury throw out a presentment twice in succession, the promoter of that work can also traverse the decision?—Yes.

2297. And yet you say the grand jury is irresponsible?—I maintain it; matters are past at the road sessions, they go before the grand jury, and without any intimation whatever to the cesspayers or the road sessions, they can throw out the work merely on the individual representation of the grand juror of the barony. All the work is being gone through at the road sessions, where the matter is investigated; then it is not made, and by the individual voice of the grand juror, it is knocked on the head. It is perfectly competent for a party, as the law says, to go before a judge when he has been refused an application on two different occasions; but I have never known any instance of any ratepayer making that application. The applications are generally for public works, for public benefit, and individuals do not like to take extra trouble and labour to promote a public work. They would take an ordinary amount of trouble, but that would be an extraordinary amount of trouble, and there is a barrier to their coming before the judge, for they have to lodge a certain amount of money before proceeding before the judge; the ratepayers do not like running that risk and trouble.

2298. *Chairman*.] Your meaning is, that the grand jurors and baronial sessions are not responsible to any constituent bodies?—Precisely.

2299. Colonel *Cooper*.] Yet they are responsible to the cesspayers, having a power of appealing before the judge?—It is very few who make use of that power.

2300. Still

2400. Still it exists?—Yes.

2401. *Earl of Mayo.*] You stated that these presentments are thrown out very often at the mere representation of a grand juror representing the barony?—Not very often, but I have known instances where they have been thrown out on the representation of the grand juror of the barony.

2402. Without any opportunity being allowed for the public to remonstrate?—If I may correct myself, without any notice to the public that it is going to be done.

2403. Are you not aware that the grand jury sitting for fiscal business is an open court?—Quite so.

2404. Do you not know that every single cess-payer and ratepayer in the barony can be present at the deliberations?—Quite so.

2405. Did you ever know an instance of a cesspayer or ratepayer, whether associated or not, being refused a hearing, on a question affecting the public interests, before the grand jury?—I never heard of it.

2406. How then can you say it is possible that, without notice or without knowledge given to the public, an important public work can be thrown out by a grand jury on the mere representation of the grand juror representing the barony?—Because, when the work is passed at the road sessions, the promoters of the work consider that no one will raise an opposition to it before the grand jury, especially the grand juror of the barony. If it was necessary for the associated cesspayers and those interested in promoting any public work to attend the grand jury, it would involve an immensity of labour and trouble, and, I may add, annoyance, in waiting for it to come on. Then the cesspayers have no notice that there is going to be such an opposition raised. They do not know who their grand juror is until they see his name published in the paper the following morning. They are ignorant of who he may be; they are ignorant of what the opposition is going to be; and I think I am justified in saying that opposition can be raised by the grand jurors of the barony behind the backs of the ratepayers, although the room is an open court and any one may appear there.

2407. Do you not know as a matter of fact that in any case which has been contested at presentment sessions, that contest and conflict is almost invariably followed into the grand jury-room, and when there has been a difference of opinion it is generally the practice for persons interested in the matter to go and express their opinions before the grand jury; does this not happen at almost every assize?—There are such cases happen, but where the case has passed the road sessions, where it is agreed to by the magistrates and cesspayers that such a work is to be done, people hardly ever think of coming to the grand jury to see if it is passed. It is generally supposed to pass as a matter of course; I could mention an instance where an important footpath was passed at a road sessions.

2408. *Colonel Cooper.*] Unanimously?—No.

2409. Was it disputed at the road sessions?—There was some dispute.

2410. There was an opposition at the road sessions?—A slight opposition; it is an important footpath leading from the city of Cork to a public cemetery; the footpath was to be made in the county; it passed the road sessions and it came before the grand jury; the grand juror of the barony opposed it; there was no opposition by the cesspayers; they knew nothing at all about it, and it was rejected by the grand jury. *W. D'Esterre Parker, Esq.* — 6 May 1868.

2411. Has that put back the making of the path?—It is only the last assizes that it occurred.

2412. Have you any knowledge of the working of grand juries out of the county of Cork?—I have not.

2413. You are aware it is rather an exceptional county from its size?—It is exceptional as regards size.

2414. Also owing to the way in which the grand jury is called?—It may be so.

2415. There are 23 baronies?—Yes.

2416. And a man must be called for each barony to represent that barony, "invited," I believe, is the term?—Yes, the law says so; sometimes a barony happens not to be represented; that may be from accident; there are very few of what we should call independent jurors in the county of Cork; they generally speaking come to represent a barony?—Generally speaking.

2417. Apparently by your practice the business of the barony is left to the grand juror?—Yes.

2418. And the other gentlemen do not seem to take much part in the business of the barony?—That is so.

2419. You are not aware whether that is rather an exceptional state of things throughout Ireland?—I do not know of any other county but Cork where that is so.

2420. Do you find at road sessions that new works generally originate with the cesspayer, or with the owner of property?—The application is generally put in the name of a cesspayer; the work is promoted by the owner of the property as a rule; the owner of the property, or those particularly interested, presiding on the bench as magistrates.

2421. Do you think a tenant taking a farm from the landlord, and asking the landlord to pay half the cess, would meet with any objection?—I really cannot say. I have been told of some landlords who pay half the county cess; I think some pay the entire cess.

2422. Even now?—I think so; I heard so, but I cannot positively say.

2423. Do you think, if the tenants generally wished to pay half the cess, an amicable arrangement could not be made with the landlord without any alteration of the law?—I do not think so; I think the law should intervene.

2424. And make it compulsory?—I think so.

2425. On all new tenants?—On all new tenants.

2426. Is your scheme for the representation of the different interests of the county dependent on the occupier paying all the rates, as at present?—My scheme is, that the occupier should pay half the rates and the landlord pay half.

2427. And still, that the occupier should be more represented than he is at present?—No, not more represented, for he is supposed to be already well represented. I do not want to get more representatives on the road sessions than the law allows; it allows 12 at the barony road sessions; I do not want to extend that number, but I want to have that number of cesspayers elected by the cesspayers; I do not extend the representation.

W. D'Esterre Parke, Esq.

5 May 1859.

2428. Earl of *Mayo*.] You say you think it would be an improvement if the associated cesspayers were elected. Have you stated by what constituency you would recommend that they should be elected?—I think the Poor Law Constituency would give a very good precedent; all ratepayers over 4 *l.* a year.

2429. With the number of votes regulated according to the valuation?—Yes.

2430. Do you think that would work satisfactorily?—I think so; it would give property its rights as regards the number of votes.

2431. In that case would you retain the present baronial divisions, or would you rather that the areas of taxation should be assimilated to the electoral divisions of poor law?—I think it would simplify it very much, if it were divided into electoral divisions; if the present electoral divisions were taken as the basis of taxation. Some of the baronies are very large, and have very little representation, and others are very small. Some are valued at 60,000 *l.* or 70,000 *l.* a year, and others at 17,000 *l.*, 18,000 *l.*, or 19,000 *l.*, and as low as 4,000 *l.*

2432. There would be this inconvenience, that in some cases the electoral divisions would break into other counties; there are, I believe, some few cases of the kind; but that, perhaps, could be altered?—Yes.

2433. Are you aware that in the formation of electoral districts originally for poor law purposes, regard was had very much by the boundary commissioners to the size of the various properties, and the boundaries of the property?—I am not.

2434. Do you think that that would be an additional reason for adopting the electoral division boundary?—My reason is that the present boundaries of the poor law unions appear to work very well for the purposes of taxation, and that, of course, they must have been regulated with more experience by the present revisers than the original formation of the baronies. The local position of the country is very much altered in many instances from what it was when the baronies were first formed.

2435. You propose that this change in the incidents of taxation should only apply to future lettings?—To future lettings.

2436. Do you propose to include in the term "future lettings" the lands now held by tenants at will?—I should say so.

2437. Do you think there would be some difficulty in the collection of the county cess, seeing that you would collect the cess principally from one class of occupiers and only partly from another class?—I think the county cess could be collected in the same way as the poor rate is, the occupier paying the entire of the county cess in the first instance and deducting the landlord's proportion.

2438. In the case you referred to of future lettings, the occupier who came under the operation of the new system would have the power to deduct half the rate from his landlord?—Yes.

2439. But the cess should be collected in the first instance from the occupier in every case?—Yes, that arrangement works well with the poor law.

2440. Do you think practically it would make much difference either to the landlord or the tenant, this mode of levying?—I do not think it would make any difference.

2441. Is it not the case now practically that the landlord pays the whole of the poor rate and the county cess?—I do not think so at all.

2442. Do not you think that in all arrangements the calculation is made as between the landlord and the tenant as to the amount of charge which is likely to be placed on the land?—Yes; as I said before the tenants really take the land without calculating the charge at all; they must take it.

2443. Do you mean to give the Committee to understand that the tenants in the county Cork take the land without reference to the amount of rent they are to pay?—I cannot go so far as that, but certainly without regard to the amount of rates they have to pay.

2444. Is not the amount of rates they have to pay really so much addition to their rent?—It is a portion of the rent.

2445. Do you think they never take into consideration whether they pay 5 *s.* an acre or 8 *s.* an acre beyond their rent?—Some may take it into consideration, but I am satisfied the general class of tenants do not.

2446. Do you mean to say that if a landlord in the County Cork had a farm to let upon which the local rate was 5 *s.* an acre, and the landlord had another farm to let of the same value upon which there were no rates at all that he would let the land charged 5 *s.* an acre for the same amount that he would let the land which had no charge on it at all?—It is very possible that he may charge more for the land that pays no rates than he would for the land that pays rates.

2447. He would get more for the land that paid no rates than for the land which paid rates?—He would try and get what he could for it.

2448. If that is the case the rates to that amount do really come out of the landlord's pocket in such a case?—Arguing in that way they do; I grant you that dividing the tax between landlord and tenant may not in a pecuniary way affect the tenant's pocket; that he may be charged more for the land, but the great point is giving the tenants some control over the expenditure of the money, controlling the expenditure of the landlord, as well as having a voice in the general disbursement of the public money.

2449. You think it is desirable that the occupier should pay a portion if it was only to give the general class of occupiers an interest in the economical and proper management of the local funds?—I think so; I think it would be unfair to allow the occupiers to have a voice unless they contributed to the expenditure.

2450. There was some misapprehension about a question I asked you with regard to the sudden breaches. You recommended, I think, that the power should be extended, and that works up to 50 *l.* should be undertaken by magistrates on the representation of the county surveyor. It escaped our memory at the time that there was an Act to that effect passed last year?—I believe there was; but whether it gave the power to the county surveyor, or made it the duty of the county surveyor to examine the works and report on the necessity of each, and the amount, I do not know.

2451. That is done by this clause, "The necessity of the same shall be certified to the magistrates by the county surveyor, and then it shall be lawful for the justices to appoint," and so on. You think that is an improvement?—Decidedly.

The

The magistrates are not judges of the expense of the work; a contractor will put in as much as he can.

2452. That Act was so lately passed as probably not to have been taken advantage of yet?—Yes.

2453. *Mr. Dawson.*] I think you omitted to state that the magistrates must see the work first?—The law says that they ought to see it, but the practice is that they do not see it; sometimes they do, but sometimes they do not.

2454. *Colonel Forde.*] You made some objections in the county Cork, principally as to the grand jurors. Colonel Cooper said there being 23 baronies and only 23 allowed on the grand jury, there were no independent grand jurors?—May I ask what you mean by the word "independent" there?

2455. In other counties not so large the sheriff has the power of summoning men who are, of course, belonging to the county, and of no particular barony?—Yes.

2456. If the county of Cork were divided into two ridings, would not that obviate the difficulty you have in view as to the grand jurors?—I do not think it would.

2457. If it were divided each riding would then have 23 grand jurors?—Each riding would divide the 23 between them?

2458. No; each riding would have 23 grand jurors?—You would have two grand jurors for each barony.

2459. No; the county would be divided into the north and south riding. There would be a grand jury for the north, and one for the south riding. Would not that give you a larger representation of the grand jurors, whom you object to, than the county?—Yes. I do not look for a larger representation. The number of the grand jury is sufficiently large.

2460. You say there are several gentlemen who ought to be on the grand jury who never are on the grand jury. Therefore, if the county were divided into ridings, those gentlemen who had property in each riding would then be on the grand jury of the particular riding in which their property was situated?—That does not follow, because the high sheriff has the power of selecting whom he likes, and may select the same gentlemen every year, and leave out the others. The high sheriff controls that.

2461. He then has a larger number to select from in the riding?—No doubt of it; it would give a better opportunity of having other gentlemen appointed; but as long as the high sheriff has the power of nominating whom he likes, he will continue to do so.

2462. You say you wish that the county surveyor should devote his whole time to the county work; do you know, by an Act lately passed, it is optional with the grand jury and the county at large sessions, having a voice in the matter, to restrict the county surveyor?—I was not aware that that was the law, but the grand jury not being a responsible body, it is not likely they would interfere.

2463. If I tell you that it is the law, and that it is perfectly optional now with the grand jury, and the county at large sessions, and then to be afterwards agreed to by the following grand jury, to regulate the salary of their county surveyors, and that they should be obliged to devote their whole time to the office, that would obviate what you object to?—Of course; if it is the law at present, there is no occasion to make any change.

2464. You said that the clerk of the petty sessions should be the returning officer for the associated cesspayers?—I think he would be a very convenient officer for that purpose.

W. D'Esterre Parker, Esq.

6 May 1868.

2465. He holds no office under the grand jury system; would not you think it should be an officer recognised under the system, who should be the returning officer?—Yes; I agree with you that it would be very desirable to have a grand jury officer. It was the petty sessions clerk who came first to my mind.

2466. Do not you think the secretary of the grand jury, like the clerk of the Poor Law Guardians, should be the returning officer, and responsible to the grand jury for the elections?—Yes, I think that would be better still, because they are generally more up to their business.

2467. You made some objections about the grand jurors selecting the cesspayers, and you stated that they sometimes did not select those they were authorised to do by the Act?—Yes.

2468. Do not they select the number, which is the full complement allowed to be associated with the magistrates?—I do not think they do.

2469. We will take it, for instance, that there are 24 names returned, out of which 18 are to be selected. The grand jurors never appoint less than 12. You stated, I think, that sometimes he only nominated 12, but is not the sessions empowered and obliged to take the number of associated cesspayers who are competent to sit with the magistrates at the sessions, that is to say, they are obliged out of those 18 to take 12?—No, they are not; I have never known an instance of it being done. They invariably take half the number selected by the grand jury.

2470. That is against the law?—Well, perhaps, you are right. I did not look particularly into that point.

2471. *Chairman.*] Does your complaint apply to the number of cesspayers fixed by the grand jury to be associated with the justices in any particular barony, or to the number balloted for by the justices at the presentment sessions?—My complaint is, that the grand juror of the barony does not generally make a proper selection of the ratepayers of the barony, that also he does not give the full number which the law allows.

2472. You are aware that the law does not contemplate that there should be the same number of associated cesspayers appointed for the barony, because it gives the grand jury a discretion between the numbers of 12 and 5?—It does.

2473. Therefore, if the grand juror for any particular barony should determine upon a number of associated cesspayers less than 12, he is not in any way violating either the law or the spirit of the law?—Decidedly they are not violating the law at all; what I complain of is the law itself; it allows too great a discretion to the grand juror in the selection of the associated cesspayers.

2474. You mean in the selection of the individuals?—Yes; as regards the district.

2475. Do you mean with respect to the number fixed upon, that in cases where, in your opinion, the barony was so large and important that the number ought to have been the full number of 12, the grand jury have fixed upon a lower number?—Precisely; and here is a very great objection to it. I am, we will suppose, an associated cesspayer: the list is sent to me previous

to

W. D'Esterre Parker, Esq.

5 May 1868.

to the sessions day; I am one of 24; it is a mere matter of chance whether I am selected or not; I go to the sessions; I drive eight or nine miles; I find my name is not called, and that I have lost my time. I think that is wrong.

9476. Colonel *French*.] Do not you think that although it may be an inconvenience in that way, it is a means of preventing a great deal of jobbing that otherwise might take place, if the associated cesspayers were known to be those who were to be associated with the magistrates beforehand?—I look upon the word "jobbing" in two different views; it may be a good job or a bad job; if it is a good job, it has a right to be done; and I think the more information the ratepayers have of whom the cesspayers are the better. They are always the promoters of a work; but at the same time, they are the opponents of a work, and it is better for both to have the fullest opportunities of voting, either for or against it. If any useful work is to be carried out, every ratepayer, with very few exceptions, will support it. I think it would be a prevention of jobbing by having every publicity given to whom the cesspayers are, and who the grand jurors are. I think the same publicity that is given to our representatives the better.

9477. Then you do not consider it as a means of stopping what I call jobbing?—I do not think the present system is the means of stopping it, but a means of encouraging it.

9478. You say yourself you do not know whether you will be called on at the sessions; therefore you cannot make any arrangement?—Suppose I have a job in hand and want to carry it out, I take very good care to attend and to get as many of my friends to attend as possible, and by so doing throw out the others; it works both for and against.

9479. The other way you would have the cesspayer to work upon during the whole time?—Yes, in the representative way you would have the cesspayer to work upon during the whole time either to promote the work or to oppose it.

9480. The cesspayer under the proposed change would be precisely in the position of a poor law guardian?—Precisely; a guardian of the land in place of being a guardian of the poor.

9481. Mr. *Herbert*.] How do the poor law guardians attend in your district?—Very well.

9482. Do the rural guardians attend as well as the *ex officio* guardians?—The rural guardians, generally speaking, attend better than the *ex officio* guardians.

9483. Can you tell the proportion?—I should say at least two to one. I should say two elected guardians to one *ex officio* guardian would attend.

9484. What number of guardians on an average attend at your board?—About 20.

9485. How many have you in the whole district?—One hundred.

9486. If there is a place to be voted for, would you have a large attendance?—They would all come in, both *ex officio* and the others.

9487. Is it not a well-known thing, that if there is what is known as a job, everyone of them come?—If there is a useful work to be carried out, or a useful thing to be done, a great many will come to promote it, and a great many would come to oppose it.

9488. Do not you think as a rule that everyone of those guardians come in, having made up their minds which way they will vote?—Well, it is very hard to say what other men think; but there is a great deal in what you say, that many of them make up their minds; some are open to conviction. I know some gentlemen who have come to oppose a thing, and when they have heard the addresses of the members, have changed their minds and have voted *for* it.

9489. That is not a very common occurrence?—I think there are a great many instances; it all depends on the impressive power of the speaker.

9490. Is it general with all the associated cesspayers elected in the way you just now mentioned, putting them in the different divisions, that one grand juror is generally accustomed to put 12 on one division and two on another; is that the general system?—Well, I think so. I know in my barony I have invariably found fault with the want of representation in my part of the district.

9491. In fact, you mean to say the grand jurors try to appoint as many associated cesspayers in their district as they can, in order to carry anything they want?—It is one of the laws of human nature.

9492. You say you do not know anything outside your own county?—Nothing.

9493. You said just now that there were several cases in which the magistrates clubbed together, and came to oppose works, or anything being done, and to outnumber the associated cesspayers?—Yes.

9494. Will you name a few of those instances; because I think it will be only fair to the magistrates?—I have known individual cases.

9495. Will you name one or two?—I should not like to mention the names. First of all, you are perfectly well aware that the law allows it; there is nothing illegal in it.

9496. Will you give me the name of the barony?—In my own barony; the barony of Kerrycurrihy. I have known more than one road session magistrate from another barony, having no property at all in the barony, coming to that road session to vote for a public work which was promoted by a friend; and I invariably got up in the public court and charged them with it, and told them it was a shame for them to come there. The result of it was, that some of them did not come there again. There are gentlemen living in the barony, who have no property beyond the yearly tenancy of a house, who have attended the road session; and I have repeatedly told them in public court, "It is not fair for you to be coming here, voting away the public money. You have no property here; do not come here; for every time you do come, I really must speak. Personally it is very unpleasant to me, because you are all intimate friends of mine; but as a matter of justice I must do it." I have done that repeatedly. There are no less than seven magistrates within the immediate vicinity of my town (Passage) that have no property at all in the town, or in the barony. It is a watering place. Gentlemen have their own property in a distant part of Ireland, and come to reside there as a nice watering place. I think it is very wrong for those gentlemen to act as magistrates on the bench and vote away our public money. I say to them, "You attend the petty sessions; it is enough for you to punish us if we do wrong; but to put your hands into our pockets for the benefit of your friends is decidedly wrong."

9497. Mr. *Maguire*.] That is not so strong a point

point as a man coming from another barony and attending your road sessions?—No.

2498. There here seem to have some combinations of claims, inasmuch as they are resident cesspayers?—Yes, but others come from other baronies.

2499. Colonel *French*.] You would not allow a magistrate, in fact, to sit at road sessions unless he had a proper qualification in the barony to which he belonged?—Decidedly not; it is only fair and right.

2500. Mr. *Leader*.] Is the barony of Kerricurrihy very close to Cork?—Yes.

2501. I believe there are more magistrates residing in that barony in proportion than in a great number of other baronies?—I should think so.

2502. It is rather an exceptional barony?—It may be so; you are a better judge of that than I am.

2503. Mr. *Maguire*.] You rather complain of magistrates coming from other baronies and dealing with the affairs of your barony with affairs that do not belong to them?—Yes.

2504. Is not that a greater abuse than that to which you referred just now?—Yes, there are some grounds for the residents attending, but there are no grounds whatever for non-residents attending.

2505. Mr. *Herbert*.] Do not you think it would be a very good thing with reference to the county surveyor, that he should print his Report before the assembling of the grand jury?—Precisely so; but what I have taken a note of was this: that he should take the initiative in any ordinary work, and make an application for doing it; the same application to be published as the ordinary applications of cesspayers are, and to come before the road session; that we should have a knowledge before hand of what he is going to apply for. The law allows him to put in applications for any work, but it is the habit of surveyors in my county not to put in any application except on some very extraordinary grounds. I think it would be well that the county surveyor should take the initiative in any ordinary work, the making or repairing of any ordinary work; that the application should be printed and come before the cesspayers at the road session; that at the road session he should have a detailed report of the state and condition of all the different roads in the district, what position they are in, and how they are circumstanced.

2506. Colonel *French*.] In that barony?—Of course in that barony; at present, as you are aware, his report comes in a very concise form before the county grand jury. The cesspayers have no notice of that.

2507. *Chairman*.] You would have baronial reports, as well as county reports from the county surveyor?—Precisely so.

2508. Colonel *French*.] Does not your county surveyor do that now?—No, he does not; he makes no report at all to the road session; the question is asked by the county secretary, "Is there any complaint against any contractor?" no individual person would get up and make a complaint against a contractor, and they are all signed, as a matter of course. I think you will say the county surveyor should be asked his opinion on every public work applied for at the road session; that he should be asked his opinion at the road session, whether that is a necessary work to be done? Sometimes he is, and sometimes he is not; and I think that is wrong.'

2509. Mr. *Herbert*.] Do you mean to say that you never heard a complaint made against a contractor at these road sessions?—Not by individuals; it is not generally done; if it is, it is the exception. I also think that he should be held responsible for the repair of all public roads, and other works, that is, so far responsible for them, that if a road is allowed to go out of repair, or out of contract, that he should be able to say, why it is so; for instance, there are many roads that are allowed to go out of contract, and remain out for three or four years. If a cesspayer takes it up the expense of putting them into repair is much more than what would keep them in repair from year to year, while at the same time the ratepayers have a bad road. "Everybody's business is nobody's business," and I think the proper officer who ought to be held responsible, is the county surveyor; he also should be held responsible for keeping open all public passages; in many places they are shut up by individuals, and no private individual likes to interfere; the county surveyor does not interfere, and the public lose the benefit of a public right.

2510. Mr. *Kendall*.] As I understood you just now, the usual mode of election of the juror for the barony, is by the high sheriff, and you object to that because there are a great many men in the baronies who ought to be jurors, who never are jurors?—Precisely.

2511. Is not the high sheriff with you an annual high sheriff?—Yes.

2512. Is he not annually nominated by the judges?—Yes.

2513. Then there can be no partisanship at all, it must be a pure accident. I ask for information. I do not see how your argument applies. I cannot see how, except by accident, any man who ought to be in the position of a juror, has not a fair chance of being nominated?—The county is a very large one; there are a number of gentlemen fully qualified to be grand jurors. How the matter is arranged by the high sheriff, or practically by the sub-sheriff, I am not actually in a position to state.

2514. The same difficulty would arise if any other person were nominated?—To remove that difficulty, what I propose is, that the grand juror of the barony should be elected by the ratepayers of the barony, the grand juror having a certain qualification of standing, and of property in the barony, as would ensure that he is a highly respectable person, and fully qualified to sit. Let him go in as the representative of the barony, in fact, the barony is, in a lesser way, the same as the House of Commons and the House of Lords here.

2515. With reference to the county surveyor, as I understand, you would have him entirely confined to that office?—I think so.

2516. From your experience, taking some of your best men, what is the relative proportion of the money they receive for the office of county surveyor, and what they receive from extraneous offices which they fill?—Their salary is 400 *l.* a year.

2517. Taking your best men, do not you think that in many instances what they get from other sources is more than 400 *l.*?—I could not say; I could not give any idea.

W. D'Esterre Parker, Esq.

6 May 1868.

2518. Have you no impression at all; it is very considerably augmented, is it not?—It is.

2519. The better the class of man, of course the more it is augmented?—No doubt.

2520. Do not you think if you confine him in that way you must as a necessary consequence have an inferior class of man to what you have got now?—Well, I do not agree with you.

2521. Do you think you would have the same men as now; I understand the competition is very considerable that man pits his wit against wit, the young men try hard to get on; do you think the same class of men would compete, if you deprive them of the chance of working their brains in both directions?—I think the salary of 400 *l.* a year would be a sufficient inducement to many clever able men to enter the profession.

2522. I do not ask you that, but do you think you would have the same class of men?—Unquestionably you would have the same class.

2523. *Chairman.*] Would you desire to go beyond the present provision of the law, which enables the grand jury if it pleases to impose that condition; would you think it necessary to make such a condition imperative upon grand jurors?—I really think it most desirable. I think where we pay a county officer, we have a right to have the services of that officer. Except in the very important work of the construction of a bridge, which very rarely happens, the ordinary repairs of the road do not require that extreme ability. It is to be hoped, as we have so many roads in Ireland, that we are not going to construct any more, particularly as the railways are coming there. We do not want those extremely talented gentlemen who may get a larger amount by their private practice than 400 *l.* a year.

2524. Mr. *Kendall.*] Can you think of any two surveyors, one who does a great deal of extraneous matter, and one who simply does the county work?—No, I cannot, I can only speak of the surveyors in my own county.

2525. You do not know two men of that kind?—I do not; their position is such that they are right in the thoroughfare of getting a good deal of business.

2526. *Chairman.*] Have you reason to complain of your own county surveyor?—No, I have not; I should be very sorry to make a complaint of him.

2527. Have you reason to think that too much of his time is occupied in private practice?—No, I think not.

2528. Mr. *Kendall.*] Now, with regard to your towns; in some of them you wish very much that they should not pay to the baronial cess; that they should have the power of having the local Acts?—Yes.

2529. Those local Acts were expensive; but of course you would limit it to a certain population, would you not?—The Towns Improvement Act limited them to a population of 1,500. It must be that, or upwards.

2530. Would you limit it to that still?—That is a very good limit, because it includes any town that is able to meet the expense.

2531. There was a point with reference to the rating of cottages which I did not understand. You would have no cottagers' houses rated?—None.

2532. I do not know what the class of men are who are the proprietors of those cottages. Are they a rich or a poor class who let to the cottagers?—The principal of the cottages throughout Ireland are owned by the landlords, the owners of land.

2533. Not by small owners?—No; then we come to the tenant.

2534. What I want to know, is the class of men who, generally speaking, let those houses, are they men of substantial means, or are they a class of men who would be likely to place the rates into their pockets by putting on an additional rent?—I do not think they would; in fact I am satisfied they would not. The rent of the cottages is almost a fixed thing.

2535. I listened with great pleasure to your evidence, but there is one thing which struck me just now, which is, that you who in Ireland are so sharp as to tenants, do not at all take into consideration the rates; that competition is so great that they care little about them; whether the rates were higher or lower, the same rent would be maintained. If it be so, in your opinion are the rents in Ireland very much too high or not?—I do not think they are too high.

2536. If that is the case, where is the competition?—You mean competition for lands.

2537. Suppose a person has got a tenement to let, you say the competition is so high, generally speaking, that men do not take into consideration what the poor rates are. Be they high or low, it matters not; they rush into the market in order to get this farm?—Yes.

2538. If that were the case, is not the rent, generally speaking, too high, because that is a sequence?—The rent, in many instances, is too high, and I will tell you why: the farmer has not the means of living in the ordinary comfort in which a farmer ought to live; it gives him as much as he can do to pay his rent and to support his family with the most humble food; he could not give them the diet of an ordinary English farmer. I certainly should be very glad to see the cottages relieved from taxation.

2539. Mr. *Leader.*] You were speaking of wishing to have the associated cesspayers elected, and also of having the present electoral divisions as the districts from which the cesspayers should be elected. Did you contemplate having one election, and the same person for poor-rate purposes and road purposes, or would you have separate elections?—Separate elections altogether; separate and distinct. The ratepayer who might wish to look after the poor might take no interest in the roads.

2540. Do you think the electoral divisions as at present would make a proper area for choosing persons to sit in the road session?—That would depend on the size of the electoral divisions as compared with the present baronies, and also on the number of cesspayers that would be named for each barony. That, I presume, would be guided in a great measure by the number of landlords residing in the barony.

2541. Do not you think it is absolutely necessary to have a re-distribution of the county Cork baronies, considering the present unequal distribution and size of the baronies?—I should.

2542. Are you aware of the different extent of baronies in the county Cork; are you aware that there is one of only 9,000 acres, and another of 200,000 acres?—I daresay there is a great difference in many of them, and the smallest barony will send a representative just the same as the largest one.

2543. Have

2543. Have you ever considered what would be the proper maximum and minimum extent of a district which would be the most suitable for holding a road session?—If you take a centre and an area of six miles from that centre, that would give a very good area; a good deal would depend upon the position of the district, for instance, there might be a town in it or there might not, some of the road session districts have no town, others have; a good deal depends upon the local position.

2544. I am supposing a re-distribution of the county, changing it altogether into new baronies, what size would you think the most suitable, how many miles long and how many miles square?—I have not given that point my attention, and I should not like to give an answer; I should consider the size of the baronies at present, and how they should be re-modelled and distributed; some of the baronies are very straggling, some are in a circle and others square, according to their peculiar geographical position.

2545. Do you think an opinion may be formed as to what is the most suitable size for each new barony, and if that could not be made up then a number of the electoral divisions as at present arranged?—Suppose in the county of Cork you agree that it is to be divided into 23 or 24 baronies, and then strike an average of the quantity of ground; it is a question I am not prepared to give an answer upon at present; bear in mind the glaring fact that some are very large and some are very small.

2546. Do you think that would be a necessary thing to remedy?—I think it would be desirable.

2547. You would wish to have a separate election for the persons to serve on the road sessions, distinct from those to serve on the poor law?—Certainly; I would not interfere with the poor law arrangements at all.

2548. Are you not aware that in Cork in some baronies it is difficult to find a grand juror, any person qualified by residence to serve?—I am not aware of it.

2549. That may account in some baronies for so many suitable men never being called upon that they are obliged perpetually to summon the same persons (from the small) baronies, it is not the fault of the sheriff but of the arrangements of the county?—Yes, it is possible. I only speak of my own barony particularly, for I am perfectly acquainted with that.

2550. Are you aware that the cesspayer has an appeal from the decision of the grand jury if he does not think he has obtained justice before the grand jury; are you aware that he can traverse it by an appeal to the judge?—Yes.

2551. In fact the grand jury is not a final court of appeal?—I should think where the grand jury throws out a work which has been passed at the road sessions, it would be useless to appeal to the judge.

2552. Is there a power?—I believe so.

2553. As well for the affirmative as for the negative?—Perhaps so, but I am not certain.

2554. It appears, in the present state of the law, as if the cesspayers had a great many protections against any injustice being done to them?—The cesspayers have a great deal of protection if the law were properly carried out, there is no question about that, but on the other hand, where the cesspayers are selected by the grand jury of a barony a great many are left out that have a right to be selected, and one portion of the barony is well represented while another portion is not; I speak of my own county.

W. D'Esterre Parker, Esq.

6 May 1868.

2555. If you take electoral divisions and choose a man from them, that would remedy that objection?—It would.

2556. Have you often attended before the grand jury in Cork?—I have.

2557. Is not the principal business conducted at the road sessions, and not at the grand jury; in fact, is not the grand jury an unimportant body in granting roads compared with the road sessions?—Most unimportant. The road sessions is the principal body in the first instance. At the grand jury they cannot originate works, at the road sessions they do.

2558. In fact, as far as roads are concerned, the acts of the grand jury are very unimportant?—Very unimportant.

2559. And it is more important to have a properly constituted road sessions than to make an alteration in the present constitution of the grand jury?—It is important to have a properly constituted road session, but it is equally important to have a properly constituted grand jury, because the grand jury can do away altogether with what the sessions have done; the one is as important as the other.

2560. There is nothing to prevent the question being brought forward again?—Persons do not like the expense and trouble of going before a judge.

2561. You are not aware of the amount of new works presented for in county Cork, or how much in the pound it would come to?—I could not tell exactly how much they come to, but some baronies are large and some small.

2562. *Chairman.*] I do not think you gave any reason for your view, that it would not do to have the same parties elected as Poor Law Guardians and as members of the baronial sessions?—The reason I gave was this, the parties who would take an interest in looking after the wants of the poor might not be inclined to take the additional work on them of looking after the interests of ratepayers at road sessions. A ratepayer may have an interest in looking after the poor and he may not have a similar interest in looking after the interests of the ratepayers at the road sessions. One gentleman may have a taste for one portion of the duty, and another for another portion. By having distinct parties, it spreads the representative system more equally over the barony or the division; you give one man the guardianship of the poor, and another the guardianship of the roads.

2563. Of course, you would not think of making the two incompatible?—No.

2564. I presume those who fill those offices would generally belong to the same class of the community?—They may or may not; but generally they would, I suppose; it all depends upon circumstances.

2565. They are generally the larger and more influential farmers in the country districts?—Generally speaking, it is all matter of taste; but generally speaking they are.

2566. As to the collection of the county cess upon the lowest class of houses, are you aware whether there is much difficulty in collecting it; do you know how far it is in practice enforced?—When first the law was enacted, putting the cess on houses, there was a great deal of difficulty in collecting it on small houses. I have known instances

W. D'Esterre Parker, Esq.

5 May 1869.

instance where a baronial constable was obliged to go round the town taking whatever he could out of the poor people's houses; the iron pot on the fire, articles of furniture, or anything else to meet the cess. The people did not feel that they had a right to pay it, but they must pawn their things to pay it. It is a miserable thing to see the rate collector go into a poor man's cabin who has not the price of a breakfast or a dinner, to take the rates; he must pawn his clothes to get it.

2567. Is that cess always paid by the occupier, and never by the landlord?—It is invariably paid by the occupier; the law says it must be paid by the occupier.

2568. But in practice?—I know in practice in some instances the landlord pays it; but that is the exception.

2569. You gave some evidence about malicious injuries; are you of opinion that the system of giving compensation for malicious injuries out of the local taxation is a sound one; do you think that it tends to the public advantage?—I do not think it makes any difference whatever. I think the injury would be committed, no matter how the compensation was paid.

2570. Do you think it to any degree checks the committal of such injuries?—Not in the slightest degree. I think if a man wishes to do an injury to another, it is no matter to him who pays for it.

2571. I understand you to propose that the payment of such compensations should be transferred from the barony to the county at large?—I think so.

2572. Are you not aware that that would cut at the very root of the principle upon which the system was founded, that system being that the immediate neighbourhood in which the outrage took place should be made to suffer for it?—That was the intention, but I think, if I may be allowed so to express myself, it was a mistaken view; I do not think it prevents the injury being done, and I think it is very hard to charge a very small portion of the community with an outrage which has been committed by perhaps a stranger; I think we have other criminal laws to guide us. If a man commits an assault upon another, and there is a prosecution, the county at large pay for it, and so again if a man commits a murder.

2573. Of course, so far as compensation to the person injured goes, it would make no difference to him where the compensation came from, but as to any check to be placed upon the commission of such malicious injuries, your proposal would make the law totally useless, your proposed transfer from the immediate locality to the county at large?—I do not think the law at present has the slightest effect upon the party committing the offence; he thinks nothing of who is to pay for it, and furthermore, in many instances, the party whose property is lost, is a large contributor towards re-imbursing himself, he not only loses his property, but he has to pay through the public cess, or public taxation, a large sum again.

2574. If no such effect is produced by the law, what justification is there for the continuance of it?—No justification whatever for the continuance of it, except that it is hard that a person should lose his property by the acts of another. If the county at large reimburses him, well and good. As regards burnings, where the party would have the power of insuring, I think they ought to avail themselves of an insurance company, and not allow their property to stand the chance of being sacrificed.

2575. What would you say to the entire abolition of the system of compensation for malicious injuries?—It is a very serious question, and I would not like to give a decided answer.

2576. You have no decided opinion upon it?—I should not like to give a decided opinion about it. There are cases where it would be very hard that a farmer should have his whole property destroyed by some evil person, and that he should be ruined for life, and no person to compensate him. I think the community at large should do it. I think it would be very hard to put it on the land or on the barony.

2577. As to any effect to be produced by the payment of compensation by way of penalty on the district in which the occurrence took place, you would put that aside altogether?—Yes; I do not think it is the slightest check.

2578. Have you heard any complaints in your neighbourhood from the road contractors of the delay in obtaining payment under the present system?—They make no complaints, because there is no use in making any complaint, but I think if the payments were made monthly the contracts would be done at a much cheaper rate, and a great economy would arise in consequence. They are not paid now, in some instances, for seven, eight, or nine months. It is a long time for them to lay out their money. Of course they must take that into consideration when contracting for the work.

2579. You think if means were provided of paying them more frequently, and within a shorter time, the county could get the work done cheaper?—Yes; you then have a more complete control over the contractor. If he is paid for his road every month he will take very good care to have that road in order. If it is not in order the money may be delayed for a while, and that would give a decided check to neglect, besides economising the entire system. In the present instance they have to borrow the money to pay for the repair of the road, and they have to pay a high interest for it; they are generally humble men who have not much capital, and in consequence they charge more than they otherwise would.

2580. Is there any difficulty in you now obtaining proper contractors for the roads?—None whatever; there is great competition generally.

2581. Have you ever had any complaints, on the part of occupiers, of materials, such as gravel being taken out of their lands without sufficient compensation?—Yes, repeatedly; I think that ought to be remedied; as you are aware the road contractor can go into any gravel pit or quarry, and take away stones or gravel without paying anything except for the surface damage. I consider that the owner of the gravel pit, or the owner of the quarry has as good a right to be paid for the market materials of that road as any other person, and that the contractor should be bound to pay for it at a price to be arranged according to the ordinary price of materials in that locality. I think it is most unfair that a road contractor should enter a man's quarry in that way.

2582. There is a system of arbitration provided by law for the purpose of fixing the compensation?—Yes, for the surface damage only, he may go down to a depth of 100 feet and pay no more for it.

2583. Do

W. D'Esterre Parker, Esq.

5 May 1868.

2563. So that there is no payment for the actual materials?—No.

2564. Colonel Cooper.] The sessions at present are obliged to accept the lowest tender, I think? —Yes.

2565. Do you approve of that system?—No, I think it is objectionable.

2566. You think a certain discretion should be allowed to the sessions?—Yes.

2567. That when a man is known to be a notoriously bad contractor he should be rejected?—Unquestionably.

2568. Although a good contractor may put in a tender a little higher?—Yes, the present system works very badly; a good contractor has a contract which expires, he has kept his road in good order, another man knows his price and puts in a tender a small trifle under him, he gets the road in good order, he makes use of the capital the former contractor has used, and he gives up the road in very inferior order; I think the present contractor, at the termination of his contract ought to have the preference of any new contractor provided he has fulfilled his contract and has given satisfaction to the county surveyor.

Friday, 8th May 1868.

MEMBERS PRESENT:

Mr. Blake.	Mr. Herbert.
Colonel Cooper.	Mr. Kendall.
Mr. Dawson.	Sir Charles Lanyon.
Colonel Forde.	Mr. Leader.
Mr. Chichester Fortescue.	Mr. Maguire.
Colonel French.	Earl of Mayo.
Mr. Gregory.	

MR. CHICHESTER FORTESCUE, IN THE CHAIR.

UNIACKE RONAYNE MACKAY, Esq., called in; and Examined.

U. R. Mackay, Esq.

8 May 1868.

2589. *Mr. Maguire.*] WHERE do you reside?—In the county of Cork.

2590. Near Fermoy?—Near Fermoy.

2591. I believe you represent two classes; you are landlord and a tenant, are you not?—Yes.

2592. You hold land and you own land?—Yes.

2593. Have you made the subject of the grand jury an object of your consideration for a considerable time?—Yes, for a quarter of a century I have been engaged in administering the law as an associated cesspayer.

2594. Has your practical administration of the law been confined to one barony, or extended to more than one?—I have had experience in three baronies, and I have property in four.

2595. May I presume that you have an accurate practical knowledge of the administration or operation of the law?—Yes, I think so.

2596. You have given the subject very great consideration?—I have.

2597. Is it your opinion that the law as it at present exists, is satisfactory?—Most unsatisfactory.

2598. Do you think it has failed, or otherwise?—I think it has failed.

2599. In what manner has it failed?—I think it is wrong in principle as regards the incidence of taxation.

2600. And as to its machinery, what should you say?—As to its machinery, it is not at all equal to the due management of the fiscal affairs of Ireland.

2601. You object to it then in principle, and to the machinery, and also to its operation?—Yes.

2602. Is the main objection that you have to it, that it violates, in your opinion, the spirit of the constitution, which requires taxation and representation to be combined?—Yes, in my mind it is a glaring violation of that principle of the constitution.

2603. That is one of your objections?—Yes.

2604. Do you also object to it on the ground that there is not a fair division of the taxes between the parties who are interested?—I think it would be very desirable that there should be a partition between both classes, the occupiers and owners; and I think very beneficial results would arise therefrom.

2605. Do you think that the two classes, the owners and the occupiers, are equally interested in the improvements effected through the expenditure?—The owner far beyond the occupier, inasmuch as he is a permanent owner, while the occupier is only a temporary owner.

2606. Do you think you, as an owner of property, have a larger interest in the improvements effected through the expenditure than you have as an occupier?—Yes; as an owner, I should say it is a capital law, but a very indifferent law for the occupiers.

2607. Suppose a gentleman owns half the land he occupies, and that he is a tenant for the remaining portion, do you think that his interest is greater in his capacity as landlord than as an occupier?—I do.

2608. Will you say why?—Because, as an owner, he has a permanent interest in the improvements made, but as an occupier of course he has a terminable interest only.

2609. Would you say that the character of that interest would be governed by the tenure of the tenancy?—Yes, it would to some considerable extent.

2610. For instance, if a man had a lease, he would have a better interest, although not a permanent interest, than a man who held from year to year?—Yes.

2611. Is that quite clear to your mind?—Quite clear.

2612. And that in every case, whether the occupier held by a lease or from year to year, the owner of that property has a larger interest in the improvements than the holder of a lease or the man who occupies from year to year?—I should say so.

2613. You are quite clear about that?—Quite clear.

2614. Will you take some of the items of the improvements effected by the expenditure, and give

give your opinion to the Committee as to in what degree the owner is more interested in the improvements, and therefore has a right to pay for them, than the occupier who now sustains the whole burden?—With regard to the first item here, new roads, I take the case for Ireland in 1866; there was in that year an expenditure of 67,179 *l.* for new roads. Of course these new roads served to open up the country or countries where roads have not been in existence, and it adds materially to the value of the landlords' property. Then there is repairs of roads, 317,159 *l.* Of course the tenants have an interest in the roads.

2615. You do not deny that the tenants have an interest?—No.

2616. It gives them greater facility in bringing their produce to market?—Yes; then there are courts and sessions houses expenditure, 4,735 *l.* Then the question is whether the higher classes or the lower classes have a greater interest in the preservation of the public peace.

2617. You think the owners have quite as much interest in that as the occupiers?—Certainly; then there are gaols and bridewells, 10,059 *l.*, and all other bridewells, 81,623 *l.*; payment to police and witnesses, 8,117 *l.*

2618. You think the one class has as much interest in that expenditure as the other?—Most decidedly; of course we are all anxious for the preservation of the public peace.

2619. As to the criminal jurisdiction, you think the owner class have as much interest as any other class of the community?—I should say so.

2620. Do you think the one class has as much interest in it as the other?—I think it is quite apparent. Then there is an item to which I wish particularly to draw the attention of the Committee; it is as to the salaries of the officers, 110,835 *l.* Now that is a very large item; it is one-ninth of the entire amount, and it is for an institution which is supposed to be administered gratuitously.

2621. We will pass over that for the moment; as to any one of these items of expenditure, is it your opinion that they ought to be defrayed by the one class as much as by the other; in other words, that the rate should be divided equally between them?—I should say so; for instance, the revision of the valuation of Ireland, in which only the landlords have an interest, amounts to 23,340 *l.*; it amounts to 1-46th of the entire amount.

2622. You say the owners have a larger interest in that than the occupiers who pay for it?—Certainly; the occupier has no land to map, while the landlord has. The public charities are 81,103 *l.*; repayment of Government advances, 65,437 *l.*; miscellaneous, 84,164 *l.*

2623. Now, as to the charities, do not you think the richer portion of the community ought to be more bound by every obligation, moral and legal, to pay for the support of the sick poor than the humbler classes?—Yes, of course a large portion of the charities ought to come from the more wealthy classes.

2624. And it ought to do so?—It ought.

2625. There is no reason, in your opinion, why the whole burden should be thrown upon one class?—No.

2626. Is there any reason why it should be thrown upon one class?—I do not see any.

2627. Are your opinions very clear and decided as to the injustice of not dividing the tax between the two parties, one of whom is at least quite as much interested as the other?—Yes, I think it would be very desirable to do so. From the good effects that have resulted from the partition of the poor rate, and from the harmony that prevailed in the administration of poor rates in Ireland, I think it would be desirable to follow that.

U. R. Mackay, Esq.

8 May 1868.

2628. Now, I ask you to give your experience to the Committee as to what is the known feeling of the occupiers or the payers of this rate throughout your county?—The feeling among the ratepayers is that of thorough indifference about this law, it has worked so much to their disadvantage.

2629. As to the division of the rate; what is their feeling about that?—Of course they would be desirous of having a partition of the rate.

2630. Has not that feeling been over and over again distinctly declared?—It has been declared repeatedly, and we have had public meetings in Ireland from time to time on the subject.

2631. Wherever opinion could be expressed on the matter it has been clearly expressed in favour of a division of the rate?—It has.

2632. There can be no doubt whatever as to that feeling?—No doubt in the world.

2633. Now as to the machinery; what are your principal reasons for objecting to the present system?—As far as I can see, from my experience, I think it is a perfect burlesque for the ratepayers to go to the presentment sessions at all; they have no voice there, at least they are outvoted there. Under the present grand jury law the very largest barony in County Cork (and we have baronies as large as some counties in Ireland; Barrymore is as large as Louth), we are entitled by the Act to a maximum number of ratepayers. I take it for granted that in a large barony in Ireland the maximum number ought to be allowed to that barony. At the sessions, preparatory to the summer assizes of 1867 for the barony of Imokilly, we had eight associated cesspayers; there were 16 nominated, but out of the 16 half the number were balloted. The valuation of that barony is 99,063 *l.* Then there is the barony of Courceys with a valuation of 6,033 *l.*, and the grand jury gave Courceys six ratepayers or cesspayers. We have the barony of Cork with only six, and with a valuation of 67,649 *l.*

2634. *Chairman.*] Is the maximum number allowed to any of the baronies?—Yes; Duhallow is a very large barony and only 11 are allowed, and in Orrery and Kilmore there are 12.

2635. *Mr. Maguire.*] Do you object to the manner in which the associated cesspayers are appointed; do you object to their being nominated by an irresponsible person?—Of course I do; of course the sessions are an emanation of the jury.

2636. Do you object, then, to the system of having those persons, who are assumed to have the practical administration of the law, nominated by an irresponsible person instead of by a person who pays the rates?—Precisely so.

2637. As to its operation, you said that the associated cesspayers were swamped; will you tell the Committee how they are swamped, and give your own experience in the matter?—In all my experience I never knew that the cesspayers were enabled to carry any proposition at the presentment sessions in Cork but on two occasions.

2638. Are you now confining your observations

U. R. Healy, Esq.

8 May 1868.

rations to the practical working of the law in your own county?—Yes.

2639. And to those baronies?—It extends no further.

2640. Will you describe to the Committee how the cesspayers are swamped at those presentment sessions?—As I told you before, for Imokilly, at the summer assizes of 1867, we had only eight cesspayers, and into that sessions court fully 300 magistrates might enter.

2641. By law they might enter?—Yes.

2642. But, practically, do they come from the neighbouring baronies?—Yes; I have known occasions when magistrates attended from neighbouring baronies.

2643. Even in the barony itself is there a large number of magistrates who would swamp the ratepayers?—Yes.

2644. How many times more would the magistrates be than the ratepayers?—I suppose six times more in that barony.

2645. In the barony itself how many magistrates would there be who might attend?—We have often been inconvenienced in the court house by the large attendance, but I never counted the magistrates.

2646. Practically did they very much exceed in number the associated cesspayers?—Yes.

2647. *Earl of Mayo.*] How many?—On some particular occasions, when particular works were to be brought forward.

2648. *Mr. Maguire.*] Would there be 20 there?—I have known a larger attendance of ratepayers than magistrates; that is, when ordinary business has come before the sessions.

2649. Whenever there is, what is popularly called a job, or a special work to be done, would there be a larger number of magistrates?—Decidedly; I never knew an instance but on two occasions in that county, when the cesspayers were able to carry out a fair legitimate motion.

2650. Some members of the Committee are anxious to get at an approximate idea of the number of magistrates that would attend on those special occasions. You say eight cesspayers were appointed by ballot; how many magistrates could you say, from your remembrance, would come on those occasions?—I have a recollection of a Bench being polled; not at those sessions, but at the previous sessions, and there were 10 magistrates and 10 cesspayers.

2651. On other occasions, have you seen a larger number of magistrates than cesspayers?—On particular occasions; for instance, if a gentleman were anxious to complete unfinished public works, on such an occasion there would be a very large attendance.

2652. What do you call a very large attendance?—A sufficient number to carry a majority.

2653. Would you say 20; double the number of cesspayers?—Well, I think there have been occasions when there were 20 at Barrymore.

2654. At any rate, the law allows the entire magistrates of the county to come if they can?—Yes.

2655. Do you object to that?—Certainly I do.

2656. Is it your opinion that the associated cesspayers, being a limited number, could be swamped in any barony by the magistrates of the barony?—In every barony in Ireland.

2657. I think you had better not go beyond the County Cork?—The magistrates from all baronies can come to any presentment sessions; there I am quite right in my answer.

2658. I am now asking for your practical experience, and I think we had better confine ourselves to the County Cork. Within your own knowledge, in any one barony in the county of Cork, the magistrates of that barony could alone, if they wished, attend and swamp the associated cesspayers?—I am not prepared to say that; there are some baronies, large mountain districts, where there probably is not a sufficient number of magistrates to swamp the ratepayers in that particular barony.

2659. Would you say in the majority of the baronies of the county, they would be able to swamp the magistrates?—Yes.

2660. Not only can all the local magistrates come to the sessions, but the magistrates of other baronies in the county can come?—Yes.

2661. You object to that?—I do; I know instances where friends of mine have been solicited to come from their own baronies.

2662. You know that as a fact?—Yes.

2663. Do you know it is a common thing for a magistrate to ask a *friend from* an adjoining barony to come and assist him on particular occasions?—I have known instances of it. I have seen magistrates from neighbouring baronies come in.

2664. Have magistrates ever told you that they have been solicited by their friends to come?—They have.

2665. And they do not consider it wrong, inasmuch as it is perfectly legal?—It is quite legal, and they take it as a matter of course. I should say this, that on one occasion, and on one occasion only, in the barony of Duhallow, I saw a gentleman from an out-barony remain seated in court; that was the only occasion in my experience; he was asked to poll and he declined to do so, stating that he was from another barony.

2666. You regard that as an exception?—Yes, and that is the only exception in my experience.

2667. Do you know practically of a magistrate coming from the western portion of the county to your portion, which is eastern, to vote, to assist his friend?—No, I know no instances of that. The county of Cork is a very wide district.

2668. You object strongly to that system?—I do.

2669. And you know that there is a very strong objection on the part of the cesspaying class?—Yes, in fact the objection is so strong that they are regardless of attending at the sessions, because they see the inutility of it.

2670. You are in favour, if I mistake not, of the elective system?—I am.

2671. Do you think that is fairly worked under the Poor Law system?—I think it is.

2672. Are you satisfied with the class of men who have been elected guardians?—Well, yes, in most cases.

2673. As a rule?—As a rule.

2674. According to your experience, do they attend fairly?—Fairly; and some of our model institutions in Ireland are principally managed by elected guardians.

2675. You would follow the poor law system, would you?—As to the incidence of taxation I would.

2676. And also as to the principle of representation?—Yes.

2677. Would you limit the right of the magistrate to interfere in the fiscal affairs of his barony

so

to those magistrates who resided in the barony?—Yes, I would.

2678. Would you have any other, and if so, what qualification?—I think the occupancy of land to the extent of 200 *l.* a year.

2679. And that should be within the barony?—Within the barony; that he should be rated to the poor to that value.

2680. Do you mean residence or occupation?—That he should be resident, and occupying land to that extent; rated to the poor to that amount; in fact he would have to pay county cess: he should be resident, and occupy land.

2681. He would have greater knowledge of, and greater interest in the affairs of the barony?—Yes.

2682. What would your qualification be for the elected representative?—I think the qualification under the Poor Law system would be ample.

2683. Are you quite satisfied with the class of men who are returned, and with the manner in which they manage the affairs entrusted to them?—Yes. I know the elected guardians are very regular in their attendance; I know very humble men who would devote one day in the week to the proceedings of the Board of which they are members.

2684. Some of the best Poor Law Unions are managed, to a very large extent, by elected guardians?—Yes.

2685. What is your idea of the number there ought to be in each district where there would be a union or a barony?—That we should have the district re-cast. If we are to follow the Poor Law boundaries, which I think would be the better way to manage, we should exclude portions of counties, and there would be some difficulty in that.

2686. As to the number in each class, how many would you have?—If we could confine the area of all to a uniform extent, the same numbers would answer.

2687. I ask you relatively the one class to the other; how many would you have; would you have them equal in number; 20 in one, and 20 in another?—I should say probably 30 for the larger districts would be ample, and 24 for the smaller.

2688. Whether the area be large or small, would you give to each class a similar representation?—That is what I am in favour of.

2689. If that were 20, you would have 10 in each, if it were 30, you would have 15 in each?—Yes.

2690. You do not wish to deprive the owner class of their share of the management of the fiscal affairs of the barony. Is not that so?—That is so. I think those numbers would be ample; there might be some expense in the election of those parties. I think it would be well to confine it to as few a number as could work the barony or district.

2691. According to your idea would you have the grand jurors also elected?—I think we should have delegates from the county boards, of which we are now speaking.

2692. Elected through what machinery?—Elected by the boards themselves to represent them on the county at large sessions.

2693. You would be in favour of a county board?—Yes.

2694. As a substitute for the grand jury for fiscal purposes?—Yes.

2695. You would not interfere with their criminal jurisdiction?—No.

2696. Have you any observations or suggestions to make to the Committee in reference to the present system of appointing grand jurors?—The present system has been to my mind a total failure. In the year 1831, when the Bill was introduced we were led to believe that the power of taxation would be vested in the presentment sessions, and in them alone.

G. E. Mahony, Esq.

8 May 1868.

2697. (*Chairman.*] How do you mean, "led to believe"?—The then secretary for Ireland was the present Earl of Derby. The Bill proposed to take away from grand jurors altogether the power of sanctioning any presentment, which the special sessions might deem unnecessary; also that it should be mandatory and compulsory on the high sheriff to select the persons from each barony in the county as grand jurors, which is not always done. I believe the spirit of the law, as laid down then, was carried out, and the Chief Baron, O'Grady, decided that such was the law; but we have had recently in my barony, at least in a case originating in my barony, Mr. Justice Keogh deciding differently.

2698. What point are you now alluding to?—To the general operation of the Grand Jury Laws.

2699. It is not obvious to the Committee what point you are alluding to, on which Justice Keogh pronounced an opinion?—With regard to a presentment ignored by the sessions.

2700. What point did Judge Keogh's ruling refer to?—It referred to a presentment that was ignored by the sessions, and that was confirmed before the judge.

2701. Colonel *Cooper.*] It was traversed in fact?—It was traversed.

2702. Colonel *French.*] What was the presentment for?—It was for malicious injury.

2703. Mr. *Maguire.*] Are you in favour of the grand jury system of compensation for malicious injury?—I am not.

2704. Are you against it?—Quite against it.

2705. What do you suggest in its place?—Of course the protection that is open to every man to resort to, namely the insurance companies. I have done so myself, and my predecessor, and I think others could do so.

2706. You would not give any compensation for malicious injury?—No; if a man is murdered there is no compensation for the loss of his life, and if his property is destroyed in many cases there is compensation. In fact, malicious injuries are becoming quite an institution in Ireland now. We have parties coming before the sessions annually with applications for malicious injury; we cannot understand them.

2707. Mr. *Gregory.*] The same party?—The same party. The case I alluded to a while ago was the second application, and it was traversed by the ratepayers at the sessions. It was not the factious opposition of an ordinary ratepayer, it was the deliberate act of the officials, those who were administering the law at sessions, and whose act was not alone ignored, but the judge actually thought fit to punish them by awarding costs against them.

2708. What do you say was a deliberate act?—Traversing it. I will tell you how it arose, the grand jury granted the presentment, and then we traversed the act of the grand jury.

2709. Colonel *French.*] Was the presentment eventually granted?—It was granted.

2710. By

U. R. Manley, Esq.

8 May 1868.

2710. By the jury under the direction of the judge?—Under the direction of the judge, and a fine actually imposed upon us, the largest amount the judge could award against us. We sat at petty sessions under the obligation of a declaration made; we acted conscientiously on the evidence adduced before us.

2711. *Chairman.*] And you rejected it?—Yes.

2712. The grand jury then passed a presentment over your heads?—Yes, and would allow no ratepayer to raise his voice in the grand jury room.

2713. You then appealed, by way of traverse, to the judge?—Yes.

2714. *Earl of Mayo.*] At what assizes did this take place?—The summer assizes of last year.

2715. Did any ratepayer propose to speak before the grand jury on the subject?—I did.

2716. And what was said?—I was told that I should not come to make a speech.

2717. Who refused, on the part of the grand jury, to hear you?—Some parties in court.

2718. It would be necessary to state their names. It is a very serious accusation against a grand jury, because they were acting illegally?—I could name a gentleman who wished to shut me up completely, upon another occasion, in the same court, and in the same way.

2719. Your statement was this, that, on the part of the ratepayers, you applied to be heard before the grand jury, and the grand jury refused to hear you; the question I ask is, what member of the grand jury stated the opinion of the grand jury upon that case, declining to hear you?—I should say that we were represented by a solicitor on the occasion.

2720. *Mr. Maguire.*] They objected to hear you, inasmuch as they heard your solicitor?—Yes; there was an observation made, that those who opposed this man's application did so because of his well known loyalty; I, of course, wished to repudiate this charge, and I was told not to make a speech.

2721. *Earl of Mayo.*] Then the statement that the grand jury refused to hear any person on the part of the cesspayers, with regard to this presentment, is not a fact?—Of course, not being represented by their solicitor, as far as the application under discussion, but I was not permitted to repel the suggestion "that the presentment was opposed on account of the applicant's loyalty."

2722. The cesspayers who objected to the presentment were represented by their solicitor?—They were.

2723. Did he state the case?—He stated the case.

2724. Did he call witnesses?—He called witnesses.

2725. Then the cesspayers placed their case in the hands of their solicitor?—They did.

2726. Did the judge not empanel a petty jury to try the case to which you have alluded?—The jury that had been trying records was in the box, and the case was referred to them.

2727. And evidence taken before them?—Yes.

2728. What was their verdict?—Their verdict was confirming the proceedings.

2729. And the judge confirmed that?—And the judge confirmed that, and imposed this fine on the ratepayers who went to sustain the act of their own court.

2730. *Mr. Maguire.*] You do not mean to represent to the Committee that the grand jury do not hear the cesspayers?—Some men of good position of course they will, but as for their listening to every ratepayer who will go in to make an objection they will not do it, nor could it be expected that they should.

2731. Of course that would be a waste of time, but where a cesspayer is appointed by the associated cesspayers, they do hear him as a matter of course, do they not?—They do.

2732. And you do not intend to represent anything else?—No, I do not.

2733. *Colonel Cooper.*] Do you consider that malicious injuries have increased of late?—Do you mean in this particular case that I speak of?

2734. No, not in this particular case, but within your knowledge have malicious injuries increased?—We have had a good many malicious injuries arising out of the unfortunate state of Ireland.

2735. But until Fenianism rather prevailed?—Certainly not; crimes, I think, of all kinds was greatly on the decrease.

2736. You say you would recommend people to insure their property?—Certainly.

2737. I want to ask you whether you are aware that insurance companies do not pay the policy if the injury is supposed to be malicious?—I think, under a new system, if the country generally went to the insurance offices with the amount of business that would be necessary it would not be so.

2738. As a fact now, are you aware that they will not pay if the injury is malicious?—No, I am not aware.

2739. *Colonel French.*] With regard to revising the valuation of Ireland, you stated that it was entirely for the benefit of the landlord; will you explain that?—There is an item here. I have calculated the expense of that from the expense in the county of Cork at 1-46th of the whole county cess of Ireland; that would be 23,000 *l.* I should say that that is for the advantage of the landlords.

2740. Are not the poor rates taken from that very same thing?—Yes, they are.

2741. Is not the Government taxation of the country taken from the very same thing?—Yes.

2742. Do not you think the county at large are just as much benefited by such a charge as the landlord?—Yes.

2743. You speak of the cess being thrown on one class, and you implied by that it was all thrown on the occupier; do you mean to state that the occupiers do not take into consideration the amount of cess along with other taxations in the country when they are taking their land?—I do not think it operates one way or the other with Irishmen, inasmuch as the great desire is to procure land; I speak generally, of course there are exceptions. Men in good positions will calculate very nicely the burdens upon land in taking a farm.

2744. Then we are to consider that all the farmers in County Cork do not consider anything about what they have to pay in the taking of land?—Indeed they do.

2745. Then how do they come to the rent?—They generally come to a very high rent; I have seen land let at the Ordnance valuation, and I have

have the greatest possible satisfaction with my tenants; some is not let at that rate.

2746. Mr. *Herbert*.] With reference to the residence, you said that a man should reside in the barony; take for instance a landlord who happens to be a resident landlord in the county who has got property in different baronies, and does not actually reside in that barony, do not you think he ought to have a voice in the matter?—I think the residents in the barony must be sufficient and ample to look after the interests of the landlord class in that barony, and then probably he would have a seat at the county Board.

2747. Colonel *French*.] You stated that you had experience of different kinds in the working of the Grand Jury Laws in Ireland, both as a landowner and as a landholder, and that you have acted frequently as an associated cesspayer?—I have.

2748. You stated in answer to a question of Mr. Maguire, generally, that the system was unsatisfactory?—Most unsatisfactory.

2749. To what do you refer; is it that the whole system is unsatisfactory in its results, or that it is unsatisfactory to particular persons?—It is unsatisfactory generally as regards the incidence of taxation, I think.

2750. Is it unsatisfactory in the results, 50,000 miles of road being kept for 400,000 *l*., and no debt?—The cost of roads is over that; it is 617,159 *l*.

2751. You are putting the new roads together?—No, it is 87,179 *l*. for new roads.

2752. It costs about half a million?—About that.

2753. And for that you have 50,000 miles of road kept in remarkably good repair?—I stated before that I think the occupiers in Ireland would be happy to pay that item, if the other items were paid by the landlords, in which the landlords have greater interest.

2754. You stated that as far as the management of the roads goes, you think there is a return made to the occupying tenants sufficient to make them satisfied with that portion of the working of the system?—I think so, provided the other items were discharged by the landlords. Generally speaking they are, but I think of late the desire is to amalgamate contracts, and have large lines of roads, which will operate very injuriously to the interests of the ratepayers. If you will allow me to explain that I will do so. For instance, in the barony of Barrymore number 30 presentment, five miles in length, 4 *s*. 6 *d*. per perch had to be given to the contractor for that road.

2755. Do you mean annually?—Four shillings and sixpence per perch annually. No. 35 presentment, in the same barony, two miles of road at 3 *s*. 6 *d*.; the difference on the five mile contract is 400 *l*.; that is, the loss to the barony would amount to 400 *l*. The annual sum for the five miles is 488 *l*. It would require a large amount of security in that case, not so much in the two miles; and what I would respectfully suggest in a case of that kind would be, that the contractor's salary should not amount to more than 200 *l*. a year, those who keep the roads in repair; the amount of money paid for the work done.

2756. Chairman.] Do you mean the amount of a contract given to any one man?—Yes; "contractors' salaries" is the technical term for it. As to the two miles of road, it is the continuation of the same road; it was the old mail road from Fermoy to Cork. Of course the railways supersede the use of it in a great measure, but still the figure is a very high one, 4 *s*. 6 *d*. a perch, that is, because there can be no competition; the man can have it at that price.

2757. Why is there no competition?—The sum is too large, and the difficulty of procuring the bail is so great for the class of persons who take roads in Ireland. In Limerick the system is being extended to the large contracts, and it will have a more injurious effect upon the expenditure.

2758. Earl of *Mayo*.] Is that Fermoy-road a yearly contract?—A yearly contract for five years.

2759. That is not what I mean; is it a contract that is let every year?—It is a yearly contract, extending over five years.

2760. Then it is a contract for five years?—Yes.

2761. Colonel *French*.] The objection that you made to the cesspayers was the general one, that the system of cesspaying being double the number nominated by the grand jury, and settled on by ballot, violates the principle of the constitution as to taxation and representation going together?—It does.

2762. Do you think, as some witnesses have stated, that it would in any way improve the system by ballot if those who were actually to serve were taken by the grand jury instead of being referred to the presentment sessions?—It would be some change in the system, but I do not see that it would be an improvement, because anything connected with that system of nomination I do not regard as an improvement; as you say it, it would. For instance, I have to ride 20 miles to attend the sessions, and I might be balloted, or I might not. If I am balloted, I can sit with the magistrates, if I am not, I must go home, and I have known men, for instance, my landlord, I have seen that gentleman snubbed by a man who got the commission; my landlord being a gentleman of high position in the county of Cork.

2763. Mr. *Maguire*.] Your landlord is not a magistrate?—He is not, although deputy vice chairman of the Fermoy Board of Guardians, and he was told he had no right to open his lips in the court, because he was not an associated cesspayer.

2764. Colonel *French*.] Is not that the law; as he was neither a magistrate, nor an associated cesspayer, had he any right?—It seems that we have a right, even before the grand inquest of the county, to make remarks. This was at an ordinary road sessions, and there he was silenced. I say that before the grand inquest, unless a man is in a very considerable position, the gentlemen sitting at that grand inquest will not hear him.

2765. There must be some power to keep order in court in the chairman of the magistrates and cesspayers?—Certainly; I agree with you there.

2766. What you would call snubbing the witness was merely an intimation that he had no right at all to address the court?—An intimation that he had no right at all to address the court.

2767. Now, you have stated in answer to Mr. Maguire, that the division of the area into two parts, would, in your opinion, be very desirable, and also that it would be very acceptable to the country at large throughout Ireland?—I should be very happy to see it effected; I should be delighted

U. S. Murphy, Esq.

8 May 1868.

U. B. *Mahony*, Esq.

8 May 1868.

delighted, though I myself, of course, would have to make a sacrifice.

2768. You lay down as the principle for that division that a certain portion of the works are much more beneficial to the landlords than the tenants?—Yes.

2769. Now, you assume that the owner of the soil makes no payment, unless he happens to be in the position of an occupier?—I should say so.

2770. Does he not, in entering into arrangements with his tenant, covenant that the tenant shall pay all the county cess?—Where a lease exists, no, he does not. It is not necessary, I believe.

2771. It is the general usage of the country?—The occupying tenant has to pay the county cess, and not alone that, but the occupiers of Ireland have to purchase sites for roads, to build the roads, to keep the roads in repair, and, after all that, they are required to pay rent for the public roads in Ireland, which I consider a most grievous wrong.

2772. Then I put it to you whether the occupying tenant does not pay any portion of these claims; whether they are not all allowed and paid for beforehand in the lease, or the possession of land given to him by the owner?—Nine-tenths, I believe, or a very large proportion of the tenantry of Ireland have no leases at all, and I look upon it as a very grievous thing; for instance, at this moment there are parties under eviction in Ireland who have subscribed to the heavy works that we have had in Cork; with their rents paid up they are about to be dispossessed, though they have contributed to the monster bridge down at Fermoy, and to some three or four large structures on the Blackwater. They have gone to the expense of those works, and now, of course, they have no longer any interest in them.

2773. What is the average of your cess for the two baronies in the county of Cork?—It is pretty close upon 1 *s*. for the half year.

2774. That is 2 *s*. for the entire year?—Yes.

2775. Do you not think in letting land, the tenant as well as the landlord takes into consideration if the land is 1 *l*. an acre and 2 *s*. for cess, that 1 *l*. 2 *s*. would be the value, and if he gets it for 1 *l*. is he not paid the entire amount?—I grant you that, under a good state of circumstances in a country, all that would be done; but in Ireland it is simply this, it is possession of land at any price, or expatriation.

2776. Would it not be a pecuniary advantage to holders of land in Ireland if half the cess were put on the landlord?—I think it would tend to great harmony between the parties.

2777. I did not ask you about harmony, but about pecuniary advantage?—Of course it would be a pecuniary advantage.

2778. Are you not aware that the landlord, as a matter of course, for his own protection in Cork, would at least put 2 *s*. on to meet the case where 2 *s*. was the amount of money to be paid?—I should hope if a principle were laid down, such as has been hitherto acted on in the administration of the Poor Law, the landlords would go with the feeling of the country in that respect.

2779. Is it your opinion that the law is at this moment, as to the Poor Law levy, that the landlord must bear one half of the taxation?—I know it is not. I know all the leases that are being entered into at the present moment do not contain that. I know the great misfortune of the present day is that legislation is going backward instead of progressing, and that that excellent law, the poor law (as good a law as ever emanated from law-makers), has been assimilated to this old rickety institution, the grand jury system, in place of the old system being assimilated to the new.

2780. Is it not the law in England, and in every other country, that the occupier who is the only person capable of giving employment, and of diminishing the rates, should be the payer of the poor rate?—Yes, I believe it is.

2781. Mr. *Maguire*.] Do you know the state of things in England?—I know with regard to our county cess.

2782. Have you personal knowledge of the state of things in England?—It is very limited indeed.

2783. Colonel *French*.] I will ask you again, is it not the law in England, and in every other country, that the occupier, who is the only person capable of giving employment and of diminishing the rates, should be the payer of the poor rate?—In Sweden the land cess is paid by the proprietors altogether. With regard to what you say of the advantage of the Irish over the English, we pay the county rates in Ireland, and that, I believe, is equal to your poor rates in England. The road rates in England are paid by the general community.

2784. There is a special levy in England for highway rate?—It is a very small one for your parish roads, which are highways, are supported by your turnpikes.

2785. Do you consider that the opening of this question, as to the half cess being paid, which offers no pecuniary advantage to the tenant, is merely opening up an additional source of difficulty between the landlord and the tenant?—I do not think so by any means, and if I thought so I should not be here to recommend it. I think from long experience of the working of the Poor Law system, up to the present moment you have harmony at all the Poor Law Boards of Ireland, but now the tenant will have to pay all the poor rates. I know men in Ireland who are subject to a 5 *s*. 6 *d*. rate at this moment. Now, I do not think it is prudent to have the weaker party subject to such a great increase in the rates. I speak now of the poor rates.

2786. You know what the Griffiths' valuation of Ireland is, and you have experience generally an opinion on it?—I do not know that I have the figures, and my memory does not serve me sufficiently to tell me what it is.

2787. From your experience in the working of that, I wish to know whether you think that valuation for which we pay so highly is of any value?—I think it is of value in this way; Griffiths' valuation includes all the improvements made by the tenantry of Ireland, as well as the value of the raw material, the soil; and I think it is of value, inasmuch as it shows what the actual value of the land is, and of course it is of great value in appropriating the taxation of the country.

2788. Would you rely on it as a standard of value yourself in any transaction?—I certainly would, inasmuch as the Act of Parliament gave to every man an opportunity of appealing from the valuation of those men if he thought he was aggrieved

aggrieved, and I think the relative value is very fairly carried out.

2788. You have stated that you are aware of one or more instances of the canvass of magistrates to attend at road sessions?—Yes, certainly.

2789. Are you aware that the magistrates, before they can act at the road sessions, must sign a declaration to administer fairly and impartially the law, and judge according to the best of their ability?—They do sign such a declaration.

2790. You said that you expected, from the Act of 1833, certain advantages. I believe you do not deny that you got the two that you named, one of which is, that no sum of money should be levied for the presentment except it originated at the road sessions?—It was supposed to be an improvement on the old system that obtained before, but we never found it so in the two instances that I gave you, where, by some fortuitous circumstances, the ratepaying element succeeded in carrying the motion at the sessions; it was annulled afterwards; it is a mockery of representation, I think. I think the sessions being an emanation of the grand jury, it is part and parcel of the old system of grand jury in Ireland.

2791. The old system was, that the cesspayers could originate, or that they could refuse to sanction a presentment, and that the grand jury had the power, which now they have not, to approve of a work rejected by the cesspayers?—I thought the law was that the taxing powers should be vested in the lower court, or presentment sessions.

2792. That is the law now, but formerly it was equally vested in the grand jury?—No; it was not vested there, for it had been tried. Chief Baron O'Grady held that it was, and Mr. Justice Keogh held that it was not.

2793. *Chairman.*] You are aware that the decision of the judge to whom you have referred applies only to one part of the county expenditure, viz., compensation for malicious injuries?—Precisely so.

2794. *Sir Charles Lanyon.*] When you speak of the power of originating at special sessions, are you not aware that if the sessions refuse a presentment twice, it is in the power of the cesspayers to appeal to the Lord Lieutenant for a commission to inquire into the presentment?—No, I was not aware of that.

2795. Being aware of that, do you still think that the sessions have not the power of originating applications?—They have the power, as you say, of demanding an inquiry. I was not aware that the Act of Parliament, the Grand Jury Act, contained any such provision.

2796. Do you not think that a very fair provision of the law, that where the sessions refuse an application, the cesspayers have the power of enforcing it by appeal?—It would seem to be so.

2797. Do you not think it essential that the representation at the sessions should be generally spread over the barony?—I think it would be desirable.

2798. That the cesspayers should not be collected from one particular locality?—It would be desirable.

2799. Have you any mode to propose in which that arrangement could be carried out?—The present system is this——

2800. I know the present system well; but have you any suggestion to make for the purpose of securing a fair representation on the part of the whole of the barony at the special sessions?—No; of course, as in the poor law administration, the best selection would be made in the district, if there was to be an election. T. E. Mackey, Esq. — 8 May 1868.

2801. Can the grand jury at the present moment originate any application whatever without its being previously approved of at the sessions?—I believe not.

2802. And if the application is refused at the sessions, the grand jury cannot present, but the sessions have the power of appeal, the cesspayers making the application?—Yes.

2803. Does not that appear to you a perfectly fair system, you not having been before aware of that power?—I was aware of that power, but I thought your question had reference to the appeal to the Lord Lieutenant.

2804. So it has?—I was not aware of that power, but I was aware of an applicant's having the power of traversing before a judge of assize. That is a very expensive process for a man to adopt, and a very uncertain one. I should never try it again, after having had a fine imposed on me for carrying out what I thought my legitimate duty, endeavouring to sustain the act of a sessions court of which I was a member.

2805. You spoke about the desirability of having small contracts?—Yes.

2806. Do you not think it very desirable and very much for the use and benefit of the public, that a class of contractors should be organised in a county, who would make it their special business to carry out these works?—The result in this particular instance was in the repairs of a road five miles in length at a loss of 400 *l.*

2807. Will you describe that; when a road has to be repaired, the circumstances under which it has to be repaired must be taken into consideration, such as the amount of traffic, does not form an element in the cost of repairing a road?—It does.

2808. The amount of material to be placed upon it?—Yes.

2809. Were those roads of which you speak exactly under similar circumstances?—I should say two miles were more unfavourably circumstanced, being nearer to the market town than the other, and of course the nearer to the town the greater the accumulation of traffic.

2810. Materials were perhaps more distant?—The materials were along the line in the five miles contract; this contract of 432 *l.* necessitated procuring bail to the amount of four times that sum, 1,728 *l.*; and I am sure gentlemen who know Ireland will agree with me in thinking that it is not very easy to get solvent men to go bail for contractors in Ireland for that amount.

2811. Do you know of any cheaper or better system for maintaining roads than the present grand jury system?—I think the roads are maintained at as low a cost as possible, but then there is more money lost by the roads than appears on the surface; the machinery costs a great deal of money.

2812. Are you not aware that the superintendence for the management of the county works is less in Ireland than the superintendence in any other country, or in any other private undertaking?—I think so, with regard to the officials, the working men, if I may so call them, of the institution; but, taking it as a whole, I do not think

D. B. Manley, Esq.

4 May 1868.

think there is anything in the world that costs so much money.

2813. I do not understand your answer?—With regard to your question, I think the superintendence, if you mean the salaries of county officials, county surveyors, and their assistants, is done cheaply and well, that is my answer; but I say with regard to the entire thing, when you come to consider that the salaries of county officers amounted to 110,233 *l.* out of 1,073,736 *l.*, you will find that that is a very large proportion of the public money to be expended for the administration of this system; I grant you, in the instance to which you have referred, the salaries of county surveyors, and the value they give for those salaries, is all that could be desired. I, myself, some time ago, had to suggest an increase of their salaries, and I was very happy the suggestion was adopted; but with regard to the salaries of others who are paid a great deal of money for doing very little, the entire salaries amount to 110,233 *l.* out of the 1,073,736 *l.* raised in the year 1866; that, to my mind, is a large expenditure for the working of the institution.

2814. Do you know anything of the auditing of the accounts before the Master in Chancery?—I have seen in the schedules that they are audited.

2815. Colonel *French.*] Do you see any use in that audit?—I know, of course, that it is to see that the accounts furnished are correct.

2816. We pay 3,000 *l.* a-year for that in Ireland?—It is, perhaps, a necessary outlay. There is another matter connected with this grand jury system which, if you will allow me, I should be glad to refer to, it is the cost of applications. Now there is a very large item for printing, for which we ratepayers pay, and all the paper that has been printed, in fact a good deal of it represents so many shillings and florins, for instance, the applicant must pay 2 *s.* for an application, contractors bond 1 *s.*, certificate accounting for his money half-yearly 2 *s.*, and for the different works there is probably, on an average, three tenders which shows a cost to the contractor of 9 *s.* for each application.

2817. Is that deemed legal?—I do not know that the Act warrants the payment of all those sums. I should say it is not legal.

2818. Mr. *Kendall.*] As I understand, just now you said that in case of a job the ratepayers had no chance, as they might be swamped by magistrates from other baronies?—Yes.

2819. How many years of experience have you had in your district?—I have been for 25 years going to sessions, as often as I was invited to go there.

2820. During that 25 years, how many instances have you known of a job that has been perpetrated; would it be one a-year during the 25 years?—I have known a job, and I can describe it.

2821. No; I want to know how many jobs in 25 years you have known; at a rough guess, one a year?—I took no note of the jobs, except at my sessions that I attend.

2822. How many sessions have you attended?—I have known jobs to be carried; I have known parapet protection walls to be run nearly half an English mile along a roadway where the descent was not three feet; coped and nicely covered over with coping stones; and I have known a very recently a job to be perpetrated in the county of Cork. One of the finest institutions there they have torn down, and it is about to be re-built, and the unfortunate ratepayers saddled with the cost of it, in order to convert one of the finest prisons in Ireland into I do not know what you call it; but they want to adopt the separate system; and with the bridewells of the country in an unfit state for the reception of prisoners.

2823. I merely want to know whether it is a frequent thing; in 25 years have you known a dozen jobs?—I must only confine myself to my own experience.

2824. By a job I mean where a legitimate thing has been required by the ratepayers, and they have been swamped by persons coming from other baronies, who had not an interest in the matter?—There are works of public utility which are largely supported. I have known instances where, during the famine years, the Board of Works have left roads unfinished; and I have known gentlemen take advantage of those lines being opened to get them completed; I have known them to work energetically in order to get those works passed.

2825. Mr. *Gregory.*] Might not those works be of utility to the public?—The ratepayers living along the roadside would much rather have them closed up; it was a great mistake those roads being opened at the time.

2826. Mr. *Kendall.*] In how many instances have you known that the ratepayers have been swamped by magistrates coming in from other baronies into a barony in which they have no interest; how many instances within 25 years?—I have no knowledge of it except when present myself. It did not often occur; I think it occurred about three times.

2827. *Chairman.*] In your own presence?—In my own presence.

2828. Mr. *Kendall.*] You can only answer for three times in 25 years?—Yes.

2829. I will ask you what were those three cases?—I must refer to official documents, then I shall be able to give you the cases; the dates and the number of the presentments. I suppose I shall be at liberty to apply to the secretary of the Grand Jury for the particular schedules.

2830. *Chairman.*] Do you refer to cases in which the wish of the ratepayers was defeated by the majority of the justices present at the presentment sessions?—I thought the question was, in how many instances magistrates in attendance from the other baronies had carried a work.

2831. Where magistrates present from other baronies had been in a majority, and had used that majority for the purpose of defeating the wishes of the ratepayers?—For the purpose of carrying a work which the ratepayers did not approve of.

2832. Mr. *Kendall.*] Where there was a division, were the magistrates all on one side, and the ratepayers on the other side?—The ratepayers being the members of the grand jurors or magistrates, several of them have gone with them in that and in other cases.

2833. *Chairman.*] In the case you refer to, the associated ratepayers did not vote in a body on the one side, and the magistrates coming from other baronies on the other side?—No.

2834. Mr. *Maguire.*] By their overriding the wishes of the ratepayers, do you mean that it was the ratepayers of the barony, or the associated ratepayers

ratepayers then present?—The ratepayers of the barony, represented by a portion of the cesspayers attending the sessions.

2835. Do you know whether the decision come to at that time, taking one of these cases, was in opposition to the general feeling of the ratepayers of the barony?—Quite so.

2836. *Chairman.*] Without going into minute particulars, could you give us the general nature of the works and the applications which in these three instances were passed, as you say, by the justices?—It was in the case of those suspended works left in an unfinished state by the officials of the Government.

2837. What are commonly called "relief works"?—Yes.

2838. In all three cases?—In all those three cases.

2839. Mr. *Kendall.*] Can you give us the time and the place to which you refer?—As I said just now, if I had the books to which I referred, I should be able to put my hands on the documents.

2840. These cases all occurred during the famine?—No, since the famine; they were roads which would never have been projected were it not for the famine, and which were useless to the public.

2841. Take one of these cases, where did it occur?—At Barrymore and Duhallow.

2842. Mr. *Gregory.*] Do you recollect the year?—I do not. I recollect in Duhallow it was, on one of these occasions, when I stated that a gentleman from a neighbouring barony attended, and who, when asked to poll, declined to vote, because he was out of his own barony.

2843. *Chairman.*] Then, in these three cases, the question was whether unfinished relief works should be completed or not?—That was the question.

2844. And upon that question the magistrates, with a portion of the associated cesspayers, were in favour of completing the work, and were in a majority, and the rest of the associated cesspayers were outvoted; is that the state of the case?—Precisely so.

2845. Mr. *Kendall.*] You gave us an instance of a friend of yours who was asked to go out of his barony for such a purpose; did he go?—He did not go.

2846. Colonel *French.*] In the relief works in the county Cork, did the landlords give up the money they were entitled to for the land which was taken by the Board of Works?—I am not aware what they did in those cases.

2847. Mr. *Leader.*] Do you recollect the time when the Tithe Commutation Act was in force?—In 1832 or 1833.

2848. Under that Act the amount of tithe was made chargeable on the land, and the landlord was made liable for it?—Yes.

2849. You wish that something of the same provision should be made now with regard to the half the grand jury cess?—To have it re-imposed as additional rent?

2850. To have a charge on the landlord, and to have it made compulsory on the landlord?—Yes.

2851. You are aware that, under the poor rate, the landlord can make the tenant pay the whole rate, if he chooses?—At present.

2852. You wish to have it made compulsory, in the same way that the landlord is made liable for the tithe commutation?—Yes.

2853. Mr. *Blake.*] Did I understand you, in reply to the Honourable Member, to say that you were not unwilling that the entire cost of the roads should be paid by the occupier, upon the understanding that the landlord should pay the entire cost of all the other charges?—I said so; and that would be a virtual partition of the thing, because it amounts to about one-half.

U. R. Mosley, Esq.

8 May 1868.

2854. Under the present circumstances, is not the landlord's property enhanced in value by the expenditure on the roads?—Unquestionably.

2855. Has he not a positive inducement, therefore, supposing that a landlord represents a barony, to put as much expenditure as possible on a barony for the purpose of having the value of his property enhanced?—Yes.

2856. You have been very often nominated as an associated cesspayer?—Yes, in the barony, I suppose, I get my turn; it is a large barony, and there are a good many ratepayers in it.

2857. Are you aware whether it is the practice in the county Cork for the grand juror representing the barony to select the highest ratepayer, or to exercise his discretion as to whom he selects?—Sometimes they are selected from a portion of the barony; sometimes they are fairly extended over the barony, when a gentleman represents the barony who knows the duty of a grand juror.

2858. The practice is to select whom he pleases, without reference to the ratepayer being a higher ratepayer than another; is that the case?—I think, as a rule, in the baronies with which I am connected, the highest ratepayers are generally selected.

2859. Have you ever known an instance where an associated cesspayer shows himself very independent upon the baronial board, that he has not been selected again; that his independence has cost him his nomination upon another occasion?—I have been rather prominent, and I have been very seldom selected in one barony with which I have to do; and in another barony, as I said, I have got my *fair* turn.

2860. Do you attribute your non-selection in the first barony of which you speak to the independence you showed as an associated cesspayer?—I certainly do.

2861. If an associated ratepayer is not agreeable to the views of the grand juror who selects him, the chances are he would not be selected again?—The chances are he would not be selected again.

2862. You are in favour, if I understand you correctly, of the entire separation of the fiscal from the criminal business?—A complete and entire separation.

2863. You would have, in the first place, a baronial board, selected by the ratepayers, that is half of the baronial board?—Yes.

2864. The others to be magistrates?—The others to be magistrates, with the qualification I stated.

2865. You would have a county board, composed of delegates from them?—Yes.

2866. Do you not think it would be as well to have the county board also selected by the ratepayers and not by the baronial board; would not it be just as easy, when the voting paper is sent round for a representative on the baronial board, to have a voting paper also sent in and returned for a representative on the county board?—Yes, if no additional expense be incurred.

U. R. Murley, Esq.

9 May 1868.

2867. There would not be much additional expense?—I think the baronial board, being the elected of the people, the selection of the delegates of the county board might be left to those representatives.

2868. You spoke, just now, of the expense that might be incurred in selecting a representative for the baronial board; is it not the case at present that, if a sufficient number of Poor Law guardians could be sent from the local districts no election takes place?—It is.

2869. May not the same thing take place with regard to the representatives for the Poor Law Board?—Yes; and I dare say the thing would settle down so.

2870. The expenses would at length become very small?—Just so.

2871. Have you ever been a Poor Law guardian yourself?—I have; I have ceased to be so for the last eight years.

2872. Was it in the Union of Cork?—No; of Midleton.

2873. Has it occurred to your union that a number of lunatics have been kept there in consequence of there not being room in the district assigned for them?—Yes.

2874. While detained in the union, the cost is equally divided between the landlord and the occupier?—Yes, except in those instances where land has been recently let, and the entire rate thrown on the tenant.

2875. When that same lunatic goes into the lunatic asylum at Cork, the entire burden is then borne by the occupier?—Yes.

2876. And he has to pay four times as much as he paid before?—Yes.

2877. *Mr. Maguire.*] It was suggested by an Honourable Member on the other side, that if the rate were equally divided between the landlord and the tenant, the tenant would have no advantage, and not only no advantage, but he would have an additional burden, for if the rate were 6 *s.* the landlord would make him pay 5 *s.*; have you any apprehension that such a state of things would occur?—Certainly not; I do not think it would.

2878. Do you think it is within the widest range of probability?—I do not think the landlord would give himself so large a margin for the probable increase of expenses as that. I think he would be disposed to go with his tenant, and I think if that change could be brought about, and the original rating clause could be restored to the Irish poor law, then we should have a prospect of being a very contented people in Ireland.

2879. The Honourable Member also spoke of opening a source of difference; is not the present state of things a source of difference?—It is; there is no confidence absolutely in the grand jury administration now.

2880. As between two classes, between the occupier and the owner, is not the effect of the one bearing the entire burden of the rate a source of difference between the two classes?—Yes.

2881. Would it not be well to remove it?—Yes.

2882. If a new law is passed, dividing the burden between both, do not you think it removes a cause of discontent?—It is removing a cause of discontent, and it will have to be done to remove a cause of great discontent. As an Irishman, I may say myself, that the only reason I have for being discontented, is the existence of the grand jury system. I may say this, that in all my experience of that system, I never knew a man who came before a Presentment Sessions of a particular creed, who did not get 20 shillings in the pound on his application, and I never knew an instance of a man of the opposite creed, the creed of the majority of the people, who got 20 shillings in the pound on his application.

2883. Your main objection to the Presentment Sessions is this, that the law permits at any time the possibility of the associated cesspayers being swamped?—Except for the humour of the thing, they might as well be without the representation.

2884. There is no sufficient protection for the one class?—No.

2885. That is your main objection?—My main objection.

2886. *Mr. Dawson.*] You mentioned this discontent as very prevalent, how is it shown?—I mean to show it in future by never entering the Presentment Sessions until this law is changed.

2887. You have acted as an associated cesspayer?—I have.

2888. And did you find that non-attendance on the part of the ratepayers general?—So general, that I believe in Barrymore on the last occasion, there were only three or four in attendance, because of the experience they had when they came before the grand jury and before the judge of assize; I look upon it as a monstrous thing, that I, who have been administering that law legitimately, because I go with men of property, men of estates in Ireland, to sustain the act of that court: I look upon it as a monstrous thing to say, that I should be actually fined in the highest amount which the law allows the judge to inflict upon a man who happened to be a ratepayer, and who did not wish to exercise factious opposition.

2889. *Chairman.*] You refer to the case of the traverse you before mentioned?—Yes.

2890. Which was tried by a petty jury?—Yes.

2891. And decided against you?—Yes, I am particularly desirous to inform the Committee of the fact how the body to whom we in Ireland owe a great deal (I mean the constabulary of the country) when they were burnt out in defending their barrack from an invasion of the Fenians, or men supposed to be Fenians; how when it comes before a grand jury in Ireland, and the officer in charge of the constabulary made an application for his losses to the amount of 100 *l.*, how the grand jury wanted to reduce that man's claim to 40 *l.* Certainly on that jury there were some high-minded men who endeavoured to get for him the full amount that he claimed; but at that assizes, men of a particular creed got 20 *s.* in the pound while every other man of an opposite creed was cut down in his application, and only a per-centage of his claim allowed.

2892. *Earl of Mayo.*] Will you have the kindness to state what that case was; was it the Ballyknockane case?—It was.

2893. *Mr. Gregory.*] Are these cases of malicious injury?—Yes.

2894. *Earl of Mayo.*] Will you state the names of the men whose applications were refused on account of their religion, and of those whose applications were granted on account of their

their religion?—"John Browne, 100 *l.* for the wilful and malicious burning and destroying a quantity of household furniture and effects, bed, bedding, wearing apparel, and other matters at Ballymacken, on the morning of the 6th March, 1867."

2895. What religion was he?—I understand a Roman Catholic.

2896. Mr. *Dawson.*] Do you know this from your personal knowledge?—I was present.

2897. Earl of *Mayo.*] How much did Browne get?—A member of the grand jury, a Mr. Payne, a land agent, moved that that man should get 40 *l.*; Captain Barry and Captain Johnson, high-minded and honourable men, said they did not see why the constabulary should not get what they were proved to have lost. There were several divisions of the jury; Mr. Payne failed in getting the jury to agree to 40 *l.*, and he then moved that the man should get 60 *l.*; ultimately, as a compromise, he got 80 *l.*, so that 20 per cent. was disaccredited.

2898. Because he was a Roman Catholic; do you adhere to that statement?—That is my experience.

2899. I am not talking about your experience; I am talking of this particular case; do you mean to assert that, to your knowledge, that man's claim was reduced from 100 *l.* to 80 *l.*, because he was a Roman Catholic?—I mean to assert that all those of his creed——

2900. I am not asking that question at all; I am asking a very simple question?—I am not going to state any such thing.

2901. Do you mean to assert that you know that that man's claim was reduced from 100 *l.* to 80 *l.* because he was a Roman Catholic?—I shall not state so positively, but that is my belief.

2902. Upon what do you ground that belief?—Upon my life-long experience. I have known men in equal position in life get every penny of the amount they sought for malicious injury. I only speak now of cases in which I was myself present, but I have known cases in which, invariably, I have divided the sessions, and I have said, "Why should not this man get as much as that man?"

2903. *Chairman.*] Are you personally acquainted with the case of this man Browne?—I was present in the court, in the grand jury room, when the case was taken.

2904. Earl of *Mayo.*] Will you go on with the next case; let us have another case where you say that a man's claim was either admitted or rejected on account of his religion?—There were four or five at least in the barrack, and they defended the barrack as long as they could, until the building was in flames above them; they descended from the barrack, and I believe, during their descent, several shots were fired at them. Captain Barry was indignant at the idea of the application being questioned at all, and he said that in cases of that kind they ought to get the full amount they claimed instantly.

2905. Mr. *Gregory.*] What Captain Barry is that?—Captain Barry, of Barryclough.

2906. Is he a Protestant or a Catholic?—He is a Protestant, and a gentleman of position and fortune; Mr. Payne, I understand, is a land agent.

2907. *Chairman.*] Do you think it is a matter of course that people should get instantly the amount of their claims in those cases?—I think that if two parties of opposite creeds come, and solemnly depose to the fact, and this man Browne was backed up by his wife, and she, poor woman, when it was thought a enormous thing for a policeman to have 100 *l.*, said, "The savings of my life, gentlemen."

2908. Earl of *Mayo.*] Was there a division in Browne's case?—There were two divisions.

2909. Are the numbers given there?—The divisions were taken; there were five applications; these gentlemen struck off so much from the sum claimed by each applicant; there were three divisions.

2910. Was the grand jury nearly equally divided, or was there a large majority on the one side or the other?—I think they were pretty equally divided in the second division.

2911. Notwithstanding that, you state it to be your opinion that the man's claim was rejected because he was a Roman Catholic?—Every one of this list almost, at least those whose creed I happen to know are Roman Catholics.

2912. Will you state the next case?—"Michael Landy 6 *l.*, for the wilful and malicious burning and destroying a quantity of clothing, effects, goods, chattels, and money at Ballymacken, on the morning of the 6th day of March 1867."

2913. What was done with his claim?—He got the same proportion.

2914. How much did he get?—He got the same proportion as the others; it was arranged under a scale.

2915. It was on a scale?—So much deducted from each man's claim.

2916. How many men were there?—Five, I think.

2917. Were they all Roman Catholics?—As far as I know they were.

2918. Are you sure they were?—I cannot say.

2919. Were they the whole number of the policemen that were in the barracks that night?—They were the four or five men who were there that night.

2920. Were those five men the whole number of the policemen who were in the barracks that night?—Four of the five were Roman Catholics but I am not certain as to the fifth.

2921. All their claims were submitted and dealt with in the same way?—Dealt with in the same way.

2922. That being the case, that all those claims were submitted to the grand jury and were dealt with in the same way, do you still adhere to the statement, that a portion of their claims were rejected because they were Roman Catholics?—I will not state it positively, but that is my belief.

2923. Would you be very much surprised to hear that one, if not two, of those men were Protestants?—I think I am positive as to four.

2924. But you would not be positive about the fifth?—No.

2925. Are you aware that there is a rule in the constabulary, that on every station in Ireland, one of the men must be of a different religion to the others?—I am not aware such a rule exists.

2926. Do not you think that is always adhered to?—I was not certain of the rule, or of the existence of it.

2927. Do not you think that the probabilities are, that one of those five men whose claims were all dealt with in the same way was a Protestant?—Yes; they were all treated in the same way, decidedly.

U. R. Manning, Esq.

8 May 1868.

2928. You

U. R. Mackay, Esq.

8 May 1868.

2928. You still adhere to your assertion, that the grand jury dealt with it upon these grounds? —From my experience through life, I do believe that the men here, and in other instances, who were Roman Catholics were cut down, and the Protestants got the full amount they claimed.

2929. Mr. *Gregory*.] In this case did the Protestants on these notices get the amount they claimed?—I speak of applicants outside this; in fact, as to the police, I am not positive; but as to four of the men, the principal man, the constable in charge, he is a Roman Catholic.

2930. *Chairman*.] You are not able to say in this particular case, as a matter of fact, that Protestant and Roman Catholic applicants for compensation, having equal claims, were differently dealt with by the grand jury; are you able in this case, as a matter of fact, to state that to the Committee?—I believe it to be so, and I know at the presentment sessions, where applicants came forward whose creed was known, my experience is that invariably the Roman Catholic applicant is cut down in his application, and there is not a word said about the application of the person of the other creed.

2931. You derive that opinion from what you consider to be your general experience?—Yes.

2932. But not from the facts of the case which you have just now brought before the Committee?—There have been claims made at the past assizes.

2933. That is not an answer to my question; I ask you whether you derive that opinion from what you consider to be your general experience, and not from the fact of the particular case which you have detailed to the Committee?—From my general experience, strengthened by the proceedings of the grand jury to which I have alluded.

2934. In this particular case?—In that and other cases before the grand jury, for most exaggerated applications were granted.

2935. I am talking of this particular case; in this case are you able to show to the Committee that there were Protestant applicants who were treated more favourably by the grand jury than the Roman Catholic applicants possessing equal claims?—I do decidedly; that is my conviction.

2936. I am not talking of any general case; I am talking of this particular case of the policemen which you have brought before the Committee?—It was quite notorious at the particular sessions I speak of, that the claims of the police should not be reduced.

2937. Do you mean to say that, in this particular case which you have brought before the Committee, there were Protestant constables who were more favourably treated than their Roman Catholic comrades?—No; I was not aware that there were any Protestant applicants. There were the constables in charge of the station, who were dealt with as I say, and I believe they were all Roman Catholics.

2938. Then the opinion which you gave to the Committee is derived from what you considered to be your general experience, not from the facts of this particular case of the Ballynockan Police barrack?—I think it is very strong in that case, under the circumstances.

2939. Earl of *Mayo*.] To leave the Ballynockan case, will you have the goodness to tell the Committee whether you know any instances of two claims for malicious injuries, one preferred by a Protestant and the other preferred by a Roman Catholic, in which the grand jury dealt with similar cases in a different manner?—There were several cases or instances of claims by persons of the two different creeds which were disposed of at that assizes in the manner I alluded to, and which the printed schedules will show.

2940. My question refers to the grand jury, if you will have the goodness to answer it?—Withdrawn.

2941. *Chairman*.] This Ballynockan case?—That and the other cases.

2942. Earl of *Mayo*.] What are the other cases?—There are several cases; there was the case of the man upon whose lands burnings had become quite an institution.

2943. Are you a Poor Law Guardian?—No, I am not; I have ceased to be so for the past eight years.

2944. Why did you cease to be a Poor Law Guardian?—I will tell you. I left the particular part of the country I was resident in, and through a gentleman very kindly offered to vacate the property on which I lived when I came to reside there, I thought as he was a very good guardian I might be quite satisfied with him, and as he stood in the position of my landlord.

2945. You never sought to be elected for your new residence?—No.

2946. Mr. *Gregory*.] I think among the jobs which you alleged against the grand jurors, was the pulling down an old prison at Cork, and building a new one for the separate system?—Yes, I opposed it.

2947. You consider that as one of the jobs which you mentioned?—I did. Several of the magistrates of the county went with me. We polled 9 to 14.

2948. Will you kindly define what you call a job?—I should say a job is that which one man gets effected at another man's expense.

2949. Was one man getting the building of that prison for his own particular purpose?—Do you mean the builder?

2950. No, I mean the grand jury; were they personally interested in that prison?—Several gentlemen who were grand jurors opposed it. Lord Bandon took a very great interest in the matter.

2951. Taking your definition of a job, do you consider that any of the grand jurors, who were in favour of building the prison upon what I may call the improved system, had any personal interest in so doing?—Well, it is one of those institutions which have been imported, and whether it will be for our advantage or not, I cannot say; it did not originate in Ireland.

2952. Do you think any of the grand juries had any personal interest with regard to that provision?—I really cannot answer for the motives that actuate the human mind.

2953. Earl of *Mayo*.] I suppose you are against the improved system of discipline in jails?—I am against the expense, as I consider it unnecessary with a decreasing population, and particularly a population becoming more virtuous every day, and crime diminishing.

2954. You prefer the old associated system to the new system of separate confinement?—A system that has, as I understand, driven men mad, I think a bad one.

2955. *Chairman*.] It was a difference of opinion upon a public question, was it not?—A difference of opinion upon a public question; but, you see, we are rather jealous of these institutions from other places besides Ireland.

2956. Colonel

2956. *Colonel Cooper.*] Were any of the cesspayers in the majority?—I think an aspirant for the magistracy voted with the majority.

2957. As far as you remember, at least one cesspayer voted with the majority?—Yes; a gentleman desirous of getting elected a justice of of the peace.

2958. *Mr. Herbert.*] You said you were a landlord?—Yes; I am a land owner. I do not say landlord, really my estate in land is so very small.

2959. Do you pay half the county cess for your tenants, as you are so much in favour of it?—Indeed I do not; but my tenants have land from me at an honest valuation, and I should be very happy if the law were made to-morrow to allow it.

U. B. Mahony, Esq.

6 May 1868.

Lord JOHN BROWNE, a Member of the House; Examined.

Lord J. Browne, M.P.

2960. *Chairman.*] Have you frequently been foreman of the grand jury of the county Mayo?—Very frequently. During the last 18 years I have attended very regularly, and, I think, I have been foreman on most occasions on which I have attended the grand jury.

2961. You have paid great attention to the working of the system?—I have.

2962. What is your general opinion of the present constitution of grand juries in Ireland?—As regards the grand jury itself, I am not now referring to the presentment sessions. I think they are on the whole a tolerably efficient body for the performance of the duties which are entrusted to them. It must be remembered what those duties are. Their functions are, as regard one portion of the taxation, the cess, exactly similar to those of the House of Lords as regards Imperial taxation; that is to say, they have no power, with a few trifling exceptions perhaps, which I will mention, of originating any taxation; their powers are solely confined to saying aye or no to presentments which have previously passed the presentment sessions, which presentments they cannot alter in any way whatever, and their powers even of vetoing are greatly limited and controlled by the 64th section of the Grand Jury Act, which in case of a grand jury refusing a presentment which has passed the presentment sessions, empowers the cesspayers to memorialise the Lord Lieutenant, who is thereupon authorised to direct the Board of Works to inquire and examine into the case in point, and if the Board of Works report that the work in question, which may either be the making of a new road, or the repair of an existing road, is necessary, then the Lord Lieutenant refers the case again to the grand jury, and if they again refuse to present, he is empowered, if he thinks fit, to order the Commissioners of Public Works to execute such repair, or to make such road, and the amount is then charged on the county at large as an imperative presentment. I think that is a very wholesome check on the despotic exercise of power on the part of the grand jury, though it has very seldom been exercised.

2963. Are you in favour of any change in the constitution of the grand jury, or are you in favour of substituting any other body for it in respect of its fiscal functions?—I think if you abolish the present system, the most desirable body to substitute for it would be a court elected by the magistrates of the county. I think a body having solely the power of veto, such as the grand jury have, is a very useful check on jobbery and on extravagance in the county. I think it is very desirable to maintain such a check on the presentment sessions.

2964. Do you think a body chosen as you describe would be an improvement upon the present system?—I rather incline to prefer it myself; but I think it would practically make very little difference.

2965. If any change were made, that is the change you would recommend?—Decidedly.

2966. As to presentment sessions, are you satisfied with the present constitution of presentment sessions, or are there any changes in that part of the system which you would advise?—I do not think the present presentment sessions are at all satisfactory; I think the cesspayers ought to be represented by elected cesspayers, and the course which to me seems simplest to carry out that object would be for the Lord Lieutenant to be given the same powers as regards the division of the county into electoral districts, as the Poor Law Commissioners have in the case of the poor laws; that is to say, the Lord Lieutenant should divide each barony into districts, in proportion to its size and population, each district returning one representative; the representative might be elected in the same way as the Poor Law Guardians, which is a very simple and inexpensive mode, and the nomination might either be made at the presentment sessions, or the grand jury, according to convenience.

2967. Then you would not adhere to the baronial divisions?—Yes; I would divide each barony into electoral districts for this purpose. It is almost unnecessary for me to say that I am entirely against a magistrate who has no interest in the barony sitting at the presentment sessions; such a thing is hardly ever done; I happen to know one case, where, I believe, it was done accidentally; a magistrate went to attend the county at large sessions, and the sessions of the barony, in which the county town was situated, were held at the same time. They asked him to take the chair, and he did it without reflection. There happened to be a close division, and there were some remarks made about it, and he was very sorry; he did it quite inadvertently, I believe.

2968. Would you provide by law for equality, or any fixed proportion between the justices and the elected members of the court?—Yes; I think it is desirable that the justices should not swamp the cesspayers in a case of that sort. It seems to me that it might be regulated by the Lord Lieutenant; it is impossible to lay down in legislation a broad line, because it must vary according to the circumstances of each barony; I think, unless the numbers of magistrates are too great, that every magistrate having an interest in the barony, not only having property, but having an interest in the barony, shall be allowed to attend the sessions; there are many cases where magistrates owning large property, and in some cases magistrates who farm 5,000 *l.* or 6,000 *l.* a year in many parts of Ireland, do not reside in a particular barony in which they have a very large interest, and

Lord *J. Browne*, M. P.

8 May 1868.

and I think they ought to be allowed to attend these presentment sessions, they having an interest in the barony, though they may not own property or reside in it.

2969. Unless you had a proportion fixed by law, and some mode of selection from out of the body of magistrates resident or possessing property in the electoral division, the cesspayers would still be likely to be outvoted by the justices?—I think the Lord Lieutenant would regulate that by apportioning the number of representatives in proportion to the number of magistrates in the habit of attending the sessions; that is a point of detail. It would be very easy to check that by saying that not more than a certain number should sit at the presentment sessions. I do not think it would be desirable that the magistrates should entirely swamp the cesspayers at the presentment sessions, or that the cesspayers should swamp the magistrates.

2970. You think that there should be an equality of numbers?—I think that there should be an approach to it; absolute equality would be difficult to attain. Magistrates go away; they leave the county, come to London, or go to Paris a great deal more than the cesspayers.

2971. *Earl of Mayo.*] There is a provision in the Poor Law that in no case can the number of *ex officio* magistrates exceed the number of elected guardians?—Exactly.

2972. You would propose a similar provision to that?—Yes.

2973. *Chairman.*] Are you in favour of an appointment of a finance committee to sit permanently between the assizes?—I am very strongly in favour of it, and I think that a very great advantage would be derived from the appointment of such a committee. I will state some of the objects for which I think that grand jury committee should be appointed. First of all I take a Parliamentary Return of 1867, No. 456; I will just give you out of it the cost of an applotment of the county cess, showing what it costs in different counties, in consequence of there being no Board, or no body having the time to look into these little matters. I find that the cost of the applotment of the cess in the county of Wexford is 200 *l.* a year; the population is 143,954, and the value is 369,000 *l.* In the county of Cork the cost of applotment is only 130 *l.*; the population, excluding the city, is 419,000, and the valuation 945,000 *l.* In King's County the total cost of applotment is only 38 *l.*; the population is 80,000, and the valuation 241,000 *l.* Well, now, if the cost of applotment in the county of Wexford were the same in proportion to the population as in King's County, it would amount to 63 *l.* instead of 200 *l.*, and if in proportion to valuation 57 *l.*; if in proportion to the population of Cork it would be 41 *l.*, and if in proportion to the valuation of Cork it would be 48 *l.* That is one of the objects for which I should propose that the finance committee of the grand jury should be appointed to look into and regulate such matters.

2974. How do you account for those great variations?—The law says that the grand jury shall present such sums as are necessary for the purpose of the applotment. The grand jury know nothing beforehand, until the county treasurer walks in with a Bill for 120 *l.* or 100 *l.* or something of that sort for the applotment of the half year. They have no means of investigating it, or time to do so. In our county it costs us 200 *l.* We remonstrated with the county treasurer, who is a gentleman in every sense of the word, and he assured us that he had actually paid that sum to the clerks. He said I assure you none of it goes into my own pocket. We had not this return before us. We did not know what it cost in other counties. We had no time to investigate it. We passed his presentment, and we have done so continuously up to the present moment. I am sure the amount might be reduced to something like the same proportion that it is in Cork, and in King's County, if there were a body that had time to look into the thing and examine it.

2975. In your opinion, you think the transitory nature of the grand jury, and the short period of time during which it sits, makes it impossible for it to exercise any control over this expenditure?—Exactly.

2976. Will you tell the Committee, in general, what are the duties which you would assign to such a finance committee?—They should have power to examine and control the accounts of the High Constable; at present the High Constable gets a warrant to collect, say, 2,500 *l.*; he is able to collect the whole of that amount, and to speculate with it, and I may say that in practice it is very commonly done; there is no doubt about it. The law requires that the High Constable should place the money in the bank whenever he has collected 100 *l.*, that he shall not keep more than that in his hands. That is practically impossible. There is a barony in my county, the chief town of which is not less than 48 miles from the county bank, and a man could not be travelling backwards and forwards with every 100 *l.* Instead of having an impossible provision of that sort, of course never attended to, which can never be enforced, and which there is nobody to enforce, if this committee were appointed, and had power to regulate and control the matter, they would see that the money was lodged as it was collected, in moderate amounts. I would give them power, in case of necessity, if they saw that there was any reason to supersede the High Constable on account of impropriety of conduct, if they had reason to believe he was about to abscond from the country, which it is perfectly easy for a High Constable and his security to do. In the county of Mayo we lost during the famine nearly 80,000 *l.* cess by insufficiency of securities and different causes of that nature, most of which would have been saved if we had had such a committee. One of the objects to which I would have the attention of this Committee drawn is, the investigation of the securities of high constables. In consequence of our having lost that large sum of money in Mayo, we have been exceedingly particular about the securities, and the result is that we direct them to submit their securities to the inspection of our solicitor, and a great many securities previously approved of have been rejected. We have lost some good collectors in consequence, and there is a great difficulty in getting good securities to attend the grand jury. According to the present law the securities must both attend together at the grand jury to perfect their bonds. Well, now the securities we have in some cases reside in Dublin, and they are put to the cost and trouble of coming all the way down from Dublin merely to perfect their bond. To remedy this, I moved the insertion of a clause in a Bill which passed the House of Commons a few years ago, but which was dropped in the House of Lords, and by that clause the bonds were authorised to

be

be taken before a master extraordinary or commissioner for taking special bail, which would have saved a great deal of this trouble, and would have prevented the necessity of the sureties travelling all the way to the grand jury. What I should recommend is, that this Committee should have power to examine into these securities, approve of them, and take the bonds, or make arrangements for taking them. A suggestion has lately been made by a high constable in my county, which is a very good one, and that is that the bond should be continuous. That is the case now with the deputy cess collector. If you look at Foot's book, page 124, you will see it is stated there that the deputy cess collectors are empowered to sign continuous bonds; it is on the note at the bottom of the page: "The bond of a surety for a deputy cess collector recited the fact of his being surety for a deputy of a high constable or collector, would collect the grand jury cess as he should be required from time to time by the collector, and for the purpose of all legal acts he might be required to perform; and was conditioned 'to collect such public moneys as he should be by the collector from time to time required, and to complete each and every collection he should be so required,' &c. one week at least before the first day of each and every assizes." Then the decision is "held that the above was a continuing security, notwithstanding that the collector's appointment was a temporary one under clause 147, and was recited to be such in the bond." There is no reason why the high constable's bond should not be continuous in the same way during his tenure of office. It might be thought desirable, as a precaution, that the grand jury should pass a resolution declaring the bond to continue in force.

2977. *Chairman*.] I suppose it would be the duty of the secretary of the grand jury to ascertain the existence and continued solvency of the securities?—I should propose that the Finance Committee should do that with the assistance of the solicitor of the grand jury. Well then I should propose that payments on account to contractors should be sanctioned by the permanent committee. I do not think it would be desirable as is done, I believe, in county Clare and other counties, that the county surveyor should have sole power to make payments to the amount of three-fourths of all the works in the whole county without some sort of control or check. At present the presentment sessions have to sanction any payment to a contractor, which afterwards goes to the grand jury, but if merely on the certificate of the county surveyor, three-fourths is to be paid by the treasurer of the county, it is depriving them of all control whatever, and I think it is putting too extensive and rather a dangerous power into the hands of the county surveyor; I think there ought to be somebody to sanction payments.

2978. Is it not the case that at present there must, on an average, be some six months between the time at which a contract is entered into and any payment which can be made on that contract?—Unfortunately the times of the grand jury are unequally divided. There is a little more than four months between the spring and summer assizes, and very nearly eight months between the summer and following spring assizes. It is very difficult for a contractor for the maintenance of roads, for instance to execute the work between the spring and the summer assizes. You are aware that he must apply for his certificate from the county surveyor ten days before the first presentment sessions. Well, the first presentment sessions were held in my county this time on the 8th May; the assizes were the 8th March, ten days before the 8th May brings it to about seven weeks after the assizes. Well that is just the time of year when everybody is very busy in the country, so I do not think there is any hardship on the contractor between the spring and the summer assizes. In fact, he is very seldom able to complete his contract, but between the summer and following spring assizes there is sometimes a hardship.

2979. Do you think contractors would be able to do their work cheaper if they were not kept so long out of their money?—I do in some cases. I would call the attention of the Committee to the 128th clause of the Grand Jury Act relative to this. It seems to me to be very defective; it authorises the payment of three-fourths of the cost of the work, but that can only be done in the event of the grand jury ordering it at the time of presenting for the work, and it says it must be done out of any funds in his hands applicable to the purpose. Now, he cannot do it out of the general funds in his hands under those words, and there is very great doubt as to how far the system of advancing money is legal under that section. Then, I should suggest, that in the event of the provisions of 19 & 20 Vict., c. 63, which have been very much discussed by the committee here, being extended and amended, that the permanent committee should have power to pay costs incurred by county surveyors in prosecuting road contractors. The county surveyor has got to pay his expenses, of course, in travelling to the court, and in the event of the contractor failing to do his duty, the county surveyor has to go twice frequently, first for the order to the contractor to execute the work, and secondly for an order levying the money by a distress on his goods. It costs him something for his travelling. I think it is hard that he should have the law costs in addition. I think it is a great impediment in the way of bringing that clause into effect. Another thing I should recommend is, that sudden damages should be under the control of this permanent committee, and particularly sudden damages to court-houses. According to the existing law, no magistrate can sign a sudden damage order for any injury to a court-house. Of course slates are blown off; sometimes part of the roof. My own is a very stormy county; windows are blown in, and all sorts of accidents may happen, and there is no power of issuing a sudden damage order for court-houses. You can do so for any other description of public works, even bridewells, which are generally attached to the court-house. These can be repaired by the Board of Superintendence up to the sum of 100*l*., but there is no provision for repairing sudden damages to court-houses. Well, then, as to bridges, I think if you had a permanent finance committee, you might go a little further in the case of sudden damages to bridges. I know the case of one valuable bridge, which could have been saved by an expenditure of 70*l*. or 80*l*.; it could not be spent, and the bridge went in consequence.

2980. *Colonel Forde*.] Have the grand jury the power to nominate a committee to carry out any works as regards court-houses?—Yes.

2981. Between the assizes?—Yes, but not for sudden damages. When a presentment is made, then

Lord *J. Browne*, M.P.

8 May 1868.

Lord J. Browne, M.P.

9 May 18[illegible].

that they may nominate a committee, but in the case of sudden damages, there is no power in the Act by which they can be repaired until the sessions. You are aware there is a section in the Grand Jury Act which gives power to grand juries, and it is one of the few cases in which grand juries can present without a previous application at presentment sessions; in all cases of sudden damages, grand juries may present without previous application to the presentment sessions for the money necessary to repair the damage, and that applies to court-houses, but, curiously enough, it does not apply to piers. Mayo is a maritime county, and therefore some of these points come under my notice. It is a curious thing that magistrates in petty sessions have power to present for sudden damages to piers, but not for sudden damages to court-houses, whereas, on the contrary, the grand jury have power to present for sudden damages to court-houses without application to the presentment sessions, and not for piers.

2962. *Chairman.*] Do you wish to say any thing as to the power to present poundage and salaries in advance?—According to the Act of Parliament, the poundages of the collectors cannot be placed on the levy till after they have lodged the cess; you do not know what the amount of it will be; it is not levied till the next assizes; supposing he has paid in the money at the summer assizes, the money is due to him then, and he is kept without it until the following spring assizes. I think they ought to have power to present a sum in advance for the purpose of paying any sums of money, such as poundages and salaries, at the time at which they are due. It is generally done, I believe, in many counties; it is done in my county, but it is quite illegal.

2963. Mr. *Dawson.*] Of course you deduct the poundage on what he is short?—We make the high constable pay in every farthing of the warrant, whether they collect it or not. We give them a high poundage, and make them lodge the whole of the money.

2964. *Chairman.*] Have you any change to propose with reference to adjourned sessions?—Yes, a very great inconvenience arises in my county from it being necessary that a magistrate should take the chair at the adjourned sessions. It has occurred at the Barony of Erris, it occurred at the very last sessions, and all the works in the barony, except continuous contracts, fell to the ground, in consequence. It has occurred within my memory, four or five times at least in that barony, and twice in another barony, and I should recommend that a cesspayer should be allowed to take the chair in the event of no magistrate being present. I also got that introduced in a clause in a Bill which passed the Commons, and dropped in the Lords.

2965. I believe the attendance at adjourned sessions both of magistrates and cesspayers is generally very inadequate?—Very, it is a mere matter of form, taking the contracts, and generally speaking, one magistrate does the whole business. Occasionally, if a cesspayer lives near he comes in. It is very seldom I have seen more than one magistrate attending.

2966. There is a probability, is there not, that elected cesspayers who have been chosen for a certain duty would be more likely to attend to their business than the associated cesspayers do now?—I think they would perhaps, for the regular presentment sessions, but for the adjourned sessions I do not think they would, because the business there is simply taking the lowest contract, and there is a very good feeling between the cesspayers and the magistrates in my county.

2967. Colonel *Forde.*] Would a power of adjournment given to the secretary, failing the magistrate being present, answer the purpose?—I think the other would be a simpler remedy, and I do not think there is any objection to allowing a cesspayer to take the chair.

2968. *Chairman.*] Are you satisfied with the present state of the law on the subject of re-presentments?—No; in fact there is no law; it is another curious case of omission in the Grand Jury Act. If a man has taken a contract and not executed it, there is no means by which that money can be applied to any purpose except the executing that same work, and there are cases where, of course, that is quite impossible. Take the case of a man who has a contract to keep a public road in repair, and he fails the last two half years in his contract, and the work is re-let to another man at a different sum of money. The money that was levied for the two half years that the contractor failed in his work remains in the treasurer's hands. There is no means of applying it to any purpose whatever according to the existing law. Take, for instance, the contract for repair of a bridge; the contractor neglects it, the bridge is swept away, it is re-built by another presentment. The money for repairing this bridge still remains in hand, and there is no mode of applying it. A common mode has prevailed in the country of re-presenting the sum of money to the credit of the district off which it was originally levied, but there is no law authorising it; and a short time ago a contractor traversed one of these re-presentments before the judge. The judge first of all inquired into the contractor's claim, and he decided that he had no claim in the world; that he had not performed his contract. Then arose the question as to what was to be done with the money. The judge looked at the Act, and he said he did not see how he could sanction our making this presentment; but at the same time it was no wrong to any one. We were doing what was for the benefit of the county, and he avoided giving a decision by telling us we had better for the future advertise all these presentments we proposed to represent, which we have done ever since (a very proper thing) and the case was dropped then, and never was revived. There is no doubt there is no law which authorises your applying it so. What I suggest is, that the 146th section of the Act should be amended by putting in after the words "It shall be applied in such a manner and under such directions as the grand jury shall appoint for the purpose of executing and completing such works," or to the credit of the district off which it was levied, or words to that effect. In this Parliamentary Return to which I have before referred, there are, I think, over 40,000 *l.* in hand in some counties for works which have never been executed. In the County Tipperary 41,000 *l.* are invested in Exchequer Bills, the greater portion of it is for works which have never been executed. It has during the last five years been invested in Exchequer Bills. In Tyrone it is 39,000 *l.* It varies in different counties.

2969. Is that the main cause of those investments?—That is one of the principal causes; the

Lord J. Browne, M.P.

8 May 1868.

the act is illegal, but it is done. In the case I mentioned, I was foreman, and I asked the judge, "Having given the notice you recommend us to give, would it be legal for us to present at the next assizes?" He said, "When the case comes before me officially, I will give a decision." He evidently intimated that the thing might be done, though it was not strictly legal; it is commonly done.

2990. You are aware that proposals have been made for the amalgamation of the offices of clerk of the Crown and clerk of the peace; have you any opinion to give on that subject?—I certainly think it is high time something should be done about these two offices; it is most monstrous, I think, those two offices remaining as they are. They could perfectly well be amalgamated I believe, and a portion of the duty should be thrown on the secretary of the grand jury. All the presentments that have passed the grand jury are sent through the office of the clerk of the Crown; he makes out a list and hands it to the treasurer within seven days of the assizes; all the checks that are signed by the county treasurer, are countersigned by the clerk of the Crown, and he calls out in public court, the names of the grand jury, and these are, as regards the fiscal business of the county, his principal duties. It seems to me, that those duties could be performed by the secretary as well as the clerk of the Crown, in fact, he is the natural man to do them. He has other duties; he keeps the Crown Book, records the verdicts of juries; he does that at the assizes, and the clerk of the peace performs that duty at the quarter sessions. It seems to me, that there is no reason why the same officer should not do it, and why the two offices should not be amalgamated. I think it would be great economy to the country, and you might abolish a large amount of fees which are paid, and which produce large salaries to these gentlemen. I might add as a general rule, that the clerks of the Crown do their duty by deputy; they do not reside in the county, they have a deputy who does the work for some small sum of money.

2991. Colonel *Forde*.] And the clerk of the peace as well?—The clerk of the peace does not in my county, but I know he does in many others.

2992. Earl of *Mayo*.] The clerk of the peace is appointed by the Lord Lieutenant of the county, and the clerk of the Crown by the Government?—Yes.

2993. In case of the amalgamation of the two offices, to whom would you propose to give the appointment?—I should say that the fairest thing would be to let them have it alternately. I do not think such a small question of patronage ought to interfere.

2994. Mr. *Dawson*.] Do you not think that all the three offices might be abolished, and that the secretary of the grand jury might perform the duties of the three offices?—No, I think not. You must have an officer for the business of the court, to keep the Crown book, and record the verdicts. I think you would be giving the secretary too much to do. If this were carried out, I should propose that the secretary should give his whole and exclusive time to the business of the county, and that he should be obliged to reside at the county town, or within a mile of it. I would give him a higher salary. The present system of fees has been very much discussed in this Committee, and I have seen that one secretary at Cork gets nearly 1,000 *l.* a year altogether. I should propose to abolish all fees, except that I would allow 6 *d.* for a tender, which I would make the secretary fill up, 6 *d.* for a copy of the specification, and 6 *d.* for a bond; I should allow no other fees; that would not amount to much; it would not be a very large tax upon the contractors. I think you should make them pay something, or else people would be coming for these documents without any purpose or object in view. That small amount of fees I would still leave to the secretary.

2995. Mr. *Gregory*.] The present fees amount to 5 *s.*?—They vary 5 *s.*, 8 *s.*, and 10 *s.*; but you do not know what the secretaries really make them pay.

2996. (*Chairman*.) You would transfer the duties of the clerk of the Crown to the secretary of the grand jury?—A portion, and another portion to the clerk of the peace; I may say the portions connected with the administration of justice. You must have one officer, the clerk of the peace or the clerk of the Crown, I do not care which you call him, to perform those duties, and I think the fiscal portion of the duties could be transferred to the secretary of the grand jury.

2997. The larger proportion of the fees taken by secretaries of grand juries at present are illegal, or rather, extra illegal, are they not?—Extra legal or illegal, it is very hard to say which.

2998. You would prohibit a secretary from taking any such fees?—I would; I would give him a larger salary than he has at present. I would impose more duties on him, make him give his exclusive time to them, reside in or near the county town, and I would prohibit him from taking any fee or payment under any excuse, except the three fees I have mentioned.

2999. Would you prohibit all county officers from acting by deputy, and require them all to reside on the spot?—I would require every one of them, including the Crown Solicitor, to reside on the spot. I am aware there is a difference of opinion about the Crown Solicitor, some prefer having a gentleman residing in Dublin, but I think it tends to a great evil.

3000. Earl of *Mayo*.] Do you approve of the alteration that has been made of late years, of dividing the office of Crown Solicitor in the way it has been divided; till lately there was a Crown Solicitor for each circuit, and the business was done by one great office, with a very large and highly competent, and paid staff. Now the office of the Crown Solicitor has been divided, and the practice is to appoint one generally for one or two counties. Do you approve of that system?—In my county there has always been one Crown Solicitor. I may say I think it is desirable that there should be a Crown Solicitor for each county, and he should reside there. He acquires local information, which is very useful in conducting prosecutions.

3001. In the case of the Crown Solicitor residing in the county, would you impose on him the duties that are performed now by the Sessions Crown Solicitors?—I think the two offices might be amalgamated with advantage. The Sessional Crown Solicitor does the same duty at quarter sessions as the Crown Solicitor does at the assizes, and I think a man residing in the county town would perform both duties with much advantage to the public.

3002. (*Chairman*.]

Lord *J. Browne*, M.P.

5 May 1858.

3002. *Chairman*.] That would practically confine the choice of the Government to the local solicitors, would it not?—That I think is very desirable; I do not know that it would do so, because I think the Government might appoint a man from Dublin on condition that he went to reside in the county. I think it better to leave it in the discretion of the Lord Lieutenant. If he resided in the county he would very soon acquire local information sufficient.

3003. Are you disposed to extend the provisions of the Act 19 & 20 Vict. c. 63, s. 17?—Yes. The Committee have already heard, and there is no doubt of the fact, I think, that the decision has been given by Sir Colman O'Loghlen, in my county, that the provisions of the 17th section of that Act were not applicable to the case of continuous contracts. I believe that anybody who reads the section will see that it was intended to be so; however that may or may not be, there have been different opinions given by different chairmen of quarter sessions. The provisions of that Act are these: that in the event of a contractor neglecting to execute his contract, the county surveyor is to summon him to the petty sessions; the magistrates then make an order that he shall execute the work within a certain time; if he fails, the county surveyor can summon him to court the second time, and then an order is made that the work shall be executed by the county surveyor, and that the costs of it shall be levied by distress warrant on his goods in the same way as any other decree of the petty sessions court. Sir Colman O'Loghlen decided that that was not applicable to continuous contracts, only to specific repairs. Different decisions have been given by different chairmen in different counties. Mr. Hollamore, who succeeded Sir Colman O'Loghlen, confirmed his decision. Subsequently he went to Tipperary, and he there reversed his own and Sir Colman O'Loghlen's decision, and gave a decision in accordance with that of other chairmen in other counties. Since that, Judge O'Brien has given a decision in favour of Sir Colman O'Loghlen's ruling. Everybody is agreed that all doubt should be removed, and that this should be extended to the case of continuous contracts. This only refers to the repairs of roads. I think it ought to be applied to the county works generally, with certain limitations; for instance, if a bridge breaks down on a public road, a man is given a contract to repair that bridge, and the whole road is stopped till it is repaired. You have no summary means of enforcing him to repair that bridge; and what I would suggest is that, instead of "the repair of any road," it might be "any county work;" and you might put some limit on the jurisdiction of the magistrates, say "any county work the cost of which does not exceed 50 *l.*," or 100 *l.* or some limit of that sort. I would make the jurisdiction higher in the case of continuous contracts, or keeping a road in repair, than a specific work, such as executing a bridge. Mr. Hill has presented a paper to the Committee, which has been shown to me, in which he proposes to give the appeal to petty sessions to an unlimited amount in the case of any work. I think it would not do to give the petty sessions magistrates power to make an order for works that perhaps cost 1,000 *l.* I think it is very desirable to retain the power, in this section, of letting the money be levied at once on the contractor's goods, by distress warrant, which practically has the effect of making the contractor execute his work as soon as the order is made. It is very seldom exercised.

3004. With respect to the bonds of contractors, do you think they ought to be entered into to the grand jury instead of, as at present, to the Crown?—It is the most extraordinary provision in the Act, that all contractors' bonds are to the Crown, and high constables' bonds are to the treasurer of the county; and the practical effect of the contractors' bonds being to the Crown is, that any proceedings under them must go through the Attorney General for Ireland. The grand jury cannot employ their own solicitor; they are obliged to employ the Crown solicitor; and the practical effect that we find in my county is, that we have to pay hundreds of pounds for these prosecutions, and we never attain a satisfactory result. After very expensive and troublesome legal proceedings, the Crown solicitor says: "Gentlemen, here is my bill for 300 *l.* or 400 *l.*" We ask, what are the results? What have they recovered? He says: "I have nothing in the world to do with that, that is in the hands of the sheriff; I have executed my part, and you must pay me my bill;" so we are obliged to pay him his bill, and the money is never recovered. Now, I believe if the bond were made to the county, that is to the secretary of the grand jury, they would employ their own solicitor, and he would act in a much simpler way, and recover the money at a very much less expense.

3005. Are you satisfied with the present system of assistant surveyors, either as to their qualifications or number?—No; there is a great difference of opinion about the assistant surveyors. My impression is, that they do nothing but take the responsibility off the shoulders of the county surveyor, who is the proper officer; and I believe with a sufficient number of county surveyors he could always do the work himself. In the County Mayo we had, until a few years ago, about ten years ago, I think, the change was made, only one county surveyor for the whole county. It is the third largest county in Ireland in extent, and there was no assistant whatever. A question arose as to appointing assistants, they had existed some years previously before I was acquainted with the working of the grand jury law, and had been found not to answer; there was great objection made to appointing assistants, and then it was agreed to request the Lord Lieutenant to appoint a second county surveyor, and we have now two county surveyors. In the southern district, the county surveyor has no assistant, in the northern district there are two assistants. There were formerly three assistants in the northern district, and the assistants in the County Mayo are paid by the barony: their salaries are levied off the barony. One of the three assistants was proved to have taken bribes from the contractors; it was one of those rare cases in which the thing can be proved; in fact the man who was dissatisfied having given a bribe, and whose work had been rejected in consequence of the observation of some of the magistrates of the district, in a moment of indignation, split, and of course the assistant surveyor was dismissed by the grand jury, and the cesspayers then expressed a desire that they should not have another; they thought that the county surveyor should do the work. I think the result of there being an assistant surveyor is that the county surveyor stays at home and does

nothing

Lord J. Browne, M.P.

8 May 1868.

nothing, and throws the onus and responsibility of anything that goes wrong on the assistant surveyor; he always says, "I have sent the assistant," whenever he is asked about such and such a road; it merely relieves him from the responsibility, and the work is not half so well done. I believe bribes are most extensively given. I have taken out of the schedule of presentments for the last assizes, the number of all the perches in every road, and turned them into miles; and the number of miles under presentment in the southern district of the County Mayo, where there is no assistant, is 638, and in the northern district, 711. Now, I believe, it is perfectly possible for one man to look after 600 or 700 miles of road himself without any assistant.

2006. Do you find it possible for an officer of the class of county surveyor to get on without the assistance of others to do the mechanical work for him?—Perfectly; the measuring of stones is the only difficulty that arises; that is one of the things particularly in which an assistant is apt to be bribed, it is so easy to do it. The way in which it is done is this; he directs the stones to be placed in heaps, with two or three boxes in a heap; he measures one heap, and then he drives along the road and marks the heaps. That is a rough mode of measuring, but it is quite sufficient for all practical purposes.

2007. Would the county surveyor be able to get through all that kind of work unassisted?—Perfectly, for 600 or 700 miles. Mr. Brett, formerly the county surveyor of Mayo, had no assistants, and the roads were never so well kept and attended as in his time. He was very particular in looking after these matters.

2008. Mr. *Gregory*.] Did he go over the road twice a year?—Yes, I believe he was in the habit of going over every road in the county before each assizes; travelling from sessions to sessions, and so on, took him over a great many roads.

2009. *Chairman*.] How many assistants are there in the northern district of Mayo?—There are two assistants; I think one would be necessary there, because it is a large mountain district, it is the extreme north-west of the county; in cases like that I would have an assistant surveyor.

2010. You do not think that a single county surveyor could do the work in Mayo without assistance?—Practically in Mr. Brett's time it was done, but I think two county surveyors are necessary in so large a county.

2011. That was an exceptional case, and he was an exceptionally active officer?—Yes, he was a very efficient man; I am perfectly satisfied with the county surveyors we have at present, but I should not like to give either of them a whole county; I think it is rather heavy work for one man.

2012. Mr. *Gregory*.] Had Mr. Brett private practice?—There is very little private practice in Mayo; there is a little, but it is a very little.

2013. *Chairman*.] Have you any opinion to give as to the protection that ought to be given to private demesnes in the making of new roads?—By the 65th section of the Grand Jury Act you will see that in making new roads protection is given to deer parks, but there is no protection given to anything else. Now, I believe in England you cannot make a new road through a man's property, even in the case of a detached farm, without his consent; I think our system in Ireland, where you can make a road through a man's property, is very much preferable; but there are limits to everything, and I think a gentleman's demesne, or orchard, or pleasure ground, or garden, or any ornamental piece of ground, ought to be protected from having a road made through them. It is curious that the fullest protection is given for taking materials for making roads under the 162nd Section of the Act, but there is no protection whatever for making a public road. It must be remembered that grand juries hitherto have been very much in the hands of the landlords; the cesspayers may have more power, and that may make a great difference.

2014. Have you ever heard a complaint made by owners or occupiers as to the compulsory power of taking road materials from their land?—Yes; the magistrates have no power, or rather the arbitrator who values the damage done when an order is given to take material compulsorily, has no power for taking the value of the materials into consideration, which I think is very hard; he can only make compensation for the damage done to the surface of the ground. Section 161 says: "And such three householders shall be sworn by such justice of the peace (previous to the damage being committed) to be appraisers of such damages as may occur, and to make a true estimate thereof, in which estimate the value of any stones, gravel, or other materials shall not be included, but only the waste committed by breaking the surface and making a passage through the land."

2015. Then you think that in the compensation the value of the materials ought to be taken into account?—I do; I think magistrates would be more willing to give orders to take materials compulsorily if they were able to give value for materials; they are very often hesitate in consequence of that.

2016. Are you aware that under the law as it stands, the occupier cannot be compelled to appoint an appraiser or an umpire on his part?—There is a difficulty about that, undoubtedly; the way that we apply that is this; we say if he does not choose to do it, the other man goes to work, whether it is legal or not I do not know; certainly it ought to be clearly defined, and it is not defined.

2017. I believe under the present law the county has no power to present for an iron bridge?—No; there is a doubt about it; I am told there has been a decision given in some western county, but there is a very great doubt about it; certainly, when an iron bridge was proposed to be built in my county, of a very important class, the sessions refused to present for it; they said the Act was perfectly clear, it said "stones, bricks, or wood."

2018. With regard to large bridges, whether iron or otherwise, would you recommend that bridges above a certain value should be charged on the county at large, and not on the barony?—I think so, decidedly. I will mention a peculiar case that occurred in my county; at present, the Grand Jury Act gives power to charge bridges entirely on the county at large or entirely on the barony, and a decision has lately been given, I understand, in the County Clare, that you can charge them half-and-half; it was doubtful whether that power existed previously; up to 1856, in the County Mayo, all bridges costing over 30*l*. were charged on the county at large; in

Lord J. Browne, M.P.

3 May 1868.

in that year, in consequence of a great many applications from one particular barony for bridges, there was a good deal of discussion, and one member of the grand jury proposed that we should put all those bridges for the future entirely on the barony; there was a division, and a good deal of angry talk about it, but it was carried by a majority, and all bridges were then placed on the barony; in the following year there was a tremendous flood in one of the mountain districts of the county, a very poor barony, and through this barony ran the main road connecting the Connemara district with Mayo; this road and the particular bridge to which I am going to refer, was made by a grant of public money from Parliament. Well, this bridge was carried away altogether, with a very large proportion of the bridges of the barony. Between this bridge and the border of the county there are only two persons occupying land; it is a mountain district; but of course they have a certain number of herds and care-takers, labourers, &c. The people of the barony said, "We do not want this bridge for baronial purposes; it is really a county bridge; it connects the two counties together; tourists going through Galway and into other parts of the county go through it. It is of more benefit to Connemara than to Mayo, and the barony refused to present for it." The grand jury said, "We have passed a resolution, and we are not going to make an exception," and the consequence of it was that the bridge remained down for five or six years at the greatest possible public inconvenience. It was only after a car being swept away and an hotel-keeper drowned in crossing through a sort of temporary ford that was made, that at last the grand jury agreed to come to a compromise. There was always a difference of opinion among the grand jury about it, and a compromise was arranged by which half was placed on the county and half on the barony.

3019. Was that legal?—It has been ruled now to be legal. There was a doubt about its legality, but it was done in some counties. The grand jury interpreted the clause in the Act, as it now turns out, correctly. A general resolution was passed, and all bridges costing over 50 *l.* each are now thrown half on the county at large and half on the barony.

3020. What change in the law would you propose?—I should recommend that all bridges costing over 500 *l.* should be thrown on the county at large. Even half the cost of this bridge on the barony was a very heavy charge; it was a very poor barony. The next largest bridge in the barony was carried away at the same time. That bridge, I believe, originally cost nearly 3,000 *l.*, but as the foundations and the abutments remained, and a great deal of the material was on the spot, it was put up again at a cost of 1,200 *l.* If the foundations and side walls had been carried away it might have cost nearly 3,000 *l.* again. I think that all bridges costing over 500 *l.* should be considered county works, and I should say all over 50 *l.* or 100 *l.* should be half on the county and half on the barony.

3021. *Earl of Mayo.*] Do you not think also it would be advisable that power should be taken in certain cases to charge adjacent baronies in different degrees?—Yes, I am aware there are cases in other parts of Ireland, though I do not happen at present to know any cases in my own county.

3022. The power might be given?—I think so; I think it would be desirable.

3023. *Chairman.*] Do you see any reason why half of the expense of maintaining the so-called mail coach roads should be charged on the county at large?—Certainly not; I think they ought to be entirely charged on their respective baronies. The practical working of it in my county is that the poorer baronies are taxed to pay half the cost of the roads in the richer baronies; those baronies in which the cess is highest have to ease the shoulders of the baronies in which the cess is lowest. Now, in the barony of Erris, a very poor barony, there was no presentment sessions, and the works were no less than 1 *s.* 0½ *d.* in the pound; all the mails in that barony were carried by foot messengers, and there is only one little bit of road in which the mail cars runs; they have no advantage from having half the cost of the mail coach road, and they have to contribute to maintaining the roads all over the county.

3024. Do you consider there are no lines of road running through a county, the expense of which might fairly be shared between the barony and the county at large?—Not at all. I think the country is rich in proportion to the traffic running through it. The practical effect is to make the poorer districts pay for the roads in the richer districts. At Erris I have seen the cess up to 3 *s.* 6 *d.* in the pound in one year.

3025. You would put an end to such a classification of the rates altogether?—I would make every barony pay for its own roads. In the case of bridges I would relieve them.

3026. Are you satisfied with the present state of the law with regard to malicious injuries?—There is only one defect in the law, and that is you have no power to exempt land in the occupation of the party injured. I think otherwise the law is as near perfection as any law can be, and works most satisfactorily in my county. All applications for malicious injuries in my county are very closely, carefully, and thoroughly investigated at the presentment sessions. They go into every point; they go into the value of the article or animal injured, and they express their opinion of the value. That is one point to which they devote their particular attention, and I believe under that section of the Act, they have full power to go into that point, though I believe some think otherwise. The presentment then goes before the grand jury, and it is again inquired into, unless it is an undoubted case of malicious injury it is very closely inquired into, and I believe there is no abuse whatever under the existing system.

3027. We have been told by a witness before this Committee, that in his opinion the system of compensation for malicious injuries has no effect in preventing the commission of such outrages, and that he would transfer the liability to payment from the barony to the county at large. What do you say to such an opinion?—I am entirely against anything of the sort. At one time in my county, we thought these malicious injuries were not sufficiently opposed or investigated by the ratepayers of the district. At that time it used to be charged either on the barony or the parish, and the grand jury adopted the rule then, that in a case where they had no reason to suspect a particular district, they put it on the town land and the adjoining town lands, and that has a very good effect in making the cesspayers of

those

Lord J. Browne, M.P.

5 May 1868.

those town lands watch the case very carefully, and we get very full evidence at the sessions and at the grand jury since that rule has been adopted.

3028. I suppose, if the rule is to have any effect at all in checking these injuries, the burthen of compensation must be a local one, and the more local the better?—It must be; of course there are good and bad all over the world; but where a man is inclined to commit a malicious injury, he is very much deterred by knowing that he would only be injuring the cesspayers of a district, instead of an individual.

3029. Whereas, I presume, if the burthen of compensation were spread over the whole county, such a motive would be entirely taken away?—Yes, and I think there would be nobody who would care to prevent these malicious injuries being perpetrated. If they know of a malicious injury likely to be committed, the compensation for which will be put upon their shoulders, they are very careful to prevent it, and it creates a public feeling against the commission of malicious injuries.

3030. The essence of the law is, that the burthen of the compensation should fall on the locality in which the outrage has taken place?—Yes; when we first made the general charge to the townland, instead of the barony, we frequently had solicitors before us say they would not oppose us if we put it on the barony. But, of course, we said that is the strongest possible confirmation of our intentions, and shows the wisdom of the rule we have adopted.

3031. Have you known of much abuse taking place in the working of the system?—I do not think there is any at all. Occasionally you will see a man whose barn has been burnt accidentally, who will apply for a compensation for malicious injury, but it is always closely investigated. Generally speaking, we look with great suspicion upon burning cases; there are not many cases of malicious injury in my county, but when they do arise, they are generally cases of a bullock, or a poor man's cow, with a knife driven into her; or a sheep is plucked or injured. There was a case of six sheep, all the poor man had, which had the backs of their necks cut, a thing which must have been malicious. We examine with great care any presentment for burning.

3032. *Mr. Gregory.*] It was stated by one of the witnesses, that most of these malicious injuries are perpetrated by strangers. According to your experience, as an old grand juror, have you not generally found that they have been perpetrated by neighbours?—I believe invariably. Of course it is impossible to speak with certainty, but very often, though you have not got legal proof, you have tolerably good reason to suspect, and we are guided by that where we place the charge for malicious injury.

3033. It was also stated that the person injured because he knows that he is to be compensated, takes very little trouble to seek out for the offender. Is the scale of compensation generally so high as to induce him to forego all endeavour to find out the offender?—No; and if he did, it would not in the slightest degree alter the case; he would be just as much entitled to compensation; I cannot see what motive a stranger would have in committing such injuries.

3034. *Chairman.*] Do you think that has any effect in preventing prosecutions?—Not the least; quite the contrary; I think it gives an interest to the parties on the land which is assessed; the cesspayers of the adjoining Crown land, to help in hunting out the criminal.

3035. *Earl of Mayo.*] Do you think it prevents parties from insuring?—No, not in the least; cattle are scarcely ever insured, and it is principally cattle which are injured; nor are those small barns and houses of the country people insured.

3036. *Chairman.*] Do you think farmers would be more likely to insure if this system were put an end to?—I do not think it would affect the question one way or the other; I believe that in law an insurance company may refuse to pay in case of a malicious injury.

3037. *Mr. Gregory.*] Do not you ever exempt the land in the occupation of the party injured?—There is no power in the world to do that; the thing used to be done, and is very frequently done, but it is quite illegal, and we have given it up in our county in consequence. There was a case at the last assizes, where I was foreman, and I asked the judge, and he said, "the law is quite clear; you have no power in the world to exempt any individual whatever." You may exempt any denomination or sub-denomination. If a man has a sub-denomination entirely in his hands, you may exempt that sub-denomination.

3038. *Chairman.*] As a whole?—As a whole; you cannot exempt any man's holding by name.

3039. That is a departure from the law which experience has proved to be useful, and which you think ought to be legalised?—Yes.

3040. Are you aware of any cases in which the court-houses of a county have been made an improper use of?—Yes, very great. I should strongly recommend that the court-houses should be placed under the control of the Board of Superintendence, with power, of course, to the sheriff to make use of them for any public purpose when he requires them.

3041. The Board of Superintendence of the county gaol?—Yes. At present the sheriff has charge of the court-houses, and he can give it for any purpose he likes. Practically, it is not the sheriff, but the sub-sheriff; and the practice prevailed extensively in my county of giving the public court-houses to all sorts of purposes, play-acting, strolling players, auctions, and all sorts of things. The grand jury passed a very strong resolution about it some years ago; some sub-sheriffs attended to it, and some did not. I should like to relate a particular case that occurred: A considerable sum of money was spent in repairing the court-house at Westport. It was exceedingly nice and newly painted; this only occurred three or four years ago, long after the resolution was passed. An application was made by a lady in the town, who wanted an auction of her furniture, to sell her furniture in the court-house. It so happened that in the town there was a large auction-room specially for that purpose, and it was solely and entirely to save paying a pound for the use of the room that she made the application. It was made to the local magistrates, and I was one, and we said the sheriff had the custody of the court-house, but we certainly would place every impediment we could in the way of its being used for an improper purpose. The lady sent back a message to say that the sub-sheriff was a friend of hers; she would get an order from him and hold it, and she did, though the

Lord J. Browne, M.P.

8 May 1868.

the grand jury passed two resolutions on the subject. I may mention that one high sheriff was greatly offended at the grand jury interfering in the matter; he said it was an infringement of his dignity passing any resolution whatever with regard to a court-house under his charge.

3042. I suppose, as the law stands, it was an infringement of his right?—It was undoubtedly: in fact, the matter came before the judge, and the judge said that the law was undoubtedly with the high sheriff, but he thought it a desecration of public justice. The sheriff said he had never the smallest intention of allowing it. That was not the same shrievalty where the court-house was used for selling the furniture.

3043. Why would you propose to place the court-house under the charge of the board of superintendence?—It is a public body; you must have them in charge of somebody. I am not at all afraid if the high sheriff would act, but in my county the sub-sheriff changes with every high sheriff, and a new sheriff comes in who does not care for the resolutions of the grand jury.

3044. Mr. *Maguire*.] For any public purpose, such as the expression of opinion on a question of public importance, you would not interfere with the privileges of the sheriff?—Certainly not, for any meeting. I see no reason why a political meeting should not be held in a public court-house. Then there is the question of payment to contractors. At present you must pay the whole sum; you cannot pay part now. A man has a contract for a large amount, and he applies for payment at the sessions; the county surveyor cannot certify, and the sessions cannot approve for part. Suppose he has left something undone, you must pay him the whole or nothing. Suppose he has left the battlements of a bridge unfinished, waiting for some cut stone, it is undesirable to leave him out of his 90 *l.* if 10 *l.* would do that work. It is often done; and if he objects to it, you cannot pass the 90 *l.*

3045. Earl of *Mayo*.] There are very large sources of expenditure which come down to the grand jury now in the shape of imperative presentments. Are there any of those classes of expenditure which you think it would be desirable to give the local body or the grand jury more power over than they have at present?—There is great difficulty about those, generally speaking. There is a most monstrous charge, in my opinion; a constantly increasing charge for the revision of the valuation.

3046. I should like to hear your opinion about that?—We cannot find out anything about it. All the information we get is an imperative presentment for a bulk sum of money expended. It is constantly increasing, and considering the small number of changes made, I cannot imagine how it costs the sum it does. It was proposed to have a new valuation; and I think the estimate was 44,000 *l.* to make a new valuation of the whole of Ireland. I am sorry I have not got the return; my impression is, the yearly valuation, which certainly does not deal with one holding out of twenty, costs 20,000 *l.* a-year; I am speaking from recollection. I think it costs 600 *l.*, or 700 *l.* a-year in County Mayo, and there is really not one holding out of twenty that is dealt with.

3047. Do you think, without perhaps interfering with the working of the central valuation office, it would be desirable that some power should rest in the local authorities of ascertaining exactly how this money is spent, and of offering an opinion as to the proceedings of the office in that respect?—I think a very great check would be placed if we had the accounts in detail sent down; not brought down the last day of the assizes; just putting them into our hands without time to examine them; but if they were published in the papers the week before hand, and people had time to look into them, stating the number of days, and the price per day paid. My impression is that a great deal of the expense is in the office in Dublin. I do not believe, from what we hear, that the men who actually do the work in the county are overpaid.

3048. There is no fault found, I believe, with the mode in which the work is done, is there?—No, we cannot expect anything of that sort to be perfect. I have known the valuing officer to persevere in doing a wrong thing, but he thought he was acting rightly.

3049. Is there any other class of expenditure that comes down in the shape of imperative presentments which you think local supervision could be advantageously extended to?—Take the case of the lunatic asylums, which is a very large item; that is regulated by a Board appointed by the Lord Lieutenant. Some people are of opinion that the grand jury ought to nominate the Board; I do not think it much signifies. I think the Lord Lieutenant always appoints the first men in the county, and if half were nominated by the grand jury it would be an improvement.

3050. You do not think, practically, there would be any great saving to the county by the adoption of a different system?—I do not think there would. I have made a note of a few things which the grand jury have power to present for without previous application to the sessions, and the only things I can think of are the court-house keepers and interpreters; they are limited to 4 *l.* for the court-house keepers, and 5 *l.* for the interpreters at each assizes. Then there are fuel and lights for the court-houses and sessions houses; those you may present for without application to the Presentment Sessions. Under section 38, sudden damages, which are an absolute necessity, may be presented for by the grand jury to any amount that is necessary.

3051. *Sir Charles Lanyon*.] That is between sessions and assizes?—Yes; well then, as to the poundage of the high constables, that is a very difficult point. I know the poundage of the high constables are necessarily very high, for several reasons. In our county, we pay a shilling in the pound, but we make the high constable lodge the full amount, whether he collects it or not, and I do not see, under the existing system, how we could reduce it without much difficulty. It is a large district, and you require to be very particular about securities. It is not very easy for a man to get security for collecting cess to the amount of 2,500 *l.*

3052. Earl of *Mayo*.] The high rate of poundage is, to a certain extent, a security for the closeness of the collection?—Yes; we get the poor rates collected for half that, but there it is collected in smaller districts. We advertise for a poor rate collector for each electoral division separately. In the electoral division in which I am chiefly interested, we get the poor rates collected for 4½ *d.* in the pound, and the collector is bound in the same way to lodge every halfpenny of the poor rate, whether he collects it

or

Lord J. Browne, M.P.

6 May 1868.

or not. The poor rate collector has not got the difficulty about security; and we find country men collect the poor rates in small districts every bit as well, and at a much less expense.

3053. What change would you propose to enable you to avail yourselves of the poor law system?—If you appointed this permanent committee, it would be a question to what extent you would extend its powers and jurisdiction; if you allow them to control the collection of the cess generally, you might allow them to divide into districts smaller than baronies, and I think by that means you would get the cess collected for smaller amounts than you do.

3054. I understand that you would suggest that the duties of this finance committee should be merely of an assenting and administering kind, and that they should not deal with any questions connected with the levying of taxation?—I should certainly give them power to control the levy (not to put a levy on, of course) not to raise money, but to control and superintend the collection.

3055. You would entrust to them all the machinery by which the regulations of the superior body should be carried out?—I would.

3056. Speaking generally, do you think that the fiscal duties performed by the associated cess-payers, and by the grand jury, are economically performed, and that the interests of the rate-payers are carefully attended to, and economy practised?—I think so, and I do not anticipate from the change which I recommend in the presentment sessions, that it would have very great practical effect, or produce much economy; but at the same time I think the cess payers have a right to be *bonâ fide* represented, which they are not at present.

3057. You think the effect of your proposal would be to give a feeling of general satisfaction more than to effect any very great practical saving to the ratepayers?—Exactly.

3058. Have you ever made any comparison between the expense of similar county works in England and Scotland?—No, I have not, and it is very difficult, so many things are mixed up in the cess.

3059. Have you any reason to believe that the expenditure for similar works in Ireland is greater than it is in Scotland or England?—I do not know what it is in Scotland or England. It ought to be a great deal cheaper in Ireland, because labour is cheaper; but there is more traffic over the roads in Ireland than in Scotland or England.

3060. Mr. *Maguire*.] There being fewer railways?—Yes; and from the habits of the country people they go and bring their cars of turf.

3061. *Earl of Mayo*.] The carriage of turf creates enormous traffic?—Yes: and then they all go to fairs and markets, &c.

3062. *Chairman*.] They are a more locomotive people?—They are.

3063. *Earl of Mayo*.] With regard to new works, I believe you live in a county where, of all counties in Ireland, if new works were likely to be set on foot, it would be that county where they would be most necessary. Looking to the future, do you think there is any very great necessity for new county works in the way of roads?—I should think very rarely. At the time of the famine, every conceivable road anybody could think of was proposed, and nobody would oppose it; it was the only way of keeping the people from dying of starvation. I believe there was not a single presentment refused at those special famine sessions; in fact, there were hundreds of acres in the county cut up with roads partly made, which have been abandoned since.

3064. Though the county of Mayo is one of the most remote districts in Ireland, you think, if there is any fault, you are more over-roaded than under-roaded?—Decidedly over-roaded.

3065. Mr. *Gregory*.] Have you ever considered the subject of the propriety of peers being allowed to sit upon grand juries?—Yes; I think it is most desirable that they should. I believe the only reason they cannot sit is because a grand jury performs criminal as well as fiscal business, and a peer theoretically, and only theoretically, has the right of sitting by the side of the judge of assize, and taking part in criminal trials, and even to charge the jury before the judge; that is a mere nominal power.

3066. Could not the difficulty as to a peer interfering in criminal business be very easily obviated?—Yes; the grand jury is re-sworn by a different oath; and reconstituted for criminal purposes, and there is no reason why peers should not take part in the fiscal business.

3067. *Chairman*.] Legally it is a different body?—Well, I do not know that it is.

3068. Mr. *Gregory*.] As the grand jury is not a political body there would be no objection on that score to a peer serving upon it?—Certainly not.

3069. You could always name a sufficient number of grand jurors to perform the criminal business, and then call the peers?—Yes: they are men of large property, and generally speaking, of independent minds, and they are less likely to be influenced by any local interests, being richer men, and in a higher position; I think their influence on a grand jury would be very desirable.

3070. With regard to coroners, do you see any very great object in continuing the situation of coroner?—I think the sooner we get rid of them the better.

3071. Do not you think inquests might properly be held by the stipendiary magistrates?—I do. I would not confine it to the stipendiary magistrates. I should say "by the magistrates," and of course if the local magistrates did not act, it would be the business of the stipendiary magistrate to do so.

3072. Have you any objection to the county cess being divided between the landlord and the tenant in all future agreements?—No; I think if it is applied to future agreements, there would be no objection in the world to it. I should be rather in favour of it than otherwise. I think to apply it to existing tenancies would create an infinity of ill-will and ill-feeling between landlord and tenant. A cess in my county averages 1s. 11½d., that will be increased by the charge for the new asylum, which will make three halfpence or two pence in the pound additional, so it would be 10 per cent. on the valuation. A great many of the largest estates in the county are let at about the Poor Law valuation; some of them I know are let under it, and on every estate you may say one-half of it goes in different expenses, and not more than one-half goes into the landlord's hands; so if one-half the cess were to be applied to the existing tenancies, it would be equivalent to deducting 10 per cent. from the landlord's income; and I think you can hardly

Lord J. Browne, M.P.

6 May 1858.

hardly expect a man to stand that; he would endeavour to recoup himself by a new arrangement with his tenant, and so to driving a landlord to make a new arrangement with every single tenant, I think it would be the most cruel, injudicious, and impolitic thing it is possible to conceive.

3073. With regard to future arrangements, you have no objection?—I think it would perfectly satisfy the wishes of those who wish to divide it.

3074. In the case of the appointment of barony constables, are you not of opinion that that appointment should be held at the first quarter sessions nearest to the barony which is vacant?—Certainly, the quarter sessions of that district; it is not clear what the law is.

3075. There is a difference of opinion with regard to the law?—A difference of opinion as to the meaning of the section.

3076. It is by some read that the appointment shall take place at the first quarter sessions in the county?—Yes.

3077. And consequently magistrates very often have to go to the extreme end of the county to vote for the appointment of a barony constable at the other end?—Yes.

3078. You are of opinion that it ought to be at the first quarter sessions of the district?—Yes, unless you give the power to the finance committee, which I have recommended. If you are to retain the existing system, it would be of great importance.

3079. Would you prefer this to having it at the first district quarter sessions, or in the first sessions in the county town?—Yes, the reason I object to the quarter sessions is this; that they are in exactly the same position as the grand jury; they do not know the securities or they have no opportunities of inquiring whether they are sufficient; I think it is a matter of vast importance. A man brings a security for collecting 2,600 *l.* of cess, you have no control over him between assize and assize, and you want security to that amount. A man produces a security and says, "Here is Mr. A," how can you tell whether the Mr. A. he produces is worth 2,600 *l.*

3080. Would you confine the voting for the barony constable to the magistrates of that particular barony, or would you throw it open to all the magistrates of the county?—Practically since we have had the cess regularly lodged, we always leave it to the parties interested in the barony, but when the money is not regularly lodged we do not do so, but all the members of the county take part.

3081. Do you consider it advisable to confine the voting to magistrates, or would you prefer the appointment of the baronial constable to be by landholders, whose property was valued at a certain rate?—I think I would leave it with the grand jury and the permanent committee. I do not think there is any objection to that; the great fault is, you have no time to examine and ascertain about the securities. I will tell you one thing that we did in our county; we made an order that any high constable retiring, should give us notice in order that we should give notice to other people to come forward; we passed a resolution that we would stop their poundage unless they give us notice beforehand; I believe we could not do so legally, but however the threat had some effect. When a man was going to retire he generally made some pecuniary arrangements with his successor, and they did us completely by saying "I did not intend to retire, but one of my securities has refused to act; I got a letter from him this morning;" so that we could not enforce the rule.

Tuesday, 12th May 1868.

MEMBERS PRESENT:

Mr. Blake.	Mr. Herbert.
Colonel Cooper.	Mr. Kendall.
Mr. Dawson.	Sir Charles Lanyon.
Colonel Forde.	Mr. Maguire.
Mr. Chichester Fortescue.	Earl of Mayo.
Colonel French.	Sir Colman O'Loghlen.
Mr. Gregory.	

MR. CHICHESTER FORTESCUE, IN THE CHAIR.

Lord JOHN BROWNE, a Member of the House; further Examined.

Lord *J. Browne*, M.P.

12 May 1868.

3082. (*Chairman.*] I BELIEVE there is something you wish to state to the Committee?—Perhaps you will permit me to correct a portion of my evidence on the last occasion. I stated that there was no power at present for magistrates in petty sessions to give a sudden damage order in the case of a court-house. That was perfectly true as regards the law up to the 20th August last, but on that day an Act of Parliament received the Royal Assent, which empowered three magistrates in petty sessions to give sudden damage orders for court-houses, the same as for other works.

3083. Mr. *Dawson.*] What was the title of that Bill?—It is called the Public Works Act, 30 & 31 Vict. c. 112.

3084. Colonel *French.*] Are you aware of a sum of money, 3 *s.* per cent., being demanded for what is called auditing the treasurer's accounts, and paid to the Master in Chancery?—Yes; I believe the chief object is to create a place that is almost a sinecure, and 3,000 *l.* a year for a gentleman in Dublin. I believe it is no audit at all. I think it is desirable that there should be some audit of the county accounts, but I do not think that the existing audit, so called, is really one.

3085. Do you remember how this so-called audit was originally introduced?—I have heard, but I do not know the facts.

3086. *Chairman.*] Why is it not a genuine and effective audit?—All that the auditor does in Dublin is this: he merely compares the papers which are sent up to him by the treasurer in a regular form. He never comes down and examines the county accounts, and never compares the different papers and documents which would be necessary for a complete audit; we know very little what he does in Dublin.

3087. What is he supposed to do; what is the designation of his office?—He is one of the Masters in Chancery, I believe, now. He used to be a man called the Chief Remembrancer.

3088. There is no local audit?—There is no local audit at all.

3089. Colonel *French.*] Now that the money that was formerly in the treasurer's hands is obliged to be lodged in the bank, do you think there is any necessity for maintaining that audit?—I think there ought to be some audit in the locality.

3090. Would you put the audit of the accounts in the hands of the foreman of the jury, or how would you propose to have an audit?—I believe that the best audit you can have for any local body is that which is followed in the case of the Poor Law: I think there are four Poor Law auditors for the whole of Ireland. They go round and spend three or four days in each poor-house in Ireland, and go through all the documents and papers most carefully, and it is the most thorough and complete audit there is anywhere in the United Kingdom. I may, perhaps, mention a fact that occurred in my county, showing how ignorant grand jurors really are about fiscal affairs in their own county. We found it necessary to obtain an Act of Parliament to re-assess a considerable portion of the county cess, which was lost during the famine. Before obtaining that Act of Parliament we went very carefully with the treasurer into the accounts of the county, and we found that there was a sum of over 6,000 *l.* which had been for a great number of years in the treasurer's hands, which nobody had ever asked for, and it was not probable that anybody ever would ask for. We excluded it altogether from our consideration, but we challenged anybody who had any claim to make it, and we never have received an application for one single farthing of that 6,000 *l.*

3091. Colonel *Cooper.*] And you have it still?—No; in obtaining the Act of Parliament to levy the arrears of cess, we excluded it from the levy, because we thought it was unnecessary, having published a notice requesting anybody who claimed any of this sum of money to come before the grand jury and substantiate their claim. Nobody did come, and therefore we excluded it.

3092. Colonel *French.*] Are you aware of a claim in 1837 sent down to the western counties for somewhere about 30,000 *l.*, which the Government

ment

Lord J. Browne, M.P.

19 May 1868.

ment said they had advanced 14 years before?—I have heard it, but I do not know the particulars.

3093. *Sir Charles Lanyon.*] In what way would you propose to constitute this new body to which you refer, instead of the grand jury of the county, for the purpose of transacting fiscal business?—If the present grand jury system were discontinued I should recommend that the magistrates of the county should elect a body of men in their place, that body of men having the same powers for the transaction of fiscal business as the grand jurors have at present.

3094. Would it be an annual election?—I should say so; that is a matter of detail; I should say once a year.

3095. Do you think that would be a better system than the present system?—Well, I do not think there would be any very material difference between them.

3096. Would you have the numbers the same?—I think so; I think it is well to have every part of the county represented in a Board of that sort. In a large county you must have men from a great many different places.

3097. *Mr. Blake.*] I would ask you whether you meant to convey that the county Board, who were to transact fiscal business instead of the present grand jury, were to be elected by the magistracy and not by the ratepayers?—Yes; the body to perform the present functions of the grand jury should be elected by the magistrates. I stated, when I was here before, that I thought it very desirable that there should be a sort of upper court, which should have the same power that the grand jury has now, which is merely of putting a veto upon works that have been previously approved of at the presentment sessions, and that that would be a check upon extravagance and jobbery. As you are aware, grand juries have no power of originating taxation at present, and I should be sorry to see them given any power of doing so, without the presentment sessions first having approved of such expenditure.

3098. *Sir Charles Lanyon.*] At all events you do not feel very strongly upon that point?—No; I think the present grand jury perform their functions very satisfactorily.

3099. With reference to the finance committee; supposing that the grand jury were to remain exercising the functions that they now exercise, do you not think it would be desirable that at the spring assizes they should appoint a permanent finance committee to perform the duties of the next year, such as you have sketched out?—I do, for the current year.

3100. You think that finance committee might be fairly appointed by the grand jury for the purpose of remaining a permanent body to superintend those works which you have described?—I do; either the spring or the summer assizes; I do not think it signifies much.

3101. With reference to the cesspayers, the proposition for dividing the county into electoral divisions is a very good one. Supposing that were done, do you not think it desirable that a list of the 10 highest cesspayers in each of those electoral divisions should be returned, instead of in the manner in which they are at present returned to the grand jury, and then that the grand jury should select one or two from each electoral division to represent at the presentment sessions by ballot?—I should prefer leaving it to the cesspayers to elect whom they chose, of course with a qualification.

3102. Do you see any very great difference between the plan you propose and that of electing by ballot the names of the cesspayers from each division to attend at the next presentment sessions?—Electing by ballot out of the highest names returned.

3103. Yes; that is, 10 being returned from each of the electoral divisions to which you refer?—On the whole, I think I should prefer the cesspayers having to choose their own representative; I think it would give more satisfaction in the country.

3104. Supposing you consider that to be the best, you would see no very great objection to the other plan?—No.

3105. And that each cesspayer so selected by ballot by the grand jury, should have the power of attending the sessions without going for a ballot, which is now a very great objection to cesspayers attending sessions, not knowing whether they will be called or not?—Exactly.

3106. *Chairman.*] The difference between your suggestion and Sir Charles Lanyon's would be this, would it not, that you would have a personal choice of representatives by a constituency, and Sir Charles Lanyon would not?—Yes; as I understand, Sir Charles Lanyon's proposition is, that the 10 highest names in each electoral division should be handed in to the grand jury, and that the grand jury should ballot among those names; my proposition is, that the cesspayers should be left perfectly free to choose whom they like, subject to a certain qualification in the representative of the electoral division.

3107. *Sir Charles Lanyon.*] Supposing that the cesspayers generally attended in the number in which they have the power of attending at the presentment sessions, would they not be generally more numerous than the magistrates; is that your experience?—No; as a general rule, the magistrates are more numerous than the cesspayers, but by no means always; I know at the last presentment sessions in my county, in one barony there were six associated cesspayers attended, and only one magistrate; and in more than one barony, I know the cesspayers were more numerous than the magistrates; but generally speaking, the magistrates are more numerous than the cesspayers; it varies in different baronies.

3108. *Chairman.*] It is a matter of chance?—Yes; I may mention with reference to taking the highest cesspayer, that there are one or two men in my own barony who, being the highest cesspayers, are always on, and who never attend; they will not take the trouble to do it.

3109. That system does not select the men who are best qualified to attend to the business?—No, I think it does not; it certainly selects the parties who have the highest interest in the cess, but I think not those who are most inclined to attend upon all occasions; though very frequently it does.

3110. Nor those individuals in whom the ratepayers would personally have the most confidence?—No; frequently it does not.

3111. *Sir Charles Lanyon.*] What is your experience as to the attendance of cesspayers in your county?—Generally speaking, it is very fair; it varies in different counties.

3112. Have you ever considered the hardship of the present mode of raising the cess by equal instalments at each assize; generally the amount of cess at each assize is about the same. Do not you

Lord J. Browne, M.P.

16 May 1868.

you think it desirable that that should be altered, so that the cess should be levied one-third in the spring, and two-thirds in the summer; so that the cesspayer would be in a better position to pay the cess during the long half-year than in the short one?—I do not think there would be any very great gain in altering the present system. The people are accustomed to it, and I think they pay the cess very willingly; I do not think it would make very material difference.

3113. You have not heard complaints as to the hardship of having to pay an equal amount of cess in the spring and in the autumn?—No; I have heard the idea discussed, but I do not think there is any feeling either one way or the other in my county about it.

3114. You said that you would do away altogether with repairing any portion of the post-roads at the expense of the county at large?—Yes.

3115. Do you not think that the same end would be attained by repairing all the leading lines of road in the county, such lines as lead from market-place to market-place, half at the expense of the county and half at the expense of the barony, so as to obtain an equalisation of cess upon the county at large?—In my county it would have precisely the reverse effect, because all the leading lines are in the richest part of the county where the cess is lowest, and the practical effect of that is that the poor baronies have to contribute towards maintaining the roads in the rich districts, and the rich districts do not help to maintain their roads. I think I mentioned one barony where the cess is 1s. 1½d., without any new works, at the last sessions. The adjourned sessions fell to the ground for the want of a chairman. There were no new works, notwithstanding which the previously existing charges on the barony were 1s. 1½d. It has to contribute to the mail-coach roads, and from being a poor barony it has hardly any mail-car roads within itself.

3116. At all events, it is your opinion that it is essential that some alteration should be made so as to equalise the cess in reference to leading lines of road?—Yes, with the view of relieving the poor districts.

3117. With reference to the assistant surveyors, you said you thought that the county surveyor could do the business without assistant surveyors?—Yes; and that we have practical experience of it in my county, a very large one, the third largest in Ireland.

3118. Do you not think that the greatest amount of deception which is practised by road contractors is in not supplying the quantity of material which they are bound to put on the different roads for which they enter into contract?—Well that a great deal depends on the county surveyor. If he does his work properly, he tells the man to put a certain quantity of material on the roadside. He then visits that material, and he tells him, "Before I come back again you must have that material spread." Perhaps he leaves a certain quantity for filling up ruts. When he comes back a second time he sees all those materials are spread. I would rather trust to a county surveyor looking after it in that way than to an assistant surveyor, between whom and the contractor there may be a great many private arrangements and understandings.

3119. Do not you think it utterly impossible for a county surveyor to measure the stones that go upon different roads?—Mr. Tracey, the county surveyor of South Mayo, has not the smallest difficulty in doing it. He says so. Mr. Brett was formerly county surveyor of the whole of Mayo, without any assistant, and I never heard that he made any complaints about the difficulty of it.

3120. Then you had not, at all events, any means of testing whether there were the right amount of material put on the roads?—The general opinion in the county is, that the roads were never so well kept in Mayo as they were when Mr. Brett was the surveyor for the whole county, without any assistants whatever.

3121. That might arise from other causes than the one to which I am referring, which is especially the desirability of ascertaining whether the quantity contracted for is placed on the roads or not; do you think it is possible to ascertain it in any other way than through the medium of an assistant surveyor?—I do. I think more efficiently by the county surveyor himself. He is a man of character and position, and quite above taking bribes. I think the great objection to the assistant surveyor is, that it relieves the county surveyor from his responsibility. When anything is wrong about a road, or any complaint made to the grand jury, the county surveyor, where there are assistants, invariably says, "I sent my assistant. I could not go myself; I had not time."

3122. With reference to presentments for the cutting off hills, do you think that the law, as it now stands, is a fair one as to placing the cost of cutting hills partly on the county and partly on the barony?—At present the grand jury have power to place it on the barony; not half-and-half.

3123. Either on the barony or on the county?—Yes.

3124. Do you think that a fair thing to do?—Well, there are cases of course where there is an enormous hill, and it might be desirable to put half on the county, but as a general rule I think I should prefer levying it as we do in my county, on the barony. There may be exceptional cases where very heavy works should be charged half on the county.

3125. (*Colonel French.*) Much would depend on the traffic of the road. If it was a very leading road, you would be more inclined to call the assistance of the county at large than if it were merely a turnpike road, for the convenience of the inhabitants?—Yes; I should also take into consideration what was the wealth or poverty of the district.

3126. *Sir Charles Lanyon.*] Do you not think that when these applications for cutting hills and filling hollows come before the sessions, consequent upon their being county at large presentments, and the barony being slightly interested in them, they do not receive the consideration they ought to receive, and are frequently passed; the parties judging of the matter having little interest in the amount of cess to be collected for them?—In my county they are all on the barony, so that case does not arise.

3127. Do you not think it would be desirable that the parties who have to pay for these works should be the parties to approve or disapprove of them?—Yes, decidedly.

3128. Therefore the cutting of hills should be put either on the barony or on the county, and considered at either of the respective sessions?—Yes; if I were to make any change I should be disposed

Lord J. Browne, M.P.

12 May 1868.

disposed to put them all on the baronies. I have no very strong feeling on the subject. It is always done in my county.

3129. Colonel *French*.] In answer to Question No. 3044, as to a Board of superintendence, you recommended that they should have the charge of the county court-house, and Mr. Maguire asked you if the sheriff could not have the privilege of letting it for meetings; why not give the whole power to a Board of superintendence; if you gave it for one purpose, why not give it for all meetings; in fact, so as to make them in charge of the county court-house?—I think whoever has charge of the county court-houses, there are certain purposes for which you must allow them to be used, and a high sheriff convening a public meeting of the whole county, I think, ought to have power to take the court-house, although as a matter of course the Board of superintendence would give permission to use it for that purpose.

3130. You think it would be better to divide the responsibility?—At present there is a divided responsibility in that sense, because the high sheriff has charge of the court-house, but the magistrates, and the cesspayers also at presentment sessions, have a right to use them for special purposes. I should have no objection to put them entirely and exclusively into the hands of the Board of superintendence. I think as the county pays for the expense of keeping them in repair and for the keepers, they ought to have some control over the purposes for which they are used. I may mention another thing which came out about the county court-house in Mayo; it turned out that the keeper was in the habit of letting lodgings in some of the rooms of the court-house; this had been going on under the present system, and the sheriff in charge had never looked after it.

3131. In answer to Question No. 3046, you referred to the revising valuation; the county through the grand jury pays the whole amount now?—They pay half the total cost; the Treasury pays the other half.

3132. It is an imperative presentment for that half which comes down from Dublin?—Yes.

3133. The Poor Law Boards now have to pay no sum which they formerly used to pay for a revising valuator?—No, but what it cost the Poor Law Board under the old system was very much less than what it now costs the county.

3134. Had they not to appoint a revising valuator each year?—No; practically we only appointed every second or third year. The Board of Guardians had power to make any necessary changes every year, and they always did that with the assistance of their collector.

3135. And did not bring in a revising valuator?—No, not every year.

3136. At all events the county virtually is, to a certain extent, relieved from a part of that charge, so that the full charge is not made in the county now?—Yes, they are relieved, but to a very small extent. I think the way in which this charge is increasing is deserving of the attention of the Committee. I moved for a return, in the year 1866, of the cost of this valuation for the three previous years. I find, in the year 1863, it was 15,000*l.* a-year. In the year 1864 it was 17,800*l.*, and in the year 1865 it was 20,000*l.* Now, I do not believe that one holding out of 20 or 30 is at all affected each year, and the only change which is made now is a change of occupancy, because the reviser has no business to change the value of land, although he may of houses. If it costs 20,000*l.* a year for making these few changes of occupancy; then to make a general valuation, instead of costing 46,000*l.*, which it is stated in this return would be the cost of a complete new valuation for all Ireland, I am sure, in the same proportion, it ought to cost 300,000*l.* or 400,000*l.* at the very least.

3137. As regards the lunatic asylums, do you think that as to a lunatic asylum, in which one county only is interested, that is, a county having a lunatic asylum for itself, the grand jury should not be empowered to take charge of it in the same manner as they now take charge of the gaols; in fact, to appoint their Board of superintendence of the county, &c., in the same manner in which they now present to the Board of superintendence in the gaols?—Yes; I think our county institutions would be more economically, and quite as efficiently managed, if there was less control on the part of those bureaucratic autocrats in Dublin, who at present interfere with every little trifling matter of detail in our county institutions. I will just mention one case; the Government, who are, in the case of lunatic asylums, virtually the inspectors, fix the number of officers and servants, and the amount of their salaries and allowances. In the county of Mayo, there is a Protestant chaplain for the asylum who gets 30*l.* a-year. About seven months ago, the Board called for a return of the number of Protestants who had been in the asylum for the last 12 months, and it was found to be seven. They then requested the Government to sanction a reduction of the salary of the Protestant chaplain to 15*l.* a-year, and I may mention, at the time the general feeling of the Board was to have abolished the Protestant chaplain altogether. I do not believe, in any other country in the world, it would be obligatory to keep a chaplain for seven poor demented wretches who could not understand one syllable he said. That request of the Board of Governors was treated with the most utter contempt, no notice whatever was taken of it, neither refusal nor acceptance, nor anything; I think it is perfectly monstrous, that if you appoint gentlemen to come and attend to the asylum Board that such trifling things as the salary of the gardener, the gate-keeper, and the steward, and things of that sort, should not be left to their discretion, but that a Board in Dublin should control them in these little trifling matters. Why should not the salary of the storekeeper be fixed by the governors of the asylum, just as well as by the Board in Dublin?

3138. *Chairman*.] Is that gentleman, the chaplain to whom you alluded, a clergyman living in the neighbourhood of the asylum?—Yes.

3139. I mean, is he a gentleman who has other duties to perform in the immediate neighbourhood?—Yes; perhaps I had better mention the different pickings he gets. First of all, he has the tithes of the parish, then he gets off the county rates for the gaol, as chaplain to the jail, then he gets off the county rates for chaplain to the poor house, then he is chaplain to the infirmary, then he gets this 30*l.* a-year for the lunatic asylum, and then he gets paid by the Government also for being chaplain to the troops in barracks.

3140. Is

Lord J. Browne, M.P. 18 May 1868.

3140. Is he a beneficed clergyman?—Yes, he is rector of the parish.

3141. Mr. *Herbert*.] How far does he live from the asylum?—He lives near; his house is within a mile of the town: but I think it is preposterous that we should be obliged to pay 20 *l.* a year.

3142. Mr. *Dawson*.] The Government first suggested a diminution of his salary, did it not?—No; the Government sent down a list of officers and salaries, and amongst others the Protestant chaplain, at 20 *l.* a year.

3143. The suggestion for the reduction came from the Government in the first instance, did it not?—No, from the governors of the asylum; the Government would not entertain the question at all; they would not even answer the letter, or take any notice of the communication.

3144. Colonel *Forde*.] Do you know the amount of that gentleman's emoluments altogether?—No, I do not.

3145. By an Act of last Session is it not provided that the Government have power to name the officers for each asylum, irrespective of the opinion of the Board of Governors?—Yes; and also all their salaries and allowances. I may perhaps be allowed to add that I think it should not be compulsory on a Board of Governors to appoint a chaplain of any religious denomination, unless there happen to be a certain number of patients of that denomination. I think it is a very unnecessary thing to be obliged to have a chaplain for six or seven of one particular religious denomination.

3146. Do not you think it would be a better arrangement to leave the appointment of the chaplains to the governors themselves, of course the opinion of the doctor in the first place being taken?—Unquestionably.

3147. Is it not the case that the doctor would have power to call in a chaplain if he considered the case of his patient such as to require it?—I should think so; I am not aware of any legislative enactment to that effect, but I should think unquestionably he could. I presume your question refers to, we will say, the case of a Presbyterian; there is no Presbyterian chaplain with us, and I presume when you asked the question you referred to the case of a patient of a religion for which there was no chaplain already existing.

3148. Would you have no chaplain at all?—I would not go so far as that; I think where you have a number of patients of any one religious denomination, it is desirable that you should have service; I should think many of the patients would be able to understand the service. In the north, I presume, the patients in some asylums are almost entirely of one religious denomination, and in the south and west almost all of another; and I certainly would have a chaplain of that denomination, whatever it might be.

3149. As to the appointment of the governors by the grand jury, you said you thought where a county had an asylum of its own, the grand jury might be empowered to take the charge of their lunatic asylum, and to appoint governors?—Yes; the governors of an asylum cannot make a contract for bread or milk, or eggs or butter, or anything, without the sanction of the inspectors in Dublin.

3150. You would give the grand jury power, in the event of a governor not attending the meetings of the Board a certain number of times, to strike off his name and to appoint another, in the hope of getting a better attendance?—I think it is most desirable. We have in our asylum a number of governors who never attend; they were put on, I think very properly, in the first instance as being the representatives of different portions of the county; but where you see that a gentleman lives at a distance, and never attends by any accident, I think it is very desirable that his name should be taken off, and somebody put on who will attend.

3151. Is it your opinion that no clergyman of any denomination should be on any of these Boards?—Certainly; I think the rule in the Poor Law Board is very advantageous in that respect.

3152. And that has made the Poor Law the complete success that it is?—It has made it work very harmoniously.

3153. As to the high constables; they are appointed by the grand jury?—They are.

3154. In the event of the grand jury failing to appoint, it is in the power of the magistrates at quarter sessions?—It is. The day after to-morrow there is to be a special session held in the county of Mayo.

3155. It need not be a special session?—In the event of a high constable either not being appointed, or his securities not being completed at the assizes, the appointment or the approving of the securities goes to the quarter sessions; and in the event of the same thing occurring at the quarter sessions, the clerk of the peace is bound to convene a special sessions for the purpose. In this case one of the high constable's securities was in Dublin, and could not come down. The taking of the securities was therefore adjourned to the quarter sessions. At the quarter sessions one of his securities, I do not know whether the same one, was taken ill; he could not attend, and therefore there is obliged to be a special sessions convened by the clerk of the peace, at very considerable inconvenience, merely for the purpose of taking the securities of this high constable.

3156. Would not you recommend that in the event of a case of that sort occurring, it should not be necessary for the two securities to be present at the same time?—Certainly; I think you ought to be able to take each security separately before a master extraordinary, or commissioner for taking special bail.

3157. Mr. *Dawson*.] You would not therefore think it necessary for the securities of these baronial collectors to be present in person at each ensuing session?—No, I think not, decidedly. I recommended before that there should be a continuing bond to obviate the necessity of their attendance at each session. It is a great expense bringing a man down from Dublin.

3158. Colonel *French*.] In case of the death of a cess collector, the law as to the grand jury, which you have stated, applies?—Yes.

3159. Colonel *Forde*.] In answer to Question 2994, as to the secretary's fees, you said there were three fees which you would allow the secretary to take. Do not you think it would be better that the secretary should have no fees whatever, but that he should be bound to fill up those documents which you recommend fees for, by stamps, to the amount to the credit of the county?—A great many people are of that opinion, but I think those fees are very small in amount, and it would be a payment to him for the trouble he takes; he would probably go to the

Lord J. Browne, M.P.
19 May 1868.

the different localities for the purpose of supplying those tenders, and would thus incur expense.

3160. Would it not be advisable that all fees in connection with the different county officers should be abolished?—We know very little about what the fees of the clerk of the Crown and clerk of the peace are. If the recommendation I made before were adopted, that the two offices should be amalgamated, and the fiscal business should be transferred to the secretary of the grand jury, then I do not see why the county should not be relieved from all charge for the payment of the officer, whether he be called clerk of the peace or clerk of the Crown, who has to perform that portion of the duties of those offices which are connected with the administration of justice; I do not see why the county should pay that. They are paid now by the county, because they form a portion of the fiscal business as well.

3161. In fact, you would wish that any fees that would be necessary for any of those offices should be credited to the county, and not to the officer who collects them?—Those fees which were taken in the quarter sessions court I would consider fees of court more than county fees.

3162. For instance, we will take the fee which is given to the clerk of the peace on licenses. I do not think that the clerk of the peace has any right to pocket that fee; that would go to the county; it is a part and parcel of his duty, for which he gets a salary?—I would rather get rid of him altogether, as far as the county is concerned.

3163. But then whoever does that duty must be paid?—Yes.

3164. If it is by fees, it should go to the credit of the county, and a proper salary should be given to whatever officer does it?—Yes, but if the county ceases to pay him any salary, it would have no claim upon fees he receives.

3165. Of course in the case of any officer whom you would appoint in his place, in the amalgamation of the two offices, you would take into consideration the double duty he would have to perform, and you would give him a salary accordingly; as you suggested that the clerk of the Crown and the clerk of the peace should be amalgamated, that officer of course would have to do double work?—As far as the administration of justice goes, but not so far as the fiscal business of the county goes. I would transfer the fiscal duty to the secretary of the grand jury, and then he would cease to be a county officer.

3166. Take, for instance, the fee which the clerk of the peace gets for licenses, would you call that fiscal, or a fee of court?—I should call it a fee of court. The grand jury have nothing in the world to do with licenses.

3167. As to the magistrates attending at the road sessions, you stated, and I think every one agrees with you, that no magistrate not having property in the barony should sit on the baronial sessions?—Yes.

3168. Would you name an amount which you think would be right as a qualification for a magistrate sitting at those road sessions?—I do not think where a magistrate is concerned it is necessary to name an amount, but there would be no objection to it if thought desirable. I think "a magistrate having an interest in the barony" would be a sufficient definition.

3169. And such magistrate might attend at the county at large sessions?—Yes.

3170. Or would you put a qualification there?—The county at large sessions is of very little importance; they have hardly anything before them; they have a few things, about which there is generally no dispute. The only question that I have seen in the county at large sessions on which a difference of opinion has arisen, is about building a new court-house; as to the county infirmary, that presentment, for instance, comes before the county at large sessions, and it is always agreed to as a matter of course. There is never a question raised.

3171. As to new works, would you think it advisable that those new works should all be brought before the sessions once a year only, and not at each road sessions?—No, I would leave it open. I think either of the two sessions. I do not see why you should not do that.

3172. Colonel Cooper.] I believe you heard Mr. Mackay's evidence the other day?—I heard part of it.

3173. And you also, I think, were here when Mr. Johnson gave his evidence?—Yes.

3174. You have heard the state of things in County Cork described?—Yes.

3175. From the exceptionally large size of that county, do you think there ought to be any special provision for it?—I certainly think the county ought to be divided.

3176. You think that would meet the difficulty?—Unquestionably; and I do not think that because you have one county of such an enormous size you should make any alteration in the general law of the country to meet a peculiar case like that when there is a much simpler way, by dividing it.

3177. You think with two grand juries of 23, the different localities would be fairly represented?—It would be exactly the same as if it were two counties; of course there are many counties in Ireland very much smaller than either of the two divisions of Cork would be.

3178. You think it may have given some dissatisfaction in that county that the localities are not sufficiently represented?—I do not know much about that county; I should think it is likely.

3179. It is possible the law may not work well in that county, although in other parts of Ireland it gives satisfaction?—Exactly.

3180. I do not think you have been asked about whether you could give any discretion at the adjourned sessions as to accepting the lowest tender?—I think you have got a discretion.

3181. You think we now possess one?—I think so; if you take Foot, at page 19, at the bottom of the page, you will see this in the note: "Five tenders were sent in; the grand jury accepted the highest, and the person who made the lowest tender applied to the court to direct the grand jury to accept it. Undeniable security having been offered, Chief Justice Doherty held that the grand jury had a discretion to deal with the different tenders, and that as they had exercised that discretion he had no authority to interfere." I think that amount of discretion is necessary, because cases very frequently occur where a contractor puts in three different tenders in three different names. His first tender we will suppose is 30*l.*, his second 40*l.*, and his third 60*l.* If anybody tenders for 45*l.*, we will say he stands upon his tender for 40*l.*;

ss

if anybody tenders for 25 l., he stands upon his tender for 20 l.; but if nobody tenders at all, then the 30 l. and 40 l. tenders are withdrawn; the parties do not appear, and the sessions are obliged to take the tender for 50 l. The way we meet that difficulty, to a great extent, in my county is this: Where a tender has been put in, and the parties do not appear, we say this is a case of fraud. There are words in the section which give us power in cases of fraud, and if we consider it to be a case of fraud, we give it to the next highest person who is not connected with this particular contractor. We can generally form a pretty good idea of that.

3182. Do you consider that tenants take into consideration the amount of the taxes on the farm they are going to take?—Undoubtedly.

3183. Where the poor rate is high, they give less rent?—Undoubtedly; it is always discussed. In taking a farm, you always hear, "What are the rates?" That is always inquired about.

3184. I do not think you have been asked whether you are in favour of superannuation in any or all of the county officers?—I think the county surveyor is very much exposed. I think if you enlarged the duties of the secretary and made him give his exclusive time, his position would be different from what it is now, but I do not think under existing circumstances I would superannuate him.

3185. Chiefly with regard to the county surveyor, who is very much exposed, and who requires to be a man of active habits, do you think it would be desirable to have a power of superannuation?—I would in the case of the county surveyor.

3186. Mr. *Dawson*.] That is in case he was the sole officer of the county, responsible for the whole of the works of the county; I think you mentioned that you would do away with the office of the assistant surveyor altogether?—I would.

3187. Therefore your view of superannuation would be dependent upon the fact that he solely performed the whole duty?—I should not go so far as to say that because the grand jury of a county wished to have one or two assistants, that therefore I would exclude the county surveyor from getting a retiring pension. I should think that would be hard upon him. He might say, "I am perfectly willing to perform all the duties myself; I had rather no assistants were taken." I think it is hard that he should be deprived of his retiring pension, because some members of the grand jury wish to have an assistant in a particular barony.

3188. Colonel *Cooper*.] You would leave it in fact to the discretion of the jury?—I would.

3189. And give them the power to superannuate the county surveyor?—Yes.

3190. *Chairman*.] Would you require the county surveyor to give his whole time to the county work?—No; I think if a county surveyor has private practice it causes him to travel over the roads and is beneficial to the county. He thereby has an opportunity of seeing the way in which the works are progressing.

3191. You would not debar him from private practice in his profession?—Certainly not.

3192. Colonel *Cooper*.] His private practice sometimes takes him out of the county, does it not?—That is another question. Private practice out of the county is a very different question. I think there is a great deal to be said in favour of preventing him practising out of the county.

3193. Colonel *French*.] When the salaries of the county surveyors were raised, was it not incumbent on them not to undertake private practice?—No, it is left optional with the grand jury to arrange it as they think fit.

3194. Colonel *Cooper*.] I think you are not in favour of deputies for either the secretary of the grand jury, or for the clerk of the Crown?—Or for any official at all except in the case of a collector. A collector in a large barony must occasionally have a deputy, and that is recognised by the Act. I would not allow a deputy in any other case.

3195. I suppose you have known instances in which the duties of the clerk of the Crown have been carried on for five years by deputy?—I believe with the exception of calling out the names of the grand jury, the general practice is for the clerk of the Crown to have his duties performed by a deputy. He resides in Dublin and he has a deputy who gets a small amount of salary and does all the work.

3196. In case of illness, it is now provided that the clerk of the peace should do the duties of the secretary of the grand jury, I believe?—It is, or in case of a vacancy occurring.

3197. If these two offices of clerk of the Crown and clerk of the peace were amalgamated, how would you enable the duties of the secretary to be carried on in case of illness?—It would be very easy to provide for that by having a meeting of magistrates to elect a new secretary the same as you do with the high constable, or if you had the permanent committee I have recommended appointed, let them appoint some one to do the duty till the grand jury meets.

COLONEL FORDE, IN THE CHAIR.

3198. Mr. *Dawson*.] You are decidedly in favour of the appointment of this finance committee?—Decidedly; I believe that if that finance committee had existed we should have been saved a very large portion of that very large amount of cess which we lost during the famine in county Mayo.

3199. Do you know how the finance committee which has been appointed by special legislative acts in the county of Dublin?—I have no personal knowledge, but I have heard from various sources that it works most satisfactorily.

3200. And it has very extensive powers, has it not?—I believe so.

3201. Do you think that an objection to the appointment of a finance committee in every county would be made on the ground that it might lead to jobbery on the part of a few individuals sitting upon that committee?—I certainly think it would not. You will find, I think, in every county, it certainly is so in my county, a certain number of gentlemen who take a leading part in everything; they attend the meetings of the county infirmary, they attend the meetings of the lunatic asylum, they attend the meetings of the Board of superintendence; those gentlemen would probably form the finance committee. They have very great influence, of course, and I do not believe they would have a bit more influence if this committee were formed

Lord *J. Browne*, M.P.
12 May 1868.

than they have at present; the only case in which their influence would not be very powerful is in the case of an appointment, where people come up from all parts of the county.

3202. Do you think there would be any difficulty in calling these gentlemen together in the county town, or wherever it was thought desirable to meet as a committee?—I think not, because the grand jury would appoint those gentlemen who lived near, and who they knew were in the habit of attending to county business.

3203. About what size would you make your finance committee, composed of how many members?—I would not have it too large. The Board of superintendence consists of 12 members, I do not know that there would be any objection to that number, but I should prefer a smaller number.

3204. Would you give to that committee a greater control over the officers of the county than generally now exists in the working of the grand jury laws, from the grand jury not meeting except at an interval of some months; would you give them any separate control?—I would give them complete control over the collectors and over the high constables.

3205. Would you give them the appointment of a collector in the case of a vacancy?—I would unquestionably, until the grand jury met, and I would give them power to examine the securities of any gentleman who tenders for the office.

3206. Do you think that the law with regard to the payment of coroners requires any alteration?—I think in Ireland, we should be a great deal better off without coroners; I think the magistrates would hold inquests much more efficiently. You have stipendiary magistrates all over the country, and if the local magistrate did not do it, the stipendiary magistrate would.

3207. Do you think there would be any difficulty in getting the magistrates to undertake the duty?—Not the least, because the stipendiary magistrate would always do it if the local magistrate did not; it would be part of his duty.

3208. In some parts of Ireland, there is no necessity for having a stipendiary magistrate. There happens to be no stipendiary magistrate in the county of Londonderry, and never has been. Is it a duty which you think you could expect the unpaid local magistrates to undertake?—I think there is a great deal of jobbing about inquests at present; inquests are held where they are quite unnecessary, very often, and I do not think the inquests are well conducted frequently; I have known very incapable men to be coroners, and it is very difficult to remove a coroner. The law says a coroner shall be removed if he does not reside in his district. Well, we had a coroner who did not reside for three years in his district; we represented it to the judge, and the judge told us the Lord Chancellor, I think, should be memorialised. Two of the magistrates memorialised the Lord Chancellor; the Lord Chancellor wrote down to request an explanation from the coroner; nobody knew what that explanation was, but he still remained in possession of his office.

3209. Do you think it desirable if you retain the coroner that he should be either a legal or a medical man?—No, decidedly not.

3210. Neither the one or the other?—I would much rather that he was neither the one or the other.

3211. *Mr. Blake.*] I understand you to be in favour of the associated cesspaying portion of the baronial board being elected by the ratepayers?—Yes, certainly.

3212. You would have combined with the associated cesspayers upon the baronial board an equal number of magistrates, I suppose?—I would.

3213. Would you have them elected by the magistrates themselves; that is, the magisterial portion of the board?—In very many baronies probably you would not have more magistrates taking an interest in the barony than would be necessary to make up the requisite number. If there was a greater number of magistrates residing than the number of cesspayers, they might either be elected by the magistrates, or you might have those that came first, or they might choose among the number when they came to the sessions.

3214. You would have a baronial board so elected to perform all the duties that would devolve upon them relating to baronial business?—I would.

3215. Can you see any objection to having a county board in the same manner; the magisterial portion of it elected by the magistracy, and the other portion elected by the ratepayers?—It must be remembered that the functions of the grand jury, or the body representing the grand jury, are solely and entirely confined to putting a veto upon works that have been previously approved of at the presentment sessions, and I think it would be a very good thing to have a differently constituted body with that power of veto.

3216. Would not the plan which you just now suggested, in reply to Sir Charles Lanyon, give a great amount of dissatisfaction, having a county board elected entirely by the magistrates?—I do not think it would at all, when you consider that they have no power of originating any taxation.

3217. Would you have them all magistrates?—It practically makes no difference. They always are magistrates.

3218. In your county, have you not people who would perform the duties of the county board very well, that are not magistrates?—I do not think it much signifies whether they are obliged to be magistrates or not.

3219. Would it not be better in principle that that county board should be elected by the ratepayers putting a certain qualification upon the person to serve, such as that he should be assessed to the value of 50 *l.* to the county; would not that ensure the selection of a person of a respectable position?—I think the object you want to secure by that second board, is to put a check upon the ratepayers for jobbing or extravagance.

3220. To perform the same functions as already are performed by the grand jury with regard to fiscal matters?—I would not let the presentment sessions choose the parties who are to check their proceedings.

3221. I do not say you should; in the first place, would you have the county board a continuous board?—I think it would be well if they were elected once a year.

3222. Would not it be desirable to have only half of them go out by rotation every year, so as to have a continuous board; may it not very often occur, that certain matters may take place in the county, between one assizes and another, what when it is desirable to have somebody like that you refer to; such matters as an inundation, the breaking down of a bridge, or the consideration of the desirability of encouraging railways in the county?—I was not contemplating that this Board should sit permanently.

3223. Not permanently, but that the body should be like a county corporation, to be called together if such a necessity as I have just spoken of should arise?—It was to meet this very case that I proposed a finance committee. That is one of the objects for which I proposed the finance committee should be constituted.

3224. If you had not a continuous county Board, that finance committee, I apprehend, could not be continuous either?—You could, by an Act of Parliament, authorise the appointment of that finance committee, the same as is done in Dublin.

3225. At the same time, might not the appointment of that county Board be very simply managed by sending out voting papers for them, at the same time that you send out voting papers for the baronial Board. Suppose the qualification for a member for the baronial Board to be 30 *l.*, and for a member of the county Board to be 50 *l.*, the two elections would occur *pari passu* without any expense or trouble, and you then would have a selection, in both instances, direct from the ratepayers; would not that be preferable to the plan you suggested of having the county Board elected solely by the magistracy?—No; I would make the county Board entirely independent of the cesspayers.

3226. Are you a member of the Board of superintendents in your county?—I am.

3227. Do you think it desirable to have a more frequent governmental inspection of prisons, instead of appointing, as very often occurs, some county gentleman to the office of local inspector of prisons who is not particularly acquainted with prison discipline and the management of prisons?—I do not know; I do not think it would. I think, myself, that we can manage these county institutions ourselves very well. I object very much to having gentlemen coming down from Dublin who are not taking part in the management of these institutions, coming in and making all sorts of alterations and changes; for instance, coming in and saying, "You have only got 100 sheets in store, I insist on your buying 20 more," and a variety of powers of that sort, which I very much object to. I would rather leave it to the local Board; I think they would manage it better, if left alone.

3228. You are a governor of the lunatic asylum in your county?—Yes.

3229. Of the new one that has been recently erected?—Yes.

3230. Were you ever the governor of a lunatic asylum before?—No; our lunatic asylum before was in Ballinasloe: it was quite impossible for anyone to attend.

3231. You were not a member of it?—No.

3232. Could you give the Committee any information as to how, after the first appointment of governors of lunatic asylums, these appointments are usually made?—They are made by the Government. I have heard complaints about it, but my own impression is that Government generally select a good class of people for them.

3233. Have you ever heard that the suggestion to the Government to nominate generally comes from the inspector of lunatic asylums?—I have heard it stated; I cannot answer for it myself, that sometimes the medical superintendent possesses influence in getting a friend of his appointed a governor, but I know nothing of it myself.

Lord J. Browne, M.P.

11 May 1868.

3234. Do you not think it exceedingly undesirable that such a suggestion should be acted upon?—I do; I think the inspector of asylums ought not to have anything to do with it.

3235. In the change of system you suggest the governors of lunatic asylums, I presume, would be entirely appointed by the county Board?—I should have no objection to letting the Government appoint a few; I think the grand jury ought to be able to appoint a certain number, say half, but I do not think it very much signifies. I quite agree with Colonel Forde, that it is desirable to alter the management of lunatic asylums. At present everything is done under the control from Dublin, and money is paid out of the Treasury in the first instance. I do not know why we should not make our own presentments, and manage it as we do our county institutions.

3236. Under the change of system, the clerk of the peace, and the clerk of the Crown, would scarcely have any fiscal duties at all to perform?—No; I propose to transfer all their fiscal duties to the secretary of the grand jury, and give him a higher salary, requiring him to reside in the county town, and to do nothing else.

3237. In the event of a separation of the fiscal from the criminal business of the grand jury, and a county Board, such as you suggest, being formed, the clerk of the peace, and the clerk of the Crown would have no fiscal duties to perform; do not you then consider that they ought to be paid out of the Consolidated Fund, the same as the other officers connected with the administration of justice, such as the Judge of Assize, the Crown Solicitor, and the Sessional Crown Prosecutor?—Yes; or out of the fees of the courts in which they act.

3238. Mr. *Maguire*.] You were asked a question with reference to what I asked you on a former day, as to the Board of superintendents and the high sheriff having the control over the court-house. Do not you think, inasmuch as a public question may come on, as it were, within the domain of political controversy, it would be far better to have the legitimate and traditional officer, the high sheriff, to call the public meeting, than to leave it to a Board of superintendents, who may, or may not, be acted upon by certain prejudices?—I should allow the high sheriff to use the court-house for a public meeting, for any purpose, that is, only for public purposes.

3239. You object to the arbitrary conduct, as I think you ought to represent it, of the Government in not allowing you to diminish the salary of the Protestant chaplain at your lunatic asylum. Would you go so far as to say that there should be no chaplain, or no salary, if the number of patients is limited to seven?—I would, most unquestionably. I do not think in any country in the world you would see seven of that class of people having a chaplain entirely to themselves; I think it is entirely unnecessary. Suppose there were seven Jews in the asylum, would you propose to appoint a minister of the Jewish religion?

3240. After all, that is a very far fetched illustration?—I will take what is not so far fetched,

Lord J. Browne, M.P.

20 May 1858.

fetched, the case of seven Roman Catholics in an asylum in Glasgow, or even in a town that has not so many Roman Catholics as Glasgow. I think it would be very undesirable to put the district to the expense of keeping a Roman Catholic chaplain.

3241. Is it not rather dangerous to draw the line; the seven to-day may be 13 to-morrow?—I should leave a discretion with the Board for that reason.

3242. Do not you think it may be establishing rather a dangerous precedent, that other Boards would say if there were 20, or 30, or 50 Roman Catholics, there is no reason why they should appoint a chaplain, that the poor demented wretches could have no possible advantage from their ministrations?—I do not think the class of gentlemen who are governors of the asylums, I do not think any class we have in Ireland administering public justice, would take such an illiberal view as that.

3243. On the whole, you do not think it would be better to have a chaplain with a very small salary than to have no chaplain at all?—No; I do not see why you are to make a difference between one religion and another. I do not see if you appoint a chaplain of the Church of England because you have seven members of that religion in an asylum, why you should not, if you have seven Presbyterians, have a Presbyterian chaplain, or if you have seven Wesleyan Methodists, why you should not have a Wesleyan chaplain.

3244. I want to ask your opinion on a matter which I do not think was put to you, but which I was urged to put before the Committee; is there power under the Grand Jury Act now to appoint a chaplain to an hospital where there are 50 or 60 beds, and take them as Catholic inmates or Protestant inmates, I do not care which?—You mean a county infirmary?

3245. Yes?—I think not; I think it is in the hands of the governors of the infirmary. The governors of the infirmary have certain funds of their own, and in addition they get the presentment in aid from the county, and it rests with the governors to pay any officers they like.

3246. Have they power under their charter, or whatever it may be, or under the grand jury laws?—No; the grand jury have nothing to say except making a presentment in aid.

3247. Have you a power to make a presentment for the purpose?—For a lump sum; the words of the Act are, "In aid of the funds of the institution, not exceeding 700*l.* at each assize."

3248. I think a Member of the Committee seems to be under the idea that the complaint from the county of Cork was rather as to the non-division of the county than the want of representation on the part of the ratepayers; which do you understand the complaint to be?—Well, really it is rather difficult to answer.

3249. You have heard Mr. Parker's and Mr. Mackay's evidence upon that point; they said nothing about the non-division of the county; do you understand that the complaint of those who represent the ratepayers or cesspayers of the county of Cork, arises from the non-division of the county or the non-representation of those classes who pay the entire of the rate?—I think Mr. Mackay, for instance, was decidedly of opinion that the cesspayers ought to be more represented.

3250. And Mr. Parker also?—I did not hear Mr. Parker's evidence, nor did I read it.

3251. Assuming that that was the burden of their complaint, I think you yourself by your evidence admit that it is a very fair ground?—Yes; I think the cesspayers ought to have more *bonâ fide* representation at the presentment sessions.

3252. And you think at the presentment sessions they should be represented by elected delegates?—Yes.

3253. I suppose you have very practical knowledge of the working of the Poor Law system in your country?—Yes.

3254. Have you acted as chairman?—Yes; I am not chairman of the Board; I am vice-chairman, but I am very frequently in the chair.

3255. Do you find the representative system work very well there?—Yes.

3256. And working well in harmony with the *ex officio* guardians?—Yes, there is the best possible feeling.

3257. Do not you think if the same were applied to the other system, the same good would result?—I do.

3258. Are you quite in favour of that?—Yes.

3259. You talk of the assistant surveyors; are you anxious that they should be done away with?—Yes; I would not go so far as to make it compulsory on every grand jury in the whole of Ireland to abolish them, but I would not sanction them in my county.

3260. What class of officers would you substitute in their place?—I would make the county surveyor do the duty himself, as they do in Mayo and I believe in Galway.

3261. Do you mean one county surveyor for an entire county?—Yes; in a large county like Mayo there are two; in Galway there are two. They have no assistants in Galway, and in the southern half of Mayo they have no assistants.

3262. Do you mean to say he should be always on the road?—As often on the road as is necessary to do his duty.

3263. And that that could be done without the aid of assistants?—Yes; I have stated that Mr. Brett was county surveyor for the whole of Mayo, the third largest county in Ireland. He had no assistant; he had the whole work on his own shoulders, and performed it most satisfactorily.

3264. I do not think I had the pleasure of hearing your evidence as to the division of the rate. I believe you are in favour of that?—Yes, in favour of it as applied to future lettings.

3265. You mean lettings by lease?—In any future lettings I should be disposed to let it be divided between landlord and tenant. I think it would create a great deal of ill-will and bad feeling if applied to any existing tenancies, whether tenants at will or not.

3266. For the future you admit the justice of the principle?—Yes; I think it would be more desirable.

3267. There is a very strong feeling in Ireland in favour of its being divided on the part of the occupying class?—I do not put it so much as a matter of justice as a matter of good policy, because I think when a man makes a bargain in taking the land, the landlord and the tenant may agree together.

3268. As a matter of good policy, you are in favour of it?—Yes, and to satisfy the general feeling.

3269. You

Lord J. Browne, M.P. 19 May 1868.

3269. You know there is a general feeling?—I do, amongst the cesspayers.

3270. You desire to satisfy that?—Yes.

3271. Now as to future lettings, I should like to understand what you mean. You would admit, I suppose, in the first instance, that a vast majority of the tenants in Ireland hold at will and not by lease?—Yes, a large majority.

3272. Suppose a man continues to hold at will liable, if the owner so desire, to be removed within a very short time. Do you think if that man hold that land under those conditions for the next 20 years, he should not have the advantage of half the rate being paid by the owner of the property?—Certainly not, unless there is another agreement made between the landlord and the tenant. The reason is this, that the rent which the tenant pays at present has been calculated and agreed to on the assumption that the tenant pays the whole of the cess.

3273. Who has the more interest in the improvements made; I do not care what they are, in the county or in any establishments created under the operation of this law, who has the more interest in their being well done and well established; is it the owner of the property or the man who at any moment, say within twelve months, may be removed from that land?—They both have an interest. If I were to make a distinction I should say in a great number of the county works the tenant has a stronger, a more individual interest than the landlord. Take the case of the lunatic asylum. We know that that is kept up for the poor lunatics, not for the rich. It is maintained for the benefit of the poor, not for the landlord class. If any of the landlord class becomes a lunatic, he is not kept in the lunatic asylum at the county expense. That is an expenditure which is solely for the tenant class.

3274. Do you mean to say the owners of property should pay nothing towards the maintenance of the lunatic asylums?—Not at all; you asked me which of the two had the stronger interest. I say there are certain institutions that are kept up for the benefit of the tenant class. I think it is quite right that the owners of property should contribute.

3275. They do not at the present moment?—They do not directly, and I have no objection in the world to applying one-half of the cess in the future.

3276. You mean the future lettings?—To future lettings solely and entirely.

3277. Those lettings may be very few in number, inasmuch as the same state of things may go on, not only with those who have leases, but those who have not leases?—I think it would be very unjust and create ill feeling, and be very impolitic to apply it to existing tenancies.

3278. After admitting the injustice of the present system, which operates, you think, unfairly, it would be only in the most infinitesimal instances where new lettings will take place, that you would give them the benefit of this division, or the principle of justice which you say you are in favour of?—I do not admit the injustice; I do not think there is any injustice where a bargain is made between the landlord and the tenant. I think, as a matter of good policy, it would be desirable to make a change. I do not think there is any injustice at all in a man keeping to a bargain he has made.

3279. Take a road through a gentleman's property, which opens up the country, which gives facility, no doubt, for the transport of produce to market, but which nevertheless opens up the country and improves his property; has not the owner of that property a greater interest in the improvements than the man who, to say the least, has a precarious tenancy, or one which is liable to be determined at the will of the owner of the property?—I do not contemplate any new roads, with very rare exceptions, ever being made in my county. There is no doubt that at the present time land in grass lets higher than it does in the hands of small tenants. There is no doubt about that in my county; and that being the case, the roads are made for the benefit of the small tenants. They are not required for land in grass. I think the tenant has just as much interest in the road as the landlord has.

3280. My question did not refer to the particular mode of cultivating the land, or the particular species of agriculture, but it referred to Ireland generally?—Well, I think the new road is to the benefit of the tenant as much as the landlord, if not more.

3281. Mr. *Herbert*.] When a road is made for the benefit of any particular property; going through any particular property; is it not very often the case that the grand jury say, "If the landlord will subscribe half, it shall be done," therefore that it does not come all on the tenants, but very often it comes on the proprietor of the land in which the improvement of the property takes place?—Not only for making new roads, new roads are very rarely made in Mayo; but even for the repairs of existing roads it is very common for the landlord to say, "I will give so much if the sessions will give so much." I do not say there is no case, but I do not recollect the case of a landlord ever making a tenant contribute to that.

3282. Mr. *Maguire*.] You are in favour of a division of the rate in future?—Yes, for future lettings.

3283. You would follow out the analogy of the Poor Law system at presentment sessions; you would have an equal number *ex officio* and an equal number of elected cesspayers?—Yes.

3284. You think that would do away with any cause of complaint that exists?—I do.

3285. Mr. *Kendall*.] As far as the lunatic asylums are concerned, the Lord Lieutenant names the Board?—He does.

3286. Is the Lord Lieutenant's power limited as to number?—No; there is no limit whatever.

3287. When a new Lord Lieutenant is appointed, does he generally add to the number?—No.

3288. He seldom interferes?—No.

3289. If there be a falling off, and you require more, is there, or is there not (I do not say it in an invidious sense), is there a party feeling in the appointment; for instance, if he is a Conservative, does he appoint a Conservative?—No; I think, practically the Executive Government are very glad to get any gentleman in the county who will take the trouble to attend.

3290. Supposing there were two of good position, would there be a conflict?—I think if there were two of good position who would attend, the Lord Lieutenant would appoint them both, and he would be very glad to do it. I never heard the idea stated of there being any distinction in that way. I happen to know that in the appointment of the Board for the Mayo Lunatic Asylum,

Lord J. Browne, M.P.

11 May 1858.

Asylum, a great deal of trouble was taken to see that the different parts of the county were represented, and that the different religions were represented.

3291. In your experience, and from what you have heard, you do not think that there is any colour in the way of politics, so far as the appointment goes?—Not the slightest.

3292. Taking the case only of sub-appointments, you have certain powers at the Board as to these appointments; is there anything like a party feeling?—Until last year the Board of Government had no power to appoint any servant whatever in the asylums, but by an Act passed at the end of last year, they were given the power of appointing servants, and all officers except the resident medical superintendent; I believe the same would follow, as in other county institutions. Occasionally, no doubt there might be a difference; a political or a religious question may come on, but I do not think it would often happen.

3293. With regard to the attendance of the Board, I believe the attendance is not large?—It is not satisfactory at all.

3294. If you were to extend their powers, and to make them more useful, do not you think that you would have a much larger attendance?—Yes, decidedly; I know that many of the governors have expressed their determination not to attend, in consequence of their being so entirely under the control of the inspectors in Dublin, and having no power of their own.

3295. You would throw a great deal more into the hands of the grand jury than in the hands of the Lord Lieutenant, in the formation of the Board, and you would give the Board a great deal more power?—I think it would be a very good thing if the grand jury appointed half. I should have no objection to their appointing the Board.

3296. You would give them the power of appointing medical men?—No; I think it is very desirable that the Lord Lieutenant should have the power of appointing the chief medical superintendent. I think when such a man is appointed, local influence should not come in, and I would rather leave the appointment of the medical superintendent to the Government.

3297. *Suppose you had a Board of eight or ten eminent men come before you, you might give the Lord Lieutenant a veto?*—I would leave the resident medical superintendent entirely in the hands of the Government; I think they have a better choice.

3298. With regard to contracts, you would let that remain with the Board?—Entirely. It is absurd that we cannot make a contract for eggs and butter without its being referred to the inspectors in Dublin to refuse or confirm the contract.

3299. With regard to the classes of insanity in Ireland, are you aware whether in Ireland, generally speaking, among the insane the larger class arises from the religious mania?—I should think they take the same proportion as in other places, but I do not know. I believe it is an undoubted fact, that religious mania is much more difficult to cure than any other description of insanity.

3300. You have given an opinion as to the impropriety of appointing a chaplain where there are only four, five, or six persons of a certain class of religion. Have you ever seen any of the English asylums, where there is a large attendance at the chapel?—I have visited the English asylums, but I know nothing about the practical working of them, so far as the chaplain goes.

3301. How often do you visit; how often does the Board meet?—Once a month.

3302. Are they well taken care of; is it an expensive matter to the county; have they a dinner prepared for them, or comforts of that kind; I mean the Board?—The Board never get an atom of anything.

3303. *Sir Colman O'Loghlen.*] As I understand, you do not object generally to appointing chaplains to lunatic asylums?—No; I think there ought to be chaplains where there are a large number of people of any religious denomination. What I object to is, having a chaplain of one particular religion when there happen to be only half a dozen of that particular religion in the asylum, particularly at the salary of 80*l.* a-year.

3304. I think I understood you to say, that you thought the governors would always have good feeling enough to appoint a chaplain where it was necessary?—I think so.

3305. Are you aware that the Board of governors, at the Belfast asylum, have refused to appoint a chaplain?—I should certainly have no objection, in a case of that sort, to the Lord Lieutenant having power to insist upon a chaplain being appointed where there are a certain number of patients.

3306. You have heard of the Belfast case?—I have only heard of it since I have been in this chair.

3307. You are aware that the Court of Queen's Bench decided they had no power to enforce it, and that consequently in the Act of last Session power is taken for the Lord Lieutenant to appoint a chaplain?—He has power to fix the number of officers, as many as he likes, and at any salary he likes.

3308. With respect to the lunatic asylums, what would you think of transferring them altogether to the Poor Law Commissioners, and putting them under the Poor Law Board?—No, I would rather leave them to the county Board; I do not see that there would be any advantage in putting them under the Poor Law Board.

3309. If you do not divide the county cess, of course, if they were not under the Poor Law Board, the expense would be paid under the poor rates; you see no advantage in that?—No.

3310. How are the accounts audited at present?—I think it would puzzle anyone to tell you that; every document is supposed to be sent over to the general Audit Office in London; and when they once get possession of the documents, we never can get them again. I would mention one case which occurred; there was a dispute as to a man's tender; the tender had gone over to the Audit Office, in London, and we requested that they would send us back the tender to see what was in it, what was the price mentioned. They wanted to know what particular purpose we wanted it for? They said it was quite unusual, and it was a curious demand to make. I think we got the tender after a good deal of correspondence on the subject; it was perfectly absurd that we could not have the tender to refer to without a correspondence.

3311. As I understand, there is no regular

audit.

audit, except by sending documents off to the Audit Board, in London?—There is that audit in London, of the extent of which I cannot form the slightest idea.

3312. There are no auditors that come round from the office in Dublin?—No.

3313. Well, now as to prisons; you were asked whether you thought it expedient to keep up the system of local inspection; do you agree with keeping it up?—I do; the local inspector in our gaol does the duty of a clerk at the meetings of the Board.

3314. Do not you think you ought to have inspectors of prisons; do you approve of Government inspectors of prisons at all?—I think it is unavoidable; you must have some Government inspection.

3315. Do not you think it very advisable that they should come round more than once or twice a year?—To tell you the truth, I think we manage our county institutions very well, if we are not interfered with.

3316. Is it of importance that there should be uniformity in all the gaols in Ireland; as to the ordinary rules of prisons, such as the admission of prisoners, and diet, and everything else, should not there be uniformity all round?—I do not think a very close uniformity is necessary; I think if there were a slight departure from uniformity it would not make any difference; I think uniformity in punishment is desirable.

3317. And in the rules of admission?—Yes, I think, in some of those things; the dietary is entirely controlled by the Government; the matters that there is not uniformity in are, I think, very trifling.

3318. With respect to the clerks of the peace and clerks of the Crown, do you see any advantage in keeping those two offices distinct, or would you amalgamate them?—I would amalgamate them; and transfer the fiscal portion of the duties to the secretary of the grand jury.

3319. Is not there some species of regulation that the appointment of the clerks of the peace should rest with the lieutenant of the county in place of the Crown?—I do not think it signifies much who has the appointment. I have heard that raised as an objection to amalgamating the two, and it is the only objection I have heard; it is a very trifling one.

3320. In Mayo, the clerk of the peace is a very good officer, I believe?—A very excellent officer.

3321. Have you heard complaints of clerks of the peace in other counties not exercising their duties in person; taking the salaries, and employing a clerk at a small sum of money?—Yes; and the same with the clerks of the Crown.

3322. In fact, clerks of the Crown seldom appear in the county?—In my county they only appear to call over the grand jury.

3323. Do you think it would be desirable to insist upon those officers discharging their duties in person, unless excused by reasonable illness, or otherwise?—Certainly, and on their residing in the county.

3324. You said, I think, that there is some difficulty in getting presentments for court-houses occasionally. Suppose you want presentments for sessional court-houses, do you find any difficulty in getting presentments for repairs and improvements?—Not for the ordinary repairs; but there is frequently objections to building new court-houses in new places. There was a proposal to build a court-house in a new place in Mayo, with the intention of having quarter sessions held there. That was one case in which there was a difference of opinion, and where it was thrown out.

3325. Do you think it necessary to give power to the grand jury to make presentments without application, at presentment sessions, for repairs of public buildings, such as court-houses?—No; I see no reason in the world why they should not (except in the case of sudden damage) go before the cesspayers.

3326. Do I understand you to say you found no difficulty in getting this kind of presentment?—Not the least, for maintaining in proper order and repair existing court houses.

3327. Are you aware that in the case of the sessional court-houses in Scotland, half the expense is placed on the Consolidated Fund?—Yes; both building and repairing.

3328. Do you see any reason why the same rule should not be applied in Ireland?—The only difficulty is that the Chancellor of the Exchequer will not agree to it.

3329. With respect to bridges, has there been any difficulty found in Mayo in getting presentments for bridges, for building or repairing them?—Yes; I have already stated the case of one particular bridge.

3330. Will you suggest whether there should be any appeal to such a body as the Board of Works, or the Court of Queen's Bench, to compel the erection of a bridge of that sort?—The Act already provides for that. The Act provides that in the event of the presentment sessions twice refusing a presentment for a work, the cesspayers may memorialise a judge who empanels a jury to try the case, and if the jury find in favour of the work, it is then referred to the grand jury.

3331. How long may that take; it may take nearly a year and a half, may it not?—No, it is done at the same assizes.

3332. I understand you to say it must be thrown out at two presentment sessions?—Yes.

3333. And meanwhile the public may be drowned, and all kinds of mischief done?—I think there ought to be some local control over the expenditure of money.

3334. You do not think there should be any superior authority to compel the making of works of that nature?—I do not; I have already stated that I think bridges of the class of Errifi Bridge, of which we are speaking, are county works, and I think all bridges of that class, costing over 500 *l.*, ought to be chargeable on the county at large.

3335. Have you considered the question of county rating?—Yes.

3336. Would you be in favour of having county rating, or of still preserving the baronial rating?—I think the baronial rating is a check on extravagant expenditure.

3337. Mr. *Herbert*.] Do you think that the members of the Board of superintendence, or half of them at least, could be compelled to reside three months in the year, so that new members should be put on; at the present time there is a difficulty; on the grand jury and the Board of superintendence the same men are appointed again and again, because there is a feeling as to who should reside and who should not?—We have a great difficulty in getting proper attendance on the Board of superintendence,

Lord J. Browne, M.P.

18 May 1858.

case, and I do not think it would be desirable to put off those five men who do attend. If they went out in rotation, they would have to go off.

3338. I know that in some cases men who are very anxious to get on the board of superintendence have not been able to get on because there was a difficulty about putting off some particular member?—If they were eligible for re-election, there would be no objection to it, but I think in a case where you have only four or five members constantly in the habit of attending, it would not be desirable to exclude them.

3339. Only for one year?—I think it would have a mischievous effect; in my county you would have a difficulty in getting men to attend.

3340. There are twelve members?—Yes.

3341. You say three or four are always attending, but the remaining eight or nine do not attend. Surely there would be some other members of the county who would like to get on?—We cannot find men to attend. We have the clerk of the peace, a solicitor. He is on the board of superintendence; he is not a member of the grand jury. We put him on because he is a man who lives in the neighbourhood, and who attends.

3342. Sir *Colman O'Loghlen.*] County Mayo is rather peculiarly situated, I believe. There are not many residents in the neighbourhood of the county town?—No, there are very few.

3343. Mr. *Herbert.*] I think you expressed your opinion about the alteration of the gaol in your county, which you have just built under the order of the Government, and the Dublin officials immediately caused the gaol to be altered and put the county to great expense?—The Chief Secretary for Ireland asked me about imperative presentments, as to what was the cause of the great expense, and whether they could be controlled in any way. I was saying that one of the causes is the constant changes made in the law, and the power which is given to controlling bodies in Dublin, such as the inspectors of prisons and asylums. They take up a particular theory, and are very hot upon it. In a few years that explodes; they take up another, and they are perfectly reckless as to the expense put on the county to carry out these theories. A gaol was built in the county of Mayo at the expense of 25,000 *l.*; that money was to be repaid by instalments. Before the whole money was paid off the fashion of gaols, so to speak, had altered, and the inspectors of prisons were very strongly in favour of the separate system, and urged upon us to adopt that system. They have no compulsory power at present. We kept it off as long as we could, until we paid off the whole of the instalments of the original cost of the prison, and then we considered the question. We found that in consequence of the plan on which that gaol had been constructed 20 years before, it was totally unsuitable to be adapted to the separate system. Every cell in the prison was of such small dimensions that it would be necessary to throw two cells into one, or else to take down the block, and widen it at an enormous expense. The original cost of the gaol, as I said, was 25,000 *l.*, and to have altered one-fourth part of the male department of the gaol to the separate system would have required an expenditure of over 3,000 *l.* We actually presented 2,000 *l.* for the purpose. We could not get any contractor to take it for less than 2,300 *l.* or 2,400 *l.*, and the thing was postponed in consequence. Now, I understand there is a great difference in opinion about the value of the separate system. I think the authorities are rather doubting about the advisability of it, and we have dropped the question. But it is quite a chance that we did not make a contract to alter the gaol to the separate system, which probably, as soon as the alterations were made, would have been discontinued.

3344. (*Chairman.*) Mr. Maguire pressed you very strongly as to the levy of the county cess half off the tenant, and as to the tenancies at will; would it not be optional for those tenants at will, if they did not like the present arrangement, to come before their landlord, and enter into a new arrangement with him, whereby the landlord could be made to pay the half of the county cess, and any arrangement might be made which might be deemed necessary between the landlord and the tenant to compensate each other?—Certainly; I think the effect of the law would be, that by degrees it would fall into the same stream; it would be done gradually, and without injustice.

3345. You see no hardship to a tenant in the tenancy at will by the present system being kept on until a new arrangement be entered into between him and his landlord?—No; there are many landlords in my county that make a sort of rule in their estate that they will not alter the terms of letting to a tenant more than once in a certain number of years. Some landlords say seven years and some 10 years. Lord Arran goes so far that he never alters a tenant's rent more than once in 21 years. He does not give leases, but he considers the tenancy to be the same thing. Now, I think a case of that sort, to put half the cost of the cess on Lord Arran's shoulders, who has many charges on his estate, would be a very great injustice to him; it would drive him to break through his existing arrangements. I am afraid there are parties in Ireland who would represent to the tenant that the landlord was trying to evade the law, and to break the law. A great deal of ill-feeling would be stirred up in that way when a landlord attempted to make a new arrangement with a tenant.

3346. You stated that, as the law is at present, the clerk of the peace is the deputy for the secretary, in the event of his illness?—Yes, or death.

3347. You do not consider that that is a good arrangement?—No.

3348. He has no knowledge whatever of the duties which a secretary has to perform?—It happens that the clerk of the peace in Mayo is also solicitor to the grand jury. He is a sharp, clever man, and knows a great deal about it.

3349. As a general rule it would not be the case?—No.

3350. In the case of illness, for the time being, of the secretary's deputy, would it not be well to have his own clerk, who is perfectly aware of all the presentments to be brought before the road sessions; that he should be, for the interim, the deputy, instead of any other officer?—Well, he might not be a capable man; he might not be a man in a position to do the work.

3351. Has not the clerk a great deal of the duty of the office to perform as it is?—That case occurred in my county. There was a vacancy, by death, of the secretary. You would always keep on the clerk of the secretary until a new one was appointed to assist him in his duties,

but

but I think a clerk is hardly a man of a proper position to be entrusted with the whole duties of a secretary of the grand jury, even *pro tem.* I would rather have somebody of a better position. If the finance committee I recommend were appointed, it would rest with them, and, if not, I think the magistrates might do it in the same way as they appoint a high constable.

3352. If that were the case, the magistrates should be called together immediately for such an appointment?—Yes.

3353. Because it might leave the county in what might be called a "fix," if such an appointment were not made?—You might leave it in the hands of the Board of Superintendence as a temporary thing. I think it does not much signify in what body the authority is vested; it is not of very great importance. There must be some body of persons to appoint an acting secretary whenever a vacancy occurs.

3354. Mr. *Blake.*] The honourable Chairman suggested that the present system with regard to tenants-at-will paying the entire cess could not be considered a grievance, as it was open to them at any time to go to their landlord to make a new arrangement; is it at all likely, in the state of things between tenants and their landlords in Ireland, that a tenant would be found to do anything of the kind; would he not rather bear the grievance than go to his landlord to make a new bargain?—I deny that there is any grievance at all, because the tenant has taken the land on the clear understanding that he has to pay the cess.

3355. I would ask you if it has not this very great disadvantage, that a tenant can never calculate with any accuracy what he will have to pay, as the amount is always uncertain?—It varies very little indeed.

3356. Assuming his landlord to be a grand juror, is not there a positive inducement offered to him to have as many improvements as possible in the barony he represents?—Practically, in the operation of the law, the landlord is always more for keeping down the cess than the tenant; I think you will find that to be the case everywhere.

3357. In your experience?—Yes; and I think you will find it is the case in other parts of Ireland too.

3358. Sir *Colman O'Loghlen.*] With respect to the clerk of the secretary, I believe he is not a recognised officer; he is not paid by the county?—No.

3359. Do you think it would be expedient, now that new duties are put on the secretary, to have a county officer?—I do not think he has any new duties.

3360. The secretary has?—It might be a question to be considered, if you impose those new duties on him by abolishing the offices of clerk of the peace and clerk of the Crown, whether you would give him an assistant or let him provide that assistant out of his increased salary.

3361. If an assistant were provided, he might be of a better class than at present?—Yes.

3362. When the Poor Law was passed, half the rates were thrown on the landlord?—Yes.

3363. Are you aware of the landlords all over the country at once increasing the rents in order to make up for the deficiency caused by the poor rates?—No; that was a different case altogether. It was the imposition of a new tax; it was quite a different case; but where you are transferring a charge that has been borne by the tenant, and which the tenant has agreed to pay, then I believe the landlord would certainly say to the tenant, "If half this charge is put on my shoulders, I must increase the rent in proportion."

3364. Mr. *Herbert.*] Are there many landlords in your county who have expressed strong opinions with reference to the division of the county cess?—No, I do not think there is a very strong feeling. I think there is a feeling amongst the tenantry, that it would be desirable that it should be divided.

3365. No landlords have expressed a strong opinion?—No.

3366. Sir *Colman O'Loghlen.*] You do not consider it a matter of justice, but you consider it a matter of expediency?—Yes; a bargain is a bargain between man and man.

3367. It is a matter of expediency to make the change?—Yes.

Friday, 15th May 1868.

MEMBERS PRESENT:

Mr. Blake.	Mr. Kendall.
Colonel Cooper.	Sir Charles Lanyon.
Mr. Dawson.	Mr. Leader.
General Dunne.	Mr. Maguire.
Colonel Forde.	Earl of Mayo.
Colonel French.	The O'Conor Don.
Mr. Chichester Fortescue.	Sir Colman O'Loghlen.
Mr. Herbert.	

THE O'CONOR DON, IN THE CHAIR.

Mr. P. BURROWES SHARKEY, re-called; and further Examined.

Mr. P. B. Sharkey.

15 May 1868.

3368. *Chairman.*] You were examined before by this Committee; upon that occasion I believe you were not able to finish the evidence which you desired to give?—No. When I was last before the Committee I had disposed of three out of the five heads under which, for the convenience of the Committee, I arranged to give my evidence, and there are two of those heads at present remaining.

3369. What are these?—First, the defects or evils of the present system, and next the amendments or the remedial measures which I would venture humbly to submit to the Committee.

3370. With respect to the first head, what do you consider to be the evils of the constitution of the grand jury?—I consider that the present mode of constituting the grand jury, having regard to the persons by whom the grand jury rate is at present paid, is not satisfactory. The grand jury is at present constituted or selected by the high sheriff. The sheriff is an officer nominated at the pleasure of the Crown, and he exercises uncontrolled discretion in the selection of his grand jury.

3371. Colonel *French.*] How do you mean that he is uncontrolled, as he is bound by law to take a certain form of selection?—I shall explain that, I hope, in the course of my evidence; and perhaps, as the Honourable Member has called attention to it, I may now explain what I mean by an uncontrolled discretion. It is true that under the present Grand Jury Act he is bound to call upon his panel a representative from each barony; but he is not bound to see that the person whom he so calls to represent the barony is to attend same, or serves upon the grand jury; therefore, I venture to think that he exercises, in the selection of his grand jury, an uncontrolled discretion. I think that that is wrong in principle, and leads occasionally, though not often, to improper persons being placed upon the panel, and, consequently, upon the grand jury.

3372. What do you mean by improper persons?—Persons who have no right whatever, either by connection with the county by property, or, if they have property, by reason of their being otherwise unfitted; and lest there should be any doubt in the minds of any of the Honourable Members of the Committee upon that point, I shall refer to a very recent case, which called forth the animadversions of one of the going judges of assize on the last spring circuit.

3373. Is that the Leitrim case?—It is. I am going to refer in support of that somewhat surprising statement (but not the less true) to the observations of Mr. Justice Keogh, in addressing the grand jury at the last Leitrim Assizes: "It is a matter of congratulation that the number requisite to make a grand jury complete are in attendance at the present assizes. On a former occasion the number was only 17; but though the requisite number is now in attendance, I wish I could congratulate you that the owners of property appeared to discharge their duties instead of their representatives. I think it is a great misfortune that the high sheriff is limited in his selection of grand jurors, as the owners of property in the county do not think proper to attend; at least owners of property who draw large incomes from the county only occasionally visit it, and systematically absenting themselves from acting either as grand jurors or magistrates. There is another matter to which I wish to call attention. I did not feel called upon to desire one of your number to stand aside, having previously been sworn, but I think it right to state that the local inspector of your gaol is not a proper person to serve on the grand jury. The local inspector is a paid officer of the county, subject to the control of the Board of Superintendence, nominated by the grand jury, and who exercise supervision over the local inspector. Is it right or proper that the grand jury should have amongst them one of their paid officers? If such a course of proceeding does not appear to the grand jury one that should not occur, no language of mine can have any effect upon them. There is another matter, also, to which I feel it is my duty to allude. I assume that he is both respectable and independent; but it is not right to place on the grand jury a gentleman who practises as an attorney at quarter sessions and at petty sessions. It is impossible that the public can have confidence in a body, one of whose number they employ daily as their agent in the local courts.

Property,

Mr. P. B. Sharkey.

15 May 1868.

Property, in this instance, has nothing to do with the matter. I see gentlemen in that box who come from the sister country, and they would find it difficult to obtain credence at the other side of the Channel, if they stated that such a practice exists here. I have observed on this before, and I shall continue to do so on every occasion when I have the honour to preside here until the sheriff discharges his duty as he should." The same learned judge, at the Galway assizes which took place subsequently, made some severe strictures upon the mode in which the grand jury of that very important county was constituted at the then assizes. The paper containing his Lordship's charge I am sure is in the Library of your Honourable House, and, if necessary, you can refer to it. I regret that I have not got it with me, but it will be found that his observations were directed to property being represented on the grand jury by means of agents, a system which he in strong terms deprecated.

3374. (Chairman.) With respect to the representation of property by agents, is not that almost necessary in consequence of the exclusion of peers from sitting on the grand jury?—That I should think is one reason, and there might be another reason added, viz., the absence from the country during the period of the year when those duties were discharged of owners of property. That is an additional reason why agents are put upon the panel to represent the owners of property, either during the absence of the principal, or on account of his being disqualified by reason of his being a peer.

3375. But the absence of the principal is not the fault of the sheriff?—The sheriff feels that he is bound to call an agent who is merely a servant, or the manager of the property. He might be, perhaps, able to find among the large ratepayers of the county the opportunity of selecting men interested in the taxation of the county who at present pay the taxes, and who are not represented.

3376. Is not that rather an objection tending to show that the sheriff is limited in his discretion, rather than that he has too much discretion?—I cannot hold that, having originally given evidence that I conceive that he has an uncontrolled discretion.

3377. In that paragraph which you read from Mr. Justice Keogh's charge, does he not refer to an undue limit placed upon the discretion of the high sheriff?—Yes. I have looked through the Acts of Parliament in force at the time when this Act came into operation, and through all the Acts since, and I find nothing whatever in any of them to fetter the discretion of the sheriff in the selection of his panel; and so, in point of law, I will venture to state that there is no Act of Parliament to control him. There may, perhaps, be in practice some moral force, or influence, which guides him; but in point of law there is no control over the sheriff.

3378. You believe, then, that the judge, upon that occasion, was wrong in alluding to some legal restraint being placed upon the discretion of the high sheriff?—It would be a bold statement for me to make; but I have only a newspaper report of what he said, and I do not know how far that statement might be controlled or explained if we had the whole of the learned judge's charge to the grand jury before us.

3379. You believe there is no legal difficulty in the way of the sheriff calling any person on the grand jury, whether he has property in the county or not?—There is no legal difficulty. He is bound, as I have already mentioned, to call a representative for each barony; but if that representative either chooses not to attend or is called, perhaps, without being apprised that the sheriff intended to call him, there is nothing to compel the sheriff to go on calling a representative from that barony until he gets one. He complies with the law by merely calling a representative, irrespective altogether whether such person is in attendance or not. The law is defective, inasmuch as it does not require each barony to be represented.

3380. He is prevented, of course, from calling a peer?—Yes, he is prevented from calling a peer. Lord John Browne, in his evidence the last day, gave a correct explanation of why it is that peers are excluded from the grand jury.

3381. Lord John Browne, I think, in his evidence stated that the reason why a peer could not be called was because, as criminal cases came before the grand jury, by some old law a peer would have a right to sit along with the judge; is there not another reason why a peer could not act on a jury on criminal cases, viz.: that, according to the law of England, every man must be judged or tried by his peers, so that a peer could not sit in trial upon a commoner?—Certainly, so long as the functions of the grand jury exist as at present, both civil and criminal, he could not do so, because the duties are so interwoven that he could not retire when the criminal business came on; but if an alteration of the law could be made, so as to make a change in that regard, I think that it would be desirable; but I wish the Committee distinctly to understand that I only object to the present mode of constituting the grand jury, having regard to the mode in which the grand jury rates are at present entirely paid by the occupiers. In point of fact, the present system is, practically, taxation without representation, which is bad in principle.

3382. Colonel French.] Do you contend that the occupier pays any portion of the cess?—I apprehend that he pays the whole of the grand jury rates.

3383. You stated that there was a limit upon the power of the sheriff; could there be any difficulty in Galway, the county to which you have alluded, in the sheriff forming a grand jury?—I should think that there ought to be no difficulty; but the sheriff who empanelled the spring grand jury appears to have left himself and the practice he pursued in empanelling that jury, open to the animadversions of the judge.

3384. Have you ever heard, or are you aware, that they could call three grand juries in the county of Galway, without going under 2,000 *l.* a year?—I am aware that, from its large extent, and the large resident proprietary which exists in the county of Galway, there ought to be no difficulty whatever in empanelling a grand jury on which property has its due, its fair, and, perhaps, as I will call it, its constitutional preponderance.

3385. Chairman.] I understand you to state that you object to the present mode of constituting the grand jury, in consequence of the unlimited power which you say the high sheriff possesses?—I do not confine it to that, though that is one of the reasons why the present mode of constituting the grand jury by the high sheriff is not satisfactory; in the next place the grand jury

Mr. P. R. Barry.

19 May 1868.

jury so constituted is not satisfactory, because it is taxation without representation; the ratepaying class in the county, the occupiers of property, are not directly represented upon that tribunal; those are the two reasons upon which I venture to base my opinion, that the grand jury, as at present constituted, is not in every respect satisfactory.

3386. Colonel *French*.] Has the grand jury any power of taxation, and has it not merely a veto on the recommendation or presentment made by the sessions?—Yes; with very trifling exceptions the grand jury has no power to initiate taxation.

3387. *Chairman*.] Would you propose that that the grand jury should be abolished altogether?—If there is not a change in the present mode of representing the ratepaying class by giving the ratepayers a better representation upon the grand jury, I would think that a change might be beneficially made; if, however, a fair share of representation is given to the payers of taxes on that body, I think that with some few points of detail being amended, the present system of transacting the fiscal business by the grand jury would answer very well.

3388. Would you propose to take it entirely out of the hands of the high sheriff?—I do not go to that length; I would suggest that if a representation were given to the ratepaying class, he should be bound to follow out that representation, so that either a person delegated in each barony, or a person elected from each barony, should be given a voice upon the grand jury, and should be called upon the grand jury.

3389. At present you are aware that the high sheriff is obliged to call somebody, but that that person need not attend; would you think it sufficient to oblige him to go on calling persons from that barony until some person attended?—That would be an amendment but it would not satisfy me; I think that to give satisfaction and to take away the outcry which at present exists, and which has existed for years against the grand jury system, the ratepaying class ought to have direct representation upon that body; I admit that there are great difficulties in that; there is great difficulty in having a frieze-coated ratepayer associated upon the grand inquest of the county with gentlemen of property and position.

3390. But do you think that is essentially necessary for a body that cannot initiate any taxation?—I do. I think it would be more satisfactory to the public at large.

3391. You merely advocate it because you think that it would be more satisfactory to the public; but you do not see any practical good resulting from it?—If the present system were amended as I suggest, I think it would work very well; but I would rather prefer that the ratepaying class should have a direct representation, whether that representation should be by the delegation of a magistrate, or of a large ratepayer or both from the sessions, to be called by the sheriff at the ensuing assizes to represent the barony, and to have some certainty by some machinery, at all events, that the barony should be represented.

3392. Colonel *French*.] But the question put to you by the honourable Chairman would secure the representation of the barony, by obliging the sheriff to go on calling until he found a representative for the barony; what is your view as to that?—That would be objectionable in this respect; that the person so called would be the nominee of the sheriff.

3393. How would he be the nominee of the sheriff, because he must be a 50 *l.* freeholder, must he not?—That was not mentioned previously; but at present, by what you propose, if he goes on calling, there can be no question, I venture to think, that the person so called is the nominee of the sheriff.

3394. You state that you think it would be very objectionable that a frieze-coated person, as you denominate him, should be associated with the magistrates and the landed proprietors at the assizes; have you ever known the magistrates, or the landed proprietors, object to act on the Poor Law Board, or the road sessions, with frieze-coated individuals?—I do not think I stated that it would be objectionable; I think I stated that it might be a difficulty.

3395. (Chairman.] Have you any other statement to make with respect to the constitution of the grand jury, beyond what you have mentioned now?—I proposed, under the first head which I mentioned, to call attention to what I conceive to be the defects, and then going back again I should under each subject point out what I submit as an amendment. Of course the Committee will take it for what it is worth; I would not venture to put it farther. I will now proceed to the mode of constituting the baronial sessions.

3396. I think that we have had the mode of constituting the baronial sessions very frequently stated before the Committee; will you, therefore, state it very briefly?—I think the intention of the Legislature in passing the Act of 1836, giving representation by the associated cesspayers at the baronial boards, was good; but in giving effect to that intention by legislation, it has not fully carried it out. The intention was to give the ratepayers such a representation at the baronial sessions as would enable them to prevent an improper or an improvident expenditure of money.

3397. Would you proceed at once to the suggestions which you make for an alteration?—I will do so. Then I propose, having regard to what I have observed upon the grand jury, that the fiscal and criminal duties of the grand jury should be separated; that the fiscal duties at present performed by the grand jury should be taken from the grand jury, and that they should be given to a county financial board.

3398. How would you constitute such a board? —I have read Lord John Browne's evidence upon that point, and I regret that upon one matter of detail I do not agree with him. He proposes to constitute the county board, which he suggests by a nomination from the justices. I do not think that that would give satisfaction, and I venture to propose that the county board first of all should consist of the justices of the peace representing the property qualification, and then that it should also be constituted of ratepayers; and whether the persons to sit upon that county board should be ratepayers elected directly from the ratepayers, or whether they should be persons delegated from the baronial sessions, is a matter of detail which might be hereafter determined, either one way or the other, to carry out my views. But in order to put some tangible plan before the Committee, I would suggest that the financial county board should consist of justices of the peace and of ratepayers, and that they should be be delegated by each baronial presentment sessions.

3399. Would you propose to confine the powers of this county board to those which are now exercised by the grand jury?—Yes; to that county board I would then transfer all the fiscal jurisdiction at present exercised by the grand jury.

3400. Do you agree with Lord John Browne in his definition of the powers of the grand jury; that they have no power of originating any taxation, and that they merely exercise a power of veto over what has been done?—I think the Noble Lord qualifies that definition and I agree with him, subject to his qualification, that except in a few particulars, they have no power of originating taxation. The powers exercised by the baronial sessions at present, I conceive, are somewhat defective, in their not being empowered to give prompt payment to the contractors; and the mode of accepting tenders at the adjourned sessions before the contract is approved of by the grand jury, I think, would admit of alteration. The accepting of tenders should take place *after* instead of *before* the contract was approved of. After the contract was finally approved of by the grand jury, the contract should then be entered into.

3401. Colonel *French*.] Not the sessions at all?—There might be a sessions for the purpose in each barony afterwards.

3402. *Chairman*.] You were speaking in the first instance, of this county board which you propose to establish; and you stated to the Committee, as I understood, that that county board should be partially elected and partially represented by the magistrates of the country?—That it should be a representation of both.

3403. Then in addition to that do you propose that there should be baronial boards?—No, I do not.

3404. Do you propose that the present presentment sessions should be continued?—I propose that the baronial presentment sessions should be continued.

3405. In the same form as at present?—Yes, but differently constituted.

3406. How would you propose that they should be constituted?—The ratepayers to sit at the baronial sessions should be elected direct by the ratepayers of the barony; that the barony, as Lord John Browne suggested, should be apportioned by the lord-lieutenant, or some other independent person, or body, into districts; and to ensure the fair distribution of the elective element, that each district should have a representative as at present in the electoral divisions under the poor law system.

3407. The baronial sessions and this county board then would be almost upon the same system, partially elected and partially composed of the magistrates?—Yes.

3408. Then, with respect to the suggestion as to the taking of tenders after instead of before the final court, I presume you refer to the continuance of the present system?—The continuance of the present system.

3409. Supposing the grand jury and the present sessions are continued, what you propose is that the tenders should be made after and not before the assizes?—My suggestion upon that point is already recommended by the Report of the Commission of 1842; they recommend that the tenders should be accepted after the assizes.

3410. Will you state to the Committee why you believe that the tenders ought to be accepted after the assizes, instead of at the presentment sessions?—At present the system is, that a contractor has to make application at three different sessions, and he has to attend at the assizes before he is certain whether he gets the contract for which he has tendered or not; therefore there is a degree of uncertainty about that at present, which has already formed the subject of observation by the Report of the Commission of 1842, and that Commission recommended the suggestion that I make in that regard, namely, that the tenders should be entered into after the assizes, thus saving a great many journeys on the part of the contractor and of his sureties, and a good deal of the expense attending the present system.

3411. At present do I understand you to say that he has to attend three sessions?—Practically it is so; perhaps I ought not to call one of them a sessions; there is in the county of Roscommon what is called a preliminary or preparatory sessions, which the secretary attends in each barony, to fill the applications for the works; he attends in the baronial town and the paper is filled by the secretary; that paper is then submitted to the presentment sessions, and having been approved of at the presentment sessions, it then comes next before the adjourned sessions, and the contractor enters into his contract there; and then he has to attend before the assizes to know whether his contract is granted or not; so that he has at all events two journeys to the sessions and one journey to the assizes, before he is able to say whether his contract is finally granted or approved of or not.

3412. By accepting the tenders after the assizes, instead of at the adjourned presentment sessions, as is done now, you would save him only one of those journeys, would you?—It would save him only one of those journeys, but considerable uncertainty as to the fate of his contract.

3413. Colonel *French*.] And you would give the sureties that additional journey?—No; it would save them that additional journey.

3414. *Chairman*.] Would you propose, then, the entire abolition of the adjourned sessions?—It is at present held before the assizes; but I propose that the adjourned sessions should take place after the assizes, and after the contract had been approved of finally. I would venture to refer the Committee on that point, in order to show that it is not a novel suggestion, to the recommendations of the Commission.

3415. Do you propose that there should be an adjourned sessions held after the assizes, and that the contractor should first go to the presentment sessions, and should then go to the assizes, and should in the third place go to those adjourned sessions after the assizes?—Yes, if his contract in the meantime was finally approved of; but in very many instances a contract approved of at the sessions is vetoed by the grand jury, and of course journeys take place in vain, because if the grand jury disapprove of the work, then all the trouble that has gone before falls to the ground.

3416. When is the sum to be presented, or how can the grand jury, without a contract being before them, know what sum to present, or is the sum to be presented after a contract is received?—I propose that when the presentment is approved of at the sessions, the county surveyor,

Mr. P. R. Sharkey.

14 May 1868.

veyor, whose duty it would be to advise the sessions, should fix the limit, and that the grand jury should then present an estimated sum, and place it upon the levy, as a fund for the payment of the contractor, that being the maximum sum.

3417. Colonel *French*.] Without specification, plan, or anything of the kind?—Yes.

3418. *Chairman*.] Is it, in your opinion, a defect, that contractors at present are obliged to attend at the assizes with their securities?—In cases where the tenders are adjourned from the sessions to the assizes, they are.

3419. But only in such cases?—Only in such cases.

3420. Where the tenders are accepted at the sessions, the contractor is not obliged to attend at the assizes, nor are his sureties obliged to attend; is not that so?—The contractor need not attend, nor his sureties, unless he goes to hear the fate of his contract.

3421. In reality, therefore, at present, he is not obliged to make this third journey?—He is not obliged to make this third journey, but in effect he does so.

3422. He does it for his own gratification, to know how his contract is likely to fare, does he not?—Yes.

3423. Colonel *French*.] Is not the presentment sessions a better body to decide the solvency of the securities than the grand jury?—I do not put that duty upon the grand jury; I think the adjourned presentment sessions are unquestionably the best body for that purpose.

3424. *Chairman*.] Have you any other suggestion to make?—I have. The first suggestion I had to make was, that there should be only one sessions during the year at which new works should be presented. First of all, that the county fiscal board should be elected for a year; that they should continue in office for a year, and that one-half of the body should go out in rotation; that the baronial sessions should in like manner be elected for a year, and that they should go out by rotation, one-half at the end of the first year, and so on.

3425. And that they should meet twice a year?—I propose that there should be only one sessions at which new works should be considered, and that no new work should be considered until full notice was given to the county surveyor, to enable him to inspect that new work, and clearly and beyond question to give his advice to the sessions as to whether it was a work which ought to be executed or not. Then I propose that those applications approved of at that baronial sessions should go to the county board at the spring or summer period of the year, according to the time they are constituted; and that that board, exercising the functions which the grand jury at present exercise, should have not only the power of vetoing it, but should also have the power of moderating it. I think that that board ought to receive more jurisdiction than the grand jury has at present; for very frequently, by the grand jury not having the power to moderate or lessen the amount granted by a sessions, a presentment falls to the ground, which would otherwise receive the sanction of the grand jury. I propose, then, after the county board approves the work, that there should be a sessions held after the spring or summer time of the year, as the case may be, at which tenders would be received for works previously approved of at the baronial sessions, and sanctioned by the county board. Then, the next suggestion I would make is, in order to meet the present inconvenience that there is by reason of the contractors not receiving prompt payment when their works are done; at present a work is executed in the month of October or November; notice is given to the county surveyor, and the work having been executed an application for payment is made for the November sessions.

3426. Colonel *French*.] There is no November sessions?—November and December; it is the same thing; it is generally December. In some counties it is November, but we will call it the winter sessions, to avoid any question. The contractor applies for payment at the winter sessions, and his application, I will assume, is allowed at the sessions; therefore in the opinion of the sessions he is entitled to payment; but he has to wait until the following assizes, the March assizes, before he reaps the fruit of his labour and expenditure before he is paid. I propose then, in order to remove that objection (which is also the subject of animadversion by the Commission of 1842, and which was one of the points that the Commission at that time condemned), that each baronial sessions should be armed with full authority, upon receiving the report of the county surveyor that the work was done, to pay the contractor either the whole or a portion of his money, instead of keeping him out of his money for a period of three, and in some cases four months, as at present.

3427. *Chairman*.] Did you hear Mr. Hill's evidence with respect to the payment of contractors before the grand jury approved of the works?—I did not hear Mr. Hill's evidence.

3428. Are you aware that there is some power at present by which advances can be made to contractors?—There is a power, but in most counties, I think (I speak certainly of two or three), it is not given effect to. There are no ways and means for giving effect to it. I am aware that the county surveyor has a power of recommending, or of advising, a payment of three-fourths of the contract; but there are no funds to pay it, and that is, I believe, one reason why that section of the Act is inoperative.

3429. Colonel *French*.] You say that you would allow the sessions to pay their contractor the full amount of his contract at the sessions?—I think either the full amount, or a proportionate part.

3430. Is not the contractor bound to keep his contract in repair from assizes to assizes?—That is because of the defects of the system.

3431. But what would become of a road, for instance, between the time that a contractor was paid and the following assizes, if it was not in anybody's hands?—If it is merely putting a road into repair, by expending so much macadam upon it; then, I think, when he has put on it that quantity of macadam, and otherwise performed his contract, it is reasonable to suppose that he would be paid just the same as for a road through any gentleman's farm.

3432. But is he not bound to keep the ruts filled in, to keep the water tables clean, and to keep the sides in proper order till the following assizes?—No doubt that prolonged duty is cast upon him owing to the present system.

3433. If you pay him you will not get him to do that, will you?—Certainly not; but if he enters into a contract to do a certain work, and he does that work at a given time, I think you have a right to pay him instead of throwing the

obligation

obligation upon him of keeping up his work for four or five months afterwards, until you, his employer, are in funds to pay him. Prompt payment would tend to diminish the cost of works.

3434. If you qualify your answer, by saying that not more than three-fourths should be paid, I will agree with you; but must you not keep something in hand to make him keep up his contract until the new contract could be entered into?—In the case of permanent contracts, which, I think, prevail generally, such a possibility as that would not arise, because the contractors are bound to keep them in repair from year to year. This would only apply to the case of bridges, or the cutting down of a hill, or other works of a like nature, which I call temporary works—the forming of a road and putting it into order, and such like. It is very hard to call upon a man, when he has executed that work to the full letter of his obligation, to keep it in perfectly good order until the following assizes until you are in a position to pay him; but if you were in a position to pay him off when he had done his work, I think it would lead to economy of expenditure, to a better performance of the works, and to a better class of contractors being obtained.

3435. Surely, if you paid a man for a bridge directly he had put up that bridge, it might be all very well to the eye at the present time, but that bridge, before the next assizes, might tumble down from some inferior work; and what are you to do then, having paid the money, and having no control over the contractor?—What would you do in the private relations of life in such a case?

3436. *Sir Charles Lanyon*.] What cause can you assign for paying contractors in a different way under grand jury presentments from every other system that is known in the country for the payment of contractors?—Perhaps the other systems, to my mind, if I knew them, might be equally objectionable; I think the closer you assimilate public to private contracts the better.

3437. Is such a thing known to a private contract, where a man is contracted to be paid the moment the work is executed?—I did not say the moment the work was executed; I said at the assizes held after the execution of the work the contractor ought to get a payment, if not of the whole of his money, certainly on account; I adopt the Honourable Member for Down's view as to the three-fourths.

3438. *Chairman*.] Your proposal, then, is, that there should be greater facility given for advancing the payment to contractors?—Certainly, when their work was either wholly or partly completed.

3439. Colonel *French*.] But why should a contractor be paid before his contract has been performed; is it not the arrangement into which he enters that he should have the work finished at a certain time, and that if it is approved of by the county surveyor he is to be paid at the coming assizes?—Yes, I think the Legislature, by the Act of 1836, affirmed the principle that it was desirable he should receive assistance by sanctioning payments on account; but, unfortunately, the Legislature in passing that Act did not provide means for carrying it into effect.

3440. But is not the contract that the work shall be performed, to be finished by a certain time, and if approved of by the grand jury, that the contractor is to receive his money at the next assizes?—It is deferred payment; he either must give bad value in the execution of the work, or he must increase the expense, in order to compensate himself for the undue length of time he will be out of his money.

Mr. F. B. [illegible]

15 May 1868.

3441. *Sir Charles Lanyon*.] In every private contract, is not a certain sum reserved until a certain time has expired after the completion of the work, so as to insure its being properly done?—Yes, certainly; and I take it to be either one-fourth or one-third. I think the Legislature has fixed one-fourth; I should say that was a reasonable sum to hold in hand, to see that the work should turn out as well as it looked.

3442. Do you propose that the Government should subsidise the contractor?—I do not propose that the Government should subsidise the contractor, but that the Board should borrow the money upon the rates from the bank, and not from the Government.

3443. I understand that you intend that they should advance money to the contractor upon the work about to be done?—Upon work actually done, by payment on account.

3444. But if the work is not done, it is not on account; you mean before the work is completed?—Before the work is completed.

3445. Is not that a kind of subsidy?—It is a payment on account of the work before execution of the entire.

3446. And if the work is never completed, how do you manage then?—Then you have a fund in hand; you must look to the county surveyor, to see that it is not overpaid.

3447. *Chairman*.] I understand you to suppose that, under the present law, advances can be made to the amount of three-fourths to contractors?—Yes.

3448. But you say that there would be a difficulty in doing that, in consequence of the want of funds?—Yes.

3449. And you propose that some means should be provided by which money could be raised before hand, so as to have a fund in hand to make those advances which at present are illegal?—Quite so.

3450. Colonel *French*.] Would it be desirable that the county surveyor should make an estimate of the probable amount which he might consider it advisable to pay when the roads were approved of by him, in order that there might be a fund presented by the grand jury, to enable him to make those payments whenever he considered them desirable?—I conceive that there ought to be an estimate made by the county surveyor, as I propose, and the district surveyor (as I shall mention in a subsequent part of my evidence) to each sessions, and that there should be a fund always in the hands of the treasurer, to be drawn upon by the advice, and upon the recommendation of the county surveyor by the baronial sessions; and that those drafts should be honoured by the person acting as treasurer, either the county bank, or the county treasurer, as the case may be; but I conceive that it is most undesirable (and the county surveyors themselves as a body, I am sure, would not wish) that you should cast upon them the duty of disbursing public money to so large an extent as that proposal of the Honourable Member must lead to throughout Ireland.

3451. *Chairman*.] The next point, I think, to which you wish to call attention, is the appointment of district surveyors instead of assistants?—Yes. With a view of having the time and attention

attention of the county surveyors directed exclusively to the business of their counties, and to seeing that the works contracted for are well performed and executed, I should first of all abolish the present system of appointing county surveyors' assistants. I do not think I need go into the reasons for that; for I think it has been set forth before the Committee in the evidence given; and I should then require that the county should be divided into districts. I would appoint to each district, according to the size and extent of the county, a district surveyor, and I should require him to give his exclusive time and attention to the duties of his office; and, in order to insure good men, or men such as at present fill the important office of county surveyor, and enable them to the full amount of confidence that the Honourable Member for Roscommon would repose in them for the disbursement of the public funds, I would pay them well. They are responsible officers, and a great deal of the expenditure of public money in the county takes place under their supervision and upon their recommendation; it is a highly responsible office; the duties should be discharged by respectable men, and they should not have too much duty cast upon them, but should be well paid for whatever duties they discharge. I conceive that they ought to be the best paid officers of the county. I would suggest that all applications to sessions for the expenditure of public money upon new works should originate with the county surveyor. I would do away with the system, which is as bad as it can be, namely, of contractors originating applications for the expenditure of money. On the attention of the district surveyor being called by one or two ratepayers to the necessity for the repair of a road, or the building of a bridge, or any other work, I would require him to inspect the work in question, and, if he thought fit, to bring forward an application in respect to that work, that he should do so at the next baronial sessions. You thus get rid of the opportunity on the part of the men who act as contractors, of hoodwinking the sessions, and passing works which turn out afterwards ought never to have been passed.

3452. Do I rightly understand you to say that you would leave it to the discretion of the county surveyor as to whether those applications for works should be made, or not?—His report to the sessions, made after personal examination, I would venture to think, ought to carry great weight with it.

3453. But do you mean to say that it should be binding upon the sessions; that in point of fact no new work could be applied for, unless the county surveyor chose to apply for it?—I will not push it to that extent, but I should think his report to the sessions ought to be given, before any application originating a work is entertained.

3454. But is not his report always given upon every work, as it comes up before the sessions present?—It is given, but in a way which I think is not satisfactory. In the first place he has to rely very much upon his assistant. Under the present law he receives notice of the intention to apply for those works. It is impossible, in a large county, for the county surveyor himself to inspect every work for which notice is given, and he must therefore trust to the opinion of his assistants, who receive 50 *l.* a-year for their services. Their opinions may not always be correct, but owing to the impossibility at present of inspecting every work applied for, he is left, in a great measure, to rely upon the opinions of his assistants.

3455. But, as I understand, that is one of the evils of the present system of assistants; if assistants were done away with, and district surveyors appointed, then there would be no further alteration in the law required?—No; because the law at present assumes that each work shall be inspected by the surveyor, but it should be an obligation upon him to report to each baronial sessions, having personally visited the work, and he should give the result of that visit in a report to the sessions, which should be circulated and published beforehand.

3456. But you will still leave it open to any person in the district to propose any new work, or any repair of works which he might think necessary?—Yes; if the county surveyor, on visiting the locality, was of opinion that it was a work which ought not to be brought forward in sessions, I should then give the ratepayer the opportunity of bringing forward his application independently; but if the county surveyor considered, on inspecting it, that it was a case in which there ought to be an expenditure of public money, I should then require the district surveyor to bring it before the baronial sessions.

3457. What would be the object of making it go directly to the county surveyor, instead of its going, as it does now, directly before the sessions from the ratepayers themselves?—The county surveyor would be very unwilling to originate any applications for new works, unless they were absolutely required; but if it is left, as at present, to the uncontrolled discretion of that class of persons called road contractors, their inventive genius will, as it is known they do now, suggest a variety of works upon which it may seem desirable to expend public money, which might just as well get on for the next 20 years without that expenditure as perhaps they had done for the 20 years before.

3458. I cannot see the difference which would take place under the change which you propose, except that the district surveyor should look at it instead of the assistant surveyor; because, under your proposal, the district surveyor would have to go and visit those works, and, if he disapproved of them, still the ratepayer would have a right to bring them before the sessions?—That is a matter of detail, and I am of course in the hands of the Committee; but, however, it does not affect the principle of the scheme which I propose.

3459. With respect to the collection of the grand jury cess, have you any proposal to make?—I have no suggestion to make as to that; but it, perhaps, might be for the consideration of the Committee whether or not some plan might be devised by which the grand jury cess and the poor rates could be collected by one and the same person, or by the same machinery.

3460. The poor rate collection in Ireland is effected now at a much lower rate than the grand jury cess, is it not?—It is.

3461. Do you see any reason why there should be a great disproportion between the charges for collection in the two cases?—I think that has been touched upon by Lord John Browne, in his evidence. The districts given to poor rate collectors are much smaller, and the difficulty in getting sureties is not so great; but, if the baronies were divided into districts as nearly as possible conterminous with the present electoral divisions.

Mr. P. B. Sharkey.

15 May 1868.

divisions, it would not be beyond possibility to devise a machinery by which all the local rates could be collected in one office.

3462. Do you not believe that if the collection of the grand jury cess were transferred to the poor rate collectors, the grand jury cess would be collected at a much lower rate than it is, and with equal security?—Certainly; I see that in the county of Roscommon, they pay at the rate of 9 *d.* in the pound, which is much higher than a landed proprietor pays for the collection of his rents; the duty is no doubt very troublesome and very onerous, but divided over the whole year it is not at all a difficult duty, and not one requiring to be paid at a high rate, except that in order to provide responsible persons as sureties, you must get responsible persons as collectors, and you must pay them high accordingly.

3463. In consequence of the great size of the districts, and the large amount of the cess?—Yes.

3464. Colonel *French.*] The poor law collectors are appointed by different bodies, are they not?—Yes; that suggestion would require a change both in the poor law system and in the grand jury system.

3465. General *Dunne.*] Are you clearly of opinion that the union of the collection of the two rates would be advantageous?—Having regard to the low rate at which the poor rate is collected, and the high rate at which the grand jury cess is collected, I think it is an alteration which would be desirable.

3466. The cess collectors very often collect the income tax also, do they not?—They do.

3467. What is the rate at which the income tax is collected?—I am not able to say.

3468. But that is united very often with the poor law rates, is it not?—Yes.

3469. And with the collection of the cess in some counties?—Yes.

3470. Do you not think that there is great inconvenience in the cess collectors coming in and giving their securities at every assizes?—There is.

3471. Would you see any objection to the law being assimilated to the poor law in that respect, and the securities being taken for a considerable time?—According to the present state of the law, there would be a legal objection to that.

3472. But if the law were changed, would you see any objection to such an arrangement?—If it could be done, I think it would be very desirable. It would lessen the expense, and the trouble and inconvenience which are thrown upon the collector and upon the collector's sureties.

3473. Are not the same securities very often renewed?—Yes, but then you have, on the other hand, to consider that, in the space of six months, a man who may be to-day a very solvent man, may become an insolvent person.

3474. Would there be any objection to taking them before the magistrates, or to any officers taking the securities?—Perhaps the poor law system might be better, to take them before a Master in Chancery; I would give facilities of that kind, guarding, of course, against abuse.

3475. Is not that annual trouble and inconvenience a great drawback to the cess collectors?—It is.

3476. *Chairman.*] Is it not the fact, that at present the collectors are not permanent officers of the county, but are merely appointed for collecting the cess between one assize and another?—Yes.

3477. Would not the change which you propose make them permanent officers, having claims upon the county for every consideration which a permanent officer has?—I understand the honourable and gallant Member to say that the appointment should continue half-yearly, as at present, but unless there was a change in the appointments, the security should be deemed continuous; I think that it might be very advantageous to impose a duty upon some officer from time to time, to see that the solvency of the securities remained the same.

3478. In what consists the appointment at each assizes of the collectors, if it does not consist in their re-entering into their securities?—It is a fiction in point of practice. They go through the form, I think. Probably the only person who would have to complain of any change would be the solicitor of the grand jury, who would be deprived of his fees every half year. I think generally speaking that you might work the system in the mode proposed by the honourable Member.

3479. Colonel *French.*] With regard to those fees to the solicitor, for taking the collector's bonds, what law is there as to that?—The general law, namely, that he is a professional man, and has to be paid for his professional services.

3480. But what does he do?—He prepares the bond.

3481. Is it not a printed form?—It might be a printed form, but I think, in most cases, the solicitors, with a view to making their proper charge, have it engrossed. That has been the practice in the county of Galway.

3482. General *Dunne.*] Is there not a great difficulty in the cess collector collecting the cess from tenants under 4 *l.*?—Yes, there is.

3483. Would you recommend that the 4 *l.* be placed under the poor rate, and paid entirely by the landlord?—I have a suggestion going further than that; but which I think, perhaps, it would be better not to mention at present.

3484. Do you think that placing the 4 *l.* upon the landlord, would not be a great advantage?—It certainly would, in my view of the case be a great advantage, and it would facilitate the collection of the rates.

3485. Is it not the fact that they do not at this moment collect the cess very often from the change of inhabitants?—I am not able to speak with authority as to that; but I think that in some counties they require the collectors to pay in at each assizes the full amount of their warrant. I do not know whether that acts injuriously upon collectors or not.

3486. If the collector pays in the full amount of his warrant, and does not collect the full amount, of course the loss must fall upon him?—It must.

3487. Assuming that to be the case, do you not think that that is one of the reasons which makes the cess collector's demand a higher rate of poundage for the collection?—It may form an element, together with the difficulty in getting respectable persons to become sureties. Unless a man has a good position in his county, he will not get persons of wealth and respectability to become sureties for him; and there is a difficulty in getting the same class of persons to collect the grand jury cess as you get to collect the Poor Law assessment.

3488. *Chairman.*]

Mr. P. B. Shirley.

15 May 1868.

3488. *Chairman.*] Following up the statement which you made with respect to its being advisable to make the landlord pay for all tenements under 4 *l.*, would you propose that the landlord should pay directly any proportion of the cess above 4 *l.*?—My opinion is, that a change in the law in that respect is very desirable. As to the benefit which the tenants would derive, it certainly is questionable. I would propose that the county rate should be divided equally between the landlord and the occupier, and although the occupier may not derive the full amount of benefit that it is supposed he would derive from that change, it would, at all events, take away what is felt to be an injustice or a grievance, whether of a sentimental character, as some persons only consider it, or otherwise, viz., that the payers of the tax have at present no voice in the disbursement of the money which is collected from them.

3489. It would give the landlords a direct interest in every alteration made in the amount of the rate, would it not?—It would; and I might call the attention of the Committee to a most important Report to Parliament upon this subject some years ago, which, I think, has not been carried in the recollection of most honourable Members. This subject was considered very fully by a Committee of this House, on which the late Lord Palmerston, Mr. Secretary Peel, Viscount Althorpe, Viscount Milton, Lord Ashley, Mr. Watkin Williams Wynn, and Mr. Vernon Smith, sat; in fact, it was a Committee constituted so as to represent the landed interest very largely. That Committee entered into the consideration of the question, and having had several meetings, and having taken a quantity of evidence, their deliberations resulted in the compilation of a Blue Book of great size; that Committee reported upon that very question of the division of the rate between the landowners and the occupiers. That was in the year 1830, and I will just read one extract from that Report. The Committee fully considered that question, and they recommended to Parliament in their Report a change in the law, to the full extent of which I do not go, for they recommended the entire payment of the grand jury rate by the landlord, and they give their reasons for so doing. The passage is as follows; it is under the heading of "Improvement of the Grand Jury Laws." "The first consideration that presents itself is, the question of the apportionment of the expenses. These taxes are imposed by the grand jurors, or principal landed proprietors; they are paid by the occupying tenants, in many cases the poorest classes of cottier peasantry; they are expended to a certain extent, in roads and bridges, which frequently add considerable value to the estates of the grand jurors, and other inheritors of land; but the pecuniary means of completing these improvements are furnished by those who have a less direct and permanent interest in the soil." They go on to say: "Your Committee have no hesitation in expressing their decided opinion, that as a check upon expenditure, and a security for the rigid examination of accounts in the execution of public works, the occupying tenant should, in the case of all future contracts, be relieved from the burthen of paying the entire county assessments, and that such assessments should, in the whole or in part, be imposed upon the landlords. It may be expected that this arrangement will render grand jurors more vigilant in preventing an undue increase of taxes which will fall directly on themselves, and it will be their interest to have the public works executed with skill and with economy, in order to obviate the necessity of new and augmented expenditure for repairs. Under this alteration of system, the imposer will also be the payer of the tax, and the person who is permanently benefited by the work, will be compelled to furnish the means for its execution. The policy of making this change has been more than once recommended to the consideration of Parliament. Your Committee not only adopt the principle with a view to the relief of the occupying tenants, and to the more perfect and economical execution of public works, but they venture to express their extreme anxiety that no time should be lost in carrying it into practical effect with the least delay."

3490. Mr. *Maguire.*] Will you give the names of that Committee?—Mr. Spring Rice (Chairman), Lord F. L. Gower, Sir J. Newport, Sir Robert Peel (who was then Secretary for Ireland), Viscount Althorpe, Viscount Milton, Lord Ashley, Mr. Brownlow, Mr. Dawson, Mr. Fitzgerald, Mr. Charles Grant, Viscount Stopford, Mr. Hope, Lord John Russell, Mr. Kennedy, Mr. Lamb, Mr. Sturges Bourne, Mr. Daniel O'Connell, Lord Oxmantown, Viscount Palmerston, Mr. John H. Parnell, Mr. Leslie Foster, Mr. Doherty (afterwards, I believe, Chief Justice); Mr. Vernon Smith, Mr. Stanley, Mr. W. Williams Wynn.

3491. Were they parties to that Report?—The Report which I have just read emanated from them.

3492. Colonel *Forde.*] Did not the Act of 1837 take that recommendation into account, and embody it to a certain extent?—I should think that it did not, inasmuch as it ignores its recommendation as to the payment of the rate by the landlord altogether.

3493. It did not ignore it altogether when it gave the cesspayers a voice at the baronial sessions, the same as the magistrates?—But the Report deals with the payment of the tax, and I think that the Act of 1836 ignores that altogether.

3494. *Chairman.*] What you have read is a recommendation upon the ground that the taxation was levied altogether at that time upon the landlords, and that the occupiers had no voice whatever in the imposition of the tax?—The grounds of that report were, first, that the tax was paid by the occupiers, who, in many cases, were the poorest class of the cottier peasantry; second, that the tax, when collected, was expended to a certain extent upon roads and bridges which frequently add considerable value to the estates of grand jurors and other inheritors of land; third, that the imposers were not the payers of the tax; and fourth, that the person permanently benefited by the work is not the person who furnishes the means for its execution. Those are the four grounds, I think, upon which the recommendation of the Committee was based.

3495. Three of those grounds were not affected by the Act of 1837, but one of them was to a certain extent?—To a certain extent.

3496. Colonel *Forde.*] You stated, did you not, in the commencement of your examination, that you object to the high sheriffs appointing the grand jury?—I said that the present system of constituting the grand jury was not satisfactory.

3497. The

Mr. P. B. Sharkey.

15 May 1868.

3497. The sheriff is an officer, is he not, who only holds office for a year?—He holds office for a year.

3498. Therefore there can be no sort of feeling that the sheriff is biassed every time by party consideration?—I did not enter into the question of party at all; I think the word did not escape my lips.

3499. I will qualify it by saying favouritism?—"Improper persons being put upon the grand jury," was the expression I used.

3500. But a sheriff being in office only a year, surely the sort of impropriety of which you speak could not naturally go on for more than one year?—Only for one year by the same officer.

3501. Do you think that the high sheriffs would all combine, so as to join in the same practice?—No, I have a higher opinion of the high sheriffs, and the mode in which they do their duty. The full extent to which I go, is that I think that the present mode of constituting grand juries is not so satisfactory as it ought to be, and as it might be.

3502. You stated, did you not, that the grand jurors have no qualification?—I think that a grand juror need not have any qualification.

3503. But he must be a 50*l.* freeholder, must he not?—No.

3504. Or the heir apparent to a certain property?—No.

3505. You will not find it in Fosse, I allow; but you will find it in the original law, will you not?—You will find some very general words used, "duly qualified according to law." If you go back to the very earliest period, when the functions of the grand jury were defined or settled by legislation, you will find you are just in the same state of doubt as to what is meant by those words. I have taken the trouble to go back, and endeavoured to find what was the proper interpretation of them; but I was unable to find that the law attaches any defined meaning to them. It gives no definition of what is "duly qualified according to law."

3506. But is it not recognised according to law that a grand juror must be a 50*l.* freeholder, or a leaseholder to a certain amount, or the heir apparent to a certain property, or an agent to a proprietor having a certain amount of property?—I do not understand how anything can be recognised as law which is not law; but practically there is that idea.

3507. General *Dunne.*] In practice, is anyone ever put on who is not connected with property in the county?—Directly, or indirectly, such as an agent, or the son of a proprietor.

3508. Colonel *Forde.*] Do you think that the grand jury are at all a check upon the expenditure which is proposed at the road sessions?—Certainly.

3509. And rather a wholesome check?—I conceive them often to be a very wholesome check.

3510. Did you not state that you would like to get rid of that check?—I would only get rid of that check for the purpose of taking away the feeling which at present exists, that it is taxation without representation.

3511. And you would take away a very wholesome check to do away with that feeling?—To create an equally wholesome check.

3512. You stated also, did you not, that you would like to give power to the grand jury to modify the presentments after they had been sanctioned by the sessions?—I would certainly, for this reason: that very often a presentment comes up from sessions in which it is found, when time is given to make better inquiries, that the sum presented is in excess of what it ought to be; and the grand jury have no power to cut it down. If they had, a very useful work might perhaps be permitted to proceed, and be executed without postponing it off for a period of perhaps six or eight months according to the period of the year.

3513. If a work of that nature had to be performed, would it be very material that it should lie over, because it can only be a very trifling work?—If you assume anything, you may as well assume that it might be an important work. I have known important works nilled at the assizes, because it was found that the amount for which the contractor had tendered for the contract was beyond that which he ought really to get for the work, and therefore the grand jury had no alternative but to nil the presentment.

3514. *Chairman.*] Have you ever known them, on the other hand, to pass a presentment which they considered to be too high, because it would cause great public inconvenience to nil it?—I cannot say that I have.

3515. But might not such a thing arise that a presentment might pass at too high a rate, in consequence of the great public inconvenience which might result from the work being neglected altogether?—I cannot say that I know an instance in which that reason operated to cause them to pass an exorbitant presentment.

3516. Colonel *Forde.*] You say that you would give power to the county surveyor to originate all new works?—I said that, in case of his having received notice, and visited the locality if he should think that it was a work to be brought forward, he should bring it forward; but that, in the event of his being of a different opinion, then the ratepayer should be able to bring forward the application at the sessions.

3517. Then you would take away the privilege which is now granted to two ratepayers of originating a work?—Subject to what I have said, I would.

3518. Do you not know that new works must come, in the first instance, before the grand jury to be certified?—That is in the case of new roads, or cutting up a man's land; but what I call a new work is a work which would require the expenditure of money, the work being already in existence, but which had got out of repair, and which required the expenditure of fresh money.

3519. That is only as to the repair of a road, is it?—That is only as to the repair of a road.

3520. But I do not call those new works?—Then we have been misunderstanding each other. I will clear that up by stating at once what I mean by new works. I have not touched in my evidence, except on the first day upon a new work which would require certification by the grand jury.

3521. I do not consider that the repair of a road is at all a new work. I consider that a new work is either cutting down a hill, or building a courthouse, or a bridge, or such things as that; would not that be your view?—In Roscommon, in the last schedule of applications for payments, they call such things as paving 150 perches of a road, and repairing 300 perches, and the building of a broken-down bridge, new works. Then to

Mr. P. B. Shanly.

16 May 1862.

distinguish them from the others, they call the others "works of maintenance," or perpetual continuance.

3522. You propose, do you not, that the associated cesspayers should be elected?—I do.

3523. How would you suggest that that should be done?—To start with, I should have the baronies divided, in the mode suggested by Lord John Browne.

3524. By whom would they be divided?—By the Lord Lieutenant, as, I think, Lord John Browne proposes.

3525. Why not by the grand jury?—The grand jury, I think, might do it, that is to say, if you continue the grand jury as at present.

3526. Then how would you propose that those cesspayers should be nominated for election?—I should assimilate as much as possible the practice of electing the ratepayers to the practice which at present exists under the Poor Law Board.

3527. You would say that when those divisions were made, a certain qualified person should be put in nomination for the office of cesspayer?—Yes.

3528. Would you say that that should be done, for instance, the day before the meeting of the grand jury for the summer assizes?—There should be timely notice given to enable the person put in nomination to say whether he will act or not, and the name should be before the constituency.

3529. That would be the case the same as it is, in fact, under the poor law system?—It would be the same as it is under the Poor Law.

3530. There the names have to be in before the 2nd of March, I think?—Yes.

3531. I suggested that they should be in the day before the meeting of the grand jury for fiscal business on the summer assizes, because there is more time between summer and spring for the elections?—I dare say that would work in practice, and there would be no difficulty in giving effect to that as a matter of detail.

3532. It is entirely to avoid expense that I am making the suggestion. Supposing there was only one nomination, they would not require an election for that barony?—No.

3533. But if there were two or more nominations, then do you think the secretary of the grand jury should be empowered to hold the election the same as the clerk of the Poor Law Guardians does now?—Yes, with the aid of the police and with written papers.

3534. And the secretary of the grand jury, in your opinion, would be the best officer to carry out that work?—I suppose you would consider him analogous in point of position and duty to the clerk of the union; in that way he would be so.

3535. The cesspayer thus nominated should act for a year, I presume?—He should act for a year.

3536. That cesspayer should not be elected for two successive years?—I think the principle of the general law of rotation would be perhaps as good as any other, as it has received the sanction of the Legislature. After a certain time he should go out of office, and a fresh person should be elected, but he should be eligible to be elected again.

3537. Would you make any provision that in case of death, or illness, vacancies should be filled up?—I should fill up the vacancies in the mode adopted under the Poor Law system.

3538. Colonel French.) You propose to vest in the grand jury a power of reducing a presentment that has been sent up from the road sessions, do you not?—I do.

3539. How would you manage where the contract has been entered into for a certain sum, and securities have been given; if the grand jury refuse that sum, of course the contract must fall to the ground?—You leave out of consideration my suggestion that the contract is not to be entered into until after the assizes.

3540. You have stated, I think, that you would propose to divide the present duties of the grand jury, fiscal and criminal, into two parts?—I would take away from the grand jury their fiscal power.

3541. Are you aware that, under the present fiscal system, at each assizes you have, without any expense, the attendance of the proprietors, the attendance of the body from whom the grand panel is taken, and by whom this business is transacted, without one penny of expense being thrown on the county?—I am aware of that, and by the plan which I propose the same result would be obtained without expense.

3542. You propose to destroy a system with the working of which at this moment every body, gentle and simple, is acquainted?—I propose only one fundamental change, and that is with respect to separating the fiscal from the criminal business, and vesting the fiscal business in an unpaid board, elected and formed in a different manner from the mode in which the grand juries are now formed.

3543. Does any reason for proposing such a change of system arise from the results of the present system?—It does.

3544. Will you tell me any evil result from the present system which would be met or remedied by your suggestion?—The change would give the ratepaying class a direct representation upon that board; and, at present, they have not a direct representation. That is one of my reasons.

3545. Is there any objection to this system; do you think that the system of roads is more expensive under the present system?—I have not said a word upon that subject. I must ask the Honourable Member to confine his questions to such evidence as I have given. I did not say a word about the expense of roads. I simply objected to the mode of constituting the grand jury at present.

3546. But you object to the fiscal system, under which the results of that system of roads come out, do you not?—I object to the present mode of constituting the grand jury, having regard to the persons who at present pay the grand jury tax.

3547. One of the results then is that you think there is some hardship on the cesspayers?—It is wrong in principle.

3548. It is merely a question of taxation without representation?—Yes; I think it is unjust that a tenant-at-will should have to make the important roads and bridges leading to his farm, which subject him to an increase of rent for the advantage of the country, and that then the landlord should obtain an extra rent for those facilities for which the tenant has paid. That is also an objection which I make.

3549. You propose to do away with an inexpensive system, and you propose to create a system

Mr. P. B. [illegible].

14 May 1868.

system of financial boards, do you not?—Certainly not; it would be no additional expense.

3550. Do you mean to say that these boards will act for nothing?—Most certainly, and they would be unworthy of their position as citizens if they did not.

3551. My own opinion is, that it will end in every member of the boards being paid?—I am not putting before the Committee the Honourable Member's scheme. I am putting before the Committee my own scheme.

3552. But how do you expect men to act without being paid?—As they do at present.

3553. It is your own private opinion that these men would act without payment?—Certainly.

3554. You think that they would come up to attend the baronial sessions whenever they were required; they, under the present system, being brought in on that business, and other business only twice a year?—At present, persons in that position, discharge the functions of poor law guardians, and they discharge the fiscal functions of grand juries, and I do not think that, because I propose to give direct representation, it is at all a fair inference that I do so at an increased expenditure. I say distinctly that I do not propose any such thing. The Bill introduced by Sir George Grey upon the system of county and financial boards and supervision upon the part of the Board of Works, over the county surveyor, or doing away with the county surveyor, and vesting the duties in the Board, then presided over by Sir Richard Griffith, was an expensive system. That system was subsequently given shape to, in a Bill introduced by Sir Denham Norreys. That was an expensive system, but I adhere strictly to the present system, modifying it in certain particulars, it being an inexpensive system.

3555. You stated, did you not, that you would compel the county surveyor to originate works and the repairs of new works, &c., in each of the baronial sessions?—I did not go to that length; I went to the extent of saying that if he, on visiting works for which notice had been previously given, thought they were of a kind to be originated, he should originate them; but that if he was of opinion that they were not so he should so state it to the person noticing, and such person should then be at liberty to bring forward his application, as at present, to the road sessions.

3556. Then you would want no alteration in the law as at present fixed?—No; in practice the law is not given effect to, because it is impossible for the county surveyor to visit every work intended to be brought forward at the presentment sessions in the 10 days before the session.

3557. But, I believe, the county surveyor is in the habit of doing so, and is prepared to be in attendance at the road sessions to state his opinion as to the cost of the work proposed?—He is, with the aids that his assistant surveyors give him; but it is utterly impossible in such counties as Roscommon, Mayo, and Galway, for the county surveyor, within the time allowed by law at present, personally to visit and properly inspect every work which is proposed to be brought forward within the succeeding 10 days.

3558. Would you call a thing impossible which has been proved to be done?—I am not sufficiently illogical to answer that question in the affirmative.

3559. Are you aware that Lord John Browne stated that every portion of that duty was done by Mr. Brett when he was surveyor of the county of Mayo, and that it is done in the other counties which you have specified?—Mr. Brett is a very efficient officer, but I think, so far as I recollect, that Lord John Browne's evidence on that point was, that Mr. Brett went over all the roads of the county; I do not think he directed his evidence to the point on which I am now speaking. I say that it is utterly impossible for the county surveyor to visit every work sufficiently frequent, and the consequence is that now there is a system of putting stones on a road when the county surveyor is expected to make his periodical visit, so that in many counties the whole of the by-roads are utterly impassable at that period.

3560. You stated, did you not, that you did not agree with some evidence which had been given, that it would be desirable for the grand jury to present a sum of money, leaving it in the hands of the county surveyor or treasurer, which would be sufficient to meet the immediate expense of the contract system?—By the plan which I propose it would be unnecessary.

3561. You do not think that that would be an improvement?—I think it would be desirable to have a fund in hand to be disbursed by the road sessions.

3562. The fund in hand being at present the mere balance of unaccounted for presentments in the treasurer's hands?—I cannot say what fund it may be, but at present the fund for the particular work would not be levied; but there ought to be some means by which a fund in aid could be obtained in this form. In many counties the banks are appointed treasurers, and there ought to be no difficulty, I apprehend, in obtaining an advance of money from the bank upon the security of the levy, if such borrowing were authorised by law. That would place the county in funds, and that recommendation I think you will find was made by the Commission who reported upon this question in the year 1842.

3563. In point of fact, you think that such a fund would be a desirable one, whether arranged by the banks, the county surveyor, or the county treasurer, and that it would be an assistance in meeting the difficulty?—I think it would.

3564. You stated, did you not, that you would not have a contract settled, or a tender put in, or opened, until after the presentment had been sanctioned by the grand jury?—Until the work had the final approval of the grand jury, or of the financial county board, as I propose.

3565. Then should the securities be given before the county board, or before the grand jury?—At a session to be called the adjourned sessions as it is, to be held subsequently to the final approval of the work.

3566. Then you do not save any trouble in that way, because you have the two sessions?—I think you save a great deal of uncertainty on the part of the contractor as to whether he will be declared contractor, or not.

3567. At present the presentment being made, the county surveyor is directed to inquire into the expense, and it is put up to tender, and to the lowest tenderer, the work, as a matter of course, is given?—That was always my impression, and as I stated in my first day's evidence;

Mr. *P. R. Sharkey.*

14 May 1858.

dence; but I have since had my attention called to a decision given in Form, by which it seems that the sessions have at present a discretionary power, but if they have not they really ought to have a discretionary power to accept the lowest tender.

3568. Do you not think it ought to be imperative that they should be bound to take, with proper security, the lowest tender?—I would rather give them a discretion; I think public bodies, where they are compelled to do a thing, do not do it as well as when they have a discretion.

3569. Do you think there would not be a great outcry of favouritism if A. was refused a tender, when he was the lower of the two, and B. got it?—I do not think so; I think it would be better to give a discretion, and I have never known an instance in which such a power has been abused.

3570. Mr. *Blake.*] Would you have the county board that you propose, perform the same functions with regard to fiscal matters as the grand jury performs at present?—That is my proposition.

3571. And be a check on the baronial board?—And be a check on the baronial board.

3572. Under those circumstances, do you not think it would be undesirable that a board, if it was to be a check upon another board, should be a delegation from that board; that representatives should be appointed from the baronial board to sit upon the county board?—The fiscal board would be formed by a combination of delegates from all the baronies, so that the county fiscal board so constituted would be a check upon the baronial board; that is, the baronial board would be supervised and controlled by the delegates from all the baronies of the county, who, according to my suggestion, would form the fiscal county board.

3573. But they would have a check upon that particular baronial board, would they not, by means of their own representatives to some extent?—They would be only as two to a much larger number.

3574. Would it not be better, under those circumstances, with the county board at large, as you suggest, that the ratepayers should have the power of directly nominating representatives on the board in the same way as they have the power of nominating representatives on the baronial board now?—It might be desirable, but that is matter of detail altogether. The great thing to be avoided is too many elections. If you could elect to the county board at the same time that you would elect to the baronial presentment sessions, and by the same machinery, and without any additional expense, I think it might be more satisfactory and better in principle to have it so arranged.

3575. Is there any reason why the two elections should not go on together?—I do not think so.

3576. Have you read a Bill which was brought in by Mr. Maguire and myself on this subject?—I have.

3577. And you saw the plan of it?—Yes.

3578. Would that answer, in your opinion?—I think it would answer.

3579. As regards the baronial boards of which you speak, would it not be desirable that, as far as possible, the persons upon those boards should be of the class whom they are supposed to represent, the farming class, for instance?—Yes.

3580. You would have a qualification for them, I suppose, of a 20 *l.* assessment?—I would have a qualification certainly, but I do not know as to the particular amount; I think I would rather follow the recommendation of the Report of 1842, "That no magistrate shall be authorised to vote at the general presentment sessions of the county, unless he be an owner or holder of land of the value of 100 *l.* a year at least within the county, and that no magistrate shall vote at any baronial sessions unless he be an owner or holder of property to an equal amount within the barony."

3581. What qualification would you have for the members of the baronial board?—Much the same as they have at present as Poor Law guardians.

3582. That is 20 *l.*, is it not?—Yes.

3583. Would it not be desirable that the qualification for a county board should be of a higher kind than that, such as, for instance, 50 *l.*?—I think it would.

3584. Under those circumstances would you not prefer to give to the ratepayers the power of sending a person having such a qualification into the county board?—That is quite a matter of detail upon which I have not made up my mind; that could be worked out in either way, I think, satisfactorily.

3585. The Honourable Member for Roscommon suggested to you that there would be probably a necessity for paying the members of this county board; under the system which you suggest, would there be any more labour on the baronial board, or on the county board, than at present?—I think not.

3586. And there would be no more reason for compensating those bodies than there is now?—No reason whatever.

3587. Is it not one of your objections against the present system, that the grand jury constitutes the tribunals which initiate the taxation?—Yes, against the present system of constituting the baronial sessions.

3588. You are in favour of the county board, as well as the baronial board, being continuous, are you not?—I merely make it a fiscal board to take the place of the grand jury; but the baronial sessions should continue the same as they are at present.

3589. But I think, if I understand you rightly, that you are in favour of having the county at large board a continuous board, one-half of the members to go out by rotation?—It should be elected for a year.

3590. But then at the end of that year you would not have all the members go out, would you?—No, I would have half go out in rotation.

3591. When the fiscal duties are separated from the criminal duties of the grand jury, could it not be so managed that the fiscal duties which are now performed by the clerk of the Crown and the clerk of the peace, might be performed by the secretary of the grand jury?—I think it would be impossible to get him to do all the fiscal duties, because there are very heavy duties cast upon the clerk of the peace at present in connexion with the registration of voters. He has to attend the quarter sessions, revising barrister's, and the jurors' sessions, and I think that it would be utterly impossible to have all the duties of the clerk of the Crown, clerk of the peace, and

secretary

Mr. P. S. Sharkey.

12 May 1868.

secretary of the grand jury discharged by one officer, unless you gave him the power to do some of those duties by deputy; of course then it would be possible.

3592. *Chairman.*] Are you aware that in one case, in Ireland, there is a gentleman who is at present discharging the duties of secretary to the grand jury, of acting or deputy clerk of the peace, and also of treasurer?—He may do it; but I cannot say whether or not the duties are discharged efficiently.

3593. If that was a fact, would it modify your statement that it is impossible to do it?—I will qualify my statement that it would be impossible to discharge all the duties now performed by the three officers efficiently.

3594. Mr. *Blake.*] Are not the fiscal duties now performed by the clerk of the Crown and by the clerk of the peace of a very trivial character?—Those performed by the clerk of the Crown may be so, but not those performed by the clerk of the peace.

3595. What reason have you for saying that the secretary of the grand jury could not perform those duties?—At present, very often the duties of the presentment sessions, of the adjourned sessions, and of the quarter sessions, are being discharged at one and the same time; and I am sure that the Honourable Member will see that it is impossible, if the same officer is not present at the different places at the same time, to discharge all those duties in person.

3596. But under the system which you propose, could you not have the meetings of the baronial boards and the other bodies connected with the county so managed that one county officer could attend them all?—Everything, it is said, is possible; but whether it could be done with due regard to the efficient discharge of the duties, is a thing to which I would rather be inclined to give an answer in the negative.

3597. You are acquainted with a great many secretaries of grand juries in Ireland, or you have heard of them; are you aware that those gentlemen perform a great deal of private business besides their business as secretaries of the county, such as the business of land agents; for instance, there is a gentleman, who is about to give evidence after you, who is secretary to a grand jury, and who is an extensive agent for land; and the secretary of the grand jury at Waterford has some very extensive agencies?—I think at present the secretary of the grand jury is not overworked, so far as the duties of the county are concerned, and that he has ample time to discharge other functions.

3598. Supposing, under the system which you suggest, that the secretary was obliged to devote his whole time to the business of the county, and was paid accordingly, could not such an arrangement be then made?—I think not. You might perhaps amalgamate the offices of the clerk of the Crown and the clerk of the peace with advantage; but I think that the increased duties which would be cast upon the secretary, even under the proposed alteration of the law, would occupy his time as much as such an officer's time need be occupied.

3599. If the present secretaries of grand juries can act as agents of extensive estates, and attend to private business, is it not only reasonable to suppose that they could perform those fiscal duties?—As I say, the secretary has some time on his hands at present, and he might be able to discharge additional duties; but if you ask me whether he would be able to discharge the entire duties of the three offices, my answer is that I do not think he would be able to do so efficiently.

3600. Might there not be such an arrangement of the sessions that no two of them need be held at the same time?—I do not think, even then, he would do it so efficiently as the duties of the respective offices ought to be discharged.

3601. You spoke of the entire payment of the rate by the occupiers being to a certain extent a sentimental grievance, did you not?—I used the word "sentimental," and what I meant was that, although the landlord might be compelled to pay a moiety of the tax in the first instance, he would in the end be relieved from the tax entirely. Even supposing the recommendation of the Report of 1830 were carried into effect, and that the landlord paid the entire tax, he would secure its being recouped to him in the form of increased rent.

3602. Is it not something more than a sentimental grievance, inasmuch as the landlord has a direct interest in having as much expenditure as possible in the place where the property is situate, and that the whole of that outlay is at the cost of the tenant?—Practically it is so; but I do not think that the landlords from my knowledge have ever pushed things so far as to give cause for an imputation of unfair or improper practices, in that regard.

3603. Is it not one of the disadvantages under which the tenant labours, that he really never knows what he has to pay?—Yes; but at the same time I am bound to say that I have known amongst the ratepayers of a barony as great a tendency to jobbing, and a greater tendency in many cases than amongst the propertied class.

3604. Is that jobbing as regards the outlay for works, or jobbing to give those works to a particular friend?—I think there is jobbing, both as regards getting a contract for a friend, and as regards having a piece of road leading to a mill, or something of that kind.

3605. Do you think that the love of jobbing in Ireland goes to the extent that a man would vote money out of his own pocket in a barony, merely for the sake of getting a contract for a friend?—The amount is so small which would come out of his own pocket, under those circumstances, that I do not think that it ever enters into his consideration.

3606. Mr. *Maguire.*] With regard to jobbing, you said that the associated cesspayers are just as likely to job as their betters, do you mean that?—I mean that.

3607. At the present moment are those associated cesspayers responsible to anybody?—They are not responsible to any person.

3608. Are they not, in fact, irresponsible, and not accountable for their acts to any person?—They are not accountable to any person, except to the good opinion of their neighbours.

3609. But if they were elected would they not be responsible to those who elected them?—Certainly.

3610. Do you not think then that if they were appointed by election they would be more amenable to public control and less liable to wander into devious paths?—Yes.

3611. But would not that be the almost inevitable tendency?—It would control it, I think, in a great measure, to make that tribunal subject

Mr. P. B. Sharkey.
15 May 1868.

to the opinions of its constituents. Constituents exercise great influence upon all representative bodies.

3612. For instance, on boards of guardians, is it not very probable that if elected guardians are found guilty of jobbing and trickery that their tenure of office is very likely to determine?—Of course they would not be returned again, but with regard to the Poor Law system, there is a controlling influence vested in the Poor Law Board, and excellently well as the Poor Law system works in Ireland, it is in a great measure owing to the advising and controlling influence of that Poor Law Board.

3613. It would not be impossible to procure such a revising or controlling system in reference to the grand jury system, would it?—It would not be possible, without increasing the expense; at the same time it is right to have attention directed to the amount of Poor Law rates which are dealt with by that body as compared with the grand jury rates.

3614. Speaking of the transference of the fiscal power of the grand jury to another board, do you know, of your own knowledge, that in many of the cities of Ireland, such as Dublin, Cork, Limerick, and others, the fiscal powers of the city grand juries have been handed over to the corporations?—I know that under both public and local Acts a large proportion of the fiscal duties of grand juries are transferred to municipal bodies, such as town commissioners or as corporations.

3615. Have you ever heard that the new bodies do not exercise their powers to the public satisfaction?—I have heard that in one or two recent cases, where a transference of those powers had taken place, there was some cause of objection.

3616. I am talking of cities and not of county towns?—I have no knowledge of county towns.

3617. It is the fact, is it not, that those powers have been transferred, in many instances, by what are termed local Acts?—By local and public Acts.

3618. As to the question of expense, is it possible that there would be any additional expense if your proposal were carried out?—Certainly not; I never contemplated any additional expense.

3619. Is it not the fact that, in every union in Ireland, the boards of guardians meet once a week?—Yes.

3620. The very highest people in the land, either as chairman, or vice chairman, or as ex officio guardians, meet there regularly once a week, do they not?—I know it to be so.

3621. Did you ever hear of such an idea being mooted in Ireland, as that any of those men, or any portion of them, were ever to be paid, or expected payment?—No, except at an exceptional period, when there were paid guardians.

3622. That was to suit a particular crisis; but the idea of payment never enters into their minds, or into the mind of the public, does it?—Certainly not; it was never in my contemplation, when I ventured to put forward the modification of the present system, as in my evidence to-day.

3623. But the Poor Law system, so far as the local administration of the law is concerned (and not talking of the officials) never cost a penny, and does not that system work both efficiently and economically?—I consider that is done.

3624. With regard to this matter of the sentimental grievance, you, in point of fact, gave the answer to Mr. Blake; but would you consider it a sentimental grievance to be compelled to pay the whole of the public rate, and to have no voice in its administration?—Certainly not; I have explained my views upon that point, but I do not think that if any change takes place, so as to divide the cess between the occupier and the landlord, the tenant will get any practical benefit by it, neither will it effect any real change beyond this; that it will take it out of the power of the tenant to make an outcry against it as at present.

3625. Do you think it fair that the tenant should not have the advantage of what the law contemplates, if it were changed to-morrow?—Yes; but it is very much surrounded by difficulties as to interference with the rights of property.

3626. But as a mere matter of principle?—As a matter of principle there can be no doubt about it.

3627. As a matter of principle, and of high justice, is it not right, according to your opinion, that some proportion of it should be borne by the man who has the largest interest in the property?—That is not only my opinion, but it was the opinion of the eminent persons who made that Report in the year 1830.

3628. Are not the leading reasons upon which the recommendation of 1830 was based, in full force at the present moment?—They are in full force at the present day.

3629. Of that you have no doubt whatever?—None.

3630. People complain, I believe, of the great expense of collecting the county cess as compared with the collection of the poor rate?—Yes.

3631. Is it within your knowledge, that there have been more defaulters amongst the collectors of the county cess than there have been amongst the collectors of the poor rate?—Certainly; to a considerable extent the defalcations have been upon the part of the collectors of the grand jury cess.

3632. And therefore the high rate of payment for collection is not the best guarantee for the security of the public, if you take the result?—The result would certainly lead to that conclusion.

3633. Then so far, that portion is administered more economically under the one system than under the other, is it not?—Far and away. The entire system of the Poor Law in Ireland bears no comparison in point of perfection with the grand jury system; and the closer you can assimilate the administration of grand jury affairs to the present system under the Poor Law, the nearer you will arrive at perfection in every detail.

Mr. Henry Wynne, called in; and Examined.

Mr. H. Wynne.

3634. (*Chairman*.) You are Secretary of the Grand Jury for the County of Wexford, are you not?—Yes.

3635. And you have come before the Committee, I believe, as representing the secretaries of grand juries in Ireland?—In some respects.

3636. They have held some meeting, have they not, with respect to the grievances under which they believe that they are labouring?—Yes.

3637. The office of secretary of the grand jury is not a permanent one, is it?—On the contrary, it is curiously the reverse. The words of the Act are unusually strong; they say that grand juries may appoint a secretary and dismiss him without even assigning a reason at each assizes.

3638. But practically, the secretary of a grand jury holds the office during good behaviour, does he not?—I believe so; at least I feel so on my own part; but, speaking as a representative, some secretaries feel that they are put in an unfair position in that way, and I was desired to put that before the Committee.

3639. They desire to have it made an office tenable during good behaviour?—We desire to have it made an office tenable during good behaviour, and for the further reason that, independently of the chances of being dismissed, we feel that its not being an office tenable during good behaviour, injures our claim for superannuation; it puts us in a worse position towards the right of superannuation than we should hold if it was an office during good behaviour.

3640. The secretaries of grand juries, I presume, are anxious to have powers given to grand juries to grant them superannuations?—Quite so.

3641. What county officers at present receive superannuation allowances?—Almost all the civil servants of the Crown to whom we wish as far as possible to be assimilated. The grand juries have the power of superannuating some of the gaol officials. Under the late Act, the county treasurers can claim superannuation.

3642. But are you aware of the reason why the county treasurer can claim superannuation; is it not because it is a gain to the county that he should resign, and because his office has been prospectively abolished?—Yes.

3643. Before that Act was passed he had no such claim?—No. I quite admit that; but we seek it as a new power to be given.

3644. You seek also, I perceive by the statement which you have handed to me, an increase of salary?—Yes; some of the secretaries pressed upon me to suggest that, as the treasurer has now the option of retiring, and having his office consolidated with that of secretary, if the treasurer do not do so, there should be a power given to the secretary to retire, and to have his office thrown upon the treasurer. The Act of last Session has established the principle that the one officer will be sufficient for the two duties; and as an option is given to the county treasurer to retire, we think that if the county treasurer do not wish to avail himself of that, an option should be given to the secretary of the grand jury to retire on a similar superannuation to what the treasurer has, and to throw his duties on the county treasurer.

3645. Do you think that would be fair to an officer who, like the treasurer, is a permanent officer, and not capable of being dismissed summarily by the grand jury?—You would give him an increase of salary as well as an increase of work, as you propose to do to us.

3646. But do you not see a great difference between throwing upon an officer like the county treasurer those duties which he might not desire, or might not be capable of carrying out, and throwing them upon an officer who is a temporary servant, and can be dismissed at once if the grand jury think proper?—That very objection will rank as one of the strong points in favour of what we press for first, viz., that our office should not be of this fluctuating character.

3647. That is for the future; but are you aware that at present the county treasurer is not in that position?—Quite so.

3648. Would you think it fair to throw upon an officer, who is not in that position, those duties which he might not wish to undertake, or which he might not be capable of undertaking?—I cannot press the point. I am merely putting it as a suggestion to the Committee.

3649. But the cases are not parallel, are they?—I cannot press the case beyond suggesting that it might be considered.

3650. Many of the county treasurers are elderly men, are they not, who would be quite incapable of acting as secretaries of the grand jury?—Yes; I believe it is considered that the secretaries are all competent to undertake the extra duties.

3651. The duties of a county treasurer are of a character which are not very difficult, but which are more ministerial, and do not require much knowledge of technicalities, but the duties of a secretary to a grand jury are of a very different class, are they not?—Yes.

3652. So that there is no parallel between throwing upon the county treasurer the duty of the secretary to the grand jury, and throwing upon the secretary to the grand jury the duty of the county treasurer, is there?—I would not press the point, but I am bound to bring before you the views which some of the secretaries of grand juries hold.

3653. Do the secretaries of grand juries also claim allowances for travelling expenses and clerks?—We bring before you the fact that we have no expenses of that kind allowed to us, and that therefore our salary ought to be made such as will clear those necessary expenses, when they are not allowed under the form of travelling expenses, and a clerk; that if not allowed in that form they should be taken into account in estimating the salary.

3654. But you are aware, are you not, that, in addition to the salaries payable to the secretaries of grand juries, they receive a large amount of emolument through the instrumentality of fees?—I am.

3655. Would you propose the continuation or the abolition of those fees?—I would propose the abolition of those fees, so far as they are received by the secretaries of grand juries. For most of them the proper term would be "customary payments," because they are not fees which can be enforced. Still a certain proportion of them are fees, but that is very small, and the bulk of the emoluments are made up of customary payments for services.

3656. Do you think that it would be a desirable thing to make it obligatory upon the secretaries of grand juries to furnish the contractors with regular forms of tenders and other applications for which they now pay fees, if the secretary's salary were increased to a reasonable degree, in consideration of furnishing those applications and other documents to the applicants for works?—I must divide the applications into two classes for that purpose. All applications for new works, and all applications for tenders, I think, should be paid for by the applicants, to prevent endless reduplication and accumulation; but the Committee are aware that the bulk of the presentments and of the applications for which we receive payment are half-yearly levies. A contract is passed for five years, we will say, for works of maintenance which consists of 10 half-yearly levies for the total,

Mr. H. Wynne.
——
19 May 1868.

total. Now I think it would be very fair that when once the original presentment was passed it should be made part of the secretary's official duty to prepare those periodical applications for the contractors; that is to say, without direct payment to himself; but I would have a payment for them which the secretary should account for, either made directly in money, or perhaps with the help of stamps.

3657. You would have payments made by the contractors such as are made now, but that they should be handed over to the credit of the county instead of being received by the secretary?—Some arrangement of that kind, but I do not pledge myself to any minute detail; I only suggest a general principle.

3658. But you believe that it would be a more satisfactory principle that the secretary's salary should be increased, and that it should be a fair permanent salary, and that those fees which ought to be continued should be paid in some shape or form to the general credit of the county?—I do.

3659. That is not alone your individual opinion, but it is the opinion of the secretaries of grand juries?—I think that it is now their opinion; but it has been the opinion of the ratepayers, the grand juries, for some time; and, at the spring assizes in 1867, my county passed a resolution (not at my instance) to the effect "That the grand jury consider it desirable that the secretary should be paid an adequate salary by presentment, the office fees to be accounted for by him, and paid in to the credit of the county rate; that a copy of this resolution be forwarded to the county and borough Members with a view of the subject being considered by the Legislature when the grand jury laws are considered." That is a resolution of the grand jury, not passed at my instance, but showing that they wish that principle to be carried out, and a similar feeling I am aware is entertained by many other grand juries.

3660. Do you not think that if such a course were adopted, in addition to having a charge made for the filling up of the documents relating to works of maintenance, it would be desirable to have a charge for filling up applications for new works, so as to prevent persons needlessly coming to the secretary?—Quite so; and I intended to convey that impression.

3661. Did you intend to convey that the charge made for those applications for new works should go to the secretary, or that it should, like the others, go to the county?—I think that it would be more convenient that all should go to the county.

3662. In that case it would be the duty of the secretary to fill up those documents for new works, as well as for the continuous presentments, would it not?—It would. One of the objections to the payment by customary fees is, that it is conceived that the amount is far larger than it is, on the principle of *omne ignotum pro magnifico*. People imagine that the secretaries to grand juries receive a great deal more than they do, which is one of the objections to the payment by customary fees.

3663. But are you aware that some of the secretaries make very large fees?—I am.

3664. Have you seen any evidence with respect to the secretary of the county of Cork?—Yes.

3665. Did you see that he received, between fees and salary, nearly 1,000 *l.* a-year?—His county is a very enormous one.

3666. There was a Return to Parliament, was there not, of the fees received by every secretary of a grand jury?—Yes, and I returned in it myself; I have never seen the general returns of last year. There was a return called for last year, asking for the emoluments of the treasurers, the clerks of the Crown, the clerks of the peace, and the secretaries of grand juries.

3667. You state that it is the general opinion that the fees which the secretaries receive are much larger than they really are. I would call your attention to the county of Cork, to which I alluded before; in this return which you have given me, I find that the fees are returned at 65 *l.*?—Those are the distinctly legal fees, and not customary payments, I presume.

3668. In this detailed return, with regard to all the emoluments which are received by the secretaries, the amount returned from the county of Cork is 65 *l.*, whereas it turned out upon examination that the amount was between 600 *l.* and 700 *l.*; can you explain it?—I can give no explanation of it.

3669. Would that lead to the belief that the idea about the fees being larger than they really are, is correct?—I can only speak from experience in my own county, that people fancy that I make a great deal more than I do. I have, in the Return of 1861, returned accurately what my whole income is. It averages from 350 *l.* to 370 *l.*

3670. In the return which you made last year, I find that you put down the average amount of fees and other payments at 220 *l.*; does that include all your fees, or is that merely the legal fees?—That includes all my fees; and then the salary besides, which is 140 *l.*, makes it from 350 *l.* to 370 *l.*

3671. Your county is a small one, is it not?—It is not a small one; it is a very populous county, and there is a great deal of grand jury business in it. There is a greater extent of mileage than in many counties which are far greater in extent, because there is a great deal of cultivable land in it, and a very large agricultural population.

3672. But the amount of fees represents the amount of presentments to a certain extent, does it not?—Certainly.

3673. So that, if your fees are small, it shows that the number of presentments is comparatively small?—The number of presentments is about 2,200 in a year. We have between 1,100 and 1,200 in a half year.

3674. Are you obliged to keep a public office in the county?—I am obliged to keep it, but I am not obliged to pay for it.

3675. Do you consider that other officers ought to be obliged to keep offices?—I do; that is to say, such officers as I consider necessary for the county, which are three.

3676. Who are they?—The secretary, the surveyor, and the clerk of the peace.

3677. Do you think that those are the only officers who are necessary?—With regard to fiscal business, I really do not see what more is necessary than the surveyor to manage all the out-door business, and the secretary to manage all the in-door machinery; and if it be not considered right that the secretary to the grand jury should hold the custody of the presentments, then they

they should be handed over to the officer who is appointed by the custos rotulorum of the county, the clerk of the peace, who keeps all the other county records.

3678. Have you heard the suggestion of throwing upon the secretary of grand jury the fiscal duties of the clerk of the Crown and the clerk of the peace?—I am not aware what fiscal duties of the clerk of the peace could be thrown upon the secretary; I do not think that with regard to the presentments, the clerk of the peace has anything at all to do with them; he has the registration of the votes; but in my county, that is quite a separate thing, and is paid for separately. In my business I only come in contact with the clerk of the Crown, and with the treasurer at present.

3679. Do you think that the duties of the clerks of the Crown could be performed by the secretary of the grand jury?—They might be so performed with some modification. I do not see that the duties of the clerk of the Crown are essential. The duties of the clerk of the Crown are to hand over to the treasurer copies and lists of the presentments which are fiated by the court and discharged, and to countersign the treasurer's cheques.

3680. Under the Act of last Session, is not the clerk of the Crown a check upon the secretary when the secretary is the treasurer?—Of course he will be so. He will then countersign the secretary's cheques, as he does now the cheques of the treasurer.

3681. Would not there be one difficulty in the way of having these two offices united in one person, namely, this—that there would be no check upon that person?—A little change of machinery would very easily provide for that. A finance committee, such as exists at present in the county Dublin, might draw cheques, countersigned by the secretary. I have not considered the details; but another way which occurs to me would be this; when the bank has, under the Act of last year, become treasurer, a return might be handed by the secretary of all presentments which had been passed, and the cheques might be drawn by him, with a number affixed, so that the bank might see that they were bound to pay them.

3682. Do you think that the banks would undertake the responsibility of making the payments in that case?—They might perhaps object; but that is only a suggestion which has just occurred to me.

3683. Have you considered whether they would be likely to take that responsibility, receiving no return for it excepting the holding of the money which they hold at present?—They might possibly object to it.

3684. Which would you think would be preferable; to unite the offices of clerk of the peace and clerk of the Crown, or, to take away from the clerk of the Crown his fiscal duties, and to transfer them to the secretary of the grand jury?—I should not be in favour of amalgamating the offices; I should remove the fiscal duties of the clerk of the Crown, and he, being then a purely Crown officer, I would have the county relieved from the payment of the clerk of the Crown's salary.

3685. But, in that case, do you not think that the clerk of the Crown could discharge at the quarter sessions all the duties which are now discharged by the clerk of the peace?—If the offices were amalgamated of course he could, but the clerk of the Crown is not generally a resident official, such as the clerk of the peace is.

Mr. H. Wynne.

19 May 1868.

3686. But it might be obligatory upon him to reside in the county, and of course he should attend the quarter sessions if such duties were thrown upon him?—Certainly.

3687. Do you see any difficulty in the way of the clerk of the Crown discharging at quarter sessions the duties of clerk of the peace, those duties being similar to what the clerk of the Crown now discharges at assizes?—I never gave my attention much to that point, but I do not see why one officer should not do it as well as another. No such point arises as was suggested with regard to the amalgamation of the offices of secretary and treasurer. There is no difference between the qualifications of the clerk of the Crown and the clerk of the peace, but I did not come prepared to give any detailed evidence upon this point.

3688. But why did you state that you believed that the only officers necessary for the county work (I presume by that you meant fiscal work) were the secretary and the clerk of the peace; what fiscal business has the clerk of the peace to do which makes you place him in that category?—He has none now; but my reason for saying that was, that if it was considered unnecessary or wrong that the presentments should remain in the custody of the secretary, they should pass to him as the custodian of all county records; they now pass out of the hands of the secretary after the assizes, and remain in the custody of the clerk of the Crown as Crown records. I propose that if the clerk of the Crown were relieved from fiscal duties, and if the county were relieved from his salary, he becoming purely a Crown officer, if it were not considered right that the secretary should retain the custody of presentments, the clerk of the peace should have them. It was in that view that I said that the clerk of the peace would be the only other officer necessary for the practical carrying out of the presentments; I consider the secretary and the surveyor are necessary, one for indoor and the other for outdoor work.

3689. (General *Dunne*.) Is there not a qualification required for the clerk of the peace; he must be a legal man, must he not?—I fancy that he ought to be an attorney, but I do not know whether any legal qualification is essential.

3690. For the clerk of the Crown there is no legal qualification, is there?—No.

3691. (*Chairman*.) But you do not state, on your own knowledge, that there is this legal qualification required for the clerk of the peace?—I do not know it, but I believe it is so.

3692. Is there any other point on which you would like to make a suggestion?—Yes; I wish to draw the attention of the Committee to the present classification of the counties in the schedule attached to the present Grand Jury Act, which we consider is not suited to the present time. Under this, as I mentioned to you, my salary is 140 *l.* as secretary of a third class county.

3693. Will you explain to the Committee your objections to that classification?—Of course; they must be chiefly, perhaps, drawn from the illustrations of my own county. We wish that the classification which was passed for the county surveyors should be adopted. That was a classification which was prepared by them with great care, taking into account all the circumstances with

Mr. H. Wynne.

18 May 1868.

with regard to the amount of fiscal work that there was in each county, and as the secretaries act *in pari materiâ* with them, we wish to press upon the Committee that that classification should be adopted.

3694. Is a different classification adopted with respect to the county surveyors from that which is adopted with respect to other county officers?—Yes, and that is the classification which we seek to have applied to us, on the ground that we work *in pari materiâ* with them.

3695. And that was adopted in a late Act of Parliament?—Yes, about six years ago. The classification of the counties has been altered since the Act of 1836, with regard to the assistant barrister. My county, which is a third class county for the secretary, is a second class county for the assistant barrister, and it is a first class county for the county surveyor. I am not prepared to state the actual grounds that there are for the classification in all the counties, but there are several points of view in which you may look at them. There is the valuation, the amount of mileage, and the amount of cultivable ground, and the number of the baronies at which sessions have to be held. In the county of Mayo, which is a first class county, the valuation is a good deal less than in my county. You suggested that you thought my county was a small county, but the mileage under presentment in my county is over 2,000 miles; it has about 900 square miles; and there is a first class county, the county of Derry, where the square mileage is only 810 miles. Kildare, which is a small county in valuation, is a fourth class county, but there are 14 baronies in it. In Donegal, which is a first class county, there are only six baronies, and there are 10 in the county of Wexford. Upon all these points I am merely indicating a few discrepancies to show that there is some ground for disputing the present classification; and then I ask for the application of the classification of the county surveyors which was very carefully prepared with a view to the amount of work to be done.

3696. But how would you deal with the case of a county which would be reduced from a second to a third class county?—There is no such case.

3697. Or from a first to a second?—There is no such case as that. The only change that is made in the county surveyor's classification by the schedule I suggest is, that wherever a county is given two surveyors, it is put into the first class in the schedule, and in every other respect it follows the classification of the County Surveyor's Act.

3698. Then how many counties does this proposed alteration affect?—I think it affects, more or less, all the counties except those in the first class. There are four classes in the schedule of the old Act, and there are but three in this. The county of Cork has always been an exceptional county.

3699. I find amongst the statements made by the secretaries that they seek for liberty to appoint an assistant, to act for them in case of unavoidable absence or illness. Was not that provided for by the Act of last Session?—It has been provided for, and I am acting under that provision at the present moment; but it is considered defective, and the point has been raised whether that does not apply solely to a secretary who has become treasurer as well. The appointment is there made subject to the approval of the Lord Lieutenant, which is a rather cumbrous mode of proceeding, and a simple application to the grand jury would be more desirable. We claim an increase of salary on the ground of the diminished value of money, and that the work has been very much increased since those salaries were originally fixed; not only the amount of presentments have been increased, but the number of sessions. Whenever a county progresses, and its business increases, for the convenience of the parties interested the baronies are divided so as to bring them within easy reach of the associated cesspayers and magistrates; and every multiplication of them, each additional barony, adds four sessions, with their attendant travelling expenses, in the year to the secretary.

3700. But would you not, if a vacancy occurred in any county in the office of secretary of the grand jury, find many eligible applicants for the office, upon the present salary and with the present work?—Am I to understand that the question refers to the present legal salary or to the proposed commuted salary?

3701. To the present emoluments; if a vacancy occurred in the office of secretary of the grand jury in any county in Ireland, without any change being made in the emoluments which the new secretary would receive, would you not find many eligible persons seeking the appointment?—I do not doubt that you would; but still I think that that is scarcely a fair way of treating the question. If the work is well done, and if it is an object to the ratepayers to have a person of integrity and honesty, surely they will find it economical as well as just to pay him well.

3702. Do you not consider the office sufficiently well paid at present to induce a person of sufficient integrity and honesty to take it?—You could not expect a person in my position to answer that question in the negative; but I think you are rather pressing that too much.

3703. I merely wish to call to your attention that you must recollect throughout the statement that you first made, that the secretary is appointed only from one assize to another, and that he can be dismissed at any time; and that, consequently, he has not the same right to cry out against work being further thrown upon him, as an officer who is permanently appointed?—Yes; but that is one of the very essential grievances of which we complain, and that is the ground for the first claim which we put forward, namely, that the office should be made permanent because it gives rise to these very suggestions, that we have no right to superannuation, and no right to complain. It takes away the force of the answer that, though our office is nominally a temporary one, still it is practically a permanent one. It has not all the benefits of permanence when a claim for increase of salary can be thus met.

3704. Colonel *French*.] What is the amount of fees that you get on each presentment?—Two shillings.

3705. Do you not get more than that; does not your office fill up the returns for the contractors?—Yes; I get 2 *s.* for that for each application.

3706. But your fees for each application are more than that, are they not?—Not for each application. My fees are 2 *s.* for the original application; 1 *s.* for the bond, which is a legal fee; 1 *s.* for each tender (that is to say, 6 *d.* is the legal fee, and 6 *d.* for filling up); and I consider,

sider, taking round numbers, there should be two tenders for each, so that that would be 5 s.

3707. Then you say you have about 2,200 presentments in the year?—I think it is about 2,000.

3708. Then your fees, according to that, are 550 l. a year, are they not?—I have only that number of applications, including applications for works of maintenance, for which the fee is only 2 s. each.

3709. But you get 1 s. on the warrant, do you not?—I get 2 s. for that.

3710. You get your 1 s. in the first instance on the tender, do you not?—Yes.

3711. And, in fact, at the adjourned sessions, you get 3 s. on each tender that is accepted?—No; I get 1 s. at the adjourned sessions for the every accepted tender; I get 2 s. in the office for the original preparation of the application; and I get, I consider, on an average, 2 s. more for tenders, because there may be, perhaps, six or seven tenders for one work, that is, on each application for a new work; but when I said there were about 2,000 presentments in the county, I meant not applications for new works, but half-yearly payments, upon each of which there is only 2 s.

3712. You are now talking about yearly contracts, are you not?—Yes.

3713. There is only 2 s. in the first instance, but then there is the filling up of the payment, taking the contractor's payments out of the warrants, so as to be paid by the treasurer; there is a fee on that, is there not?—I have only one fee. I only make one fee of 2 s. for each half-yearly payment; it is given in detail in that return which the Chairman has.

3714. You say that you have 5 s. on each presentment?—By the time that each single presentment for a new work passes out of its inchoate into its perfect stage, I shall have perhaps received that amount; if it is a single presentment, I shall receive no more; if it is a presentment for permanent works for five years, I then receive for each application that I make for future levies 2 s.

3715. And the other 3 s. is only paid on the first application?—Yes; when I said there were about 2,000 presentments, I meant that there were 2,000 on which I received the 2 s.

3716. General *Dunne*.] What is the law by which those fees are levied?—There is no law for it; it is our customary payment for the work that we do.

3717. Does not it differ in every county?—I believe it does; and one of the reasons why we have brought this strongly before the Committee is, that there is a strong feeling among the public in general, that it is not a proper way for officers to be paid by fees of that kind, which we could not recover if people ran rusty.

3718. Any man can fill up his own application, can he not, if he chooses?—Yes.

3719. *Chairman*.] I suppose you do not give out these forms until you are paid?—In my case I do; I have always endeavoured to suit the convenience of the public as much as I can, and I never ask the contractors for payment until the sessions when they are in funds, so that it is no grievance to them.

3720. Colonel *Cooper*.] Do you afford any advantages to the public by going about the country and holding offices?—Yes; I localise the office and bring it within easy reach of contractors before the sessions. I go to three or four of the most important central towns.

3721. And that is quite optional on your part?—That is quite optional on my part.

3722. And it is a very great convenience to the public?—It is a very great convenience to the public.

3723. And that is partly paid by those fees?—It is partly paid by the fees. It saves contractors both travelling expenses and time, and I must say that the bulk of them recognise that they derive great advantage from it, and they do not grumble. A circumstance occurred lately at one of the last sessions at which I was; there was a gentleman from the county of Wexford, who was examined before the Committee, Mr. Leigh. He was the chairman of our road session, and he had a good number of renewals of contracts, some 19 or 20. Mr. Leigh proposed at a full bench of ratepayers that the contracts should be taken for seven years instead of five years, because he said that they would get contractors on better terms, and that they would get better contractors by their having a longer interest; and one of the rate-paying farmers who was there, got up and said, "Well, I think we ought to do this if it will benefit us, and if we think we can get better terms; but, gentlemen, you ought to increase the salary of your secretary if you do so, for you are taking away his fees." Mr. Leigh is a very good friend of mine, and he said, "Mr. Wynne will be able to take very good care of himself. He is going over to London, and all this will be brought out before the Committee, and a very good argument it will be for him;" so that I am almost giving you Mr. Leigh's evidence as well as my own upon that point.

3724. Colonel *Forde*.] How many new contracts have you in the year, on an average?—I should say about 100 at each assizes; but you will not bind me to that; the numbers vary.

3725. Have you contracts for five years generally?—Generally for five years, except when they are made shorter for an exceptional purpose, which is also taking away our fees, and this is throwing two or three contracts into one.

3726. *Chairman*.] I find by this return of the year 1881, that the fees are 6 s. upon new works; there is, first, the forms of tender, 6 d.; bonds, 1 s.; supplying forms of presentment, 2 s.; filling form of tender, 6 d.; and 2 s. for application for payment?—That is a subsequent matter that is done for each of the half-yearly payments afterwards. In the case of a single presentment, there would be the fees by the time it was ultimately paid for, but there is only 5 s. on the original starting of the presentment until it reaches its perfect form, having passed the grand jury. My fees are 4 s. or 5 s., according to the number of tenders. Then the presentment is not paid for without an application being made to the sessions, and coming before the assizes; it then becomes a matter of subsequent payment.

3727. Then your fees upon a presentment, in the first instance, before it is finished, are between 4 s. and 5 s., and subsequently, when an application for payment comes in, there is an additional fee of 2 s.?—That is quite correct.

3728. Mr. *Blake*.] You are in favour of having a fixed salary for officers in your position, are you not, instead of deriving part of your income by fees?—Yes.

3729. What are your present receipts from fees;

Mr. H. Wynne. — 15 May 1868.

fees; about 200 *l.* a year?—Somewhere about, or more.

3730. A portion of that 200 *l.* a year is derived from the voluntary act of the persons seeking presentments, and giving you the filling up of the forms?—Nearly all of it.

3731. If all the emoluments from fees were to go into the county fund, and if you were paid by salary, would not there be likely to be a loss to the county fund, generally speaking, from the inducement being taken away from officers in your position to take upon themselves the trouble of seeking to fill up these forms?—No, I do not think so, because I would have the fees paid, whether or not. I do not anticipate that any appreciable loss could accrue to the counties in that manner.

3732. Is it not rather considered a favour if a party comes to you to pay 2 *s.* in one instance and 2 *d.* in another, for the filling up of these forms, instead of going anywhere else?—They never go anywhere else in my county.

3733. But they might do it elsewhere, might they not?—But it is never done in my county.

3734. Have you not heard that it is done elsewhere?—I have heard so.

3735. Would there not be an actual loss to the county rates then?—I think it would be very inappreciable and very ideal.

3736. Supposing that the grand jury were to require you to devote your whole time to the performance of your duties, and to compensate you adequately, do you think that you would be able to perform, in addition to your own, all the fiscal duties which are performed by the clerk of the peace and the clerk of the Crown?—The clerk of the peace has no fiscal duties connected with us at present. We asked that the provisions of the County Surveyors' Act should be carried out in one respect, and we would ask that it should be so in another respect. By that Act it was left optional to the employers, whether the whole time of the officers should be required or not. It was not made imperative in the Act, but a power was given which has been exercised by some grand juries, but not by others, of insisting upon the whole time of the officers being devoted to their official duties. The officer in my county was not required to do it, but in another county where a friend of mine was appointed, he was required to give his whole time, and he did not accept the situation. In another county, the surveyor was given the option of 400 *l.* a year with private practice, or 500 *l.* a year without it, and he accepted the lower salary; and I believe he has done his work to the perfect satisfaction to the county.

3737. If you were required to devote your whole time to the business of the county to which you belong, would you consider that you were over-burdened with work, if you did the fiscal duties which appertain to those officers as well as your own?—Certainly not. When I spoke of the fiscal duties of the clerk of the peace, I did not allude to anything which he does at quarter sessions.

3738. Might it not be so arranged by having a proper rotation of presentment sessions, that you could attend, and do everything which the clerk of the peace does now?—Yes; but the clerk of the peace does nothing now. The clerk of the peace has no fiscal connection with us now.

3739. But the clerk of the Crown has?—The clerk of the Crown has.

3740. Could you do his business?—I suppose so, if there were some change in the machinery of his business as to the countersigning of the treasurer's cheques.

3741. But the machinery could be so arranged that everything could be satisfactorily done by you?—I presume so, so far as the amount of work is concerned. Of course, I am speaking of fiscal duties.

3742. How many years have you been in your present position?—Nearly 12 years.

3743. And you have a very extensive acquaintance with the working of the system, and the feeling of the people with regard to it?—Yes.

3744. Do you think that it would be desirable that there should be a direct representation from the ratepayers upon the baronial boards?—I have no hesitation in saying that it would be most desirable; I think that they have a constitutional right to it, and I think that it would give satisfaction. There are objections to the mode in which the present cesspayers are appointed, which they feel very much, though in my county, which is the only one of which I have experience, it is but right to state that the parties do not meet as in hostile camps, the one trying to impose taxation on the other, but they meet on fair and friendly terms as business men assembled to impose taxation for the common benefit, and they meet on very good terms, and act very harmoniously together.

3745. But speaking of Ireland as a whole, do you think that the change would be desirable?—Yes, and in my county also; because I know that there are objections to the present mode of appointing the cesspayers.

3746. Do you think that in all future lettings, it would not be both desirable and just, that there should be a division of the county rate between the landlord and the occupier?—That is a question upon which I have never been able thoroughly to make up my mind; I think that the change would be popular as implying a community of interest in burdens between the landlord and the tenant; but future lettings would seem to me to cover yearly holdings; now, as a matter of practice, yearly tenancies are not revised from year to year, and still they would strictly come under the term. If I understand you rightly, nothing but existing leases would be excluded by such a case as you put.

3747. I mean all future lettings, both as regards leases and tenants-at-will?—It would be attended with some delicacy in its operation with regard to yearly lettings; where lands have been over-rented or let at high rents on yearly lettings, it certainly would be an immediate and just benefit to the tenant, but where lands have been let at a low rent, the immediate burden would be thrown upon the landlord. Ultimately, we might expect that the politico-economical principle would work itself out, that all taxation was indirectly borne by the land, but as an immediate effect a burden would be thrown upon the landlord, and the most indulgent landlords would be the least likely to take advantage of the power which they had of resisting this burden, which would be a re-adjustment of the rent. An immediate raising of rent would look almost as if it were flying in the face of the principle established for the benefit of the tenant by Parliament.

3748. Regarding

3748. Regarding it as a matter of principle in future transactions, you would be rather in favour of it?—Yes; the difficulty would be, that future transactions seem to include yearly lettings; as to leaseholds, I should have no doubt whatever about it. In my own county, the principle has been adopted in two cases, and without any prospective effect; it has been retrospective; those have been the cases of the Wexford Bridge, for which a large rate was levied, and of the Ross Bridge, which has not yet been raised, but under which a very large tax will be raised. In both those cases, it was considered desirable to give the power of dividing the rate.

3749. Colonel Cooper.] Do the cesspayers attend the sessions regularly in your county? Certainly, in most cases they attend.

3750. Are any excluded generally from the ballot?—I could scarcely say that we very often have the full number.

3751. But very seldom more than the number?—I have very seldom come to the end of the list, though I have done so.

3752. If it was an elective body, do you think that there would be as much competition for the office of associated cesspayer as for that of a poor law guardian?—I scarcely think there would; they meet more seldom, and there is not constant work.

3753. And unless there was any large or new work contemplated they would probably not attend?—I think that they always attend in fair numbers, and watch the taxation of their barony; but one of the objections to the present arrangement is that very question of the ballot. Large yeoman farmers have said to me that they do not like having their time taken up and coming on the chance of being excluded. The only feeling of soreness that I know of is as to that. They say, "We may come, but if we are a little late we cannot come in at all, whereas a magistrate can come in at any time of the sessions." Those are two of the objections to the present system of having double the number appointed.

3754. Do you think that there would be any objection on the part of the magistrates to having the associated cesspayers an elective body?—I think not.

3755. It is your belief that the magistrates and cesspayers pull very well together?—That is my opinion, and increasingly so.

3756. Are you a solicitor?—No.

3757. In some counties the offices of secretary to the grand jury and solicitor to the grand jury are held by one person, are they not?—The fact is, that in my county the solicitor of the grand jury has very little to do. Occasionally, if it is suggested that a case should be sent to counsel, or a traverse attended, it is through him that it is done. I am not a solicitor, but I was a barrister before my appointment; and I think the grand jury generally look to me for advice, not that they have not the highest opinion of their solicitor, but they do not think it necessary to employ a solicitor.

3758. But they have a great advantage in your being a barrister; in some counties it is necessary to refer matters to a solicitor?—I can only answer from my own experience.

3759. (Chairman.] The solicitor to the grand jury is only paid for whatever work he does?—Quite so.

3760. Colonel Cooper.] I think he has a salary of 40 *l.* a-year?—Not in our county.

3761. Colonel Forde.] With regard to the election of cesspayers, what would be the most convenient time for the election to take place?—I do not know exactly what time.

3762. Of course I would consider that you, as the secretary of the grand jury, would be the returning officer?—Certainly; I should say that the autumn would be the most convenient time.

3763. That is to say, that the return should be sent in at the summer assizes, and, if there was likely to be an election, that the secretary should hold it between that and say the road sessions?—Yes; or as near the road sessions as possible, so as to allow them a little vacation.

3764. But he must have his return made out in proper time, so that the cesspayer may know that he is elected for the office?—Quite so.

3765. Would you allow the associated cesspayers to be re-elected the following year?—I certainly would. I do not see any objection to that. I think that, if once a good elective board is constituted, there is no reason why they should not continue. You might as well apply the principle of alternate exclusion to the magistracy. I assume the best men will be selected as ratepayers, and then they will be on a par with the magistrates.

3766. Then do you assume that the magistrates will be elected as well?—No, I do not; but the cesspayers are associated with the magistrates.

3767. Chairman.] Do you believe that the elective board will be a more independent and respectable body than the present cesspayers?—Not more respectable; they could not be more respectable than they are in my county.

3768. Do you think they would be more independent?—I think not. Probably they will consist of the same class of people; but they will be appointed in a manner which will give more satisfaction.

3769. Colonel Forde.] Do your cesspayers ever outvote your magistrates?—Yes, frequently. There is one barony in which they must almost always do it. There are only three or four magistrates in this barony. The number of cesspayers must always largely predominate; when once they are selected, except that the chairman has a casting vote, and that none of them can be re-appointed, they are on a full equality in my county.

3770. They are not subservient to the magistrates in the least?—Not at all.

3771. Have you ever, in your recollection, known the case of a board pretty nearly equal, as regards magistrates and cesspayers, on which the cesspayers outvoted the magistrates?—Yes.

3772. So that they are under no sort of surveillance of the magistrates?—No, there is no feeling of that kind.

3773. Chairman.] Do you think that the elected ratepayers would be more under that feeling, and that they would be more, in fact, the representatives of the landlords than the present ratepayers?—I do not think so; I do not see how that would come about.

3774. Do you not think that any large landed proprietor could have any man whom he chose elected as an associated cesspayer?—Such an abuse might possibly arise.

3775. You do not think it has ever arisen under the poor law system?—I would not go so far as to say that abuses have not arisen.

Mr. H. Wynne.

15 May 1868.

3776. Has it ever come under your notice that guardians have been returned, in fact, by the landlord?—I could not go so far as to say that.

3777. But it is not an impossibility?—It is not an impossibility; undue influence may be used, and that is undue influence, of course.

3778. You do not think that the landed proprietors would take advantage of any power which they might possess of having any one they wished elected as a representative of the cesspayers?—I do not think they would in my county, because, as I have stated, they act very harmoniously together. The cesspayers who are nominated are of an extremely high class, some of them gentlemen on the grand jury, the master of the hounds, and some others of high standing, and they are nominated because they are the largest ratepayers. At the same time, the leading magistrates who are associated with them in my county are generally the leading agriculturists, who pay in their own persons the largest amount of cess.

3779. Do you not think that having ratepayers elected would put it in the power of the large landed proprietors to have their nominees returned?—There is a possibility of that of course, but one objection to the present system is that there is no representation, very often, of different parts of a barony. In some baronies in my county there are large towns, and there all the highest ratepayers are probably the leading merchants of that town, who would not take the trouble of attending a sessions out of that town; so that there is no representation.

3780. Colonel *Forde*.] Is it usually the case that no representative is taken from a county district there?—The practice differs. Some judges have held that you must take the highest on the list, and I think that most of our grand jurors have followed that practice, though, I must say, against my opinion.

3781. That decidedly you think is objectionable?—Yes; I think the whole number should not belong to one corner, and that corner, perhaps, a corner that will take very little interest in the business.

3782. In the event of a barony being divided into different districts, and an associated cesspayer being elected for each of those districts, that would obviate what you object to, would it not?—It would.

3783. Mr. *Blake*.] You have spoken of the harmonious feeling between the magistrates and the associated cesspayers; those cesspayers being the nominees of the grand jury, is it not also a fact that there has been a considerable agitation in the county of Wexford amongst the ratepayers for grand jury reform, by reason of their dissatisfaction with the present system?—I think that that has a good deal died away. There was some agitation, and there is still some talk that things ought to be improved, but there is a better tone of feeling now, because, as a matter of practice now, the magistrates in my county confine themselves to their own baronies.

3784. But a witness who preceded you, Mr. Leigh, who was high sheriff of your county, took an active part in grand jury reform, did he not, by reason of the dissatisfaction which the ratepayers felt about the system?—He did; that was some years ago.

3785. Was not that agitation joined by persons of high position in the county?—Yes. The agitation did not go to any great extent; Mr. Leigh, I think, was one of the chief promoters of it, and there were some large yeomen farmers and gentlemen associated. Some of them have since become magistrates.

3786. That discontent was caused by the system of representation and non-division of the rate, was it not?—I believe so.

3787. *Chairman*.] Do you think that if the system of having elected ratepayers were adopted, it would throw much additional trouble upon the secretaries?—I fancy it would; I have not exactly experience of the amount of occupation which it has thrown upon the clerks of the unions, but I know that they are paid for acting as returning officers.

3788. Could you give the Committee any idea of whether or not the Poor Law elections are expensive?—They are not very expensive; I think that 20 *l.* a year is what is paid in my county to the clerk of our union; there are four unions.

3789. Colonel *Forde*.] You think that each barony if it chooses to go to an election, should pay its own expenses on that occasion, and not put them on the county at large?—I think it should.

3790. *Chairman*.] Do you not think then that there would be very few contested elections?—I do not think there would be any contest carried out with great acerbity, or even with very great zeal.

3791. I am not at all referring to that; but do you think that there would be many occasions upon which it would be necessary to send out voting papers, and to go to the expense of holding an election?—I should not like to give a decided answer as to that.

3792. If that were to be the case there would be considerable expense, would there not?—Not considerable expense; there would be some expense.

3793. The secretaries to the grand juries would expect an increase to their salaries, would they not in that case?—Of course they would. They would probably be paid as the clerks of the unions are paid.

Tuesday, 19th May 1868.

MEMBERS PRESENT:

Mr. Blake.	Mr. Herbert.
Colonel Cooper.	Mr. Kendall.
Mr. Dawson.	Sir Charles Lanyon.
General Dunne.	Mr. Leader.
Colonel French.	Mr. Maguire.
Mr. Chichester Fortescue.	The O'Conor Don.

THE O'CONOR DON, IN THE CHAIR.

Mr. EDWIN SADLEIR, called in; and Examined.

Mr. E. Sadleir. 19 May 1868.

3794. (Chairman.) YOU are Secretary of the Grand Jury of the County of Tipperary, are you not?—Yes.

3795. And you are also acting now as treasurer for that county?—Yes.

3796. And I believe you also act in the capacity of deputy clerk of the peace?—For a short period.

3797. For how long have you been so acting?—Until the return of the clerk of the peace, who is supposed to be back in, may be, 12 months.

3798. Has he been absent long?—About four or five months; he will be with me by about June.

3799. The county of Tipperary is divided into two ridings, I believe?—Yes.

3800. And there are two grand juries, are there not?—There are two grand juries.

3801. And you discharge the duties which you have mentioned in both ridings, do you not?—I do.

3802. How many presentment sessions are there in the county of Tipperary which you have to attend?—Six in the north and six in the south, half-yearly.

3803. I suppose that, as treasurer, and as acting as deputy clerk of the peace, you are able to give the Committee some information as to the duties of the clerk of the peace?—I am, but not as to all of them.

3804. Has the clerk of the peace any fiscal duties?—No.

3805. What are the duties which he has to discharge?—The criminal business of the county, and the registry of freeholders, if you call that fiscal, and preparing lists of voters.

3806. The preparation of the list of voters is a special duty for which he receives special payment, is it not?—He is paid the expenses of it, but I do not think that he gets very much.

3807. But in addition to that particular duty for which he receives a specific payment, what are his general duties for which he receives his salary?—Attending at the different quarter sessions, and keeping an account of the decrees or orders of the courts.

3808. Have you since you have been discharging the duties of deputy clerk of the peace had to attend at the quarter sessions?—Yes.

3809. Have you found that compatible with your duties as secretary to the grand jury?—Yes.

3810. The quarter sessions do not interfere with the presentment sessions?—No, I have generally the appointment of the sessions; I have never been interfered with, so I fix my own days, and they have in no way clashed.

3811. Do you know anything of the duties of the clerk of the Crown?—Yes, they are almost similar to those of the clerk of the peace, but they are merely confined to the assizes.

3812. Does the clerk of the Crown discharge the same duties at the assizes as the clerk of the peace discharges at the quarter sessions?—Yes, with regard to criminal business.

3813. The clerk of the Crown has some fiscal duties, has he not?—The presentments go through his hands; the presentments which are passed by the grand jury are fiated by the judge and delivered to the Crown Office, and the clerk of the Crown then gives the secretary or the treasurer a copy of the presentments fiated.

3814. And he also countersigns the treasurer's cheques, does he not?—He does.

3815. Do you see any difficulty in uniting the two offices of clerk of the Crown and clerk of the peace?—I do not.

3816. The duties which one has to discharge at the assizes would not interfere with those discharged at the quarter sessions by the other, would they?—Certainly not.

3817. Do you think that the fiscal portion of the duties of the clerk of the Crown might be done away with, or handed over to the secretary of the grand jury?—As far as I have gone, I look upon it as a great drag-chain to do the business; I would rather have nothing to say to it.

3818. Under the Act which was passed last year, and under which you are acting as treasurer, the secretary of the grand jury is also the treasurer of the county, practically, is he not?—Yes.

3819. And the clerk of the Crown is now a check upon the secretary of the grand jury when he is treasurer?—To speak candidly, he is supposed to be a check; but I really do not think that he is a check.

3820. Why do you say so?—There is a great confidence among officers; the clerk of the Crown will depend upon me, and I depend upon the clerk

Mr. *E. Sadleir.*

19 May 1868.

clerk of the Crown, and there is a great question if one is a check upon the other.

3821. But if the duty of countersigning the cheques were taken away from the clerk of the Crown, there would be no check whatever upon the secretary acting as treasurer, would there?—There would be a check.

3822. What would that be?—A good salary is a check; a man who is well paid will not commit errors or faults.

3823. But except the check of the fear of losing his office there would be no check upon him?—Surely the auditor of the accounts is a check, and he can be made a greater check, perhaps, than he is at present.

3824. Do you know particularly how the accounts are audited at present?—I do not, for I have not passed any accounts as yet; I was only appointed the last assizes.

3825. I presume you are aware that the accounts are audited only twice a year?—I think they are audited twice a year, but they have not been audited with me yet.

3826. They are audited in Dublin, are they not?—Yes.

3827. It has been proposed by some witnesses before the Committee that the fiscal duties of the clerk of the Crown should be transferred to the secretary of the grand jury; would you approve of that transference?—Certainly.

3828. And that the clerk of the Crown for the future should have nothing whatever to do with the fiscal business of the county?—I approve of that.

3829. And then that the offices of clerk of the Crown and clerk of the peace should be amalgamated, and that one officer should discharge the two sets of duties, both being essentially connected with criminal affairs; do you think that that is a plan which could be carried out?—Certainly; I should have no objection to it; these done not interfere.

3830. As secretary of the grand jury, you receive a certain salary, and also I believe you receive a certain amount of fees?—I do.

3831. There was a return moved for last year of the salaries and fees of the various officers connected with the county presentments in Ireland, and I see in the county of Tipperary returned to you the sum of 320 *l.*; does that include all the fees which you receive, both those which are called customary fees and legal fees?—That is about on an average what I generally make; for this coming year, 1868, I shall make about 10 *l.* or 20 *l.* more; but on an average it is about from 250 *l.* to 320 *l.* That includes all fees.

3832. Upon an average upon each presentment there are fees charged to the amount of about 5 *s.*, are there not?—I will explain how the fees are; there are what we call the legal fees; there is 1 *s.*, which I charge for a tender, and 1 *s.* for a bond; those are the legal fees; as customary fees I charge 2 *s.* 6 *d.* for filling up an application to be laid before the bench, which two cess-payers are to sign, and I serve the notices required by law.

3833. Have you another fee for that?—No; the 2 *s.* 6 *d.* does all that; that saves the people coming may be 20 or 30 miles to the office; I go into each barony and hold a sessions for that purpose, and they all flock in to me; then, when payment is to be applied for for the works, they come to me and pay me 2 *s.* 6 *d.* for the application for payment, for which I serve a notice on the county surveyor, and I produce his paper at the sessions and get it approved.

3834. Colonel *French.*] That is 7 *s.* on every presentment, is it not?—Exactly; 7 *s.* on every presentment.

3835. *Chairman.*] Do you not think it might be better to do away with those fees, and to give the secretaries a larger salary, at the same time obliging them to fill up those forms for the applicants?—I am afraid there would be a great many applications filled up that would be perfectly useless which would flood the sessions with unnecessary work.

3836. Supposing a charge was made in the form of stamps upon every application that was made, those stamps to go to the credit of the county, how would that work in your opinion?—I think it would pay very well; that was the original way in which we had it before the Act of 6 & 7 Will. 4 came in.

3837. Would not that be better than having the secretary of the grand jury himself receiving those different fees, of which no regular account is kept?—I do not know; I think that those that are interested are the fair persons to have to pay it.

3838. How do you mean those that are interested?—If a person is anxious to become a contractor for the repair of a road, I think it is fairer for him to bear any little expense attending it.

3839. You misunderstand me. The proposal of the Committee is that each contractor for the future should have a right to go to the secretary and to call upon him to give those forms, but that upon those forms there should be a stamp, and that stamp the contractor, or applicant, whatever he might be, should pay for, and then the receipts from those stamps would go to the credit of the county, the secretary receiving no fee whatever: would that arrangement, in your opinion, work well?—I think that it would do very well.

3840. But would it not be more satisfactory to have the secretary's salary fixed at a known amount than to have it in this uncertain character, so that few people can know what it is, or would you as a secretary prefer that it should remain as it is?—I would legalise the fees; the fees make a public officer very obliging.

3841. Does it not give the secretary an interest in cutting up contracts?—In no case; I have been engaged in county business 35 years, and in no case have I interfered in cutting up contracts whatever.

3842. But it would be your interest to do so, would it not?—It would, certainly.

3843. Do you think it desirable that it should be the interest of any public officer to have things done that might not be for the benefit of the county?—I do not; I approve of a high salary.

3844. The clerk of the peace also receives certain fees, does he not?—He does.

3845. Would you explain to the Committee what those fees are, and what they are for?—He gets 3 *d.*, I think, for an entry; and he gets 3 *d.* for a decree, that is 6 *d.* Then he gets on an ejectment about 2 *s.* 6 *d.*, I think; but I am not very well up as to the fees he gets, because I have only been a very short time in office, though my father was clerk of the peace for 30 years.

3846. You are not in a position to state very accurately to the Committee how the fees received

Mr. *R. Keating.*

19 May 1868.

ceived by the clerk of the peace are made up?—I am not; but I would not hold the office, acting as deputy clerk of the peace, for the fees, except to pay the man the compliment. I would do it for nothing.

3847. You have been receiving these fees, I suppose?—Yes; and they hardly pay the expenses.

3848. What are the expenses?—I must go myself and bring my clerk to an hotel, and stop out a week or so during sessions.

3849. I see the fees returned for the county of Tipperary are 340 *l.*; do you mean to say that would not pay the expenses of going to quarter sessions?—Yes, but a great deal of that expense is caused by the registry of the fees on ale-houses. These are the only fees that are worth talking about. I suppose he gets about 100 *l.* a-year for that.

3850. I asked you to give the Committee an account of all the fees that he received; will you state exactly the whole amount of the fees that he receives for ale-houses and everything?—I should say he receives about 100 *l.* a year for ale-houses, and about 100 *l.* a year for the registry of voters; that is as far as I can judge.

3851. Mr. *Leader.*] Does that include the money received for the entry of processes?—I think that is about 100 *l.* a year.

3852. (*Chairman.*] Can you give the Committee in detail the particular amount that he receives upon each particular item?—I could not. I could only give a rough guess at it.

3853. I do not want you to give the entire absolute amount received in a year, but I want you to give the Committee the amount received upon each license and upon each ejectment, and upon each of these different items, and the different items upon which he receives fees?—He receives for the licenses 6 *s.* 6 *d.* On entering processes in the registrar's book he receives 3 *d.*, and if there is a decree pronounced he receives 3 *d.* more. I think he gets 2 *s.* 6 *d.* altogether for the ejectments, but it is really all guess-work.

3854. I thought you were receiving these fees yourself at present?—I was not appointed until my predecessor had got them. He first got them up to a certain time last November, and from that time there were no fees paid on the ale-houses except a few at quarter sessions for new cases.

3855. But you have since then been in receipt of them, have you not?—Yes, but that is a mere trifle.

3856. It may be a mere trifle in the aggregate amount, but I presume that upon each individual item it is the same fee?—The fees are paid annually in November. In November he gets 100 *l.*

3857. Who pays them?—The different publicans that have been licensed. When they are licensed, they are obliged to serve a notice upon the clerk of the peace, and give him a fee of 6 *s.* 6 *d.*

3858. What you have said latterly regards the license alone, does it not?—That is all.

3859. But with respect to the processes, decrees, and ejectments, of which you have spoken, you are certainly accurate as to the amount which he receives upon each of them?—Yes.

3860. For the registration of voters you say that he receives 100 *l.* a year?—About 100 *l.* a year.

3861. He is supposed to receive for that only what it costs him, is he not?—I think he is paid for the trouble and expense attending it. He has to compare every item; he must employ clerks to be sure to fill them up; and then he has to compare them himself to see that they are correct.

3862. To compare them with what?—With what the clerk writes.

3863. Are you aware what fees the clerk of the Crown receives?—I am not aware.

3864. Is he resident in Tipperary?—One is resident and the other is not.

3865. Are there two clerks of the Crown then in the county of Tipperary?—Yes, and the salary is divided between the two of them.

3866. There is a payment made to the treasurer for the applotment of the county cess, is there not?—Yes.

3867. This payment varies, does it not, in different counties?—I suppose it does; the extent of the county has a good deal to do with it.

3868. Is that payment left entirely to the discretion of the treasurer to charge what he likes?—The late treasurer explained to me that I think he charged 2 *s.* for every 100 names contained in the applotment book for copying; and the following session he charges 1 *s.* 6 *d.*; then I think he told me he had about 20 *l.* over to pay himself for having them examined and compared.

3869. The amount I see stated here is 150 *l.*?—It is so; that is for the two ridings.

3870. Have you seen this return that was presented last year of the different sums received by the various county officers?—No, I have not.

3871. If the secretary of the grand jury were to receive an allowance for a clerk, might he not be obliged when acting as treasurer to make this applotment, without any particular payment for it?—I think it would be quite impossible for one man to do it.

3872. In what consists the difficulty of this applotment?—In the amount of manual labour in the way of writing.

3873. How long would it take a clerk to write out all the names?—Really, as I tell you, I am a novice in it at the present moment, but I offered very nearly the same amount to clerks in Clonmel to do the work, and they would not do it at less than what the late treasurer gave.

3874. You have done it, I suppose, since you undertook the office of treasurer?—I am doing it at present.

3875. Are you giving to the clerks the amount that is stated here in this return?—I am not.

3876. This manual labour is done by them then at a less price than this 150 *l.*?—It is, but I have not included what it will cost myself in time; I have to compare every item myself.

3877. It is the same work that is done by every clerk of the union, I suppose, as regards the poor rates?—It is not the same amount, but it is the same description of duty that each clerk of the union does with respect to his own union.

3878. It is the same description of duty that each clerk of the union does with respect to his own union without any special payment for it, is it not?—I do not know what they are paid.

3879. You are aware that the collectors of the counties cess are obliged to lodge the money that they have received as soon as it amounts to 100 *l.*?—I am aware of it.

3880. Is there any way of enforcing that obligation

Mr. [illegible]. [illegible] May [illegible].

gation at present?—I do not think it is enforced, or I am not aware that there is any way of enforcing it.

3881. Would it not be possible through the instrumentality of the treasurer to enforce that obligation, by making him look after it and see that it was lodged?—If a collector says, "I will not collect," he may rest on his oars for some time, and then he may commence again all of a sudden and do great hardships.

3882. There is no obligation, at present, to make the collector collect it at any particular time; but there is an obligation that if he collects it he should lodge it; that is to say, that he should not collect it from the people, and then use it for his own private purposes. Would it not be very easy for the treasurer to see that, if the man had collected the money, it should be lodged, as the Act of Parliament directs it should?—The treasurer could only take the *ipse dixit* of the collector. How am I to find out, as treasurer, that a collector has collected 5 *l.* or 500 *l.*?

3883. Has not the collector got collecting books?—Yes.

3884. Have you ever seen the collecting books that the poor-rate collectors have in which they enter the receipt upon one portion (just in the same way as in private check-books), and in which there are blocks kept of each receipt given to the person paying the rate?—I have not seen them.

3885. Might not these collectors of public cess be checked in that way very easily?—If they gave an honest block-book they might.

3886. But would not they run a very great risk if they gave a dishonest one?—I do not know.

3887. Supposing that they represented in their book that a certain man had not paid up, whereas he had paid, would they not run a great risk of that individual coming forward and stating that he had paid?—Yes, but the collector may have a true report in his own desk, and he may not give me a true report of what he has received.

3888-9. But if he were obliged to enter into this block-book every payment that he has received, would not that be a check?—Supposing he has two block-books, and made a few entries in each and sent one to me, what am I to say.

3890. Have you never seen a poor-rate collector's book?—I have not, nor the constable's collecting books.

3891. Supposing it were the case that the poor-rate collectors were obliged to keep books of that description and to enter upon the block which they retained the names of the men to whom they gave the receipt, that was torn out of the book, and the amount of the receipts, and supposing that were done by the county cess collectors, would not that be a means of checking them and showing what money they had received?—It certainly would.

3892. If such a means as that could be adopted, would it not be very easy to oblige the collectors to come in, say, once a month, to the treasurer, and to show him their collecting books, so that it might be known what money they had collected, and what money they had lodged?—Yes.

3893. Do you think that some means of that description might be adopted to enforce the present law?—Yes, I think it could.

3894. What do the county cess collectors receive in the county of Tipperary for the collection of the rate?—Ninepence in the pound.

3895. What do the poor-rate collectors generally receive in the same county?—I do not know what it is; I only pay my own poor rates, and I do not care about what anybody receives for collecting them.

3896. How are the cess-payers selected in the county of Tipperary to attend at presentment sessions; do they take the highest cesspayers, or do they scatter them over the different baronies?—They take the highest cess-payers.

3897. No matter from what part of the barony they come?—No matter what part of the barony they come from, under the Grand Jury Act.

3898. Do you think the present constitution of presentment sessions satisfactory?—I do.

3899. Do you find that the cess-payers attend regularly?—They do not attend well.

3900. Do you think that that is a proof that they consider the system satisfactory?—I do not know that we can; I can explain why they do not attend so regularly as they should; that is very simple.

3901. Why do you think that they do not attend?—Because they are not sure, after coming a long distance, whether they will be selected or not.

3902. You think that the uncertainty of the ballot at the presentment sessions is one of the great causes why they do not attend?—I do, certainly.

3903. And if their being called to sit at the presentment sessions were a certainty, do you believe that under the present system of selection they would attend?—I do.

3904. You do not consider that it would be an improvement to have them elected as the poor law guardians are elected?—No; the mistake was in not having the ballot at the assizes and not at the sessions. If the ballot took place at the assizes for the 10 or 20 cesspayers, whatever the number is, they would know then who was to attend, and they would attend then, I am sure.

3905. But would not the rule of taking the highest cesspayers very often result in their all being taken from one particular part of the barony, and in the rest of the barony being left unrepresented?—It may so happen.

3906. But may it not very often happen in a barony where one part is very fine, good grass land with a great number of large occupiers, that all the highest cesspayers would come from that part?—I am sure that they would be very proper persons to represent the barony.

3907. But the poorer portions of the barony would be entirely unrepresented then?—No, because you have magistrates in every locality, who pay taxes as well as the ratepayers, and those localities are therefore equally represented with the others.

3908. Then those poorer portions would be represented merely by magistrates?—Exactly.

3909. And you think that that is sufficient?—I think so; I do not find our county is so far gone as all that.

3910. Mr. *Dawson*.] Would you unite the offices of treasurer and of secretary of the grand jury?—Yes; I am not acting permanently as clerk of the peace; I am acting as secretary, and I am doing the duty of the treasurer, for which duty I am paid about 125 *l.*, for what he was paid 600 *l.* for.

3911. Have you been appointed since the Act

of

of last year, which abolished the office of county treasurer?—It is within this last six months.

3912. Colonel *French*.] But how do you mean that you receive 126 *l.*?—That is all they are paying me now under the new Act; but the Lord Lieutenant can give me, I believe, to the amount of one-third of the salary of the late treasurer.

3913. *Chairman*.] Has he not done so?—To be candid, I have not memorialised him yet, but I think the payment is so little for the work done, that I do not think I can look after that.

3914. But did he not give you the two-thirds?—I did not apply to him.

3915. Supposing he does give it you, would it not be a great deal more than 126 *l.* a year?—I cannot say it.

3916. What was the salary of the treasurer?—It was 400 *l.* a year; and then he had 200 *l.* a year interest money, so altogether it came to about 600 *l.* a year.

3917. Do you mean to tell the Committee that two-thirds of 400 *l.* is only 126 *l.*?—It is not much more, I think.

3918. Mr. *Dawson*.] I suppose that is not counting the interest of the money?—No.

3919. Colonel *French*.] You stated, did you not, that you did not think that there was any additional security in the treasurer's check being countersigned by the clerk of the Crown?—I do not think there is very much.

3920. Do you think that the treasurer's signature alone is equal to that of the two officers?—I do.

3921. And that there is no provision against the treasurer's misappropriating the funds?—I do not see how he can misappropriate any funds.

3922. If his cheques were paid to his own order solely, could not he misappropriate any portion of the funds lodged in the bank?—Yes; but he has to give security; he would not do it.

3923. Does not everybody give security who is appointed under the grand jury?—Not the secretary of the grand jury, for I never gave any security.

3924. The secretary of the grand jury had to give security for a large sum of money in former times, had he not?—The treasurer gave security, but the secretary never gave security.

3925. You said that the cheque which was required might be had through the auditor?—Yes; I should think so.

3926. Are you aware that the treasurer's accounts are not sent up to the auditor until the assizes are terminated?—Yes; but they would be checked then.

3927. If the treasurer misappropriated the money, if he levanted with it, for instance, he would be safe out of the country long before the accounts came to the auditor, would he not?—Yes.

3928. You stated that you had certain fees as clerk of the peace; do you know anything of the origin of those fees?—I do not.

3929. Are you aware that when salaries were given to the clerk of the Crown and the clerk of the peace it was in lieu of their services as well as their fees?—That is not the Act, certainly.

3930. Will you show that it is not?—I am sure that it is not; they got a certain amount.

3931. I think I can make it out that it is so, and that there is a misappropriation of all the fees of those officers, inasmuch as they ought all to have been paid to the credit of the county?—I believe it is the law that they should be entitled to receive a certain fee.

3932. Are they not to hand it over to the credit of the county?—Certainly not.

3933. Then you have never handed, as far as your experience goes, any fees which you have received to the credit of the county?—There are some fees which are specified; for instance, the copy of the registry, I think, for the barony.

3934. I merely want to know whether you have ever handed any fees over to the county?—I know that the clerk of the peace did hand over those few shillings which he received for copies of the registry, but no fees, such as the fees which he receives for entering processes or other ordinary fees; those are regulated by the Act.

3935. You have not done so, and, in your opinion, the law does not require those fees to be lodged to the credit of the county?—Certainly not; the salary of the clerk of the peace was greatly reduced at that time.

3936. Several questions were put to you by the Honourable Chairman as to the possibility or advisability of compelling the cess collectors to pay in the 100 *l.* which the law requires them to do, and of the treasurer seeing that that was done; is that, in your opinion, a good plan?—I think it would be a very good plan; if he collects 50 *l.* he can show me that he collects 50 *l.*, and if he collects 100 *l.* he can show me that he has collected 100 *l.*

3937. *Chairman*.] In the questions which I put, you did not understand me to mean that he should be obliged to collect it, but merely that when it was collected he should be obliged to lodge it?—Yes; I think that that is very fair.

3938. Colonel *French*.] Do you find great difficulty in your own mind in seeing how a check could be established that would compel him to do so?—I am not very well up to the meaning of it; if I understood thoroughly well the meaning of it I could give you an answer.

3939. If the collector had collected 99 *l.* and then stopped, the law does not compel him to lodge that 99 *l.*?—If it is not confined to any sum, I think it is possible; the collectors could make me a return weekly of how much they receive.

3940. *Chairman*.] You stated to the Committee that you expected to receive only 126 *l.* for discharging the duties of treasurer?—Yes, that is about two-thirds of 400 *l.*, or 270 *l.*

3941. Do you mean to tell the Committee that 126 *l.* is two-thirds of 400 *l.*?—I declare I never troubled my head with what I was saying; I have been very much occupied.

3942. And you have given evidence before the Committee without taking any trouble to ascertain its correctness?—I said it was about that.

3943. It is more than twice that amount, is it not?—It is 266 *l.*

3944. Mr. *Leader*.] You at present appear to be secretary for the whole county?—I am.

3945. Is it arranged that, supposing you resigned your post, there should be one secretary only, or two secretaries?—I think two secretaries would be a great improvement.

3946. But then the county would be at the expense of two, instead of one as at present?—Yes, I think it would be a great improvement taking into consideration that he is acting as treasurer now.

3947. *Chairman*.] When you say that you think it would be a great improvement, have you found that your duties in one riding interfere with your duties in the other?—It is not as regards my duties that I complain, but the county

Mr. E. Smith.

19 May 1858.

is extensive it is, say 60 miles long; I reside in the county town of the south riding, and if any ratepayer wants to come to me, he has to come actually 60 miles. Some men are not satisfied until they see me in person; no letter writing will satisfy them.

3948. Mr. *Leader*.] What bank acts as treasurer to the county now?—The Provincial Bank.

3949. What do they charge for their trouble?—I do not know how it is done; it is a running account; I do not think they are paid beyond the advantage of having the money in their bank.

3950. Do they lodge any money in Exchequer Bills?—Yes, that comes through the auditor of the accounts. There is no much interest loaded to the county on the Exchequer Bills.

3951. Was there no arrangement made with the Provincial Bank when they became treasurers, except merely that they should have a certain balance of that character?—I think they were only paid just the same as in the case of any other private account. Sometimes the money in the bank will run very close; the bank will have very little money, and sometimes the cheques will exceed it.

3952. *Chairman*.] Under the Act which was passed last year, there was no duty whatsoever thrown upon the bank beyond that which it had before of receiving from the collectors the amount which they collect; is not that the case?—There is a sort of additional duty put upon them.

3953. What is that?—That is seeing that the proper person signs these drafts.

3954. Is there any responsibility thrown upon the bank if they make a payment on a cheque which is signed by some other person besides the secretary of the grand jury beyond the responsibility which they incur with every private individual who keeps an account with them?—I do not think that there is.

3955. All the duties of the office of treasurer are thrown upon the secretary of the grand jury, are they not?—Yes, but the bankers know the signature of the person who takes money on a private account.

3956. But in this case they know the signature of the secretary of the grand jury, do they not?—They do.

3957. And they can make no payment unless the cheque be signed by the secretary of the grand jury and countersigned by the clerk of the Crown?—No.

3958. And beyond that there is no responsibility whatever thrown upon them?—There is, certainly.

3959. What is it?—As to the identity of the man who has drawn the money. Suppose I give a draft to Tom Ryan and that Tom Ryan gives it to his brother, or cousin, another Tom Ryan, this man goes and draws the money and the other man does not get it.

3960. But that is a responsibility which exists with respect to every private account which they have, is it not?—Yes, but individually it is not very much. When numerous payments are made by the bank, there is, I think, great responsibility thrown upon the bank to see that they are paying the money for the proper person. The order may be good, but how are they to know the individual?

3961. How were they paid before when there was a particular individual acting as treasurer?—The treasurer got the receipt from the individual.

3962. He got the receipt from the individual, and he gave that individual a cheque upon the bank?—He kept that receipt in his possession and gave a draft.

3963. And he gave a cheque upon the bank?—Yes.

3964. Was not that bank in exactly the same position as regards responsibility as the present banks are now?—Not so, because they could fall back on the receipt which was held by the treasurer.

3965. Who could?—The county bank could.

3966. Cannot they fall back now? There is no receipt given now.

3967. Will you explain what you mean by no receipt being given now?—The receipt is on the back of the draft. I have been acting as secretary, and here is a draft for Tom Ryan, and I give it to him and he takes it away; he brings it to the bank. I do not see Tom Ryan sign his name to it, but the bank sees Tom Ryan's name, or they ought to see it.

3968. Have you heard that any of the banks object to any of the responsibility which is thrown upon them?—They did at first, but afterwards I heard no complaints.

3969. But with respect to what the Honourable Member for the county of Cork asked you as to lodging money in Exchequer Bills, the bank have nothing in the world to say to that, have they?—I think not.

3970. It is the secretary of the grand jury now who will have to do that in case it is necessary, is it not?—Yes.

3971. And all the actual duties of the treasurer have been transferred to the secretary of the grand jury, have they not?—Yes.

3972. Mr. *Blake*.] You are secretary for the whole county of Tipperary, and treasurer also, are you not?—I am.

3973. I believe you are a land agent also, are you not?—No, I am nothing at all, but simply secretary or treasurer.

3974. Have you no other avocation?—None whatever, and I never had any other.

3975. You recommended just now that in the county of Tipperary for each of the Ridings there should be a secretary, did you not?—I do, for the good of the cesspayers, not for myself, certainly.

3976. Could the whole of the duties which are performed now continue to be performed by you satisfactorily?—They could.

3977. Is there much disadvantage arising to the cesspayer from your performing all the duties now?—No, not much.

3978. Do you know the clerk of the Crown and the clerk of the peace for the county of Waterford?—I do not know him.

3979. Are you aware that he performs the duties of the clerk of the Crown and clerk of the peace for the county of Waterford, and also of clerk of the Crown for the county of the city of Waterford?—There is very little to be done by the clerk of the Crown. It is merely done during the assizes. I suppose that in the county of Waterford the duty of the clerk of the Crown is only for a day, or two days.

3980. Could you, without much stress upon yourself, perform all the fiscal duties appertaining to grand juries which are at present performed by the clerk of the Crown if you were properly compensated?—Certainly.

3981. And

Mr. B. [illegible]. 19 May 1868.

3981. And you have no doubt, from the example of the county of Tipperary, which is a very extensive one, that the whole of the fiscal duties might fairly be put upon officers in your position without any apprehension that the public service would suffer in consequence?—I should think it would be far better. I have been asked about the check, but I say that two badly paid officers may put their heads together and rob the county.

3982. It is quite possible to perform the duties under such circumstances as you mention, being properly compensated?—Certainly, even in the mode of doing business now, it appears to me an absurdity. I hand over a list of presentments to the clerk of the Crown, and what does he do? He gives back to me a copy of what I gave him. If he makes a mistake, it is not he who will be blamed, but I should be blamed.

3983. From your long experience as a county officer, do you see any objection in any future letting that the rates should be divided between the landlord and the occupier?—To be candid with you, I never considered anything about it one way or the other.

3984. Do you see any objection either to the associated ratepayers being directly appointed by the cesspayers, instead of being nominated, as they are at present, by the representatives of a barony upon the grand jury?—I think that they are far better represented by the grand jury.

3985. Have you ever heard any dissatisfaction expressed in your county at that mode of appointment?—It would end, I think, in this way: that a large road contractor would fix on his man to be a representative of the barony.

3986. Could he carry his man?—I think he could. Any man who agitates a bit can carry a great deal.

3987. Even though the cesspayers would pretty well know that it was for the purpose of a job?—Even so; indeed they would.

3988. Your answer then is, that a contractor wishing to get a job in a barony, and that fact being known, could carry any man he pleased as against the rest of the cesspayers?—I think so.

3989. Mr. *Dawson*.] Do you think that if there was any change in the way in which these associated cesspayers are nominated, they could be the same individuals as the poor law guardians, and that you could have men elected for the two offices?—I really do not understand the poor law guardians; I never trouble my head about them.

3990. But from your general knowledge of the working of the grand jury laws, do you think that the present clause for malicious injuries should be maintained; in your county, which is a very large one, do you see that there is any serious additional tax inflicted upon the public by the present clause allowing applications to be made for damage and compensation?—I think it is a very great advantage.

3991. Is there any flax grown to any extent in the county of Tipperary?—There is not.

3992. I will read you an extract from a letter which I received this morning on that subject, and I will ask your opinion upon it: "Sir,—As I see you are on the Committee on the grand jury laws, I hope you will contrive to get the clause for malicious injuries done away with, as the burning of flax mills in this county is becoming quite a tax of itself, and now that insurance can be effected, I consider that the duty of every one having a flax mill is to insure it, and if he does not do so, let him bear the consequences." Now I can confirm that as regards the county of Londonderry where a great deal of flax is grown, and the county cess is very much increased by these applications for malicious injuries, which are generally speaking recovered. Is there anything of that kind in the county of Tipperary?—Nothing whatever.

3993. *Chairman*.] You stated, did you not, in answer to the Honourable Member for Londonderry, that you believed that these presentments for malicious injuries were very desirable?—Yes, for those who have suffered injury.

3994. Is not the principle of these presentments making the innocent pay for the guilty?—It is hoped that it will have the effect of checking guilty parties.

3995. Do you think that it has the effect of checking such offences?—That is questionable.

3996. But what is your opinion?—I certainly think it has.

3997. Do you think it has the effect of leading to the discovery of the perpetrators of these crimes?—No, we have never found out the perpetrators in Tipperary since I have been secretary, or for a long time before that.

3998. Therefore it does not appear at all to tend to the discovery of criminals?—Not to the discovery.

3999. Has it a tendency in the opposite direction?—We have not so many malicious injuries now as we used to have.

4000. But when you have malicious injuries, you say that the perpetrators are very seldom discovered?—I do not recollect one.

4001. Do you think that the fact of the sufferers having the power of going to the grand jury and the presentment sessions, and of getting compensation for these malicious injuries, has a tendency to make them careless about the person who has committed the crime?—I do not, because they are well scrutinised by the sessions, and afterwards by the grand jury.

4002. Supposing an application to be very well scrutinised at the presentment sessions and by grand jury, still has not the fact that a man has a means open to him of getting repaid for any loss which he may suffer, a tendency to make him careless about searching out the individual who has committed the crime?—His sole object is to be paid.

4003. If there were no such payment, he would have an object in discovering who injured him, would he not?—Yes, he would.

4004. Which is deadened at least by the present system?—Certainly.

4005. Are you aware that no such system of payment for malicious injuries exists in England?—I am not aware of that.

4006. You may take that as a fact. Should you be surprised if you heard that the number of persons apprehended for malicious injuries in Ireland was only 5 per cent. upon the offences, while in England, according to the criminal statistics for similar crimes, the number of persons apprehended was over 50 per cent.?—I am not surprised at that.

4007. And yet, in England, no such system of compensation exists; if that were the case, would not these proportions lead you to believe that this system of getting compensation for malicious injuries greatly did away with the desire of persons to discover the criminals?—No. When I know that the people of England, to a man, try to find out

Mr. E. Gulkin.

19 May 1852.

out the guilty party, and when I know that the people of Ireland, to a man, try to conceal the guilty party, it does not surprise me.

4008. Do you apply that statement to all the crimes committed in the country, or merely to those particular malicious crimes?—You may extend it to all crimes.

4009. Are you perfectly certain that that is a correct statement?—You asked me for my opinion.

4010. But upon what do you support that opinion?—Upon my knowledge, and the times in which I have lived.

4011. Should you be surprised, then, to learn that there is a greater percentage of apprehensions in Ireland upon all crimes than there are upon all crimes in England?—No.

4012. Supposing that all the crimes of Ireland were put down on one side, and the number of persons apprehended for those crimes on the other, and if the same were done for England, should you be surprised to learn that there was a greater per-centage of persons apprehended for crimes in Ireland than there were of persons apprehended for crimes in England?—I should not be surprised.

4013. And yet you stated a moment ago that you believed every one in England, immediately a crime is committed, did their best to discover the criminal, but that in Ireland it was just the reverse?—Yes.

4014. And yet in the country in which people do so little to discover the criminals, there is a greater per-centage of criminals apprehended on the crimes than there is in England?—The police do so much in Ireland.

4015. Ought not the police to do equally as much with respect to this particular class of crimes?—They do their best.

4016. And their best, in this class of cases, is that they apprehend only 3 per cent.?—You know it is very hard to catch a man, and the police cannot do everything.

4017. But do you not believe that many of those malicious injuries which are brought before the grand jury are really occurrences which happened by accident?—In any case which has even the semblance of accident the cesspayers and magistrates at the baronial sessions invariably disallow it.

4018. But the application is made?—There may be some applications, but very few.

4019. You think that very few applications are made, except where there is a really good case?—Very few. There is a certain amount of money to be spent, such as lodging affidavits and serving notices, and travelling here and there, and attending road sessions, and men will not lose their time on a mere chance.

4020. Mr. *Kendall.*] As I understand you, you say that the private information in the case of crime, which is given in England, is much larger than the private information given in Ireland, but that, at the same time, the police in Ireland are so much superior to the police in England, that the per-centage of apprehensions on the number of crimes is greater in Ireland than in England?—Yes.

4021. *Chairman.*] But is not the private information with respect to these particular classes of crimes less than with regard to any others?—I do not think it is; I do not think it varies.

4022. If a man loses his money and is robbed, will he not immediately go off to the police and do his best to assist the police in discovering the man who has robbed him?—Yes; certainly he will.

4023. But if his corn-stack is fired, or some injury is done to his cattle, his whole object would be to go to the grand jury to show that that burning or injury was done maliciously, and he will not care in the slightest degree to find the man out who committed the crime, will he?—I think they do try. Their first duty is to go to the police and to gain a good countenance at the road sessions. The police will be there to prove whether this man is doing his best to support his claim.

4024. Mr. *Dawson.*] Are there many cases of malicious injury in the county of Tipperary?—No, not very many.

4025. How many do you suppose on an average, at each sessions are presented?—There are generally about two in each barony, and sometimes none.

4026. Colonel *French.*] You were asked whether levying the amount of the injury done on the town land, or on whatever district the grand jury may decide, was not punishing the innocent for the guilty; would it in case a house was burnt, or a turf rick was burnt, of a tenant who came in and took lands from which there had been an ejectment, be punishing the innocent for the guilty?—It would to a certain amount; all the people in the locality had no hand in it.

4027. But has not that been done *primâ facie*, in order to prevent a new tenant coming in, by the rest of the holders, or with their sanction on the town land?—They should use their influence to prevent it, but they know nothing at all about it.

4028. *Chairman.*] Are you aware that up to a comparatively recent period presentments were granted in Ireland, to persons for losses sustained by means of robbers; and that if a man was robbed, he would have a right to go to the grand jury and seek a presentment for it?—That has not occurred in my county for 36 years.

4029. Are you not aware that an Act of Parliament existed so late as the year 1848, enabling persons to do so?—I am not aware of it; it was never acted upon in our county, even where money was burnt in a house; latterly they granted it where a poor man had 10 *l.* in his house, and his house was burnt; but formerly they would only give him the value of the house.

4030. Colonel *French.*] In some stages of civilisation, it is necessary to force the people to have a pecuniary interest in preserving the law of the country, is it not?—It is.

4031. Mr. *Lanier.*] Supposing that a vacancy occurred in the post of secretary for the county of Tipperary, who would elect him?—The grand jury would have the appointment.

4032. But there are two grand juries, which of them would elect him?—It is given to the South Riding Grand Jury.

4033. Then the South Riding have the power of appointing a secretary for the North Riding?—Yes.

Mr. HENRY BRETT, called in; and Examined.

Mr. H. Brett.

10 May 18[illegible].

4034. *Chairman*.] You are the county surveyor for the county of Wicklow, are you not?—I am.

4035. And before holding that office in the county of Wicklow, you held it in several other counties, did you not?—I held that office in the counties of King's County, Mayo, and Waterford.

4036. And before you became county surveyor, you were connected with the county of Sligo, were you not?—I was connected with the county of Sligo for several years.

4037. In what capacity?—As surveyor and supervisor of roads and as overseer, and in various capacities under the grand jury.

4038. With regard to your own office, you are acquainted of course with the mode in which applications for presentments are made, and the forms to be gone through?—I am.

4039. Do you believe that many of those forms are quite unnecessary?—It appears to me that they are very complex, and that they might be greatly simplified.

4040. Will you state to the Committee in what points you think they might be simplified?—In all the cases of continuous contracts which are usually for three or five years, it is mere routine to have them approved of again; and it appears to me that those applications might be scheduled, and that all the applications by cesspayers ought to be as far as possible confined to new works, such as hill cuttings, and bridges and special works requiring public notification.

4041. Would you have them confined exclusively to new works?—Yes, except in very special cases.

4042. At present it is obligatory upon the applicant to post a notice upon the police barracks, is it not?—Yes.

4043. Do you believe those notices are of any use whatever?—In most cases they are not posted, and when they are posted they are of very little use.

4044. If they are not so posted is the application formal?—It ought to be done, as required by law, but the session in most cases, seeing the inutility of it, very rarely, according to my experience, inquire into the service of notices, except in cases of new works, or special works.

4045. Would you not require some notice to be given before-hand of an intention to apply to the next sessions?—I would; I think a notice of 20 or 30 days might be given to the county surveyor, and I would let him tabulate or make schedules of the applications according to the order, or merits of the works, and those schedules should be printed and posted on the police barracks, and sent to all the magistrates and cesspayers.

4046. That, you think, should be done by the county surveyor?—I think it should be done by the secretary, but that the county surveyor should arrange all the documents. He might either himself do it, or he might assist the secretary to do it.

4047. Would you do away with the fees paid to the secretary at present for those applications?—I would, most assuredly. It appears to me that the secretary is in a very anomalous position; he is first the officer of the grand jury, and he is next, to a great extent, the agent of the contractor in filling documents; and in that way he is placed in a position in which he ought not to be.

4048. I presume that the contractor would require certain forms to be filled up on certain occasions?—I would make the secretary furnish copies of all documents upon stamps; the stamps to be collected into a fund as they are in commissions, and to go to the credit of the county.

4049. The Committee have received a good deal of evidence as regards the presentments of roads, half on the county and half on the barony; do you believe that those presentments are desirable as they are at present carried out?—In my judgment the roads of each county should be classified according to the order of their importance. The regular mail-coach roads, and great arteries of the country to sea ports and leading towns ought to be in one class by themselves, and should be kept in the very best order. The second class of roads are to market towns, and to great lime-works and quarries, and large bogs and coal fields. The minor roads ought to be kept in a different way altogether, at a smaller expense.

4050. Would you have any of those roads put upon the county at large?—I would have the first class roads put, either upon the county; or partly on the county and upon districts of the county; I will instance the county of Wicklow, where we have two leading roads, one at the sea-side, and one at the western side of the mountains, both of which were mail-coach roads. The railway on one side has done away with the necessity of a mail-coach road at that side between Dublin and Wexford, and though the traffic on the road continues the same in extent, the baronies through which that line runs are charged solely with its maintenance, while a similar road on the western side of the county is charged half on the county at large and half on baronies, and that is felt to be a very great grievance. Either they ought to be altogether abolished as charges on county or the leading arteries at both sides of county, as, I say, ought to be charged half on the county at large, and half on the districts.

4051. The character of the mail-coach roads has very much varied from what it was formerly, has it not, since railways have come into operation?—In most cases they are now mail-car roads, but I speak of actual mail-coach roads, not mail car-roads under new arrangement.

4052. And they are very often very small unimportant roads, are they not?—They are.

4053. Would you give power to the grand jury, or to whatever body managed the finances of the county, to deal with a road in another county?—I would; I will give the Committee an instance. Between the county of Wicklow and the county of Kildare, there is a portion of mail-coach road which I referred to, and the boundary is in the centre of the road for probably about a mile, and then there are detached corners of a few yards belonging to the county of Kildare. The cesspayers of that county feel no interest whatever in the road, and in most cases they do not grant presentments for it.

4054. You mean to say that half the breadth of the road is in one county and half in the other?—Half is in one county, and half in the other; one half is kept in repair, and the other half is

frequently

Mr. *H. Brett.*

19 May 1859.

frequently totally disregarded, and nothing is done for it. It is a source of very great inconvenience, and it appears to me that either the county which has the major part of the road ought to have the care of it entirely, charging the adjoining county with its proportion of the expense, or it should be divided in two by a committee, or joint commission, from both grand juries.

4055. And you would make this co-operation of the two grand juries compulsory, I suppose?—I would.

4056. Colonel *French.*] Is not that compulsory in the case of bridges joining two counties?—It is; but it is subject to a great deal of difficulty, for the law provides that the one should make presentments at the same time as the other, a matter which is a physical impossibility.

4057. Then when the county in which the larger proportion of the work is, makes a presentment for it, it is compulsory upon the other county also to make a presentment for it?—Yes.

4058. *Chairman.*] Would you permit one county to subscribe towards the expenses of a bridge situated altogether in another county, although it might be very useful to the first mentioned county?—I would, and for roads also. There is a road in the county of Waterford through the corner of a small poor barony, between Clonmel and Knockloftv. That barony has no interest whatever in the road, being purely for the benefit of the counties of Limerick and Cork; I say that the people interested in that road ought to be compelled to contribute towards it.

4059. At present, if they are willing to contribute to it, they have no power to do so, have they?—They have no power to do so.

4060. And the difficulties arising from that are very great, are they not?—Very great.

4061. Do you think the power of the county surveyor for enforcing the completion of contracts, is sufficient?—It is not.

4062. Have you read a paper which has been handed in by Mr. Hill, with regard to that?—I have.

4063. Do you consider that the proposals that he makes for remedying that evil are sufficient?—I disagree with a portion of what Mr. Hill puts forward. So far as regards acting under the 54th section, that is, that upon a ten days' notice the surveyor may repair the road, if the funds are available, I think that is very salutary; I would be strongly disposed to mix it up with the proposal about going before petty sessions, but I do not think that in cases of maintenance contracts there ought to be summonses twice over. It appears to me that a second adjournment, such as Mr. Hill proposes, would be most objectionable.

4064. You think that at most there ought to be only two adjournments?—I think there ought to be no adjournment: it might be arranged in this way; that in all cases where it becomes necessary for the county surveyor to interfere he should, in the first instance, serve a 10 days' notice on the contractor and if it was a maintenance contract the magistrates should then and there authorise the repair or make a mandatory order on the contractor for a penalty. For instance, in the county of Wicklow, after snows, and during frosts and floods, we are subject to great casualties. The roads suddenly break up and great inconvenience arises; and notwithstanding all the efforts made to make the contractors attend to them, if we are to wait for summoning and re-summoning, a great deal of injury might be caused to the public by the delay. I think there ought to be summary means for providing for cases of that sort.

4065. You would permit the road to be repaired in some summary way, and give summary jurisdiction?—I would.

4066. Particularly in mountain districts?—Particularly in mountain districts. I would allow the magistrates to hear a second summons, and give some little time. When a man, by inadvertence, took a contract for a lower sum than was sufficient, I would not press too hardly; but, in repairs of bridges and maintenance contracts, I would take the most summary means of having them carried out.

4067. You would not in those latter cases, allow the magistrate any jurisdiction to give any further time?—In the cases of neglect of maintenance of roads, I would give them no power to postpone at all. If the case was proved after 10 days' notice, I would call upon them to make a mandatory order on the contractor, or to authorise the county surveyor to repair the road at once.

4068. You are aware that the bonds entered into by contractors are made out to the Crown at present?—They are, and that gives rise to another cause of difficulty. In many of the applications put forward by the cesspayers one cesspayer signs the names of both; those applications go before the sessions, but they are not very strictly inquired into, and they are approved of. Then contracts are entered into, and when it becomes necessary to proceed before the chairman of the county or any of the superior courts, the whole legal question as to the validity of all documents is raised, and it becomes a very serious obstacle indeed. The signatures of the parties to the application, to the communers, to the tenders, and to the bonds are all questioned, and when the county surveyor is asked to show that the proceedings are strictly legal, difficulties present themselves at every step. This ought to be provided for by a provision that the documents should be *primâ facie* evidence of their validity.

4069. And that the onus should rest with the other party?—The onus should be on the contractor; to show that he was not liable; I have been turned round several times lately within the last two years in very important cases, and have completely failed.

4070. In consequence of not being able to prove the signature of the parties who went security for the bond?—Precisely.

4071. You are also obliged to get the permission of the Attorney General to take any of these proceedings, are you not, in consequence of these bonds being made out to the Crown?—These bonds are at present made out to the Crown.

4072. Ought not all these bonds to be made out to some officer of the county?—I think they ought.

4073. Would you suggest any other alteration with respect to the method of proceeding against contractors for non-compliance with their contracts?—I think that the amendment which I propose would go a great way to meet the difficulty, viz., if the documents connected with the contract were declared to be valid until proved to the contrary, and if the magistrates were obliged to make a mandatory order after notice in cases of neglect of maintenance contracts, and in other cases to proceed in the ordinary way. I think that would go a great way to meet the difficulties, means being provided to pay for the outlays.

4074. As

Mr. H. Brett.

19 May 1868.

4074. At present there is no fund, is there, out of which those legal expenses can be met in the first instance?—There is no fund either for the legal expenses or for the outlays which ought to be made upon the roads neglected by contractors.

4075. What outlays upon the roads?—Supposing the county surveyor found it necessary, under the 54th section, to employ another contractor, or to employ an overseer and labourers, he must either pay them out of his own pocket or he must get them to wait until the next assizes, until the amount expended be deducted out of the contract, and so unless he agrees to pay an extravagant price, the chances are he cannot get work done at all. I say that means ought to be provided to meet those outlays at once, and that immediate payments be made by the county secretary or the county treasurer.

4076. You think there ought to be a particular sum voted for that purpose?—I think there ought to be a "general purpose fund."

4077. You think there ought to be a general purpose fund voted for contingencies between one assizes and the other?—Yes; it might be done in a very simple way; it might commence at the summer assizes, when the dog tax comes in, that and any surplus sum that may have been collected and not discharged or otherwise applied might be applied to this general purpose fund, and also the sums levied in excess. In each applotment made by the treasurer there is a small margin; the treasurer does not make out his applotments to the precise amount that is to be levied, but in almost every case there are some few pounds over and above in each barony, and are collected and paid into the county bank. All those sums every two or three years are re-credited back again to the districts, and these might at once be applied to the general purpose fund.

4078. Would you draw upon that fund for any other purpose than the one you have mentioned?—I would apply it to the provision for sudden damages and for outlays in cases of default, and for any contingency that might arise from any casualty in the county.

4079. Do you think that there is sufficient provision at present made for making advances for works in progress?—The grand jury in most cases do not order advances unless they are applied for by the contractor; they have power to order three-fourths to be advanced, but the rule heretofore has been not to act upon that until the treasurer has actually a fund available. Supposing at the summer assizes, a bridge costing 1,000 *l.* is presented, and the grand jury authorise the contractor to receive instalments not exceeding three-fourths of the money; but in nearly all counties the treasurer will not advance until he has that 1,000 *l.* actually in hand, and that causes a great delay; all the funds in the treasurer's hands, or, at all events, the general purpose fund, ought to be applicable to those advances to enable the contractor to execute the works.

4080. Would you oblige the collector to collect the money immediately?—I would, and I would have his books and checks all audited, as they are under the Poor Law, fortnightly or monthly, and see that the moneys collected were paid into the county bank.

4081. Who do you propose should look after the collectors to see that they collect the money, and pay it in when collected?—I should say, certainly, the treasurer, or whoever has to do with the accounts as treasurer.

4082. Do you think that that is a duty which he could very well perform?—I do; it appears to me that the treasurer ought to be put in a position to do three things, viz., to make the applotment, to pay incidental outlays upon roads, and to aid the contractors by advances. Of course the grand jury would enable him to appoint a clerk or a deputy for that purpose, but I would put the responsibility upon the treasurer. I would not create a new office, but I would make it obligatory upon the secretary or treasurer to discharge those duties.

4083. Of course you would have to give him an increase of salary for that purpose?—Certainly.

4084. How do you suppose that he could verify the collector's accounts?—Precisely as it is done for every board of guardians, weekly or fortnightly, or monthly, as the case may be, by the production of the block receipt books, each collector being obliged to furnish printed receipts to the cesspayers, and from a comparison of the block receipts with his collection book there would be no difficulty whatever in checking his accounts.

4085. You would oblige the collectors to come into the treasurer periodically?—Yes; once a month, or oftener, as need be.

4086. Have you found any difficulty as county surveyor in having to pay the men whom you employ to repair roads or other works for the county?—Very great difficulty. In the first place, as the law now stands, the surveyor must find funds, and it is exceedingly objectionable and irksome, and a great loss of time for him or his assistant to have to pay those moneys to workmen and labourers; the moneys ought not to pass through his hands at all.

4087. You believe that the payments ought to be taken away from him altogether?—Certainly. You should put the responsibility of executing the works upon him, and put the responsibility of paying parties upon another officer altogether.

4088. You would put that duty and responsibility upon the county treasurer?—I would.

4089. At present the grand jury have no power to alter a contract, have they?—They have not, and this causes very great inconvenience. Sometimes parties take contracts at sums that are too high. In some baronies the magistrates and cesspayers allow a large limit for competition; by management among the contractors that limit is very frequently not reduced, and when the contract comes before the grand jury the amount is very often found excessive, and they have no alternative, but either to pass it or to reject it, and to leave the road without a contract. In other cases the contracts are very much too low, and persons who are notoriously defaulters, come forward and take contracts, giving securities, but having, nevertheless, no means or qualification for executing the works. Sometimes it happens, as in the county of Wicklow, at last assizes, that a man gets a contract by fraud by purchasing the lower tenders of other parties. In that case he passed an I O U for the sum of 10 *l.* to induce a lower tenderer to get out of the way while he got the contract; but when the person who had the I O U came to sue for it, the contractor pleaded that it was a fraudulent transaction, and the chairman of the county was forced to dismiss the case; and he called my attention to it. It went before the grand jury, and they thought they had no power; but, however, the Chief Baron

Mr. H. Brett.

19 May 1868.

Baron decided that as it was a fraudulent transaction from the beginning, he had the power, and nulled the presentment. Then the difficulty arose as to what we were to do for the repair of the road. Fortunately the road was in good order, and we were able to leave it for a few months up to the summer assizes without a contract, and it has not suffered much.

4090. Do you think it desirable, therefore, to give the grand jury power to alter contracts, both as regards raising and lowering them?—I would give them power to make temporary arrangements to annul the contract if it is too high, or too low, and to make temporary provision for a few months to try and get an eligible contractor again.

4091. You would empower them to annul the contract, and hand the road over to the county surveyor, we will suppose, until the next presentment sessions?—Yes, to go before the next presentment sessions again.

4092. Are you aware that that is done at present by some grand juries?—I believe it is done.

4093. It is not legal to do it, is it?—I apprehend that it is not legal.

4094. Did you hear Mr. Tait's evidence with respect to the difficulty which contractors experience in getting materials of a certain description for roads?—I did not hear his evidence, but I read an outline of it.

4095. Do you concur in his statements?—I do; I find very great difficulty myself in procuring materials; the power ought to be simplified and extended to get materials of every kind.

4096. At present it is confined to stones and gravel, is it not?—It is; there is a great difficulty about getting earth, and some magistrates are very unwilling to exercise their powers in many cases, so that great difficulties arise.

4097. Have you any observation to make with respect to the certificates granted by county surveyors at presentment sessions for the completion of any works?—I think all the certificates ought to be allowed at the sessions to give credit for the period up to the assizes; the applications for payment ought to be approved at the sessions, but the certificate itself ought to be given before the grand jury.

4098. Will you explain the difficulties which arise sometimes under the present system of having a certificate given at the presentment sessions?—Sometimes the judges hold that the certificate cannot be given for a maintenance contract until an entire half-year has elapsed; and the result of that would be that a contractor could get nothing until the end of the 12 months. Others of the judges hold, that it is the duty of the surveyor and of the sessions to allow the application for payment to pass at the first sessions, though the half-year has not expired; and it is desirable to simplify this to declare what is really the meaning of the law, and to enable the sessions and grand jury to deal with the question. It appears to me that the application ought to be allowed to pass, giving credit for the period up to the assizes, and that then the grand jury should be allowed to deal with it finally when it comes before them.

4099. A maintenance contract is to keep the road in repair from the summer assizes until the spring, is it not?—Yes, for part of a year.

4100. And then the presentment sessions occur several months before?—Yes, before spring assizes.

4101. And it is impossible for the county surveyor to certify several months before that the road has been kept in order until a certain period which had not yet expired?—Yes, and frequently it becomes his duty to report a neglect of parties between the sessions and the assizes, and it is to explain the law and to give power to facilitate payments that I say the certificate, although allowed at sessions, ought to be revised at assizes.

4102. Is it legal to withdraw it?—It is not legal, but it is customary sometimes.

4103. Do you approve of the mode in which county surveyors are at present appointed?—Up to the present time they have been appointed under the law passed in 1833. All the lists are now exhausted, but in my opinion the mode provided for the examination, under the civil service commissioners, is not a good one; I consider that one of the examiners ought to be a practical engineer, conversant with county duties, or a county surveyor.

4104. Did you hear Mr. Tait's evidence upon that point, or did you read it?—I read it.

4105. Do you agree with him that there ought to be a certain number of persons on a list, always ready to step into a vacancy, which might arise?—I do, and for this reason; the law as it now stands, enables the county surveyor to appoint what is called a deputy, an officer who is entirely different from an assistant; as matters now stand, there is no one on the list eligible for that office, and any county surveyor might be taken suddenly ill, and he would have no person to appoint to the office; I would, therefore, recommend that there should be three names placed on a list, and that the Lord Lieutenant should appoint the first on the list, and that when another vacancy occurs he should appoint the second, and that as soon as the list came down to one, there should be a fresh examination and two more names should be added, so as never to have more than three nor less than one; very great inconvenience would arise if a vacancy occurred, just before sessions or assizes, if there were no means of appointing men rapidly. As the law now stands, notice should be given, and a long time must elapse before an examination, and the county interests would be very seriously prejudiced by following out what is contemplated by the recent Act.

4106. Can county surveyors be moved from one county to another at the will of the Lord Lieutenant?—They can.

4107. Is that extensively acted upon?—It is.

4108. Without an express wish of the county surveyor to leave the county in which he is?—I believe it has been recently acted upon, in some cases without the knowledge or application of the parties; I do not know all the circumstances, but the belief is that the officer was removed in a manner which I had reason to apprehend was not very satisfactory.

4109. Does such a thing exist among the county surveyors, as promotion from a third class county to a first class county?—Heretofore there was but one class, and all the salaries were alike; now that they are classified; in my opinion, when a vacancy occurs in a first or second class county, the existing officers ought to have the preference in promotion before the new officers coming in, and that the latter ought to take their chance in the lower class of counties; that would be a great inducement to exertion, and to a better discharge of the duties.

4110. Colonel

Mr. *H. Brett.*

19 May 1868.

4110. Colonel *French.*] According to the experience and abilities of the officers who have been in before?—Yes.

4111. Would you leave the promotion in the hands of the Lord Lieutenant?—I would leave it in the hands of the Lord Lieutenant; but instead of appointing an entirely new officer who might be a young man just from college, with no great experience, to a large county with extensive works, it would be but reasonable to place in such county an experienced officer, and but a matter of justice to the experienced officer himself, that he should get the promotion.

4112. *Chairman.*] But would not that always leave the third class counties in the care of inexperienced men?—That does not follow.

4113. As a general rule it would follow, I suppose?—Of course I would let the grand jury have a voice in the matter.

4114. Then supposing that a county surveyor wished to be transferred (as he naturally would wish) to a better county, and the Lord Lieutenant thought that he was an excellent man, and promoted him to a better county, what discretion would be left to the grand jury?—They might object to receive the new officer if he was not an eligible person.

4115. But how would you define his being an ineligible person?—I think that would be greatly controlled by having one of the examiners conversant with county duties and of practical experience; a portion of his duties should be to inquire not merely into the candidates' acquirements, but into their general fitness for the office; and therefore no great inconvenience would arise.

4116. No one would be selected but one who would be eligible; but you must admit that there would be a great difference between a young man who was inexperienced in discharging the duties of county surveyor, and an experienced officer who had given his time for many years to this particular duty?—I admit that.

4117. And the third class counties, I apprehend, would always be in the hands of those young and inexperienced men?—I admit that difficulty would arise.

4118. And, therefore, would not the third class counties consider it an injustice that they should never have the chance of having an experienced officer?—To meet that I would give the third class counties the power in some way to make it worth the while of their officers to remain with them.

4119. You would, in fact, give a third class county the power of increasing the salaries, and of raising them up to the salaries of second or first class counties?—Precisely.

4120. Do you believe that the county surveyors' assistants are necessary?—I think they are.

4121. Did you hear or read Lord John Browne's evidence with respect to them?—I heard a small portion of it.

4122. Are you aware that he stated that in the county of Mayo, when you were county surveyor there, you discharged the whole duties of county surveyor, without any assistance, in a most satisfactory way?—That was for a limited period; I did so for one year, before the assistants were appointed, and again for two years before I left the county. That was after a famine year, when the grand jury, from motives of economy, discontinued the assistants; and the post then became so laborious and onerous that I was glad to leave the county for that reason alone.

4123. You think it impossible for the county surveyor to inspect all roads and works that come under his notice?—I think it would not be possible. I know that it is the practice in several counties that the surveyor only goes round periodically, perhaps just before the sessions and the assizes, and founds his report thereon. I think that there should be more frequent inspections, and that the inspecting casually before the sessions or assizes, is not sufficient to see that the roads and works are maintained; and that in order to oblige the contractors to do their duty, there should be frequent reports and examinations by the assistants monthly, or oftener, as the cases might require. Even in the smallest county I do not think that a county surveyor could discharge his duties without assistance, to look after numerous minor details.

4124. The question of whether, or not, county surveyors' assistants were required, was very fully inquired into in the year 1857, was it not?—It was.

4125. And the Committee which inquired into it at that time came to the conclusion that they were necessary?—They did. All the circumstances connected with them were very fully and amply inquired into.

4126. The question between appointing assistants and appointing district surveyors, was raised before that Committee, was it not?—It was.

4127. And the decision of the Committee was then unanimously in favour of having assistants, was it not?—It was. It arose in this way. The authorities of Trinity College, Dublin, wishing to find a means of employing the young men trained up at their engineering school, brought the matter under the notice of the present Secretary of the Treasury, Mr. Hamilton, and a Committee was appointed to inquire whether it would be better to have district surveyors, dividing the counties into several portions, and to have young men of a higher class of education appointed to those districts; and the result of the inquiry was, that the present mode of having county surveyors and assistants was in every way better and more economical.

4128. And you do not concur with Lord John Browne in believing that it would be possible for a county surveyor to attend himself, without assistance, to a large county?—It is not possible for him to do it with advantage to the public. It would be physically impossible for him to do it, no matter what amount of energy or exertion he might bring to discharge his duties, where numerous details have to be looked after.

4129. Have you known any inconveniences or disadvantages to counties to arise from their being no power to grant superannuation to county officers?—Very great inconvenience, and it exists at this moment. Of the officers appointed in the year 1834 (34 years since), there are seven at present in office, and of that number one, at least, has been entirely incapacitated for some years past.

4130. And he is continued in office still?—He is continued in office still. In the county of Galway, a gentleman was kept on for several years. The grand jury, acting with kindness and consideration, and not wishing to throw a man upon the world, kept him on until it became impossible to continue. In another case, in the south of Ireland, the grand jury, some 20 years ago, discontinued the officer; he is still living in the county, but subsisting on the charitable contributions of a few surveyors and friends, who endeavour to

Mr. H. Brett.

19 May 1868.

support him. In both cases, that is to say, in Galway and in Donegal, the grand jury passed the strongest resolutions in favour of the parties. They did not discontinue the surveyors from any fault, but from their inability to discharge their duties, and the grand jury regretted not having the power to superannuate them. In Galway the grand jury passed a resolution that if the superannuation could be granted, even after the officer had retired, they would be very glad to avail themselves of the power to grant it with a view of benefiting the public service, as well as to see that the officer was not thrown penniless on the world.

4131-2. You believe that it would be found more beneficial to the public service if the grand jury were given the power of granting superannuation to their officers after a certain period?—I do.

4133. Do you believe that great detriment sometimes happens in consequence of their inability to do so, and continuing officers who were really incapable of discharging their duty properly?—I have no doubt whatever of it; the grand jury, as a body, while they have due regard to economy, wish to act kindly and considerately to those who have discharged their duties fairly towards them for a number of years.

4134. With regard to the general grand jury system, do you believe that the present constitution of grand juries is satisfactory; have you heard complaints made against it throughout the country?—I have had 40 years' and upwards experience, and I can say with truth that in my judgment, and from all that I have heard, I believe that it is not possible to get any system that will give greater satisfaction than the present grand jury system, with some little modifications. I am acquainted with some of the most experienced grand jurors in various parts of Ireland, and I have conferred from time to time with them. This morning I have received a letter from a gentleman of very great experience, who is very often foreman of the grand jury of the county of Wicklow, that is Sir George Hodson, and he says: "After a long and practical experience of the working of the grand jury system under the 6 & 7 Will. 4, c. 116, I am very much in favour of maintaining all its leading provisions, and I believe, as a whole, it has worked well and efficiently." Another gentleman, who was in the room to-day, our county Member, came here prepared to give you similar testimony; he is very often foreman of a grand jury.

4135. Do you extend what you have stated with respect to the grand jury, to the presentment sessions?—I would make some change there. With regard to the grand jury, it appears to me that one improvement would be certainly necessary, that is, that a representative should, if possible, be provided for each barony, and if not a resident proprietor, at all events a freeholder; that the sheriff should be obliged to have some person resident in the barony called on the grand jury.

4136. Do you believe that if there was a representative from each barony on the grand jury, then that body would be a satisfactory one, acting as a body to veto or otherwise the works that come from the presentment sessions?—I do for this reason, that though the grand jury sometimes changes (and in a large county particularly it is not possible to have always the same gentlemen on the grand jury) still as a whole they are so balanced, and the opinions pro and con are so well divided over the county, that I think the greatest possible amount of fair play is shown in every matter that comes before them.

4137. Then you think, on the whole, that the grand jury represents the landed proprietors of the county?—I have no doubt of it.

4138. And you believe that it is desirable that there should be a body existing as a check upon the original presenting body, the presentment sessions?—I do.

4139. And you are of opinion that the grand jury as at present constituted, is as satisfactory a body as you could expect to be formed for that purpose with the alteration which you have mentioned?—I do not think any elected body could give greater satisfaction to the cesspayers of the counties generally, than the grand juries do at present with the modification I spoke of.

4140. With respect to the presentment sessions, do you think they are properly constituted at present?—I believe that very considerable alteration ought to be made in constituting the presentment sessions. I would certainly recommend that the present mode of selecting the cesspayers should be discontinued.

4141. Would you propose, in lieu of it, an election by the cesspayers, or anything else?—In my opinion a simple ballot at the assizes would answer all purposes. I would not select the 100 highest cesspayers, but would make it compulsory on the collectors to return five or six from each parish. I would not take the highest from the barony as a whole by any means, because they might be all in one corner of the barony. The highest in one parish might not be more than one-fourth or one-fifth as to the amount of those in another part of the barony; but I would take the highest, such as they are in various parts of the barony, and I would ballot for them.

4142. And you consider that that would form a more satisfactory body than a body elected directly by the cesspayers?—It appears to me that a body elected by the cesspayers would be pretty much like the poor law guardians, the same continuous body year by year, and that it would be more satisfactory to the cesspayers to have a new body every year. In my judgment it would be cheaper and equally efficacious, and I believe at least equally satisfactory.

4143. But it would not be a direct representative body?—It would hardly be a direct representative body, but I know very many districts in Ireland where, if the representative system were adopted, the representative would be the mere nominee of the landlord. The bailiff or some person in that capacity would, in all probability, be elected.

4144. You think, if the cesspayers were elected in the same way as poor-law guardians, in many districts the body returned to sit at the sessions would be much more under the control of the great landed proprietors than the present cesspayers?—I have no doubt of it.

4145. In point of fact, in some cases those elected cesspayers would be the mere nominees of the landlord, would they not?—I have no doubt of it; I could name a dozen such cases.

4146. And therefore, you think it more desirable that the highest cesspayers should be selected by ballot, rather than that they should be nominally elected by the cesspayers, but really returned by the landed proprietor?—I think it would be more economical, that it would be

simpler,

simpler, and that it would in all probability give persons who would freely maintain and represent the views of their co-cesspayers; and that it would give very great satisfaction to the ratepayers at large.

Mr. H. Brett. — 19 May 1868.

4147. On the other hand, do you believe that there is a very strong feeling among the public in Ireland that those who pay the taxes should be represented by elected individuals in the body that votes the taxes?—I know that feeling does exist; it is a question of difficulty in either way, but what occurs to me is, that some simpler mode such as I speak of would be found perfectly satisfactory; still, if an election was preferred, I do not see that there would be any objection to it, except that in some cases the elected cesspayers would be the nominees of the proprietors, and that certainly would appear to me to be very objectionable.

4148. It would be different in different parts of Ireland, I take it?—It would.

4149. In some parts you would have a very independent body returned, really representing the wishes of the electors, whereas in other parts of Ireland you would have persons merely representing the wishes of the landlords who put them on?—Certainly; no doubt; but I would have a person selected by ballot from each parish, or each portion of the barony.

4150. Are you aware, from your long experience in county matters, whether a strong feeling with respect to the division of the county cess does not exist in Ireland?—I think that as regards the repair of roads the feeling is not very strong; but with regard to new roads, bridges, lunatic asylums, and permanent institutions, I know it is felt to be a hardship to have the cess paid altogether by the occupiers.

4151. Do you not think that it would give general satisfaction if at least in all new lettings there was a division made of the payment of the county cess?—I think it would give satisfaction; I am not quite sure that the amount of benefit that is expected would be derived, but still I think it would give satisfaction.

4152. Even supposing that the landlord really pays for these county works in a diminished rent, still you are aware that there is a general feeling in the country that the landlord does not pay; and would it not be desirable that that feeling should be removed by having him directly contribute at least half the expense that is incurred on these public works?—I think it would give satisfaction in that way; and I think it is also believed by many of the cesspayers that the proprietors do not exercise sufficient control at present, but that they would do so if they were obliged to pay half of it themselves.

4153. The division would give them a direct interest in every alteration which took place in the rate, would it not?—It would.

4154. With respect to malicious injuries, do you believe that that is a desirable class of presentment?—It is a question of great difficulty. I have heard, very recently, cases which, in my judgment, were purely cases of accident, and which the sessions looked upon as cases of presumed malice, though none could be proved; and it seems to me that the malicious injuries ought to be treated with a great deal more care if the principle of compensation is to be preserved at all.

4155. Is not the principle of those malicious injuries making the innocent pay for the guilty?—Yes; except that many persons would most likely be injured by persons having malicious intentions against them. If the parties were not aware that some redress would be given. If malicious persons knew that no compensation would be made to persons injured by their acts, it is probable that injuries would be more common than at present; but I think that compensating persons who have suffered injuries does not lead either to the repression of crime, or to the detection of offenders.

4156. You do not think it either leads to a diminution of those offences, or to the detection of the criminals?—I do not think it does.

4157. Then upon what ground is it justified; why should you have those presentments for injuries done to individuals levied upon the whole townland, or parish, or barony; and, therefore, upon many innocent persons?—It is a question of great difficulty; it is merely as a matter of expediency to deter evil-doers.

4158. But you say that you do not think that it produces the effect of diminishing the number of those malicious offences?—I think there would be more malicious offences if the compensation were done away with.

4159. You think that it has then the effect of diminishing them?—Indirectly, I think it has.

4160. Do you think that it has the effect to such an extent as to justify this otherwise unjustifiable proceeding of making the innocent pay for the guilty?—I think that is a very bad principle, but it is only in the way that I speak of that indirectly it prevents the party from carrying out his malicious feelings.

4161. Are you aware that no such system exists in this country?—I was not aware of it.

4162. Colonel *French*.] Do you not consider that the grand jury have cause of complaint in being made the instruments of levying money off their counties in the form of compulsory presentments, about which they have no knowledge, and over which they have no control?—I am quite aware of it, and I can give you two instances. I know that about the year 1835 or 1836, the county of Mayo, and, I believe, the county of Sligo (and I have a document in my hand referring to the county of Roscommon) were obliged to pay for advances purporting to have been made many years before in a time of distress, there being then different occupiers, different proprietors, and a different state of things altogether. Compulsory presentments were sent down from the Treasury; the grand jury refused to pass them; and the judges put them on as mandatory presentments, and the amounts were levied off the county.

4163. In the county of Roscommon I think it amounted to over 6,000 *l.*?—It did. I do not recollect what it amounted to in Mayo, but it amounted to a very considerable sum.

4164. I think it was about 30,000 *l.* on all the Connaught counties, was it not?—I believe so.

4165. The presentment was alleged to be for money advanced by the Government in 1822, which they were never asked for, but which they sent down on account of the state of the country to stop the collection of the cess; and in 1837 they made the first demand?—I am quite aware of the circumstances; I recollect the advances being made; but for 12 or 14 years afterwards no demand was made by the Treasury, and then orders were ultimately sent down, and the counties had to pay.

4166. It was levied by the order of the judge of assize, Judge Burton, was it not, the grand jury

Mr. *R. Stevt.*

23 May 1859.

jury denying the debt, and having refused to levy it?—Yes.

4167. Are you aware that the same principle extends to buildings, and supporting of lunatic asylums?—Yes.

4168. The grand jury have no control over their erection, or over their management, have they?—Not further than the appointment of commissioners, or of the Board of Control.

4169. But those are appointed by the Lord Lieutenant, are they not?—I do not know that the grand jury have any voice in the matter.

4170. But a presentment is sent down, signed by the Under Secretary, and the grand jury are compelled to present whatever that sum may be, are they not?—Yes.

4171. Are you aware that at the last assizes of Roscommon, there was an increase in a few months of the expenditure to the amount of 800 *l.*?—I am not aware of it.

4172. The same system obtains as to the building of gaols, and as to the Government advances for buildings of all kinds, does it not?—Yes.

4173. It is the same in bridges under arterial drainage, and it was the case, I believe, in the works carried on in the Shannon?—It was.

4174. That money advanced by the Government, amounting to several millions of money, was levied, I believe, by the counties at an interest of 5 per cent.?—Yes.

4175. The Government themselves having borrowed the money at about 3 per cent.?—Yes.

4176. Was there, to your knowledge, any loss whatever experienced by the Government during the time that the system of making advances to the counties was in operation?—Not a farthing; I may add that at the last assizes for the county of Wicklow a question arose as to the extra force of police. On inquiry into this subject the grand jury found that the county was entitled to a certain standing force, but that they had not that standing force; they were short by some 20 or 22 men; and notwithstanding their being short of the Parliamentary number, they were still charged for an extra force of police, though the standing force was incomplete, and they looked upon that as a very great hardship.

4177. The Government also, when they alter the number of police in a county, can send down a compulsory presentment for a certain number over, can they not?—Yes, and in this case we had not the full number.

4178. Mr. *Maguire*.] You were asked by the Honourable Chairman as to the feeling throughout the country, with respect to the division of the rate; and as I understood you said that the occupiers who now pay the rates consider it a grievance to have to pay for new roads, but that for all the other matters which form the great bulk of the expenditure they think that it should be divided between the owners and the occupiers?—As to new roads, bridges, and works of a permanent nature, my experience is that the cesspayers look upon it as being a great grievance to have the whole paid by the occupiers.

4179. Would they be content entirely to pay any portion of it themselves?—They would for the ordinary maintenance of the roads.

4180. Does that form the larger portion of the expenditure?—It is usually about half of the entire cess, or a little less than half the entire cess.

4181. May I ask whether you ever saw an authorized expression of opinion in favour of the occupier bearing the entire burden even of that portion of the cess?—I have formed that opinion from conversations with them at sessions and at assizes in my tours through the counties of Wicklow, Mayo, and Waterford.

4182. Are you prepared to give that as the expression of the opinion of the cesspayers throughout those counties?—That is my belief.

4183. Is it founded upon experience from actual observation?—It is founded upon my experience of 40 years.

4184. Did you ever hear distinct and solemn declarations made by those people at public meetings, and afterwards expressed in petitions to this House, in favour of a division of the whole rate, as between the owner and the occupier, without making any discrimination between one item of expenditure and another?—I cannot say that I have, but I know that there is great diversity of opinion; I have taken frequent opportunities of trying to elicit the general opinion upon the subject.

4185. But they are very strongly opposed to paying for those other items of new roads, bridges, lunatic asylums, gaols, and all those other matters, are they not?—Yes; they very strongly object to all those.

4186. They object to have the whole burden thrown upon themselves, do they not?—They do most strongly.

4187. Does your own feeling go with theirs upon that matter?—It does.

4188. Mr. *Herbert*.] With regard to the making of new roads, is it not generally the case in most of the grand juries in Ireland, that if a new road is made the landlord whose property is benefited by that new road generally subscribes, and very often gives half the cost of the road?—In some few cases the landlords behave with very great liberality; in certain cases the proprietors give the land gratuitously, but except in a few cases where the new roads are for opening up mountain districts or in a boggy country, or places of that kind, the proprietors do not usually subscribe.

4189. Mr. *Maguire*.] You say that in many instances the owners do not subscribe; are there not many instances where the owners insist upon being paid for the road?—No doubt of it.

4190. In several instances they have been so paid, have they not?—They have.

4191. Is not that a road for which the owner is paid, oftentimes included and measured in the farm rent?—In some counties it is so, but in others it is not.

4192. In some counties the very road on which the proprietor has insisted for payment, and which is as hard as iron, and on which they never can grow a blade of grass, is measured within the farm of the tenant, and is charged to him in the shape of rent, is it not?—It is.

4193. Do you not think that it is rather a hardship that, the road being given up to the public for which the owner is paid, the man who has to pay for that road in the shape of rent, has to pay for it in the shape of maintenance?—The road ought not to be charged to the tenant, but I think he ought to pay for its maintenance.

4194. But it ought not to be measured in his farm as arable, or pasture land, ought it?—I think it ought not.

4195. Is it not rather hard that, where the one man has all the value of that road and the other has

has gone, save the pecuniary occupation, he should have to maintain it?—I think it is.

4196. It is a very grave hardship, is it not?—I think it is.

4197. If you were in the position of an occupier, and that road were included in your own farm, you would consider it a very serious grievance, would you not?—No doubt; but on the other hand that is not always the case; there are a great many exceptions to that rule, I could point out some scores of cases.

4198. Then, although you do not anticipate that a very great benefit would result from the legal partition of the burden between the occupiers and the owners, still you think that it would give a large amount of satisfaction?—I have no doubt that it would. I think it would give satisfaction in this way, that the cesspayers would then be of a different opinion from what they are now, and that they would be under the impression that the proprietors and the grand juries, as representing the proprietors, would be more economical, and would look more closely into the application of the cess than they do at present.

4199. You are very enthusiastic in your praise of the grand jury system, of which, I think, you are a very able officer from all I have heard; and, in point of fact, you said that it was not possible (and you spoke from the experience of 41 years) to have any better system; but that you would be inclined to make some small modifications in it; I think you would be inclined to make rather large modifications in the system, would you not?—I do not think that I should.

4200. The division of the rate is rather essential, in your opinion, is it not?—That, I think, has nothing to do with the constitution of the grand jury.

4201. I suppose you admit that there are very good roads in Ireland?—Generally speaking.

4202. As good roads as are generally to be found in any part of the world?—Generally speaking.

4203. Do you think that the use of the ballot, in the appointment of the associated cesspayers, would be quite as useful in its result as if they were elected?—I think, generally speaking, it would. In very many of the districts I think there would be great difficulty in having annual elections. It would tend to considerable expense, and I do not see the advantage of it.

4204. Did you not say that the same people would very likely be constantly elected, and therefore where would be the expense of the annual elections?—I take it that it would involve as much as under the poor-law system, the sending out of voting papers.

4205. Is not that a very simple machinery?—Still it costs a good deal of money.

4206. Can you state what is the expense of an election in any ordinary electoral division?—I suppose from 10 *l.* to 15 *l.*

4207. Do you know that of your own knowledge?—I think it amounts to that; I think that I heard that at a poor-law meeting which was lately held in the county of Wicklow.

4208. Unless there is a contest, there is no expense, is there?—No.

4209. Are there not, in many instances, no contests whatever?—That would very much depend upon the mode of conducting the election.

4210. Supposing that the payers of the rate, or supposing that, under the new system, the payers of half the rate were allowed to elect a representative, and they found a good man, who was regular in attendance, and was vigilant and economical; do you mean to say that they would send him adrift at the end of the year?—I mean that the expense of the contest would be that.

4211. But there would be no expense where there was no contest, would there?—I suppose not.

4212. Do you apprehend that there would be any contest, you having said yourself that you apprehend that the same people would be always elected?—I think that when it came to the elections, influence would be exercised in favour of bailiffs and such people.

4213. What would the expense of the system be if your apprehensions were realised?—The cesspayers who are not under the control of the landlords might express a wish to be elected.

4214. Is it not very proper that they should do so?—Certainly.

4215. Is not the electoral system in the country far more healthful and far more satisfactory for the public, generally speaking, than nomination, or the chance of a ballot?—I do not like the present system of nomination; I give that up.

4216. Then you get to that half-way house, as it were, ballot for the grand jury. Do not you think that the elective system would give far greater satisfaction?—I do not think it would.

4217. Have you any objection to the working of the poor-law system?—They are the same round of people all through.

4218. Do they not work very well?—I think the law is administered very well, but I think that it is an expensive law.

4219. Is it not the best imaginable result of any law contemplated by the Legislature that it should work well?—It is my opinion that the grand jury law works well now. I think it is more economical, and that more value is given to the public. I think that less satisfaction is given by the poor law to the public, and that more money is consumed in official salaries and less money goes to the poor than goes in proportion to the repair of the roads.

4220. No doubt when a pauper swallows his meal in the morning you do not see much of the result of it afterwards?—No.

4221. But everything done by the grand jury is seen in the construction of roads or public buildings?—More benefit is given to the public. I merely recommend that as less expensive, but I do not see any very great objection to the election.

4222. But at the same time you would like to give as much satisfaction as possible?—Certainly.

4223. Do you think that there is any reason why the elective system should not be tried?—I see no reason whatever.

4224. And if the gentry of the county were sufficiently represented as they are on the Poor Law Board, do you not think that it would be satisfactory?—No doubt of it.

4225. Would you be against the system of having any magistrates outside the barony take part in the proceedings of another barony?—I think the magistrates ought to be confined to the baronies where they reside, or have property.

4226. Is it a bad system to allow the possibility of such an abuse as a number of gentlemen coming

Mr. *H. Brett.*

13 May 1858.

Mr. *H. Brett.*

19 May 1862.

coming from one place, in which they have an interest, to swamp those who may be said to represent a special interest in their own locality?—I think it is a bad system. After a long experience I can say this, and with truth, that the magistrates, as a rule, are far more economical than the cesspayers; that the cesspayers are more anxious to expend the money than the magistrates are.

4227. Did you ever hear of magistrates coming from a distant barony for the purpose of carrying a job?—I have witnessed it.

4228. Is not that a very gross and wanton abuse?—No doubt, but it is quite a common thing for a leading contractor to have influence among the cesspayers, and the cesspayers are very anxious to have considerable sums expended upon the roads in their neighbourhood, where a less sum might do; so that the magistrates, on the whole, are more economical.

4229. If those cesspayers were amenable to constituents, do you not think that they would be more economical?—I do.

4230. *Sir Charles Lanyon.*] Although I fully agree as to the necessity of some alteration in the mode of representation, do you think there is an exact analogy between the Poor Law Guardians and the cesspayers at presentment sessions?—I do not think there is altogether.

4231. Do you not think that a cesspayer who may be at the presentment sessions is a person who may have a great personal interest in the works which are brought before those sessions?—Certainly.

4232. And if he wanted to obtain a little job in his own immediate neighbourhood, being a person of influence, he could easily command his election as a cesspayer to the presentment sessions, could he not?—Yes, and more particularly if he was connected with the great proprietors of the district.

4233. Under those circumstances, can you imagine any more satisfactory plan for the purpose of providing a fair representation of the cesspayers at the sessions than the system proposed by Lord John Browne, as to the division of the baronies into what may be called electoral divisions, or something tantamount to that, a cesspayer being returned by ballot for that division by the grand jury themselves?—It appears to me that it would answer all purposes.

4234. Do you not think that it would be the very best system that could be invented for the purpose of promoting a fair representation of the cesspayers, and preventing the possibility of a job?—I think so.

4235. Do you not think that the appointment of assistants materially tends to economy as well as to the better execution of the public works in the county?—I do.

4236. Do you not think that they tend very materially to prevent deception and fraud on the part of contractors, in the quality of the materials which they are bound to supply?—I do.

4237. Do you think it possible, without assistance, that you can get a fair return for the amount of money presented for the execution of works in the county?—I think it is not possible, but I would add to that that the assistants should be entirely amenable and responsible to the county surveyor, who should be responsible to the grand jury; and that he should have the power of removing them and complete control over his assistants. I myself have had on several occasions a good deal of difficulty with assistants who did not give satisfaction, and when I applied to the Lord Lieutenant to assist me to remove them, I was referred to the grand jury, and the grand jury had to remove them.

4238. If the cesspayers were elected by ballot by the grand jury from each electoral division as suggested by Lord John Browne, do you not think that it would ensure them a full attendance of the cesspayers at every sessions?—I am sure it would. At present, in many cases, they do not attend, though generally speaking they attend fairly enough in the county of Wicklow. The parties are not certain whether they will be chosen in the ballot.

4239. You spoke of the promotion of county surveyors from one county to the other being desirable, and the chairman made some objection to that consequent upon the small class counties always having the new appointments; would it not be better that a small class county should have a new surveyor than that a large class county should have the new surveyor?—Certainly.

4240. Therefore, the public interest would be benefited by the power of transferring a surveyor from one county to another, would it not?—I think so.

4241. With regard to the appointment of county surveyors under the new Act, can you describe how the commission is to be constituted?—Entirely of Civil Service Commissioners.

4242. Have those Civil Service Commissioners any practical man upon the Board?—I am not aware that they have; it occurs to me that provision ought to be made now that some practical men be associated with the Civil Service Commissioners.

4243. Do you think it possible for purely theoretical men properly to test the capabilities of a man as to his efficiency for a county surveyorship?—I think it is not possible.

4244. Do you not think it desirable that some practical man, such as an engineer, should be on that Board, and that it should not be left to the Civil Service Commissioners?—No doubt; the Select Committee of the year 1857 recommended that a professional engineer of high standing like Sir Richard Griffith, or a man in that position, and a man of high literary attainments, mathematical and scientific attainments, together with a county surveyor, should form the Board of Examiners; but I think that if a practical man were associated with the Civil Service Commissioners, results might be arrived at which would be all that need be desired; but if it is left entirely to the Civil Service Commissioners, I do not see how they are capable of judging of the fitness of a candidate for the office of county surveyor, for the duties he will have to discharge.

4245. With respect to the certificates, I understand you to say that those certificates should not be lodged at the special sessions?—So I say as to certificates for maintenance contracts.

4246. That the mere passing of the accounts at the special sessions, should be a matter of form, and that the certificates should be finally attached at the assizes?—Just so.

4247. *Chairman.*] Do you mean to say that there should be no sort of certificate at the presentment sessions?—No; I do not mean that, I

mean

 189

same that there should be power to allow the contractor's claim provisionally.

4248. *Sir Charles Lanyon.*] Do you not think that it would be desirable that the certificate, lodged at the sessions, should be a conditional one, with power to withdraw?—That would answer the purpose equally well; I might add that in cases of special works for bridges, hill cuttings, and new roads, I would not give the final certificate in any case until the works were completed; I would allow no presentment to pass the sessions for them, but merely for the maintenance contracts.

4249. The conditional certificate to which you refer, should merely have reference to works of maintenance?—Precisely.

4250. New works and matters of that description should be completed prior to the sessions?—Quite so.

4251. But still if they were completed prior to the sessions, you should have the power, in case of failure, to withdraw at the assizes?—Of course.

4252. With regard to the power of the grand jury to alter contracts, do you think that it is desirable that, in the case of a high contract, the grand jury should have the power of presenting a lower sum?—I do not; I did not mean that.

4253. Did you mean that the grand jury should have the power of presenting any sum to the county surveyor that he might think desirable, and that he should have the power of getting the work executed?—Yes, up to the next period of presenting.

4254. With reference to low contracts, do you think it would be desirable to give the grand jury the power of annulling a low contract, even though it might be so reported by the county surveyor?—I do; I am suffering at this moment, in the case of a very important second class road in the county of Wicklow leading to a railway station. The sum limited was 1 *s.* a perch, and a small farmer took it at 3½ *d.* or 4 *d.* a perch. It is utterly impossible that a man can do it at that price; he is a little above the class of paupers, and the result is very great inconvenience.

4255. Do you not think that if the law were amended by the introduction of such clauses as those to which you have already referred, which have been handed in by Mr. Hill, those clauses consequently upon the power which they would give, would have the effect of very soon weeding out from the people who now execute the contracts of the county, the men who are inefficient or incapable of doing the work properly?—In this way perhaps it would; if out of the general purpose fund, the county surveyor was authorised to expend up to the amount allowed at the sessions, and if that power were given to the county surveyor to sue the contractors for the difference between the contract and the amount approved at sessions, as matters stand at present the bonds and contracts are little better than a nullity.

4256. Mr. *Maguire.*] Why are they a nullity?—For two reasons; first, in most cases the magistrates take very little trouble to scrutinise the solvency of the securities; and secondly, the difficulty of recovering on the bonds is such that it is a practical impossibility to turn them to account.

4257. Sir *Charles Lanyon.*] Supposing a work is presented at an assizes, and that the contractor fails to proceed with that work, will not the clauses to which we have referred give you the power of proceeding against the contractor, and compelling him to execute that work within a reasonable period?—They will, if you add to Mr. Hill's suggestions that which I suggested myself, that is, in the case of works of maintenance not to make it obligatory to have adjournments or more than one sessions, but to adopt some means to put the onus of proof of non-liability upon contractors themselves, and to improve the arrangements for executing works.

Mr. E. Brett. 19 May 1868.

4258. General *Dunne.*] But when there is no contract at all, must the work fall to the ground?—Not necessarily.

4259. Sir *Charles Lanyon.*] Would it not be desirable in the case of no contract being sent in for the execution of a public work, approved of at the sessions, that the county surveyor should have the power to execute that work, a presentment being made to him by the grand jury?—Certainly.

4260. *Chairman.*] Has not the grand jury that power at present?—They have.

4261. Sir *Charles Lanyon.*] Will you amend the clause to which you refer, as having been handed in by Mr. Hill, in such a way as you think would meet the difficulty which you experience in reference to it?—I shall have great pleasure in doing so; I think that if that were done it would meet all the difficulties.

4262. As to the general purpose fund, is there not a large amount of money always in the hands of the county treasurer for unpresented works, which could be applied as a general purpose fund from which to supply the funds necessary for the execution of works under the new sections?—In some counties that is not the case, but in most counties there is an abundant fund.

4263. At all events it is absolutely necessary, is it not, that some fund should be provided for the time when the treasurer is not in funds for the purpose?—I think so, and that means should be provided to disburse from those funds.

4264. The system of classification of roads by county surveyors is one which I have always considered the most desirable, and which would do away with an enormous amount of inconvenience. Into how many classes would you propose to divide them?—I propose to divide them into three classes; as regards the first class roads, I would empower the grand jury to contract for materials upon them separately, from the maintenance, and then, either to contract for their maintenance by skilled labourers, or to employ overseers or whatever mode seemed to be best, and I would give them the power to have those contracts annual or triennial, so that the road should be kept in the best repair at all times; those charges to be partly on the district and partly on the county at large, as the commissioners or the committee of the grand jury should decide.

4265. Do you not think that it would be a very much better and fairer system that each barony should maintain its own roads, than that any portion of the leading roads should be repaired by the county at large?—I think it would answer the purpose if, instead of confining it to the barony, you include the district which might be benefited. In many cases the road passing for a small distance through a barony, the great bulk of the barony has no actual advantage at all, while the district beyond would be very much benefited.

4266. But would not the system generally be a fair

Mr. *H. Brett.* — 19 May 1868.

a fair one to limit the presentment for the repair of the roads in every barony, those roads which the greatest amount of money would be required to repair, being generally through the property of those who are best able to pay for them?—It certainly would be fairer to charge some of them on the baronies.

4267. Is it not the case that many of the poorer mountain districts have now to pay more than one-half of the expense of maintaining roads 40 or 50 miles away from them, which run through properties of considerably more value?—No doubt, that is the fact.

4268. Therefore, do you think that the best mode of levying the cost of maintaining the roads would be altogether upon the baronies?—Either upon the baronies, or a portion on the county at large; but, at all events, I would distribute it, and possibly in most cases it would answer the purpose to levy upon the barony itself.

4269. Have you anything to suggest with regard to an appeal from the sessions in cases where parties making applications may be refused by the sessions?—I think they ought to have the power of immediately appealing to the assizes. There is a mode provided by the Grand Jury Act after two such refusals; but it is a very cumbrous mode, and I think that a simpler mode might be provided by a memorial to the grand jury, the case being heard by the grand jury before a judge in a summary way.

4270. Do you not think that the power of trying it as a traverse would be tried, would be a very simple mode of giving an appeal from the decision of the sessions?—It would answer all the purposes. I would ask the Committee to consider the propriety of considering that the presentments are generally made for the summer assizes. The cesspayer between spring and summer has to pay the cess, and the larger amount of presentments are generally made in the spring, and levied at the time when they can be least afforded. If it could be arranged that the major part of the presentments should be made when it is easiest to pay the cess, or that they should be divided in the proportions of three-fifths and two-fifths, that would be a great relief.

4271. *Chairman.*] Do you propose that the maintenance contracts should be entered into in the summer?—I think that the maintenance contracts ought to be entered into in summer. The eight months' maintenance would require a larger pay, but you might provide for three-fifths being levied after the summer assizes, and two-fifths after the spring assizes.

4272. When a maintenance contract is entered into at the spring assizes, very little work is done upon it until the summer assizes, and yet the contractor has a right to receive the whole half-yearly payment, provided he keeps the road in repair during that time?—I try in practice to make him give value for the money; I am very slow to pay him unless I think that he has earned it.

4273. You do not pay him the half-yearly allowance upon the time between the spring and summer assizes?—Not unless I find the work done, but it would greatly simplify matters to have the contractor's claims date from the summer assizes, and to have a larger levy made at that time.

4274. Suppose a contract is made to keep a road in repair for three or five years at the spring assizes, and the contractor keeps it in repair from the spring to the summer assizes, which is only four months, do you allow him at the summer assizes a half-yearly payment upon that road?—I do, if he puts out a sufficient quantity of metalling, and does a sufficient quantity of repairs to justify it.

4275. That four months being one-third of the year, and not half?—Yes; that appears an objectionable mode, though they obviate that in some counties. They only present three months' pay at the March assizes; they present eight or nine months' pay at the summer assizes. It appears to me that if the Committee would recommend in their report that a larger levy should be made at the summer assizes, and that if possible all contracts should be started with at the summer assizes, that would greatly simplify the matter.

4276. Mr. *Herbert.*] Do you not think that the making of a new road through a property very much enhances the value of the property through which it goes?—No doubt.

4277. Both to the occupier and to the landlord?—No doubt.

4278. Do you not think that, as a general rule, the amount of increase of value and convenience which that road gives to the tenant compensates the tenant very well for the amount of land which he may lose by the making of that road?—Not in all cases.

4279. But generally, is it not so?—In a great many cases if it passes through a wet or boggy district, and the land is of no great value, he may be compensated for it no doubt, but if it runs through a piece of valuable land, and he has to pay rent for that, I do not think that it follows in all cases that making the road would compensate him for losing the land. He may be served well enough by the old road for the purposes of his farm; so that, as a general rule, I would not say that in all cases the tenant is sufficiently compensated.

4280. You were talking about the magistrates coming to carry a job (I think that the word was not exactly expressed), and swamping the cesspayers at the meeting of the Road Sessions; can you tell me how many cases during the last five years you have known in which the magistrates have come from other districts in order to carry such a job?—Probably one or two.

4281. In fact, it is a very rare occurrence, is it not?—It is very rare.

4282. Mr. *Kendall.*] As I understand, your opinion is, that under the present grand jury laws the county expenditure is much more economically managed than the expenditure under the poor law?—I think so.

4283. In that case there must be some great defect in the poor law; what special defect would you point out?—The number of officials and the nature of the law itself; that is to say, it is not possible to give the amount of benefit to poor people that the grand jury law does, which provides a large measure of employment, and is to some extent reproductive.

4284. Have you ever made a rough estimate as to the per-centage for superintendence, and buildings, and plant, and so on, connected with county matters, and for superintendence, and buildings, and plant, and so on, as connected with the poor law?—I can merely answer for my own department.

4285. Can you give the Committee any idea of the per-centage of the cost of plant, and superintendence tendance, and so on, in the one case as compared with the other?—The cost of supervision under the poor law is about 60 per cent., and under the grand jury law I take it to be 15 or 20 per cent.

4286. Mr. *Maguire.*] Is there any analogy between the repair of a road, and the care of a number of children in a school, or people in a hospital?—Hardly any, or very little.

4287. General *Dunne.*] Can you conceive any cheaper administration than the present grand jury system?—I cannot; I am not aware of any.

4288. Nor more expensive than the poor law?—Not more expensive than the poor law.

4289. Have you any doubt that the general tenantry who pay the cess, would much rather have the whole of it removed?—I have no doubt whatever of that.

4290. And in fact it is the general feeling of people, is it not, not to like taxation, but to feel it irksome?—There is no doubt of it.

4291. Lunatic asylums are placed on the counties, are they not?—They are.

4292. Are they not entirely for the benefit of the poor?—Quite so.

4293. And almost all the county establishments are for the benefit of the poor, or the public, are they not?—Quite so.

4294. Is it not the case that the generality of roads are more useful directly to the people and indirectly to the landlords?—That is the fact, and the bulk of the cesspayers feel it to be so.

4295. Have you ever seen at these different presentment sessions any ill-feeling between the magistrates and cess-payers; is not that very rare?—I have been present at more than one thousand sessions of one kind or another, and I can say that I never observed anything of the kind amongst people of all classes of politics and opinions.

4296. Have you not observed in general that the object of the magistrates is rather to keep down expense than to increase it?—No doubt of it; that is my experience.

4297. And the grand jury are very severe, are they not, in their examinations of any proposal to expend money?—My experience is that they are extremely economical.

4298. The honourable Chairman asked you about malicious inquiries; have you any doubt that whatever the abstract justice may be, the infliction of punishment on a district tends to make people very watchful as to those inquiries being malicious?—It may have that effect; but, nevertheless, I really cannot find in my experience that it tends much to the discovery of the perpetrators of the crime.

4299. But does it not tend to the prevention of crime?—I think it tends to the repression of it.

4300. But do not the people of the locality generally come forward to oppose it, if they possibly can?—They do.

4301. And that therefore makes it very hard, does it not, to make good anything but malicious injuries?—It does; but I know several cases which appears to me to be purely accidental, or done by wanton mischief, where no malice could be assigned.

4302. Can the grand jury give a presentment unless malice is proved?—I have known presentments granted where malice was not proved.

4303. But it is contrary to law, is it not?—I should say that it is. Mr. H. Brett.

4304. Are not the grand jury generally very severe in their examination upon these points?—Generally speaking they are. 19 May 1868.

4305. As to the payment for roads, do you not think that it is very rare that a public road, or any part of it, is paid for by a tenant?—Yes; but there are such instances.

4306. But in private roads it is not uncommon?—I cannot answer for that, but I can answer for roads laid out by myself, which I know are charged to the tenants.

4307. Is that a custom in the counties with which you are connected?—Not in my present county, but in counties with which I have been connected.

4308. But you are not able to say whether it is universal?—I think it is not universal.

4309. Mr. *Leader.*] Do you think that the division of the baronies in most of the counties with which you have been acquainted is tolerably judicious?—I think it is in most cases; some few of them require revision, but in most cases they answer the purpose very well.

4310. You perhaps are not aware of the difference of their extent in the county of Cork?—I am not.

4311. Some baronies have 260,000 acres more than others; do you think that an alteration ought to be made there?—I think so.

4312. Mr. *Blake.*] In answer to the honourable Member for Cork, I think you stated that the occupiers would be satisfied to pay for the cost of the roads if the other portion of the county expenses, such as gaols and lunatic asylums, were borne by the landlords?—I think so; I do not mean to say that the entire burden of the other part should be borne by the occupiers.

4313. I understood you to say that you thought that the occupiers would be willing to pay for the cost of roads, provided that the landlords bore the other portion of the county expenses, such as gaols and lunatic asylums; was I correct?—That is in the same proportion which they pay under the Poor Law; that is, exclusively.

4314. Do you mean exclusively for the whole?—No; exclusively for the public institutions and new roads.

4315. And that the occupiers themselves are to pay all the costs of the roads?—Yes; and I do not think they would object to it.

4316. Is not the landlord quite as much benefited by the making of a road on his property as the occupier?—He is, undoubtedly.

4317. Do you not think that, upon that principle, he ought to bear a portion of those expenses?—Certainly, for making the roads and bridges, but I mean for keeping them in repair.

4318. Do you think that they ought to be kept afterwards by the occupier?—I think so.

4319. Is it not his interest to have them kept in a good state also?—I think that the landlords in many cases do not use the road so much as the occupiers, but in some cases they do.

4320. But is it not a very important thing; will not a farm set much better if it has good, well maintained roads leading to it, than if the case was otherwise?—No doubt.

4321. On that principle, ought not that portion of the rate to be equitably borne between them?—I think that when the proprietors are ratepayers themselves, they look upon it that they pay their fair share, and that the maintenance would be

Mr. H. Eben.

19 May 1864.

more reasonably divided by leaving it according to the present arrangements, and that all permanent improvements, such as new roads, bridges, asylums, gaols, and county institutions, should be divided; but I cannot say that I have heard any complaints in my experience from the ratepayers as to the necessity of dividing the maintenance of the roads with the landlords.

4322. Mr. *Maguire.*] Perhaps they would be glad to get any instalment of what they considered justice, and they would be satisfied with that modicum?—No doubt; of course they would like to get rid of the whole if they could.

4323. Colonel *Cooper.*] With regard to new roads, do you think that half the cost might be borne by the landlord?—Yes, I do.

4324. Would you draw a clause for that purpose, or would you leave it to the option of the presentment sessions to say how the road is to be constructed?—I did not mean that; I meant that the cost for the construction of that road should be borne exclusively by the proprietors in the same way in which the poor rate is borne.

4325. Do you think that that should be the law?—I do.

4326. Do you think that that might not be met in this way: that a proprietor is anxious to have a road made through his property, which will cost 1 *l.* a perch, and he says that he is willing to undertake that road if the presentment sessions will present 10 *s.* a perch for it?—It might be met in that way.

4327. Would you not think it a good thing to leave it open to the presentment sessions as I suggested, to say how much they will present for making a new road, and that if the landlord chose to bear half, the county might bear half?—Yes; but that would be subject to the objection that the landlord might make arrangements to contribute a portion and to carry out the work himself, and I have known cases where promises sometimes were made and afterwards not carried out; so that if a promise of that sort, and an obligation is undertaken to pay a certain sum, it ought to be paid into the county funds; it ought to be done in the ordinary manner; I would not present a sum to a proprietor for a road.

4328. But do you think the difficulties might be met as between the landlord and the occupier, by the landlord paying, or agreeing to pay, a proportion of the sum required to make the road?—I do.

4329. With regard to the town of Bray, it has been taken out of the jurisdiction of the county by a Local Act, has it not?—It has.

4330. Part of the town of Bray is in the county of Wicklow, is it not?—Yes, the major part.

4331. Do you know anything of the working of that Local Act?—I do.

4332. Has it increased or decreased the rates?—It has increased the rates.

4333. Very much?—Very much.

4334. Do you know that of your own knowledge?—I know it of my own knowledge, for I have the management of the township.

4335. Have the ratepayers of the town of Bray as much control over the expenditure under that Local Act as they had under the grand jury laws?—I think they have; but the difficulty is that they start with the cost of the Act, which was in one shape or another considerably over 2,000 *l.*, and they are proceeding to execute large waterworks, and to expend the sum of 3,000 *l.* on them, and 3,000 *l.* on drainage, and there are some other works, so that, practically, they start with 10,000 *l.* of debt.

4336. Have they power to raise that money?—They have the power to raise it under that Act, and I am at present carrying it out for them, and the result of that is, that where formerly they used to be taxed at the amount of 1 *s.* 4 *d.* in the pound, they will now be taxed at 3 *s.* 6 *d.* in the pound.

4337. There is, I suppose, a maximum rate in the Act?—3 *s.* 6 *d.*, I think it is.

4338. Did they borrow the money from the Government?—No; from private sources.

4339. Are the roads as economically repaired now as they were formerly?—They are not.

4340. They cost more per perch than they did?—They do.

4341. Are they better kept in repair than they were?—There is a little more attention paid to them, but, in my opinion, the people of Bray would have been much better off if they had remained as they were.

4342. Can you say you are acting as the township surveyor?—I am.

4343. Do you think that there ought to be a power for towns to separate themselves from the jurisdiction of grand juries without coming to Parliament for a private Act?—I think that in large towns, such as Kingstown and Rathmines, where there is a large area of taxation of 50,000 *l.* or 60,000 *l.* a year, it might be an advantage; but in a small township like Bray, with only 15,000 *l.* or 20,000 *l.*, it is a very unwise measure to adopt.

4344. But if they wish to separate themselves from the county now, they must come to Parliament at a large expense to get a private Act, must they not?—Yes.

4345. Do you think there ought to be provision made in the grand jury law, to enable a township of a certain population to separate if they please from the grand jury?—I think there ought to be.

4346. It would obviate the expense of a private Act?—I think that they ought not to have that expense.

4347. And that provision would obviate the necessity of a town coming to Parliament each time to separate?—Yes, I see no difficulty in it.

4348. And you think that it would be a great benefit to the towns wishing to separate?—Provided they had a sufficient area of taxation.

4349. Have you had considerable experience on that subject?—Very great.

4350. What do you say is the least value at which a town should be separated from the county?—I think their valuation should be at least 40,000 *l.* a year. If it is anything less than that, it must necessarily embarrass them by a higher figure of rating.

4351. *Chairman.*] When you say that you think it would be an advantage to permit towns to separate themselves from the county without going to Parliament for that purpose, what tribunal would you substitute for Parliament; would you allow them to separate themselves without any inquiry?—No; I think that they might do it through the Lord Lieutenant and the Privy Council in Ireland, so as to have marked out the boundaries and separate the areas of taxation for each, and make an adjustment of the roads to be kept inside and outside the township.

4352. But

4352. But it would require the substitution of some tribunal for the Houses of Parliament?—Certainly.

4353. What is the present law with respect to towns which are under the Towns Improvement Act, and have town Commissioners; how are they charged for the county expenses?—They have to pay the same as the rural districts.

4354. The streets there are kept up by the county, are they not?—They are; the towns of Wicklow and Arklow are rated the same as any county village, and they have to pay their share, and all their roads and footpaths are kept in repair; one of the great advantages of leaving the towns to manage their own affairs is with regard to the sanitary measures; there is a very great doubt as to whether anything as to sewage proper can be done under the grand jury law; anything which relates to the roads, such as gullets or drain pipes for carrying away water, may be done, but when you come to sanitary matters, the grand jury have no power.

4355. Colonel *Cooper*.] Are you quite certain of that?—I am quite certain of it; I have heard it argued before the judges for the inhabitants of Bray before they got their Act of Parliament; they contributed a certain sum, and the grand jury made a presentment in aid of that sum, and it was traversed before the judge, and it was only on showing that the floods of the sea did injury to the roads, and it was by a great effort that that presentment was carried.

4356. Mr. *Maguire*.] Could the grand jury have provided waterworks for that town?—No; but in a very simple way under the Sanitary Act it could have been done.

4357. Colonel *Cooper*.] There was a public Act under which they might have got the water without going for a private Act?—Yes.

4358. Did you say that the grand jury had no power where towns are under town commissioners, to construct sewers?—Nor in any case; the grand jury have no power over sewers at all except for the purpose of making gullets or drains for the safety of the road, but for anything which can be construed as a sewer for sewage purposes, there is no such power whatever.

4359. *Chairman*.] Have the grand jury or the county authorities any power of breaking up the streets in towns for laying down gas-pipes?—I do not think there is any such power, because there is the General Gas Companies Act; there are certain public Acts called the Waterworks Clauses Act, the Gas Works Clauses Act, and the Lands Clauses Act, and those Acts give general powers to gas companies which are constituted under them, that they may, with the concurrence of the grand jury, or of the town commissioners, as the case may be, break up the roads.

4360. Can any gas company break up the roads without having a special Act of Parliament constituting them a gas company for those purposes?—They must put themselves under the Gas Clauses Act.

4361. But they need not come to Parliament for a special Act?—Certainly not.

4362. Cannot boards of guardians, under the Health of Towns Act, construct sewers?—They can; they are the authority under the Sanitary Act.

4363. In all but corporate towns?—In all but corporate towns. The corporate authorities are the parties there, and the grand jury have nothing whatever to say to it except as to gullets for taking away water which is injurious to roads.

0.39.

4364. *Chairman*.] Would you look at this return which was furnished to the Committee in 1857 of the expenses of roads up to that period (*handing a paper to the witness*); do you think that we could get a return similar to this to the present day?—No doubt of it.

Mr. *H. Brett*.

19 May 1868.

4365. Can you furnish such a return?—I think I can; the only thing for which I may be at a loss, is the length of the mileage of the roads, but I think that might be obtained from the county surveyors if you would give me a few days on going home to enable me to do so.

4366. That return, I believe, was prepared by the county surveyors at that time?—It was.

4367. And the county surveyors have probably kept somewhat similar statistics since?—I have no doubt most of them have done so. I do not think that there would be any great difficulty in doing it.

4368. You stated, did you not, in answer to some questions which were asked you with respect to the substitution of the present poor-law guardians for the cesspayers, that you do not consider that it would be desirable?—I think it is not desirable.

4369. And as to your answer to the honourable Member for Cork, when he asked you whether you did not consider the elective principle better than the nomination principle; may I take it that your objection to the elective principle was, that you believed it would be more a nomination principle in many instances, than the present system?—That is my belief.

4370. Do you believe that in many parts of Ireland, if you had the poor-law system transferred to the cesspayers, you would have in fact a really nomination system established?—In a great many districts, I have no doubt whatever that that would be the result.

4371. Then your objection was not to the general principle of election, but rather to its degenerating into a simple nomination in many cases?—Precisely.

4372. You suggested, did you not, that the cesspayers should be selected by ballot, and not out of the 100 highest names, but that certain names should be returned from each parish?—From the parish or some other district as the committee might think fit.

4373. Some honourable Member of the Committee suggested electoral divisions; what do you think of that?—It appears to me that the parish would suffice at present without going to any trouble, and that there might be a return from each parish of four, five, or six, according to the circumstances of that parish, but so that each parish or district should be represented.

4374. Are you quite certain that the parishes are conterminous with the baronies?—Parishes are not conterminous with baronies in every case.

4375. The electoral divisions are not?—They are not.

4376. That would be a difficulty in substituting electoral divisions, would it not?—It would. In case of the failure of the magistrates attending, I would suggest that the cesspayers ought to be allowed to hold the sessions themselves, and that they ought to be allowed to act whenever they come in.

4377. Do you think that a disadvantage has arisen from the fact that the grand jury is not a permanent body, and that between one assizes and the other there is no permanent body repre-

senting

Mr. *H. Hunt.*

19 May 1863.

occupying the county?—My judgment is, that there ought to be for special cases some board of superintendence or committee; for example, in building a court-house, or in any case of a large work being executed. I do not know that it would be necessary to have it at all times, but there ought to be power, whenever the grand jury thought fit, to nominate a committee to represent them, and to report to the following assizes.

4378. Are you in favour of having a permanent or standing finance committee?—I do not see the necessity of it.

4379. Mr. *Maguire.*] Would you relieve the very humble and poor class, whose tenements are valued at 2 *l.* or 3 *l.* a year, from the payment of the rate?—I think it would be a very great improvement.

4380. Do you know that great hardship has attended the collection of the rate from that class?—Great difficulty.

4381. Have you heard an opinion expressed in favour of freeing them from the liability to the tax?—I think that the very small tenements ought to be relieved from liability to the cess.

Mr. Edwin Sadleir recalled; and further Examined.

Mr. *E. Sadleir.*

4382. Have you any other suggestion to make to the Committee?—I have placed on the table a paper which contains my suggestions.

4383–5. You propose that the county surveyor should make the applications for all descriptions of work, and give a list of such applications to the secretary of the grand jury, who should send copies to the magistrates and cesspayers?—Yes.

4386. Secondly, you propose that there should be no competition for works, but that the magistrates and cesspayers should fix the amount to be given for any work, and then that it should be tendered for?—Yes.

4387. What do you mean by there being no competition?—I would allow a sum not to be lowered by any competition; I would have no competition. An adjourned session to be held, and instead of their calling for tenders, to propose for doing the work they should ask me for cards of proposals; on these proposals they should put merely their names and their securities. These cards should be put into a balloting box; the chairman should draw one out, and the first name which came out should be the contractor.

4388. What objection have you to competition?—That it is not honest.

Friday, 22nd *May* 1868.

MEMBERS PRESENT:

Mr. Blake.	Mr. Gregory.
Colonel Cooper.	Mr. Herbert.
Mr. Dawson.	Mr. Kendall.
General Dunne.	Sir Charles Lanyon.
Colonel Forde.	Mr. Leader.
Colonel French.	Mr. Maguire.
Mr. Chichester Fortescue.	The O'Conor Don.

THE O'CONOR DON, IN THE CHAIR.

Mr. WILLIAM BOLSTER, called in; and Examined.

Mr. *W. Bolster.* 22 May 1868.

4389. *Chairman.*] YOU are a Cesspayer of the county of Limerick, are you not?—Yes.

4390. And you frequently act as such at the presentment sessions?—Yes.

4391. I believe you are Chairman of the Farmers' Club in Limerick?—I am.

4392. That is a club which takes in other counties besides the county of Limerick, does it not?—We have taken in the counties of Clare and Tipperary.

4393. You have had, I presume, some experience in the working of the grand jury laws?—I fancy I have a very practical knowledge of it.

4394. Do you object to the present system?—Very much indeed.

4395. What are your chief grounds of objection as regards the constitution of the grand jury?—There are two important points which we consider very objectionable, viz., not equalising it in the same as the poor rate; and even a greater point, I think, is want of representation.

4396. Do you think that the great objection to the system is, that there is not a proper representation?—Certainly.

4397 The grand jury does not profess to be a representation of the cesspayers in any way?—Certainly not. Several members sit on our grand jury who are not ratepayers at all, and who, in fact, have no property in the county. I know some absentee landlords who never come to sit on the grand jury, and they nominate their agents, who, perhaps, have not more than an acre of land, and even that acre may be perhaps set to other people.

4398. But those agents on the grand jury represent the land, do they not?—They represent the property, of course.

4399. Is it not the case that the grand jury have not much power of initiating any taxation, and that they can pass very few presentments which have not previously been approved of at presentment sessions?—Of course, they are generally brought forward at the presentment sessions, but they have it all their own way at the presentment sessions.

4400. But confining your evidence first to the grand jury; as a fact, the grand jury have not the power of initiating, that is to say, of originating any, or much, county taxation?—Not unless it comes before the road sessions.

4401. But there are one or two exceptions to that, are there not?—Yes.

4402. They have the power of settling the salaries of the county officers, have they not?—Yes; as to the large sums which go on the county at large. I think that the grand jury, without the road sessions, have all the power.

4403. Mr. *Gregory.*] Those are imperative presentments, are they not?—They go under the heading of being on the county at large. We are not represented at all on the sessions of the county at large. Each barony is only allowed one cesspayer there, but they never think of attending.

4404. *Chairman.*] With respect to the grand jury powers; the grand jury, without any application to either the county at large sessions, or the baronial sessions, have the power, have they not, of settling what payment is to be made; for instance, for the collection of the county cess?—Certainly, and all the other officers' salaries.

4405. And you do not think that that is satisfactory?—I think that a great deal of discontent is caused in the county by the fact of our paying all the tax, and having no means in the world of cutting down the salaries.

4406. With respect to the constitution of presentment sessions, do you consider that the cesspayers are properly represented there?—It is no representation.

4407. Why do you say that it is no representation?—Because, if the cesspayers do attend at the road sessions, the magistrates have the power of coming from the whole county in such a body that the cesspayers might just as well not be there at all. We say that no magistrate has a right to vote in any barony at the road sessions, unless he has a qualification in that barony.

4408. Mr. *Gregory.*] Do magistrates in your county often come in from other baronies and vote at the road sessions?—I have seen it very often done.

4409. Do they vote in a barony where they have no property or interest?—Certainly.

4410. Have you known many instances of it?—It is some years ago. At the time of the famine in Ireland they frequently came when new roads were required in the county to employ the people. There have been cases where roads would be useful for advancing the value of the property, and which they thought would be opposed at the road sessions, and they have brought magistrates from all the districts to help to carry the matter.

Mr. F. Baister. —— 27 May 1868.

4411. But in ordinary times have you found it to be generally the case that magistrates do come from other baronies and vote at presentment sessions?—I have not a doubt about it.

4412. Where they have no interest or property?—Yes.

4413. *Chairman.*] But, at all events, such power exists?—Such power exists.

4414. And you do not believe that it is satisfactory that it should exist?—We do not think so, because it does away altogether with our representation.

4415. Do you consider that the cesspayers are represented by the associated cesspayers at the presentment sessions, and that that is a proper representation, irrespective of the magistrates altogether?—I think the grand juror has the sole appointment of the cesspayers. I have always heard, and I think myself, from my practical knowledge that, if any particular work has to be carried at the following sessions, the grand juror takes particular pains in summoning the cesspayers who he thinks would not be likely to oppose him.

4416. But the grand juror has the power of putting on any one whom he likes, has he not?—Yes; the collector returns 100 names, and the grand juror has his choice from those 100 names.

4417. Mr. *Gregory.*] Does he not take the highest?—He does not. I was not on the three last road sessions, and I am one of the highest cesspayers, and men far below me have been on.

4418. Colonel *French.*] You could not be on twice in succession, could you?—Not in the same year.

4419. *Chairman.*] Were you on the list returned by the collector?—I fancy I must have been.

4420. Were you nominated by the grand juror?—I never heard that I was.

4421. Do you receive a list?—I was never nominated.

4422. Do you find that the associated cesspayers attend well, in the county of Limerick, at the road sessions?—They do not attend at all; perhaps out of the number summoned only two attend, and sometimes none at all.

4423. To what do you attribute their non-attendance?—To their idea that it is quite useless for them to go where they have no power.

4424. Do you think that if all the cesspayers attended, or if the maximum number of cesspayers attended the presentment sessions, as a general rule, there would be more magistrates there?—Yes, I fancy there would be; but even if the cesspayers did attend the road sessions, and out-voted the magistrates, the grand juries still have the power at the assizes to undo what the majority of the associated cesspayers might have done at the baronial sessions.

4425. They have not the power of passing any work which was not approved of at the presentment sessions, have they?—No; but they have the power of throwing out any work which might be carried.

4426. Their power is a negative one, and not initiative, is it not?—Yes.

4427. Have not the cesspayers a remedy, if the grand jury throw out a presentment more than once?—They can bring it before the judge at the assizes, I believe.

4428. What would you propose to substitute for the present mode of nominating the associated cesspayers; would you say that they should be elected, or that they should be balloted for?—With regard to the associated cesspayers, as they are at present, so far as their election is concerned, I should say that the best way to do it would be to have the barony collector furnish 100 names, say of the highest cesspayers in the barony, and let these be drawn by ballot, or something of that kind, and take the first men that come out.

4429. Would there not be this objection to that; that if the 100 names were taken from the entire barony the men who came out might all be from one particular locality of the barony?—That might be an objection.

4430. Would it not be desirable if any scheme of that sort were adopted, that instead of 100 names being returned from the whole barony, there should be a certain number of names returned from each parish, or each electoral division?—That would be a better arrangement by far.

4431. Do you think that, if that were done, it would be a satisfactory system?—I think, so far as it goes, it would be; but I do not think it is sufficient.

4432. Mr. *Gregory.*] Would you do that by election?—I do not know that it would be worth the trouble of going to an election; I think the ballot would be almost sufficient as far as the road sessions are concerned.

4433. *Chairman.*] Would you think that the grand jury should be continued?—I think that the present system should be altered so as to satisfy the people that they are represented, they believing, as they do, that they pay the whole of the tax unless the landlord is the occupier; I think the people will not be satisfied unless they have some representation in the disbursement of the moneys which they pay.

4434. But would they not have a representation in the disbursement of the monies which they pay, if they had this representation at the presentment sessions?—No, because the grand jury have the power, as I said before, of undoing at the assizes what the cesspayers may carry.

4435. But could any tax be imposed which had not been voted by the representatives?—No, but the magistrates could still out-vote them at road sessions; even the magistrates in the barony.

4436. Do you think that the number of magistrates who should attend at presentment sessions should be limited; that there should not be a greater number of magistrates, for instance, than cesspayers?—Exactly; if that were done there would be representation to some extent.

4437. Would there not be a representation to this extent; that no tax could be levied which had not been voted by this representative body of cesspayers and magistrates?—Yes, there would.

4438. In that case would you think it necessary that the constitution of the grand jury, which should be a body merely for passing a vote, or not, upon the presentment sessions should be also altered?—I do not think that it is satisfactory as it is.

4439. What alteration do you think would be necessary?—My idea, and the idea generally, I think, of my division of the county is, that we ought to have the same representation in disbursing the amount of the grand jury cess as we have at the different Poor Law Boards; we are equally constituted *ex-officio* elected cesspayers at all the Poor Law Boards, and the thing works

very

very well in my mind; it gives the occupier an advantage which I consider in Ireland to be a very great one, i. e., of mixing in the different local Boards with the landlord; they understand each other very well at those Boards; I happened to be vice-chairman of the Kilmallock Union for 10 or 15 years, and I found very great advantage myself as a ratepayer in meeting all the noblemen and landlords about me.

4440. But would not that exist in the baronial sessions?—Not to the same extent.

4441. Do you think that it would be necessary to have a county board constituted in the same way?—I think a county board should be so constituted. We do not require to have anything to say to the criminal business of the county. I think you might have a grand jury for that if you wish it. We get quite enough criminal business from being on the common juries.

4442. Would that board be appointed by election?—By election, the same as the guardians.

4443. Then, would the county board be appointed by election, and the baronial board by ballot?—Election, perhaps, would be better for both.

4444. Do you see any great necessity for the existence of this county board at all?—There is a very great necessity, because the ratepayers have no confidence at all in the present state of things.

4445. But if the present state of things were altered, and if the ratepayers had an equal share in settling the presentments at the baronial board, do you see any necessity for having another elected board appointed merely for passing a veto on those presentments?—I do not think it would be sufficient to satisfy the ratepayers. I think we have a right to a voice in the disbursement of the general funds of the county, as being the parties who pay them.

4446. What do you mean by general disbursements?—The disbursement of whole grand jury cess. In the election of officers we have no voice, and we contend that we have a right to a voice in the election of an officer.

4447. You consider that this county board would be necessary for the purpose of electing those officers?—Yes, and for the disbursement of monies.

4448. What do you mean by disbursing the monies?—Disbursing the whole amount of the grand jury cess, which the grand jury have the power at present of distributing without any voice of ours.

4449. Under your proposal the grand jury, or the county board, or whatever you like to call it, would not have the power of disbursing any monies which had not been previously voted by you?—They have with great respect. There are items which we contend ought to be immediately divided between landlord and occupier.

4450. We will come to that afterwards, but will you now confine yourself to this particular point?—We will take the printing of the county, which is a very big item. The baronial sessions have nothing to say to that.

4451. It comes before the county at large sessions, does it not?—It comes before the county at large sessions.

4452. It cannot be passed before the grand jury, can it, unless presented by that county at large sessions?—There is no representation at the county at large sessions.

4453. But, supposing that your proposal with respect to the baronial sessions should be adopted, then you would have control over all those presentments to which you refer, would you not?—It would be an improvement upon the present state of things, but I do not think that it would be sufficient.

Mr. W. Sclater.

21 May 1868.

4454. Will you state to the Committee exactly in what point you consider that it would be deficient?—One point is, that I know gentlemen in my neighbourhood who are, some of them, farming 1,200, 1,400, and 1,600 acres of land, and their position is just as good as, and better, than that of a great many of the grand jurors; and I know that a great jealousy exists with those that they are never summoned on the grand panel of the county, although they are universally large cesspayers, while an absentee's agent, who has nothing to do in the world with the property, is summoned.

4455. But that is a grievance which does not so much refer to the taxation which is raised upon the county; that is rather a grievance of certain gentlemen considering themselves not to be placed in that social position in the county that they ought to occupy, is it not?—So far, it is.

4456. Is it not a social grievance rather than one connected with the levying of the taxation of the county?—It is a general grievance with the whole of the occupiers.

4457. How do you mean that it is a general grievance with the whole of the occupiers?—We believe that we have a right to be represented as we are at the poor law boards, both at the baronial sessions and before the grand jury.

4458. Supposing that you had these baronial boards formed in the manner you suggest, giving ample representation both to the occupiers and to the owners, would there be any necessity for the grand jury, or any county board, or any board of any description whatever beyond them?—I think that the county board for general purposes should exist.

4459. Are the general purposes which you mean the election of the county officers?—Yes, and the winding-up of the whole thing; what occurs at baronial sessions. I think you ought to have a general board to fiat presentments, and all that sort of thing.

4460. Would not each barony fiat the presentments for its own barony; and, at present, do not the contractors come before the presentment sessions and have their contracts certified there?—They are certified by the county surveyor.

4461. If you had a baronial board, could not all that be done finally?—Perhaps so.

4462. Do you see any necessity for having another body constituted who would have no power whatever of initiating taxation, and who would be merely a sort of supervising body over the other?—I think that that would be a very good thing.

4463. And you think that the grand jury, as at present constituted, would not be a satisfactory body for carrying out that object?—No; I would have somebody else, of whom the occupiers would be more independent.

4464. Would you prefer having a body partially composed of the occupiers themselves?—No; I would prefer being under such a body as the Poor Law Commissioners.

4465. You would propose having a check upon the baronial board by the constitution of a Government board?—I prefer it to a local grand jury.

4466. You

Mr. W. Baker. 21 May 1862.

4466. You have stated that the appointment of the collectors of the county cess rested with the grand jury, and that the settlement of the amount to be paid for the collection rested with them; do you consider that the amount paid for the collection of the county cess at present is excessive?—I think it is too high.

4467. It is very much higher, is it not, than what is paid for the collection of the poor rates?—4½ d. to 5 d. is about the amount paid for collecting the poor rates, and for the county cess they get 9 d.

4468. Do you not believe that there would be many eligible persons who could give the best security, and who would be quite willing to collect the cess for a less amount?—Quite as good, and better; and you would get men to collect the grand jury cess much cheaper than at present, because the majority of the collectors at present are gentlemen, who hold the office as a sinecure, and collect the cess by deputies, and I think you would get working men, who could give ample security, who would be very glad to advance themselves by doing it, and at a much cheaper rate than the present collectors.

4469. *Mr. Gregory.*] I suppose you would have a strict supervision, so that the county cess collectors should pay in the sums as fast as they receive them?—Certainly.

4470. Are you aware that the high rate of security which is required for those constables arises in consequence of the large sums of money which remain in their hands from assizes to assizes?—I think strict supervision would be a very good thing; but I also think that the fact of the present collectors doing their work, principally by deputies, is one of the great causes why the whole of the cess is very seldom collected off each barony; that is the fault of the collectors, and not the fault of the people who have to pay the cess, because every cesspayer in the country knows that he has to meet at every assizes his barony rate; and it is the fault altogether of the collector if any man's rate remains unpaid.

4471. Colonel *French.*] But has not the collector, if it is uncollected, to pay it out of his own pocket?—He has, and that is one of his excuses for asking a high rate of payment; but I contend that the whole cess could be collected.

4472. Would you see any objection to dividing the baronies into parishes, in order to secure a greater number of people qualified to give the security for the collection of the cess?—That would hardly be worth doing, I think.

4473. *Mr. Gregory.*] Would you propose that the cess collector should pay in every 100 *l.* as he receives it?—Yes, just the same as the poor law collectors.

4474. Colonel *French.*] Are not the owners of land represented on the grand jury?—Frequently not, the owners being absentees.

4475. But where they were represented, you would give a double representation to that property, would you not, to the exclusion of other properties?—I believe that the high sheriff in choosing the grand panel of the county, is quite satisfied if he puts on the panel any gentleman who has any qualification as a freeholder in that barony.

4476. *Chairman.*] You state that you are aware that there are many eligible persons who could give the best security who would be willing to collect the county cess; would it be fair to ask you (as you mentioned yourself) whether you would undertake the collection of the county cess at a lower rate than is now paid?—I would only be too happy to have it. I wish I had the chance.

4477. Would you collect it at the same rate as the poor rate is collected?—I should be very glad to do it for 6 d., whereas, 9 d. is paid at present. It would be very well worth my while to attend to it, and do it myself.

4478. *Mr. Gregory.*] What is the charge for collecting the poor rate in your union?—For the first two-thirds we give 5 d. as an inducement to the collectors to pay in, and then for what remains after that we only give 4½ d.

4479. *Chairman.*] Of course you speak of the barony in which you reside?—I would take any barony in the county.

4480. And you could get the best security?—Yes.

4481. Have you ever heard of the county cess collectors failing?—Yes.

4482. Do you not think that that just as often happens with regard to them as with regard to the poor law collectors?—It does not happen so often to them as to the poor law collectors, because you have a number of barony constables, who are men of large property in the county, and who are generally some of grand jurors.

4483. But when any one of them fails, there is generally a greater loss, is there not, than in the case of poor rate collectors?—They have security for the barony constables.

4484. Have not those securities sometimes turned out to be worthless?—That is the fault of the grand jury, I think, who made a bad selection.

4485. Are you aware of the county ever being at a loss in that respect?—I never heard of it. I have known one collector, a gentleman who broke down, but his securities paid.

4486. Do you think that the collection of the poor rate and of the county cess could be amalgamated, and that the same person could do both?—I think it would be too much for one man to do; I think it would be quite enough for one man to take either, unless he were allowed a deputy.

4487. *Mr. Gregory.*] Would not the one call on the part of the collector do for both?—You have to call several times; you would not get the money the day you call, and although you have the power of distress, still you do not like, if you find you can get the amount within a reasonable time, to go to cross purposes with the people.

4488. *Chairman.*] Have you seen a paper which has been put in by the barony cess collector to your county, in which he states the differences between the duties thrown upon the barony cess collector and upon the poor rate collector?—Yes.

4489. I find he first says that, "The barony cess collector receives the valuation-book, with poundage rate, and names and valuations of occupiers, the amount payable by each must be calculated by the collector." Whereas the poor rate collector has not to make any such calculations?—No, his calculations are made by the clerk of the union.

4490. Do you think that that is a very formidable objection?—No, the calculations are very simple.

4491. The barony collector also pays for printing the account-books, notices, &c.; and the poor rate

rate collector has his stamps and notices paid for, is that so?—I doubt very much whether the baronial constable has to pay for the printing; I am almost certain as to that, though I could not speak from authority.

4492. Has he to pay for the stamps on the receipts which he gives?—I am not certain.

4493. And the poor rate collector has not?—No.

4494. The baronial collector has also to furnish lists of jurors to the clerk of the peace, has he not?—Yes. That is very simple.

4495. That is a duty which has nothing to do with the raising of the tax, but which is, in fact, a sort of criminal duty imposed upon him?—It is a criminal duty. He has the cesses before him, and there is no difficulty in doing that.

4496. He has also to collect from the occupiers rated below 4 *l.*, has he not, whereas the occupiers rated below 4 *l.* do not pay poor rate at all?—Yes; but those are very isolated cases, I should say. In my neighbourhood I do not know many.

4497. Are there not many occupiers in Ireland rated below 4 *l.*?—Not in my neighbourhood, or in my county. There are numbers of poor people living under me, but they are all taken in the general rating, and I pay the whole of the grand jury cess for them.

4498. Is there any difference between the responsibility of county cess collectors and of the poor rate collectors with regard to paying the full amount of the levy?—Yes; the barony constable, I believe, must make his accounts square at the assizes, unless he can show that there is no means for collecting it.

4499. But must not the poor rate collector do the same?—The poor rate collector also must do the same; but his time is extended for doing it. The guardians will allow a poor rate collector, if he is in arrears, to take a longer time to get in the rate, but the barony constable must, I think, make his warrant good at the assizes.

4500. What is the length of time that the barony cess collectors have for collecting the levy?—At the July assizes the warrants are issued for the cess; and the next assizes follow, perhaps, in March.

4501. Have they not a very long time for collecting the cess?—They have lots of time; and I am quite satisfied that they could make the collection good.

4502. Have they not practically as long a time as the poor rate collector?—No; in our union we always make a 12 months' rate. We make a rate to carry us through for 12 months, and, consequently, the poor rate collector has the whole 12 months to make his collection.

4503. Colonel *Forde.*] Do you mean to say that your guardians do not insist upon your rate collector returning the amount of his rate before a certain time?—We hold out an inducement; we give him a higher poundage on the first two-thirds of the rate; and upon any that remains after that we reduce the poundage.

4504. Does it take the whole year to do it?—It does not take the whole year to do it; but a good deal goes on for a long time after the striking of the rate.

4505. Mr. *Gregory.*] The greater portion of the rate is collected pretty soon, is it not?—The greater portion of the rate is collected within the first four months.

4506. *Chairman.*] But on the whole, whether, or not, the county cess could be collected by the same individual as the poor rate, you feel quite confident that eligible persons could be got to collect the county cess at a much lower rate than at present?—I am quite satisfied of it.

Mr. W. [illegible]

[illegible] May 18[illegible].

4507. To what do you attribute the fact that these persons do not come forward to do so?—Because the barony constable is the friend or nominee of the grand jury, and the people outside that board have no influence.

4508. There is a feeling that there would be no chance?—No chance whatever.

4509. And that is one reason why the cesspayers want representation on the grand jury?—Yes. I also think that the public works of the county ought to be tendered for.

4510. You refer, I presume, to printing, and such things as that?—Yes, that is one of the principal items.

4511. Is not the printing in your county tendered for?—It is never tendered for. It has been in the hands of one man since before I was born, certainly.

4512. Do the grand jury present to him any sum which they think proper?—The grand jury pay him very liberally. I do not like mentioning names, because it is unpleasant; but I happen to know the gentleman very well. However, I fancy I am doing a public duty, and I mention it on that account. I think it would be done a great deal cheaper if it were tendered for.

4513. Colonel *Cooper.*] Is there any fixed sum for printing?—No; it is a very large item.

4514. Does it vary much in different years?—Scarcely at all; I think it is exactly the same.

4515. *Chairman.*] In the county of Limerick is there no such thing as tenders for the county printing?—There is not.

4516. It comes before the county at large presentment sessions first, does it not?—Yes.

4517. And it is passed there as a matter of course?—Yes, it has been passed there for, I suppose, 60 or 70 years.

4518. You do not consider that there is anything like adequate representation upon that county at large sessions?—I am certain that there is no representation at all at the county at large sessions; magistrates from the whole county attend there, and, of course, even if one cesspayer from each barony did go it would be of no use, but they never go; I have very often been at the head of the associated cesspayers myself, but I never dreamt in my life of going to the county at large sessions.

4519. Mr. *Gregory.*] Do you think that, if there was equal representation on the county at large sessions, on the part of the magistrates and cesspayers, there would be a larger attendance of the cesspayers?—I am quite satisfied that if we felt that there was a chance of preventing those things which we feel to be grievances, the cesspayers would attend.

4520. Colonel *Forde.*] What sums come before the county at large sessions upon which there is any necessity to take a vote?—The printing comes before them, and the appointment of county officers all comes before them.

4521. They are imperative presentments, are they not; they are laid down by Act of Parliament?—Yes, but they have to pass the county at large sessions.

4522. Mr. *Gregory.*] But whatever was the representation, you could not vary them in any way, could you?—I could vary the printing account;

Mr. W. Fisher.

20 May 1858.

county; for the half-year it was 275 *l.*; I am quite satisfied that, notwithstanding only that 275 *l.* appearing in the county book, there are a great many more perquisites which go to the printer.

4523. Does that include advertisements?—I would say it does.

4524. *Chairman.*] Is there a regular contract made with the printer?—Yes.

4525. Is there ever a charge made in the county of Limerick, or does he ever send in a bill for additional expenses outside the contract?—I should say not.

4526. Colonel *Forde.*] Will you state any other items in the county at large accounts as to which you think the cesspayers ought to have a voice?—The making of bridges all generally goes on the county at large. That is the practice; they are too heavy sometimes to put on barony.

4527. But they go before the baronial sessions, do they not?—Yes, but it is county at large rating. I fancy they have to pay for doing it. I do not know that there has been a bridge built in the county during this year, but I have known bridges to be made, and I have known the expenses to be put entirely upon the county at large.

4528. But it had passed your baronial road sessions in the first instance, had it not?—Yes.

4529. Then you are the parties who passed it, subject to its being put upon the county at large? —The magistrate at the road sessions have it, but we do not.

4530. *Mr. Gregory.*] But, under an altered state of things and a better representation, would you have the power of deciding those points?—We have no fancy, no pride, or anything of that kind as to being on the grand panel of the county; in fact it is not our position; we do not at all fancy it in that way; but I think if we got protection and were properly represented, even at the baronial sessions, it would be the means of allaying a great deal of discontent which at present exists.

4531. *Chairman.*] With respect to the division of the county cess at present, the entire of the county rate is paid directly by the occupier, is it not?—Yes.

4532. Do you not believe that a great deal of dissatisfaction exists in Ireland upon this ground? —Certainly.

4533. Even though the cess may be paid indirectly by the landlord, through his giving the land to his tenant at a diminished rent, still there is a strong feeling, is there not, amongst the occupiers, that it is unjust, that the whole of this tax should be paid directly by them, the chief part of the regulation of it being in the hands of the landlord?—I would not go so far as to say that the tax is at all paid indirectly by the landlord. I do not think it is; I think that the tax is paid altogether by the occupier. I will give you an example, if you will allow me. When the clergyman's rent-charge was first altered in Ireland, it was taken off the occupiers, of course protecting the proprietors where leases did exist, and in any lettings which have been made since, the occupier does not pay the rent-charge, but it is paid solely by the landlord; and I doubt very much if that has not done more good in Ireland than any alteration of any law which has been made for years. It has allayed discontent in the country, because the occupier does not pay.

4534. But let us take the example which you have given of the rent-charge. You state, do you not, that you believe that the county cess is not paid indirectly by the landlord?—I do.

4535. And you give, as an example to prove that, the case of the tithe rent-charge?—Yes; I will give you an example in my own person; My father had the lease of the lands which I hold now, and in that lease he paid 10 guineas a year rent-charge. I have got a new lease, and I pay no rent-charge, and I pay a lesser rent.

4536. Has the farm deteriorated in any way? —I have improved my farm very much myself.

4537. What is the reason why you pay a lesser rent now?—Because I got my lease in the year 1850, when prices were not so high as now.

4538. You got your lease under exceptional circumstances?—Yes; but if my lease expired to-morrow, I have not the slightest expectation that my rent would be advanced.

4539. Supposing that your lease expired to-morrow, and that your landlord put your farm up to-morrow, do you think that the landlord would not get a greater rent for it than you are paying?—I think that you would get any amount of rent promised for land in Ireland.

4540. Do you not think that as good and solvent a tenant as you are could be got to give a higher rent for your land?—There might be a trifle more rent got; but I think that to get any interest out of the land, I could not pay more.

4541. Then yours is an exceptional case, and not a fair case to test the law upon, because in the first place your old rent was exceptionally high, and your present rent was fixed at an exceptional time?—Yes; but it is right for me to state that my land was set to me after a large amount of drainage, which was done by my landlord under the Board of Works, the superintendence of it being managed by myself; and in the years 1849 and 1850 I laid out 500 *l.* in permanent works in the way of drainage, which my landlord allowed me; I was complimented by the Board of Works for the manner in which I did the work.

4542. *Mr. Gregory.*] What is the length of your lease?—It was a 31 years' lease.

4543. *Chairman.*] Taking a case, which is not exceptional like yours, such as for instance the case of an ordinary farm of 50 acres at present, set at 2 *l.* an acre, in a barony in which the county cess is 2 *s.* in the £., and supposing that the landlord of that farm received for it 100 *l.* a year, which is at the rate of 2 *l.* an acre, the tenant pays for it in reality 110 *l.*, because he pays 100 *l.* to the landlord, and 10 *l.* for the county cess. Supposing that that farm were put up for competition, and that a law were passed that all the county cess should be paid by the landlord, would not that landlord get 110 *l.* for that farm, instead of 100 *l.*?—£. 10 is a very small advance on a farm.

4544. But would it not be worth the same to the tenant after the passing of that law as before? —Decidedly.

4545. And would not the tenant therefore, supposing the farm were put up for competition (which is the only fair way to test it), be willing to pay the 110 *l.*, the same money as he had paid before?—I am quite certain that he would.

4546. Would not the landlord then receive 110 *l.* rent?—Yes, but notwithstanding all that I think the thing would work better; I have not a doubt that the tenant would be satisfied to pay the 10 *l.* extra.

4547. Therefore, at the present time, when the

the landlord receives only 100*l.* for this farm, he is in reality bearing the loss of 10*l.*, is he not, in consequence of the tenant having to pay the county cess?—No, I think not; I cannot see how he can show a loss.

4548. Is not that a proof that indirectly the landlord, even where he has let his land to the highest bidder, pays indirectly the county cess?—Perhaps when the letting was made first by the landlord, the county cess might not have been half what it is now; I think the county cess is increasing very much.

4549. But in the first instance when it was let, would it not be so?—In the first instance, I agree with you altogether.

4550. The chief disadvantage arising from the whole payment of the county cess being made directly by the tenant is, that although the landlord may pay indirectly, through his rent being lowered, yet that no variation in the tax affects him in any way; and that an increase in the rate does not affect his rent?—No.

4551. And therefore, when once the rent is settled, he has no direct interest in any alteration which is made in the amount of the rate, has he?—When once he makes the setting, if the grand jury cess is 10*d.* in the pound he may indirectly, perhaps, pay that 10*d.* in the pound; but if the grand jury cess went up to 3*s.*, or 3*s.* 6*d.* in the pound, he is not indirectly paying any advance.

4552. And you consider that that is not a desirable state of things to exist?—I think so.

4553. Do you think it would be more desirable that every alteration which should take place in the county cess should be felt directly by the landlord?—I think, if the alteration was made, and land was put up to be set, it must meet its own value; and if it were set for its value, on that value of course the calculation is made that the county cess is added to the rent. It would work better, I think, if it were equally divided, as the poor rates are, notwithstanding the fact that the tenant would be the whole time paying the whole of it.

4554. But even allowing that in all new lettings that would be considered, you still hold that it would be more satisfactory to the public feeling of the country that a certain portion of the tax should be paid directly by the landlord?—Certainly.

4555. And in addition to satisfying the public feeling, by the landlords contributing directly a portion of the rate, would it not also give the landlord a direct interest in every variation that took place in the rate?—I am quite satisfied that, although the grand jury cess might be added to the rent by the landlord, still if the landlord was liable for half the rate, our grand jury would look a great deal more sharply after their work than they do at present.

4556. Mr. *Gregory.*] As far as your experience goes, when a tenant takes a farm in your county, does he generally make inquiries and calculate the average of what the county cess is?—Of course, a practical man would do so.

4557. But as a general rule is it done?—As a general rule they never calculate about land in Ireland.

4558. But do you not think that the Irish tenant farmers are shrewd enough in taking a holding to make some estimate in their own mind of what the average of the county cess is?—I am sorry to tell you that I think that the only thing which the Irish farmers, as a body, calculate is how they can best go into possession. They have no other resources; they can turn themselves to nothing else; and they all depend upon land for their livelihood. I know several men who have been broken, who had made money in other countries, and had come over to Ireland to farm, and paid high fines and exorbitant rents, and who have smashed in two years.

Mr. W. Baker.

24 May 1868.

4559. *Chairman.*] Do you think that it would be sufficient to provide that, in all future lettings, there should be a permission for the division of the rate between landlord and tenant?—Most decidedly. Of course, I would not meddle with existing leases; because I think that it would be very unfair if I got a lease for 15 years ago, my landlord understanding that I was to pay the whole of the charge, for me to say, "You must pay half of the county rate now."

4560. Would you apply the same rule with respect to tenancies from year to year?—Most decidedly; I would insist upon a division. I think that it would induce men to give their tenants leases. If the grand jury cess was divided, half and half, the landlord might say, "Come, Jack, you have never had a lease, and you shall have a lease now." Jack would be delighted to get a lease, and in giving the lease the landlord might very easily slip in the grand jury cess; and I think that would be perfectly satisfactory.

4561. Do you think that they would be satisfied with that?—I am sure that there is no tenant in Ireland of 100 acres of land who would not willingly pay 20*l.* or 30*l.* a year more for a lease. You may talk about the tenant right question, and all that kind of thing, but the only tenant right that I think is required in Ireland for the industrious tenant is a lease. That is my notion as a practical farmer.

4562. Mr. *Kendall.*] A lease for many years?—That is another question. I think that if I take a farm, and I have to build a house, and I have to drain it at my own expense, and the landlord does not make any improvements for me, I ought at least to get a 61 years' lease, if I do all the work myself.

4563. Mr. *Gregory.*] That is a building lease?—That is a building lease, and draining, which is the most important thing in Ireland; but if the landlord, on the contrary, does these things himself, I think it would be very fair to give no lease at all, or it might be better to give a 21 years' lease.

4564. *Chairman.*] There are certain charges upon the county rates at present for lunatic asylums, and county infirmaries, and charges of that sort, which are rather public charity charges; do you not think they ought rather to be charged upon the poor rate?—We consider them pauper institutions, and that they should come fully under the Poor Law Act; the rate for the county asylum, in Limerick, for the half year was 2,494 *l.* 11 *s.* 11 *d.*; that is nearly 5,000*l.* a year which we pay for the asylum, which is a pauper institution.

4565. And the charge for the lunatic asylum has been increasing very much of late years, has it not?—Yes, we have to pay a portion to Clare and Kerry, but they both have now asylums of their own. There has been some change in the cost of keeping lunatics.

4566. The lunatic asylums have been increased in number very much, have they not?—Very much.

Mr. W. [illegible].

[illegible] May 1862.

4567. Formerly there was only one asylum for several counties, and now each county has an asylum for itself?—Yes. Then there are in each county in Ireland two officers, whose posts are almost sinecures. One is the clerk of the Crown, and the other is the clerk of the peace. I think there would be a great saving if those two offices were made into one.

4568. There is very little fiscal business attached to either office, I believe?—Very little; we never see the clerk of the peace in the county of Limerick; he has a deputy who does his work for him, and the clerk of the Crown also does his work by deputy. Those offices are mere sinecures, and it is a great hardship on the cesspayer who pays the rate.

4569. Are you aware what fiscal duties the clerk of the Crown has to discharge?—I should say his fiscal duties are solely paying off witnesses at assizes, and all that sort of thing; I do not think his duties can go, so far as fiscal business is concerned, much further than that. Of course he has to do with the criminal business of the county.

4570. He has to countersign the cheques for prosecutors, has he not?—Yes; and he has to countersign all the receipts for money paid to witnesses, and all that sort of thing, at the sessions.

4571. Do you not think that, if the offices of clerk of the peace and clerk of the Crown were united, that one officer would be an officer concerned with the criminal business of the county?—Yes.

4572. And that the fiscal duties attached to either office should be taken away from that officer, and handed over altogether, say to the secretary of the grand jury?—Most decidedly; I am quite sure that it would be very easy to unite the offices of clerk of the Crown and clerk of the peace, and if you amalgamated both you would get just as efficient men to do the duties of both for the salary of one.

4573. Mr. *Gregory*.] Then you would have that man, I presume, to reside in the county?—Certainly, and to do his own business.

4574. *Chairman*.] Would you not think it desirable that that officer should be a professional man, the business he would have to do being criminal business?—Most decidedly; I do not think any man but a professional man ought to hold either post.

4575. Are you in favour of county infirmaries, as at present constituted?—I think the poor law infirmaries are the best, or at least as good as any that we have.

4576. Is there no desire evinced on the part of the poor people in your part of the world to go to the central establishment of the county infirmary, instead of being treated in the workhouse?—I think a pride exists in the poor people, and that you will not induce them to go to a workhouse, as they call it, where you can induce them to go to the county infirmary.

4577. The county infirmary is governed by the subscribers to its funds, is it not?—A portion is levied off the county, but it is so governed. There is another great advantage in the county infirmary which you have not in the workhouse, that you have a great number of clever physicians attending the county infirmary, whereas the medical staff of the workhouse hospital is confined to a man who may be a country practitioner, and perhaps of no great skill.

4578. Mr. *Gregory*.] I suppose county infirmary cases are generally cases of a particularly difficult description, which cannot be treated in the workhouse hospitals?—Yes; and they have the great advantage of having the first physicians from the city always attending.

4579. Do you approve of the mode in which county infirmaries are governed at present?—I think so. I do not think they could be made better.

4580. The grand jury have nothing to say to the government of these county infirmaries, have they?—Yes, there is a committee of the grand jury formed to inquire into the subject.

4581. But who make all the appointments in the county infirmary?—The governors.

4582. Who are the governors?—The men who have subscribed, I believe, originally for the infirmary; but I am not exactly certain as to that.

4583. Do you think that that is a satisfactory system for the government of those establishments?—I am quite satisfied that the county infirmary in Limerick could not be better governed than it is.

4584. But do you think it is a good principle that any one who pays 1 *l.* a year can have a vote for the appointment of the officers?—I think it is.

4585. You do not think that it leads at any time when there is an election for any important officer in those institutions to a gentleman's going in and paying a guinea for that year, in order to have a vote?—I never heard of its being done; but there is a committee of every grand jury on the county infirmary.

4586. Colonel *French*.] With regard to the county infirmaries, the private subscriptions are doubled by the grand jury, are they not?—I believe so.

4587. That is the only charge that the grand jury have to pay, is it not?—Yes.

4588. As regards the county at large charges, printing was the one to which you referred, and you did not refer to any others at the time; will you state any others?—I do not see that there are any others.

4589. It appears that it is only in your county that that is a charge that does not come before the county at large sessions?—I am not aware that it is acted upon in any other county, but I am quite satisfied that it is not advertised for in my county, because I am sure that if it was, several other printers would have been at it.

4590. Colonel *French*.] Have you ever heard of complaints being made that the County Infirmary, which is a superior establishment to all the other medical establishments in the county, is nearly exclusively for the benefit of those in its neighbourhood?—I never have; I live 13 Irish miles from Limerick, and I have frequently got tickets of admission for the poor people in my district to go into the County Infirmary.

4591. Mr. *Gregory*.] You have a railway, have you not?—Yes; but when we had not a railway, it was just the same.

4592. *Chairman*.] But that is not a very long distance, is it?—It is nearly the two extreme ends of the county; the county of Cork is within five miles of me.

4593. Is there no point of the county of Limerick more distant from the city than 13 miles?—Castle West, I suppose, would be about 23 miles.

4594. But the distance of some portions of the county

county from the county town is much greater than that, is it not?—Certainly; on the whole, I think county infirmaries are very useful institutions.

4595. You would not propose the abolition of county infirmaries?—I would not.

4596. General *Dunne*.] You say that it would give satisfaction to public feeling if half the cess was taken off?—Yes.

4597. Would it not give much greater satisfaction if the whole of it was taken off?—That would be unreasonable to expect; but I believe it would give very great satisfaction.

4598. But would they not like it much better?—Certainly, but I think it would be unreasonable.

4599. Colonel *French*.] Why would it be unreasonable?—It would be unreasonable for me to expect that the landlord should pay the whole of the cess.

4600. *Chairman*.] You have been asked by the gallant general whether you do not believe that the public would be better satisfied if the whole of the county rate were placed upon the landlord. If the landlord paid the entire rate directly, might not the landlord in that case claim to have the entire management of the roads and expenses of the county?—Most decidedly. We should never wish to interfere with them.

4601. General *Dunne*.] The landlord pays every tax laid upon the land, does he not?—I do not think so.

4602. How do you think there is a difference made in the lettings?—I do not think that in letting land those nice calculations are entered into.

4603. For instance, when the tithe rent-charge was placed on the proprietor, do you not think that an alteration (I do not say immediately) took place in a rise in the value of land?—I do not pay either priest or minister, and I hold my land cheaper now than I did then.

4604. Mr *Maguire*.] Though you say that the tenant would be more pleased if the landlord paid the entire of this tax, did you ever hear such a demand made on the part of the tenants of Ireland, as that the landlord should pay the entire grand jury tax?—I know an agent in my neighbourhood who is adopting a course similar to having the landlord to pay all the taxes.

4605. But did you ever hear, on the part of those representing the occupiers of Ireland, any such demand as that implied in the question asked you?—I never did.

4606. There is no such demand made?—I never heard of it.

4607. Do you maintain that they would be quite satisfied if the tax were divided equally between landlord and occupier?—Perfectly so. I never heard a tenant in my life make any application to have the whole tax paid by the landlord.

4608. Colonel *Cooper*.] Did you ever hear a demand that half the tax should be paid by the landlord?—I do not know that that demand has ever been made personally to a landlord; but it is the opinion of the people that it should be so paid.

4609. Mr. *Dawson*.] How would you provide a direct representation of the cesspayers?—In the same way as at the Poor Law Board.

4610. Do you think the same individuals could serve both as poor law guardians and as representing the cesspayers?—It does not follow that they would be the same, because they would be elected by the ratepayers of the different counties.

4611. Do you think it desirable that they should be the same, so as to avoid multiplicity of elections?—I think if you could keep the whole thing under the poor law it would work as well.

4612. Do you think that the two rates could be collected by the same individual?—I think it would be too much for one individual, unless he was allowed deputies, as they have under the grand jury system.

4613. Colonel *Cooper*.] I suppose a better class of persons make use of the county infirmary than the ordinary poor people?—Yes, certainly.

4614. It is a very great convenience to the farmers, is it not, to have such good medical assistance?—There are many decent people in the country who could not afford to pay a physician in their own houses.

4615. Of the class of farmers?—Of the small class of farmers. They would object to go into a workhouse hospital, and they avail themselves of the facility of going into the county infirmary.

4616. On those grounds you think that a county infirmary is a great convenience and benefit to the county?—Yes; that coupled with the extra skill of the physicians who attend it.

4617. Do the grand jury appoint a committee to examine into charitable accounts at each assizes?—They do. As regards the county infirmary, the statement is this: "The committee appointed to examine the accounts of this county infirmary have found them quite correct, and recommend a presentment of 400 *l.* to be granted," and so on; and that is signed by three of the grand jurors.

4618. And they also audit the accounts of the lunatic asylum, do they not?—Yes; there are lunatic asylum committees, gaol boards, and county infirmary committees.

4619. If they thought there was extravagance anywhere, they would control that expenditure, would they not?—I dare say they would; but, at the same time, I am quite sure that they allow everything to be very extravagant in all the institutions.

4620. Mr. *Dawson*.] When you speak of their controlling the expenditure, you mean that they report to the grand jury upon it?—Yes; they report fairly, I think, but everything goes too high we fancy.

4621. Have the expenses increased lately?—Yes, the cess is increasing all over Ireland.

4622. But are the expenses of the lunatic establishments increasing?—We have more lunatics, I think, than we had.

4623. Colonel *Cooper*.] They go into asylums more than they used to do, do they not?—They do.

4624. Do you think the asylum is extravagantly managed?—With regard to the inmates of the asylum, comparing them with paupers, of course they are a great deal better fed than the workhouse paupers; it might be, after all excusable to give an unfortunate lunatic better care and feeding than a pauper, but they are three times as well fed as the paupers; they get plenty of good beef and plenty of good soup, and all of that sort of thing; in fact, I think they are fed as well as I am myself.

4625. Colonel *French*.] Do you see any reason why the grand jury should be called upon to make presentments for lunatic asylums, they having

Mr. *W. Holmes.*

21 May 1868.

having nothing to say to the management of the lunatic asylums?—I think the public charities should be all worked under the guardians of the poor.

4626. Do you not think that it would be a fair claim to put upon the Consolidated Fund the expense of all the lunatic asylums?—If we could put it all on the Consolidated Fund it would be a very good thing; that would be the best.

4627. Mr. *Kendall*.] As I understand from you just now, the cesspayer is ill at ease because he fancies he has not got the voice he ought to have, and he is angry because the grand jurors have the veto; but is it not the case that nothing can originate with the grand jury, and that all must originate with the cesspayer?—I think not.

4628. After all is arranged the grand jury can say no to any expenditure, can they not?—Yes, they can.

4629. And that is what you do not like?—Yes, but nothing originates with the cesspayers; it is with the magistrates and the grand jury that most of the expenditure originates.

4630. In your experience who are the most careful over the public funds, the cesspayers or the grand jury?—I cannot answer that question, for this reason, that the cesspayers take no interest at all in the expenditure; they leave it altogether to the magistrates.

4631. But there is an appeal to the judge; is that ever resorted to?—It is an appeal that is very seldom attempted.

4632. Why is it seldom attempted?—It is expensive in the first place. You have to fee counsel to go before the judge.

4633. Colonel *Cooper*.] Do the cesspayers in the county of Limerick object to the present law for malicious injuries?—No, I think it is very fair.

4634. Do you think that it gives satisfaction?—I do.

4635. You think the system a fair one of levying a cess for malicious injuries?—Most decidedly, and I think the grand jury in that case carry out the law very strictly and very fairly.

4636. Do you think also that the cases are strictly investigated at the road sessions?—Very fairly.

4637. And you think the law on that subject is good?—I do.

4638. And you do not wish to see any change in it?—I think it stops malicious injuries in the counties.

4639. Mr. *Dawson*.] Are there any flax mills in the county of Limerick?—None at all. There is one in Limerick, but it is not working.

4640. Mr. *Gregory*.] Do you think that these malicious injuries are generally committed by persons in the neighbourhood, or by total strangers?—By persons in the neighbourhood.

4641. Then, under those circumstances, would you not be prepared to levy the charge for malicious injuries upon the neighbourhood, rather than throw it over the county at large?—It is generally levied on the parish where it occurs; it is never on the barony at large.

4642. *Chairman*.] But is not the principle of the payment for these malicious injuries making the innocent pay for the guilty?—But it has this good effect on the other hand; that if a bad class of man wants to burn my house down at night, and he knows that I shall be re-imbursed by the county, he says: "What is the use of doing this? I am only serving him instead of injuring him, because he will get compensation for it."

4643. Mr. *Gregory*.] If an ill-conditioned man wishes to do you an injury, and it becomes known to the neighbours, they will all do their best to prevent it, will they not, because they will object to have to pay for it?—No doubt.

4644. *Chairman*.] Do you think it has any effect in repressing crime of that nature, or in leading to its discovery, or the reverse?—It is very hard to get information in Ireland as to such crimes.

4645. Do you think that is owing, in some degree, to the fact, that the man who suffers the injury looks rather to procuring compensation from the grand jury than to discovering the crime?—I think so.

4646. Do you not think that the fact of his having the capability of going before the sessions and the grand jury for compensation, makes him rather indifferent about discovering who committed the injury upon him?—I do not know that I am correct in saying so, but I believe that, if the offender was found out, a prosecutor's compensation does not lie at all.

4647. Is that a general belief?—Yes.

4648. And does not that belief, at least, make the person who suffers the injury very indifferent as to finding out who did it?—I would not say that it did. If I were paid compensation for such an injury it would not lessen my ardour to find out the criminal.

4649. But if there were a general belief (as you said just now there was) that the discovery of the offender would be a bar to your receiving compensation, would not that operate in at least deadening the desire for the discovery of the offender?—If my own house were burnt at night, I would much sooner be paid for it than have the satisfaction of giving penal servitude to the fellow that did it.

4650. And if you knew, or thought that on discovering the offender you would not receive the compensation, would you take as much trouble to find him out?—I think I should.

4651. But would other people do so?—I cannot answer for them; but I would like to find out the offender if I possibly could.

4652. Mr. *Gregory*.] Do you not think that the present system has this effect, that if an ill-disposed fellow wishes to do an injury to another person, he being one of his neighbours, he does not do it from remembering, in the first place, that this man will be compensated for the loss; and, in the second place, that the part of the payment for that compensation will fall upon himself?—Decidedly.

4653. *Chairman*.] Do you think that, as a rule, the compensation for malicious injuries falls upon the perpetrators, and that the perpetrators, in fact, are occupiers of land, generally speaking?—I do not think that at all.

4654. Therefore, as a rule, it is innocent people who pay this compensation, is it not?—Just so.

4655. So far, then, as a man has the fear of having to pay any amount of the compensation himself, that very seldom comes into operation?—Very seldom. It is generally the very lowest class of society that perpetrates those offences.

4656. Mr. *Gregory*.] Have not many instances come under your knowledge of a malicious injury being done to a person by a neighbour, owing to some squabble about the land, or something of that kind?—I never knew an instance where a person really an occupier and himself subject to taxation, or any of that class of men, was charged

with

Mr. W. Bolster. 21 May 1868.

with a malicious injury to another. He may get it done, no doubt, by another, but I have never heard of his doing it himself.

4657. *Chairman.*] Are you aware that up to a comparatively recent period there existed power in Ireland to levy compensation for robberies suffered by individuals?—It does not extend to robberies, I believe.

4658. But are you aware that, up to a comparatively recent period, it did?—No; I think it would not be a wise thing.

4659. Sir *Charles Lanyon.*] Do you not think it is generally known in a parish who are the parties perpetrating a malicious injury?—There may be a strong suspicion, but I do not know that it is known.

4660. Colonel *French.*] Particularly when a stranger has come into some land, the feeling being rather against a new man coming in, instead of the farmer who had been ejected, or does not some idea of that kind operate in the minds of the offenders?—No doubt suspicion generally attaches to those parties. The whole of the offices of a neighbour of mine was burnt down the other day, and at the last sessions a presentment was passed for compensation to him. The reason assigned for that was, that he had parted with a labourer, and of course the suspicion all rested upon that labourer, but there was no evidence to bring him to trial.

4661. *Chairman.*] But you believe sufficient grounds exist in Ireland for making (as you say happens in ordinary cases) the innocent party pay for the crime of the guilty?—I think it is a good arrangement that compensation should be made.

4662. Do you think it prevents crime?—I do.

4663. Mr. *Chichester Fortescue.*] I suppose you would say that that effect would be entirely destroyed if the compensation were to be levied upon the county at large, instead of on the district in which the outrage took place?—I think the parish is better. It brings it into a narrower area.

4664. *Chairman.*] But, as I take it, your chief reason for believing that this system of presentments is good is, that the previous knowledge that a man will be compensated prevents the party from committing the offence?—Yes, that, together with the sentiment of the people, who know well that the tax will fall upon themselves, may have the effect of preventing a thing of the kind being done.

4665. Mr. *Dawson.*] Do you think it desirable that the grand jury should have the power of assessing this damage over any district such as a barony, a parish, or even a town land?—I believe they have the power, but it is mostly confined to the parish.

4666. As you are in favour of the principle, do you not think that it is desirable to retain that power?—If it was a tremendous amount, I think it would be a hardship to put it upon the parish; but if it was a small amount, I think it ought to be put on the parish. If it were a very large amount, I think it should be extended over the barony at least.

4667. Mr. *Gregory.*] Do you not think that it would be advisable that the law should be made perfectly clear that the person who has suffered injury should be exempted from the taxation that was levied for the purpose of compensating him?—I think it would be a very good thing, and a very fair thing; but at the same time the tax comes so light upon everybody that it would be hardly worth while to make the distinction.

4668. Except that it would be carrying out the principle?—Yes.

4669. General *Dunne.*] Do you find that your neighbours, the farmers generally, are very strict in inquiring into the circumstances of the case to prevent anything of the kind?—They take a very great interest in those subjects; I know that in almost all those cases before the grand jury the cesspayers assemble and subscribe to fee attorneys to defend the barony before the grand jury.

4670. Is there not sometimes a disposition among people to make out to be a malicious injury, what is really a pure accident?—I have known, from my own experience, several burnings brought before the baronial sessions which were purely accidental, and the attempt always failed to carry them.

4671. And so strong is the feeling of the people, that they actually fee lawyers to prevent injustice being done?—Yes; I have seen it done frequently before grand juries.

4672. Mr. *Herbert.*] Is it your opinion that the way in which dispensary tickets are given by the poor law guardians is a good system?—I think it is a capital system.

4673. Have you ever known tickets given to people who ought not to receive them?—Not to my knowledge; if it is done, the donor has the power of bringing before the guardians the person who does it, and having the tickets cancelled; I issue a great many tickets myself as a guardian; but there are a number of other people who also have the power of distributing the tickets.

Mr. John Lentaigne, called in; and Examined.

Mr. J. Lentaigne.

4674. *Chairman.*] You are one of the Inspectors General of Prisons in Ireland, are you not?—I am.

4675. As such, I presume, you have become acquainted with the general working of the prisons throughout the whole country?—Yes; it is my duty to inspect every second year half the gaols and bridewells of Ireland, and to make a report upon them.

4676. There are two Inspectors General, are there not?—There are two Inspectors General, with equal powers, and under the Act of Parliament we have two districts, and we make alternate inspections of each district, north and south; so that each of the inspectors visits each prison once every two years, or oftener, of course, if necessary.

4677. The expenses of the prisons in Ireland are borne by the county rates, are they not?—They are borne by the county rates, except that a sum of 3*s.* a week is allowed by the Treasury for each prisoner convicted under certain sentences.

4678. Is that an allowance in aid of the county rates?—That is an allowance in aid of the county rates.

4679. Are you acquainted with an officer called the Local Inspector of Prisons?—I am.

Mr. *J. Lentaigne.*

22 May 1863.

4680. Is there a local inspector for every prison in Ireland?—Yes; there must be under the present Act.

4681. This local inspector is appointed by the Board of Superintendence, is he not?—Yes, he is both appointed and dismissed by the Board of Superintendence.

4682. Will you state to the Committee what are the duties of that officer?—The statutable duties under the Act of Parliament are the general supervision of prisons; the regulation of the procuring and providing of food and other necessaries for prisoners. He is to see that the prison regulations, bye-laws, and rules are observed and carefully carried out. He is to visit every prison under his inspection twice, at least, in every week, and at each visit to go into every room in the prison; and if any complaints are made by a prisoner against the gaoler or his assistants, immediately to inquire into such complaint; and if the same shall appear well founded, he is to report accordingly to the Board of Superintendence, and afterwards to the inspector general. He is to report specially, on oath, the state of the prison to the judge at each assizes, or, in the county or city of Dublin, to the Queen's Bench; and in his report he is to insert, at full length, a copy of the 24 rules which are mentioned in the 109th section of the Prisons Act, with a separate column opposite each rule; he is to certify how far each rule has been observed and complied with; and he is to state, as to any other regulations directed in other parts of the Act, whether they are complied with, especially with regard to food, clothing, bedding, &c. He is further to report to the inspectors general the decision of the Board of Superintendence on the complaints of prisoners; and when an officer shall resign, or a prisoner shall die, he is to furnish a report as to the resignation of the officer, or the cause of death of the prisoner. He is, once in each quarter, or oftener if necessary, to report whether any epidemic disease has appeared in the prison under his inspection; whether there has been riot, or mutiny, or escape, or attempt at escape; or whether a prisoner has changed his religious profession. He is to add any observations respecting the health, discipline, and order of the prison, and keeping the books. He is *ex officio* to be inspector of the bridewells belonging to his district; and they are specially under his supervision. He is to make some returns under the Act with regard to the sentences of prisoners, and to certify the fitness of probationary officers. Those are all the statutable rules; but in some prisons there are more rules added to those. In some prisons he keeps the accounts; but in one prison it is the secretary to the board of superintendence, who is also secretary to the grand jury who keeps the accounts.

4683. With respect to those duties, are not the majority of them duties which ought rather to devolve upon the governor than upon any one else?—The majority of them might and ought to devolve on the governor; but there are some which must be done by an inspector, as a check over the governor, such as visiting every cell and every room in the prison twice in a week, and inquiring as to whether there is a complaint of a prisoner. That should be done by some person quite independent of the governor.

4684. Do you think it necessary that that should be done so often as twice in a week?—It is better to have it done twice in a week, or it should be done once at least in a week.

4685. Do you believe that that is a provision which is in practice carried out?—The inspector states on oath that it is carried out, unless where he states otherwise in the column for observations; but I visit a prison so seldom, that generally I cannot tell whether or not it is carried out. There is one case where I know an inspector has been ill for the last three years, and he could not have done it, and he has not done it.

4686. How did he comply with the provision as to declaring upon oath in reference to the condition of the prison?—I spoke to him about it, and he told me that he writes his reply in the column opposite the query, "This rule has only been partially observed." The rule is, that he shall visit every prison, and shall go into every room and inquire; but he does not go through the rooms, because he is invalided, and he is not able to walk up stairs.

4687. He merely goes to the prison and goes home again, and then he considers he has done his duty?—No; he looks at the books and makes inquiries, and remains a long time in the prison; and I suppose any prisoner who complains is brought before him. I referred to this matter in my last report, and he said then that he would be well very soon; but the prison is not under my inspection this year, and I do not know whether he is now well or not.

4688. But you say that for three years he has been in this state?—In the year 1860 he was invalided. He had met with an accident to his knee, and he could not walk upstairs. I found that his son had died, and that he had met with misfortune, and I did not report on it that year; but last year I found that he had not recovered. However, he tells me that he is getting quite well; and I suppose that by this time he is able to do his duty; but I merely wish to show that the duty has not always been done.

4689. Do you consider that it is necessary in every county to have a local inspector for every gaol?—My colleague and I are both of opinion that if there were district inspectors appointed by the Government, it would be a great deal better. They would not then be appointed by the same Board which appoints the subordinates, and they would not be placed in constant contact with the officers.

4690. You do not think it satisfactory that this officer, who has to exercise a sort of supervision over the other officers, should be a nominee of the same body who appoints those other officers?—I think that it would be better that he should be an independent man, like the inspectors of the constabulary, and of other bodies, and it would be a saving of about 2,000 *l.* a year.

4691. How many district inspectors would be necessary for all Ireland?—There are 39 local inspectors at present, but I think four district inspectors would be quite sufficient to discharge those duties.

4692. And they would probably be of a better class, and more independent, would they not?—I think that amongst the local inspectors are some of the most honourable men in Ireland, who are most strict in carrying out all their duties. The case which I have mentioned is that of a gentleman who has met with an accident, and it is an exceptional case.

4693. But the present state of the law with respect to those local inspectors, you do not consider

sider to be satisfactory; do you consider them at present to be useful and beneficial officers as at present appointed?—There should be some officer to inspect the bridewells, and also to look after the prisoners; but I think that it would be much better to have district inspectors appointed by the Government, and paid for out of the consolidated funds. The cost would be about 8,000 *l.*, I suppose, instead of 4,000 *l.* Mr. *J. Lentaigne.* 11 May 1868.

4694. Do you think that these four district inspectors would be sufficient to visit all those prisons and bridewells often enough?—There are 39 gaols and 113 bridewells.

4695. Could they be visited once a week by those four inspectors?—There are railways to all the gaols, and I should see no difficulty in that.

4696. Do you not think that the number of prisons in Ireland is greatly in excess of the requirements of the country?—It is greatly in excess. In Maryborough gaol, which is in a large district, there were the other day two women, one on remand, and the other imprisoned for some trifling offence, and there were, including debtors and a drunkard, 16 male prisoners in charge.

4697. How many prisoners is Maryborough gaol capable of holding?—One hundred and eight male and 20 female criminal prisoners, besides 24 debtors, being accommodation for 152 prisoners of all classes.

4698. Could you give the Committee an idea of what the cost per head per annum of the prisoners in some of the gaols in Ireland is, in consequence of the small number of prisoners, taking the King's County, for instance?—In King's County each prisoner costs 85 *l.* 6 *s.* for the year 1866. We have not the return for the year 1867. That is the average, including staff charges.

4699. Is the number of prisoners there so small that the general expenditure of the prison being calculated upon the number of prisoners makes that the cost of each individual prisoner?—Yes; whilst in Antrim, where there are a large number of prisoners, and where there are industrial works, it is only 13 *l.* 3 *s.* 2 *d.* The table of expenditure which I hold in my hand does not include the whole cost of the prisoners, because there was in 1866, 16,000 *l.* laid out in improving the gaols, and then there were the bridewells; altogether there was about 100,000 *l.* laid out upon the gaols in 1866.

4700. What is the per centage of the establishment charges in the prisons in Ireland?—The total cost of officers is 44,008 *l.* 11 *s.* 10 *d.*; the daily average number of prisoners is 3,638; the average rate per head, 16 *l.* 11 *s.* 1 *d.*

4701. Do you consider on the whole that a great advantage would arise from an amalgamation of the prisons in Ireland, and that in fact there is not a prison required for each county?—Very great advantage would be derived from it, and a very considerable saving effected, perhaps, as much as 40,000 *l.* a year, but this is only a rough estimate, and I do not pledge myself to it.

4702. Would 40,000 *l.* a-year be saved by amalgamating the prisons in the country?—The saving would be considerable; my colleagues and I, in our report for the year 1865, referred to this at pages from 58 to 61. We there state that there are 38 county gaols and borough gaols in Ireland provided with a staff, comprising local inspectors, chaplains, medical officers, governors, and inferior officers. The amount of salaries alone in 1865 was no less than 43,564 *l.* 6 *s.* 4½ *d.* If, however, the chaplains and medical officers were fully salaried, as in England, and if the keepers of the bridewells received fair remuneration, the burden on the rates would be very largely increased. The chaplains get, generally, 30 *l.* a year, and the highest they can get is 50 *l.* a year, except in Dublin. The salaries of some of the bridewell keepers are only 10 *l.* or 15 *l.* a year. The medical officers are, in some gaols, very badly paid, and if they were paid adequately to their duties it would increase the expenses very materially.

4703. All this staff has to be kept up, no matter what number of prisoners are in the gaol?—Yes.

4704. For instance, in that case which you have mentioned where there were only seven prisoners, this staff of local inspector, governor, turnkeys, chaplains, and all the rest of the officers has to be kept up for those seven prisoners?—Yes.

4705. When you say that an amalgamation of the prisons would be an advantage, would you propose that several counties should club together for one prison to which all the offenders should be sent; or, on the other hand, would you propose that offenders sentenced to a certain term should be transferred to the Government prisons, and that there should be left in the counties only those who had committed light and trivial offences?—What my colleagues and I desire is, that all the grave offenders should be transferred to one central prison, as in Scotland, and that there they should all be treated in the same way, and that there should be the same punishment for a particular offence, instead of having 39 separate forms of punishment in the 39 gaols; a short term of confinement in one gaol is much more severely pressed than a long term in others. The late Mr. Justice Hayes told me that he never sentenced a prisoner without studying the quantity of punishment in the particular gaol before he sentenced him. He took a great deal of trouble about it, because he found punishment in the gaols was so unequal.

4706. Is there great dissimilarity in the punishment which is given in the different gaols?—As great as possible.

4707. If this central prison were established, should you still think it necessary that there should be a central prison for the minor offenders in each county?—Not in each county, but in each district. The counties should associate together and form district prisons.

4708. You would propose, in the first place, that the grave offenders should be transferred to a central prison, and, in the next place, that for the minor offences, district prisons would be sufficient?—Yes; that is Lord Mayo's idea, and it is our idea also. Lord Mayo has studied it a good deal, and he has proposed to bring in a Bill to that effect.

4709. Would that be a very great saving to the counties?—A very great saving.

4710. And in that case the multiplication of prison officers would in many cases not be required?—No; it would be a great saving of prison officers.

4711. Could those four district inspectors easily look after the district prisons which you propose should be established?—I think so.

4712. Mr. *Herbert.*] With reference to that saving

Mr. *J. Lentaigne.* 22 May 1863.

saving of 40,000 *l.*, have you taken into consideration the amount which it would cost to remove these prisoners to and from the district prisons? —Generally the prisons are in towns on railways, and the expense would not be considerable.

4713. You said that you would save 40,000 *l.* per annum; but in that calculation was the amount of travelling expenses incurred by these prisoners and their escort taken into consideration?—I am of opinion that the saving would be so great as to render the expense of transmitting prisoners, for which purpose railways would be generally available, comparatively of inconsiderable amount.

4714. *Chairman.*] Are you not aware that at present grand juries have the power of agreeing together for having one prison for different counties?—Yes, they have under the 50th and 51st sections of the Prisons Act, passed in 1826, they have the power, but it has never been acted upon.

4715. Are there not some very strong cases where such an amalgamation seems almost inevitable, such as the cases of the city and county of Limerick, and the town and county of Galway? —In the city of Limerick they have spent a large sum of money in rebuilding their gaol, although they have a very good gaol in the county, within half a mile of it, which is quite capable of containing more than all the prisoners committed from both the county and the city.

4716. And in spite of that, they have gone to a very great expense in repairing and altering their own gaol?—They have about 5,000 *l.*

4717. *Mr. Maguire.*] On what plea has that been done?—The two Boards could not agree; I did my best in the matter; I went down several times, but they could not agree. Colonel Monsell asked me to go down, and we had two or three meetings of the Board, but we could not agree on the terms.

4718. General *Dunne.*] Was not a Bill brought in some years ago with the same object of amalgamation, which was very much debated among grand juries at the time?—There is the 19th and 20th of Victoria, under which they have the power as regards the counties and towns, or cities and the adjoining county; but the power is permissory, and in the case of Limerick, the power not being compulsory, although we were very anxious that it should be done, they would not do it.

4719. Has not the permissive power been discussed by a great many grand juries?—It does exist, and it has been discussed.

4720. Has it ever, in any case that you are aware of, been used?—Twice in Waterford and Kilkenny, and at Galway they are now going to do it.

4721. Are you aware that in King's and Queen's Counties there was a discussion of the same kind?—Not since I have been in office.

4722. But still it has been discussed, has it not?—It has been discussed, over and over again.

4723. And only in two instances have the permissive powers been adopted?—In two instances only, and Galway will adopt it.

4724. Does the Prison Bill contemplated by the present Irish Government make it compulsory? —I am not aware.

4725. However, it is not before the House, as yet?—It is not.

4726. Mr. *Dawson.*] Is there a uniform salary attached to this office of inspector?—There is not; I can state the salaries of the different inspectors. In Antrim, it is 150 *l.*; in Armagh, 90 *l.*; in Carlow, 60 *l.*; in Cavan, 100 *l.*; in Clare, 100 *l.*; in Cork County, 200 *l.*; in Cork City, 100 *l.*; in Donegal, 130 *l.*; in Down, 111 *l.*; in Dublin County, 130 *l.*; in Dublin City, 300 *l.* but there is some change now); in Fermanagh, 90 *l.*; in Galway County, 153 *l.*; in Galway Town, 40 *l.*; in Kerry, 160 *l.*; in Kildare, 100 *l.*; in Kilkenny, 80 *l.*; in King's County, 70 *l.*; in Leitrim, 100 *l.*; in Limerick County, 120 *l.*; in Limerick City, 75 *l.*; in Derry, 110 *l.*; in Longford, 80 *l.*; in Louth, 75 *l.*; in Drogheda, 10 *l.*; in Mayo, 100 *l.*; in Meath, 35 *l.*; in Monaghan, 97 *l.*; in Queen's County, 60 *l.*; in Roscommon, 93 *l.*; in Sligo, 100 *l.*; in Tipperary, North Riding, 90 *l.*; South Riding, 120 *l.*; in Tyrone, 150 *l.*; in Waterford, 170 *l.*; in Westmeath, 80 *l.*; in Wexford, 100 *l.*; and in Wicklow, 90 *l.*

4727. Mr. *Blake.*] Is it not the case, that the local inspector at Waterford has another office which gives him a further emolument, as being Secretary to the Board of Superintendence?—That includes it all. He gets 140 *l.*, as local inspector, and 30 *l.* as Secretary of the Board of Superintendence.

4728. Mr. *Dawson.*] Is it necessary for these officers to make a daily inspection of the gaol?—They must do it twice a week by the Act of Parliament.

4729. What power is there as to their removal? —The Board of Superintendence have absolute power of removal.

4730. And only the Board of Superintendence?—The Lord Lieutenant can remove them under a very complicated section of an Act of Parliament with a previous inquiry, but it fails sometimes. In Limerick City we were anxious to act upon it, but we could not do so.

4731. Is there any superannuation attached to the office?—Yes.

4732. Have the Board of Superintendence the power of awarding superannuation?—The mode of procedure in awarding superannuation is defined by the 125th section of the Act 6 & 7 Will. 4, cap. 116.

4733. Mr. *Maguire.*] Is that power permissive or compulsory?—The presentment can always be thrown out by the ratepayers; it is not compulsory.

4734. Colonel *French.*] You said that the Secretary to the grand jury was sometimes obliged to keep the gaol accounts; is that the case?—Yes. In Louth, the secretary of the grand jury does so, but he is also secretary to the Board of Superintendence.

4735. Is he local inspector as well?—He is not local inspector. It is not one of the assistable duties.

4736. Of course he gets a salary for it?—He does; as Secretary to the Board of Superintendence he receives 25 *l.* per annum.

4737. Is it not usual sometimes for the deputy governor to keep the accounts, with a head turnkey as a clerk under him?—It is.

4738. Would you recommend that this local inspector, or the deputy governor with a head turnkey as a clerk should be the person to keep the accounts?—The books ought of course to be kept

by

Mr. *J. Lentaigne.*

7 May 1868.

by the deputy governor, when there is a deputy governor.

4739. Then, is there no deputy governor in Louth, where the secretary acts?—There is not; only a Chief Warder. In many gaols the Deputy Governor keeps the accounts.

4740. Could you state the expense of the 33 local inspectors in gross?—Yes, for 1866, it was 4,017 *l.* 10 *s.* 9 *d.*

4741. You propose that four district inspectors should do that work, do you not?—Yes.

4742. What salaries would you give those gentlemen?—500 *l.* a year each.

4743. And that would be 2,000 *l.*; what about your travelling expenses?—I suppose that would include travelling expenses.

4744. You, as inspector general, 1,000 *l.* a year, and your travelling expenses, do you not?—I get 935 *l.* 10 *s.*, without any allowance for travelling expenses. The district inspectors might also get their travelling expenses, but that certainly would not be more than 100 *l.* a year each. I think that the district inspectors should be Government officers. I do not think that they ought to be paid out of the rates.

4745. General *Dunne.*] Are not the inspectors at present paid a much lower rate in Ireland than in England?—Yes, I think so; we get 935 *l.* 10 *s.*, including all our expenses, and we get nothing else.

4746. But are not the English inspectors paid much more?—Yes; the inspectors of lunatic asylums are paid much more, they get their travelling expenses and a guinea a night, personal expenses when absent on duty, and salaries rising from 800 *l.* to 1,200 *l.* a year, by increments of 50 *l.*

4747. Sir *Charles Lanyon.*] I think I understood you to say that although the local inspectors might be superseded by district inspectors, yet that local inspection of some kind is desirable?—Inspection is absolutely necessary for bridewells, and also as a check.

4748. Then it is merely as to the system which you would propose an alteration, and not as to the office itself?—Not as to the office itself, for there must be inspection.

4749. Have you any schedule which you could hand in as part of your evidence to the Committee which would show the expenses of the different prisons throughout Ireland, so that we might have the opportunity of seeing the higher per centage in those districts where there are few persons confined, as compared with other prisons, so as to give us some idea whether or not it would be advisable that an amalgamation should take place?—I could do so.

4750. General *Dunne.*] Is it not the case that prisons are empty at one time, and at other times a flow of crime springs up which you are not prepared for, so that you could not always judge from the present state of a prison what the requisites of the districts are?—Not always; but there are districts where there is no crime such as Carlow.

4751. And where there is not likely to be crime?—There is not likely to be crime.

4752. Sir *Charles Lanyon.*] Have you any returns showing for the last 10 years the maximum and the minimum of the different prisons?—We have. We publish a report every year, and all those returns are contained in that report; I wish to say that some of the most honourable, efficient, and excellent men in Ireland are local inspectors, and, therefore, I would not in the least have it imagined that those do not do their duties quite as conscientiously as the inspectors general.

4753. Mr. *Blake.*] Is it not the fact that the local rules of the different boards vary considerably?—They do, and that is a fault. The present systems of rules are different in every gaol. There ought to be but one system of rules.

4754. The direct control which you and your colleagues possess over those prisons is very little indeed, I think?—Very little.

4755. In the case of the illegal treatment of a prisoner, either as regards undue severity or undue leniency, that might go on for a very long time unchecked, even after you became aware of it?—It is our duty to report it to the Lord Lieutenant, and he then orders an inquiry on oath, and, under the 82nd section of the 19 & 20 Vict., he can, after the Board of Superintendence have inquired into it and reported, if he sees right, dismiss the officers.

4756. But you cannot of yourselves direct a change of treatment when any complaint arises?—No; but we can report any illegality which is ascertained.

4757. With regard to a question which the Honourable Chairman asked you as to having a central prison, do you mean that this central prison should be like the prison at Perth, in Scotland?—Yes.

4758. And that all prisoners sentenced for periods of more than six months should be sent there?—Yes.

4759. Then, would the other prisoners be kept in the county prisons?—Yes, or in district prisons; and then, in every centre of population, there ought to be something corresponding to a district bridewell, where prisoners on remand should be detained, and very short sentences be carried out, so as not to have the expense of moving prisoners.

4760. Is it not the fact, that a vast number of the gentlemen who are at present appointed to the office of county inspector, are country gentlemen, wholly unacquainted with prison discipline, or the proper mode of treating or looking after the prisoners?—It is not their duty; they are only over the governor and the officers to see that the prisoners are treated fairly, and that the Act is carried out.

4761. If you want to change that system, and to have the district inspectors, would you not be disposed to impose more duties in the way of inspection on the chaplains than they have to perform at present; they have to perform a certain amount of inspection at present, have they not?—They have to inspect the food; but I do not think that it ought to be a part of the duty of the chaplains. They are so badly paid that unless you increase their pay you could not impose additional duties upon them.

4762. Would you be disposed to have them do something more in the way of inspection, increasing their salary if you will?—If the long-sentenced prisoners were taken away, I do not think that it would be necessary.

4763. If the long-sentenced prisoners were removed, and those district prisons instituted, there would then be a very considerable saving of expense, would there not?—There would then be a very considerable saving of expense, and, at the same time, I believe that the Treasury—and, in fact,

Mr. *J. Lentaigne.*

29 May 1868.

fact, it has been shown that the Treasury would not lose by it, even if they paid the expense. There was a paper drawn up by the directors of convict prisons which would show that, by having the prisoners together in one central prison, the Treasury would not lose, because the 5 s. a head, for maintenance now paid out of the Consolidated Fund, added to the value of the work of the prisoners, would pay the expense. At the same time, there would be an enormous gain to the county rates. There would be fewer officers, and a different staff, and a different system for short sentences.

4764. And the classification could be carried out in a better manner, could it not?—Yes; there would be fewer classes of prisoners, and we should not have men for one, two, three, or, as I have known, four years in a county prison.

4765. Mr. *Maguire.*] What are you to do with the 39 prisons which exist now?—Part of them could be used as county bridewells, but there would be no expense of staff. There should always be prisoners for trial kept in them during the assizes, and they would do for prisoners on short sentences immediately in the district, but longer sentences should be removed.

4766. You would diminish the staff, and make the staff less expensive?—Much less expensive.

4767. Would you have a governor?—I would have a responsible officer, but I would have no schoolmaster, for instance.

4768. In other words, you would not demolish the prisons, but you would retain them with a diminished staff?—I would retain them with a diminished staff.

4769. And, of course, at less expense?—At less expense.

4770. Mr. *Dawson.*] I suppose that they are all attached to quarter sessions towns now?—They are not in quarter sessions towns, but in assize towns.

4771. Sir *Charles Lanyon.*] Then would you propose to have such a staff as the bridewells now have?—We find that the bridewells have not a sufficient staff, but I would have a sufficient staff.

4772. General *Dunne.*] At this moment could not the Government take any convict prisoner and put him where they liked?—They could not unless he was sentenced to penal servitude; even in the case of the Fenian convicts they cannot do so.

4773. Mr. *Dawson.*] You stated just now the salaries of these local inspectors. Are these salaries fixed by an Order in Council issued by the Lord Lieutenant, or how is it arranged as to the separate salaries?—The grand juries under the 56th section of the Prisons Act, give any reasonable sums as salaries they choose.

4774. There is it not arranged according to first and second-class counties?—No.

4775. How often do the Board of Superintendence meet?—They always meet monthly.

4776. What is the average attendance at them, generally speaking. Is there one third of the members present?—About one third. In some counties there is a very good attendance, and in others there is a very bad attendance. It just depends upon local circumstances.

4777. Are there in many parts of Ireland gentlemen appointed on Boards of Superintendence, who do not live in the neighbourhood, which makes their attendance very difficult?—There are a few; the Board is generally composed of gentlemen living in the neighbourhood, who are available, from the proximity of their residences, but not always.

4778. But there is no complaint of a deficiency of attendance, is there, in any particular part of Ireland?—There must be at least six member of the Board attending to confirm an appointment.

4779. Colonel *Cooper.*] Do you propose to reduce the number of assize towns in Ireland?—No, I have nothing to do with that.

4780. Then what would you do with prisoners committed for trial?—They would be removed to the county town to the present prison during the assizes.

4781. But if a man is committed two or three months before an assizes, where would you put him?—If he was a grave offender, and if it was a serious crime, and there was a danger of escape, he might be removed to Dublin; we propose that the Lord Lieutenant should have absolute power to remove him.

4782. But the ordinary class of offenders who are committed for trial would be sent to the county gaol, as at present?—Yes.

4783. And they would be kept there until they were tried?—Yes; we propose that the Lord Lieutenant should have discretion to remove.

4784. And anybody convicted, and sentenced to imprisonment for six months and under would be committed to the county gaol?—To a county or a district gaol, according to the sentence.

4785. I understand you to say that you would not move any person under six months?—Not to a central prison; Lord Mayo proposes a central prison as in Scotland, like the prison at Perth.

4786. And then a district prison also?—Then a few districts would be grouped together, for shorter sentences.

4787. But would you not still require a county prison?—Yes, there must be in every centre of population a place to commit offenders to, so as to save the expense of conveyance.

4788. With a certain staff?—Yes.

4789. You would require very much the same staff as at present, would you not?—No.

4790. What reduction could you make?—A very great reduction.

4791. A man waiting for trial would require his chaplain; would you keep the chaplains as at present?—The chaplains generally get 80*l*. a year.

4792. You could not reduce that sum?—No, you could not.

4793. What does a governor get, on the average?—He gets from 100*l*. to 300*l*.

4794. Could you reduce that much?—Yes, you could, but not below 100*l*., I suppose.

4795. There would be a medical officer to the gaol, would there not?—Yes.

4796. And he is badly paid at present, is he not?—He is often badly paid at present. In some counties he receives no remuneration for his professional services in the gaol, being also medical officer of the county infirmary.

4797. Could you reduce his salary?—In some cases I could, but in others I could not. He need not attend where there are short sentences so frequently as he would in long ones.

4798. But you could not reduce his salary much?—I do not like to give a definitive opinion upon these subjects which I have not prepared.

4799. What

4799. What do you think is the amount of saving which we could effect in the prison management?—It would require a very elaborate calculation, founded on a comparison of many years, to furnish a complete answer to the question. But I beg to refer to a Table (*marked No. 2, in Appendix*), which would enable the Committee to form a proportionate estimate.

4800. Was the nature of the difficulty in *Limerick* as to the proportion which each party should pay to the expenses of the staff, or to the maintenance of prisoners?—I do not know; the boards did not seem to pull together. We had great difficulty in Galway, but that has been got over, and they have now agreed.

4801. What was the difficulty?—That was entirely as to the proportion of the expenses, and the number of members who were to be on the board; but that has been all settled satisfactorily.

4802. Would those difficulties exist if the district system was adopted?—I think not.

4803. Mr. *Maguire*.] With regard to an answer which you gave just now, I understood that it was that a prisoner charged with murder, for instance, and not tried, might be removed to Dublin previous to his trial?—Yes.

4804. Do you think that that would be a fair thing to do?—The Lord Lieutenant has power now to do it.

4805. Does he exercise that power?—He exercises it in the case of political prisoners.

4806. But we are talking of an ordinary murder. Supposing that a man was charged with murder in the county of Cork, would you think it advisable that that man should be sent to Dublin instead of being kept in the county of Cork, where his advisers or friends come to him?—I would not deprive him of his advisers.

4807. But would you not deprive him of his advisers if you sent him 200 miles off?—I would not do it in that case.

4808. Would not that apply to many parts of Ireland?—No doubt.

4809. Do you not think that it would be practically an unfair thing to remove a man away?—A man to be tried should have every opportunity to prepare his defence.

4810. But he would not have every opportunity if he was sent to Dublin?—The Lord Lieutenant has the power now.

4811. But the Lord Lieutenant does not exercise it; as a matter of fact, did you ever hear of a case where a murder, even of the most heinous character, was committed, in which the Lord Lieutenant sent a man up to Dublin, away from his friends?—I am not aware of it.

4812. Why should he do it now?—I do not say that he would do it. That power is only exercised when there is danger of the escape of political prisoners; those are all the cases to which I refer, and that has been done.

4813. *Chairman*.] You speak merely of that power existing?—The power at present exists, and I would not deprive the Lord Lieutenant of it.

4814. Mr. *Maguire*.] Did you not say that you would have a special institution, amongst other advantages, for the reception of persons who have not yet been tried, but who have been charged with heavy offences?—I am afraid the Honourable Member has misunderstood me; I did not mean that; what I mean is a central prison, where prisoners sentenced should be removed, that they might all have the same quality of punishment.

4815. That I distinctly understand, but in answer to the Honourable Member near me, did you not state that an untried prisoner, with a heavy charge hanging over him, might be sent away from his own county?—I do not mean that; I do not mean that the prisoners should not have every opportunity.

4816. *Chairman*.] You only meant that as at present the Lord Lieutenant has power to remove those untried prisoners in certain cases where he thinks it desirable to do so; if he thought it desirable to exercise that power, he might remove them to the central prison which you would establish?—Yes, in a case of danger and risk, as to political prisoners.

4817. Colonel *Cooper*.] As I understand you you propose to reduce the county gaol staff very considerably?—Yes.

4818. Appointing an inferior class of officers?—Perhaps so, in some instances; but always of a trustworthy character.

4819. Do you think it desirable to commit prisoners perhaps for three or four months to a bridewell awaiting their trial?—No; it would never answer.

4820. Where would you commit them?—I think that any officer in a county gaol who could have charge of prisoners after trial, would be quite sufficiently trustworthy to take care of prisoners waiting for trial.

4821. General *Dunne*.] Have not prisoners in cases of epidemics and fevers frequently been removed by the order of the Lord Lieutenant?—There are special powers in the Act of Parliament to remove prisoners in case of dilapidation, in case of alterations of the prison, and in case of epidemics. They are frequently removed, and there is no practical inconvenience, because every person gets sufficient opportunity to prepare his defence, and I am sure I would not deprive him of such opportunity.

4822. *Chairman*.] You have been also, I believe, a grand juror in several counties for several years?—I have.

4823. You have served as grand juror for the county of Dublin, have you not?—I served in the county of Dublin formerly, but not latterly. Since I have taken office, my time is so much occupied, that I have not been on the county of Dublin grand jury for a good many years; but I still attend in my own county of Monaghan.

4824. Would you be prepared to give the Committee any information upon the grand jury laws in general, or would it be unfair to ask you questions regarding them?—I will answer any question which is put to me.

4825. With respect to the county of Dublin, that county is peculiar, is it not, differing in many respects from the other counties in Ireland?—Yes; it is the only county in which there is a finance committee, and only one presenting term for both the city and county. The finance committee does the business during the whole year.

4826. Do you think that the system of finance committees works well on the whole, and that it is an improvement on the working of the grand jury system in the county of Monaghan, with which you are acquainted?—I think that it would be very desirable to examine either the committee

Mr. *J. Lanigan*.

—

21 May 1868.

Mr. *J. Lentaigne.*

[illegible] May 18[illegible].

secretary of the grand jury or some of the finance committee on that point. I was only one year on the finance committee of the county of Dublin, and I know so little of the working of it, that I should not like to give an opinion on it.

4827. (*General Dunne.*) Is the allowance granted for convict prisoners in Ireland the same as it is in England?—No; in Ireland it is lower.

4828. Mr. *Maguire.*] What do you understand by the word "allowance?"—Three shillings a week, paid by the Treasury to the county for certain classes of prisoners convicted.

4829. (*General Dunne.*] Does that pay the actual expense?—It does not.

4830. Therefore the counties lose on convict prisoners?—At present they do, as I have already explained in a former answer.

Mr. Blake.	Mr. Herbert.
Colonel Cooper.	Sir Charles Lanyon.
Mr. Dawson.	Mr. Maguire.
General Dunne.	The O'Conor Don.
Colonel French.	Sir Colman O'Loghlen.
Mr. Gregory.	

THE O'CONOR DON, IN THE CHAIR.

Mr. MACARTHY DOWNING, called in; and Examined.

Mr. Macarthy Downing. [illegible] May 18[illegible].

4831. Mr. *Maguire*.] FROM what part of the county of Cork are you?—I reside at Skibbereen.

4832. In which riding is that?—In the West Riding of the county of Cork.

4833. Are you a landed proprietor?—I am.

4834. And an occupier?—And an occupier.

4835. In what baronies do you possess property?—I possess property in three baronies; in the baronies of the east division of West Carbery, of the west division of West Carbery, and of the west division of East Carbery.

4836. You hold land also as an occupier, do you not?—I do.

4837. What is your rating as an occupier?—£. 125 a-year.

4838. Then you may be classed amongst the high ratepayers of your barony?—Yes.

4839. What barony is that?—That is the east division of West Carbery.

4840. You also, I believe, are vice chairman of the board of guardians of the Skibbereen Union?—I am.

4841. How long have you been an elected guardian of the Skibbereen Union?—I have been 25 years an elected guardian.

4842. How many years have you been vice-chairman of your board?—Three years.

4843. You have a perfect knowledge, at any rate, of the operation of the poor law system in your district, have you not?—I think I have.

4844. You say that you are rated to the grand jury at a valuation of 155 *l.* a-year, and that you are amongst the highest rated occupiers of your barony; have you often been returned as a selected ratepayer?—No; I think I have only been returned four times within eight years.

4845. How do you account for that?—It is a very difficult thing to account for it. It is in the hands of the grand juror of the barony to select as many ratepayers as are to sit at the road sessions, and I do not wish to attribute any motive to any grand juror; but there is the fact that I think I was better entitled to be more frequently on the road sessions than men who have been returned nine or ten times during the same time.

4846. If I mistake not, public report attributes to you the possession of more property than several of the grand jurors of the county of Cork possess?—I believe that is the case.

4847. At any rate you are amongst the highest ratepayers of your barony, and you say that you have been selected only four times?—Only four times.

4848. As to the mode in which the barony is represented, would you tell the Committee whether all portions of that barony are fairly represented, or whether you think that there is a capricious nomination?—The barony in which I reside consists of 11 parishes. I may, perhaps, illustrate what may occur at each presentment sessions by showing what occurred at one. In the east division of the barony of West Carbery in the year 1865, there were 56 cesspayers returned; that is the lowest number which can be selected. There were 10 returned and five to be selected. Of those, two had been on the previous sessions and could not serve; another had been four years bedridden, which was very well known to every one connected with the administration of the fiscal business of the barony, and a fourth was neither a ratepayer nor a householder.

4849. Then how came he to be on the rate-book?—He was put on the rate-book, and the result was that there was not a single associated ratepayer at that presentment sessions sat with the magistrates.

4850. When was that?—That was at the spring presentment sessions of the year 1865. That is a very large barony, there are generally from 12 to 15 or 16 magistrates assembled there, and there was not a single associated cesspayer sat at that sessions. At the very last presentment sessions for that barony, there being 11 parishes, there were but seven associated ratepayers; of those seven *four* were from one parish, two from another, one from a third, and eight parishes were totally unrepresented.

4851. How many magistrates sat at that presentment sessions?—There were only seven, which was very unusual.

4852. What you complain of in that case is the non-representation of a very large portion of the barony?—Yes; and it is the case in almost every barony. I see there was a meeting the other day at Macroom with regard to the barony of West Muskerry, where they showed that out of the nine parishes there were six unrepresented, and that of the number of cesspayers returned for the coming sessions there were eight who had been on the last presentment sessions, and who were therefore disqualified.

Mr. *M'Carthy Downing.*

26 May 1868.

4853. Is that abuse, as far as you know, common?—Quite so.

4854. Have you perceived it very often?—Yes, frequently.

4855. Is it a matter of public remark and complaint?—A man gets up and says that his parish is not represented at all; that he has no one to say anything about the interests of such a road in his parish. To show how the grand jurors discharge their duty in the selection of ratepayers, I might mention to the Committee, that at a very late sessions in the county of Cork, out of 12 ratepayers the grand juror returned four clergymen, who are disqualified by law.

4856. In what barony was that?—The west division of West Carbery.

4857. Then does the mode of nomination of the associated cesspayers give dissatisfaction?—Great dissatisfaction. Why should it not give dissatisfaction? The grand jurors for my barony selects from 100 of the highest ratepayers, and no one else interferes; I dare say that the grand jurors for my barony are just as pure and just as much above suspicion as those of any other barony of the county. Of course we all carry with us some feelings which may prejudice our opinion, but I do not see why I should be excluded by the caprice, or the prejudice, or coloured views by the favour of a grand juror who selects out of 20 names the 10 that he wishes. If he was a corrupt man and wished to carry a job, he could select 10 men who would vote exactly as he pleased.

4858. Of what class are the associated ratepayers generally?—We have perhaps three or four intelligent men; three or four may have been elected guardians, who are in the habit of sitting with the *ex officio* guardians, and three or four of them may sometimes sit; but as regards the rest they are men not fit to take part in the discussions, because they are under the control of the large landed proprietors.

4859. Are they more or less, in fact, than the mere nominees of the grand juror?—They are so to a great extent.

4860. From your own experience, do those men who have acted as elected guardians generally make the best associated cesspayers, and perform the public business better?—They are the persons amongst the associated ratepayers who really take an independent part, and who will often lead the other cesspayers.

4861. In fact, the training in the board-room makes them acquainted, more or less, with the management of public business, does it not?—Clearly.

4862. What is your opinion as to the manner in which the associated cesspayers attend?—They attend very badly. They are sometimes a class of men who really will say yes or no, according as they may be asked before, and they do not take any very great interest in the matter; they are very ignorant, a great many of them. Another reason why they do not attend, I know myself, is, that, they often come a very long distance, and have been disappointed in the ballot; 10 names are drawn out of 20, and, of course, some must be disappointed, they go away, and they do not again come.

4863. Do they then take it for granted that they will not be drawn in the ballot at a future time?—Yes; they say, "I shall not be drawn, I will stop away."

4864. Whereas if they were elected and were responsible to any constituent body they really would attend?—They would attend then, or they would not be returned again, and you would have this great advantage, that you would have every parish in the barony represented; if you had the elected guardians to sit with the magistrates at the presentment sessions you must have every parish in the barony represented by a man who is responsible to the ratepayers.

4865. Then you are in favour of the elective system and of an equal representation of all the divisions of a barony or of a county?—Yes; I proposed, 20 years ago, at my board of guardians, and it was carried by a very large majority, that the elected guardians should sit with the magistrates.

4866. I am not going to ask the question whether party, or religion, enters into the question of the election of the associated cesspayers, but if there be any strong bias on the part of the gentleman who has the power of nominating under this law, has he not the power of gratifying his peculiar feelings and of selecting those whom he likes, and rejecting those to whom he has an objection?—Clearly; I do not know whether it enters into the mind of the grand juror or not, but I know that the result is very striking; in the east division of East Carbery at the last presentment sessions, there were 16 magistrates and nine cesspayers, and there was not a single Catholic amongst them.

4867. Are there highly rated Catholic cesspayers in the barony?—Very highly; in the west division of West Carbery there were 11 magistrates and six ratepayers, and only three Catholics out of the 17.

4868. Are there many qualified Catholics in that barony?—Clearly; I should say that probably of the largest cesspayers they are about equal; I am now giving you the very last presentment sessions.

4869. You have the official returns there?—Yes; for the east division of West Carbery, there were seven magistrates, and seven cesspayers, twelve being Protestants and two being Catholics; in the west division of West Carbery there were eleven Protestants and three Catholics.

4870. In all those cases could they have obtained a sufficient number of Catholics who were qualified by rating to be amongst those to be selected?—Certainly.

4871. You do not attribute any motive, but you state the fact?—I do not attribute any motive, but I think that every man carries with him certain feelings, and really he does not know sometimes that he possesses them, or that he is influenced by them in the discharge of certain duties. He might have thought the men he selected were really the better men, and more intelligent.

4872. But, at any rate, you would like a change to be made in a law which gives power to a man, if he wishes to gratify caprice or prejudice, to do so?—Certainly.

4873. Mr. *Herbert*.] Was the grand juror who chose the cesspayers in these cases a Protestant, or Roman Catholic?—Protestant in every case.

4874. Mr. *Maguire*.] You are not attributing any motive, but you are only stating a *fact*?—Exactly. I entertain a very high opinion of the integrity and impartiality of the gentlemen of my barony; but, as I said before, I might myself be influenced

influenced in the same way, and I rather think, perhaps, I would be.

4875. Have you any remarks to make with reference to the present mode of conducting business at the ordinary road or presentment sessions?—I do not think that there is much to complain of, except that there is generally a very great hurry and not sufficient inquiry.

4876. At any rate, you do complain of the want of interest which is generally manifested by the associated cesspayers in the discharge of the duties which they are called upon to perform?—Clearly. They are not considered anything at the presentment sessions.

4877. As far as you know, do they feel that, under the present state of things, they lack responsibility?—Of course they do, and that is the reason that they do not attend.

4878. As to presentment sessions for the county at large, do you wish to make any remark?—I think that that presents even a more extraordinary state of things. There are 23 baronies in the county of Cork, and it is to be supposed that each barony would be represented at the session for the county at large. I have taken the average for eight years, and there have been only five of the 23 baronies represented at the county at large sessions; and at the very last presentment sessions there was but one barony represented by a cesspayer, and that was the smallest barony in the county, the barony of Kinsale, which is valued at 6,000 *l.* a year. Now, if the Committee will allow me to illustrate how this may operate, I will take the liberty of doing so. There is for the next county at large presentment sessions an application for 15,000 *l.*

4879. What is the nature of the work?—The nature of the work is the repair of a bridge from Youghal to the Waterford side of the Blackwater. £. 7,300 of that is to be presented on the county at large. If the representation upon the county at large presentment sessions is only what it has been for the last eight years, there may be but one, or only five cesspayers to defend the interests of the county. If the grand juror would put the leg of a compass, if I may say so, upon Youghal, and make a circle, and put the other upon the extreme western part of the county of Cork, he would find that, by making that circle, he would take in the whole of the towns of Galway and Ballina; so that the West Riding of the county of Cork has to pay a portion of 7,300 *l.* for a bridge from Youghal to Waterford, with which they have as much connection as a person living at Ballina, or at Galway, the distance being quite as great.

4880. How do you account for the non-attendance at those county presentment sessions?—As I said before, there is no responsibility whatever. I may be selected, as a cesspayer, to attend, but I am not accountable to any one for my conduct, and I do not go.

4881. Then, representation is as necessary there as the road session?—Clearly; quite so.

4882. Responsible representation?—Certainly.

4883. Do you wish to give any farther illustration of your view?—I would carry that representation still further. I do not want to interfere with the present system of the grand jury, but at the same time I have reason to complain that the grand jurors for the county of Cork are selected from a very small number, and from the same families over and over again, which, I think, is a great wrong, and creates very much dissatisfaction.

4884. Would you substitute an election by the ratepayers, instead of nomination by the sheriff to the grand jury?—Before I answer that, I say that I would not interfere with the present system of the grand jury, but I would carry representation into the grand jury room; I would have the elected guardians of each barony, who, according to my plan, would be the associated ratepayers at the presentment sessions, elect either one or two of their own body, as may be necessary to sit with the grand jury upon fiscal business, and I would thereby carry into the grand jury room, representation, as well on the grand jury as on the road sessions, and then you would stop all complaints.

4885. As I understand, you leave the grand jury to be nominated as they are nominated under the present system?—Yes, by the sheriff.

4886. But you would bring the representative element into the grand jury room?—Yes; that is to say, that I would have 4 l. instead of 23 for fiscal business in the county of Cork grand jury room.

4887. For each barony you would have a representation?—Yes.

4888. Sent in specially by the ratepayers?—Yes; and, of course, qualified to any extent which may be considered fit and proper, say a rating of 50 *l.* a year.

4889. But as I understand, by whatever means your ideas may be carried out, the great thing which you are anxious to form is representation at every board, and in every department?—Certainly.

4890. And you, as having had 26 years' knowledge as an elected guardian of the operation of the Poor Law system in your district, and being obliged to observe it more closely for three years as vice-chairman, are in a position to say whether the class of people who are generally returned as elected guardians are really a good working class?—Exceedingly.

4891. Are they attentive?—They are very attentive.

4892. You contemplate that it is from that class that you would have the representation?—Yes. To prove that one of the great advantages which I consider would be gained by having the elected guardians the associated ratepayers would be, that you would secure attendance. I have taken for the last three years the attendance at my board, for the years 1866, 1867, and 1868. The *ex officio* guardians and the elected guardians are equal in number, there being 34 of each, that is 68. In the year 1866 the attendance of *ex officio* guardians was 173, and the number of elected guardians for the same year was 325. In the year 1867 the attendance of the *ex officio* guardians was 190, and of elected guardians for the same period, 341. In the year 1868 the attendance of the *ex officio* guardians, 133, and of elected guardians, 276. That shows that the attendance of the elected guardians, because of their responsibility, is nearly twice that of the *ex officio* guardians.

4893. The *ex officio* guardians not being bound to attend, and being, in fact, not responsible to any one for attendance, or non-attendance?—Yes.

4894. Do you find from your experience that that represents the state of things in the county of Cork, West Riding, generally?—Yes.

4895. Are

4895. Are there several boards of guardians in the West Riding of the county of Cork?—There are.

4896. And do you find that there is about the same proportion of attendance upon those boards?—Very much the same, as far as I have been able to ascertain.

4897. So far as attendance is concerned, you have clearly proved that there is superiority on the part of those who are responsible to some person for their conduct?—That is quite clear.

4898. As to their intelligence, are they fit to conduct the affairs which are entrusted to them?—Quite so. Our board of guardians is conducted with great decorum and harmony, and it would be merely transferring the fiscal business over to a board really constituted by carrying out what I recommend.

4899. Is the fiscal business of the grand jury, or at least that portion of it which falls within the province of the associated cesspayers, more important than the business which the elected guardians have to transact weekly?—Clearly it is much larger, so far as the amount of money distributed is concerned.

4900. But is it not more important for the country; that is to say, it does not require greater intelligence for its conduct, does it?—I think not.

4901. You would have no apprehension that the affairs of the county would not be well managed if they were handed over to that class?—Clearly not. I think it must come to that sooner or later. You will find that the fiscal business will be handed over to the board of guardians. Call them what you will, county boards or baronial boards, or whatever it may be, you may rest assured that eventually the fiscal business of the barony will be discharged through the boards of guardians.

4902. Do you consider that the grand jury, as at present constituted, give satisfaction?—No. I said before that I thought not; and that the reason that it does not give satisfaction is because the same men are empanelled over and over again. I think there are men in the county of Cork who are as well entitled by intelligence and property to be put on the grand jury, who never are put on.

4903. Without disturbing the present system, which I understand you do not contemplate, how would you improve it; in fact, how could you correct that abuse?—It merely strikes me in this way: that if the sheriff were still to return the grand jury, I do not see why he might not take, and be obliged to take, his grand jury from a certain number of proprietors whose names are put in the rate-book to the amount of, say 200 *l.* a year; and that he should take in rotation the men who are rated as landed proprietors, taking them from the first to the last, and going over the list in that manner.

4904. Mr. *Gregory.*] Should peers and noblemen be included?—I do not see any objection to that.

4905. Mr. *Maguire.*] Will you proceed with your suggestion?—I do not suggest it; I merely say that it would be a way of meeting the complaint, if the sheriff was obliged by law to take 60 or 70 or 100 men, who were valued in the poor rate-books at, say 100 *l.* or 200 *l.* a year, or anything you liked, taking from the first to the last, so that if he took, say 23, for the spring assizes, he must take the next 23 for the next assizes, and so exhaust the whole list.

4906. Colonel *French.*] Would you do away with the power which now compels the sheriff to name one person from each barony?—Not at all; I think that is essentially necessary.

4907. Mr. *Maguire.*] But even if the sheriff did continue to nominate as he now does (and perhaps capriciously, as certain facts might show), you would still think that the whole system might be greatly corrected by bringing representation from the people, as it were, the ratepayers into the grand jury room?—It would satisfy the ratepayers, and it would silence the objection that exists at present to the mode in which the grand jury is selected.

4908. Have you anything else to say with reference to the grand jury system?—No; I am not at all one of those who complain of the way in which the grand jury discharge their duty; I think they do it generally very fairly; but I say this, that they have not time to discharge their duties; it is a perfect mockery to say that they discharge the business of the county when there are but four days allowed for the disposal of the enormous business which comes before that grand jury, who dispose of 45,000 *l.* or 46,000 *l.* at one presentment sessions, and they admit it, and they cannot help it.

4909. Would you extend the period of their existence?—Certainly, something is required; my suggestion would be, in the first place, to have a finance board, consisting of the board of guardians, who would discharge the greater portion of the business of the grand jury.

4910. You would transfer that business?—I would.

4911. But supposing there was no such transfer, what would you recommend?—If there was not, they must give more time to the discharge of their duties; we suffer enormously in the county of Cork beyond any other county. The county of Cork is 110 miles long and 70 miles wide. My idea is, that a great portion of the fiscal business which is now discharged by the grand jury, may be discharged by the board of guardians, sitting upon a given day as a board of guardians, but made a county board for fiscal purposes connected with the grand jury; but I have not entered into the question in detail.

4912. You have not a matured plan?—Not at all.

4913. Colonel *Cooper.*] Have you seen Dr. Hancock's plan?—I have not.

4914. Mr. *Maguire.*] At any rate, supposing there is no transfer of the fiscal business of the grand jury to the board of guardians, you say that you are in favour of the extension of their existence; for, in other words, that you would have a permanent committee?—Yes; and I would have the time enlarged for the grand jury to discharge the fiscal business; it is now hurried over in a way that they really cannot avoid.

4915. Would you make it compulsory that they should exist for a greater time?—I would have the law altered; the law at present says that they shall not continue, I think, beyond four days.

4916. You think that four days is much too short a time?—Quite so, for the county of Cork.

4917. To what time would you extend it?—I have not an idea upon that; I would let them be summoned 10 days before the assizes commenced.

4918. If they were summoned 10 days before the assizes commenced, and existed for a certain

number

number of days afterwards, do you think that would meet your objection?—Only to that extent; but I think the only remedy is really dividing the county of Cork. I do not know whether it comes within the province of this Committee, but if it came within the province of the Committee I should like to state my opinion as to that; I can say that there is no grievance that I know of, of such an extent as that which the people suffer in the West Riding of the county of Cork, from the fact of being obliged to go, upon every occasion connected with fiscal business, to the city of Cork. A man has to travel 70 miles to serve his notice in Cork, he has to go 70 miles to get his order for payment, he has to go 70 miles if he enters into a bond; he is obliged to travel sometimes two days before he can get to a railway; he is obliged to stop, perhaps, in Cork three or four days before he can be attended to, from the hurry in the office, and in that way there really can be no competition with regard even to contracts. People will not go to Cork and lose their time, and lose their money; and it is, I think, a most monstrous thing that the county is not divided. If the county of Cork was divided into equal moieties there are only three or four counties in Ireland that would be larger in area than either of the divisions afterwards, and only three or four that would be larger in valuation. The county of Tipperary is divided, and why it is that the county of Cork is not divided I cannot comprehend.

4919. *Chairman.*] Why do you say that the people are obliged to go into the city of Cork for all these different applications, does not the secretary of the grand jury go into the different baronies?—He merely goes to the presentment sessions, but he does not go there for the purpose of making payments. A man is obliged to go to Cork to get his order from the Clerk of the Crown, and he presents that, signed by the treasurer, and he goes to the bank to get paid. That is all done in the city of Cork.

4920. But that is the only thing for which he is obliged to go into the City of Cork, is it not?—No; to serve his notice he must go there; he must serve a notice upon the secretary of the grand jury for all presentments; he must serve a notice upon him with regard to malicious injuries; he must serve a notice upon him with regard to almost everything under the Grand Jury Act.

4921. Mr. *Maguire.*] Is that done by post, or personally?—Probably the secretary of the grand jury will take it by post; but I should be sorry to advise a man to rely upon his accepting it by post; besides, look at the enormous expense of taking witnesses to the city of Cork, from places like Castletown, and Bearhaven, and Skibbereen; and there are places 24 miles beyond Skibbereen. Look at the transmission of prisoners, and everything of that kind; whereas if the county was divided, there would be an immense saving in the county cess.

4922. Where would you have the assize town?—I would have the assize town at Skibbereen, as being the most important town in the West Riding.

4923. If you have any detailed statement as to the inconveniences that you imagine arise from a non-division of the county into ridings for assize purposes, will you hand it into the Committee?—I will do so; and I am much obliged to the Committee for allowing me to do so.

4924. As to the division of the rate, do you think it would be wise to make the same distribution of the burthen as is made under the Poor Law system?—I have been of that opinion for 25 years. I got a petition to Parliament, signed, I think, about 20 years ago, which was presented by the present Lord Fermoy. That petition, I think, was signed by every *ex officio* guardian in the union who was present on that day, and there were a great many; and it prayed Parliament to pass a law that the county cess should be paid as the poor rate is paid. It was signed by the chairman of the day, a Mr. Townsend, and several other large landed proprietors.

4925. Whatever may be the opinion of the *ex officio* guardians, I believe there is no doubt that the feeling of the ratepaying class is in favour of the division?—I know no grievance which is considered so intolerable by the people as that.

4926. You know that that feeling is strongly entertained, and that it has been entertained for a very long time?—I know that it is strongly entertained, and it has been entertained for a long time, and I know that it has caused a good deal of discontent.

4927. Do you think that the discontent is rendered, as it were, more natural because they see the poor rate divided between the landlord and the occupier?—I think they feel beyond that the injustice of it. They feel that really there is a tax imposed by one class (I may say entirely by a class, because I do not look upon the associated ratepayers as exercising any material control at presentment sessions), and they think it is paid by another class almost exclusively, if not entirely, certainly principally. I consider that the class which imposes the tax, is the class which derive almost the entire benefit of it. I think those facts must make any man discontented with it.

4928. Is there any result of the county expenditure which, in your opinion, is not so much to the advantage of the owner of property as to the momentary occupier?—In the first place, every important road that opens a large extent of country is calculated, of course, to improve very largely the fee simple value of that property. Who pays for that? the occupier, who is a tenant from year to year; a tenant that may within six months, or 12 months, be turned out.

4929. According to the law?—According to the law.

4930. Though at the same time the man may remain for his whole life, still the law is such?—Yes. It is a very common thing that if there is a very heavy expenditure on a road, it is made payable by, say, six or eight instalments; and the occupying tenant pays that for three or four years. I will suppose (what may occur) that he is turned out from one cause or the other. The occupying tenant pays for the whole of that improvement, and just after he has paid for it, and the landlord has all the benefit of it, he is turned out. But that is not the only grievance connected with it; that road very often goes through the best portion of the occupier's land.

4931. Is not that included in his rent?—Yes, he complains of it. I have known them myself come to presentment sessions with a memorial and present it to the presentment sessions, praying that the roads should not be made, as it would go through the best part of their land. It does go through the best part of their land, and they still pay the same rent; there is never an abate-

Mr. *Maurice Downing.*

26 May 1868.

cent of a shilling, while all the benefit accrues to the landlord.

4932. The landlord derives a benefit in the enhancement of the value of his property; but does it not frequently happen that the landlord has been paid by the county for the land that that road occupies?—No doubt very frequently that has been the case; but latterly that is not so much the case. Juries empanelled to try traverses for damages are very chary of giving damages where the landlord derives much benefit; they take that very much into consideration.

4933. But at any rate you do not consider that the occupying tenant derives a larger benefit than the landlord, who is the owner in fee simple?—No; then there are the bridges and gaols, and the transmission of prisoners, in all which the landlord has, of course, a much larger interest than the occupying tenant.

4934. As maintaining the order of society?—Yes.

4935. Is it not rather hard also upon the occupying tenant that, if a poor man becomes a lunatic, he has to bear the entire burden of a costly cess?—It is a most extraordinary thing. One lunatic asylum has cost at least 70,000 *l.*, and I believe that an addition has been made to it.

4936. And the city also has a large proportion to pay for it, has it not?—It has. We are paying now about 9,500 *l.* a-year to support it, besides paying, I think, 18,000 *l.* a year in instalments.

4937. Those are compulsory presentments, are they not?—Those are compulsory presentments. I believe the grand jury have no control whatever over them.

4938. But it is too hard, you think, to make the occupying tenant pay for the entire support of these lunatics?—I consider it to be a great injustice.

4939. You seem thoroughly to share the feelings entertained by those who are the large class of the community with respect to what you consider this injustice?—Certainly.

4940. And you are anxious that the rate should be divided?—I do not see why we should not do in this country what is done in Scotland, where the heritor pays altogether for the support of the gaols, the transmission of prisoners and all that class of expenses to which I have been just referring; he also pays all the local and county charges, except the road money, which is divided equally between the landlord and the tenant; that is the law in Scotland, and I cannot conceive why it should not be the law in Ireland.

4941. Mr. *Herbert.*] Have they not turnpike roads almost all over Scotland?—Yes; but there is a road cess also paid, half by the landlord and half by the tenant; but every other tax is paid by the owner of the land.

4942. It is all paid by the occupier in England, is it not?—I believe in England it is all paid by the occupier.

4943. Mr. *Maguire.*] With regard to Ireland it ought not, you think, to be paid by one class alone?—I am quite sure that it ought not.

4944. You say that the *ex officio* guardians of the landlord class in your part of the country are in favour of its division?—They are, at this moment. I have a letter here from a gentleman who was high sheriff two years ago, and who has been constantly one of the grand jurors, and he says: "By all means enforce upon the Committee the necessity of dividing the cess between landlord and tenant."

4945. Mr. *Herbert.*] You stated, did you not, that you were a landed proprietor yourself?—I did.

4946. Do you act so with your tenants?—I do not; nor do I think you will get any landlord to do so until the law is changed.

4947. Mr. *Maguire.*] But you would do it when the law is changed, I presume?—I would do it most willingly, and I would extend it to every occupier of land, whether he has a lease or not; that is, to every occupier occupying his own farm and working it.

4948. You would not limit its operation merely to tenants at will?—I would not; that was always my opinion. I speak now entirely from my own district; I know that it would be a very small inducement to give the tenants in my district half of it where the rents are so excessively high over the valuation.

4949. But generally speaking for the country, I believe the rents are, as you know, considerably over the valuation?—In my barony they are in many cases double the valuation.

4950. A doubt has been expressed by persons giving evidence before this Committee that if the law were changed, dividing the cess equally between the owner and the occupier, the occupier would really not get the advantage of it; do you believe that that would be the case?—I think in many cases he would not get the advantage, but that in a great many cases he would; but in cases where he would not get the benefit of it he could not be injured, he would be served to the extent that he would know then what he would have to pay, and he would not have this county cess increasing year after year, as an additional rate upon him; because, I suppose, the Committee are aware how enormously the county cess has risen in Ireland.

4951. (*Chairman.*] You state that the county cess has increased enormously; could you give the Committee any statistics to prove that?—Certainly.

4952. Mr. *Maguire.*] Do you mean that it has increased locally or generally?—Generally. I will give it you in the county of Cork, which I think is a very fair test for the rest of Ireland. I will give it in decennial periods, which I have taken from a Return made to Parliament, which I suppose is the best authority. In the year 1775 the cess for the whole county of Cork was 9,780 *l.*; in the year 1785 it was 8,263 *l.*; in the year 1795 it was 20,269 *l.*; in the year 1805 it was 48,108 *l.*; in the year 1815 it was 56,889 *l.*; in the year 1825 it was 82,116 *l.*; in the year 1835 it fell to 63,555 *l.*; in the year 1845 it was 88,601 *l.* I am not able to give you what it was in 1858, but I can answer that it was much larger, because in the year 1848 the cess for the county of Cork rose to the enormous amount of 187,000 *l.*

4953. *Chairman.*] But was not that an exceptional period, owing to the famine and the desire of employing the people?—It was; but now for the last 10 years ending in 1865, it was over 90,000 *l.* a-year.

4954. Mr. *Gregory.*] Could you state how much that is in the pound on the valuation in those different periods?—I could not do that, but I could tell you how much it is at present. The average is now about 1 *s.* 10 *d.* in the pound all over the county of Cork. Before I leave that, I may perhaps be allowed to state a circumstance which is rather important. The county cess upon contracts alone for maintaining roads and public works between the years 1824 and 1849 increased

from

Mr. *M'Carthy Downing.*

25 May 1868.

from 4,700 *l.* in 1826 to 17,400 *l.* in 1849, and it is now over 20,000 *l.*

4955. *Mr. Maguire.*] But you do not object to the roads being kept in perfect order, and to useful public buildings being erected?—Not at all; but I say that the tenant does not really know what his rent is, because there is an increase upon him year after year for county cess. If you look at another item in the expenditure you will find how every thing is increasing. If you take malicious injuries on an average for five years ending in 1838, the levy in the county for malicious injuries was 166 *l.* The average in 1848 was 600 *l.*; and at the last spring assizes for the half year it was 363 *l.*, or 726 *l.* for the year.

4956. *Chairman.*] Was there any exceptional case in that last half-year?—There was.

4957. Will you take the year before when there was no exceptional case?—Then it was 600 *l.*, and that is, I think, one of the reasons which shows how unjust it is to make the tenant pay all the county cess.

4958. *Mr. Gregory.*] Was the year 1838 at all exceptionally low as regards malicious injuries?—It was not. The period before was low; but taking that exceptional case alluded to by the Honourable Chairman, I think that it is one of the strongest possible reasons why the county cess should be divided between landlord and tenant. At those presentment sessions which are now being held for the barony of Barrymore, the very man who got a presentment last year for 850 *l.* (a man of the name of Hassan, who was a witness at some of the Fenian trials), has a presentment for 400 *l.*, and they put it on the parish, which will raise the rate upon that parish to 1 *s.* 1½ *d.* in the pound, in addition to the ordinary county cess, although the crime might have been committed by a man from London, or from Glasgow, or from anywhere else, if malicious at all.

4959. *Mr. Maguire.*] With regard to this division of the rate, you say that whether a man had a lease or not, you would divide the rate between him and his landlord?—I would.

4960. But if you do that, do you not think that there is a stronger reason why you should divide it at once in the cases of all those tenants who do not hold leases under landlords?—Of course; I would be very glad to see it done with regard to occupying tenants at once. I would not stop the legislation because it would not be extended to leaseholders.

4961. Do you wish that the law should come into operation at once, after the law is passed, with respect to all occupiers who do not hold leases?—I would apply it to every occupier in Ireland; because I think, if I have read rightly some of the proceedings before this Committee, some Honourable Members, as it appears from their questions, would only divide it with reference to future lettings, and that would be doing nothing whatever.

4962. Taking a certain barony, though a number of the tenants there hold from year to year, and though any year their tenancy may be determined by the landlord, yet there may be practically no new letting for their whole lives; and therefore the law would never come into operation for their benefit?—Of course not.

4963. Would that be fair?—It would not be fair.

4964. Would anything be more unfair than that a man who has a precarious tenancy and a precarious interest should pay all the burden of this rate?—No; but do not be surprised at my saying that I would extend it to men who hold by lease. You will find that that has been recommended by a Committee of this House. I do not refer to the Committee to whose Report Mr. Sharkey referred; but I refer to the Town Lands Committee of 1844, which recommended that it should be extended to all occupiers of land.

4965. Will you state what that recommendation was?—They recommended strongly that the county cess should be divided between landlord and tenant, extending it to all occupiers of land.

4966. But you are of opinion that there would be no appreciable advantage if it did not at once apply to occupiers?—Clearly.

4967. If the law did not embrace all at once, and if it was limited merely to new lettings, you think there would be no advantage in it?—Clearly; I do not apprehend that there is any matter which has received so large an amount of testimony in its favour as this very question. If you refer to the testimony given before the Devon Commission, you will find that landed proprietors, judges, land agents, and of course the farmers, all recommended that that should be done; I have a list of witnesses here, every one of whom gave the strongest testimony upon that point.

4968. As being a measure of justice to the farming classes?—Yes, and some even went beyond that, and said that they would put it all upon the landlord, and let him deal with the tenant; but I think the division of it would be better for many reasons.

4969. Will you state the reason why you think division would be better than placing the burden upon the landlord class?—I think that if you placed the whole burden upon the landlord, you would place it eventually upon the tenant; I think that if you placed it all upon the landlord, you would exclude the ratepayers from any active participation in the administration of the law; and I would think it much more advisable and better for the interests of the county at large, that all classes should have an interest in carrying out the law with satisfaction to the public at large.

4970. Is there, as far as you know, any demand upon the part of the occupying class, that the landlords should bear the entire burden?—No; on the contrary, they never ask more than that the same allowance should be made, as is made in the case of the poor rate.

4971. They never asked for more, did they?—I never heard of it.

4972. And you would have heard of it if they had, would you not?—I should have heard of it.

4973. All they ask is for what seems to them to be simple justice?—Quite so.

4974. Would you exempt the poorer class from the payment of the rate?—Decidedly; I would exempt every tenement which was not valued at 4 *l.*; I think the imposition of the rate on that class is the most cruel thing in the world; I have known a poor widow, with a little cabin, to be threatened with distraint for 5½ *d.*, which I discharged myself; I have known even as small a sum as 2½ *d.* to be recovered, and I think that is cruel.

4975. These poor people are utterly unable to pay any tax, in fact, are they not?—Utterly unable.

Mr. *Maunsell Dunning.*

26 May 1852.

4976. Mr *Gregory*.] It adds even to the expense of collection, does it not?—It adds to the expenses of collection, and it adds largely to the sums which cannot be recovered, and which are re-presented, which is a most unfair thing, because it is throwing upon other people the payment of that which ought to be paid by the landlord of the small tenants. It is unjust in its operation, it is cruel to the occupier, and it is a wrong upon the general ratepayer.

4977. Mr. *Maguire*.] Is the solution of the question, in your opinion, striking off altogether the smaller class, and putting the tax upon those who own the property?—Certainly. Another thing which I think most unfair is, that the owner of an unoccupied house is obliged to pay the county cess for it, whereas he is not obliged to pay the poor rate.

4978. Then would you recommend an assimilation of the two laws in that respect?—Certainly.

4979. As to malicious injuries and the present system of investigating them, have you any information or suggestion to give to the Committee?—The only observation that I have to make upon that is, that if you have my plan carried into effect, and have elected guardians sitting with the magistrates; and if the magistrates should not exceed (which I strongly recommend) the number of elected guardians, you may depend upon it that you would not have so many malicious injuries presented for as there are.

4980. You think that the application of the elective system would be a check in such cases?—It would be a great corrective. I need not tell the Committee that if there is any idea that things are done maliciously, the magistrates are quite alive to putting those sort of things down, and they would be satisfied with evidence with which I would not be satisfied

4981. Do you think that if there were representatives of the ratepayers present at those tribunals, they would investigate each case more rigidly?—Certainly; and their minds would not be so ready to receive impressions.

4982. Have you any other suggestions which you would wish to make as to the amendment of the law in any way?—I think I have suggested what appears to me to be desirable. I am very strongly in favour of having the elected guardians. For instance, in the barony of the east division of West Carberry there are resident 17 elected guardians. From those 17 you would select, by ballot amongst themselves, 12; and I certainly would not have the magistrates come in at any time they please at the road sessions, though an associated ratepayer, if he is not there when he is balloted for, and comes in two minutes afterwards, will not be allowed to sit; nor would I allow the number of magistrates to exceed the number of associated ratepayers.

4983. Does an evil, in your opinion, arise from the present system, which permits all the magistrates of a barony, or of a neighbouring barony, to come in and swamp the associated ratepayers?—I cannot state that I have ever seen anything of that kind occur, unless the magistrate who came in had property in the barony.

4984. But have you seen a preponderating number of local magistrates?—Certainly.

4985. And do you think that unfair?—Perfectly unfair; it will never give satisfaction while you have more magistrates than ratepayers.

4986. But under any circumstances a law which gives power to neighbouring magistrates to come in and increase the number of local magistrates, you think is very much open to abuse, and should not exist?—Certainly.

4987. As to the surveyors or secretaries, have you any suggestions to make?—The only suggestion which I have to make upon that point is, that I do not think the deputies of the county surveyors are at all taken from the class from whom they ought to be taken. They are very often intelligent farmers, who know nothing whatever about road making, and who know very little, indeed, of fiscal business. I would have them trained persons, persons taken from the office of the Board of Works, or some persons of that kind.

4988. Would you have them competent to become surveyors afterwards if necessary?—I would have them competent to be surveyors according to their merits; I believe that the office of treasurer is quite unnecessary. I would have all the payments go through the secretary of the grand jury, and I would have the secretary of the grand jury responsible for the legality of those payments as the clerk of the union is at present under the Poor Law system.

4989. You have no treasurer for the union, have you?—No; we have a banker which, of course, the county will have also.

4990. *Chairman*.] Are you aware that an Act was passed last year doing away with the office of county treasurer prospectively?—I am aware of it; I would have the whole of the fiscal business done through the secretary.

4991. Mr. *Maguire*.] As to the fees paid to the secretary of the grand jury for various offices at the present moment, what do you say?—I would certainly abolish them.

4992. There is a complaint, is there not, that they are excessive?—A very great complaint; they amount to a very large sum.

4993. Would you make them moderate and substitute payment by stamps for payment in money?—I think the mode ought to be that after notices of applications had been served locally upon, say, the clerk of the union, who should be obliged to transmit them to the secretary of the grand jury, there should be a stamp of, say, one shilling, which should go to the benefit of the county, instead of the parties being obliged as at present to go to the city of Cork and lose both time and money; I would give them every facility.

4994. I believe you have a letter from Mr. Mackie, who wishes to correct a statement which he made in his evidence as to the discontent which has arisen from the present law which places the entire burden upon the occupier?—Mr. Mackie says that he only meant when he said that that was the only cause of discontent in Ireland that it was in reference to taxation.

4995. *Chairman*.] You commenced your evidence by telling the Committee that you are a rated occupier to the amount of 125 *l*.; what are we to understand exactly as regards that; do you mean to say that you pay 125 *l*. cess, or that your land is valued at the amount of 125 *l*.?—My land is valued at the amount of 125 *l*. a year.

4996. And you have never been returned as a cesspayer except four times during eight years?—Only four times during eight years.

4997. By being returned you mean being put upon the list, out of which you might be selected by ballot?—Yes.

4998. You

Mr. *McCarthy Downing.* — 26 May 1868.

4998. You do not mean to say that you have served four times?—I rather think I have not; I think probably I have served about three times.

4999. You have informed the Committee that the number of cesspayers returned in your barony was, in the year 1865, limited to 10, that being the lowest number that could be returned by law; and that out of these 10 a very large proportion were disqualified?—Yes, quite so.

5000. Your objection, then, to what took place at the grand jury with regard to presentment sessions is an objection rather to the mode in which the present law is carried out, is it not, than to the present law itself, because, according to the present law, those men should not have been returned?—They should not.

5001. And the grand jury on that occasion acted illegally?—They acted illegally.

5002. It was not, then, a fault in the law, but it was a fault in the mode of carrying it out, was it not?—I think that it was a fault in the law to place it in the power of any man to make so great a mistake as that when a system can be introduced which will render it impossible.

5003. In the county of Cork I presume the grand jurors select from the number of cesspayers that are returned any person they like from any part of the barony not taking the highest rated cesspayers?—They select any one out of the 100 that they choose.

5004. Your chief objection, as I take it, to the law in that respect is, that it leaves too great a discretion to one individual?—Just so.

5005. But would not that objection be got over if the grand jurors were obliged to take the highest cesspayers?—I do not think that that would at all meet the objections which I make.

5006. That would meet that particular objection, would it not?—It might meet that particular objection, but I raised other objections.

5007. But supposing that, instead of being obliged to return the 100 highest cesspayers from the whole barony, the collector was obliged to return a smaller number of the highest cesspayers from each parish, and that out of that smaller number returned from each parish a certain number of the highest cesspayers should be balloted for, would not that do away with your objection?—I think not, because they are not at all the class of men fitted for the discharge of the duties at the presentment sessions.

5008. You do not think that the persons who pay the highest cess are the best fitted persons for discharging the duties at presentment sessions?—I do not; I know there are a great many of them who do not read or write English.

5009. And who pay a higher cess?—And who pay a higher cess.

5010. Did you not state that those cesspayers are quite under the control of the landlords?—I do not say that all of them are; I say that if I was a grand juror, and if in my barony I wish to carry a road, or any other matter in which I had an interest, I could select from the 100 ratepayers who were returned to me as many cesspayers as I was sure would vote for me.

5011. But supposing that the law were changed in the way suggested to the Committee by other witnesses, you could not do so, could you?—I think I could, because I think that in every parish I would find as many persons as I could influence.

5012. But the suggestion which has been made to the Committee by other witnesses is, not that the grand jurors should have any selection whatsoever, but that there should be a ballot held at the assizes out of the highest cesspayers returned by the collectors from each parish, what would be your view as to that?—Then there would be no responsibility upon the men to attend, and that is what I look to.

5013. But you stated as one of the chief reasons why they did not attend, the uncertainty of their being allowed to sit, and that uncertainty would be done away with, would it not?—Yes; if they were selected at the assizes and notice were immediately given to them, that would get rid of that objection.

5014. You have another objection: that if a man was not responsible to anybody, he would not think it necessary to attend?—Just so; he would not.

5015. You say that the grand juror who selects the cesspayers at present, can very easily select those whom he knows will vote as he wishes at the presentment sessions?—Quite so.

5016. Do you not think that if the law were changed, and an election substituted for the present system in very many baronies in Ireland, the landlords could return any persons to the presentment session whom they chose?—I think not.

5017. You are speaking, I presume, merely from your experience in the county of Cork?—I think, when I speak of the county of Cork, I speak, as an Honourable Member of the Committee knows of, a portion of Ireland where the landlords probably exercise the greatest influence, viz., in the Carbery's, in the West Riding, and though the landlords have returned their nominees frequently, yet whenever there is a matter of importance, and wherever there is any issue between them and the people with regard to the return of an elected guardian the people always return their favourite.

5018. But in the matter of an elected guardian, when there is an issue raised, it is some issue in which the feelings, and, if I may use the expression, the passions, of the people are implicated; but do you think that, in the matter of the expense of roads, and such things as that, there would be sufficient feeling in the people to counteract the influence of the landlords?—I think so. I think that nothing would touch the feelings of the people more than that question.

5019. Then, your experience would lead you to believe that the elected guardians of the poor in that part of Ireland are more careful in keeping down expenditure than any other class in the country?—I do not say that.

5020. Do you believe that those associated cesspayers, elected as you propose, would be more careful in keeping down expenditure than the present magistrates and cesspayers are?—I think that the magistrates would be equally anxious, perhaps, to keep down taxation as the elected guardians, provided that the landlords paid a portion of the county cess; but my contrast was as between the elected guardians and the present associated ratepayers, the men who are associated with the magistrates; I drew no contrast between the magistrates and the elected guardians.

5021. Do you think that the associated cesspayers, if elected, would be more likely to keep down the county cess than if they were the highest ratepayers of the barony?—Much more so, I think, because they would be responsible to the men who returned them, just in the same

Mr. M'Carthy Downing.

[illegible] May [illegible].

same way as a Member of Parliament responsible to his constituents.

5022. But in your evidence in chief, was not the point upon which you insisted principally that every parish ought to be represented at the sessions?—Certainly; and that by an elected associated ratepayer.

5023. With respect to the presentment sessions of the county at large, you say those are, generally speaking, very badly attended, and you gave some instances to prove it; as a general rule, what sort of presentments come before the county at large sessions?—The repair of court houses is one thing; for instance, the Youghal Bridge which I spoke of a short time since.

5024. But those are not presentments that come usually before the county at large sessions; they are extraordinary presentments, are they not?—They are.

5025. Will you inform the Committee what are the usual presentments which come before those sessions?—I think the repair of the county court-house and the repair of the bridewells.

5026. Are those generally large items at every sessions?—They are not very large.

5027. What are the large items which come before those sessions?—At some sessions they may be very large, and at others they may be very small.

5028. But, generally speaking, is it not the fact that nearly all the presentments which come before the county at large sessions, are presentments of a formal character, which must be passed?—Generally speaking that is the case, but not always. I think I gave a very strong fact to show that that is not the case in the sessions now pending.

5029. Generally speaking, the presentments which come before those sessions are of rather a formal character, are they not?—They are.

5030. May not that, to a certain extent, account for the fact of their being badly attended?—Possibly it may be so.

5031. Do you expect that at these next sessions when this large presentment is to come before them the attendance will be as bad?—No, I think it will be better.

5032. Do you not think that, upon all occasions when those large presentments are known to be likely to come before the county at large sessions, people will then attend to their business?—I think that where there is an extraordinary item of this kind, it is probable that they will; but I think it must be something extraordinary to bring people a distance of 70 or 80 miles.

5033. People naturally will not go 70 or 80 miles to a presentment sessions, where they have no duties to discharge, but only to vote monies which they are obliged to vote?—I do not know that they would be obliged to vote.

5034. They are obliged to vote the salaries of the county officers, and the expenditure upon the public buildings, are they not?—They do not always vote those presentments. They refused in one case to vote for the repair of a bridewell, for a number of years, though representations were made by the chairman of quarter sessions that the galleries were coming down.

5035. The county of Cork, of course, is a very exceptional county?—It is an exceptional county so far as its extent goes.

5036. And you propose, as I understand, that the county of Cork should be divided into two ridings, and that the assizes should be held in a different town for one riding, from that in which it is held for the other?—Certainly.

5037. Is it not a fact that any town in the western division of the county of Cork would be as inconvenient to certain portions of the western division as the city of Cork is to that western division, in consequence of the railways not all reaching that town, as they do the city of Cork?—There are portions, no doubt, of the West Riding which are nearer to Cork.

5038. *Mr. Maguire.*] And which border upon the city?—Yes.

5039. *Chairman.*] It has been represented to this Committee by almost every witness who came from the county of Cork, that there would be great inconvenience in having the assizes in any other place than in the city of Cork, because the railways all converge to the city of Cork, and it is much easier for jurors and others to get to the city of Cork from any other portion of the county, than to get to Skibbereen, for instance, or to any other town in the county?—I do not think that is correct by any means. I am quite certain that every official who has been examined before the Committee, would be adverse to any change; but I venture to say that the gentlemen of the West Riding of the county of Cork would give very different evidence. How could it be said that to the whole district along to Bantry, to Bearhaven, and to Crookhaven, it would not be a great convenience to have the assize town at Skibbereen?

5040. Do the railways go to Skibbereen?—You have a railway to Dunmanway, so that the people of Dunmanway will have only an hour's ride from Dunmanway to Skibbereen.

5041. How far from Dunmanway is Skibbereen?—About 16 English miles.

5042. To get from Dunmanway to Skibbereen people would have to drive 16 miles, would they not?—At present they would, but there is a railway in contemplation.

5043. On the whole you believe that it would be much more convenient to have an assize town in the West Riding than to have the county of Cork divided, and the assizes for both divisions held in the city of Cork?—Certainly.

5044. Even in the latter case there would be a convenience in having two grand juries, and then a greater representation of county interest?—You would have that; but I do not look to that as the important matter.

5045. And you would also have this other great convenience, would you not, that the assizes for one division would be held first, and for the other division afterwards, and the jurors for one division would not be required to come into the city of Cork until the assizes for the other division had been held?—No doubt.

5046. *Mr. Maguire.*] Is not that done at the present moment?—That is done at the present moment.

5047. The inconvenience was so great, I believe, that arrangement was come to under the advice, I believe, of Chief Baron Pigott.

5048. *Chairman.*] You stated, did you not, with regard to the constitution of the grand jury, that your objection to the grand jury itself was that the same men were put upon the grand jury over and over again?—Yes; while there are men of much larger properties who are not put on.

5049. Would not that objection be equally strong against those elected boards; would they

not

not be the same men over and over again?—It does not at all follow; but even so I do not see any objection to that, because they are the representatives of the ratepayers, which the grand jury are not.

5050. But what would be the objection to having the same men on the grand jury, if there be no objection to having the same men for the ratepayers?—I think it causes dissatisfaction in the minds of others. I might state, as an instance, that the west division of West Carbery was represented at one time by a man who never had a single acre of land in that barony, and never had a residence in the barony, and who knew no more about it than a stranger, save that he had been for three years before, the agent to a nobleman for property of about 2,000 *l.* a year.

5051. Was he on it successively?—No; he was only on it once.

5052. I am speaking now of your objection to having the same man repeatedly on the grand jury?—I think that is an objection; it causes dissatisfaction; if you find there are one hundred gentlemen in the West Riding who may fairly expect to be on the grand jury, and that it is confined to 10, I think that makes the other 90 very much dissatisfied.

5053. Your objection is one touching a matter of feeling?—It is a matter of feeling.

5054. You do not object to the body as being an incompetent body?—I do not think they are incompetent; on the contrary, I think they are very competent; I have no fault to find with the mode, generally speaking, in which the grand jury discharge their duties.

5055. You say that four days are quite insufficient for discharging the fiscal duties of the grand jury?—Yes; and the grand jury have repeatedly said so.

5056. But I presume that in the other counties of Ireland four days would be amply sufficient?—I should think so.

5057. And if the county of Cork were divided that objection would not exist, would it?—It would not.

5058. Mr. *Dawson.*] How long do they sit now?—Only four days; they are constantly obliged to apply to the judge to allow them to take up presentments and other matters during the Crown business.

5059. *Chairman.*] You have given a very strong opinion in favour of a division of the county cess, and I think you referred to the case of Scotland where you said that all the county expenses were thrown upon the owners, except the money for the roads, and that that was divided; but are you aware that in Scotland a system exists, generally speaking, of 19 years' leases, and that at the end of that 19 years' lease, the land is put up again to the highest competition?—I am aware of that.

5060. In such a system as that, is it not the fact that the owner must, speaking economically, bear the whole of the burdens of the taxes upon the land?—I know political economists say so; but if that is to be carried out, let it be done at once, and let the landlords in Ireland pay all the rates, and let the land be let to the highest bidder: if the landlords take upon themselves the payment of all the rates, let them let the land afterwards as they best can; the tenants would be perfectly satisfied with that.

5061. You think the tenants would have no objection to having their rents raised all over the country?—It would find its own level, I think.

5062. Mr. *Dawson.*] If you know the system in Scotland, do you not know that, on the expiration of these leases it is almost invariably the case that the rents are raised?—I believe they are raised sometimes. I happened to be in Scotland in the Lothians, and I happened to converse there with some of the very large holders of land, one paying 1,000 *l.* a-year, and another 800 *l.* a-year, and I asked them what will be the result upon the termination of their leases, and they said they never had any difficulty in arranging with the proprietor.

5063. Are you aware that in the county of Fife the average letting of land is four guineas an acre all over the county?—I was not aware of it.

5064. *Chairman.*] You go so far in favour of a division of the county rate, do you not, that you propose that it should be extended to all holders of land, whether by lease or otherwise?—That is my own individual opinion; but I do not think that would be well received, generally speaking, by the proprietors.

5065. Do you think that it would be fair, supposing a landlord let a farm to a tenant at a fair rent, on the understanding that the taxes should be paid by the tenant, that by subsequent legislation the same should be thrown upon the landlord?—In that abstract view it would not be fair.

5066. But would not that place the man who had given leases to his tenants at a great disadvantage, as compared with the man who had not given leases?—It would, no doubt.

5067. Would not that be a great discouragement to proprietors giving leases?—It would.

5068. Would you, therefore, advocate that proposal?—I do not advocate it very strongly; but I think it would be a very agreeable thing in the present state of the country if all the tenants felt that the proprietors were inclined to deal liberally with them; and in my own district I think any reduction of that kind may very well be made in consequence of the high rents which are paid.

5069. But any landlord who desires to encourage this good feeling can reduce his rent at any time, can he not?—No doubt.

5070. Would you advocate imposing this penalty upon the men who had granted leases to their tenants at moderate rents?—I do not advocate it, as a matter of right; but as a matter of individual feeling, I would be glad to see it done.

5071. You stated also, did you not, that you would place the county cess upon tenements below 4 *l.* upon landlords?—I would; upon the immediate lessor.

5072. That would, amongst other things, save a great deal of expense of the cost of collection, would it not?—Very great, indeed.

5073. Do you think that the cost of collection of the county cess in Ireland is excessive?—It is very excessive. It amounts in the county of Cork to over 3,000 *l.* a-year; it is 9 *d.* in the £., while the poor rate is collected at 4 *d.*

5074. Do you not think that the county cess could be collected at a much lower rate than 9 *d.*, when the poor rate is collected at 4 *d.*?—I am quite sure the collectors of the poor rate would be very glad to get the collection of the county rate at the same rate as that at which they collect the poor rate, and think it would be a very great advantage.

Mr. *Macarthy Downing.*

10 May 1868.

Mr. Macarthy Downing.

29 May 1868.

6075. Is it not a great disadvantage to the occupiers to have those small sums collected from them three or four times a year by different persons?—Yes; there is very often a race between the two to know who will have it first; but the one collector would suit the occasion; he would deal with the tenants in a different way altogether.

6076. It has been been suggested to the Committee that it would be inadvisable to appoint the poor rate collectors as collectors of the county cess, because the baronies are so very large, and because they might find it difficult to get securities to the large amount that the county cess collectors get; do you see the force of that objection?—There may be some difficulty in getting security; but in my union there is no man who gets security as a collector of the poor rate for 3,000*l*., or 4,000*l*., who would not get security for a larger amount.

6077. Do you not think that if that difficulty did exist it might be got over by dividing the baronies, for collecting purposes, into smaller districts?—That might be done; but I do not think that difficulty would be found to exist at all.

6078. You have stated that you do not consider the assistant county surveyors to be persons at all qualified to discharge their duties, and you thought they ought rather to be men trained by the Board of Works; are not the deputy surveyors at present obliged to undergo an examination before they are appointed?—Not that I am aware of. I do not believe it to be so.

6079. You do not believe that there is any qualification whatsoever required for the assistant surveyors?—There may be an examination by the county surveyor himself, but I never heard of it. I know men who have been taken from the farming classes, superior farmers. It certainly is not so in all counties.

6080. Do you think you would get men of this higher class that you speak of who could, as I understand you, be promoted to the office of county surveyor to serve in the counties for the very low salaries which are at present paid?—Perhaps not; but I think there would be a saving if you had a superior class of men who would understand applications, and presentments, and matters of that kind. I would make the county surveyor responsible for every man under him; and, if you like, I would give him a larger salary. I forgot to mention, what I think is essentially necessary, viz., that every county surveyor ought to be bound to reside in his district, and to have his office there.

6081. But what I want clearly to understand is your proposal with respect to these deputy surveyors. At present they are subject to the county surveyor. He is the responsible officer, and they are appointed by him, are they not?—I think they are appointed by the grand jury.

6082. Are not the assistant surveyors at present appointed by the county surveyor, being removable by the grand jury?—Probably that is so; but I was under the impression that they were elected by the grand jury.

6083. Do I rightly understand you to state, that you would propose that this higher class of men, whom you wish to have in the counties, should be in the same position, subject to the county surveyor?—Certainly.

6084. And appointed by him?—I think it would be better; I think he should be responsible.

6085. You could hardly expect that he would be responsible, could you, unless he had both the power of appointing and removing those people?—That is very true.

6086. Do you think you would get men of the position you mention, who would undertake the duties under those circumstances?—I think the men that are now sent out by the Board of Works under the Valuation Acts are not paid very highly, and yet they are men of intelligence and men who are very competent to discharge that duty; their salaries are not very large; they are sent out for the purpose of the annual revision of the valuation of land.

6087. With respect to malicious injuries you say that the presentments for these in the county of Cork have increased enormously of late years; do you think that that is due to a real increase of crime in the county?—I do not think it is; for the last three presentment sessions, unfortunately, one man has had three presentments for malicious injuries of nearly 400*l*. each, because he was a witness upon some Fenian trials. I must tell you that I read the case very carefully, and if I had been on it I should have pronounced that there was not a particle of evidence to show that there was anything malicious; but, however, they found otherwise.

6088. Do you think that this principle of granting compensation for malicious injuries is a good one in itself?—I do not.

6089. Is it not making the innocent pay for the guilty?—Decidedly.

6090. Do you think it has the effect of leading to the discovery of offenders?—I never knew an instance of it.

6091. And when a man has his house, or stack, burnt, is not the first thing that he seeks compensation from the grand jury, and not the discovery of the offender?—Clearly.

6092. And he does not much care, does he, whether, or not, the man who burnt the house, or the stack, is ever found out?—Quite so.

6093. When a man is robbed, on the contrary, does he not immediately try to find out who has robbed him?—He goes and lays an information, and does his best to discover the thief.

6094. But when one of these injuries is done, is it not the case that he takes no trouble about it?—None, whatever; on the contrary, very often the dogs that give information are put up before the injuries are committed. I suspect that two-thirds of these cases are not malicious injuries at all.

6095. You believe that two-thirds of the applications are applications where there is no malicious injury at all?—Yes.

6096. On the other hand, do you believe that this system of compensating people for malicious injuries leads to a repressing of that offence in Ireland?—I do not.

6097. You do not think it has any effect of that kind?—Not the slightest.

6098. Supposing that it were right to have compensation given for malicious injuries, is the tribunal before which the matter is brought at present a proper tribunal to try it?—I should say not at all.

6099. Do you not think it ought to be brought before a jury and a judge and tried regularly?—I would rather have it tried before the chairman of quarter sessions, and have a jury, if you like; but I would rather leave it to him, because he is unprejudiced, and he has a legal mind.

6100. Are

Mr. M'Carthy Downing.

—

[illegible] May 1868.

5100. Are the presentment sessions and the grand jury in your opinion proper tribunals before which to bring proceedings of this quasi criminal character?—I should say not at all. I think it has a very injurious operation, and that it has a tendency to increase those applications.

5101. Mr. *Dawson*.] With regard to the division of the county, I presume your evidence is simply addressed to the case of the county of Cork; has it reference to any other county in Ireland?—No, not to any other county in Ireland. Tipperary, as the Committee are aware, has been divided.

5102. As to the division of the county cess, when a contract is already in existence, would you divide the cess between the landlord and the tenant, the contract being of course an agreement between the landlord and the tenant about the letting of the landlord's land?—Yes; but the contract may be a letting from year to year. If you put it in that way, I would certainly divide the cess.

5103. If it were in a case of a lease of any kind, would you divide the cess?—Not in the case of an existing lease.

5104. You also mentioned that you would prevent the number of magistrates attending at the presentment sessions from exceeding in number the associated cesspayers, how would you equalise the numbers of the attending magistrates and of the associated cesspayers?—At 12 o'clock, which is the time when the chair is taken, that might be regulated.

5105. Would you make the chairman veto the appearance of any magistrate after a certain time?—Certainly; if for instance, at 12 o'clock, so many magistrates and so many ratepayers were present, and if there were a larger number of magistrates let the magistrates be balloted for, or *vice versâ*.

5106. Do you see any probable advantage in collecting both the poor rate and the county cess in one year, in the month of November, and do you think the two rates could be advantageously collected by one officer, at a rate not exceeding 1*s*. in the £. for both collections?—I think it would be very desirable to have but one collection. In our union we strike but one rate in the year, and we strike that before the 29th of September, so as to give the tenant the right to deduct it from the rent falling due; I think that the Honourable Member's suggestion is an admirable one as to the collection of the rate, and as to the amount to be paid for the collection.

5107. Have you ever heard of the proposition of creating a standing committee of the grand jury, to sit during the interval between the assizes?—I think it is very desirable.

5108. What powers would you give the members of that committee?—In the first place I would give them the power which is exercised now by two magistrates, where sudden breaches occur. I would give the necessary order in that case, signed by that standing committee, or whatever you may call it, to have those sudden breaches made good; I would have them also pay the money quarterly to the contractor, which I think is very necessary; I think contractors have great cause to complain now of the way in which they are now paid.

5109. Would you give them power to take any cognizance of complaints against the county officers?—They might take the complaint and hear evidence upon it, but I take it for granted that the grand jury would have eventually to decide upon that complaint.

5110. Do you think there would be a difficulty in getting an effective committee like that from want of attendance, or do you think it would create a liability to jobbery amongst certain individuals, who would always endeavour to be members of the committee, and so on?—My idea goes beyond that, because I would have what you call a finance committee in every barony, whereas you would have it only for the whole county.

5111. Do you think that one county committee would not be sufficient?—I do not think it would be of much benefit to meet the objections which exist at present to the mode in which people are obliged to go to Cork.

5112. Do you think it would be better to have a baronial committee?—I do, and in that view I am sustained by a good many of the grand jurors.

5113. And that they should report to the grand jury?—They should report to the grand jury.

5114. Mr. *Blake*.] I understand you to be in favour of the baronial boards being composed of elected associated ratepayers in an equal number with the magistrates?—I would make the elected guardians the associated ratepayers; they are elected by the ratepayers, and they represent at the board of guardians the ratepayers; they would also represent them at the presentment sessions; in fact, they might walk from the board of guardians into the court-house, where the presentment sessions are being held, and then you have the same men who have been in the habit of acting together, and who understand each other, and who have habits of business.

5115. Would it not be desirable to allow small farmers, say those rated at 20*l*. a-year, to send in men of their own class upon the baronial board, if they thought proper?—That is the very power that I give them. Supposing that a man is now a candidate for the position of an elected guardian, if the law was passed, as I now take the liberty of suggesting, it would be known at the time that the same man would be the associated ratepayer at the presentment sessions, and he would be voted for in both capacities, and he would be returned with two objects, both to represent the ratepayers at the Poor Law Board, and to represent them at the road sessions.

5116. For the person whom you would send in to sit upon the grand jury, would you not have a somewhat higher qualification than the qualification that you would require for a member of the baronial board?—I said that they might have a qualification of 50*l*. a-year, which is the present qualification for a grand juror, I think.

5117. But would not that qualification exclude a great number of very intelligent men who might be very desirable to sit upon the baronial board?—I do not want to go so high; but I thought the Honourable Member suggested that the qualification should be increased. According to my plan any man who was an elected guardian would be qualified to be selected to sit with the grand jury. The Poor Law Commissioners have fixed what that qualification is. No man can be returned as an elected guardian of the poor in my district who is not rated to the poor at 30*l*. a-year. It varies in different unions; in some unions it is 20*l*., according to the number of persons to be found; so that no one can be an elected guardian of the board, of which I am vice-chairman, who is not rated to the poor at 30*l*. a-year.

Mr. McCarthy Downing.

26 May 1868.

5118. Would it not be better to give them an opportunity of sending members direct in to the county board, instead of having them selected from the baronial board?—I would be quite satisfied with that. I do not care how you do it, provided you give the ratepayers the opportunity of selecting. I would prefer that the ratepayers themselves should select a man living in the barony to represent them on the grand jury.

5119. Would it not be desirable, in your opinion, to separate the criminal from the fiscal business of the grand jury, and to give to the sheriff the summoning of the grand jury as heretofore, for criminal purposes; and for fiscal purposes to have a distinct county board?—I quite agree in that.

5120. Would it not be also desirable, in your opinion, from your experience as a country gentleman, to have that board a continuous one, instead of its being terminated at each assizes?—I think you would find it very hard to find men always ready to discharge public business. I do not see how that could possibly be done.

5121. Of course I mean that the board is only to be called together as occasion might require?—I agree with the Honourable Member entirely, that the meetings ought to be more frequent than they are; I think that if they were held quarterly, instead of twice a-year, it would be a great advantage.

5122. Between one assizes and another will it not often occur that matters will arise in which it will be desirable to have some such body?—Clearly. As I said before, I think there ought to be a baronial board who would have certain powers between the two assizes.

5123. But, if an inundation took place in the county, or some large drainage works were contemplated, or a guarantee for a railway throughout the county were required, would it not then be desirable to have some body, like a county corporation, which could be called together for the purpose of discussing the desirability of, or necessity for, matters of that kind?—My recommendation would be that the board of guardians should be that body, who meet every week.

5124. Have they not sufficient duties at present, as a board of guardians, without imposing upon them that additional duty?—I do not think they would object to it at all; I think, on the contrary, that they would be very anxious to have the power of controlling the expenditure in their barony; and I think it would be a very desirable thing. You have them there constituted without any alteration in the law.

5125. But you must have two boards in the county; you must have the baronial board, and you must have the board of the county at large; how would you make the board of guardians perform the functions of both these bodies?—I do not propose that they should do so. The Honourable Member asked me the question as to whether it would not be necessary to have some constituted body between the assizes to entertain certain applications which might become necessary between the two assizes; I replied that I thought you had a board constituted in the board of guardians that would do so.

5126. But how will your baronial board be constituted; you will then have your board of guardians both as the board of the county at large, and as the baronial board?—The county at large sessions meet at given periods, and they meet in a different place, and you have so many magistrates there who might not be guardians at all.

5127. But I want to understand your plan; you say that the board of guardians now could perform all the functions that are at present performed by the baronial board, and you also say that the board of guardians could perform the functions of a fiscal board for the county at large; how could you get the same body to perform both functions?—I did not say that. The Honourable Member asked me whether there ought not to be some board that would take up and entertain matters arising between two assizes, and I said that the board of guardians are now constituted in such a way that I think it may be the board that would entertain those questions between the two assizes; I did not say that they were to be what you call the county board, or the grand jury, for fiscal purposes.

5128. Are you going to form your baronial board out of the board of guardians?—Yes.

5129. How are you going to form your county board out of the board of guardians?—I have answered that question already by allowing the ratepayers to select one representative to sit on the grand jury; I prefer the Honourable Member's plan to the one which I have myself suggested.

5130. And you would have the board of guardians to act as a baronial board?—Yes.

5131. And for the purposes of a county at large board, you would have them elected by the ratepayers distinct from the board of guardians?—Distinct from the board of guardians.

5132. *Chairman.*] I understood you to state to the Committee that there was a qualification required for being put upon the grand jury?—I was wrong if I put it in that way; what I meant to say was, that the Legislature considered that a man who was a 50 *l.* freeholder was fit to sit upon the grand jury, and that if he had a 50 *l.* freehold he should be selected in preference to anyone else; so far it is a qualification.

5133. Do you mean to say that the sheriff, after having called a 50 *l.* freeholder, or a 100 *l.* leaseholder, as a representative from each barony, is obliged by any Act of Parliament to call any particular person upon that grand jury?—He is not; but I say he is bound to have a representative from the barony who is a 50 *l.* freeholder, if he is in the barony and resident.

5134. He is bound to call him, but the person called need not attend?—He need not attend.

5135. After having called that 50 *l.* freeholder, may not the sheriff then call a person with no property whatever in the county?—He may, but he must be resident in the barony.

5136. The representative of the barony must be a resident?—Yes, he must.

5137. But after that representative has been called, may not an individual be called who is not resident and who has no property?—I think so; I think that is the construction of the law.

5138. How many poor law unions have you in the county of Cork?—I could not exactly state that at this moment.

5139. Are there a dozen?—There are a great many more.

5140. How many baronies are there in the county of Cork?—Twenty-three.

5141. Could those unions perform the baronial duties?—I think so, very well; there would be no difficulty about that; I have given that subject a good deal of thought.

5142. *Sir Colman O'Loghlen.*] I think you stated

stated that there are 23 baronies in the county of Cork?—Yes.

5143. Therefore, in fact, the sheriff in the county of Cork must have each barony represented?—Yes, he must.

5144. According to the Act of Parliament the barony representative must have lands to the value of 50 *l.*, or hold lands on lease to the value of 100 *l.*; were you not speaking of Cork alone when you said that a qualification was necessary?—Yes.

5145. In reference to the gentleman who was agent to the absentee nobleman, had he land to the value of 50 *l.*?—He had not an acre of land in the barony.

5146. How was it then that he happened to be on the grand jury?—You must ask the sheriff, or under sheriff that question.

5147. In that particular case there was no legal representative of the barony, as you say?—None at all.

5148. I have understood, from some questions that the Chairman has asked you, that you are in favour of dividing the county of Cork for fiscal purposes?—Certainly.

5149. I believe it is quite impossible that the fiscal business of the county can be done within the four days as it is now?—It is not done, and it is quite impossible to do it.

5150. Do you see any objection, if they divided the assize business, to its all being done in the city of Cork?—I object to that; but at present it would be of very great benefit to adopt what you suggest.

5151. Assuming that it could be done (though you are of course in favour of Skibbereen), do you think that it would be an advantage to divide the county of Cork even if you had two assizes held in the city?—It would be a decided advantage. I understand you, of course, to mean that you would have an assizes for the West Riding, and assizes for the East Riding, and two grand juries to meet in the county.

5152. With respect to the county officers you spoke about assistant county surveyors and county surveyors in general; do you know in your county, of county officers being kept on, and discharging their duties when they have become incapable from old age, or illness; have any cases of that kind occurred in your county where the grand jury did not wish to discharge them?—I am not aware of any case of that kind.

5153. But are you aware in the county of Cork of persons who are unable to discharge their duties being kept on, because there was no means of superannuating them?—I am not aware of any such case.

5154. In the county of Cork, does the clerk of the peace do his duty in person?—I don't know if I ever saw him at quarter sessions.

5155. Does he do his business by deputy?—He does his business by deputy.

5156. Can you tell me roughly what the total emoluments of the clerk of the peace in the county of Cork are supposed to be, including his salary and fees?—I should say that the clerkship of the peace must be worth, at the very lowest calculation, from 1,600 *l.* to 2,000 *l.* a year.

5157. And you say that he never attends to his business in person?—Never.

5158. Has he one deputy, or two deputies?—He has two, one for the East Riding and one for the West.

0.58.

5159. Are they paid by salary, or by fees, or how are they paid?—They are paid by salary.

Mr. Moriarty Downing.

26 May 1868.

5160. Can you tell the Committee what those salaries are?—I cannot; but I suspect that they are very small.

5161. Have you ever considered whether the clerks of the peace should not be bound to do their duty in person?—I always considered it to be a most extraordinary thing that clerks of the peace did not do their duty in person. It is a very important office.

5162. It is a most important office, so far as civil bill proceedings are concerned, is it not?—It is a most important office; but the answer to that is, that it would be impossible for him to do his duty in person, because there is only one clerk of the peace for the whole county.

5163. Are you aware that in other parts of Ireland great complaints are made that clerks of the peace do not do their duty in person?—I am aware of that.

5164. Do you think that in any new arrangements it should be made obligatory upon the clerk of the peace to do his duty in person, unless prevented by illness, or by any other sufficient reason?—I think so.

5165. The clerk of the Crown is a very efficient officer, is he not?—He is.

5166. He does his duty in person, does he not?—He does his duty in person.

5167. Have you ever considered the question of amalgamating the two offices of clerk of the peace and clerk of the Crown?—Yes.

5168. Do you think that one officer could do the two duties?—I think that he would be quite competent to do them.

5169. Would it be your opinion that the two offices should be in future amalgamated in any change in the law?—I think so; I would transfer the present fiscal duties of the clerk of the Crown to the secretary's office, and I would have all the fiscal business done there.

5170. That is to say, that you would transfer the fiscal business of the clerk of the Crown to the secretary, and the Crown business you would transfer to the new officer, either to be called the clerk of the peace or the clerk of the Crown?—I would.

5171. It has been suggested to me by Colonel Vandeleur that the clerk of the Crown acts as a kind of check upon the grand jury's secretary as regards the accounts, is that the case?—But with regard to the accounts, I would have the accounts audited as the poor-law union accounts are audited.

5172. I believe that the grand jury accounts are all audited now in the main?—Yes; but that is not satisfactory.

5173. Is it your opinion that there ought to be a more efficient audit of the accounts?—Yes; the accounts ought to be audited at the county court house, where every person would have an opportunity of attending.

5174. When you are speaking about the amalgamation of the two offices of the clerk of the Crown and clerk of the peace, of course you are aware that those two offices at present are appointed differently, the one by the Lord Lieutenant of the county and the other by the Crown?—Yes.

5175. Do you think that if those offices were amalgamated the new officer should be a person appointed by the Crown, and not by the Lord Lieutenant of the county?—I should not like to

deprive

Mr. *Maurice Downing.* — [illegible] May [illegible].

deprive the present Lord Lieutenant of the county of Cork of any privilege which he has; but of course the appointment ought to come from the Crown decidedly.

5176. Do you not think that, speaking generally, you would be more likely to get by that means a more efficient officer than you would get through the private influence of any nobleman or gentleman?—Certainly.

5177. You have given an opinion, have you not, as to the advisability of dividing the grand jury cess between landlord and tenant?—I hold a very strong opinion upon that point.

5178. And I understand you that your chief reason is not so much the natural justice of the case as that you think it would be an acceptable deference to public opinion in Ireland?—Yes.

5179. And so far as you are aware of the public opinion in the county of Cork, would it be in favour of dividing the cess?—Yes; take away that burden and they will say that it shows that Parliament is willing to hear them and to help them.

5180. And you think, without regard to the strict principles of political economy, that it is a boon which would be recognised as such by the people of Ireland?—Certainly.

5181. With regard to leases, you have stated that it would be a hardship upon the persons who had granted the leases if they were to be rendered liable for the whole of the county cess; but would not that hardship be done away with if you put a clause in the Act that in leases made before the passing of the Act the division should not apply?—Certainly.

5182. Supposing the law were to declare that you might deduct it from landlords who made leases, do you think that even that injustice would be more than compensated by the general satisfaction which it would give to the country?—I do.

5183. And I believe you yourself have given leases on some of your property?—I have made a good many leases.

5184. You would have no objection to pay the county cess?—Not the slightest.

5185. Supposing that all kinds of tenants, whether holding leases or not, were entitled to deduct half the grand jury cess, of course you would not apply that to leases for ever?—No; only to persons who occupy their own land.

5186. The reason why you would deduct it from landlords, is because they are interested in the improvement of the soil; but of course, where a landlord has made a lease for 100 years, he has no substantial interest; and therefore, you would not deduct it from those kind of leases?—I would not; I would say that in the case of any lease which was over 60 years, or which had 60 years to run, I would not deduct it.

5187. Have you ever in your professional experience observed the defect of the grand jury law, about compensation for consequential damages, which does exist at present?—I am aware that no such compensation can be given.

5188. In a case in which a new bridge was built, the road being raised up to the bridge, and the houses at the sides being by that means put in a hollow; is it not the case, that at present, the owners of those houses, the houses not being taken, can get no compensation?—It is.

5189. And it has often occurred that damage has arisen from public works, for which the persons injured could get no compensation under the grand jury law; but you are aware that under the Lands Clauses Consolidation Act, you can get compensation for such damage?—Yes.

5190. Do you think that it would be an improvement, if under the grand jury law the owners of houses and land should be entitled to get compensation for consequential damage, as well as for land, or buildings actually taken?—Certainly, I think that it would be very desirable that under the grand jury laws, persons should have the same power of obtaining compensation for damage as under the Lands Clauses Consolidation Act.

WILLIAM WENTWORTH FITZWILLIAM DICK, Esq., a Member of the House; Examined.

W. W. F. Dick, Esq. M.P.

5191. *Chairman.*] You are a Member of the House of Commons, and represent the county of Wicklow, do you not?—Yes.

5192. You have been a grand juror and a magistrate of the county for many years, I believe?—Between 30 and 40 years.

5193. And therefore you have had an opportunity of seeing the working of the grand jury laws?—Yes.

5194. Have you also resided a good deal in England, and do you possess property in England? I have a great deal.

5195. And are you acquainted with the way in which the roads and public works in England are carried out?—Not, of course, so well as in Ireland; but tolerably well.

5196. From your experience as a grand juror, what is your opinion of the grand jury system in Ireland?—My opinion of the grand jury system in Ireland as compared with any other system in England or Europe, with which I am acquainted, and I have seen a great deal of Europe, is that it is eminently and by far the best system that I know, subject, of course, to defects which I see no difficulty in remedying.

5197. Do you think that it is not an expensive system, considering the work that it accomplishes?—I do not think that it is an expensive system, when you come to consider the return which is given for the outlay, and also the great increase in the property upon which the tax is levied.

5198. Do you consider that, although the actual amount raised under the grand jury presentments has increased, still considering the great increase in the value of property in Ireland, the rate of taxation has not increased?—I do. From my observation in my county in my time, I know practically that property has increased in value more than one-third, and I do not think that the taxation has increased at all in that proportion, whilst I know that the public works have been greatly extended, and that the roads and bridges are in a much better state.

5199. Do you believe that the roads, and bridges, and public works in Ireland are carried out as well as in any country which you know?—I do, but you will please to observe that though I know a great deal of Ireland, and in particular I know a great deal of the Counties Kildare, Carlow, Wexford, and Dublin, of course I am speaking particularly of Wicklow, wherein my experience has principally been acquired.

5200. You

5300. You are probably acquainted also with the working of the poor-law system as a guardian?—I am, but of course not to the same extent, because I have served a vast deal longer as a grand juror, and I have given those duties more attention.

5301. Which do you believe to be the more expensive, the grand jury system or the poor-law system?—I myself believe that the poor-law system is extremely expensive, in comparison with the return which is got for it. Taking into consideration the staff, the buildings, and the whole thing, speaking of that with which I am acquainted, namely, the union in the County of Wicklow, I should say that of the two, so far as my experience goes, there is not much difference in point of expense. I think that the staffs of both (if I might apply the term "staff" to the officers of the grand jury, the county officers), are pretty much upon an equal scale, as far as my experience goes, in the County of Wicklow.

5302. (General *Dunne*.) Is it not the case that with regard to the poor-rate, 6 *d.* out of every 1 *s.* is paid for management?—Not only is 6 *d.* in every 1 *s.* paid for management, but there are electoral divisions in the union, within which my principal property lies, wherein if the money that is raised upon the electoral division was expended upon the paupers of that division, we might send a fellow about in a carriage, and keep him upon beef and claret.

5303. Therefore, it is a much more expensive administration, is it not?—Yes, I speak of a particular case, where there is one old woman in a very rich electoral division, and the rate of course levied for the maintenance of that old woman would be very trifling if it was merely for her maintenance, but then you have the rate levied for the union at large, with the expenses and staff, and so forth. That old woman might be sent about in a carriage, as I tell you, if her electoral division was relieved of those expenses, and she might be kept like a lady.

5304. Mr. *Dawson*.) What union is that?—It is the union of Baltinglass, of which I am speaking.

5305. *Chairman*.) You are aware, of course, as an experienced grand juror, that grand juries have very little power of initiating taxation at present?—They have very little power.

5306. The powers of a grand jury are chiefly confined to passing a veto on, or approving new works which have been approved at the presentment sessions?—It is very much so.

5307. Do you believe it to be desirable, that a body, such as a grand jury, should exist which is composed in the main of the landed proprietors for the purpose of considering those works which have been passed at presentment sessions?—I do not consider it advisable to establish any body in connection with the grand jury, either as superior to it in authority, or emanating from it, nor do I think that there is any necessity for it. I think that it would lead to a great deal of confusion, and that it would be productive of no good.

5308. I think that you misunderstood my question. What I meant to ask you was this, whether you considered it desirable that there should exist in every county in Ireland some body, let us suppose the grand jury, composed of the landed proprietors who would have the power of over-hauling the proceedings of the presentment sessions?—I do not see the necessity of it, or the good of it.

5309. You do not see therefore any good in the existence of the grand jury?—Yes, I see in it very great good.

5310. What is the use of the grand jury at present?—I think that the grand jury is a superior power controlling the expenditure of the county.

5311. And do you consider it desirable that that body should exist?—I do; and I think that there is an advantage in its not being always the same body of men, that is to say, there being some little variation from time to time which must always arise from some men not attending, and others being called in their place. I think that it infuses new blood occasionally. It is not known exactly who attends, and who does not attend.

5312. Would you approve of any alteration in the constitution of the grand jury?—Very little.

5313. What alteration would you suggest?—I think if it were practicable (here there is the difficulty), every barony ought to be represented where it can be represented consistently with having the proper class of men on it. Now, I will take a case in point in my own county. There is the barony of Shillelah, which, I think, belongs to one man; it is very desirable that there should be a representative for that barony, but I do not think it would be desirable to put any man from the barony upon the grand jury. I think that he ought to be an educated man, and a man who knows something of what he is about. I do not think that it would do to take an ordinary farmer or an ordinary cesspayer, and put him there. It would be giving him too much authority. He has quite enough in the lower House, if I might so call it; in the road sessions, where the associated cesspayers represent him.

5314. Mr. *Dawson*.) Is the proprietor in this barony, to which you allude, resident in the county?—It is Lord Fitzwilliam. He is represented by his agent, and his agent is generally called; and when the agent can attend, I think it is very desirable that he should, but sometimes the agent does not attend, and then they try to have a first-class tenant. If they can get a first-class tenant, which occasionally they can do, it is very well, but I would not make it imperative upon the high sheriff, in the event of his failing to get a first-class tenant, to call somebody.

5315. *Chairman*.) How would you define a first-class tenant, except by the amount of his rent, or by the amount of taxation which he paid?—It is so difficult to define it that I say I would not alter materially the present constitution of the grand jury.

5316. You would not think it advisable to oblige every barony to be represented on the grand jury?—I think that it is very desirable; but I think that, as from the necessities of the case you can have nothing perfect, you must leave it very much to the judgment and the option of the high sheriff.

5317. So that you would leave it very much as it is at present?—Very much as it is at present.

5318. Would you approve of any alteration in the constitution of the presentment sessions?—Very little. The only alteration that I would recommend, if any, is, that the cesspayers should be elected by ballot. At present they are balloted for at the assembling of the road sessions

W. W. F. Dick, Esq., M.P.

2d May 1868.

dens from a list returned by the grand jury. I would have no objection to have the list, which is returned by the grand jury taken by ballot from a list returned by the county officer, who now returns it, and which should comprise the principal cesspayers of the barony; but care must be taken that you do not, if you are drawing them by ballot out of a hat, for instance, get all from one corner of the barony. There would be the difficulty. Supposing that this table before me represented a barony, you should have them from the different districts, because, by the ballot, you might have all the cesspayers from one particular spot, and then there would be an evil arising. I think the associated cesspayers ought, as much as possible, to be scattered.

5219. Would you think it a satisfactory proposal if the collector, instead of being obliged to return the hundred highest cesspayers from the whole of the barony, were obliged to return the hundred highest cesspayers from each parish, and if out of those there should be a ballot?—I should have no objection whatever to that so long as the parish is in the county; but a parish may go into two or three counties. I would keep it within the county.

5220. Are there instances of parishes going into two or three counties?—Plenty of them.

5221. (General *Dunne*.) But are not the parishes generally conterminous with the baronies?—In my county, on my property where I reside, the parish is called the parish of Kiltegan, and the parish of Kiltegan runs into the county of Carlow. Then, again, there would be a difficulty to define the Roman Catholic and the Protestant parishes, which have not always strictly the same boundaries, but I would object in any case to go outside the boundary of the county.

5222. Could not that be done by keeping to the barony?—Yes, by keeping to the barony.

5223. (Mr. *Dawson*.) Or the town land?—Or the town land; that would be better still; but the objection to the town lands is, that some of them are extremely small, though some of them are large enough.

5224. (*Chairman*.) Do you not think that the cases of those parishes which go into two counties might be met by some provision, and that, as a general rule, the parish would be a fair area to take?—I think it might be met; but if a parish went into two counties there must be so small a portion in one county that it would be practically not worth sending a representative from.

5225. Do you think that there would be any harm, in such cases, in allowing the whole of that parish to be considered in the county in which the larger portion was?—I do not know that there would.

5226. Are the electoral divisions always conterminous with the baronies?—Not always. The union of Baltinglass extends into Kildare and Carlow.

5227. (Mr. *Dawson*.) The different electoral divisions are confined to the county, are they not?—That I could not say.

5228. (*Chairman*.) But, at all events, what you suggest is, that there should be some smaller division of the baronies, and that the cesspayers should be balloted for out of those smaller divisions of the baronies to attend at the sessions?—I think that would be very desirable, taking, of course, the *bonâ fide* large cesspayers. I would not go below a certain limit to the lowest of the cesspayers. You must strike a line below which you would not go; but those are little matters of detail.

5229. I suppose, as you state so strongly your approval of the present grand jury system, that you would be opposed to the setting up of any system of baronial or county boards?—I would. I think that it would lead to an increase of expense. I think that it would lead to extravagance. I think it would lead to a great deal of party work, a great deal of evil, and to no one good.

5230. Could you mention to the Committee any reasons for believing that there would be greater extravagance at this board than at the grand jury, or at sessions? If you will kindly give me more clearly than you have done what the nature of the board is which you would suggest being set up, I will endeavour to answer the question. I presume that you mean a body of elected persons.

5231. It has been suggested to the Committee by Mr. M'Carthy Downing, and by other witnesses before the Committee, that it would be desirable to have baronial boards partially elected and partially composed of magistrates, such as the Poor Law Boards are at present; and that there should be also county boards of a somewhat similar composition, partially elected, and partially the representatives of property; would you approve of that?—I would disapprove of it, first, because I think it is useless; you sweep away the present grand jury system altogether, and I think that the evil arising from it would be this, that the body of gentlemen who would be elected as cesspayers, would be in many cases the instruments of the great proprietors; for instance, take a case in point; on my estate (I openly say that in my own defence, I would do it), a candidate would be started in my own district, and I should naturally put out my strength to have a man elected who I felt would view matters in the same light as I do; and I believe that the same feeling would operate throughout the length and breadth of the land.

5232. Do you believe that the elected members of these boards would be in many instances the nominees of the landed proprietors?—Of a great landed proprietor, or of half a dozen small ones united, and I do not believe that any good will arise in any case.

5233. Would your argument upon this point apply equally to a proposal to have the cesspayers at the sessions elected, instead of being chosen by ballot as you propose?—No, I object to election for the same reason; if I was only to consider the interests of the class to which I myself belong, I would say, let them be elected, because I am quite sure that in my county, as a rule, we should elect men who would cooperate with us, but if you elect them by ballot, then it would be a matter of chance.

5234. You consider that the substitution of election for the principle of selection by ballot, would lead to strengthening the hands of the landed proprietors?—I do; and I am quite satisfied with the strength they have already, if it is left with them.

5235. Do you not believe that a strong feeling exists in Ireland that the taxpayers should be directly represented by persons elected by themselves?—I think that is a very beautiful theory, but I think in practice you would find it as I stated, namely, that the representatives would be

the

W. H. F. Dick, Esq., M.P.

26 May 1868.

the nominees of the principal men in the district, whereas if you did it by ballot that objection would be obviated.

5236. Do you not consider that even if they were the nominees of the proprietors, in many instances it would satisfy that public feeling which exists to a certain extent?—It may be throwing dust into their eyes.

5237. Do you not think that the proprietors would be able as you say to protect themselves?—In that case they certainly would be, and I think that, as it is, they can do so.

5238. You have probably heard of another suggestion, namely, the division of the payment of the county cess between landlord and tenant?—I have.

5239. Would you approve of that?—I would not. It is not because I want to throw a burden upon the tenant and to relieve the landlord, but because I believe that it would be the same in the end. You could not in justice throw upon a landlord, whose lands were let under lease at present, any of the tax, because the lands are let subject to it, and in all future cases the landlord would naturally cover the tax, by an addition to the rent of 1 s. or 1 s. 6 d., and in my belief it would, if anything, be a little more, for the land-landlord would take care to be upon the right side as a rule throughout the kingdom. It is but the law of human nature that he should be.

5240. But do you not consider that if in future the system, as you say, righted itself, and the landlord received an increased rent for his land, it would be desirable that, as he has so much the guidance and control over the expenditure of the county, he should have a direct interest in every variation which takes place in the county rate?—As I before said, I do not think that any good would be derived from it, whilst this evil to my mind would arise. I believe that of the two classes of people the cess paying or farming class and the landlords or upper class, the lower class is a much more extravagant class. I believe that if it was left to themselves, they are more under the influence of contractors for roads and their friends than the upper classes are; and I believe if they were even in imagination (for it would only be that) relieved of the taxation by the landlord being called upon to pay the whole of the rate, they would be more disposed, assuming that they have influence upon the Board or upon the cess-payers their representatives, to an increased expenditure.

5241. That is on the supposition of the landlord paying the whole of the tax is it not?—In reality, I deny that he would ever have to pay it. Where the lands were held from year to year, I maintain that he would cover the tax by an addition to the rent.

5242. You do not mean to say that he would change his rent every year?—No; but I mean upon an average over the whole of his estate. His agent or himself would pretty well understand what the taxation of the whole property was, and he would strike an average; one man might pay a few pence more than another, but upon the whole the tenantry would pay the rate. It is the same with tithes at this moment.

5243. But when once the average was made, and the rent fixed, would not the landlord afterwards, if he paid half the county cess, have a direct interest in every variation which took place in the rate?—I think that the landlord has now a double interest; he has an interest, first of all, of course, in controlling the expenditure; and then he has an interest in seeing that the highways and byways of the county are kept in good order. He would not have a bit more interest under the proposed alteration.

5244. At present, when the rent is fixed, it is of no consequence to the landlord whether the county cess be 1 s., or 9 d., or 1 s. 6 d., or 2 s. in the pound, as far as the payment of the tax goes. His rental is not diminished in the slightest degree by the increase of the tax, nor is it increased by the diminution of it?—I think that he has a very great interest, because if the tenantry are overburthened with taxation it will ultimately reach him.

5245. If the taxation were increased to a very large amount it would be so; but do you think that a change from 1 s. to 1 s. 6 d., for instance, would have that effect?—I think every shilling cess put upon the tenant's back over and above what is sufficient for the wants of the district, of course, must affect the tenant, and must affect his status, and in the end must affect the landlord.

5246. But it does not directly affect the landlord in each individual case, does it?—Not directly; but practically I find that the landlords are always very jealous of excessive taxation.

5247. Would your objection to this division of the county cess apply to cases of new lettings?—I do not suppose that you could with justice apply it where there are leases. I only see one good which would arise from it, and that is, that the collecting would be easier, like the tithe. Instead of collecting in driblets, you would collect from the agent or the landlord the whole sum.

5248. Mr. *Dawson*.] Are not the landlords occupiers of farms on their own lands to a great extent?—Certainly. I do not know a single resident landlord in my county, nor do I know of any in Ireland, with the exception of one or two, and even they are non-residents, who are not occupiers in their own persons.

5249. Therefore they must all be interested, must they not?—They must be interested. We are obliged all of us to farm. I only know of one man who does not do so; and he lets his land to his agent.

5250. Do you not consider it rather an unfair thing to charge the landlords over Ireland, generally, with being indifferent as to the extent of the county cess?—I am sure of it. As I said just now to the honourable Chairman, my experience has been that magistrates and landlords, and grand jurors have always been jealous of excessive taxation, and if (as I hold to be almost practically impossible under the present law, as I may afterwards explain) if an attempt is made to carry what is technically known as a job, you will carry it with the greatest ease if you come to deal with the nominated cesspayers, but the moment that you come before the grand jury, that moment your difficulties spring up, and there you are stopped *in limine*.

5251. *Chairman*.] But to return to the question of the division of the county cess; as I understand you, you hold that at present the landed proprietors in reality pay the whole of this tax, it being a tax upon the land directly or indirectly?—I hold that the land pays it, no matter who is the instrument; out of land you cannot get more than a certain sum, a portion being rent, and a portion bearing the tax.

5252. That being the case, and the landlord paying

W. W. F. Dick, Esq., M.P.

28 May 1858.

paying the whole of the taxation which is placed upon land, and as you are aware a popular impression existing in Ireland that he pays none of it, would it not be desirable to make him pay at least a portion of that which he now pays directly instead of indirectly?—You have assumed a thing which I cannot admit, namely, that it is popularly assumed that the landlord pays nothing, and that the tenant pays it all. From my experience I do not think that the men of my country are such geese as that; in my experience they know very well how the real fact is, and that if they were relieved from taxation it would be put upon him by the landlords. Of course there is a stratum of very wretched creatures who live in hovels at the foot of mountains, who are scarcely reached by taxation, but the moment you come to a *bona fide* farmer he knows very well the real state of the case.

5253. But do you not think that in other parts of Ireland, putting your own county aside, there is a popular impression that this taxation is borne by the occupiers?—I know that it is said so.

5254. Then supposing it to be the case that a great number of people in Ireland, the great bulk of the occupiers in certain parts of Ireland, believed that they paid the whole of the tax, and supposing it also to be the case as you hold that the landlords are in reality the payers of the tax, would it not be desirable in such a case for the landlords to pay directly what they are now paying indirectly, and thereby to do away with this impression if it exists?—I do not think it would. I do not think that the sentimental relief which the tenant would receive, because after all it is only sentimental, would amount to such a gain as would make it desirable to effect that change.

5255. What harm would it do to the landlord?—The harm that it would do to the landlord would be, as I before said, that the moment that those men come in imagination (because after all it is only in imagination) to think that the landlord was paying it, they themselves will be less disposed to economy than if they thought they were paying the whole thing.

5256. But supposing that that were coupled with the system of having elected representatives, would you say that the landlords would not be able to protect themselves against any extravagance?—I think they would, but I would not drive them to that unnecessarily; I think that it would be a very mischievous thing to drive men into such a position that they must arm themselves at every point to defend themselves against such evils.

5257. Do you think that if the cess were divided between landlord and tenant the extravagance of the cesspayers would become so great as to injure the landlord?—I think that the cesspayer is a less careful and more unreflecting man than the landlord, and I think that he is more open to influence as to expenditure. I always remark in my county that in cases of repairs, or the making of new roads, or other such matters, our contractors always try to canvass the representative cesspayers, or those who they imagine will be so. They never attempt, or very rarely attempt, to influence the magistrates or the gentry before the day comes. They know that they would not be listened to; I speak, of course, as a rule.

5258. Your objection to the division of the county cess would be the fear that the cesspayers would be still more extravagant if that system were adopted?—I think so, and I do not want to give them more power than they have at present.

5259. But were it not for that, do you not think that it would be desirable, supposing that a feeling exists such as I mentioned before, that the landlord should pay directly what he now pays indirectly?—As I before said, I do not think that any real advantage would accrue except that it would make the collection of the county cess an easier matter because it would be collected in bulk from each landlord instead of in detail from the tenants.

5260. Have you any observation to make as to injuries done to bridges, and filling up watercourses, and a variety of works of that description?—That would very much apply to the question of malicious damages; there is a great deal of injury done in my county to the bridges and watercourses, but in particular to the bridges by turf carriers from the mountain districts to the towns; they throw the cut stone off the battlements, and there is scarcely an assizes where there are not presentments put in for the repair of bridges which were only repaired a year or two before; I think that that is done from sheer maliciousness; I do not think that it is done particularly to make work for masons.

5261. What would you propose to do to remedy that?—That is rather a difficult question to answer, because I do not know how it is to be remedied; if you are to try to remedy it by something on the principle of malicious damage, I do not think that that would succeed; I do not think you would ever get an Irishman, as a rule, to give evidence against any fellow for malicious injury, merely by levying a little tax; he would rather pay his extra shilling than give evidence.

5262. Do you approve generally of the principle of granting compensation for malicious injuries?—In general I do; I think the good arises in this way; if a man wishes to injure another, and he knows that the man will get compensation he will be less disposed to do it; but I do not think that it leads to the discovery of the crime, because you will never get the district which is to be taxed either to watch, or if they found it out, to tell.

5263. You do not consider, then, that the existence of this system of compensation for malicious injuries leads to the discovery of the offenders?—No; but I think it prevents the injuries being committed very frequently.

5264. Do you not think that very often applications are made for compensation for malicious injuries where there was no malicious injury suffered at all?—I am sure of it, and there comes the difficulty in dealing with malicious injuries by burning; in the case of malicious injuries such as houghing cattle, hamstringing horses, cutting their tails off, or putting their eyes out, or cutting the teats off cows, those horrible things which I have known done, there can be no mistake about their being malicious, and in all those cases I would make it imperative and instantaneous; but the burning of cabins and outhouses and haggards is a very nice question, because there is no man in the world more careless than our countryman; it is not two years ago that I went into my own haggard, and I saw one man on a rick thatching with a pipe in his mouth, and a fellow attending him carrying straw, up to his middle in loose straw, smoking also; they will all do that, and then if their houses get burnt and there is in the

wide

wide world a man who they think is their enemy, they will try and put it upon him; but that only applies to those cases of burning.

5265. Mr. *Dawson*.] Are there any flax mills in your neighbourhood?—There are no flax mills; in my county; the magistrates are excessively jealous before they will present for malicious injuries; if it is for the burning of a thatched house it must be shown past all doubt, but the moment you come to deal with injuries to cattle there can be no mistake about their being malicious.

5266. *Chairman*.] I understand you, then, to advocate the continuance of the system of compensation for injuries to cattle, but not with regard to burning?—I will not say with regard to burning, because then it would be always burnings, whereas now it is sometimes injuries to cattle, but I think that if it could be restricted, it would be advantageous.

5267. Do you not think that it would be better to have these cases of malicious injury tried before a court, such as the court of quarter sessions?—I think that it might be desirable; perhaps it might be more sifted there.

5268. General *Dunne*.] Can they not try it by a jury at the assizes?—It can be so tried.

5269. *Chairman*.] But it cannot be tried now, can it, excepting some parties subscribe towards the expense of the traverse?—That is the case.

5270. Mr. *Maguire*.] The general impression which I receive from your evidence is, that you do not place very much reliance upon the associated cesspayers, either as regards their wisdom or their economy?—Very little; to tell you the truth, the only advantage which ever I saw arise from their associating first of all, was a sentimental one; they were pleased at it, and then they were able to give information, coming from a district which they knew something about, and which the magistrates, perhaps, might not know.

5271. As a rule, I believe they do not attend very well?—As a rule, they are very careless about attending.

5272. And you say that they are less reflective than any other class?—So I think.

5273. And that, generally speaking, they are not economical or careful?—They are not as economical, careful, or reflecting as the upper class.

5274. These men are selected by chance, at the present moment, more or less. First of all they are nominated by a grand juror, who acts under no responsibility?—First they are nominated by the county officer.

5275. A grand juror, who is responsible to no person, selects a number of names, does he not?—The grand jury, not the grand juror.

5276. Does not the grand juror select for his his own barony?—Not as a matter of course; the grand jury selects the highest ratepayers, generally speaking, as much as possible, I have always observed; taking them so that, they would represent different districts of the barony.

5277. But do they mostly select the most intelligent and trustworthy men?—I have found them in Wicklow always do it.

5278. You speak from knowledge of your own county, when you say that the most intelligent and trustworthy men are selected, and yet you have found that they are generally unreflecting and extravagant?—As a body they are so, but the most intelligent of that body are selected.

5279. They take care to consider who is the most intelligent man; do they consider who is the most independent in the formation of his opinion, or in his conduct?—They select whom they consider to be the best man to represent the district, that is to say, they try to scatter them over the whole district.

W. W. F. Dick, Esq., M.P.

16 May 1868.

5280. And unhappily the result of this great care on the part of the grand jury is, that they select a thriftless, extravagant, and unreflecting set of men?—I do not say that; I say that the body as compared with the educated and upper class, are less reflecting and less economical, but from that less reflecting and less economical class, I say that the grand jury, according to my experience, have selected the best 12 men from the list put before them to represent the barony.

5281. Supposing that they select a certain number, it is left to chance, is it not, whether the best men of that number afterwards have the management of the affairs of the barony?—Then after that it is balloted.

5282. Is not that a very blundering system. Supposing that there are, on an average, 12 men, but that six of these are better men than the other six, would it not be far better to have these selected distinctly, than to leave it to the blundering accident of the ballot to pick them out?—I apprehend that the motive of the Legislature in adopting that second ordeal of the ballot was to prevent any partiality, first of all, by making the county officer send in a list of 100 of the highest cesspayers, and then for the grand jury to select 12 or 24, whichever the number may be, of the best men for it; and then again there is the ordeal of selection by ballot.

5283. But does the ballot, in point of fact, select the six best men. Supposing six to be taken out of 12?—Of course, in anything done by ballot there can be no choice. You first take 12 of the best men, and it does not follow that, supposing that you take six out of the 12 by ballot, you will get the best six. That is a matter of chance.

5284. Do not you yourself think that if these men were elected by the ratepayers, who certainly have a very strong interest in having the best men chosen, as they are the payers of the tax, it would be far better than that they should be appointed under the present system?—I do not, because, as I stated before, I believe that the influence of the great proprietors of the district would return their nominees.

5285. You are in favour of the present system, and you say that you are so from consulting the interests of the occupiers?—The interests of all parties.

5286. You said that you would less consult the interests of the occupiers if you were in favour of election. Are not the occupiers quite entitled to form an opinion of what is their own interest?—I think they are, but I think there are other interests besides the tenants' interests.

5287. As regards the occupiers, generally speaking, above a certain standard, do you not think they are as acute and intelligent a set of people as any in the world?—I think they are as acute and intelligent set of people.

5288. And do they not understand their own interests quite as well as the landed gentry understand theirs?—I think they understand their interests very well.

5289. Is this such an abstruse mystery that they cannot understand at once what is their real interest in this matter?—I think that it is a very

W. W. F. Dick, Esq. M.P.
16 May 1862.

abstruse mystery. It is an abstruse mystery of the organization of humanity. I think that the operation of a man's interest tells the moment his superior comes in contact with him, and I believe that those acute and intelligent men, of whom you speak, are so acute and so intelligent that the moment their superiors, and their landlords, come in contact with them in a question of that sort, they would feel their own interest to be such that they would go with the landlord in the election of the officers.

5290. You have knowledge and experience of the operation of the poor law system, have you not?—Yes.

5291. Have you seen the class of men who are elected guardians in the rural districts, or in towns?—Yes.

5292. Have you heard any complaints of their want of intelligence, their want of capacity, their want of punctuality in attendance on their duties, or of their want of fairness or independence?—I have heard complaints.

5293. Generally?—I have. I myself have taken part in removing guardians by our legitimate influence at the next election, for incapacity, and in putting in efficient men.

5294. But it is not in the power of the constituent body if they found a man a blundering fool, or a sycophant, or in any way unworthy of their confidence to remove him?—It is in their power.

5295. Have those who pay the rates any power whatever over the selection of the man who is to be associated with the magistrates in imposing those rates upon them?—Of course he is elected only for the moment.

5296. He is not responsible to them for his conduct, is he?—Certainly not.

5297. He may blunder; he may be a fool; he may be incapable; he may be extravagant, or he may be ill-reflecting, but they cannot remove him?—Of course; but he is only temporarily there, and the other is elected permanently.

5298. May not the same man be put on again?—No.

5299. When may he be put on again?—The year after that again; he may, or he may not be put on again.

5300. At any rate they have no control over him whatever?—No.

5301. But if an elected guardian does not satisfy those who have elected him, they have the power of removing him, have they not?—Of course they have; but not until the end of 12 months; they have the power of not electing him again at the next election, whenever it is.

5302. Is not that every 12 months?—They have the power to remove him at the next election.

5303. As to the division of the rate, you say that if the cess were divided between the occupier and the landlord, the landlord would re-impose it in the shape of rent on the tenant?—I believe he would.

5304. Do you think that is fair?—I do, and I think that you would do it if you were in that position, and I think you would be justified in doing it.

5305. We have had a landlord before us to-day who said he would not do it?—I would do so.

5306. Do you not think that the landlord derives as much benefit from all the county improvements as the occupier does?—I do not think he derives nearly so much.

5307. From roads, for instance, through his property?—I do not think that he derives so much; I think that the farming class derive more benefit, and I do not think that they themselves are aware of the benefit which they derive, because there are certain things which they never look into. There is the wear and tear of carts and horses from the bad roads, upon which they do not reflect.

5308. With regard to roads only, is it the fact that the spaces upon which the roads are made, are very frequently included in the rent of the tenant?—That, I believe, is a custom which obtained in my county in olden times. I find it in leases on my estate which were granted 100 years ago, but it is not done so in my day.

5309. I am not speaking of an individual case at all; but is it a general rule, on the contrary, that roads are included in the rent of the tenant?—I do not think that in all new roads now it is so included.

5310. Is not the landlord generally compensated for the road?—No, it is the tenant.

5311. In all cases?—In all cases that I have ever known; that is to say, where a new road is run through a farm in the occupation of A. B., the landlord is not always compensated, but the tenant generally is. The landlord would say that otherwise he would resist the road being made; and if his influence was sufficient, of course there would be an end to it; but if it is made with the landlord's consent, I have always found him to give up the right of the land.

5312. Is not the rent of the land for the road included afterwards in the rent of the tenant?—Certainly not in my experience.

5313. Should you be surprised if you heard witnesses speaking of other parts of the country, and even surveyors stating that that practice was adopted in their district?—I should not be surprised, because I think that it is very likely it is so in many cases.

5314. If that were the case, do you think that the tenant would have so much interest in the maintenance of the road as his landlord would have?—I think he would.

5315. You do not think that it would be fair to put any portion of the charge upon the landlord?—Assuming that a new road is made through a district, the tenant gets compensation for the land taken from him, and, getting that compensation, he ought to pay the rent that you speak of.

5316. But, according to your opinion, supposing that the law were changed, and that the cess were divided equally between the landlord and the tenant, the tenant would have no advantage practically, inasmuch as it would be put upon him in the shape of rent?—I think so. It is so practically in the case of the tithe.

5317. (Colonel Cooper.) You stated, did you not, with regard to dividing the cess between landlord and tenant, that it might effect a saving in the collection?—I do not think you would save a farthing.

5318. Do you think it would be more easily collected?—If you threw the whole burden of the payment on the landlord, I think then that it would be more easily collected.

5319. I understood you to say that if you divided the cess you thought it would be easier to collect it?—No; because if that were done, then the cess-collector would have, of course, to collect the moiety.

5320. He would collect it, I presume, as he collects

lects the poor rate; collecting the whole from the occupier, who deducts half from the landlord when he pays his rent?—It would be easier if you collected the whole of the county cess from the landlord, because of course the collector, who would have but a few individuals to call upon for payment, would receive it in bulk, with half the labour, and it ought, therefore, to be done more cheaply.

5321. With regard to injuries to the parapets of bridges, would it not be possible to make the contractors responsible for all bridges and parapets on their section of the road?—At present we are trying to do that in Wicklow.

5322. Would not that meet the difficulty which you have suggested?—When they propose for contracts for repairs, we oblige them to include all damages of that sort; but then they immediately put it on, so that, practically, the cost of the damage is still borne by the county.

5323. With regard to the road sessions, generally speaking, the magistrates are large occupiers in your county, are they not?—Yes.

5324. And, in fact, the interests of the landlords and of the occupiers are common?—They are in my county, certainly.

5325. Is not that the case throughout the greater portion of England and Ireland?—Throughout Ireland their interests are in common.

5326. Is it not very seldom in a division that the magistrates are all one way and the cesspayers another?—I have always said that they are in the same boat.

5327. Have you ever known an instance in which the whole of the magistrates voted one way and the cesspayers another?—Never.

5328. A presentment may be disputed, but you will find the magistrates and the cesspayers pretty equally divided in the majority or in the minority?—True; I never knew them separated into two distinct parties.

5329. The presentment sessions are considered now to be irresponsible to anybody, but does not the right of traverse, if a certain job is perpetrated, give a certain control to the occupiers of the barony?—They are responsible to one another and to themselves as a body in general. I do not think it is possible now, if men do their duty, for a job to be perpetrated. Let us take a case in point, such as the making of a new road or of a bridge. First of all, they have to placard the churches and chapels and police barracks, and places of public resort with the applications for presentment to execute the new work, to give it publicity. Then it has to come before the magistrates and associated cesspayers, and there it is discussed. Then it has to go before the grand jury, and there it is discussed; and then it is not carried; it must go back again and wait another year, and be again published at the public places of resort, and again come before a fresh body of associated cesspayers (not the same body which existed before), and it must again be approved of by them, and then go before a new grand jury, and be there canvassed, and be there approved of; and, finally, it is passed, for it is liable to be traversed before the judge of assize.

5330. The judge is the final authority, is he not?—The judge is the final authority.

5331. It is not passed until the judge fiats the presentment?—Not until the judge fiats the presentment.

5332. Do you not consider that that gives a very considerable indirect control to the cesspayers of the district?—I do not think that human ingenuity could devise any greater control to prevent jobbing.

5333. Do you think that the elected guardians or cesspayers would give more control?—Nothing would give more control than the existing system to prevent jobbing.

5334. Mr. *Dawson*.] With reference to the question put by the honourable Member for Cork about the roads, the same thing exists in England, does it not?—I understand it does, but I cannot speak from a knowledge of England as I do from a knowledge of Ireland. I am a large landed proprietor in England, but I am not well acquainted with the working of it yet.

5335. As to extravagance, or possible extravagance, on the part of those associated cesspayers and the body which they represent principally, do you find that the application for new roads generally proceeds, in the first place, from the cesspayers themselves?—I think that applications for new roads and repairs proceed more frequently from the cesspayers than from the magistrates, from my experience.

5336. With regard to the collection of rates, do you think that the poor-rate and the county cess could be collected together at one period of the year, instead of twice in the year?—That is a question upon which I should not like to give a decided answer; unless I saw my way clear, I should not like to make a change in the present system, though perhaps the two rates might be collected together.

5337. It is said that their being separate now causes great extra expenditure in the collection of both rates, whereas, if they were simultaneously collected, they might be collected by one person, at a reduced rate; what would be your view as to that?—They might be, but whether the farming class would like to pay the whole in one payment rather than two, I am not prepared to say; that would entail careful accounts to keep the two items of the poor-rate and the cess distinct.

5338. Do you know the way in which the poor-law accounts are audited now?—Yes.

5339. Do you think that that is superior to the way in which the audit of the county expenditure is conducted?—When I give an opinion, I like to be very decided, and I am not certain as to that, but I think that it would be very desirable to abolish the office of treasurer in counties.

5340. Prospectively it is already done?—It is.

5341. You believe that the duties can be very efficiently performed by a county bank?—Certainly.

5342. Do you think that there could be any further amalgamation and reduction of the county officers?—Yes; I think that great economy might be effected in many ways. I think that the clerk of the peace and the clerk of the Crown, as far as I can see, might be one; in my county I am sure that they might.

5343. Do you think the lunatic asylums could be transferred from the present boards to the Poor Law Commissioners?—I do; I think that amalgamation might be carried out in many instances with most beneficial effects, and great saving. I think that the tendency of the present day is extravagance in respect to staffs, and all public officers' salaries.

5344. Do you think that a good case could be made

W. W. F. Dick, Esq., M.P.

3d May 1858.

W. W. F. Dick, Esq., M.P.

26 May 1862.

made out for transferring to the consolidated fund the cost of gaols and court houses, these being for imperial purposes?—I do.

5345. [*Sir Charles Lanyon.*] With regard to the grand jury, do you not look upon the grand jury more as a court of appeal than in any other light?—I do.

5346. It can originate nothing?—Very little; I will not say that it can originate nothing; but practically speaking, it is so.

5347. Would you not think it desirable that there should be some little alteration in the mode in which the cesspayers are appointed, and that it would be better to elect them by ballot at the grand jury, instead of at the sessions?—I gave that opinion before.

5348. Would you not think it desirable that all applications for works of maintenance for the repair of roads, and bridges, and works which are necessary works, and not new works, instead of being made as they are now by the cesspayers at the sessions, and by interested parties, should be divided into districts, and into classes, and should be applied for by the county surveyor?—I am a great advocate for giving county surveyors power and authority. I think that if a county surveyor is an honest and efficient man, and a man of education, you cannot do better than give him great authority. He is the man who is really responsible; he is the man who is, or who ought to be, constantly on the spot; he knows what ought to be done, and he ought to know the best way and the cheapest way of doing it, and I think that frequently, if they had authority, which they now have not, they might save great expense; for instance, in the case of sudden damages, and many other things, the county surveyors going along see things which ought to be done; but he has not authority to give orders about them.

5349. The point which I want to come to is this: The applications are made at the present moment generally by the contractor, first for small portions of road, or districts of road, lying in their immediate neighbourhood, so that works may be contracted for in which they are interested, to prevent competition and so forth; and very often roads of little consequence are applied for, when roads of greater consequence are not applied for; therefore, would it not be very much better to compel the county surveyor to make applications for the repairs of every road, and that those applications should only be made once in a year, or two years, or three years, according to the class of the road which would have to be repaired, instead of acting on the present system?—That is a thing which I had never thought of before; but as you put it to me upon the first blush of the thing, I think with you, that it would be a very desirable thing. The fact is, that it comes back to what I before said, that I would give the county surveyor more power and authority than he already possesses.

5350. With regard to elected guardians, do you consider that the duties of an elected guardian are analogous to the duties of an elected cesspayer?—I wish that to be very distinctly understood, that I think they are not analogous, and not being analogous, the comparison does not apply.

5351. Is there the same reason for electing a cesspayer to attend the sessions as for electing poor law guardians?—Certainly not.

5352. Colonel *Cooper.*] Do you consider that the lunatic asylums are extravagantly managed?—I have not sufficient experience of the working of lunatic asylums to give an opinion, which I would expect the Committee to take as worth anything; but, as a general rule, I am afraid that by boards of guardians there is a great deal of money spent that might be saved upon the staff, and machinery, and houses, and all the details which apparently goes to the credit of the unfortunate inmates, whereas, in reality, it does not.

Friday, 5th June 1868.

MEMBERS PRESENT:

Mr. Blake.	Colonel French.
Colonel Cooper.	Mr. Gregory.
General Dunne.	Mr. Leader.
Colonel Forde.	Earl of Mayo.
Mr. Chichester Fortescue.	The O'Conor Don.

THE O'CONOR DON, IN THE CHAIR.

Mr. NEAL DAVIS, called in; and Examined.

Mr. N. Davis. 5 June 1868.

5353. *Chairman.*] ARE you Clerk of the Peace for the County of Mayo?—I am.

5354. And are you also a solicitor?—I am.

5355. Are you solicitor to the grand jury?—I am solicitor to the grand jury, and member of the board of superintendence; and I hold some other trifling situations in the county.

5356. Are you also a member of the board of guardians in your union?—I am a member of two boards of guardians; I am vice-chairman of one, and a member of the other.

5357. The clerks of the peace are appointed by the custodes rotulorum of the counties, are they not?—They are appointed by the custodes rotulorum of the counties.

5358. What are the duties of the clerk of the peace?—The duties are very multifarious; his duties are both on the criminal and on the civil side of the court of quarter sessions. On the criminal side he has to act as registrar to the chairman and to the justices; he has also the delivery of spirit licenses. He has to get in all informations, and to prepare the indictments from them for the court; that is to say, that he is registrar to the court of quarter sessions. He has to swear the grand jury, and to swear the petty juries at the quarter sessions; he has to issue cheques for the payment of witnesses; he has to make out the returns as to parties convicted for the governors of prisons, and sundry other Returns which are called for by the Government and by this House; he has to arrange for the summoning of the common juries of the county, and of the grand jury who preside at the quarter sessions; he has to issue the precepts to the high constables, to make returns for preparation of the jury lists of the county, and to make out copies of the returns made by them, and to have them printed and posted through the county, and to issue notices where they are to be revised, and to attend at those several places with the magistrates to see them revised, and to give any information in his power upon them; he has, after the revision is over, which takes place in three different parts of the county, to make out a general list, arranging the names according to rank and property, and to lay that before the justices, and the justices presiding sign that, and deliver it over to him, upon which he makes a second list, which he delivers to the sheriff, and it is from that that the different panels in the county are called; he has the regulation as to fines upon jurors and prosecutors, and issuing notices to them and warrants against them if they do not pay the fines, and afterwards he renders accounts of all moneys received by him to the fines and penalties office. That is so far as the criminal side is concerned; there are some small matters which I have not given in detail here.

5359. With respect to the civil side of the quarter sessions court, what are the duties of the clerk of the peace?—With respect to the civil side of the quarter sessions court, he has, first, to arrange the lists of the general quarter sessions, and to submit them to the chairman of the county for his revisal; he has to attend the day previous to each quarter sessions, to take up all the causes which are to be entered at the sessions; he has to enter them in alphabetical order, both the defended cases and the undefended cases; and he has afterwards to attend the court and swear the witnesses, and to perform other duties there. After the court is over, he has daily to compare his book which he keeps with a book which the chairman keeps, in case of any mistakes; and when the entire court is over, decrees are sent to him, which he signs, and gets the chairman to sign, and which he then delivers to the various parties who are entitled to them.

5360. These are duties which in superior courts are discharged by the registrar of the judge, are they not?—They are, but the former are very small in comparison. From a list which I have here, it appears that the registrar of the judge may have eight or ten cases for trial at an assizes. Now, in the half-year ending with the summer assizes, 1867, we had 806 civil bill decrees to be delivered out, and signed and certified, through the county; and in the following half-year we had [illegible], making a total 1,700, which we had to check and to deliver out; and we had to enter 1,101 in one sessions, and 1,350 in another sessions, besides ejectments and different other things. I have not taken ejectments into account there.

5361. Will you proceed with the statement of the other duties of the clerk of the peace?—The sheriff, under a late Act of Parliament, gets certain fees as compensation, and he is appointed the collector of those fees for the sheriff upon all the

Mr. *N. Davis.*

5 June 1852.

the business which is done in the court, and he has to collect those fees and to pay them over to the sheriff. He is also the registrar of the insolvent debtors' court, which is a part of the civil side of the quarter sessions court. The schedules are sent down to him from Dublin, and he has to enter them in a book of record which is kept, to compare the affidavits of service, to report the services, if proper, to the chairman, and to take down the orders of the chairman, whatever they may be, either for the dismissal of a petition, or for the discharge of a prisoner, or a remand, and all those orders he sends back to the insolvent court at Dublin. At the assizes he has to attend on the judges on appeals, and to keep a book there as to the appeals which are entered, and the witnesses who are examined. Then he has to keep the register of the voters of the county, which is a very serious duty, and occupies a very considerable time. He has another duty, which seldom occurs, of the registration of trees.

5362. Mr. *Gregory.*] Has that often occurred in your experience?—Not very often, but it has occurred in my experience. There was at the very last quarter sessions a case where a lease expired, and the party came to make an offer to pay for the trees rather than let them be cut down, and they had to get the different documents in my office. There was a trial to be had, but there was a compromise upon it.

5363. *Chairman.*] Does the clerk of the peace receive any payment upon that?—He receives one shilling upon each affidavit, and a shilling if each party comes for an affidavit afterwards, but they are very seldom applied for. We are obliged to keep our office open from 10 o'clock to 3 o'clock to answer all questions. We have also a duty which gives a great deal of trouble as to the appointment of petty sessions clerks. Where a petty sessions clerk dies, the clerk of the peace has to issue a notice to the different magistrates residing within the district, and also publish it in the papers, and some question has arisen as to who is entitled to vote upon it. I do not know how it was settled between them. They have not come to any decision exactly as to who was entitled to vote for the election of petty sessions clerk, but it is not my business.

5364. Mr. *Chichester Fortescue.*] Was the question as to what magistrates were qualified?—Yes. The Act of Parliament says those usually attending or are residing within the district are to vote. What "usual attendance" is I cannot arrive at at present; but, however, it is for the Government to decide that. Some say that three days in three years is the usual attendance.

5365. *Chairman.*] Are those the principal duties of the clerk of the peace?—Those are the principal duties of the clerk of the peace; but I have also to make returns of the militia officers of the force.

5366. General *Dunne.*] Will you describe what duties the clerk of the peace has to discharge with regard to militia officers?—I have to return the names of the several officers, and I have also to make a return to the Government of the different appointments which are made.

5367. Have you anything to do as to the qualification?—I do not know that I have anything to say as to qualification.

5368. Colonel *French.*] Are you not bound to state what the qualification of an officer appointed is?—I do not think that I have ever been called upon to state that; I think that is a matter between the Government and the person to whom the commission is granted.

5369. General *Dunne.*] Has he ever to send in a certificate to you?—Yes; if he is a captain, it is 200 *l.*, I think, and this is kept filed. Then, as to railways and fisheries, the clerk of the peace has to keep all documents which are lodged in his office for inspection.

5370. *Chairman.*] Have you any special remuneration for the militia duties?—I made inquiries upon the subject (as every officer will, I suppose, make the most of his office) here in England, and I was told that the clerk of the peace in England, or as he is here called the clerk of lieutenancy, is entitled to three guineas on one commission, and two guineas on another; I never got it but in one instance. In the case of one lieutenant colonel I refused it, but he insisted on my taking it, and I set about inquiring whether I had a right to it.

5371. General *Dunne.*] Is there a special presentment by the grand jury for that purpose?—I never got it; I never had any fee upon it.

5372. *Chairman.*] Will you put in a statement of the duties of the clerk of the peace?—I will do so. (*The same was delivered in, vide Appendix.*)

5373. Could you state, generally, to the Committee how much time those respective duties, which you have mentioned, occupy?—I think from three to four months I am travelling and attending the quarter sessions; that is exclusively of my attending the juries and attending other different duties connected with it.

5374. Could you state to the Committee for which of those services which you have mentioned in this document, you receive particular fees?—I receive 3 *d.* in the entry of each civil bill, and then 3 *d.* also upon the decree, if the decree is granted; and upon ejectments.

5375. Do you receive fees for those licenses of which you have spoken?—I do; I receive 2 *s.* 6 *d.* annually on each, and when they come to apply I get a fee of 2 *s.* 6 *d.*

5376. Do you receive any fees on the duties which you discharge upon the criminal side of the court?—Nothing, but on the issuing of Crown summonses, and if informations are called for; but they are never called for, and I have got none. A party who has taken up a private prosecution might call upon me for a copy of the information, and I should be entitled to 3 *s.* 4 *d.* upon it; but in upwards of 20 years I do not think that I have got 3 *l.* on the whole from that.

5377. Then in a general way for most of the duties which you discharge upon the civil side of the court, you receive particular fees upon each particular duty discharged?—Exactly.

5378. But the duties which you discharge on the criminal side of the court are paid for by your salary?—With the exception of matters which Government pay for, such as bench warrants and Crown summonses. Those two things the Government pay me; according as I send in the account, and it is checked by the local Crown solicitor, and that is sent in to the clerk of the Crown and paid to me. It amounts to perhaps 8 *l.* or 10 *l.* a year; sometimes more, and sometimes less.

5379. Then when you state to the Committee that you had such a large number of decrees and of ejectments in different years in your county,

of

of course the more documents you have, the greater remuneration you receive?—Decidedly, and the more trouble I have too.

5380. Have you received any fees or additional remuneration for the trouble put upon you under the Act which obliges you to collect the fees for the sheriff?—Yes, there is a fee of 1 d. in the 1 s., I think. In one-half year the fees came to 8 l. 1 s. 6 d., and in another half-year to 8 l. 18 s. 4 d. That is about 17 l. a year.

5381. With respect to the duties imposed upon you in the making out of voters' lists, do you receive a peculiar remuneration for that?—No.

5382. Is there not a particular presentment made by the grand jury to remunerate the clerk of the peace for the discharge of that duty?—There is for the outlay, and that is a matter which the different clerks of the peace in Ireland are endeavouring to get remuneration for under the Act. In England I think that under the new Act there is a remuneration given to the officer who does the duty, but none is given to us; we have to send in before the special sessions an account of the outlay, but the Act of Parliament gives no remuneration.

5383. What do you understand by the outlay?—First of all I pay 20 l. a-year to my clerk as remuneration for looking after that specially; and I pay different other clerks; I have perhaps five clerks employed sometimes. It is a very arduous duty, for the error of one letter in a man's name at one time gave me an excessive degree of trouble. We have to attend before the chairman when he is correcting the list, and I put down my expenses in going and attending there as an outlay.

5384. Then you are paid for all the manual work which is done, and you are also paid your expenses for attending at the sessions, are you not?—No; I am paid for what I pay others to do; but I am not paid anything for what I do myself for my supervision, or regulation of it; I in fact pocket nothing out of the transaction; it goes amongst different other people.

5385. But the work is all done by your clerks, is it not?—No, by special clerks whom I bring in for the occasion only for that purpose. The clerk under me said that it was a hardship on him to be employed in doing this, and I gave him 20 l. additional for looking after that specially.

5386. As I understand you, the work which is required to be done in this registration of voters, is done by special clerks, whom you pay for the purpose?—It is done by my clerk whom I have specially agreed to pay for his additional trouble, and to others specially employed.

5387. And the grand jury pay you that additional, and they pay also those clerks, do they not?—They do.

5388. Supposing that you did that work yourself, instead of employing a clerk to do it, would not they pay you equally?—I could not do it; it would be out of my power to do it; there is a great deal of time occupied in copying of lists, and great particularity is required; and it must be done within a particular time; and if the slightest mistake occurs an action lies against the clerk of the peace if a voter loses his right to vote by that mistake; I was threatened with it once myself.

5389. In point of fact you are paid for everything in connexion with this registration of voters, except for your overlooking your clerks?—Exactly.

5390. And you consider that the clerk of the peace ought to be paid for overlooking what is done by others, and which is paid for by the grand jury?—I am obliged to go all over it again and to compare it; there is not a list which goes from my office of the freeholders of the county which I do not compare, and frequently cross-compare, for they very often come back from the printers with mistakes in them; the clerk of the peace, or whoever the officer is in England, has it under the late Act of Parliament. It is right for me to mention that before this Act came into force the clerk of the peace got 1 s. on every 40 s. freeholder, who was registered, and that was considered to be one of the principal emoluments of the situation; I got it, I think, on the 10 l., 20 l., and 50 l. freeholders for a short time, but under the 13th and 14th Victoria I think it is, we get nothing except what I tell you, and that is where we consider that there is a grievance.

Mr. H. Davis.

5 June 1868.

5391. Do you know anything about the duties of the clerks of the Crown?—I would rather let them speak for themselves, but I will tell you so far as I know.

5392. Are not the duties of the clerk of the Crown at the assizes, in a general way, similar to those which you discharge at quarter sessions?—They are on the criminal side of the court much the same.

5393. Have you any fiscal duties to perform as clerk of the peace, in connection with the county business?—None.

5394. Does not the clerk of the peace act as secretary to the grand jury, if a vacancy occurs?—That is only in the case of the death or illness of the secretary. On one occasion when the secretary died, for half-a-year I executed his duties, for which I was paid by the grand jury.

5395. Are there any other occasional duties of the clerk of the peace in connection with fiscal business?—Not that I recollect.

5396. You stated that you were solicitor to the grand jury?—I am, and have been so for many years.

5397. What do you understand by solicitor to the grand jury; it is not an office which is paid a particular salary, is it?—He is not recognised by law at all, but I do not know how the grand jury can well get on without having some officer of the kind.

5398. Mr. Chichester Fortescue.] Are you employed by the grand jury as any other solicitor might be?—They might employ any other solicitor, but I have been employed now for 40 years as their permanent solicitor.

5399. Chairman.] Do you prepare the bonds for the collectors of the county cess?—I do; I have brought one of the bonds here to show the Committee.

5400. Are you paid by the grand jury for preparing those bonds?—I am, and that is the only standing salary, if I may so call it, that I have. Some cases have arisen from time to time. I have an Act of Parliament here for the grand jury which I brought through the House.

5401. Do you know under what Act of Parliament the grand jury are justified in passing a presentment for preparing the bonds of the collectors?—I think a section of the present Grand Jury Act allows them to pay law expenses when duly taxed and certified.

5402. But ought not the preparation of a bond for a collector to be an expense borne by himself?—At one time it was borne by the collectors.

Mr. *N. Davis.*

5 June 1868.

lectors, and I think they remunerated with the grand jury. It was very immaterial to me from whom I got it, but the grand jury thought it better to pay it, and they do pay it.

5403. As a matter of fact, in the county of Mayo, the grand jury make a particular presentment for the expenses of preparing bonds for collectors?—They do.

5404. Do the grand jury cause you to inquire into the solvency of the securities?—They so far do so, that they throw the whole responsibility upon me, and the result was that at the last summer assizes, the foreman of the grand jury who is now present at the time, I tendered my resignation. I was prevailed on to hold it over, but at the next assizes I intend to give it up. I thought the responsibility was too great and the payment too small.

5405. How do you mean that the responsibility was too great and the payment too small?—They stated that they held me responsible for the solvency of the securities, which I thought was too great a responsibility.

5406. But how can they hold you responsible? —I do not say that they can do so, but it is an unpleasant thing to be impeached afterwards, if I take security which I conceive to be good. It is very difficult to get securities. I will give two instances of that: one gentleman whom I know to be a correct collector, from having some difference with his surety, would not ask that surety, nor would he ask anybody else to be security for him, and he wanted me to take some security which I refused, and I compelled him to lodge the entire amount of the cess, before the warrant was delivered to him. He handed me a bank deposit for the entire amount of the cess; this I handed in to the treasurer, and then the warrant was given to the collector. In the very last assizes a gentleman was required to do the same to the extent of over 1,000*l.*

5407. Do you always require the money to be lodged?—I only require it in cases where I consider that the security is not such as I can approve of.

5408. However, the grand jury take your word?—I am sorry that they throw it upon me to take my word, but I certainly will not do it again for any remuneration.

5409. Do you think it desirable that such a responsibility should be thrown upon the solicitor, who is not a regular officer of the grand jury?—I do not think it is just, or it is very hard, at all events. What I proposed was that they should appoint a committee, and that the names should be laid before them for the committee then to decide upon whether the securities were solvent or not. There was some reason or other given against that, and they said that they had got through with me so long that they would continue to hold me, but, however, they will not hold me beyond the next assizes. It is but fair for me further to add, perhaps, that the payment for taking the bonds is the only salary that the nominal solicitor of the grand jury has. It is about between 40*l.* and 50*l.* a year in Mayo.

5410. You stated, did you not, that there was great difficulty in getting security from the collectors?—There is very great difficulty.

5411. Do you not think that difficulty could be very much got over if the baronies were divided into districts for the purpose of collection, and the collection was of smaller amount?—I think if it was done much in the same way as the poor law collection, it would be easier to get security. The amount being smaller, the risk would be less.

5412. The amount being smaller, and the difficulty of getting security being less, do you not think that the cess could be collected at a lower rate than at present?—I think it might; the only reason that I think it might is that it is collected at a much lower rate by the poor law guardians. In some places I know that it is collected for 4½*d.*, and I think for 6*d.* in the county of Mayo.

5413. And you pay, I understand, 1*s.*?—We pay 1*s.* for collection of our county cess.

5414. Mr. *Chichester Fortescue.*] Do you know whether the boards of guardians in the county of Mayo find any difficulty in obtaining solvent collectors?—I know they do not; but the amount is small, and that is the reason of it.

5415. Do you attribute the comparative readiness with which the boards of guardians obtain good collectors to the fact that the collection is only for a limited district, namely, the union?—I have no other reason to give than that.

5416. (*Chairman.*] The collectors of the poor rates are obliged to lodge their collection within a certain time, are they not?—They are; but it is best for me to remark that there is a supervision over the accounts of the collectors of the poor rates, which there is not in the case of the grand jury cess. The accounts are called for, I cannot say whether weekly or monthly, and there is a book kept; and I think the clerk of the union reports to the guardians whether there is unnecessary arrear or not, and if there is, the collector is called up and made to account for it.

5417. Is not the collector's account placed before the board of guardians at every meeting and examined by the chairman?—It is so; but if there is an unnecessary arrear, the collector is called and made to account for it. Before the grand jury, when the warrant is given by the treasurer to the collector, there is no supervision whatever, that I am aware of, for either four months or eight months. He gets his warrant, and he may collect it in a week after the assizes, or he may not do so (which is very generally the case), till a few days before the assizes. At all events I know that it is seldom if ever lodged to the credit of the county until a few days before the assizes. One of the difficulties that arose from that was, that in my own time one of the collectors died; his securities were not very solvent at the time, or at least they were not reachable. Some of their property had, unfortunately, travelled into the court for the sale of Irish estates; but there was a sum of 700*l.* found to be lodged in the bank, and there is no doubt whatever that it was county money, but it was not lodged to the credit of the county, and the executor drew the money, and the county lost it.

5418. Are you not aware that by a section of the Grand Jury Act the collectors are obliged to lodge their collection when it amounts to 100*l.*? —I know that they are, but who is to call them to account for it; they are bound by the Act to do so; but I do not know that it is the duty of the treasurer to see that they do lodge it, and there is nobody that I know of that does.

5419. Do you not think it would be very easy to oblige the collectors to make an account of their collection to either the secretary of the grand jury, or the treasurer, once a month, or at some

fixed

Mr. *N. Dunn.*

5 June 1868.

fixed period?—It would; but I do not think you would get either the secretary of the grand jury or the treasurer, unless it was part of his duty to do it.

5420. Mr. *Gregory.*] If you had a standing committee to examine accounts, might not they do it?—I think it would be highly advisable, and I think that would be one of the principal reasons for a standing committee.

5421. Do you not think that one of the causes of the difficulty of the constables obtaining security is the fact of their being allowed to hold, and to make use of such large sums in their hands for a considerable time?—There is no doubt of it; if I was called on to-morrow I would not enter into security for a high constable for that reason. On one occasion, one of the very best high constables, found a difficulty in getting security in the county, and when he found one she was a lady, for I sometimes take ladies if I can find them responsible.

5422. Mr. *Chichester Fortescue.*] If there was a constant supervision over the proceedings of collectors, as in the case of the poor law, the question of security would not be of such vital importance, would it?—Decidedly not.

5423. *Chairman.*] Do you think that such a supervision could be effected without the establishment of something like a finance committee?—There must be either that or some public officer, but he must have somebody to report to, to call the collectors to account, for the only penalty would then be that if the man did not lodge his collection, as he was bound to do, he would not be elected at the following assizes.

5424. Would he not incur any penalty under his bond?—He might, but I do not think juries are much inclined to give damages in a case of that kind.

5425. You do not think its being entered in the bond is of much consequence?—I do not think it would be; I should be afraid to advise them to bring an action upon it. In one case, being very anxious to keep an officer in his place, finding him a very good officer, I went round with him, at his request, to the different insurance offices, and they told me they would insure for a bank clerk, but that they would not insure for a county collector, and the only reason was, I believe, what I mentioned, viz., that there is no supervision of the accounts.

5426. Mr. *Chichester Fortescue.*] Has it ever been your own duty to conduct an action against a defaulting collector?—Unfortunately, it was on one occasion.

5427. *Chairman.*] Did you recover on that occasion?—I did not, but it was certainly the fault of the grand jury themselves; they were a little too hasty, for they passed some praises or encomiums on the collector, forgetting that he was in arrear, and these were read as evidence against them afterwards.

5428. Mr. *Chichester Fortescue.*] As condoning the offence?—Exactly.

5429. *Chairman.*] Did you not state it as your opinion that no county officer could exercise this supervision, and enforce this payment of the collection when made?—I do not say that, but I do not think so as they are at present appointed.

5430. You know that the secretary of the grand jury is appointed only at the pleasure of the grand jury, from one assize to another?—That is so, no doubt.

5431. He not being a permanent officer, they may make any regulation respecting his duties, may they not?—Yes; but I do not think it would be fair with the salary he gets; he has very arduous duties, I must say.

5432. But supposing that the salary of the secretary of the grand jury was revised, and that this was made one of his duties, do you think that he could efficiently discharge it without the institution of a finance or standing committee?—I do not know how it may be in other parts of Ireland, but I know that our present secretary of the grand jury is a very efficient officer, and I am sure he could do it, but of course he would expect to be remunerated.

5433. But you think an efficient officer could do it?—I have no doubt he could do it, but at the same time, if he did do it, I would like to know what the penalty would be. It could be done by the secretary of the grand jury as regards ascertaining whether this man was in arrear or not; but finding him in arrear, if he had no permanent body to apply to, either to remove the collector, or to call upon his sureties, it would become a nullity in fact, because then he would have only to report to the grand jury the fact of this man not having complied with the law, and in the meantime the man might have all the cess in his pocket and leave the country.

5434. But at present, without any supervision at all, is it not the fact the counties very seldom lose through the barony cess-collectors not paying in?—Since the loss that I mention, they have not lost 1 *s.*, but that is thanks to what they do, for they make the collector pay in every shilling, whether he collects it or not.

5435. The barony cess-collector's securities are very well looked into now, are they not?—They are as well looked into as I can look into them; but some of them I am not quite satisfied with.

5436. Therefore, at present, without any supervision whatsoever, the counties do not in the end lose any of the county cess?—I am only speaking of the county of Mayo.

5437. But, so far as your experience goes, it very seldom happens that the counties lose through the barony cess-collectors?—I think, during the last six years, there has not been 1 *s.* lost. If a man gets a warrant for 1,000 *l.*, he must pay that 1,000 *l.*; and if there happened to be 200 *l.* uncollected by him in consequence of deserted premises, or anything of that kind, the grand jury will not take that excuse, but he must pay it frequently out of his own pocket. The way in which he recoups him is, that he makes an affidavit before the grand jury, and the grand jury make a re-presentment upon those special premises, and then he gets it. I know in one barony it has been represented for some time.

5438. Do you not think that if the barony cess-collectors were obliged to bring in their accounts to the secretary of the grand jury once a month, or at certain periods, that would make them more careful to pay in the money to the credit of the county as soon as it was collected?—It would, I think; but at the same time if a man desired to be a defaulter, I do not know whether the penalty would lie upon him if he became contumacious.

5439. But your difficulty would only refer to men who desired to be defaulters in the end?—Yes.

5440. But taking the case of the present collectors,

Mr. *N. Davis.*

5 June 1868.

lectors, who are not defaulters, and who have good security, and who become defaulters, the county has plenty of security to fall back upon in their cases, and this check of the secretary of the grand jury will oblige them to pay in the money as soon as collected, would it not, which in many instances they do not do now?—Yes, or to stand under the odium of being defaulters.

5441. That is the alternative which would be presented to them?—Yes.

5442. If a collector refuse to pay in this 100*l.* when called upon to do so by the secretary of the grand jury, he would not be appointed a collector at the next assizes?—No; and being aware of that he would make arrangements to leave them, and not with an empty hand.

5443. Mr. *Gregory.*] You had a standing committee with power to dismiss a collector not fulfilling the conditions, could that difficulty to which you have alluded arise?—I think not.

5444. *Chairman.*] You say that if there were a committee, or anybody who had power to discharge a collector who did not lodge the 100*l.* when collected, the difficulty would not arise; supposing that collector to be a defaulter who was going away with the cess, would not the difficulty equally arise?—I think not, because then the direction from that committee might go immediately to sue his sureties.

5445. Mr. *Gregory.*] And the sum being comparatively small, I presume there would be less difficulty on the part of the sureties in paying it?—Yes; and there would be less difficulty in getting sureties.

5446. Have you a collector at this moment in gaol on account of being in arrears in your county?—Yes, for four or five years, I am sorry to say; but it was only 140*l.* or 150*l.*

5447. Were not the sureties forthcoming?—My recollection is that they were not; I think that one of them is dead, and the other is not forthcoming, and I think it is since that very case that they have become so strict in throwing the burden of approval upon me.

5448. Are you in favour of the present system of having fresh bonds from the constables at each assizes?—I believe that the Poor Law Act now allows continuous bonds.

5449. But that is not so in the case, I think, of the county cess?—Decidedly not.

5450. Would you see any practical difficulty at all in substituting, for the present system, one of continuous bonds?—I should not; but I think that there would be great difficulty in getting people to enter into continuous bonds.

5451. Would the difficulty arise with regard to the sureties, or with regard to the constables themselves?—With regard to the sureties, many men would become security for one assizes who would not like to have a charge upon their estate by reason of a continuous security.

5452. Is it the practice in your county to enter judgment upon the bond?—No, you cannot enter judgment until there is a default; but there is an Act now under which you can register the bond as a notice to the public, to avoid bankruptcy or insolvency; that I am paid for, and I do it every assizes, and I think the dread of that makes people somewhat more cautious about becoming security, because the statute applies.

5453. Do you register the bonds?—I do.

5454. Have you ever been applied to not to register those bonds?—I would not listen to such an application.

5455. But I presume that you have been asked, have you not?—No; they have frequently said that it was a hardship, but I have told them that I had nothing to do with hardships.

5456. *Chairman.*] Do you think that the offices of clerk of the peace and clerk of the Crown could be amalgamated?—There is not a doubt of it.

5457. The duties which the clerk of the Crown has to discharge at the assizes would not interfere with his duties as clerk of the peace, would they?—Not in the slightest degree; so far from it I think that it would facilitate the duties of both; the reason for it is this: that when informations the chairman of the county thinks do not come within his province to try, he sends to the assizes; and vice versâ what the judge of assize thinks trivial, he sends to the sessions.

5458. There would be, in fact, a saving of trouble, would there not, if the offices were united?—I think so; but I do not say that if you put it upon the clerk of the peace additional payment would not be required, and that you should not make allowance for a staff.

5459. Mr. *Gregory.*] Will you enumerate the returns which you have to make for Imperial purposes as to that?—They are multifarious. There is a new office created in Dublin, and a Mr. Hancock, the public officer who holds that office, gives a great deal of trouble in making the returns. I do not know whether he is recognised or not, but he is in some situation under the Castle.

5460. Do you think that you could specify those particular returns which you have to make?—I do not think that I could specify them, but one return which I had to make was a return of the number of electors in each county and city in the year 1841, and immediately after the Act of Union. That is a Parliamentary Return of the year 1799.

5461. When had you to make that?—I had to make that a very short time ago; in April last.

5462. Do you get any extra pay or emolument for making up those returns?—Not a farthing. I have a Return here to so much of an Order of the House of Commons, dated the 6th of April, as related to the questions whether I was a professional man, whether I discharged my duties by deputy or in person, and, if by deputy, at what salary, the number of criminal indictments at all the quarter sessions of the county from 1840 to 1844, from 1830 to 1834, and from 1860 to 1867, amounting to 1,500 odd.

5463. Do those returns which you have to make to the Government occupy a considerable portion of your time?—They do; but in a well-regulated office they can be met, to a great extent, by keeping the returns constantly up; and by falling back upon them we make them up much more easily than perhaps we otherwise should. Still they occupy a great deal of time and a great deal of particularity. I never had one thrown back upon me yet for want of particularity, but I have numberless returns to make out.

5464. Colonel *French.*] Do you consider yourself as clerk of the peace to be a Government officer?—I do not.

5465. Do you consider it a hardship under these

those circumstances to be called upon to make Returns to the Government without any remuneration?—I do consider it a great hardship, and to be bound by those Returns.

5466. Mr. *Chichester Fortescue*.] Are you aware that the return which you have just mentioned, is not a Return to the Government, but a Return to the House of Commons?—It is.

5467. Colonel *French*.] You have been for a considerable number of years, clerk of the peace for the county of Mayo, have you not?—I have been so for 20 years, from October 1848.

5468. Could you state the amount of salary receivable from the Government half-yearly?—It is 370 *l.* a year, I think.

5469. Could you state what is the amount of fees annually on an average?—I have brought accounts with me, and now produce them so as to afford the Committee every information. We are obliged to make an affidavit at each sessions to lay before the grand jury or the judge, and they return them to me, and I keep them. I have the two last, those which I now produce, for the spring and summer assizes, and these give the whole history of everything which I get, as I swore to them. The amount of the fees from the spring assizes, and ending the summer assizes, 1867, was 80 *l.* 7 *s.* 9 *d.*; and from the summer assizes, 1867, to the spring assizes, 1868, it was 143 *l.* 12 *s.* 1 *d.*; the total being 223 *l.* 19 *s.* 10 *d.*

5470. You, having held the office for only 20 years, are not aware when the salary was first given to the clerks of the peace, and clerks of the Crown?—No, not from recollection; but I could have traced it out.

5471. You are bound to make a return as you have stated, at each assizes of the amount of the fees?—Yes.

5472. Do you hand that in to the grand jury?—Yes.

5473. Does the county cess get any credit from that?—No.

5474. Do you consider it to be your legal right to retain those fees?—Undoubtedly. I do not think that the clerk of the peace would be sufficiently remunerated, even with that. The clerks of the peace are considered to be very well paid. When I got the office I was told that I should have 1,000 *l.* a year; but I am sorry to say that I never could bring it to that, and I am nearly four months away from home living in hotels.

5475. What is your opinion as to the legality of those fees?—I think that the law is with the clerks of the peace, and I think that they will maintain it.

5476. Could you state where that law is to be found?—I think that it is the 14th and 15th Victoria, the present Quarter Sessions Act. It certainly gives the clerk of the peace a sum of 5 *d.* on the entry, and 3 *d.* on the decree.

5477. You have stated that you have thought that there would be no difficulty in amalgamating the offices of clerk of the peace and clerk of the Crown in the same person; is not one of those officers appointed by the Government, and the other by the *custos rotulorum* of the county?—Yes.

5478. In whom would you propose to leave the appointment of the one officer who is to do the duties which are at present performed by the two?—I stated what was wrong when I said that there was not a difficulty, because I think that is the difficulty, and the only difficulty, which there is in it; but I think it might be done turn-about by the *custos rotulorum* and the Government.

5479. But should the nomination to the office be vested in the Lord Lieutenant of Ireland, or in the executive Government; ought not the payment of that office to come out of the Consolidated Fund, and not from the grand jury cess?—No doubt; if they take the patronage, I think they ought to pay for it.

5480. Do you know anything of the audit of grand jury presentments which was established by Mr. Antony Blake, the Accountant General?—I think I know as much of it as others, and that is very little. I do not think that anyone knows anything about it; at least I never could understand that there was any investigation about it.

5481. Do you think that there is any necessity for such an office, at 1,400 *l.* a year appointed to by the Government?—I think, as I said in answer to a former question, that if the county have to pay all the expenses, they have a right to have their own audit.

5482. Do you not think that the Poor Law Auditors, who are paid by the Government already, could, in addition to their duties, audit twice a year the grand jury accounts, as is now done by a Master in Chancery?—I think they would do it more to the satisfaction of the grand jury; but at the same time I do not think they would consider it to be their duty, and I doubt if the Poor Law Commissioners would allow it to be done.

5483. The Poor Law Auditors are very well paid now; would it be adding very much to their duty?—No; I think that the grand jury, or that some members of the grand jury themselves ought to have the opportunity of investigating the accounts equally with any public officer, and that the accounts ought to be laid before them as well as before any public officer.

5484. Colonel *Fortescue*.] I do not see, in this list of your fees, anything about the spirit licenses; are they in it?—They are; that is what makes the difference between 140 *l.* and 80 *l.*

5485. Do you get a fee on the transfer of a license from one person to another, as well as upon the new licenses, or do you reckon them as new licenses?—From anyone who comes in by notice we get a fee, and we get a fee of 1 *s.* on every other.

5486. What do you get on the insolvent debtors?—I get half-a-crown on them; but everything is included in that return, with the exception of one thing, which I do not consider to be a fee. The Chairman said that some person gave evidence here that the fee for the registration of freeholders was included in our list of fees; I did not include it, because I do not take it to be a fee, as I take it to be an actual payment of expenses.

5487. Is it usual in other counties for the solicitor to the grand jury to take a fee on the bonds?—I do not know; I never knew attorneys to do anything without being paid for it.

5488. (What do the attorneys do it?) is not the bond a printed document?—The bond is, but I am not paid for the bond alone, I think; but, as I said before, for looking into the securities, for the registration of the bond, and for the preparation of the bond, and attending before them, just as I should be paid by any individual. If I got a printed form from any gentleman here and attended, I would charge him very nearly the same as a private individual.

5489. Why

Mr. M. Davis.
—
5 June 1868.

5489. Why could not the grand juror representing a barony take that bond and be responsible for the sureties for his barony, and not leave it to the solicitor to the grand jury?—I do not think that it would be a legal thing for any private gentleman to act as a solicitor in the preparation of a bond, and perhaps there might be a penalty attached to it as it is.

5490. But it is a printed bond, is it not?—It is a printed bond in part, and the names and the amounts and the sureties belong to be filled up.

5491. And do you think that any gentleman filling that up would be liable to an action?—I think that he would be stepping out of his way to do it, though I should be sorry to say that he was liable to an action. I attend the grand jury from the commencement of the meeting of the grand jury to the end, and if any questions arise upon the construction of any law I am there to answer them. That I never charge for, and I have no means of charging for; and the only remuneration which I receive for that constant attendance at the grand jury is the fees on the bonds.

5492. Colonel *French*.] Both for that and for the examination of the securities?—Both for that and for examining securities, and in some very few instances when I was in doubt, I searched the register to see whether the parties had property, or not; I was paid a small amount for that in addition.

5493. General *Dunne*.] I think you said that you would have difficulty to find the collectors' securities if you made them continuous, as the Poor Law securities are?—Yes.

5494. But if they did find securities that were deemed sufficient, do you not think that it would be a great convenience to prevent at every assizes the necessity of the formation of a new bond?—I think that it would be a convenience; but still you should have some officer who would look very closely to see whether those securities had not died off, and left you without security. A man might be originally a very good security, and at the end of 10 years he might not be so.

5495. But would greater convenience arise there than in the case of the Poor Law where that continuous security is accepted?—It is only lately that it has been done, I believe, and I cannot tell you how it works.

5496. You say that the examination of the securities is entirely put upon you?—It is.

5497. Do you recommend that a committee of the grand jury should be formed for that purpose?—Yes, I do.

5498. Are you aware that that is done in some counties?—I believe it is; I know that it is done in the county of Galway, for I made inquiries.

5499. Is that done in the county of Mayo?—It is not done in the county of Mayo: I may have been wrong in recommending it generally; but I recommend it for Mayo.

5500. The sums of money in the hands of the collectors may be different at different times of the year, may they not, according to the time at which they choose to collect?—Yes; the moment the collector gets his warrant he may collect if he likes, or he may let it lie over till a few days before the assizes.

5501. Are the warrants usually issued until the money of the previous collection is reported as lodged?—No. What is done at the grand jury of the county of Mayo is this: I attend at the treasurer's office, and I get from him a certificate of the amount being paid in; I then produce that, and the grand jury authorise me to take the bond, if I approve of the security, and the sum mentioned in the collector's warrant is paid to the full amount, whether the collector has received it or not.

5502. Would it not be much better to do it as it is done under the Poor Law, and not to charge the persons holding small tenements but to charge the landlord up to 4*l.*?—I do not feel myself competent, without consideration, to answer that question.

5503. Is not the deficiency in payment chiefly in that class?—It is, I believe.

5504. Have you ever heard the collectors make any complaints of that kind; that from the change of lodgers they cannot collect?—I have heard complaints of that kind.

5505. Are the process servers in any way connected with your duty?—Yes.

5506. Do you think that the present payment of process servers is satisfactory?—I have not heard much complaint about it.

5507. They are paid by salary now, are they not?—They are paid by salary and by fees.

5508. What are the fees?—I think it is 6*d.* on the service of a process.

5509. Then do you think that the salary and the service fees are a sufficient remuneration?—I think they are so far a sufficient remuneration, that the chairman of my county refers a good deal to my judgment (whether I am worthy of it, or not) in the selection of the process servers; and a vacancy never arises for which I have not four or five applicants.

5510. Are they a trustworthy class?—They are; we have not found a single fault with them, they are kept very strictly to their duty; it is only six weeks before the sessions that they have anything to do; their salary is about 10*l.*, and they get about 10*l.* more by the services they effect.

5511. Do you get for that a person of a good class?—I believe so.

5512. And they were not formerly persons of a very superior class, were they?—No.

5513. Do you think that, under the Act which gave them those fees, the class of process servers is improved?—It is by the great check which there is over them. They are obliged to attend at my office on the first day, and if I do not see them in order, or if in any way hear complaints, I report them.

5514. Then you think any complaints which may exist are not justified?—I think not; I think that, considering the class of persons from whom you select them and the salary they get, they do their duties very fairly.

5515. Mr. *Chichester Fortescue*.] Will you look at the Act of the 16 & 17 Vict. c. 136, sec. 4, and say, whether, or not, you consider that to be the section, under which the grand jury is entitled to present the expense of legal proceedings, and under which, therefore, you are employed?—That is the section, "That in addition to the purposes for which grand juries may now by law present, it shall be lawful for the grand jury of any county, county of a city, or county of a town, to present to be levied off the county at large, such sum, or sums of money as may be incurred in defending such county on the trial of any traverse or other proceedings in which such grand jury may consider the rights of the cesspayers should be defended and protected, and also such sums as may be necessary for any

[illegible]

costs incurred in the conduct and management of any matter of business which any such grand jury may consider right and proper for the interests or benefit of such county should be confided to, and conducted by any counsel, solicitor, or agent, provided however that no such presentment shall be made, unless there shall have been laid before such grand jury, a bill, duly taxed and certified by the proper taxing officer, of the costs incurred for any of the purposes aforesaid, for which such presentment shall be required." There was a section in the previous Act of Parliament, but it was not so extensive as that.

5516. *Chairman.*] I do not exactly understand you, as to whether you are in favour of continuous bonds to the collectors of county cess?—There is a good deal for and against it. As I said before, if they were looked very strictly after perhaps it might be done, but then you do away with the solicitor (and I am speaking now somewhat disinterestedly, for I do not intend to hold the office any longer), for you have no other means of compensating him, except by that side-wind.

5517. If those bonds were made continuous, would you not by that Act make those collectors permanent officers of the grand jury?—No doubt you would.

5518. At present they are merely appointed from one assize to another to collect the cess?—Yes.

5519. And they have no claim whatever as officers of the grand jury?—No.

5520. But if you entered into continuous bonds for the collection of the county cess, would you not by doing so place them in the same position as other officers appointed by the grand jury?—They would not be subject to removal, except for improper conduct I should say.

5521. Colonel *French.*] But under the poor law system, to which you propose to reduce the area of collection, you say that the bonds are continuous?—I am told that they are at present, but they were not so.

5522. Why should they not be so, if the area was reduced?—If the area was reduced, I do not see any reason against it, if you get good securities. The only thing as I say is to see that the people do not die off. A man may be a very good security in the year 1867, and in the year 1868 or 1869, he may be a very bad one.

5523. *Chairman.*] If the baronies were divided into districts for the purpose of collection, would you see any objection to having collectors for those districts appointed by the presentment sessions and approved of by the grand jury?—I would rather leave it in the power of the grand jury altogether.

5524. Do you not think that the parties living in the locality, the gentlemen and the ratepayers, who might meet together at the presentment sessions, would be in a better position to judge of the securities of those small districts than the gentlemen who meet together on a grand jury only for a few days, and who then have a great deal of business to transact?—In that way they would.

5525. And if the districts were made smaller, it would be very easy, would it not, to get ample security for those small districts?—No doubt of it; I would go security for many a man for 50 *l*, when I would not for 500 *l*.

5526. General *Dunne.*] In those districts would the remuneration be sufficient to induce any man to accept the duty?—I think they do it under the Poor Law.

5527. *Chairman.*] Do you find that under the Poor Law, there are collectors easily found for collecting the cess in each electoral division?—I find them sometimes underbidding each other in the amount when they accept it.

5528. And the result of that is that the poor rate is collected at one half the cost of the collection of the county cess, is it not?—Yes; or at one-third of the cost.

5529. General *Dunne.*] Are not the electoral divisions often of smaller area than the baronies?—Yes.

5530. Are not the baronies most unequal in their area?—Yes; and they are very unequal in their amount of cess.

5531. *Chairman.*] But, in the smaller baronies, where the amount of cess would be very trifling, it would be very easy, would it not, to get security for the collectors?—I do not think that it is small in any instance in the county of Mayo, and I cannot speak of any other county.

5532. If, as the gallant General suggests, in some parts of Ireland the baronies would be very small, would not the amount of cess for which the collectors would be responsible be proportionately small?—To be sure it would.

5533. And would it not, therefore, be proportionately easy to get security for the collection of that small amount of cess?—I should say so, and it would be unnecessary to divide it there.

5534. And there would be no necessity in that case for paying a higher rate than the poor rate collector for an electoral division of the same size would be paid?—No, I think they advertise under the Poor Law for the collection of the rates, and tenders come in.

5535. Do you not think that it would be very desirable to have a similar system with respect to the county cess?—I do not think that it could be done in large baronies.

5536. The difficulty of doing it arises at present from the largeness of some of the baronies, does it not?—It does.

5537. But if the large baronies were divided, as I have suggested, and the small baronies left as they are, that difficulty would not arise, would it?—No; I think you might advertise them.

5538. Colonel *French.*] Are you not aware that the baronial collector in many cases gets 9 *d.*, or probably as much as 1 *s.*, and that he pays his deputy, who actually collects it, only 3 *d.*?—I do not know it, but I firmly believe it; because if he did not get it collected for a great deal less, he would not hold it.

5539. Colonel *Forde.*] Would it not be a great convenience, supposing that the sureties were not obliged both to be present at the time of taking securities at the assizes, and if the sureties might be completed at a future time?—They are at a future time in very many instances.

5540. Is it absolutely necessary for them to be both together at the grand jury?—Yes, I consider it so.

5541. Would it not be made a great deal easier supposing that the two were not obliged to be together at the same time?—I think so.

5542. And without any detriment to the bond?—I do not see any detriment to it, as in the case of any private individuals entering into a bond, one may enter into it before one class of witness, and another before another class of witness, and it is equally binding.

0.46. I I 3 5543. Would

Mr. N. Davis.

5 June 1868.

5543. Would not that simplify matters very much?—It would. One gentleman in the county of Mayo has two sureties, one of whom resides in the city of Dublin, and that gentleman has to travel from Dublin to attend the grand jury in the county of Mayo; whereas, if there was competent authority to take it in Dublin, he would not be put to that trouble.

5544. *Mr. Gregory.*] It might be taken in Dublin before a Master in Chancery, might it not?—Not under the present law, but it might be so taken.

5545. *Chairman.*] Would you not think it desirable that the clerk of the peace and the clerk of the Crown should be resident in the county?—I do not know as to the clerk of the Crown, but I would certainly say as to the clerk of the peace that he should be resident, for every day applications are made to his office.

5546. If those two offices were amalgamated, do you not think that the officer appointed should be bound to discharge his duties himself and not by deputy?—Not a doubt of it. When I was appointed there were only three conditions put upon me as honourable conditions by the custos rotulorum. The first was, that I should be resident in the county; the second was, that I should take such fees only as should be attached to the office; and the third was that, in the case of ill health, if I appointed a deputy, he was to have the revision of the deputy, so that no improper person could be placed in that position.

5547. Have you any list of clerks of the peace and clerks of the Crown in Ireland who have deputies?—There is a list in Thoms' Almanac, but I do not say that it is correct in every respect, because there was a gentleman who acted as an assistant to me at one time, and he was put down in it as my deputy. I was doing the duty myself, and I did not want to have it understood that I was doing the duty by deputy; and therefore I insisted upon having it struck out. I have a clerk to whom I pay a fair salary, but he has no authority to sign my name. I must sign everything myself, and therefore he is no deputy; but there are instances in Ireland where the deputies sign every document and the clerk of the peace signs none.

5548. *Mr. Gregory.*] In the case of the death of a barony constable in your county what is the practice; is the election for the new barony constable held at the first quarter sessions which occur in the county, or is it held at the district quarter sessions?—I know that there was one case of the kind, but I could not say with certainty how that is; I think that in the case of death it is to be reported to the treasurer by the clerk of the peace, and a special sessions is then called. It is under the 11 & 12 Vict. c. 20, s. 1.

JOHN NUGENT, Esq., M.D., L.R.C.S.I., called in; and Examined.

J. Nugent, Esq., M.D.

5549. *Chairman.*] YOU are a Commissioner of Control in Lunacy, and Inspector General of Lunatic Asylums, are you not?—I am.

5550. You have held that, or a similar office, for how many years?—I have been inspector of lunatic asylums for about 22 years, and a commissioner of control for about eight years.

5551. Lunatic asylums are at present supported by presentments made by grand juries, are they not?—They are.

5552. Will you state to the Committee, as briefly as you can, the origin of those asylums, and how they came to be supported by grand jury presentments?—The first public asylum which was erected in Ireland was in the year 1815, towards the close of the reign of George the Third. It was a public asylum, erected by the Government at a cost of about 75,000 *l.*, and it was intended for the lunatics of Ireland generally, the Government itself paying for the building, and not charging it at all; subsequently, in the years 1820 and 1821, there was a Committee of the House of Commons, and an Act was afterwards passed the 1 & 2 Geo. 4, c. 33, which enabled the Lord Lieutenant of Ireland in Council to erect any number of asylums he might deem fit, and to associate as many counties together forming districts as might be advisable. Under that Act there were nine public asylums built in Ireland, and the total cost of them was 210,000 *l.*

5553. Colonel *French.*] Was any assent of the counties required?—None was required, an absolute power was given to the Lord Lieutenant in Council to erect asylums as he thought fit in any locality, and to associate as many counties as he thought fit to form each district.

5554. *Chairman.*] Those asylums were built by money contributed out of the Consolidated Fund in the first instance, were they not?—The advances were made from the Consolidated Fund, for, under the same Act of Parliament, the Lord Lieutenant had the power of ordering such advances as might be requisite.

5555. Those first asylums were built under the direction of certain Commissioners, were they not?—Yes; a Board of Commissioners was appointed at the time of the passing of the Act, and eight Commissioners shortly after nominated in an Order of Council.

5556. After the asylums were built the Commission ceased, did it not?—That Board ceased its duty when the nine asylums were built; and fully furnished. The asylums were then transferred to Board of Governors, selected also by the Lord Lieutenant in Council from the gentry, the principal grand jurors, generally speaking, of each district.

5557. On what terms were those advances made then?—On no terms whatsoever. There was no interest charged upon the sums advanced, but still, acting under the power which was given to the Lord Lieutenant, he could fix any period of time for the repayment; and he then fixed 14 years, the repayments to be made twice a year by the grand jury, and in fact there were 28 half-yearly instalments paid in the course of 14 years.

5558. Had the Lord Lieutenant the power to arrange whatever period he thought desirable?—Yes; he could extend or diminish it, as he thought fit.

5559. And the Lord Lieutenant in Council fixed upon this period of 14 years?—Yes.

5560. General *Dunne.*] Why did he fix upon that period?—That is a question which, of course, I could not answer; but it was at the rate of about 7½ per cent. per annum, to pay off the debt.

5561. *Chairman.*] These asylums were built before any Poor Law was established in Ireland, were they not?—These asylums were built before the

the Poor Law was established in Ireland. The first of these asylums erected at Armagh, was occupied in the year 1825, and the last of them occupied in 1834 or 1835 (I cannot say which) was at Waterford. That was anterior to the Poor Law Act, and there being no Poor Law at that time, of course the asylums became chargeable upon the only available means which then existed, viz., the county cess.

5562. Could you tell the Committee what asylums have since been built, and under what circumstances?—These asylums, I should say, were built only for 960 patients, so that in the course of a few years they became filled, and the result was, that many apartments which were intended for other purposes were converted into day-rooms and sleeping-rooms. When the number increased to 1,700 patients, it was found necessary to make additions to them, and those additions, which cost, one way or another, from 60,000 *l.* to 70,000 *l.*, not being sufficient, seven new asylums were directed to be built in the year 1846, and they were terminated in the year 1854. These seven asylums were built by the Board of Works. I have mentioned that the original Board had ceased, and the Board of Works became their representatives, and it was under the Board of Works that the seven asylums, forming the second batch of asylums, were built at a cost of 316,000 *l.*

5563. Were those second asylums built without any requisition from the counties to have them built?—Those second asylums were built, I cannot say without a requisition, because it was with the knowledge and approval of the grand juries, but they were built totally irrespective of any controlling power on the part of the grand jury, because it was still under the 1 & 2 Geo. 4, c. 33, which originally empowered the Lord Lieutenant to build asylums, and which also empowered him, at any time when he thought fit, to divide districts, and to increase the number of asylums. It was under that Act that he built the seven asylums to which I have just referred, merely changing the Commissioners for building, they being, in the latter instance, the Board of Works.

5564. Subsequently to the building of those latter asylums which you have mentioned, the building of asylums was taken out of the hands of the Board of Works, was it not?—Yes, because when those seven asylums were built and handed over to the governors, they found fault with many of the parts of the buildings in detail. They considered that many of them were extravagant, and that they were badly built; and the result was that in the year 1858 there was a Committee of the House of Commons, Mr. Horsman being then Chief Secretary, and I believe I was the only witness examined with reference to the erection of those asylums. Subsequently a Commission was appointed, and two English architects and one of the Commissioners of Lunacy in England were sent over to report upon the state of those asylums, and it eventuated in a concession by the Treasury of 29,000 *l.*, which was deducted out of the 316,000 *l.* the primitive cost of the buildings. Since then, in consequence probably it may be of that allowance, the Government thought it more advisable in the year 1860 to abrogate the power of the Board of Works, so far as the building of asylums was in question; and they appointed four Commissioners, of whom the two Inspectors constituted a moiety, the two others being members of the Board of Works, the chairman and one other member.

J. Nugent, Esq., M.D.

5 June 1868.

5565. Under this new board, how many asylums have been built?—Under this new board we have built now six asylums.

5566. Can you state to the Committee the total amount expended on the building of asylums under the three different boards?—Yes, but perhaps I may anticipate the answer by stating that the last board, or the Board of Control, as it at present exists, made it one of their arrangements to consult on every occasion with the local gentry, that is to say, with committees of the grand juries, and so to proceed *pari passu* with the grand juries in the building of asylums, in order to obviate as much as possible any misunderstanding when the asylums should be handed over to the local authorities.

5567. Colonel *French.*] Had you any sanction from the grand jury for the building of any asylum?—Yes.

5568. Can you produce it?—I can produce it, but the Committee will probably accept my word as the fact. The total cost of those asylums now finished amounts to about 960,000 *l.* I do not include in that the 75,000 *l.* for which, as I mentioned to the Committee, the Richmond Asylum was built as a general asylum for Ireland. The Government, in the year 1830, transferred, by a free gift, the whole of that Richmond Asylum, for which they had paid 75,000 *l.*, to a district comprising the city of Dublin, the county of Dublin, the county of Meath, the county of Louth, the county of the town of Drogheda, and the county of Wicklow.

5569. *Chairman.*] So that in point of fact, nearly a million of money has been spent upon the building of those asylums?—Yes, and more than a million will have been spent in the course of a couple of years, because at the Richmond Asylum there will be an expenditure of probably 25,000 *l.*, and there have been additions lately ordered at Omagh, Maryboro', and various other asylums, which may cost 100,000 *l.* more; so that we may say that the expenditure will finally extend to 1,020,000 *l.*

5570. And all that has been repaid, or is in course of repayment from the county rates?—I think the amount repaid is about 340,000 *l.*

5571. Earl of *Mayo.*] Does that include interest as well as capital?—There is no interest.

5572. *Chairman.*] With respect to the maintenance of those asylums, how is that contributed?—Under the 1st & 2nd Geo. 4, the Lord Lieutenant can advance any sum of money not exceeding 10,000 *l.* to any district half-yearly; thus the maintenance of lunatic asylums at present is thus effected: the money is advanced from the Consolidated Fund, not paying any interest, and, as it is expended by the Board of Governors, from one half year to another, it is repaid at the next subsequent meeting of the grand jury, the amount so expended being sent down certified from the Privy Council Office.

5573. The amount is sent down and then it becomes an imperative presentment on the grand jury?—It is an imperative presentment on the grand jury.

5574. Are you aware what would be the rate in the pound of those payments?—Taking the valuation on which the rate in Ireland is levied to be about 12,000,000 *l.* or 13,000,000 *l.*, as I believe it is, the cost within another year will be as nearly as possible for the maintenance alone

J. Nugent, Esq., M.D.

9 June 1858.

3 d. in the pound on the whole valuation of Ireland, but it will vary very materially in some districts, for example, in the rich counties and in the counties where the population is sparse, being comparatively small; and in other counties very large. I will adduce a case in point: in the county of Meath the population is a little over 110,000 inhabitants, and the rateable property is about 580,000 l.; the result is that about 1½ d. in the pound clears the maintenance of lunatics for the county of Meath. If you take the county of Mayo, the population of the county of Mayo is about from 360,000 to 380,000 persons, and the rateable property is 310,000 l., so that you have considerably more than double the population, and but little more than half the income of the county of Westmeath; the maintenance, therefore, in the county of Mayo comes to about 4½ d. in the pound.

5575. *Earl of Mayo.*] When you make use of the word "maintenance," do you mean the whole annual cost of the asylum?—The whole annual support. I have drawn a distinction between the primitive cost of the asylum and the current maintenance from year to year.

5576. Colonel *French.*] How much will have to be paid in the county of Mayo?—That depends; if the county of Mayo has to pay, as other counties have, at the end of 14 years it will have liquidated its expenses. The cost of its asylum is about 35,800 l.; to meet a portion of which the county of Roscommon and the county of Galway will have to pay an *ad valorem* amount for the benefit which the county of Mayo had in the Galway Asylum. That will be deducted from the 35,800 l., so that probably between repayments for buildings and the current expense of maintenance it will be about 6½ d. in the pound while it continues. If the repayments be limited to 14 years, it will certainly be 6½ d. per annum in the pound.

5577. Is it in contemplation to erect any more of these asylums?—No; but we must make additions to some of them; we must increase the Richmond Asylum and various others.

5578. (*Chairman.*] Are the lunatics, confined in these asylums, paupers?—I do not think that pauperism is the test of admission into a lunatic asylum.

5579. Do you mean to say that in these lunatic asylums, supported at the public expense, lunatics are kept who are able to pay for themselves?—They are not able to pay for themselves. Pauperism is the test of admission into a poorhouse. A farmer cannot go into the poorhouse as a farmer; but if a farmer, who pays a rent of 30 l. or 40 l. a year, and who has his family to support, becomes insane, surely it would be a cruelty to deny him the advantage of a lunatic asylum, for the maintenance of which he has been perhaps paying for 20 or 30 years. Pauperism is the test of admission into a workhouse, but the legitimate test of admission into a lunatic asylum is that the party has not the means sufficient to support himself outside as a lunatic, or to support himself in a private licensed asylum.

5580. *Earl of Mayo.*] What is the term used in the Act?—Poor persons who are unable to support themselves.

5581. The definition is the same used in the Medical Charities' Act?—Precisely.

5582. *Chairman.*] The cost of a lunatic in the asylum is very much greater than the cost of a pauper in the workhouse, is it not?—The total cost, last year, was 100,000 l., and there were 4,200 lunatics; that is about 21 l. 10 s. per annum. It varies from one year to another, as provisions are cheaper or dearer. The cost of a pauper is about 9 l., I suppose.

5583. It is more than double?—Decidedly.

5584. Are not a great number of paupers transferred from workhouses to these asylums?—A great number of paupers are so transferred, and that is the majority of the case.

5585. Do you not think that these charges for lunatics, being for paupers, or for poor persons unable to support themselves, are charges which more correspond to the charges usually borne by the poor rates, than to the charges borne by the county rates?—The fact of the matter is, as I stated in the beginning, that when the lunatic asylums were built the only way they had of being paid was out of the county cess, and that has continued ever since. I presume that the parity of payment that they would adopt would be adopted in like manner, as is now the case in England. Lunatics in England are paid for by their parishes.

5586. In the same way as paupers who receive out-door relief are paid for?—Precisely.

5587. Do you not believe that if this charge were transferred to the poor rates and taken away from the county cess, it would lead to more circumspection on the part of boards of guardians and others in sending persons to lunatic asylums who might as well be retained in the workhouse?—Unfortunately the workhouse authorities throughout Ireland, with whom I have a very extensive acquaintance, always seem to desire to get rid of their lunatics, and by that means they escape an immediate charge; but still what one poorhouse does in one district the next poorhouse is doing in another, and it comes to an equality; so taking the total outlay thus incurred on the district at large no saving can be effected.

5588. Are not many persons sent from the workhouses to asylums who would be just as well in the workhouse?—Yes, that is a very important question; I think the legitimate object of an asylum is twofold; first as a curative institution, and secondly, as harbouring people who, though incurable, still require constant supervision to prevent themselves, and to protect society at large. That is the class of people for whom I think the lunatic asylum is essentially requisite; but then there is an immense mass of insane people who, with a little care and a little attention, could be very well maintained in the workhouses at one-half the expense, if a proper system were arranged.

5589. Are there many persons sent to lunatic asylums who are harmless idiots?—Yes, many of them are harmless idiots, who could be very well treated, I think, elsewhere. The very practice I now refer to is occurring to such an extent in England, that boards of visitors of asylums have are taking it into most serious consideration. I was speaking yesterday to the Commissioners of Lunacy in England; they have 58,000 lunatics of all grades and classes. From time to time I have visited different English asylums, and I find it reported at the last which was opened for the county of Surrey, at Brookwood, that out of 300 there are not 20 curable cases in it. The board of visitors are almost at a loss what to do, for in the county within the past 10 years the population of lunatics has increased from 1,400 to 2,300.

5590. *Earl of Mayo.*] Have they any lunatics in

in the poorhouses in England?—They have; as regards, for example, the asylum at Wakefield, in Yorkshire, the physician there reports that within the last few years a comparatively small portion of the original lunatics were remaining in the asylum, and that they were obliged to get rid of the rest by placing them in workhouses.

5591. *Chairman.*] Do you not think that if the Poor Law guardians had to pay a proportion of the expenses of the lunatic asylums for all the lunatics that went from each union, they would be more careful in not sending, to those asylums, that class of patients that could be treated as well at the workhouse?—They might, certainly.

5592. At present you have stated that the boards of guardians think that they get rid of an expense by sending them away?—Certainly; I think they were obliged to get a rider on to the Poor Law Act to meet the necessity of receiving lunatics in England.

5593. Mr. *Chichester Fortescue.*] Do you know what the definition is in England at the present time?—I do not know what it will be; I think if they have 50,000 lunatics in England, according to the unanimous decision of the judges the other day they will have 100,000 before long. The case was simply this: a physician had a lunatic to live in his house, he did not give information of the fact to the Commissioners in Lunacy, and they instituted proceedings against him. The effort which he made was that the man was not a lunatic, that he had been a very rational man all through life, and that he never had a delusion; the replication to the plea on the part of the Commissioners in Lunacy was, that the patient was incapable of taking care of himself to the extent that he ought, and that the defendant had received money for taking charge of him, the judges held that the man was insane; the affection being probably that imbecility which supervenes on advanced life, in many instances.

5594. Earl of *Mayo.*] There has been a correspondence lately, has there not, between the Poor Law guardians, and the inspectors of lunatic asylums, with respect to the power of removal of lunatics from lunatic asylums to poorhouses?—There has.

5595. Will you state to the Committee the circumstances of that particular case?—The board of guardians of a poorhouse can refuse the acceptance of a lunatic sent from a lunatic asylum into the poorhouse as a lunatic.

5596. *Chairman.*] Even though he may be a pauper?—Even though he may be a pauper. The Commissioners of the Poor Law are anxious, as far as possible, in consequence of the Act which the Earl of Mayo passed last Session to assist the inspectors in getting rid of lunatics out of gaols, and as there are a number of worn out cases in the lunatic asylums, we are desirous to provide for them elsewhere. Many poorhouses are willing to receive them, but others peremptorily refuse.

5597. Do you think that if the expense of keeping these paupers in lunatic asylums was paid out of the poor rate that difficulty would exist on the part of boards of guardians in receiving those paupers?—It would certainly make them more cautious about sending them.

5598. But if a pauper is supported in a lunatic asylum, he will cost more than twice what he will cost in the workhouse, will he not?—Certainly.

5599. Do you not think that that would be a very strong reason to induce the guardians to take them into the workhouse rather than to have them kept in the asylum?—Certainly, it would be an argument.

J. Nugent, Esq., M.D.

5 June 1868.

5600. All the medical charities in Ireland are paid under the poor law and by the poor rates, are they not?—They are.

5601. And this charge for lunatics is exactly the same class of charge, is it not?—It is, but on the other hand there is the objection raised by the landlords. They say that the tenant takes his ground cognizant of the fact that he has to support the lunatic poor.

5602. You are referring now to the question of the payment of poor rates being divided and the county cess not being divided; but quite irrespectively of that, do you think that the charges correspond?—I do.

5603. Have you any suggestion to make to the Committee with respect to the length of time allowed by the Government for the repayment of the advances made for buildings?—I think in some instances it comes very heavy; I should like if it were possible, the period of extension to be increased. Those institutions are built to last for centuries almost; of course the cost of construction is large, and I think it is very hard upon the present occupying tenants that they should have to pay for the building of institutions that will be good for centuries to come, and when they have ceased to have anything to do with the property of the county.

5604. Earl of *Mayo.*] Has there been any general demand for the shortening of the time?—I do not know that there has.

5605. General *Dunne.*] Was not the 14 years made upon a calculation of the valuation some years ago?—I do not know upon what principle it was made.

5606. Mr. *Chichester Fortescue.*] If the mode of charging for the expenses of lunatics in Ireland, were to be assimilated, or as nearly as possible assimilated to that of England, the expense would be charged to the electoral divisions, would it not?—It would.

5607. That would be the nearest parallel to the English parochial system of charging, would it not?—Certainly.

5608. *Chairman.*] Would you see any objection to dividing the charge of the lunatics between the different electoral divisions, or unions; would you see any difficulty for instance in dividing the establishment charges of the lunatic asylum?—I would charge the establishment charges upon the unions at large.

5609. You would see a difficulty in dividing the establishment charges over the electoral divisions?—I think so; there are no establishment charges, but we will say the maintenance charges.

5610. You would prefer charging the whole upon the union at large, and not assimilating it to the English system, of charging it upon the electoral division?—No, I think it is more congenial with the feelings of the Irish Poor Law Board in those cases, to have the union at large, pay a certain amount.

5611. When you say a certain amount, what are the Committee to understand by that?—I mean that the full amount of the annual cost of maintenance, should be paid by the union at large.

5612. And what do you understand by maintenance?—We will say the 21 *l.* 16 *s.* a year.

5613. Does that include a proportion of the establishment

J. Nugent, Esq., M.D.

5 June [illegible]

establishment charges?—It includes everything; it clears off every item of expenditure, except the building.

5614. Mr. *Chichester Fortescue.*] Then you would not propose to have any electoral division charge, corresponding to the parochial charge in England?—No, I would make it more general, I would make it a union at large charge; but I would observe that there is a difficulty in the way, one arising from the fact, that while unions embrace portions of two or more counties, lunatic districts are strictly confined within the limits of a county.

5615. But the motives against sending the paupers into the lunatic asylums would be weaker in the case of the guardians of the union at large, would they not, than they would be in the case of the guardians of a particular electoral division?—Yes, but then you have already the union fully represented, and perhaps the electoral division might not be represented on the occasion when the charge was made.

5616. Are there any paying patients in Irish lunatic asylums?—Yes; but the number of paying patients in the asylum is, indeed, very minute. For example, of the 120,000 *l.* that was paid last year for the maintenance of lunatics, not more than 1,600 *l.* was received from paying patients.

5617. What is the rule applicable to that subject?—Strictly speaking I do not think it is legal to receive paying patients; but still if there is a vacancy in an asylum, and a person is unable to pay outside, it is very hard to deny him the benefit of it.

5618. But you doubt its legality?—I think so. We have the opinion of the law officers, and they say that it is not legal, because the asylum is built for the insane poor; but still that privilege is extended occasionally.

5619. Are you aware that it is legal in this country, and that it is practised to a considerable extent?—You have in this country what we have not in Ireland, viz., licensed houses for parochial purposes.

5620. But I am speaking of the county asylums?—The county asylums have auxiliary asylums, as it were, in these licensed houses.

5621. But are you not aware that paying patients are admitted into the county asylums in England?—No, not as private patients.

5622. Earl of *Mayo.*] Do those persons who pay in the asylums pay the full charge?—Not as a rule.

5623. Is there any rule about it?—No; it may be however that at a board meeting a man comes in and says, "My son, gentlemen, is very ill, and I am willing to pay something for his support. Will you admit him? I will give 10 *l.* a-year. It is as much as I can afford, and when you wish I will take him away;" and the board say, "Very well, we will take him at 10 *l.* a-year." There is no rule; it is an *ad misericordiam* appeal in every case.

5624. Mr. *Chichester Fortescue.*] Do you think it would be desirable to put that matter upon a legal footing under any proper regulations?—I think it would. Lord Kimberley asked me at one time what I proposed to do about it; and I said I would make two rules, either that a person should pay the full amount, or that he should pay half the full amount instead of huckstering, as they occasionally do, and saying, "Cannot you pay 5 *l.* or 4 *l.*?"

5625. Earl of *Mayo.*] Is it your opinion that when the asylums which are now in course of construction are finished, there will then be ample room for the treatment of the lunatic poor that are likely to become fit subjects for the lunatic asylums?—I should think there would if great discretion is used.

5626. You are aware, I presume, that in the report of the Royal Commissioners they stated that to give proper accommodation to the cases which were fit for the reception in an asylum that accommodation ought to be nearly doubled? —They did.

5627. Does your experience coincide with that opinion which they expressed in that report?—I do not think it is necessary to go to all the expense of the arrangement of a regularly constituted asylum for a class of persons who are not likely to benefit by it, or who would not be able to appreciate the advantages of it. In our office we got this very year a return of every aged and imbecile lunatic all through the county. There are 256 police districts in Ireland, and we got at the end of the year in one day a return from the police of the number of lunatics, and they amounted to 7,500, exclusive altogether of those in poorhouses or in asylums. We know the locality and the townland, and we know their names and everything connected with them; I went very minutely through it, and I think five-sixths of them might be classified under the terms of imbecile idiots and epileptics. The building of an asylum costs per head a very large amount; it cost about 160 *l.* each bed, and in England I suppose it costs about 210 *l.*, so that every place, every bed, is represented by an interest of 9 *l.* or 10 *l.* a year added to the cost of maintenance.

5628. Then when you speak of this large number of persons that you have ascertained are still not in receipt of relief, is it your opinion that their position is one which is satisfactory, and that really they would not be the better for being placed in lunatic asylums?—I think they would be the better for being placed in some safe receptacle; but I do not think it would be necessary to go to the expense of building asylums for them; the way in which I would meet that difficulty would be this: there are many poorhouses that are unoccupied; and where they are in a wholesome, healthy situation, and where there is a quantity of ground attached to them, I see no difficulty whatever in adding to them a certain number of rooms, and putting one or two attendants to every 40 or 50 patients, and to the patients' having a better dietary than is afforded to the ordinary paupers of the institution. They could be maintained, perhaps, in that way for 10 *l.* or 11 *l.* per head, whereas in the ordinary lunatic asylums they would cost double that amount, totally irrespective of the cost of building accommodation for them.

5629. Mr. *Chichester Fortescue.*] That would be a special ward for imbeciles and idiots in the workhouse, under special regulations and with special diet?—It would.

5630. Earl of *Mayo.*] You would not propose to do that in every workhouse, would you?—Certainly not.

5631. You propose to select a workhouse suitable for it, and to make a lunatic ward in that workhouse for a union of unions?—Precisely. In the county of Kilkenny the Board of Governors of the Kilkenny Asylum adopted my advice on that subject, and they have made arrangements, and they send their lunatics to

where

J. Nugent, Esq., M.D.

9 June 1868.

where they are very well and very kindly treated, both in the workhouses at Kilkenny and Thomastown; independently of which, at Callan there is a workhouse half unoccupied, with about 10 acres of ground, which would make a very suitable asylum for chronic cases. Then I may observe with regard to the extensive county of Cork. The County of Cork Asylum was built for 600 patients, and within the last six months, the number of patients has been increased by 60. It is quite clear that the asylum is too small, and you must do one of two things; you must either make increased accommodation for another class of lunatics, or you must build another asylum in the western part of the county. Adjoining the asylum, at Youghal, there was an immense establishment for an agricultural school, with fine buildings utterly unoccupied, and with 30 acres of ground. Why should not that be taken and made a receptacle for hopeless chronic cases?

5632. Mr. *Chichester Fortescue.*] What is the nature of that agricultural school?—It was intended as an agricultural school, but it was given up.

5633. Was it under the National Board?—I do not know whether or not it was under the National Board.

5634. Earl of *Mayo.*] It was in connection with the poorhouse, was it not?—It was.

5635. It was one of the poorhouse farms, I believe?—Yes.

5636. Will you tell the Committee what you consider to be the nature of the present treatment of the lunatics in workhouses in Ireland?—I must say that there is a great amount of kindness of feeling displayed towards them. In the North Dublin Union, there are 140 of those lunatic inmates, and in the South Dublin Union there are the same number. I go there four or five times a year, and I must say that they are attended to with the greatest kindness. The only drawback is the want of a little more ground for exercise; but they are well fed, and their personal cleanliness is strictly attended to. The board pay a few attendants to look after them; and except, as I have mentioned, the want of ground for recreation, I do not see that they would be better off in the asylum.

5637. Is it the practice in those unions where there are such large numbers to send bad cases to the lunatic asylums?—Certainly.

5638. Is that constantly done?—Certainly; whenever a bad case is sent to them, they send it to the asylum, and it is accepted. If by legislation lunatic poorhouses should be established in each district, I think it should be an understood thing to give and take; and that if the lunatics become very violent in the poor-house, they should be at once drafted off to the asylum, and that those poorhouses should be visited from time to time by the resident physician, who has become cognizant of the cases which have been removed from his asylum, so that he may see how they are getting on; and if he sees that they are falling back, either mentally or corporeally, from the treatment in the poorhouse, they should be brought back to the lunatic asylum.

5639. Then you would suggest that power should be given to the board of governors of lunatic asylums to send a certain description of patients to the poorhouse lunatic ward?—Certainly.

5640. That would give the board of governors the power of sending persons who are not destitute, to be chargeable to a certain union where they have perhaps been brought up, and from which they have come, so that it would have the effect of introducing a principle into the Irish Poor Law which would be, to a certain extent, contrary to the principle on which the law of settlement has been founded?—Yes; but the only way to obviate that would be to do it by making it a special principle as regards lunatics.

5641. But so far as lunatics are concerned, it would be an alteration of the fundamental principle on which the Irish Poor Law was founded, would it not?—Certainly, except that you might meet it by making the Poor Law authorities pay so much for the maintenance of those lunatics, and let the governors of the asylum refund out of grand jury presentments, the expenditure upon those lunatics who had been so removed to the poorhouse.

5642. That would be a different mode of payment, because that would be really giving power to the boards of governors to farm out to the poorhouses a portion of their patients?—Certainly, as your Lordship very fairly puts it, as I stated, you would then have two different establishments in the same house, but the only way to meet that would be that we should not interfere if they are in a particular part of the establishment, and if that is the lunatic ward. I will give you a case in point. Up to the year 1853 we paid the Poor Law Board for patients which we had supported in the Dublin district at the auxiliary workhouses of Island Bridge and at the Hardwick cells. They were incurable lunatics, which we drafted off from the Richmond Asylum, whenever a great pressure from curable lunatics occurred. The Poor Law Board gave us up those two localities, and got payment regularly for the maintenance of the patients in them.

5643. Mr. *Chichester Fortescue.*] Then would you have those lunatic wards in poorhouses inspected by the inspectors of lunatic asylums over and above the ordinary Poor Law inspection?—Of course. In fact, my colleague and I from time to time visit nearly all the poorhouses in Ireland. We have the right of visiting every place where a lunatic is kept, either private or public.

5644. Earl of *Mayo.*] If you think that those poor lunatics can be kept so much more cheaply in the poor houses, why would it not be possible to establish in the lunatic asylums themselves a description of treatment similar to that which is pursued in the poorhouses, and which you say is sufficient for a certain class of lunatics?—They attempted that on a large scale in England, and they found great difficulty in doing it. It is much better to have a class of people in one house all receiving nearly the same treatment, than to have different gradations of treatment in the same asylum, for they say: "Here are a certain proportion of incurables; we will feed them worse, and not look after them so much as the curable cases." I think it is bad in principle. Besides, then you would have to take additional ground, and erect additional buildings.

5645. From your great experience of lunatics, do you think that it is easy to draw the line between a lunatic who is absolutely incurable, and a lunatic to whom constant medical treatment might, at all events, afford a considerable amount of alleviation of suffering?—Yes, there are a certain class of whom you can predicate that they never will be cured, who are utterly demented, and

J. Nugent, Esq., M.D.

5 June 1859.

and merged into idiotcy or imbecility, or whose minds have become affected from long-continued attacks of epilepsy, and who are affected both corporeally and mentally. That class of patients afford no hope of recovery. At the same time, I do not mean to say that every individual so circumstanced is a person who does not require the most remote care and attention, because many of these people are the very class of patients for whom all the auxiliaries and all the improved treatment that an asylum can afford are necessary; but there is a certain limited number who are quiet and inoffensive, and who will sit in a corner and spend the whole day in thoughtless existence, incompetent to do anything.

5646. Do you not think that if this system were adopted, there would be a considerable temptation held out to the authorities in those institutions to relieve themselves of the expense of a large number of their patients by sending to places where they would be more cheaply kept, and where the medical treatment would be less active, persons who might probably be better relieved in an asylum, and who required daily medical attendance, such as they would receive there?—But you have the controlling power in the executive body who will visit those asylums, and who will see that they are proper houses; and further, you have the physician of the asylum, who becomes responsible for the class of people sent to those places. The inspectors in their visitations would see that no abuse was committed, and no person should be transmitted from an asylum to a poor-house without an intimation to the central office, stating the circumstances under which he was so sent, and without the authority of the inspectors being obtained for his removal.

5647. Do you think that that would be a sufficient check on any evils which might arise?—Perfectly sufficient.

5648. Is it your opinion that if those evils did arise they would be very serious?—Most serious.

5649. Do you think that in those lunatic wards which you have described, you will be able to command a sufficient amount of medical experience and talent for the proper treatment of those patients?—I think so.

5650. Your opinion, I presume, is that all lunatics require more or less medical treatment and inspection?—They do; as a rule in all the poorhouses, they should be visited daily, whether they require it or not.

5651. Is that the rule now?—That is the rule now.

5652. Does that rule obtain in all workhouses where there are lunatics?—It does when they are numerous.

5653. General *Dunne*.] Do you not think that if some of these harmless incurable lunatics were allowed to live at home, a small pension being granted for their support, that would be very satisfactory, both to the people and to their families?—I think that it would be open to abuse, because if you give to a family 4 s. or 5 s. for the support of an imbecile, it is out-door relief.

5654. But are there not at this moment a great number of that class, whom their families keep and do not send to the asylum?—There are; but in that case it is the worse for the families; I would have the lunatics always under governmental inspection.

5655. Have you ever compared the charges of the system of maintenance of lunatics in Ireland and in England?—Yes; our charges are considerably less than elsewhere. I will take the Dundrum Criminal Lunatic Asylum, which is altogether under the control of Government inspection; we have from 160 to 170 criminals there; they have about 25 acres of ground perfectly open and clear, and the expense there is not more than 23 l. per head per annum, everything included; whereas at Broadmoor, which partakes more of the character of an insane prison, it is fully a half more.

5656. Are the salaries of the officers different?—Yes; the salaries of the Broadmoor Asylum officers are very much larger.

5657. What is the salary of the medical superintendent?—Our medical superintendent's salary is 360 l. at Dundrum, at Broadmoor it is, I apprehend, 1,200 l.

5658. In the various asylums throughout Ireland, is the scale of salaries on the *same* ratio as in England?—The salaries are not as good in Ireland as in England.

5659. Is that the case with regard to your own salary?—We are far below the English inspectors in that respect; after 22 *years'* service, my salary is 1,050 l. only a year.

5660. Can you tell me the reason why they should be better paid in England than in Ireland?—I cannot tell, but I should be very glad if there were no necessity for asking the question.

5661. Are the duties the same?—Without wishing to underrate the services of the English commissioners we have, I think, greater and more varied duties, for in addition to visiting and inspecting, we have the whole fiscal superintendence of asylums, and the whole control of the criminal asylum at Dundrum, which costs about 3,000 l. a year at the outside; besides we are joint trustees and commissioners, as already stated, for the building, furnishing, &c. of all public asylums.

5662. The whole administration in Ireland therefore is much less expensive than in England?—Yes; the asylums in Ireland, I may say, are essentially governmental institutions, and in England they are local institutions. Of course, in Ireland, the Government hold the inspectors in a great measure responsible for any advice which they give, or any information which they afford.

5663. Then the counties have very little more to do with it than to pay for it?—They have very little to do but with the fiscal arrangements.

5664. Have they any power to examine into the accounts?—All the expenses of the asylum are paid by the governors.

5665. But can the board of governors examine into the details of the accounts, if they think proper?—Certainly; and they are bound to do so.

5666. *Earl of Mayo*.] As a rule, do the boards of governors exercise a practical superintendence over the economy of these establishments?—I believe they do. I have been for 22 years connected with lunatic asylums, and I think that the system of expenditure in lunatic asylums is the best that can possibly be devised; nothing is done except by contract, and no contract is made until the contracts have been sent up to the office of the inspectors, and approved and entered there; we then send over to the Audit Office the name of the party who has entered into the contract and the amount of money payable for each individual article;

ments; and then the money is advanced by the Lord Lieutenant in Council, and paid to the credit of the board of governors of each asylum. Then, as to the items of expenditure, the boards of governors meet once a month, and sometimes more frequently, and they then examine the accounts, and the applications for payments are examined and vouched for at this board, and at the next board the payment is ordered; the vouchers are then sent over to the Audit Office through our office for all the expenses, and anything which is irregular is discovered at once at the Audit Office.

3667. But do the governors exercise in the original making of the contract a practical supervision?—I think they do.

3668. Are you aware that it has been alleged publicly that for all practical purposes the making of contracts originally is very much in the hands of the resident medical superintendent, and do you think that that is a fair statement of what occurs?—Conscientiously I do not think that it is; and if it did occur, I think that the board would be abdicating its functions.

3669. Do you think that as a rule they do not do it?—I think, as a rule, honestly, truly, and conscientiously, the utmost integrity is exercised by the boards of governors in making just contracts; and that they examine fairly, honestly, and correctly, all the accounts.

3670. When a contract comes to you to be ratified, do you ever make any objection to it, or suggest alterations in it?—Constantly; all the contracts accepted are sent to us; very often, for instance, we see a tender for bread for 7¼ d., and another man's tender accepted at 7½ d.; in that case we should at once write down to know why the tender at 7¼ d. was not rejected, and the tender at 7½ accepted, and there is always a satisfactory answer given, either that the person had failed in performing a contract, or that his character was not sufficiently good, or that his security was not such as could be relied upon.

3671. So that in addition to the check which there is over the making of contracts by the local bodies, you have, in the case of lunatic asylums, additional check of a central authority over every contract?—Certainly; very often the contractors write complaining of the board's conduct towards them, and of course in a case of that kind we transmit to the board a copy of the letter which we get from the complaining contractor, and request the board to explain the circumstances.

3672. General *Dunne*.] Speaking generally, do you not find that the board of governors and the inspectors agree very well and act harmoniously together?—I do.

3673. What is your opinion of the local inspectors?—We have no local inspectors; I think they would be merely a useless expense. In the opinion of the public at large it is well that to an institution, such as a lunatic asylum, which is not so open as others, there should be an external officer, such as a visiting physician.

3674. And you would continue those officers?—I would.

3675. They are in communication with the governors, and with the local authorities, are they not?—They are.

3676. Are they satisfactory to them?—I believe they are, but I am speaking more of the principle than of the particulars.

3677. Colonel *Forde*.] Do I understand you to suggest a new officer for lunatic asylums in the shape of a local inspector?—Certainly not.

3678. Is not the visiting physician appointed for that purpose?—The visiting physician is constantly meeting the governors of the asylum. He mixes with the public, and is always amongst the most respectable practitioners in the locality.

3679. Mr. *Blake*.] In order that a poor person should get into a lunatic asylum, is it not essential that his next of kin should make a declaration that the person's means are insufficient to support him in a private asylum?—Yes.

3680. With the exception of Dr. Steward's asylum at Lucan, where he takes a few patients at exceptionally low rates, is it not a fact that a person cannot be maintained in any private lunatic asylum in Ireland for less than 50 *l.* or 60 *l.* a year?—That I believe is the minimum.

3681. In your experience, have you heard that there are persons in lunatic asylums, supported out of the rates who would be able to pay the cost charges in the asylum, but who escape from it by reason of the declaration of their friends that they cannot support them in a private asylum?—Certainly.

3682. Under those circumstances, do you not think it very desirable to have a change in the law, so as to enable persons whose means or the means of whose *friends* are inadequate to support them in a private asylum, to be maintained in the district asylum at the cost charges?—I think it would be but just.

3683. Do not many of their friends, where those persons have, for instance, 25 *l.* a year, and when they hear that they could not be maintained in a private asylum under 40 *l.* a year, save their consciences by making a declaration that they are unable to support them in a private asylum?—Certainly.

3684. So that under those circumstances the rates are often charged for the maintenance of persons who legitimately could pay?—Certainly.

3685. With regard to the suggestion which you have offered as to the desirability of having certain workhouses arranged for the reception of incurable and harmless lunatics, would it not be essential to give those people a somewhat different treatment from the ordinary paupers?—I would look upon it as essential.

3686. Are there not a great number of harmless patients in the poorhouses of Ireland who have not the advantage of such treatment?—There are; but I think a manifest improvement is taking place generally speaking, in the treatment of the lunatic classes in Ireland in poorhouses; I am quite aware that there are some poorhouses where they are badly treated; but still I think a benevolent feeling is now arising on the subject, and boards of guardians, from the subject being constantly brought under their notice, are becoming more liberal in their ideas; indeed, I think the parties responsible for the lunatics not being properly looked after in poorhouses are the medical men themselves.

3687. Are there many charitable institutions in Ireland for the maintenance of poor lunatics?—There are two; the first is Swift's Hospital, which is a foundation in which people of small means are admitted and people of large means pay largely, and the difference between the two meets the deficiencies of the one. Then there is a very creditable establishment near Dublin, superintended by a religious community, in which I think

J. Nugent, Esq. M.D.

5 June 1868.

J. Nugent, Esq., M.D.

3 June 1858.

I think they have now about 140 female patients, the surplus beyond the cost of the maintenance of the rich going for respectable persons who cannot afford to pay the absolute charges, but who pay in part.

5688. What is the average cost in Swift's Hospital?—The average cost I would say is about 60 guineas a year.

5689. Is that the lowest for which it could be done?—I do not think, taking the whole asylum together, you could do it under 56 guineas. They have very good living, and are very well looked after.

5690. Do not the Society of Friends look after their own lunatics?—They do; and I never saw an asylum on the whole superior to the Quakers' Retreat near Dublin, which is a voluntary institution.

5691. Is there not a very great want in Ireland of asylums for a class of patients who could pay from 30*l.* to 40*l.* a year?—It would be advantageous; but you have not in Ireland what there is in England, a class between the gentry and the poor. In Ireland we have absolute paupers; then we have the farmers, and then we have the rich men; but in England you have two or three grades between those classes, and I do not think that we have those grades in Ireland.

5692. In your inspection of private asylums in Ireland, have you not found several persons there whose friends are absolutely in distressed circumstances?—Occasionally.

5693. Would it not be not only advantageous to the ratepayers to have such a class of people taken into the district lunatic asylums at something over the cost price, but also most advantageous to that class of people themselves?—Certainly; and I look ultimately to that being the result. If we can disembarrass the lunatic asylums in Ireland of all classes except those whose residence is necessary, for their own protection or the protection of society, it will leave a margin for the class of people to which you refer, who will pay the average cost of their maintenance in the institution.

5694. Is it not the practice of the boards of governors of some lunatic asylums in Ireland absolutely to refuse any stipend whatever with the patients?—Yes; in Belfast they will not receive anything; but in fact, out of 120,000*l.* paid for the maintenance of lunatics last year, only 1,600*l.* was received as part payment from their friends, which is little more than one per cent.

5695. Are not some of the large towns in Ireland, and particularly some of the maritime towns, placed in a very disadvantageous position by getting a large proportion of lunatics who frequently do not belong to the town at all?—Yes; Dublin suffers materially from that.

5696. Has it ever occurred to you that it would be desirable to transmit the patients who may become insane in some maritime town, and to make them chargeable to the unions to which they belong?—In Ireland, to our credit, I must say, that I never knew a lunatic belonging to England to be sent out of a lunatic asylum in Ireland; but we occasionally get them sent over to us from England, and frequently from Scotland.

5697. With regard to the appointment of governors of lunatic asylums in the first instance, the gentlemen so appointed were named by the Lord Lieutenant and the Privy Council, were they not?—Yes.

5698. But I suppose that in a great measure now the Lord Lieutenant adopts those gentlemen whom you and your colleagues may suggest as being most desirable?—No, I am not much consulted; they are generally appointed without reference to me.

5699. Mr. *Chichester Fortescue.*] Is it not the case, that in Irish workhouses there is a considerable class of lunatics to whom the technical condition of destitution is not legally applicable, namely, the class of patients in the infirmaries?—Yes. Under Sir Robert Peel's Act, which was a most beneficial one, persons who are not paupers, but who are not well to do, can take advantage of hospital accommodation and hospital treatment. There never was a wiser or more benevolent Act than that.

5700. So that already with regard to that particular class, the condition of destitution has been dispensed with?—Yes; and if you take insanity as a disease, it appears to me that it must follow as a corollary, that it should be similarly treated.

5701. Mr. *Blake.*] Is there a settled dietary in lunatic asylums?—We have not a settled dietary.

5702. Is it not the case that the diet really varies very considerably?—It varies considerably, but with the exception of Cork, I think that it is nowhere under par. If you take the dietary given to the lunatics in Ireland, and take the dietary given to lunatics in England, I think that the dietary given in Ireland is on the whole quite as good; and certainly if you take the treatment of the lunatic in a lunatic asylum in Ireland, and contrast his position with what it was before he entered the asylum, you will find that you have brought him as it were from a hovel into a palace; because in England comfort is indigenous to the family of the lunatic, but in Ireland it is unfortunately the reverse.

5703. Do you not consider from your experience and knowledge of the treatment of insanity, that a particular kind of dietary is very essential for the curative treatment of patients?—That depends upon the condition of the patients; I cannot answer the question generally, because each individual patient presents peculiar phases of the disease which you must meet accordingly. A liberal dietary of animal food, as a rule, is requisite.

5704. But is it not the fact that in some of the asylums in Ireland there is a smaller quantity of meat and soup given to the whole of the patients than is given to the whole of the patients in another asylum?—Yes; I have said that there is a variation; but still, taking the average dietary in Ireland, no one can at all take any objection to it; you might improve it slightly, but as a rule I think that the Irish lunatic is well fed, and nothing can be better than the care bestowed upon him.

5705. Would it not be desirable that an officer in your position should have the same power as the Poor Law Commissioners have of directing the question of dietary?—We have the power to do it under the Privy Council rule, but if there is no absolute deficiency it becomes rather invidious to tell a board of governors that they are not giving enough to their patients; we do it indirectly through the medical man, but as I said before, the scale of dietary, with the exception of Cork, where I was the other day, and where they promised to increase it, it is very good.

5706. Do

J. Nugent, Esq., M.D.

5 June 1868.

5706. Do you think that a board of governors, which chiefly consists of country gentlemen, who cannot have any practical or perhaps any theoretical ideas about the treatment of insanity, ought to have the power of deciding whether any officers, such as chaplains, ought to be appointed or not?—I think that is a lapsed question, because there is only one asylum in Ireland where they have refused to appoint chaplains, and I had a letter the other morning stating that they had unanimously resolved to appoint chaplains.

5707. Do you think for the due treatment of insanity a board of governors of a lunatic asylum which, as I have just stated, consists of a body of gentlemen who may not have any practical or theoretical knowledge of the treatment of insanity, should have the power of saying that they would have a certain officer, such as a chaplain, or that they would dispense with him altogether?—It is a delicate question; but I myself think that there are certain officers who ought to be appointed to asylums. That is my own personal conviction, and I do not mean to say that I am right, but I think that certain officers ought to be attached to asylums, and should as a matter of course be necessary ingredients of the staff of asylums totally irrespective of whether they are allowed or disapproved of; I am simply expressing my opinion, but that is the law.

5708. If that be the law, why is it that in one asylum, at least in Ireland, the board of governors persistently persevered in not allowing the appointment of a chaplain?—Perhaps they acted upon their conscientious convictions.

5709. Do you not think that for the due treatment of the insane the judicious ministrations of a chaplain are very essential?—I have very strong convictions on that point; I think that no asylum should be without a chaplain. In the very first annual report upon the English asylums, that question of religious ministrations in asylums is dealt with, and my own conviction, from observation, is that it appears to be almost an injustice to deny to any person whom you keep immured, and who has not the power of going out, the privilege of attending religious ministrations, or the benefit of his clergy. Insanity may take ten thousand different forms. A person may be insane on one subject and sane on others. It may be my weakness to imagine that I shall die in a poorhouse, but that does not debar me from being able to appreciate the benefits of religion, and it should not debar me from indulging in the gratifications of religious worship. A person's mind may be as clear as possible on every point, except one. I do not pretend to any party at all, but on Sunday last I was at the Cork Asylum, and I went down in the morning, though I am a Roman Catholic myself, to see the Protestant chapel. About 40 of the patients and attendants were present, and I never saw better behaved people in my life, or people who seemed to be more interested in the sermon which was preached to them, and they came out of their little chapel in the grounds, and walked away seemingly quite happily.

5710. Is it not rather a failure of duty in point of law, on the part of the Lord Lieutenant of Ireland, when there is not a chaplain appointed in an asylum in Ireland, to allow such a state of things to go on?—I would not venture to give an opinion upon that point. A great deal is left to the discretion of his Excellency.

5711. *Earl of Mayo*.] There is only one asylum, I believe, in Ireland, where there are no chaplains?—There is another besides the one to which reference has been made, namely, Armagh. The late Primate of Armagh gave out of his own pocket 60 *l.* a year to a clergyman to act as chaplain to the asylum, and the Roman Catholic bishop also appointed a clergyman, but those gentlemen are paid by the bishops of their Churches and are not regularly salaried. I know of no asylum in England or Ireland except those two which is without a clergyman.

5712. *Mr. Blake*.] The Lord Lieutenant has the absolute appointment of the resident medical officer, has he not?—He has.

5713. Does he ever consult you and your colleagues as to the eligibility of the persons who are appointed?—Generally.

5714. From the answer which you have just given, that you consider that the chaplain is an essential officer in an asylum, should you consider that an aspirant for the office of resident physician of an asylum who gave a contrary opinion was fit for such a position?—I disagree with him in the opinion, but it might be a matter of conscience. He might think that it would be injudicious.

5715. If spiritual consolation to some of the lunatics in an asylum, at all events, is essential in a curative point of view, should you not consider that if a person entertained a contrary opinion upon that point, his idea was not a correct one?—I would say that it was not a correct idea.

Tuesday, 9th June 1868.

MEMBERS PRESENT:

Mr. Blake.	Mr. Kendall.
Colonel Cooper.	Sir Charles Lanyon.
General Dunne.	Mr. Leader.
Colonel French.	Earl of Mayo.
Mr. Gregory.	The O'Conor Don.

THE O'CONOR DON, IN THE CHAIR.

Mr. HENRY BAKER, called in; and Examined.

Mr. *H. Baker.* — 9 June 1868.

5716. *Chairman.*] YOU are Secretary of the Grand Jury of the County of Dublin, are you not?—I am.

5717. And you have been so since the Act under which the grand jury system was established?—Yes.

5718. The system in the county of Dublin differs from that in other parts of Ireland, does it not?—It does.

5719. You have there only one assize in the year, I believe?—That is all.

5720. And there is practically no criminal business transacted by the grand jury of the county of Dublin, is there?—Rarely, or never.

5721. The criminal business of the county of Dublin is done at a commission, is it not?—Yes.

5722. There is also but one presentment sessions in the year in the county of Dublin, I believe?—Yes, and an adjourned sessions.

5723. The adjourned sessions in the county of Dublin is held after the assizes and not before, is it not?—Yes.

5724. The system there is that you have first the presentment sessions, then the assizes, and then the adjourned sessions?—Yes.

5725. Tenders are received and contracts entered into at the adjourned sessions, are they not?—Yes.

5726. And no contract is entered into until the work has been approved by the grand jury?—And previously by the original sessions.

5727. Colonel *French.*] Then you have two meetings of the sessions?—Yes.

5728. *Chairman.*] You have the same number of meetings of sessions as other counties, the difference being that the adjourned sessions are held in the county of Dublin after the assizes, instead of before?—Exactly.

5729. Do you see any advantage in that?—Yes; I understand that practice in other counties is that the contracts and recognizances are all entered into previous to the grand jury considering each presentment; and that then if they do not approve of a presentment, you are obliged to cancel the whole proceeding; whereas the contracts not being taken in the county of Dublin until after the grand jury have approved of them, no contracts are taken except what are acted upon *bonâ fide*, subsequently.

5730. Contracts then, as contracts, do not come before the grand jury at all?—Not at all.

5731. How are the cess-payers selected in the county of Dublin to attend the Presentment Sessions?—There is a list of 100 of the highest cesspayers for each barony furnished by the county cess collectors to the secretary; and, the number being previously fixed by the grand jury of the cess-payers who are to attend, 12 being the maximum allowed by the statute, take 36 names from the head of the list, excluding, in the first instance, those who have been acting for the preceding year. Then the 36 names are put into a ballot-box, and the foreman of the grand jury, in open court, draws 12 names, and those 12 names are published, and they are the cess-payers for the ensuing year.

5732. Is the ballot taken at the assizes?—The ballot is taken at the assizes.

5733. And it is a ballot out of three times the number who are eligible to sit?—It is.

5734. Are those cess-payers selected for each barony?—They are selected for each barony. There are 36 names for each barony.

5735. Do you find that the cess-payers thus selected attend the presentment sessions regularly?—Not well.

5736. Do they attend as well as the magistrates?—Generally speaking they do not.

5737. Mr. *Gregory.*] Is there any attempt made to get the different parts of the barony represented, or do you merely take them as they come?—I merely take them as they come on the list. They are put in the order of the amount of cess which they pay, the highest coming first.

5738. *Chairman.*] Then you ballot for the 12 simply out of the 36 highest cess-payers?—Yes, for each barony.

5739. Might it so happen that those 12 who came out of the ballot, might come from one particular portion of the barony?—Quite so.

5740. General *Dunne.*] Is there a special grand jury enactment for the county of Dublin?—There is.

5741. *Chairman.*] In the county of Dublin at the adjourned sessions, the magistrates and cess-payers are not obliged to accept the lowest tender, are they?—No.

5742. Will you state to the Committee what is the exact difference in that respect?—There have been words introduced into the county of Dublin Act, to the effect that they are not obliged to take the lowest tender if they see any reason for not doing so.

5743. What is their general practice in that respect?—Their general practice in that respect is to take the lowest tender, unless there is an objection made; the usual objection upon which they

they act in, the man having been previously a contractor, and having done his work badly.

5744. Do they rely a good deal upon the opinion of the county surveyor with respect to contractors applying for works?—I think that the magistrates, generally speaking, have some knowledge as to the character which he holds, either through members of the finance committee, or from being members of the finance committee themselves.

5745. Are those adjourned sessions where the contracts are entered into, well attended?—No, generally speaking, they are not nearly so well attended as the original sessions; they look upon it more as a matter of form as to taking the recognizances than originating works.

5746. Is it so much a matter of form when there seems to be so much discretion left to them as to what tenders should be accepted?—That is the only way in which I can account for the very great difference in the attendance.

5747. Do you find that there is in Dublin as there is in other parts of Ireland, a very great difference in the attendance?—A very great difference.

5748. You have also in Dublin a standing finance committee, have you not?—Yes.

5749. By whom was it appointed?—By the grand jury.

5750. And of whom does it consist?—The greater part of it is generally taken from the grand jurors, and the remainder from the ratepayers of the county.

5751. Must they necessarily be members of the grand jury?—No, the Act describes no qualification whatever for being a member.

5752. Are they generally the same persons who are re-appointed year after year?—Generally three or four are changed at the end of the list, being those who have given the least attendance during the preceding year.

5753. How often does this committee meet?—Regularly once a month, and occasionally oftener, as circumstances may render it desirable.

5754. Will you state the exact duties which they have to discharge?—Paying the contractors, and receiving the reports of how the collection is made by the collectors every month; but the disbursement of the public funds is their principal duty.

5755. Are not other matters very often referred to them by the grand jury, if any matter for discussion arises?—If any point of question arises that the grand jury find that they have not time to dispose of during the time, they always refer it to the finance committee.

5756. I suppose that the finance committee is looked up to and depended upon a good deal by the grand jury?—Very much so indeed.

5757. Colonel *French*.] Of what number does the finance committee consist?—Twelve.

5758. *Chairman*.] Practically, you may say that the finance committee is the grand jury?—I should very much say so. The leading members of both bodies are generally the same.

5759. They meet, I suppose, in the city of Dublin?—Yes; at the Court of Queen's Bench.

5760. I think that you have a return here of the number of meetings?—I have.

5761. Will you hand that in?—I will do so. (*The same was delivered in.—vide Appendix.*)

5762. What is the average attendance?—Seven at each meeting during the year for the last 10 years.

5763. Mr. *Gregory*.] Is that the annual or the average attendance?—That is the average attendance, taking all the meetings together.

Mr. H. Baker.

9 June 1868.

5764. *Chairman*.] Is there any quorum necessary for the transaction of business?—Three form a quorum.

5765. This finance committee, you state, make all the payments to contractors?—Yes.

5766. Do they require the certificate of the county surveyor upon works?—Not necessarily. They can pay on any evidence they please.

5767. But the surveyors are obliged to attend the meetings, are they not?—Yes; and of course they always take their evidence.

5768. Have they, in Dublin, assistant surveyors?—No.

5769. How many county surveyors are there?—Two.

5770. The county is divided into two districts, is it not?—It is.

5771. And those two districts look after themselves?—Yes.

5772. How often are the payments made by the finance committee to the contractors?—Once a month. They meet once a month to pay anybody who puts in a claim, and the time they have regulated for the payment of contractors on works of maintenance is once a quarter.

5773. Colonel *French*.] Where do they get the funds to pay them?—All the county funds are to their credit in the Bank of Ireland, and they can draw upon them.

5774. *Chairman*.] Are the collectors obliged to bring in their accounts to this finance committee at every meeting, once a month?—Yes.

5775. And they are obliged to lodge their collection?—They should lodge their collection as soon as they have collected 100 *l.*

5776. Do you not think that with regard to the finance committee, the county of Dublin is differently situated from other counties in Ireland?—I should think so. I should think that it was easier to obtain advantages in the county of Dublin than in other counties.

5777. Because the grand jurors chiefly reside in the city of Dublin, and they can go down to the four courts?—Yes, it is a central place, and has many attractions besides the meeting of the Committee.

5778. Supposing that such a committee were adopted in other parts of Ireland, in your opinion, would it be as well attended?—I should not have the same confidence in the attendance.

5779. In the county of Dublin as you stated practically, the finance committee is the grand jury of the county, and whatever they wish is done?—There is very seldom a difference of opinion.

5780. There is no treasurer in the county of Dublin at all, is there?—No.

5781. Has there ever been a treasurer?—Yes, up to the commencement of the operation of this Act.

5782. You, as secretary of the grand jury, sign the cheques, do you not?—I countersign the cheques.

5783. They are first signed by the chairman of the finance committee, are they not?—Yes, and two members.

5784. Do you receive any fees besides your salary as secretary to the grand jury?—I receive 6 *d.* on each recognizance which is prepared, and brought to the adjourned sessions, and 3 *d.* for each form of tender issued.

5785. Do

Mr. *H. Baker.*

9 June 1858.

5785. Do you not receive any customary fees as they are called?—There is 1 *d.* charged for each form which is given out of the office, which I keep printed for the public convenience, and for my own; and if these forms are filled up by my men in the office (though they take nearly as many without their being filled up as filled) I think there is 6 *d.* charged for filling them up.

5786. Is that all?—That is all.

5787. Are those forms printed at the public expense?—No.

5788. How is the collection of cess made in the county of Dublin?—The poundage is 1 *s.* in the pound.

5789. Is it collected by collectors appointed by the grand jury?—Yes.

5790. Are you aware what is paid in the county of Dublin for the collection of the poor rates?—In the district in which I reside, I think the average is four per cent.

5791. Is there any difference in the law with respect to the power of the county surveyor in enforcing contracts in the county of Dublin?—I believe that the 57th section which enables him to go in on a ten days' notice, and execute the work himself, where a contractor is in default, does not exist in other counties: that is to say, if he lets his road go out of repair, the surveyor may serve him with a ten days' notice, and after the expiration of those ten days, if the road is not in perfect order, the contractor has power to execute the works himself, and apply to the finance committee for payment, which is taken out of the sum which would be to the credit of the contractor.

5792. Is that considered sufficient to provide against defaulting contractors?—There are other resources open to the county surveyor to proceed on afterwards. That is an additional one in the County of Dublin. They can put their recognizances in suit, and they can also apply to petty sessions.

5793. Has any difficulty arisen in prosecuting defaulting contractors for not having tried, in the first instance, this remedy, of the county surveyor repairing the road himself?—Yes, there was a case tried in the court of Queen's Bench, and the court ruled that they did not think that the county surveyor should have proceeded on the recognizance against the contractor until he had exhausted the means given him under that section, that is to say, until he had spent all the money which was to the credit of the presentment.

5794. In many cases would not that make the contractor rather careless?—It would have that effect, and it is the opinion of the Finance Committee, I think, that it had that effect.

5795. When was the Act passed for regulating the county of Dublin grand jury?—It came into operation in January 1844.

5796. Can you tell the Committee the relative expenditure in the county of Dublin, before that Act came into operation and since?—The rate in the pound before the operation of the Act was 11½ *d.* In the present year it is 1 *s.* 6 *d.* in the pound. Then there is a certain proportion of that accountable for by the turnpike roads which in the year 1856 were transferred from the turnpike trustees, and thrown upon the county to the amount of about 6,000 *l.* a year.

5797. Could you state what was the amount spent in the year 1843, and in the last year?—The amount of the cess in the year 1843 was 25,525 *l.*, and in the present year it is 33,380 *l.*

5798. In the present year is it the same area which is dealt with by the grand jury; is the 33,000 *l.* spent over the same area as the 25,000 *l.* in the first year which you mentioned?—No.

5799. What is the difference?—There was a much greater area in the year 1843 than there is in the year 1858.

5800. There has been a great deal of the county of Dublin taken out of the grand jury arrangements since then, has there not?—A great deal has been practically taken out by the local Acts of Parliament forming townships which are now taken away from the county, so far as baronial assessment is concerned.

5801. And those townships manage their own roads and bridges, and everything else of that description, do they not?—Yes.

5802. They pay a certain proportion to the public charges, do they not?—They remain a constituent part of the county for county at large assessments.

5803. Have you any county at large assessments connected with roads, or bridges, or works of that kind?—Very rarely; there is no such thing for roads. Occasionally there is a large bridge put on, but it is very rarely.

5804. Is there no such thing in the county of Dublin as mail car and coach roads, payable half by the county at large?—No.

5805. Does each barony pay for its own roads?—Each barony pays for its own roads.

5806. And do those townships pay all such expenses?—They pay all such expenses.

5807. Then the only portion of the county expenses to which those townships contribute are the institutions and county at large expenses of that description?—Salaries and all those things are placed on the county at large.

5808. The cess in the county of Dublin has enormously increased since the year 1843, has it not?—It has.

5809. Both as regards the poundage and the total amount?—Yes.

5810. Has it increased in the same proportion in the townships?—I am not prepared to say. I do not exactly know what the rates in the townships are. They report themselves as being better off.

5811. There has been a strong desire to separate themselves from the county, has there not?—There has.

5812. All you have said refers strictly to the county of Dublin?—Exclusively to the county.

5813. The city being under quite a distinct arrangement?—Quite so. The corporation of Dublin manage that.

5814. This finance committee, as I understand, pays the contractors at least quarterly?—Yes.

5815. Do you think that any advantage has arisen from that, in the way of getting contracts taken at a lower rate?—I think so. I think that being able to give the contractors their money at short periods is a great assistance.

5816. As a matter of fact, are the contracts in the county of Dublin lower than in the neighbouring counties?—I am not prepared to speak as to that. I do not know of my own knowledge how that is.

5817. You do not know, for instance, whether the contracts in the county of Dublin are lower than in the county of Wicklow, which is next to it?—I do not. I have no information as to that.

5818. Your idea then, with respect to the advantage

Mr. *G. Baker.*

9 June 1868.

advantage of those quarterly payments, is merely a general one, is it not?—I have known individual cases where men have taken contracts, and where they could not carry on their contracts if they were kept, say six months, out of their money.

5819. Do you think that that must have led to the contracts in the county of Dublin being lower than in other places?—It ought to do so; but whether as a matter of fact it does so or not I do not know.

5820. Would you be surprised if you heard that the fact was the other way, and that in the county of Wicklow they were much lower than in the county of Dublin?—I would not, because I think there are many circumstances that render Dublin very expensive in that way. In many parts of the county of Dublin material is getting very scarce, and there is a great indisposition, on the part of landowners and proprietors, to allow contractors to go for material to convenient places.

5821. Would that apply to (we will suppose) whatever barony lies next to the county of Wicklow?—I do not know that it would apply to that particularly.

5822. At all events, you know nothing about the expense of contracts in other counties?—I do not.

5823. How do you account for the very large increase in the cess in the county of Dublin since the year 1843?—In addition to what I mentioned before, the price of labour has increased very much indeed.

5824. Has it increased comparatively more in Dublin than in other parts of Ireland?—I am not prepared to say that; but so far as my knowledge goes, it has increased 30 per cent. in Dublin.

5825. Colonel *French.*] What extent of turnpike road was thrown in addition on you to keep up?—Ninety-two miles.

5826. Do you attribute the increase of the cess to the 92 miles of turnpike road, and to the high price of labour?—The increase, as far as the turnpike road goes, is specifically set out as being about 6,000 *l.* a year.

5827. General *Dunne.*] Is that by the loss of the tolls?—That is by the loss of the tolls.

5828. Colonel *French.*] Had you a compensation rate levied annually off the county?—There were some mortgages to pay off and debentures.

5829. Are there any compulsory presentments since the change that came in, such as for lunatic asylums, or things of that kind, that have increased?—Yes; they are increased to a certain extent, and the gaol is considerably increased.

5830. All that accounts then for the cess increasing?—Yes.

5831. *Chairman.*] Has the cess increased in the county of Dublin in a greater or lesser proportion than in other parts of Ireland?—That I am not prepared to say.

5832. Colonel *French.*] It does not exceed 1 *s.* 8 *d.* in the pound at this moment, does it?—No.

5833. *Chairman.*] With regard to the clerk of the Crown in the county of Dublin, has he any fiscal business to discharge in connexion with the grand jury system?—He takes charge of the presentments, and gives me a copy of the presentment book.

5834. Does he countersign the cheques?—No.

5835. Does he swear the grand jury?—No.

5836. Then the only fiscal duty he has to discharge in the county of Dublin is keeping the county books and records?—That is all that occurs to me.

5837. Who swears the grand jury?—The clerk of the Crown of the Court of Queen's Bench, who is a distinct officer altogether.

5838. He is not paid by the county, is he?—No.

5839. Colonel *French.*] Do you pay for auditing the accounts in Dublin at the Master in Chancery's Office?—We do.

5840. General *Dunne.*] Do you not find that the cesspayers who are elected under that system are generally the same people within one or two?—They vary within the 36 or 40 names.

5841. Do you think you are bound by Act of Parliament to take the highest?—No.

5842. Would it, in your opinion, be better to ballot, and throw the whole number in, in order to get different classes elected?—I do not know what my answer should be if I was asked why I went out of the top of the list.

5843. *Chairman.*] Are you obliged to take the number 36 to ballot for out of the list?—Yes; the Act defines that you are to put into the ballot three times the number appointed by the grand jury to sit.

5844. Colonel *French.*] In other counties it is only twice the number, is it not?—Yes.

5845. *Chairman.*] And in other counties the ballot is at the sessions, and not at the assizes?—Yes. One great advantage in the county of Dublin is, that they know many months before who is eligible.

5846. And when a cesspayer comes into presentment sessions in the county of Dublin, if he comes in after the court has met, is he allowed to sit with the magistrates?—Certainly.

5847. No matter at what time he comes in?—Certainly.

5848. General *Dunne.*] You say that the finance committee is not necessarily composed of grand jurors?—No.

5849. Is any qualification whatever required, such as being a 50 *l.* freeholder?—No.

5850. May they take a man who is really without a qualification at all, and choose him merely for being a man of business?—Yes.

5851. In practice, are any persons taken who are not interested in the county?—I should say not. They must be interested so far as being ratepayers goes, and generally large ratepayers are selected.

5852. In the country, do you not think that it would be very difficult to get men to meet together so often as once a month?—I should be afraid that it would be very difficult.

5853. Have you found any advantages as regards sudden breaches and damages, by having this finance committee; have they any powers to repair such damages?—Yes; they can pay the expenses of sudden damage at any time, on a magistrate's order.

5854. Then the magistrate's order would be necessary?—Certainly.

5855. Is it confined, as in other counties, to 50 *l.*?—It is.

5856. But they do not do it on their own authority; they merely supply the funds?—They merely supply the funds. It must be done on the order of two magistrates and on the certificate of the county surveyor.

5857. But they supply the funds at once, in-

Mr. *H. Baker.*

9 June 18[illegible].

stead of waiting, as in other counties, till the sessions?—Yes.

5858. That is the advantage, is it?—That is the advantage.

5859. Have they anything to do with the payments for gaols and lunatic asylums during the intervals between the meetings of the sessions? —They have.

5860. You have a Board of Superintendence in addition, have you not?—Yes.

5861. And the Board of Superintendence merely gives an order or an estimate to this financial committee?—Yes.

5862. In the proceedings against defaulting contractors, have you found the inconvenience which has been experienced in other counties, from the difficulty as to the law of proceeding against the defaulting contractor?—We have found some inconveniences, and I think the law might be amended.

5863. What amendments would you suggest; will you point out any peculiarity in the law affecting the county of Dublin grand jury, that you are aware of?—One was that under the 10 days' notice a surveyor can go in and repair a work if it is let go to default; but the Court of Queen's Bench have ruled that you cannot put the recognizance in suit until that is done. The finance committee think that is an evil.

5864. That is applicable to all counties, is it not?—I believe not; I believe the general Act does not give that power at all.

5865. Then, even as you have it in the county of Dublin, it is an advantage over the law as it obtains in other counties, is it not?—It is.

5866. Then what further amendment would you propose?—It would be desirable to be able to put a recognizance in suit more than once.

5867. Who looks to the solvency of the sureties?—The adjourned sessions.

5868. Is there any officer appointed for the purpose, or is it merely the members of the sessions, the magistrates and the associated cesspayers, who look into it?—Nothing more.

5869. There is no professional man appointed to do it?—No.

5870. Are they generally found to be sufficient? —Frequently not.

5871. Therefore is not the system in the county of Dublin faulty in this respect, that there is no means of ascertaining the solvency of those men? —I would not say exactly that, because if they were sworn to their property before they were made sureties, I think the evil would be checked in a great measure.

5872. Then they are not sworn?—They are not sworn.

5873. Do they not make a declaration, equivalent to an oath?—No, they do not; they are sometimes asked the question.

5874. But are they not bound by a declaration, and do they not sign a declaration as to that?—They do not.

5875. Mr. *Gregory.*] Are the members of the finance committee chosen at all to represent different localities, or are they merely selected as being particularly good men of business?—Generally, care is taken that each barony is represented on the finance committee.

5876. Mr. *Blake.*] The standing committee of the county of which you speak, perform the most important of the fiscal duties of the grand jury, do they not?—Yes.

5877. Then, so far as the administration of the fiscal business is concerned, I suppose that standing committee may be looked upon very much as the grand jury itself, may it not?—I think so.

5878. Do you consider that the administration of the grand jury system would suffer, by separating the fiscal from the criminal business altogether?—I should think not in the least.

5879. That standing committee having answered so well as you have represented, do you not think that it would be advantageous to have a distinct body appointed for the purpose of transacting the fiscal business of the counties, only leaving the criminal business to be performed by another body to be summoned for that purpose by the sheriff?—In the county of Dublin it is virtually so at present, because the grand jury in the county of Dublin do no criminal business.

5880. Would you see any objection to having such a body as you speak of appointed by the ratepayers, and voted for by them?—I do not think the business could be better done than it is at present, but a great many of the ratepayers in Dublin would be better satisfied if it were so.

5881. Then would you see any objection to it? —No, I should see no objection to it.

5882. That is, so far as a financial Board for the county at large is concerned. With regard to the Baronial Boards, I presume that on the same principle, you would see no objection to having them also appointed by the ratepayers?—No. The ratepayers, virtually, might have great influence in the arrangement of the presentments if they attended, but they do not attend.

5883. But the selection of the ratepayers at baronial sessions at present is by the grand jury, is it not, and not by the votes of the ratepayers? —Quite so.

5884. Do you not think that a change in that system would be desirable?—It would be popular amongst the ratepayers.

5885. And you would see no objection to that, yourself?—I do not see, virtually, any objection to it.

5886. In all future lettings do you think that the division of the rate between the landlord and tenant would be a desirable thing?—I think it would.

5887. Colonel *Cooper.*] If I understand you rightly the finance committee cannot originate a new work?—No, except under very special circumstances; that is to say, if the necessity for a work arises subsequently to the sessions.

5888. Do you mean a sudden drainage work, or some other work?—Sometimes (as in the case of the Lambay Pier) there is a special provision by which they grant 100 *l.* for a special work, where there is evidence produced that it has arisen since the last presentment sessions, and that it would be detrimental to the county to let it lie over to the next sessions.

5889. That is because the grand jury meet but once a year; it would have to wait at least a year?—Yes; I take it that it would be the same for six months.

5890. Do you suppose that any of those sudden emergencies, or the sudden necessity to execute a new work could arise in the six months?—Yes; for instance, we have a great many sea walls, and leaving them exposed for 10 days sometimes, is dangerous.

5891. But that would come under the head of sudden damage, would it not?—Yes; but sudden damage is limited to 50 *l.*

5892. And

5892. And your finance committee can go so far as 100 *l.*?—For special work, on evidence on oath.

5893. How do the townships contribute towards the general county expenditure; take Kingstown, for instance?—They pay exactly as if there had been no alteration in the Act concerning county at large charges; they are taxed on their valuation exactly as every other part of the county.

5894. And not in any way as to the number of prisoners, or lunatics, or people that come in?—No, nothing of the kind; they remain to all intents and purposes a constituent part of the county, so far as county at large charges go.

5895. With regard to the way in which the cesspayers are chosen, it depends really more upon their qualifications as ratepayers than on any power of the grand jury, does it not?—I should say so.

5896. The grand jury, if I understand your explanation correctly, do not interfere in any way in putting the 36 names in?—Not in the least.

5897. They leave it to you, do they not?—They do.

5898. So that they really cannot tell who the first 12 would be?—Not in the least.

5899. So that in that way they are impartially chosen?—Quite so.

5900. *Chairman.*] There is no selection of the 36 cesspayers, is there?—None whatever beyond taking them from the head of the list as they are in the list.

5901. Has this finance committee the power of appointing any public officers?—None except *ad interim*, if a vacancy occurs in the surveyorship, they appoint an officer to do the duty until the next meeting of the grand jury; it is in the same way with barony cess collectors.

5902. Does the finance committee appoint a barony cess collector *ad interim* if a vacancy occurs?—Exactly.

5903. Mr. *Gregory.*] To be confirmed by the grand jury afterwards?—Either to be confirmed by the grand jury, or another person may be substituted as the grand jury please.

5904. Has it often happened that another person has been so substituted?—I think not.

5905. Colonel *French.*] You have stated that you think it would be advisable to divide the cess between the owner and the occupier; is that your opinion as a matter of justice, or as a matter of expediency on account of the cry which is now raised by the press and by some other persons?—I should say on both grounds.

5906. Would you consider it so desirable that you would deem it expedient to violate the contracts that are at present entered into between the owner and the occupier, that the occupier should pay the entire of the cess?—I presume that it would not be retrospective.

5907. Do you imagine that it would be any pecuniary advantage to the tenant, or that it would be the reverse?—It would be an advantage to him, so far as this, that he would be confident that all those voting for the imposition of the rate were equally interested with himself.

5908. But do you not think that the landlords, as a matter of prudence, would increase the rent sufficiently to secure to themselves the amount for which they were rendered liable?—I suppose it would ultimately be the case.

5909. In Dublin you pay now an average cess of 1 *s.* 6 *d.* in the pound, do you not?—Yes.

5910. Do you not think that the landlord, if the change in the law took place, would be very apt to add to the rent at least 9 *d.* in the pound to cover himself against any future increase of expenditure?—No, so far as my judgment goes. I think that the landlord in the first instance, and for many years to come, would be a sufferer. Mr. H. Baker. 9 June 1868.

5911. Do you not think that this proposal is merely starting an additional subject of difference between landlord and tenant, after the cess has been for more than a century paid always by the occupier, and those charges being paid in every other county (this county amongst others) by the occupier?—I am not prepared to say that anybody has started it with that object.

5912. Do you think that it would lead to a further ejectment from the small holdings, there having been a very great diminution of this settlement of the small holdings in Ireland?—I do not think that it would.

5913. Do you think then that the landlord would be content to pay the additional charge for all the small holders under 4 *l.*?—Where he was able, I think that he would.

5914. And you think that there would be no farther cause for ejectment from small holdings?—I should not think it would have that effect.

5915. Do you think it has had that effect under the poor law?—No.

5916. *Chairman.*] In the county of Dublin, are the recognizances entered into by the contractor to the Crown?—They are to the Crown.

5917. Has not inconvenience sometimes arisen from the fact that they are made to the Crown; must not the Attorney General prosecute?—Yes.

5918. Do you not think that it would be better if they were made directly to some county officer?—I believe that the proceedings would be simpler.

5919. Is there any limit upon the number of magistrates who can attend presentment sessions in the county of Dublin?—No.

5920. Can a magistrate from any barony attend in any other barony?—I believe that there is nothing to prevent their doing so, but it is not the practice.

5921. How many baronies are there in the county of Dublin?—There are nominally nine.

5922. Mr. *Gregory.*] Why do you say "nominally"?—There is virtually one barony absorbed by a township.

5923. As a matter of practice, do magistrates attend in baronies in which they have not property in the county of Dublin?—Unless in the case of agents representing property, I think not.

5924. *Chairman.*] Has the county of Dublin suffered from the withdrawal of the townships?—I should say that the portions of the baronies in which those townships have been formed, which are still left in the county, have suffered.

5925. It is the richer portion which is withdrawn generally, is it not?—It is.

5926. Colonel *French.*] These townships include Kingstown, I suppose?—They include Kingstown, Rathmines, and all those districts.

5927. General *Dunne.*] I understood you to say, in answer to the honourable Member for Roscommon, that in time the tenant would be charged the difference of the cess which would be remitted to him now?—Yes, as a matter of opinion.

5928. Then, in fact, at this moment is not the landlord the person who really is taxed for the county

Mr. *H. Baker.*

9 June 1868.

county cess, and does he not, in fact, pay it ultimately?—Ultimately, I think he does.

5929. Then the only advantage in putting it on him would be as a matter of justice; I want to understand what will be the justice of it?—He takes an active part in the laying on of the cess.

5930. But you say also that it comes ultimately out of his own pocket, so that he is just as directly interested now as he would be at any time, is he not?—I think that he would be more directly interested if he had to pay the half of it.

5931. Do you consider that, as a fact, the landlords are extravagant in the expenditure of the county cess at this moment?—No; quite the reverse.

5932. Have you found that the cesspayers have a much stronger inclination in that way, or not?—I should not say that they were inclined to be extravagant either.

5933. But not more so than the landlords?—I think not.

5934. Therefore they are equally concerned at this moment, and they equally wish to keep down the expenses?—Yes, so far as I can form an opinion.

5935. (*Chairman.*] The gallant General has asked you whether the landlords at present do not pay the county cess through a diminution in their rent; supposing the landlord at present does pay the county cess through getting a lower rent in consequence of the tenant having to pay it, on the other hand, when once the rent is fixed, the landlord is not in any way affected, either by a rise or a fall in the county cess, is he?—He is not.

5936. Whether there is a rise in the cess or not, in tenancies-at-will or in tenancies under lease, when the rent is fixed the landlord receives the same rent every year, does he not, whether the rate be 1 *s.* or 1 *s.* 6 *d.* in the pound?—No doubt.

5937. Do you not think it one of the advantages which would arise from a division of the cess, that every direct alteration of the *rate* would be at once felt by the landlord?—I should say so.

5938. That is in reality the advantage which would arise from this division, is it not?—I should say so.

5939. The proprietors themselves who have so much control in the expenditure, would themselves pay every alteration in the *rate*, and would feel every change, would they not?—They would feel every change.

5940. At present they do not feel every change, do they?—Quite so.

5941. Mr. *Blake.*] At present, has not the landlord very often a positive interest in having as much expenditure on public works as possible in the barony in which his property is?—I do not see in what way he would have such an interest.

5942. For instance, in the making of roads, and bridges, and other works, which are calculated to enhance the value of his property, he would have an interest in encouraging as large an expenditure as possible in that way, would he not?—His interest would appear to me to be too remote to influence him much in the matter, unless he wants to open building ground, or something of that kind.

5943. If he has a farm to be set to a tenant, is it not his interest to have good roads made in the neighbourhood?—Unquestionably.

5944. The tenant, as it stands at present, has no control over the expenditure in that way; he cannot do anything in the way of sending in a representative to check the expenditure?—No; he has only the associated ratepayers.

5945. And they may be chosen by the landlord himself, may they not, if he represents the barony on the grand jury?—Of course.

5946. General *Dunne.*] They are not chosen in Dublin by the grand jury, are they?—They are chosen by ballot in the way which I have described.

5947. Mr. *Leader.*] Are there not many matters which act as a check upon the expenditure?—Yes.

5948. Mr. *Blake.*] The gallant General has asked you if the associated cesspayers are not chosen by ballot; that is the practice in the county of Dublin; but are you aware that in other counties it is a matter of selection?—I am.

5949. (*Chairman.*] Could you give the Committee any information with regard to the rates in the £. in those townships?—I know that in some of the townships they are limited to 2 *s.*

5950. Colonel *French.*] The high sheriff, I presume, selects the grand jury in the county of Dublin, as well as in the other counties in Ireland?—He does; he summons them.

5951. Have you ever heard any complaints made that the selection is a partial one?—I have constantly heard complaints made by gentlemen who have not been high enough on the panel.

5952. From your official experience, have you any reason to suppose that that charge is well founded?—I am quite sure that the different sheriffs are in the habit of making different arrangements in the panel; but their motive in doing so of course I cannot tell.

5953. But the sheriff is changed every year, so that it would seem to be a universal complaint against the sheriffs?—I think it is by somebody.

5954. *Chairman.*] Do you see any use in the county of Dublin grand jury, considering that everything is done by the financial committee?—Yes, indeed I do see a great use in it.

5955. What does the grand jury of the county of Dublin do which could not be done by the finance committee?—They are an effectual check upon the sessions in the whole county, because they are open to receive any complaints of presentments passed at the different sessions which ought not to be passed.

5956. Do they generally act upon that, and do they frequently reject presentments?—Whenever there is a case made out, they are in the habit of hearing it very patiently, and according to the best of their judgment, either confirming or rejecting it.

5957. Do they never refer such cases to the finance committee?—They never refer such things to the finance committee if they are in a position to dispose of them themselves.

5958. They do not refer it for want of time?—No.

5959. Mr. *Leader.*] Has your attention ever been directed to the question of establishing financial boards in some of the large counties of Ireland?—I have often heard the question mooted.

5960. Do you think that in some of the counties which are extensive, you could have a constant and large attendance of persons appointed to act on a financial board who reside in remote districts?—

districts?—I always had a doubt as to the practicability of it in other counties from that reason, and also from the great evils which might result from a few individuals attending constantly.

5961. Sir *Charles Lanyon*.] When you spoke of the dissatisfaction as to the sheriff, I think that you said it was owing principally to the manner in which the gentlemen were placed upon the panel, as to whether they are high up, or low down?—Quite so.

5962. It was not with reference to dissatisfaction as to the selection of the men, but with reference to their position on the panel that you gave your answer?—Quite so.

Mr. *H. Baker*.

9 June 1868.

5963. General *Dunne*.] Are they obliged to put a 50 *l.* freeholder first on the panel before calling any one else?—I think not.

5964. *Chairman*.] Has the sheriff perfect discretion as to the whole panel of the grand jury?—I think so.

Mr. John Edmund Roach, called in; and Examined.

Mr. *J. E. Roach*.

5965. *Chairman*.] You are a Solicitor in Dublin, are you not?—I am.

5966. And member of the finance committee of the grand jury of the county of Dublin?—Yes.

5967. You have also been a grand juror of that county, have you not?—Occasionally I have. I am very low on the panel, but the sheriff occasionally has called me. The Committee are aware that there are four grand juries sworn in Dublin in the year, one of them being the presenting grand jury; and I think that I have been twice on it, and on others occasionally; but I am not on the finance committee as a grand juror. It is a ratepayers' committee.

5968. The finance committee, as we have heard, is not necessarily confined to members of the grand jury?—No; it is a ratepayers' committee, with some small qualification; I think a rating of 10 *l.* a year, or something of that kind. I think that there is a statutable qualification of some 50 *l.* a year required for a member of the finance committee.

5969. But there is no qualification required for being a grand juror, is there?—No.

5970. You are also clerk of the Crown for the County of Wexford, are you not?—I am.

5971. And you reside in Dublin, do you not?—Yes.

5972. Have you heard the evidence of Mr. Baker, with respect to the working of the finance committee in Dublin?—Yes.

5973. Do you coincide in what he has stated?—Yes; he has exhausted the subject, I think.

5974. Have you any other information to give with respect to the working of that finance committee in the county of Dublin?—No; I heard a good deal of Mr. Baker's evidence, and I do not think I can add anything to it.

5975. Do you find the attendance on that finance committee satisfactory, generally speaking?—Very good; it is never less than six, and it is more often nine.

5976. I see by a return which I have before me, that you are a very regular attendant yourself?—Yes, it is a kind of hobby or amusement to me. I understood the working of the grand jury laws otherwise, and I have been there pretty regularly.

5977. Are matters ever referred to this finance committee, which are outside the mere question of finance?—The grand jury will sometimes make a recommendation to them upon some particular matter, which they say they would be glad if the finance committee would attend to, and then it has happened occasionally that unexpected emergencies have arisen, such as railways, township bills, and so forth, as to which damage might occur on the county, unless somebody attended to it; and then the finance committee, though perhaps strictly having other functions, take action upon it to prevent injury arising to the county.

5978. But are such questions as whether certain presentments should, or should not, be ratified by the grand jury, ever referred to the finance committee?—They are out of their province altogether. They are a mere committee, and they do pretty much what is done by the treasurer in other counties.

5979. This committee, as we are informed, pays the contractors quarterly?—Yes, as a matter of convenience to the contractors.

5980. Do you believe that that has led to the contracts being taken at a lower rate in the county of Dublin?—I cannot say that. What occurs is this: on any application being made in the ordinary way by two ratepayers, and so forth, as happens in all the other counties at the road sessions, the surveyor attends, and he gives his estimate to the magistrates and to the cesspayers assembled, and the surveyors complain to me that the road sessions do not deal liberally with them; that is to say, that they always take something off whatever their estimate for the work may be. Then they are put in this difficulty, as they say, that they must shape their specification either for the reduced amount which the road sessions give them, and thereby not do the thing in the way in which it is wished, or if they make it what it ought to be, and so advise the sessions, no one will bid for the work, because they cannot do it for what is allotted to it by the sessions.

5981. Does not the county surveyor examine the specification beforehand?—Yes; the county surveyor advises the road sessions that such a work, or the maintenance of such a road, would amount, say, to 100 *l.*, and the road sessions say, "That is a thing that ought to be done, but could not you to do it for 80 *l.*?" He says, "I cannot." Then they say, "We will only give you 80 *l.*," and then he says, "I am put in a difficulty, because if I prepare a fitting specification to do that work no person will bid for it." Then arises this state of things: it is what is called thrown upon the surveyor, and that puts him out of what the finance committee consider to be his proper office; that is to say, the supervision of work done, and he has to undertake it himself without having a proper staff to do the work.

5982. Have you found, as a matter of fact, that there are very few tenders to do work at a lower rate than that which is fixed on by the sessions and makers?—For a good deal of the maintenance of roads where the contracts are not very large (I was alluding before to where they were large), the tendency in our county is that the surveyors increase the length of the contracts by putting several small contracts together; but where the contracts are of small length

Mr. J. E. [illegible]. — 9 June 1868.

length, then invariably a man is found, although the sessions have diminished the amount, to take it for less. He will get security, no doubt, but the road is not done.

5983. Do you think that the contracts are taken at too low a figure?—Yes; in very many instances they will underbid each other, no matter what it is offered for, and it leads to a bad system of things, because the surveyor then has to go on on a ten days' notice, and the contractors have to be sued, and so forth; and in the meantime the public have not got a new road.

5984. Do you believe that that is more the case in the county of Dublin than in other parts of Ireland?—I cannot say that. As regards the roads, so far as I have seen them in other counties, although they were very good some years ago, yet my humble opinion is that they are not improving; but, however, that is a matter of individual opinion.

5985. On an average, has the county surveyor very often in each year, to take a part of the road upon this ten days' notice?—It is a kind of thing which he does not admire doing, because he, as he says, has no staff to do it; of course, as Honourable Members are aware, he has no assistants, as they have in other counties; and then he is obliged to get some kind of staff together, and very often he is obliged to employ the contractor, and the contractor's son, and the contractor's cart, and the contractor's horse, and the contractor's heap of stones, and so forth.

5986. But in the county of Dublin, as we are informed, the sessions are not obliged to accept the lowest tender?—The Act is the same, though they may give a different construction to it; though I yield at once to Mr. Baker on the subject, because he is quite familiar with it.

5987. Mr. Baker informed the Committee that in the county of Dublin there was an exception to the rest of Ireland with regard to the lowest tender, and that in the county of Dublin they were not obliged to take the lowest tender, though they generally did so?—The words in the Act, with which no doubt the Committee are familiar are, "fraudulent or unfair," in my recollection.

5988. These are the words in the general Act extending to all Ireland, are they not?—That is what I am applying my mind to now; I was not aware that there was a difference, but it is quite likely that there is; but whether or no in the county of Dublin, unless the contractor be a man of bad reputation as a contractor, a man, for instance, whose sureties they had had to sue, they take the lowest tender.

5989. As a matter of fact, are you able to state that the contracts in the county of Dublin are taken at a comparatively lower rate than in other counties in Ireland?—I am not informed as to that.

5990. Then are you aware whether they are taken at a lower or at a higher rate than in the neighbouring county of Wicklow, for instance?—No, I am not aware even as to Wexford.

5991. The county cess in the county of Dublin has very largely increased since the passing of this Act, has it not?—So I have gathered from a return which I heard Mr. Baker mention.

5992. Are you aware of any immediate cause for that great increase?—No. Of course the price of labour has a good deal increased in Dublin, and the prices of living and so forth. There were some 10 or 12 years ago some 90 or 100 miles of road thrown on the county, and they had been worked out by the trustees, who knew that the time was coming, and they were left in such a state that no contractor would take them for years; and there the surveyors were obliged to take them into their own hands, and to work them at an inconvenience, to say the least of it, to the other roads in the county, because their personal care and time were taken up in doing the business of a contractor.

5993. But those roads have, I presume, been put into repair for several years?—For some years, so that contractors can be gotten for them.

5994. Has the expenditure, in consequence of that, very much diminished since this extraordinary expenditure upon the roads when they first took them up?—I should not like to say that, but those roads are roads of great traffic, such as what are called the Great Western roads, and the road from Limerick, and so forth. I suppose that probably they are let, speaking loosely, at some 70 *l.* or 80 *l.* a mile; but I am not giving that as an exact sum, though I think you will find that it is about that.

5995. But you state that when those roads were taken up from the turnpike trusts they were in a very bad state, and required an extraordinary outlay; are you aware whether since then that outlay has diminished after that extraordinary occasion had passed?—It may have diminished, but I do not know that it has.

5996. Colonel *French*.] Are you aware whether those roads are kept by contract now, or whether they continue repairing by presentment?—They are kept by contract now. When they were put into heart, if I may use the expression, contractors were then gotten for them.

5997. You stated that you were Clerk of the Crown for the county of Wexford; will you state to the Committee, in a general way, what are your duties as Clerk of the Crown; in the first place have you any fiscal duties in connexion with the grand jury?—Yes; the fiscal duties of the Clerk of the Crown of course are to attend at the assizes, and to attend at the fiating of the presentments by the court, and to the traverses, if any such there be; and he is obliged, within seven days, to furnish a copy of the presentments, verified on oath. He is also obliged to furnish a list of queries to the grand jury, which must be discharged by the grand jury; and he cannot countersign a draft until that is properly certified by the grand jury. The secretary of the grand jury attends in court, as the Committee are aware, and attending in court with some of the members of the grand jury; formerly they had to go through each presentment. That is not exactly adhered to now, and the presentment is fiated or struck according to its merits. Of course, practically, very few of them are struck; the discussion arises upon them before the judge, and it is the business of the clerk of the Crown to record the results of those matters before the court; and, having done so, of such of the presentments as are fiated, he has to give, within seven days, a copy of such, attested on oath, to the treasurer.

5998. Is there any portion of the duty which could not be discharged by the secretary of the grand jury?—Of course there is no impossibility in the secretary to the grand jury discharging it. The old theory about the clerk of the Crown (whether it exists now or not I do not know) is this; they used always to want, as clerk of the Crown

Mr. J. E. [illegible]

9 June [illegible].

Crown to a county, a stranger, who was supposed to stand indifferent to all local interests, and the Committee will see pretty well what was the object of giving him the custody of those presentments.

5999. Is it in the range of possibility for the clerk of the Crown to go over and verify all those multifarious presentments?—Yes; they have a triple process about the presentments. First, as regards the presentments of the particular sessions, whatever the number may be (in my county it is 1,200 or so), the clerk of the Crown is obliged, before he can verify them on oath, to compare the copies which are furnished with that which has been fiated by the court; the county at large books and the barony books. Having done so, he then delivers that as the foundation of the treasurer's warrant to levy the amount on the county. That is the first process. But he has another process to go, which is this: of the presentments of the last sessions he sends a query book to the grand jury, and they are obliged to discharge each and every one of the payments. There is just the same number of payments and the same number of accounts, in which a mistake may be made; he has to see that they are all discharged by the grand jury before he can countersign his name to a single cheque for the amount; and if, by any little oversight, a half-yearly payment which ought to have been made has escaped from any mistake, he is precluded from countersigning it.

6000. But, as a matter of fact, does he not generally sign them upon the signatures which are there before?—No; they are signed by somebody else on his signature. I am only speaking of my own practice; the thing is quite simple. The query book is, in fact, an abstract or copy of the accounts, and it is indirectly and shortly a description of the presentments passed at the last sessions. That is sent to the grand jury, and I will not countersign one until I have the word "discharged," written either by a member of the grand jury with respect to all the undischarged queries, or with respect to the works of maintenance by the secretary.

6001. Upon the discharge of the secretary you do it?—With respect to works of maintenance I do it upon the discharge of the secretary, as the officer of the grand jury. He hands it down with the other papers to the judge, and it comes into my custody in that manner; it is, in fact, fiated. The duty of the clerk of the Crown is to write on that query book, "Be paid as discharged," and he hands to the treasurer a copy of the query book as given to him by the grand jury, and that is the authority of the treasurer to pay the money.

6002. As a matter of course, upon those presentments, signed by the secretary of the grand jury, and fiated, as you say, as a matter of course, the clerk of the Crown writes his name?—I am speaking now of the query book. If you will allow me to popularise, it is just this: a certain quantity of presentments have been made at the antecedent assizes, and the amount of them is sent out by the treasurer's warrant, to be collected amongst the ratepayers. Then the clerk of the Crown, as the officer of the court at the next assizes, sends to the grand jury a list of all that they have presented money for, and asks them simply, "What have you done about so and so"? They say, "Discharged," or "Not discharged." Of all that are discharged he makes an exact copy in the query book, and he writes at the end of the copy of that which he makes for the treasurer, "Be paid as discharged," and that is the treasurer's authority.

6003. But could not that be done quite as well by the secretary to the grand jury?—That is done substantially by the finance committee, or by the chairman and the secretary in the county of Dublin.

6004. But in other counties, where there is no financial committee, do you think that it could be sufficient to have that done by the secretary to the grand jury?—I am not saying a word that is offensive as regards any officer, but the clerk of the Crown is supposed, in theory, to stand between the secretary and the treasurer as a check upon them. That is the old abstract idea of what the clerk of the Crown is in respect to finance matters.

6005. That, of course, is the theory of this duty of the clerk of the Crown; but do you think that, practically, it is of any great utility?—The practice, as far I know (and I know the practice of more counties than my own), is as I have told you. In my county there are 1,200 presentments, of which I have to give copies at the sessions, and 1,200 queries which I have to send up to the grand jury; but besides that to the Audit Office, Master Fitzgibbon's Office, I am obliged to send abstracts and lists of every one of those presentments which have been discharged. He would not issue to the treasurer, unless he had a certificate under the hand of the clerk of the Crown that each and every of those presentments were discharged at the session. I am not attempting to impress upon the Committee the multifarious nature of the duties of the clerk of the Crown, but I wish you really to know what they are. With respect to each presentment there is a triple duty performed. One is the inception of it by sending it out to be collected; another is by asking the grand jury what they have done with the similar presentment the last time; and the third is certifying to the Receiving Master the presentments which have been discharged at the last assizes. The Committee will perceive that I am obliged to certify that they have been discharged by the Court at the last assizes. The grand jury discharge them; they are laid before the judge, and he, through the clerk of the Crown, issues an order that they be paid.

6006. The Committee are perfectly aware that all that must be done under the present law, but the point to which I wish to direct your attention is, whether you believe that any practical utility arises from that obligation, and whether things would not be quite as safe without requiring the signature of the Clerk of the Crown?—Of course, if you are beginning another system de novo, anything of that kind could be done; but so long as you adhere to the present system, I humbly conceive that it is no harm to have an independent officer, if he be a respectable officer, who would not be swayed to the right or to the left—I am not saying that the secretary or the treasurer would do so—but if the Clerk of the Crown does his duty, he acts between them.

6007. As I understand it, when those documents come down to the Clerk of the Crown, all that he has to do is to see that they have been signed and discharged by the grand jury and by the secretary of the grand jury; and if he sees that they are properly carried out, he puts his signature to them?—With respect to the dis-

Mr. J. E. Beach.

9 June 1868.

charged queries in the case of each grand juror holds the book of each barony, it is awarded as a kind of duty put upon them, that he is the person who discharges the query book. With respect to works of maintenance, it is on the certificate of the surveyor that they are discharged, or not; and I apprehend (though I do not know) that the manner in which that is done at the grand jury is, that the county surveyor says that payment is to be passed, it having gone before the adjourned road sessions, and that then the secretary of the grand jury discharges it himself.

6008. With respect to the other duties of the Clerk of the Crown, he acts at the assizes with regard to criminal matters in Ireland, as the registrar of the judge does in the superior courts in Dublin, does he not?—Yes.

6009. These are chiefly his duties?—Yes; and if there be any English Members on this committee, as I suppose there are, I may say he, as the clerk of arraigns and the clerk of indictments, does in this country.

6010. Has he anything to do with the civil side of the court at assizes?—Nothing whatever.

6011. Does the clerk of the Crown receive any fees?—He does.

6012. On what?—On informations. His fees are principally on copies of information which he furnishes to the Attorney General through the Crown Solicitor. These are provided by an Act of Parliament of the year 1809, the 49th of Geo. 3.

6013. What is the exact fee received upon an information?—Six shillings and twopence for the copy of the information.

6014. Is that the only fee which the clerk of the Crown receives?—No; if he is asked to search for an information he has 2s. for the search, and 2s. 6d. for a rule entered in court. When a prisoner is arraigned, and when he is tried, and when he is convicted and sentenced, there is a rule on each of them. That is also provided for by the Act of Parliament.

6015. Do you see any difference between the duties discharged by the clerk of the Crown at the assizes and the duties discharged by the clerk of the peace at quarter sessions?—No; they are quite analogous.

6016. Do you not think that these offices might be amalgamated, as far as the criminal duties are concerned, and discharged by one officer?—They could. Of course it is a mere question of arrangement, and a question of remuneration. There is no legal incapacity. The clerks of the Crown are practising solicitors, and the clerks of the peace are not so, a great number of them being private gentlemen.

6017. Must the clerk of the Crown be an acting solicitor?—I do not say that he must be so, because the Crown have means under an Act of Parliament of 40 years ago, of appointing any person to be a solicitor in any thing which they require; but the fact is, that I think, with one exception, every clerk of the Crown in Ireland is a solicitor.

6018. Do the clerks of the Crown, as a general rule, act in person?—Yes.

6019. Are there not many counties in Ireland where they never appear, but where they do their duties by deputy?—I think there are but two such instances to my knowledge.

6020. But you think there would be no clashing of business between the clerk of the Crown and the clerk of the peace, if the one officer were appointed to discharge both duties, that is to say, the criminal duties exclusively?—I do not see that there can be any clashing.

6021. The quarter sessions and the assizes do not interfere with each other, do they?—No.

6022. And it would be very easy, would it not, for the same officer to attend at the assizes, and to attend at the quarter sessions?—Clearly there is no physical impossibility in that.

6023. The clerks of the Crown are appointed by the Crown, are they not?—They are.

6024. (General *Dunne*.) The clerk of the Crown pays the witnesses, does he not?—It is the duty of the clerk of the Crown to pay the witnesses.

6025. On what authority does he pay those witnesses?—Properly speaking, he is the officer of the court, and the court allows him to measure (which I believe is the technical phrase) the amount of the expenses?—If any question arises about medical witnesses, or otherwise, he speaks to the judge, and says, "There is such-and-such an application. Ought I to do so-and-so?" and the authority emanates from the judge.

6026. Does he pay also for the maintenance of prisoners before trial?—He has no ministerial office, as regards the payment for convicts.

6027. He is the executive, is he not?—He countersigns the cheques.

6028. There is a certain allowance from the Treasury for certain classes of prisoners and witnesses, is there not?—I cannot give evidence as to that. That is, in fact, before they take them off the county, before they take them to the Government gaol. What is done practically, is this, the proper officers in Dublin send the amount which they ascertain by some of their departments, and have it lodged in the county bank to the credit of the county; and that, in fact, is what originates the interference of the clerks of the Crown. He gets an intimation that there is 89*l*., for instance, for the maintenance of prisoners, and as a matter of convenience, it being mixed up with the other money, he is obliged to sign it.

6029. Then he is merely mixed up with the county, because the county receives a certain assistance from the Treasury?—Yes, it is, in fact, a fault (if I may use the expression) on the part of the Government to put it there at all; but when it is found there it would be an unfair exercise of discretion on the part of any officer to say, "I will not help you to get it out, though I have the key to open it."

6030. Has the clerk of the Crown any knowledge whether that sum is a proper sum, or not?—No. If the Government tell me that they have lodged such a sum amongst the county funds, and request me to sign that amount in favour of the county treasurer, I have no discretion; I am their officer. It is put there for safety, and I suppose they think that it is as well to have as many checks upon it as possible.

6031. Therefore you know nothing of the amount?—No.

6032. Are the witnesses for felonies supported by the Crown, or by the county?—I can only speak popularly of that; I believe they are supported by the county.

6033. Have the grand jury any means of inquiring into any of those payments, or is it an imperative presentment?—As to the payment for convicts, that was a different thing; that was a credit.

6034. But

6034. But have the grand jury any power of controlling or knowing what amount is paid by the Government in support of those convicts?—I do not know the elements on which they proceed. With regard to this finance committee, they have something similar with respect to the reformatory schools. When a demand is made on that committee with regard to a reformatory school they send the Bill; that is, I send them by the reformatory school committee to the governor of the gaol, and he checks it; and on the governor of the gaol certifying as to the number of days, the factors of the calculation, being right, they then pay it, and they will not do it without.

6035. That is in Dublin, but what happens in Wicklow, for instance?—I really cannot say; that is outside my duty.

6036. How do you get the authority as to the amount for which you give those cheques for the payment for any prisoners, either Crown, or otherwise?—I have nothing to do with the payment of prisoners at all; I apprehend that the manner in which that is done is, that it is paid by the Board of Superintendence, but that is a mere hypothesis of mine; I do not know it; I get a letter from the proper officer saying, "59 *l.* 15 *s.* has been sent down, and you will countersign a cheque for the local inspector for that amount," and I must do it. I have the custody of the safe.

6037. This amount, as I understand it, is sent from the Government officer to the inspector of the gaol?—I take it to be so, but I know nothing of his duties. As I explained to you before, if I may use the expression, I have one of the keys of the safe.

6038. In fact you do nothing but get a requisition from the Government?—I merely get a requisition from the Government, and I would not sign a cheque without it. It is outside my duties, properly speaking, because they might have put any other names there for any other purpose, and said, "You must countersign a cheque for it."

6039. The clerk of the peace is not always a professional man, is he?—He is not.

6040. And yet he conducts prosecutions at the quarter sessions, does he not?—That is his duty, but it is sometimes performed by deputy. The duty, if I may mention it now, of the clerk of the Crown, is to prosecute all cases at the assizes; I do not wish to go into a long list of my duties, because the Committee are quite familiar with them, and there are heaps of reports and returns about them, but it is the duty of the clerk of the Crown to prosecute every case returned for trial at the assizes. The practice in Ireland, which has grown up with different Attorneys General is, that the Crown intervenes in serious cases, and they employ their own professional men, their own solicitor; and the Attorney General employs his own counsel, and sometimes he comes himself specially; but in any cases which are not prosecuted by him, it is the duty of the court to discharge the gaol, and it is the duty of the clerk of the Crown to examine the witnesses, and so forth; but in practice it is only done, except in cases of common assault and larceny, and so on, because all the serious cases are properly taken up by the Crown, and prosecuted. With respect to the clerk of the peace, the serious cases in Ireland are prosecuted in a different manner, or under a different system from what takes place here. There is an Act of Parliament in England which prescribes that certain offences must be tried at the assizes which cannot be tried at quarter sessions; but in Ireland there are on record with the different clerks of the peace and clerks of the Crown, written instructions from the Castle, saying that such cases must be prosecuted at the assizes, and such others must not; but sometimes the Attorney General varies that, by saying that a particular description of offence, such as cattle stealing, is to be prosecuted at the sessions, and not at the assizes.

Mr. *J. H. Sand.*

9 June 1868.

6041. Are the fees of the clerk of the peace analogous to those of the clerk of the Crown?—No, because the fees of the clerk of the peace are principally made up on his civil duties. The chief fee of the clerk of the peace, or at least the chief of the fees as returned, is a fee of this nature; that he gets 2 *s.* 6 *d.* on the renewing of licenses of publicans in the county; and the number of publicans in the county multiplied by half-a-crown, makes a very large item in his fees.

6042. Has he anything to do with the civil bills?—Yes, but his fees on all those are very small fees; and, as far as I have ever understood, the clerk of the peace has as much as he can do since the registration has been put upon him; he has a very onerous office.

6043. Does he not get a salary for acting as the clerk of Lieutenancy does in England in reference to militia registrations?—I do not know anything about that.

6044. Do you know anything about the process servers?—I do not.

6045. *Sir Charles Lanyon.*] With reference to this finance committee, are you of opinion that its existence in any way dispenses with the necessity for the existence of the grand jury with respect to the fiscal business of the county?—I should say not; as the finance committee of the grand jury of the county of Dublin is constituted, as I mentioned to the Committee, their primary duty is to pay the contractors from day to day, if I may use the expression, if necessary; but they are ready to pay them when their work is done. That of course is a great relief to the contractors, and possibly it may absolutely lessen the amount of taxation upon the county, though I will not say that it has that effect, but it is all in favour of the contractors.

6046. At all events you are not of opinion that the grand jury of the county of Dublin could be dispensed with consequently upon the existence of the finance committee?—The existence of the finance committee in the county of Dublin could in no way be made available to dispense with the grand jury for the county of Dublin with respect to those fiscal matters.

6047. Do you know, and can you suggest any better court of appeal or court of decision upon fiscal matters, than the grand jury of the county?—As I understand the grand jury, I do not consider it to be exactly a court of appeal; I understand that the grand jury exercises a veto; you may call a thing by another name, but, after all, I really look upon the grand jury system as it exists in Ireland, as being a code of laws for regulating the roads; and from what experience I have had of it (and I have been for some considerable time in the county of Wexford, and I have been a shorter time in the county of Dublin) I think that you can improve it in a great many minor matters; but, as a general system, it has worked very well.

6048. Are you of opinion that the present grand jury laws work very efficiently and well,

but

Mr. J. H. B[illegible]. 9 June 1868.

but that they merely require some little oiling or lubrication of the machinery to make an efficient system?—That is my opinion.

6049. General *Dunne*.] With regard to expense, have you any idea whether the grand jury system is an expensive system of administration or not, and could the expense be lessened?—From the drift of some of the questions which the honourable Chairman has asked me about the consolidation of offices, I presume that, by the consolidation of offices, you might lessen the expenses, but you must give something more to the officer who does the business of the two offices, and, I think, that in the end it would not be found to be a great saving.

6050. *Earl of Mayo*.] Do you think that there is greater economy in the county of Dublin under the system which prevails there than there is in the other counties of Ireland, where a somewhat different system prevails?—I cannot say that there is; Mr. Baker, who is a most intelligent officer, and on whom all classes have the greatest reliance, and who has a very considerable estate in the county, is paid 450 *l.* a year as salary.

6051. But, as regards the general expenses of the county, in consequence of the system which prevails in the county of Dublin, do you think that there is any diminution of expenditure in the general works of the county, as compared with other counties in Ireland?—I do not.

6052. Sir *Charles Lanyon*.] Do you think that you get your contracts more cheaply executed in consequence of the existence of the finance committee, from the regularity of the payments?—The thing is not so prominent that I could state that the result is either one way or the other.

6053. *Earl of Mayo*.] Do you think that there is any substantial difference in favour of economy as between the two systems?—Certainly not; the grand jurors in the county of Dublin, who have been on the finance committee for many years, are all the first gentlemen of the county, and they take a great deal of pains about it; I do not wish to say that they are not liberal, but I must say that in many cases they are illiberal; the only liberal thing which I ever knew them do, was raising the poundage of the barony constables.

6054. *Chairman*.] Was that raised by the finance committee?—I was on the grand jury there, and from having a good deal of experience of the working of the system, one of the gentlemen on the grand jury said to me, "There are some arrears going on here, and it is a continual yearly grievance and annoyance; do you not think that we might get a better class of men if we gave a little more?" I said, "You might try the experiment;" and they made it 1 s., making at the same time a bargain that the collectors were to pay in the whole amount, but that there should be no arrears; and from that time we have had no run-away contractors, we have had no arrears, and we get the entire amount of our cess without any trouble.

6055. But was that increase in the rate of collection granted by the finance committee, or by the grand jury?—By the grand jury; but the Committee will quite understand that where some eight or nine of the influential members of the grand jury are also members of this finance committee, there is a kind of transfusion of experience from one to the other.

6056. Sir *Charles Lanyon*.] You spoke of the expense in the cost of works in Dublin; are you not aware that that arises to a great extent from the turnpike roads being now repaired at the county expense, instead of being repaired by the turnpike trusts?—Yes; either Mr. Baker or I myself, have already mentioned to the Committee that there was about some 90 miles and upwards of roads, costing about 70 *l.* a mile added to the county, and that we really got them in a scandalous state.

6057. Are you not also aware that the price of labour has very much increased?—I am.

6058. Is it not also a consequence of the increase in the price of labour, that there is not nearly the same amount of competition for those small jobs amongst country contractors as there used to be; and therefore, that the prices that prevail are not so low as they used to be?—Yes; and this also has happened: formerly we had two or three large contractors, men of capital, and I do not know how it is, but within the last eight or ten years they have disappeared. One of them was a contractor of the name of Plunkett, who had been with Mr. Dargan, and who had several very large contracts; but they have all disappeared, and we have not gotten them. With respect to the small contractors it is a very difficult thing; they will undertake to do anything, and they make a pitiable case afterwards to the committee for payment, and it is a very unpleasant duty not to pay them.

6059. With reference to the difficulty of which you speak, as to the works having very frequently to be undertaken by the county surveyor, do you not think that that difficulty could be very easily remedied by some greater facility being provided for proceeding against defaulting contractors, and that if there were some easier mode of proceeding against defaulting contractors, you would not have the same class of men proposing for your works, and consequently not the same difficulty?—The finance committee have invariably endeavoured to impress upon their surveyors that they ought to sue road contractors, or that they ought to sue them with more energy than the finance committee think they do sue them with. The surveyors say that it is a complicated and difficult thing. The very first thing that occurs is this: the surveyor says, "I have instructions to do so and so, and I shall have an attorney against me when I go before the magistrate." The committee say to him, "It is your duty to do it." He says, "Will you allow me to employ an attorney?" They reply, "We will not; but if you proceed against those parties properly, and we see at the end of the whole proceeding that you proceeded earnestly and zealously in the matter, we will recommend the grand jury to pay you." But they do it at the imminent risk of having to pay the costs out of their own pockets; and of course the more simple the process, the more likely they would be to have recourse to it.

6060. If greater facilities were given for the purpose of prosecuting defaulting contractors, do you think it would tend greatly to improve the execution of the public works of the county?—No doubt of it.

6061. Mr. *Lawder*.] Are you aware that an Act was passed last Session prospectively abolishing the office of county treasurer in Ireland?—I am aware that there was such an Act, and I saw the Bill, but I will not undertake to say that I know much about the Act.

6062. Do you not think that, in consequence of

Mr. J. H. Roach.

9 June 1868.

of the Act being passed, there should be some person who would control the acts of the secretary, and not allow him to have the sole power of issuing his warrant for the amount on the county?—I am now speaking, perhaps, wrongly from not having the Act before me. I assume that the treasurer is either dead or has resigned, and that then the secretary is acting as both treasurer and secretary. As the code is at present I merely hand him the levy, and he could not put into it anything else than what is handed to him by the clerk of the Crown.

6063. You have a check upon the treasurer at present?—At present there is such a check.

6064. And do you think is necessary that some check of that sort should continue?—It has up to this time been the spirit of the law, and I think every one will consider that the more reasonable checks there are, no matter how respectable any public officer is, the better for the public and for himself too.

6065. Mr. *Blake*.] The finance committee, of which you are a member, partakes very much of the character of a financial county board, does it not?—Originally it had no characteristic of the kind, except that it exercised a certain power over the surveyor and some of the county officers; but the practice which I mentioned to the Committee has crept in, which makes it, not a county board, but perhaps the nearest expression that I could use, would be a kind of county standing committee of the grand jury.

6066. But you perform a good deal of the duties of the grand jury, do you not?—No; the only thing we do is, that when the contractors bring in their bills for payment, we pay them?—If a complaint is made of the state of a road, we have the surveyors in and ask them all about it, and if they say, "We cannot satisfy you as to this," then we call upon them for a written report at the next meeting.

6067. Are you appointed at every assizes?—Every assizes, or presenting term, the grand jury appoint a fresh committee; that is to say, they take off the four gentlemen whose attendance has been worst, and they appoint four in their place.

6068. What is the whole number?—Twelve, three being a quorum.

6069. Then four go out and eight remain in?—Yes.

6070. Do you not consider that such a Board as that could very well discharge the whole of the fiscal duties of the county if they were confided to them?—I should think it would be a hazardous thing to entrust those duties to a body of twelve with a quorum of three. I think the number is too small.

6071. You may make them larger if you like; but could not a board of the same character perform those duties?—That would be a grand jury, only giving it a different name.

6072. Should you see any objection to separating the criminal from the fiscal business of the grand jury, leaving to the sheriff the power of summoning a body of gentlemen to discharge the criminal business, and leaving to the cesspayers the privilege of appointing the baronial and county boards?—If I rightly understand the Honourable Member's question, he means that the baronial boards would manage the affairs of the barony, and that the county boards would manage the affairs of the county at large.

6073. I mean that they would act as the grand jury do now, so far as fiscal affairs are concerned?—I do not exactly understand what is meant by baronial boards.

6074. By baronial boards, I mean bodies similar to the associated cesspayers and magistrates, the road sessions. Would it not be desirable to have such a body as that appointed by the cesspayers?—That is, in fact, that instead of the grand jury exercising the function of appointing the associated ratepayers, the cesspayers should do it.

6075. What is your opinion about that?—It is a matter which I have not considered. Anything of that kind may act very well; but as far as I have had experience (and I have had experience now for some years), the present system has worked well. I can quite understand the principle which is involved in the honourable Member's question, which is this: that the payment of rates should be accompanied by representation. After all, of course this Committee has heard over and over again that substantially the landlord pays the rate. From what I myself have seen of the landlords in different counties, they are just as economical as, if not more so, than the ratepayers, and I think the Committee will see that there is a very good reason for that, because anything that raises the taxation, whether it is of a house, or of a farm, diminishes the amount of rent, the rent and taxation being a compound quantity which you cannot much exceed. If you increase the taxation, you undoubtedly diminish the rent. The landlord, therefore, has a direct interest in keeping down the taxation; but in the counties of Dublin and Wexford, they are certainly not by any means liberal.

6076. Supposing that you take a farm, and that you agree to give a landlord 30 *s.* an acre for it, and that at the time you have taken it the grand jury cess may be 1 *s.* in the 1 *l.*, but that owing to improvements in the barony, it rises from 1 *s.* to 1 *s.* 6 *d.*, that does not increase the rent which you pay to the landlord, does it?—Unquestionably, the contract between the landlord and the tenant being to the effect that the tenant undertakes to pay a rent of 50 *l.* a year, over and above all taxes whatever; if he be kept to that contract he has no power at all to influence the taxation; but after all, if he keeps to his contract, that is his undertaking.

6077. Under the circumstances would it not be just in principle to give the tenant a voice in sending in the parties who are to impose the taxation upon him?—As a matter of principle, of course that is so; I do not, of course, attempt to argue against that, but as a matter of practice, the present system has worked pretty well.

6078. But as a matter of justice in all future lettings, would you not be in favour of the rate being divided between the landlord and the tenant?—I can see no objection to that. It is a matter of arrangement between them. Practically every one knows what the result would be. The same thing took place with the tithe rent-charge; the tithe rent-charge was always added to the subsequent rent.

6079. If you approve of the members of the baronial board under these circumstances being elected by the ratepayers, upon the same principle do you not think that the board for the management of the county at large ought to be elected in the same way?—I said that the alteration possibly would make it as good as it is now; but I did not say that if I were to have the meeting

Mr. J. E. Hunt.

9 June 1858.

carting out of it I would make the alteration; because at present we have a thing producing a good result, a fair administration of the roads; and with great respect, what the honourable Member is just now mentioning, though it is a good abstract principle, is to a certain extent speculative; that is to say, it may turn out worse, or better than, or only equal to, the present system; but that the ratepayer ought to be represented, and that a man who pays taxes ought to have something to do with the distribution of them, I cannot contend is not a right principle.

6080. Do you not think that it would be desirable to have such a body of the grand jury for fiscal purposes; a continuous body, and one that could be called together in the interval between the assizes, whatever emergency arose, instead of a body beginning and ending at every assizes?—In fact, the grand jury's existence having ceased, a subsequent grand jury is not the same body in theory, and it may upset all that they have done.

6081. But would it not be desirable for county purposes to have a body which is entrusted with the administration of the fiscal affairs a continuous body, instead of a body that ends at each assizes?—I do not know whether the honourable Member means that the making of presentments would be continuous and current from the beginning of the year to the end; that is to say, that that body would have the power of making presentments according as it suited the convenience of the county, or whether all the presentments should be made at one period, there being a continuous grand jury for the purpose of meeting any emergencies that might arise. I dare say several advantages might arise from having a continuous grand jury; but there may be great disadvantages also.

6082. Assuming that there are advantages, could such a state of things be established under the present system of summoning the grand jury by the sheriff?—I think there was a Bill brought in last session by a member of this Committee to make what his called a Standing Committee of the present grand jury, and that would apparently meet the difficulty which the honourable member suggests.

6083. But they would have very limited powers, would they not?—They would, of course.

6084. Under circumstances of that kind, might not, and would not a continuous body be desirable?—I must confess that I cannot see what object there would be in not having all the presentments either once or twice a year. By that system you concentrate at that one period the entire intelligence of the county in the place of having it spread over a period of 12 months, because, unquestionably, they can exercise a greater discretion and judgment over the presentments if they are all brought before them once or twice a year than if they are brought before them every week or every month. If they were brought before them in that manner there might be times when it might be convenient to bring in a presentment and get it passed when all the parties could not be present.

6085. In the very county where you are clerk of the Crown an important bridge was broken down some time ago between one assizes and another, and there was no power, was there, to bring a body together to consider what ought to be done in that case of emergency?—No; but that was a private bridge, if I remember rightly. I presume it was the New Ross Bridge to which the honourable Member alludes.

6086. They are going to build a public bridge now. Supposing that that bridge was swept away between the summer and the winter assizes, between which there is a period of eight months, would it not be exceedingly awkward that nothing could be done in cases of a disaster of that kind, or in case of an inundation taking place in the county, or in case of the desirability of the county aiding the railways going through it; and might not many cases of that kind arise where it might be desirable to have some standing body that might be consulted, and that could act in cases of that kind?—No doubt it would. The nearest example that I can give to you of that is another similar bridge, the only bridge that has been built in my time in Wexford, which they call the Wexford free bridge. When I went down to Wexford in the year 1846, it was a matter of discussion between the grand jury and the different parties, and they had the benefit, I think, of about 16 or 18 years of discussion before it was built, so that they had 36 grand juries on it, and that did not advance them one bit, through having a continuous number of half-yearly grand juries. I do not know whether having a grand jury every month, or every quarter, would make them better, but the Wexford free-bridge was under discussion for that length of time, and it is now built. I do not know how long the Ross Bridge will take.

6087. Colonel *Greville*.] With regard to matters referred by the grand jury to the finance committee, if matters are so referred to the finance committee, can they carry them out if they approve of them?—Taking what the honourable baronet was speaking about with regard to the state of the roads in such a barony; we recommend to them to keep a close supervision over the roads, but they do not depute any authority whatever to do any act. The only thing is, as I mentioned, that if it is necessary to get a *locus standi* here by reason of there being a bill injurious to the county passing through Parliament, the finance committee would take upon themselves to instruct a parliamentary agent to do what is necessary expecting that they would get an act of indemnity as they always do from the grand jury afterwards.

6088. Do you prefer large contracts, for maintenance, or small ones?—I was at one time very much in favour of the surveyor's having large contracts in Dublin. They make the contracts either longitudinally large by putting six or seven miles together in one straight line (for instance, from Dublin to the Scalp), or they have another manner of doing it, which is by a central process, that is to say, they will take one particular village or place, and give to one contractor all the roads, say within a radius of a quarter or half a mile of that particular locality. That would appear to be an economical process, but it embarrasses the Finance Committee very much, because if one end of a road seven miles long, is left to get out of order, then it is very hard to deal with it, because you must either stop the whole, or you cannot well pay the man for seven miles of a road.

6089. But then you can desire the county surveyor to go in and repair that short bit, can you not?—No doubt.

6090. Do you yourself like the large contract system

system or the small contract system?—The large contract system is the best, I should think.

6091. Which do you think is the cheapest?—I cannot say much about the cheapness. Before these large contractors came in, and at the commencement of the time when the Grand Jury Act came into operation, the roads were ugly roads, but they had a great deal of material in them. They were not nicely shaped, but they had so much materials that the first of these large contractors put very little materials upon them. He took portions out from the water tables, and so on, and he made very nice green edgings, and it looked very nice, and was very nice, no doubt, but knowing his business, he made a good deal of money out of the large contracts you allude to, and he left the road very near the yellow clay, and then he retired. I cannot tell you as to the comparative expense, but that is one of the evil effects of these very large contracts.

6092. For short length of contracts you have more competition I presume?—Just so, and you have an unskilled workman to deal with; but taking them altogether, perhaps the large contracts may be better. There is much more competition and much more litigation with the small ones, and much more trouble in enforcing a contract.

6093. Are you aware that the surveyors worked the mail-coach roads more cheaply than they are managed at present?—There are no mail-coach roads, by that name, in the county of Dublin.

6094. But are you aware that the turnpike-roads were managed more cheaply by the surveyors than they are at present?—That is to say, that they were managed more cheaply by the trustees than they were managed by the county, but when the surveyor took them into his own hands to work, I cannot say that they were worked cheaper. Although the surveyor, being put to that kind of work, ought perhaps to do them cheaper, inasmuch as what he does includes the profit to the contractor, whatever it would be, yet practically, from his not having a sufficient staff to do the work, and to supervise it, I cannot say that they are much more economical. On the contrary, what is complained of by the Committee is, the surveyor is taken from his legitimate duties to do that for which he was not intended.

6095. I think you stated that so far as your knowledge extended, there were only two counties where the clerk of the Crown never attends?—That is where he acts by deputy.

6096. Is Sligo one of those counties?—It is; and the other is a northern county.

6097. Who verifies all the presentments in those counties?—The clerk of the Crown is, in his patent, allowed to appoint a deputy. I find by the Act of Parliament which one of the members of the Committee referred to me last year, that there is now power to appoint a deputy; for instance, I have received within the last 10 days a letter from Sir Thomas Larcom, saying that the secretary has power to appoint a deputy in case of necessary absence, which throws me into great difficulty, because it puts upon me the difficulty of finding out what necessary absence is.

6098. Can the deputy appointed by the clerk of the Crown do the whole of the clerk of the Crown's work?—Clearly.

6099. From one end of the year to the other?—Yes; clearly.

6100. Must the grand jury present the whole of his salary to the clerk of the Crown, although he may never come near the county?—Yes; if the duty be done and no complaint is made.

6101. It is proposed by some people to amalgamate the offices of clerk of the Crown and clerk of the peace, and also that any fiscal duties which these officers have hitherto performed should be handed over to the secretary of the grand jury, who would countersign the cheques; would you see any objection to that?—There would be no responsible officer to do it. The clerk of the peace has no fiscal duties whatever to perform. That is some little error that has crept in. Under the general grand jury law, the clerk of the peace in the case of the illness of the secretary of the grand jury does the duty, and is paid out of the salary or paid by the secretary for his work and labour in so doing. You may call these fiscal duties, but that is the only thing approaching to fiscal duties that he has to do.

6102. *Chairman.*] Except the registration of voters?—With great respect, that does not come under the definition of fiscal business; that is a duty put upon him. For instance, these fiscal duties of the Clerk of the Crown, of which the Committee have heard so much, are put upon him without fee or reward; he is not paid for one of those duties. His salary arises from a totally different source. Seventy or 80 years ago, and for many years before that, the clerk of the Crown had no salary, but he was paid by what were called prosecutors' fees and prisoners' fees. The prisoners' fees were a great grievance two or three generations ago, and we know nothing of them now, but they were the chief part of his emoluments; and as those fees were abolished, the grand juries were directed by the same Acts that abolished the fees to make to the clerk of the Crown a presentment for the amount of the prosecutors' and prisoners' fees, which he was entitled to be paid by those prosecutors and prisoners. The prisoners were relieved from it, and he got the amount presented on his affidavit. That went on till, I think, the 3 and 4 Geo. 4, and then, for the first time, he was given a salary. A commission, sitting at that time on that subject, took the different counties, and ascertained what the presentments were, and they classified the counties, partly from that, partly from the extent of the county, and partly from the population, and out of that have arisen the presentments for the salary of the clerk of the Crown. For instance, in my county, which is a very large county, I have 820 *l.*, and my fees come to 50 *l.*, or 60 *l.*, or 70 *l.* a year. I do not complain, but I assure you that I earn them.

6103. Supposing the fiscal duties were withdrawn from the Clerk of the Crown, do you see any difficulty in providing a check upon all payments?—The thing is actually in existence in the county of Dublin; the check is this, that the chairman and two members of the committee sign the cheques.

6104. Then do you think that a county would require something like a finance committee if the fiscal duties were taken away from the Clerk of the Crown?—Undoubtedly they would require some controlling body, and if it was contemplated to have representative bodies, I think that it would be found to be impossible to go on without some controlling body; I do not say the Poor Law Commissioners, but something analogous to them.

Mr. *J. H. [illegible].*

9 June 1868.

Mr. J. E. [illegible]. 9 June 1868.

them; of course you take the Judge of Assize with the clerk of the Crown; the committee are of course aware, that although a case may not arise, there is a great benefit in having a judge to settle any real difficulty that exists. I may mention that, according to the Act of Parliament, it is the business of the clerk of the Crown when the Judge of Assize comes into a town (though it is not now so necessary as it was formerly), to wait upon the judge with every one of those applications for presentments for malicious injuries; the obvious object of that was, that the judge might have the opportunity of going through the papers himself with the grand jury, and of either expressing his assent or dissent to what they had done. The thing is now in such good working order that that is hardly ever done, but that is a portion of the duty of the clerk of the Crown.

6105. Do you know anything of the various townships in the county of Dublin?—Yes, of course we must all know more or less of them.

6106. Has the taxation risen much in those townships since they were separated from the county?—I should not like to say; but taking Kingstown and Rathmines, and so forth, they take the best portion of each of their baronies. What they said was, that a portion of their money was spent in that barony for the farmers' roads and their dung carts, and so forth, and they said, "We have villas, and we do not keep any carts or horses, or anything of the kind, and it is not fair to spend our money on roads for farmers," and then they took the roads into their own hands. Their allegation was, that for what they paid the county for the roads they could have either water or light, or something else; but in their Acts I think it will be found that there is a maximum of taxation which they cannot exceed.

6107. Are you aware whether or not their taxation is heavier than it was under the grand jury?—It would be very difficult to say, because there are other elements altogether. The best of them is Rathmines, and with respect to representation there, of course the ratepayers elect the commissioners; and practically, if any one takes a house there the landlord now always pays the taxes.

6108. Does that give the landlord the vote?—It gives him the vote; the tenant pays no taxes; that is to say, he takes the house for 60 *l.* a year, including all taxes, and he has nothing to do with them.

6109. So that practically the landlords have the nomination of the commissioners?—That is the premises. I do not wish to draw any conclusion from it, but the question is many-sided, and you can look at it on every side, and that is one side of it.

6110. You referred to the fact of the secretary of the grand jury having power to appoint a deputy under an Act passed last year; are you aware that he can only appoint that deputy from one assize to the other, and that it must come before the grand jury at the first assize after the appointment?—That is not conveyed in the letter which I received from Sir Thomas Larcom. Of course I would not presume to say a word as to what the Act of Parliament is, but the phraseology of the Act of Parliament which I received was "during his necessary absence."

6111. The secretary of the grand jury under that Act has the power of appointing a deputy, with the approval of the Lord Lieutenant, to act during illness or necessary absence, from one assize to the other; but it must be brought before the grand jury at their meeting, and he cannot continue that deputy without the express approval of the grand jury; is that not so?—As I read the letter, it was a continuous appointment, but of course I stand corrected, if you say that it is only from from one assize to the other.

6112. An Honourable Member asked you about the difficulties which might arise in case the offices of clerk of the Crown and clerk of the peace were amalgamated, and the fiscal duties transferred to the secretary of the grand jury, do you not think that, if a difficulty of that sort arose, the officer who would be appointed to discharge those two duties might countersign the cheques, if it were thought desirable, in the same way as the clerk of the Crown now does?—Of course he might do so.

6113. That would get over the necessity of appointing a finance committee, would it not, if it were not thought desirable?—I cannot follow the argument so far as that, but there is no doubt whatever that if any officer were appointed to do the duties of the consolidated office, he could countersign cheques just as well as the clerk of the Crown or the clerk of the peace does, or as they did jointly until 30 years ago.

6114. May I ask you how many days or how many weeks in the year you are occupied with your duties as clerk of the Crown?—In Wexford from 10 days to a fortnight at each assizes; that is, for the local actual duties, but the work is prepared by me in Dublin and done in Dublin.

6115. What is the work that is prepared in Dublin?—Those query books that I spoke of; and any cheques, and so forth, that are to be signed in the interim, of course I have to do as well. There are cheques continually turning up, we will say, for instance, under what is called the 129th Section, which, as the Committee are aware, contains something analogous to this very finance committee; that is to say, they are payments out of the surplus funds of particular presentments, which the grand jury think it right that the contractors should be kept in funds with.

6116. Do these come up to you to sign?—I must keep an account of them; I must take very good care that they are not signed for more than three-fourths of the amount.

6117. Are they very numerous?—Yes; of late years the grand jury have, so far as they can, exhausted the surplus, because it is no benefit to them that it should lie in the bankers' hands.

6118. Can you give the Committee any idea of how many presentments you have of that description?—I should not like to make an absolute statement as to that; but there are a good number of them.

6119. Are there 50 on an average?—No.

6120. Are there 20?—Perhaps there are, but there are certainly not 50.

6121. Do you think there are 20?—I should say so, but I do not like to give a hap-hazard answer in that way; but you asked me whether there were any cheques to sign in the interim, and I state that that is the kind of thing; now also the witnesses' expenses at petty sessions in certain prosecutions are sent up, and they have to be signed; there is a duty going on from one assize to the other all the time. The question which I was asked as I understood it was, whether

Mr. J. E. Reed. — 9 June 1868.

whether I thought that all these duties were comprised in a month in the year; for instance, the furnishing of the informations.

6122. But upon this furnishing of the informations you receive a specific payment, do you not?—No doubt.

6123. You are paid individually for each information and for your trouble in regard to it, are you not?—No doubt; the only view which I wish to convey to the Committee on that subject is this, that the salary which the clerks of the Crown receive is not a salary for doing the fiscal duties, but a salary for the criminal duties, and it is in lieu of what was presented to them in place of the fees which they received formerly. The criminal business is what we are paid for really, and the other duties are given to us without payment. It is something analogous to the registration which is put upon the clerk of the peace by Parliament, without giving him any countervailing remuneration for it.

6124. But the number of prisoners of late years has been very small, has it not, as compared with what it used to be?—Yes; but however it was very large, some 15 to 20 years ago.

6125. It was very large when the salaries were arranged?—Possibly, but that is 50 years ago.

6126. Though the duties have diminished so much of late years, the clerks of the Crown still continue to receive the salary which was fixed when the business was very heavy?—No doubt; in the years 1846, 1847, and 1848, I was obliged to have four or five clerks, and I dare say for 10 days I have myself been up until two o'clock in the morning preparing those indictments, and my salary was not increased for that; I did as much business in that one year as I do now in four or five years.

6127. Colonel *Cooper*.] But you gained in fees, I suppose?—No; they were prosecutions for stealing potatoes and things of that kind.

6128. Colonel *French*.] Why should the salary be paid by the grand jury, when the officer is not appointed by the grand jury, and when his duties relate to criminal matters?—That is a question between you and the Consolidated Fund.

6129. Do you not think it would be fairer to put it upon the Consolidated Fund as a portion of the criminal expenses of the county, than to compel the grand jury by compulsory presentment to raise the money?—You have an analogy in this, that at the time of the alteration of the Corn Laws the witnesses' expenses were intended to have been paid out of the Consolidated Fund, as they are in England, and of course you are aware that those expenses, though they were put on the Estimates for four or five years, were never called for, and it was not until the year 1853 or 1854 that they were paid out of the Consolidated Fund. Anterior to that, you are aware that they were paid by the counties, and it would appear to have been even a greater hardship that they were obliged to pay those witnesses' expenses which were always paid by the Treasury here.

6130. Colonel *Cooper*.] Are you obliged to keep an office open in the assize town?—Yes, I have no office in the court-house; I pay for my office; but I do not mention that as a grievance. I have no deputy, but I have a person who attends there; but I do not wish to endeavour to impress the Committee with the duties of the clerk of the Crown, because all Honourable Members are themselves familiar with them; and, as I said before, there are heaps of Returns on the subject.

ROBERT S. HAYES, Esq., M.D., called in; and Examined.

R. S. Hayes, Esq., M.D.

6131. (*Chairman*.) ARE you a Medical Man?—I am.

6132. And you are a coroner, I believe?—I am one of the coroners for the county of Kildare.

6133. You have come here, I believe, on behalf of the general body of the coroners of Ireland?—I have.

6134. How are the coroners at present appointed in Ireland?—They are elected by the freeholders, or Parliamentary electors of the county, the same way as a Member of Parliament.

6135. And in what way are they paid?—They are paid by fees; 30 s. for each inquest, with 6 d. a mile forward, and nothing back.

6136. Is there not a limit placed to the amount that each coroner can receive?—There is; it is not to exceed 50 *l.* at each assizes.

6137. What are the coroners bound to do; what are their functions?—The chief duties are the holding of inquests. First we issue a precept, and send out summonses for the jury and witnesses; we then attend and hold the inquest; we have to furnish the constabulary with a copy of the verdict; we have to furnish the Registrar of Births and Deaths with the particulars of each case, and to keep a copy of the same; we have then to keep a statistical Return of all the inquests during the year for the Government; we have to furnish the Board of Superintendence with a monthly account of the expenses of each inquest; we have to advance the medical fees and other expenses; we have to furnish the grand jury at each assizes with an abstract of each case.

6138. Colonel *French*.] Is there any limit to your medical fees?—Yes; it is discretionary with the coroner whether he examines a medical man or not; we are obliged to attend the grand jury at each assizes during the fiscal business, and we are obliged to attend the judges during the assizes. We are sometimes sent for to hold an inquest, and having travelled perhaps 30 or 40 miles, on hearing the circumstances, we consider an inquest unnecessary; we get but 6 *d.* forward for that, and we lose our whole day, and there is no fee.

6139. *Chairman*.] Are you obliged to attend whenever you are sent for?—Yes; whenever the police send for us. The Act of Parliament directs the police to send for us.

6140. Of what is it that you complain?—We complain of our being paid by fees instead of by salary; we are subject to a great deal of trouble and annoyance by being found fault with by the grand jury sometimes, for holding an unnecessary inquest, and sometimes for other things, and our mileage, we consider, is quite insufficient. We should be much better pleased to have a fixed salary, and with that view, a meeting of the coroners which was called in Dublin, resolved on drawing up a short bill, which I believe was sent to most of the Members of this Committee.

6141. Could

R. S. Hayes, Esq., M.D.

9 June 1862.

6141. Could not those duties which you have stated as being discharged by the coroner be discharged just as well by the stipendiary magistrate?—I should say not.

6142. Why not?—First, because a stipendiary magistrate is liable to be removed on duty constantly; our stipendiary magistrate in Kildare has been away at Howth lately for a month or five weeks, and they are sometimes sent to the north when party processions take place, and to the assizes, and so forth, and you could not depend upon them attending at all.

6143. Do you not think that in such cases the local magistrates could hold inquests?—They could hold the inquest certainly, but I do not know whether you could depend upon their always attending like a paid officer, such as the coroner, who is obliged to be resident in the county.

6144. Colonel *French*.] But are the magistrates not in the habit of holding inquests under particular circumstances?—The Act of Parliament authorises two magistrates to hold an inquest where the coroner does not attend for 48 hours.

6145. And they report that to the petty sessions of the district, do they not?—No, the police have the power of calling upon the magistrates to attend.

6146. And it is reported to the clerk of the Crown, is it not?—Yes; they are bound to lodge the inquest with the clerk of the Crown, as we are also.

6147. *Chairman*.] Do you think that if a provision were made for the absence of resident magistrates, the local magistrates would be found wanting in the discharge of their duties; might not the same provision as is at present made, if the coroner be absent, be made, if the stipendiary magistrate were absent?—It might.

6148. Is it not the fact that the coroners very often reside a long way from the places where they have to hold inquests?—They are obliged to reside within their districts.

6149. But some counties are very large?—In Cork and Galway they may have to travel 30 miles; in my district, the longest distance which I have is 24 miles.

6150. Would it not be much more convenient to get a resident magistrate, generally speaking, than a coroner?—I do not think so. The coroner, as I need not state to the Committee, is one of the oldest officers under the Crown, being equal in antiquity to the sheriff.

6151. Is there any qualification required for the coroner?—He must be a 50 *l.* freeholder, or 100 *l.* leaseholder.

6152. He need not be a medical man, need he?—He need not be; but the general feeling in the present day is, that medical men are the most fitting men for the office, for many reasons. There are 86 coroners in Ireland, and there are 73 medical men amongst them.

6153. Have the coroners always been paid in the way that they are now paid?—Always, I think, by fees.

6154. Colonel *French*.] It was formerly limited to 40 *l.* at each assizes, was it not?—Under the old Act, I believe, it was limited to 40 guineas.

6155. *Chairman*.] Is there any other point to which the coroners object, except to payment by fees?—Yes; we ask for the power of appointing deputies, as the coroners in England can do. We have not that power in Ireland, nor have we the power of taking bail, in cases of manslaughter, as the coroners in England have. We also think that a coroner, when he arrives at 70 years of age, ought to be obliged to retire from his office, and be superannuated. We also think that the mode of election is very troublesome and very expensive. We have had instances of it; and when I was informed that I was to be examined here, I sent out a circular to every coroner in Ireland, asking for information on certain subjects, and I am able to give the Committee some statistics on the subject. I received answers from four coroners whose elections cost them 250 *l.* each; from one coroner whose election cost him 300 *l.*; from one coroner whose election cost him 400 *l.*; from two coroners whose elections cost them 500 *l.* each; from one coroner whose election cost him 600 *l.*; from one coroner whose election cost him 964 *l.*; and from one coroner whose election cost him 1,000 *l.*

6156. Are they elected by the Parliamentary electors?—By the Parliamentary electors over the whole district.

6157. Are they the electors resident in the district, or those who have Parliamentary votes in the district?—Those who have Parliamentary votes in the district. I was elected without a contest. My Lord Mayo was kind enough to propose me, and I was elected without any opposition, and it did not cost me, of course, anything like that; it only cost me 30 *l.* or 40 *l.*

6158. Would the coroners think it better that they should be appointed either by the Government or by the grand jury, or by some body, and not elected?—Yes; but there is a difference of opinion as to what body should appoint, if the change were made.

6159. Earl of *Mayo*.] Have you ascertained the opinions of the coroners generally upon that point?—I have; my suggestion would be, if the change was made at all, that it should be in this way: the Chief Justice of the Queen's Bench is the Chief Coroner for Ireland; and I think that, if a vacancy occurred, a candidate might come forward, by counsel, and apply to the Court of Queen's Bench to be appointed coroner. Let as many candidates as like come forward; let the Judges of the Court of Queen's Bench hear the statements, and examine the candidates, if they wish; and let them appoint whom they consider to be the fittest person.

6160. Is there any analogous appointment to that now made?—The Commissioners of affidavits and Commissioners in Chancery are appointed in that way. The judges hear the case, and they are recommended, either by the grand jury, or by the law officers of the Crown, or by the Counsel who go the circuit, and the judges act upon those recommendations. There may be two or three candidates before them, and they always make a selection. In this case, if it were thought right that the appointment should be made by the Queen's Bench, there being four judges on the bench, the appeal might be left to the Lord Chancellor if the numbers were even.

6161. *Chairman*.] Do you consider that the position of the Commissioners of Affidavits is analogous to that of coroners?—I do not. One is a judicial office, and the other is simply a ministerial office.

6162. Colonel *French*.] Do you think it is desirable

sirable that there should be an additional qualification, and that the coroners should, *for instance*, like yourself, be medical men?—I think that it would be very necessary and useful if they were examined in medical jurisprudence and the law of evidence; that, I think, would be quite sufficient for a coroner.

6163. You mentioned, I think, that there were more occasional disputes between coroners and grand juries?—Yes.

6164. Did these occur after the Act of Parliament, enabling the coroner to give fees without any limit to the medical men whom he thought necessary to examine?—We are strictly limited; we can only give one guinea to a medical man, and, in the case of a *post mortem* examination, two guineas.

6165. Have you ever heard of coroners bringing about medical men with them, and not calling upon the medical man of the dispensary of the district where the death had occurred?—The general practice is to employ the dispensary medical man.

6166. Do you think that it ought to be made imperative upon them to employ him?—I do not think it should be imperative.

6167. *Earl of Mayo*.] What do you do yourself generally?—I generally employ the dispensary medical officer; but some of the dispensary medical officers are very young and inexperienced men, and, if it was a serious case, I should like to have a good opinion.

6168. Colonel *French*.] Do you think that the discretion ought to be left with the coroner?—I think so.

6169. Of the expense of the election, considering the very small amount of remuneration, you think it exceedingly advisable to get rid of?—I think so.

6170. Because, if you expended 1,000 *l.* in the election, and the income is not above 80 *l.* a year, you could not expect to get respectable persons to fill the office?—Exactly; the salary being so small, and so uncertain, and subject to those unpleasant collisions with the grand jury, we would much rather have a small fixed salary, even if you did away with the mileage.

6171. *Chairman*.] If a fixed salary were resolved upon, would the coroners be satisfied with a salary, as at present proposed?—Yes; that Bill fixes the salary at 100 *l.*, with 9 *d.* a mile mileage.

6172. Colonel *French*.] Are you aware that certain grand juries in Ireland, have been in the habit of presenting larger sums to the coroners than is allowed?—I never heard of it.

6173. *Chairman*.] On an average, does the amount received by coroners come up to the 50 *l.*?—In some cases it does.

6174. Is it usually the case?—Not always. I have sometimes been up to my maximum, that is to say, 49 *l.* 10 *s.* for 33 inquests. My brother coroner's salary is generally up to it, because he has the camp in his district, which gives him a good many additional inquests.

6175. Would it not vary very much in different districts in Ireland?—Of course it would.

6176. Would it be a proper system to have a fixed salary for every part of Ireland?—I think it would. As the coroner is a judicial officer, and is liable to be called upon, and is obliged to reside in the district, I think that an even salary to every coroner, no matter what his inquests were, or what they were likely to be, would be the simplest and fairest mode.

R. S. Hayes, Esq., M.D.

9 June 1868.

6177. This salary I understand you would fix at what would be a proper remuneration for the coroner in the district where most trouble was given?—We mean 50 *l.* half-yearly as the maximum.

6178. Would you oblige the counties in which there were, perhaps, only a dozen inquests all over the county to pay the same amount?—I think that there are no counties like that.

6179. Are there not some counties which do not come at all up to the maximum number?—There are some counties where there are four coroners, and there are five in others; Galway has five.

6180. In counties where you have a large number of coroners, would you have each coroner get his maximum of 100 *l.* a year?—Yes, 50 *l.* at each assizes.

6181. Would you have the same number of coroners?—No; I think that some of the counties might be reduced; there are nine counties which have more than three; I think that three would be enough for any county. Eight counties have four, and one has five, so that if those were struck off as they died away, it would reduce them by 10.

6182. But would not those counties, which are of greater extent require that there should be a greater number of coroners, in order to have them at convenient distances?—That would be, but three would be enough for any county. Two is the general number, and Carlow has only one, it being a very small county.

6183. Are you not aware that, at the present moment in many counties in Ireland, a maximum of 50 *l.* is very seldom reached?—I cannot speak for any counties but my own.

6184. Supposing that that were the case, would you give the 100 *l.* salary and a mileage in addition?—That is in this Bill, and that was agreed to at the meeting of which I have spoken; but from the queries which I sent out, and to which I got answers, I have ascertained that the majority of the coroners in Ireland are willing to take 100 *l.* a year, without any dispute as to mileage or anything else. They wish to have themselves placed on a respectable footing, and not to be paid by fees; they think that it is derogatory to the office. And if the office is to be maintained, they think that it ought to be maintained by a salary.

6185. Have you any statistics of the number of inquests held in different counties in Ireland?—I have not.

6186. *Earl of Mayo*.] Have you any statistics as to the average remuneration?—The amount of coroners' fees in the county of Kildare for the last five years was 641 *l.* 8 *s.* 6 *d.* between my brother coroner and myself.

6187. Are you aware that the English coroners are paid by an average of five years, and that their inquests often amount to 200 *l.* or 300 *l.* a year?—I believe that is so. The London coroners have 1,200 *l.* a year.

6188. Colonel *French*.] You say that *for most* counties in Ireland two coroners would be sufficient, and in the largest three, and that each coroner would be content with a salary of 100 *l.* a year?—Yes.

6189. In the county where there are three, that is, trebling the present amount levied for coroners, and where there are two, it is doubling

R. S. Hayes, Esq., M.D.

9 June [illegible].

it; is not that so?—No; each coroner, at the present moment, may, if his inquests amount to so much, receive 100 *l.* a year.

6190. Is it not the case, under the clause to which you refer, that the grand jury is limited as to all the coroners, not to exceed a grant of 50 *l.* a year?—No; the 9 & 10 Victoria, chapter 37, section 23, says, "That it shall and may be lawful to and for the grand jury of any county, riding, or division, when they shall have examined and approved of such abstracts and accounts as aforesaid, to present for the payment of any coroner within such county, riding, or division, the sum of 1 *l.* 10 *s.* sterling for each and every inquest held by him respectively since the preceding assizes, or since his last application for a presentment, but such sums not to exceed in the whole the sum of 50 *l.* sterling at any one assizes; and such grand jury shall present, in addition thereto, and over and above such payment, such further and other sums at the rate of 6 *d.* per mile for every mile which such coroner shall have been obliged to travel from his usual place of residence for the purpose of taking such inquest: Provided always, that whenever any coroner shall have held more than one inquest on the same day, then in respect of every such inquest taken after the first, the said sum of 6 *d.* per mile shall be computed and paid to such coroner for every additional mile only which he shall have been compelled to travel in consequence of holding more than one inquest on the same day." With reference to mileage, the judges have decided that it is only forward.

6191. But by the Grand Jury Act, the grand jury cannot grant more than 50 *l.* to all the coroners, can they?—That is repealed long ago. This Act repeals it formally in the preamble: "So much of an Act passed in the sixth and seventh years of the reign of his late Majesty King William the Fourth, intituled 'An Act to consolidate and amend the Laws relating to the Presentment of Public Money by Grand Juries in Ireland,' as relates to the Payment of Coroners and of Medical Witnesses," is repealed.

6192. *Chairman.*] You do not think that there should be any classification of the counties, or difference in the salaries, in different parts of Ireland, but that there ought to be a uniform salary for coroners all over Ireland?—I think that a uniform salary would be more satisfactory to all, and more acceptable.

6193. Although in some counties coroners would have more than five times the number of inquests than in others?—I really cannot see how that can be.

6194. But you stated that your colleague, having the Curragh Camp in his district, had a larger number than yourself?—Yes; he has a few more than I have.

6195. Are there not exceptional circumstances of that kind in all parts of Ireland?—I scarcely know of one in Ireland, except the camp.

6196. Do you not think that where there is a dense population in large towns, the number is greater?—Yes; but every coroner has those towns in his district. I have three or four towns in my district, and Dr. Carter has towns in his district; but happening to have the camp, there are rather more inquests there than there would be otherwise. Our chief anxiety to get the salary is to do away, as I have said before, with the unpleasant collisions which we sometimes have with the grand jury. I myself had had one very unpleasant incident some years ago. I sent in my abstract for 24 *l.* for inquests, and 11 of those inquests were struck out of my presentment. It happened at the time that I was the only coroner in the county. There was a vacancy, or something of that kind, and I was called upon to do the extra duty. Some of those inquests were held previously to the previous assizes, and on that ground the grand jury struck them off, and I was obliged to employ a solicitor and counsel to go before a judge; and he at once saw the unfairness of it, and ordered the money to be presented to me.

6197. *Colonel French.*] The grand jury having struck them off on the ground of their not being lawful on account of the assizes having passed since the inquest was held, did the judge put them in?—Yes. Here is the whole report of the case:—"Mr. Curran, who appeared for Dr. Hayes, said that gentleman was fairly and fully entitled to 1 *l.* 10 *s.* each for those 11 inquests, otherwise he would not be dealt fairly with according to law. There was a space of four months' difference between the summer and spring assizes, and the spring and summer assizes, and he could not be allowed for more than 33 inquests at either period, even if he had 56; therefore if he was not allowed to bring forward the surplusage from the long to the short period, if there should be any, it would be doing him a great injury, and prevent him from receiving that remuneration to which he was evidently entitled, according to the plain reading of the section of the Act of Parliament, by which provision was made for such cases. Mr. Curran here quoted the 9 & 10 Vict. c. 37, which stated that the inquests should be enumerated from the previous assizes, or from the last application for presentment, which at least should be ten days previous to the assizes, and that that sum should not exceed on the whole 50 *l.* sterling at any one assizes." Then the Court asked, 'Was not Dr. Hayes's last application made at the last assizes? (*Mr. Curran.*) It was made, my lord, a certain time previous to the presentment sessions.' Mr. Curran, in continuation, called his *Lordship's* attention to the disjunctive phrase, 'or since last application.' He then referred to the 41st section of the same Act. On further reference to the 21st section, he stated that Dr. Hayes had lodged his previous application before those 11 inquests were held; the law had left the time of lodgment of such application discretionary with him, so that it was at least 10 clear days before the assembling of the grand jury. (*Court.*) Then in fact, when did he lodge the application? (*Captain Hervey.*) Four months before the assizes. His Lordship read the Act bearing on the subject, and said he thought the fair remuneration for a coroner was 100 *l.* a year; that it could not exceed that, no matter what extra amount of inquests he might hold within the year. As to lodging his application ten days before the assizes the law gave him every latitude, and he could lodge it at any period previous to that; there as the year, with regard to holding assizes, was unequally divided, one being double the interval of the other, it was very likely there would occur two-thirds the number in one interval, and one-third during the other; then it would be a great hardship to an officer entitled to 100 *l.* a year, to have his remuneration cut down, because the larger portion of the year's inquests occurred

before

R. S. Hayes, Esq., M.D.

9 June 1868.

before the assizes, preceded by the long interval of time, the law not allowing more than 50 *l.* to be levied at each assizes. If he did lodge his application, and after that if the 11 inquests took place, it would be a hardship to have them disallowed, providing the inquests presented for at the spring and summer assizes did not exceed 100 *l.* a year. Mr. La Touche said, the grand jury having had their doubts on the subject, referred it for his Lordship's opinion. (*Court.*) My opinion is, that he should have 100 *l.* a year, if he had a sufficient number of inquests within that period to warrant the presentment; and I think he is fairly entitled to the presentment now under consideration."

6198. Who was the Judge?—It was Judge Crampton, I think.

6199. *Chairman.*] So that the coroners, it would appear, have the power of dividing their inquests between two assizes?—Yes, if you get up your number to 33, which makes 49 *l.* 10 *s.*

6200. Has not that been overruled by Judge Keogh, and one or two others?—The words of the Act are plain; the moment you get your number you lodge your application for a presentment; and then you carry on your presentment to the next half-year; if you get your full number, you can lodge them whenever you have arrived at that number.

6201. Earl of *Mayo.*] Do you think that the mode of inquiry before a coroner as to the cause of death is always very satisfactory?—I do; at least I speak for myself.

6202. In cases of crime, do you think it satisfactory?—Yes, I find no difficulty whatever in discovering crime, and no difficulty in procuring witnesses; medical men, of course, if it be a serious case, make a post-mortem examination, and declare the cause of death.

6203. I am not speaking so much of the discovery of the cause of death as of the guilty parties by whom the crime has been committed; have you observed in your experience as a coroner in serious cases, that the course of inquiry which takes place before the coroner is not of a very satisfactory nature?—I have not; I can hold as searching an inquiry as any one provided the police secure the attendance of the witnesses.

6204. Have you had any serious cases?—Certainly.

6205. Do you find that the police assist?—Always; they are most particular; in fact they have stringent instructions to that effect.

6206. I am alluding now to that portion of your inquiry which is not an inquiry into the cause of death, but which is an inquiry in a case of outrage, as to the parties by whom the death has been occasioned?—Our inquiry is when, where, how, and by what means, a certain person came by his death. That enables me to go into all questions.

6207. Do you think it would be desirable to limit the inquiry before a coroner simply to the cause of death, as to whether it arose from violence or from natural causes; leaving all matters connected with the administration of justice, and the bringing home of the crime to the guilty parties to the magistrates, and the Crown solicitor, and other persons entrusted with the administration of the law?—I do not see what advantage there would be in merely declaring the cause of death.

6208. Is it not very often the case that at the same time that a coroner's inquest is going on an inquiry is going on by magistrates, very much partaking of the same nature, conducted by different persons, and the result of which very often is, to throw a great deal of doubt upon evidence which may hereafter be produced?—In England the magistrates hold a concurrent inquiry into cases with the coroner, but it is not my experience that it is so in Ireland.

6209. But in Ireland the inquiry before the coroner does not prevent the investigation into the crime taking place before the magistrates, does it?—Unless some special circumstances are reported to the Government, and they order an inquiry, I do not know of the magistrates holding an inquiry into a case after the coroner had disposed of it.

6210. But it may be actually going on at the same time, may it not?—I never knew it.

6211. Is it not very often the case that a prisoner, on a charge of murder, is committed by the magistrates as well as by the coroner?—No; if he was first committed by the coroner there would be no further committal.

6212. Might he be committed by the magistrate first?—That cannot take place, because the inquest must be the first inquiry; the moment the death occurs it is reported by the police; I have never known it otherwise in Ireland.

6213. Inquests are very frequently adjourned in serious cases. In the case of an adjourned inquest, may not an investigation in the meantime take place before a magistrate, and the magistrate commit a man for trial?—I know it is the case frequently in England, but I never knew such a case occur in Ireland.

6214. Do you not think that if such things do occur, it must occasion constant clashing?—I think it would, but certainly my experience in Ireland is to the contrary. I was about to read to the Committee the directions to constables: "It is the duties of the constabulary to inform the coroner of all cases of sudden death, although from the notoriety from certain facts, it may appear that an inquest may be nothing more than a matter of form, but still it is a form, the regular observance of which is equally required by law and policy."

6215. Have you ever known instances of the constabulary requesting an inquest to be held, when the inquest was deemed not to be necessary afterwards?—They are always bound to report, and to mention in full, the circumstances as far as they can be found out, to the coroner, and the discretion generally lies with the coroner, as to whether the inquest shall be held or not. The instructions in the Act of Parliament are, "That when any dead body shall be found, or any case of sudden death, or of death attended with suspicious circumstances shall occur in any district, the sub-inspector of the constabulary of such district, or the constable or sub-constables acting in and for the place where such dead body shall be found or such death happen, shall give, or cause to be given, immediate notice thereof to the coroner of such district, together with such information as he or they shall have been able to obtain, touching the finding of such dead body or such death. And the said coroner shall, if upon receipt of such or other sufficient notice and information, he shall deem it necessary to hold an inquest on such dead body, issue his precept to the sub-inspector of such district, or, in his absence,

R. S. Hayes, Esq., M.D.

9 June 1858.

stant, to the head constable or other constable acting for him."

6216. Do you think that that is a duty which ought to be left to a man in the position of a sub-constable?—Unless the constable is absent on duty, it is always the constable who writes to me.

6217. Are you aware that certain cases have arisen, where inquests have been demanded, where much pain has been caused to parties, and where really there was no ground for an inquest, and it was not at all desirable?—If the coroner or the police were to mind the feelings of the people in that way, there would be very few inquests, because there is a general feeling against an inquest; but at the same time I have been coroner of Kildare 18 years now, and I do not remember one single case where the parties were offended or annoyed at my going; if the thing is done decently and in order, and quietly, there is no objection raised.

6218. Do you think that, speaking generally, those complaints are well founded?—I do not.

6219. Practically, is it generally the constabulary officers, or the subordinate members of the force who send for you?—Chiefly the constables. Some constabulary officers require the constables to send a report to them first, and then they communicate with the coroner; but I think that the Act of Parliament means that it should go direct from the constable to the coroner, but sometimes the magistrates interfere with us in our duties.

6220. How is that?—In Celbridge, some years ago, two children were drowned in the Liffey, and a magistrate ordered the children to be buried and the police not to report the case to me.

6221. He was not acting according to the law in that case, was he?—He was not.

6222. Do you think that giving remuneration to coroners in the shape of salary, instead of paying them by fees, as is done now, would induce a better class of men to engage in the occupation?—It is clearly my opinion, and the opinion of all the coroners in Ireland, that it would get a better class of men.

6223. In that case would you require any specific qualification beyond a knowledge of medical jurisprudence and the laws of evidence?—I think that would be quite sufficient.

6224. Would you require a money qualification?—I would continue the qualification of the Act of Parliament.

6225. How would you propose to ascertain the competency of the candidates in regard to those two points which you have mentioned?—With regard to the property qualification, the Act of Parliament appoints how that is to be done. The candidate is to lodge the certificate with the Clerk of the Crown. With regard to the other points, it might be very well to make the candidate for the coronership submit to an examination.

6225*. Do you think that that would be desirable?—I certainly do. I think it would improve the class of men very much.

6226. You expressed yourself in favour of superannuation; I apprehend that in case the alteration which you suggest was made, it would not have the effect of making the coroner's men, who devoted their whole time to their business, because there would not be sufficient employment for them?—No.

6227. I presume that you are aware that in all the modern rules of superannuation it is supposed to be necessary to entitle persons to superannuation that they should devote their whole time to the public service?—I do not think that follows in every case; for instance, the clerks of petty sessions are fixed on a salary of 100 *l.* a year, and I believe that they are entitled to superannuation. It affects the clerks of unions.

6228. You are aware that that is the general rule in the public service?—Yes.

6229. And if superannuation were given to coroners, it would, of course, be a departure from that rule?—Yes.

6230. Do you not think that there should be a limit of age fixed, so that in all cases coroners should be obliged to retire from the public service at a certain age?—That is what I said; at 70.

6231. Do you not think that that ought to be made a condition of their appointment?—Yes.

6232. Irrespective of superannuation as regards future appointments?—I think that would be a hardship.

6233. Is it possible that a man, generally speaking, after reaching the age of 70 years, can perform the duties of a coroner efficiently?—I know that sometimes they have very long journeys in all weathers.

6234. And occasionally the duty is very severe, is it not?—It is very severe sometimes. I have before me a Parliamentary Report of the year 1839, which is rather ancient, certainly, but it is like the office of coroner in that respect. The Commissioners say, "The coroner's duty on inquisitions is often attended with much trouble and loss of time, being frequently delayed for want of jurors, or by the absence of a surgeon, whose attendance is generally necessary, and whose arrival he must in such case await. As the inquest must always be taken upon view of the body by the coroner and jurors, should such body have been buried, it is necessary for the coroner to have it disinterred and inspected. The absence of witnesses occasionally requires an adjournment, which leads to a repetition of attendance and trouble. It frequently becomes the duty of the coroner to commit persons who, by the verdict of the jury, are found guilty of murder or manslaughter, or who appear to him to have been guilty, or to have been accessary before the fact, or accomplices therein; he is also required to bind witnesses, who have given evidence at the inquest, in recognizances, to attend at the assizes or commission. In conducting the inquiry, he is expected to take down in writing the substance and import of the testimony of every witness examined on the inquest; to read the evidence so taken down to the witnesses, and have it authenticated by their signature and by his own. He may also be required to explain to the jurors the legal effect of the evidence, in order to enable them to specify in their verdict the precise nature of the offence, which, in some cases of homicide, requires much discrimination."

6235. In the case of inquests which go on for a great number of days, do you get any remuneration for that extra duty?—No.

6236. I believe that on one occasion you conducted one of the most important inquiries ever held before a coroner, where 13 people were killed?—Yes; the great accident on the Great Southern and Western Railway occupied me eight days.

6237. And

R. S. Hayes, Esq., M.D.

9 June 1868.

6237. And that really resolved itself into a trial of the working of the whole railway system of Ireland, did it not?—It did; every line of the evidence of 85 witnesses was written by my own hand.

6238. Was there no additional remuneration for that?—Nothing but my fees.

6239. But what is the qualification for a coroner?—He must be a 50 *l.* freeholder, or 100 *l.* leaseholder.

6240. Do you think that every 50 *l.* freeholder, or every 100 *l.* leaseholder, would be a qualified person to hold such an investigation as that?—I do not at all.

6241. Do you consider, therefore, that a person appointed solely upon that qualification of being a 50 *l.* freeholder, or a 100 *l.* leaseholder, is a proper person to hold the appointment?—No; that is the reason why I suggest that the appointment should be vested in a judge, and should not be in the hands of the electors. I need not tell the Committee that religious or political feelings will operate one way or the other.

6242. At present any man who is a 50 *l.* freeholder, or a 100 *l.* leaseholder, is eligible?—Yes.

6243. And he may be called upon to discharge the important duties which you had to discharge upon that occasion?—Yes; I have a return here of the time occupied by various coroners in holding inquests, and the remuneration they received. There were eight coroners occupied for three days in holding the one inquest, and received only a fee of 1 *l.* 10 *s.*, four were occupied four days, and received a fee of 1 *l.* 10 *s.*; five were occupied for five days, and received only 1 *l.* 10 *s.* There was one inquest, which occupied 16 days, that was in the Six-mile Bridge affair, where there were six deaths, and the coroners' fees were only 9 *l.* for 16 days' work; and Mr. Hosty, of the county of Galway, was three weeks employed on one inquest, off and on, and 1 *l.* 10 *s.* was his fee.

6244. Colonel *French.*] You have stated that your opinion was that the coroner was entitled to receive a fee of 1 *l.* 10 *s.* for every inquest held by him?—Yes; provided his fees do not exceed 50 *l.* at each assizes.

6245. Irrespective altogether of the mileage?—Irrespective altogether of the mileage.

6246. Are you aware that the Court ruled at the Sligo assizes that the grand jury had the power to diminish the coroners' fees, if they considered that they had sufficient reason to do so?—Yes, they can swear the coroner to the truth of his statement.

6247. Are you aware that the Court has also ruled that grand juries are compelled, and have no choice but to present the amount of money paid to medical men by the coroner?—Yes; that has been decided by two or three of the judges.

6248. If the coroner, for instance, gives 2 *l.* where the grand jury consider that 1 *l.* would have been sufficient, they must present the 2 *l.*, must they not?—He cannot give 2 *l.* unless the surgeon makes a post-mortem examination.

6249. But if he gives 2 *l.* where the grand jury are of opinion that 1 *l.* would be sufficient, and that there ought to be no post-mortem examination, that cannot be diminished, can it?—A discretionary power is given by the Act to a coroner as to whether he will have a post-mortem examination or not.

6250. But, if there is a post-mortem examination, the 2 *l.* must be paid?—Yes.

6251. You used the phrase "advanced by the coroner;" are you aware of any coroner advancing, out of his own pocket, the fees?—Out of my pocket I have advanced the fees at every inquest.

6252. Do you never give an order on the treasurer?—Never; the Act is mandatory on the coroner to pay the money.

6253. Do you believe that it is carried out?—I do not in all cases.

6254. You yourself are in the habit of carrying out the law?—Yes.

6255. Then you are out of the money from the period when the inquest is held until the ensuing assizes, are you not?—No, only for a month; the Board of Superintendence pay every month; there is a certain sum presented in advance for the Board to meet the incidental expenses of coroners' inquests.

6256. Is there any duty attached to the office of coroner which could not with proper arrangements be discharged by the resident magistrates?—Certainly.

6257. What is the duty which the resident magistrates would not be able to perform?—The coroner himself must be constantly resident in his district, and the same obligation could not be enforced on magistrates, or even on stipendiary magistrates; the coroner has to act in the place of the sheriff in selecting juries, whenever the high sheriff or sub-sheriff is disqualified from acting; the coroner is the officer to whom writs and executions are issued whenever the sheriff neglects his duty or cannot perform it; the coroner is the only officer who can execute legal process against the sheriff himself.

6258. Those are cases of debt, are they not?—Yes, civil process.

6259. The coroner also, if a warrant is given to him to arrest a person for debt, can without communication with the sheriff, carry it into effect?—He can; but he never has to do that unless the sheriff returns the writ, and says *nulla bona* or *non est inventus*, or something of that kind.

6260. Are you aware of any advantage accruing to the county from that power being vested in the coroner?—The coroners frequently execute writs when the sheriffs cannot or do not; I have done it myself.

6261. And do you think that is a power which ought to be preserved?—I think so; some one must do it; if the sheriff is engaged in a lawsuit himself, then the coroner has to strike the special jury for him.

6262. Earl of *Mayo.*] With regard to mileage, did you say that you thought that there ought to be a regular payment, or would you think it better to continue the present system of paying by the mile?—If the Committee please to approve of the 100 *l.* a year, I would rather take it and have no mileage, and have no trouble about it.

6263. Do you think that that would enable people to say that coroners had not sufficient inducement to be very keen in attending inquests?—No, I think, on the contrary, it would place the coroner in a better position, and make him a more respectable officer.

6264. And you think that it would not interfere with the performance of his duty?—I think not.

R. S. Hayes, Esq., M.P.

9 June [illegible].

6265. Mr. *Blake*.] You stated that the same qualification which enables a person to vote for a Member of Parliament enables him to vote for a coroner; is it not the fact also that the coroner is not prevented by any legal enactment from employing any bribery or treating, if he chooses, at the election?—I do not know that there is anything in the Act to prevent it.

6266. Are you aware that it is the fact that he is not prevented from bribing?—I am not aware.

6267. Did you hear, some time ago, that at an election for coroner for a southern county, two persons who voted for him, by reason of his treating them, were drowned, and that they were the two first persons on whom he held an inquest?—I never heard that. If men come in to vote for a man, I think there is no great harm in his giving them refreshments; but to make them drunk was wrong.

6268. Have you ever heard that great bribery has gone on occasionally in elections for the office of coroner?—In older times I think that the office was often bought, but I have never heard of it of late years.

Friday, 12*th June* 1868.

MEMBERS PRESENT:

Mr. Blake.	Mr. Kendall.
Mr. Dawson.	Sir Charles Lanyon.
General Dunne.	Mr. Leader.
Colonel French.	Mr. Maguire.
Mr. Gregory.	The O'Conor Don.

THE O'CONOR DON, IN THE CHAIR.

Mr. JOHN DUIGNAN M'DERMOT, called in; and Examined.

Mr. J. D. M'Dermot. 12 June 1868.

6269. *Chairman*.] YOU are a Solicitor in the county of Roscommon, are you not?—Yes.

6270. You are also, I believe, Chairman of the Town Commissioners and a Magistrate of Boyle?—I am.

6271. And a Poor Law Guardian?—Yes.

6272. Have you for many years been Deputy Chairman of the Board of Boyle?—For about three years, I think.

6273. Have you given lately any attention to the annual charge made under the grand jury presentments for the revision of the valuation?—I have.

6274. Would you state to the Committee what has been the annual charge for revision in the county of Roscommon within the last five or six years?—From the 1st of May 1863 to the 30th of April 1864, I find from the county book that the charge made was 278l. 8s. 9d. I may state that the charges are in the different years, from the 1st of May to the 30th of April all through. The next is for 1864, 378l. 11s. 10d. For the year 1865, it is 476l. 11s. 10d. For the year 1866 to 1867, it is 330l. 13s. 1d. It is only at the summer assizes that those sums appear in the county books, and, therefore, for the year 1868, has not been finished yet. The total is 1,464l. 5s. 6d., paid by the county for four years.

6275. And the total annual revision costs twice that amount, does it not?—Twice that amount; the Treasury, I suppose, pays the other half, making a total of 2,928l. 11s.

6276. Have you ascertained any statistics with respect to the changes in the valuation over the county in any particular year?—I have; in the year 1863 I found by the county book that the valuation was 294,003l. 12s., and in the year 1864 it was 293,927l. 10s., being a decrease of 76l. 2s. between the years 1863 and 1864. In the year 1865, the valuation by the same authority, the county book, was 294,281l. 17s., the difference as between 1864 and 1865, being an increase of 354l. 2s. on some baronies, and a decrease on others of 86l. 4s., making the total amount of change 330l. 6s. In the year 1866 the valuation was 294,148l. 1s., the difference between the valuations for the years 1865 and 1866, being a decrease of 133l. 11s. In the year 1867 the valuation was 294,134l. 13s., the difference between the years 1866 and 1867 being a decrease of only 13l. 8s. The difference between the years 1863 and 1867 in the valuation is only 131l. 1s.

6277. Taking your own union of Boyle, what was the total valuation last year?—The last valuation of the union of Boyle is 73,553l. 17s. There is of that 22,548l. 19s. in the county of Sligo. The year before the valuation for the same union of Boyle was 73,643l. 4s., there being only a difference on the entire union of 90l. 7s.; in the preceding year 1866-67, the difference was only 18l. 6s. 9d.

6278. In the year 1866, what do you state was the total amount charged for the annual revision of the county?—The expense was 476l. 11s. 10d. from the 1st of May 1865 to the 30th of April 1866.

6279. That is only half the expense, is it?—That is only half the expense, the expense payable by the county; the total was 953l. 3s. 8d. That was the expense of the annual revision for the year 1866.

6280. Could you explain to the Committee in what consists this annual revision?—The poor rate collectors are required in November in each year to furnish to the clerks of the unions, lists of any changes, such as changes of occupancy, houses down, houses built, increase or decrease of farms, to be laid before the guardians. The clerk of the union then transmits that list to the Valuation Office. A valuator is sent down, and a day is appointed to meet the poor rate collectors to go over the lists; and the chief portion of his duty (at least judging from what has occurred in the Boyle Union for the last three years) appears to be to make changes where there has been the substitution of one occupier for another; and that information is supplied in the manner which I have stated; it is only necessary for him, as I understand, to go to the different holdings, and personally to inspect them whenever a house has been built, or a farm has been added to, or the portion of it previously held, lessened; but in regard to change of occupancy, there is no necessity for him to go, neither is there if houses are down, because there is nothing to do except to strike his pen across the entry, in case of houses being down.

6281. Could you state to the Committee how many days the revisers have been engaged in the union of Boyle in the last three years in discharging that duty?—I have taken the dates from the clerk of the union, and it appears that in the year 1866, the reviser was in Boyle from the 24th of January to the 28th of February; in the year 1867, from the 6th of February to the 11th or 12th of March; and in December 1867, for the present valuation from the 4th to the 31st.

Mr. J. D. M'Dermot.

19 June 1868.

6282. In some of those years was he there more than a month?—In one instance it is a little more, namely, in 1867, from the 6th of February to the 11th or 12th of March; that would be about five weeks.

6283. How many unions are there in the county of Roscommon?—There is the Boyle Union, the Roscommon Union, the Castlerea Union, the Strokestown Union, and the Athlone Union.

6284. Could you mention to the Committee how many town lands in the Union of Boyle had the reviser in this year actually to revise and go over the land and change the value?—I have myself, with the clerk of the Boyle Union, gone over the books which are furnished to the guardians by the valuator, and I can only speak personally in reference to the books for the last valuation and the one before, for this reason, that I understand the practice to be that one set of books lasts for three years; the valuator makes his valuation for the first year, say, in black ink, and, if there are any changes the next year, they are made in red or blue ink, and the third year in different coloured ink; after the third year they are sent to the Valuation Office, and the one for the three past years is, therefore, not in the workhouse at Boyle; but for this present valuation, and the one before I have myself, with the clerk, gone over the books; and, as far as I can perceive, and personally from the information which I received from the clerk in the year 1866, there was but one townland which there was any necessity to visit for the purpose of revision.

6285. Eighteen hundred and sixty-six was the year in which this very large sum was charged, was it not?—So I understand; in 1867 I understand that there was but one townland also revalued, the valuation of it being 212 l. 15 s. this year, and 213 l. 5 s. the year before; but on the last occasion, namely, from the 4th of December to the 21st of December, that is, for the rate which is to be struck this year, there were five townlands in one division of the county of Sligo revised; they are small, the total valuation being 369 l. at present, as against 375 l. 13 s. the former valuation; there was also one alteration in value in the townland of Boyle, and there was another division in the county of Roscommon revised, the valuation of it being 147 l. 15 s., as against 146 l. 15 s. The five townlands, of which I have spoken as being revised, were in the county of Sligo, so that in the county of Roscommon, in this period, there were very few townlands in the Union of Boyle revised.

6286. There is a portion of the union of Boyle in the county of Sligo, is there not?—Yes; the valuation of the entire union is stated to be 72,622 l. 17 s., of which 29,848 l. 12 s., are in the county of Sligo, leaving for the Roscommon portion of the union, 42,774 l. 5 s.

6287. You have stated to the Committee that, in the county of Roscommon, there are five unions; may Boyle be taken as being very much the same in area and extent, or as being at least as large in area and extent as the other unions?—I should say so. It is larger than some of them.

6288. And the changes in that large union have been of that very trifling character?—They have been of that character.

6289. In the Boyle Union also, there are a great many townlands very much cut up into small holdings, are there not?—There are.

6290. So that in every respect it is a fair standard to judge by?—I think it is. In Castlerea it appears that the difference between the last and previous valuations is only 13 l. 10 s., that being a decrease; and in the county of Mayo portion of it, there is an increase of 6 l. 6 s.

6291. You stated, did you not, that the Valuation Office do not furnish each year a new list?—They do not.

6292. The reviser merely corrects in the old book the alterations that have occurred since the previous year, for three years?—Precisely.

6293. Do you think that this sum of 933 l., which was charged for the annual revision of the valuation in the county of Roscommon for 1866, was excessive?—I do. I think it is excessive for any of the years. I should state that the number of changes are, perhaps, chiefly changes of occupants. The last time the number of changes in the Union of Boyle were about 775, of which 359 were in the county of Roscommon. In the previous year the number of changes were about 471, of which 301 were in the county of Roscommon.

6294. Do those changes include mere changes of names?—I may say so.

6295. Are you aware that in a return for the year 1866 it is stated that the changes of occupancy in that year, in the county of Roscommon, were 2,012?—I am.

6296. Were those changes in occupancy principally, as you have stated, changes of name?—Precisely.

6297. The total changes in that year in the county were 740, were they not?—Yes.

6298. And amongst those 740 are included, of course, all the changes that might arise in one particular townland?—Of course.

6299. In fact, the revision of one townland might fill up a considerable number of changes of occupancy, might it not?—It might.

6300. Looking at the whole of that return, what are the portions of it in which the reviser had any real work to do?—With regard to the first, which appears to be the chief item of the changes of occupancy, he had no necessity at all to go the lands, because he was supplied with that information by the collector. As to the next item, with regard to changes in the area and valuation, it was necessary for him to go where the amount is 740. But as to the number of houses down, 163, that was supplied to him by the collector. The number of houses built, 30, he should go to see; and as for the gasworks, the last item, eight, it is so insignificant that I need not refer to it.

6301. The number of houses built and changes of area, and valuation or the consolidation of farms, were the only items upon which he really had any manual labour to perform?—So I take it.

6302. But is it not your decided opinion that most competent officers could be got in each county to discharge the duty of this annual revision at a very much reduced cost?—My opinion is that the county surveyor, who has a very high salary, could discharge the duty. In fact, the salary of the county surveyor is the highest in the county. The county surveyor of Roscommon has 500 l. a-year; he has 60 l. a-year for a clerk and office, and 150 l. for assistants, making a total upon the county of 700 l. a-year; and considering the figures to which I have referred, the amount of work done, say, in the Boyle Union, and the return of Sir Richard Griffith, I think

Mr. J. D. M'Dermot.

18 June 1868.

think that the county surveyor could, without interfering with his other duties, discharge this duty, with the aid of the collectors of the county cess, and, if necessary, of the poor rate collectors; but I think that the collectors of the county cess, perhaps, would be sufficient; and I think that he could do the whole business of the county of Roscommon in one month easily.

6303. But even if it were thought desirable that it should be done by some other officer independent of the county surveyor, is it your opinion that very competent professional men, surveyors, could be got who would discharge this duty annually for a very much reduced sum?—I am certain of it; I am certain that they would get a person above the class of a surveyor, because it must be a responsible person who would be above any suspicion. I should say that you would get a person to do it for from 60 *l.* to 100 *l.* a-year at the very outside.

6304. The presentment for the expense of this annual revision comes down to the grand jury as an imperative presentment, does it not?—It does.

6305. And the grand jury have no power of inquiring into how the expense arises, or in what it consists, have they?—None whatever; they have no check whatever; the reviser is entitled to a guinea a-day hotel and travelling expenses, and the grand jury have no power whatever of checking him; he may spend any time he likes about it.

6306. In fact, as far as the county is concerned, there is no check whatever on the charge, is there?—None whatever; the Commissioner sends down the particulars to the grand jury: he takes them from the gentleman who goes down upon the work, and the grand jury must act upon that.

6307. Colonel *French*.] Is the assent of the county through the grand jury, or by any other means, required before the reviser undertakes this work?—No; they know nothing about it before he comes down. All they know is by a detail of expenses, which the Commissioner is bound to send them down before the summer assizes.

6308. (*Chairman*.] And there is no means of finding out what the actual work done by these revisers is even at the different offices of the unions?—In the way that I have stated I think there is, because I have shown the length of time that those gentlemen were occupied, and from the books the work that was done; but the counties have no means of ascertaining it, except by making these inquiries, and I very much doubt whether, even if they had the same information that I have tried to convey, they could enter into any discussion with the Commissioner as to the reasonableness, or otherwise, of those charges.

6309. There is no means at all of finding out, in fact, on what account those charges are made upon the county?—No.

6310. And it can only be discovered by a great deal of trouble, and by collecting the facts at the different workhouses?—That is all.

6311. And, of course, even then it is imperfect, because there is a great deal which it is impossible for an individual to find out with regard to what is done in Dublin?—It is so; but, as far as the counties are concerned, I understand that the duty is simply this: in addition to what I have already stated, a certified list of the valuation of the town lands is sent to each union, not including the names, because the book, as I have already stated, is used for the three years; but there is a certificate, as I believe it is called, which contains the gross valuation of the different town lands. Then, with regard to the work that is done in the Dublin office, there is from the revisions applicable to the unions a county book made out, which is transmitted to the treasurer.

6312. Are you aware whether there is a new book containing a list of all the names of the occupiers of tenements furnished to the treasurer each year?—I cannot state that positively; but I should say by analogy to the practice in the unions the same system is adopted, namely, of making the book last for two or three years, because I think if it saves trouble in one instance it would do so in another.

6313. Colonel *French*.] Do you consider, from the position of the county surveyor and the knowledge that he officially has, that there would be no very great additional labour in his discharging all that duty that is now done by the reviser?—I think he could discharge the duty.

6314. Are you aware that the counties complain very much, not alone of this charge, but of the whole system of compulsory presentments?—I believe they do.

6315. Sir *Charles Lanyon*.] Do you suppose that the county surveyor could perform those duties without any increase of staff, or some one specially appointed for the purpose of attending to them?—The only additional staff that possibly might be required would be a clerk; and considering that he is paid for that, and the amount of salary that he has, I really think the duty ought to be done by the county surveyor.

6316. Do you think it would be fair to put this additional duty upon the county surveyor without giving him any additional remuneration?—I do, considering the amount of salary which he receives, and which is higher than that of any other officer in the county.

6317. General *Dunne*.] Does it ever occur, or does it seldom occur, that the increase of valuation repays the expenditure?—It never repays it. The difference between the valuations from the county books from 1862 to 1867, I make to be only 185 *l.* 1 *s.*

6318. And what was the expense of valuation?—£. 1,144. 5 *s.* 6 *d.* to the county.

6319. And therefore, by the valuation, the county lose the difference?—Of course.

6320. In fact, it is a losing concern, is it not?—It is, but at the same time it is necessary of course to have an accurate valuation and revision, I think.

6321. But in a pecuniary sense it is a loss to the county, is it not?—Decidedly.

6322. And it could be done in a very easy way without any loss, could it not?—Yes.

6323. Is it not the fact, that those valuators really do nothing, but that the work is done by the clerks of the unions and the barony constables?—The collectors do the chief work, because they supply nearly all the information.

6324. Are you aware that, frequently the valuator never go near the land at all?—It is shown by these returns, that he does not, but there were a few instances in which it was necessary in those three years for him to go.

6325. Mr. *Leader*.] It appears by this return, that the whole expense of valuation is 20,316 *l.* a-year,

Mr. J. D. M'Dermott.

18 June [illegible].

year, half of which is payable by the counties; is that so?—Half the expense of the valuation is paid by the county.

6326. Can you state to how much in the £. this valuation comes in the whole upon the rental of Ireland, or of each county?—I have not made a calculation of it.

6327. If you understood that it was considerably less than a farthing, and not much more than half a farthing in the £., would you consider that excessive?—If, on principle, it is wrong to give even a half farthing, I should say it was excessive.

6328. *Chairman.*] If it could be done as well for one-tenth of the sum, you think it should be done for it?—Certainly.

6329. You have had a good deal of experience, I presume, in grand jury matters in general, as a practising solicitor in the county of Roscommon?—I have had.

6330. And you are also very frequently engaged at the presentment sessions, are you not?—Yes.

6331. Do you know anything about the offices and duties of the clerk of the Crown, and the clerk of the peace?—I have read the evidence of a witness in reference to the duties of the clerk of the Crown, and perhaps it may not be necessary to go over them; but I may state that, so far as the county is concerned, there is very little done for it. I am not aware of anything that the clerk of the Crown does for the county except to give copies of the presentments to the treasurer, and to send a copy to the receiver masters' office in Dublin, and to countersign cheques at the assizes.

6332. That duty of giving a copy of the presentments to the treasurer, and to the office in Dublin, is not a very onerous duty, is it?—No; the duties of the clerk of the Crown are discharged in the county of Roscommon in a couple of days at each assizes. There is an office opened by a deputy, and his business is simply to receive informations when they are sent there, but the business of the clerk of the Crown is transacted in four or five days in the county.

6333. The business of the clerk of the Crown in criminal matters, has very much fallen off of late years, has it not?—It has.

6334. Has not the number of criminals tried at the assizes been very much diminished?—It is much less.

6335. And it was for that duty, was it not, that the salary of the clerk of the Crown was fixed at the amount at which it was fixed?—Yes; and considering that the chief portion of the duties, in fact, I may say, all the duties, of the clerk of the Crown are in connexion with the administration of justice, I cannot see upon what reasonable ground the county should pay him. I think, if he is to be retained as a Government officer, he ought not to be paid by the grand jury.

6336. Do you see any difficulty in uniting the offices of the clerk of the Crown and the clerk of the peace?—I think both duties could be discharged by one individual. Considering that there are very few appointments open to members of my profession, I would not wish to be understood as expressing a decided opinion that they ought to be amalgamated; but I rather incline to the opinion that if the Government wish to retain the privilege of appointing those gentlemen, they ought to pay them, and not the county. If I am to express an opinion, irrespective of the consideration to which I have already referred, then I unhesitatingly say that the duties can be discharged by one man.

6337. And the duties discharged by that one man, with the exception of this countersigning of cheques, and giving these copies of the presentments, would have nothing whatsoever to do with the fiscal business of the county, would they?—No, they would be entirely in reference to the criminal business.

6338. With respect to the applotment of the county cess, there is a payment made for that to the county treasurer, is there not?—There is a payment made for that to the county treasurer; I think it is 30 *l.* or 40 *l.*

6339. That, I believe, is not a fixed charge throughout Ireland?—No; as I understand by Act of Parliament, it is entirely discretionary with the grand jury as to what they will allow for it. An applotment, as I take it, consists in merely apportioning the sum upon the baronies; for instance, if a barony is valued at 50,000 *l.*, how much is that in the 1 *l.* upon A. B.'s or C. D.'s holding? It is very easy to calculate how much in the 1 *l.* it is. That is what I understand to be the applotment, and it does not take very long to do it, I fancy.

6340. A list of the occupiers and of the tenements is furnished to the county treasurer?—Yes.

6341. And all he has to do in this applotment is, after having ascertained what the poundage rate is, to apportion it out?—Precisely.

6342. That does not seem to be a very arduous duty?—No.

6343. Might not that duty be very easily discharged by the secretary of the grand jury?—I think so.

6344. Have you ever known instances of magistrates going out of their district to attend presentment sessions?—I have; I know an instance which occurred about six months ago, at the presentment sessions at Strokestown, where two magistrates went out of their barony in reference to a certain application which created some public interest.

6345. Of course you do not think it desirable that that power should remain, of magistrates acting out of their district?—Certainly not.

6346. Mr. *Dawson.*] Do you happen to know in that instance, whether the associated cesspayers attending were swamped by the attendance of those magistrates from a distance?—I did not take down the numbers; it was out of my barony; I was professionally engaged there, and the application was withdrawn by me on account of an informality in the signing of the application; but the gentlemen to whom I have referred, I know proposed to go on with the merits of the case, and immediately after the application was over, both those gentlemen left the court.

6347. Mr. *Leader.*] Is that the only instance of the kind that you have known?—I cannot from memory state other instances, but when there is the power of doing it at all, I take it that even if it has not been very much acted upon, still it is highly objectionable.

6348. Those men did not vote, did they?—No; for the application was withdrawn; but they took a very active part in it.

6349. You are not quite sure whether they would have voted, or not?—I have not the shadow of a doubt that they attended for that one application,

plication, and immediately it was over they retired.

6350. (*Chairman.*) In consequence of what was the application withdrawn?—In consequence of an informality.

6351. *Sir Charles Lemon.*] Over what number of years does your experience extend?—I have been practising over 30 years.

6352. Is this the only case in which you are aware of its having occurred during those 30 years?—I cannot charge my memory with any particular cases beyond that, and therefore I do not like positively to say, but my impression is that it has occurred in other instances, in the county.

6353. *Chairman.*] What is paid in the county of Roscommon for the collection of the county cess?—I think it is 9*d.* in the pound.

6354 Do you not believe that that rate of collection could be very much reduced by a division of the baronies into collecting districts?—I think there would be more competition then, because the amount of security would not be so great.

6355. It would be easier to get security for the smaller amount, would it not?—It would be easier to get security for the smaller amount.

6356. If the baronies were divided into districts for collecting purposes, would you think it advisable that those collectors should be appointed by tenders, as under the Poor Law?—I should think so.

6357. Should they be appointed at the sessions or by the grand jury?—I should say at the sessions.

6358. Colonel *French.*] They would find it easier to get security having smaller districts to collect from, would they not?—They would.

6359. *Chairman.*] With respect to the present system of applying for malicious injuries, have you any observations to make to the Committee?—I think that the interval of three days for the lodgment of an information stating whether the person injured knows the person who committed the act, is rather short; and I have known instances where a *bonâ fide* application fell through in consequence of that informality in the information. If the information does not disclose that fact, it can never be remedied, because the application must be made at the next presentment sessions, if there be time, and the information must be within three days; or, if there be any informality in the notices, I do not believe that that can be rectified either.

6360. Do you consider that this system of granting compensation for malicious injuries leads to the discovery of the criminals in such cases?—I cannot charge my memory with a case where a person charged with malicious injury was found out; but there is this to be borne in mind, that if it be really a malicious injury, it is very difficult for the person upon whom the injury is committed to detect it; because, generally speaking, it is at night that those things are done, and the matter is tested by what I may call circumstantial or inferential evidence, given at the presentment sessions, as to the animus entertained towards the man. The onus lies upon him of showing it.

6361. Do you think that, on the other hand, it tends to a repression of those malicious injuries?—I think that it ought to do so, because the tendency is, I think, to limit the area for the payments as much as possible; and I think that in that way the punishment follows as severely almost, I should say, as well can be.

6362. But do you think that the punishment falls upon the guilty parties, generally speaking?—I do not think it does. I think that the town lands where the person is supposed to live is made to pay; he pays a share of it, but it is very little, compared with what he ought to pay if he could be found out.

6363. In all cases the great bulk of the payment is made by innocent parties, is it not?—It is made by persons in the town land, on the principle, I suppose, of not watching suspicious persons.

6364. And in very many cases I presume that the guilty party suffers nothing at all?—I am sure he does not. For instance, if he is a person that has been evicted, and has no place to go to, except, perhaps, the workhouse, he pays nothing.

6365. The most of this compensation is payment by the innocent for crimes committed in their locality?—It is paid by the persons residing in the townland or townlands suspected. There is a power, of course, to spread it farther.

6366. And you say that you do not know a single instance in which it has led to the detection of the criminal?—I cannot charge my memory with any such instance.

6367. Colonel *French.*] If the criminal were detected, there could be no presentment made, could there?—There is nothing specific I think in the Act to preclude it, but the information requires it to be stated whether the person is known or not.

6368. *Chairman.*] If it were the fact that the discovery of the criminal would prevent the injured party receiving compensation, would not that be the strongest possible inducement to his not giving any information which would lead to the discovery of the criminal?—Of course it would influence him; but an application at the presentment sessions for compensation is never granted upon the mere *ipse dixit* of the person injured. There is general evidence given as to the feeling entertained towards him in the locality; there is evidence given, perhaps, of his [illegible] some person in a holding of land, or of any other cause of difference, and, generally speaking, the constable, whose business it is to visit the scene of the outrage, is examined on those cases, and his opinion is taken as to whether it is malicious or not; and in the examination of those cases I think the presentment sessions are exceedingly strict. I take it from what I have seen, that there is rather a tendency against granting those applications, unless they are coerced to do so from being satisfied as to the malicious feeling.

6369. I am not now referring to any investigation into the question as to whether the injury was malicious, or not; but if it be the fact, or the impression in the county, that the discovery of the criminal would bar the compensation; is not that a bonus against the discovery of the criminals in such cases?—No doubt it would appear so.

6370. If it be the law, or if it be the impression that it is the law, supposing that a man sees a person firing his house, or committing some malicious injury upon him, and supposing he catches the criminal *in flagrante delicto*, would it not be his interest to say nothing whatever about it, because he is under the impression that it is the law, or because it is the law that he can receive

Mr. J. D. M'Dermott.

20 June 1839.

ceive no compensation if he discovers the criminal?—Yes; but from my experience I have always seen a willingness to direct the attention of the presentment sessions and of the grand jury to some particular individual residing in some particular townland.

6371. But without bringing the crime home to him in such a way as to have him convicted?—No; but I think it is going very far to suppose that a man would be a party to another man setting fire to his house, or injuring his cattle, upon the mere chance of being repaid.

6372. I am not speaking of his being a party to it; but supposing that a man went into his field and found his cow injured, or his horse maimed, and that he saw a man who he knew was his enemy, going away from the field, and that he followed him and discovered upon him an implement with which he would have been likely to have committed the injury; do you imagine that if that man supposed that his discovering this criminal would lead to his receiving no payment for his horse or cow, it would not induce him to refrain from giving information as to this individual?—I think he should give some evidence as to when the offence occurred, if it occurred in daylight, but generally speaking, those things occur at night.

6373. Supposing that the information barred his receiving compensation, do you think that any man would give it?—It would depend upon the character of the witness; but, generally speaking, I should say that he would disclose the facts in reference to it.

6374. But according to your evidence, he might then as well not apply for compensation, because it would bar his receiving compensation?—I don't believe that it is so, but I am not quite certain.

6375. In that case, do you think that the man would prefer having the offender convicted, to receiving compensation?—He ought to do so.

6376. But do you think that humanity in general is so constituted that that would be the result?—As I said before, it depends entirely upon the character of the person.

6377. But is it not a direct bonus given to the injured party not to make any effort to discover the man who has injured him?—It would appear like it certainly, assuming that the law is so.

6378. If the law be not so, but if it be the impression in the country that it is so, would it not have the same effect?—It would.

6379. Are you not aware that it is the general impression in the country that if the criminal is discovered, the man cannot receive any compensation for the injury?—It is generally considered so; but I do not know whether I am right as to the law.

6380. Colonel *French*.] Are you aware that the generality of the presentments which come before the road sessions, if refused by the associated cesspayers and magistrates, cannot be presented for by the grand jury?—I believe that is so.

6381. Do you see any reason why presentments to be made for malicious injuries should stand on a different footing?—I think that that is a case which requires what I may call more sifting. It sometimes goes before three tribunals; the presentment sessions, and the grand jury, and if it is traversed, before a judge and jury in court.

6382. That would be the ordinary course of every presentment if approved of at presentment sessions, would it not?—Yes.

6383. But in the case of malicious injuries, the decision of the presentment sessions is not final, is it?—No.

6384. If it is thrown out by the associated cesspayers and magistrates on the ground that there is no malice in the transaction, it still comes before the grand jury, does it not, to be either presented for, or rejected by them?—It does.

6385. If the grand jury, following the example of the presentment sessions, reject the presentment, that is not final, is it?—I take it that it rests with the judge; after it is thrown out by the presentment sessions, the grand jury approving of it.

6386. You doubt that they can have a trial by a petty jury?—Yes, I think so; I doubt much whether the power exists of having it tried by a judge and jury in a case where it is rejected by both the presentment sessions and the grand jury. At all events, I do not think that a judge, if he had the discretionary power, would exercise it, unless a very strong case was shown.

6387. In your own experience, have you not many cases in which, after the decision of the grand jury, you have contested it before the judge?—Yes.

6388. Had you to apply in those cases to the judge for permission?—Yes, I had. I assume then that the power does exist, and that I was wrong in stating that it did not exist, but it is discretionary, I take it, with the judge.

6389. Do you think it advisable (it not being a part in the English law) to retain the power of making those presentments for malicious injuries?—I think that it ought to be retained, and that if a man is maliciously injured, he ought to be repaid for that injury. I should say that it is advisable to retain the power of payment out of some fund.

6390. General *Dunne*.] Is it not one of the oldest of English practices, extending even from Saxon times?—I believe so.

6391. It is a kind of rough justice which cannot be logically defended on some points, but is it not generally effective?—I think so.

6392. *Chairman*.] Do you know whether or not it is the practice in England?—I cannot speak with reference to the practice in England.

6393. General *Dunne*.] Have you ever heard any proposal to apply it, in the case of murders, to the compensation of families?—I have not.

6394. Do you think that it might be made effective in checking those murders?—I have not known a case of that sort. There is power, I believe, in the grand jury law to apply for it in certain cases of murder.

6395. Is not murder excepted?—It may be so, but I have not known a case of the sort, at all events.

6396. Colonel *French*.] Do you know when originally the salaries were given to the clerk of the Crown and the clerk of the peace?—I cannot speak as to that.

6397. Then you cannot say how they were originally remunerated?—I cannot.

6398. Mr. *Blake*.] You know something of the working of the grand jury system with regard to the associated cesspayers, do you not?—A little.

6399. Do you think it would be desirable that the associated cesspayers should be nominated

by

by the ratepayers, in the same way as the poor law guardians?—I think it would be a very good plan.

6400. With regard to the grand jury, from your knowledge and experience in the county of Roscommon, do you not think that it would be very desirable that the fiscal business should be separated from the criminal business, and that a county board should be appointed, having only fiscal business to perform?—I think that it would be a good plan.

6401. Do you not think that it would be a good plan that such a body as that should also be appointed by the ratepayers, the same as the baronial boards?—I do; because I think that at present the ratepayers are not sufficiently represented on the question of taxation. In the county of Roscommon, I know several gentlemen who farm from 1,000 to 2,000 acres, and they are never upon the grand jury.

6402. Would it not be also very advantageous to have the grand jury a continuous body instead of a body whose existence terminates at the end of each assizes?—I do not know that. If it is to be an elective body, I would not say that it should be a permanent one, because, if there were any persons that did not give satisfaction, they are in for a certain time, without any means of getting rid of them.

6403. But I mean by a continuous body, that their existence as a body should never cease, but that one-half, or one-third of them should go out by rotation every year?—I have not considered that matter, but I suppose that there could be no great objection to it.

6404. Would you also be in favour, in all future lettings, of the division of the rate between landlord and tenant, as the poor rate is divided?—I certainly think that the landlord ought to pay his portion of the county cess; and I only wonder that it has existed so long otherwise.

6405. As the law is at present, the landlord not paying any of the rates, and having the advantage of all the improvements, is there not a kind of positive bonus held out to him to have as large an expenditure in his barony as possible?—I must say that I think that as regards the question of expenditure at the assizes, from my experience the grand jurors take as much pains as they possibly can do to save expense; but at the same time they are dealing with the money of others, no doubt, those others not having a voice in its application, or at least not to any reasonable extent.

6406. When a tenant takes a farm now he has no direct control over the expenditure, has he, so far as naming the parties that are to control it is concerned?—He has not, either at the presentment sessions, or at the assizes.

6407. Do you consider that to be a bad system?—I do, decidedly; I think it is very unjust.

6408. Mr. *Dawson*.] With regard to the county board, would you have it entirely elected, or would you have the magistracy represented by a portion of their body?—I do not see why a magistrate *ex officio*, and who may not have any property, or very little property, should be put above a man who pays 20 times as much cess.

6409. Then you would have the whole of this county board elected?—I should say so; I do not see why a magistrate should be upon the county board who may not have a couple of pounds a-year taxes to pay, to the exclusion of a gentleman who might have 800 *l.* a-year to pay.

6410. Mr. *Maguire*.] In case a man who has the administration of public funds does not give satisfaction, you think it well that he should be removable?—Certainly.

6411. Do you not think that there would be more protection in the elective system than in the nomination system for your principle?—I think so; it was in regard to the elective system that I was speaking.

6412. But you seemed to apprehend that there was some little danger because the elective person might remain in so long?—There would be no means of checking him if he was left in for a certain period, of course.

6413. At the present moment there is no check whatever upon him, is there?—There is no check whatever, at present.

6414. A man may shew himself to be foolish, or extravagant, or thoroughly unable to perform his duty, and the juror of the barony may put him on over and over, may he not, according to the present system?—Yes.

6415. Therefore, according to that, those who pay the rates have no control whatever?—They have not.

6416. Would you not rather have them elected distinctly by the ratepayers, and make them responsible to those who pay the rates?—That is the idea which I wish to convey.

6417. You are so anxious to have responsibility, that you would only elect those men for a short time?—I was merely asked whether the body should be continuous, and I misunderstood the question, but following out the idea of the Honourable Member who commenced examining me on the point, there is an analogous case to this under the Towns Improvement Act; under that Act the commissioners are elected, we will say, and they go out annually in threes, and the corporations are in the same way.

6418. Do you think that that would be too long a term of office?—I think that three years would be too long, and that if the system of election was adopted it ought to be analogous to the election of poor law guardians, who remain in office for 12 months, and it may be longer when they are not opposed.

6419. But you think that it would give more satisfaction to have people elected to discharge so important a duty as that?—I do.

6420. Is there, so far as your experience goes, a strong feeling on the part of the payers of the rate that injustice is done to them?—Yes; there can be no other feeling.

6421. Does that feeling exist upon two grounds; first of all, that there is no responsibility, because there is no election; and, in the second place, that the rate is not divided?—Precisely.

6422. Is there a strong feeling, to your own personal knowledge, upon this point?—I believe that there is, and since this question was mooted, I have never heard any one advance any *bonâ fide* argument at all in favour of the payment of the rate as at present.

6423. Then may we understand that the reasonable and calm public sentiment of the county is in favour of an equitable division of the rate?—Decidedly.

6184. There is no appeal to passion about the matter, is there?—No.

6123. It does not admit of it?—No.

Mr. J. E. M'Dermot.

10 June 1852.

6426. It is a mere matter of pounds, shillings, and pence, is it not?—It is a mere matter of pounds, shillings, and pence.

6427. And it is a matter which even the humblest members of the community may, and do distinctly understand?—I think so.

6428. With regard to malicious injuries, and particularly to burnings, is it not the result of your observation, that a great many people get compensation where they really ought not to get it?—No, on the contrary, I think that the inclination is not to give them payment, unless a very clear case is made out.

6429. Then you think that in all cases there is a very severe scrutiny?—I do; I think, first, that at the presentment sessions the matter undergoes a very strict investigation, or at least, in the county of Roscommon it certainly does; and then it goes before the grand jury again.

6430. But do you not think that altogether it would be better to have the matter sifted before a judge and jury than to have it tried as it is at the present moment?—I do not know that it would; I think there are a great many circumstances in a locality which a cesspayer, or a magistrate, if he is one, may be aware of, and without interfering with the law of evidence in a question of this sort, which is merely a question as to the opinion entertained of a particular individual; I think that circumstances of that sort would justify me in saying that the present system might be better in that view of it, because there might be on the jury 12 men from a different place altogether, whom it might be hard to convince, perhaps, that there was such a feeling.

6431. As a mere matter of fact, do not many of these investigations (if I may so call them) come before the presentment sessions without the assistance of a legal man on either side?—From my experience in the county of Roscommon, wherever there is a case of any importance there are professional men employed on both sides. It is a matter of importance to a poor man to lose a cow, or anything of that sort.

6432. Supposing it were a large amount, do you not think that the attendance of a professional man, he having experience in the mode of eliciting facts, would be very useful?—I think it would be absolutely necessary.

6433. Is it not the case that that is not always obtained at the presentment sessions, whereas it may be or would be invariably obtained before a judge and jury?—I think, for the reasons I have stated already, the practice being to have them, that the same facilities are afforded, because it is open to them to have a man to attend for them, either at the presentment sessions or at the assizes.

6434. You would not alter the present system? —I cannot state instances in which I have found difficulty to arise.

6435. But have you come to the opinion that it is very necessary to have every case of the kind thoroughly sifted, not only because it is right to give compensation to a man if he is wilfully injured, but because at the same time it is necessary to vindicate the character of the community if it is assailed by a false charge?—Yes.

6436. Do you think that it is absolutely necessary that there should be such investigation on public as well as on individual grounds?—Certainly.

6437. *Chairman.*] Do you believe that the claim to this compensation is a right which each individual ought to possess when injured maliciously, and do you believe that the proper tribunal to decide upon that right is a tribunal composed of the representatives of the party who have to pay the compensation?—I conceive that the persons from the locality who are aware of the feeling entertained towards the man, and of the facts of the case, are very competent to form an opinion upon the subject; and, although I have seen those cases very thoroughly sifted, whenever there was fair ground for satisfying reasonable men that the act was done maliciously, I never found the body at the presentment sessions to hesitate to give compensation.

6438. But still you must admit that if the presentment sessions represent the cesspayers of a particular barony or district, they are in fact trying their own case and becoming judges on their own cause, though they may act very fairly? —That is so. I was at the presentment sessions in the county of Leitrim within the last month or so, and there were a number of magistrates and cesspayers there, and there was an application for compensation for malicious injury in cutting the tails off five or six head of cattle. On that occasion I found that the cesspayers to a man voted that it was malicious along with the magistrates. It was insinuated by some (and there was a professional man employed to oppose the claim) that it was not done maliciously, but that it was done by the man himself; but the cesspayers considered that the feeling towards him was so strongly proved that, if I recollect rightly, they unanimously voted in favour of its being malicious.

6439. *Chairman.*] Do you consider that it is consistent with the general principles of British law that persons, however much disposed to act fairly, should be judges in their own case?—Of course not, but indirectly in a great many instances those feelings do operate whether it be a civil or a criminal case. Those feelings would exist in one instance, I should say, the same as in another; but still, generally speaking, my opinion is that jurors in the county of Roscommon discharge their duties fairly, both as cesspayers at presentment sessions, at assizes, and at sessions.

6440. Do you not think that in all cases of injury by fire to buildings of a greater amount than 50 *l.*, security against any injuries ought to be provided by insurance, and that anyone having buildings or houses of the value of more than 50 *l.* ought to insure his premises; and that if he does not do so, he ought not to be compensated for their loss?—Possibly that may be so, but I do not know whether there would be an insurance for cattle, though possibly there might be.

6441. I am speaking now of buildings and injuries done to them by fire; do you not think that they stand in a different category from injuries to cattle, and other injuries of that description?—I do not at present see the difference.

6442. Is there not the difference that those buildings can generally be insured?—They can be insured.

6443. Mr. *Deasy.*] Have you any experience with regard to the mills; do you know the way in which they are generally built?—I am not very well acquainted with them; in my locality there is but one.

6444. Would you not say that they ought always

always to be insured on account of their ignitable qualities?—The only flax mill in the neighbourhood of Boyle was burnt down some time since, and I asked the owner why he did not insure, and he told me the insurance company would not insure it for him.

6445. Is there much flax grown in the county of Roscommon?—In the union of Boyle there was last year about 300 acres only; Strokestown is the chief portion of the county in which flax is grown. In Strokestown they have generally about 1,000 acres under flax, and in the Strokestown Union I believe there are two or three flax mills; I doubt whether the insurance company would insure them, or if they did insure them I expect they would put a very high figure on them. I remember seeing in one of the county papers an advertisement from one gentleman stating that the flax was insured, and that persons sending there would be sure to get compensation if there was any fire.

6446. Have you known any applications made in regard to malicious injuries in connection with the burning of flax mills?—I have.

6447. Mr. *Maguire*.] Would it not be well to have a judge preside at such investigation, he being a man of ability and strict impartiality?—At the presentment sessions a magistrate is chairman, and I think he has sufficient knowledge to decide upon a matter of the sort; it is simply a question of animus and the question of amount, and I think it is very easy, from all the surrounding circumstances, to form an opinion upon it.

6448. Is not animus just the thing above all others that might lead a tribunal astray?—I do not see how a body of intelligent men could not form an opinion as to whether there was a malicious feeling towards a man or not.

6449. Are not intelligent men among the most likely to be a little carried away by the popular belief of the time?—Possibly it may be so.

6450. At any rate, a judge is not likely to be swayed by the same prejudices as people locally affected, is he?—Certainly not; but I have never known chairmen of the presentment sessions to have any strong feeling upon the subject.

6451. Mr. *Dawson*.] Have you ever known an instance of a decision of a grand jury about these malicious injuries reversed afterwards by the same case being placed before a petty jury?—I think so, though I cannot refer to any particular instance; and I have known the amount to be changed.

6452. *Chairman*.] Do you remember a particular case, which excited a good deal of interest in the county of Roscommon, with regard to a flax mill that was burnt near Boyle; Mr. Cox's mill; was not the decision in that case reversed by a petty jury?—Yes; that was, I believe, alleged to be a malicious injury.

6453. Mr. *Dawson*.] The grand jury are the only people who can assess the amount of damage and place it upon a particular locality, but the finding may be reversed by a petty jury?—It could be reversed by a judge and jury, of course, but I forget the facts of that particular case.

6454. *Chairman*.] Was it not the fact in that case that the presentment was passed by the grand jury, and then traversed before the judge and tried by petty jury, and thrown out?—I think so.

6455. Do you not remember other cases in which similar results have taken place?—I cannot charge my memory with them.

6456. Mr. *Maguire*.] In that case, at any rate, it was important to have the supervision of a judge, was it not?—Of course it is an advantage to have an experienced judge, but that may have been the act of the jury, because the judge merely put it to them as a question of malice, or no malice.

6457. But the judge comments upon the evidence, and puts the bearing of the evidence upon the case before the jury, and guides the jury, does he not?—He does.

6458. And if there were anything like fraud or concealment, or trickery, it would be the duty of the judge to point it out to the jury, would it not?—It would; I would not wish to be understood as objecting to have such a tribunal. I only say that I have known instances where fair decisions have been arrived at by the magistrates and cesspayers on the question of malice.

6459. But do you not think that it is most important to have a highly experienced, competent, and important person to preside at such trials?—I should have no objection to have it tried in that way.

6460. Mr. *Leader*.] With regard to the necessary forms for serving notices to recover compensation for malicious trespasses, are they not very cumbersome?—I think they are; there must be first the information within three days; then there must be the notices to the high constable, the churchwardens, and the nearest police station, within six days, and then there is also the notice ten days before the presentment sessions to the secretary of the grand jury, and at the police station, &c.

6461. Do you think that all these notices are requisite?—I think that the more publicity is given to the matter the better, but I think, perhaps, too much particularity is required, especially in reference to the precise time for serving the notices, because it may so happen that a person not acquainted with it would let the time pass and then be without a remedy.

6462. Is it easy to find out the churchwardens in some parishes in Ireland?—It is not.

6463. Have you ever heard of applications being dismissed on the ground of the policeman not allowing the notices to be affixed to the board at the police station?—I have not known any instance of that sort, but I know that, in strict law, it is required to be posted on a board.

6464. Therefore if the board was inside a police barrack, and the policeman would not allow the notice to be posted on it, and if the claim was refused on that ground, do you think it would be just?—I think it would be very unjust, but still according to the strict letter of the law, it should be posted on the police barrack.

6465. *Chairman*.] Are you aware whether the grand jury have the power of granting presentments for diocesan schools?—I know they have; but I do not know an instance where it has been acted upon.

6466. Have they the power to grant those presentments without applicating to the presentment sessions?—Yes, under the 96th section of 6 & 7 Will. 4, c. 116, "It shall and may be lawful for the grand jury of any county in which any

Mr. A. D. M'Dermott.

—

11 June 1868.

Mr. *J. D. M'Dermott.*

10 June 1858.

any diocesan school or district school, or the site appointed for the same shall be situate, to present, to be levied off such county, any sum or sums which they shall think proper for purchasing, providing, building, or repairing any such schoolhouse," &c. It does not appear by that, that it is necessary to go to presentment sessions at all for it.

6467. Mr. *Leader.*] Are you aware that at present, supposing a bridge is proposed to be built, the cost of which should be levied on the county at large, that presentment does not come before the sessions of the county at large?—I am not aware of it, but I know that with regard to bridges which appear upon a river flowing between two counties, there is a difficulty in obtaining presentments, inasmuch as the grand juries of both the neighbouring counties must concur before it be passed. There is a wooden bridge on the border of the counties of Leitrim and Roscommon, which I remember since I was a child, as having always been in almost the same state. It is wholly unprotected and dangerous, and I believe there have been difficulties in obtaining presentments in reference to it; I should say that in the case of a bridge between two counties, where one county passes the presentments, it ought to be imperative upon the other county to pay a like amount, to do it. That principle is recognised in reference to bridges upon roads upon which the mails are carried, and the Commissioners of Drainage have, as I take it, power under certain circumstances to have presentments of that kind passed; but at present there is great difficulty for the reason I have stated, and I think that, if one county pass such a presentment, it ought to be imperative upon the other to do so.

6468. But I am speaking of bridges in the interior of the county, for which the presentments come before the barony, and do not come before the county presentment sessions, although the tax is levied on the county; do you think that that is fair?—I do not think it is.

6469. *Chairman.*] Are you aware that unoccupied houses at present are subject to the county cess?—I am, and I think it is unfair; unoccupied houses, I take it, would not be taxed under the Poor Law.

6470. And you think that they ought to be equally exempted under the county cess?—I do, on the same principle; I think that until the 19 & 20 Vict., you might for six years recover arrears due upon premises, even supposing they were not occupied. Now, it is limited to two years, for the person primarily liable to pay, but I think that if the premises are unoccupied, it is unfair to charge for them.

6471. Are you aware that the recognizances of the contractors are entered into to the Crown, and not to the county?—I am, and I think it is most objectionable. The recognizances of the road contractors are to the Attorney General, whilst the bonds of the high constables, or collectors for much larger amounts, are payable to the treasurer of the county. I cannot understand what difference there is, or why the Attorney General should have anything at all to do with these cases, which are purely fiscal matters. I have known, in the county of Roscommon, in the last 12 months, a number of cases against road contractors for non-fulfilment of the terms of their bond; and the Crown solicitor stood up in Court and objected to their being heard, as he was the representative of the Attorney General. The cases went off upon another point, because the solicitor of the grand jury happened not to be in attendance; but I believe that at the coming sessions of the county of Roscommon there are civil bills issued at the suit of the Attorney General, for the recovery of amounts against defaulting road contractors. Before the name of the Attorney General can be used permission must be got, and I suppose his clerk gets a fee upon that; but I do not see what the Attorney General has to do with them at all, and I think the recognizances ought to be to the treasurer of the county, or to the county board, the grand jury, or whatever it may be.

6472. Mr. *Maguire.*] Would you exempt persons under 4 *l.*, in fact the poor, from the payment of this rate?—I think when they are exempted under the poor laws, by analogy they ought to be exempted under the grand jury laws.

6473. Do you know that there is great hardship, frequently, in the collection of the rate from very poor people?—I think there is, and in fact, that the county cess ought to be payable by the landlord in cases where the tenements are so small.

6474. It is very difficult to collect the cess from the poor people, is it not?—It is very difficult.

6475. General *Dunne.*] Do you not think that the difficulty of collecting the cess from persons occupying tenements at a rental of less than 4 *l.*, from the fluctuation in the holdings, tends to increase the expense of collecting the cess?—I am certain that it does. If it were not for those small holdings the cess would be collected for a smaller amount, because I have known that to be used by cess collectors as a strong argument as to the class of district in which they had to collect.

6476. In the east of Ireland, no doubt, the holdings are not so small as to create inconvenience; but is it not the case that in the west of Ireland the whole population rent at such low rates that such an arrangement would throw the whole of the cess upon the landlord, in various parts of Connaught, for instance?—I have already wished to convey that if holdings under 4 *l.* are exempted, it might, possibly, be a serious question whether the landlord should have to pay it or not; but I certainly think that the whole of the occupiers of 4 *l.* holdings ought to be exempted.

6477. But, if both were exempted, would it not cause a very large deduction in the amount of the cess in certain counties?—It would.

6478. But what I understood the proposition of the Honourable Member to mean, and what I mean is, that the cess in the case of tenements under 4 *l.* should be paid by the landlords, would you see any objection to that?—There would be no objection to that. All that I say is, that I think that the occupiers of tenements rated at 4 *l.* or under 4 *l.*, ought not to pay the county cess.

6479. It is very difficult, is it not, to collect the rates in towns from lodgers who continually fluctuate?—It is.

6480. Mr. *Leader.*] With regard to traverses on presentments, I presume you are tolerably conversant with the practice in those cases?—I am.

6481. Do you think that there is sufficient time now given for serving the notices as to those traverses?—The Act says, "That every person intending

intending to traverse any presentment or payment for which it is by this Act required, that application shall be made at the presentment sessions, shall give notice in writing of such intention to the secretary of the grand jury within two days after the first day of such sessions." I think that that is entirely too short.

6482. What period would you fix?—Two days is certainly too little. There must be 10 days given to the secretary to put it upon the list; but it might be within a month after if it did not interfere with the coming session, or, say, within 14 days, but two days is entirely too short.

6483. Would you think that where presentments for malicious injuries are rejected on account of informalities, the grand jury should have the power of judging whether the formalities were unnecessary or not?—If the Act of Parliament says that you must within a certain time do a certain thing, I do not see how the grand jury could well get rid of it. I would rather extend the time for doing it, but I would give them the power to decide whether the presentment sessions had arrived at a correct conclusion on those points as well, and they have that power, because the grand jury do inquire into those things.

6484. How many notices do you think ought to be served?—I do not see the value of serving notices on the churchwardens, because it gives no great publicity at all to the matter. I think that service upon the magistrates at the next petty sessions and service at the police station would be sufficient.

6485. And at the Poor Law Board?—I think that would be a very good arrangement.

6486. And the places of worship in the parish?—Yes; churches and chapels; but I do not see the use of serving the notices upon the churchwardens and the high constables.

6487. *Chairman.*] Do you wish to make any further observation with respect to the evidence which you have given?—If you please; having spoken about the offices of the clerk of the Crown and clerk of the peace, and having expressed an opinion in reference to the appointment of clerk of the Crown, I wish to say that in regard to the clerk of the peace I think that a portion of his salary ought also to be paid by the Government; because a good deal of his work is in reference to the administration of justice also.

6488. But for the work of his office connected with civil matters, he is paid by fees, is he not?—His entire salary is paid by the county for both, and he gets certain fees.

6489. But does he discharge any civil business for which he does not receive fees or some separate payment?—He receives some fees, but they would not be sufficient, I should say, to pay him. For instance, he receives 3 *d.* upon the entry of civil bill; he is obliged to make out two sets of books at each sessions, one for himself and one for the chairman, containing all the civil bills, and also an ejectment book in duplicate, and a book in which spirit licenses are entered, and also the Crown book; he has no fees for the Crown book.

6490. But has not this civil business been placed upon him since his salary was fixed; the salary is for criminal business, is it not?—I suppose it is.

6491. And the civil business is paid for, or supposed to be paid for, by the fees, is it not?—It is supposed to be so.

6492. Consequently, if his criminal duties ought to be paid for by the Crown, the whole of his salary ought to be paid by the Crown?—It would appear so; I think it is unfair that the county should have to pay it. As to his appointment, it appears to me to be odd that the *Custos Rotulorum* of the county should have the appointment. I do not understand why it should be so, because the *Custos* is really a myth, he has nothing whatever to do. I wish also to say, that in reference to the fees paid to the secretaries of grand juries, they generally get fees (though not referred to in the Act of Parliament) for preparing applications and tender, recognizance and specification, amounting to 4 s. 6 d. on the part of road contractors.

6493. Mr. *Leader.*] Is not that on the whole thing?—I understand that it is so; 1 s. is allowed by the Act of Parliament for preparing the recognizance, but in regard to the filling of the application, &c., there is no fee stated in the Act of Parliament; and I believe that in the county of Roscommon the fees for filling the application, &c., are what I have stated. The secretary of the grand jury attends on certain days previous to each presentment sessions, for the purpose of receiving those applications in the different baronies; and for the preparation of them, I understand the fees to be as I have stated. It is a common thing for persons to make several applications, and very many of them are refused; I think that there would be a greater number of applications if the fees were smaller, and if they were fixed by law as they ought to be.

6494. *Chairman.*] Do you mean to say that the fee upon the application alone, exclusive of the tender, is 6 s.?—I mean upon all 4 s. 6 d.

6495. Upon each presentment before it finally passes through all the stages through which it has to pass, are there fees to the amount of 5 s. paid to the secretary?—I infer 4 s. 6 d., which I should have said. I understand there is also 1 s. 6 d. charged on the application for payment when the work is done, making in all 6 s.

6496. You do not mean upon the first application?—No.

6497. Is there any other point upon which you wish to give evidence to the Committee?—I was asked a question as to whether I thought that it would be fair to ask the county surveyor to do the extra duty as to the revision of the valuation, without any additional payment, and I replied in the affirmative. Of course it would be only fair that he should be paid for books, and any outlay of that sort; but I think that the present allowance to him for a clerk ought to be sufficient, and then he ought to discharge the duty without any payment, beyond the outlay for books, and things of that sort.

Mr. JOHN O'REILLY, called in; and Examined.

Mr. J. O'Reilly.

11 June 1869.

6498. *Chairman*.] You are a Valuator, Land Surveyor, and General Civil Engineer, are you not?—I am.

6499. Were you for many years employed under the General Valuation Office?—I have been so employed upwards of 20 years.

6500. Could you state to the Committee the total cost of the valuations which have taken place in Ireland, taking first the townland valuation, and, secondly, the tenement valuation?—The total cost in this return, furnished on the 11th May 1869, of the townland valuation, is 159,970 *l.*, and of the tenement valuation, 325,133 *l.* 11 *s.* 11 *d.*

6501. Could you tell the Committee what was the cost per acre of the valuation, calculated over the whole of Ireland?—Taking both together, it is about 5¼ *d.* an acre.

6502. And what is the tenement valuation by itself?—I have not made a calculation of what the tenement or townland valuation would be separately; but I have a statement here of counties in which no townland valuation was made. Those counties are Cork, Dublin, Kerry, Limerick, Tipperary, and Waterford. The total cost of the valuation in those counties was 138,056 *l.*, or 6¼ *d.* an acre.

6503. From your experience, as a valuator, do you think that that was a very excessive cost for valuing?—It is fully three times what it ought to be.

6504. You have valued some counties under the Valuation Office, have you not?—I have been employed as an office assistant before it was centralised, and when there were district offices in the country. In a part of the county of Monaghan, in the barony of Cremorne, in which there were 83,489 acres, the cost was about 385 *l.* There was no cost incurred except the salaries of the valuator and myself. I did all the office work at the first commencement, and the whole of the work was done in one year. Our salaries both together amounted to 366 *l.* 13 *s.*, and that was the whole cost. There were no travelling expenses, or any other expenses incurred, except postage and the wages of a labourer attending upon the valuator, which was 7 *s.* 6 *d.* a week.

6505. How much was that per acre?—It was 1 *d.* an acre. This was on the townland valuation, and the whole valuation was complete, with the exception of making one fair copy for the grand jury, and another for lodgment in the archives of the castle, which would be very small; I think one-eighth of a penny would cover the expense of making the two copies.

6506. Was that for the townland valuation?—That was for the townland valuation.

6507. What do you think ought to be the expense of making a tenement valuation?—It ought not to be more than the townland valuation.

6508. Is there not more labour in making the tenement valuation?—No; because on the townland valuation the land had to be very carefully travelled over, in order to distinguish the different qualities and mark it out into lots.

6509. Have you not to make the distinction of the qualities in the tenement valuation?—It is not so particularly made as in the case of the townland valuation. It was more a view valuation, than a valuation of the soils and subsoils.

6510. The whole cost of those valuations was paid by the counties of Ireland, was it not?—It was.

6511. There has been also a charge for the annual revision of the valuation, has there not?—Yes.

6512. Up to a certain period, was not the whole of that annual revision charge paid by the counties?—Up to the passing of an Act in the year 1858 or 1859, the whole of the revision was charged to the counties. Since that it is divided between the Government and the counties.

6513. Could you tell the Committee whether there was any estimate made by the Commissioner of Valuation as to what the probable annual charge of this annual revision would be before the Bill was passed under which it was made?—I have a copy of a letter which was written by the Commissioner of Valuation, Sir Richard Griffith, to Lord Naas, on the rejection of a Bill which was introduced in the year 1857, explaining the nature of the Bill, and replying to some discontent which was caused by it, and to some objections which were taken to it in the newspapers; and he states in this letter, that if the Bill had passed, he would be enabled to make the annual revisions for 130 *l.* on an average for each county in Ireland, or 4,160 *l.* for the entire of Ireland, saving, he said, a sum of 326 *l.* for each county, which it would cost by the mode of operation under which they carried on the revisions before that time.

6514. According to that letter of Sir Richard Griffith, it would appear that in the year 1857, he estimated that the annual cost of the revision of the valuation for each county in Ireland might be so low as 130 *l.* for each county?—He stated rather positively that it would be no more than 130 *l.* for each county.

6515. Under the Bill, to which allusion was made in that letter, was it proposed that the counties should be furnished with applotment books ready prepared from the Valuation Office?—Yes, for the grand juries, and also for the boards of guardians, ready for the collection of rates.

6516. Are any such applotment books furnished now?—No, nothing is furnished now, except the tables of valuation.

6517. Was it not proposed under that Bill that the expense of the field work of this revision should be charged on the Consolidated Fund?—It was.

6518. In the statement that was then made by Sir Richard Griffith, was it contemplated that the cost of that field work would exceed 130 *l.* for each county?—I made an estimate of the cost of the field work, of the annual revision at that time, and according to the rates of the salaries which were paid to the field revisers, and by a close and approximate calculation, I found that the field work would amount to only about 8,000 *l.*, and that the cost incidental to the office work would be, according to the rates of the salaries, and the then expenses of the valuation, about 11,000 *l.* or 12,000 *l.*; and I wrote some letters commenting upon this letter of the Commissioner at the time, showing the bad arrangement which was proposed to be made by the charging of field work to the Government, and the office work to the counties, and stating that it would not be a fair division of the expenses, and that it would place a great deal more upon the counties than a just or fair proportion.

6519. What

Mr. *J. O'Reilly.*

19 June 1868.

6519. What has been the actual cost of the annual revisions, taking the last years, 1863, 1864, 1865?—The cost of the annual revision in 1863 was 14,919 *l.* 13 *s.* 5 *d.* by Colonel French's return; for the year 1864, it was 18,084 *l.* 14 *s.* 7 *d.*; for the year 1865, it was 20,806 *l.* 17 *s.* 8 *d.*; for the year 1866, it was 21,606 *l.* 4 *s.* 3 *d.* I have not the amount for the year 1867.

6520. The cost of the annual revision then, in the year 1866, was nearly three times as much as it was estimated at in 1857 by Sir Richard Griffith?—Very nearly three times as much.

6521. Of what does the annual revision consist?—The annual revision of the field work consists in correcting the changes of names of the occupying tenants; any changes that may have occurred in the division or the consolidation of farms must be also rectified; houses thrown down are struck out in the lists of valuation, and houses built and improved are valued. Railways, gasworks and telegraphs are re-valued, but the labour of these is unimportant.

6522. Taking the case of the county of Roscommon, as to which a return was presented to Parliament, what would you calculate as the actual number of days which ought to be employed in doing the work mentioned in that return for the county of Roscommon?—I have revised a good deal myself during the time that I have been in the valuation office, and, I should say, from the extent of the county of Roscommon, and the number of changes which I see here that 40 days ought to have been sufficient to do the whole county.

6523. How many days does it appear that the gentlemen were occupied in revising it?—One hundred and forty days were occupied by the three revisers that are here mentioned; one was 60 days, one 53 days, and one 27 days.

6524. Calculating the expense of the actual field work of this revision upon the salaries paid to these gentlemen, what was the actual amount paid for the field work?—Calculating it upon the salaries appended to the names, and the number of days which each of them spent, I make it out to be 74 *l.* 16 *s.* 6 *d.*

6525. Is 74 *l.* 16 *s.* 6 *d.*, the amount which would be paid for the time they were occupied in the revision, calculating it upon their actual salary?—Yes.

6526. What was the charge upon the county of Roscommon that year for that annual revision?—By this return it was 692 *l.* 4 *s.* 1 *d.*, in the year 1866.

6527. So that the difference between 692 *l.* 4 *s.* 1 *d.* and 74 *l.* 15 *s.* 6 *d.* is charged for office expenses?—For office work and incidental expenses.

6528. Do you not think, considering that the time employed in the field work would only cost 74 *l.* 16 *s.* 6 *d.*, this is a most extravagant charge for the office work?—By the showing of this return that is all that it cost, and the office work must have cost the difference, which is certainly extravagant.

6529. What would be the actual office work in connexion with the annual revision of the county?—The reviser is obliged to make all the alterations in the list of valuation, and to set them up so that there is nothing to be done in the office but to transcribe them, making two fair copies of them, one for the grand jury, and the other for the board of guardians.

6530. Are you aware whether there is a fair copy made every year for the board of guardians, or whether they do not merely correct the old copy?—There is not a fair copy made every year. I know myself that I have used a copy of the board of guardians the third year, interlining the changes which have occurred.

6531. Would you refer to the other side of this return, and state to the Committee what is the total amount of the expenses of the valuation office in Dublin?—The total amount of salaries by this return is 18,305 *l.*

6532. Comparing that with the total amount of what is called the cost of the annual revision, is there not a difference?—There is a small difference of 2,303 *l.* for office incidentals, I suppose such as rent, and fuel, and lights, and certain other things.

6533. The difference you presume is for stationery and these incidental expenses?—Yes.

6534. Do you think that this annual expense of the revision of the valuation which appears to be every year increasing, is likely to go on increasing or to diminish?—It must increase; it will require this staff of 104 persons to maintain the annual revisions, though they have not active work for more than about six months.

6535. Is there a very large staff kept, although there is only work at a particular season of the year?—Precisely.

6536. And the salaries of these officers are fixed upon a sliding scale which increases, are they not?—They are taken in at a certain minimum salary, and they go on increasing according to their different classes to the maximum.

6537. Are there many of those officers mentioned in this return, who have reached the maximum at present?—Very few; in the first class there are 13, and 12 of these have yet to reach the maximum.

6538. And until this maximum is reached it is presumed that this expense will go on increasing every year?—It will go on increasing every year; there is an increase of 10 *l.* per annum on each salary of the first and second-class assistants, and 5 *l.* per annum of third class.

6539. The grand jury of the county have no control whatever over the expense of these revisions, have they?—None whatever.

6540. Does it come down to them as an imperative presentment, without their having any power of inquiring into it?—All the power they have is to require a return of the cost with which they are supplied.

6541. Do you not think that this revision could be carried out on a much cheaper scale if the grand jury had authority to appoint revisers themselves?—Any arrangement of a local nature would be much more inexpensive than the centralisation of the office in Dublin. If the appointment of revisers were vested in the grand jury it would be done for less than half the amount.

6542. I believe that you have some scheme prepared for having Ireland divided into districts?—I have a sort of sketch, which might be modified, so as not to increase the expense: I have given the maximum which I think is ought to cost the country.

6543. What is the amount for which you think the annual revision could be accomplished, paying very handsomely for it?—Paying well for it, according to a division which I have made here, the whole revision of districts, I conceive, could be done, and the officers well paid for 10,830 *l.*

6544. In

Mr. L. O'Reilly.

10 June 1868.

6544. In that estimate which you have made, could you give the Committee an idea of the average salary which you would pay to each of those revisers?—For the county of Down I have estimated it at 450 *l.*; for the county of Antrim I have estimated it at 500 *l.*, Belfast coming into it; for Derry I have estimated it at 400 *l.*; for Armagh, Monaghan, and Louth, I have estimated it at 500 *l.*; for Donegal I have estimated it at 450 *l.*; for Cavan and Fermanagh I have estimated it at 550 *l.*; for Tyrone I have estimated it at 350 *l.*; for Leitrim and Sligo I have estimated it at 420 *l.*; for Mayo I have estimated it at 450 *l.*; for Galway I have estimated it at 450 *l.*; for Roscommon, Longford, and Westmeath, I have estimated it at 600 *l.*; for Meath and the county of Dublin I have estimated it at 600 *l.*; for the city of Dublin and townships of Rathmines, Pembroke, Kingstown, and Sandymount, I have estimated it at 350 *l.*; for Kildare and Wicklow I have estimated it at 360 *l.*; for King's and Queen's Counties, and Carlow I have estimated it at 460 *l.*; for Kilkenny and Waterford I have estimated it at 450 *l.*; for Kerry I have estimated it at 420 *l.*; for Limerick I have estimated it at 400 *l.*; for Clare I have estimated it at 400 *l.*; for Tipperary I have estimated it at 600 *l.*; for Cork I have estimated it at 700 *l.*; and for Wexford I have estimated it at 300 *l.*; one-half being charged to the Consolidated Fund and one-half to the counties.

6545. Could not very first-class men be got to discharge the duties of the valuation for the salaries which you have mentioned?—I would do any single one of those districts for the sum which I have mentioned, and I am as capable of revising as any officer on the valuation establishment.

6546. And yet paying those very high salaries which you have mentioned, the annual revision would cost something less than half of what it costs at present?—Less than half, and it would not increase.

6547. If the counties had the appointments of those revisers they would then have a control over the expenditure, would they not?—Certainly.

6548. At present there seems to be no control over what those revisers do except the control which is exercised by the Commissioner of Valuation?—There is no local control whatsoever.

6549. There is no control as to how many days he stops in the district, or as to what he does, or as to the manner in which he performs his duty when he comes there?—Certainly not.

Mr. WILLIAM MALCOLMSON, called in; and Examined.

Mr. W. Malcolmson.

6550. *Mr. Blake.*] Are you one of the firm of Malcolmson Brothers?—I am.

6551. And you are chairman of two or three railways, are you not?—I am.

6552. Are you also a proprietor of land in fee and a tenant of land?—I am.

6553. And I think that you have also had some experience in the working of the grand jury laws?—Some little experience.

6554. Do you consider that it would be advantageous to the country that the fiscal business should be separated from the criminal business, and that a board for the discharge of the first should be appointed, one-half of magistrates appointed by the magistracy, and the other half appointed by the ratepayers?—Decidedly.

6555. And you would have a board analogous to the present road sessions, appointed by the ratepayers in the same way, I presume?—Yes.

6556. Would you be disposed to give such a board as you suggest some additional powers to those which are now possessed by the grand jury?—I do not know in what way the question leads.

6557. At present the duties of the grand jury are usually confined to the making of roads and bridges, and other works of that character, but if you had the board formed into a species of county corporation, would you be disposed to invest them with further powers for works calculated to improve the county?—I would; I consider that it would be a great benefit to the counties for such a board to exist with larger powers.

6558. Will you be kind enough to give some particular instance of what increased power you would give them, and for what purpose?—I believe that in counties surrounded by the sea, this board could, with much advantage, assist both pecuniarily and by its influence in obtaining greater facilities for small piers and harbours which are wanted; and in the interior counties of Ireland there is required a very large amount of arterial drainage, in which I think they could be very usefully employed.

6559. With a view to arterial drainage, would you form drainage districts?—I would form drainage districts.

6560. Then would you have the work performed by the county and the district, or would you have the proportion improved charged in proportion to the advantages which they derived from it?—There would be several ways of providing for the taxation, but I think that the plan might be very well adopted of charging according to the advantage obtained by the locality.

6561. But you, I presume, do not calculate that in any instance any proportion of the expense should be borne out of the pockets of the ratepayers?—No.

6562. You would give the county board compulsory power to drain where they deemed it essential, and then you would have the parties benefited by such drainage charged *pro ratâ* according to the advantage derived?—It is that compulsory power which is required in Ireland in many localities; in fact, in every county there is a larger or a smaller portion of land in which, from the deficiency of united action on the part of the occupiers, this arterial drainage is not carried out; and I feel certain that a county board, having powers to compel the arterial drainage to be carried out, would benefit the entire county very largely.

6563. Do you think that such a county board as you mention ought to be a continuous board?—Decidedly.

6564. And, as a continuous board, would it, in your opinion, be eminently useful in regard to such works as you have spoken of for the improvement of the county?—Yes; parties interested in the improvement of the locality could, before

before this county board, submit plans for the general improvement of the county which we have not the opportunity of doing before the present uncertain grand jury boards.

6565. At present, as you are aware, peers are prevented from acting as grand jurors; would you be in favour of having peers upon these boards?—I should be in favour of having peers upon these boards.

6566. Have you ever given thought to the subject of a division of the rate between the landlord and the occupier, as the poor rate is divided?—I have.

6567. Would you be in favour of that separation?—I should.

6568. And would you consider it right in principle, that where there is taxation there ought to be representation?—I should.

6569. Mr. *Maguire*.] At any rate you are not in favour of the present system of the nomination of the cesspayers by the grand jury?—No; I think it is very undesirable.

6570. In fact, I suppose, according to your opinion, those really who have the administration of the public money are not responsible to those who pay the tax?—They are not sufficiently responsible.

6571. Is there a strong feeling about that in Ireland, or in your district?—I think that there is an increasing feeling.

6572. Do you think that it is a reasonable and sound feeling?—I think it is.

6573. One that is not fictitious or got up by excitement, or anything of that kind?—No.

6574. It is based upon reason and fairness?—Upon reason and justice.

6575. Have you a very strong opinion yourself that the rate ought to be divided?—I have.

6576. Do you see any reason why the owners of property who share in the advantages of the improvements, should not bear a proportion of the burden?—No.

6577. You yourself, as a landlord, would willingly do it, I suppose, if the law were changed?—I would willingly do it.

6578. Do you think that if the law was changed, a considerable number of owners of property in Ireland would not charge the rate again in the shape of rent upon their tenants?—I think they would submit to the law.

6579. Do you think that though many might not do so, a great many would do so?—Not being a large landlord I could not give an opinion, but I believe from the general practice of the letting of land it would not enter largely into the calculations of the letters of land.

6580. At any rate you do not believe that a considerable number of landlords would not only put upon the tenant in the shape of rent what they have to pay in the shape of taxation, but that they would actually put more upon the tenant?—I can hardly give an opinion, but I do not think that they would as a class increase the rent in the proportion of any taxation of this sort.

6581. Do you think it just as fair to divide the burden for the county cess as to divide the burden for the support of the poor between the two classes?—Quite as fair.

6582. And that is not objected to either by the landlord or the tenant, is it?—No.

6583. They both submit to their share of that burden, but are you very strong as to the necessity of those persons who have the administration of that fund being elected, just as guardians are elected now, by the ratepayers?—I have held that opinion for a long time.

6584. Do you find from your own knowledge that the class of men who are now guardians work generally very well, and that they manage the administration of the Poor Laws?—They do it fairly.

6585. They take a fair share of the work, and have a fair share of intelligence, have they not?—Yes.

6586. And do they perform their duties on the whole satisfactorily?—I believe so, so far as I know.

6587. Supposing that the same class of men had to administer the county rate, and to discharge a duty almost analogous to that of the Poor Law guardians; do you not think that they would give satisfaction in that capacity as elected cesspayers?—I should think so; I expect they would.

6588. At any rate there would be the satisfaction that the ratepayers would have control over them?—Yes; much more than at present.

6589. What possible control have they at present?—None.

6590. Of course the constituents of a guardian at present have control over him, have they not?—They have.

6591. If they find that he is an imprudent or rash or dishonest person, they will not elect him again, as a matter of course?—No.

6592. Is not that a very salutary control?—It is.

6593. It works well under the Poor Law, and it would work well under any other system, would it not?—I should expect so.

6594. Do you not think that it would be important to have something like a continuous board, or something different from the present grand jury, which appears and vanishes once in six months?—I think that a continuous board would be most important for the efficient working of the county board.

6595. Do you think that under the special circumstances of our country, which need improvement in various ways, a permanent board might apply itself to a great many objects of utility?—I am of that opinion.

6596. Do you feel strongly upon that point?—I do.

6597. And do you think that the grand jury is altogether unsuited to discharge many of these duties from its being so purely ephemeral in its nature?—I think that a county board could have many matters, such as new tramways and other general improvements in the county, laid before them which at present, from the short time during which the grand jury sit, and from their ephemeral character, we cannot bring with satisfaction before them.

6598. In course of time might not a great many new and important duties, which they would be suited to discharge, rise up?—I am quite of that opinion.

6599. Do you think that they could be trained to great account both locally and nationally?—I believe that locally they could.

6600. Would you exempt the very poor from the payment of this rate, or do you know anything of the circumstances of its collection from very poor people?—I have not given the subject sufficient thought to be able to give an opinion upon it.

Mr. W. Malcolmson.

16 June 1868.

0.59.

6601. But

Mr. W. Malcolmson.

11 June 1852.

6601. But if there be in these cases very great difficulty in collection, and if the collection be very small, and if the circumstances to which I have referred make the cost of collection greater, you would get rid of those objections, would you not?—I think that would be desirable.

6602. (*Chairman.*) Are you in favour of the abolition of the grand jury and the appointment of two sets of permanent boards, a county board and a baronial board?—Clearly.

6603. Do you contemplate that that county board should take the place of the present grand jury, or that it should take the place of the county at large sessions?—The county grand jury having more power, I think the county board should have greater power than the present county jury have.

6604. Do you contemplate that that county board should have the revision of everything passed at the baronial board?—Yes.

6605. Would you have the baronial board supreme with regard to roads and matters in its own barony?—I would have the county board supreme in everything connected with the county.

6606. But would you have the baronial board final and supreme with regard to everything connected with the barony?—I think it would be better to submit everything to the higher tribunal of the county board.

6607. Would you have the presentment, say, for roads and works in a barony, first come before this baronial board and be approved of by them, and then go to the county board?—Yes.

6608. What power would you give the county board with respect to those works approved of by the baronial board?—I would give them the power of negativing them if the majority judged that they were undesirable from the expense, or from the locality not fully requiring them. At present grand juries reject cases coming up from what we call the road sessions, and perhaps they continue to do so for some time, and ultimately they pass them. It is well that particularly large outlays should not be entered into too rapidly.

6609. Would you restrict the power of this county board to the rejection or approval of works passed at the baronial board, or would you allow them to alter them, or to grant works which were not passed at the baronial board?—I think that there are works which might be charged on the county at large, which might not come up from the baronial board.

6610. But I am speaking now of works charged upon the baronies; would you leave them exactly in the same position as they are in now, only substituting this county board for the county grand jury?—That is what I propose.

6611. With regard to the works charged on the county at large, would you have this baronial board take the place both of the grand jury and of the county at large sessions?—Yes.

6612. You would have no tribunal intervening between it and the works charged upon the county at large?—No.

6613. Do you believe the present grand jury system to be an expensive one, and do you think it is extravagant?—I am not sufficiently acquainted with the details to give a correct opinion from my own personal knowledge.

6614. You recommend then the appointment of these county and baronial boards rather as a question of principle than because you are aware of any practical disadvantage arising from the present system?—I believe the present system not to be a good one.

6615. You believe it theoretically not to be a good one, but are you able to give the Committee any facts as to its being extravagant or working badly?—I am not prepared with any particular facts, but from having lived in the country all my life and knowing the general working of the grand jury system, I believe such an improvement as is proposed would be a large benefit to the country.

6616. When you say that it would be a large benefit, do you mean that it would lead to diminished expenditure or to works being better carried out?—I think it would lead to more careful expenditure and to the works also being well carried out. I believe the county surveyors require more supervision than at present they have with regard to the grand jury. I believe that the county surveyors as one class of the officials of the county do not receive that immediate supervision that as officials of the county they should receive.

6617. Do you believe that in consequence of that either the roads are extravagantly worked or that they are badly looked after?—I have seen outlays made in connexion with bridges and repairs of walls and other things of that nature, which, I think, if the outlay was more carefully looked after would not have been gone into.

6618. And do you think that it would be more carefully looked after, and that there would be a diminution of extravagant expenditure (if it exists) under the proposed change to elective boards both for the lower and higher tribunals?—I do.

6619. From your experience of grand juries and presentment sessions, do you find that the cesspayers or the magistrates are more inclined to extravagance?—I have not often enough attended these sessions to be able to give a correct opinion.

6620. When you speak of the expenditure being more carefully looked after under your proposal, you of course remember that the grand jury at present have no power of adding to the expenditure that is proposed at the presentment sessions with regard to roads and public works of that description?—I believe that the originating of the presentments, if done by a representative body, would be more carefully looked after than it is at present.

6621. Supposing the presentment sessions were made representative, and that the grand jury were still continued without any change being made regarding them, would not all the originating of works come from a representative body?—I think there would be an advantage in both bodies being representative.

6622. But at present when you speak of the extravagant expenditure which exists now as compared with what would exist under your proposed scheme, you are aware, of course, that the grand jury have no power of adding to any expenditure upon works of that description?—They have the power of declining to fiat the presentments.

6623. That is a power of diminishing the expense, is it not?—That is a power of diminishing the expenditure.

6624. They have no power of initiating any presentment for works, have they?—Not at present; but that power could be given to them in certain cases.

6625. As regards such works as roads and bridges,

bridges, and works of that description, is it not the case that they originate, not with the grand jury, but with the presentment sessions, because the grand jury have no power of adding to the expense at all?—That is so.

6626. *Mr. Gregory.*] Under your system of county boards, you would permit those county boards to originate great works, would you not?—Any works of public utility which the locality required.

6627. Would you require any check over those boards; and, if so, what check would you propose?—It never occurred to me that any such machinery would be required.

6628. Under the present system, is there not a double check with regard to works: first of all, the presentment sessions of the ratepayers, and then afterwards what you may call the supreme court of the grand jury; so that under the present system you have a greater check upon expenditure than you would have under the proposed county boards?—I think the elected members of the road sessions, and people of a similar class, would be more careful in what they would pass, and that anything extravagant in the way of expenditure would not be likely to be submitted to the county board.

6629. Then in all cases where there were fresh works, you would wish that they should be submitted to and approved of in the first instance by the road sessions?—By the road sessions.

6630. *Chairman.*] Even when they referred to the county at large?—I think that so far as they are interested in the area for which the road sessions administered the taxation (if I may so call it), it should pass that district sessions.

6631. As I understand you, you propose to do away altogether with the tribunal, corresponding to the presentment sessions for the county at large, because you propose to have but two tribunals. Now, with regard to expenses relating to the county at large, they would only come before the one tribunal, and there would be no court of appeal or court of revision with regard to them, would there?—There would not; but I think that the consent of the associated ratepayers ought to be had before a work for the county at large should pass the county board.

6632. Then if you required that, a work of course for the county at large would be payable proportionately by all the baronies of the county, how would you manage in case some baronies approved of it, and others disapproved of it?—Some legislation would be necessary by which you would say that three-fourths of the consent should be had, or some proportion, as to which I am not prepared to give an opinion.

6633. As I understood, in your evidence given in answer to the Honourable Member for Waterford, you proposed to give this county board most extensive powers for drainage purposes and different public works; would it not be very dangerous to entrust all those powers to one board without any supervision or check?—When I mentioned arterial drainage, of course the drainage would pass almost always through more than one barony; and it would be necessary to have the consent of the locality to that drainage taking place. With regard to a pier or harbour, the barony in which that would be constructed would be much more largely benefited than the county at large, and their consent, I think, ought to be had in both cases.

6634. You do not think that difficulties would arise in the apportionment of the expense and in acquiring the consent of the different baronies to their county-at-large works?—I have not considered the details, but I think it is quite possible to legislate that a proportion of those interested should have a casting vote as to whether the thing should be carried out or not.

Mr. W. Malcolmson.

14 June 1868.

6635. *Mr. Gregory.*] From your own experience, have you ever remarked that improvements are retarded by the present grand jury system?—I cannot say that I think that we should blame the grand jury system for it, but from my intimate knowledge of the several counties through which our railways run, I believe there is a large amount of improvement in the direction which I mentioned, namely, of arterial drainage to be carried out, and for which I think the county boards could very usefully be occupied in arranging. At present, from what cause I know not the drainage of the country generally is not going on.

6636. With regard to the election of the ratepayers, it has been stated by some witnesses here that in their opinion balloting would be almost a safer system than election, because election would be accompanied by the preponderating influence of the landlords in many cases, or else by the preponderating influence of the contractors, who would endeavour to return their own nominees; do you think that objection holds good?—I would be in favour of voting papers.

6637. But still the influence of the landlord and of the contractor would remain the same, whether you used voting papers or open voting, would it not?—Yes.

6638. *Chairman.*] When you speak of voting papers, do you mean secret voting papers, or voting papers such as they have under the Poor Law?—Voting papers such as they have under the Poor Law.

6639. *Mr. Gregory.*] Do you think that in electing those representative ratepayers the influence of the contractors would be great?—I do not think it would.

6640. An Honourable Member asked you whether it was not the case that jobbing Poor Law guardians lost their election; does it tally with your experience that jobbing Poor Law guardians lose their elections generally in Ireland?—I do not think so, as a class. There is not a very great change in them; but occasionally a better man is put in for one that does not give satisfaction.

6641. Do you not think that we look rather venially in Ireland upon jobbing guardians, and that that offence is rather condoned by other guardians who have a little tendency in the same way themselves?—That may be so; but I think there is less jobbing now than there was at first.

6642. Do you not think that is still exists?—To some extent.

6643. With regard to the division of the cess between landlord and tenant, do you contemplate that it should be a prospective arrangement; that is to say, that it should take place in all future agreements, or that it should come *de facto* at once in the case of all existing agreements?—It would be more just to have it prospective.

6644. *Mr. Blake.*] It is quite your intention, is it not, to convey to the Committee that such a board as you would suggest, and elected in the way you suggest, meeting more frequently than the grand jury meet at present, might perform, not only all the functions which the grand jury perform now, but might also discharge the functions now discharged by the county sessions at large?—Yes.

Tuesday, 16th June 1868.

MEMBERS PRESENT:

Mr. Blake.	Mr. Kendall.
Mr. Dawson.	Mr. Lawler.
General Dunne.	Mr. Maguire.
Colonel Forde.	Earl of Mayo.
Colonel French.	The O'Conor Don.
Mr. Gregory.	

THE O'CONOR DON, IN THE CHAIR.

Mr. ROBERT BODKIN, called in; and Examined.

Mr. R. Bodkin.

16 June 1868.

6645. Mr. *Gregory*.] YOU are a Grand Juror of considerable experience in the county of Galway, are you not?—I have been for 30 years, with two exceptions, attending grand juries in the county of Galway.

6646. Are you a magistrate of the county?—Yes.

6647. And you are a Poor Law guardian, I think?—Yes; I am a Poor Law guardian of three unions.

6648. You have been chairman and vice chairman, have you not?—I have been chairman for a time.

6649. And consequently I may take it for granted that you have had considerable experience of both systems?—Yes; I have had some experience.

6650. Before going into more specific questions, do you think, as a general rule, that the Poor Law system is conducted with greater attention to economy than the fiscal system of the grand jury?—I think not.

6651. In regard to presentment sessions, you may have seen from the evidence which is published, that some dissatisfaction exists, and, indeed, general dissatisfaction is stated to exist with regard to the mode of choosing the associated cesspayers; do you think that is the case?—I think there has been dissatisfaction, and I quite agree as to the dissatisfaction.

6652. Do you think that the dissatisfaction is well founded?—I think it is.

6653. As far as your experience goes, in the county of Galway, is it the habit there to take the highest cesspayers returned by the barony constable for each barony?—The grand jury of the county of Galway believed that they were compelled to select the 10 highest cesspayers supplied by the barony constables, and that then they were to be balloted for afterwards at the presentment sessions.

6654. Do you think that the system of taking the highest cesspayers, even if it were strictly and honestly carried out, is a bad system?—I think it is a bad system, and if you will allow me, I will illustrate it in this way: at the very last Galway assizes, in the largest barony in the county, in fact, the barony which I represent on the grand jury out of the 10 highest cesspayers who were elected, there were six who were very nearly connected; I think there were three brothers, and they were all very nearly related; and out of the six I dare say there were not more than two who ever had or ever would attend presentment sessions; and to add to the objectionable complexion of the matter they happened to be all of the same name.

6655. I believe that another objection is this: that, under the present system, the representative cesspayers may be all taken from one portion of the county instead of being selected from various portions of the county with different interests to be represented?—That might or might not happen. If they happened to be the highest cesspayers there would be no reference to their position in the barony.

6656. Still it is a matter of chance, is it not?—Quite so.

6657. Do you think it right that that uncertainty should prevail with regard to the representation of places?—I should think not.

6658. Two modes have been proposed before the Committee for remedying this alleged defect in the present system, the one being that the associated cesspayers should be chosen by election, and the other being that they should be chosen by ballot at the meeting of the grand jury; do you adhere to either of those systems, and, if so, which you do prefer?—I could not recommend the electoral division system, because the electoral divisions are not always conterminous with the barony boundaries, but of the two I should prefer their being balloted for by the grand jury, provided there was some alteration made as to the manner in which the high constable was to submit the names; that is to say, so that we should have every district within a barony represented.

6659. Would it suit your views that the barony should be divided into a certain number of districts, from which the barony constable should return a certain number of names, or would you take as it were, parochially?—I have never considered it in a parochial view, but any mode which you could suggest, which would give a representation from each portion of the barony, would be what I would recommend and desire.

6660. Then do you think, on the whole, that the principle of ballot at the grand jury would be preferable to the principle of election?—Certainly it would be preferable to the present plan, because then there would be a certainty as to the people who would be balloted for; now, out of the 10 who are selected only five can act, because it is the five who come first in the ballot who act.

6661. Does

6661. Does that uncertainty very often prevent the cesspayers from attending at the presentment sessions?—Thus, and I am afraid more indifference to it than we could wish.

6662. Therefore, I presume that you would be satisfied by the choice, either of the ballot system at the grand jury, or of the elective system, provided the baronies were properly divided, so that adequate representation might be afforded to all portions of the barony?—I should.

6663. Have you ever heard any objections alleged with regard to the system of election upon the ground that if the associated cesspayers were chosen by election they would be more under the immediate control of the landlords, or that they would probably be elected by the influence of the contractors?—I have never heard any such objection raised, but I have always felt that the associated cesspayers were more anxious to vote with the landlords than to exercise any discretion of their own, unless they came for some particular purpose. I think they rely more upon the landlords than they do even upon one another.

6664. Do you think that a contractor would exercise much influence upon the elections in a barony?—Of course, where his particular friends were there would be a certain influence exercised I dare say, but I do not apprehend any great evil from that.

6665. Does that consideration of undue influence (if I may so call it) determine you more to the system of ballot than to the system of election with regard to the choice of the cesspayers?—The difficulty as to election is how it could well be done. If I were quite sure that they could be elected by the cesspayers I should very much prefer that to the grand jury having anything at all to say to it; but the ballot at the grand jury would still be a great improvement upon the present system.

6666. In short you would be very well satisfied, I presume, if you got either one or the other?—I think so; I think either would be a great improvement.

6667. From your experience is it the habit of magistrates to attend road sessions where they have no particular interest in that particular locality; have any instances of that kind come to your knowledge?—Yes; I know many instances where magistrates have attended, and from a very great distance, who have had no interest in that locality, either in the way of holding landed property, or in the way of paying rates or cess.

6668. I presume that you are of opinion that it is not advantageous that that mode of procedure should be continued?—Certainly not; I have always myself acted on the rule of never attending in any barony in which I had not property.

6669. And I presume that you would, therefore, confine the attendance of magistrates to those who either possess property, or occupy property in a particular barony?—There may be people who are deeply interested in the rates having large farms, or something of that sort, as ratepayers, who certainly might be permitted to attend.

6670. I have received from the secretary of our grand jury this morning a letter, from which I will read you an extract. Referring to the case of adjourned road sessions where no magistrate attends, he says: "I had instances of this in the baronies of Leitrim, Longford, and Ross last November, and in the barony of Dunkellin last Saturday. A certain price is fixed at the special sessions, and then tenders are taken at adjourned sessions from contractors not to exceed the price allowed. The magistrate who attends is bound to take the lowest, and surely the secretary of the grand jury could do this where there is no magistrate, particularly as it has to be ratified by the grand jury at the next assizes before it becomes a contract. But as the law is at present, if no magistrate attends there can be no adjourned sessions; and when there is no adjourned sessions the grand jury cannot take tenders, and all contracts fall to the ground for the half-year. For instance, now any roads whose term of contract may have expired at this assizes in the barony of Dunkellin will have to remain out of contract till after the spring assizes in 1869; and where a road is out of contract for six months, particularly in winter, it very quickly goes into a bad state of repair, and requires a larger price when contracted for again;" is the last portion of that statement strictly correct?—No; because I think by the 20th or 21st of Victoria the grand jury have the power of placing works in the hands of the county surveyor.

6671. At the adjourned sessions, in order to remedy this defect, would you propose in the mode suggested by the secretary of our grand jury that the secretary should take contracts to be ratified by the grand jury, or would you propose that a cesspayer should take the chair where no magistrate was present, provided the cesspayer himself was one of those who were present at the presentment sessions?—I certainly would prefer that to the sessions not being held; if a cesspayer had attended in the absence of a magistrate I think we should allow him to hold the sessions.

6672. Would you have a cesspayer in the chair?—I do not see how you could have the sessions without you had something of that sort. With the permission of the Committee I will mention what I consider to be rather an anomaly in the law with respect to presentment sessions; if the presentment sessions are held, even though there may be no tender sent to them, the grand jury can receive a tender. It appears to me strange (though the going judges of assize have ruled it over and over again) that where there are no sessions held the grand jury are then precluded from receiving tenders; but if there were sessions, though a tender may not be presented to the sessions, nevertheless the grand jury can receive a tender.

6673. *Chairman*.] I understand you to say, a short time ago, in answer to the Honourable Member for the county of Galway, that, if there were no adjourned sessions held through the non-attendance of magistrates, in such cases the grand jury could present the works to the county surveyor?—So they could. That has nothing to do with it.

6674. But could they receive a tender for them; that is, provided there were no sessions; but if there were sessions held, and if there were no tender at the sessions, then it would be competent for the grand jury to receive a tender?—That has been ruled by the going judge of assize over and over again.

6675. Colonel *French*.] Have you ever known a case where the road sessions have referred the tenders to the grand jury?—I have.

6676. That is rather objectionable in one point of view, is it not, because the grand jury are not

Mr. *R. Hodkin.*

16 June 1868.

Mr. R. [illegible]. — 16 June [illegible].

so capable of judging of the solvency of a security as the cesspayers and the magistrates in the neighbourhood?—Generally speaking, I think they are not.

6677. Mr. *Gregory*.] Are you in favour of invariably taking the lowest tender in contracts?—I am.

6678. Would you make no exceptions?—No.

6679. Taking for instance the case where a contract had been put in by a man who had been a notoriously bad contractor before, would you allow that to be an exceptional case?—You throw great discretionary power into the hands of the presiding magistrate by doing that. I find that the grand juries have sometimes not bound themselves to take the lowest tender; but then they rely upon the Act, which says, that under certain circumstances the security not being good, or something of that sort, you are not bound to take the lowest tender, and I think the grand jury of Galway have occasionally acted upon the advice of the county surveyor as to not taking tenders where the sum named, or the means of the contractor were quite inadequate to perform the work.

6680. But still, are you of opinion that, upon the whole, it is more advisable that the principle should be rigidly carried out of taking the lowest tender, rather than of admitting exceptional circumstances?—At sessions, most assuredly. I would not exercise the power, even myself, at adjourned sessions, though I might have confidence in my own integrity. I think that you cannot be too stringent.

6681. Colonel *French*.] Would not the only check be the solvency of the security?—Yes, certainly. I think you may exercise a very wise discretion there. Of course, the insolvency of the security would be a very good reason for rejecting a tender.

6682. Mr. *Gregory*.] With regard to the grand jury itself, suggestions have been made that there should be a financial board established, chosen by the grand jury, to sit between assizes and assizes to perform certain functions connected with county business; have you considered that subject?—I think that it would be very desirable if there could be something of the sort effected.

6683. Would you think it advisable that a certain number of gentlemen should be chosen by the grand jury to sit between assizes and assizes, and to conduct such fiscal business as should come before them?—I take it, that the selection should be made from the grand jury of the best business men, having reference to localities.

6684. One objection which is urged to that is, that gradually the functions of the grand jury might merge in a small clique, as it were, of country gentlemen, and that it would become, in short, a very narrow representation; do you think that that objection holds good?—I cannot think so, inasmuch as I believe that they would be a deputation of the grand jury, just as a board of superintendence or any other body appointed by the grand jury is, and then they would be amenable to the grand jury. In fact, they would do nothing which would not be ratified by the grand jury.

6685. Mr. *Dawson*.] With reference to a question put to you by the Honourable Member for the county of Galway, do you conceive that such a committee is desirable, as part of the present system of the grand jury, or were you referring to a wholly different kind of county board in place of the grand jury?—No; I know of no county board that I ever heard of which would be preferable to the grand jury.

6686. Are you, therefore, satisfied with the constitution of the grand jury as it is at present?—Perfectly, with those alterations which we are speaking of.

6687. Then your answer would refer to a committee of the grand jury under the present system?—Precisely.

6688. Colonel *French*.] Do you think that the danger of their interfering with the duties of the grand jury would be put a stop to if this financial board were confined, like the board of superintendence, or anything else, merely to executive duties?—That is what I mean.

6689. Mr *Gregory*.] Might you not obviate the objection as to this body becoming a clique by making provision that a certain portion of them should not be eligible for re-election within a certain period?—Anything of that sort would be very desirable. Perhaps the Committee will allow me to say that the reason why I recommend these boards would be, that many circumstances occur, between assizes and assizes, which it would be very desirable should be dealt with by the grand jury, if it were in existence, or by a deputation from them. If a barony constable, for instance, dies, or levants, or anything of the sort, we are in a very awkward position. You have to go on to the first sessions of the county, very often at a very extreme distance. He is brought before an assistant barrister, who knows nothing whatever of the securities that are offered; and I know several cases where there have been great defaults in consequence of the want of knowledge in that way. In the case of the roads the contractors might be defaulters, and the county surveyor might be called upon to interfere. He would have then an opportunity of referring to the body of which I spoke; but the county surveyor is now perfectly powerless, so far as money or means are concerned, to be able to do what he ought to do when those roads are placed in his hands.

6690. Colonel *French*.] Is it not the case that the difficulty as to barony constable can only occur if the vacancy happens between the two grand juries?—That is all.

6691. Mr. *Gregory*.] You mentioned the board of superintendence in one of your answers; do you not think that that instance would rather militate against a financial board, such as you have been describing, inasmuch as I do not believe the attendance of members of the board of superintendence is remarkably regular?—I do not know that the numbers are very great, but three form a quorum; and I scarcely ever remember a board falling through for want of numbers.

6692. I presume that a board of this description, such as you have sketched out, dealing with county interests, would naturally pay more attention to them than to a mere question of prison discipline, or prison regulations?—No; I feel it to be my duty to attend invariably at the board of superintendence, and I know that a great many other gentlemen feel coerced by the same sense of duty.

6693. Perhaps, as a general rule, the county gentlemen would not be so conscientious as yourself, and perhaps the attendance upon this board might be rather slack, in which case there might be some difficulties, might there not?—I should think that their duties would not be very onerous.

It

It would only be in cases of necessity that they would be called upon to act, I take it.

6694. *Chairman.*] Is it not the fact that, although generally speaking there is a quorum of the members of the board of superintendence, yet that quorum consists of the gentlemen who live near the county town, and that the quorum is nearly always composed of the same members; and, in fact, it is not the board of superintendence, instead of being a large body, a small body composed of the gentlemen who reside near the county town?—I can only speak of the county of Galway, and that does not apply to the county of Galway. I live 12 miles from Galway, and I know one gentleman who lives 18 miles from it, and they are some of the most constant attendants.

6695. In some of the other counties of Ireland, you are aware that that is not the case?—I am.

6696. Mr. *Gregory.*] I presume that you would entrust to such a board as this, in the case of a vacancy in the appointment of barony constable, the power of appointing another *ad interim*?—I would give that board no power, except conditionally on its being confirmed by the grand jury.

6697. I am only speaking of an *ad interim* appointment; would you give such a board the power of making such an appointment?—Certainly.

6698. This board would examine the accounts of the barony constables, would it not?—Yes, I think a half-yearly examination might be sufficient for that purpose.

6699. Do you not think that an examination of the receipts of the barony constables, in order that they should not retain too large a sum of money in their hands, would be a very valuable function of this board?—Yes, but it would be attended with this difficulty; that they do not proceed with the collection till a month or two before the assizes, and some of the largest cess-payers do not pay them until the assizes.

6700. Do you not think it advisable, at all events, that there should be some machinery to enable the county to prevent the accumulation of large sums in the hands of the barony constables, in case those amounts should get there, by the payment in of all sums, say, exceeding 100 *l.*, as soon as the collector received them?—It might be desirable, but I think it would be attended with some difficulty; and I do not see how you could compel a barony constable to do so.

6701. Is it not the law at present, that he should pay it in as soon as he gets 100 *l.*?—Yes, but you would find it very hard to carry it out, I think.

6702. Colonel *French.*] In the event of a vacancy occurring in the office of barony constable between one assizes and another, the successor is elected by the magistrates of the county, is he not?—He is, and it is a very objectionable mode of election.

6703. Mr. *Dawson.*] As to the appointment of barony constables, have you heard that the attendance of it is a grievance, of which they complain, that they have to produce their sureties *in propriâ personâ* at every ensuing assizes, and that they think it is unnecessary, and might very easily be obviated by an affidavit of their existence and of their solvency; do you think that would be sufficient?—Then you should alter the law which appoints them *de novo* at every assizes, though they really remain on from time to time, as long as they conduct themselves properly.

6704. I do not think they would object to being appointed at every succeeding assizes, if the same security were held as necessarily good?—But the bond that would apply to one case would not apply to another succeeding case.

6705. Then in fact you see an objection to the alteration?—I think it might be done; if you proposed to do it for any length of time, you might take a great amount of security which would cover the amount of cess, which would be collected within that time.

6706. Mr. *Gregory.*] Taking the case of a continuous bond in the place of a temporary bond, would that obviate the objection?—I think it would be very desirable that they should not have to renew their security at each assizes, but in the present state of things you could not do otherwise.

6707. Mr. *Dawson.*] I myself have seen gentlemen brought up to complete these securities in a very debilitated state of health, where it was evidently a matter of great suffering and privation to them; and I have presented a memorial from all the baronial collectors of the county which I represent, viz., Londonderry, and I think it is a very great grievance. From an experienced gentleman like yourself, I should like to know whether your opinion agrees with that?—As at present the bonds are constituted, they only give security for the amount that is then presented for; but if there was any mode of giving security that would cover the cess for one or two or three years, or whatever time you define; it would be better perhaps than to leave them subject to the annoyance of which you speak.

6708. Mr. *Gregory.*] Presuming things to remain as they are at the present moment, do you think it would be possible for the contractors' sureties to enter into their bond before some authority in the locality where they live, instead of being brought down to do so at the town where the grand jury is sitting?—His sureties might do it of course before any responsible officer of the county; but what I understood the Honourable Member for Londonderry county to allude to was, that he should not at every half-year have to enter into a new bond.

6709. General *Dunne.*] Could they not be allowed to perfect their bonds locally before any magistrate in the neighbourhood, and would not that be a great convenience?—Upon having a certificate from the treasurer that they had discharged the last bond, I think it might be done by any responsible officer.

6710. At this moment?—Yes.

6711. Mr. *Gregory.*] Would not one of the difficulties connected with the continuous bond, be this; that persons would be extremely unwilling to become security for a very large sum of money for an indefinite period of time?—I think it would be a difficulty.

6712. It would influence you very much in becoming a security, would it not, whether you were to become security for six months, or for a considerable number of years?—It would, I admit.

6713. There has been a recommendation to this committee that all tenements under the annual value of 4 *l.* should be exempted from the county cess; are you of that opinion?—I am not.

6714. Will you give your reasons to the Committee?—I hold, perhaps, peculiar opinions, but I hold that every man in the community should

Mr. R. [illegible]. 26 June 1868.

contribute

Mr. R. [illegible].

18 June [illegible].

contribute towards the taxation of the country for the maintenance of the laws to which he owes his protection. Of course I know that, under the poor law rating, 4 *l.* occupiers are exempted, but I know many estates where the tenants are obliged to pay as a matter of agreement for the 4 *l.*, even though the landlord may allow it to them afterwards, and I do not see any reason for exempting them. It comes to a very small sum indeed, and I cannot say that I would recommend it.

6715. Does it not become a case of very great hardship in towns where those infinitesimally small sums are levied upon people who have really hardly the means of paying them, and does it not put the collector in a very awkward position, even to the degree of increasing the charges for the collection?—It would, of course, facilitate the duties of the collector very much, there is no doubt, for under the tenement valuation, the 4 *l.* comes to a very small sum indeed. Some of them are rated at 3 *l.*, and I have known a house rated at as little as 10 *s.* They all pay now under the tenement valuation.

6716. Do you think that insisting upon taking from those poor people those small sums inspires them with any desire for economy in the general administration of the fiscal affairs of the county? —I do not see any reason for exempting them more than for the landlord's exempting them from the payment of rent.

6717. Except, I presume, that it is a question of greater convenience on the one side, and that it would be a question of very great inconvenience on the other?—The convenience applies solely in my mind, to the person who is collecting it.

6718. But is there no inconvenience on the part of the payer?—No more than in the case of any other payment. I believe that payment is inconvenient to everybody occasionally.

6719. With regard to a broader question than that, what is your opinion as to the division of the county cess between the landlord and the tenant? —I have no hesitation in stating to the Committee, that I would be opposed to any alteration of the present arrangement.

6720. Are the Committee to gather from that answer of yours, that you would be opposed to any alteration of the present system, presuming that that alteration was confined altogether to future agreements?—That is my view.

6721. Even if it should not be applicable to existing agreements, and that it should not have a retrospective effect?—I think it would be equally objectionable as regards the present arrangement. My principal reason is, that I think it would tend very much to disturb the relations between landlord and tenant. I think there is no landlord who would be letting land who would not leave a very large salvage for this increased assessment, and that perhaps the tenant would suffer much more than the landlord. Besides that, it would unsettle things. Many men leave their estates as they are, but if they were to disturb them at all, it would be against the tenant, more than the landlord. That is my conscientious opinion.

6722. But I have pre-supposed a case in which there would be no disturbance, and in which it would have entire reference to prospective agreements; would your objections hold equally to that?—Equally, because I think the landlord would make greater provision for it, even than the cess would ever come to; because the cess is variable, and the landlord would naturally provide himself against the possibility of any loss. I have heard many tenants complain of the poor-rates, of which the landlords pay half, and I have scarcely heard an instance (though I have great experience in the letting of lands, as I manage my own estate), of an objection to the grand jury cess.

6723. Have you never heard an objection to the whole of the grand jury cess being paid by the tenant?—No. Of course since there has been an agitation about it, I have heard it mentioned, but I do not know that any tenant has ever asked me yet to abate his rent, putting it on those grounds, though many have complained as to the poor-rate, of which they pay but half.

6724. In letting your land have you ever been applied to by the tenant to pay your share of the county cess?—Never in my life.

6725. But, looking at the question abstractedly, or taking for instance a case which occurred in our own county, where we bound ourselves to repay a deficiency which might arise from the construction of a railway running through Galway, that repayment to be made out of the county cess, do you not think that a great public undertaking of that description was certainly quite as much for the benefit of the owner of the land as for the benefit of the occupiers of the land, and that in a case of that description, it would have been fair that the owners of the land should have borne their proportion of the liability for a work of such exceeding importance to all classes of the community?—You are speaking of the operation of a Bill for which no provision of that sort was made. There was no provision in the county cess to relieve the occupiers of half the cess for that particular object.

6726. Do you not think that a new imposition of that kind coming at once upon the occupiers alone has rather a one-sided appearance?—No, because I look upon the tenant as having his share proportionately in all improvements of that sort equally with the landlord.

6727. Then the tenant having his share equally with the landlord, would it not be fair that the landlord should pay his share?—I do not know; the tenant takes the land, and holds it subject to those charges; he considers all that.

6728. He takes the land subject to what he knows, and subject to what the average is; but supposing any new imposition comes, which he has not foreseen (take, for instance, this very case of the railroad), is it not then a hardship upon the tenant that he should have a new imposition put upon him alone, which he has never previously contemplated?—You put a very extreme case, but that would apply to any new road equally, which he never expected would have been passed.

6729. With regard to the subject of superannuation, are you of opinion that officers connected with the grand jury should obtain superannuation after a certain period of service in cases where they have not devoted the whole of their time to the service of the county?—I should be very slow to recommend superannuation in a general system of that sort.

6730. Do you adhere to the recommendation of the Poor Law Commission of 1861, which laid down the principle that officers connected with the Poor Law should not receive superannuation, except in cases where they had devoted their

their whole time to that particular service?—That would be my opinion.

6731. Do you think that that is applicable to the county officers?—I think it is.

6732. There has been some evidence taken before this Committee upon the subject of malicious injuries; are you satisfied with the state of the law as it exists at present with regard to that matter or not?—As regards malicious injuries the present system does not produce the detection of crime, but I think that to a great extent it prevents it; for people will be very slow indeed to do an injury in the neighbourhood if they knew that the district around would have to compensate the injured party.

6733. The neighbours would be slow to permit an act of vengeance to be done, would they not, if they knew that the person who was to be assailed would be compensated for his loss, and that they would have to pay for it?—I think so.

6734. Do you think, therefore, that the present system is a great deterrent to offences of that kind?—I think so; and it is very carefully watched, because it goes before the sessions and before the grand jury, and not unfrequently before a judge and petty jury afterwards; and I find that people are always alive to their own interests, and that if there is any objection to the claim they come and oppose it.

6735. I have received a letter to-day from a very active landowner and magistrate in the county of Waterford, Sir John Keane, and he says: "In cases of malicious injury by fire, or otherwise, you should recommend that power be given both to the applicants for compensation and to the opponents of the presentment, particularly to compel the attendance of witnesses (say by summons signed by two justices of the peace) at presentment sessions and before the grand jury. I make this suggestion because at our last sessions at Lismore witnesses in opposition to the presentment were afraid to come forward, inasmuch as the bailiff of the estate had given warning that there must be no opposition on the part of the tenantry to the application. The burning, however, was clearly malicious, and eight justices of the peace and eight ratepayers so voted it. I may say here that in this county we summon 20 ratepayers, 10 to sit if answering their names at the appointed hour." Is there no power at the present moment to summon witnesses in the case of a malicious injury, either before presentment sessions or before the grand jury?—I have never known the necessity to arise in our county.

6736. Have you generally found witnesses very ready to attend?—Very ready.

6737. I suppose that the neighbours, if there is any doubt at all about the malicious injury, will take very good care to be present and to oppose it?—They will take pretty good care to be present and to oppose it, and very often they are represented by a solicitor; indeed, both sides are generally represented by solicitors in an important case.

6738. That shows that they would be very ready to put a stop to it if they got a chance, does it not?—Certainly; but I hope there will be no alteration made as to the power of the grand jury. It is only in a few cases that the grand jury have any control over the sessions, and very properly, too; but there the grand jury have the power, as the Committee are aware, of putting it on the townland, or upon the parish, or upon the half barony, or upon the barony; and I think that that power should still be left to the grand jury, for I have often myself had reason to change my mind between the sessions and the assizes, as to where it ought properly to be placed.

6739. What is your practice in Galway as to exempting the property of the party aggrieved, from contributing to the assessment?—We always intend to exempt it, and I think it is generally done.

6740. Do you think that you are justified by law in doing that?—Yes, it is not to be presumed that a man will destroy his own property.

6741. The law, I am afraid, sometimes presumes things which are not perfectly correct. Are you quite certain that you are warranted in exempting the injured man's property?—If we are right in the law we have the power of putting it wherever we like, and we have always done it, I think.

6742. *Chairman.*] Do you exempt a particular holding, or is it the townland which you exempt?—A very important exception occurred at the last assizes, and I do not know whether it was done by design or by mistake; but we were in the habit of passing presentments on all lands, save and except those occupied by the applicant. That is the wording generally on the back of the presentment. We have been very often told by the judge of assizes that usage was even stronger than law.

6743. Mr. *Gregory.*] You can exempt any sub-denomination if any such sub-denomination exists; but you cannot exempt the holding, I believe?—We have been doing it these 30 years.

6744. Can you suggest to this Committee at all any mode in which increased economy and diminution of expense could be obtained in our grand jury system?—I think that all our institutions, such as our lunatic asylums, are conducted with a great deal of expense. I think that we have a very unnecessary annual expense for revision; I think, too, that the offices of the clerk of the Crown and clerk of the peace, might be very advantageously amalgamated, and I am quite sure that now, with a stipendiary magistrate in every district the duties of the coroner could be very well discharged by the stipendiary magistrate attending at an inquest instead of a coroner.

6745. Mr. *Dawson.*] There are counties in Ireland without any stipendiary magistrate, are there not?—In those cases that would not apply. My evidence entirely applies to my own county of Galway.

6746. Mr. *Gregory.*] Might you not have a local magistrate, or, failing him, a sub-inspector of police?—I have never tried it. I only thought that a stipendiary magistrate would be a very fair substitute for the coroner, and that it would lessen the expense.

6747. Is the revision to which you allude a very expensive operation?—I think that the last revision cost about 630 *l.*, which was assessed upon the county; but I think it is an increasing expense. It is rather an anomaly in one way, inasmuch as the revision is made for poor law purposes in every union. There are 10 unions in the county of Galway. The revision is generally made about Christmas, and the rate which is afterwards made upon that revision is not made until the following autumn, say about September. I could not venture to say exactly whether the revision should be made every three years, or every five years, or at what intervals; but I have no doubt that an annual revision might be dispensed with, and that with the poor law clerk on the one side, and an intelligent barony constable on the other, the duties might be very well done.

6748. Do you think that the large sum expended might be considerably diminished?—I think it might.

6749. Are there any other topics upon which you would like to be examined before the Committee?—If you recollect I said that I would not be for interfering with the system of accepting the lowest tender; but if I did that, I would give the county surveyor of the county a much more stringent mode of compelling the fulfilment of contracts. Nothing can be more objectionable than the present mode. The county surveyor withholds his certificate, the road is left out of repair, and then the grand jury, or a committee of the grand jury, who revise these things in our county, are obliged to recommend a prosecution, which is attended with very considerable expense, and very often with very doubtful results. You have to bring the secretary of the grand jury, and the county surveyor, and all those parties to the sessions, and in the end very likely the contractor gets off, or if he does not get off the whole of the work gets out of order in the meantime. What I would respectfully suggest to the Committee is, that instead of executing the bonds as they are at present executed, they should be executed to the secretary of the grand jury, or to some officer of the county; and that in default of the contract, and the county surveyor reporting against the road, he should be authorised to bring the defaulting party before a bench of magistrates, and to punish him as you would for any other offence, for a breach of contract.

6750. Instead of the 10 days' notice?—You can bring him before a bench of magistrates by 10 days' notice, and the county surveyor may put the road in repair; but I would summon them before the petty sessions, and you would find that both securities and contractor would be immediately made amenable, and would look after the work. The present system has worked exceedingly ill.

6751. You stated, I think, that one objection which you have to the present system is, that the bonds of contractors are made to the Crown, and not to the grand jury?—Precisely; and thereby you get a clumsy and expensive machinery.

6752. And the power of the county surveyor to enforce contracts is insufficient, is it not?—It is; and there is no fund at the present moment at the disposal of the county surveyor. That was one of the reasons why I suggested a standing committee; that in case of urgency of that sort funds might be supplied through that body.

6753. You do not mean to place those funds, I presume, in the hands of the county surveyor himself? Are you of opinion that all payments should be made, not by the county surveyor, but by some more direct agent of the grand jury?—Certainly. I look upon it as most objectionable to place funds or roads in the hands of the county surveyor, if it could be possibly avoided.

6754. During your long experience as a grand juror for, I think, 30 years, have you ever found any instance in the county of Galway in which you consider that a decision of the grand jury has been influenced in any degree, either by religion or by politics?—Never. I am happy to say that we have never had anything but the most friendly feeling upon our grand jury; and, in fact, we never inquire what a man's religion or his politics are in the discharge of our duty, or in our social intercourse.

6755. You are a Roman Catholic, I think?—I am.

6756. *Chairman.*] You stated, in answer to the Honourable Member for the county of Galway, with respect to the constitution of the presentment sessions, that you would prefer having the cesspayers balloted for, rather than selected, and as I understood you, you preferred the ballot, because you considered that there would be a difficulty in having the election?—Precisely.

6757. What difficulties do you see in the way of having an election?—I do not know how we could have them elected so as to have each portion of the barony represented. In a very large barony I should like to see every district represented.

6758. But how do you propose to accomplish that object by means of the ballot?—The Honourable Member for the county of Galway, as I understood, asked me whether by the barony constable sending to the grand jury a certain number of names from each district, that object might not be secured.

6759. The expression, "From each district," implies that the barony should be divided into districts, does it not?—Yes.

6760. That would be necessary in the case of the ballot, as well as in the case of election, would it not?—Yes; if they could be elected irrespective of the grand jury, I should prefer it.

6761. If the barony could be divided into districts, for the purpose of returning cesspayers, you would prefer that those cesspayers should be elected, rather than that they should be selected by ballot out of those districts?—I would rather that the grand jury should have nothing to say to them, if it could be avoided; but I should prefer the ballot to the present system.

6762. But you would prefer election to either mode, if the baronies could be divided, so as to render it easy?—Precisely.

6763. With regard to this finance committee, in favour of which you expressed an opinion, would you explain to the Committee the exact functions which you would give that committee, or to what would you limit its functions; you stated one duty which it might perform, namely, the appointment of a barony constable, in case of a vacancy; is there any other duty which you think it might perform?—Not only in the case of a vacancy, but as the gallant general said, it does so happen that specials do not come in, or sometimes even the barony constable, until the judge discharges the grand jury, and then they have to go to the sessions, and as the law at present stands, it is the first sessions in the county, be it for ever so remote a district. In that case the finance committee would discharge that duty. Then they would assist the county surveyor in the case of roads and public works, which were, perhaps, in operation, which he could not certify for at the grand jury, but for which they could, between assizes and assizes, perhaps

perhaps give a contractor a portion of the money.

6764. Would you empower that committee to pay for those works, afterwards certified by the surveyor?—Only in a very limited way, by direction of the grand jury, the grand jury telling them that there were a certain amount of new public works only, because the county surveyor can always certify for a portion in case of new works.

6765. Would you have this committee to meet regularly at fixed periods, or would you have it called together only when some extraordinary occurrence necessitated its being assembled?—I think that I would have two or three meetings fixed between assizes and assizes. My reason for that is, that in the disastrous times, in the famine times, Galway, like many other counties in Ireland, was in great arrear. All the barony constables could collect no cess, and under the authority of the judge of assize (I think it was the late Chief Justice Lefroy), we were allowed to appoint a committee, of which I was a member, with, I think, five or six others. We met three times, I think, between assize and assize, and in that way we got in nearly the whole of the cess, which would not otherwise have been done, or the contractors would not have been paid. There was no money to pay contractors, or anybody, except in that way.

6766. That was a very extraordinary case, was it not?—It was an exceptional case, certainly.

6767. But for ordinary occasions, I understand you to express an opinion that the functions of this committee should be extremely limited?—Very limited. I do not want to give up any of the duties which could be discharged by the grand jury, but only to supply the want which is often felt between assizes and assizes, of a body to discharge those duties.

6768. It was suggested to you that this Committee might overlook the accounts of the collectors, and might see that they complied with the Statute in lodging 100 *l.* as soon as 100 *l.* was collected, and you saw a difficulty in the way of their duty. Did that difficulty relate to making the collectors collect the money or lodge it?—I think the collection is generally so good that I do not see any great object in it, though I am only speaking of my own county. I know that we should have considerable difficulty in getting the collectors first to collect the money, but I dare say that if they collected it we should have less difficulty in obliging them to lodge it.

6769. Would you see a difficulty in obliging them to lodge it when it was collected?—No, we could oblige them to lodge it, or we would not re-appoint them.

6770. At present the collector is not obliged to collect any of the money until before the assizes, is he?—I do not know what his obligation is, but that is his practice.

6771. But there is an obligation, is there not, in the Grand Jury Act, that if he collects a sum up to 100 *l.* he is to lodge it?—In our county that has been a dead letter.

6772. Do you not believe that that statutory obligation could be enforced by making the collectors come before this finance committee, say once a month, and show whether they had collected any money or not, and by obliging them, if they had collected money to the amount of 100 *l.*, to lodge it?—Certainly, that could be done, but I think that the collectors would be still more tardy then; I think they would not collect.

6773. If the collectors do not collect this county cess, the money is in the hands of the ratepayers, and it is for their benefit; but if the collector on the other hand collects it, and uses it for his own advantage, the public lose the whole advantage of it, do they not?—No doubt.

6774. Would it not be desirable then, either that the collector should leave the money in the hands of the public, or that if he collects it, he should lodge it to the credit of the county?—Certainly.

6775. And you think that a finance committee would accomplish one or other of those objects?—I do.

6776. What is the rate paid for the collection of the cess in the county of Galway?—Nominally it is 9 *d.*; but in those times that I spoke of, we gave an additional 3 *d.* as a sort of premium, and that state of things has continued; they get 1 *s.*

6777. You are a poor-law guardian, are you not?—I am, in three unions.

6778. Are you aware what is paid for the collection of the poor rate on an average?—It varies in different places. It is 6 *d.* in some places, and 5 *d.* in others; and I think that I am connected with one union where it is 4 *d.*

6779. But it is, generally speaking, not more than 6 *d.*?—No.

6780. Do you believe that there is any really valid reason why the county cess should cost twice as much for collection as the poor rate?—There is one reason, and that is the 4 *l.* people, who are exempted under the Poor Law. Upon every tenement, no matter how small it is, even if it be a house valued at 10 *s.*, the grand jury collector, the barony constable, must collect the county cess. I think it is much more onerous than the collection of the poor rate.

6781. Do you not believe that if the baronies were divided into districts, instead of having a collector for the whole barony, there would be persons got who would collect the county cess at a much lower rate than that at which it is collected at present?—I will answer that question by saying that I have no doubt that you would get people to do anything for much less than the persons at present employed.

6782. Giving ample security?—Very likely; but I should not advise the division of the district.

6783. Do you not believe that one of the reasons why the collection of the county cess is more expensive than that of the poor rate is, that it is very difficult for persons to get security for the large amount required in the barony; and that in consequence of the security required being so great, very few persons can come into the field and offer to collect the county cess?—That may be one reason; but generally speaking it is a very much higher class of person, and a much more respectable class of person who collects the grand jury cess than those who collect the poor rate, and they have a staff, too.

6784. Is not that one of the reasons why it is so expensive; is it not the fact that most of the barony cess collectors do not collect the rates at all themselves, but have sub-collectors who collect for them?—There are a great many such cases, I dare say.

6785. If the baronies were divided into smaller districts, could you not get persons of smaller means who would be able to get ample security for the smaller districts, and who would, collecting the cess themselves, be able to collect it at a much lower rate than those gentlemen who have to employ deputies?—I am quite sure of that.

6786. Should you see any objection to that?—I do, in this way; I have always thought, even at the board of guardians, that we ought to see what would be a fair price. I would never advertise for tenders for the collection of the cess. You would get men to propose to do it for 4 d., and even for 3 d., to get into the thing, as they say. I should always think what hire the labourer was worth, and I should give them that, not giving too much. I think that 1 s. is too much.

6787. If ample security were given for the collection and payment of this rate, why should the county be at a loss by paying a higher rate than it could be done for by men who gave ample security?—I can only answer that question by saying, that I am quite sure that you would get men to tender for very much lower terms than at present, and not only for that, but for every office.

6788. But do you not think that you would not only get men to tender, but that you would get men by whom the collection would be done in the most satisfactory manner, and whose security would be amply sufficient if any defalcation arose?—I am sure you would.

6789. Do you not believe then that men could be got to collect the county cess to the utmost satisfaction at a much lower rate than is at present paid for collection, if the baronies were divided into smaller districts?—I am quite sure that you would, and I am quite sure that the present collectors would collect at a lower rate if it were put up to competition in that way.

6790. You also consider, do you not, that the levying of the county cess upon tenements under 4 l. in value, is one cause, and a very strong cause, why a higher rate should be paid for the collection of the cess than for the collection of the poor rate?—Yes; it is a more troublesome business.

6791. Nearly all the arrears and bad debts under the county cess, arise in these very small tenements, do they not?—I do not say that; I think that they are sometimes the best paid.

6792. Although they are the most difficult in collection?—They are the most difficult in collection, because they have to go to such a number of small holdings; it is not the amount, so much as the great number which causes the difficulty; I think that class of people very often pay wonderfully well.

6793. Is it your opinion that it is the tenant, or the landlord, who pays the county cess in reality?—The landlord.

6794. Do you consider that the landlord pays the whole of it in every instance?—I think he does.

6795. Then how am I to understand your argument against exempting those occupiers under 4 l.; you stated, did you not, in answer to the Honourable Member for the county of Galway, that you objected to exempting those occupiers under 4 l., because you considered that every man should contribute to the taxation of the country?—Exactly.

6796. If it be true that the landlords are the parties who pay this tax, and that the occupiers in reality do not pay it, why do you say that they should not be exempt from the payment, because every man should contribute to the taxation of the country?—I mean that that is calculated in the amount of rent that they pay. I hope that you did not think that I meant that they directly paid it; but I say that the landlord indirectly pays it, because I think that in the case of a man who takes a 4 l. holding, the landlord calculates all the charges and everything upon that, and he lets it to him upon that calculation.

6797. Therefore at the present moment the tenants of those small holdings in reality do not contribute to the taxation of the country?—They pay, of course, like anybody else, in the same way as the largest tenant does.

6798. But if this tax were done away with, the landlord's rent would be the same, would it not?—I think so.

6799. It is the landlord, therefore, who really pays it, is it not?—Yes; but not immediately.

6800. Then the difference in the adoption of the proposal for exempting those men would be merely this: that the landlord pays it at the present moment, as you say, and that if the Honourable Member for the county of Galway's suggestion were carried out, he would still continue to pay it; but that he would pay it directly instead of paying it indirectly?—Yes. Perhaps the Committee misunderstood me; but what I intended to convey was, that the landlord makes, or ought to make, his calculations upon the different charges, and the tenant in the same way, whether paying 3 l. or 100 l., should make his calculations as to the charges affecting that holding. In that way I intended to convey that the landlord and the tenant calculate it in letting and taking land.

6801. Therefore the landlord at present in reality pays the county cess for those holdings under 4 l. in a diminished rent, does he not?—It is equally applicable to any other holding.

6802. Of course it is; but I only want to confine your attention to those 4 l. holdings at present; does not the landlord now in reality pay the county cess for those small holdings in a diminished rent?—He does.

6803. Why then do you see any objection to asking the landlord to pay that sum directly which he now pays indirectly?—For the very reason which I stated, viz., that I think that every one in the country ought to contribute to the taxes, and to be aware that there are taxes to which they should contribute. It makes little difference to me whether the man pays 4 l. or 100 l.

6804. Are you also against the division of the cess in the case of tenements over 4 l.?—Yes.

6805. Is it upon the same principle that you are against it in that case?—I think I stated that it would very much disturb the relations between landlord and tenant.

6806. That is with regard to past contracts; but, with regard to future contracts, is your objection on the same ground?—With regard to future contracts, I think it would be worse for the tenant, because I think the landlord would make a calculation which would be very often detrimental rather than advantageous to the tenant.

6807. But do you think the landlord has any power of exacting any rent he likes for a new farm?—I have a sensitive feeling that he has not.

6808. The tenant will not pay more than it is worth, will he?—The landlord will make his calculation.

Mr. E. Smith.

16 June 1868.

calculation, and so will the tenant. It will be a bargain between them.

6809. But in the case of a farm out of lease, which is put up to the highest bidder, the tenant makes his calculation, and the landlord makes his calculation; in what way would the tenant be injured by the landlord having to pay the county cess on this farm, because the tenant will not give more than it is worth in any case?—I see no reason for giving half more than the whole.

6810. But will you explain to the Committee in what way this candidate for a tenancy is injured by the landlord being obliged hereafter to pay half the county cess upon this farm which is put up to competition?—There are a great many lettings at present that men are disposed to leave as they are; but if there were new arrangements made, I think there would be, perhaps, an increase of rent, as well as a calculation of this tax, to which you allude.

6811. You refer to existing tenancies; but supposing that such existing tenancies were excepted, would there not be a strong inducement to the landlord to leave existing tenancies as they were; because, in existing tenancies, they would not have to pay any of the county cess?—Supposing that they were tenants at will, tenants that had no leases, how would you deal with them?

6812. Supposing that existing tenancies from year to year were not included in the operation of the law, would you have any objection to having the cess being divided in all future contracts where a new tenant came in?—One of my objections to it would be the dissatisfaction which it would cause with the neighbouring holders; those men who had not the advantage which the other men would have, or would be supposed to have. They would naturally suppose it to be an advantage, and a great advantage if they got half the cess allowed them by their landlord, and I think there would be a disturbance of their relations.

6813. But is not that a dissatisfaction which could be very easily settled, by the tenant coming in and offering to make a new agreement with the landlord?—Of course; there is nothing of that sort that could not be settled in that way.

6814. Is not that a disadvantage which they could themselves terminate immediately?—Of course.

6815. And the landlord would probably be very glad to enter into a new arrangement, would he not?—I think that a great many new arrangements would be rendered necessary by that step.

6816. Necessary, in consequence of the tenants desiring it?—No; but necessary in consequence of the imposition upon the landlord of the payment of half the cess.

6817. In all new agreements?—I think that in all new agreements it would create great dissatisfaction amongst the old holders.

6818. But, as I suggested, they could put themselves on the same footing, could they not?—Of course they could; but I do not think they would benefit by it.

6819. You do not think, therefore, that many of them would do it?—I do not think they would.

6820. Therefore, you do not see any great reason why there would be any great disarrangement of existing tenancies, if such a law were passed?—I do not thoroughly understand the Honourable Member's question; but I think I cannot state it more distinctly to the Committee than that I think it would not be to the advantage of the tenant, and that I think it would very much disturb the relations between the landlord and the tenant; and I see no reason to alter that opinion.

6821. With regard to malicious injuries, I understood you to say that you considered that this system of granting compensation for malicious injuries did not lead to the discovery of the criminals in many cases?—I do not think it does often, or perhaps at all.

6822. Is there an impression in your part of the country, that if the criminal was discovered, the claim for compensation would fall to the ground?—I think not.

6823. Do you think that the present system prevents the commission of these crimes?—I think it does.

6824. In what way do you think it has a deterrent effect?—I do not think that neighbours would like to commit a malicious injury if they thought they were themselves to be obliged to contribute to the payment of compensation for it.

6825. Do you think those malicious injuries are generally speaking committed by neighbours who would have to pay compensation for them eventually?—I cannot give an accurate opinion upon that; but it is generally somebody in the neighbourhood. Probably it is about land taken by another party. We always believe that there must be malice, though we are very seldom able to trace the offender.

6826. Is it not very often done by a person who pays no tax at all?—That may be the case.

6827. Is it not a very usual case that an evicted tenant commits injury of this kind against the man who takes his farm after him?—Yes; but it is so seldom detected that that is all matter of surmise.

6828. If you compel the neighbours to contribute to the payment of compensation in the case of a malicious injury, do you not thereby assume that it is the neighbours who have committed the crime?—We punish the neighbours at all events, because it is generally put in the immediate locality, but it does not follow that the neighbours even if they do not commit the crime may not be in some way accessory to it.

6829. Mr. *Gregory*.] Is not the evidence which you receive before the grand jury generally to the effect that suspicion lights upon some of the neighbours?—Yes.

6830. *Chairman*.] Do you think that it rests with the whole townland that you put it on, or the whole barony, or parish?—It is always dealt with as such.

6831. Do you deal with it on the belief that you make the guilty parties pay?—That is our general belief, because it is only in that way that we should have reason to alter the imposition of it on any particular place.

6832. So you believe that these malicious injuries are generally the work of a large body of people, and not of one individual who may happen to have a spite against the injured party?—I do not say that; one individual might do it, but it is seldom, as I said before, that we have any means of knowing who has done it, though there may be suspicion.

6833. But you go upon the assumption, which you

0.68. R R

Mr. R. Ruthven. — 28 June 1858.

you cannot of course prove, that is generally speaking has not been the work of one, but that it has either been the work of many, or of one, supported by many?—Yes, or connived at by many.

6834. And that is the justification for charging it upon the neighbours?—Upon the immediate locality. That is the only justification that I know of.

6835. If that justification did not exist, would you consider this system to be a fair one?—I should say not; in that case I might as well charge another barony with it.

6836. For instance, if a criminal were discovered and he were found to be an evicted tenant who had no interest in the building, and no relative there, and the case was proved against him, do you consider that it would be fair in that case that the surrounding townlands should have to pay for his crime?—That is a question which is very difficult to answer, for I would not like to punish an unoffending party, and yet I should not like to deprive an injured man of any compensation.

6837. Do you not think that in the case of buildings of the value of, say 50*l*., or 100*l*., persons ought to be protected against injury by fire by insurance rather than by coming upon the county for compensation?—It would be most desirable; but these people, I suppose, have never heard of insurance in their lives, and thatched cabins are generally not likely to be insured.

6838. Are thatched cabins generally worth 50*l*. or 100*l*.?—I never saw a thatched cabin that was worth 50*l*. or 100*l*.

6839. My question referred to buildings of considerable value?—I think it would be very desirable in such cases if insurance could be substituted.

6840. Do you not think that in such cases parties should have no claim for compensation for injury by fire?—Certainly not.

6841. (General *Dunne*.] How could you compel them by law to insure?—In the case of large buildings, I think, it would be very desirable if they were insured.

6842. *Chairman*.] With regard to the question of their being compelled by law to insure, I presume that you understand me to mean that they should have no claim for compensation, leaving it to themselves to insure or not, as they thought proper?—Of course, I did not understand you to mean that it should be compulsory.

6843. In fact, that would be in the nature of an indirect legal penalty on the man who did not insure, would it not?—It might be considered to be so.

6844. Colonel *French*.] Did I rightly understand you, in answer to the Honourable Member for Galway, to state, that when at the adjourned sessions there was no magistrate present all the tenders could be brought before the grand jury, and be taken before them in the same manner as at the adjourned sessions?—No; what I intended to convey was, that where, there were adjourned sessions, and where there were no tenders submitted to the adjourned sessions, then it would be competent for the grand jury to receive those tenders that never were sent to the adjourned sessions; but when there were no adjourned sessions, no tenders could be received by the grand jury; that, I think, is rather an anomaly. I am stating to you the result of my experience of its having been decided by successive judges of assize. The question was first raised in the county of Mayo, and afterwards raised in the county of Galway, and the judges decided that the sessions not having been held the grand jury could not receive the tenders.

6845. The secretaries of grand juries are paid now by a salary, together with fees, are they not?—They are.

6846. Do you think that an advisable plan?—No; I think it would be better to give them a stated salary.

6847. What suggestion would you make with regard to the present fees?—Something like the stamps that are used in the petty sessions courts might be adopted, so that the country should not lose anything by the change; I think it would be very easy to compute what their fees are, and to give them a salary in lieu of them.

6848. But you would keep up the present fees by way of stamps put to the credit of the county? —I would keep up the present fees by means of stamps. If the county was to pay an additional sum I think the contractors could very easily contribute the payments which they do now in the form of fees to the secretary.

6849. Then you think that the present fees should be placed to the credit of the county, and you still think it advisable that the contractors should pay those fees?—I think so.

6850. *Mr. Gregory*.] It would be much more satisfactory to the secretary himself, would it not? —I am sure it would.

6851. Is it not rather an undignified position for him to be exacting fees from applicants for his own private use?—I am sure it is. The other plan would be much more desirable.

6852. Colonel *French*.] As to the management of lunatic asylums, have you a lunatic asylum for your own county separately?—It was a district lunatic asylum, but by degrees we are getting separated from all the counties. We were joined with Mayo, and we have the county of Roscommon still associated with Galway.

6853. Do you see any reason why the lunatic asylums, particularly where there is one for a county, should not be under the same control, and the same management as regards pay, &c., as the gaols under the present system?—I think it would be very desirable to give a representation upon the management to the different counties interested.

6854. But, as far as the money is concerned, you know now that the present system under the Board of Control in Dublin is, that the money is sent down every three months for the payment of the bills of the asylums, and that there are compulsory presentments at each assizes to pay those sums back to the Board of Control?—Yes.

6855. In your opinion would it not be better to levy those sums which are requisite for the support of the lunatic asylums in each half year upon a warrant, and that they should be placed in the hands of the treasurer, as at present the money for the support of the gaols is placed, and to the credit of the Board of Superintendence?—I think it would be a great improvement.

6856. Do you think that the grand jury (we will say) should have the nomination of the governors for the asylum in the same way as they have the nomination of the Board of Superintendence?—That would be very desirable. The gallant colonel knows, I think, very well how the presentment is sent down, and we know nothing more about it.

6857. General

6657. General *Dunne*.] It is an imperative presentment, is it not?—It is.

6658. Colonel *French*.] You have been a grand juror for a considerable number of years, have you not?—I have.

6659. And you are fully acquainted with the entire system under which the county fiscal business in Ireland is managed, are you not?—I think I am.

6660. Are you aware that it is the most inexpensive system of any country in Europe?—I think it has been managed with great care and attention, and with as much economy as we can manage.

6661. But at the grand jury you have the advantage of the local knowledge and the personal interest, &c. of the chief persons in the county, have you not?—We have.

6662. Without any expense whatever?—Certainly.

6663. You are aware that the proceedings of the grand jury are in open court?—I am; that is to say, the fiscal business.

6664. The greatest possible publicity is given to it, is it not?—Certainly.

6665. You are aware, that under the system, should there be anything considered to be illegal without any expense any cesspayer can appeal to the judge to refuse his fiat?—Most assuredly.

6666. A question has been put to you as to the advisability of classifying the cesspayers, whether parochially, or according to the Poor Law unions; do you consider that to be necessary?—I consider the present system to be objectionable, as I have already stated.

6667. But do you believe that any cesspayer paying a high cess in the barony has not full knowledge of the state of all the roads in his district?—He can have full knowledge if he likes.

6668. Generally speaking, he does like, does he not?—He does.

6669. Is it not to his advantage to know, for two reasons; one being that he has to bear a proportion of the expense, and the other being that the state of the roads is of material interest to him in sending his produce to market?—Yes.

6670. A question has been put to you by the Chairman as to the division of the cess, and you have stated (and I think you gave very full reasons for that statement) that you see no advantage, at least to the tenant, in the division of the cess; is that your opinion?—That is my conscientious opinion.

6671. The question put to you was, whether a tenant, a man of capital, would not insist that he would not give more than the rent which he considered the land to be worth, and you answered that he would not; but on the other hand, in making a calculation of the cess, do you think that the landlord would take less for his land than he considers to be the value of the land and the cess together?—I am sure he would not.

6672. Do you think that it would be an advantage, in order to secure a better attendance of the cesspayers, that a ballot out of 100, or out of a certain number of names, should take place at the grand jury?—I said that I preferred that to the present system, but to the Chairman I stated that if it could be done in any way, so as to secure a representation from each portion of the barony, I would prefer it.

6673. But in relation to the present system, do you think it would be advisable that there should be no doubt as to who the cesspayer was that was to serve?—I think that it is very desirable.

6674. And that it should be published at the same time, and that instead of a ballot to be drawn out of the number of cesspayers, the actual number appointed should be named?—Certainly.

6675. You are of opinion that it would be desirable (and in that I believe everybody agrees with you) if at a fair expense we could have representation even in the small thing of taxation, to keep the two together?—I think so. I would like to see representation.

6676. Therefore any proposal for the election of the associated cesspayers would, *primâ facie*, meet your view, would it not?—Quite so.

6677. The system that is complained of as regards the grand jury is, that they are not a permanent body; do you think that by appointing a certain number of men as a board between sessions and sessions, who would meet, say monthly, and go into all the questions as to how the collection was going on, and as to the amount of money that they would be empowered to draw upon the certificate of the county surveyor for contractors, all that complaint would be sufficiently met?—I think it would. I think it would be very desirable to have a standing committee.

6678. The division of the county cess, in your opinion, would involve, and must involve, necessarily, a pecuniary loss to the tenant. If, for instance, the half cess on a tenancy of 3 *l.* was 1 *s.* in the £., it would be 1 *s.* 6 *d.* that he would have to pay. Do you not think that the landlord would put on double or treble that, in order to meet contingencies?—I think he would have a margin which would not be advantageous to the tenant.

6679. And do you not think that it would be an advisable and a sensible thing on his part to do so?—Of course it would be wise on the part of the landlord; I think that the landlord would look after his own interests in the same way as the tenant would look after his.

6680. Do you not think that even a tenant under 4 *l.*, having to pay 6 *d.* or 8 *d.* in the £., which would be about the average, would have a kind of interest in preserving public works?—I stated at first that I thought every one ought to bear his share of the taxation of the country.

6681. And do you not think that he gets full value in the use of roads, and everything else, for the small amount that he pays?—Every man in the community that ever goes from his house, must feel the advantage of the roads.

6682. Do you think that this question, raised between landlord and tenant, will tend very much to disturb the relations which have hitherto existed between them?—I endeavoured to convey that I thought it would have that effect.

6683. Do you think that it must necessarily tend towards the ejectment of tenants from those small holdings under 4 *l.*?—I do not know; I have not had much experience of ejectments; I never evicted a man in my life.

6684. But I believe it is generally the case as between landlord and tenant in the Province of Connaught, that ejectments are very rare, and that the same families go on for hundreds of years under the same landlords?—I think so.

6685. There was a question put to you by the Chairman, as to putting up a farm to be let to the highest bidder; is that the custom of letting in the West of Ireland?—No.

Mr. R. [illegible].

16 June 1868.

6886. Is not the landlord always desirous if he can keep the same tenants at the expiration of the lease?—I have had tenants for years, and I should never think of disturbing them, though I could get a higher rent.

6887. A question has been put to you as to superannuation, and the demands which are lately coming up from every person connected with the fiscal business of the county for superannuation; do you consider that persons who do not give up the whole of their time to county business are entitled to superannuation?—I should say not.

6888. Do you conceive, for instance, to take the case of a Bill before the House, that a clerk in the office of a Master in Chancery, to whom this Master in Chancery has given the audit of the county accounts in Ireland should be entitled to superannuation?—That is a matter upon which I can give no opinion.

6889. Do you consider that every person connected with the Poor Law, either as a medical man, or otherwise, is entitled to superannuation?—I think not; but I think all these cases depend upon circumstances.

6890. Mr. *Gregory*.] Is it your opinion, that where persons do not give their full time to the duties of their office, they are not entitled to superannuation?—That is my opinion; but a man who may be worn out in your service I think has a claim.

6891. *Chairman*.] Do you think that any disadvantage has arisen to the public service from the inability to grant superannuation, and the consequent retention in office of men who are really unfitted to discharge their duties; and are you aware in the county of Galway, at any time of an officer being retained in his office on account of there being no ability to grant him a superannuation allowance?—I am aware of such an instance, but it did not remain very long. We had a county surveyor, whose infirmity of health and declining energies made it very desirable that he should retire; I think he had been with us for over 30 years; that I should have looked upon as an exceptional case, and I should have been very glad if we had had the power to grant him a superannuation.

6892. Colonel *French*.] That no longer exists, does it?—It exists no longer.

6893. *Chairman*.] But occasionally do not instances happen where officers are retained where they are really incapable, in consequence of there being no power of granting them a superannuation allowance?—I can only tax our county with that one instance, which did not remain very long.

6894. Mr. *Gregory*.] Which do you think would be the greater inconvenience; to establish a new system of quartering a number of people upon the county, or that we should have suffered temporary inconvenience by the retention of this county surveyor?—I think the case which the Honourable Chairman put to me is an exceptional one, and I should not be in favour of a general superannuation. We could find very many active men who would very soon become very inactive.

6895. Colonel *French*.] I believe you were asked whether you did not think that a power should be given to compel the attendance of witnesses in the case of malicious injuries?—I do not think that that question was put to me. It was in reference to a letter which was read by the Honourable Member for the county of Galway. I said that we had no necessity for it in Galway, and that, therefore, I had never turned my attention to it.

6896. Are you aware in your experience of any difficulty in having witnesses up on malicious injuries?—No, I have never found any difficulty.

6897. On the contrary, in several cases do not the people in the neighbourhood pull together and fee counsel to oppose the presentment?—Generally that is my experience.

6898. Mr. *Gregory*.] If the power did not exist, would you object to that power of summoning witnesses being given?—A case might arise in which there might be intimidation, and in that case I think it would be very desirable that the power should be given if it does not exist; but it is a case in which, as I say, I have had no experience.

6899. Colonel *French*.] Do you not think that if a malicious injury is presented for by the grand jury, and the presentment sessions, it is more likely to carry out the object if it is placed on a small locality; for instance, if it is placed on certain town lands, where the outrage is supposed to have originated, is it not much better than if it is placed on the parish, or on the county at large?—We never place it on the county at large.

6900. That would render it perfectly inefficient as a measure of punishment to the adjacent town lands, would it not?—Quite so.

6901. You stated, did you not, that you are in Galway (but I am afraid not legally) in the habit of exempting from the incidence of the fine the land which belongs to the person injured?—We have been in the habit of doing that, and I heard to-day for the first time that it was not legal.

6902. You have been asked some questions in relation to the annual revision, do you consider that annual revision, which is very expensive, to be at all necessary?—No, not as an annual revision.

6903. Do you think that once in about seven years would be sufficient for a revision, and that in the mean time the clerks of the unions could make any alteration that was necessary?—I should not like to fix any time, but I should say from five to seven years might be allowed to elapse.

6904. But you would have it at much longer intervals than a year?—Certainly.

6905. These presentments come down compulsorily upon the grand jury, do they not?—Yes.

6906. They are sent down from Dublin, and they must be levied?—They must be levied.

6907. There is no explanation which is at all satisfactory to the members of the grand jury, is there?—Not a word.

6908. Are you aware what the original cost of the revision in Ireland was; for instance, could you state what it was in the county of Galway?—In the county of Galway, if you will allow me to refer to a memorandum, I can state what the revision has cost. In the year, down to the 1st of May 1861, it cost 332 l.; in the year 1867 it was 630 l. 5 s. That is only half of the cost, the other half being paid by the Government.

6909. Only half of the expense of the revision is paid by the counties, I believe?—So I understand.

6910. So that whatever the amount charged to the counties is, the actual cost was double that amount?—It was.

6911. Do you agree with the general attacks which

which have been made upon the result of the Irish Grand Jury Law?—I do not.

6912. Are you aware that upwards of 50,000 miles of road in Ireland, public roads, and what they call private roads here, are kept in repair for a very moderate sum of money, amounting to less than half a million?—I do not know the exact sum.

6913. Twenty-six thousand miles of road in this country were bankrupt for 6,000,000 *l.* I do not think we owe any money in Ireland, on double the extent of road. Have you turned your attention at all to this officer who has been forced upon the grand jury, called an auditor of grand jury accounts, and are you aware that compulsory presentments are sent down twice a year to pay a Master in Chancery for this business, which he tells us he discharges, and do you see that the counties get any value for their money?—I do not think they do.

6914. General *Dunne.*] You would have an audit of the accounts, of course?—Yes.

6915. Colonel *French.*] Would it not be a very small addition to the work which the Poor Law Commissioners do, who are paid out of the Consolidated Fund, to audit the grand jury accounts twice a year?—It would.

6916. Are you aware that the first batch of lunatic asylums were originally built without any communication with the counties, or with the parties by whom the expenses were to be borne?—I was not quite aware of it, but it is very likely.

6917. Are you aware of the rapid way in which the expense of those asylums is increasing?—I can tell you what it has cost the county of Galway, though the comparison which I am drawing is not strictly correct, inasmuch as we have to reimburse the county of Mayo for their contribution to our buildings. In the year 1855 it was 1,811 *l.*; in the year 1866 it was 3,365 *l.* 15 *s.* Then, I suppose, we began to pay our share to the county of Mayo, for I find that, in the year 1867, it is 4,061 *l.*, and in the last spring assizes, which is but a half-year, I find it has reached to 2,904 *l.* 17 *s.* 6 *d.*, which would be over 5,800 *l.* for the year. It is gradually increasing.

6918. Are you aware of any reason why the expense of lunatic asylums should be thrown upon the grand jury levy?—I am not, indeed; but it is a tax which we have been long paying, and over which the grand jury have no control.

6919. Why should they be made the medium of levying large sums of money upon the county for those purposes?—Very few members of our grand jury know anything at all of the expenditure upon the lunatic asylum.

6920. It has been stated that lunatic asylums ought not to be local charges, but that they ought in England, Scotland, and Ireland to be paid for from the Consolidated Fund; what is your view of that?—I should be exceedingly happy if that could be carried out.

6921. In fact, our lunatic asylums cost ten times as much as keeping the same portion of our poor people. The same objection refers to all presentments being compulsorily sent down by the Board of Works, does it not?—Yes.

6922. There was a question put to you as to why the collector of the grand jury cess should have a higher salary, or a higher rate of poundage than the poor collector; is there not one reason which has not yet been stated, and which is that the collectors of the county cess, before any presentment can be made for the payment of their fees, are obliged to lodge to the credit of the county all the money which they have not collected, so that, in fact, there should be no deficiency in the amount which they are bound to levy?—I do not quite understand that question.

6923. Must they not, out of their own resources, pay up any amount which may be deficient?—To enable them to get the 1 *s.* in the £., they must make up any deficiency in the collection. They may leave the collection until very near the assizes; they still hold the warrant, which is operative, I think, for two years, but they do lodge the money very often in advance.

6924. But the collector could get no presentment for his salary without paying in the full amount, could he?—No presentment could be got.

6925. In fact, would it not be contrary to the law if the judge fiated the presentment under those circumstances?—I am not sure that he might not give something on account, but I am quite sure that he would not give the 1 *s.* in the pound.

6926. Is not another reason why the collection of the poor rate is lower than the collection of the county cess the smallness of the area on which the collection has to be made in the one case as compared with the area in the other case?—Yes; and I mentioned also the numerous holdings to which the collector of the grand jury cess is obliged to go in excess of what the poor rate collector has to go to.

6927. In the Poor Law collection, I believe, it is the universal custom for the collector to do the work himself?—I believe so.

6928. And he has a greater facility for getting security, has he not, the sum being so much smaller?—Yes.

6929. And are not the sureties better off; because he is forced to pay in every 100 *l.* as soon as he has collected it?—Yes; but I forgot to state that another reason is, that there are greater facilities afforded for enforcing the payment of poor rates from the occupiers than there are under the grand jury laws.

6930. If the collectors of the county cess were, immediately on the warrants being put into their hands, to levy the entire amount, and were bound to lodge it in the bank, what benefit would that be to the county?—I stated before that I did not see any great advantage in enforcing an immediate collection.

6931. If it is in the bank to meet the cheques which are signed by the treasurer and the clerk of the Crown it is ample time, is it not?—Quite so.

6932. And that is much more a bank question than a county question, is it not?—Quite so.

6933. General *Dunne.*] With regard to those 4 *l.* tenements they are much more numerous in the west of Ireland than in the east?—I take it that they are.

6934. And therefore any feeling with regard to getting rid of 4 *l.* tenements, which are generally in towns in Leinster would, perhaps, not obtain so strongly in Connaught; is it not the case that the 4 *l.* tenements of which the collectors complain as finding it difficult to collect the cess from them, are chiefly in towns with us, and not in the country?—There are many with us in the country; but, of course, the greater number are in towns.

6935. Do you find any great objection to the way in which the process servers are appointed now?

Mr. *R. Bodkin.* 15 June 1868.

Mr. R. [illegible]. 16 June 1868.

now?—It is the assistant barrister who does that.

6936. Mr. *Blake*.] I understood you, in your replies to the Honourable Member for the county of Galway, to say that even with regard to future lettings you would be against the division of the cess between the landlord and the tenant?—That is my opinion.

6937. Is not one of the disadvantages under which the tenant labours under the present cess system that he never knows exactly what he has to pay, and that he is never able to calculate with any precision the amount which he may have to pay?—I think that he makes a very probable calculation. We know pretty nearly what our county cess is; it does not vary more than 1 *d.* in the pound, I think, at any time.

6938. But may not circumstances arise sometimes, such as the breaking down of bridges, the construction of new works in the county, or the building of gaols and lunatic asylums, and things of that kind, which may increase the amount of the cess?—It is quite possible.

6939. When once a landlord makes an agreement with the tenant as to the rent which he is to pay him, does it matter to the landlord what the county cess may be after that, as the whole of it is paid by the occupier?—I think that the landlord has, or at least ought to have, a very great interest in everything affecting his tenant; and I think that the landlord feels almost as anxious to keep down the cess as the tenant himself.

6940. Very often is it not rather an object to the landlord to have as large an outlay as possible in the barony in which he may have his property, in the way of roads and other works, as being calculated to enhance the value of the property?—I have never known an instance of that influencing any landlord.

6941. But as a matter of fact, may it not be his interest to have a considerable outlay, for instance, in making improved roads in the barony in which his property is, or in the building of bridges, and other works of that character?—What I understand you to say is, that improvements in a barony are a greater object to a landlord than to a tenant. If that is the question put to me, it might, perhaps, be so, because the tenancy is not permanent; but I think that the tenant has a proportionate interest in everything concerning the county as much as the landlord.

6942. The landlord's object, then, is not to prevent outlay, is it?—My experience is, that the landlords as grand jurors are as careful and as anxious to prevent expenditure as if we were to pay the whole of it ourselves.

6943. As you are in favour of the whole of the tax being paid by the tenant, do I understand you correctly that you are in favour of the ratepayers nominating their own representatives upon the baronial board?—I should be delighted. I stated, I think, to the Honourable Member for the county of Galway that I would prefer the ballot in the the grand jury to the present system; but if the barony could be so divided that the grand jury or the landlords would have nothing to do with the election, I would prefer that the cesspayers themselves should make their own selection.

6944. Would you have the baronial boards composed of representatives from the magistrates and of ratepayers elected by the ratepayers?—Yes, by the ratepayers; I should have no objection if it were wished, to exclude the magistrates from any voice at all in the question.

6945. You also expressed an opinion in favour of the grand jury being a continuous board, did you not?—A delegation of the grand jury; I am in favour of some body which would act between assizes and assizes, in the discharge of the duty which may suddenly or unexpectedly arise.

6946. Could not that be satisfactorily performed by the county board, or the grand jury (call it whichever you please), provided it was a continuous county board?—I prefer the old system of the grand jury.

6947. If you give to the ratepayer the privilege of sending his representative upon the baronial board, upon the same principle would you not also give him the privilege of electing his representative upon the county board, which is to check the expenditure by the baronial board?—The very reason for my giving him representation in that way would induce me to allow property to have its representation upon the grand jury.

6948. But would not property have its representation, if you required from a member of the larger board a certain qualification, say to be rated at 50 *l.* a year?—My experience is, that in the representation of property, the more intelligent class, and the higher class of man that you have upon the grand jury, the safer the ratepayer is in his hands.

6949. But in your own barony, for instance, would not a gentleman of your position and property be likely to be elected to represent the barony by the ratepayers?—You will excuse my answering a question about myself; but I should have no personal fear of not having always a sufficient representation in the barony; at the same time I tell you fairly that I should prefer the present system of election by the sheriff, each barony being represented.

6950. With regard to the maintenance of the pauper lunatics, I infer from some of your answers that you are of opinion that it is unfair that the occupier should pay the whole of the maintenance of the pauper lunatics, as he does at present?—I do not know that I was asked any question relating to it.

6951. What is your opinion about it?—I think we pay a very large sum of money to the lunatic asylum, without having any control over it.

6952. Are you aware that at present where the occupier only pays half the cost of the maintenance of a sane pauper, he pays the whole cost of the maintenance of the insane pauper?—I am aware that it is levied off the county as the grand jury cess, and not as the poor rate.

6953. In principle is it not unfair that where the occupier only pays half the amount for the sane pauper, he should pay the whole amount for the insane pauper?—It is assuming all through that it is right that the payment should be divided.

6954. Do you think that in that instance it ought to be divided?—I do not; I do not see any particular reason for it in that particular instance, for the reason I stated before, that it would all find its level in another way.

6955. Mr. *Maguire*.] Do you not think that it would be more satisfactory to the occupier to have the rate divided by law, between him and the owner of the property?—I do not.

6956. Would you, yourself, think it expedient to have the whole burden of the poor rate, for instance,

instance, placed upon one class?—It would come back to what I stated before. If it were originally so, the same thing would apply. If I were asked to-morrow whether the Poor Law ought to be divided, I would say that there was the same reason for putting the whole upon one class, as for putting half.

6957. That is, in other words, that the owners of property, the rich portion of the community, should not sacrifice anything towards the maintenance of the poor?—I do not mean that. My objection to the division of the cess entirely rests upon the belief that a landlord in letting his land makes his arrangements, and that the tenant makes his arrangements.

6958. But as a matter of abstract justice, and independently altogether of what the results would be at one time, or the other, do you not think that the burden, which is a public burden, ought to be divided equally between all classes of the community?—I do not; I think it is divided, but not directly divided.

6959. Under any circumstances the county cess is not, either directly or indirectly, divided; but it is put upon one class and upon one class alone, is it not?—It is just like rent.

6960. But as a matter of fact, is it not so?—One class pays it ostensibly.

6961. A suggestion was made in a question which was asked (and you seemed quite to agree with it), that it was about one of the most inexpensive systems in any country in the world?—I did not say in the world. I think the gallant colonel, the Member for Roscommon said, "in the world;" but I do not profess any knowledge on the subject.

6962. You said, I think, that it was an inexpensive system when well and economically worked?—You will understand me to have only spoken from my own experience, and as comparing it with the management of the Poor Law system, of the expense and inconvenience, of which I have a good deal of experience. I think it is as economically and well worked.

6963. Is it not a most inexpensive system to the owners of property in the country, and not inexpensive to the other class, who have to pay the entire burden?—You assume that it is on one class, and I do not admit that.

6964. At any rate, there are 50,000 miles of road in Ireland, according to the gallant colonel's statement, and I believe they are very well maintained?—So he stated.

6965. Am I right in saying that, according to the view of the ratepayers of the country, these roads have been made, and are maintained solely by the occupying class?—There I differ from you again.

6966. But at any rate, they ostensibly pay for it, do they not?—Exactly.

6967. What was exactly the meaning which you attached to an answer which you gave, in which you seemed to think that there was some advantage in having the humbler classes taxed, because it gave them an interest in maintaining the public works of the country?—I did not say the public works. I stated in answer to the Honourable Member, who asked the question, that I would like, that every man in the community should pay his proportion of the tax, whatever it may be, in the support and maintenance of those laws to which he owed his protection.

6968. Then as to the public, did you not say that it was a useful thing to tax a poor man, in order that he might have a keener appreciation of the value of public works, and therefore a greater interest in maintaining them?—We would all like to be exempt from taxation if possible.

6969. That is not the question that I asked you; what public works are there which it is necessary to preserve through this kind of interest, that is to say, by the taxation of the poor man, in order to give him a personal interest in it?—What apprehension would there be if a poor man paying under 4 *l.*, if you like, was freed from all taxation, either a road, or a bridge, or a gaol, would be in danger of being injured, either through his neglect, or through his malfeasance?—I do not mean to say that they would be at all injured.

6970. *General Dunne.*] Are not the roads made by the poorer classes, and do they not receive all the benefit of the expenditure?—Yes.

6971. Are not the roads as much used by them as by the rich?—Of course.

6972. *Mr. Maguire.*] Do I rightly understand you to say that the occupiers receive all the benefit of the roads and bridges and other works?—I did not intend to convey that.

6973. Of course the owners of property are benefited by those improvements?—Of course.

6974. You yourself as a landlord know that your property is improved, and that the country is generally improved by them, is it not?—No doubt the country generally is improved by them.

6975. Which of the two classes really has the larger interest in those improvements, or in the preservation of them?—I have always considered that we have all our proportionate interest, though of course the interest of a man at 8 *l.* a year is very small as compared with that of a man who has 4,000 *l.* or 5,000 *l.* a year.

6976. Taking it in that way, the man of 4,000 *l.* or 5,000 *l.* a year has a large interest, but is not his interest permanent and never ceasing, while that of the other man may cease to-morrow?—Yes, but then he ceases to pay taxes.

6977. But he originally helped to make the improvement, did he not?—Certainly.

6978. His interest may determine to-morrow, whereas the interest of the man who owns the property continues; and, therefore, is there not every reason in equity and justice, why the man who really has the larger interest, because it is a permanent or enduring interest, should pay a portion of that expenditure?—I cannot see it in that light, and I assure you it is from no unfriendly feeling towards the tenant.

6979. That I thoroughly believe, but I am endeavouring to get some explanation. Under any circumstances then, you go this length, that you think it is fair, inasmuch as no doubt the occupying class do pay, from your point of view, a very large proportion of the expenditure, that they should have the right of nominating their own representatives?—I should be very glad to see it.

6980. Would you exempt a man under 4 *l.* from paying the county cess?—I would not.

6981. Is not the collection attended with great hardship, from the poverty of the class, and with great difficulty to the collector?—As I endeavoured to explain to the Honourable Chairman, there is a great deal of difficulty to the collector, but

but it would surprise you, from what I hear, how that class of people do pay those taxes. They pay them far more readily than their rents.

6982. You would not exempt them, then?—That is my opinion now.

6983. At the baronial presentment sessions, would you allow a magistrate from another barony to come and interfere with the presentments of that barony?—I would not. I will illustrate that if you will allow me. I am very much opposed to allowing any magistrate to take part in the taxation of a barony in which he has not property. I made it a rule myself never to sit upon any presentment sessions in a barony where I had not property.

6984. But the law allows you to do so, does it not?—The law allows me to do it, and I always thought that that was a mistake.

6985. Then you would change the law?—I would change the law, because I would practice what I preach.

6986. Would you have, under any circumstances, an equal number of magistrates and an equal number of elected cesspayers?—I am always glad to meet as many cesspayers as have an interest.

6987. But supposing that you made an alteration in the law, would it not be a fair thing to have an equal number of both classes?—I think so. I do not object to a farmer attending at sessions, though he may not have landed property in the barony, if he pays taxes to a certain amount.

6988. Do you not think that if the cesspayer were elected, and if he were responsible to a constituent body for his actions, he would have a stronger sense of personal responsibility than he has as being only nominated?—I would much prefer seeing him elected.

6989. Mr. *Leader*.] Supposing the present law to be maintained for recovering compensation for malicious injuries, do you think the road sessions is the best tribunal to decide upon whether an injury is malicious or not, or would you let it go before the court of quarter sessions?—I think I should prefer the road sessions, and then I would have it go before the grand jury, because, as I stated before, we very often get more information between the sessions and the assizes; and then the grand jury exercises the power which they have over the sessions of changing it to the barony, or the half barony, or the parish, and then if the people are not satisfied with it, it is very constantly brought before a petty jury, so that it goes through three ordeals.

6990. Then you are in favour of retaining the investigation, as at present, before the road sessions?—There may be a better tribunal, but I would prefer it to the court of quarter sessions.

6991. Mr. *Dawson*.] I think you gave an answer from which we may judge what your opinion is upon the subject; but I wish to ask you if you are satisfied with the way in which the grand jury of the county is at present appointed?—I think I am; I live in one of the largest counties in Ireland, and we have, what few counties can say, a sufficient number of gentlemen to constitute three grand juries waiting in the box to be called; and I think, though there is sometimes a little heartburning in respect to the preferences given by the sheriff, when each barony is represented, we all feel satisfied.

6992. Do you think that the grand British first principle of taxation and representation going together is sufficiently exemplified in the present mode of choosing grand juries to have the control of a large county levy?—I have occasionally had to regret certain districts not being represented, parties not answering to their names, though the sheriff has complied with the Act; but, as a general rule, I think it has been satisfactory.

6993. Are you satisfied with the way in which the county surveyor's duties are generally performed in a county?—I am satisfied, generally speaking, though, of course, in a very large county there are very often complaints, and the county surveyors are very often held responsible for acts over which they have no control.

6994. Do you think that the county surveyor gives sufficient personal control and superintendence over the roads himself, taking into consideration the fact that he has a staff of assistant surveyors under him?—In our county, I think, generally speaking, they do so; we have two county surveyors.

6995. Mr. *Gregory*.] Do you think that they visit the roads, generally speaking, once or twice a year?—They must visit them once before every assizes; they must visit them twice a year, certainly, but they ought to visit them oftener.

6996. Mr. *Dawson*.] In evidence before this Committee the county surveyor of Clare said that he could not personally inspect the roads in his county more than once in two years; is that the case in the county of Galway?—I should not be at all satisfied with an answer of that sort; but Galway is a much larger county. I think that they should visit them very frequently, and I do not think that once every half-year is sufficient.

6997. Do you think that the present appointment of county surveyors by the Government is satisfactory?—I do not know that my opinion upon that subject would be of any consequence; but we never had but three county surveyors; two of them have been very good men, and the other has been superannuated.

6998. Mr. *Gregory*.] How do you account, as you have considerable experience in this matter, for the roads in your county being so inferior to the roads the moment you cross the border of the county of Clare; those in Clare being extremely well kept, and those in Galway being in some cases, and sometimes was abominable?—One reason which our county surveyors give for the roads not being so well kept in Galway is, that we do not give so good a price for the roads. I do not mean to say that that is a very valid excuse, but they say so.

6999. I presume that there is no difference between Galway and Clare as to the mode of taking the lowest tender, is there?—I have not experience of Clare, but I suppose not; I suppose they comply with the Act.

7000. Is there not equal facility for obtaining all the metal and material for making and maintaining roads?—The law empowers that. I will not go the length of saying that our roads are very bad; I think our roads in the western part of the county are very much improved of late.

7001. Some of them are extremely bad, but others are bad in comparison, are they not?—I think so.

7002. Do you not perceive a most marked difference in the roads the moment you pass the frontier of Galway and get into the county of Clare?—Yes; the roads in Clare are much better.

7003. But

Mr. R. Baffin. 16 June 1868.

7003. But you cannot give the reason why this difference exists?—I cannot; perhaps it is from the county surveyor not paying sufficient attention to them. If ever a road is bad in my neighbourhood, I appeal at once to the county surveyor. I think it would be very desirable that there should be some uniformity as to the scale of payment of county surveyors.

7004. *Chairman.*] Where does the difference exist at present?—I think the Act of the 19th and 20th Victoria gave power to the grand jury to raise the salaries of the county surveyors. Before that they got 300 *l.* a year, and 60 *l.* a year allowed for an office. By this Act it is optional with the grand jury to raise their salaries; in many counties they have done so, and it has created a jealousy in those in which it has not been done; and I would much prefer seeing that there was a uniform scale for every county, and that they were well paid and obliged to do their work properly.

7005. Before that Act passed, was it obligatory upon all grand juries to give a fixed sum?—Yes; I believe the maximum was 300 *l.* a year.

7006. What was the minimum?—Some counties did not give as much.

7007. Then the law is the same now as it was before, is it not, except that the maximum is different?—There is no limit now, I believe.

7008. There is a maximum salary now, is there not?—I think not.

7009. Have you looked at the scale under the late Act?—I have not; but there may be a maximum. I was speaking of what different grand juries have done. Some have raised it to 500 *l.*, and some to 600 *l.* a year.

7010. The maximum is all which the Act of Parliament fixes, and it is in the power of the grand jury to give the maximum or not; are you aware that that was the case before the Act passed, only that there was a different maximum?—I did not know that there was a maximum now.

7011. Do you object to allowing any discretionary power to grand juries to fix what the salary is to be?—The discretion which I would prefer would be to deduct from the salary where the work was not done; but I would prefer the salary being fixed by the Government, according to a schedule or scale.

Mr. JOHN ADAMS, called in; and Examined.

Mr. J. Adams.

7012. *Chairman.*] YOU are a Justice of the Peace for the county of Londonderry, and a Linen Merchant, are you not?—I am.

7013. And you were high sheriff of the county in the year 1863, were you not?—I was.

7014. Have you frequently been a member of the grand jury?—Yes.

7015. Have you also acted at the presentment sessions?—I have.

7016. And you have been selected by the cesspayers of the county of Londonderry to represent their views to this Committee, have you not?—I have.

7017. Do the cesspayers of the county of Londonderry object to the present grand jury system?—They do.

7018. What are their principal objections; what is the ground-work of their objections?—The two chief objections are to taxation without representation, and also that they have the whole burden of the cess to bear.

7019. Do they believe that neither on the presentment sessions nor at the grand jury is there any *bonâ fide* representation?—They do not think that it is elective.

7020. What alteration do you, on their behalf, propose to be made?—The alteration which the cesspayers feel should be made is, that elections of cesspayers should take place for the baronial boards.

7021. That the cesspayers who sit at the baronial sessions should be elected by the ratepayers?—By the ratepayers.

7022. Do they desire that that board should be composed exclusively of elected representatives?—Yes, of cesspayers elected by the cesspayers, and of magistrates elected by the magistrates.

7023. Do they also propose to supersede the grand jury?—They propose that there should be a separate fiscal board for the county to meet at the assizes, so as to separate the criminal from the fiscal business of the county.

7024. And that the county board should be equally elected?—The county board should be elected by the baronial boards.

7025. Is this proposed county board to take the place of the grand jury, or to take the place of the county-at-large sessions?—The intention in my mind is, that it should take the place of the grand jury.

7026. And should there be any subordinate tribunal corresponding to the county-at-large presentment sessions?—The feeling with the ratepayers is, that as they have to pay the taxation throughout the baronies for works upon the county at large, all those presentments for the county at large should be brought before each baronial sessions to have the opinion of those sessions upon them, so that the representatives from those baronial boards, when they went up to the county fiscal board, could have an opportunity of attending to them, and discussing them the better; and of either passing them, or rejecting them, or reducing them, as they thought right, through their representatives at the county fiscal board.

7027. But they would come before the baronial board merely to be discussed?—To be discussed. They might express an opinion, but the final decision would be through the representatives when they went to the county board.

7028. It is proposed that the cesspayers sitting at the baronial board should be elected; it would be necessary, then, to divide the baronies into districts, would it not?—They considered that they should be elected at the same time, and something in the same manner as the boards of guardians; but that is not exactly my own opinion.

7029. Would it not be satisfactory to them to have the associated cesspayers at the sessions elected, and to leave the grand jury as it is?—They would prefer having a fiscal board, and allowing the grand jury to attend to the criminal business of the county.

7030. But you are aware that the grand jury at present have no power, or a very trifling power, of initiating taxation at all?—There are some cases in which they have power, without the presentments coming through the road sessions, as in a case of the collection of the county cess, and some other things which I do not recollect at present.

7031. But the great bulk of the presentments must be passed by the presentment sessions before they can be passed by the grand jury, must they not?—Yes.

7032. If those baronial and county boards were established and the grand jury done away with, would it not be necessary to establish some independent body which would control those elective boards?—My view upon that subject would be that a board should be elected, perhaps taken from a section of the Board of Works, who are parties conversant with county affairs, to act in a somewhat similar capacity to that in which the Poor Law Commissioners act at present. I consider that one cause of the success of the Poor Law has been, that it is under the control of a Board of Commissioners who are free from any local prejudices. We could have the whole affairs managed in a similar manner throughout the whole kingdom; and my opinion is, that if such a board were established it would have a salutary effect in the management of the grand jury laws.

7033. Do you think that if those elective county boards were established, it would be necessary to have some controlling or directing power outside the county?—It would be better, I think, to have some board corresponding to the Poor Law Board.

7034. How would you propose that this commission should be paid?—In the same way as the Poor Law Commissioners are paid, by the Government. I do not see why they should pay the one and not pay the other. If they have the management and the appointment, I think it would be very fair that they should pay the cost.

7035. What powers would you give to this commission?—Somewhat similar powers to those that the Poor Law Commissioners have.

7036. Is the present system of county surveyors approved of by the ratepayers in your district?—No. I think there should be a better class of deputy surveyors, and that instead of there being one or two for each barony, there should be one man elected, after due advertisement had been made, by a competitive examination, and that the man should get a good salary of 150*l.* or 200*l.* a-year, and that he should attend exclusively to the business of the barony for which he is appointed.

7037. Are you aware whether the present county surveyors' assistants undergo any examination before their appointment?—I do not know whether they undergo any examination or not; but I think not.

7038. But if they did undergo an examination, would you consider that that would be satisfactory?—I think not; for I do not think that you can get a good-enough class of men at the salary given.

7039. Do you think that the salary given to the assistant surveyors is too low to ensure a good class of men for the office?—I think so.

7040. And do you think that the county surveyor should be altogether abolished, then?—Of course, during the existence of life interests, I should not interfere with the present system; but afterwards what I would call provincial inspectors should be appointed from a superior class of men, and those men should take a circuit or province, as the case might be; and they should have the superintendence of all extensive works, such as any works in the county at large, gaols, or court-houses, or new public roads, or new improvements.

7041. How would those men be paid?—would pay them proportionately by each county to which they attended. If they got a salary of 1,000*l.* or 1,200*l.* a-year, and they attended to seven or eight counties, that would not be more than 150*l.* to each county.

7042. Do you think that such abuses have arisen under the present system of county surveyors that it is necessary to make such an alteration?—I think that this would be a better system.

7043. Do you say that because you believe, theoretically, that it would be better, and not because you have seen any great disadvantage to arise from the present system?—I do not think that the roads are attended to as well as they should be by the assistant surveyors.

7044. Do you think that the roads have been worse looked after since the appointment of those assistant surveyors than before, when the county surveyors had no assistants?—I do not recollect so long as that; for we have had assistants in the county from which I come for a very long time. The assistants latterly got an addition to their pay; that is all the difference.

7045. What is the payment made in the county of Londonderry for the collection of the county cess?—One shilling in the pound.

7046. And what is the general cost of the collection of the poor rate in the same county?—I should suppose about an average of 6*d.* in the pound.

7047. Do you not think that the cost of the collection of the county cess would be very much diminished if the baronies were divided into districts for the purpose of collection?—I think it is likely that it would.

7048. What are the reasons why the cost of the collection of the county cess, at present, is so much higher than the cost of the collection of the poor rate?—It is a higher class of men who are required for it, and they are required to give a much larger amount of security.

7049. Is that in consequence of the greater extent over which the collection is scattered?—Yes.

7050. Would that be the case if the baronies were divided for the purpose of the collection?—It would not be so likely to occur.

7051. And it would be easier to get security for the smaller amount, would it not?—I should say so.

7052. In consequence of that, do you believe that the collection of the county cess could be made at a cheaper rate if this system were adopted?—I think it is likely that it could be.

7053. Do you recommend that the collection of the county cess should be tendered for?—Yes.

7054. What is the practice, on that point, with regard to the collection of the poor rate at present?—It is done by tender. With regard to the county cess collection, although it is a half-yearly appointment, in the county of Londonderry it is looked upon as a permanent appointment, so long as the collector gives proper security, and does his work properly; and I consider that it would be some hardship upon those individuals to be thrown out of their situations; and I think that they should get the benefit of the present law so long as they are eligible.

7055. But

7055. But do you think it is fair to the county to continue paying so much more for the collection of the cess than it is really worth?—I think that considering that life-interests are so generally respected, some regard should be had to the circumstances to which I have referred.

7056. Do you consider that to be a life-interest?—I cannot call it a life-interest, but it is the custom. I never knew a baronial constable changed since I have been upon the grand jury, except by death or by voluntary resignation.

7057. Would you think it fair to reduce the amount now paid to the collectors?—I would leave the option as it is at present; the grand jury have the power to reduce the poundage if they like.

7058. Do you consider that that would be fair?—I consider that it would be fair towards those men, but I think the ratepayers would prefer to have it reduced at once.

7059. Do you think it would be fair towards those men to reduce the poundage?—I think it would.

7060. But not to take the collection away from them altogether?—No, so long as they chose to collect it for the sum which the fiscal board chose to give them, and so long as they gave proper security.

7061. Do you think that the office of coroner is a necessary office?—I do not; the feeling is that there is a great deal of abuse under it, by there being more inquests held than are necessary.

7062. Would you approve of the coroner's fees being changed into a fixed salary?—By no means; that would make it worse, because they would do nothing then.

7063. Have the coroner's fees in the county of Londonderry, generally speaking, reached the maximum which each coroner is entitled to receive?—On the last grand warrant, which I have beside me, I think it was about 30 *l.* in the half year on the average for the four coroners, that would be 60 *l.* a year.

7064. The maximum is 100 *l.* a year, is it not?—I do not know what the maximum is; I think it is seldom as much as that in the county of Londonderry.

7065. Would you consider it fair to give the coroners all over Ireland a salary of 100 *l.* per annum?—I would not; I think it would be quite extravagant; I would not give them a salary at all, because then I think there might be a far greater complaint of their neglecting their duty than there is now of their overdoing it.

7066. As I understand, there are no stipendiary magistrates in Londonderry?—There are none resident in the county; there is one in the county of Donegal, who occasionally comes into the county of Londonderry when required, but there are no stipendiary magistrates for Londonderry.

7067. If the office of coroner were abolished who would do the duty of the coroner?—The local unpaid magistrate in some districts might do the duty very well. In mountain districts, where magistrates are scarce, it might be rather putting too great a burden upon such magistrates as were resident; but in any part of the country, where there were magistrates, I do not think there would be any difficulty or hardship in it.

7068. Do you think the local magistrates would cheerfully undertake this additional duty?—Perhaps they would just as soon let it alone; but I think there would be no objection to taking it in turn.

7069. But how could you oblige them to do it?—I think a man who receives the commission of of the peace from Her Majesty ought to do all the duties that are expected of him, as far as he can.

7070. Do the presentment sessions for baronies at present pass any presentments leviable upon the county at large?—Sometimes they do.

7071. Do you approve of that system?—The baronial sessions often pass works, such as the cutting of hills, that may be placed either upon the barony or upon the county at large; and in some cases they will ask the county at large to do it; but it is very rarely that the grand jury do that, they generally put it upon the barony.

7072. Do you think that any alteration of the law is required in that respect?—I think not; I think that the grand jury or the fiscal board would attend to that very well.

7073. Colonel *French.*] It is only in cases where they tax themselves, is it not, that at the same time they tax the county at large?—Just so.

7074. *Chairman.*] With respect to the division of the payment of the county cess, what is the view that you represent?—The view of the ratepayers throughout the county of Londonderry is very strong on that subject. They are decidedly of opinion that the county cess should be paid upon the same system as the poor-rate; that is to say, that there should be a division between the landlord and the tenant.

7075. Do they consider that the cess on land and tenements under a 4 *l.* rating should be altogether paid by the owner?—Yes, in the same way as it is paid under the Poor Law.

7076. Would you apply that principle to existing tenancies?—My constituents (as I think I may call those who sent me here) would go further upon that point than I do. I would respect existing leases.

7077. Would the bulk of the ratepayers in the county of Londonderry extend that principle to existing tenancies?—I think they would extend it to all tenancies.

7078. Would you yourself propose to extend it to all existing tenancies not under lease?—Yes.

7079. To all tenancies from year to year?—Yes.

7080. Do you think that any inconvenience would arise from that, in consequence of the landlords trying to repay themselves for this additional tax thrown upon them?—I do not think that in my county very much inconvenience would arise from it. If the landlords chose to protect themselves, I do not think the tenants would find much fault.

7081. Do you think that the tenants would object to having their rents raised in consequence of the landlords having to pay this tax?—I do not think they would, though I am sure they would rather not have their rents raised; but I do not think that would create any bad feeling.

7082. Is it the general feeling, so far as you are aware, throughout the county of Londonderry, that the whole of this cess is paid by the occupier?—It is paid by the occupier primarily. There are few of that class of people who are able to see very clearly that it is paid ultimately by the landlord, and they look upon it in a very serious light, considering that they have to pay so much

for

Mr. J. Adams.

16 June 18[illegible].

for the support of public institutions, such as gaols, lunatic asylums, infirmaries, and so on, and for other large public works and they also look upon it as being somewhat hard upon them to have to pay for all new roads, and so on, when the owners of the properties are the people who generally are most benefited by those roads permanently.

7083. Although it may be true that in the long run the landlords bear this tax through diminished rent, yet is it very hard to convince the occupiers, who pay it directly, that such is the case?—I think so.

7084. And in consequence of that, is there a general feeling among them that they are not fairly treated in consequence of being obliged to pay the whole of the tax?—That is their feeling.

7085. With respect to the expenses of lunatic asylums, county infirmaries, and expenses of that description, are they not charges that ought rather to be made upon the poor rates than upon the county cess?—Decidedly; unless the Grand Jury Law is put upon the same principle as the Poor Law; otherwise they should be taken off the county rates and placed upon the poor rates. These public charitable institutions, such as lunatic asylums and infirmaries, are, in my opinion, far more connected with the Poor Law than with the county affairs.

7086. The grand jury or the presentment sessions have no control over those institutions at all, have they?—I think they have very little control; they have the accounts submitted to them.

7087. And the persons relieved are either paupers, or persons corresponding to those who are relieved under the Medical Charities Act, that is to say, persons who are unable to pay for themselves, are they not?—Yes.

7088. So that the charges in reality correspond to the charges at present raised under the poor rate?—Yes. The cost of maintaining a lunatic in the asylum is generally double as much as the cost of maintaining a pauper in the union workhouse.

7089. Do you not believe that if these charges were transferred to the poor rate, and if each union were obliged to pay for the support of their own lunatics in the lunatic asylums, the guardians of those unions would be more careful in seeing that only fit persons were sent from their respective unions to the asylums?—I think that the guardians could effect a more economising control and examination than the grand jury or the magistrates could do.

7090. The grand jury have no power whatever, in any shape or form, either directly or indirectly, in regard to the expenses of those asylums, have they?—I think not.

7091. But the boards of guardians would look after the inmates of asylums in the interests of their own union, would they not?—Yes.

7092. Have you any other suggestion to make to the Committee?—I mentioned that my system for electing the representative at the baronial board would be different from that which accords with the feeling of the ratepayers generally. My system would be that, say, 10 names from each electoral division should be sent up to the grand jury, or to the fiscal board, by each electoral division, annually at each summer assizes. Supposing that there were four electoral divisions in a group, one man should be balloted for from each of those four electoral divisions by the county fiscal board; and out of those four a second ballot for one to represent the district at the baronial sessions.

7093. Do you think that that would be more satisfactory than having those elected directly by the ratepayers?—I think so. I think it would prevent the possibility of anything like favouritism.

7094. Do you apprehend that if they were elected, sometimes the influence of the landlord, and at other times the influence of the contractor might affect the election?—There is a liability to that construction being put upon it.

7095. And you think, upon the whole, that it would be fairer, and that it would work better if they were taken in this way by ballot out of each electoral division?—I do. In that way you would have one to represent each group at this second ballot on the baronial board, and then the baronial board would elect their own men by ballot also, to send up to the county fiscal board.

7096. Would the county fiscal board, both as regards magistrates and as regards cesspayers, be elective?—It would be elective, both as regards magistrates and cesspayers.

7097. The magistrates electing magistrates, and the cesspayers electing cesspayers?—Yes, for both boards.

7098. Mr. *Dawson*.] At those different meetings was this the arrangement that appeared to be preferable; that each county should be divided into baronial districts; and that the presentment sessions for each district should be constituted in the following way: that the cesspayers of each baronial district should elect, in the same way as the Poor Law guardians are now elected, six cesspayers to represent them on the baronial board, and that the magistrates and landowners residing in the district, and having certain property qualifications, should choose six of their number to represent them on the board; that the baronial board so constituted should choose a certain number of cesspayers and an equal number of landowners to represent them on the fiscal board; and that the persons so chosen by the several baronial boards should constitute the fiscal board of each county with power to elect their own chairman?—I did not attend those meetings, but that was the view taken by those who did attend the meetings.

7099. *Chairman*.] Have you any other suggestion to make to the Committee?—I consider that the fact of the landlord and tenant being interested in the payment of the county cess, as they are in the payment of the poor rates, would have a very salutary tendency. I think that the representative system has a very good effect in bringing classes more together, and in showing them that their interests are identical, which I think is very desirable, and which would be accomplished by the division of the county rate.

7100. Giving both parties a direct interest in every alteration made in the rate?—Yes, both in the levying of it and in the expenditure of it.

7101. Earl of *Mayo*.] You propose very extensive changes altogether in the grand jury system; would you state to the Committee whether your reasons for suggesting those changes are that the system which you propose in your opinion would be abstractedly better

than

than the present one, or that there are serious and crying evils connected with the administration of the law as it stands which require alteration?—I think the system that I am suggesting would be better, provided you had a controlling board, such as I have described.

7102. What are the particular evils in the present system which you wish to correct?—The chief evil is the want of the baronial boards being properly formed; that the magistrates by far out-number the cess payers, and that the cess payers are not elected, but appointed at the assizes.

7103. But is it your opinion that there is any extravagance or unnecessary outlay of money in the administration of the present system?—I would not say that there is; but still there might perhaps be more economy.

7104. Do you think that the roads in the county of Londonderry are generally pretty economically kept?—I think they might be better kept.

7105. Do you think that the roads in the county of Londonderry are as well kept as they are in other counties?—I do not think they are as well kept as they are in the adjoining county, the county of Antrim; at least, so far as regards the leading roads.

7106. What reason can you give for that?—I cannot tell you that exactly; one reason, perhaps, may be that the county of Antrim roads have been better made originally; a great many of them were made under Sir Charles Lanyon, and they may be more easily kept in order on that account; and, perhaps, in some cases, the material used may be more easily got, or it may be of better quality.

7107. Do you think that the contracts that are settled by the baronial sessions in the county of Londonderry are generally too high?—I do not think the contracts are too high if they were properly carried out.

7108. Would you approve of the principle of taking the lowest tender?—I think so, when the party tendering gives proper security.

7109. Then, as you adopt the principle of taking the lowest tender, there would not be much saving in the contracts under your system, I apprehend?—I do not know.

7110. With regard to the other public works, such as bridges and the like, do you consider that they are generally constructed economically and well under the present system?—I cannot express a very decided opinion upon that point, either one way or the other, but I suppose they are fairly done.

7111. Do you think there is any favouritism shown to any parties by the different bodies who have charge of the administration of the law?—It is unpleasant to make insinuations when one cannot give any special cases; but there is a very general feeling that the deputy surveyors do not attend to their business as well as they should do.

7112. But with regard to the associated cesspayers and the grand jurors, does any such feeling exist?—I never heard any insinuation of the kind with regard to them.

7113. Then do you think that the administration on the whole is very pure, and that there have been no allegations of corruption or of favouritism?—I have heard no such direct allegations. I have heard of people perhaps getting

a road that the cess payers considered unnecessary; perhaps I may have done so myself.

Mr. *J. Adams.*

16 June 1868.

7114. But, however, the law gives ample means does it not, for the persons who feel themselves aggrieved in such matters to come in, and by traverse, and in other ways, to oppose a presentment to which they object?—Yes, they have an opportunity of coming in by traverse, but that is a matter which I think is not so well arranged under the present law as it should be. There is a cost of about three guineas additional put on the traverse, and it comes forward at a time when the county surveyor is very much otherwise occupied, and in my opinion it would be much better that the traverse should be at the quarter sessions, if any change in the law took place.

7115. But under your system of electing the cesspayers and the baronial board, would you propose to abolish the system of traverse?—I would not; but I would bring the application for it forward at the quarter sessions, instead of at the assizes.

7116. Do you think the constitution of the quarter sessions court is altogether of such a nature that the trial of an important traverse would be as satisfactorily conducted there as it would be in the presence of one of the judges of the land and a large bar?—I do, and much better; because the important circumstances of the case and of the locality would be much better known in the court of quarter sessions; and it would be much easier to get witnesses at the quarter sessions than it would be at the assizes.

7117. But if a traverse came before the court of quarter sessions, it would be tried before an inferior judge and an inferior bar, would it not?—I suppose I may admit that; but you could still give an appeal to the assizes if it was necessary.

7118. But that would increase the expense very much, would it not?—It would.

7119. You stated that you thought that in the event of your plan being adopted there should be a central authority somewhat similar to the Poor Law Commissioners; will you describe a little more in detail what you consider would be the duties of this central body?—The duties of that central body would be to control the general management of the county affairs in a somewhat similar way to that in which the Commissioners of the Poor Law control its action and working.

7120. But are not the laws and system which a board of guardians have to administer very different in their nature from the laws and system which one of your baronial boards would have to administer?—No doubt they are; but there would be a different class of men to deal with. The portion of the Board of Works who I propose should be constituted for the purpose, I take it, would be scientific men, engineers or otherwise, who understand matters of the kind.

7121. Would you state in a little more detail what are the precise matters in which you would propose that this central board should interfere?—They should regulate the system being carried out similarly throughout the kingdom by all the grand juries; that if there was any difficulty between another officer and the local board an appeal should be made to them; that they should have the appointment of officers, after a competitive examination before them, and so on.

7122. Then, so far as I can gather, you propose that this central body should have the

power

Mr. J. Adams.

26 June 1878.

power of appointing a considerable number of gentlemen who would act as inspectors, and go about the country and inspect the roads?—They would have the appointment of the baronial surveyors, and of the provincial engineers.

7123. Would you propose that the central body should appoint the baronial inspectors?—Yes, and also the provincial surveyors, or circuit surveyors.

7124. Then you would propose to take out of the hands of the local board the appointment of their own officers?—I think the appointments of the officers, if they were made in the way that I speak of, would be better than the local appointments.

7125. Then would your proposal be this, that the baronial and county boards should have the administration of the funds, but that all their officers should be appointed by a central board?—Yes; but subject to dismissal by the baronial and county fiscal board, with the approval of the commissioners.

7126. Do you think that that is a proposal which would be generally popular in the north of Ireland?—I do not know; it is only my own idea.

7127. Of what number of persons do you propose that this central body should consist?—My idea is that the central board of commissioners should consist of two or three individuals.

7128. What salaries would you propose to give them?—I could not tell what salaries are given to the Poor Law Commissioners.

7129. Would you put them upon the same footing as the Poor Law Commissioners?—I would.

7130. You say that you would have provincial surveyors?—Yes.

7131. What would be their duties?—Their duties would be to look after the more important works in the counties for which they would be appointed; such as any leading roads, and any new buildings, court-houses, or gaols, or infirmaries, or bridges, or anything of an important nature that required the skill and knowledge of scientific men to plan and to superintend.

7132. And what salary would you propose to give them?—The salary that I would propose would be a high salary.

7133. And who is to pay them?—The counties to which they would attend. There might be one for each circuit of, perhaps, seven or eight counties; and the salary should be divided over them in proportion to the extent and the valuation of the counties; perhaps on an average it would be about 160 *l.* a year to each county; and supposing that the superior class of engineers that I suggest were appointed, they should have a salary of from 1,000 *l.* to 1,200 *l.* a year.

7134. Would these officers have control over the local surveyors?—I think it would be well, if there was any necessity for calling their attention to anything, and, if the local boards thought it necessary to get some advice, these officers should be the persons to give it.

7135. Then this provincial surveyor would, I presume, have a controlling power over the local county surveyors?—He would have a control over them when called upon to exercise that control; but they would be more under the control of the county fiscal board and of the local board.

7136. But these provincial surveyors would be under the control of the central board, I apprehend?—Yes, they would, for matters having reference to the county at large.

7137. In point of fact, you would have every local surveyor under the threefold control of the local board, of the provincial surveyors, and of the central body?—Yes.

7138. Do you think that that would be likely to produce harmonious action and efficiency in the administration of affairs?—I think that the work would be better done, and that they would attend better to the contracts being all performed properly than is the case at present.

7139. Have you ever calculated what would be the expense to the counties under this plan?—No; except in the case of our own county of Londonderry. That is a small county, and it would be divided, according to my plan, into four baronial districts. In that way there would be 800 *l.* for the salaries of the baronial surveyors, and, say, 150 *l.* for the provincial surveyor, that makes 950 *l.*, while at present the work costs about 1,250 *l.* It would therefore effect a saving of about 300 *l.* Of course I am always excepting existing interests. I do not wish to interfere with the present county surveyors.

7140. How many assistant surveyors are there at present in the county of Londonderry?—There are seven.

7141. Do you think that they do not do their duty?—I can bring no direct charge against them; but there is a feeling abroad that they do not attend to their duty as well as they should.

7142. Do you think that the roads would be better inspected by those two or three gentlemen who would visit them occasionally?—Yes; I think four would do the work much better than seven, because the four would be selected from the class of young men in engineers' offices, after competitive examination, who are anxious to get themselves forward into a better situation, and I have no doubt they would do the work better.

7143. Do you think that it requires any very high order of education, or any very great amount of engineering knowledge, to perform the duties of an assistant surveyor, who will never be called upon to carry out or to design a public work, but who will have merely to look to the repair of the ordinary county roads?—I do not think it requires a man of very high engineering knowledge; but he ought to have sufficient engineering skill to know whether the plans are carried out properly according to the specification.

7144. Do you not think that it would be quite enough to have one official for each district who would be competent to design new works, but that for the repair of common roads no such person is required?—I think he is not required for common roads; but there is a difficulty if you have not some head man for planning and seeing the large works on the county at large carried out.

7145. Do you propose to make many new roads in the county of Londonderry?—I do not know that it is intended to do so.

7146. Do you not think that the public is amply provided with roads in the county of Londonderry?—It is pretty well provided with roads. Still, some people think it might be better, and I dare say there are some localities where I would say myself that it would be better to have new roads.

7147. But still is it the case that any new works

works of any extent are likely to be carried on? —I think not at present.

7148. You stated, did you not, that you disapproved altogether of paying the coroners by fixed salaries?—I did.

7149. You stated, did you not, that you think that the general rule as to fixed salaries is, that people do very little for them?—As far as regards the coroners, I think that would be so.

7150. Did your observation apply only to coroners?—It may apply in other cases also.

7151. But do you not think that the county would gain by paying a small fixed salary to the coroner, the allegation being that some of these gentlemen sometimes hold inquests which are unnecessary, for the purpose of increasing their remuneration?—I have explained already that I think that then you fall into the other extreme.

7152. Do you think that holding an inquiry into the cause of death where violence is suspected is necessary in all cases?—I think that if there is any suspicion of any foul play having occurred, it is quite necessary that an inquiry should be held.

7153. Do you think it would be possible or desirable to do away with those inquiries?—I do not think it would be desirable to do away with them altogether; but I think that if they were left to men who were not particularly anxious to make money out of them for themselves, there might be a great many less inquiries than there are at present.

7154. But do you think that for the purpose of avoiding the few unnecessary inquiries which may take place, it would be desirable to give those duties over either to unpaid persons or to men who would probably have no experience of such matters, and who would only be called upon to hold an inquest here and there?—I think there are very few magistrates who have not more experience and more ability to conduct an inquest than most of the coroners; and I think that now, with the assistance of the police, and the information which they would get through the police, there would be very little difficulty in deciding whether it was a case requiring an inquest to be held or not, without even going to the place. They could send for witnesses and have them examined before them, and they could determine pretty well whether it was a case for an inquest or not.

7155. Still you could not force any man to go to a place without paying him for it, could you? —I do not say that you could; but you might as well say that you could not force a magistrate to go to petty sessions or to take a dying declaration.

7156. But the duties are not exactly the same; the one is an absolute necessity, and the other may be postponed or done by somebody else. You lay great stress, do you not, upon the division of the county cess between the landlord and the tenant, making it analogous, in that respect, to the poor rate?—I do.

7157. Do you think that there is any other grievance in the matter, or is it merely a general opinion on the part of the occupiers that they are harshly treated?—I am sure that the occupiers and ratepayers in my neighbourhood think it a great grievance. I have already explained that they cannot see it in the light in which other people see it, who may look farther into it and more disinterestedly at it, and who believe that it falls upon the landlord, ultimately.

7158. All they know is that they pay it?—All they know is that they pay it. They think they pay for improvements which improve the landlords' property more than theirs.

7159. Would you propose at once to make the alteration which you consider desirable?—I think so.

7160. Irrespective of the existing leases and agreements?—I said that my own opinion was that I would respect existing agreements.

7161. With regard to tenants at will, and all future lettings, would you immediately assimilate the payment of the county cess to that of the Poor Law?—Immediately.

7162. Supposing that the tenants at will found that the landlords increased their rent in proportion to the amount of county cess, which they would be called upon to pay, do you think that that would alter their opinion upon the matter?—I do not think it would alter it much. As I have said already, they might feel a little about it, but I do not think that it would get up any commotion, or any unpleasantness.

7163. Still you think that no alteration could be made with regard to existing contracts and leases?—In our county it frequently occurs that lettings are made at will, and it is supposed that there will not be an increase of rent for a number of years; that has been the practice for some time past, and I suppose it would be found that that is the case now. Most of the property in the county of Londonderry, as the Committee are aware, belongs to London companies. Their system is a valuation about every 21 years. I suppose that the tenants think that they would not take advantage of altering the rent until the usual time for altering it.

7164. In fact, in the contemplation of this question, they trust to the generosity of the landlord not to make any alteration, do they not?—Just so.

7165. But I presume the London companies, like every other landlord when letting their land, take into consideration the charges in the way of rates and taxes to which the land is subject?—I suppose that the valuators who are sent down to the estate, do so.

7166. And the tenant in making his contract, I presume, equally takes that matter into consideration?—I should say so.

7167. *Earl of Mayo*.] It is a common custom in the county of Londonderry to hold the land by lease or agreement, is it not?—No, it is held at will, as a rule; leases are the exception.

7168. Then it would be in the power either of the London companies or of the existing landlords to make a different arrangement with regard to rent, would it not, in case there was a new law affecting the levying of the county cess?—It would.

7169. Do you think that if the cesspayers were elected, they would attend better at the meeting of the sessions than they do?—In my plan I provide for their attendance; I would have them summoned after their election. I would have the ballot previously, so as to enable the secretary of the grand jury to summon them under a penalty of 20 *l.* for non-attendance, without sufficient cause; and then I would have the sheriff summon for the county fiscal board also, requiring their attendance, under a higher penalty, perhaps, of 30 *l.* or 40 *l.*

7170. Do you propose that the cesspayer should be elected in the same way as the Poor Law

Mr. *J. Adams.*

16 June 1868.

Law guardians?—That is the opinion of my constituents, if I may call them so, but I think that they should be elected by ballot.

7171. Who should be the constituents of these future representatives of the cesspayers?—Their names would be returned as they are now; that is to say, 10 of the highest, we will say, should be returned from a greater number from each electoral division, and sent forward to the county fiscal board at the summer assizes annually, and then one balloted out of those 10 for that electoral division; that would go on, say, for four electoral divisions, and there would be four names. Then a second ballot would take place, and out of these four names one would come down to the baronial board to represent it; the electoral divisions would be placed together as a group in one locality.

7172. But I am not talking about the baronial boards; I wish to ascertain what your plan is for the election of the representatives of the cesspayers at the meeting, which is to represent the present baronial session?—I perhaps do not make myself clearly understood; it would be just similar to what it is by law at present. A number of names of the highest cesspayers are sent up to the grand jury by the collector of the public rate; and instead of one grand juror and another crossing those names, I would send up a fewer number of names, say 10 of the highest, to the county fiscal board or the grand jury through the secretary by the rate collector from each electoral division.

7173. But I thought that you proposed to do away with the fiscal power of the grand jury altogether?—The first election must be by the grand jury if the law were altered.

7174. Then do you propose that the county board should elect the members of the baronial board?—No, not at all; it is just the reverse. The baronial board would first be elected out of the names sent up by the collector by ballot instead of being crossed off as they are at present by the grand jury.

7175. But who is to ballot for them?—The grand jury, as at present, would ballot the names, taking one out of the 10.

7176. But when you talk of ballot, do you mean voting by ballot, or do you mean putting all the names into a box and having the man whose name first comes out elected?—Yes; the same as is done now at road sessions.

7177. Would not the effect of that be, that it would be a mere chance who was the gentleman elected to serve?—It would; but the chance would be that one must come out of every district; that, according to my system, cannot be avoided.

7178. Then would not those proposed representatives be really elected by chance, and not in regard to their business-like habits or knowledge of affairs?—No; they would be supposed to be more eligible, because the names sent up would be those of the highest cesspayers.

7179. But the highest cesspayers are not always the most intelligent, I am afraid?—Not always, but I would say that they ought to be.

7180. Then, in fact, it is not a system of election at all, but a system of selection by chance, is it not?—It is a system of selection by ballot.

7181. (Chairman.] Is not that your own proposal, and not that of the cesspayers?—No; the proposal of the cesspayers is election as under the Poor Law.

7182. Colonel *Forde.*] Are you a Poor Law guardian?—I am now an *ex officio* guardian, and I acted, previously to being a magistrate, as an elected guardian.

7183. From your knowledge of the economy practised by the Poor Law Commissioners, do you suggest that a like body should have the control of the fiscal business of the county?—Yes.

7184. Have you never found that the Poor Law Commissioners generally err on the side of increasing the expenses of the Poor Law rather than of decreasing them?—I do not think they do so, perhaps, more than what is necessary.

7185. Are they not always very anxious to have the salaries of the different officers increased?—The increase of the salaries always is awarded by the boards of guardians, except the chaplains', I believe. They are the only persons whom they appoint.

7186. Do the Commissioners ever send down an order for the guardians to take into consideration certain subjects of that sort, such as the increase of salaries, or the increase of accommodation, or anything of that sort?—They may do so, sometimes; but I have known very few instances of it in the union to which I belong.

7187. Do you consider that a Board of Commissioners, say in Dublin, would be likely to transact the fiscal business of each county in Ireland more satisfactorily than those who are locally interested, and who know all the circumstances of the county?—I do not consider that they would interfere locally at all; they would only have an overruling control if it were necessary. The local machinery would go on still as usual.

7188. But they would be a controlling power, would they not?—They would be a controlling power.

7189. And do you think that they would be better able to do that than the gentlemen and the cesspayers of the county?—I do not think it is likely that the gentlemen and the cesspayers of the county, and the Commissioners would fall foul of each other in any way; but by having a general rule laid down by the Commissioners, you would insure a uniform management all over the counties in Ireland.

7190. In your direct examination by the Honourable Chairman you complained, did you not, that the cesspayers had no representation upon the county at large sessions?—They have a representation, but the county town is entirely at one side of the county, so that the county sessions are very badly attended.

7191. That is the fault of the associated cesspayer who is elected, is it not?—Yes; there is one appointed, if anyone will consent to go, from each baronial district.

7192. Where would you propose that county fiscal board should meet?—At the county town, at the time of the assizes, as the grand jury meet now.

7193. Do you think that those who are elected or appointed at the baronial sessions, would be more likely to attend at the fiscal boards, which you propose, than they are now?—It is very hard to say, but my feeling is that they would.

7194. On what grounds?—Being representatives, they would make it their business to attend more regularly and more closely to their duties than now, that they are irresponsible.

7195. But surely a man is a representative man, when he is chosen as a representative from the

Mr. *J. Adams.*

16 June 1868.

the baronial sessions, to attend at the county at large sessions, is he not?—Yes.

7196. And he is in the same position as the representative man that you propose, is he not?—I may not have made myself understood by the Honourable Member. I would do away with the presentment sessions for the county at large.

7197. But you would appoint a fiscal board, which is the same thing, would you not?—Yes; as I have mentioned already, I would summon them, and make it imperative upon them to attend.

7198. If you did that with the present system, would not that do as well?—The present system is, that they are summoned by the sheriff.

7199. That is the grand jury; but I am talking of the associated cesspayers; would not those whom you would elect be in the same position as the associated cesspayers are now?—They would for the baronial boards.

7200. And for the county?—Yes; there would be representatives sent forward to the fiscal boards from the baronial boards also.

7201. What would be the difference between the two representative bodies, the present associated cesspayers, and the representatives at the county at large board, appointed in the manner in which you suggest?—Under the system which I suggest, there would be representatives from each of the baronial boards to comprise the county fiscal board, which I would say, might be the same in number as the grand jury are at present.

7202. General *Dunne.*] Where is all this system which you are proposing, to be found?—It is a new system.

7203. Is it totally the work of your own imagination?—Yes.

7204. You do not find fault with the old system, do you?—I do find fault with the old system.

7205. Do you think that this is better?—That is my opinion.

7206. Mr. *Blake.*] At the baronial boards you would have the cesspayers upon it who are not magistrates, as near as possible to the class of the present persons who are nominated by the grand jury, would you not?—Yes.

7207. They are generally of the farmer class, are they not?—Generally.

7208. And there are some small farmers amongst them, are there not?—They may be, some of them, small farmers.

7209. Would you not consider that, for a person to serve upon the baronial board as a cesspayer, a qualification of the value of 20 *l.* in the county would be sufficient?—That would do very well in my locality; but I think, according to the Poor Law, a variation, according to the extent of the holdings in the districts, would be advantageous. Under the Poor Law, I think, it extends from 15 *l.* to 30 *l.*, but a person assessed at 20 *l.* I think should be eligible.

7210. Would not the county fiscal board which you have spoken of, be intended to be a species of check, as the grand jury is now on the presentment sessions; and do you not think that it would be desirable to have the minimum qualification for it fixed at 50 *l.*?—I think that if you did it in some districts, you would have very few men eligible.

7211. But you would have sufficient to form a respectable fiscal board in the county, would you not?—I cannot say as to that, but if there are sufficient, I think it is all the better to have a high qualification.

7212. Under those circumstances, would it not be more desirable to have the members of the county board elected directly by the ratepayers, instead of being elected directly from the baronial boards, as you have proposed?—That would occasion additional machinery, and I think that if they were taken from the baronial boards, they would be better acquainted with the working of the system, and with things which would have come before them at the baronial board; and, therefore, I consider that it should be men from the baronial board that should be taken for the fiscal board.

7213. But when you render the members of the baronial board eligible for the county board also, do you think that it would be desirable that they should be elected as a matter of course from the baronial boards, as it is the intention that they should be a check over them?—I do not see that there would be any objection to the baronial board electing representatives upon the fiscal board.

7214. With regard to the county cess, does it not frequently occur that when once the landlord agrees with the tenant for the rent which he is to pay him, it makes no difference to the landlord what amount of county cess the tenant may have to pay afterwards, and he does not lose anything by it?—The landlord does not lose anything, whether the cess is higher or lower.

7215. Is it not very often absolutely the interest of the landlord that there should be a considerable outlay in the barony in which he may have property, as being calculated to enhance the value of that property?—That is my opinion, though it is different from that which the previous witness expressed.

7216. As things stand at present, is not the landlord, who may be generally supposed to represent the barony, able to lay, and is he not influenced very often to lay, as much taxation as possible on the tenant, without the tenant having any control over the expenditure?—He has the power to do it, but I do not say that he has any wish to oppress his tenantry; but if the matter had to come through the presentment sessions, it might be checked to some extent.

7217. And having so enhanced the value of his property, the letting of his land is also enhanced, is it not?—It is.

7218. Does it not sometimes occur that the land being so enhanced in value, an increased rent is required from the tenant-at-will for it?—That is the tendency when a valuation takes place; but as I have mentioned already, the rents are not changed very frequently in the county of Londonderry.

7219. Going outside of the county of Londonderry, where the landlords may not be disposed to do it, may it not occur that the very outlay for which the tenant has been compelled to pay is the very thing which increases the amount of his own rent afterwards?—That is my opinion.

7220. And so far do you consider the present mode of levying the rate to be unjust and wrong in principle?—I think that all public improvements are more for the landlord's interest than the tenant's, because the landlords have a permanent interest and the tenants only a fluctuating one.

7221. As you are disposed to separate the fiscal from the criminal business of the grand jury,

Mr. *J. Adams.* 10 June 1862.

jury, confining that body, as it was originally intended, to the transaction of the criminal affairs of the county, do you not think that it would be better to have other machinery than what you suggested in the way of a county board, called together by a summons from the sheriff; and do you not think that the secretary of the board might summon them?—The secretary should summon the baronial board, and he might be made to summon the county fiscal board also.

7222. Do you not consider that the mode of electing the county fiscal board and the baronial boards might be managed by voting papers, the same as in the election of the Poor Law guardians, done in an inexpensive way?—That is the idea that the cesspayers of the county have as to the way in which they should be elected. It was the desire to prevent the possibility of any suspicion of favouritism that induced me to suggest the system of balloting out of the highest ratepayers.

7223. Though, on your own representation, the landlords of the county of Londonderry are very just and good ones, do you not think that a change in the present grand jury system, even for the county of Londonderry, is called for?—I could not say that I could give instances where undue influence has been made use of; but it is quite possible that such might be the case; and in making a new law I would endeavour so to frame it, that it would be impossible, even if there was an inclination, though I do not say that there would be an inclination, to do anything wrong.

7224. But the ratepayers of the county of Londonderry and the tenants felt a change such as you suggest to be so essential, that they were assembled together and were willing to pay the cost of two witnesses to come over and express those opinions which you have expressed to-day?—They assembled together at different parts of the county, and they had different meetings, and felt very much upon the subject; they had large placards and advertisements of it in all parts, and they entered into a subscription to pay witnesses. They told me that my expenses would be paid by the committee, but they sent another gentleman here for the purpose of giving me any assistance which was necessary in the way of any information which I might want to obtain.

7225. Although the grand jury system in the county of Londonderry, you consider, is as fairly administered as in any other part of Ireland?—I think so. I think that justice has been very fairly administered by the grand jury: I have never seen anything else since I have been on it but what is fair and reasonable.

7226. But do the people of the county think that such changes are imperatively called for?—They think so; they think there should be representation.

7227. And all the other things which are mentioned in your paper?—Yes.

7228. *Mr. Maguire.*] Is the expression of opinion which you put forward here to-day on the part of the ratepayers of Londonderry, the result of what is popularly called agitation and inflammatory appeals?—There is very little agitation about it; I have not heard of any speech-making or anything of that nature, but it may be called a public meeting.

7229. Is it not really the result of strong conviction?—It is the result of strong conviction.

7230. There is nothing factitious in it, is there?—No.

7231. Or merely got up for the occasion?—Not at all.

7232. But is it the result of a strong conviction that the state of things is not just?—It is in my opinion entirely that.

7233. Is that an opinion which you are authorised to give in the name of the ratepayers of the county generally?—Yes; they sent me here in that capacity.

7234. And that you know to be their strong feeling?—Yes.

7235. Putting aside your plan altogether, would those whom you represent, and on whose behalf you speak here, be satisfied with this alteration; a system of representation, instead of the present system of nomination, and a division of the rate; if these two things were granted, would they be more or less content with the existing state of things?—I think those are the two principal points; all the others are mere matters of detail.

7236. In fact the rest is, as it were, a kind of scientific or speculative arrangement for a future time, is it not?—You may say so.

7237. Is there any desire, on the part of the cesspayers whom you represent that the landlords should pay the entire of the cess?—By no means; I never heard such a thing expressed, even by the most out-and-out of the class. I never heard them express a wish to put all upon the landlord.

7238. Is all that they want a fair partition?—All that they want is fair play, as they think, and to get the landlord's interest to be identical with theirs.

7239. And to adopt the same principle as is adopted in the arrangement of the Poor Law tax?—Yes.

7240. As to attendance you have had long experience as a Poor Law guardian, have you not?—I have.

7241. I suppose that under any system by which the cesspayers would be elected, about the same class of persons would be returned as those who are returned now as Poor Law guardians?—They would be somewhat similar.

7242. Have you had experience of that class?—I have.

7243. Do you find, as a rule, that they attend as well as the *ex officio* guardians?—I think they do. In our union the elected guardians attend better than the *ex officio* guardians.

7244. Are they remarkable for intelligence and shrewdness?—Most of them are shrewd sharp enough men.

7245. Are they quite enough up to discharge their duties fairly to those whom they represent?—Quite so.

7246. Do you find that they are generally speaking thrifty and economical?—They are.

7247. Are they quite as much so as others?—They are. I would say that they are more so of their class.

7248. Do they not mostly act under a considerable sense of responsibility, because they are elected and must answer to others for their conduct?—I think they do. It is a very common thing in our union, that if a man does not give satisfaction, he is turned out at the next election for guardians.

7249. If the associated cesspayer was made a really representative man, if he showed either incapacity, or corruption, he would be sent about his business at the next election, would he not?

not?—I think that he would not be elected again.

7250. Then he would act under a sense of responsibility, would he not?—He would.

7251. He would have a constituent body to whom he should be responsible?—Yes.

7252. Do you think that that would be a great advantage?—I think so; that I think is one of the principal advantages.

7253. Do you imagine that it would be very injurious to the occupiers of the county, who now pay the rates, if the law was changed so that the landlord should pay half of the cess?—I think not. I have stated in my evidence that I would except existing leases, and so far as the other contracts go the landlords have it in their power to change them at any time.

7254. Do you imagine that the landlord would not only recoup himself of the rate if he were compelled by law to pay it, but that he would get something additional?—I do not think that the landlords in my county would do so.

7255. Do you not think, plainly speaking, that it is rather a slander upon the character of the landlords to anticipate such a state of things?—I would say so; I think that landlords and tenants ought to have such good feeling towards each other that one would not try to do towards the other anything which was not just and proper.

7256. But you distinctly say that you express the feelings of the ratepayers when you say that there ought to be representation, and that there ought to be a division of the rate?—I do, decidedly.

7257. And this is not a mere matter of vulgar agitation, but of strong conviction, is it not?—It is a matter of strong conviction.

7258. Mr. *Dawson*.] Since the progress of this inquiry, has there not been a deep feeling throughout the whole county of Londonderry about the progress of it, and a desire to appear and give evidence here?—There has.

7259. And at the several baronial meetings which have been held, have not the different resolutions been passed almost unanimously?—They have; or, at least, to the best of my knowledge they have; but I was not at the meetings there.

7260. I presume that the division of the county cess was universally adopted as the groundwork for a desirable change?—Yes.

7261. May I ask whether the majority of the landlords, in your opinion, would raise their rents by the amount of the half of the cess which would be remitted by law?—My opinion is that some of them would; but I think that others would not until whatever time their usual valuation would take place, and then no doubt they would take it into consideration that they had half the cess to pay.

7262. Do you think that they would be justified in raising the rents?—I think so if they think proper.

7263. Do you think that the tenants would still wish for this division of the cess if they thought their rents might be subject to such an alteration?—I think on the whole they would even under the risk of that.

7264. You know that in our county we have a principle of tenant-right (I am happy to say, to which I myself am very favourable); but where that tenant-right prevails it is acknowledged, is it not, that the tenants have a permanent interest in the land?—They have no legal claim, but that is the custom, and it is looked upon as being as good as if it were legal by those wishing to get into new holdings.

7265. Then do you not think that under the circumstances in a county where tenant-right exists, as it does in the county of Londonderry, it is rather unfair to say that all the improvements which have been made, and which are being made, are merely for the benefit of the landlord?—No doubt the tenant gets a share of the benefit; but I think that ultimately the landlord gets a greater share, because his property is permanently improved, whereas the tenant's holding is only for a short period, and he is then liable to an increase of rent for his own improvement. Therefore I consider that the advantage is decidedly in favour of the landlord.

7266. Colonel *Forde*.] What do you get for tenant-right there?—Various sums. You cannot fix it at any particular sum.

7267. Is it anything near the fee-simple of the property?—I have known it sell at above that, even where there was no lease. People are sometimes so foolish as to give these fictitious sums when they wished to acquire perhaps a piece of land adjoining a farm which they have already, or something of that kind.

7268. Mr. *Maguire*.] Is that custom universal in the county of Londonderry?—By no means. There are restrictions put upon it now by several landlords.

7269. But it does not exist throughout the whole county, does it?—I think that it does, but not to the extent which I am describing now. I am describing to the Committee rather an extreme case.

7270. Mr. *Dawson*.] It is a generally admitted fact that tenant-right is accepted throughout the county of Londonderry, is it not?—It is; but frequently now instead of one tenant selling to another, they have to submit to the price or terms that the office or agent will give them for it, and then that agent will put in whom he likes.

7271. In the cases where leases are given, a division of the county cess would not affect the tenants until the expiration of those leases, according to the opinion which you gave just now?—No, I would except existing leases. With regard to leases, tenants are sometimes afraid to take them, because they are told by the agent that they will be held to the strict letter of the law regarding those leases; that is to say, that they must give up the land altogether to the landlord. It is by law at present his property, and it is liable to be given up to him; but, according to the custom, they have always been allowed to dispose of it by tenant-right. But they have been told that if they are going to take leases, it ceases at the end of the lease, and that deters tenants from taking leases I have heard.

7272. Do you think that the offices of the clerk of the peace and the clerk of the Crown might be amalgamated with advantage, and one officer appointed, whose salary alone should be paid by the grand jury?—I do. I think that there is no necessity for the two officers.

7273. Do you think that those county fiscal boards should have power given by the new Act to buy up the head rents of all county court-houses, bridewells, and other public buildings, supported by public rates, which I see is one of the resolutions?—That is a mistake. What was intended was compulsory power to purchase lands for the sites of court-houses and bridewells, and so on?—I think that is necessary.

7274. Do

7774. Do the elected Poor Law guardians generally attend regularly?—They attend very well in the Coleraine Union.

7775. Are you of opinion that the elected cesspayers would attend better now if they were called up?—I think so. The present plan is so uncertain that they will not go merely upon the chance of being put on.

7776. Is the irregularity of the attendance of those associated cesspayors confined to the county of Londonderry, or do you know what is done in other counties?—I do not know how it is in other counties. There is one matter here which I should like to refer to; with regard to the salary of the secretary, the last witness said that he should have nothing in addition to his salary, but my feeling is that it would be better to let it remain as it is, and that the secretary should get the fees which he now gets for the papers which he puts out for applications for presentments, and so on. My reason for that is, that the parties who make these applications do not think anything of paying for them, and it saves the ratepayers the payment of so much of the county secretary's salary.

7777. (*Chairman.*) The proposal made by the last witness, and by other witnesses before the Committee, was that the secretary should get a fixed salary, and that these payments should be made by the contractors, and should go to the credit of the county; would that meet your objection?—If it went to the benefit of the county, it would do very well.

Friday, 19*th June* 1868.

MEMBERS PRESENT:

Mr. Blake.
Colonel Cooper.
General Dunne.
Colonel Forde.
Colonel French.
Mr. Gregory.
Mr. Kendall.
Sir Charles Lanyon.
Mr. Leader.
Mr. Maguire.
The O'Conor Don.

THE O'CONOR DON, IN THE CHAIR.

Mr. JOHN BALL GREENE, called in; and Examined.

Mr. *J. B. Greene.* 19 June 1868.

7378. *Chairman*.] YOU are Superintendent of the Valuation Department in Dublin, are you not?—I am.

7379. Will you inform the Committee what was the original cost of the tenement valuation?—£. 335,000 *l.*

7380. Before the tenement valuation, there were several other valuations in Ireland, were there not?—There was an original valuation made in town lands, which I think commenced somewhere about the year 1830.

7381. Was the 335,000 *l.* paid by the counties?—It was entirely paid by the counties.

7382. What was the cost of the preceding townland or Ordnance valuation?—In round numbers, 160,000 *l.*

7383. Were there not, previously to that, different valuations under the poor law?—Not previously but subsequently; the Ordnance valuation was commenced in the year 1825.

7384. When were the poor law valuations made?—On the introduction of the poor law into Ireland it became necessary to have a tenement valuation, and the townland valuation was superseded, and then an Act passed, the 9 & 10 Vict. c. 110, to make a tenement valuation; that is the valuation made by the department of which I am superintendent.

7385. What was the cost per acre of that tenement valuation?—The cost of that tenement valuation varied, I think; about 5½ *d.* or 6 *d.* per acre all round; I have not the papers before me, but I should say that it amounted to that.

7386. When was it commenced?—It was commenced about the year 1846.

7387. And when was it finished?—It was finished in the year 1864.

7388. How many counties were completed in the year 1851?—I am unable to answer that question.

7389. There were not very many finished then, I presume?—There were not.

7390. Were there many left incomplete in 1851?—No; Ulster was the last province valued, and that was completed in 1864.

7391. I see that you state in a paper which you have handed in to me, that the expense of the valuation was very much increased in consequence of the changes of occupiers between the years 1841, 1851, and 1861; that the population has very much diminished, and that in consequence of that diminished population, there have been great changes in the territorial arrangements of Ireland.

7392. But is it not the case that the changes which took place between the years 1841 and 1851 could have had very little effect, since the valuation of very few counties was completed before the latter period?—Yes; but the population, I should have said, has continued to decrease from 1851 nearly in the same ratio, or, indeed, in a greater ratio, and in consequence of the incomplete state of the revision of the Ordnance survey of some counties, considerable additional cost was incurred, the valuation surveyors having been obliged, by actual measurement, to survey and compute the areas of farms, the fences of which were not represented on the Ordnance plans.

7393. After the completion of the valuation, was the staff of the valuation office much diminished?—It was reduced from 413 persons to 100 persons who now form the staff.

7394. What is your opinion as to the necessity for having an annual revision of the valuation?—The annual revision appears to me to be necessary in the present state of the country. The changes going on are so very numerous that if they were allowed to accumulate for two, three, or four years, the repairing of a work such as this, which is based on the Ordnance survey, and on which every tenement is accurately laid down and surveyed with a field book containing the quality of each particular soil within each field and farm, would involve such an amount of work that the staff should be temporarily increased to do it. To illustrate which, I can give the number of changes in the west of Ireland which have taken place during the present year.

7395. What is your opinion with respect to the division of Ireland into revising districts, as has been proposed by some persons?—I think that it would destroy uniformity, and I think that there would not be full confidence in a number of people being employed having local interests and local influence; whereas, I believe

Mr. J. B. Greene.

29 June 1868.

believe that the present system does possess confidence, inasmuch as we endeavour to carry it out with fairness and impartiality. Ireland is already divided into districts by our department, and I beg to submit to the Committee a map showing the divisions (*handing a map to the Committee.*)

7296. According to this map certain districts are given to certain individuals?—Yes, whom we call field valuers.

7297. General *Dunne.*] Is that merely for surveying purposes?—Yes, merely for surveying purposes.

7298. *Chairman.* Do you believe that the appointment of local valuators of districts or counties would not give satisfaction?—I am quite satisfied that it would not.

7299. If they have no duty to perform, except to allocate the valuation amongst the owners of land, why do you say that it would not give satisfaction?—It is a very serious thing, because if a man was entrusted with a district, say, one of 20 districts, and the maps of our department were handed over to him, an accurate field survey of every change should be laid down on the plans. Supposing that two or three acres were taken from one man and given to another, that must be accurately marked on the map, and then the valuator would refer to the book and ascertain the value of that portion as given in the original field book. Of course that could be done, but I am afraid that in a very short time it would grow perhaps into a loose system, whereas there is such supervision at present that nothing of the sort can take place.

7300. In what consists the supervision?—The field men are allowed to remain as short a time as possible in the field. They are urged to get over the work in order to save expense. They are allowed a certain amount of expenses while they are out of town, and they are allowed their travelling charges. All that they do is to mark out every change on the map, and to send the map to Dublin, and we compute and make all the necessary calculations in the office, they being paid less in the office in Dublin than in the country.

7301. What is the proportion of the annual cost of the revision upon the whole valuation of Ireland?—It is about one-fifth of a penny.

7302. This valuation is used for Imperial as well as for local purposes, is it not?—It is.

7303. And one half of the annual revision is paid by the Treasury, is it not?—It is.

7304. Sir *Charles Lanyon.*] Is that one-fifth of a penny on the valuation, or per acre?—On the valuation.

7305. What is the cost of the actual copying out of the lists of the annual revision?—We make two new copies every year. There are 1,800,000 lines to be copied, and if we take the price allowed to the Poor Law Guardians for that, it would amount to about 2,280 *l.* for each copy. We do not give a new copy every year to the Poor Law Guardians, because we think that we can economise by correcting it; but I calculate that once in every three years they must have a new copy. The copies altogether would amount to about 5,000 *l.*

7306. Do you calculate, then, that in the Valuation Office you pay for this valuation at the same rate as the Income-tax Commissioners?—Very nearly, including the copying and comparing.

7307. Do you think it could be done for a lower price than that?—It could not be done by scriveners, because when we tried it we found so many errors. It is a peculiar class of work, to perform which accurately requires a person to be very conversant with the duty.

7308. With respect to this annual revision, what was the expense of it in the year 1864, 1865, and 1866, up to the last year?—We have it in each county, and I can give it for the years 1864, 1865, and 1866, but it is not totted; for 1866 the total is 21,507 *l.* for all Ireland, half of which is paid by the counties, and half by the Treasury.

7309. It appears from a Return presented to Parliament in the year 1866, that the expense of this annual revision has been progressively increasing since 1863, the date of that Return. In 1863 it was 15,300 *l.*; in 1864 it was 17,842 *l.*; in 1865 it was 20,546 *l.*; and now you state that in 1866 it was 21,507; is that so?—Yes. If you will refer to that Return, you will find that several of the counties were not revised in some of the years and were not completed, as Armagh, Fermanagh, and Down; Down is a very heavy county, and the revision of those three counties is not in that Return, because the original, or primary valuation, was not completed.

7310. It was not completed in what year?—They were completed in 1864, I think; of course they could not be revised until 1865, and they are included in 1865.

7311. But according to the two returns, the increase is still progressively greater in 1866 than 1865, is it not?—Yes, and I should say that the increase will continue for a little while; for, according to the Treasury Regulations the staff commence at a small salary of 80 *l.* a year, and they increase annually by 7 *l.* 10 *s.*; of course there is an addition every year.

7312. Have those officers reached their maximum?—All have not reached their maximum yet.

7313. Is it not the case that very few of them, in point of fact, have reached the maximum?—I cannot say how many of them have reached it.

7314. Before we proceed further, will you explain what is the reason that those two returns, one having been furnished in the year 1866, and the other in the year 1867, giving the expense of the annual revisions, differ as regards almost every county in Ireland?—That is very easily explained. One return is made out for what we call the financial year: that is to say, from April to March, counting 12 months from April; and the other is made out, as it was required by the heading of the returns, for the year from January to December, so that they could not be alike.

7314*. How does it appear that there was that difference in the order for the returns?—It says, "For each year, from 1860 to 1866, both inclusive." Then the other is only "A return of the cost of the valuation in each county for the last three years." I presume that the accountant, finding it easier to make it out for the financial year by just putting together the two half-yearly sums that are sent to the grand jury, accordingly made it out; whereas the other return is made out from January to December, which was supposed to be the form required.

7315. This return for 1867 gives the salaries of the different officers and the staff in Dublin for that year; could you state to the Committee the total amount of the expenses of salaries and of of the office in Dublin in that year?—I could not give that at once.

7316. May we assume that the expenses of the salaries of these officers, printing, stationery, and other incidental matters shown in this sheet, are the charges for which this annual revision expense was laid upon the counties?—Certainly.

7317. Are we to assume that these officers whose salaries are mentioned here discharge all the duties of the annual revision, and copying, and everything else connected with the annual revision?—Certainly.

7318. You have stated to the Committee that these officers are appointed under a regulation of the Treasury, and that they have an annual increase in their salary until it reaches a maximum; I presume, therefore, that they are permanent staff officers who cannot be dismissed without compensation?—No, there is a provision in the 23 Vict. c. 4, for superannuating the entire staff by the Lords of the Treasury.

7319. They are, in fact, permanent staff officers, are they not?—They are a permanent staff.

7320. Then is the annual cost of the revision a fixed sum, excepting as regards this increase in the salaries, according to the length of the service of the officers?—It is not exactly a fixed sum, because it will vary according to the amount of work to be done. If it be necessary to keep a man in the country for seven months instead of four or five months, the expense will be increased in proportion.

7321. But, with the exception of that addition of expense for paying a man in the country, rather than in Dublin, the expenditure is a fixed sum, is it not?—It is.

7322. If that be the case, no matter whether the number of changes in the arrangement of land in Ireland fluctuates or not, this annual charge for revision will still remain at this high figure, will it not?—It would if it continued, and the staff were not reduced and superannuated. If a general revision of the valuation of certain counties in Ireland were necessary, the staff would be available for the duty of revaluation.

7323. But laying aside altogether this question of re-valuing, if this staff be kept up for the purpose of the annual revision, is it not the case that whether there is much or little work to be done in the counties, the salaries of all these officers will still have to be paid?—Yes, except that the staff at present are very hard worked to do it. These copies are very laborious things, and we must have them out by the assizes, and we have very heavy work to do it.

7324. According to the estimate which you have made of the expense of this copying, it is not one-fourth of the whole expense, is it?—It is a little less than one-fourth.

7325. And the other three-fourths of the expenditure must remain the same, must it not, whether the change made by the proprietors on their estates are great or small?—I should say so, according to the present arrangements; but if the staff was found to be in excess, a reduction of the least efficient hands would be recommended.

7326. In this paper which you have handed to me, you state that if the changes in the county of Roscommon in the year 1869 be very few, the charges against that county might not exceed 80 l. or 100 l.?—It would be considerably less.

7327. I presume that the great bulk of the charges for the annual revision are the payment of the salaries of this permanent staff?—Yes; supposing that there is no necessity in one year's annual revision for any change in Roscommon, we can only charge for supplying the copies to them, and of course the Government would have to dispense with some of the officers. I do not see any other way of doing it.

7328. With regard to the expense of the staff in Dublin, I have added up the figures in this return, and I find that the expenditure on salaries in the office in Dublin, in the year 1866, was 20,584 l., was that so?—That must be the gross or entire expenditure.

7329. Was that the entire expenditure for the salaries of these permanent officers and for printing?—Yes.

7330. That is the permanent charge upon it already?—Yes.

7331. And that must remain?—Yes.

7332. And that will exist in the year 1869, will it not, whether great or small changes are made in the counties in Ireland?—I should say so, unless, as I said before, the changes cease, of which I do not see much probability, because they are greater this year than they were last year.

7333. Supposing that in the county of Roscommon the proportion of changes in the coming year are very small, and that in the other counties of Ireland they are on the same scale as they were in preceding years, if the result of that be that the county of Roscommon has to pay only 80 l. or 100 l., it follows, does it not, that the other counties will have to pay a very largely increased proportion, although their changes have not at all increased?—Unless the staff is reduced, there being these reductions in the works, I do not see any other way of meeting it.

7334. But you inform the Committee, as I understand, that the staff cannot be reduced without superannuation?—No, they must be superannuated, or you must find other duties for them.

7335. The expenditure, therefore, of the counties really does not depend, as stated in a note to this return, upon the actual number of changes that have been made in them?—To a certain extent it does, as the time occupied in the field and the office will be charged to the county where the greatest number of changes occur, and which will reduce proportionally the cost of the other counties.

7336. As long as that staff is permanent whether the changes are greater or smaller, each county will have to bear its proportion of this 20,584 l. a year, will it not?—Each county will have to bear its proportion, having regard to the number of changes made in one county over that of another.

7337. With respect to this note attached to the Return of 1867, which states that the expenditure involved in making the annual revision fluctuates in proportion to the number of the changes made by the proprietors in their estates, that reference does not apply to this 20,584 l. a year, does it?—It does to a proportion of it.

7338. Does it not merely apply to the difference between that sum and the total cost of the annual revision, namely, 21,500 l., or to less than 1,000 l. a year divided over the whole of Ireland?—Yes.

7339. Do you think it is a fair thing for the Valuation Office to send a return to Parliament with

Mr. J. B. Greene.

19 June 1868.

Mr. J. B. *Greene.*

29 June 1868.

with this case appended to it, which would easily lead the public to believe that the whole expense of the annual revision fluctuated in proportion to the changes that took place?—I think it was contemplated that it would fluctuate, because we have a number of hands that have been a very long time in the service, and as we found the work sometimes decreased we have applied to the Treasury, and said, that so-and-so had been 25 years in the service, and that we could dispense with his services, and he has been superannuated.

7340. But if you had him superannuated, he would have still to be paid a certain amount for doing nothing, would he not?—Yes; but out of the Consolidated Fund, and not at the expense of the counties.

7341. Taking the actual cost of valuation in the county of Roscommon for the year 1866, there was a Return presented to Parliament with respect to that, was there not; will you first state to the Committee what was the total cost of the annual revision in that county for that year?—£. 692. 1 s. 1 d., nearly 700 *l.*

7342. It appears that there were three revisors appointed in that county, and that one of them spent 60 days, another 63 days, and another 27 days, in that revision?—Yes.

7343. Were those men employed solely in the county of Roscommon?—No, they may have been during the year employed elsewhere, but for that period they must have been in the county of Roscommon exclusively.

7344. Are those revisors sent to particular unions?—Yes.

7345. Are you aware that the unions embrace different counties?—Yes, but they are only charged for their portion. The accounts are kept separately and accurately, and they must return the number of days and the portion of the union in each county.

7346. Taking each of these revisors separately, it appears that the first gentleman spent 60 days, and that his salary is 140 *l.* a year; that is to say, that he spent two months in the revision?—Yes.

7347. Two months at 140 *l.* a year would be about 23 *l.*, would it not?—Yes.

7348. The next gentleman was occupied for 63 days, and his salary is 210 *l.*; supposing that we consider him as having spent two months there also, his salary for that work, in the same proportion, would be 35 *l.*, would it not?—It would.

7349. And the last gentleman was occupied for 27 days, or one month, at a salary of 143 *l.*, and that would be about 12 *l.*, would it not?—It would.

7350. If you add those amounts together, you will find that the salaries of those gentlemen, for the time during which they were employed in that valuation, would not be very much more than 70 *l.*?—It would be about 70 *l.*

7351. Would 70 *l.* calculating the time that they spent in the county of Roscommon, be the remuneration that they would receive in proportion to their salaries?—Just so.

7352. If we take their office duties in connection with that particular revision, do you think it ought to be greater than the salary which those particular revisors receive for the time they were in the field?—In addition to that, you must put down 43 *l.* that they were paid for lost expenses, and 49 *l.* for travelling expenses, and 7 *l.* for labourers, which make up 168 *l.*, which was the cost of their work during the time they were in the country.

7353. I suppose only a small amount of that would come to Roscommon?—The accounts are kept so accurately that that is the exact amount chargeable against Roscommon.

7354. If we add to that 70 *l.*, what will be the total?—The total salary and expenses of three persons in Roscommon amount to 168 *l.*

7355. Was the rest of the 700 *l.* charged for office expenses in Dublin?—To office expenses and the copying of the returns. There are 40,000 lines in Roscommon.

7356. The cost of copying, as you have told us before, is about one-fourth of the entire expense?—Of the gross expense. The copying in Dublin amounted to 120 *l.* added to that, that is to say, the full office copies of 40,000 lines, and the totting and comparing the amounts for the county of Roscommon.

7357. Was the copying of Roscommon much greater in proportion than in other counties?—I estimate that there were 40,000 lines to be copied on a form of this nature (*producing a form*).

7358. What do you make that cost to be?—Two copies of that, one for the county treasurer, and another for the office, which is done every year, come to 60 *l.*, computing it at the same rate.

7359. Then what is the total charge for copying?—The total charge for copying is estimated at about 120 *l.*

7360. And what is the total cost of the annual revisor's salary?—The revisor's salary and expenses are 168 *l.*

7361. That makes 288 *l.*, does it not?—Yes.

7362. For what was the rest of the 700 *l.* charged?—There is another duty that is required to be done all the year, and it is done in the office, that is to say, the renewal of the maps showing every tenement, no matter how minute it is, in the county. Those maps get worn out by constant action in the field, and wet weather, and so on, and from the frequent changes those maps become perfectly useless. We have then to employ draughtsmen to get fair Ordnance sheets from the Phœnix Park, and to transfer to them the tenement boundaries, both in town and country, and they are principally employed in that way.

7363. Are those maps renewed every year?—No, about every third year; that is the field maps. Of the office maps we do a portion every year.

7364. But, according to your statement, the actual work in the field, and the copying of the annual revision in the county of Roscommon in the year 1866, cost only 288 *l.*?—Yes.

7365. To that you have to add the expense of this renewing of maps, have you not?—There is the renewing of the maps, and there is the calculating of all the changes and alterations that the revisor makes in the field, which is not included in either of those items. I think I have explained that the revisor marks out the new tenements on the map, and transmits those maps to town, and we compute them there, and refer to the original field books and see the severable portion of the value taken from or added to the holding, and that occupies a considerable time; in fact, the whole thing is done in a very systematic manner, which requires great care and accuracy.

7366. Supposing that this work was done by the county themselves, or by the district revisors, the

the chief work that they would have to do would be to do this work in the field, and to make these copies, would it not?—Certainly.

7367. Would not that be the principal part of the revision?—Yes.

7368. And yet for this principal part of the work the expenditure is not one-half of what was charged to that county in the year [illegible]?—Yes; but I imagine the person who would revise a district of two or three counties in Ireland would have a staff to do all this sort of work, to assist him. It would be utterly impossible for one person to do it.

7369. Do you consider that the actual work of the reviser in the different counties, and the making out of these copies of that revision, is one-half of the work that is required to be done?—I will not say that exactly, but I have made an estimate here of the draughtsmen's salaries, in addition to that for all the computations and maps that they have to make of all the towns, and for the fair plans which they have to draw, and they amount to 175 l., in addition to that. If you add 175 l. to [illegible] l., it makes [illegible] l.

7370. What is the duty of these draughtsmen?—They are professional surveyors and map draughtsmen, who calculate the areas of the holdings of so many acres, roods, and perches; and then we have tables by which to calculate the value of the land; if it is, for instance, 110 acres, 2 roods, 22 perches, at so much an acre.

7371. Is not that calculation made by revisers in the county?—No, it is sent up to town to be done. The maps are sent up to town with the information as to the changes, and the computation of the area and value is made by draughtsmen.

7372. Would not the man who is sent down, and who is on the spot, and who knows its real value, be quite competent to do it at the same time?—He is not permitted to do it. He would destroy the uniformity of the system if he were allowed to judge for himself. The valuation exists, and must stand for 14 years unaltered; that is the gross valuation.

7373. But supposing that a farm in the original valuation is all in one, and is valued at 100 l., and that it is divided into two, and that the reviser comes and goes over the land, and makes a division of the farm into two, there is a boundary line drawn across it, and he estimates what is the value of the one side and what is the value of the other, does he not, upon the land?—Certainly not. The farm is valued at 100 l.; but there might be 30 or 40 qualities of soil, varying in value from 5 s. an acre to 20 s. or 30 s. an acre, and the qualities of the soil are laid down in our maps at the office, and numbered in the field book. The reviser on the ground only marks the line dividing it into two portions, and he transmits that to the office. We then get the draughtsmen to calculate to ascertain the number of acres of each quality that have been added to one farm and taken from the other; and to compute that at the prices originally determined by the field valuer years ago.

7374. Sir *Charles Lanyon*.] Have you one of those maps here?—I have. (*The Witness produced a map, and handed it to the Committee.*)

7375. *Chairman*.] How is the difference in the soil marked out on this map?—It is marked out here. (*The Witness described the map to the Committee.*) It would not do to guess it, or to allow the valuer to do so, because he might take a different view, and then the uniformity would be destroyed.

7376. Then all that the reviser does is to mark upon the map the lines marking the change of boundaries?—Yes, and to put in correct names and all the information that is necessary to furnish new lists.

7377. As regards the changes of names, those are sent in by the barony poor rate collectors, are they not?—Certainly not.

7378. Are not the collectors obliged to furnish to the clerks of the union, at certain periods of the year, all the changes that have been made?—Yes, but they never do it; we tried several times to enforce it, but we never could do so; we should be very glad to do it, because it would be a great saving. We always issue a circular.

7379. If the collectors do not do it, how is it found out that changes have been made?—We generally insert a notice in the newspaper to landlords, ratepayers, and agents, stating that the reviser will be there, and requesting that, as it is important, the lists being now used for so many purposes, that they should be correct, and they will attend and give the reviser as much information as possible. The lists are extremely defective; the fact is that the lists that are sent in to us from the Poor Law guardians are only nominal lists. The collectors do not go to the trouble to ascertain the changes in the course of the collection; and, therefore, our officer has to note the changes that have taken place. There would be endless complaints if our officer merely acted upon the return which he receives from the clerk of the union.

7380. Is it not the fact that it is the duty of the clerk of the union to send in those returns?—Yes, the clerk of the union sends them in; but it is not the duty of the clerk of the union to collect them; it is the duty of the Poor Law collector to do so.

7381. And you say that they do not discharge that duty?—They do not.

7382. At what time does this revision usually commence?—The Act of Parliament requires it to be commenced after November, so that we can take in generally the May and November changes of tenancies. We do not like to send the revisers to the field until after Christmas, when the days begin to get a little longer, and they can do more work; and then we are generally able to take in the changes in May and November, unless the revisions are wanted before May; but frequently we are able to ascertain the changes. A great number of changes take place in November.

7383. By what time must it be completed?—The Act requires it to be completed the first day before the quarter sessions in each year.

7384. So that this work takes from about Christmas time until June?—Yes.

7385. What are all these revisers, and clerks, and draughtsmen doing all the rest of the year?—They are, I may say, repairing an edifice that has been damaged. The maps are injured, and the field books are injured by continual wear and tear in being carried about; and there is such reference to our office now for information, that we must keep an office copy and a fair set of maps for information in the office at Dublin. We have to keep those maps and copies in constant repair; and the clerks are employed throughout the year, as busily as men could be, in preparing the maps, and making new maps of towns and cities (which are very important), and in preparing and amending the lists for the next year's revisions.

7386. I presume

Mr. J. B. Greene.

19 June [illegible].

7386. I presume then that this staff in Dublin have so very much to do, at present in this annual revision, and this keeping up of maps and other works connected with the office, that it would be utterly impossible for them to undertake a new valuation of Ireland without an immense increase of the staff?—If the changes which I have here in a return received this morning from Dublin continue in Ireland, they could not do it.

7387. At present you state that this large staff is fully occupied by the annual revision?—Yes, in the annual revision. There is one thing that would facilitate it; they could contribute very much to assisting in the revision of the valuation, or in a re-valuation, because, supposing that the annual revision takes place immediately before they correct the maps, they would be available to put into the hands of temporary valuers; we would not have to send over the ground again, but we could at once use the revision maps for the re-valuation.

7388. Colonel *French*.] Then it would not be required to bring them up to what they stand at in the tenement valuation?—It would not.

7389. *Chairman*.] Are these changes in the occupation of land at all diminishing?—In some places they are diminishing, and in other places they are not.

7390. On the whole of Ireland, are they diminishing?—In the north of Ireland I do not think the changes are so frequent as they were.

7391. What control is there over the time which these revisers spend in the country in this field work, or other work which is entrusted to them?—There is this control; in the first place, they are obliged to keep a daily journal, and to record the day of the month, the number of hours they have been in the field, the ten maarks they have visited, and the number of tenements altered. They have also to give a return of the distance they have travelled, and of the expenses of travelling and the cost of the car hire; that is the supervision, but of course I cannot say that sometimes there are not mistakes made.

7392. As far as the grand jury, or the county authorities are concerned, have they any control or supervision over these revisers?—They have not.

7393. Have they any control or supervision whatever over the expenditure of this annual revision?—They have, because the 40th section of the Act requires that the Commissioners shall transmit on, or before, the first day of the assizes to the grand jury an account of the costs and particulars; that is the only control which they have.

7394. What are the costs and particulars which the Commissioners furnish to the grand jury?—They furnish, I think, a general detail of the costs under the same heads that are furnished to the Audit Office in London.

7395. What are those details?—I think they give the salaries, and I think they give hotel and bus expenses, and stationery and printing, as well as I recollect. The accountant, I think, furnishes those particulars.

7396. Are you quite certain that they furnish all those details to the grand jury?—I think that the Act of Parliament is complied with.

7397. But is it the obligation under the Act of Parliament that they are to furnish those details which you have mentioned?—Yes.

7398. Does the Act specifically set out all those particular points which you have mentioned?—It does not; it uses merely the word "details."

7399. But is this word "details" interpreted as the Commissioner of Valuation thinks proper?—No, it is interpreted, I think, according to the view of the Audit Commissioners in London. They desire the accounts to be kept under certain heads, and I think those are the heads which are adopted.

7400. But beyond that have the grand jury any control or discretion whatsoever in the matter?—I think not.

7401. It comes to them as an imperative presentment, which they must pass, and they have no discretion, have they?—None.

7402. Do you think it satisfactory that a very large charge of this description should come down annually upon the county without the county authorities having any means of ascertaining whether it is a justifiable charge, or not?—I think that it entirely depends upon the question of value; if the counties get value it is fair, and if they do not, then it is not fair.

7403. Do you believe that the most competent valuators could not be obtained in each county who would undertake to do all the work that those annual revisers do in the different unions, for a very much smaller sum than is paid to them?—I am quite sure that you would get people to do it for any sum.

7404. But would you get the most competent men?—No, I do not think so; because we find it extremely difficult to get competent men.

7405. Do you not think that those men who are at present engaged in the valuation office in this work would accept those positions in the counties if they were offered to them at much lower salaries than the counties at present pay?—Probably if they were dismissed, they would be very glad to undertake it.

7406. You do not think then that a man who is in the office now would do it?—He might be got to do it.

7407. Are you quite convinced that none of those revisers, whom you at present send down to the counties, would undertake to do the whole work of copying, and laying out of these lines upon the map, and all the rest for a very much smaller sum than is charged to the counties at present?—I think that you could not get parties to do it accurately for a smaller sum than is charged at present; but I am sure you could get parties to undertake it at any price.

7408. I am not speaking of parties generally, but of the individual reviser, whom you send down to do the work?—I do not think that they would be calculated to do the work under the system that is at present adopted, because I would not allow them to make calculations, for I am perfectly certain that they would slur it over, and do it as rapidly as possible, and in three years I am sure the valuation, which cost £25,000l., would not be worth three halfpence.

7409. Colonel *French*.] Do you give them a retiring pension when they leave your service?—Yes; the Treasury award the pension, none of which is charged to the counties.

7410. *Chairman*.] Do you mean that the valuation would be worthless on account of the alterations which would be made in the maps?—Yes; it is rather a scientific and nice work; the work is altogether done, as is generally known, with care and accuracy, and it requires skilled men to do it.

7411. You

7411. You do not think that one skilled man could be got to do the different duties, but that it requires, in fact, all these different officers through whose hands it passes at present?—Certainly; it requires to pass through two or three hands to have the thing done with accuracy; I think it would be very unfair if the valuation were not equally apportioned among the tenants, and I think that would be the case if it were distributed over Ireland in the hands of a number of local revisors.

7412. Upon what principle was this tenement valuation originally made; was it done by a comparison of the soils in each particular field?—It was based upon a scale of the prices of agricultural produce, which, at the time the average was taken, were near the fair prices of the produce. That is an average, say of seven years, for instance, wheat 25 s. a barrel and so on. It was on the basis of those prices that the valuation was fixed.

7413. When you say that it was on the basis of those agricultural prices that the valuation was fixed, how was the particular value of one field ascertained relatively to those prices?—The valuer went into a field and dug up the soil and examined the sub-soil. He then estimated what that soil was best adapted for. Of course he did not do that in every case, but he calculated it in this way; there are 10 acres in this field that would produce, say seven or eight barrels of wheat per acre. He took the amount given in the scale, 25 s. a barrel, and made a gross sum, and from that he took out all the outgoings, and took out the landlord's rent. That is the way in which the whole thing has been done. It has been done on a scientific principle throughout Ireland.

7414. Was each field done in that way throughout Ireland?—If two adjoining fields were of the same quality they were grouped together, and the numbers dotted on the map and the areas computed.

7415. (Colonel *French.*) You stated that during the last year there were more changes than usual, did you not?—Yes; I have a return here as to several counties, particularly in the west of Ireland, where I think the changes are more numerous than in Leinster and elsewhere.

7416. Have you not, during these last three or four years, had representations from several grand juries as to the incorrectness of the different returns which have been sent down?—I have not.

7417. Have there not been representations as to the incorrectness of the names of the different parties holding different lands?—No; we have had some complaints, but very few. Perhaps in all Ireland we might have had a dozen letters from individuals requesting to know why their names were not put upon the valuation lists; and upon inquiry we found that the reason was that they gave no notice themselves, or did not apply to the revisor or the clerk of the union.

7418. Is it not the case that the county of Down grand jury have represented that the returns, as far as names were concerned, were not so correct as they ought to be?—Not that I am aware of; there has been no complaint made from any grand jury that I recollect, with the exception of Mayo.

7419. Your revisors attend at the different Poor Law unions, do they not?—They do.

7420. Is it not the case that the collectors are warned in to attend on the days on which the revisors appear at each union, to give the necessary information to your officers on the subject?—That is the case.

7421. You stated, did you not, that you could not rely upon the information which you got, and that your officers had to make further inquiries?—What I mean is, that we cannot rely upon the lists which are sent in upon the 20th of November in each year, purporting to come from the collectors, but that list is sent in, and perhaps, in the whole union, there would not be many changes. The revisor goes round and says to the clerk of the union, "Will you kindly send for the collectors?" and he sends for the collectors, and from them they obtain further information as regards the changes in the occupation.

7422. Then are the Committee to understand that the return, which you say is not complete, is the one which is obliged to be forwarded to your office, say, in November, or at whatever date it may be?—That is so.

7423. The Chairman asked you as to the expense in the different counties for the offices in Dublin; how do you apportion the expense of the office to each county?—The general establishment charges are apportioned in respect to the gross amount of the valuation.

7424. Can you state the amount of the general establishment charges?—I should say that they are about 5,000 *l.* a year. I do not think they can be more. That is Sir Richard Griffith's salary, my salary, and that of the solicitor and chief clerk and accountant. Then there is the proportion of the office rent, which is not very much; 250 *l.* spread over all Ireland.

7425. Then are there the salaries of the other establishment clerks?—No, the other clerks are kept at each county; they are only charged for the work they do in each county.

7426. But that is really for a certain number of days, is it? The revisor will be there, say, four or five months in the year. Then a certain number of clerks in town are apportioned to these revisors, who are kept constantly in the county, and those clerks regulate and amend the maps and keep the books in order, so that everything may be perfectly straight.

7427. Then you have a system of clerks in your office whose business it is to attend merely to the county to which they are attached?—Precisely so. Of course sometimes, if it is more convenient, we change them from one county to another, and charge accordingly.

7428. What would be the expense for each county for these clerks who are allotted to the different counties?—Roscommon is the only one as to which I have made that out.

7429. In that sum of 175 *l.*, were the salaries of those clerks who were attached to Roscommon included?—Not in the 120 *l.*, but 465 *l.* was the entire amount of salaries which I made out for Roscommon; and then the proportion of the establishment to that was 175 *l.* for clerks constantly at work, making, amending, and repairing books and maps for Roscommon.

7430. Is the remainder for the revisor when he goes down?—The remainder is for the revision. Then there are a number of copying clerks for making the copies for the treasurer, and the Poor Law guardians, and the municipal bodies.

Mr. J. B. *Greene.*

10 June 1869.

7431. How could that expense be lessened, assuming that there were not so many alterations to be made, so that the expense for the next year on the county of Roscommon, as you stated, would be only 100 *l.*?—I was calculating it in this way; that we should only have to supply them with the lists that we had copied; that is to say, that we should have to send the treasurer, and the clerk of the union, and others in Roscommon, copies, and only charge them for those copies, and I calculated that the charge would be reduced in that way; but from the way in which the honourable Chairman put it to me just now about the establishment, I think that I was probably a little astray in my calculations; but I think if there were an uniform system of assessment in each county, as in Dublin and Belfast, then one copy of the valuation only would be required, and a consequent saving would follow in this respect.

7432. Colonel *French.*] How long have you been connected with this office?—I have been connected with it for 17 years.

7433. It is about 40 years since its commencement, is it not?—I think it is.

7434. I should suppose, from the constant inquiries which are going on at the office, that the nature and value of the soil of the different counties can be very fairly estimated now by the officers in your department?—The books in the office represent the nature and quality of the soil in each county in Ireland.

7435. But you have had a great many opportunities of testing the correctness of those documents, so that I presume that you are pretty well satisfied now as to the information which you have in your books?—It is the information which was collected a number of years ago, and it represented at that time the nature of the soil, but whether the circumstances of the country are altered or not, that will not show.

7436. But if there be any question creating a doubt as to the value of land, I presume that you have at different times investigated and made up your own mind as to whether the complaint was well founded or not?—I presume so.

7437. Is the system in your office promotion from one class to another?—It is, but not by seniority.

7438. It is by efficiency?—Yes, that is the rule laid down by the Treasury.

7439. Is there any check over the appointments, or have you them in your own hands?—We have nothing whatever to say to the appointment now. It is done by nomination and competitive examination.

7440. *Chairman.*] But the Chief Commissioner has the nomination, has he not?—He has the nomination; that is to say, he can recommend an individual, but the Treasury may reject the nomination.

7441. But is anybody eligible for this competitive examination unless he is nominated by the Commissioner?—They are nominated by Sir Richard Griffith.

7442. The Chief Commissioner, therefore, has in fact a considerable power in the appointment of those persons, has he not?—He has the nomination.

7443. Colonel *French.*] He can name the persons who go up for examination?—He names the persons for examination.

7444. But he could not recommend to the Treasury to appoint a man who had passed an inferior examination to other persons, could he?—No; after they go up for examination he never interferes in the slightest degree.

7445. Could you give any estimate of what you consider to be the difference between the rated value and the rental value of the country generally; it was supposed at first that the rate was either one-third or one-fourth under the actual rental value if it was screwed up to the average; do you consider that that is the case now?—No; if I were to go over all Ireland I would say that you could not add more than 15 per cent. There are places, I must admit, which have been changed in circumstances, where you could safely add 25 per cent. to arrive at a fair live-and-let-live rent.

7446. Do you think that it will be necessary to increase the valuation of Ireland as it now stands, at your next revision?—I should say so.

7447. Sir *Charles Lanyon.*] After the valuation is made in the field, the work, I take it, in the office becomes purely mechanical work, does it not?—Quite so.

7448. It is merely a reference to figures and work, which anyone trained to it can do, is it not?—It is so.

7449. Do you not think that the work can be very much better carried out under the present system of a division of labour, by having surveyors first employed in the field, and the work being then sent to the central office to be examined and checked, according to the original documents, than by the appointment of any separate officer in each county?—Unquestionably I do.

7450. Do you not think that the whole of the system of the valuation of Ireland would be very greatly interfered with, if not altogether destroyed, by any alteration of the present arrangements with reference to both the out-door and the in-door work?—I have stated that if any interference with it took place I do not think that in three years the country would look upon it as anything but a perfectly useless document.

7451. General *Dunne.*] Without the annual revision?—Yes.

7452. Sir *Charles Lanyon.*] Do you not think that the annual revision is a cheaper mode of proceeding than it would be to allow the alterations to accumulate for three years and then to make that revision?—I think it would be next to impossible to carry it out, because the effect of that would be, that if you allowed the alterations which have taken place in the western counties to continue at the present rate, which is 74,000 changes per annum, the same staff could not possibly get over the ground and amend the documents and set them forth to the public for the purposes for which they are used, viz., for a fair levy of the county rate and of the poor rate; and for arrangements between the owners and occupiers of land, and for the elective franchise. It would require an additional staff, and then for three years that staff should be disbanded, and got up again at the expiration of another three years.

7453. Is your staff at the present moment fully occupied?—They are fully occupied, and most heavily worked.

7454. With regard to the expense of 700 *l.* connected with Roscommon, there appears to be a little discrepancy in the statement of the cost

of

of the central office; the figures that I took down were 288 *l.* for the field expenses, and 175 *l.* for the staff expenses in Dublin, making altogether 463 *l.*; now if there be no other expenses to be charged specially to the county, that would make the difference between the 463 *l.* and 700 *l.*, viz., 237 *l.*, the charge for the central office, would it not?—There is a proportion for the cost of supervision; there are law expenses which are not included; there is stationery, and there are other incidental charges which make it up; but I should add that there is 80 *l.*, which I have calculated amounts to something like the proportion for the general establishment, and then there are law and other costs.

7455. What do you suppose for those costs, which are specially applicable to the county of Roscommon, should be added to this sum of 463 *l.*?—The charge for advertisements is 6 *s.* 10 *d.* Printing and stationery happens to be rather a heavy item here; I think it is 63 *l.* Then there is postage; that is really only a trifle. Carriage of parcels costs 4 *l.* 11 *s.* Proportion of office rent, 11 *l.* 9 *s.* Light and fuel, 11 *s.* Law expenses only 19 *s.* It amounts altogether to about 80 *l.*

7456. Then we have to add 80 *l.* for special expenses connected with Roscommon?—Yes; and then there is the proportion which I have not given, of Sir Richard Griffith's salary and my salary, and the chief clerk's.

7457. But is not that included in the 8,000 *l.* for the central office?—Yes; but I have not added that to this.

7458. Of this sum of 700 *l.* which was charged for Roscommon, how much was specially applicable to that county without reference to the general expenses. It is 543 *l.*, is it not?—It is.

7459. What was the gross amount chargeable to the county of Roscommon at the last session?—*£.* 692.

7460. Then the difference would be 149 *l.*, which, according to that estimate, is the gross amount of the sum chargeable to the county of Roscommon for the central office, the rest being the special expenses incurred for the revision of the county of Roscommon?—I am afraid that there must be some other charge which I have not included there.

7461. *General Dunne.*] Could you put in a return of it?—I will do so.

7462. *Sir Charles Lanyon.*] When the 700 *l.* is spoken of as the cost of the revision for the county of Roscommon, or for any other county, it is desirable that it should be seen how far those expenses apply specially to that county, and what are the general expenses. Supposing that there are 32 counties in Ireland, and that those expenses were 100 *l.* for each county, they would amount altogether to 3,200 *l.* Then you say that that is in proportion to the valuation, so that Roscommon being one of the highest counties, it would not be so high as that in some of the other counties; can you ascertain that?—I will ascertain that.

7463. *Chairman.*] What are the particular items of the printing of which you spoke?—I think that this sum of 63 *l.*, which is the charge for printing, is not in other counties so much as it is in Roscommon; but I imagine that it is a portion of an instalment that is due to the Government for the original printing, which has been spread over a number of years. The Government only collected the money by a series of instalments spread over a number of years, and there might be a proportion of an instalment in this amount.

Mr. *J. B. Greene.*

19 June 1868.

7464. *General Dunne.*] Did you say that the original valuation cost 825,000 *l.*, and that you do not think it is worth three-halfpence?—No; I said that it would be rendered utterly useless, if the revision of the valuation of Ireland was distributed into independent hands.

7465. At this moment do you think that the valuators who are sent down to the districts to revise, go to every place?—Certainly not; their instructions are not to go to any place unless they are satisfied that some change is absolutely necessary to render the lists more perfect.

7466. But they are bound to go, are they not, if there is any report of a change?—Certainly.

7467. Do they not generally take these changes from the books of the Poor Law Guardians?—No; their instructions are particularly not to do so, because we find that very frequently there are most erroneous names and sub-divisions represented, which really do not exist, and the instructions are that the reviser must satisfy himself of the accuracy of the returns given. For instance, since I came here I have received a letter as to a revision of the Union of Tipperary, to say that there were 37 houses thrown down in one street in the town of Tipperary, and that the reviser had not attended to it. I said that this was very strange, and I sent the letter over, and I got an answer to say that the 37 houses are standing still unoccupied.

7468. Therefore, if he does not go, of course he is liable to censure if he is reported to you?—Yes, unless he is perfectly satisfied.

7469. The reviser has nothing to do, has he, but to state the facts as to a change of tenement, or a change by death?—He has to see if there is a change of position, or a change by subdivision, or by the consolidation of farms; and if there is such a change, he has to put it down.

7470. But how is he to obtain information as to changes by death or succession from father to son?—We have directed them to endeavour to see the receipt from the landlord in whose name he takes the rent.

7471. Would it do to take it from the county cess collectors?—No.

7472. Do you think that would not be sufficient?—We could not trust it at all; they have no idea of maps, and they would be telling us that one holding was altered, whereas it was another one.

7473. The expense of the revision that you have given for the county of Roscommon, I suppose, would be applicable to any county in Ireland, according to the size of the county?—No; some landlords carry on more stripping than others; they go right in a straight line, across hedges and ditches, and they put us at a very great expense in re-surveying and re-applotting the valuation.

7474. In those cases, do you send down surveyors to re-survey?—Yes.

7475. Do you think, as has been proposed in some places, that if each poor law union kept a competent surveyor of their own, who merely sent up the bonds to you, that would be a more inexpensive way?—No; I do not think that we should like to have anything to say to him, because then we should be relying upon a surveyor, over whom we had no control, and the work could not be supposed to be accurately, or justly, done; and in Ireland people look so much to the

Mr. J. B. Greene.

15 June 1869.

the land, and to the accuracy of the returns, that we could not carry out that system.

7476. Could not the men employed locally be placed under your command, so that you might have the power of insisting upon their being correct?—Yes; but I do not see the advantage of leaving those men there for 12 months going over the county privately; I think that once a year is enough.

7477. But could you not employ them each year for a certain time in the revision, as several gentlemen have proposed?—I think not with proper regard to accuracy.

7478. Do you think that it would be much cheaper?—I think it might be cheaper, perhaps, for one year, but I think after two or three years it would be found not to work at all well, and that a great deal of work would have to be done over again; we should have no check upon them.

7479. You stated, did you not, that you considered that the difference between the valuation and the rental was about 15 per cent.?—Yes; that is taking the average of all Ireland.

7480. Do you think that the valuation throughout Ireland is tolerably even, comparatively speaking?—I think that in the north of Ireland the valuation is higher than in the south, or the west.

7481. Then it approximates more to rent there?—It does; the reason of that is, that the Act of Parliament required us to deduct certain rates at the time the valuation was made; those valuations were made in the year 1848, and up to 1858, when things were very low, and taxes were very high; the valuations made at that period are relatively lower than the valuation of Ulster, which is only just completed, and where the taxation is comparatively less.

7482. Do you think that the variation is so great that it requires a re-valuation of the whole country?—No; but I think that in equity such places as were valued some time ago ought to be revised and placed upon the same standard of taxation as Ulster.

7483. The last valuation cost 325,000 *l.*; how much do you think that a revision of that kind would cost?—I should say that it ought to cost not more than 50,000 *l.*

7484. Do you think that the result of such a re-valuation would be worth 50,000 *l.*?—That is a question which I cannot answer.

7485. Would the result be so valuable for the locality for general taxation, and for poor law purposes?—It would not be an advantage to the locality, because they would have to pay, I suppose, higher taxes.

7486. But is it any great matter whether the valuation is high or low, so far as paying the taxes is concerned, because the rate would be either high or low proportionately?—If you levy over a certain space within a poor law boundary, that is the effect; but if the area of taxation is extended over the whole country, as in the case of the income-tax, it ought to be fairly and equitably done.

7487. Therefore, do you not think that it is merely for income-tax, and for purposes of imperial taxation, that this revision would be useful?—I think that, for poor law purposes, and for the grand jury cess, and so on, it is necessary to have the valuation uniform over Ireland.

7488. But within a poor law union, for instance, where the tax is levied, is it any matter whether it is high or low, so that it is uniform within the area on which the tax is levied?—Yes, it would make a very serious difference. For instance, there might be in one county a uniform valuation where the rates were high, and the deduction, of course, proportionate, and in the next county the rate might be low. Then the grand jury cess is not levied within similar areas to the poor law unions, and it would be very unfair and unjust.

7489. Are those variations very frequent?—I have known, in the county of Clare, 8 *s.* or 9 *s.* deducted in one poor law union, and, perhaps, 4 *s.* or 5 *s.* in another.

7490. But generally the rise of the valuation would be for the purpose of imposing the income-tax, would it not?—That is one of the purposes.

7491. In the case of rent-charge, would there be any difference?—No.

7492. Are you aware of the way in which England is valued?—England is not valued upon a uniform system. I have heard great complaints as to that, and I believe it was at one time endeavoured to put it under the same arrangement as Ireland.

7493. But it is not so now, is it?—I believe not.

7494. Have you any knowledge as to how the deductions are made, and how, in fact, the valuation is made?—I believe that in England the tenant pays the taxes. He pays, say, 100 *l.* a year rent, and he pays 30 *l.* or 40 *l.* taxes. They put down the rent as the amount that goes into the landlord's pocket; they do not take the taxes into account. In Ireland we take the gross value, and then from that we deduct the rates, taxes, repairs, and insurance.

7495. And half is charged to the landlord?—Yes.

7496. But in England do you not think that the difference between the real letting value and the actual valuation on which the tax is levied is much greater than in Ireland?—I do not think there is very much difference.

7497. Have you seen a return in which such a comparison is given?—I have not.

7498. Then you would not recommend the English system for Ireland?—No, I would recommend the Irish system for England.

7499. Could you put in a paper giving the average expense of the annual revision in each county in Ireland?—This paper, which I have before me, gives the cost in each county.

7500. Mr. *Blake*.] In reply to an honourable Member, I think you stated that, between the valuation and the letting value of the land, there was a difference of about 15 per cent.?—That is the average, taking the whole of Ireland.

7501. But does not the actual rental, on an average, go considerably beyond that?—In some places I know the valuation is 25 per cent. below the actual letting value, and that is owing to the deductions that are made; but if you take the whole valuation of Ireland at 15 per cent. you come very near the true live-and-let-live rent of the country.

7502. That is so far as the difference between the letting value and the valuation is concerned?—Yes.

7503. But then is there not a much greater disparity than that between the actual rental paid and the valuation?—Yes, I think the actual rental paid in Ireland is pretty smart.

7504. Could you give an approximate idea as

to

to the difference between the rent actually paid and the Government valuation?—I am sure the actual rent paid is 25 per cent. altogether over the Government valuation on an average.

7505. Did you ever hear in Ireland of places where the rent actually charged by the landlord is 50 per cent. over your valuation?—I have heard of such cases.

7506. Could you give the Committee any idea as to whether the rent and the valuation in England more nearly approximate than in Ireland?—I think the rent and the valuation in England more nearly approximate than in Ireland.

7507. *Chairman.*] Upon what ground do you say that the rent and the valuation in England more nearly approximate than in Ireland?—I think the rents in Ireland are higher in proportion, generally speaking, than the rents in England.

7508. Have you examined into the relative proportions of the rental and valuation in England?—Yes, I have had occasion to do so. I was sent by the Government over to the north of England to inquire into places there, and I found that rents were paid on soil of from 30 s. to 35 s. an acre; and in some places in Ireland I have known it to be quite up to that for similar soils.

7509. Are you not aware that the valuation in England differs immensely in different parts of the country?—I was speaking rather of the rental of the two countries.

7510. Do you consider that the rent of Ireland is, on the whole, higher than the rental of England?—I think it is as high.

7511. Could you tell me whether there was any estimate made of what the cost of this annual revision would be before it was commenced?—I cannot recollect.

7512. Are you aware whether or not the Chief Commissioner, in the year 1857, stated that it would not cost more than 10,000 *l.* a year?—I do not recollect that.

7513. You say that the valuation at present made would be worthless if district revisers were appointed; but those district revisers could not alter the general valuation of the country, or of the townland at all, could they?—They could do so gradually, unless there was great supervision over them; they could really practically do whatever they pleased, which they cannot do now.

7514. The actual value of a townland can never be changed from year to year, can it?—No.

7515. The townland valuation, then, would remain the same, would it not?—Yes, supposing that the interior of that townland has been changed two or three times, how on earth is anyone to discover whether that has been equitably apportioned or not.

7516. Does not the difficulty merely extend to the equitable apportionment within that townland?—Within the townland, during the duration of the valuation.

7517. Do you mean to tell the Committee that you believe that the whole general valuation of Ireland, even if it were equitably apportioned, would be worthless?—Certainly; because I think that the maps give the occupiers a true notion of the quality of the land. If the quality of the land, the divisions of the lands, and the value to be put to them, are not accurately ascertained and uniformly adhered to, I am quite sure that the valuation would be perfectly worthless, because you would find one property valued a great deal too high, and another too low.

Mr. J. B. Greene.

19 June 1868.

7518. Within a townland?—Within a townland the whole valuation would, of course, remain the same.

7519. At present there is an appeal, is there not, from the decision of the valuators?—Certainly.

7520. If such an appeal were left to the tenants, or other occupiers of those holdings, in case they thought themselves aggrieved, would not that remedy any difficulty that would arise from disproportionate applotment within the townland in case district revisers were appointed?—Of course the tenants would appeal, as at present; but I think the tenants of Ireland, if I may be allowed to say so, would much rather have an independent body. We really have no appeal, because if there is anything conceived to be wrong, the very instant we discover it we send another man to the ground to correct it. In consequence, the people are so well satisfied with the fairness with which the system is conducted, that they seldom appeal.

7521. Would not an appeal provide against this unfairness to particular tenants?—In some measure it would; but I do not believe that they would ever avail themselves of the quarter sessions, unless there was something very gross.

7522. At all events, the only disadvantage that could arise, supposing the thing to be done in the worst possible manner, would be that within the limits of a townland, the occupation of which had been altered, discrepancies might arise between one valuation and another?—Yes.

7523. That is the total amount of inconvenience that could arise, even if this annual revision was carried out on the very worst possible principle?—Yes, but I believe as regards the tenant, that would extend to all districts; every townland, I believe, would become the same.

7524. Have you a return with respect to the size of the baronies in the county of Cork?—I have. (*The same was delivered in, vide Appendix.*)

7525. *Mr. Leader.*] You are aware, I suppose, of the size of the different baronies in Ireland?—I am.

7526. Do they vary very much?—Very much indeed; and I think they vary more in the county of Cork than perhaps in any part of Ireland. For instance, in the barony of Barrymore there are 153,000 acres, and in the barony of Barretts there are only 31,000 acres. The valuation of one barony is 60,000 *l.*, and of the adjoining one it is only 5,000 *l.*

7527. *Mr. Blake.*] Would it not be almost impossible to support an appeal against valuation, inasmuch as the question would be one of relative value as compared with other land?—Yes; it would be difficult to do it, because they should employ valuators to go over it to see whether it was relative or not.

7528. As you mentioned that it would save expense to have local valuators, what objection have you to their appointment, if they were placed under the control of your department?—If you leave a person locally there, I do not see how his time is to be employed the whole year. We get the field work done in five months, and save an immense expense by doing so; but if you leave a man in the field all the year, I do not think you would have the same control to see that everything is accurately done, because the

Mr. J. B. Greene.

the valuation must be made in a most minute way to keep it up with accuracy, and to have the tenant equitably and fairly taxed.

7529. Could you not look over the work of the local people?—If the local man sent up his maps to our office, shewing the whole subdivision in a townland, we should not know that he had surveyed it accurately unless we went and had it done again. We should have to take it for granted that it was all right.

7530. Mr. *Gregory*.] You mentioned that in some cases the rent was double the amount of the taxation; are there many such cases?—No, the only cases that have come before me have arisen where there was a large amount deducted for taxes during the famine year, and the year's valuation was consequently very greatly reduced. As I stated, I know some places where 6 s. or 8 s. in the £. were deducted.

7531. Those, then, are purely exceptional cases to which you have referred?—They are purely exceptional cases; I do not know any districts in which that is the case.

7532. *Chairman*.] You stated, did you not, that you believed that the cost of a new valuation of Ireland would be only about 50,000 *l.*?—Yes, but only the portion that requires to be re-valued at once would be done for that amount.

7533. What do you mean by the portion that requires to be re-valued?—Ulster and parts of Leinster do not require to be re-valued, because they have been done recently.

7534. Then that 50,000 *l.* does not extend to the whole of Ireland?—It would extend to Munster, and part of Leinster and Connaught.

7535. I understood you to say that the cost of the new valuation for the whole of Ireland would be 50,000 *l.*?—No, because I do not think that Ulster requires any addition at all made to it.

7536. Mr. *Gregory*.] Do you consider that successive revisions of the valuation would be less costly?—I think that a revision once a year would cost less than a revision made every third year.

7537. Mr. *Blake*.] Could you give the Committee an idea of the comparative per-centage of the actual rental in Ulster, and of the valuation?—In Ulster it would be about 10 per cent.

7538. Could you state what is the proportion in the south and west of Ireland?—I am sure that the rent is from 15 to 25 per cent. more than the valuation.

7539. Mr. *Gregory*.] Does that arise from the reduction of the taxes, which are now less than they were before?—Mainly from that; the south and west were valued early, and Ulster, as I have stated, was only valued recently.

7540. If there was to be a new valuation, therefore, in the south and west of Ireland, I presume that the valuation would be considerably raised?—Yes.

7541. And you would make it more in conformity, probably, with the rents?—More in conformity with the rents, and equal to the scale of Ulster.

Mr. John Hardiman, called in; and Examined.

Mr. J. Hardiman.

7542. *Chairman*.] You are deputy clerk of the peace for the county of Limerick, are you not?—Yes.

7543. How long have you held that office?—I was first appointed very nearly six years ago.

7544. Could you mention to the Committee in how many counties in Ireland there are deputies appointed for the clerks of the peace?—In 24 counties in Ireland.

7545. And in those counties the clerks of the peace themselves do not discharge the duties at all, do they?—No; having the deputies, the clerks of the peace never do the duties themselves.

7546. The deputy is appointed by the clerk of the peace, is he not?—He is.

7547. And he is responsible alone to him, is he not?—He is.

7548. His tenure of office of course depends upon the tenure of office of the clerk of the peace?—Upon the will and pleasure of the clerk of the peace.

7549. And of course it terminates with the death or resignation of the clerk of the peace?—Yes, if not before.

7550. Are the deputy clerks of the peace in any way officially recognised by the authorities in the county?—Yes; in the Act of Parliament of the 14th and 15th of Victoria, it is set out that the deputy clerk of the peace, or the deputy who is thereby required to perform duties in the absence of the clerk of the peace, is to do all things necessary to be done by the clerk of the peace, and in that way the deputy clerks of the peace are recognised.

7551. Are they appointed by any legal instrument?—Yes, under a stamped document; in fact I can shew the Committee an appointment if they would wish to see one (*producing a document, and handing it to the Committee*).

7552. I see by this document that they are merely appointed during the will and pleasure of the clerk of the peace?—During the will and pleasure of the clerk of the peace.

7553. A proposal has been made to the Committee to amalgamate the offices of clerk of the Crown and clerk of the peace, as you are, I presume, aware. If such a proposal were carried out, the deputy clerks of the peace would of course lose their present appointments, would they not?—They might still retain their appointments as deputies, if the Committee so reported, provided deputies were not done away with. It does not follow that upon the amalgamation of the offices, the deputations must be annulled.

7554. But suppose that an Act were passed obliging the new officer to discharge his duty in person, those gentlemen then, of course, would lose their appointments?—Then they would all lose their appointments, of course.

7555. But, as I take it from your evidence, those appointments are merely upon the will of the present holders of the office?—That is so.

7556. Therefore those gentlemen really have no vested interest in this office which they can put forward as against the counties, or as against the public?—They have no vested interest except, as I said before, in being recognised by the Government, or by the official authorities, and as doing the duties and being obliged to enter into a heavy sum as security to the clerk of the peace for the due performance of those duties to the clerk of the peace.

7557. They enter into this engagement with this

the individual who at present holds the office, do they not?—They do.

7558. And they do not enter into any engagement with the public, do they?—No.

7559. And they have no responsibility to the public?—No; but they have to the clerk of the peace, who is also bound to the Government in a large sum.

7560. The clerk of the peace is the official recognised officer who is responsible for all those duties, is he not?—He is.

7561. I understand that the deputy clerks of the peace in Ireland believe that they have some claim for compensation from the counties, in case those offices were amalgamated and the deputies were done away with; will you mention to the Committee on what ground they base this claim?—On the simple grounds of having been, some of them, a very long time in office, and having devoted their time to learning the business of the office. Some of them may now be incapable of taking other situations; they are too old, perhaps, to learn professions, or to stand competitive examinations for any other appointments.

7562. But are not those claims which they will have upon the present clerks of the peace, who appointed them, they being their servants?—It is on the clerks of the peace who appointed them that they would have those claims; but then it is optional with the clerks of the peace, either to send them adrift, or to give them any sum which they may wish to give; they can treat them in any way they wish, inasmuch as a clerk of the peace, under one of those deputations, might to-morrow cancel the deputation, and say, "It is my will and pleasure to discharge you; your time is up now, and I do not require you any further."

7563. If it were left optional with the existing clerks of the peace to appoint deputies or not, but if it were required that in all future appointments the clerks of the peace should discharge their duty in person, would then the deputy clerks of the peace have any complaint to make?—They would, inasmuch as of course they would all lose office; the 34 deputy clerks of the peace who are now acting would all be thrown out of office.

7564. I do not think that you understand my question; supposing an enactment were passed that with respect to all the existing clerks of the peace they should be left in the position in which they are at present, but that with regard to all new appointments to the office of clerk of the peace, such new officers appointed should discharge their duties in person, would the deputy clerks of the peace then consider that they had any ground for complaint?—That might be very hard to say; that might all depend upon the lives of the present clerks of the peace.

7565. But their tenure of office at present depends upon the lives of the present clerks of the peace, as you mentioned before?—It certainly does.

7566. Their claim does not extend beyond the lives of the present occupants of the office, does it?—It does not.

7567. And if the present occupants were left in the same position as they are in at the present time, the deputy clerks of the peace would have no ground to complain, would they?—They would not except that they were in office at the time that the new incoming clerks of the peace were appointed, and that they would know the duties.

7568. Mr. *Gregory*.] They would have no claim upon them, would they?—Certainly not.

7569. (*Chairman*.] And they would have no claim upon the public?—No.

7570. At present they have no claim upon the public, but they have a claim upon the men who appointed them?—Yes.

7571. In instances where deputy clerks of the peace are appointed, is it their duty to prepare the list of voters for the different counties?—It is.

7572. Do they receive the whole of the remuneration for the performance of that duty?—It is all a matter of arrangement as to their remuneration or salary with the clerks of the peace. They receive a certain salary from the clerks of the peace, which is merely a matter of arrangement. They, of course, are bound to account for all the fees and presentments and salary of the office.

7573. In fact, there are private arrangements between each deputy and each clerk of the peace?—That is so.

7574. And those arrangements may be different in different counties?—Yes.

7575. And the deputy clerks of the peace are, on the whole, the mere servants employed by the clerks of the peace, are they not, with whatever arrangement between them they may think proper to adopt?—Just so.

7576. Do you think, that if it were considered desirable for the public good that the offices of clerk of the peace and clerk of the Crown should be abolished, and that a new office should be created, the duties of which should be transacted by one individual, it would be possible that any cognizance could be taken, in an Act of Parliament or otherwise, of these gentlemen who are merely servants of public officers, and who are in no way either appointed or recognised by the public except as his servants?—Of course, except on the ground, as I before stated, that they are losing office, and are being thrown out of employment, they have no cause of complaint as against the public.

7577. And the cause of complaint in that case would be against the men who employed them, would it not, and not against the public?—It would, except that they are recognised by the public and the officials, and that they have done the duties for a length of time, and that the answers to all communications coming from the Government, and even from this honourable House, are returned by those deputy clerks of the peace, and signed by them, and acknowledged by the officials.

7578. But they are so signed and made out by those deputies merely as the appointed servants of the clerks of the peace, are they not?—Decidedly so, and in no other capacity.

7579. And if any mistake were made in those documents, is it not the clerk of the peace who would be responsible for it?—I do not know that, because, as I said before, the words of the Act of Parliament are these: "And any deputy hereby authorised to act for the clerk of the peace." Whether that would bring in the deputy clerks of the peace of themselves to be accountable, I cannot say.

7580. Primarily, the clerks of the peace would be responsible, would they not?—In the first instance they would.

Mr J. Hardiman.

19 June 1852.

7581. And they might be able to make the deputy responsible to them afterwards?—They might do so.

7582. Mr. *Leader*.] What duties does your principal perform now?—He does not perform any duties; I do the whole thing.

7583. He has a sinecure, has he?—He is like a great many others, perhaps, in that respect.

7584. *Chairman*.] You need not answer this question if you do not like, but would it be fair to ask you what salary you receive?—I have no objection to answer it; the salary is about 300 *l.* a year.

7585. And for that do you discharge the whole of the duties?—The whole of the duties.

7586. Does the clerk of the peace receive all the fees?—I account with him, and give him a return at the end of the year of all the monies which I receive for him.

7587. Mr. *Leader*.] Can you state how much his salary is?—I could not state the salaries in the different counties. They have very much decreased latterly; the fees are decreasing.

7588. *Chairman*.] What fees does the clerk of the peace receive?—There are a great many fees; they are divided into two classes, civil and criminal fees. There are fees for the entry of civil bills, on those they receive the sum of threepence, that is for the entry and for the order and the hearing. Then they receive on signing a decree threepence more for checking that decree and signing it, and seeing that it is all correct.

7589. Do they receive fees also on ejectments?—On ejectments they receive a fee of 1 *s.* 6 *d.* on the entry, and then on the signing of the decree and checking it they receive 1 *s.* It varies; if the rent is over 30 *l.*, then they get an extra sixpence on that, but there are very few of those.

7590. Do they receive fees on spirit licenses?—They do; there are fees for signing the certificate, then there are also fees every year for renewing those licenses, which the clerk of the peace gets.

7591. Do you, as deputy, receive any advantage from the increase of those fees?—I do.

7592. I understand you to say that the arrangement in your particular case was that you received 300 *l.* a year, and that you did all the duties?—It is about 300 *l.* a-year.

7593. But does your salary vary in proportion to the fees?—It does: the greater the fees and the income, the greater my salary is.

7594. Mr. *Leader*.] Cannot you state how much the fees are in your county?—The whole income of the office is generally about from 620 *l.* to 640 *l.*

7595. General *Dunne*.] Is there a regular salary?—Yes, the salary is 370 *l.* a-year; that is 400 *l.* Irish.

7596. There is a table of fees, is there not?—Yes; those are the fees that I am enumerating.

7597. Are there not some customary fees besides the legal fees?—No, except for the registry and the making out the jurors' book.

7598. Are there no fees by prescription, or is nothing paid to the clerk of the peace for registry?—No, except for the registry of trees, on which they get a small sum.

7599. They are entitled to them by law, are they not?—They are.

7600. But they are entitled to no fees by prescription?—They are not.

7601. *Chairman*.] Is your salary, upon the whole, about 300 *l.* a year, including the amount you receive through those fees?—It is.

7602. It appears by this Return of the salaries and emoluments of the different county officers, that in Limerick the salary of the clerk of the peace was 370 *l.*, and that the fees amounted to 371 *l.*; do you discharge the whole of the duties of this office for about 300 *l.* a year?—Yes.

7603. And the rest the clerk of the peace receives for doing nothing; is that so?—That is so.

7604. Colonel *Cooper*.] But then he has the expense of an office, has he not?—No; all public officers are bound by law to have offices in the court-house, where offices are provided for them.

7605. Colonel *Farde*.] You state that your chief, the clerk of the peace, pays you a certain sum in the way of salary; will you state what that sum is?—I mentioned that it was about 300 *l.* a year.

7606. Does that include your fees?—That is taking in everything.

7607. You need not answer this question unless you like; but does he not give you a certain amount irrespective of the fees, say 100 *l.* a year?—My arrangement is, that I am to receive all the income from fees, and every other source in the office, and I give him so much, and I keep so much myself: there are certain private arrangements generally made.

7608. *Chairman*.] You are acquainted, I presume, with the duties of the office of clerk of the Crown?—I am.

7609. Do you see any difficulty in the two offices being united in one person?—I do not see any difficulty in the world. It may be right for me to mention, that the clerks of the peace are, for some portion of the year, obliged to be away in different quarter session towns, and if parties came in, or inquiries were made, or documents were required which should be signed officially by them, they might at the time be away, and it might be very inconvenient if those documents could not be signed by anybody else but themselves.

7610. Could you mention to the Committee how the expenses for the registration of voters are calculated. The clerk of the peace, as you are aware, at present receives remuneration for expenses incurred under the Registration of Voters Act?—He does.

7611. How are those expenses made up, and upon what basis does he send in his bill for them?—Some years ago there was a regular table of expenses drawn out, and put before the grand juries of the different counties, and a certain sum was named which was to be thenceforward paid each year to the clerk of the peace, and that sum is received every year in the county of Limerick.

7612. Does that sum remunerate them for all the expense and trouble which the registration of voters have thrown upon them?—I would not say that it is a sufficient remuneration, because it is very low in the county of Limerick, but that is the only sum which they receive for remuneration in that respect.

7613. But still is it not more than the actual cost which this registration of voters has put them to, and is there not supposed to be included in that sum a remuneration for the clerk of the peace's trouble?—There is; but it must be a very

small

small sum to pay the expenses, for there is a great deal of trouble in preparing the registry.

7614. Colonel *French*.] Does not the clerk of the peace after each revision send his regular bill of costs to the grand jury at the assizes?—He does not; he has one stipulated sum, as I before said.

7615. Is that by private arrangement between the grand jury and your clerk of the peace?—Yes, that arrangement was made some six or seven years ago.

7616. *Chairman*.] The clerk of the peace is appointed by the custos rotulorum of the county, is he not?—He is.

7617. And of course in appointing the clerk of the peace he is aware of the Act which permits the clerk of the peace to do his work by deputy?—He is perfectly well aware of it.

7618. Is there any other point in connexion with this subject upon which you would wish to remark to the Committee?—There is nothing that strikes me now except this alone, that if the offices of clerk of the peace and clerk of the Crown were amalgamated, and the office given by Government to a certain individual, he might be looked upon with discredit as regards the preparation of the registry, because it would be in his hands in a great measure to prepare the registry. If he were biassed in any way for a candidate, it might perhaps be looked upon as objectionable.

7619. But would not that difficulty exist at the present time; what is the difference with respect to that matter which would ensue, if there was this union of the two offices?—Certainly the same difficulty would exist now. The clerk of the peace not being himself acting, and the deputy being under the direction of the chairman, there might be more control over him than there would be otherwise.

7620. But in the other case, this new officer (whatever you like to call him) would be under the control of the chairman, would he not?—He certainly would.

7621. And of course holding the two offices, he would be a man having a higher salary, and presumed to be in a higher position than the present deputies?—Decidedly.

7622. Why therefore do you imagine that there would be any greater danger in case this new officer was appointed than there is at present?—I would not say that there would be any greater danger, but I merely say that being the creature of, or being appointed by, the Government, the objection might possibly arise.

Mr. J. Hardiman.

19 June 1868.

7623. I understand from a document which I have seen, which emanated from deputy clerks of the peace, that in case the offices of clerk of the peace and clerk of the Crown were united, they have some proposal as regards the salaries; what is that proposal?—They would be quite willing to do the duties if they were allowed to continue, and to pay the clerks of the peace if they were obliged to retire, a certain sum, whatever the Committee might think proper, provided they were allowed themselves to continue doing the business during their lives, and then of course when they died out there would be new appointments.

7624. Have you any other suggestion to make to the Committee?—I merely desire to say that it would be a great matter if the deputies could be recognised in some way. If the office is abolished, the hardship will fall upon the deputies and not upon the clerks of the peace, who do not perform the duties themselves now.

7625. General *Dunne*.] Supposing that the deputies were allowed to die out, there would be no claim for compensation, would there?—Certainly not.

7626. If the clerks of the peace got compensation, would they not be bound to share that with the deputies?—That would be a matter of private arrangement; they might be bound in honour to do so, but it would not be compulsory upon them.

7627. *Chairman*.] Your case is, that if the clerks of the peace were abolished, they would receive compensation for the abolition of their office while the acting men would receive no compensation?—I would not say that the clerks of the peace would not give their deputies compensation, but they would be left at the mercy of the clerks of the peace to treat them as they wished.

7628. And you believe that there ought to be some provision which would oblige the clerks of the peace, in case the deputies were not continued, to give them a certain proportion of the compensation, whatever it might be, which was allowed to themselves?—Most certainly. When we have worked, and acted, and earned that compensation for the clerks of the peace, it would be hard upon us then if we were sent adrift without some provision being made for us.

LIST OF APPENDIX.

Appendix, No. 10.

Appendix, No. 11.

Appendix, No. 12.

Appendix, No. 13.

Appendix, No. 14.

Appendix, No. 15.

Appendix, No. 16.

Appendix, No. 17.

APPENDIX.

Appendix. No. 1.

PAPER put in by Mr. *John Hill.*

DRAFT BILL.

I. In all cases in which the county surveyor shall consider it necessary to proceed under the 54th section of the said recited Act of the 6 & 7 Will. 4, c. 116, the treasurer shall from time to time, in such manner and under such regulations as the grand jury may direct, out of any monies in his hands applicable to the general purposes of the county pay and advance such sums to contractors, artificers, or workmen, as may be duly certified by such surveyor, not exceeding the amount at the time on the levy and unpaid in respect of the contract, in connexion with which the proceedings are being taken, and such monies so advanced shall be replaced by the monies raised and levied under the presentments in favour of said contract.

II. If, in the opinion of the county surveyor, the contractor for any county work shall be guilty of neglect to commence or to proceed with his work, or shall be executing it with improper materials, or in an improper manner, it shall be lawful for such surveyor to summon the said contractor and his sureties, by summonses left at their usual places of residence, before the justices at petty sessions of the district in which such work, or the greater part thereof, may be situate; and if such charge be established before such justices, it shall be lawful for them to make an order directing the said contractor and his sureties to execute his contract within a period to be stated in such order, and to pay the cost of the proceedings together with such penalty for the default, not less than 10 *s.* nor more than 10 *l.*, as to the said justices shall seem right; and if at the expiration of such order the county surveyor shall still see reason for being dissatisfied with the manner in which such work has been executed or proceeded with, it shall be lawful for him again to summon the contractor and his sureties before the justices at petty sessions, and the justices shall thereupon proceed to inquire into, and finally adjudicate upon, the complaint; and if it shall appear that such work has not been commenced or has been insufficiently executed, or executed contrary to the terms of the contract, it shall be lawful for such justices, having ascertained the amount which it may require for the completion or execution of such work according to the contract, to authorise such surveyor to complete or execute the same at a cost not exceeding the amount of the recognizance for said contract; Provided, that in those cases in which such surveyor shall so recommend, it shall be lawful for such justices to postpone the giving of such authority, and to extend the time for completion, and at the time of so doing to impose such further penalty not less than 10 *s.*, nor more than 10 *l.*, with costs, and such conditions as to further like penalties or to the issuing of authority to the surveyor to have the work completed or executed, as to them shall seem right.

III. In every case in which authority to the county surveyor to complete or execute a work shall have been so given as in the last section mentioned, the petty sessions clerk shall forthwith send a certified copy of the ruling to the county treasurer's office, and the treasurer shall thereupon from time to time in such manner and under such regulations as the grand jury may have directed, out of any monies in his hands applicable to the general purposes of the county, pay and advance such sums to contractors, artificers, or workmen as may be duly certified by such surveyor, not exceeding the amount authorised in the said ruling, and at the ensuing assizes such surveyor shall report to the grand jury all such cases, in order that, if considered desirable, proceedings against the contractors and their sureties may be directed.

IV. Whenever, in pursuance of the requirements of the preceding section, the treasurer shall have paid on foot of any contract an amount greater than that at the time on the levy, and to the credit of it, he shall submit to the grand jury at the ensuing assizes a statement of any such, and of all such, amounts so paid in excess; and it shall be lawful for the grand jury, having regard thereto, to present, to be raised off the county at large, or the barony, or half barony thereof chargeable with the work, in respect whereof the excess shall have occurred, the amount or amounts so paid in excess, if not otherwise recovered from the defaulting contractor and his sureties.

V. It shall be lawful to recover in any suit on a recognizance for the due fulfilment of a county contract, such sum of money as shall have been applied, or as it shall be necessary to apply, to the execution of the work in respect whereof the forfeiture shall have accrued, and in the case of contracts extending over one or more years, to sue on such recognizance for each and every or any forfeiture when and as same shall occur; Provided always, that the aggregate of the monies recovered in any suit or suits in any one year of the term of the contract, shall not exceed the penal sum therein mentioned, and that the re-

App. No. 1.

covery of any monies in any one year shall not affect the power to recover the full amount of the recognizance in any subsequent year of the term.

VI. All monies recovered under such recognizance shall be forthwith paid over to the treasurer of the grand jury of the county, county of a city, or county of a town, within which the forfeiture of such recognizance may have arisen, and may be applied under the direction of the said grand jury, either in aid of the presentments of the county at large, or barony, or half barony, chargeable with the contract in respect whereof the forfeiture shall have occurred, or for the purpose of the completion or execution of said contract, under the superintendence of the county surveyor.

VII. Whereas the limitation to the sum of 5 l., in section 80 of the said recited Act of Will. 4, of the amount which may be presented for the erection of direction posts, milestones, milkposts, and depôts for materials has been found inconvenient, and productive of disadvantage, be it enacted that the same be hereby repealed, and that it shall be lawful henceforward for any grand jury to present for any such purposes such sum or sums as shall appear to be necessary.

VIII. Nothing herein contained shall extend to any work or presentment in the county of Dublin or county of the city of Dublin, nor in any way repeal, alter, or vary the provisions of said recited Acts, save the 17th section of said Act of the 19th and 20th years of Her Majesty's reign, chapter 63, which is hereby repealed; and save so far as same are otherwise hereby expressly repealed, altered, or varied.

In addition to the powers given to the justices at petty sessions in the foregoing sections, I would recommend that they should have authority to void or determine a contract for maintenance, in case of gross neglect, at their discretion.

John Hill, 2 April 1858.

Synopsis of Mr. Hill's Clauses.	Objections.	Mr. Brett suggests—	Advantages.
MAINTENANCE OF ROAD CONTRACTS:			
Two justices necessary - - -	Loss of time to all concerned; it would lead to adjournment, and [illegible] proceedings being taken.	Proceedings able to all cases. One justice of the peace to have jurisdiction up to 5 l. penalty. Two justices of the peace, from 5 l. to 10 l., maximum penalty to be [illegible] expenses of county officers.	Simplicity. Great saving of officers' time, and [illegible] quantity or amount. [illegible]
Summons, penalty, minimum 10 s., costs. Maximum 10 l., and costs.	As petty sessions cases should not exceed 10 s., officers might be heavy in taking proceedings, and the object should be defeated.		
Justice of the peace's order to county surveyor, to enter on work.	The [illegible] of the peace may not be the best judges, and they may not be [illegible].	One proceeding only - - -	Saves much time, and quicker remedy.
SPECIAL WORKS:			
Two justices - - - - -	Objection as above.	Every such work to be [illegible] with county surveyor, if work be of public necessity to be [illegible].	County surveyor being then [illegible] responsible, [illegible] of work to be of public utility. [illegible]
Summons and penalty, minimum 10 s., and costs.	Ditto.		
Maximum 10 l., and costs. - -	Ditto.		
Second summons and penalty - -	This tedious mode of proceeding would certainly prevent officers from acting; proceedings would probably occupy every [illegible] of time.		
Order to proceed by justices - -	As the justices act under the county surveyor, the latter will not give him the chance, especially in any work not imperatively necessary; and so that the [illegible] will be a dead letter.	County surveyor to visit by court, and to apply to contractor and [illegible] of his opinion on work or not.	Full responsibility on county surveyor, and [illegible] fairly given to the parties concerned.
		If neglect continued by contractor, [illegible], penalty, and [illegible] may be repeated, as often as may be necessary, until bond is satisfied.	The knowledge of this "[illegible]" will [illegible] contractor to work.
On recommendation of surveyor, justice may extend time and [illegible] time.	The adjournment a second time being allowed, for a third and [illegible] time (perhaps a fifth or sixth time) from previous adjournments, county surveyor will not recommend.	Justice to enforce penalty on bond -	Will be evidence how far the bond is attended, if future proceedings taken.

10 May 1858.

Henry Brett, C.E.,
County Surveyor, Wicklow.

Appendix, No 2.

EXTRACTS from a LETTER from Dr. *John Hancock*, of Lurgan, expressing his Views with respect to the Reform of the Grand Jury Laws.—17 May 1868.

To The O'Conor Don, Chairman of Grand Jury Committee.

Sir,

AFTER nearly 30 years' experience, I have come to the conclusion that the present grand jury system is indefensible; I am inclined, therefore, to recommend that the grand jury be in future relieved from all fiscal duties, that the management of the repairs and making of roads and bridges be transferred to Boards of Guardians and Town Commissioners respectively.

That the lunatic asylums be transferred from the management of the present Boards to the Poor Law Commissioners, and supported by a group of unions adjacent to each asylum; the Board of Governors to consist of a certain number of representatives from each union.

The cost of gaols and constabulary being a part of the administration of justice, to be charged to the Consolidated Fund.

The offices of clerk of the Crown and Peace to be united, and discharged in person by a gentleman resident in each county.

The county surveyors to be transferred to unions.

The office of barony constable to be abolished.

County infirmaries to be sold for the benefit of the counties, as there is a complete system of medical relief without them.

Salaries of judges' and barristers' criers to be abolished.

The cost of militia and reformatories charged to the Consolidated Fund.

Registration of county voters to be charged to unions, and borough voters to boroughs.

Traverses for damages and liability to be heard by assistant barristers.

The Guardians to meet twice a year for the disposal of road business in public, and after due notice, under such regulations as the Poor Law Commissioners may by sealed order direct.

Payments to contractors once a month on certificate of surveyor; by this means the grand jury cess would be amalgamated with the poor rate, and a large saving in collection effected.

The Poor Law system of audit is excellent, and would of course apply.

The present cost of lunatics in the asylum is very high, and a considerable saving would be effected by uniform management; the asylums would then be useful for acute and dangerous cases, and harmless and chronic cases would be kept in the workhouses.

Under this arrangement, the Board of Superintendence of Lunatics in Dublin Castle might be consolidated with the Poor Law Board.

The Board of Superintendence of the Gaol should be appointed by the Lord Lieutenant, and the County Inspector of Constabulary might be made the local inspector.

There are 163 unions in Ireland, and 325 baronies, so that each union would represent about two baronies; but the unions being of recent formation, are much more symmetrical, and a Board of Guardians could well and efficiently manage the roads, and there would be constant supervision and control. Landed property would be safe in the hands of the Guardians, as half of each Board at least must be magistrates.

The one collection of the double tax in November would be a great relief to the farmer, instead of the present collection of cess in spring and summer, and the efficiency and economy of the proposed system would compensate the landlords for their contribution to the cess. I do not know whether you concur in these views; but if time permitted, I could give satisfactory reasons for their adoption.

The Commissioners of Public Works should be empowered to advance money on liberal terms to Boards of Guardians and Town Commissioners on a mortgage of the rates for works of permanent and public utility.

Appendix, No. 3.

App. No. 3. LETTER from Mr. *Gerald FitzGibbon*, to the Right Hon. *Chichester Fortescue*, M.P.

Sir, Office, Four Courts, Dublin, 16 May 1868.

MY attention has been called to a report in "*Saunder's*," of yesterday, of the proceedings before a Select Committee, sitting on the Irish Grand Jury System, of which you are the Chairman.

Lord John Browne is reported as stating that the audit of Treasurer's accounts is at a charge of 5 s. per cent. It is also reported that Colonel French remarked that the present system of audit costs 6,000 *l.* a year.

If anything depends on the cost of the audit, I hope the Committee will not think me obtrusive when I state that by a rule of the Lord Lieutenant in Council, made in 1842, the limit of expense was settled at 3 *s.* for every 100 *l.*, being 2 *s.* less than the maximum allowed by the Act.

I state on next page the accurate cost of the audit each year since I came into office in November 1860, by which it appears that the expenses, when greatest, amounted to 1,510 *l.* 4 *s.* 10 *d.* in the year 1864. That they did not amount to 1,500 *l.* in any other year, and that the average of eight years was 1,460 *l.* 19 *s.* 5 *d.*

I have, &c.

The Right Hon. Chichester Fortescue, M.P. (signed) *Gerald FitzGibbon.*

		£.	s.	d.
1861 - -	Total Expense of Audit - - -	1,457	15	3
1862 - -	- ditto - - ditto - - - -	1,478	18	4
1863 - -	- ditto - - ditto - - - -	1,485	8	1
1864 - -	- ditto - - ditto - - - -	1,510	4	10
1865 - -	- ditto - - ditto - - - -	1,466	8	3
1866 - -	- ditto - - ditto - - - -	1,410	2	9
1867 - -	- ditto - - ditto - - - -	1,430	7	8
1868 - -	- ditto - - ditto - - - -	1,427	1	8

All ending 25th March each Year.

Appendix, No. 4.

PAPER delivered in by Mr. *William Johnson.*

COUNTY OF CORK.

RETURN of the ATTENDANCES of MAGISTRATES and CESSPAYERS at the PRESENTMENT SESSIONS for the Barony of *Barrymore* for the last Five Years.

1863.	1864.	1865.	1866.	1867.
SPRING SESSIONS.	SPRING SESSIONS.	SPRING SESSIONS.	SPRING SESSIONS.	SPRING SESSIONS.
Magistrates: Lord Fermoy. G. Standish Barry. Wm. J. Sheehy. Cornelius O'Callaghan. George A. Wood. Denis Morrogh. John Carmichael. Edward Morgan. Captain Hayes. Captain Barry.	*Magistrates:* Wm. J. Sheehy. G. Standish Barry. Richard Morris. Hon. Robert Hare. Simon Dring. Sampson T. W. French. Cornelius O'Callaghan. Denis Morrogh. John N. Beamish.	*Magistrates:* Wm. J. Sheehy. Sampson T. W. French. Cornelius O'Callaghan. Denis Morrogh. John N. Beamish. Thomas Gallwey. Captain Stewart. Wm. H. Barry.	*Magistrates:* Lord Fermoy. Sampson T. W. French. John N. Beamish. Wm. J. Sheehy. Cornelius O'Callaghan. G. Grubb. Captain Moran. John G. Nason. Thomas Tarrant. Richard Morris.	*Magistrates:* Lord Fermoy. George A. Wood. Richard Morris. Wm. J. Sheehy. Lieut. Col. Beamish. Lieut. Col. Wood. Henry Mansfield. Simon Dring. Captain Stewart. Cornelius O'Callaghan. Edmond Burke. Alex. W. Lowe. Robert Martin.
Cesspayers: Richard G. Campion. John Wakeham. Patrick Clereen. Thomas Donovan. Wm. Cashman. Edward Heard. Edmond Murphy. Richard Cleary. Wm. O'Connell. James Dunlea.	*Cesspayers:* Richard G. Campion. Wm. Cashman. Denis Cantillon. Richard Barry. David Barkley. John Fenton. Michael Flynn. Henry Wilson.	*Cesspayers:* Joseph B. Wakeham. Uniacke R. Mackey. Richard Fell. Wm. Cashman. John Peard.	*Cesspayers:* Uniacke R. Mackey. James Higgins. Wm. O'Connell. Richard Cleary. Patrick Glavin. Henry Wilson. John Wakeham. James Kent. Henry Ellison.	*Cesspayers:* Henry Wilson. John Hanson. Nathaniel C. Martin. Hugh Delany. Richard Fell. S. K. Farsey.
SUMMER SESSIONS.	SUMMER SESSIONS.	SUMMER SESSIONS.	SUMMER SESSIONS.	SUMMER SESSIONS.
Magistrates: Wm. J. Sheehy. Sampson T. W. French. G. Standish Barry. Denis Morrogh. Wm. H. Barry. Cornelius O'Callaghan. Freeman Crofts. Benjamin S. Wood. George A. Wood. John Carmichael. John G. Nason.	*Magistrates:* Wm. J. Sheehy. Thomas George French. Simon Dring. John N. Beamish. G. Standish Barry. George A. Wood. John G. Nason. Abraham J. Devonsher. Wm. Barry.	*Magistrates:* Wm. J. Sheehy. Cornelius O'Callaghan. George A. Wood. Benjamin R. Wood. Denis Morrogh. Thomas Gallwey.	*Magistrates:* Lord Fermoy. Wm. J. Sheehy. George A. Wood. Abraham J. Devonsher. John G. Nason. Henry Mansfield. Thomas Gallwey. Cornelius O'Callaghan.	*Magistrates:* Lord Fermoy. George A. Wood. Richard Morris. Col. Beamish. Wm. J. Sheehy. John N. Beamish. Cornelius O'Callaghan. A. W. Lowe. Henry Mansfield. Thomas H. Tarrant.
Cesspayers: John Martin. Charles Aldworth. Edmond Farrell. Denis Murphy. Timothy O'Regan. Edward Hayes. Wm. Barry. John Haynes. Richard Verling.	*Cesspayers:* Michael Burke. Michael Flynn. Daniel Cashman. Daniel Barkley.	*Cesspayers:* John Martin. S. K. Farsey. Wm. Barry. Wm. Hayes.	*Cesspayers:* John Martin. Patrick Hegarty. Michael Dunlea. George Logan. Richard Martin. Thomas Adams. John Peard. James Hughes. David Kent.	*Cesspayers:* John Peard. Edmond Farrell. Jeremiah Delany. James Kent. Wm. M'Carthy. Wm. O'Connell. John Kennedy. George Logan. Uniacke R. Mackey. Denis Cashman. Richard Martin. Patrick Hogan.

Wm. Johnson, Secretary, Grand Jury.

Appendix, No. 5.

PAPER handed in by Mr. *Henry Brett.*

Grand Jury (Ireland) Laws.

Suggestions as to Constitution of Special or Baronial Sessions.

In order to insure full representation, it is essential to divide each barony into districts, to be represented each by some one person paying cess for property in his occupation therein. Each district to be of the value of not less than 5,000 *l.*, nor more than 10,000 *l.*, according to valuation of barony.

Cess collector to return to clerk of Crown lists of highest cesspayers in each district, two for each 1,000 *l.* value (not being disqualified as in Sec. 7 of Grand Jury Act).

Clerk of Crown to prepare cards with names of highest cesspayers therein, and draw out in open court before the judge of assize, district by district, and name for each district.

The cesspayers so drawn for the several districts in a barony to constitute with justices the baronial sessions.

Justices to sit, resident in barony or qualified by property therein in possession, or as heirs or agents thereto.

Justices of the peace present to choose a chairman from among themselves, if more than two in attendance.

If only two justices of the peace present, senior to preside.

If only one justice of the peace, he is to preside.

If no justice of the peace present, cesspayers to choose a chairman from among themselves if more than two; if two only, the first drawn by secretary by lot to preside, and if only one cesspayer, such cesspayer to preside.

Chairman to have in addition to his vote a casting vote.

Justices may act alone, cesspayers may act alone, qualified justices of the peace, and associated cesspayers eligible to act whenever he comes in, in like manner as justices of the peace.

If no justice of the peace or cesspayer attend, within hours named, county secretary to adjourn such session to a future day, giving notice thereof.

If business not completed within hours named, sessions to have power to adjourn such sessions, but no application not in the list to be entertained.

If no justice of the peace at adjourned sessions for receipt of tenders for works, tenders taken by associated cesspayer to be valid.

No justice of the peace or associated cesspayer to become contractor for, or to be pecuniarily interested in any county contract; penalty, 100 *l.*

No contractor eligible to sit at any presentment sessions; penalty, 100 *l.*

County sessions shall consist of the following, one justice of the peace for each barony, present at baronial sessions, and elected by the justices present.

One associated cesspayer for each barony, present at baronial sessions, and elected by the cesspayers present.

If at any baronial sessions only one justice attend, such justice, and if only one cesspayer, such cesspayer, shall sit at county sessions for such barony.

Justices of the peace present to choose a chairman from among their number, and if no justices of the peace present, cesspayers present to choose a chairman from among themselves.

At county and large sessions, like proceedings in all respects as at baronial sessions.

To decide upon all applications for works chargeable in whole, or in part, upon the county at large.

To

Chargeability.

To settle chargeability of roads and bridges as between adjoining baronies, and as between baronies and county at large.

Division.

To divide baronies into cesspayers' districts, and on memorial of baronial sessions, to vary them from time to time, if the county sessions think fit.

Vacancies in county offices.

To elect to vacancies in county offices, subject to approval of grand jury.

Grand Jury.

It has been ruled that the sheriff is not bound to go on calling persons until each barony is represented. (Foot's Grand Jury Laws, page 27.) It is desirable to enact—

Qualification.

That the qualification of persons capable of acting on a grand jury shall be a resident in occupation of a 50*l.* freehold, or 100*l.* leasehold.

Mode of empanelling.

The sheriff shall prepare baronial lists of all qualified persons, and continue calling persons therein, barony by barony, until one person appears for each barony in the county, if any such person be in attendance. The first answering to be foreman.

Having thus, if possible, secured the representation of every barony, he shall begin again, taking first the barony of highest value in the county, and so on, barony by barony, in order of value, and so on, until the full number (23) be filled up.

The persons so answering shall be the grand jury of the county, and in all fiscal matters shall decide by a majority of *those present*, provided not less than 12 be in attendance at the time. The foreman to have in addition to his vote a casting vote.

Power to compel witnesses to attend.

The several administrative bodies, namely, the baronial sessions, the county sessions, and the grand jury, to have power to compel the attendance of witnesses by summons signed by the county secretary.

Imperative presentments.

All imperative presentments should, having been laid before the grand jury, be put on the fiat by the court, if legal, and printed in a separate chapter in the abstract of presentment.

County works.

It is desirable to make the following alterations in the works presentable by sessions and grand jury:—

To authorise the use of iron and brick in bridges; the alteration of stream courses for site of bridge, and without varying chargeability of bridge to be built.

To authorise the construction of sewers, &c., through presented streets (with power to arrange chargeability).

To authorise the making of a new road through a stone or brick house, and through an office of an inhabitant of such house.

To limit presentable roads to those not less than 18 feet wide in the clear of fences or gripes, and in cases of "turn-again roads," to those which offer the only means of ingress and egress to tenements valued over *£*.

The provisions as to county printing contracts require revision.

Grand Jury Laws (Ireland).

Suggestions for Amendment.

Application for works. By whom.

Application to be made by one cesspayer. *County surveyor* to make application for necessary repairs or improvement of presented roads, bridges, &c., if not already provided for by presentment.

When.

Cesspayers applications to be lodged with county secretary 30 days before first presentment sessions for the county; and county surveyor's applications at like time, but such requirement not to take away power to apply at sessions for any such work as above, if omitted through informality or insufficiently applied for.

Notices not required, except in certain cases.

County secretary to list all applications, and such list to serve instead of notices, except notices on occupiers, in cases of making new roads and widening and stopping up old roads.

Where.

Applications to be made where works locally situate.

If expense, or any part of it, be proposed to be placed upon county at large, such application to be submitted to county sessions.

Applications for making or repairing existing roads, situate in two or more baronies, to be made in the barony off which larger portion of expense is proposed to be raised, and like for bridges, and to go before county sessions for apportionment.

App. No. 3.

In all contracts for maintenance, one-fourth of the yearly amount to be presented after spring, and three-fourths after summer assizes; chargeability of county roads as between county and baronies, to be settled by county at large sessions, and similarly as to bridges, if proposed to be placed upon the county in whole or part.

Incidence of county cess.

If one baronial sessions agree to present two-thirds of cost of bridge over barony stream, or one-third of total cost of new road in adjoining barony, the balance to become compulsory on the second barony, if so decided by county sessions.

If of two adjoining counties one shall present two-thirds of cost of bridge over county stream, or one-third of repairs of road in adjoining county, the balance to become compulsory on the other, and the apportionment of such amount to rest with the county sessions of the respective counties.

On all holdings rated under 4 *l.* *the cess ought not to be levied on the occupier.*

Bonds.

Bonds to be made to county secretary, minimum amount 10 *l.*, one surety for sums under 20 *l.*, and two or more for larger sums.

The amounts now required for works over 10 *l.* to be reduced, a special bond for maintenance contracts to be good for each and every year of the term, and amount in all cases to have reference not to the contract price, but to the limit allowed by sessions, and in special cases (nominal presentments) to special sums to be named by sessions.

Proceedings on bonds for neglect, &c., petty sessions.

One justice of the peace to have jurisdiction, if penalty sought do not exceed 5 *l.*; two justices of the peace, if over 5 *l.*; power of justices of the peace to extend to *penalties* only; production of bond, specification, and tender, to be evidence.

Penalty to be not less (if case proved) than actual expenses of county officers in attendance as witnesses, nor more than 10 *l.* at any one time, and amount to be endorsed on bond by justice of the peace.

If penalty inflicted, county surveyor to have power to enter upon work, if, in his opinion, necessary for the public convenience, notifying to the contractor and sureties present in court whether he elects so to do, or will leave the work in their hands; in which case, if neglect continued, penalty shall be again recoverable.

Penalties to be paid over to county secretary (or treasurer), and balances placed to credit of "General Purpose Fund."

All county works to be included; any such proceedings not to nullify contract until bond fully satisfied.

Unexpended balances.

Balances uncertified to be placed to credit of barony or county (as the case may be), or in cases reported by the county surveyor as of great public utility, may, by order of grand jury, be expended in completion of the work; county balances may be allocated to general purposes.

Payment for works in charge of county surveyor.

Tender of resignation of contract for sufficient cause shown, if recommended by county surveyor at sessions, and allowed thereat, may, if approved by county sessions and grand jury, be accepted.

County treasurer, on receipt of "abstract of presentments," to pay on works given in charge all sums certified by the county surveyor as expended out of General Purpose Funds.

And similarly on neglected works, on receiving copies of conviction of contractor.

The amounts not in the former case to exceed the limit of sessions, or in the latter the sum conditioned in the bond.

Treasurer *to pay on the works*, and to be allowed a reasonable poundage therefor.

Uncertified balances as above.

Grand jury may present for difference between amount of contract and limit of sessions, or so much as has been expended, if not recovered at quarter sessions.

What works may be given in charge.

The works to be given in charge to the county surveyor shall be those of repairs and improvements reported by him as necessary to prevent public inconvenience or loss, and shall include any such work for which either there has been no tender, or such tender as the grand jury may think it better not to accept.

Security for sub-contracts.

On any work on which the county surveyor enters, justices of the peace in petty sessions to have power to ratify sub-contract and take bond to treasurer, for sufficient amount, subject to like conditions, powers, and penalties with ordinary contracts, &c., at special sessions.

Proceedings on bonds for neglect, &c. Quarter sessions.

Powers of chairman at quarter sessions to extend not only to recover pecuniary loss, but also inconvenience caused by neglect or delay. Proceedings at quarter sessions to be taken, if so ordered, by county sessions or grand jury.

"General Purpose Fund."

All monies in hands of county treasurer not ordered for payment at the preceding assizes, to be available for general purposes.

Grand jury may allocate county at large balances or funds coming to credit of county at large, to General Purpose Fund, or may present for such fund a sum not exceeding 500 *l.*

Fund and monies available to be drawn upon by county treasurer to pay advances to contractors, and to make payments on works in charge of county surveyor, and fund to be recouped out of presentments for such works as they come in.

Payment to contractors.

Advances on certificate of county surveyor may be made on all county works over 20 *l.* in amount, including maintenance contracts, not exceeding three-fourths of the amount presented at each assizes for such work.

Works

Works certified and allowed at sessions, if approved by grand jury, may be paid in full. — *App. No. 6.*

Maintenance works, if favourably reported on by county surveyor and allowed at sessions, may, if certified by county surveyor at sessions, and approved of by grand jury, be paid for to full up to the amount.

Notice of traverse. — In cases of "traverse," notice to be served on applicant and county secretary 12 days before the empannelling of the grand jury for fiscal business.

Proceedings in work twice disallowed. — If any work applied for be twice disallowed at sessions or by grand jury, or if the price allowed be such as no tender can be procured for, there should be an appeal to a petty jury, as in a traverse, with like notice to county secretary.

Procuring materials. — Power should be extended to the carrying away materials through lands, and by that passage which can be made the most direct.

Among the materials should be included clay, earth, or sods, and the provisions should extend to all county works.

To simplify the provisions of the Grand Jury Act, c. 109, it is necessary to provide that, after previous inspection by any one or more of the appraisers of compensation, contractor (or surveyor) may proceed to raise, &c.

Nuisances, trespass, or injury on public roads. — It is most desirable to bind under a penalty, the occupiers of land adjoining a public road,—

To keep the fences along same in repair.

To scour drains at the back of such fences.

To allow water to pass off road.

To remove, at all seasons, boughs, &c., obstructing; to plash hedges to, say, 4 feet high, compulsorily, and in a similar way to prevent him from turning water from his lands upon the road or roadsides.

Temporary occupation of land. — During the progress of a county work, power to be given to occupy lands temporarily for a substituted road, or for preparation of materials, compensation to be assessed as in case of materials.

Appointment of county surveyor. — To ascertain the fitness of candidates, a practical engineer conversant with county matters and works, or a county surveyor, ought in all cases to be one of the board of examiners.

At present there is not, and until a vacancy occurs there cannot be, any person "qualified" to act as county surveyor, though at any moment an emergency requiring such may arise through the illness or death of one of these officers.

To prevent the serious inconvenience and great loss which such an occurrence might cause, an examination should be held at once, and a list made of the candidates "qualified," not exceeding two to be placed in the order of merit, and whenever the list is reduced to one, an examination should be held, and the best qualified candidate be added to the list; in all cases the person at the top of the list to be appointed.

Promotion. — As well to stimulate the zeal of the officers as to make the most suitable arrangements for the discharge of the arduous duties in the first class counties, it seems desirable in filling up vacancies to carry out a system of promotion.

Dismissal. — The power of dismissal seems of an unnecessarily arbitrary character, "at the pleasure of the grand jury." It seems reasonable that if complaints arise, they should be referred to a tribunal not connected with any of the parties.

Removal from county to county. — Some check should also be placed upon the arbitrary power of removal from county to county.

Superannuation. — The arduous duties of the office seem to require, not only in justice to the officer, but for the benefit of the public service, that a superannuation allowance should be granted.

Assistants. — The surveyor to have power to employ an assistant for every 250 miles of road presented for, and to regulate the salaries of these officers, but so as that the total amount shall not exceed 6 s. 8 d. per mile.

It would appear in many respects desirable that the county surveyor should, if he so thought fit, employ his assistants to oversee the roads "in charge" at a small percentage allowance, to be paid out of the presentment for the work.

The surveyor should have not only, as now, power to appoint his assistants, but also to remove or dismiss them; and thus the whole responsibility should devolve upon him, as head of his department.

It would be useful in heavy works, such as a large bridge or county building, that power should be given to county sessions and grand jury, to authorise the employment of a clerk of works or temporary assistant.

Amalgamation of offices. Clerks of Crown and peace. — The offices of clerk of the peace and clerk of the Crown might with advantage be amalgamated; the fees abolished, and remuneration made by salary only, according to a classification of counties.

Clerk of the crown. — The documents on which fees are paid should be stamped, and the proceeds go to the credit of the county.

The first vacancy in either office not to be filled up; the survivor to hold both.

Subsequent vacancies to be filled by votes of the members of the county [illegible], subject to the approval of the grand jury.

Officer

Officer may appoint a deputy (subject to approval of county sessions and grand jury) to act in cases of illness or other unavoidable necessity, but not otherwise.

Deputy, if vacancy occur, to act until a successor be appointed, and receive thereafter a rateable proportion of salary.

These offices (of which the latter was recently abolished on death or resignation of county treasurer) should be amalgamated as above proposed, and like rules made as to first and subsequent vacancies, salaries, fees, and stamps, and also as to the appointment of a deputy.

The salary should be such as to remunerate the officer for the increased duties and responsibilities, as well as for the abolition of fees.

He should fill up all applications and notices and supply copies of tenders, and be responsible for the accuracy of all bonds and copies of specifications, which he should be bound to supply, but not copies of maps or sections.

He should make the applotments of the county cess, issue warrants for its collection, and audit the collectors' accounts monthly.

He should make all payments on works in charge of the county surveyor, and furnish to the grand jury accounts of the expenditure on each work.

He should attend at all proceedings against contractors for default, and produce the necessary original documents in his custody on a notification from the county surveyor.

He should convene extraordinary meeting of county sessions, on requisition of three members, or of the county surveyor.

The persons qualified to attend to be those who were qualified to sit in the next preceding sessions, for the county at large.

To fill vacancies in county offices.

To provide for sudden damages of large amount to roads, bridges, or county buildings.

To take measures for the protection of the interests of the county, and order proceedings, if they find it necessary.

Classification of Counties.

Three Tables of classification obtained at present.

Of these, the Tables in the Grand Jury Act and that regulating the salaries of the treasurers of counties, appear very faulty, and wholly inapplicable.

The Table in the County Surveyor's Act (1862) was made for that office alone, and does not seem applicable to the other county offices, and, even for the county surveyor, it does not meet the varying circumstances of that officer in the larger counties.

It is desirable that a Table of classification on some stated principles should be made, calculated to meet the alterations in the different county offices, and to meet any changes which the law may permit.

(signed) *Henry Brett*, Clerk,
County Surveyor, Wicklow.

28 May 1868.

Appendix, No. 6.

PAPER handed in by Mr. *Neal Davis*, 5 June 1868.

STATEMENT of the DUTIES of CLERKS of the PEACE.

CLERKS OF THE PEACE.

Appointment by Custos Rotulorum and dismissal by justices for improper conduct under 1 Geo. 4, c. 27, s. 420.

Duties

In Ireland are equal to those of clerks of the Crown at Crown side, and register of judges in Ireland at civil side, and to the clerk of the peace, clerk of the Lieutenancy, and register of county courts in England, with sundry other duties which they have not to perform. He is the register of almost all acts in the county, all returns being made to him, and he having to make all returns to the Government.

Salary.

The counties in Ireland are divided into four classes, the salaries of the clerk of the peace varying from 310 *l.* to 277 *l.*, according to the class he belongs to, excepting Cork, where the salary is 554 *l.*—6 & 7 Will. 4, c. 116, s. 160.

Criminal Court—his Duties.

To act as register to the chairman and justices at the criminal side of the court.

Spirit Licenses.

1. To receive all notices of applicants therefor.

2. To enter same in a book of record kept for that purpose.

3. To call out the names of applicants. To inform the justices and chairman if parties have applied before, and why licenses not granted, and then to take down the order of the justices as to granting and refusing; if the latter the grounds thereof.

4. To issue certificates to all parties when granted.

5. To take in from the officers of Inland Revenue annually the names of all holding licenses in the county, and to enter same in a register in alphabetical order.

Informations and Indictments.

1. To receive all informations and send facts therefor to clerks of petty sessions.

2. To prepare all indictments for the grand jury.

3. To call and swear grand jury.

4. To enter in criminal book all cases found by the grand jury, and to make out similar book for the court.

5. To swear petty juries, and take down their findings in criminal book, as also sentences of the court.

6. To issue cheques for payment of witnesses' expenses.

7. To make out return of parties convicted for governor of prison, and deliver same.

8. To make out returns in duplicate of all persons returned for trial, and their sentences for the Government, quarterly.

9. Also a general annual return for like purpose.

Jurors.

1. To issue to the several high constables precepts to make returns of persons fitting to serve on juries.

2. To make out copies of those returns when made.

3. To have same printed and posted through the county.

4. To issue notices of time and place of holding revisions, and have same in like manner posted.

5. To be at such places, and have such revisions made and signed by the several justices attending, and when all made—

6. To make out one general copy of all parties selected, arranged as to rank and property, and have same at future meeting signed by the justices who attended the revision.

7. To have copy thereof again made, and then to deliver same to the sheriff, which thereupon becomes the list of jurors of the county on which all trials must be had.

Fines.

Under 14th and 15th Vict. c. 90, s. 401.

1. To enter all fines on jurors and prosecutors who do not attend.

2. To issue notices to them of their being fined.

3. To receive and enter all petitions for remission of fines; to take down the chairman's order thereon.

4. To issue warrants to sheriff for the levying of all fines not remitted, and to pay into the fines and penalties' office all fines paid.

5. To make quarterly returns of fines to the Government.

Civil

App. No. 6.

Civil Side.

To make out and submit draft of the lists of the times and places of holding the general quarter sessions of the county for the coming year, and when revised by the chairman to have same printed and published quarterly, and posted in the several divisions of the county.

1. To attend the day previous to each general quarter sessions in each county town to receive from the several attorneys the several civil bills entered for trial, and all defences thereto, as also all ejectments.

2. To enter same in a book of record kept for that purpose, with names of action and amount sued for, and leases sought to be ejected, with names of attorneys for plaintiff and defendant, with duplicate book for chairman.

3. To attend in court daily, and to take down the names of all witnesses examined and orders made by the chairman as to decrees or dismissals.

4. Each evening to compare book kept by chairman with that kept by clerk of the peace lest of any discrepancy therein, and to confer with him, if necessary, thereon.

5. To compare all decrees and dismissals when given in by the several attorneys; to sign same; then to lay them before the chairman, and obtain his signature thereto, and to issue same to the several attorneys concerned.

Sheriff.

To collect all fees payable to the sheriff on such entries and decrees under the recent Act, and to account to him therefor.

Insolvent Debtors.

The Insolvent Court in Dublin sends down the schedules of such parties as are to be brought up before the court.

1. The clerk of the peace then enters same in a book of record kept for that purpose.

2. Compares the affidavits of services of notices on creditors, and reports thereon to the chairman.

3. Attends and takes down the names of witnesses examined, and the order of discharge, dismissal of petition, or remand.

4. Makes out order of discharge for the governor of the gaol.

Appeals.

Attends on the judges at each assizes with list of appeals and documents, and [illegible] thereof, and takes down order made thereon.

Registration of the Freeholders of the County.—13 & 14 Vict., c. 69.

1. To issue requisition to the several clerks of the several Poor Law Unions, to make returns of all persons qualified since last revision, and to send them copies of former registry lists for that purpose.

2. To receive from them these lists, with their objections thereto, and to have same printed, with the clerk of the peace's objections (if any).

3. To attend at the several divisional towns, and have same posted; also, to send to the several police stations to have same lodged there.

4. To have notices posted in like manner for all parties whose names may be omitted, to make claims.

5. To have notices posted of lists of all parties claiming, and notices to send in objections thereto.

6. Then to prepare a general [illegible] list of contents of all the above for revisal by the chairman of the county.

7. To issue notices through the public papers in the county, and also to have same posted of the times and places of holding the general revision sessions.

8. To attend at the several courts of revision in the different parts of the county, and, when these lists are revised, to deliver them to the printer, and to compare and revise carefully the same; and, when same are finally printed, to deliver a signed copy to the sheriff of the county from which the election of the members takes place, and to keep copies for distribution, and to account with the treasurer for the sale of them.

Registration of Trees.

To receive affidavits of planting, &c., to read same out the following sessions in open court.

To enter them in book of record, and to give certified copies to any parties applying.

Further Duties.

The clerk of the peace is bound to keep his office open daily from 10 to 3 o'clock. He is also bound to attend at the several sessions of the county, and this alone takes him absent from home for three or four months, besides his attendance on sundry other occasions. He must, for the carrying on efficiently of the business, keep an intelligent clerk, and during the time of the registration of the county, employ others also.

Petty Sessions Clerks, &c.

He has to summon the justices of the district on their appointment, and to keep a return of each petty sessions district and its extent and boundary.

Justices of the Peace.

Also to keep a record of them.

Militia.

Also of the officers and strength of the regiment.

Railways and Fisheries.

Also to keep all maps, &c., thereof lodged with him for inspection.

Returns.

Also to make same whenever required by Parliament or other authorised parties.

Appendix, No. 7.

PAPERS put in by Mr. *John Lentaigne*, and referred to in his Evidence, 23 May 1868.

TABLE, No. 1.—Showing the Expenses of County and Borough Gaols in Ireland in the Year 1867.

(Referred to in Q. 1746.)

County and Borough Gaols.	Total Expense of Gaols.	Profit from Sale of Work.	Net Expenditure.	Average Daily Number of Prisoners, Debtors included.	Average Total Cost of each Prisoner. Per Diem.	Average Total Cost of each Prisoner. Per Annum.
	£. s. d.	£. s. d.	£. s. d.		s. d.	£. s. d.
Antrim - - - -	4,700 – 5	641 18 10	3,058 7 6	188·62	– 10·5	18 8 7·42
Armagh - - - -	1,697 9 8	45 19 2	1,651 9 11	64·84	1 5·79	25 10 11·76
Carlow - - - -	1,155 1 5	- - -	1,149 4 4	29·31	2 7·34	19 – 8·07
Cavan - - - -	1,847 16 –	- - -	1,847 16 –	44·85	1 0·88	27 16 9·83
Clare - - - -	1,841 4 3	16 7 5	1,824 16 10	65	1 6·61	28 12 4·96
Cork County - - -	5,180 8 –	37 9 8	5,142 14 10	142	1 9·61	36 – 11·5
„ City - - -	2,277 7 1	72 11 10	2,203 15 8	116·67	1 0·28	18 4 8·86
Donegal - - - -	2,127 10 5	– 10 8	2,127 8 8	46·78	2 7·38	45 10 8·49
Down - - - -	2,230 1 4	6 18 10	2,271 4 6	39·75	1 8·75	32 7 8·17
Dublin County - -	4,647 4 2	30 7 3	4,625 17 5	138	1 8·5	33 10 0·91
Dublin City:						
Richmond B. - -	7,833 5 3	625 8 7	7,208 4 2	257	1 6·04	27 8 –
Grangegorman P. -	4,787 16 7	36 10 8½	4,740 16 4½	142	1 10·6	64 8 11·16
Fermanagh - - -	1,300 6 8	5 5 1	1,165 8 5	34	2 0·55	37 8 11·89
Galway County - -	1,775 7 1	34 8 5	1,740 18 5	42·83	2 3·23	39 17 5·75
„ Town - - -	728 14 10	18 14 8	714 – 8	15	2 7·5	47 18 0·5
Kerry - - - -	2,468 6 7	32 11 5	2,434 14 11	57·61	2 3·8	42 5 7·15
Kildare - - - -	2,061 12 4	29 19 10	2,031 12 6	32·2	1 10	63 10 6
Kilkenny County - -	1,579 10 7	- - -	1,579 10 7	24·35	3 4·91	62 8 8
„ City - - -	546 3 7	- - -	546 3 7	12·44	2 5·32	54 11 11·5
King's - - - -	1,674 6 7	- - -	1,674 6 7	27·33	3 1·85	67 11 11·4
Leitrim - - - -	1,189 7 7	- - -	1,189 7 7	21·29	3 2·07	40 7 6·48
Limerick County - -	2,327 5 8	71 14 1	2,255 11 11	27·3	1 7	79 8 10
„ City - -	1,198 11 7	26 16 6	1,172 16 1	31·7	1 6·73	38 9 9·75
Londonderry - - -	2,035 2 8	229 1 11	1,806 – 8	43	1 10·73	41 14 7·84
Longford - - -	1,311 4 4½	4 17 9½	1,306 6 1½	22·75	2 1·73	57 7 10·6
Louth - - - -	1,443 15 –	42 6 3	1,401 12 10	41·67	1 10·4	34 2 10·3
Drogheda Town - -	430 7 4	16 17 6	413 9 10	14·18	1 7·48	29 13 2·2
Mayo - - - -	1,844 4 8	5 – 11½	1,839 3 8½	61·39	1 4·64	29 16 7·49
Meath - - - -	1,940 18 11	- - -	1,940 18 11	26·37	4 2·8	73 18 11·61
Monaghan - - -	1,186 3 5	12 14 6	1,169 8 3	37·83	1 8·67	31 4 5·84
Queen's - - - -	1,811 11 10	9 4 11	1,802 6 11	22·27	2 10·61	83 9 7·46
Roscommon - - -	1,631 10 6	5 3 7	1,626 7 11	36·17	2 6	44 19 1·55
Sligo - - - -	1,671 9 11½	16 8 9½	1,654 19 4	30·88	2 11·75	54 1 8·35
Tipperary, N. Riding -	2,011 8 1	16 8 5	1,994 19 8	40	2 9·33	49 17 11·3
„ S. Riding	3,253 5 1	158 9 9	3,165 15 4	49·84	1 8·2	64 9 11·30
Tyrone - - - -	2,033 11 5	41 7 6	1,942 8 9	54·6	1 9·5	35 15 11
Waterford, County and City	3,214 2 9½	139 11 –	3,075 8 9½	82	1 10	37 9 8·39
Westmeath - - -	1,482 15 4	45 18 7	1,431 1 8	32·0	2 6·75	46 14 4·9
Wexford - - - -	2,529 3 11	18 3 –	2,510 – 11	37·42	1 6·37	32 1 8·78
Wicklow - - - -	1,569 6 –	- - -	1,569 6 –	33·99	2 6·38	46 8 4·83
Total 1867 - - - - £.	87,101 6 1	2,682 11 –¼	84,418 15 –¾	2,658·16	1 8·89	31 16 9·05
Total 1866 - - - - £.	84,043 18 6½	2,249 1 4¼	81,804 18 –¾	2,646·72	1 8·39	30 17 8

App. No. 9.

TABLE, No. 2, showing the Daily Average Number of Prisoners, the Total of Staff Charges, and the Rate per Head of Staff Charges, in the following Gaols:—Sligo, Leitrim, Longford, Cavan, Roscommon, and Westmeath.

(Referred to in Question 1798.)

—	Daily Average Number of Prisoners.	Total of Staff Charges.	Rate per Head of Staff Charges.
		£. s. d.	£. s. d.
Sligo - - - - - - -	[illegible]	[illegible] 8 10	21 6 7
Leitrim - - - - - - -	24	789 11 11	32 16 10
Longford - - - - - - -	[illegible]	510 11 7	25 1 10
Cavan - - - - - - -	46	927 11 8	16 8 8
Roscommon - - - - - - -	28	[illegible] 16 7	26 10 11
Westmeath - - - - - - -	31	[illegible] 11 4	20 15 9
TOTAL - - -	201	5,20[illegible] 4 5	56 4 4

The above table may assist the Committee in forming a notion of the principle of grouping, containing as it does six gaols of counties lying contiguous to each other, the assize towns of which are all connected by railway communication, except that of Roscommon, which is only 14 Irish miles distant from Longford, the locality which would seem from its position to be the most desirable site for a district prison embracing these jurisdictions.

Mullingar is distant by railway time (the rate of the Midland Railway trains being very moderate) from Longford one hour, Carrick one hour, Cavan one hour and a half, and Sligo two hours and a half.

The daily average number of prisoners confined in the whole group is 201, but, if the lunatics, who have hitherto constituted an important element of gaol population, and the prisoners sentenced to hard labour for periods exceeding six months, be deducted, the average would be probably reduced by 25 per cent., *i. e.*, to 150, for whom, if the most liberal calculation of salaries be adopted, the sum of 1,200 *l.* would be ample, thus establishing a saving of 4,000 *l.* a year on this aggregate of prisons.

Appendix, No. 8.

PAPER handed in by Mr. *Greene*, 19 June 1868.

ELECTORAL STATISTICS (COUNTY OF CORK).

NAME OF BARONIES.	Gross Area, Statute Acres.	Valuation in 1867.	Population in 1861.
EAST RIDING.		£.	
Barretts - - - - - - - -	61,769	17,377	5,897
Barrymore - - - - - - -	142,236	109,716	39,419
Condons and Clangibbon - - - - -	78,051	60,137	29,619
Cork - - - - - - - -	47,985	180,246	173,[illegible]
Duhallow - - - - - - -	228,770	91,511	48,048
Fermoy - - { exclusive of Borough	121,195	56,150	25,[illegible]
Fermoy - - { including Borough -	121,[illegible]	72,317	29,432
Imokilly - - { exclusive of Borough	84,073	65,616	41,250
Imokilly - - { including Borough -	85,218	87,[illegible]	46,754
Kerrycurrihy - - - - - -	24,346	30,910	11,069
Kinalea - - - - - - -	40,911	31,219	10,945
Kinnatalloon - - - - - -	27,310	15,071	4,995
Kinsale - - { exclusive of Borough	11,715	10,590	8,071
Kinsale - - { including Borough -	12,832	16,234	5,[illegible]
Muskerry, East (part of) - - - -	94,781	61,183	29,138
Orrery and Kilmore - - - - -	63,346	56,006	16,900
TOTAL (exclusive of Parliamentary Boroughs) - - - - -	991,904	£. [illegible]	248,[illegible]
TOTAL (including Parliamentary Boroughs) - - - - -	1,046,[illegible]	£. 677,831	356,[illegible]*
WEST RIDING.			
Bantry - - - - - - - -	59,216	14,070	9,210
Bear - - - - - - - -	88,[illegible]	16,840	16,519
E. Carbery, E.D. - { exclusive of Borough	67,179	[illegible]	16,[illegible]
E. Carbery, E.D. - { including Borough -	67,[illegible]	44,987	15,535
E. Carbery, W.D. - - - - - -	100,148	41,874	23,[illegible]
W. Carbery, E.D. - - - - - -	90,919	33,[illegible]	24,[illegible]
W. Carbery, W.D. - - - - - -	109,179	26,740	26,186
Courceys - - - - - - - -	6,011	8,033	3,867
Ibane and Barryroe - - - - -	34,310	33,735	13,987
Kinalmeaky - { exclusive of borough	28,155	27,[illegible]	9,804
Kinalmeaky - { including borough -	30,[illegible]	36,879	11,714
E. Muskerry (part of) - - - -	39,144	10,196	4,430
W. Muskerry - - - - - - -	160,497	43,426	20,[illegible]
TOTAL (exclusive of Boroughs) - -	808,[illegible]	£. 368,[illegible]	171,[illegible]
TOTAL (including Boroughs) - - -	837,[illegible]	£. 397,[illegible]	176,[illegible]
TOTAL of County Cork (exclusive of Boroughs) - - - -	1,800,[illegible]	£. 948,207	410,[illegible]*
TOTAL of County Cork (including Boroughs) - - - - -	1,8[illegible]	1,074,[illegible]	544,818

* Not including [illegible].

General Valuation of Ireland,
Dublin, June 1868.

0.58. 3 E 2

Appendix, No. 9.

PAPER handed in by Mr. *Henry Baker*.

COUNTY OF DUBLIN.

GRAND JURY PRESENTMENTS (IRELAND).

RETURN showing the Amount of the Grand Jury Cess now as compared with what it was before the Act 7 & 8 Vict. c. 106, County of Dublin Grand Jury Act.

	£.	s.	d.
1843:			
Amount of County Cess - - - - - - - -	15,923	11	10
Amount of valuation per Poor Law Returns, being the first valuation received as basis for cess rating - - - - - - -	458,311	–	–
Poundage rate on above valuation - - - - - - -	–	–	8¼
1868:			
Amount of County Cess leviable on county exclusive of townships -	38,389	15	6
Total value of county exclusive of townships - - - - -	385,601	–	–
Poundage rate on above valuation - - - - - - -	–	1	8
Amount of County Cess leviable on townships - - - -	6,837	10	6
Value of townships in the County of Dublin - - - - -	258,488	10	–
Poundage rate on above valuation - - - - - - -	–	–	6¼

Appendix, No. 10.

PAPERS handed in by Mr. *John Lentaigne*.

Table, No. 1.

GAOLS AND BRIDEWELLS, IRELAND.

	£.	s.	d.	£.	s.	d.
1st April 1851. Balance due to Exchequer by counties for alterations in gaols and bridewells - - - - - - - - - -				86,875	18	6
Advances in year 1851–52 - - - - - -	11,[illegible]	–	–			
" " 1852–53 - - - - - -	[illegible]	–	–			
" " 1853–54 - - - - - -	8,[illegible]	–	–			
" " 1854–55 - - - - - -	16,476	–	–			
" " 1855–56 - - - - - -	10,[illegible]	–	–			
" " 1856–57 - - - - - -	4,[illegible]	10	–			
" " 1857–58 - - - - - -	2,[illegible]	10	–			
31st March 1858. Balance due by counties - - - - - -				67,[illegible]	17	8

Table, No. 2.

(Table taken from Report of Inspectors General of Prisons for 1867.)

RETURN showing the Number of Prisoners of all classes in custody in the county and borough Prisons of *Ireland* from 1851 to 1867 inclusive.

Forty-sixth Report of Inspectors General of Prisons in *Ireland*, page 8.

No. 1.—Number of Prisoners in Gaols (of all Classes).

On 1st January 1851 - - -	10,684	On 1st January 1860 - - -	2,[illegible]
Ditto - 1852 - - -	9,[illegible]	Ditto - 1861 - - -	2,[illegible]
Ditto - 1853 - - -	7,[illegible]	Ditto - 1862 - - -	2,316
Ditto - 1854 - - -	6,746	Ditto - 1863 - - -	[illegible]
Ditto - 1855 - - -	4,[illegible]	Ditto - 1864 - - -	[illegible]
Ditto - 1856 - - -	3,[illegible]	Ditto - 1865 - - -	2,747
Ditto - 1857 - - -	3,116	Ditto - 1866 - - -	[illegible]
Ditto - 1858 - - -	3,[illegible]	Ditto - 1867 - - -	[illegible]
Ditto - 1859 - - -	2,844	Ditto - 1868 - - -	2,463

Table No. 1 records the number of prisoners of all classes in custody on each 1st day of January from 1851 to 1868, and by reference to it we learn that the number in confinement on the 1st day of January 1868, viz., 2,463, is the lowest in the whole table, with the exception of the year immediately preceding, and less than one-fourth of the aggregate in custody on the 1st January 1851, when our gaols contained no less than 10,684 inmates.

No. 2.—Return of the Numbers (of all Classes) in Gaols on the 1st day of each Month in the Years

	Jan.	Feb.	March.	April.	May.	June.	July.	August.	Sept.	Oct.	Nov.	Dec.
1851 -	10,684	11,630	11,464	10,697	11,646	10,227	10,222	10,469	9,465	9,436	9,867	9,461
[illegible] -	9,565	9,367	9,871	9,544	9,669	9,377	8,834	8,621	7,486	7,466	7,494	7,[illegible]
[illegible] -	7,[illegible]	8,214	8,161	7,359	7,401	7,374	7,051	6,[illegible]	[illegible]	[illegible]	6,471	[illegible]
[illegible] -	5,735	6,166	6,453	5,775	5,656	5,577	5,514	[illegible]	5,417	[illegible]	4,[illegible]	5,[illegible]
[illegible] -	[illegible]	5,[illegible]	4,799	4,760	[illegible]	[illegible]	4,343	[illegible]	4,148	[illegible]	3,747	3,844
[illegible] -	3,161	[illegible]	[illegible]	[illegible]	[illegible]	[illegible]	[illegible]	[illegible]	[illegible]	[illegible]	3,444	[illegible]
[illegible] -	3,[illegible]	3,315	3,477	[illegible]	[illegible]	[illegible]	[illegible]	[illegible]	3,572	[illegible]	[illegible]	[illegible]
[illegible] -	[illegible]	[illegible]	[illegible]	[illegible]	[illegible]	[illegible]	[illegible]	[illegible]	[illegible]	[illegible]	[illegible]	[illegible]
[illegible] -	[illegible]	[illegible]	[illegible]	[illegible]	[illegible]	[illegible]	[illegible]	[illegible]	[illegible]	[illegible]	[illegible]	[illegible]
[illegible] -	[illegible]	[illegible]	[illegible]	[illegible]	[illegible]	[illegible]	[illegible]	[illegible]	[illegible]	[illegible]	[illegible]	[illegible]
[illegible] -	[illegible]	[illegible]	[illegible]	[illegible]	[illegible]	[illegible]	[illegible]	[illegible]	[illegible]	[illegible]	[illegible]	[illegible]
[illegible] -	[illegible]	[illegible]	[illegible]	[illegible]	[illegible]	3,149	[illegible]	[illegible]	[illegible]	[illegible]	[illegible]	[illegible]
[illegible] -	[illegible]	[illegible]	[illegible]	[illegible]	[illegible]	2,813	[illegible]	[illegible]	[illegible]	[illegible]	[illegible]	[illegible]
[illegible] -	[illegible]	[illegible]	[illegible]	[illegible]	[illegible]	[illegible]	[illegible]	[illegible]	[illegible]	[illegible]	[illegible]	[illegible]
[illegible] -	2,767	[illegible]	[illegible]	[illegible]	[illegible]	[illegible]	[illegible]	[illegible]	[illegible]	[illegible]	[illegible]	[illegible]
[illegible] -	[illegible]	[illegible]	[illegible]	[illegible]	[illegible]	[illegible]	[illegible]	[illegible]	[illegible]	[illegible]	[illegible]	[illegible]
[illegible] -	[illegible]	[illegible]	[illegible]	[illegible]	[illegible]	[illegible]	[illegible]	[illegible]	[illegible]	[illegible]	[illegible]	[illegible]

TABLE, No. 3.

(Appendix to Forty-sixth Report of Inspectors General of Prisons in *Ireland*.)

TABLE XV.—AMOUNT of ACCOMMODATION in the several County and Borough Gaols on the 31st December 1867.

County and Borough Gaols.	Cells for a Single Prisoner. 9-feet long, 6-feet wide, and 9-feet high, &c.		Of Larger Size.		Of Smaller Size.		Cells to contain Three Persons.		Sleeping Rooms. Number.		Number of Beds in same.		Hospital. Number of Rooms or Wards.		Number of Beds or cribs.		Number of Ward Closets.		Number Gaol can accommodate. Debtors.		Criminals.		Total.
	M.	F.	M.	F.	M.	F.	M.	F.	M.	F.	M.	F.	M.	F.	M.	F.	M.	F.	M.	F.	M.	F.	M. & F.
Antrim	[illegible]	[illegible]	[illegible]	[illegible]	[illegible]	[illegible]	[illegible]	[illegible]	[illegible]	[illegible]	[illegible]	[illegible]	[illegible]	[illegible]	[illegible]	[illegible]	[illegible]	[illegible]	[illegible]	[illegible]	[illegible]	[illegible]	[illegible]
Armagh	[illegible]	[illegible]	[illegible]	[illegible]	[illegible]	[illegible]	[illegible]	[illegible]	[illegible]	[illegible]	[illegible]	[illegible]	[illegible]	[illegible]	[illegible]	[illegible]	[illegible]	[illegible]	[illegible]	[illegible]	[illegible]	[illegible]	[illegible]
Carlow	[illegible]	[illegible]	[illegible]	[illegible]	[illegible]	[illegible]	[illegible]	[illegible]	[illegible]	[illegible]	[illegible]	[illegible]	[illegible]	[illegible]	[illegible]	[illegible]	[illegible]	[illegible]	[illegible]	[illegible]	[illegible]	[illegible]	[illegible]
Cavan	[illegible]	[illegible]	[illegible]	[illegible]	[illegible]	[illegible]	[illegible]	[illegible]	[illegible]	[illegible]	[illegible]	[illegible]	[illegible]	[illegible]	[illegible]	[illegible]	[illegible]	[illegible]	[illegible]	[illegible]	[illegible]	[illegible]	[illegible]
Clare	[illegible]	[illegible]	[illegible]	[illegible]	[illegible]	[illegible]	[illegible]	[illegible]	[illegible]	[illegible]	[illegible]	[illegible]	[illegible]	[illegible]	[illegible]	[illegible]	[illegible]	[illegible]	[illegible]	[illegible]	[illegible]	[illegible]	[illegible]
Cork County*	[illegible]	[illegible]	[illegible]	[illegible]	[illegible]	[illegible]	[illegible]	[illegible]	[illegible]	[illegible]	[illegible]	[illegible]	[illegible]	[illegible]	[illegible]	[illegible]	[illegible]	[illegible]	[illegible]	[illegible]	[illegible]	[illegible]	[illegible]
" City	[illegible]	[illegible]	[illegible]	[illegible]	[illegible]	[illegible]	[illegible]	[illegible]	[illegible]	[illegible]	[illegible]	[illegible]	[illegible]	[illegible]	[illegible]	[illegible]	[illegible]	[illegible]	[illegible]	[illegible]	[illegible]	[illegible]	[illegible]
Donegal	[illegible]	[illegible]	[illegible]	[illegible]	[illegible]	[illegible]	[illegible]	[illegible]	[illegible]	[illegible]	[illegible]	[illegible]	[illegible]	[illegible]	[illegible]	[illegible]	[illegible]	[illegible]	[illegible]	[illegible]	[illegible]	[illegible]	[illegible]
Down	[illegible]	[illegible]	[illegible]	[illegible]	[illegible]	[illegible]	[illegible]	[illegible]	[illegible]	[illegible]	[illegible]	[illegible]	[illegible]	[illegible]	[illegible]	[illegible]	[illegible]	[illegible]	[illegible]	[illegible]	[illegible]	[illegible]	[illegible]
Dublin County	[illegible]	[illegible]	[illegible]	[illegible]	[illegible]	[illegible]	[illegible]	[illegible]	[illegible]	[illegible]	[illegible]	[illegible]	[illegible]	[illegible]	[illegible]	[illegible]	[illegible]	[illegible]	[illegible]	[illegible]	[illegible]	[illegible]	[illegible]
Dublin City:																							
Richmond B.	[illegible]	[illegible]	[illegible]	[illegible]	[illegible]	[illegible]	[illegible]	[illegible]	[illegible]	[illegible]	[illegible]	[illegible]	[illegible]	[illegible]	[illegible]	[illegible]	[illegible]	[illegible]	[illegible]	[illegible]	[illegible]	[illegible]	[illegible]
Grangegorman F.	[illegible]	[illegible]	[illegible]	[illegible]	[illegible]	[illegible]	[illegible]	[illegible]	[illegible]	[illegible]	[illegible]	[illegible]	[illegible]	[illegible]	[illegible]	[illegible]	[illegible]	[illegible]	[illegible]	[illegible]	[illegible]	[illegible]	[illegible]
Fermanagh	[illegible]	[illegible]	[illegible]	[illegible]	[illegible]	[illegible]	[illegible]	[illegible]	[illegible]	[illegible]	[illegible]	[illegible]	[illegible]	[illegible]	[illegible]	[illegible]	[illegible]	[illegible]	[illegible]	[illegible]	[illegible]	[illegible]	[illegible]
Galway County	[illegible]	[illegible]	[illegible]	[illegible]	[illegible]	[illegible]	[illegible]	[illegible]	[illegible]	[illegible]	[illegible]	[illegible]	[illegible]	[illegible]	[illegible]	[illegible]	[illegible]	[illegible]	[illegible]	[illegible]	[illegible]	[illegible]	[illegible]
" Town	[illegible]	[illegible]	[illegible]	[illegible]	[illegible]	[illegible]	[illegible]	[illegible]	[illegible]	[illegible]	[illegible]	[illegible]	[illegible]	[illegible]	[illegible]	[illegible]	[illegible]	[illegible]	[illegible]	[illegible]	[illegible]	[illegible]	[illegible]
Kerry	[illegible]	[illegible]	[illegible]	[illegible]	[illegible]	[illegible]	[illegible]	[illegible]	[illegible]	[illegible]	[illegible]	[illegible]	[illegible]	[illegible]	[illegible]	[illegible]	[illegible]	[illegible]	[illegible]	[illegible]	[illegible]	[illegible]	[illegible]
Kildare	[illegible]	[illegible]	[illegible]	[illegible]	[illegible]	[illegible]	[illegible]	[illegible]	[illegible]	[illegible]	[illegible]	[illegible]	[illegible]	[illegible]	[illegible]	[illegible]	[illegible]	[illegible]	[illegible]	[illegible]	[illegible]	[illegible]	[illegible]
Kilkenny County and City	[illegible]	[illegible]	[illegible]	[illegible]	[illegible]	[illegible]	[illegible]	[illegible]	[illegible]	[illegible]	[illegible]	[illegible]	[illegible]	[illegible]	[illegible]	[illegible]	[illegible]	[illegible]	[illegible]	[illegible]	[illegible]	[illegible]	[illegible]
King's	[illegible]	[illegible]	[illegible]	[illegible]	[illegible]	[illegible]	[illegible]	[illegible]	[illegible]	[illegible]	[illegible]	[illegible]	[illegible]	[illegible]	[illegible]	[illegible]	[illegible]	[illegible]	[illegible]	[illegible]	[illegible]	[illegible]	[illegible]
Leitrim	[illegible]	[illegible]	[illegible]	[illegible]	[illegible]	[illegible]	[illegible]	[illegible]	[illegible]	[illegible]	[illegible]	[illegible]	[illegible]	[illegible]	[illegible]	[illegible]	[illegible]	[illegible]	[illegible]	[illegible]	[illegible]	[illegible]	[illegible]
Limerick County	[illegible]	[illegible]	[illegible]	[illegible]	[illegible]	[illegible]	[illegible]	[illegible]	[illegible]	[illegible]	[illegible]	[illegible]	[illegible]	[illegible]	[illegible]	[illegible]	[illegible]	[illegible]	[illegible]	[illegible]	[illegible]	[illegible]	[illegible]
" City	[illegible]	[illegible]	[illegible]	[illegible]	[illegible]	[illegible]	[illegible]	[illegible]	[illegible]	[illegible]	[illegible]	[illegible]	[illegible]	[illegible]	[illegible]	[illegible]	[illegible]	[illegible]	[illegible]	[illegible]	[illegible]	[illegible]	[illegible]
Londonderry	[illegible]	[illegible]	[illegible]	[illegible]	[illegible]	[illegible]	[illegible]	[illegible]	[illegible]	[illegible]	[illegible]	[illegible]	[illegible]	[illegible]	[illegible]	[illegible]	[illegible]	[illegible]	[illegible]	[illegible]	[illegible]	[illegible]	[illegible]
Longford	[illegible]	[illegible]	[illegible]	[illegible]	[illegible]	[illegible]	[illegible]	[illegible]	[illegible]	[illegible]	[illegible]	[illegible]	[illegible]	[illegible]	[illegible]	[illegible]	[illegible]	[illegible]	[illegible]	[illegible]	[illegible]	[illegible]	[illegible]
Louth	[illegible]	[illegible]	[illegible]	[illegible]	[illegible]	[illegible]	[illegible]	[illegible]	[illegible]	[illegible]	[illegible]	[illegible]	[illegible]	[illegible]	[illegible]	[illegible]	[illegible]	[illegible]	[illegible]	[illegible]	[illegible]	[illegible]	[illegible]
Drogheda Town	[illegible]	[illegible]	[illegible]	[illegible]	[illegible]	[illegible]	[illegible]	[illegible]	[illegible]	[illegible]	[illegible]	[illegible]	[illegible]	[illegible]	[illegible]	[illegible]	[illegible]	[illegible]	[illegible]	[illegible]	[illegible]	[illegible]	[illegible]
Mayo	[illegible]	[illegible]	[illegible]	[illegible]	[illegible]	[illegible]	[illegible]	[illegible]	[illegible]	[illegible]	[illegible]	[illegible]	[illegible]	[illegible]	[illegible]	[illegible]	[illegible]	[illegible]	[illegible]	[illegible]	[illegible]	[illegible]	[illegible]
Meath	[illegible]	[illegible]	[illegible]	[illegible]	[illegible]	[illegible]	[illegible]	[illegible]	[illegible]	[illegible]	[illegible]	[illegible]	[illegible]	[illegible]	[illegible]	[illegible]	[illegible]	[illegible]	[illegible]	[illegible]	[illegible]	[illegible]	[illegible]
Monaghan	[illegible]	[illegible]	[illegible]	[illegible]	[illegible]	[illegible]	[illegible]	[illegible]	[illegible]	[illegible]	[illegible]	[illegible]	[illegible]	[illegible]	[illegible]	[illegible]	[illegible]	[illegible]	[illegible]	[illegible]	[illegible]	[illegible]	[illegible]
Queen's	[illegible]	[illegible]	[illegible]	[illegible]	[illegible]	[illegible]	[illegible]	[illegible]	[illegible]	[illegible]	[illegible]	[illegible]	[illegible]	[illegible]	[illegible]	[illegible]	[illegible]	[illegible]	[illegible]	[illegible]	[illegible]	[illegible]	[illegible]
Roscommon	[illegible]	[illegible]	[illegible]	[illegible]	[illegible]	[illegible]	[illegible]	[illegible]	[illegible]	[illegible]	[illegible]	[illegible]	[illegible]	[illegible]	[illegible]	[illegible]	[illegible]	[illegible]	[illegible]	[illegible]	[illegible]	[illegible]	[illegible]
Sligo	[illegible]	[illegible]	[illegible]	[illegible]	[illegible]	[illegible]	[illegible]	[illegible]	[illegible]	[illegible]	[illegible]	[illegible]	[illegible]	[illegible]	[illegible]	[illegible]	[illegible]	[illegible]	[illegible]	[illegible]	[illegible]	[illegible]	[illegible]
Tipperary, N. Riding	[illegible]	[illegible]	[illegible]	[illegible]	[illegible]	[illegible]	[illegible]	[illegible]	[illegible]	[illegible]	[illegible]	[illegible]	[illegible]	[illegible]	[illegible]	[illegible]	[illegible]	[illegible]	[illegible]	[illegible]	[illegible]	[illegible]	[illegible]
" S. Riding	[illegible]	[illegible]	[illegible]	[illegible]	[illegible]	[illegible]	[illegible]	[illegible]	[illegible]	[illegible]	[illegible]	[illegible]	[illegible]	[illegible]	[illegible]	[illegible]	[illegible]	[illegible]	[illegible]	[illegible]	[illegible]	[illegible]	[illegible]
Tyrone	[illegible]	[illegible]	[illegible]	[illegible]	[illegible]	[illegible]	[illegible]	[illegible]	[illegible]	[illegible]	[illegible]	[illegible]	[illegible]	[illegible]	[illegible]	[illegible]	[illegible]	[illegible]	[illegible]	[illegible]	[illegible]	[illegible]	[illegible]
Waterford County and City	[illegible]	[illegible]	[illegible]	[illegible]	[illegible]	[illegible]	[illegible]	[illegible]	[illegible]	[illegible]	[illegible]	[illegible]	[illegible]	[illegible]	[illegible]	[illegible]	[illegible]	[illegible]	[illegible]	[illegible]	[illegible]	[illegible]	[illegible]
Westmeath	[illegible]	[illegible]	[illegible]	[illegible]	[illegible]	[illegible]	[illegible]	[illegible]	[illegible]	[illegible]	[illegible]	[illegible]	[illegible]	[illegible]	[illegible]	[illegible]	[illegible]	[illegible]	[illegible]	[illegible]	[illegible]	[illegible]	[illegible]
Wexford	[illegible]	[illegible]	[illegible]	[illegible]	[illegible]	[illegible]	[illegible]	[illegible]	[illegible]	[illegible]	[illegible]	[illegible]	[illegible]	[illegible]	[illegible]	[illegible]	[illegible]	[illegible]	[illegible]	[illegible]	[illegible]	[illegible]	[illegible]
Wicklow	[illegible]	[illegible]	[illegible]	[illegible]	[illegible]	[illegible]	[illegible]	[illegible]	[illegible]	[illegible]	[illegible]	[illegible]	[illegible]	[illegible]	[illegible]	[illegible]	[illegible]	[illegible]	[illegible]	[illegible]	[illegible]	[illegible]	[illegible]
Total for Males	[illegible]	-	[illegible]	-	[illegible]	-	[illegible]	-	[illegible]	-	[illegible]	-	[illegible]	-	[illegible]	-	[illegible]	-	[illegible]	-	[illegible]	-	-
Total for Females	-	[illegible]	-	[illegible]	-	[illegible]	-	[illegible]	-	[illegible]	-	[illegible]	-	[illegible]	-	[illegible]	-	[illegible]	-	[illegible]	-	[illegible]	-
Total for M. and F.	[illegible]		[illegible]		[illegible]		[illegible]		[illegible]		[illegible]		[illegible]		[illegible]		[illegible]		[illegible]		[illegible]		[illegible]

* This Return does not include the accommodation for prisoners now being provided in Cork County Gaol; that prison being now in progress of alteration, no return has been received from it.

Appendix, No. 11.

SUGGESTIONS by Mr. *James Lambert*.

The following Suggestions are respectfully recommended to the attention of the Grand Jury Laws Committee by the undersigned.

Grand Jury Laws.

The present system has, on the whole, worked well for a period of 30 years, and it has the recommendation of being simple, and easily understood by the county contractors. I believe that it would be far safer to amend it by removing the objections which long experience has discovered in it, and effecting certain direct improvements which would render it more safe and beneficial, than to substitute any revolutionary scheme, which might be attended with a great deal of inconvenience at the commencement, and which might not prove near as good after all.

I believe that what has been said about "jobbery" is greatly exaggerated; at all events, I have been connected with the fiscal business of this county (*Wicklow*) for many years, and I have no recollection of any flagrant "job" having been perpetrated. The fact is, that if anything of the kind took place at the presentment sessions, it would be sure to become known, and then a full opportunity is afforded to any cess payer to complain before the grand jury (at the assizes), and ensure the throwing out of the presentment. I know that in this county the grand jury, in the case of any presentment where a doubt is entertained as to its necessity, invariably lean to the side of the cess payer by disallowing it.

After all, it is very doubtful whether there might not be more real abuses under the proposed "Electoral Board" system, and more expense and inconvenience incurred, than under the present one, which, with certain amendments and improvements, ought to get a further trial.

Suggestions Recommended.

1. *Every barony* in the county ought to be represented on the grand jury.

2. The cess-payers to be associated with the magistrates at the several presentment sessions ought to be balloted for before the grand jury out of the lists—of 100 or other number—furnished by the high constables, such lists to be composed of cess-payers in *every parish* (or other district) in the barony. No magistrate to attend out of his own barony.

[*N.B.*—I am of opinion that these two simple improvements would remove all complaints as to "jobbery."]

3. An additional payment to be made to contractors between Summer and Spring Assizes, say in the month of November, so that there would be *three* general payments in each year, at an interval of *four months* between each.

[*N.B.*—This would be a great boon to the contractors, and it would tend to get works done more promptly.]

4. The county surveyor to have power to certify at each assizes (as well as at the presentment sessions), so as to be able to pay contractors who had worked well between the presentment sessions and the assizes.

5. The signatures to contractors' bonds to be taken (in any action at law) as the *bona fide* signatures of the parties whose names are attached; and the *onus probandi* to lie with the parties themselves to show that they are not their signatures. The declarations in court at adjourned sessions by contractors, acknowledging the signatures to be theirs, to be taken as final against them.

[*N.B.*—This would simplify and facilitate legal proceedings, and prevent the breaking down of a prosecution.]

6. The lowest tender not necessarily to be received, if the contractor is a pauper, or in any way an unfit or ineligible person to get the work.

[*N.B.*—At present many paupers and indolent individuals get works which they are not able or willing to execute, and so cause confusion and disappointment. There should be a remedy for this state of things.]

App. No. 11.

7. The offices of Clerk of the Peace and Clerk of the Crown might be amalgamated.

8. The county cess should be equally divided between landlord and tenant.

[*N.B.*—I hardly know of anything that would give more universal satisfaction than this. It would be a considerable relief to the tenant farmers, as the county cess comes high, and in bad years is very much felt. Besides it is to be noted that the two payments must be made within a period of about four months, and they must be paid promptly. I would strongly recommend this alteration, as the present state of things has a one-sided and apparently unjust appearance, whereas the equal payment between landlord and tenant would remove all grumbling, and induce the belief that the grand jury would be the more careful in passing the presentments. I am decidedly of opinion that it would be a wise and politic arrangement.]

General Valuation Office.

The expense of this system is upwards of 20,000 *l.* a year, and is annually on the increase, while the work is but imperfectly done; whereas the business can be far better performed by the following plan, at about *half the amount*, or at the utmost from 10,000 *l.* to 12,000 *l.* a year.

1. Let the county applotment be taken out of the treasurers' and secretaries' hands, and appoint a county applotter for each county, who shall also be the reviser of valuation, and I would also say the valuation of new buildings, &c. He could likewise make out the valuation lists for treasurers, poor law unions, &c., so that the entire business for each county could be done in the county.

[*N.B.*—As the amalgamating principle is now being acted on, this would be a very natural and proper amalgamation of offices. A thorough business man, with his own assistants, could do everything that is now done in the Valuation Office. Of course each county would (as at present) pay the expense of applotting the county cess; but is it not manifest that the applotter should do the other work also. Having all in his own hands, he could work the cheaper. I may remark that some of the scrivenery (*i.e.*, valuation lists) is actually done by women.]

2. Make the high constables (or collectors of county cess), instead of the poor rate collectors, furnish the lists of alterations in holdings, changes of names, &c., which they could do with the greatest facility on each collection.

[*N.B.*—The high constables are the proper men to furnish these returns, as they would themselves be interested in the correctness of the valuation lists, on which their applotments are founded. They might be allowed a very small remuneration for their trouble.]

3. One commissioner might be kept to settle disputes in respect to valuation; also to assist in particular valuations, such as mines, mills, railways, &c.; say at a salary of 500 *l.* a year and his travelling expenses.

By this plan the whole work could be localised, and a great saving to the counties and the Treasury effected, and besides by the conjoint exertions or labours of the local officers and the high constables, it would be done more correctly. It is not likely that there would be any objection taken to local valuators, especially when the right of appeal existed.

I would estimate the expense at from 300 *l.* to 350 *l.* a year for each county (at an average), whereas the present rate is 625 *l.* a county, and it is still increasing.

Wicklow, 29 June 1868. *James Lambert.*

Appendix, No. 12.

STATEMENT put in by Mr. *McCarthy Downing*, of Prospect House, in the County of Cork, by Permission of the Committee. App. No. 12.

The people of the County of Cork have long felt the grievances under which they have suffered, in consequence of there being but one assize town for the county, and that its fiscal business is disposed of by one grand jury, and one set of public officers in the City of Cork.

These grievances the people have for many years agitated to be relieved from, but the influence of interested parties, and the spirit of centralization, have hitherto been successful in preventing their redress.

The necessity for a division of the county for fiscal purposes is now almost universally acknowledged, and it is a matter of surprise that the existing abuse has been so long tolerated.

The area of the county is 1,846,333 acres; a population of near 600,000; and its valuation more than 1,000,000 *l.*

To discharge the smallest matter requiring personal attendance, hundreds of the population are obliged to travel as great a distance as 80 miles, to reach the City of Cork.

The expense and loss of time thus incurred is often ruinous to those possessing only humble means.

I have, in my evidence before the Committee, given other reasons, and anticipating the recommendation of the Committee that a division of the county should, with the least possible delay, be effected, I take the liberty of stating why I consider that it is essential to the entire removal of the grievances complained of, and to the prosperity of the western division of the county, that a separate and distinct assizes should be held in the town of Skibbereen.

Supposing that the present divisions of the county into ridings will be adopted for assize purposes, the West Riding will consist of more than 800,000 acres, a population of 176,000, and a valuation of 295,000 *l.*, and will be exceeded in population and valuation by only 11 other counties; and amongst those 11 is included the County of Tipperary, which is divided for assize purposes and has two distinct assize towns.

The Committee will observe what an immense extent of country lies to the west, north-west, east, and south-east of the town of Skibbereen, extending in the first direction more than 60 miles, and in the second more than 25 miles, and includes the important harbours of Castletown, Berehaven, Dunmanus, Long Island, and Crookhaven.

The Committee will further observe that Skibbereen is surrounded by a group of small towns and villages, calculated to make it the centre of commerce and attraction; on the east it has Rosscarbery, Leap, Glandore, and Union Hall; on the south Castletownsend, Baltimore, Sherkin, and Cape Clear; on the west Crookhaven, Goleen, Schull, Ballydehob, and Aughadown; and on the north and north-west, Caheragh, Drimoleague, Cahiragh, and Drinagh; the inhabitants of which pour into Skibbereen, as their weekly market town.

It is, moreover, to some extent a maritime town, as vessels of 400 tons burden unload at a distance of little more than two miles, while lighters of 50 tons burden load and unload at its very quays.

It has been put forward by the interested parties before referred to, that holding assizes in the Town of Skibbereen, would entail enormous expense, by the building of a second county gaol, and second county court house.

This I take the liberty of denying, because there would be no such necessity.

Skibbereen at present has a court house capable of accommodating 500 persons, with all the necessary accommodation for juries and public officers. It possesses a district bridewell, capable of being enlarged, if necessary, at a small expense, but with railway communication from the City of Cork to Dunmanway, which, I believe, will be completed to Skibbereen within a short period. It appears to me that an enlarged gaol would be unnecessary, because the principal part of the criminal business is disposed of at quarter sessions, and when the area is confined to the West Riding, few cases of that importance will arise requiring the discipline of a large county gaol, and should cases arise there is nothing to prevent the transmission of such criminals to the present county gaol, for the erection and support of which the West Riding has hitherto paid two-fifths of the whole.

The Committee will observe, that lunatics from the most distant parts of the county are at present transmitted to the county asylum in the City of Cork.

I trust the Committee will permit me to say, that it is desirable that in so immense a county as Cork, that a second large or county town should exist, and that no town is better calculated to increase in size, population, and commercial importance, than Skibbereen, which is distant from the City of Cork 53 miles. It is the head of the customs' department, and the port extends 275 miles of the sea coast; comprises 13 coast guard stations, the inspecting commander of which resides near the town; it has its custom house and bonding stores; possesses two banks, two good hotels, and good lodgings to any extent; it is placed under the operation of the Towns Improvement Act; is as well lighted by its public gas lamps, and has probably the largest and best supply of water from its public fountains of any town in Ireland. It has also two telegraph offices, one in connexion with Cape Clear, the other with Crookhaven; two most important points in the map of Ireland in a national point of view, and it has also the advantage of having a public Journal published weekly therein, which is the only paper published in the county.

For the reasons which, by permission, I have had the honour to lay before Your Honourable Committee, I trust that it may be a recommendation in Your Report, not only that the County of Cork should be divided for assize purposes, but that the assizes for the West Riding of the county ought to be held in the town of Skibbereen.

I have, &c.
(signed) *McCarthy Downing.*

RETURN of Extent of Cost of Works, Executed under Grand Jury Presentments in *Ireland*, for ... in the respective

COUNTIES.	Years.	A. Roads under Contract for Repairs, including Widening, Fencing, Filling Gaps, and Making Footpaths. Length.	A. Amount.	B. Roads under Contract for Maintenance. Length.	B. Amount.	Cost per Perch.	Totals of Columns A. and B. Length.	Totals Amount.	C. New Roads. Length.	C. Amount.
		m. p. y.	£. s. d.	m. p. y.	£. s. d.	d.	m. p. y.	£. s. d.	m. p. y.	£. s. d.
ANTRIM	[illegible]	[illegible]	[illegible]	[illegible]	[illegible]	[illegible]	[illegible]	[illegible]	[illegible]	[illegible]
ARMAGH	[illegible]	[illegible]	[illegible]	[illegible]	[illegible]	[illegible]	[illegible]	[illegible]	[illegible]	[illegible]
CARLOW	[illegible]	[illegible]	[illegible]	[illegible]	[illegible]	[illegible]	[illegible]	[illegible]	[illegible]	[illegible]
CAVAN	[illegible]	Returns not yet received.								
	[illegible]	[illegible]	[illegible]	[illegible]	[illegible]	[illegible]	[illegible]	[illegible]	[illegible]	[illegible]
CLARE	[illegible]	[illegible]	[illegible]	[illegible]	[illegible]	[illegible]	[illegible]	[illegible]	[illegible]	[illegible]
CORK, EAST (North Division).	[illegible]	Return not yet received.								
	[illegible]	[illegible]	[illegible]	[illegible]	[illegible]	[illegible]	[illegible]	[illegible]	[illegible]	[illegible]
CORK, EAST (South Division).	[illegible]	Return not yet received.								
	[illegible]	[illegible]	[illegible]	[illegible]	[illegible]	[illegible]	[illegible]	[illegible]	[illegible]	[illegible]
CORK, WEST	[illegible]	[illegible]	[illegible]	[illegible]	[illegible]	[illegible]	[illegible]	[illegible]	[illegible]	[illegible]
DONEGAL (North Division).	[illegible]	[illegible]	[illegible]	[illegible]	[illegible]	[illegible]	[illegible]	[illegible]	[illegible]	[illegible]
DONEGAL (South Division).	[illegible]	[illegible]	[illegible]	[illegible]	[illegible]	[illegible]	[illegible]	[illegible]	[illegible]	[illegible]
DOWN (North and South Divisions).	[illegible]	[illegible]	[illegible]	[illegible]	[illegible]	[illegible]	[illegible]	[illegible]	[illegible]	[illegible]
DUBLIN	[illegible]	[illegible]	[illegible]	[illegible]	[illegible]	[illegible]	[illegible]	[illegible]	[illegible]	[illegible]
	[illegible]	Footpaths, &c., included in Column B.								
	[illegible]	[illegible]	[illegible]	[illegible]	[illegible]	[illegible]	[illegible]	[illegible]	[illegible]	[illegible]

[illegible] the Years 1834, 1844, 1854, 1864, and 1857, compiled from the County Presentment Books, by the Surveyors [illegible] Counties.

D. Cutting Hills and Filling Hollows. Amount.	E. Bridges, Gullets, and Road Buildings. Amount.	Total of Columns A, B, C, D, and E. Amount.	Cost of Superintendence. Amount.	Per-Centage of Cost.	Gross Number of Miles of New Roads made from 1834 to 1857. Length.	Amount.	Number of Surveyors.	Number of Assistants.	OBSERVATIONS.
£ s. d.	£ s. d.	£ s. d.	£ s. d.		m. f. p.	£ s. d.			
[illegible]	[illegible]	[illegible]	[illegible]	[illegible]	[illegible]	[illegible]	[illegible]	[illegible]	
[illegible]	[illegible]	[illegible]	[illegible]	[illegible]	[illegible]	[illegible]	[illegible]	[illegible]	
[illegible]	[illegible]	[illegible]	[illegible]	[illegible]	[illegible]	[illegible]	[illegible]	[illegible]	
[illegible]	[illegible]	[illegible]	[illegible]	[illegible]	[illegible]	[illegible]	[illegible]	[illegible]	
[illegible]	[illegible]	[illegible]	[illegible]	[illegible]	[illegible]	[illegible]	[illegible]	[illegible]	
[illegible]	[illegible]	[illegible]	[illegible]	[illegible]	[illegible]	[illegible]	[illegible]	[illegible]	Maintenance of turnpike [illegible] included with roads in returns for years 1834 and 1844.
[illegible]	[illegible]	[illegible]	[illegible]	[illegible]	11 from 1844 to 1854		[illegible]	[illegible]	
[illegible]	[illegible]	[illegible]	[illegible]	[illegible]	[illegible]	[illegible]	[illegible]	[illegible]	
[illegible]	[illegible]	[illegible]	[illegible]	[illegible]	[illegible]	[illegible]	[illegible]	[illegible]	
[illegible]	[illegible]	[illegible]	[illegible]	[illegible]	[illegible]	1854 to 1857	[illegible]	[illegible]	
[illegible]	[illegible]	[illegible]	[illegible]	[illegible]	[illegible]	[illegible]	[illegible]	[illegible]	Large presentments for cutting hills were made in some of the intermediate years.
[illegible]	[illegible]	[illegible]	[illegible]	[illegible]	[illegible]	[illegible]	[illegible]	[illegible]	
[illegible]	[illegible]	[illegible]	[illegible]	[illegible]	[illegible]	[illegible]	[illegible]	[illegible]	
[illegible]	[illegible]	[illegible]	[illegible]	[illegible]	[illegible]	[illegible]	[illegible]	[illegible]	
[illegible]	[illegible]	[illegible]	[illegible]	[illegible]	[illegible]	[illegible]	[illegible]	[illegible]	
[illegible]	[illegible]	[illegible]	[illegible]	[illegible]	[illegible]	[illegible]	[illegible]	[illegible]	
[illegible]	[illegible]	[illegible]	[illegible]	[illegible]	[illegible]	[illegible]	[illegible]	[illegible]	
[illegible]	[illegible]	[illegible]	[illegible]	[illegible]	[illegible]	[illegible]	[illegible]	[illegible]	Considerable amount of work, consequent upon the drainage operations, has not to be presented for in this county; [illegible] miles of roads [illegible] [illegible], a body previously [illegible] [illegible] by the Commissioners of Public Works.
[illegible]	[illegible]	[illegible]	[illegible]	[illegible]	[illegible]	[illegible]	[illegible]	[illegible]	
[illegible]	[illegible]	[illegible]	[illegible]	[illegible]	[illegible]	[illegible]	[illegible]	[illegible]	
[illegible]	[illegible]	[illegible]	[illegible]	[illegible]	[illegible]	[illegible]	[illegible]	[illegible]	
[illegible]	[illegible]	[illegible]	[illegible]	[illegible]	[illegible]	[illegible]	[illegible]	[illegible]	
[illegible]	[illegible]	[illegible]	[illegible]	[illegible]	[illegible]	[illegible]	[illegible]	[illegible]	
[illegible]	[illegible]	[illegible]	[illegible]	[illegible]	[illegible]	[illegible]	[illegible]	[illegible]	
[illegible]	[illegible]	[illegible]	[illegible]	[illegible]	[illegible]	[illegible]	[illegible]	[illegible]	
[illegible]	[illegible]	[illegible]	[illegible]	[illegible]	[illegible]	[illegible]	[illegible]	[illegible]	
[illegible]	No return of Contractors	[illegible]	[illegible]	[illegible]	[illegible]	[illegible]	[illegible]	[illegible]	
[illegible]	[illegible]	[illegible]	[illegible]	[illegible]	[illegible]	[illegible]	[illegible]	[illegible]	
[illegible]	[illegible]	[illegible]	[illegible]	[illegible]	[illegible]	[illegible]	[illegible]	[illegible]	
[illegible]	[illegible]	[illegible]	[illegible]	[illegible]	[illegible]	[illegible]	[illegible]	[illegible]	
[illegible]	[illegible]	[illegible]	[illegible]	[illegible]	[illegible]	[illegible]	[illegible]	[illegible]	
[illegible]	[illegible]	[illegible]	[illegible]	[illegible]	No means of making this Return.		[illegible]	[illegible]	
[illegible]	[illegible]	[illegible]	[illegible]	[illegible]			[illegible]	[illegible]	
[illegible]	[illegible]	[illegible]	[illegible]	[illegible]			[illegible]	[illegible]	
[illegible]	[illegible]	[illegible]	[illegible]	[illegible]	[illegible]	[illegible]	[illegible]	[illegible]	
[illegible]	[illegible]	[illegible]	[illegible]	[illegible]	[illegible]	[illegible]	[illegible]	[illegible]	
[illegible]	[illegible]	[illegible]	[illegible]	[illegible]	[illegible]	[illegible]	[illegible]	[illegible]	General total and average for county.
[illegible]	[illegible]	[illegible]	Cannot be ascertained.		[illegible]	[illegible]	[illegible]	[illegible]	The [illegible] of miles of road repaired in 1834 cannot be ascertained, the documents being confined to the [illegible] [illegible] state.
[illegible]	[illegible]	[illegible]	[illegible]	[illegible]	[illegible]	[illegible]	[illegible]	[illegible]	
[illegible]	[illegible]	[illegible]	[illegible]	[illegible]	[illegible]	[illegible]	[illegible]	[illegible]	
[illegible]	[illegible]	[illegible]	[illegible]	[illegible]	[illegible]	[illegible]	[illegible]	[illegible]	
[illegible]	[illegible]	[illegible]	[illegible]	[illegible]	[illegible]	[illegible]	[illegible]	[illegible]	
[illegible]	[illegible]	[illegible]	Cannot be ascertained.		[illegible]	[illegible]	[illegible]	[illegible]	Present Grand Jury Act in this county came into force in 1843. At present the [illegible] for road [illegible] include turnpike and, [illegible], [illegible] [illegible]. On [illegible] January [illegible], [illegible] of turnpike [illegible], [illegible] to [illegible] of the [illegible] [illegible], became chargeable upon the county for the first time, the presentments passed for [illegible] [illegible] repair of which that year amounted to [illegible].
[illegible]	[illegible]	[illegible]	[illegible]	[illegible]	[illegible]	[illegible]	[illegible]	[illegible]	
[illegible]	[illegible]	[illegible]	[illegible]	[illegible]	[illegible]	[illegible]	[illegible]	[illegible]	
[illegible]	[illegible]	[illegible]	[illegible]	[illegible]	[illegible]	[illegible]	[illegible]	[illegible]	
[illegible]	[illegible]	[illegible]	[illegible]	[illegible]	[illegible]	[illegible]	[illegible]	[illegible]	

Appendix, No. 18.—Return of Extent and Cost of Works, executed under Grand Jury Presentments in Ireland,

COUNTIES.	Years.	A. Roads under Contract for Repairs, including Widening, Building, Filling Gripe, and Sinking Footpaths. Length	A. Amount	B. Roads under Contract for Maintenance. Length	B. Amount	Cost per Perch.	Totals of Columns A and B. Length	Totals Amount	C. New Roads. Length	C. Amount
		m. f. p.	£. s. d.	m. f. p.	£. s. d.	d.	m. f. p.	£. s. d.	m. f. p.	£. s. d.
Fermanagh	[illegible]	[illegible]	[illegible]	[illegible]	[illegible]	[illegible]	[illegible]	[illegible]	[illegible]	[illegible]
Galway, East	[illegible]	[illegible]	[illegible]	[illegible]	[illegible]	[illegible]	[illegible]	[illegible]	[illegible]	[illegible]
Galway, West	[illegible]	[illegible]	[illegible]	[illegible]	[illegible]	[illegible]	[illegible]	[illegible]	[illegible]	[illegible]
Kerry	[illegible]	[illegible]	[illegible]	[illegible]	[illegible]	[illegible]	[illegible]	[illegible]	Included in Column B	
Kildare	[illegible]	[illegible]	[illegible]	[illegible]	[illegible]	[illegible]	[illegible]	[illegible]	[illegible]	[illegible]
Kilkenny	[illegible]	[illegible]	[illegible]	[illegible]	[illegible]	[illegible]	[illegible]	[illegible]	[illegible]	[illegible]
King's County	[illegible]	[illegible]	[illegible]	[illegible]	[illegible]	[illegible]	[illegible]	[illegible]	[illegible]	[illegible]
Leitrim	[illegible]	[illegible]	[illegible]	[illegible]	[illegible]	[illegible]	[illegible]	[illegible]	[illegible]	[illegible]
Limerick, East	[illegible]	[illegible]	[illegible]	[illegible]	[illegible]	[illegible]	[illegible]	[illegible]	[illegible]	[illegible]
Limerick, West	[illegible]	[illegible]	[illegible]	[illegible]	[illegible]	[illegible]	[illegible]	[illegible]	[illegible]	[illegible]
Londonderry	[illegible]	[illegible]	[illegible]	[illegible]	[illegible]	[illegible]	[illegible]	[illegible]	[illegible]	[illegible]
Longford	[illegible]	[illegible]	[illegible]	[illegible]	[illegible]	[illegible]	[illegible]	[illegible]	[illegible]	[illegible]
Louth	[illegible]	[illegible]	[illegible]	[illegible]	[illegible]	[illegible]	[illegible]	[illegible]	[illegible]	[illegible]
Mayo	[illegible]	[illegible]	[illegible]	[illegible]	[illegible]	[illegible]	[illegible]	[illegible]	[illegible]	[illegible]
Meath	[illegible]	[illegible]	[illegible]	[illegible]	[illegible]	[illegible]	[illegible]	[illegible]	[illegible]	[illegible]

[illegible] the Years 1841, 1844, 1844, 1854, and 1857, compiled from the County Presentment Books, &c.—continued.

D. [illegible] and [illegible] Repairs. Amount.	E. [illegible], Lodges, and [illegible] Buildings. Amount.	Totals of Columns A, B, C, D, and E. Amount.	Cost of Superintendence. Amount.	Per-Centage of Cost.	Gross Number of Miles of New Roads made from 1841 to 1857. Length.	Gross Number of Miles of New Roads made from 1841 to 1857. Amount.	Number of Surveyors.	Number of Assistants.	OBSERVATIONS.
£. s. d.	£. s. d.	£. s. d.	£. s. d.		M. F. P.	£. s. d.			
[illegible]	[illegible]	[illegible]	[illegible]	[illegible]	[illegible]	[illegible]	[illegible]	[illegible]	New roads were laid out, [illegible], and marked on the ground by surveyor [illegible], without any additional cost to the public.
[illegible]	[illegible]	[illegible]	[illegible]	[illegible]	[illegible]	[illegible]	[illegible]	[illegible]	One surveyor is [illegible] for the entire county. 64 miles of roads added in [illegible], which previously had been maintained by the Commissioners of Public Works.
[illegible]	[illegible]	[illegible]	[illegible]	[illegible]	Exclusive of other works.	[illegible]	[illegible]	[illegible]	184 miles of public roads added in [illegible], which previously had been [illegible] by the Commissioners of Public Works, and [illegible] miles of [illegible], which, prior to 1845, had not been [illegible] by the county. [illegible] miles of roads were added [illegible] under 16 & 17 Vict. c. 136, previously [illegible] by Commissioners of Public Works.
[illegible]	[illegible]	[illegible]	Not in county returns.	[illegible]	[illegible]	[illegible]	[illegible]	[illegible]	There were [illegible] miles of roads not contracted for in 1854. [illegible] miles of [illegible] roads [illegible] chargeable on the county on 4th January 1855. No return received for 1854 or 1857.
[illegible]	[illegible]	[illegible]	[illegible]	[illegible]	[illegible]	[illegible]	[illegible]	[illegible]	
[illegible]	[illegible]	[illegible]	[illegible]	[illegible]	[illegible]	[illegible]	[illegible]	[illegible]	In 1844 there were [illegible] miles of public roads not under contract, the cost of maintenance of [illegible] would amount to [illegible] l. [illegible] s. [illegible] d.
[illegible]	[illegible]	[illegible]	[illegible]	[illegible]	[illegible]	[illegible]	[illegible]	[illegible]	[illegible] Surveyor's forms in this county much improved by the Acts 14 & 15 Vict. c. 72, and 16 & 17 Vict. cap. 137.
[illegible]	[illegible]	[illegible]	[illegible]	[illegible]	[illegible]	[illegible]	[illegible]	[illegible]	One surveyor in 1854 for the entire county. Previous to 1854, only about [illegible] the [illegible] of roads were under a surveyor [illegible], and as well as all other county works, they were most imperfectly and inefficiently managed.
[illegible]	[illegible]	[illegible]	[illegible]	[illegible]	[illegible]	[illegible]	[illegible]	[illegible]	
[illegible]	[illegible]	[illegible]	[illegible]	[illegible]	[illegible]	[illegible]	[illegible]	[illegible]	
[illegible]	[illegible]	[illegible]	[illegible]	[illegible]	[illegible]	[illegible]	[illegible]	[illegible]	Surveyor's duties considerably increased by [illegible], [illegible] miles of [illegible] roads completed under superintendence of county surveyors.
[illegible]	[illegible]	[illegible]	[illegible]	[illegible]	[illegible]	[illegible]	[illegible]	[illegible]	[illegible] miles of roads have been under contract for maintenance and repair in the county. No return received in [illegible] or [illegible].
[illegible]	[illegible]	[illegible]	[illegible]	[illegible]	[illegible]	[illegible]	[illegible]	[illegible]	
[illegible]	[illegible]	[illegible]	[illegible]	[illegible]	[illegible]	[illegible]	[illegible]	[illegible]	

COUNTIES	Years.	A. Roads under Contract for Repairs, including Widening, Fencing, Railing, Gripe, and Making Footpaths. Length.	A. Amount.	B. Roads under Contract for Maintenance. Length.	B. Amount.	Cost per Perch.	Totals of Columns A. and B. Length.	Totals of Columns A. and B. Amount.	C. New Roads. Length.	C. New Roads. Amount.
		m. f. p.	£. s. d.	m. f. p.	£. s. d.	d.	m. f. p.	£. s. d.	m. f. p.	£. s. d.
Monaghan	[illegible]	[illegible]	[illegible]	[illegible]	[illegible]	[illegible]	[illegible]	[illegible]	[illegible]	[illegible]
Queen's County	[illegible]	[illegible]	[illegible]	[illegible]	[illegible]	[illegible]	[illegible]	[illegible]	[illegible]	[illegible]
Roscommon	[illegible]	[illegible]	[illegible]	[illegible]	[illegible]	[illegible]	[illegible]	[illegible]	[illegible]	[illegible]
Sligo	[illegible]	[illegible]	[illegible]	[illegible]	[illegible]	[illegible]	[illegible]	[illegible]	[illegible]	[illegible]
Tipperary, North	[illegible]	[illegible]	[illegible]	[illegible]	[illegible]	[illegible]	[illegible]	[illegible]	[illegible]	[illegible]
Tipperary, South	[illegible]	[illegible]	[illegible]	[illegible]	[illegible]	[illegible]	[illegible]	[illegible]	Included in column A.	
Tyrone	[illegible]	[illegible]	[illegible]	[illegible]	[illegible]	[illegible]	[illegible]	[illegible]	[illegible]	[illegible]
Tyrone, East	[illegible]	[illegible]	[illegible]	[illegible]	[illegible]	[illegible]	[illegible]	[illegible]	[illegible]	[illegible]
Waterford	[illegible]	[illegible]	[illegible]	[illegible]	[illegible]	[illegible]	[illegible]	[illegible]	[illegible]	[illegible]
Westmeath	[illegible]	[illegible]	[illegible]	[illegible]	[illegible]	[illegible]	[illegible]	[illegible]	[illegible]	[illegible]
Wexford	[illegible]	[illegible]	[illegible]	[illegible]	[illegible]	[illegible]	[illegible]	[illegible]	[illegible]	[illegible]
Wicklow	[illegible]	[illegible]	[illegible]	[illegible]	[illegible]	[illegible]	[illegible]	[illegible]	[illegible]	[illegible]

in the Years 1834, 1844, 1854, 1856, and 1857, compiled from the County Presentment Books, &c.—*continued*.

D. [illegible]	E. Bridges, Gullies, and Road Buildings.	Totals of Columns A, B, C, D, and E.	Cost of Superintendence.	Per-Centage of Cost.	Gross Number of Miles of New Roads made from 1834 to 1857.		Number of Surveyors.	Number of [illegible].	OBSERVATIONS.
Amount.	Amount.	Amount.	Amount.		Length.	Amount.			
£ s. d.	£ s. d.	£ s. d.	£ s. d.		m. f. p.	£ s. d.			
[illegible]	[illegible]	[illegible]	[illegible]	[illegible]	[illegible]	[illegible]	[illegible]	[illegible]	
[illegible]	[illegible]	[illegible]	[illegible]	[illegible]	[illegible]	[illegible]	[illegible]	[illegible]	
[illegible]	[illegible]	[illegible]	[illegible]	[illegible]	[illegible]	[illegible]	[illegible]	[illegible]	
[illegible]	[illegible]	[illegible]	[illegible]	[illegible]	[illegible]	[illegible]	[illegible]	[illegible]	
[illegible]	[illegible]	[illegible]	[illegible]	[illegible]	[illegible]	[illegible]	[illegible]	[illegible]	One surveyor to 1856 for entire county.
Included in column A.		[illegible]	[illegible]	[illegible]	Cannot be ascertained.		[illegible]	[illegible]	Return for year 18[illegible] not received. [illegible]
[illegible]	[illegible]	[illegible]	[illegible]	[illegible]	No means of making this return correctly.		[illegible]	[illegible]	The return from that county was incomplete.
[illegible]	[illegible]	[illegible]	[illegible]	[illegible]	[illegible]	[illegible]	[illegible]	[illegible]	
[illegible]	[illegible]	[illegible]	[illegible]	[illegible]	[illegible]	[illegible]	[illegible]	[illegible]	
[illegible]	[illegible]	[illegible]	[illegible]	[illegible]	[illegible]	[illegible]	[illegible]	[illegible]	
[illegible]	[illegible]	[illegible]	[illegible]	[illegible]	[illegible]	[illegible]	[illegible]	[illegible]	Gross sum from 1834 to 1855 of column A - - - £ [illegible]; Ditto - ditto - D - [illegible]; Ditto - ditto - E - [illegible]
[illegible]	[illegible]	[illegible]	[illegible]	[illegible]	[illegible]	[illegible]	[illegible]	[illegible]	
[illegible]	[illegible]	[illegible]	[illegible]	[illegible]	[illegible] Carried.				

Since the appointment of County Surveyors in 1834, these [illegible] have been greatly [illegible]—by the [illegible] which have been made in the [illegible] of roads [illegible] [illegible], and by the County [illegible] of Public Works and of Turnpike Trustees, and with the repairs and construction of [illegible] and [illegible], also by the [illegible] of Bridges rendered necessary by the Drainage Works.

Select Committee on Grand Jury Laws, by Henry Brett, County Surveyor, Wicklow.

Appendix, No. 14.

PAPER handed in by Sir Charles Lanyon, D.P.

App. No. 14.

Constitution of Presentment Sessions to be held conjointly by magistrates and cess-payers.

Except in cases hereinafter provided for.

Magistrates not qualified to sit at baronial sessions unless resident in the barony in and for which they propose to act, or unless they possess freehold or leasehold property, or are heirs apparent to such property, or are agents to the owner of a property situated in the barony in or for which any of the aforesaid propose to act, and with regard to agents they should only sit and act when the owners are not present.

The amount of qualification need not be nearly so large as that for grand jurors. Freehold or leasehold property of the annual value of 20*l.* to 30*l.* might be sufficient.

Declarations to be made.

The number of magistrates so qualified and eligible to act for each barony being ascertained, a similar number of cesspayers to associate with them in sessions should be eligible and might be selected as hereinafter suggested.

Parishes would not do, being often of very unequal size, representation would not be sufficiently secured.

Electoral divisions under Poor Law would not do, as their boundaries are not co-equal with county or baronial divisions.

Road Districts.—Baronies might be divided into districts, to be called "Road Districts," of such size, having regard to area, population, or valuation, as would best secure general representation of the cesspayers, by the union of a number of contiguous townlands for the purposes of the Act, not dividing a townland in any case.

The collector of cess could do this in the first instance, and the baronial sessions might revise or alter, if necessary, afterwards, on the application of cesspayers.

This would secure representation from every locality, and place the representation in the hands of the ratepayers themselves.

It would also do away with the uncertainty as to representatives at present complained of.

Election of Cesspayers—To associate with justices at presentment sessions.

The five highest cesspayers from each of these road districts being noticed by the collector of cess might attend a general meeting of such cesspayers in each barony to be held within or for the barony. At this meeting, and from the five cesspayers noticed to attend, whether they should be present or not, one or more as may be considered necessary should be selected by ballot to represent the road district at the next presentment sessions of the barony, and so on for each of the districts.

If the number so selected were found to exceed the number of magistrates eligible for the barony, the names of the cesspayers so drawn, for the whole barony, should be put into the box and the name or names first drawn, to the number of those in excess of the eligible magistrates, shall be struck off the list of the eligible cesspayers. And on the other hand, if they should fall short of the number of eligible magistrates, then the names of all the unsuccessful cesspayers of the whole barony shall be put into the box, and the first drawn name or names, to the required number, shall be added to the list of eligible cesspayers.

See 6 & 7 Will. 4, c. 116, s. 12.

When Work is in Two or more Baronies.—At present application is made in that barony off which it is proposed that the larger portion of the expense of such work is to be raised, without making the same at the presentment session for each of such baronies.

It would be an improvement to permit the magistrates and representative cesspayers of the other barony or baronies to attend and vote at the sessions held in the barony where the application is taken into consideration; but to vote only in the particular case or cases affecting their barony and in no other.

6 & 7 Will. 4, c. 116, s. 36.

County at Large Works.—There are some works, the expense of which may be levied off the county at large, and yet the applications for them be considered at the baronial sessions—lowering hills, filling hollows, building bridges, &c. It would not be unfair in such cases to permit any magistrate or any cesspayer of the county, qualified to act at any other sessions to come in and vote in such cases, seeing that every barony pays a proportion of the county at large charges.

The Grand Jury, though not constituted at present in what is by many deemed a sufficiently representative or popular way, is perhaps practically as fair a board and as efficient as any that would be obtained by any other system. If, however, it is determined upon by the committee to recommend the representative system in this body, I think the following plan might secure representation, and the high character of present grand juries at the same time.

Persons in each barony possessing a certain amount of property in the county (not necessarily magistrates) or who may be heir apparent to such amount, or who may be agent to a person possessing a certain amount, &c., eligible to be on fiscal grand jury.

The

The qualifications required for justices attending presentment sessions under 19 Geo. 3, c. 84, s. 2, revised might suit, viz.:

App. No. 14.

1. Freehold estate or estates in fee simple or in fee tail, or for life (situate in any part of the county) of the annual value of 200 *l.*

2. The heirs apparent to any person so seised.

3. Leasehold estate or estates for life, of the annual value of 300 *l.*

4. Ditto for years not less than 14, being unexpired, 400 *l.* yearly.

5. Ditto for life and years combined, of annual value of 400 *l.*

For counties.

6. £. 10,000 above just debts, and justice resident in county.

7. Agent to the owner of an estate of annual value of 4,000 *l.*; agent eligible only as agent when owner is not on grand jury.

For counties of towns or cities?

Persons so eligible to meet together on due notice being given them, in their respective baronies in which they may have a part or the whole of the property from which they qualify, and elect by ballot or otherwise as they may think proper one or more of their number to represent such barony on the "fiscal grand jury."

That this fiscal grand jury need not necessarily be limited to 23.

The 23 grand jurors for indictment business might be selected by the sheriff out of the fiscal jury, and the remainder be discharged when fiscal business finished.

That if any barony shall fail to return a grand juror, the high sheriff may invite or summon some person qualified as aforesaid to represent that barony.

Those originally elected, subject to penalty if they neglect or refuse to attend without giving notice   days before the assizes to the high sheriff, who should be empowered to make up the deficiency out of qualified persons.

For Mode of making Application to Presentment Sessions, &c.—See printed Report by county Antrim Grand Jury, and Appendix by their secretary at Spring Assizes, 1868.

Sessions for a Barony might be held in another barony, or even in an adjoining county, if found more convenient. For example:—In the county of Antrim the county of the town of Carrickfergus is situated almost in the centre of the barony of lower Belfast, and the town of Carrickfergus would be the most convenient place for that barony if legalized.

Places for holding Sessions.—In some baronies there are not petty sessions houses, and places for presentment sessions are sometimes obtained on sufferance for the day. I have seen a school designed to allow sessions to be held in the school-room. There is no power to rent such, or any place, unless under the petty sessions clause, which requires that four petty sessions should have been held within the four previous months. This, of course, cannot be stated respecting places other than petty sessions houses.

In one case used, I remember the accommodation consisted of a little pulpit-like box, which held, not very conveniently, three magistrates. The cesspayers and officers had no table, and but one little "keg," or barrel, as a seat, among them. In the adjoining barony, a very few miles off, indeed within five minutes walk of the boundary of the barony, there is a most commodious court-house, but it could not be legally used, because in a different barony.—*See* printed Appendix, p. 8.

Petty Sessions Houses should be of a much better kind than they often are. The amount of rent allowed for them should be larger, and a certain amount of accommodation made obligatory.

Reserves or Depôts for Road Materials.—Amount limited for these in present Act too low.

Rollers, &c.—There should be power to present for road rollers, and for proper central places in each district, to keep them safely.

Our county of Antrim roads take the lead of most other roads I have seen in Ireland, or even England or Scotland; but the French roads, which I never saw till lately, are very superior, and I attribute this a good deal to the free use of the "rollers" and the "rammers." Scarcely a loose stone was to be seen, even in the districts most distant from the leading towns.

Payment of Contractors might be three times a year, instead of twice, with advantage; in addition to the payments after the Spring and Summer assizes, a third time, say, in November, midway in the long interval between Summer and Spring Assizes, would do. This was formerly the case after the October Quarter Sessions; unless the whole system be altered for a still more prompt payment.

Fees to Secretaries.—I quite concur with those who prefer a fixed salary to payment by fees. I dislike the collecting of them, and although little is said against them by contractors, they very often shirk them. Stamps, as has been proposed, would be a better plan for collecting them for the credit of the county. They should be retained in this way, on tenders at least, to curb over competition, which would be reckless without some check.

Superannuation. Power to appoint deputy in case of illness, &c., and allowance for a clerk of [illegible] only just.

In

In settling the amount of salary, returns for two or three years only should not be made the basis, but for at least 10 years; and the depreciation in the value of money, or increase of value of labour (by 60 per cent., perhaps) should be taken into account.

Clerks of the Crown and Treasurers would have a great increase of business thrown upon them, if the prompt payment system be introduced generally.

Sites for Militia Barracks, &c.—Power should be given to grand juries, or somebody, to take premises for militia accommodation, and pay for them such sums as might be awarded by an inquisition jury, such as, under the 7th of Geo. 4, c. 74, is permitted for obtaining sites for prisons. A difficulty in this county suggests the proposition.

The place most convenient, everything taken into account, and used already after some expenditure to accommodate the militia on premises belonging to the county, could be extended by the purchase of other premises adjoining; but the proprietor, knowing the facts, asks much more than is considered a reasonable price. Such power as is suggested would fix the price in a fair way between the parties.

The above and foregoing are some of the most prominent points in the grand jury system which occur to me as most worthy of notice just now.

John Coates,
Secretary to the Grand Jury of the County of Antrim
for nearly 47 years.

Appendix, No. 16.

Memorandum.

In 1814, during the Chief Secretaryship of Sir Robert Peel, the Act 54 Geo. 3, c. 131, was passed. It empowered the Lord Lieutenant to declare by proclamation any county, barony, or baronies, to be in a state of disturbance, or to require an extraordinary establishment of police, and thereupon to appoint a chief magistrate of police, with a salary of 700l. per annum, house and furniture, a clerk, a chief constable, and not exceeding 10 constables; on the district being restored to peace and good order the offices of these persons were to cease.

All the expenses were to be defrayed by advances from the Consolidated Fund, to be repaid by Grand Jury Presentments.

The establishments formed under this Act were called the Peace Preservation Police.

In 1822, the Constabulary Act, 3 Geo. 4, c. 103, was passed. It empowered the Lord Lieutenant to appoint a chief constable for every or any barony, and by proclamation to require the magistrates for any county to assemble and nominate a number of constables and sub-constables, to be specified, not exceeding 16 for each barony. In default of the magistrates nominating, the Lord Lieutenant was empowered to appoint. The number might be increased on certificate of magistrates at quarter sessions. Houses were to be provided for the residence of the chief and other constables. General superintendents and inspectors, not exceeding four, were to be appointed by the Lord Lieutenant.

Resident magistrates might be appointed by the Lord Lieutenant, on the application of three or more magistrates assembled at general or special sessions. All expenses (including magistrates' salaries, and the superannuation of chief and other constables) were to be advanced from Consolidated Fund, and repaid by Grand Jury Presentments; but sums levied for fines and forfeited recognizances were to be allowed as part of such payment.

On this Act being carried into effect in any county, the Act 54 Geo. 3, c. 131, was to stand repealed as to such county.

This Act was carried into effect, except where it was considered necessary to continue the police establishments formed under 54 Geo 3, c. 131. Both these Acts ceased to be in force when the Constabulary Act, 6 Will. 4, c. 13, was brought into operation in 1837. That Act vested all appointments in the Lord Lieutenant, and charged the counties with only a moiety of the expenses, excepting the salaries, &c., of the inspector general, his deputies and clerks, the magistrates, the receiver, and the paymaster. Pensions were to be paid from a superannuation fund, formed by deductions from pay; but in the event of the fund being insufficient, authority was given for charging the counties in which the pensioners had served with a moiety. (This, I believe, was never done.)

In 1839, by 2 & 3 Vict., c. 75, authority was given for the formation of a reserve force, which might be temporarily sent into counties by the Lord Lieutenant, and a moiety of the expenses charged to such counties.

In 1846, by 9 & 10 Vict., c. 97, the counties were relieved from the charge of a moiety of the expenses of the constabulary, except in the cases of (1). Additional force applied for by magistrates in special sessions. (2). Reserve force sent into counties; or (3). Additional force appointed by the Lord Lieutenant in a district proclaimed as disturbed.

The number of men which each county should be entitled to have free of charge was defined by 11 & 12 Vict., c. 72 (1848); and altered by 20 & 21 Vict., c. 17 (1857); and 28 & 29 Vict., c. 70 (1865).

3 July 1868. *R. N. M.*

www.ingramcontent.com/pod-product-compliance
Lightning Source LLC
Chambersburg PA
CBHW051741300426
44115CB00007B/652
9783741105098